Lecture Notes in Computer Science 8602

Commenced Publication in 1973
Founding and Former Series Editors:
Gerhard Goos, Juris Hartmanis, and Jan van Leeuwen

T0172032

More information about this series at http://www.springer.com/series/7407

Anna I. Esparcia-Alcázar et al. (Eds.)

Applications
of Evolutionary Computation

17th European Conference,
EvoApplications 2014
Granada, Spain, April 23–25, 2014
Revised Selected Papers

 Springer

Editors

see next page

ISSN 0302-9743　　　　　　　　　　　ISSN 1611-3349　　(electronic)
Lecture Notes in Computer Science
ISBN 978-3-662-45522-7　　　　　　　ISBN 978-3-662-45523-4　　(eBook)
DOI 10.1007/978-3-662-45523-4

Library of Congress Control Number: 2014956223

LNCS Sublibrary: SL1 – Theoretical Computer Science and General Issues

Springer Heidelberg New York Dordrecht London

Cover illustration: Designed by Laura Pirovano

Printed on acid-free paper

Springer-Verlag GmbH Berlin Heidelberg is part of Springer Science+Business Media
(www.springer.com)

Volume Editors

Anna I. Esparcia-Alcázar
S2 Grupo, Spain
aesparcia@s2grupo.es

Antonio M. Mora
Universidad de Granada, Spain
amorag@geneura.ugr.es

Alexandros Agapitos
University College Dublin, Ireland
alexandros.agapitos@ucd.ie

Paolo Burelli
Aalborg University Copenhagen,
Denmark
pabu@create.aau.dk

William S. Bush
Vanderbilt University, USA
william.s.bush@vanderbilt.edu

Stefano Cagnoni
University of Parma, Italy
cagnoni@ce.unipr.it

Carlos Cotta
Universidad de Málaga, Spain
ccottap@lcc.uma.es

Ivanoe De Falco
ICAR-CNR, Italy
ivanoe.defalco@na.icar.cnr.it

Antonio Della Cioppa
University of Salerno, Italy
adellacioppa@unisa.it

Federico Divina
Universidad Pablo de Olavide, Spain
fdivina@upo.es

Rolf Drechsler
German Research Center for Artificial
Intelligence, Germany
drechsle@informatik.uni-
bremen.de

A.E. Eiben
VU University Amsterdam,
The Netherlands
a.e.eiben@vu.nl

Francisco Fernández de Vega
University of Extremadura, Spain
fcofdez@unex.es

Kyrre Glette
University of Oslo, Norway
kyrrehg@ifi.uio.no

Evert Haasdijk
VU University Amsterdam,
The Netherlands
e.haasdijk@vu.nl

J. Ignacio Hidalgo
Universidad Complutense
de Madrid, Spain
hidalgo@fis.ucm.es

Paul Kaufmann
University of Paderborn, Germany
paul.kaufmann@gmail.com

Trung Thanh Nguyen
Liverpool John Moores University, UK
T.T.Nguyen@ljmu.ac.uk

Petr Pošík
Czech Technical University,
Czech Republic
petr.posik@fel.cvut.cz

Robert Schaefer
AGH University of Science
and Technology, Poland
schaefer@agh.edu.pl

Kevin Sim
Edinburgh Napier University,
UK
k.sim@napier.ac.uk

Anabela Simões
Polytechnic Institute of Coimbra, Portugal
abs@isec.pt

Giovanni Squillero
Politecnico di Torino, Italy
giovanni.squillero@polito.it

Ernesto Tarantino
ICAR-CNR, Italy
ernesto.tarantino@na.icar.
cnr.it

Andrea G.B. Tettamanzi
Université de Nice,
Sophia Antipolis, France
andrea.tettamanzi@unice.fr

Neil Urquhart
Edinburgh Napier University, UK
n.urquhart@napier.ac.uk

Mengjie Zhang
Victoria University of Wellington,
New Zealand
mengjie.zhang@vuw.ac.nz

Nur Zincir-Heywood
Dalhousie University, Canada
zincir@cs.dal.ca

Preface

Evolutionary computation (EC) techniques are efficient, nature-inspired planning and optimization methods based on the principles of natural evolution and genetics. Due to their efficiency and simple underlying principles, these methods can be used in the context of problem solving, optimization, and machine learning. A large and continuously increasing number of researchers and professionals make use of EC techniques in various application domains. This volume presents a careful selection of relevant EC examples combined with a thorough examination of the techniques used in EC. The papers in the volume illustrate the current state of the art in the application of EC and should help and inspire researchers and professionals to develop efficient EC methods for design and problem solving.

All the papers in this book were presented during EvoApplications 2014, which incorporates a range of tracks on application-oriented aspects of EC. Originally established as EvoWorkshops in 1998, it provides a unique opportunity for EC researchers to meet and discuss application aspects of EC and has been an important link between EC research and its application in a variety of domains. During these 16 years new workshops and tracks have arisen, some have disappeared, while others have matured to become conferences of their own, such as EuroGP in 2000, EvoCOP in 2004, EvoBIO in 2007, and EvoMUSART in 2012.

EvoApplications is part of EVO*, Europe's premier colocated event in the field of evolutionary computing. EVO* was held from April 23 to 25, 2014. Granada, Spain, home to 'The Alhambra' UNESCO World Heritage Site provided the setting, with the Universidad de Granada, Departamento de Arquitectura y Tecnología de los Computadores representing the venue, and included, in addition to EvoApplications, EuroGP, the main European event dedicated to genetic programming; EvoCOP, the main European conference on evolutionary computation in combinatorial optimization and EvoMUSART the main International Conference on Evolutionary and Biologically Inspired Music, Sound, Art and Design. The proceedings for all of these events in their 2013 edition are also available in the LNCS series.

The central aim of the EVO* events is to provide researchers, as well as people from industry, students, and interested newcomers, with an opportunity to present new results, discuss current developments and applications, or just become acquainted with the world of EC. Moreover, it encourages and reinforces possible synergies and interactions between members of all scientific communities that may benefit from EC techniques.

EvoApplications 2014 consisted of the following individual tracks:

- *EvoCOMNET*, track on nature-inspired techniques for telecommunication networks and other parallel and distributed systems,
- *EvoCOMPLEX*, track on evolutionary algorithms and complex systems,
- *EvoENERGY*, track on EC in energy applications,

- *EvoFIN*, track on evolutionary and natural computation in finance and economics,
- *EvoGAMES*, track on bio-inspired algorithms in games,
- *EvoIASP*, track on EC in image analysis signal processing and pattern recognition,
- *EvoINDUSTRY*, track on nature-inspired techniques in industrial settings,
- *EvoNUM*, track on bio-inspired algorithms for continuous parameter optimization,
- *EvoPAR*, track on parallel implementation of evolutionary algorithms,
- *EvoRISK*, track on computational intelligence for risk management, security, and defence applications,
- *EvoROBOT*, track on EC in robotics
- *EvoSTOC*, track on evolutionary algorithms in stochastic and dynamic environments, and
- *EvoBIO*, track on EC and related techniques in bioinformatics and computational biology.

EvoCOMNET addresses the application of EC techniques to problems in distributed and connected systems such as telecommunication and computer networks, distribution and logistic networks, interpersonal and interorganizational networks, etc. To address the challenges of these systems, this track promotes the study and the application of strategies inspired by the observation of biological and evolutionary processes that usually show the highly desirable characteristics of being distributed, adaptive, scalable, and robust.

EvoCOMPLEX covers all aspects of the interaction of evolutionary algorithms (and metaheuristics in general) with complex systems. Complex systems are ubiquitous in physics, economics, sociology, biology, computer science, and many other scientific areas. Typically, a complex system is composed of smaller aggregated components, whose interaction and interconnectedness are non trivial. This leads to emergent properties of the system, not anticipated by its isolated components. Furthermore, when the system behavior is studied from a temporal perspective, self-organization patterns typically arise.

EvoFIN is the only European event specifically dedicated to the applications of EC, and related natural computing methodologies, to finance and economics. Financial environments are typically hard, being dynamic, high-dimensional, noisy, and co-evolutionary. These environments serve as an interesting test bed for novel evolutionary methodologies.

EvoGAMES aims to focus the scientific developments in computational intelligence techniques that may be of practical value for utilization in existing or future games. Recently, games, and especially video games, have become an important commercial factor within the software industry, providing an excellent test bed for application of a wide range of computational intelligence methods.

EvoIASP, the longest-running of all EvoApplications tracks which celebrates its 15th edition this year, has been the first international event solely dedicated to the applications of EC to image analysis and signal processing in complex domains of high industrial and social relevance.

EvoNUM aims at applications of bio-inspired algorithms, and cross-fertilization between these and more classical numerical optimization algorithms, to continuous optimization problems. It deals with applications where continuous parameters or functions have to be optimized, in fields such as control, chemistry, agriculture, electricity, building and construction, energy, aerospace engineering, and design optimization.

EvoPAR covers all aspects of the application of parallel and distributed systems to EC as well as the application of evolutionary algorithms for improving parallel architectures and distributed computing infrastructures. EvoPAR focuses on the application and improvement of distributed infrastructures, such as grid and cloud computing, peer-to-peer (P2P) system, as well as parallel architectures, GPUs, manycores, etc., in cooperation with evolutionary algorithms.

EvoRISK focuses on challenging problems in risk management, security, and defence, and covers both theoretical developments and applications of computational intelligence to subjects such as cyber crime, IT security, resilient and self-healing systems, risk management, critical infrastructure protection (CIP), military, counter terrorism and other defence-related aspects, disaster relief, and humanitarian logistics.

EvoSTOC addresses the application of EC in stochastic and dynamic environments. This includes optimization problems with changing, noisy, and/or approximated fitness functions and optimization problems that require robust solutions, providing the first platform to present and discuss the latest research in this field.

EvoBIO brings together experts across multiple fields, who draw inspiration from biological systems in order to produce solutions to complex biological problems.

And finally, a General track including those papers dealing with applications not covered by any of the established tracks.

This year's edition of EvoApplications had 128 submissions, with 55 papers accepted for oral presentation and 24 for poster presentation.

Many people have helped make EvoApplications a success. We would like to express our gratitude first to the authors for submitting their work, to the members of the Program Committees for devoting their energy to reviewing those papers, and to the audience for their lively participation.

We would also like to thank the Institute for Informatics and Digital Innovation at Edinburgh Napier University, UK, for their coordination efforts.

The papers were submitted, reviewed, and selected using the MyReview conference management software. We are sincerely grateful to Marc Schoenauer of Inria, France, for his great assistance in providing, hosting, and managing the software.

We would like to thank the local organizing team: Juan Julián Merelo Guervós, Victor M. Rivas Santos, Pedro A. Castillo Valdivieso, María Isabel García Arenas, Pablo García Sánchez, Antonio Fernández Ares, and Javier Asensio. We thank Kevin Sim from the Institute for Informatics and Digital Information, Edinburgh Napier University for creating and maintaining the official Evo* 2014 website, and Pablo García Sánchez (Universidad de Granada, Spain) and Mauro Castelli (Universidade Nova de Lisboa, Portugal) for being responsible for Evo* 2014 publicity.

We would also like to express our sincerest gratitude to our invited speakers, who gave the inspiring keynote talks: Prof. Thomas Schmickl of the University of Karl-Franzens University, Graz, Austria, Prof. Federico Morán of Universidad Complutense de Madrid, Spain, and Prof. Susan Stepney of the University of York, UK.

We especially want to express our genuine gratitude to Jennifer Willies of the Institute for Informatics and Digital Innovation at Edinburgh Napier University, UK. Her dedicated and continued involvement in Evo* since 1998 has been and remains essential for building the image, status, and unique atmosphere of this series of events.

April 2014

Anna I. Esparcia-Alcázar
Antonio M. Mora
Alexandros Agapitos
Paolo Burelli
William S. Bush
Stefano Cagnoni
Carlos Cotta
Ivanoe De Falco
Antonio Della Cioppa
Federico Divina
Rolf Drechsler
A.E. Eiben
Francisco Fernández de Vega
Kyrre Glette
Evert Haasdijk
J. Ignacio Hidalgo
Paul Kaufmann
Trung Thanh Nguyen
Petr Pošík
Robert Schaefer
Kevin Sim
Anabela Simões
Andrea G.B. Tettamanzi
Neil Urquhart
Mengjie Zhang
Nur Zincir-Heywood

Organization

Organizing Committee

EvoApplications Chair

Anna I. Esparcia-Alcázar   S2 Grupo, Spain

Local Co-chairs

Juan Julián Merelo   Universidad de Granada, Spain
Víctor M. Rivas   Universidad de Jaén, Spain

Proceedings Chair

Antonio M. Mora   Universidad de Granada, Spain

Publicity Co-chairs

Pablo García-Sánchez   Universidad de Granada, Spain
Mauro Castelli   Universidade Nova de Lisboa, Portugal

Webmaster

Kevin Sim   Edinburgh Napier University, UK

EvoCOMNET Co-chairs

Ivanoe De Falco   ICAR-CNR, Italy
Antonio Della Cioppa   University of Salerno, Italy
Ernesto Tarantino   ICAR-CNR, Italy

EvoCOMPLEX Co-chairs

Carlos Cotta   Universidad de Málaga, Spain
Robert Schaefer   AGH University of Science and Technology,
                 Poland

EvoENERGY Co-chairs

Paul Kaufmann   University of Paderborn, Germany
Kyrre Glette   University of Oslo, Norway

EvoFIN Co-chairs

Alexandros Agapitos   University College Dublin, Ireland
Andrea G.B. Tettamanzi Université de Nice Sophia Antipolis, France

EvoGAMES Co-chairs

Paolo Burelli   Aalborg University Copenhagen, Denmark
Antonio M. Mora   Universidad de Granada, Spain

EvoHOT Co-chairs

Rolf Drechsler   German Research Center for Artificial Intelligence,
                         Germany
Giovanni Squillero   Politecnico di Torino, Italy

EvoIASP Co-chairs

Stefano Cagnoni   University of Parma, Italy
Mengjie Zhang   Victoria University of Wellington, New Zealand

EvoINDUSTRY Co-chairs

Neil Urquhart   Edinburgh Napier University, UK
Kevin Sim   Edinburgh Napier University, UK

EvoNUM Co-chairs

Anna I. Esparcia-Alcázar S2 Grupo, Spain
Petr Pošík   Czech Technical University, Czech Republic

EvoPAR Co-chairs

Francisco Fernández de Vega University of Extremadura, Spain
J. Ignacio Hidalgo   Universidad Complutense de Madrid, Spain

EvoRISK Co-chairs

Anna I. Esparcia-Alcázar S2 Grupo, Spain
Nur Zincir-Heywood   Dalhousie University, Canada

EvoROBOT Co-chairs

Evert Haasdijk   VU University Amsterdam, The Netherlands
A.E. Eiben   VU University Amsterdam, The Netherlands

EvoSTOC Co-chairs

Anabela Simões   Polytechnic Institute of Coimbra, Portugal
Trung Thanh Nguyen   Liverpool John Moores University, UK

EvoBIO Co-chairs

William S. Bush   Vanderbilt University, USA
Federico Divina   Universidad Pablo de Olavide, Spain

Program Committees

EvoCOMNET Program Committee

Mehmet E. Aydin   University of Bedfordshire, UK
Frederick Ducatelle   IDSIA, Switzerland
Luca Gambardella   IDSIA, Switzerland
Rolf Hoffmann   Technical University Darmstadt, Germany
Farrukh Aslam Khan   National University of Computer and Emerging
                        Sciences, Pakistan
Kenji Leibnitz   National Institute of Information and
                        Communications Technology, Japan
Manuel Lozano Marquez   Universidad de Granada, Spain
Domenico Maisto   ICAR-CNR, Italy
Davide Marocco   University of Plymouth, UK
Roberto Montemanni   IDSIA, Switzerland
Enrico Natalizio   Université de Technologie de Compiègne,
                        France
Robert Schaefer   AGH University of Science and Technology,
                        Poland
Georgios Sirakoulis   Democritus University of Thrace, Greece
Pawel Topa   AGH University of Science and Technology,
                        Poland
Jaroslaw Was   AGH University of Science and Technology,
                        Poland
Lidia Yamamoto   University of Strasbourg, France

EvoCOMPLEX Program Committee

Anca Andreica	Babeş-Bolyai University, Romania
Tiago Baptista	University of Coimbra, Portugal
Antonio Córdoba	University of Seville, Spain
Carlos Fernandes	Technical University of Lisbon, Portugal
Carlos Gershenson	UNAM, Mexico
Juan Luis Jiménez Laredo	University of Luxembourg, Luxembourg
Iwona Karcz-Dulęba	Wrocław University of Technology, Poland
Joshua Payne	University of Zurich, Switzerland
Katya Rodríguez-Vázquez	UNAM, Mexico
Maciej Smołka	AGH University of Science and Technology, Poland
Marco Tomassini	University of Lausanne, Switzerland
Alberto Tonda	Politecnico di Torino, Italy

EvoENERGY Program Committee

Andy Tyrrell	University of York, UK
Frank Neumann	University of Adelaide, Australia
Jan Ringelstein	Fraunhofer Institure for Wind Technology and Energy System Technology, Germany
Kalyan Veeramachaneni	MIT Computer Science and Artificial Intelligence Laboratory, USA
Konrad Diwold	Fraunhofer Institute for Wind Technology and Energy System Technology, Germany
Maizura Mokhtar	University of Central Lancashire, UK
Martin Middendorf	University of Leipzig, Germany
Peter Palensky	Austrian Institute of Technology, Austria
Ralph Evins	Laboratory of Building Science and Technology, Switzerland
Sanaz Mostaghim	Karlsruhe Institute of Technology, Germany
Una-May O'Reilly	MIT Computer Science and Artificial Intelligence Laboratory, USA

EvoFIN Program Committee

Eva Alfaro Cid	Technical University of Valencia, Spain
Anthony Brabazon	University College Dublin, Ireland
Shu-Heng Chen	National Chengchi University, Taiwan
Wei Cui	University College Dublin, Ireland
Manfred Gilli	University of Geneva and Swiss Finance Institute, Switzerland

Ronald Hochreiter   University of Vienna, Austria
Mak Kaboudan   University of Redlands, USA
Piotr Lipinski   University of Wrocław, Poland
Dietmar Maringer   University of Basel, Switzerland
Serafin Martinez-Jaramillo   Bank of Mexico, Mexico
Wing Lon Ng   University of Essex, UK
Michael O'Neill   University College Dublin, Ireland
Nikolaos Thomaidis   University of the Aegean, Greece
Ruppa Thulasiram   University of Manitoba, Canada
Garnett Wilson   Afinin Labs Inc. and Dalhousie University,
                                         Canada

EvoGAMES Program Committee

David Camacho   Universidad Autónoma de Madrid, Spain
Antonio J. Fernandez Leiva   Universidad de Málaga, Spain
Pablo García Sánchez   Universidad de Granada, Spain
Antonio González Pardo   Universidad Autónoma de Madrid, Spain
Francisco Luís Gutiérrez Vela   Universidad de Granada, Spain
Johan Hagelback   Blekinge Tekniska Hagskola, Sweden
John Hallam   University of Southern Denmark, Denmark
Erin Hastings   University of Central Florida, USA
Philip Hingston   Edith Cowan University, Australia
Pier Luca Lanzi   Politecnico di Milano, Italy
Federico Liberatore   Invited Researcher at Universidad de Granada,
                                         Spain
Edgar Galvan Lopes   University College Dublin, Ireland
Simon Lucas   University of Essex, UK
Rodica Ioana Lung   Babes Bolyai University, Romania
Penousal Machado   University of Coimbra, Portugal
Hector P. Martínez   IT University of Copenhagem, Denmark
Patricia Paderewski   Universidad de Granada, Spain
Mike Preuss   TU Dortmund, Germany
Jan Quadflieg   TU Dortmund, Germany
Jacob Schrum   University of Texas at Austin, USA
Noor Shaker   IT University of Copenhagen, Denmark
Moshe Sipper   Ben-Gurion University, Israel
Terence Soule   University of Idaho, USA
Julian Togelius   IT University of Copenhagen, Denmark

EvoHOT Program Committee

Marco Gaudesi   Politecnico di Torino, Italy
Antonio M. Mora   Universidad de Granada, Spain
Julio Perez   Universidad de la República, Uruguay
Ernesto Sánchez   Politecnico di Torino, Italy
Alberto Tonda   Politecnico di Torino, Italy

EvoIASP Program Committee

Lucia Ballerini	University of Dundee, UK
Leonardo Bocchi	University of Florence, Italy
Oscar Cordón	Universidad de Granada, Spain
Sergio Damas	European Center of Soft Computing, Spain
Laura Dipietro	Massachusetts Institute of Technology, USA
Francesco Fontanella	Université degli studi di Cassino, Italy
Spela Ivekovic	University of Strathclyde, UK
Mario Koeppen	Kyushu Institute of Technology, Japan
Jean Louchet	Inria, France
Evelyne Lutton	INRA, France
Pablo Mesejo Santiago	University of Parma, Italy
Luca Mussi	University of Parma, Italy
Youssef Nashed	University of Parma, Italy
Ferrante Neri	De Montfort University, UK
Gustavo Olague	CICESE, Mexico
Riccardo Poli	University of Essex, UK
Sara Silva	INESC-ID, Portugal
Stephen Smith	University of York, UK
Kyoshi Tanaka	Shinshu University, Japan
Andy Tyrrell	University of York, UK
Roberto Ugolotti	University of Parma, Italy
Leonardo Vanneschi	Universidade Nova de Lisboa, Portugal

EvoINDUSTRY Program Committee

Bahriye Basturk Akay	Erciyes University, Turkey
Maria Arsuaga Rios	CERN, Switzerland
Jason Atkin	University of Nottingham, UK
Sima Etaner-Uyar	Istanbul Technical University, Turkey
Gurhan Kucuk	Yeditepe University, Turkey
John Levine	University of Strathclyde, UK
Nysret Musliu	Vienna University of Technology, Austria
Sanja Petrovic	University of Nottingham, UK
Nelishia Pillay	University of KwaZulu-Natal, South Africa
Rong Qu	University of Nottingham, UK
Sanem Sariel	Istanbul Technical University, Turkey
Shengxiang Yang	De Montfort University, UK

EvoNUM Program Committee

Wolfgang Banzhaf	Memorial University of Newfoundland, Canada
Hans-Georg Beyer	Vorarlberg University of Applied Sciences, Austria
Xavier Blasco	Universidad Politécnica de Valencia, Spain
Ying-ping Chen	National Chiao Tung University, Taiwan
Bill Langdon	University College London, UK
Salma Mesmoudi	Institut des Systèmes Complexes, France
Christian Lorenz Mueller	New York University, USA
Boris Naujoks	Cologne University of Applied Sciences, Germany
Ferrante Neri	De Montfort University, UK
Mike Preuss	WWU Münster, Germany
Ivo Fabian Sbalzarini	Max Planck Institute of Molecular Cell Biology and Genetics, Germany
Guenter Rudolph	TU Dortmund, Germany
P.N. Suganthan	Nanyang Technological University, Singapore
Olivier Teytaud	Inria, France
Şima Uyar	Istanbul Technical University, Turkey
Darrell Whitley	Colorado State University, USA

EvoPAR Program Committee

Jose Manuel Colmenar	Universidad Complutense de Madrid, Spain
Gianluigi Folino	L'ICAR-CNR, Cosenza, Italy
Malcolm Heywood	Dalhousie University, Canada
Juan L. Jiménez	University of Luxembourg, Luxembourg
William Langdon	University College London, UK
Francisco Luna	University of Extremadura, Spain
Una-May O'Reilly	MIT Computer Science and Artificial Intelligence Laboratory, USA
Jose Carlos Ribeiro	Politechnique Institute of Leiria, Portugal
Marco Tomassini	Lausanne University, Switzerland
Garnett Wilson	Afinin Labs Inc. and Dalhousie University, Canada

EvoRISK Program Committee

Hussein Abbass	UNSW@Australian Defence Force Academy, Australia
Robert K. Abercrombie	Oak Ridge National Laboratory, USA
Rami Abielmona	University of Ottawa, Canada
Anas Abou El Kalam	École Nationale Supérieure d'Ingénieurs de Bourges, France
Nabendu Chaki	University of Calcutta, India
Mario Cococcioni	NATO Undersea Research Centre, Italy

Josep Domingo-Ferrer	Rovira i Virgili University, Spain
Stenio Fernandes	Federal University of Pernambuco (UFPE), Brazil
Solange Ghernaouti-Hélie	University of Lausanne, Switzerland
Miguel Juan	S2 Grupo, Spain
Rabinarayan Mahapatra	Texas A&M University, USA
Antonio Manzalini	Telecom Italia, Italy
Owen McCusker	Sonalysts, USA
David Megias	Universitat Oberta de Catalunya, Spain
Javier Montero	Universidad Complutense de Madrid, Spain
Frank W. Moore	University of Alaska Anchorage, USA
Srinivas Mukkamala	New Mexico Tech, USA
Srini Ramaswamy	ABB Corporate Research Center, India
Martin Rehak	Czech Technical University, Czech Republic
Kouichi Sakurai	Kyushu University, Japan
Guillermo Suarez de Tangil	Universidad Carlos III de Madrid, Spain
Shamik Sural	Indian Institute of Technology, Kharagpur, India
Kay Chen Tan	National University of Singapore, Singapore
Vicenç Torra	CSIC, Spain
Shambhu Upadhyaya	State University of New York at Buffalo, USA
Antonio Villalón	S2 Grupo, Spain
Xinyuan (Frank) Wang	George Mason University, USA
Xin Yao	University of Birmingham, UK

EvoROBOT Program Committee

Nicolas Bredeche	Institut des Systémes Intelligents et de Robotique, France
Jeff Clune	Cornell University, USA
Stephane Doncieux	Institut des Systémes Intelligents et de Robotique
Marco Dorigo	Universite Libre de Bruxelles
Heiko Hamann	University of Paderborn, Germany
Jean-Marc Montanier	Norwegian University of Science and Technology, Norwey
Jean-Baptiste Mouret	Institut des Systémes Intelligents et de Robotique, France
Stefano Nolfi	Institute of Cognitive Sciences and Technologies, Italy
Claudio Rossi	Universidad Politécnica de Madrid, Spain
Sanem Sariel	Istanbul Teknik Universitesi, Turkey
Thomas Schmickl	Karl Franzens University Graz, Austria
Juergen Stradner	Karl Franzens University Graz, Austria
Jon Timmis	University of York, UK

Andy Tyrrell   University of York, UK
Berend Weel   Vrije Universiteit, The Netherlands
Alan Winfield   University of the West of England,
                                   UK

EvoSTOC Program Committee

Enrique Alba   Universidad de Málaga, Spain
Peter Bosman   Centre for Mathematics and Computer
                                   Science, The Netherlands
Juergen Branke   University of Warwick, UK
Lam Bui   Le Quy Don Technical University, Vietnam
Hui Cheng   University of Bedfordshire, UK
Ernesto Costa   University of Coimbra, Portugal
Andries Engelbrecht   University of Pretoria, South Africa
Sima Etaner-Uyar   Istanbul Technical University, Turkey
Yaochu Jin   University of Surrey, UK
Shayan Kavakeb   Liverpool John Moores University,
                                   UK
Changhe Li   China University of Geosciences, China
Michalis Mavrovouniotis   De Montfort University, UK
Jorn Mehnen   Cranfield University, UK
Ferrante Neri   De Montfort University, UK
David Pelta   Universidad de Granada, Spain
Hendrik Richter   HTWK Leipzig University, Germany
Philipp Rohlfshagen   SolveIT Software, Australia
Renato Tinos   Universidade de São Paulo, Brazil
Krzysztof Trojanowski   Polish Academy of Sciences, Poland
Shengxiang Yang   De Montfort University, UK
Xin Yao   University of Birmingham, UK

EvoBIO Program Committee

Jaume Bacardit   University of Nottingham, UK
Jacek Blazewicz   Poznan University of Technology, Poland
Florentino Fernández   University of Vigo, Spain
Alex Freitas   University of Kent, UK
Mario Giacobini   University of Turin, Italy
Raffaele Giancarlo   University of Palermo, Italy
Rosalba Giugno   University of Catania, Italy
Casey Greene   Dartmouth College, USA
Jin-Kao Hao   University of Angers, France
Ting Hu   Dartmouth College, USA
Mehmet Koyuturk   Case Western Reserve University, USA

Penousal Machado	University of Coimbra, Portugal
Elena Marchiori	Radboud University Nijmegen, The Netherlands
Marco Masseroli	Politecnico di Milano, Italy
Brett McKinney	University of Tulsa, USA
Pablo Moscato	The University of Newcastle, UK
Alison Motsinger-Reif	University of North Carolina Raleigh, USA
Vincent Moulton	University of East Anglia, UK
Carlotta Orsenigo	Politecnico di Milano, Italy
Michael Raymer	Wright State University, USA
Simona Rombo	ICAR-CNR, Italy
Marc Schoenauer	Inria Saclay Ile-de-France, France
Ugur Sezerman	Sabanci University, Turkey
Marc Smith	Vassar College, USA
Leonardo Vanneschi	ISEGI, Universidade Nova de Lisboa, Portugal
Andreas Zell	University of Tübingen, Germany
Zhongming Zhao	Vanderbilt University, USA

General Track Program Committee

Marco Gaudesi	Politecnico di Torino, Italy
Spela Ivekovic	University of Strathclyde, UK
Luca Mussi	University of Parma, Italy
Ernesto Sánchez	Politecnico di Torino, Italy
Giovanni Squillero	Politecnico di Torino, Italy
Alberto Tonda	Politecnico di Torino, Italy

Sponsoring Organizations

- Free Software Office (OSL) of the University of Granada.
- Granada Excellence Network of Innovation Laboratories (GENIL).
- Institute for Informatics and Digital Innovation at Edinburgh Napier University, Scotland, UK.
- The EvoCOMNET track has been technically sponsored by the World Federation on Soft Computing.

Contents

EvoENERGY

EvoFIN

EvoGAMES

EvoHOT

EvoIASP

EvoRISK

EvoROBOT

EvoSTOC

EvoBIO

General Track

EvoCOMNET

Evolving a Trust Model for Peer-to-Peer Networks Using Genetic Programming

Ugur Eray Tahta[1,2(✉)], Ahmet Burak Can[1], and Sevil Sen[1]

[1] Department of Computer Engineering, Hacettepe University, 06800 Ankara, Turkey
eraytahta@gmail.com
[2] ASELSAN, 06370 Ankara, Turkey

Abstract. Peer-to-peer (P2P) systems have attracted significant interest in recent years. In P2P networks, each peer act as both a server or a client. This characteristic makes peers vulnerable to a wide variety of attacks. Having robust trust management is very critical for such open environments to exclude unreliable peers from the system. This paper investigates the use of genetic programming to asses the trustworthiness of peers without a central authority. A trust management model is proposed in which each peer ranks other peers according to local trust values calculated automatically based on the past interactions and recommendations. The experimental results have shown that the model could successfully identify malicious peers without using a central authority or global trust values and, improve the system performance.

1 Introduction

In the last decade, with the fast expansion and improvement of peer-to-peer (P2P) systems, malicious activities have become a major security problem in P2P systems. Due to openness of P2P systems, unreliable users may occupy considerable portions of P2P populations. Trust management in such open environments is an important and difficult research problem. Trust management models generally aim to exclude unreliable peers from P2P systems. However maintaining true trust relationships without a priori knowledge is a very hard problem. It is difficult to distinguish malicious peers from innocent ones with a certainty in such environments. Thus, most of the proposed trust models in the literature offer approximate decision guidelines about peers.

Trust management can be accomplished by a central authority, such as eBay. Participants in eBay can rate each other at the end of auctions and information about auctions is stored in the central server. However, having a central authority conflicts with the nature of P2P systems. Thus peers need to organize themselves to manage and store information about their trust relationships [1–3]. In pure P2P networks like Gnutella [4], peers flood trust queries to the network in order to obtain trust information about others. In such a network, all peers store trust information about neighbors according to the past interactions [2,5,6]. Queries enable to collect recommendations about the queried peer and make a decision about it. Some models use distributed hash tables (DHT) to store

© Springer-Verlag Berlin Heidelberg 2014
A.I. Esparcia-Alcázar et al. (Eds.): EvoApplications 2014, LNCS 8602, pp. 3–14, 2014.
DOI: 10.1007/978-3-662-45523-4_1

trust information [1,3,7]. Each peer stores the trust information about other peers determined by a DHT algorithm, which enables efficient access to the information. Thus peers can learn the global trust information about others without flooding queries to the whole network.

Trust management in P2P systems is a difficult problem due to the lack of a central authority and uncertain information collected from peers. P2P trust models should be able to recognize complicated behavioral patterns of malicious peers and make smart decisions to distinguish malicious peers from benign peers using this uncertain information. Using machine learning techniques might be a good choice for such a complex problem. In this paper, we propose a genetic programming (GP) based trust management model. Our model intends to determine characteristics of malicious and benign peers using the features derived from peers. Two kinds of information are collected by peers: interactions and recommendations. Peers store their past interactions with other peers and collect recommendations about peers from their neighbors. These two types of information provide bases for the feature set. A trust model is evolved with these features by using genetic programming in order to measure trustworthiness of peers. Peers do not collect information about all other peers. A peer creates a view with the peers interacted in the past or intended to interact with. Each peer ranks other peers according to the trust values generated by the model which is evolved by using genetic programming, and makes download decisions using these values. Using the generated trust values, malicious peers are excluded from the system.

The paper is organized as follows. Section 2 discusses the related research. Section 3 introduces the proposed trust model. Section 4 presents the simulation environment and gives the experimental results. Section 5 summarizes the conclusion.

2   Related Work

P2P systems offer sharing environments for common resources by improving diversity, prevalence and easy accessibility. On the other hand, these characteristics make them vulnerable to many attacks. P2P systems can be divided into two groups; structured and unstructured [8]. In the unstructured overlay networks, queries are flooded in the network, such as in Gnutella [9]. The structured P2P networks generally utilize DHTs for indexing information on peers selected by the DHT algorithm. For example, Chord system [10] proposes a decentralized network with a distributed lookup primitive on a circular Chord ring. Peers on this ring are charged to store information determined by the Chord's algorithm.

Most of the prominent trust models use the reputation concept and statistical models to make decisions on trustworthiness of peers. Reputation generally relies on peer's past experiences and recommendations from other peers, such as in XRep [11] or P2PRep [12]. EigenRep [3] uses transitivity of trust to calculate trust values. Conner et al. [13] proposed a reputation-based trust management framework supporting synthesis of trust-related feedback from different entities.

In [14], an effective way of calculating reputation has been presented. The model considers several features such as number, age, or frequency of transactions, how frequently a given peer attends a common vendor, and the number of common vendors between the pairs. It aims to investigate the characteristics of transactions executed by malicious peers.

Detecting malicious peer behaviors with the help of machine learning techniques is another promising approach for generating trust management models. Weihua Song et al. [15] uses neural networks and derives trust values from heterogeneous agents based on recommendations. The agents classify recommendations as qualified or unqualified for choosing the providers. In [16], support vector machines are used to reduce the cost of communication with less query and to improve the success rate. In [17] a generic trust framework is proposed by using linear discriminant analysis and decision trees. An agent uses its own previous transactions (with other agents) to build a knowledge base and distinguishes successful transactions from unsuccessful ones.

There are some applications of evolutionary computation techniques to computer and network security in the literature. One of the mostly employed area is intrusion detection in which either genetic programming (GP) or genetic algorithm (GA) is mainly used. The first GP application to intrusion detection is given by Crosbie and Stafford [18]. Since then there are many useful applications to the field. In [19], Abraham and Grosan compare the genetic programming technique with other machine learning methods for intrusion detection [19] and show that genetic programming techniques outperform other techniques and are lightweight. The grammatical evolution technique is successfully employed for intrusion detection on wired networks [20] and on ad hoc networks [21]. Sen and Clark [22] employ multi-objective evolutionary computation (MOEC) techniques in order to show how energy usage and detection ability can be traded off for resource-constrained networks. Moreover, they show the significant potential of evolutionary computation techniques to explore the suitable intrusion detection architecture by taking into account the objectives of cooperative intrusion detection programs. The MOEC techniques are also used to explore how intrusion detection system sensors could be best placed on a network in [23].

Even though there are many applications of evolutionary computation techniques to the intrusion detection problem, as far as we know there is only one application of genetic algorithm in order to detect attackers in P2P domain. A peer profile based trust model proposed by Selvaraj et al. [24] uses genetic algorithm. This model combines peer profiling with an anomaly detection technique. It establishes trust using only local interaction data of the peer. There is a trusted central authority which manages the peer list to secure peers' IDs. Our model have used both interaction data from peer's own experience and recommendation data collected from other peers. Additionally, our model does not depend on a central authority to calculate trust values. This is believed to be a more suitable approach for P2P systems.

3   The Model

The proposed trust model uses genetic programming to make trusting decisions on peers. Genetic Programming (GP) is a common evolutionary computation technique, which is introduced to the machine learning community by Koza [25]. Banzhaf [26] comes up with an assertion that GP could produce more successful results comparing to other machine learning techniques and programs written by people.

In GP, functions (operators, program statements etc.) and terminals (features, constants etc.) build a GP tree. Each GP tree represents an individual. Basically, a group of individuals which are the candidate solutions to the problem are generated by GP in each generation. How well the individuals solve the problem is evaluated by using a fitness function.

3.1   Feature Sets and Operators

Selecting the right feature set is a difficult problem and a key point to obtain successful results in GP and other machine learning techniques [27]. In our model, the information collected from past interactions and recommendations of neighbors form the feature set.

Interaction based features are obtained from the peer's past experiences with other peers. These experiences occur directly between two peers who interacted in the past. Interactions can be any activity specific to the P2P application, such as file sharing, CPU sharing, and storage sharing. Interaction based features are listed in Table 1.

Table 1. Interaction Based Features

Feature	Symbol
number of interactions	f1
number of successful interactions	f2
average size of downloaded files	f3
average time difference between last two interactions	f4
average weight	f5
average satisfaction	f6

Satisfaction and weight parameters are calculated as in [28]. Successful interactions are the interactions that the file download is finished successfully. Satisfaction parameter is calculated based on average bandwidth, agreed bandwidth before the interaction, online, and offline period values of the uploader:

$$Satisfaction = \begin{cases} (\frac{AveBw}{AgrBw} + \frac{OnP}{OnP+OffP})/2 \ if \ AveBw < AgrBw, \\ (1 + \frac{OnP}{OnP+OffP})/2 \qquad otherwise \end{cases} \quad (1)$$

Weight parameter is calculated based on file size, number of uploaders of the dowloaded file, number of uploaders of the maximum uploaded file:

$$Weight = \begin{cases} (\frac{size}{100MB} + \frac{\#Uploaders}{Uploader_{max}})/2 \; if \; size < 100MB, \\ (1 + \frac{\#Uploaders}{Uploader_{max}})/2 \quad\quad otherwise \end{cases} \tag{2}$$

The second set of features is recommendation based features. When a peer wants to interact with another peer, it asks its own neighbors about their experiences. The neighbors who have information about the peer requested send their recommendations. These experiences about another peer are called recommendations. A recommendation contains the following information: average number of successful interactions, average satisfaction of interactions, average weight of interactions, and calculated trust value of the queried peer. The recommendation based features are listed in Table 2:

Table 2. Recommendation Based Features

Feature	Symbol
number of recommendations	f7
average of neighbours' average number of successful interactions	f8
average of neighbours' average satisfaction values	f9
average of neighbours' average weight values	f10
average of trust values	f11

In our genetic model, we use simple operators to generate a formula for trust calculation. The operators used in our model are addition, subtraction, division, multiplication, inverse, log, square root, and square.

3.2 Fitness Function

The fitness function is one of the important factors affecting the performance of evolutionary computation techniques. The fitness function determines how well a program is able to solve the problem [25, 29]. In the evolved trust model, a fitness function based on the reduction in the number of attacks is used. In other words, if R_{trust} denotes the number of attacks with our trust model and $R_{noTrust}$ denotes the number of attacks without any trust model, then our fitness function is;

$$fitness = R_{trust}/R_{noTrust}. \tag{3}$$

If the generated individuals can mitigate the number of attacks, the value of fitness function decreases and the success of the model increases. Thus, the fitness function is aimed to be minimized in our genetic model. At the end of the evolution, the most successful individual is selected as the solution.

4   Experiments and Analysis

The experiment environment consists of two integrated modules. First one is a file sharing simulation program implemented in Java language to asses the evolved trust model in P2P environments against malicious attacks. The second one is the ECJ 21 toolkit [30] for the GP implementation. It is integrated with the simulation program to train the trust model. In the experiments, the population and generation sizes are chosen as 100 and 300 respectively. The other parameters are equal to the default parameters of the ECJ toolkit.

4.1   Simulation Module

The simulation module is adapted from the program used in [28]. Each simulation takes 50.000 cycles, where each cycle represents 10 minutes of network activity. There are 1000 peers in each simulation. Basically, peers interact with each other for sharing a file and build a reputation according to their behaviors. At the beginning of the simulation, peers are strangers to each other. When a peer uploads a file to another peer, it becomes a neighbor of the peer. A neighbor is preferred over a stranger if they are equally trustworthy.

Peers build an interaction history while downloading and uploading files. If a peer intends to download a file, it gets the list of file providers. Then, it calculates the trust values of these file providers using its own interaction history and recommendations from its neighbors. Trust values are calculated based on the formula generated by the genetic programming module using the features and the fitness function explained in Section 3. If a peer has neighbors in the file provider list, it prefers the one with the highest trust value. Otherwise, it downloads the file from the stranger who has the highest trust value. At the end of a download process, if the file provider uploads a virus infected or an inauthentic file, it is marked as a malicious peer and is never interacted again.

4.2   GP Module

The GP module works in an integrated manner with the simulation module. It trains our trust model against various attacker types and tries to find the best individual in order to evaluate trust values of peers. In the training process, GP creates individuals by using the features and the operators given in Section 3.1. Each individual runs the file sharing simulation from start to finish. Reduction in the number of attacks represents the success of an individual. When the best individual is found, it is tested on various attacker models on the simulation module. The general steps of the GP Module are listed in Algorithm 1.

4.3   The Problem

Generally, a P2P network consists of good peers and malicious peers (attacker). A good peer always gives fair recommendations and uploads authentic files.

Algorithm 1. How Gp Module Works

initialize population
while current generation $<=$ maximum generation **do**
    for all individuals in the current generation **do**
        execute simulation
        evaluate the fitness function
    end for
    apply genetic operators (selection, crossover, reproduction, mutation, etc.) to the individuals
    create new population
end while

However, a malicious peer may upload inauthentic files or give unfair recommendations to harm the system. Reducing the number of inauthentic/infected file uploads and unfair recommendations is the aim of a trust management model.

In our simulation, malicious peers are considered to behave in two different ways: naive and hypocritical. If malicious peers perform unaccompanied attacks and do not aware of other malicious peers, they are called individual attackers. Individual attackers can behave as described below:

- *Naive:* The attacker always uploads virus infected/inauthentic files and gives unfair recommendations to others [31].
- *Hypocritical:* The attacker perform attacks by uploading inauthentic files or giving unfair recommendations with x% probability. Otherwise, it acts like a good peer [3,5].

If a group of peers know each other and attack to other peers as a team, they are called collaborators. Collaborators always upload authentic files to each other. If a good peer requests a recommendation from a collaborator about another collaborator, the collaborator might give high recommendations unfairly in order to improve the queried collaborator's trust value. The types of attack carried out by collaborators are be described as follows:

- *Naive:* Collaborators always upload virus infected/inauthentic files to good peers and gives unfair recommendations to good peers.
- *Hypocritical:* Collaborators perform attacks by uploading inauthentic files to good peers or giving unfair recommendations with x% probability. Otherwise, it acts like a good peer.

4.4   Experiments

In the experiments, the model is trained for all types of individual attackers firstly. Training is done with a network setup in which 10% of the peers is malicious. The best results of 10 runs is chosen for each attack type. Then, the trained model is tested with 10%, 30% and 50% malicious peers ratio in the networks. During the experiments, the attack probability of hypocritical attackers is chosen as 20% in all interactions. If a peer uploads a virus infected or inauthentic file, it is counted as a file-based attack. Initially, the simulation is executed without the trust model for each network setting in order to figure out

Table 3. Success ratio of the trust model against individual attackers for the file-based attacks

	10%	30%	50%
Naive	83.8	78.9	73.6
Hypocritical	71.8	57.7	47.1

the number of attacks when a trust model does not exist. Then the simulations are run with the evolved trust model. Success of the trust model is assessed by the number of attacks prevented with the model.

Table 3 shows the success ratio of the evolved trust model against individual attackers according to varying malicious peer populations in the network. The model has a notable success against individual naive attackers. Since identifying a naive attacker is easy after the first interaction, a high percentage of these attacks can be prevented. Our model has a good success ratio for individual hypocritical attackers, which is 71.8% in a network in which 10% of the peers is malicious. In the network in which 50% of the peers is malicious, the trust model could prevent nearly half of the attacks as shown in Table 3. In such extremely malicious networks, this is a good success ratio for hypocritical attackers.

Convergence speed of the trust model is important to identify attacks in a reasonable time. Figure 1 shows the decrement in the number of attacks by naive and hypocritical individual attackers when the evolved trust model is used.

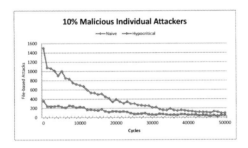

Fig. 1. File-based attacks over time in a network consisting of 10% individual attackers

Unfair recommendations given by malicious peers are considered as recommendation-based attacks. The evolved trust model has also good performance on recommendation-based attacks. Figure 2 shows the decrement in the recommendation-based attacks over time. In the model, if a peer intends to collect recommendations about another peer, it firstly requests recommendations from its trustworthy neighbors. Therefore, unfair recommendation rate is mitigated over time as peers gain more neighbors. However, unfair recommendations do not drop as quickly as file-based attacks since determining an unfair recommendation is not easy as determining an infected/inauthentic file.

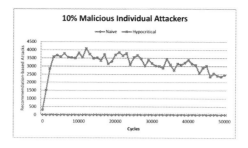

Fig. 2. Recommendation-based attacks over time in a network consisting of 10% individual attackers

The second step of the experiments is done with collaborative attackers. Like individual attackers, at first the model is trained against the collaborators, and then tested on various malicious network setups. Collaborators attack to other peers as a team and give fair recommendations to each other. The attack probability of hypocritical attackers is chosen as 20% in all interactions in the experiments. The team size of collaborators is set to 50 peers.

Table 4. Success ratio of the trust model against collaborators for the file-based attacks

	10%	30%	50%
Naive	79.3	75.1	71.9
Hypocritical	61.7	46.3	39.5

Table 4 shows the success ratio of the trust model against collaborators in networks consisting of varying malicious peer population. Naive collaborators are identified by good peers after the first interaction. Hence they can not disseminate high recommendations about each other and can not take advantage of collaboration. The success ratio of preventing attacks in naive collaborators is 79.3% in a network in which 10% of the peers is malicious and, this performance drops to only 71.9% even the ratio of malicious peers is increased to 50%. However, hypocritical collaborators are more effective than naive ones. Detection of hypocritical collaborators is more difficult since they perform attacks intermittently. A hypocritical collaborator can disseminate high recommendations about its team mates before being identified by good peers. Since the collaborators help each other in order to evade detection, their identifications become very difficult. However, the trust model could still prevent 61.7% of file-based attacks carried out by hypocritical collaborators in a network in which 10% of peers is malicious. Figure 3 shows the number of file-based attacks over time in a network consisting of 10% collaborators. The model decreases the number of effective attacks carried out by naive and hypocritical collaborators dramatically.

Recommendation-based attacks carried out by collaborators are presented in Figure 4. High recommendations given by collaborators unfairly are also counted

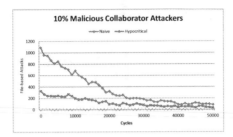

Fig. 3. File-based attacks over time in a network consisting of 10% collaborators

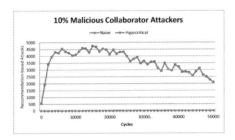

Fig. 4. Recommendation-based attacks over time in a network consisting of 10% collaborators

as recommendation-based attacks. Collaboration increases the number of misleading recommendations slightly. However, the trust model still mitigates the number of recommendation-based attacks. It also prevents misleading recommendations to increase over time.

5   Conclusion

This paper proposes a trust model evolved by using genetic programming. Trust values of peers are calculated by a formula generated by this model. Malicious and benign peers are distinguished from each other based on these trust values. The experimental results show that the model could distinguish different types of attacks from benign behavior of good peers successfully. Naive and hypocritical attacker models are studied with individual and collaborative behaviors. The model is trained against these types of attacks and evaluated on various network setups containing different ratio of malicious peers. Naive attackers are identified easily in both individual and collaborator scenarios. Hypocritical attackers are more difficult to deal with and more successful when they collaborate. The evolved trust model has decreased the number of file-based attacks in all scenarios with promising success ratios. Recommendation-based attacks are mitigated but not decreased as much as file-based attacks due to the difficulty of recognizing misleading recommendations. The evolved model showed that genetic programming could be employed to build a trust model in peer-to-peer networks.

References

1. Aberer, K., Despotovic, Z.: Managing trust in a peer-2-peer information system. In: Proc. 10th International Conference on Information and Knowledge Management (CIKM). ACM (2001)
2. Cornelli, F., Damiani, E., di Vimercati, S.D.C., Paraboschi, S., Samarati, P.: Choosing reputable servents in a p2p network. In: Proc. of the 11h Int. World Wide Web Conf., May 7–11 (2002)
3. Kamvar, S.D., Schlosser, M.T., Garcia-Molina, H.: The eigentrust algorithm for reputation management in p2p networks. In: Proc. of the 12th International Conference on World Wide Web, WWW 2003, pp. 640–651. ACM (2003)
4. Clip2, The gnutella protocol specification v0.4 (document revision 1.2) (2001). http://www.clip2.com/GnutellaProtocol04.pdf
5. Selcuk, A.A., Uzun, E., Pariente, M.R.: A reputation-based trust management system for p2p networks. In: Proc. of the IEEE International Symposium on Cluster Computing and the Grid, CCGRID 2004, pp. 251–258. IEEE Computer Society (2004)
6. Zhou, R., Hwang, K., Cai, M.: Gossiptrust for fast reputation aggregation in peer-to-peer networks. IEEE Trans. on Knowl. and Data Eng. 20(9), 1282–1295 (2008)
7. Xiong, L., Liu, L.: Peertrust: Supporting reputation-based trust for peer-to-peer electronic communities. IEEE Trans. on Knowl. and Data Eng. 16(7), 843–857 (2004)
8. Xiao, L., Liu, Y., Ni, L.M.: Improving unstructured peer-to-peer systems by adaptive connection establishment. IEEE Transactions on Computers 54(9), 1091–1103 (2005)
9. Stakhanova, N., Ferrero, S., Wong, J.S., Cai, Y.: A reputation-based trust management in peer-to-peer network systems. In: ISCA PDCS, ISCA, pp. 510–515 (2004)
10. Brunskill, E.: Building peer-to-peer systems with chord, a distributed lookup service. In: Proc. of the Eighth Workshop on Hot Topics in Operating Systems, HOTOS 2001, p. 81. IEEE Computer Society (2001)
11. Damiani, E., Vimercati, D.C.D., Paraboschi, S., Samarati, P., Violante, F.: A reputation-based approach for choosing reliable resources in peer-to-peer networks. In: Proc. of the 9th ACM Conference on Computer and Communications Security, pp. 207–216. ACM Press (2002)
12. Damiani, E., De Capitani di Vimercati, S., Paraboschi, S., Samarati, P.: Managing and sharing servents' reputations in p2p systems. IEEE Transactions on Knowledge and Data Engineering (TKDE) 15(4) (July/August 2003)
13. Conner, W., Iyengar, A., Mikalsen, T.A., Rouvellou, I., Nahrstedt, K.: A trust management framework for service-oriented environments. In: WWW 2009. ACM, pp. 891–900 (2009)
14. Prasad, R.V.V.S.V., Srinivas, V., Kumari, V.V., Raju, K.V.S.V.N.: An effective calculation of reputation in p2p networks. JNW 4(5), 332–342 (2009)
15. Song, W., Phoha, V.V., Xu, X: An adaptive recommendation trust model in multiagent system. In: IAT. IEEE Computer Society, pp. 462–465 (2004)
16. Beverly, R., Afergan, M.: Machine learning for efficient neighbor selection in unstructured p2p networks. In: Proc. of the 2nd USENIX Workshop on Tackling Computer Systems Problems with Machine Learning Techniques, SYSML 2007, pp. 1:1–1:6. USENIX Association (2007)

17. Liu, X., Tredan, G., Datta, A.: A generic trust framework for large-scale open systems using machine learning, CoRR, abs/1103.0086 (2011)
18. Crosbie, M., Stafford, G.: Applying genetic programming to intrusion detection. In: Proc. of AAAI Symposium on Genetic Programming, pp. 1–8. Cambridge, MA (1995)
19. Abraham, A., Grosan, C.: Evolving intrusion detection systems. In: Genetic Systems Programming: Theory and Experiences, vol. 13, pp. 57–79. Springer (2006)
20. Wilson, D., Kaur, D.: Knowledge extraction from kdd'99 intrusion data using grammatical evolution. WSEAS Transactions on Information Science and Applications **4**, 237–244 (2007)
21. Sen, S., Clark, J.A.: A grammatical evolution approach to intrusion detection on mobile ad hoc networks. In: Proc. of the Second ACM Conference on Wireless Network Security, pp. 95–102. ACM (2009)
22. Sen, S., Clark, J.: Evolutionary computation techniques for intrusion detection in mobile ad hoc networks. Computer Networks **55**(15), 3441–3457 (2011)
23. Chen, H., Clark, J.A., Tapiador, J.E., Shaikh, S.A., Chivers, H., Nobles, P.: A Multi-objective Optimisation Approach to IDS Sensor Placement. In: Herrero, A., Gastaldo, P., Zunino, R., Corchado, E. (eds.) CISIS 2009. ASC, vol. 63, pp. 101–108. Springer, Heidelberg (2009)
24. Selvaraj, C., Anand, S.: Peer profile based trust model for p2p systems using genetic algorithm. Peer-to-Peer Networking and Applications **5**(1), 92–103 (2012)
25. Koza, J.R.: Genetic Programming: On the Programming of Computers by Means of Natural Selection. MIT Press, Cambridge (1992)
26. Banzhaf, W., Francone, F.D., Keller, R.E., Nordin, P.: Genetic programming: an introduction: on the automatic evolution of computer programs and its applications. Morgan Kaufmann Publishers Inc., San Francisco (1998)
27. Hall, M.A.: Correlation-based feature selection for machine learning, Ph.D. dissertation (1999)
28. Can, A.B., Bhargava, B.: Sort: A self-organizing trust model for peer-to-peer systems. IEEE Trans. Dependable Sec. Comput. **10**(1), 14–27 (2013)
29. Cramer, N.L.: A representation for the adaptive generation of simple sequential programs. In: Grefenstette, J.J. (ed.) ICGA, pp. 183–187. Lawrence Erlbaum Associates (1985)
30. Ecj 21: A java-based evolutionary computation and genetic programming research system (2013). http://www.cs.umd.edu/projects/plus/ec/ecj/
31. Dellarocas, C., Immunizing online reputation reporting systems against unfair ratings and discriminatory behavior. In: Proc. of the 2nd ACM Conference on Electronic Commerce, EC 2000, pp. 150–157. ACM (2000)

A Hybrid Primal Heuristic for Robust Multiperiod Network Design

Fabio D'Andreagiovanni[1,2]([⊠]), Jonatan Krolikowski[2], and Jonad Pulaj[2]

[1] DFG Research Center MATHEON, Technical University Berlin,
Straße des 17. Juni 135, 10623 Berlin, Germany
[2] Department of Optimization, Zuse-Institute Berlin (ZIB),
Takustr. 7, 14195 Berlin, Germany
{d.andreagiovanni,krolikowski,pulaj}@zib.de

Abstract. We investigate the Robust Multiperiod Network Design Problem, a generalization of the classical Capacitated Network Design Problem that additionally considers multiple design periods and provides solutions protected against traffic uncertainty. Given the intrinsic difficulty of the problem, which proves challenging even for state-of-the art commercial solvers, we propose a hybrid primal heuristic based on the combination of ant colony optimization and an exact large neighborhood search. Computational experiments on a set of realistic instances from the SNDlib show that our heuristic can find solutions of extremely good quality with low optimality gap.

Keywords: Multiperiod Network Design · Traffic Uncertainty · Robust Optimization · Multiband Robustness · Hybrid Heuristics

1 Introduction

The design of a telecommunication network can be essentially described as the task of establishing the topology of the network and the technological features (e.g., transmission capacity and rate) of its elements, namely nodes and links. The dramatic growth that telecommunications have experienced over the last ten years has greatly increased the complexity and difficulty of the corresponding design problems. The growing need for taking into account data uncertainty, such as that of traffic volumes, has made things even more complicated. In this context, the traditional design approach of professionals, based on a combination of trial-and-error and simulation, may lead to arbitrarily bad design solutions and thus the need for optimization-oriented approaches has arisen.

In this paper, we focus on the development of a new Robust Optimization model to tackle traffic uncertainty in a Multiperiod Network Design Problem

This work was partially supported by the *German Research Foundation* (DFG), project *Multiperiod Network Optimization*, by the DFG Research Center Matheon (www.matheon.de), Project B3, and by the *German Federal Ministry of Education and Research* (BMBF), project *ROBUKOM* [1], grant 05M10PAA.

© Springer-Verlag Berlin Heidelberg 2014
A.I. Esparcia-Alcázar et al. (Eds.): EvoApplications 2014, LNCS 8602, pp. 15–26, 2014.
DOI: 10.1007/978-3-662-45523-4_2

(MP-NDP). This problem constitutes a natural extension of a classical network design problem, in which we want to decide how to install capacity modules in the network in order to route traffic flows of communications generated by users. The extension implies the design over a time horizon made up of multiple periods. Moreover, traffic uncertainty is taken into account to protect design solutions against deviations of the traffic input data, that may compromise feasibility and optimality of solutions. To the best of our knowledge, the (MP-NDP) has received little attention and just a few works have investigated it (primarily, [2] and [3]). These works point out the difficulty of solving multiperiod problems already for just two periods and (easier) splittable-flow routing [2], and for a pure routing problem in satellite communications [3]. Our direct and more recent computational experience confirmed this behaviour, even for instances of moderate size considering a low number of time periods and solved by a state-of-the-art commercial mixed-integer programming solver.

In this work, our main original contributions are:

1. the first Robust Optimization model for Multiperiod Network Design. The formulation is developed to tackle traffic uncertainty, modeling data uncertainty by Multiband Robustness [4–6], a new model for Robust Optimization recently introduced to refine the classical Bertsimas-Sim model [7];
2. a hybrid solution algorithm, based on the combination of an exact large neighborhood search called RINS [8] with ant colony optimization [9];
3. computational experiments over a set of realistic instances derived from SNDlib, the Survivable Network Design Library [10], showing that our hybrid algorithm is able to produce solutions of extremely high quality associated with very small optimality gap.

The remainder of this paper is organized as follows: in Section 2, we review a canonical network model for joint routing and capacity installation; in Section 3, we introduce the new formulation for Robust Multiperiod Network Design; in Sections 4 and 5, we present our hybrid metaheuristic and computational results.

2   Capacitated Network Design

The *Capacitated Network Design Problem* (CNDP) can be described as follows: given a network and a set of demands whose flows must be routed between vertices of the network, we want to install capacities on network edges and route the flows through the network, so that the capacity constraint of each edge is respected and the total cost of installing capacity is minimized. The CNDP has been a central and highly studied problem in Network Optimization, that appears in a wide variety of real-world applications. For an exhaustive introduction to the topic, we refer the reader to the well-known book [11].

The CNDP is commonly formalized in the following way: we are given 1) a network represented by a graph $G(V, E)$, where V is the set of vertices and E the set of edges; 2) a set of commodities C, each associated with a traffic flow d_c to route from an origin s_c to a destination t_c; 3) a set of admissible paths P_c

for routing the flow of each commodity c from s_c to t_c; 4) a cost γ_e for installing one module of capacity $\phi > 0$ on edge $e \in E$. Using this notation, we can model the problem as an *integer linear program*:

$$\min \sum_{e \in E} \gamma_e \, y_e \hspace{4cm} \text{(CNDP-IP)}$$

$$\sum_{c \in C} \sum_{p \in P_c : e \in p} d_c \, x_{cp} \leq \phi \, y_e \hspace{2cm} e \in E \hspace{1cm} (1)$$

$$\sum_{p \in P_c} x_{cp} = 1 \hspace{3cm} c \in C \hspace{1cm} (2)$$

$$x_{cp} \in \{0, 1\} \hspace{3cm} c \in C, p \in P_c$$

$$y_e \in \mathbb{Z}_+ \hspace{3.5cm} e \in E \,,$$

The problem uses two families of variables: the binary variables x_{cp} (*path-assignment variables*) and the non-negative integer variables y_e (*capacity variables*). A path-assignment variable x_{cp} is equal to 1 if the entire flow of a commodity $c \in C$ is routed through path $p \in P_c$ and 0 otherwise. A capacity variable y_e represents instead the number of capacity modules installed on edge $e \in E$. The objective function minimizes the total cost of installation. Capacity constraints (1) impose that the summation of all flows routed through an edge $e \in E$ must not exceed the capacity installed on e (equal to the number of installed modules represented by y_e multiplied by the capacity ϕ granted by a single module). Constraints (2) impose that flow of each commodity $c \in C$ must be routed through a single path.

Remark 1. This is an unsplittable version of the CNDP, namely the traffic flow of a commodity $c \in C$ *cannot be split* over multiple paths going from s_c to t_c, but must be routed on exactly one path. Moreover, the set of feasible routing paths P_c of each commodity is pre-established and constitutes an input of the problem. This is in line with other works based on industrial cooperations (e.g., [12]) and with our experience [1], in which a network operator typically considers just a few paths that meet its own specific business and quality-of-service considerations.

3   Multiband-Robust Multiperiod Network Design

We introduce now a generalization of the CNDP, designing the network over multiple time periods and taking into account traffic uncertainty. The multiperiod design requires the introduction of a time horizon made up of a set of elementary time periods $T = \{1, 2, \ldots, |T|\}$. From a modeling point of view, in the optimization problem we simply need to add a new index $t \in T$ to the decision variables, to represent routing and capacity installation decisions taken in each period (we stress however that this greatly increases the size and complexity of the problem).

Concerning traffic uncertainty, we assume that for each commodity $c \in C$ the demand d_c is *uncertain*, i.e. its value is not known exactly, but lies in a known range. More specifically, we assume to know a nominal value of traffic $\bar{d}_c$ and maximum negative and positive deviations δ_c^-, δ_c^+ from it. The actual value d_c thus belongs to the interval: $d_c \in [\bar{d}_c - \delta_c^-, \ \bar{d}_c + \delta_c^+]$.

Example 1 (traffic uncertainty). We are given two commodities c_1, c_2 with nominal traffic demands $\bar{d}_{c_1} = 100$ Mb, $\bar{d}_{c_2} = 150$ Mb and we know that these values may deviate up to 10%. So the maximum negative and positive deviations for c_1, c_2 are $\delta_{c_1}^- = \delta_{c_1}^+ = 10$ Mb, $\delta_{c_2}^- = \delta_{c_2}^+ = 15$ Mb, respectively. The actual values of traffic are then $d_{c_1} \in [90, 110]$ Mb, $d_{c_2} \in [135, 165]$ Mb.

The presence of uncertain data in an optimization problem can be very tricky: it is well-known that even small variations in the value of input data may make an optimal solution heavily suboptimal, whereas feasible solutions may reveal to be infeasible and thus completely useless in practice [13]. As a consequence, in our case we cannot optimize just using the nominal demand values $\bar{d}_c$, but we must take into account the possibility that demands will vary in the ranges $[\bar{d}_c - \delta_c^-, \ \bar{d}_c + \delta_c^+]$ that we have characterized. We illustrate the bad effects of input data deviations by providing an example.

Example 2 (infeasibility caused by deviations). Consider again the commodities of Example 1 and suppose that in some link we have installed exactly the capacity to handle the sum of their nominal values (i.e. we have installed $100+150$ Mb of capacity). This capacity dimensioning neglects that the demands may deviate up to 10%. It is sufficient that one demand increases, while the other remains the same to violate the capacity constraint of the link, making the design solution infeasible in practice.

Over the years, many methods such as *Stochastic Programming* and *Robust Optimization* have been proposed in literature for dealing with data uncertainty in optimization problems. We refer the reader to [13] for a general discussion about data uncertainty and its effects and for an overview of the most studied methodologies to deal with them.

In this paper, we tackle data uncertainty by Robust Optimization (RO), a methodology that has gained a lot of attention over the last decade [7,13]. RO essentially takes into account data uncertainty by including additional hard constraints in the optimization problem. These constraints eliminate those solutions that are not protected against deviations of the input data from their nominal values. So a robust optimization problem considers only those solutions that are completely protected against specified data deviations. The data deviations that are considered are specified through a so-called *uncertainty set*. More formally, suppose that we are given a generic linear program:

$$v = \max \ c'x \ \text{with} \ x \in \mathcal{F} = \{Ax \le b, \ x \ge 0\}$$

and that the coefficient matrix A is uncertain, i.e. we do not know exactly the value of its entries. However, we are able to identify a family $\mathcal{A}$ of coefficient matrices that represent possible valorizations of the uncertain matrix A, i.e. $A \in \mathcal{A}$. This family represents the uncertainty set of the robust problem. Then we can produce a *robust optimal solution*, i.e. a solution that is protected against data deviations, by considering the *robust counterpart* of the original problem:

$$v^{\mathcal{R}} = \max \ c'x \ \text{with} \ x \in \mathcal{R} = \{\tilde{A}x \le b \ \forall \tilde{A} \in \mathcal{A}, \ x \ge 0\} \ .$$

The feasible set $\mathcal{R}$ of the robust counterpart contains only those solutions that are feasible for all the coefficient matrices in the uncertainty set $\mathcal{A}$. Therefore, $\mathcal{R}$ is a subset of the feasible set of the original problem, i.e. $\mathcal{R} \subseteq \mathcal{F}$. The choice of the coefficient matrices included in $\mathcal{A}$ should reflect the risk aversion of the decision maker.

Providing protection entails the so-called *price of robustness*, namely a deterioration of the optimal value of the robust counterpart w.r.t. the optimal value of the original problems (i.e., $v^{\mathcal{R}} \leq v$). This is a consequence of restricting the feasible set to only robust solutions. The price of robustness reflects the features of the uncertainty set: uncertainty sets expressing higher risk aversion will take into account more severe and unlikely deviations, leading to higher protection but also higher price of robustness; conversely, uncertainty sets expressing risky attitudes will tend to neglect improbable deviations, offering less protection but also a reduced price of robustness.

Example 3 (protection against deviations). Following example 2, a simple way to grant protection would be to install sufficient capacity to deal with the peak deviations of each commodity. So we should install 110+165 Mb of capacity.

3.1 A Robust Optimization Model for Traffic-Uncertain Multiperiod Network Design

If we denote by $\mathcal{D}$ the uncertainty set associated with the demands of the commodities, we can finally state the general form of the robust counterpart of the multiperiod network design problem as follows:

$$\min \sum_{e \in E} \sum_{t \in T} \gamma_{et} \, y_{et}$$

$$\sum_{c \in C} \sum_{p \in P_c : e \in p} \bar{d}_{ct} \, x_{cpt} + DEV_{et}(x, \mathcal{D}) \leq \phi \sum_{\tau=1}^{t} y_{e\tau} \qquad e \in E, t \in T \qquad (3)$$

$$\sum_{p \in P_c} x_{cpt} = 1 \qquad c \in C, t \in T$$

$$x_{cpt} \in \{0, 1\} \qquad c \in C, p \in P_c, t \in T$$

$$y_{et} \in \mathbb{Z}_+ \qquad e \in E, t \in T \,,$$

Besides the addition of a new index $t \in T$ in the decision variables to represent decisions taken in each time period, the modifications of the model concentrates in the robust capacity constraints (3). Each of these constraints considers: 1) the sum of *nominal* traffic demands $\bar{d}_{ct}$ of commodities using the edge e in period t; 2) the overall maximum positive deviation $DEV_{et}(x, \mathcal{D})$ that demands may experience on edge e in period t and are allowed by the uncertainty set $\mathcal{D}$ for a routing vector x; 3) the overall capacity installed in e since the first period of the horizon (so we sum up the integer variables $y_{e\tau}$ from period 1 to t and multiply them by the basic capacity ϕ of a module).

Structuring the Uncertainty Set $\mathcal{D}$. We now have a general definition of the robust counterpart of the multiperiod problem. A question that is still open is how to structure the uncertainty set $\mathcal{D}$ and deciding which deviations from the nominal traffic values $\bar{d}_{ct}$ to take into account to produce robust solutions.

To characterize $\mathcal{D}$, we use *Multiband Robustness*, a new model for Robust Optimization recently introduced to refine and generalize the classical Γ-robustness model by Bertsimas and Sim [7], while maintaining its accessibility and tractability. For a detailed explanation of Multiband Robustness we refer the reader to [4–6]. Here we directly discuss the adaption of the model to our specific case.

According to the multiband framework, we build a *multiband uncertainty set* as follows:

1. for each commodity $c \in C$ and time period $t \in T$, we know the nominal value $\bar{d}_{ct}$ of the traffic coefficient and maximum negative and positive deviations $\delta_{ct}^-, \delta_{ct}^+$ from it. The actual value d_{ct} is then such that $d_{ct} \in [\bar{d}_{ct} - \delta_{ct}^-, \ \bar{d}_{ct} + \delta_{ct}^+]$;
2. the overall deviation range $[\bar{d}_{ct} - \delta_{ct}^-, \ \bar{d}_{ct} + \delta_{ct}^+]$ of each coefficient d_c^t is partitioned into K bands, defined on the basis of K deviation values:
$$-\infty < \delta_{ct}^- = \delta_{ct}^{K^-} < \cdots < \delta_{ct}^{-1} < \delta_{ct}^0 = 0 < \delta_{ct}^1 < \cdots < \delta_{ct}^{K^+} = \delta_{ct}^+ < +\infty;$$
3. through these deviation values, K deviation bands are defined, namely: a set of positive deviation bands $k \in \{1, \ldots, K^+\}$ and a set of negative deviation bands $k \in \{K^- + 1, \ldots, -1, 0\}$, such that a band $k \in \{K^- + 1, \ldots, K^+\}$ corresponds to the range $(\delta_{ij}^{k-1}, \delta_{ij}^k]$, and band $k = K^-$ corresponds to the single value $\delta_{ij}^{K^-}$;
4. for each capacity constraint (3) defined for an edge $e \in E$, period $t \in T$ and band $k \in K$, a value $\theta_{etk} \geq 0$ is introduced to represent the number of traffic coefficients of the constraint whose value deviates in band k. Of course, $\theta_{etk} \geq 0$ must be less or equal than the number of traffic coefficients that are present in the constraint.

Given the previous characterization of the multiband uncertainty set, the maximum positive deviation of traffic $DEV_{et}(x, \mathcal{D})$ of a constraint (3) can be found by solving a binary linear program (see [4] for details). Since the polytope associated with the binary program is shown to be integral, by considering its relaxation and by exploiting strong duality, it is possible to reformulate the original trivial robust counterpart as the following *linear and compact* robust counterpart (we refer the reader to [4] for a formal proof of the result):

$$\min \sum_{e \in E} \sum_{t \in T} \gamma_{et} \, y_{et} \qquad\qquad \text{(Rob-MP-CNDP)}$$

$$\sum_{c \in C} \sum_{p \in P_c : e \in p} \bar{d}_{ct} \, x_{cpt} +$$

$$+ \sum_{k \in K} \theta_{etk} \, w_{etk} + \sum_{c \in C} \sum_{p \in P_c : e \in p} z_{ecpt} \leq \phi \sum_{\tau=1}^{t} y_{e\tau} \quad e \in E, t \in T$$

$$w_{etk} + z_{ecpt} \geq \delta_{ctk} \, x_{cpt} \qquad\qquad\qquad e \in E, c \in C, p \in P_c : e \in p,$$
$$t \in T, k \in K \qquad\qquad (4)$$

$$w_{etk} \in \mathbb{R} \qquad\qquad\qquad\qquad e \in E, t \in T, k \in K \qquad (5)$$

$$z_{ecpt} \geq 0 \qquad\qquad\qquad\qquad e \in E, c \in C, p \in P_c : e \in p, t \in T$$
$$(6)$$

$$\sum_{p \in P_c} x_{cpt} = 1 \qquad\qquad c \in C, t \in T$$

$$x_{cpt} \in \{0,1\} \qquad\qquad c \in C, p \in P_c, t \in T$$

$$y_{et} \in \mathbb{Z}_+ \qquad\qquad e \in E, t \in T \ ,$$

This formulation includes additional constraints (4) and variables (5),(6) which are derived from the dualization operation that allow to linearly reformulate the original (non-linear) problem including the term $DEV_{et}(x, \mathcal{D})$ in each capacity constraint (see [4] for details).

In principle, we can get a robust optimal solution for (Rob-MP-CNDP) by using use any commercial mixed-integer programming software. However, as showed in the computational experiment section, getting feasible solutions to this problem may be a challenge even for a state-of-the-art solver like IBM ILOG CPLEX (http://www-01.ibm.com). In the next section, we thus propose a hybrid exact-ant colony primal heuristic that is able to find solutions of very high quality.

4   A Hybrid Primal Heuristic for the Rob-MP-CNDP

Attracted by the effectiveness of MIP-based and bio-inspired heuristics in hard network design problems (see, for example [9,14–16]), we present an original hybrid primal heuristic based on the combination of Ant Colony Optimization (ACO) and an exact large neighbourhood search. ACO is a metaheuristic originally proposed by Dorigo and colleagues for combinatorial optimization [17] and later extended to integer and continuous problems (e.g., [9]). Over the years several refinements of the basic algorithm have been proposed (e.g., [18,19]). ACO was inspired by the behaviour of ants searching for food and is essentially based on the definition of a cycle where a number of feasible solutions are iteratively built in parallel, using information about solutions built in previous executions of the cycle. An ACO algorithm presents the following general structure:

1. UNTIL an arrest condition is reached DO   (Gen-ACO)
   (a) Ant-based solution construction
   (b) Pheromone trail update
2. Daemon actions

We now proceed to detail each phase of the previous sketch for our hybrid ACO-exact algorithm for the (Rob-MP-CNDP). Our approach is hybrid since the canonical ACO construction phase is followed by a daemon-action phase, based on an exact large neighborhood search formulated as a mixed-integer linear program.

Ant-Based Solution Construction. In the step 1 of the cycle, $m \geq 0$ *ants* are defined and each ant iteratively builds a feasible solution for the optimization problem. At every iteration, the ant is in a *state* corresponding with a *partial solution* of the problem and can further complete the solution by making a *move* and thus fixing the value of a new non-fixed variable. The move is chosen prob-abilistically, evaluating pheromone trail values. For a more detailed description of the elements and actions of step 1, we refer the reader to the paper [19] by Maniezzo. This paper presents ANTS, an improved ANT algorithm that we have taken as reference for our work. We considered ANTS particularly attractive as it proposes a series of improvements for ACO that allow to better exploit polyhe-dral information about the problem. Furthermore, ANTS is based on a reduced number of parameters and uses more efficient mathematical operations.

Before describing how our ANTS implementation is structured, we make some preliminary considerations. The formulation (Rob-MP-CNDP) is based on four families of variables: 1) the path assignment variables x_{cpt}; 2) the capacity variables y_{et}; 3-4) the auxiliary variables w_{etk}, z_{ecpt} coming from robust dual-ization. Though we have to deal with four families, we can notice that routing decisions taken over the time horizon entirely determine the capacity installation of minimum cost. Indeed, once the values of all path assignment variables are fixed, the routing is completely established and the worst traffic deviation term $DEV_{et}(x, \mathcal{D})$ can be efficiently derived without the auxiliary variables w_{etk}, z_{ecpt} [4,5]. So we can derive the total traffic D_{et} sent over an edge e in period t in the worst case. The minimum cost installation can then be derived through a sequential evaluation from period 1 to period T, keeping in mind that we must have $\left\lceil \frac{D_{et}}{\phi} \right\rceil$ capacity modules on e in t to accommodate the traffic. As a conse-quence, in the ant-construction phase we can limit our attention to the binary assignment variables and we introduce the concept of *routing state*.

Definition 1. *Routing state (RS): let* $P = \bigcup_{c \in C} P_c$ *and let* $R \subseteq C \times P \times T$ *be the subset of triples* (c, p, t) *representing the assignment of path* $p \in P_c$ *to commodity* c *in period* $t \in T$. *A routing state is an assignment of paths to a subset of commodities in a subset of time periods which excludes that multiple paths are assigned to a single commodity. Formally:*

$$RS \subseteq R : \nexists (c_1, p_1, t_1), (c_2, p_2, t_2) \in RS : c_1 = c_2 \ \wedge \ p_1, p_2 \in P_{c_1} \ \wedge \ t_1 = t_2 .$$

We say that a routing state RS is *complete* when it specifies the path used by each commodity in each time period (thus $|RS| = |C||T|$). Otherwise the RS is called *partial* and we have $|RS| < |C||T|$.

In the ANTS algorithm that we propose, we decided to assign paths con-sidering time periods and commodities in a pre-established order. Specifically, we establish the routing in each time period separately, starting from $t = 1$ and continuing up to $t = |T|$, and in each time period commodities are sorted in descending order w.r.t. their nominal traffic demand. Formally, this can be sketched through the following cycle that builds a *complete routing state*:

FOR $t := 1$ TO $|T|$ DO
    1. sort $c \in C$ in descending order of $\bar{d}_{ct}$.
    2. FOR (sorted $c \in C$) DO
        (a) assign a single path $p \in P_c$ to c;
    END FOR
END FOR

For an iteration (t, c) of the above nested cycles, the assignment of a path to a commodity corresponds with an ant moving from a partial routing state RS_i to a partial routing state RS_j such that: $RS_j = RS_i \cup \{(c, p, t)\}$ with $p \in P_c$. We note that by the definitions of routing state a sequence of moves is actually a sequence of fixings of decision variables, as done in [19].

The probability that an ant k moves from a routing state i to a more complete routing state j, chosen among a set of feasible routing states, is defined by the improved formula of [19]: $p_{ij}^k = \frac{\alpha\,\tau_{ij}+(1-\alpha)\,\eta_{ij}}{\sum_{f \in F} \alpha\,\tau_{if}+(1-\alpha)\,\eta_{if}}$, where $\alpha \in [0, 1]$ is a parameter assessing the relative importance of trail and attractiveness. As discussed in [19], the trail values τ_{ij} and the attractiveness values η_{ij} should be provided by suitable lower bounds of the considered optimization problem. In our particular case: 1) τ_{ij} is derived from the values of the variables in the solution associated with the linear relaxation of the robust counterpart (Rob-MP-CNDP); 2) η_{ij} is equal to the optimal solution of the linear relaxation of the nominal multiperiod network design problem, i.e. the problem that does not consider the traffic uncertainty. The optimum of this problem can be quickly computed and its computation becomes faster as more variables are fixed.

Daemon Actions: Relaxation Induced Neighborhood Search. At the end of the ant-construction phase, we try to improve the quality of the feasible solution found by executing an *exact local search* in a *large neighborhood*. In particular, we adopt a modified *relaxation induced neighborhood search* (RINS) (see [8] for an exhaustive description of the method). Let $(\bar{x}, \bar{y})$ be a feasible solution of (Rob-MP-CNDP) found by an ant and (x^{LR}, y^{LR}) be an optimal (continuous) solution of the linear relaxation of (Rob-MP-CNDP) Moreover, let $(\bar{x}, \bar{y})_j, (x^{LR}, y^{LR})_j$ denote the j-th component of the vectors. Our modified RINS *(mod-RINS)* solves a sub-problem of (Rob-MP-CNDP) where:

1. we fix the variables whose value in $(\bar{x}, \bar{y})$ and (x^{LR}, y^{LR}) differs of at most $\epsilon > 0$, i.e.:
$$(\bar{x}, \bar{y})_j = 0 \ \cap \ (x^{LR}, y^{LR}) \le \epsilon \implies (x, y)_j = 0$$
$$(\bar{x}, \bar{y})_j = 1 \ \cap \ (x^{LR}, y^{LR}) \ge 1 - \epsilon \implies (x, y)_j = 1$$
2. impose a solution time limit of T.

A time limit is imposed since the subproblem may be difficult to solve, so the exploration of the neighbourhood may need to be truncated. Note that in point 1 we generalize the fixing rule of RINS, in which $\epsilon = 0$.

Pheromone Trail Update. At the end of each ant-construction phase h, the pheromone trails of a move $\tau_{ij}(h - 1)$ are updated according to an improved formula proposed in [19]:

$$\tau_{ij}(h) = \tau_{ij}(h - 1) + \sum_{k=1}^{m} \tau_{ij}^k \quad \text{with} \quad \tau_{ij}^k = \tau_{ij}(0) \cdot \left(1 - \frac{z_{curr}^k - LB}{\bar{z} - LB}\right), \quad (7)$$

where the values $\tau_{ij}(0)$ and LB are set by using the linear relaxation of (Rob-MP-CNDP): $\tau_{ij}(0)$ is set equal to the values of the corresponding optimal decision variables and LB equal to the optimal value of the relaxation. Additionally, z_{curr}^k

is the value of the solution built by ant k and $\bar{z}$ is the moving average of the values of the last ψ feasible solutions built. As noticed in [19], adopting formula (7) allows to replace the pheromone evaporation factor, a tricky parameter, with the moving average ψ whose setting has been shown to be much less critical.

Algorithm 1 details the structure of our original hybrid exact-ACO algorithm. The algorithm includes an outer loop repeated until a time limit is reached. At each execution of the loop, an inner loop defines m ants to build the solutions. Pheromone trail updates are done at the end of each execution of the inner loop. Once the ant construction phase is over, mod-RINS is applied so to try to get an improvement.

Algorithm 1. Hybrid ACO-exact algorithm for (Rob-MP-CNDP)

1. Compute the linear relaxation of (Rob-MP-CNDP) and initialize the values of $\tau_{ij}(0)$ by it.
2. UNTIL time limit is reached DO
    (a) FOR $\mu := 1$ TO m DO
        i. build a complete routing state;
        ii. derive a complete feasible solution for (Rob-MP-CNDP);
        END FOR
    (b) Update $\tau_{ij}(t)$ according to (7).
3. apply mod-RINS to the best feasible solution.

5   Experimental Results

We tested the performance of our hybrid algorithm on a set of 15 instances based on realistic network topologies from the SNDlib [10] defined in collaboration with industrial partners from former and ongoing projects. The experiments were performed on a machine with a 2.40 GHz quad-core processor and 16 GB of RAM and using IBM ILOG CPLEX 12.4. All the instances led to very large and hard to solve robust multiperiod network design problems. We observed that even a state-of-the-art solver like CPLEX had troubles identifying good feasible solutions and in all the cases the final optimality gap was over 90%. In contrast, as clear from Table 1, in most cases our hybrid primal heuristic was able to find very high quality solutions associated with very low optimality gaps.

After executing preliminary tests, we found that an effective setting of the parameters of the heuristic was: $\alpha = 0.5$ (balancing attractiveness and trail level), $m = 3$ ants, $\psi = m$ (width of the moving average equal to the number of ants), $\epsilon = 0.1$ (tolerance of fixing in mod-RINS), $T = 20$ minutes (time limit in mod-RINS). The overall time limit for the execution of the heuristic was 5 hours. The same time limit was imposed on CPLEX when used to solve the robust counterpart (Rob-MP-CNDP). Each commodity admits 5 feasible paths, i.e. $|P_c| = 5, \forall c \in C$ and 3 positive deviations bands including the null deviation band. For each instance, in Table 1 we report its ID and features ($|V| =$ no. vertices, $|E| =$ no. edges, $|C| =$ no. commodities, $|T| =$ no. time periods). Moreover, we show the performance of the hybrid solution approach, that is denoted by the three measures $c^*(\text{ACO})$, $c^*(\text{ACO+RINS})$, gapAR%, which represent the value of the best solution found by pure ACO, the value of the best solution found by ACO followed by RINS and the corresponding final optimality gap). We also show the performance of CPLEX, which is denoted by measures $c^*(\text{IP})$ and gapIP% representing the value of the best solution found and the corresponding final optimality gap.

The best solutions found by our hybrid algorithm have in most cases a value that is at least one order of magnitude better than those found by CPLEX (2700% better on average). The results are of very high quality and, given the very low optimality gap, we can suppose that some of these solutions are actually optimal. We notice that in most cases executing RINS after the ant-construction phase can remarkably improve the value of the best solution found by the ants.

Table 1. Experimental results

ID	$|V|$	$|E|$	$|C|$	$|T|$	$c^*(\text{ACO})$	$c^*(\text{ACO+RINS})$	gapAR%	$c^*(\text{IP})$	gapIP%
				5	1.16E07	5.68E06	29.8	1.37E08	97.1
Germany50	50	88	662	7	2.12E07	9.02E6	15.5	3.48E08	97.8
				10	6.66E07	5.75E08	96.2	1.25E09	98.2
				5	5.89E06	2.34E06	1.3	9.52E07	97.6
Pioro40	40	89	780	7	1.42E07	5.10E06	3.1	2.40E08	97.9
				10	4.78E07	1.62E07	0.4	8.45E08	98.1
				5	6.41E06	3.04E06	23.0	6.01E07	96.1
Norway	27	51	702	7	1.44E07	5.73E06	12.8	1.47E08	96.6
				10	4.91E07	1.74E07	7.7	5.15E08	96.9
				5	1.55E06	6.04E05	2.2	1.74E07	96.6
Geant	22	36	462	7	3.61E06	1.29E06	1.6	4.32E07	97.1
				10	1.23E07	4.30E06	0.5	1.24E08	96.5
				5	2.55E05	1.02E05	4.9	1.50E06	93.5
France	25	45	300	7	5.97E05	2.18E05	2.2	3.01E06	92.9
				10	2.00E06	6.81E05	1.0	1.62E07	95.8

6   Conclusion and Future Work

We studied a Robust Optimization model for the Multiperiod Network Design Problem to tackle uncertainty of traffic demands. Robust solutions are deterministically protected against deviations of input traffic data, that may compromise the quality of produced solutions. The increase in complexity and dimension of the problem caused by considering multiple periods and robustness prevents state-of-the-art commercial solvers from finding good quality solutions, so we have defined a hybrid heuristic based on the combination of ant colony optimization and an exact large neighborhood search. Computational experiments on a set of realistic instances from the SNDlib showed that our heuristic can find solutions of extremely good quality. As future work, we plan to refine the heuristic (for example, by improving the ant-construction phase) and to integrate it with a branch-and-cut algorithm to enhance its computational performance.

References

1. Bauschert, T., Büsing, C., D'Andreagiovanni, F., Koster, A.M.C.A., Kutschka, M., Steglich, U.: Network planning under demand uncertainty with robust optimization. IEEE Communications Magazine **52**(2), 178—185 (2014). doi:10.1109/MCOM.2014.6736760
2. Lardeux, B., Nace, D., Geffard, J.: Multiperiod network design with incremental routing. Networks **50**(1), 109–117 (2007)
3. Gamvros, I., Raghavan, S.: Multi-period traffic routing in satellite networks. Europ. J. Oper. Res. **219**(3), 738–750 (2012)
4. Büsing, C., D'Andreagiovanni, F.: New Results about Multi-band Uncertainty in Robust Optimization. In: Klasing, R. (ed.) SEA 2012. LNCS, vol. 7276, pp. 63–74. Springer, Heidelberg (2012)
5. Büsing, C., D'Andreagiovanni, F.: A new theoretical framework for robust optimization under multi-band uncertainty. In: Helber, S., et al. (eds.) Operations Research Proceedings 2012, pp. 115–121. Springer, Heidelberg (2014)
6. Büsing, C., D'Andreagiovanni, F., Raymond, A.: 0–1 multiband robust optimization. In: Huisman, D., et al. (eds.) Operations Research Proceedings 2013, pp. 89–95. Springer, Heidelberg (to appear, 2014)
7. Bertsimas, D., Sim, M.: The price of robustness. Oper. Res. **52**(1), 35–53 (2004)
8. Danna, E., Rothberg, E., Le Pape, C.: Exploring relaxation induced neighborhoods to improve mip solutions. Math. Program. **102**, 71–90 (2005)
9. Dorigo, M., Di Caro, G., Gambardella, L.: Ant algorithms for discrete optimization. Artificial Life **5**(2), 137–172 (1999)
10. Orlowski, S., Wessäly, R., Pioro, M., Tomaszewski, A.: SNDlib 1.0 - survivable network design library. Networks **55**(3), 276–286 (2010)
11. Ahuja, R., Magnanti, T., Orlin, J.: Network Flows: Theory, Algorithms, and Applications. Prentice Hall, Upper Saddle River (1993)
12. Bley, A., Grötschel, M., Wessäly, R.: Design of broadband virtual private networks: Model and heuristic for the b-win. vol. 53. DIMACS SDMTCS, pp. 1–16 (2000)
13. Ben-Tal, A., El Ghaoui, L., Nemirovski, A.: Robust Optimization. Springer, Heidelberg (2009)
14. D'Andreagiovanni, F.: On Improving the Capacity of Solving Large-scale Wireless Network Design Problems by Genetic Algorithms. In: Di Chio, C., Brabazon, A., Di Caro, G.A., Drechsler, R., Farooq, M., Grahl, J., Greenfield, G., Prins, C., Romero, J., Squillero, G., Tarantino, E., Tettamanzi, A.G.B., Urquhart, N., Uyar, A.Ş. (eds.) EvoApplications 2011, Part II. LNCS, vol. 6625, pp. 11–20. Springer, Heidelberg (2011)
15. D'Andreagiovanni, F., Mannino, C., Sassano, A.: Negative Cycle Separation in Wireless Network Design. In: Pahl, J., Reiners, T., Voß, S. (eds.) INOC 2011. LNCS, vol. 6701, pp. 51–56. Springer, Heidelberg (2011)
16. Kambayashi, Y.: A review of routing protocols based on ant-like mobile agents. Algorithms **6**(3), 442–456 (2013)
17. Dorigo, M., Maniezzo, V., Colorni, A.: Ant system: Optimization by a colony of cooperating agents. IEEE Trans. Syst. Man Cybern. B **26**(1), 29–41 (1996)
18. Gambardella, L.M., Montemanni, R., Weyland, D.: Coupling ant colony systems with strong local searches. Europ. J. Oper. Res. **220**(3), 831–843 (2012)
19. Maniezzo, V.: Exact and approximate nondeterministic tree-search procedures for the quadratic assignment problem. INFORMS J. Comp. **11**(4), 358–369 (1999)

A Trajectory-Based Heuristic to Solve a Three-Objective Optimization Problem for Wireless Sensor Network Deployment

Jose M. Lanza-Gutiérrez[✉], Juan A. Gómez-Pulido,
and Miguel A. Vega-Rodríguez

Department of Computers and Communications Technologies,
Polytechnic School, University of Extremadura, Campus Universitario s/n,
10003 Caceres, Spain
{jmlanza,jangomez,mavega}@unex.es

Abstract. Nowadays, wireless sensor networks (WSNs) are widely used in more and more fields of application. However, there are some important shortcomings which have not been solved yet in the current literature. This paper focuses on how to add relay nodes to previously established static WSNs with the purpose of optimizing three important factors: energy consumption, average coverage and network reliability. As this is an NP-hard multiobjective optimization problem, we consider two well-known genetic algorithms (NSGA-II and SPEA2) and a multiobjective approach of the variable neighborhood search algorithm (MO-VNS). These metaheuristics are used to solve the problem from a freely available data set, analyzing all the results obtained by considering two multiobjective quality indicators (hypervolume and set coverage). We conclude that MO-VNS provides better performance on average than the standard algorithms NSGA-II and SPEA2.

Keywords: Coverage · Energy efficiency · Multiobjective optimization · NSGA-II · SPEA2 · Relay node · Reliability · VNS · Wireless sensor network

1 Introduction

At the moment, Wireless Sensor Networks (WSNs) are one of the most emerging wireless technologies. They are applied in many fields, such as precision agriculture, industrial control, robotic, rescue operations or forest fire detection [18].

A traditional WSN is composed of a set of sensors capturing information (i.e. physical variables), and a sink node collecting all this information [4]. There are some important factors that encourage the use of WSNs, where for other technologies the deployment of the network would be more expensive or impossible. Some of them are the use of power-autonomous low-cost devices and the absence of wires. However, WSNs also have important shortcomings affecting important factors like energy costs and Quality of Service (QoS).

© Springer-Verlag Berlin Heidelberg 2014
A.I. Esparcia-Alcázar et al. (Eds.): EvoApplications 2014, LNCS 8602, pp. 27–38, 2014.
DOI: 10.1007/978-3-662-45523-4_3

Because of sensors are often powered by batteries, WSNs are particulary sensitive to energy expenditure. The sensors send all the information captured to the collector node, implying an energy cost. In a star topology, this energy consumption is similar in all the sensors. However, in a multi-hop topology is habitual the existence of bottlenecks: some sensors are subject to a higher energy cost. These bottlenecks adversely affect the behavior of the network. With the aim of avoiding this situation, a new type of device specialized in communication tasks called router or relay node was added to WSNs recently [16].

The efficient design of WSNs is defined in the literature as an NP-hard optimization problem [22]. Consequently, non-conventional techniques are often used, such as heuristics and metaheuristics. Heuristics are techniques designed to solve an specific problem. Metaheuristics are procedures to solve very general types of problems. We find two main lines of research for WSNs, works optimizing traditional WSNs, and works adding relay nodes to traditional WSNs, the so-called Relay node Placement Problem (RNPP). Taking the first approach, there are some relevant contributions using heuristics. Cardei et el. [1] split WSNs into disjoint set of sensors, deciding which must be active to optimize the network lifetime. Cheng et al [2] assigned different power transmission levels to the sensors to reduce the energy consumption. Other authors considered metaheuristics from the Evolutionary Computation (EC) for the same purpose. In this line, Konstantinidis and Yang assigned power transmission levels to the sensors as in [11], but optimizing network lifetime and coverage. Hu et al. [10] maximized the network lifetime splitting WSNs (as do [1]). However, this research line has two main shortcomings. Firstly, it is habitual the use of redundant sensors to maximize the network lifetime, implying costly networks. Secondly, network size is limited because of more sensors implies a higher energy cost.

The works taking the second approach try to overcome these shortcomings by adding routers. Beginning with heuristics, Wang et al. [22] considered routers with processing limitations to optimize the energy cost and Han et al. [9] optimized the fault-tolerance. On the other hand, other authors considered EC. Perez et al. [19] optimized the number of routers and the energy expenditure and Zhao and Chen [23] optimized both average path length and energy cost.

Our work follows this second line of research. We add relay nodes to previously established static WSNs in order to optimize three important factors: average energy consumption, average coverage and network reliability. The following contributions are presented in the curse of this paper:

- The three-objective approach for the RNPP is solved by using three different metaheuristics: two well-known genetic algorithms NSGA-II [6] and SPEA2 [24], and a multiobjective version of the Variable Neighborhood Search algorithm (MO-VNS) [8].
- All the results obtained are analyzed in depth thought a widely recognized statistical methodology. Using as quality indicators two multiobjective metrics: hypervolume and set coverage.

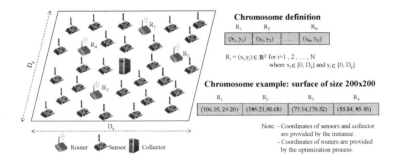

Fig. 1. Network definition considered in the RNPP

- In the current literature, some papers use randomly generated data set or non-public ones. In this work, we consider a freely available data set, implying that this work can be replicated and improved by other authors.

The remainder of this paper is structured as follows. In Section 2, a formal statement of the RNPP is provided. Algorithms used appear in Section 3. Experimental results are discussed in Section 4. Finally, our concluding remarks are left for Section 5.

2   A Realistic Approach for the Relay Node Placement Problem

The WSN considered in the RNPP is composed of three types of wireless static devices placed on the same 2D-surface of size $D_x \times D_y$: a sink node (also called collector node), M sensors and N routers or relay nodes (see Fig. 1). Each sensor obtains information about the environment with a sensibility radius R_s on a regular basis. This information is sent to the sink node, being this node the only connection point of the WSN to the outside. The routers only relay all the received information to the collector node. All the devices communicate among them with a same communication radius R_c. The routers and the collector node have an unlimited power supply, and the sensors are powered by batteries. Thus, a sensor is alive if its battery is not exhausted.

The routing protocol used by sensors and routers is the same. It is based on the minimum-distance path between devices provided by Dijkstra's algorithm [3]. In addition, we consider a perfect synchronization and a perfect medium access, ensuring that there are no collisions among devices.

Let C and S_r be the collector node and the set of routers, respectively, and let $S_s(t)$ be the set of alive sensors at time t. With the aim of modeling the energy expenditure suffered by the sensors, the energy model proposed by A. Konstantinidis et al. [11] is considered. Then, according to this model, the transmission power needed by a sensor $i \in S_s(t)$ to reach another device $j \in S_s(t) \cup S_r \cup C$ at time t is given by

$$P_i(t) = \beta \cdot d_{i,j}^\alpha \qquad t > 0, \tag{1}$$

where $\beta > 0$ is the transmission quality parameter, $d_{i,j}$ is the Euclidean distance between i and j, and $\alpha > 0$ is the path loss exponent. Thus, the residual energy of the sensor i at time t is given by

$$E_i(t) = E_i(t-1) - [(r_i(t)+1) \cdot P_i(t) \cdot amp \cdot K], \qquad t > 0, \tag{2}$$

where $r_i(t)$ is the number of packets that the sensor i receives and relays to the collector node at time t, the $+1$ term is the information packet that the sensor i captures at this time and sends, amp is the energy consumption per bit of the power amplifier, and K is the information packet size. Initially, all the sensors start with the same energy charge IEC in their batteries. Hence,

$$E_i(t) = IEC \qquad \forall i \in S_s(t), \ t = 0. \tag{3}$$

When the residual energy of a sensor equals 0, the device cannot capture more information or be linked again. Following this energy model, we assume the energy expenditure depends only on the most expensive task: the sending. The receiving, processing and sensing tasks are considered negligible.

The network lifetime (LF) is an important concept in this type of network. It is the amount of time units over which a WSN is able to provide enough information about its environment. For this purpose, a coverage threshold (CV) is often used. If the coverage provided by the alive sensors is lower than CV, we consider that the network lifetime has come to its end.

In a previous work two important factors were optimized [15]: average energy consumption and average coverage . Such as in [14], in this paper we include a third factor which provides a better realism to this problem definition: network reliability. These three factors are defined as:

– Average energy consumption(AEC, to minimize): It is the average energy expenditure of the sensors over LF (in Joules), that is

$$f_1 = LF^{-1} \left[\sum_{t=1}^{LF} \sum_{i \in S_s(t)} \left(\frac{E_i(t-1) - E_i(t)}{|S_s(t)|} \right) \right], \tag{4}$$

where $|S_s(t)|$ is the cardinal of the set $S_s(t)$.
– Average coverage(AC, to maximize): It is the percentage of the surface area covered by the sensors over LF. There are two main ways to obtain this value in the literature [21]. Some authors consider that a sensor covers a circumference of radius R_s. Hence the global coverage is the union of the M areas. Other authors place a matrix of binary demand points on the surface, where a demand point equals 1 if there is some alive sensor at a distance lower than R_s, and 0 otherwise. Finally the activated points are

counted. We consider the second approach. Although the first one is a little bit accurate, the second one is less hard to compute. Thus, AC is given by

$$f_2 = LF^{-1} \left[\sum_{t=1}^{LF} \sum_{x=1}^{\lceil D_x \rceil} \sum_{y=1}^{\lceil D_y \rceil} \left(\frac{R_{x,y}(t)}{\lceil D_x \rceil \times \lceil D_y \rceil} \right) \right], \tag{5}$$

where $R_{x,y}(t)$ is the demand point placed at the coordinates (x,y) of the matrix of $\lceil D_x \rceil \times \lceil D_y \rceil$ binary demand points at time t.

– Network reliability(NR, to maximize): It is the average network fault-tolerance, showing the probability that the sensors successfully send information to the sink node. Let Re_i be the reliability of the sensor i defined in [5] as

$$Re_i = 1 - \prod_{l=1}^{P}(1 - (1 - Err)^{h_l}), \tag{6}$$

where P is the number of disjoint paths between i and the sink node given by Suurballe's Algorithm [20], h_l is the number of hops in the l-th disjoint path, and Err is the local channel error. Thus, NR is defined as

$$f_3 = \sum_{i \in S_s(t)} \left(\frac{Re_i}{M} \right) \qquad t = 0. \tag{7}$$

To summarize, the RNPP is defined as an NP-hard multiobjective optimization problem. The objective is to place N routers to optimize a traditional WSN defined by the parameters D_x, D_y, R_s, R_c, IEC, K, CV, α, β, amp, Err and the positions of the collector node and the M sensors.

3   Multiobjective Optimization: The Algorithms Used

As stated before, the RNPP is an NP-hard optimization problem. This type of problem is solved through approximated techniques. Accordingly, we consider three different metaheuristics. NSGA-II and SPEA2 belong to genetic algorithms, a subtype of evolutionary algorithm characterized by encoding their individuals as chromosomes. An individual is a possible solution to the optimization problem. The remainder is a trajectory algorithm, solving methods whose search process follows a trajectory in the search space.

NSGA-II uses two populations P_t and Q_t of the same size PS. P_t saves the parents of generation t, and Q_t saves the offspring generated by individuals in P_t. Initially, P_t is randomly generated and Q_t is empty. So long as the stop condition is not reached, both populations are combined in a new set R_t of size $2PS$. Then, according to both rank and crowding measures, the best PS solutions of R_t are inserted into the new parent population P_{t+1}. Next, a new Q_{t+1} is generated based on P_{t+1}. To this end, and so long as Q_{t+1} is not filled, a pair of individuals are selected from P_{t+1} though binary tournament method. Then, a new individual is generated and inserted into Q_{t+1} through crossover

Algorithm 1. MO-VNS with perturbation mechanism

1: *add a random solution to the emply population P_v*
2: *generate the set of neighborhood structures N_s*
3: **while** *not stop condition* **do**
4:     **while** *there are solutions non − used during the search in P_v* **do**
5:         *a ← randomly pick a non − used solution from P_v*
6:         n_{s_k} *← randomly pick a neighborhood structure, $k \in 1, \ldots, k_{max}$, $n_{s_k} \in N_s$*
7:         **while** $k <= k_{max}$ **do**
8:             *ã ← generate a neighborhood solution of a in n_{s_k}, marking a as used*
9:             *add ã to P_v and remove all the dominated solutions*
10:            **if** *ã $\in P_v$* **then**
11:                *$k \leftarrow 1$ and $a \leftarrow \tilde{a}$*
12:            **else**
13:                *$k \leftarrow k + 1$*
14:            **end if**
15:        **end while**
16:     **end while**
17:     *perform perturbation in P_v to avoid local minima*
18:     *reset all the marks of P_v*
19: **end while**

and mutation operators,. As crossover operator, we consider the usual one-point crossover. As mutation operator, we assume a greedy strategy: router coordinates are randomly changed, but only changes that provide a better individual are accepted. The same encoding is used for the three algorithms. A chromosome is a 2D-coordinate list of M routers (see Fig. 1).

SPEA2 uses an auxiliary population $\overline{P_t}$ where the best solutions are saved along generations, and a regular population P_t with sizes $\overline{PS}$ and PS respectively. Initially, P_t is randomly generated and $\overline{P_t}$ is empty. So long as the stop condition is not reached, the fitness value for each individual in $P_t \cup \overline{P_t}$ is obtained. This fitness is based on the Pareto dominance concept and additional density information. The best solutions according to this fitness are inserted into the new $\overline{P_{t+1}}$. Next, a new P_{t+1} is generated based on $\overline{P_{t+1}}$, using the binary tournament, mutation and crossover strategies as discussed for NSGA-II.

MO-VNS performs local searches by using neighborhood structures. Let a neighborhood structure be the maximum displacement that a router experiences during the local search. Thus, the set of neighborhood structures N_s is given by

$$N_s = \left\{ n_{s_k} \in \mathbb{R} \ / \ n_{s_k} = \frac{min(D_x, D_y) * k}{dv * k_{max}} \right\} \qquad n_{s_k} < n_{s_{k+1}}, \qquad (8)$$

for $k = 1, \ldots, k_{max}$, where k_{max} is the number of neighborhood structures, dv is a factor which delimites the displacement, and $min(D_x, D_y)$ provides the minimum value between D_x and D_y.

As outlined in Algorithm 1, MO-VNS uses a population P_v where only non-dominated individuals are kept. Each individual in P_v has a flag which determines if the solution was used during the search. Initially, a random solution is added to P_v (line 1). Then, so long as the stop condition is not reached, a non-used solution $a \in P_v$ and a neighborhood structure $n_{s_k} \in N_s$ are randomly selected (lines 5-6). Next, a new solution is generated through a local search using $a \in P_v$ as base solution (line 8), marking $a \in P_v$ as used. The local search

Table 1. Instances used in this paper

Instance	$D_x \times D_y$	M	HO_AEC	HO_AC	HO_NR
100x100_15_30	100x100	15	0.1091	89.24%	95.67%
200x200_15_30	200x200	57	0.2791	87.10%	93.23%
300x300_15_30	300x300	128	0.4225	76.44%	85.28%

Table 2. Hypervolume reference points

Instance	Ref_AEC		Ref_AC		Ref_NR	
	ideal	nadir	ideal	nadir	ideal	nadir
100x100_15_30	0.02	0.10	1.00	0.60	1.00	0.50
200x200_15_30	0.10	0.30	1.00	0.60	1.00	0.50
300x300_15_30	0.04	0.50	1.00	0.60	1.00	0.50

Table 3. Parametric sweep

NSGA-II		
Parameter	Value	Range
Mutation	0.80	0.05,0.10,0.15,...,0.95
Crossover	0.80	0.05,0.10,0.15,...,0.95
SPEA2		
Parameter	Value	Range
Mutation	0.70	0.05,0.10,0.15,...,0.95
Crossover	0.60	0.05,0.10,0.15,...,0.95
MO-VNS		
Parameter	Value	Range
Mutation	0.10	0.05,0.1,0.15,...,0.95
k_{max}	10	3,4,5,6,7,8,...,14
dv	2	1,1.5,2,2.5,3,3.5,...,6.5

is given by

$$R_{\tilde{a}_z} = R_{a_z} + \left(\frac{n_{s_k}}{2} - rand(n_{s_k}) \right) \qquad n_{s_k} \in N_s, \ k \in 1, \ldots, k_{max}, \qquad (9)$$

for $z = 1, \ldots, N$, where R_{a_z} and $R_{\tilde{a}_z}$ are the routers placed on the z-th gene of the solutions a and $\tilde{a}$ respectively, and $rand(n_{s_k})$ is a random number between 0 and n_{s_k}. Next, the new solution is added to P_v, removing all the dominated solutions (line 9). If $\tilde{a} \in P_v$, the local search provided a good solution, and then the local search is repeated again using a k value of 1 and taking $\tilde{a}$ as base solution (line 11). Otherwise, k is increased, so long as k takes the maximum value k_{max} (line 13). Once all the solutions are explored, the marks are reset, and then all the individuals are eligible for a new selection again (line 18). Before starting the search process again, a perturbation mechanism is performed to avoid local minima (line 17). To this end, the greedy mutation operator discussed for NSGA-II and SPEA2 is used for each solution in P_v.

4 Experimental Methodology

As stated before, non-public data set was found that fit this problem definition. Hence, in order to study the performance of the metaheuristics, we consider a data set defined by ourselves in [13]. This data set is composed of three traditional WSNs (a set of sensors and a collector node). The number of sensors is the minimum value to cover the whole surface, being placed by a monoobjective genetic algorithm optimizing the coverage offered by the sensors (see Table 1). The collector node is placed in the center of the scenario. We assume the following network parameters: $R_c = 30m$ and $R_s = 15m$ from [17], $K = 128KB$, $CV = 70\%$, $Err = 10\%$, and the energy parameters $EC = 5J$, $\alpha = 2$, $\beta = 1$ and $amp = 100pJ/bit/m^2$ from [12]. In a previous work [15], two different R_c values were assumed, 30 and 60 meters. However, it makes no sense to consider $R_c = 60m$ for our problem definition, since the network reliability is almost 100% for all the cases.

This data set is optimized by adding relay nodes. We assume the addition of these devices increases the network cost. Hence, we decide not to include

Table 4. Hypervolume and standard deviation for each algorithm and test case

NSGA-II ($\overline{Hyp}$ %, std.dev)					
Test case	Evaluations (Stop condition)				
Instance (routers)	50 000	100 000	200 000	300 000	400 000
100x100_15_30(2)	41.01%, 0.0030	41.25%, 0.0024	41.47%, 0.0002	41.48%, 0.0001	41.48%, 0.0000
100x100_15_30(3)	53.54%, 0.0050	54.15%, 0.0018	54.46%, 0.0019	54.56%, 0.0011	54.63%, 0.0005
200x200_15_30(2)	32.49%, 0.0100	33.22%, 0.0042	33.53%, 0.0025	33.64%, 0.0018	33.74%, 0.0021
200x200_15_30(4)	41.46%, 0.0180	43.21%, 0.0167	45.07%, 0.0109	45.57%, 0.0134	45.96%, 0.0116
200x200_15_30(6)	48.75%, 0.0345	53.12%, 0.0193	55.65%, 0.0161	57.00%, 0.0168	57.68%, 0.0156
200x200_15_30(9)	57.14%, 0.0254	61.82%, 0.0223	65.57%, 0.0211	67.45%, 0.0194	68.31%, 0.0174
300x300_15_30(6)	28.35%, 0.0074	29.44%, 0.0068	30.42%, 0.0061	30.81%, 0.0060	31.05%, 0.0057
300x300_15_30(12)	29.84%, 0.0068	31.53%, 0.0100	32.86%, 0.0098	33.81%, 0.0107	34.37%, 0.0112
300x300_15_30(18)	31.26%, 0.0061	32.92%, 0.0088	34.30%, 0.0107	34.99%, 0.0097	35.41%, 0.0099
300x300_15_30(24)	33.40%, 0.0060	34.99%, 0.0137	36.51%, 0.0157	37.22%, 0.0133	37.86%, 0.0132

SPEA2 ($\overline{Hyp}$ %, std.dev)					
Test case	Evaluations (Stop condition)				
Instance (routers)	50 000	100 000	200 000	300 000	400 000
100x100_15_30(2)	41.07%, 0.0021	41.24%, 0.0016	41.31%, 0.0015	41.46%, 0.0002	41.46%, 0.0002
100x100_15_30(3)	53.76%, 0.0038	54.27%, 0.0029	54.56%, 0.0011	54.61%, 0.0007	54.64%, 0.0007
200x200_15_30(2)	32.56%, 0.0054	32.88%, 0.0053	33.21%, 0.0032	33.38%, 0.0031	33.47%, 0.0026
200x200_15_30(4)	42.41%, 0.0150	44.03%, 0.0148	45.03%, 0.0153	45.54%, 0.0141	45.72%, 0.0130
200x200_15_30(6)	53.35%, 0.0180	55.98%, 0.0179	57.53%, 0.0072	58.57%, 0.0124	**59.09%**, 0.0084
200x200_15_30(9)	61.49%, 0.0179	65.42%, 0.0200	67.85%, 0.0184	68.99%, 0.0165	**69.70%**, 0.0132
300x300_15_30(6)	29.45%, 0.0062	30.55%, 0.0071	31.19%, 0.0072	31.54%, 0.0068	**31.78%**, 0.0055
300x300_15_30(12)	31.58%, 0.0071	33.19%, 0.0106	34.62%, 0.0116	35.41%, 0.0113	**36.00%**, 0.0115
300x300_15_30(18)	33.44%, 0.0089	35.22%, 0.0086	36.73%, 0.0092	37.68%, 0.0080	38.34%, 0.0093
300x300_15_30(24)	35.43%, 0.0077	37.04%, 0.0094	38.63%, 0.0076	39.45%, 0.0082	40.20%, 0.0093

MO-VNS ($\overline{Hyp}$ %, std.dev)					
Test case	Evaluations (Stop condition)				
Instance (routers)	50 000	100 000	200 000	300 000	400 000
100x100_15_30(2)	41.76%, 0.0003	41.79%, 0.0002	41.81%, 0.0002	41.82%, 0.0002	**41.82%**, 0.0001
100x100_15_30(3)	54.96%, 0.0037	55.21%, 0.0037	55.31%, 0.0019	55.56%, 0.0033	**55.61%**, 0.0033
200x200_15_30(2)	31.76%, 0.0241	34.04%, 0.0088	34.60%, 0.0126	35.22%, 0.0080	**35.92%**, 0.0017
200x200_15_30(4)	42.81%, 0.0189	44.38%, 0.0184	45.24%, 0.0165	45.78%, 0.0155	**46.14%**, 0.0166
200x200_15_30(6)	54.46%, 0.0197	56.37%, 0.0146	56.99%, 0.0127	57.27%, 0.0139	57.47%, 0.0136
200x200_15_30(9)	63.48%, 0.0155	64.21%, 0.0116	65.33%, 0.0104	65.87%, 0.0109	66.45%, 0.0102
300x300_15_30(6)	30.36%, 0.0043	30.93%, 0.0057	31.19%, 0.0050	31.34%, 0.0058	31.40%, 0.0057
300x300_15_30(12)	33.82%, 0.0063	34.56%, 0.0071	35.31%, 0.0070	35.68%, 0.0056	35.83%, 0.0056
300x300_15_30(18)	37.04%, 0.0068	37.83%, 0.0061	38.48%, 0.0056	38.83%, 0.0038	**39.01%**, 0.0048
300x300_15_30(24)	40.14%, 0.0098	40.91%, 0.0072	41.48%, 0.0067	41.79%, 0.0054	**41.95%**, 0.0048

more than 20% of routers regarding to the number of sensors. Thus, 10 different test cases are defined as shown Table 4. Each test case follows the notation *instance_name(number of routers)*.

Before optimizing the data set, the three algorithms were configured by a parametric sweep [15]. The range of values considered for each parameter is shown in Table 3, as well as the configuration obtained through this tuning. After this step, 31 independent runs are performed for each algorithm in order to obtain statistical validity. With the purpose of studying the convergence of the algorithms, five different stop conditions are considered: 50 000, 100 000, 200 000, 300 000 and 400 000 evaluations. The solutions obtained are evaluated through hypervolume metric, considering the experimental reference points shown in Table 2. Thus, average hypervolumes and standard deviation for each

Table 5. P-values obtained through Wilcoxon-Mann-Whitney's test comparing among hypervolumes

Instance (routers)	MO-VNS vs SPEA2					SPEA2 vs NSGAII				
	50 000	100 000	200 000	300 000	400 000	50 000	100 000	200 000	300 000	400 000
100x100_15_30(2)	0.0000	0.0000	0.0000	0.0000	0.0000	0.2505	0.9060	1.0000	1.0000	1.0000
100x100_15_30(3)	0.0000	0.0000	0.0000	0.0000	0.0000	0.0486	0.0182	0.0188	0.0370	0.1032
200x200_15_30(2)	0.3431	0.0000	0.0000	0.0000	0.0000	0.3920	0.9938	0.9999	0.9995	0.9999
200x200_15_30(4)	0.1376	0.2843	0.3086	0.2215	0.0871	0.0273	0.0410	0.5530	0.6136	0.7949
200x200_15_30(6)	0.0094	0.1815	0.9750	0.9996	1.0000	0.0000	0.0000	0.0000	0.0001	0.0001
200x200_15_30(9)	0.0000	0.9920	1.0000	1.0000	1.0000	0.0000	0.0000	0.0000	0.0008	0.0005
300x300_15_30(6)	0.0000	0.0099	0.3646	0.8787	0.9953	0.0000	0.0000	0.0000	0.0000	0.0000
300x300_15_30(12)	0.0000	0.0000	0.0079	0.2257	0.7012	0.0000	0.0000	0.0000	0.0000	0.0000
300x300_15_30(18)	0.0000	0.0000	0.0000	0.0000	0.0010	0.0000	0.0000	0.0000	0.0000	0.0000
300x300_15_30(24)	0.0000	0.0000	0.0000	0.0000	0.0000	0.0000	0.0000	0.0000	0.0000	0.0000

Instance (routers)	MO-VNS vs NSGA-II					SUMMARY				
	50 000	100 000	200 000	300 000	400 000	50 000	100 000	200 000	300 000	400 000
100x100_15_30(2)	0.0000	0.0000	0.0000	0.0000	0.0000	MO-VNS	MO-VNS	MO-VNS	MO-VNS	MO-VNS
100x100_15_30(3)	0.0000	0.0000	0.0000	0.0000	0.0000	MO-VNS	MO-VNS	MO-VNS	MO-VNS	MO-VNS
200x200_15_30(2)	0.4691	0.0000	0.0000	0.0000	0.0000	NONE	MO-VNS	MO-VNS	MO-VNS	MO-VNS
200x200_15_30(4)	0.0038	0.0148	0.2997	0.2215	0.2299	NONE	NONE	NONE	NONE	NONE
200x200_15_30(6)	0.0000	0.0000	0.0006	0.2223	0.6455	MO-VNS	NONE	SPEA2	SPEA2	SPEA2
200x200_15_30(9)	0.0000	0.0000	0.6764	0.9996	1.0000	MO-VNS	SPEA2	SPEA2	SPEA2	SPEA2
300x300_15_30(6)	0.0000	0.0000	0.0000	0.0009	0.0203	MO-VNS	MO-VNS	NONE	NONE	SPEA2
300x300_15_30(12)	0.0000	0.0000	0.0000	0.0000	0.0000	MO-VNS	MO-VNS	MO-VNS	NONE	NONE
300x300_15_30(18)	0.0000	0.0000	0.0000	0.0000	0.0000	MO-VNS	MO-VNS	MO-VNS	MO-VNS	MO-VNS
300x300_15_30(24)	0.0000	0.0000	0.0000	0.0000	0.0000	MO-VNS	MO-VNS	MO-VNS	MO-VNS	MO-VNS

test case, stop condition and algorithm are shown in Table 4. The highest hypervolumes for 400 000 evaluations are in bold.

Analyzing Table 4, we may note that MO-VNS seems to provide better results. However, we do not known if the differences are significant. To this end, we assume a widely used statistical methodology. The first step is to study if the data follow a normal distribution through *Shapiro - Wilk's* and *Kolmogrov - Smirnov - Lilliefors's* tests with the hypothesis: H_0 if data follow a normal distribution, and H_1 otherwise. P-values lower than 0.05 were obtained for all the cases. Hence, we cannot assume data follow a gaussian distribution. Consequently, the median (Me) must be used as average value. The second step is to check if there are differences among the algorithms. To this end, *Wilcoxon - Mann - Whitney*'s test (samples do not follow a normal distribution and are independent) is used with the hypothesis: H_0 Me_i is worse or equal than Me_j, and H_1 Me_i is better than Me_j, with $i = 1, 2, 3$, $j = 2, 3$, $i < j$, 1=MO-VNS, 2=SPEA2 and 3=NSGA-II. The P-values obtained are shown in Table 5. Values exceed 0.05 are shaded, because of differences are considered not significant.

Based on these p-values, the algorithm which provide the best performance in each case appears in the part summary of Table 5. Analyzing this summary, we observe as MO-VNS provides the best results in complex and simple test cases, but it does not in medium ones. Furthermore, we check as MO-VNS is quicker than NSGA-II and SPEA2 on average. It is necessary a less number of evaluations to get similar results, but when the number of evaluations is

Table 6. Average set coverage C(A,B) among algorithms

Instance (routers)	A MO-VNS		NSGA-II		SPEA2	
	B NSGA-II	SPEA2	SPEA2	MO-VNS	NSGA-II	MO-VNS
100x100_15_30(2)	98.56%	98.29%	63.26%	0.00%	75.81%	0.00%
100x100_15_30(3)	87.89%	89.89%	39.95%	3.17%	33.10%	1.72%
200x200_15_30(2)	72.29%	76.06%	49.24%	12.36%	42.85%	14.50%
200x200_15_30(4)	70.57%	72.56%	43.05%	9.76%	43.68%	8.17%
200x200_15_30(6)	76.56%	45.83%	17.04%	15.43%	77.67%	30.40%
200x200_15_30(9)	40.41%	17.38%	5.89%	35.33%	77.39%	63.40%
300x300_15_30(6)	85.74%	56.88%	17.67%	4.67%	61.09%	18.19%
300x300_15_30(12)	73.02%	50.02%	11.89%	12.70%	71.56%	31.04%
300x300_15_30(18)	92.48%	67.69%	8.70%	5.53%	75.78%	16.91%
300x300_15_30(24)	96.86%	86.30%	17.94%	0.60%	67.81%	13.51%
Partial average	**79.44%**	**66.09%**	**27.46%**	**9.95%**	**62.68%**	**19.78%**
Average	**72.76%**		**18.71%**		**41.23%**	

increased, this advantage is reduced. On average, MO-VNS is the best a 62%, SPEA2 a 16%, NSGA-II a 0%, and none of them a 22%.

In addition to hypervolume, we consider the set coverage C(A,B). That is the percentage of solutions from the algorithm B that are weakly dominated by A. To this end, we obtain the set coverage between each pair of algorithms, test case and stop condition. For this purpose, we use the medium front of the distribution of 31 samples. The average set coverage between each pair of algorithms during the 400 000 evaluations is shown in Table 6. Analyzing this table, we reach similar conclusions as for hypervolume. MO-VNS provides the best coverage relation (72.76%), followed by SPEA2 (41.23%) and in the tail NSGA-II (18.71%).

Finally, some implementation details. The algorithms were programmed by ourselves in C++, using the Lemon library for graphs (*http://lemon.cs.elte.hu*). The IBM SPSS software was used to get the *Shapiro-Wilk's* and *Kolmogrov-Smirnov-Lilliefors's* tests. Finally, the *Wilcoxon−Mann − Whitney's* test and hypervolume were taken from [7].

5   Final Remarks

In this paper, we study the addition of relay nodes to previously established WSNs, with the aim of optimizing three important factors: average energy consumption, average coverage and network reliability. This is the so-called relay node placement problem, which is an NP-hard optimization problem. To solve this problem, we consider three different metaheuristics, two well-known genetic algorithms (NSGA-II and SPEA2), an a novel multiobjective approach of the VNS. These algorithms are used to optimize a freely available data set. Analyzing all the obtained results in depth, and using two known multiobjective indicator: hypervolume and set coverage. As a result, MO-VNS provides the best behavior on average, followed by SPEA2, and in the tail NSGA-II.

As future lines of research, it would be interesting to consider other metaheuristics. One of our aim is to find an algorithm providing good results in general terms. In addition, it would be a good idea to consider a greater number of test cases, and conduct real world-experiments.

Acknowledgments. This work was partially funded by the Spanish Ministry of Economy and Competitiveness and the ERDF (European Regional Development Fund), under the contract TIN2012-30685 (BIO project), and by the Government of Extremadura, with the aid GR10025 to the group TIC015.

References

1. Cardei, M., Du, D.Z.: Improving wireless sensor network lifetime through power aware organization. Wireless Networks **11**, 333–340 (2005)
2. Cheng, X., Narahari, B., Simha, R., Cheng, M., Liu, D.: Strong minimum energy topology in wireless sensor networks: Np-completeness and heuristics. IEEE Transactions on Mobile Computing **2**, 248–256 (2003)
3. Cormen, T.H., Leiserson, C.E., Rivest, R.L., Stein, C.: Introduction to Algorithms, 3rd edn. The MIT Press (2009)
4. Dargie, W., Poellabauer, C.: Fundamentals of Wireless Sensor Networks: Theory and Practice. Wiley (2010)
5. Deb, B., Bhatnagar, S., Nath, B.: Reliable information forwarding using multiple paths in sensor networks. In: Proceedings of IEEE LCN, pp. 406–415 (2003)
6. Deb, K., Pratap, A., Agarwal, S., Meyarivan, T.: A fast elitist multi-objective genetic algorithm: Nsga-ii. IEEE Transactions on Evolutionary Computation **6**, 182–197 (2000)
7. Fonseca, C., Knowles, J., Thiele, L., Zitzler, E.: Performance assessment tool suite. http://www.tik.ee.ethz.ch/pisa/?page=assessment.php
8. Geiger, M.J.: Randomised variable neighbourhood search for multi objective optimisation. In: Proceedings of the 4th EU/ME Workshop 0809.0271, pp. 34–42 (2008)
9. Han, X., Cao, X., Lloyd, E.L., Shen, C.C.: Fault-tolerant relay node placement in heterogeneous wireless sensor networks. IEEE Transactions on Mobile Computing **9**, 643–656 (2010)
10. Hu, X.M., Zhang, J., Yu, Y., Chung, H.H., Li, Y.L., Shi, Y.H., Luo, X.N.: Hybrid genetic algorithm using a forward encoding scheme for lifetime maximization of wireless sensor networks. IEEE Transactions on Evolutionary Computation **14**, 766–781 (2010)
11. Konstantinidis, A., Yang, K., Zhang, Q.: An evolutionary algorithm to a multi-objective deployment and power assignment problem in wireless sensor networks. In: Proceedings of IEEE GLOBECOM, pp. 1–6 (2008)
12. Konstantinidis, A., Yang, K.: Multi-objective k-connected deployment and power assignment in wsns using a problem-specific constrained evolutionary algorithm based on decomposition. Computer Communications **34**, 83–98 (2011)
13. Lanza-Gutierrez, J.M., Gomez-Pulido, J.A., Vega-Rodriguez, M.A.: Instance sets for optimization in wireless sensor networks. http://arco.unex.es/wsnopt (2011)
14. Lanza-Gutierrez, J.M., Gomez-Pulido, J.A., Vega-Rodriguez, M.A.: A new realistic approach for the relay node placement problem in wireless sensor networks by means of evolutionary computation. Ad Hoc and Sensor Wireless Networks (2013) (accepted)

15. Lanza-Gutiérrez, J.M., Gómez-Pulido, J.A., Vega-Rodríguez, M.A., Sánchez-Pérez, J.M.: Relay Node Positioning in Wireless Sensor Networks by Means of Evolutionary Techniques. In: Kamel, M., Karray, F., Hagras, H. (eds.) AIS 2012. LNCS, vol. 7326, pp. 18–25. Springer, Heidelberg (2012)

16. Lloyd, E.L., Xue, G.: Relay node placement in wireless sensor networks. IEEE Transactions on Computers **56**, 134–138 (2007)

17. Martins, F., Carrano, E., Wanner, E., Takahashi, R., Mateus, G.: A hybrid multi-objective evolutionary approach for improving the performance of wireless sensor networks. IEEE Sensors Journal **11**, 545–554 (2011)

18. Mukherjee, J.Y.B., Ghosal, D.: Wireless sensor network survey. Computer Networks **52**, 2292–2330 (2008)

19. Perez, A., Labrador, M., Wightman, P.: A multiobjective approach to the relay placement problem in wsns. Proceedings of IEEE WCNC **1**, 475–480 (2011)

20. Suurballe, J.W.: Disjoint paths in a network. Networks **4**, 125–145 (1974)

21. Wang, B.: Coverage problems in sensor networks: A survey. ACM Comput. Surv. **43**, 32:1–32:53 (2011)

22. Wang, Q., Xu, K., Takahara, G., Hassanein, H.: Device placement for heterogeneous wireless sensor networks: Minimum cost with lifetime constraints. IEEE Transactions on Wireless Communications **6**, 2444–2453 (2007)

23. Zhao, C., Chen, P.: Particle swarm optimization for optimal deployment of relay nodes in hybrid sensor networks. Proceedings of IEEE CEC. **1**, 3316–3320 (2007)

24. Zitzler, E., Laumanns, M., Thiele, L.: Spea 2: Improving the strength pareto evolutionary algorithm. Tech. rep., Computer Engineering and Networks Laboratory (TIK), ETH Zurich (2001)

Optimizing AEDB Broadcasting Protocol with Parallel Multi-objective Cooperative Coevolutionary NSGA-II

Bernabé Dorronsoro[1]([⊠]), Patricia Ruiz[2], El-Ghazali Talbi[1], Pascal Bouvry[2], and Apivadee Piyatumrong[3]

[1] LIFL, University of Lille 1, Villeneuve-d'Ascq, France
bernabe.dorronsoro_diaz@inria.fr, el-ghazali.talbi@lifl.fr
[2] Faculty of Science, Technology and Communication, University of Luxembourg, Walferdange, Luxembourg
{patricia.ruiz,pascal.bouvry}@uni.lu
[3] National Electronics and Computer Technology Centre (NECTEC), Klong Luang, Pathumthani 12120, Thailand
apivadee.piyatumrong@nectec.or.th

Abstract. Due to the highly unpredictable topology of ad hoc networks, most of the existing communication protocols rely on different thresholds for adapting their behavior to the environment. Good performance is required under any circumstances. Therefore, finding the optimal configuration for those protocols and algorithms implemented in these networks is a complex task. We propose in this work to automatically fine tune the AEDB broadcasting protocol for MANETs thanks to the use of cooperative coevolutionary multi-objective evolutionary algorithms. AEDB is an advanced adaptive protocol based on the Distance Based broadcasting algorithm that acts differently according to local information to minimize the energy and network use, while maximizing the coverage of the broadcasting process. In this work, it will be fine tuned using multi-objective techniques in terms of the conflicting objectives: coverage, energy and network resources, subject to a broadcast time constraint. Because of the few parameters of AEDB, we defined new versions of the problem in which variables are discretized into bit-strings, making it more suitable for cooperative coevolutionary algorithms. Two versions of the proposed method are evaluated and compared versus the original NSGA-II, providing highly accurate tradeoff configurations in shorter execution times.

Keywords: Multiobjective optimization · Cooperative coevolutionary algorithms · Communication protocol · Energy efficiency

1 Introduction

Mobile ad hoc networks, hereinafter MANETs, are spontaneous wireless networks that are created between mobile devices without any previously existing infrastructure. In such networks, devices can appear or disappear at any time,

© Springer-Verlag Berlin Heidelberg 2014
A.I. Esparcia-Alcázar et al. (Eds.): EvoApplications 2014, LNCS 8602, pp. 39–50, 2014.
DOI: 10.1007/978-3-662-45523-4_4

quickly change their location, or suddenly adopt a selfish behavior and consequently stop collaborating on the network performance. Additionally, packets can be dropped because of the presence of physical obstacles that weaken the signal (or provoke its reflection or diffraction), collisions in the shared medium, or any other physical phenomena that might affect communications (e.g., the Doppler effect or fading). Because of all these issues, the topology of MANETs is highly dynamic and unpredictable.

As a result of the mentioned peculiarities of the topology of MANETs, the design of communication protocols for this kind of networks is a difficult task. The behavior of the protocol is highly sensitive to both small changes in the set of configuration parameters and the network it is tested on. Therefore, fine tuning the parameters for optimally configuring a communication protocol is a difficult task. Additionally, because of the important drawbacks present in MANETs there is not a single goal to be satisfied but several (usually in conflict) like network resource use, QoS, energy consumption, etc.

Due to the intrinsic broadcast nature of wireless networks, broadcasting is one of the most suitable protocols for them. Indeed, many high level applications and even other protocols assume the existence of broadcasting as a low level operation. In wireless networks, these dissemination algorithms are generally associated with the broadcast storm problem [11]. However, due to the recently appearance of MANETs, and all the drawbacks inherited from them, the main problem in broadcasting is not only reducing the number of forwardings, but also trying to overcome all these undesirable aspects.

In this work, we tackle the problem of fine tuning the adaptive enhanced distance based broadcasting algorithm (AEDB) [12] parameters for its optimal performance on MANETs. AEDB is an energy-aware broadcasting algorithm that uses a cross-layer design to reduce the energy consumption. In our previous work [13], AEDB was optimized using two well known Evolutionary Algorithms (EAs): a cellular genetic algorithm hybridised with a differential evolution, CellDE [7], and the Non-dominated Sorting Genetic Algorithm II, NSGA-II [3]. However, due to the high computational requirements of the network simulator and its stochastic behavior (requiring a number of independent simulations to evaluate a given protocol configuration), experiments take too long (over 280 hours per algorithm execution in the densest network). In the current work, we propose for the first time the use of a parallel cooperative coevolutionary multi-objective algorithm (CCMOEA) to both speed up the optimization process and find better configurations of the protocol. CCMOEAs are recent techniques that decompose the problem into several smaller sub-problems by simply splitting the solutions representation, and they have proved to be highly accurate and fast for a number of continuous and combinatorial multi-objective problems [4,5].

The contributions of this paper are detailed next. First, we apply for the first time a parallel CCMOEA to the AEDB protocol optimization problem to find accurate solutions in much shorter execution times than those of the previously existing works. Because the CCMOEA decomposes the solution representation into several smaller ones and AEDB has only five variables to tune, we here propose a novel definition of the problem in which variables are discretized. Two different discretization levels are considered, and we evaluate their impact on the performance of the CCMOEA, this was never studied before [4,5]. Another contribution with respect to those works is the study of the behavior of the CCMOEA on this highly noisy real-world optimization problem, compared versus an state-of-the-art technique (the NSGA-II [3] algorithm). Finally, we compare the performance of the optimized parameter configurations of AEDB with the different algorithms on a large number of networks.

The paper is organized as follows. We revise in the next section the most relevant works in the literature on protocols optimization for MANETs. Section 3 describes the AEDB protocol and the optimization problem tackled in this work. The cooperative coevolutionary optimization method is introduced in Sect. 4. The experimental analysis and results are reported in Sections 5 and 6, just before formulating the conclusions and main lines for future work in Sect. 7.

2   Related Work

A complete recent survey on the use of evolutionary algorithms for optimizing different aspects of mobile ad hoc networks can be found in [6]. Focusing on the protocol optimization problem, as the one we deal with in this paper, we can find a few papers in the literature. In all cases, the optimization is an offline process that (usually) looks for the optimal configuration of the protocol to enhance some aspect of the network, such as QoS, the network use, or the energy used, as it is the case considered in our work. The first study in this line was probably the one by Alba et al. [2], in which a broadcasting protocol for MANETs was optimized using a multi-objective genetic algorithm.

Different metaheuristics have been applied to solve the minimum energy broadcast (MEB) problem in wireless ad hoc networks (Particle swarm optimization, ant colony optimization, evolutionary algorithms and hybrid evolutionary algorithms) [10,15]. All of them are offline techniques that are limited to static networks. Abdou et al. [1] optimized a probabilistic broadcasting algorithm in terms of the local density. The multiobjective optimization focuses on minimizing the channel utilization as well as the broadcasting time.

The optimization of the AODV routing protocol for vehicular ad hoc networks is presented in [8]. Another routing protocol, OLSR, is optimized with a parallel EA in [14] in order to minimize the energy used by the algorithm, subject to acceptable QoS requirements. Both works deal with single-objective problems.

Ruiz et al. [13] optimize the performance of AEDB using two well known multiobjective algorithms (CellDE and NSGA-II), by maximizing the coverage achieved in the dissemination process and minimizing both the time and the energy used.

3   AEDB Protocol Optimisation

The AEDB protocol [12] is a broadcasting algorithm that reduces the transmission power for disseminating a message, aimed at saving energy in both sparse and dense networks. As in any distance based algorithm, nodes are candidates to forward the message if the distance to the source node is higher than a predefined threshold. Thus, there exists a forwarding area, and only nodes located in it are potential forwarders. In this case, a crosslayer technique is used to inform the upper layers about the signal strength of messages received. Therefore, the decision is not taken in terms of distance but power. This predefined value for the energy is called the *borders_threshold*. Before forwarding, the node sets a random delay in order to avoid collisions with neighbor devices.

AEDB saves energy by reducing the transmission power when forwarding the message. The new transmission power is the one that reaches the furthest neighbor. This is estimated according to the reception energy detected in the beacons exchanged (every 1 second). In order to be aware of the nodes mobility, an extra fixed amount of energy, the *margin_threshold*, is added to the one estimated.

In denser networks, the probability of having a node close to the transmission range limit is higher. This would highly reduce the energy saved in such networks. Indeed, when the network is very dense the connectivity is usually very high. Thus, reducing the transmission power allowing the loss of some one hop neighbors will save energy without any detriment in the performance of the broadcasting process. Contrary, when the network is sparse, the node must maintain the network connectivity, as not doing so would make more difficult to spread a message through the whole network. AEDB is able to adapt its behavior to the network density. If many nodes located in the forwarding area are detected (the *neighbors_threshold*), the transmission range is reduced and some one hop neighbors are discarded. Next we are describing the problem at hands.

3.1   Problem Description

The performance of a broadcasting algorithm in MANETs is usually related to some standard metrics. We consider here the most common ones: i) *coverage*: the number of devices that after the dissemination process receive the broadcast message; ii) *energy used* by the broadcast process: the sum of the energy every device consumes to forward the message; iii) number of *forwardings*: the amount of nodes that after receiving the broadcasting message decide to resend it; and iv) *broadcast time*: the time needed to spread a message in the network, since the source node sends the message until the last node receives it. Long delays might affect the validity of the message, as it can be outdated.

From the point of view of the broadcasting algorithm designer, the higher the number of objectives the more complex the optimisation process and the decision making. Therefore, as it was previously done in [13], in this work AEDB is optimised in terms of three objectives: coverage, number of forwardings, and energy used. The broadcasting time is included as a constraint: any solution longer than 2 seconds is considered not valid [13].

```
 1: t ← 0
 2: {⊐ means parallel run}
 3: ⊐i ∈ [1, I] :: setup( P⁰ , i ) {Initialize every subpopulation}
 4: sync() {Synchronization point}
 5: {∀ means sequential run}
 6: ∀i ∈ [1, I] :: broadcast( P⁰ , i ) {Share random local partial solutions in every subpopulation}
 7: ⊐i ∈ [1, I] :: evaluate( P⁰ , i ) {Evaluate solutions in every subpopulation}
 8: sync()
 9: while not stoppingCondition( ) do
10:    ⊐i ∈ [1, I] :: generation( Pᵗ , i ) {Perform one generation to evolve the population}
11:    sync()
12:    ∀i ∈ [1, I] :: broadcast( Pᵗ , i ) {Share best local partial solutions in every subpopulation}
13:    t ← t + 1 {Increase generations counter}
14: end while
15: mergeParetoFronts( ) {Merge the Pareto fronts found in the subpopulation into a single one}
```

Fig. 1. Parallel CCMOEA framework

The main goal of this work is to tune the main AEDB parameters (*borders_threshold*, *margin_threshold*, *max* and *min delay*, and *neighbors_threshold*) using multi-objective techniques based on Pareto dominance in order to obtain the best possible protocol behavior, considering the three objectives explained.

Our problem is to optimize F, given by Eq. 1, where s is an AEDB configuration, simulated using the ns3 network simulator on 10 different networks, and e, c, f, and bt stand for the average energy saved, coverage, number of broadcastings, and broadcasting time out of the 10 simulations, respectively.

$$F(s) = \begin{cases} min\{e\} \\ max\{c\} \quad ; \text{s. t. } bt < 2 \\ min\{f\} \end{cases} \tag{1}$$

4   Cooperative Coevolutionary NSGA-II

The CCNSGAII algorithm we are using in this work was presented in [4,5]. A pseudocode is given in Fig. 1. As previously mentioned, CCNSGAII splits the solution vector and evolves each subset of the solution using NSGA-II, in so-called sub-populations. In order to evaluate the partial solutions in the sub-populations, the algorithm needs to somehow construct a whole solution that can be evaluated on the original problem. In CCNSGAII, this is done in the following way. Every sub-population is sharing a number of local best solutions, randomly chosen from the best non-dominated solutions found so far. Then, to build a global solution, the sub-population takes the corresponding part from the solutions shared by the other sub-populations, chosen at random. An example of how one sub-population, P_1, shares four of its best solutions (i.e., $N_s = 4$) with the other two populations is presented in Fig. 2. In case the local contains less than N_s non-dominated solutions, randomly chosen individuals are taken from the rest of the population to complete the set of N_s solutions.

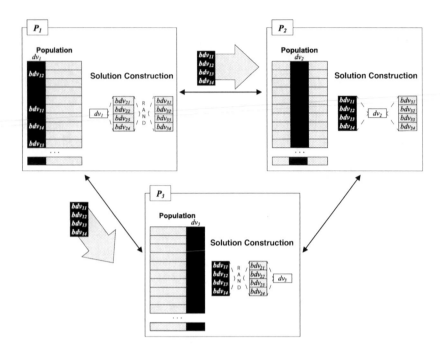

Fig. 2. In the CCNSGAII, every population (for example, $P1$) shares with the other coevolving populations (P_2 and P_3) its four best partial solutions (bdv_{11} to bdv_{14}). The partial solutions are evaluated by building complete solutions with random partial solutions of the other two subpopulations (bdv_{2X} and bdv_{3Y}).

5   Experimental Analysis

We summarize in this section the results obtained by NSGA-II algorithm and two versions of CCNSGAII (differing on the discretization granularity of the problem) on the optimization of AEDB for three different network densities. As mentioned in Sect. 3.1, we use ns3 simulator to evaluate the performance of the AEDB configurations given by the individuals in the algorithm. In order to have confident results, we evaluate each solution in 10 different networks and the fitness value of each objective is defined as the average value of the 10 runs. These 10 networks are always the same for evaluating every solution.

The configuration of the studied algorithms is given in Table 1. The chromosome of NSGA-II is composed by the five variables introduced in Sect. 3.1. All of them are treated as real variables, and the value of *neighbors_threshold* is rounded to the closest integer one for the simulations. Variables were discretized to solve the problem with CCNSGAII. We studied two different precisions for the four real variables of AEDB, namely 16 and 32 bits, while 8 bits were used to codify the only integer variable. This makes two different discretization levels (of 72 and 136 bits chromosomes) to represent the same problem in CCNSGAII-short and CCNSGAII-long, respectively.

We use 8 subpopulations that run on 8 different threads for CCNSGAII algorithm, and every subpopulation shares 20 solutions, randomly chosen from its local Pareto front. All subpopulations are composed by 100 solutions (as the population of NSGA-II). They are randomly initialized, and binary tournament is used to choose solutions for recombination. The operators implemented are the two points recombination and the bit flip mutation for the two CCNSGAII, while the recommended SBX and polynomial operators are used for NSGA-II.

The termination condition of all algorithms is fixed to 50,000 evaluations performed, and 30 independent runs of every algorithm are done for each problem. We use the inverted generational distance (IGD), spread (Δ), and hypervolume (HV) to quantify the quality of the different Pareto front approximations found by the algorithms [6], according to accuracy of solutions, diversity, and both of them, respectively. Because the optimal Pareto front is not known for the considered problems, and some of the used metrics need it, we build a reference Pareto front, composed by selected solutions from all the Pareto front approximations provided by the different algorithms (100 solutions were selected by the Adaptive Grid technique), and use it in place of the optimal one as in [6]. Additionally, these reference Pareto fronts are used to normalize the fronts provided by the algorithms, in order to avoid any bias in the results given by the different order of magnitude of the objectives.

Table 1. Algorithms configuration

Numb. of subpop.*	8
Cores used	8 (1 for NSGA-II)
Number of threads	1 per subpopulation
Population size	100
Final archive size	100, from all subpops.
Migration policy *	20 random
Max. evaluations	50,000
Pop. initialisation	Random
Selection	Binary tournament
Recombination	DPX
	(SBX for NSGA-II)
Probability	0.9
Mutation	Bit Flip
	(Polynomial for NSGA-II)
Probability	$\frac{1}{number\_of\_variables}$
Independent runs	30

* Not applicable for NSGA-II

Table 2. Configuration of ns3

Devices/km^2	100-200-300
Speed	[0, 2] m/s
Size of the area	500 m × 500 m
Default trans. power	16.02 dBm
Dir. & speed change	every 20 s

Table 3. Domain of the variables

minimum delay	[0, 1] s
maximum delay	[0, 5] s
border_Threshold	[-95, -70] dBm
margin_Threshold	[0, 3] dBm
neighbors_Threshold	[0, 50]

The configuration of ns3 for the simulations performed is summarized in Table 2. The mobility model used is the random walk [9]. The simulation environment used is a square area of 500 m side. The speed of the nodes can vary from 0 to 2m/s (i.e., between 0 and 7.2km/h). We study three different network densities in the optimization process. They go from a spare to a dense one, with 100, 200, and 300 devices/km^2.

In the simulations, the network evolves for 30 seconds in order to have the nodes uniformly distributed in the area. Then, after these 30 seconds, a node starts the broadcasting process. The simulation stops after 40 seconds.

In order to limit the search space, we defined reasonably large intervals for each of the parameters we are optimising. They are shown in Table 3.

6   Results

In this section, we summarize the results we found after the experiments done. We provide in Table 4 the average results computed by the three considered metrics over 30 independent runs of the algorithms. In order to get statistical confidence in our comparisons, we performed the Wilcoxon matched-pairs signed-rank test. In the table, we show the results of this pairwise test in the comparison of the algorithm in the current column versus the others in the left-hand columns. Symbol ∇ states that the algorithm in the current column is statistically worse, while $\blacktriangle$ means that the algorithm is statistically better. Finally, '$-$' is used in the cases where no significant difference was found.

Table 4. Comparison of the performance of the algorithms according to the three metrics. Average and standard deviation values.

		NSGA-II	CCNSGAII-short	CCNSGAII-long
HV	100dev	$5.60e-01_{3.0e-03}$	$5.54e-01_{3.5e-03}$ ∇	$5.53e-01_{2.9e-03}$ ∇ $-$
	200dev	$5.70e-01_{2.3e-03}$	$5.56e-01_{3.3e-03}$ ∇	$5.56e-01_{3.8e-03}$ ∇ $-$
	300dev	$5.68e-01_{3.5e-03}$	$5.53e-01_{3.5e-03}$ ∇	$5.52e-01_{5.5e-03}$ ∇ $-$
△	100dev	$8.72e-01_{6.2e-02}$	$7.94e-01_{6.6e-02}$ $\blacktriangle$	$7.85e-01_{6.2e-02}$ $\blacktriangle$ $-$
	200dev	$9.75e-01_{5.6e-02}$	$8.41e-01_{6.0e-02}$ $\blacktriangle$	$8.27e-01_{6.7e-02}$ $\blacktriangle$ $-$
	300dev	$1.06e+00_{3.8e-02}$	$9.08e-01_{9.3e-02}$ $\blacktriangle$	$8.73e-01_{9.0e-02}$ $\blacktriangle$ $-$
IGD	100dev	$4.15e-03_{4.8e-03}$	$4.26e-03_{2.7e-03}$ ∇	$5.03e-03_{3.4e-03}$ ∇ $-$
	200dev	$5.84e-03_{6.1e-03}$	$8.44e-03_{3.8e-03}$ ∇	$9.18e-03_{6.4e-03}$ ∇ $-$
	300dev	$3.42e-03_{3.4e-04}$	$8.79e-03_{5.5e-03}$ ∇	$1.16e-02_{6.3e-03}$ ∇ ∇

From Table 4, we can clearly observe the good performance of the CCNSGAII algorithms with respect to NSGA-II. In terms of HV, the differences on the results provided by the three algorithms are very low, less than 3% in all cases. Despite that, NSGA-II statistically outperforms the CCNSGAII algorithms.

The two CCNSGAII versions provide more diversified Pareto front approximations, compared to NSGA-II. We found statistical significance on all comparisons between NSGA-II and the two CCNSGAII versions, while there is no statistical difference between the two CCNSGAII algorithms in any case. CCNSGAII-long improves the diversity values obtained by NSGA-II by 9.98%, 15.18%, and 14.33% for the sparse, medium, and dense networks, respectively.

According to IGD metric, we found that the NSGA-II algorithm outperforms the two cooperative coevolutionary ones in terms of accuracy of solutions. Differences become larger with the network density, up to one order of magnitude for the densest network.

If we compare the two CCNSGAII algorithms, we can see that CCNSGAII-short provides more accurate results than CCNSGAII-long, with 15.31%, 8.06%, and 24.22% better values for IGD metric for 100dev, 200dev, and 300dev densities, respectively. Similar values were found by the two CCNSGAII for HV. In the case of Δ metric, CCNSGAII-long gets 2.21% better values than CCNSGAII-short, in average.

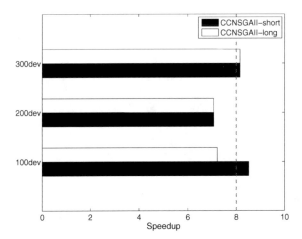

Fig. 3. Speedup results of CCNSGAII-short and CCNSGAII-long with respect to the original NSGA-II

We show in Fig. 3 the speedup results obtained by the CCNSGAII algorithms. They are computed as the execution time of the original NSGA-II over the time of the corresponding CCNSGAII algorithm. The red dashed line indicates the linear speedup value. As it can be seen, the CCNSGAII algorithms provide close to linear speedups for all network densities (always over 7), and super-linear in half of the cases. The best speedup value obtained is 8.52, by CCNSGAII-short.

In order to compare the quality of the AEDB configurations each algorithm found, we are selecting five of the best non-dominated solutions reported by every evolutionary algorithm. For that, we built the reference Pareto front for every algorithm, as explained in Sect. 5, but only taking into consideration all solutions from the same algorithm. As we are dealing with a broadcasting algorithm, we are interested in configurations that are actually able to disseminate the message. Thus, we discarded from the reference Pareto front all solutions with less than 80% coverage. From the remaining solutions we kept only those with less than 30% of forwarding nodes. The five selected solutions are the ones with better energy saving results from this set.

The selected five solutions for every algorithm are compared in Table 5 on a large set of 100 different networks. The table shows the average energy used (E), and the average percentages of coverage (C) and number of forwardings (F) obtained on these 100 networks. We used the Wilcoxon test to look for statistical significance on the comparison of the performance of all solutions. Those results with dark grey background are said to be consistently better than the others

Table 5. Average values of energy used (E), and percentages of coverage (C) and number of forwardings (F) of a number of selected AEDB configurations over 100 networks

		NSGA-II			CCNSGAII-short			CCNSGAII-long		
		E	$\%C$	$\%F$	E	$\%C$	$\%F$	E	$\%C$	$\%F$
100dev	Sol1	114.69	80.16	30.44	106.85	74.44	26.92	123.17	**82.00**	30.96
	Sol2	111.97	77.56	29.48	109.64	75.40	29.08	107.98	77.96	28.44
	Sol3	**96.21**	72.84	24.88	116.02	81.20	116.03	97.10	73.40	25.36
	Sol4	116.45	80.64	30.68	108.33	76.40	28.28	99.11	78.48	29.76
	Sol5	113.20	78.40	29.92	**88.78**	68.64	**22.52**	104.36	73.72	25.68
200dev	Sol1	91.98	76.18	11.68	138.77	89.00	17.34	98.10	78.58	12.46
	Sol2	110.91	82.02	14.26	90.81	74.92	11.58	128.37	85.16	16.44
	Sol3	91.45	73.06	11.66	113.70	84.00	14.46	149.80	**93.00**	18.74
	Sol4	87.71	72.48	11.16	145.49	**93.70**	18.34	153.58	**94.20**	19.52
	Sol5	75.80	66.42	**9.60**	71.48	63.22	**9.06**	88.69	73.14	11.26
300dev	Sol1	102.34	79.91	8.53	**80.10**	69.16	**6.73**	89.42	74.27	7.48
	Sol2	101.40	78.69	8.45	91.99	73.97	7.67	165.85	**95.63**	14.09
	Sol3	134.24	90.64	11.17	90.85	73.45	7.57	97.24	77.16	8.11
	Sol4	91.48	75.72	7.64	93.12	74.99	7.76	88.58	74.08	7.39
	Sol5	88.93	72.83	7.41	171.93	**98.25**	14.47	116.43	84.27	9.80

(meaning that they are at least statistically better than one other solution and never statistically worse than any other). Solutions that are consistently worse than all the others (they are statistically worse than at least one solution and not better than any other solution) are emphasized with light grey background. The results in bold face are those dominating the highest number of other solutions for every density.

We can see that the solutions found by the CCNSGAII are better in coverage than those of NSGA-II, with 5 consistently best solutions for CCNSGAII-short, 6 for CCNSGAII-long and 4 for NSGA-II. Indeed, none of the solutions provided by NSGA-II is consistently better than any other one for the 200 and 300 devices/km^2 densities. The overall best solutions (those statistically better than the highest number of solutions) were always found by CCNSGAII-long, together with CCNSGAII-short in the denser density. We found that NSGA-II provides only one solution with 90% coverage, while there are 5 solutions from the CCNSGAII algorithms with higher values, reaching up to 98.25% coverage.

The differences on the results provided by the three algorithms are not so important in terms of the number of forwardings and energy used. In both cases, the three algorithms provide 3 solutions that are consistently better than the others (except CCNSGAII-long for energy used, that provides 2 consistently better solutions). However, the overall best solutions are in these cases found by CCNSGAII-short for all networks.

Finally, we found that Sol1 provided by CCNSGAII-short for 300dev networks stands out as the only one that is consistently better than all the others in some objectives and is not consistently worse for any other: it is consistently better for energy used and number of forwardings. The configuration of this solution is: *minimum delay* = 0.26344701304646373; *maximum delay* = 0.8817425803006027; *border_Threshold* = −94.14015411612115; *margin_Threshold* = 0.15202563515678644; and *neighbors_Threshold* = 41. If we analyze this configuration, we observe that the value of the *neighbors_Threshold* is high, i.e. it is unlikely that AEDB discards 1-hop neighbors, thus no energy reduction will be performed. However, such low value of the *border_Threshold* means that the forwarding area is very small, and thus, the number of potential forwarding nodes. If we compute the average of the percentage of the energy saved per forwarding node for this specific configuration, we obtain 45.92% (in mWatt).

Analyzing the results provided by the solutions, we observe that all the algorithms behave as the designer of a broadcasting algorithm desires. That is, for sparse networks the solutions provided by the algorithms promote high coverage, sacrificing the number of forwarding nodes and energy savings. However, for denser networks, the solutions obtained by the algorithm pay more attention to the energy savings, as disseminating the message is easier but reducing the energy is more difficult.

7   Conclusions and Future Work

We propose in this work the use of a parallel cooperative coevolutionary multiobjective algorithm to solve the problem of fine-tuning a broadcasting protocol for mobile ad hoc networks for optimal performance. The number of devices receiving the broadcasted message, the network use for that, and the global energy consumption during the process are the three objectives to optimize. The broadcasting process time was set to be less than 2 seconds, as a constraint of the problem.

The problem was discretized with two different precisions for real numbers (namely 16 or 32 bits encodings) in order to being able to handle them with cooperative coevolutionary techniques. We found no statistical difference between the algorithms using these two encodings. In the comparison of NSGA-II with its cooperative coevolutionary versions, we found that the former was better for IGD metric, and worse in terms of diversity of solutions provided. Regarding the hypervolume metric, all algorithms found very close results, even though NSGA-II was found to outperform the others with statistical significance. However, the cooperative coevolutionary algorithms are able to find solutions with super linear speedups in many cases, with respect to NSGA-II. This is an important issue, since one fitness evaluation implies 10 simulations in ns3, taking among 10 and 94 seconds, depending on the network density, and 10,000 fitness evaluations are performed in every run. We observed that the solutions found by CCNSGAII-long are the best ones in terms of coverage, while CCNSGAII-short provides the solution with better values of forwarding and energy use. We were able to find a single best overall solution for all objectives.

As future work, we plan to include robustness to the optimization process in order to cope with the high uncertainty intrinsic to this problem.

Acknowledgments. B. Dorronsoro acknowledges the support by the National Research Fund, Luxembourg, under AFR contract no 4017742.

References

1. Abdou, W., Henriet, A., Bloch, C., Dhoutaut, D., Charlet, D., Spies, F.: Using an evolutionary algorithm to optimize the broadcasting methods in mobile ad hoc networks. Journal of Network and Computer Applications **34**, 1794–1804 (2011)
2. Alba, E., Bouvry, P., Dorronsoro, B., Luna, F., Nebro, A.J.: A cellular multi-objective genetic algorithm for optimal broadcasting strategy in metropolitan MANETs. In: Nature Inspired Distributed Computing (NIDISC), p. 192b (2005)
3. Deb, K., Pratap, A., Agarwal, S., Meyarivan, T.: A fast and elitist multiobjective genetic algorithm: NSGA-II. IEEE Trans. on Evol. Comp. **6**(2), 182–197 (2002)
4. Dorronsoro, B., Danoy, G., Bouvry, P., Nebro, A.J.: Multi-objective Cooperative Coevolutionary Evolutionary Algorithms for Continuous and Combinatorial Optimization. In: Bouvry, P., González-Vélez, H., Kołodziej, J. (eds.) Intelligent Decision Systems in Large-Scale Distributed Environments. SCI, vol. 362, pp. 49–74. Springer, Heidelberg (2011)
5. Dorronsoro, B., Danoy, G., Nebro, A.J., Bouvry, P.: Achieving super-linear performance in parallel multi-objective evolutionary algorithms by means of cooperative coevolution. Computers & Operations Research **40**(6), 1552–1563 (2013)
6. Dorronsoro, B., Ruiz, P., Danoy, G., Pigné, Y., Bouvry, P.: Evolutionary Algorithms for Mobile Ad Hoc Networks. Wiley/IEEE Computer Society (2014)
7. Durillo, J.J., Nebro, A.J., Luna, F., Alba, E.: Solving Three-Objective Optimization Problems Using a New Hybrid Cellular Genetic Algorithm. In: Rudolph, G., Jansen, T., Lucas, S., Poloni, C., Beume, N. (eds.) PPSN 2008. LNCS, vol. 5199, pp. 661–670. Springer, Heidelberg (2008)
8. García-Nieto, J., Alba, E.: Automatic Parameter Tuning with Metaheuristics of the AODV Routing Protocol for Vehicular Ad-Hoc Networks. In: Di Chio, C., Brabazon, A., Di Caro, G.A., Ebner, M., Farooq, M., Fink, A., Grahl, J., Greenfield, G., Machado, P., O'Neill, M., Tarantino, E., Urquhart, N. (eds.) EvoApplications 2010, Part II. LNCS, vol. 6025, pp. 21–30. Springer, Heidelberg (2010)
9. Groenevelt, R., Altman, E., Nain, P.: Relaying in mobile ad hoc networks: The brownian motion mobility model. J. of Wireless Networks, 561–571 (2006)
10. Hsiao, P.-C., Chiang, T.-C., Fu, L.-C.: Particle swarm optimization for the minimum energy broadcast problem in wireless ad-hoc networks. In: IEEE Congress on Evolutionary Computation (CEC), pp. 1–8 (2012)
11. Ni, S., Tseng, Y., Chen, Y., Sheu, J.: The broadcast storm problem in a mobile ad hoc network. In: Conf. on Mobile Comp. and Networking, pp. 151–162 (1999)
12. Ruiz, P., Bouvry, P.: Distributed energy self-adaptation in ad hoc networks. In: Proc. of IEEE Int. Workshop on Management of Emerging Networks and Services (MENS), in Conjunction with IEEE Globecom, pp. 539–543 (2010)
13. Ruiz, P., Dorronsoro, B., Bouvry, P.: Finding scalable configurations for AEDB broadcasting protocol using multi-objective evolutionary algorithms. Cluster Computing **16**(3), 527–544 (2013)
14. Toutouh, J., Nesmachnow, S., Alba, E.: Fast energy-aware OLSR routing in VANETs by means of a parallel evolutionary algorithm. Cluster Computing **16**(3), 435–450 (2013)
15. Wolf, S., Merz, P.: Evolutionary Local Search for the Minimum Energy Broadcast Problem. In: van Hemert, J., Cotta, C. (eds.) EvoCOP 2008. LNCS, vol. 4972, pp. 61–72. Springer, Heidelberg (2008)

Improving Extremal Optimization in Load Balancing by Local Search

Ivanoe De Falco[1], Eryk Laskowski[2]([✉]), Richard Olejnik[3], Umberto Scafuri[1], Ernesto Tarantino[1], and Marek Tudruj[2,4]

[1] Institute of High Performance Computing and Networking, CNR, Naples, Italy
{ivanoe.defalco,umberto.scafuri,ernesto.tarantino}@na.icar.cnr.it
[2] Institute of Computer Science, Polish Academy of Sciences, Warsaw, Poland
{laskowsk,tudruj}@ipipan.waw.pl
[3] Computer Science Laboratory, University of Science and Technology of Lille,
Villeneuve-d'Ascq, France
richard.olejnik@lifl.fr
[4] Polish-Japanese Institute of Information Technology, Warsaw, Poland

Abstract. The paper concerns the use of Extremal Optimization (EO) technique in dynamic load balancing for optimized execution of distributed programs. EO approach is used to periodically detect the best candidates for task migration leading to balanced execution. To improve the quality of load balancing and decrease time complexity of the algorithms, we have improved EO by a local search of the best computing node to receive migrating tasks. The improved guided EO algorithm assumes a two-step stochastic selection based on two separate fitness functions. The functions are based on specific program models which estimate relations between the programs and the executive hardware. The proposed load balancing algorithm is compared against a standard EO-based algorithm with random placement of migrated tasks and a classic genetic algorithm. The algorithm is assessed by experiments with simulated load balancing of distributed program graphs and analysis of the outcome of the discussed approaches.

Keywords: Distributed program design · Extremal optimization · Load balancing

1 Introduction

The paper presents Extremal Optimization (EO) [1] based load balancing algorithm for distributed systems. The proposed algorithm is composed of iterative optimization phases which improve program task placement on processors to determine the possibly best balance of computational loads and to define periodic migration of tasks. The EO algorithm discovers the candidate tasks for migration based on a special quality model including the computation and communication parameters of parallel tasks. The paper presents an improved load balancing algorithm comparing the algorithm given in [2], which was based on

© Springer-Verlag Berlin Heidelberg 2014
A.I. Esparcia-Alcázar et al. (Eds.): EvoApplications 2014, LNCS 8602, pp. 51–62, 2014.
DOI: 10.1007/978-3-662-45523-4_5

classical Extremal Optimization approach. In the classical EO the fully random selection of a new improved partial solution in the neighbourhood of the solution being modified is done. The fully random selection has been considered unsatisfactory, since for a big number of executive processors a degradation of the quality of obtained result (the parallel speedup of the applications) was observed. Therefore, we have improved the applied EO algorithm by a replacement of the fully random selection of the target computing node in migration by the stochastic selection performed with the guidance by some knowledge of the problem properties. The guidance is based on a formula which estimates how a migrated task matches the given processor in respect to the global computational and communicational balance in the system. It should be stressed that we have maintained the nature-inspired solution improvement but done in the way which speeds up the convergence of the algorithm. As a result we have obtained a correct behavior of the algorithm when the cardinality of processor set in the system increases.

The algorithm is assessed by experiments with simulated load balancing of distributed program graphs. In particular, the experiments compare three algorithms: the proposed load balancing method including the EO with a guided stochastic selection of the improved solution, an EO with fully random selection of the improved solution and a genetic algorithm (GA). The comparison shows that the quality of load balancing with the guided EO is in most cases better than with fully random selection and with the GA.

The paper is organized as follows. In Section 2 the related works in load balancing based on nature inspired algorithms are reported. In Section 3 the EO principles are shortly explained, and the EO with guided state changes is introduced. Section 4 describes the theoretical foundations for the discussed algorithm, explains how the EO is applied to the dynamic processor load balancing. In Section 5 the experiments which assess the proposed algorithms are presented.

2   Related Works

A huge quantity of papers exist in literature dealing with dynamic load balancing in parallel and distributed systems. Good reviews and classifications of classic load balancing methods are presented in [3–6].

Genetic algorithms have been the first nature–inspired optimization method to be used with reference to this issue. Munetomo et al. [7] are among the first to present a genetic algorithm for stochastic environments and show its application to dynamic load balancing in distributed systems. Zomaya and Teh [8] investigate how a genetic algorithm can be employed to solve the dynamic load balancing problem. To address the problem of dynamic load balancing in a processing pool, Uyar and Harmanci [9] apply an improved genetic algorithm called *damGA* (diploidy-aging-meiosis Genetic Algorithm). Very recently, Lin and Deung [10] face dynamic load balancing in cloud-based multimedia system using a genetic algorithm. More recently, other nature–inspired optimization methods have been investigated for dynamic load balancing, including Particle

Swarm Optimization (PSO). A good review of several such methods can be found in a very recent paper [11].

At the best of our knowledge, no other authors have attempted to use EO for dynamic load balancing. We feel, instead, that EO has all the desired features useful to efficiently tackling this problem. Firstly, EO is perfectly suited to face combinatorial optimization problems where solutions are represented by integer values. Secondly, evaluating each component of a solution on its own and changing a bad component only, rather than the whole solution, is highly desirable when an incremental improvement is necessary. GA or PSO would modify the solution as a whole, possibly destroying good issues too. So, the proposed approach has clear originality features and enables making profit of EO advantages such as low computational complexity and limited use of memory space.

3   Extremal Optimization Algorithm Principles

Extremal Optimization was proposed by Boettcher and Percus [1], following the Bak–Sneppen approach of self–organized dynamic criticality [12]. It represents a method for NP–hard combinatorial and physical optimization problems. EO is based on improvements of a single solution S consisting of a given number of components s_i, called species. Each component is a variable of the problem. A local fitness value is assigned to each component. At each time step, S is evolved by randomly updating the worst variable only in respect to ϕ_i, to a solution S' belonging to its neighbourhood $Neigh(S)$. After each update, a global fitness $\Phi(S)$ is computed and the modified solution S' is registered if its global fitness is better than that of the best solution found so far.

We apply a probabilistic version of EO based on a parameter τ, i.e., τ–EO, introduced by Boettcher and Percus, which prevents the solutions from staying in a local optimum. For a minimization problem, the components are first ranked in the increasing order of local fitness values. Then, a distribution probability k over ranks is considered as follows: $p_k \sim k^{-\tau}$, $1 \le k \le |S|$ for a given value of τ. At each update of S, a rank k is selected according to p_k so that the species s_i with $i = \pi(k)$ randomly changes its state and the solution moves unconditionally to $S' \in Neigh(S)$.

3.1   Extremal Optimization With Guided State Changes

During our experimental research on load balancing of distributed applications, reported in [2], we have revealed that EO is able to provide the best results for almost all combinations of system and application parameters.

However, we have noticed that, when the number of neighbour states of rank k increases (i.e. the number of processors is higher), the algorithm starts struggling with the problem of too many possible moves. The probability of "good" state change decreases. To alleviate this problem we incorporate more problem-specific information into the algorithm. It is implemented as a local target function ω_s, which is computed for all neighbours $Neigh(S)$ of rank k. Then

---

Algorithm 1. τ–EO algorithm with Guided State Changes (EO–GS)

---

initialize configuration S at will

$S_{\text{best}} \leftarrow S$

while total number of iterations $\mathcal{N}_{\text{iter}}$ not reached **do**

    evaluate ϕ_i for each variable s_i of the current solution S

    rank the variables s_i based on their fitness ϕ_i

    choose the rank k according to $k^{-\tau}$ so that the variable s_j with $j = \pi(k)$ is selected

    evaluate ω_s for each neighbour $s' \in Neigh(S)$, generated by s_j change

    rank neighbours $s' \in Neigh(S)$ based on the value of target function ω_s

    choose $S' \in Neigh(S)$ according to the exponential distribution $\text{Exp}(\lambda)$

    accept $S \leftarrow S'$ unconditionally

    if $\Phi(S) < \Phi(S_{\text{best}})$ **then**

        $S_{\text{best}} \leftarrow S$

    end if

end while

return S_{best} and $\Phi(S_{\text{best}})$

---

the neighbours are sorted according to the increasing value of ω_s. The new state $S' \in Neigh(S)$ is selected randomly using the exponential distribution $\text{Exp}(\lambda)$ over the sorted neighbours $Neigh(S)$. Thus, the stochastic local search towards "better" neighbours (according to the value of ω_s) is performed. The bias to the "better" values is controlled by the λ parameter of the exponential distribution. The scheme of the Extremal Optimization with Guided State Changes (EO–GS) is shown in Algorithm 1.

4 Load Balancing Based on Extremal Optimization

The proposed load balancing algorithm is meant for distributed application programs composed of T indivisible tasks which are threads (single-thread processes). Each task is composed of sequences of computational instructions (blocks) separated by communication instructions with other tasks.

We assume a centralized program execution environment which means that the executive system works under control of some load balancing infrastructure responsible for organizing optimized execution of programs. The executive system is a cluster of N processor aka computational nodes interconnected by a message passing network.

Our load balancing problem is formally defined in the following way: during program execution dynamically map each task t_k, $k \in \{1 \ldots |T|\}$ of the program to a computational node n, $n \in [0, N-1]$ in such a way that the total program execution time is minimized, assuming the program and system definition as stated earlier in this section. Dynamic task mapping to computational nodes can change during program execution by means of task migration.

The load balancing method proposed in the paper, consists in execution of a series of indivisible pairs of two main steps: the detection and the correction of processor load imbalance. The load imbalance detection step employs some measurement infrastructure to monitor the states of the executive system and the application program relevant for the detection of system load imbalance. In parallel with the execution of an application program, computing nodes periodically report their loads to a load balancing monitor which evaluates the current system load imbalance value. Depending on this value, the second step (i.e. the imbalance correction) is done or step one is repeated. In the second step, we execute the EO-based algorithm described in next sections, which determines the set of tasks for migration and the migration target nodes. Based on that, the physical task migrations are executed and the algorithm goes to step one.

4.1   Detection of Load Imbalance

Two parameters are used to evaluate the state of the system:
$Ind_{power}(n)$ – computing power of a processor node n, which is the sum of nominal computing powers of all cores on the node, in MIPS, MFLOPS or similar, $Time^{\%}_{\text{CPU}}(n)$ – the current CPU time availability i.e. percentage of the CPU computing power currently available for application threads on the node n, periodically estimated by load observation agents on computing nodes.

A load imbalance LI (a boolean) is defined based on the difference of the current CPU time availability between the most heavily and the least heavily loaded computing nodes:

$$LI = \max_{n \in P}(\mathit{Time}^{\%}_{\text{CPU}}(n)) - \min_{n \in P}(\mathit{Time}^{\%}_{\text{CPU}}(n)) \geq \alpha$$

where P is the set of all computing nodes. The detection of load imbalance equal *true* requires a load correction. α is determined using an experimental approach (in our experiments we have set it between 25% and 75%).

4.2   Correction of Load Imbalance

The application is characterized by two metrics, which should be provided by a programmer based on the volume of computations and communications in tasks:

1. COM(t_s, t_d) is the communication metrics for a pair of tasks t_s and t_d,
2. WP(t) is the load weight metrics introduced by a task t.

COM(t_s, t_d) and WP(t) metrics can constitute exact values, e.g. for well-defined tasks sizes and inter-task communication in regular parallel applications, or only some predictions, e.g. when the computation depends on the processed data as in irregular parallel applications.

A task mapping solution S is represented by a vector $\mu = (\mu_1, \dots, \mu_{|T|})$ of $|T|$ integers from the interval $[0, N-1]$, where the value $\mu_i = j$ means that the solution S under consideration maps the i–th task t_i of the application onto the computing node j.

The global fitness function $\Phi(S)$ is defined as

$$\begin{aligned} \Phi(S) = {}& attrExtTotal(S) * \Delta_1 + migration(S) * \Delta_2 + \\ & + imbalance(S) * [1 - (\Delta_1 + \Delta_2)] \end{aligned} \tag{1}$$

where Δ_1, Δ_2 parameters control the weight of components of the global fitness, $1 > \Delta_1 \geq 0, 1 > \Delta_2 \geq 0$ and $\Delta_1 + \Delta_2 < 1$. The function $attrExtTotal(S) \in \{0,1\}$ represents the impact of the total external communication between tasks on the quality of a given mapping S. The function $migration(S) \in \{0,1\}$ is a migration costs metrics. It is equal to 0 when there is no migration, when all tasks have to be migrated $migration(S) = 1$. The function $imbalance(S) \in \{0,1\}$ represents the numerical load imbalance metrics in the solution S. It is equal to 1 when there exists at least one unloaded computing node, otherwise it is equal to the normalized average absolute load deviation of tasks in S.

The local fitness function of a task $\phi(t)$ is designed in such a way that it forces moving tasks away from overloaded nodes, at the same time preserving low external (inter-node) communication. The γ parameter ($0 < \gamma < 1$) allows tuning the weight of load metrics.

$$\phi(t) = \gamma * load(\mu_t) + (1 - \gamma) * rank(t) \qquad (2)$$

The function $load(n)$ indicates whether the node n, which executes t, is overloaded (i.e. it indicates how much its load exceeds the average load of all nodes). The $rank(t)$ function governs the selection of best candidates for migration. The chance for migration have tasks, which show low communication with their current node (attraction) and low load deviation from the average load. The load balancing parameters mentioned above are explained in full details in [2].

4.3   Guided Target Node Selection for State Changes

In the standard EO algorithm (see [2]), any neighboring state could be selected randomly using the uniform probability distribution. The idea of a guided state changes is based on some "biased" random selection, to enable preferring some neighbors over others. At each update of rank k, nodes $n \in N$ are sorted according to $\omega(n1, n2)$ function and one of them is selected using the exponential distribution $Exp(\lambda)$. The bias to the "better" values, i.e. lower values of $\omega(n1, n2)$ in our case, is controlled by the λ parameter of the exponential distribution.

A "biased" random selection uses formula similar to those used for the local fitness calculation to qualify the computing nodes for migration of task j:

$$\omega(n1, n2) = \begin{cases} relload(n1) - relload(n2) & \text{if } relload(n1) \neq relload(n2) \\ attrext(j, n2) - attrext(j, n1) & \text{otherwise} \end{cases}$$

where:

$$attrext(j, n) = \sum_{e \in T(n)} (COM(e, j) + COM(j, e)), \text{ normalized vs. } \max_{e \in N}(attrext(j, e))$$

$$relload(n) = \frac{loaddev(n) - \min_{m \in [0, N-1]} loaddev(m)}{\max_{m \in [0, N-1]} loaddev(m) - \min_{m \in [0, N-1]} loaddev(m)}$$

$$loaddev(n) = NWP(S, n) / Ind_{power}(n) - \overline{WP}$$

and $T(n) = \{t \in T : \mu_t = n\}$ — the set of threads, placed on node n, $NWP(S, n) = \sum_{t \in T : \mu_t = n} WP(t)$, $\overline{WP} = \sum_{t \in T} WP(t) / \sum_{n \in [0, N-1]} Ind_{power}(n)$.

When $\omega(n1, n2)$ has a low value, the computational load of node $n1$ is lower than that of node $n2$ or the task j has stronger attraction to node $n1$. This is the preferred target of migration. High values of $\omega(n1, n2)$ indicate overloading of node $n1$ or no communication to this node from task j.

5   Experimental Results

We describe below experimental results obtained by simulated execution of application programs with the proposed method of load balancing in a distributed system. The assumed program parallelization model corresponds to parallelization based on message-passing, using the MPI library for communication. The experiments were run in a simulated cluster of multi–core processors. Each processor had its own main memory and a network interface. At the level of the network interfaces data transfers and communication contention were modeled.

In the experiments, a set of 10 randomly generated synthetic exemplary programs was used. Their general structures were phase-like, in which they resembled MPI-based parallel programs which corresponded to numerical computations or simulations of physical phenomena. The programs were represented as a set of phases (see Fig 1), each composed of parallel tasks (threads). Tasks of the same phase could communicate. At the boundaries between phases there was a global exchange of data which corresponded to external communication between processes. Application programs contained from about 60 to 550 tasks. Their communication/computation ratio C/E was in the range $[0.05, 0.20]$.

Based on the time properties of tasks two types of applications were distinguished: regular and irregular. Regular applications had fixed task execution times. Irregular applications had the execution time of tasks depending on the processed data. They showed unpredictable both execution times of tasks and the communication schemes. With irregular tasks, system load imbalance could

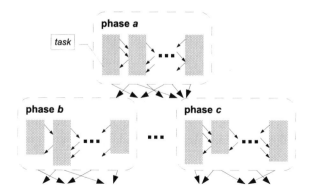

Fig. 1. The general structure of exemplary applications

occur even without variations in computing nodes availability. With regular applications system load imbalance could occur due to the suboptimal placement of tasks on processors or when runtime conditions had changed. The properties of the proposed load balancing algorithm for both types of applications were comparatively examined.

For comparison purposes, the same simulated parallel environment and the set of graphs were used. We compared EO and EO–GS to genetic algorithm (GA) which used the same global fitness function. GA used binary-encoded chromosomes, in which an allele at position i was the processor number of the task i. Two genetic operators were used: single-point crossover and mutation. The selection was based on roulette-wheel scheme. We used the following GA parameters: the size of population – 50, the probability of mutation – 0.015, the probability of crossover – 0.25, the number of iterations – 500. Half of the chromosomes of the initial population was generated randomly, the second half was initialized through cloning of the current placement of application tasks.

5.1   Performance of the Presented Algorithms

In the first series of experiments, load-balanced execution of phase-like applications was studied in systems containing from 2 to 32 homogeneous processor nodes. The following parameters for load balancing control were used: $\alpha = 0.5, \Delta_1 = 0.25, \Delta_2 = 0.25, \gamma = 0.5, \tau = 1.5$, for EO–GS $\lambda = 1.0$. The number of iterations for EO and EO–GS was set to 500. The results correspond to averages of 5 runs of each application. For each run 4 different methods of initial task placements (random, round-robin, METIS, packed) were tested. METIS is a graph partitioning optimization software [13]. The packed method consists in round-robin mapping of equal groups of tasks. In total, 20 runs were executed for each parameter set to produce an averaged result.

The speedup of both EO–based algorithms and the genetic algorithm as a function of the number of processors is shown in Fig. 2. For regular applications (upper curves) the speedup improvement due to EO–based algorithms is generally bigger (not worse or better) than that of GA. Our exemplary irregular applications (lower curves) give smaller speedup than regular ones (with or without load balancing) what is an expected result, since parallel execution of such applications is less efficient. However, for irregular applications the EO-GS algorithm is generally the best comparing all the others. It should be stressed that EO-GS gives much better results than EO and GA especially for a bigger number of processors. It is due to completely random placement of migrated tasks on processors in EO and GA, not supported by any knowledge of the system and program state. EO-GS uses a more thorough migration target selection.

Since migration costs can be very different (a single migration can be as short as a simple task activation message, but also it can involve a transfer of the processed data, which is usually very costly), we decided to keep the generality of our experiment results and to approximate the imposed load balancing costs by the number of task migrations, Fig. 3. The number of migrations is decidedly higher for irregular applications (upper curves). The average cost imposed by EO–GS algorithm is generally lower than the cost introduced by other approaches. For irregular applications the migration number with EO-GS is lower than with the EO and GA. For regular applications the number of task migrations in both EO-based algorithms is almost halved comparing GA. Experiments revealed that the GA approach can not work out an efficient migration decision for irregular applications run on bigger number of processor, thus we notice sudden drop in the GA (irg) curves both in Fig. 2 and 3.

To generalize comparisons of performance of the discussed load balancing algorithms, we have computed the average speedup improvement of the considered

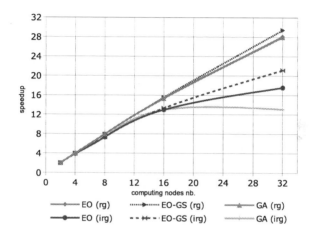

Fig. 2. Speedup for different number of nodes for tested algorithms

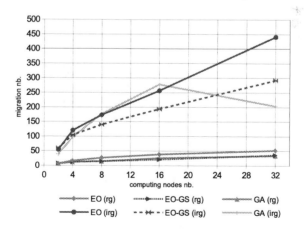

Fig. 3. Cost of the dynamic load balancing as the number of task migrations per single execution of an application

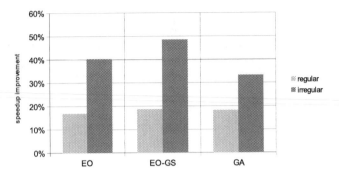

Fig. 4. Average speedup improvement for different algorithms due to load balancing

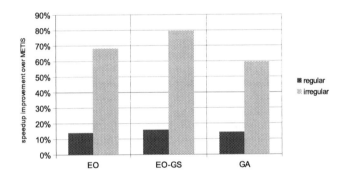

Fig. 5. Comparison of speedup obtained by different algorithms and METIS initial task placement

algorithms over execution without load balancing. The speedup improvement is calculated as $S_b/S_u - 1$, where S_b is the speedup obtained when load balancing algorithm is active, S_u is the speedup of the unbalanced execution. The best speedup improvement over the unbalanced execution for both irregular and regular applications is provided by EO–GS algorithm (see Fig. 4).

To justify the quality of the results, we have compared the speedup obtained for dynamic load balancing using the analysed algorithms to the speedup based on static task placement obtained by METIS graph partitioning algorithm. To do so, we executed regular and irregular applications with initial task placement by METIS and the same applications starting from imbalanced, random initial placement with the dynamic load balancing switched on. For regular applications the improvement due to load balancing with static initial METIS placement is small (in the range 12% – 16%, see Fig. 5). The improvement indicates that the compared algorithms are able to work out profitable migration decisions even

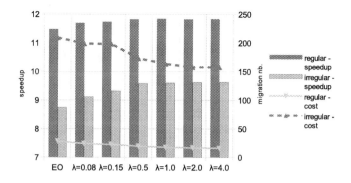

Fig. 6. Average application speedup and migration number (load balancing cost) for different values of EO–GS parameters as a function of λ

after METIS initial optimisation of regular applications, resulting in their balanced execution. For irregular applications METIS initial optimisation is not sufficient for efficient balanced execution up to the end of their task sets. For irregular applications speedup improvement after METIS initialisation due to dynamic load balancing is on average several times higher than for regular applications. We can see that the EO–GS algorithm gives here the best results, better than other studied algorithms by 15%.

5.2   The Algorithm Parameter Setting

The influence of the setting of λ parameter on overall performance of EO–GS algorithm is shown in Fig. 6 (EO denotes here the results for the standard EO algorithm). Increasing value of λ results in a noticeable increase of the speedup for irregular applications, at the same time reducing the cost of load balancing (i.e. the number of migrations). Although the cost initially decreases slowly, for $\lambda = 0.5$ or more is much smaller than in the standard EO algorithm. For regular applications λ has almost no impact on the average speedup (there is a slight increase) and slightly reduces the number of migrations. Note that regular applications show already high speedup for standard EO, thus improvement is possible only through reduction of the number of migrations. For both types of graphs increasing λ above 1.0 has no longer a significant effect on the results.

6   Conclusions

The paper has presented the dynamic load balancing in distributed systems based on application of the Extremal Optimization approach. The proposed load balancing algorithm is an improved version of the classic Extremal Optimization, in which we replaced the completely random computing node selection by the stochastic selection where node selection probability is guided by some knowledge of the problem. Our approach proved to be an efficient method for load balancing, distinguished by low computational complexity and limited use of memory space.

The proposed algorithm has been assessed by experiments with simulated load balancing of distributed program graphs. In particular, the experiments compare load balancing with EO with guided search against the classic EO and genetic algorithm based on equivalent theoretical foundations. The comparison shows that the quality of the improved EO-based load balancing outperforms in most cases that with classical EO and the genetic algorithm.

References

1. Boettcher, S., Percus, A.G.: Extremal optimization: methods derived from coevolution. In: Proceedings of the Genetic and Evolutionary Computation Conference (GECCO 1999), pp. 825–832. Morgan Kaufmann, San Francisco (1999)
2. Olejnik, R., De Falco, I., Laskowski, E., Scafuri, U., Tarantino, E., Tudruj, M.: Load Balancing in Distributed Applications Based on Extremal Optimization. In: Esparcia-Alcázar, A.I. (ed.) EvoApplications 2013. LNCS, vol. 7835, pp. 52–61. Springer, Heidelberg (2013)
3. Barker, K., Chrisochoides, N.: An evaluation of a framework for the dynamic load balancing of highly adaptive and irregular parallel applications In: Proceedings of the ACM/IEEE Conference on Supercomputing, Phoenix. ACM Press (2003)
4. Willebeek-LeMair, M.H., Reeves, A.P.: Strategies for dynamic load balancing on highly parallel computers. IEEE Trans. on Parallel and Distributed Systems 4, 979–993 (1993)
5. Xu, C., Francis, C., Lau, M.: Load balancing in parallel computers: Theory and Practice. Kluwer Academic Publishers, Norwell (1997)
6. Khan, R.Z., Ali, J.: Classification of task partitioning and load balancing strategies in distributed parallel computing systems. International Journal of Computer Applications **60**(17), 48–53 (2012)
7. Munetomo, M., Takai, M.N.K., Sato, Y.: A stochastic genetic algorithm for dynamic load balancing in distributed systems. In: Proceedings of the IEEE International Conference on Systems, Man and Cybernetics, vol. 4, pp. 3795–3799. IEEE Press (1995)
8. Zomaya, A.Y., Teh, Y.-H.: Observations on using genetic algorithms for dynamic load-balancing. IEEE Trans. on Parallel and Distributed Systems 12(9), 899–911 (2001)
9. Uyar, A.S., Harmanci, A.E.: Application of an improved diploid genetic algorithm for optimizing performance through dynamic load balancing. In: Proceedings of 2002 WSEAS International Conferences. WSEAS Press (2002)
10. Lin, C.-C., Deng, D.-J.: Dynamic load balancing in cloud-based multimedia system using genetic algorithm. Chang, R.-S., et al (eds.) Advances in Intelligent Systems & Applications, SIST 20, pp. 461–470. Springer, Heidelberg (2013)
11. Mishra, M., Agarwal, S., Mishra, P., Singh, S.: Comparative analysis of various evolutionary techniques of load balancing: a review. International Journal of Computer Applications 63(15) (2013)
12. Sneppen, K., et al.: Evolution as a self-organized critical phenomenon. Proc. Natl. Acad. Sci. **92**, 5209–5213 (1995)
13. Karypis, G., Kumar, V.: Multilevel graph partitioning schemes. In: Proc. 24th Intern. Conf. Par. Proc., III. pp. 113–122. CRC Press (1995)

Studying the Reporting Cells Planning with the Non-dominated Sorting Genetic Algorithm II

Víctor Berrocal-Plaza[✉], Miguel A. Vega-Rodríguez, and Juan M. Sánchez-Pérez

Department of Computers and Communications Technologies, University of Extremadura Escuela Politécnica, Campus Universitario S/N, 10003 Cáceres, Spain {vicberpla,mavega,sanperez}@unex.es

Abstract. This manuscript addresses a vital task in any Public Land Mobile Network, the mobile location management. This management task is tackled following the Reporting Cells strategy. Basically, the Reporting Cells planning consists in selecting a subset of network cells as Reporting Cells with the aim of controlling the subscribers' movement and minimizing the signaling traffic. In previous works, the Reporting Cells Planning Problem was optimized by using single-objective metaheuristics, in which the two objective functions were linearly combined. This technique simplifies the optimization problem but has got several drawbacks. In this work, with the aim of avoiding such drawbacks, we have adapted a well-known multiobjective metaheuristic: the Non-dominated Sorting Genetic Algorithm II (NSGAII). Furthermore, a multiobjective approach obtains a wide range of solutions (each one related to a specific trade-off between objectives), and hence, it gives the possibility of selecting the solution that best adjusts to the real state of the signaling network. The quality of our proposal is checked by means of an experimental study, where we demonstrate that our version of NSGAII outperforms other algorithms published in the literature.

Keywords: Reporting Cells Planning Problem · Mobile location management · Multiobjective optimization · Non-dominated Sorting Genetic Algorithm II

1 Introduction

In the Public Land Mobile Networks, the desired coverage area is divided into several smaller regions known as cells, among which the available radio-electric resources are distributed and reused [1]. In this way, these networks are able to provide service to a huge number of mobile subscribers with few resources. Therefore, it is obvious that this cell-based architecture requires of a system that controls the subscribers' mobility in order to locate the callee terminals and redirect the incoming calls. Furthermore, the proper mobile location management is

© Springer-Verlag Berlin Heidelberg 2014
A.I. Esparcia-Alcázar et al. (Eds.): EvoApplications 2014, LNCS 8602, pp. 63–74, 2014.
DOI: 10.1007/978-3-662-45523-4_6

a critical issue in current mobile networks due to the exponential increment in the number of mobile terminals that has occurred in the last decade.

There are several strategies to manage the subscriber mobility [2], all of them consist of two main procedures: the subscriber location update (LU) and the paging (PA). The subscriber location update is the procedure whereby a mobile station (or subscriber's terminal) updates its location in the location register databases according to a method pre-established by the network operator. Never Update, Always Update, Reporting Cells, and Registration Areas are examples of static location updates (static location updates are more used than dynamic ones because they require fewer network capabilities [3]). In this work, we study a popular location update: the Reporting Cells strategy [4]. This strategy controls the subscriber mobility by selecting a subset of network cells as Reporting Cells (a mobile station only updates its location when it moves to a Reporting Cell). On the other hand, the paging procedure is the method used by the network to know the exact cell in which the callee subscribers are located [5]. The different paging procedures could be classified into two main groups: probabilistic and non-probabilistic. In this work, we use the same paging procedure as in [6–9]: the Blanket Polling paging, a non-probabilistic paging in which all the network cells that have to be paged are polled simultaneously.

The Reporting Cells Planning Problem defines a multiobjective optimization problem with two conflicting objective functions: minimize the location update cost (LU_{cost}) and minimize the paging cost (PA_{cost}). However, in recent literature, this multiobjective optimization problem was tackled by means of different single-objective metaheuristics [6–9]. For it, these two objective functions were linearly combined into a single objective function. The linear aggregation of the objective functions allows simplifying the problem but has got associated several drawbacks (see Section 3).

With the aim of avoiding such drawbacks, we propose the use of multiobjective optimization for finding quasi-optimal configurations of Reporting Cells. This is a novel contribution because, to the best of our knowledge, there are no other works in the literature that tackle the Reporting Cells Planning Problem with a multiobjective approach.

The rest of the paper is organized as follows. The related works are discussed in Section 2. Section 3 shows a formal description of the Reporting Cells Planning Problem. Section 4 defines the main features of a multiobjective optimization problem and presents a detailed explanation of our proposal. Section 5 gathers the experimental results and comparisons with other works published in the literature. Finally, our conclusion and future work are discussed in Section 6.

2   Related Work

In the literature, there are several works that tackle the Reporting Cells Planning Problem (RCPP). This problem was firstly formulated by A. Bar-Noy and I. Kessler in [4], where the authors demonstrated that the RCPP is an NP-complete problem. And subsequently, different methodologies were proposed with the aim of solving this location management problem. A. Hac and X. Zhou presented in [10] a heuristic method to find quasi-optimal solutions of a simplified RCPP (the RCPP was simplified by considering the paging cost as a constraint). R. Subrata and A. Y. Zomaya proposed in [6] three artificial life techniques of the single-objective optimization field: Genetic Algorithm (GA), Tabu Search (TS), and Ant Colony Optimization (ACO). In these algorithms, the RCPP objective functions were linearly combined with the aim of simplifying the optimization problem. The same strategy was used in [7–9], where the RCPP was studied with the algorithms: Geometric Particle Swarm Optimization (GPSO) [7], a combination of the Hopfield Neural Network with a Ball Dropping mechanism (HNN-BD) [7], Differential Evolution (DE) [8], and the Scatter Search algorithm (SS) [9].

In contrast to these related works, we propose the use of multiobjective optimization to avoid the drawbacks associated with the linear aggregation of the objective functions. This approach is a novel contribution because, to the best of the authors' knowledge, there are no other authors that tackle the RCPP with multiobjective optimization.

3   Reporting Cells Planning Problem

The Reporting Cells is a static location management strategy which was proposed by A. Bar-Noy and I. Kessler in [4]. This strategy controls the subscriber mobility by selecting a subset of network cells as Reporting Cells (RCs). In this way, a mobile station only updates its location when entering a Reporting Cell. On the other hand, the paging procedure is only conducted in a subset of network cells (all the network cells of this subset are paged simultaneously). This subset is determined by means of the vicinity factor $(V(i))$, which can be defined as the maximum number of network cells that must be paged to locate a callee subscriber [6–9]. For an RC (RC_i), $V(i)$ corresponds to the number of non-Reporting Cells (nRC) reachable from this RC (RC_i) without passing over other RC (RC_j), and including the RC in question (RC_i). And for an nRC (nRC_i), due to the fact that an nRC might be in the vicinity of several RC, $V(i)$ corresponds to the maximum vicinity factor of all the RC reachable from this nRC (nRC_i). Fig. 1(a) and Fig. 1(b) show an example of the vicinity factor calculation for an RC and an nRC respectively.

Therefore, the challenge of this location management strategy is to find the configurations of Reporting Cells that minimize the location update cost (LU_{cost}) and the paging cost (PA_{cost}). Formally, these two objective functions could be expressed as Equation 1 and Equation 2 respectively, where N is the number of network cells. ρ_i is a binary variable that is equal to 1 when the cell i is an RC, otherwise ρ_i is equal to 0. $N_{LU}(i)$ is the number of location updates of the cell i. $N_P(i)$ is the number of incoming calls of the network cell i. And $V(i)$ is the vicinity factor of the cell i.

$$\boldsymbol{f}_1 = min \left\{ LU_{cost} = \sum_{i=0}^{N-1} \rho_i \cdot N_{LU}(i) \right\}, \tag{1}$$

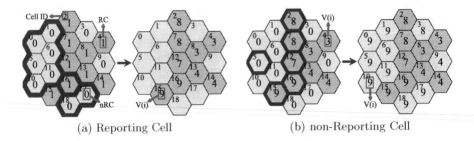

(a) Reporting Cell   (b) non-Reporting Cell

Fig. 1. Calculus of the vicinity factor

$$\boldsymbol{f}_2 = min\left\{ PA_{cost} = \sum_{i=0}^{N-1} N_P(i) \cdot V(i) \right\}. \tag{2}$$

Note that these two objective functions are conflicting. The LU_{cost} is reduced to a minimum when all the network cells are nRC (i.e. there is no location update). However, in this case, the PA_{cost} is maximum because the callee subscribers should be searched in the whole network. On the other hand, the PA_{cost} is minimum when all the network cells are RC (i.e. $V(i) = 1 \forall i \in [0, N-1]$), but in this case the LU_{cost} is maximum because a location update will be performed whenever a mobile station moves from one cell to another.

In previous works [6–9], this problem was tackled by using different meta-heuristics of the Single-objective Optimization (SO) field. For it, the optimization problem was simplified by means of the linear aggregation of these two objective functions, see Equation 3. However, this technique has several drawbacks. Firstly, a very accurate knowledge of the problem is required when configuring the weight coefficient ($\beta \in \Re$). Secondly, the appropriate value of such coefficient might be different for different states of the signaling network. And thirdly, a single-objective optimization algorithm must perform an independent run for every value of β.

$$\boldsymbol{f}_3^{SO}(\beta) = min\left\{ \beta \cdot LU_{cost} + PA_{cost} \right\}. \tag{3}$$

In this work, we propose a multiobjective approach with the aim of avoiding these drawbacks (a multiobjective optimization algorithm treats each objective function separately). Furthermore, a multiobjective approach gives the possibility of selecting among a wide range of solutions the one that best adjusts to the real state of the signaling network.

4   Multiobjective Optimization

Formally, a Multiobjective Optimization Problem (MOP) could be defined as the optimization problem in which two (or more) conflicting objective functions must be optimized simultaneously [11] (e.g. the Reporting Cells Planning Problem). In

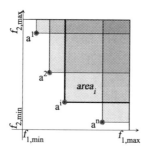

Fig. 2. Hypervolume for a minimization problem with two objectives

a MOP, the main challenge is to find a wide range of solutions (each one related to a specific trade-off between objectives) evenly distributed in the objective space. These desired solutions are commonly known as non-dominated solutions, and the set of non-dominated solutions is referred as Pareto Set. If (without loss of generality) we assume a minimization bi-objective problem (as the RCPP), a solution $\mathbf{x}^i$ is said to dominate the solution $\mathbf{x}^j$ (expressed as $\mathbf{x}^i \prec \mathbf{x}^j$) if and only if $\forall k \in [1,2], f_k\left(\mathbf{x}^i\right) \leq f_k\left(\mathbf{x}^j\right) \wedge \exists k \in [1,2] : f_k\left(\mathbf{x}^i\right) < f_k\left(\mathbf{x}^j\right)$.

There are several multiobjective indicators to measure the quality of a set of non-dominated solutions (whose representation is the Pareto Front). In this work, we use one of the most popular indicators: the Hypervolume (I_H). This multiobjective indicator is discussed in Section 4.1. Section 4.2 presents our version (in terms of our evolutionary operators specific to the RCPP) of the Non-dominated Sorting Genetic Algorithm II (NSGAII).

4.1   Hypervolume: $I_H(A)$

Assuming a minimization bi-objective MOP, the $I_H(A)$ indicator measures the area of the objective space that is dominated by the Pareto Front A, and is bounded by the reference points [11]. These reference points are calculated by using the maximum and minimum value of every objective function. In the RCPP, this could be done by evaluating the extreme configurations of Reporting Cells: Never Update (when all the network cells are non-Reporting Cells, LU_{min} and PA_{max}), and Always Update (when all the network cells are Reporting Cells, LU_{max} and PA_{min}). Due to the fact that the main target of a multiobjective optimization algorithm is to find a wide range of solutions evenly distributed in the objective space, the I_H establishes that the set of solutions A is better than the set B when $I_H(A) > I_H(B)$. Fig. 2 shows an example of the $I_H(A)$ calculation for a minimization bi-objective MOP, which can be formally defined by means of Equation 4.

$$I_H(A) = \left\{ \bigcup_i area_i \mid \mathbf{a}^i \in A \right\}. \tag{4}$$

Algorithm 1. Pseudo-code of NSGAII

---

1 % *Initialize the parent population*
2 Ind ← Initialization (N_{pop});
3 % *Evaluate the parent population*
4 Ind ← ObjectiveFunctionsEvaluation (Ind);
5 Ind ← FitnessEvaluation (Ind);
6 % *Main loop*
7 **while** *stop condition* $\neq$ *TRUE* **do**
8   % *Crossover operation*
9   Off ← Crossover (Ind, P_C, N_{pop});
10   % *Mutation operation*
11   Off ← Mutation(Off, P_M);
12   % *Evaluate the offspring*
13   Off ← ObjectiveFunctionsEvaluation(Off);
14   % *Evaluate all the individuals*
15   [Ind, Off] ← FitnessEvaluation (Ind, Off);
16   % *Selection of the fittest individuals*
17   Ind ← NaturalSelection (Ind, Off);
18 **end**

4.2   The Non-dominated Sorting Genetic Algorithm II

The Non-dominated Sorting Genetic Algorithm II (NSGAII) is the multiobjective evolutionary algorithm proposed by K. Deb et al. in [12]. Basically, the
NSGAII is a population-based algorithm in which the evolutionary operators of
biological systems (recombination of parents, mutation, and natural selection)
are iteratively applied with the aim of improving a set of solutions. Algorithm
1 shows the pseudo-code of NSGAII, where N_{pop} is the population size, P_C is
the crossover (or recombination of parents) probability, and P_M is the mutation
probability. As we can observe in this pseudo-code, the first step in NSGAII is
the initialization and evaluation of the first population of parents (each individual of the population is an encoded solution of the problem). Subsequently, a
new set of solutions (offspring) is generated by using the crossover and mutation operations. And finally, the best individuals found so far are selected as the
parent population of the next generation. This last is done by using the natural
selection operator.

Individual Representation. As we mentioned in Section 3, a network cell
might be in two possible states: Reporting Cell (RC) and non-Reporting Cell
(nRC). Therefore, a possible individual representation could be a vector that
stores the state of each network cell, e.g. 1 if the network cell is an RC, and
0 otherwise. In this work, every individual of the first population of parents is
randomly generated by using the discrete uniform distribution.

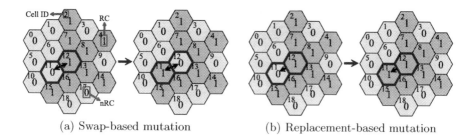

(a) Swap-based mutation   (b) Replacement-based mutation

Fig. 3. Mutation operations

Crossover Operation. The crossover is an evolutionary operator which is performed with probability P_C to generate a new population of N_{pop} individuals (the offspring) [11]. In this work, we use an elitist crossover where the maximum number of crossover points is equal to 4. This evolutionary operator consists of the following steps: firstly, four individuals (parents) grouped in pairs are randomly selected. Secondly, we generate two offspring by recombining the best parents of both groups. And thirdly, only the best of these two new individuals is stored in the offspring population.

Mutation Operations. This operator is performed with probability P_M to modify the genome of the offspring [11]. In this work we have defined two mutation operations specific to the RCPP. The first one consists in swapping the value of two neighboring cells that belong to different states (i.e. RC and nRC). Fig. 3(a) shows an example of this operation. And the second one consists in replacing the value of a network cell by the value of one of its neighboring cells belonging to the other state (see Fig. 3(b)). The mutation operation has been configured such that these two mutation operations cannot be applied over the same individual simultaneously.

Natural Selection. The natural selection is the evolutionary operator by means of which the best individuals (of the whole population, i.e. parents and offspring) are selected as the parent population of the next generation. In [12], K. Deb et al. define a fitness function to determine the quality of a solution (or individual) in the multiobjective context. This fitness function has two main terms: the non-dominated sorting and the crowding distance. The non-dominated sorting is used to arrange the solutions in fronts by using the dominance concept. And the crowding distance is used to estimate the density of solutions surrounding a particular point of the objective space. For more information about these two procedures, please consult [12].

Table 1. Statistics of Hypervolume (I_H)

	Test Network											
Ref. points	TN1	TN2	TN3	TN4	TN5	TN6	TN7	TN8	TN9	TN10	TN11	TN12
LU_{max}	11480	11428	11867	30861	30237	29864	47854	46184	42970	54428	49336	49775
LU_{min}	0	0	0	0	0	0	0	0	0	0	0	0
PA_{max}	125184	124576	125248	256500	256788	255636	691008	680000	690112	1691300	1666400	1676400
PA_{min}	7824	7786	7828	7125	7133	7101	10797	10625	10783	16913	16664	16764
Statistics of I_H												
Aver.(%)	60.59	61.44	62.58	71.78	71.93	72.73	75.89	76.71	76.95	78.50	79.80	79.65
Dev.(%)	0.00	0.00	0.00	0.04	0.01	0.03	0.16	0.11	0.17	0.28	0.26	0.30

5 Experimental Results

In this section, we present the experimental study conducted to evaluate the quality of our proposal. For it, we have tested our version of NSGAII in 12 test networks of different complexity: TN1-TN3 (test networks of 4x4 cells), TN4-TN6 (test networks of 6x6 cells), TN7-TN9 (test networks of 8x8 cells), and TN10-TN12 (test networks of 10x10 cells). These network instances were firstly published in [7], and were also studied in [8,9]. The reasons why we use these network instances in our study is because they cover a wide spectrum of the problem (12 test networks of different complexity) and because the 12 test networks were generated by using realistic subscriber's call and mobility patterns (in contrast to previously published network instances, where the mobile activity of every network cell was randomly generated according to a normal distribution [7]).

Furthermore, we have compared our results with those obtained in other works published in the literature [7–9], where different single-objective metaheuristics were applied to optimize the same set of test networks: Geometric Particle Swarm Optimization (GPSO) [7], Hopfield Neural Network hybridized with the Ball Dropping technique (HNN-BD) [7], Differential Evolution (DE) [8], and Scatter Search (SS) [9]. This comparative study is discussed in Section 5.1.

Another novel contribution of our work is the use of a high-performance solver: the IBM ILOG CPLEX Optimizer [13]. A comparison with this well-known optimizer is also presented in Section 5.1.

With the aim of performing a fair comparison, our proposal is configured with the same population size (N_{pop} = 175 individuals) and the same stop condition (*Maximum number of generations* = 1000) as in [8,9]. Regrettably, a runtime comparison cannot be conducted because the execution time of SS, DE, HNN-BD, and GPSO is not available. The other parameters of NSGAII (crossover probability (P_C) and mutation probability (P_M)) have been configured by means of a parametric study of 30 independent runs per experiment. The parameter combination that maximizes the Hypervolumen (I_H) is: $P_C = 0.75$ and $P_M = 0.25$. Table 1 shows statistical data (mean and standard deviation) of the I_H indicator for this configuration. This table also gathers the reference points for each test network (see Section 4.1). And Fig. 4(a)-Fig. 4(l) show the Pareto Fronts associated with the mean I_H for each test network. These figures reveal that our proposal achieves good Pareto Fronts, because they extend from the

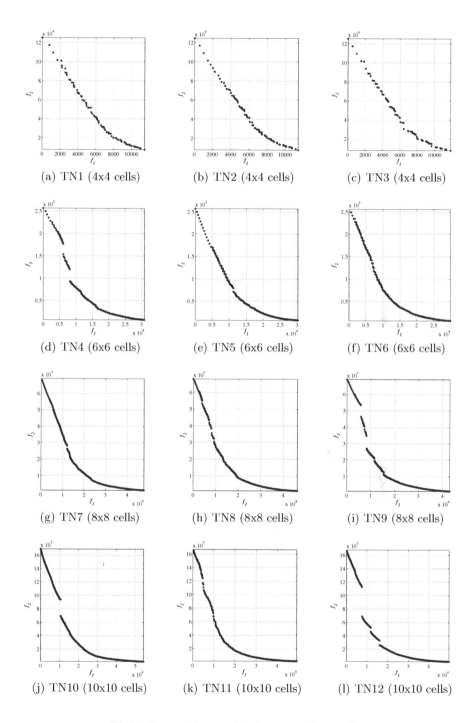

Fig. 4. Pareto Fronts with the mean Hypervolume

Table 2. Comparison with other works: f_3^{SO} (10). We indicate with "-" the information that is not available in the corresponding reference

Algorithm		TN1	TN2	TN3	TN4	TN5	TN6	TN7	TN8	TN9	TN10	TN11	TN12
								Test Network					
NSGAII	Min.	98535	97156	95038	173701	182331	174519	308702	287149	264204	385927	357368	370868
	Aver.	98535	97156	95038	173701	182331	174605	308859	287149	264396	387416	358777	371349
	Dev.(%)	0.00	0.00	0.00	0.00	0.00	0.13	0.05	0.00	0.09	0.20	0.16	0.15
CPLEX	Min.	98535	97156	95038	181677	200990	186481	375103	351505	407457	514504	468118	514514
	Aver.	98535	97156	95038	181677	200990	186481	375103	351505	407457	514504	468118	514514
	Dev.(%)	0.00	0.00	0.00	0.00	0.00	0.00	0.00	0.00	0.00	0.00	0.00	0.00
SS[9]	Min.	98535	97156	95038	173701	182331	174519	307695	287149	264204	385927	357714	370868
	Aver.	-	-	-	-	-	-	-	-	-	-	-	-
	Dev.	-	-	-	-	-	-	-	-	-	-	-	-
DE[8]	Min.	98535	97156	95038	173701	182331	174519	308401	287149	264204	386681	358167	371829
	Aver.	-	-	-	-	-	-	-	-	-	-	-	-
	Dev.(%)	-	-	-	-	-	-	-	-	-	-	-	-
HNN-BD[7]	Min.	98535	97156	95038	173701	182331	174519	308929	287149	264204	386351	358167	370868
	Aver.	98627	97655	95751	174690	182430	176050	311351	287149	264695	387820	359036	374205
	Dev.(%)	0.09	0.51	0.75	0.56	0.05	0.87	0.78	0.00	0.18	0.38	0.24	0.89
GPSO[7]	Min.	98535	97156	95038	173701	182331	174519	308401	287149	264204	385972	359191	370868
	Aver.	98535	97156	95038	174090	182331	175080	310062	287805	264475	387825	359928	373722
	Dev.(%)	0.00	0.00	0.00	0.22	0.00	0.32	0.53	0.22	0.10	0.48	0.20	0.76

Never Update to the Always Update (the two extreme configurations of Reporting Cells). However, it is noteworthy the existence of gaps in the mean Pareto Front of the test networks TN4, TN9, TN10, and TN12. The study of such gaps would be a good challenge for a future work.

5.1   Comparison with Other Works

In this section, we compare our proposal with other algorithms published in the literature: Geometric Particle Swarm Optimization (GPSO) [7], Hopfield Neural Network hybridized with the Ball Dropping technique (HNN-BD) [7], Differential Evolution (DE) [8], and Scatter Search (SS) [9]. Regrettably, all of these algorithms belong to the single-objective optimization field (to the best of the authors' knowledge, there is no other work in which the Reporting Cells Planning Problem is tackled with a multiobjective approach). So, in order to perform such comparison, we have searched in our Pareto Fronts the solution that best fits the objective function used in these works (which is Equation 3 with β equal to 10: f_3^{SO} (10)).

This comparative study (of 30 independent runs per experiment) is summarized in Table 2, where we present: the minimum cost (Min.), the average cost (Aver.), and the deviation percentage (Dev.(%)) from the minimum cost [7]. This table highlights that our proposal is very interesting because it achieves a wide range of solutions (each one related to a specific trade-off between objectives) in a single run (see Fig. 4(a)-Fig. 4(l)) and, at the same time, it provides better (in average) and more stable results than the single-objective metaheuristics published in [7]. And also better minimum cost than [8], mainly in the more difficult networks (TN10, TN11, and TN12). This is far from trivial because we are comparing with metaheuristics specialized in finding only one solution (the one that best fits f_3^{SO} (10)).

Furthermore, we have optimized each test network by using the IBM ILOG CPLEX Optimizer [13]. In this study, we have limited the execution time of the IBM ILOG CPLEX Optimizer to be 10 times higher than the execution time of our algorithm (which is approximately of 7 minutes for the most complex test networks: TN10, TN11, and TN12). This comparison (see Table 2) confirms the virtues of the evolutionary computation, because the IBM ILOG CPLEX Optimizer is only competitive in the less complex test networks (TN1, TN2, and TN3).

6   Conclusion and Future Work

In this manuscript, we propose a multiobjective approach for finding quasi-optimal configurations of Reporting Cells (a strategy to manage the subscribers mobility in the Public Land Mobile Networks). For it, we have adapted the Non-dominated Sorting Genetic Algorithm II (NSGAII) [12]. This approach is a novel contribution because, to the best of the authors' knowledge, there are no other works in the literature that tackle this problem with multiobjective optimization techniques. With a multiobjective approach, we avoid the drawbacks associated with the linear aggregation of the objective functions and, at the same time, we obtain a wide range of solutions among which we could select the one that best adjusts to the real state of the network.

By means of an experimental study, we have demonstrated that our algorithm is very promising because it achieves good Pareto Fronts and outperforms (in average) the results provided by single-objective metaheuristics. In this experimental study, we have tested our algorithm in 12 test networks of different complexity.

As a future work, it would be interesting to adapt other multiobjective metaheuristics and compare them with our version of the NSGAII. Furthermore, it could be a good challenge to study the nature of the gaps that appear in the Pareto Fronts of the test networks TN4, TN9, TN10, and TN12.

Acknowledgments. This work was partially funded by the Spanish Ministry of Economy and Competitiveness and the ERDF (European Regional Development Fund), under the contract TIN2012-30685 (BIO project). The work of Víctor Berrocal-Plaza has been developed under the Grant FPU-AP2010-5841 from the Spanish Government.

References

1. Agrawal, D., Zeng, Q.: Introduction to Wireless and Mobile Systems. Cengage Learning (2010)
2. Mukherjee, A., Bandyopadhyay, S., Saha, D.: Location Management and Routing in Mobile Wireless Networks. Artech House mobile communications series. Artech House (2003)

3. Taheri, J., Zomaya, A.Y.: A combined genetic-neural algorithm for mobility management. J. Math. Model. Algorithms, 481–507 (2007)
4. Bar-Noy, A., Kessler, I.: Tracking mobile users in wireless communications networks. IEEE Transactions on Information Theory **39**(6), 1877–1886 (1993)
5. Boukerche, A.: Handbook of Algorithms for Wireless Networking and Mobile Computing. Chapman & Hall/CRC Computer & Information Science Series. Taylor & Francis (2005)
6. Subrata, R., Zomaya, A.Y.: A comparison of three artificial life techniques for Reporting Cell planning in mobile computing. IEEE Trans. Parallel Distrib. Syst. **14**(2), 142–153 (2003)
7. Alba, E., García-Nieto, J., Taheri, J., Zomaya, A.Y.: New Research in Nature Inspired Algorithms for Mobility Management in GSM Networks. In: Giacobini, M., et al. (eds.) EvoWorkshops 2008. LNCS, vol. 4974, pp. 1–10. Springer, Heidelberg (2008)
8. Almeida-Luz, S.M., Vega-Rodríguez, M.A., Gómez-Pulido, J.A., Sánchez-Pérez, J.M.: Applying differential evolution to the Reporting Cells problem. In: International Multiconference on Computer Science and Information Technology, pp. 65–71 (2008)
9. Almeida-Luz, S.M., Vega-Rodríguez, M.A., Gómez-Pulido, J.A., Sánchez-Pérez, J.M.: Solving the Reporting Cells Problem Using a Scatter Search Based Algorithm. In: Szczuka, M., Kryszkiewicz, M., Ramanna, S., Jensen, R., Hu, Q. (eds.) RSCTC 2010. LNCS, vol. 6086, pp. 534–543. Springer, Heidelberg (2010)
10. Hac, A., Zhou, X.: Locating strategies for Personal Communication Networks: A novel tracking strategy. IEEE Journal on Selected Areas in Communications **15**(8), 1425–1436 (1997)
11. Coello, C.A.C., Lamont, G.B., Veldhuizen, D.A.V.: Evolutionary Algorithms for Solving Multi-Objective Problems (Genetic and Evolutionary Computation). Springer-Verlag New York Inc., Secaucus (2006)
12. Deb, K., Pratap, A., Agarwal, S., Meyarivan, T.: A fast and elitist multiobjective genetic algorithm: NSGA-II. IEEE Transactions on Evolutionary Computation **6**(2), 182–197 (2002)
13. ILOG Inc: ILOG CPLEX: High-performance software for mathematical programming and optimization (2006). http://www.ilog.com/products/cplex/

Impact of the Topology on the Performance of Distributed Differential Evolution

Ivanoe De Falco[1], Antonio Della Cioppa[2], Domenico Maisto[1(✉)],
Umberto Scafuri[1], and Ernesto Tarantino[1]

[1] ICAR-CNR, Via P. Castellino 111, 80131 Naples, Italy
{ivanoe.defalco,domenico.maisto,umberto.scafuri,
ernesto.tarantino}@na.icar.cnr.it
[2] Natural Computation Lab, DIEM, University of Salerno,
Via Ponte don Melillo 1, 84084 Fisciano, SA, Italy
adellacioppa@unisa.it

Abstract. Migration topology plays a key role in designing effective distributed evolutionary algorithms. In this work we investigate the impact of several network topologies on the performance of a stepping–stone structured Differential Evolution model. Although some issues on the control parameters of the migration process and the way they affect the efficiency of the algorithm and the solution quality deserve further evaluative study, the influence of the topology on the performance both in terms of solution quality and convergence rate emerges from the empirical findings carried out on a set of test problems.

1   Introduction

Evolutionary Algorithms (EAs) [1–4] have proven to be very effective in dealing with hard optimization problems whose solution space is so large as to make an exhaustive search unviable [5,6]. Nonetheless, their main disadvantage is related to the convergence speed. A popular way for contrasting this drawback and achieving a speedup is to implement structured versions where the population is divided into multiple semi–isolated subpopulations (*demes*) connected each other according to a particular network topology. These subpopulations evolve independently and interact by means of a migration operator used to exchange individuals. The number of individuals that are sent to (received from) other demes is determined by the *migration rate*, while a *replacement function* defines how to include the immigrants into the target subpopulation. Besides, the *migration interval* establishes the exchange frequency among neighboring subpopulations [7]. Concerning the network topology, this distributed framework may be categorized as following either the *island model* (fully connected demes) or the *stepping–stone model* (interaction restricted to customized logical or physically connected demes) [8]. The connectivity degree of the topology beneath determines the number of the neighboring subpopulations and its diameter is the most important factor influencing the propagation of good individuals [9].

© Springer-Verlag Berlin Heidelberg 2014
A.I. Esparcia-Alcázar et al. (Eds.): EvoApplications 2014, LNCS 8602, pp. 75–85, 2014.
DOI: 10.1007/978-3-662-45523-4_7

The separation of demes serves as a natural way to maintain the diversity reducing the possibility of population stagnation [9], may guide the evolution in many directions simultaneously, and may allow speedup in computation and improve solution quality with respect to a single EA evolution [10,11].

Originally developed for Genetic Algorithms (GAs) [1,3], the distributed approach has been employed also for different paradigms. Among these paradigms, distributed Differential Evolution (dDE) has been the subject of significant research [12–18]. The choice of DE [19] is due to its simple but powerful searching capability, and to its overall performance with respect to other stochastic and direct search global optimization techniques on a wide range of benchmark problems [20] and real world problems [21].

In the following we make reference to the stepping–stone dDE model. To assess the impact of the migration topology on a dDE algorithm, simulations have been performed on a range of test problems and for several network topologies by making use of a standard dDE algorithm, *i.e.*, DDE [22].

Paper structure is as follows: Section 2 illustrates the state of the art; Section 3 presents a description of the parallel framework. In Section 4 the experimental findings are shown and discussed together, and a statistical analysis is performed. The last section contains final remarks and future works.

2   State of the Art

Since the distributed models were introduced in connection with parallel GAs, it is not surprising that all the issues involved, including the migration topology, have been studied in this context. Several surveys have been published in the nineties [7,23]. Although in some case the influence of the migration topology has been neglected [7], research was conducted to analyze its impact [10,24]. Naturally the distributed approach has not been investigated exclusively in relation to GAs. There is a wide research on the dDE models which can be characterized on the basis of the neighborhood topology, the migration policy, the selection function and the replacement function.

In [12] the migration mechanism as well as the algorithmic parameters are adaptively coordinated according to a criterion based on genotypical diversity. An adaptive DE is executed on each subpopulation for a fixed number of generations. Then a migration process, based on a random connection topology, is started: each individual in each subpopulation can be probabilistically swapped with a randomly selected individual in a randomly chosen subpopulation (including the one containing the initial individual).

Tasoulis et. al [13] propose a dDE, named PDE, characterized by unidirectional ring topology, a selection function that picks up the individuals with the best performance and, with a given probability, send these individuals to the neighboring subpopulations. When the migration occurs, the migrating individuals substitute random individuals of the target subpopulations.

In Apolloni et al. [15] a distributed version, known as IBDDE, is presented: the migration policy is based on a probabilistic criterion depending on five parameters. The individuals to migrate are randomly selected and the individuals arriving from other islands replace randomly chosen local individuals only if the former ones are fitter. The topology is a unidirectional ring in which the individuals are exchanged with the nearest neighbors.

In De Falco et al. [22] a distributed version of DE, called DDE, has been proposed. It consists of a set of classical DE schemes, running in parallel, assigned to different processing elements arranged in a torus topology, in which each generic DE instance has four neighboring communicating subpopulations. The individual sent is the best one and it randomly replaces an individual in the neighboring subpopulation, except the local current best one.

In the paper by Ishimizu and Tagawa [17] a structured DE approach still based on the stepping–stone model is presented. Different network topologies, ranging from ring to torus and hypercube, are taken into account. The migration takes place every fixed number of generations and the exchange involves only the best individual which migrates towards only one of the adjacent subpopulations on the basis of the topological neighborhood and randomly replaces an individual, except the best one, in the receiving subpopulation.

An improved version of PDE algorithm which entails the employment of four different scale factor values within distributed differential evolution structures is advanced in [18]. The subpopulations are arranged according to a ring or a torus topology. Although proper choice of a scale factor scheme appears to be dependent on the distributed structure, any of the proposed simple schemes has proven to significantly improve upon the single scale factor distributed differential evolution algorithms.

In [25] a structured DE which uses a biological invasion inspired migration strategy is advanced. The subpopulations are displaced in a torus topology. During the migration the individuals with the fitness better than the average fitness in their subpopulation are sent to all the neighboring subpolulations and a replacement strategy is performed to keep unchanged the size of each subpopulation.

3   The Distributed Model

Our Distributed DE (DDE) algorithm is based on the classical coarse–grained approach to EAs [7] in which a collection of networked subpopulations cooperate in the solution of a problem by a migration operator. It consists in a locally–linked strategy, known as *stepping stone–model* [8], in which each DE instance is connected to a number of instances according to the connectivity degree of the topology beneath. Each subpopulation can communicate with the other ones only through its neighbours.

Decision must be taken for the migrant selection, i.e. the choice of the elements to be sent, and replacement, i.e the individuals to be replaced by the migrants. Different strategies can be devised: the migrants can be selected either according to fitness or randomly, and they might replace the worst individuals or substitute them only if better, or they might finally replace any individual (apart from the very best ones, of course) in the neighbouring subpopulation. Consistently with the biological events, it was noted that the number of migrants should not be high and the migration should occur after a period of stasis otherwise the subsearch in a subpopulation might be very perturbed by these continuously incoming elements [7, 26].

This mechanism allows attaining both *exploitation* and *exploration*, which are basic features for a good search. Exploration means to wander through the search space so as to prevent premature convergence to local optima. Exploitation implies that one area is thoroughly examined, so that we can be confident to state whether this area is promising. In such a way, good solutions will spread within the network with successive diffusions, so more and more demes will try to sample that area (exploitation), and, on the other hand, there will exist at the same time clusters of subpopulations which will investigate different subareas of the search space (exploration). Therefore, a suitable percentage of migrants each subpopulation sends to its neighbours, called *Migration Rate* (M_R), and an appropriate exchange frequency between neighbouring subpopulations every M_I generations, named *Migration Interval*, are to be introduced to exploit at the best the potential of this cooperating stepping–stone model. A rigorous theoretical analysis that leads into new insights into the usefulness of migration, how information is propagated in island models, and how to set parameters such as the migration interval is reported in [27]. This study is corroborated by empirical results that investigate the robustness with respect to the choice of the migration interval and compare various migration topologies using statistical tests.

Within this general framework we have implemented a distributed version for DE, which consists of a set of classical DE schemes, running in parallel, assigned to different processing elements arranged in several topologies in which each generic DE instance has a different number of neighbouring communicating subpopulations.

4   Experiments

To investigate the influence of the network topologies in DDE we have compared their performance on a set of benchmark thirty–dimensional functions as defined in [28]. Namely, the unimodal functions F_1 and F_3, and among the multimodal, the basic functions F_6 and F_{10}, the expanded functions F_{13} and F_{14}, and the hybrid composition functions F_{16} and F_{22} have been taken into account. Among these, F_1, F_3, and F_6 are separable. As suggested in [29], throughout the experiments, the values for the DE parameters have been chosen as follows: *scale factor* ($F = 0.9$) for all the functions and the *crossover ratio* (CR) has been set to 0.1 for all the separable functions and 0.9 for all the other functions. The $DE/rand/1/bin$ [19] mutation mechanism has been used. As topologies a Ring, a bidirectional ring (Bring), an incomplete binary tree (IBtree), a Torus, a WK–recursive (WK), and a Hypercube, each constituted by a total of 16 nodes, have been investigated. Some of these topologies are outlined in Fig. 1.

The total population size has been chosen as 160, which results in sixteen subpopulations with 10 individuals. The number of generations has been set

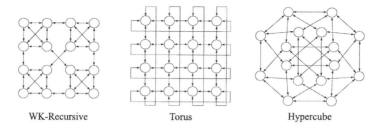

WK-Recursive   Torus   Hypercube

Fig. 1. The network topologies

Table 1. Best migration interval and related average final value for each problem

Problem	Ring		Bring		IBtree		Torus		WK		Hypercube	
	M_I	$\langle\phi_{b_f}\rangle$	M_I	$\langle\phi_{b_f}\rangle$	M_I	$\langle\phi_{b_f}\rangle$	M_I	$\langle\phi_{b_f}\rangle$	M_I	$\langle\phi_{b_f}\rangle$	M_I	$\langle\phi_{b_f}\rangle$
F_1	10	$5.68\cdot10^{-14}$	10	$3.18\cdot10^{-14}$	10	$4.32\cdot10^{-14}$	10	$4.09\cdot10^{-14}$	10	$4.09\cdot10^{-14}$	10	$5.00\cdot10^{-14}$
F_3	10	$4.85\cdot10^{+5}$	10	$3.62\cdot10^{+5}$	10	$3.62\cdot10^{+5}$	10	$3.40\cdot10^{+5}$	10	$2.89\cdot10^{+5}$	10	$6.41\cdot10^{+5}$
F_6	30	$4.37\cdot10^{+1}$	40	$3.66\cdot10^{+1}$	20	$4.67\cdot10^{+1}$	10	$3.74\cdot10^{+1}$	10	$3.53\cdot10^{+1}$	10	$7.47\cdot10^{+1}$
F_{10}	30	$5.07\cdot10^{+1}$	40	$5.10\cdot10^{+1}$	50	$5.40\cdot10^{+1}$	50	$5.34\cdot10^{+1}$	50	$5.31\cdot10^{+1}$	50	$5.84\cdot10^{+1}$
F_{13}	50	$2.17\cdot10^{0}$	50	$1.98\cdot10^{0}$	40	$2.15\cdot10^{0}$	50	$2.64\cdot10^{0}$	50	$2.43\cdot10^{0}$	50	$2.81\cdot10^{0}$
F_{14}	50	$1.24\cdot10^{+1}$	40	$1.26\cdot10^{+1}$	40	$1.27\cdot10^{+1}$	50	$1.26\cdot10^{+1}$	40	$1.26\cdot10^{+1}$	50	$1.27\cdot10^{+1}$
F_{16}	50	$9.21\cdot10^{+1}$	50	$9.36\cdot10^{+1}$	50	$9.93\cdot10^{+1}$	50	$9.81\cdot10^{+1}$	50	$9.86\cdot10^{+1}$	50	$9.39\cdot10^{+1}$
F_{22}	50	$8.68\cdot10^{+2}$	50	$8.75\cdot10^{+2}$	50	$8.77\cdot10^{+2}$	50	$8.83\cdot10^{+2}$	50	$8.84\cdot10^{+2}$	50	$8.81\cdot10^{-2}$

to $1,875$, so as to have a total number of fitness evaluations equal to $300,000$, following the rules widely used to face those testbeds, as for example in [29].

The parallel algorithm, which uses the Message Passing Interface is written in C language. All the experiments have been carried out on a Vega cluster constituted by 16 Pentium 4 processors with a frequency of 1.5 GHz and 512Mb of RAM, interconnected by a FastEthernet switch.

A first phase of our investigation has aimed at finding the best possible value for the migration interval M_I for each function and for each topology. We have considered a given range of possible values, i.e., 10, 20, 30, 40, and 50. For any such value 25 runs have been effected for each function and each topology, and the averages $\langle\phi_{b_f}\rangle$ of the best final fitness values over the 25 runs have been computed. Table 1 reports the best values of M_I, together with the corresponding values of $\langle\phi_{b_f}\rangle$.

Examination of the results shows that for the easiest functions F_1 and F_3 the best value for M_I is obtained at the lowest tested migration interval. For the most difficult problems the results are better and better as the migration interval increases, and this holds true until a given value for M_I is reached; after this value, the performance worsens more and more as M_I further increases.

4.1   Statistical Analysis

To compare the algorithms from a statistical point of view, a classical approach based on nonparametric statistical tests has been carried out, following [30]. To do so, the ControlTest package [31] has been used. It is a Java package developed to compute the rankings for these tests, and to carry out the related post–hoc procedures and the computation of the adjusted p–values.

Table 2. Average Rankings of the algorithms

Topology	Friedman	Aligned Friedman	Quade
Ring	3.000	24.125	3.083
Bring	2.313	17.938	2.667
IBtree	4.125	25.125	3.944
Torus	3.688	24.813	3.764
WK	2.563	18.688	2.125
Hypercube	5.313	36.313	5.417
statistic	14.286	6.822	4.148
p–value	0.014	0.234	0.005

The results for the one–to–all analysis are reported in the following. Table 2 contains the results of the Friedman, Aligned Friedman, and Quade tests in terms of average rankings obtained by all the topologies. The last two rows show the statistic and the p–value for each test, respectively. For Friedman and Aligned Friedman tests the statistic is distributed according to chi–square with 5 degrees of freedom, whereas for Quade test it is distributed according to F–distribution with 5 and 35 degrees of freedom.

In each of the three tests, the lower the value for an algorithm, the better the algorithm is. Bring turns out to be the best in two out of the three tests while WK is the best according to the Quade test. Among the other four topologies, their order is in all the tests the following: Ring is always the third best heuristic, Torus is the fourth, followed by ITree, and finally the Hypercube is the sixth.

Furthermore, with the aim to examine if some hypotheses of equivalence between the best performing algorithm and the other ones can be rejected, the complete statistical analysis based on the post–hoc procedures ideated by Holm, Hochberg, Hommel, Holland, Rom, Finner, and Li has been carried out following [30]. Moreover, the adjusted p–values have been computed by means of [31].

Table 3 reports the results of this analysis performed at a level of significance $\alpha = 0.05$. In this table the other algorithms are ranked in terms of distance from the best performing one, and each algorithm is compared against this latter to investigate whether or not the equivalence hypothesis can be rejected. For each algorithm each sub–table reports the z value, the unadjusted p–value, and the adjusted p–values according to the different post-hoc procedures. The variable z represents the test statistic for comparing the algorithms, and its definition depends on the main nonparametric test used. In [30] all the different definitions for z, corresponding to the different tests, are reported. The last row in each sub–table contains for each procedure the threshold value Th such that the procedure considered rejects those equivalence hypotheses that have an adjusted p–value lower than or equal to Th.

Summarizing the results of these tables, the equivalence hypothesis between WK and Bring cannot be rejected by any test and by any post–hoc procedure. The hypothesis of their equivalence to the Hypercube, instead, is rejected by all post–hoc procedures, and that with IBtree in many cases. Finally, their equivalence with Torus and Ring is always excluded by Li post–hoc procedure.

Table 3. Results of post–hoc procedures for Friedman(top), Aligned Friedman (center), and Quade (bottom) tests over all tools (at $\alpha = 0.05$)

i	Algorithm	$z = (R_0 - R_i)/SE$	p	Holm/Hochberg/Hommel	Holland	Rom	Finner	Li
5	Hypercube	3.207	0.001	0.010	0.010	0.010	0.010	0.011
4	IBtree	1.938	0.053	0.013	0.013	0.013	0.020	0.011
3	Torus	1.470	0.142	0.017	0.017	0.017	0.030	0.011
2	Ring	0.735	0.462	0.025	0.025	0.025	0.040	0.011
1	WK	0.267	0.789	0.050	0.050	0.050	0.050	0.050
Th				0.013/0.010/0.013	0.013	0.011	0.020	0.011

i	Algorithm	$z = (R_0 - R_i)/SE$	p	Holm/Hochberg/Hommel	Holland	Rom	Finner	Li
5	Hypercube	2.625	0.009	0.010	0.010	0.011	0.010	0.004
4	IBtree	1.027	0.305	0.013	0.013	0.013	0.020	0.004
3	Torus	0.982	0.326	0.017	0.017	0.017	0.030	0.004
2	Ring	0.884	0.377	0.025	0.025	0.025	0.040	0.004
1	WK	0.107	0.915	0.050	0.050	0.050	0.050	0.050
Th				0.013/0.010/0.013	0.013	0.011	0.020	0.004

i	Algorithm	$z = (R_0 - R_i)/SE$	p	Holm/Hochberg/Hommel	Holland	Rom	Finner	Li
5	Hypercube	1.983	0.047	0.010	0.010	0.010	0.010	0.013
4	IBtree	1.096	0.273	0.013	0.013	0.013	0.020	0.013
3	Torus	0.987	0.323	0.017	0.017	0.017	0.030	0.013
2	Ring	0.577	0.564	0.025	0.025	0.025	0.040	0.013
1	Bring	0.326	0.744	0.050	0.050	0.050	0.050	0.050
Th				0.010/—/0.010	0.010	—	0.010	0.013

4.2   Behavior of the Topologies

A very interesting remark is that the migration frequency corresponding to the best performance for any given topology has a strong relationship to the degree of difficulty of the problem: the simpler the problem the lower the value for M_I, the harder the problem the higher the value. This holds true for all the topologies and for all the problems. Just to give some examples, Fig. 2 shows four different situations. Namely, the top–left pane deals with the quite easy function F_3 for the bidirectional ring: the lower the value for M_I the better the performance. Top–right pane reports on the behavior of WK topology over F_6 function: this is a quite easy one, and same conclusions as before hold true. The bottom–left pane, instead shows the behavior over the more difficult F_{13} function: now the situation is reversed, and the higher the value for M_I the better the performance. Similarly, the bottom–right pane sketches the behavior of WK over the difficult F_{22} problem: same considerations as before hold true. This seems to imply that as the problem becomes more and more complex to solve, the demes should exchange individuals less frequently, probably because each deme needs now to more deeply perform exploitation.

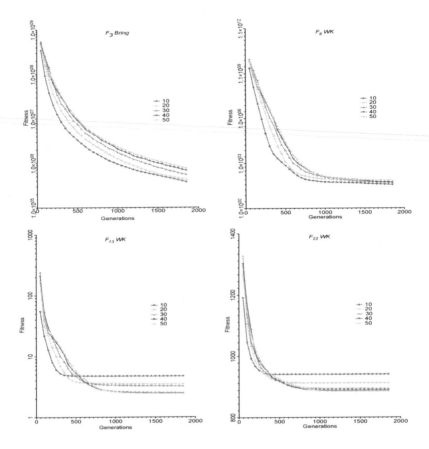

Fig. 2. A few examples of behavior of some topologies over some functions supporting the hypothesis that the harder a function, the higher the best value for M_I

A second feature worth noting is that WK and Torus topologies have faster convergence capability to suboptimal solutions than the other topologies. This takes place in general for any given function, and for any value of M_I. It is interesting to note that this holds true also in the circumstances in which these two topologies do not reach the best values at the end of the evolutions, rather they are overtaken by other topologies that start more slowly. Figure 3 shows this feature for four exemplary situations. Its top–left pane deals with F_3 function at $M_I = 30$, the top–right one reports on F_{10} at $M_I = 50$, the bottom–left one sketches the situation for F_{14} at $M_I = 50$, and finally the bottom–right pane shows F_{16} test case at $M_I = 50$. In all the cases Ring topology is the slowest. This feature could be profitably used whenever speed becomes of paramount importance in solving a problem: WK and Torus are very appealing, if a good suboptimal solution is needed in a very low amount of time.

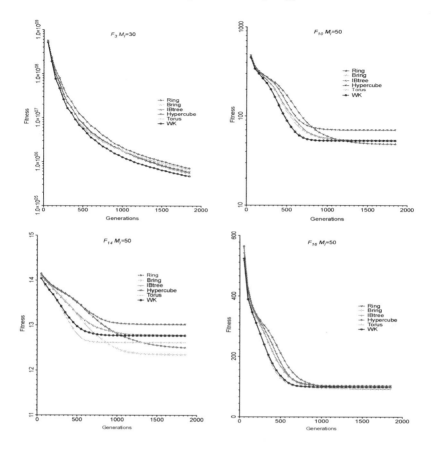

Fig. 3. Some examples of the faster convergence achieved by WK and Torus

5   Conclusions and Future Works

A distributed DE algorithm has been considered to evaluate the impact of the migration topologies on the stepping–stone model. The simulation results performed on a set of classical test functions and their statistical analysis have been shown to compare the performance of the different network topologies.

Future works will aim at carrying out a wider evaluation phase. This will be accomplished by performing sets of experiments with other DE operators, so as to ascertain that the performance are unchanged independently of the DE scheme chosen.

References

1. Holland, J.: Adaptation in natural and artificial systems. The University of Michigan Press, Ann Arbor (1975)
2. Schwefel, H.: Numerical optimization of computer models. Wiley & Sons (1981)

3. Goldberg, D.: Genetic algorithms in search, optimization, and machine learning. Addison-Wesley Professional (1989)
4. Koza, J.: Genetic programming. MIT Press, Cambridge (1992)
5. Bäck, T., Fogel, D.B., Michalewicz, Z. (eds.): Handbook of Evolutionary Computation. Oxford University Press, Oxford (1997)
6. De Falco, I., Cioppa, D.A., Iazzetta, A., Tarantino, E.: An evolutionary approach for automatically extracting intelligible classification rules. Knowledge and Information Systems **7**, 179–201 (2005)
7. Cantú-Paz, E.: A summary of research on parallel genetic algorithms. Technical Report 95007, University of Illinois, Urbana-Champaign, USA (1995)
8. Mühlenbein, H.: In: Rawlins, G. (ed.) Foundations of Genetic Algorithms. Morgan Kaufmann, San Mateo (1991)
9. Tomassini, M.: Spatially structured evolutionary algorithms. Springer (2005)
10. Cantú-Paz, E.: Efficient and accurate parallel genetic algorithms, vol. 1. Kluwer Academic Publisher, Norwell (2000)
11. Alba, E., Tomassini, M.: Parallelism and evolutionary algorithms. IEEE Trans. on Evolutionary Computation **6**, 443–462 (2002)
12. Zaharie, D., Petcu, D.: Parallel implementation of multipopulation differential evolution. In: Proceedings of the Nato Advanced Research Workshop on Concurrent Information Processing and Computing, pp. 223–232. IOS Press (2003)
13. Tasoulis, D., Pavlidis, N., Plagianakos, V., Vrahatis, M.: Parallel differential evolution. Proceedings of the Congress on Evolutionary Computation. **2**, 2023–2029 (2004)
14. De Falco, I., Della Cioppa, A., Scafuri, U., Tarantino, E.: A distributed differential evolution approach for mapping in a grid environment. In: Proceedings of the Fifteenth EUROMICRO International Conference on Parallel, Distributed and Network-Based Processing, pp. 442–449. IEEE Press (2007)
15. Apolloni, J., Leguizamón, G., García-Nieto, J., Alba, E.: Island based distributed differential evolution: an experimental study on hybrid testbeds. In: Proceedings of the Eight International Conference on Hybrid Intelligent Systems, pp. 696–701. IEEE Press (2008)
16. Weber, M., Neri, F., Tirronen, V.: Distributed differential evolution with explorative-exploitative population families. Genetic Programming and Evolvable Machines **10**, 343–371 (2009)
17. Ishimizu, T., Tagawa, K.: A structured differential evolution for various network topologies. International Journal of Computers and Communications **4**, 2–8 (2010)
18. Weber, M., Neri, F., Tirronen, V.: A study on scale factor in distributed differential evolution. Information Sciences **18**, 2488–2511 (2011)
19. Price, K., Storn, R.: Differential evolution. Dr. Dobb's Journal **22**, 18–24 (1997)
20. Price, K., Storn, R.M., Lampinen, J.: Differential Evolution - A Practical Approach to Global Optmization. Springer (2005)
21. Nobakhti, A., Wang, H.: A simple self-adaptive differential evolution algorithm with application on the alstom gasifier. Applied Soft Computing **8**, 350–370 (2008)
22. De Falco, I., Della Cioppa, A., Maisto, D., Scafuri, U., Tarantino, E.: Satellite Image Registration by Distributed Differential Evolution. In: Giacobini, M. (ed.) EvoWorkshops 2007. LNCS, vol. 4448, pp. 251–260. Springer, Heidelberg (2007)
23. Alba, E., Troya, J.: A survey of parallel distributed genetic algorithms. Complexity **4**, 31–52 (1999)

24. Alba, E., Luque, G.: Theoretical models of selection pressure for dEAs: topology influence. In: Proceedings of the IEEE International Conference on Evolutionary Computation, pp. 214–221 (2005)

25. De Falco, I., Cioppa, D.A., Maisto, D., Scafuri, U., Tarantino, E.: Biological invasion-inspired migration in distributed evolutionary algorithms. Information Sciences **207**, 50–65 (2012)

26. Skolicki, K., De Jong, K.: The influence of migration sizes and intervals on island models. In: Proceedings of the Conference of Genetic and Evolutionary Computation, Association for Computing Machinery Inc, pp. 1295–1302. ACM (2005)

27. Lässig, J., Sudholt, D.: Design and analysis of migration in parallel evolutionary algorithms. Soft Computing **17**, 1121–1144 (2013)

28. Suganthan, P., Hansen, N., Liang, J., Deb, K., Chen, Y., Auger, A., Tiwari, S.: Problem definitions and evaluation criteria for the CEC 2005 special session on real-parameter optimization. Technical Report 201212, Zhengzhou University, China and Nanyang Technological University, Singapore (2005)

29. Rönkkönen, J., Kukkonen, S., Price, K.: Real-parameter optimization with differential evolution. In: Proceedings of the IEEE Congress on Evolutionary Computation, vol. 1, pp. 506–513. IEEE (2005)

30. Derrac, J., García, S., Molina, D., Herrera, F.: A practical tutorial on the use of nonparametric statistical tests as a methodology for comparing evolutionary and swarm intelligence algorithms. Swarm and Evolutionary Computation **1**, 3–18 (2011)

31. García, S., Fernández, A., Luengo, J., Herrera, F.: Advanced nonparametric tests for multiple comparisons in the design of experiments in computational intelligence and data mining: Experimental analysis of power. Information Sciences **180**, 2044–2064 (2010)

Modeling the Offloading of Different Types of Mobile Applications by Using Evolutionary Algorithms

Gianluigi Folino[✉] and Francesco S. Pisani

Institute of High Performance Computing and Networking (ICAR-CNR),
Rende, Italy
{folino,fpisani}@icar.cnr.it

Abstract. Modern smartphones permit to run a large variety of applications, i.e. multimedia, games, social network applications, etc. However, this aspect considerably reduces the battery life of these devices. A possible solution to alleviate this problem is to offload part of the application or the whole computation to remote servers, i.e. Cloud Computing. The offloading cannot be performed without considering the issues derived from the nature of the application (i.e. multimedia, games, etc.), which can considerably change the resources necessary to the computation and the type, the frequency and the amount of data to be exchanged with the network. This work shows a framework for automatically building models for the offloading of mobile applications based on evolutionary algorithms and how it can be used to simulate different kinds of mobile applications and to analyze the rules generated. To this aim, a tool for generating mobile datasets, presenting different features, is designed and experiments are performed in different usage conditions in order to demonstrate the utility of the overall framework.

1 Introduction

Modern smartphones boosted their capabilities due to the increasing coverage of mobile broadband networks, to the new high-performance processors, to the large-volume storage and to new different types of sensors. All these capabilities together make it possible for mobile devices to handle much more complex tasks and to execute different kinds of applications. On the other hand, that consumes a lot more computing and networking resources and therefore demands much more energy, while the battery technology has not developed as fast as mobile computing technology. A possible solution to alleviate this problem is to offload part of the application or the whole computation to remote servers, as explained in [4], where software-based techniques for reducing program power consumption are analyzed, considering both static and dynamic information in order to move the computation to remote servers.

In the last few years, the emergence of the Cloud Computing technologies and the consequent large availability of cloud servers [1], encouraged the research

© Springer-Verlag Berlin Heidelberg 2014
A.I. Esparcia-Alcázar et al. (Eds.): EvoApplications 2014, LNCS 8602, pp. 86–97, 2014.
DOI: 10.1007/978-3-662-45523-4_8

into the usage of offloading techniques on cloud computing platforms. A number of papers were published trying to cope with the main issues of the process of offloading, mainly oriented toward a particular problematic, i.e. Wifi [7], network behavior and bandwidth [9], the tradeoff between privacy and quality [8].

In [3], a framework is presented for the automatic offloading of mobile application using a genetic programming approach, which attempts to address the issues listed above. The framework comprises two parts: a module that simulates the entire offloading process, and an inference engine that builds an automatic decision model to handle the offloading process. The simulator and the inference engine both apply a taxonomy that defines four main categories concerning the offloading process: user, network, device and application. The simulator evaluates the performance of the offloading process of mobile applications on the basis of user requirements, of the conditions of the network, of the hardware/software features of the mobile device and of the characteristics of the application. The inference engine is used to generate decision tree based models that take decisions concerning the offloading process on the basis of the parameters contained in the categories defined by the taxonomy. This is based on a genetic programming tool that generates the models using the parameters defined by the taxonomy and driven by a function of fitness, giving different weights to the costs, time, energy depending on the priorities assigned.

However, the offloading cannot be performed without considering the issues derived from of the nature of the application, i.e. multimedia, games, communications, which can change the resources necessary to the computation and the type, the frequency and the amount of data to be exchanged with the network and consequently the energy consumption profile.

In this paper, we extend the framework, building a generator of artificial datasets, which using the categories defined in the above-cited work, permits to simulate different kinds of mobile applications, which present different characteristics in terms of the amount of computation, of the type, the frequency and the amount of computation and the amount of data to be exchanged. The generator permits to analyze both the effectiveness of the models built by the decision-tree based GP approach and the interpretability of the models themselves. In addition, the analytical model, showing how the cloud simulator and the mobile simulator model the different types of applications is shown.

The rest of the paper is structured as follows. Section 2 presents the entire framework used to perform the offloading process. In Section 3, the mobile simulator is illustrated. In Section 4, we show how the artificial datasets are generated. In Section 5, some experiments are conducted to verify the effectiveness of the approach and to analyze the models obtained. Finally, Section 6 concludes the work.

2   Background: A GP-based Framework to Perform the Offloading of Mobile Applications

In this section is presented the framework that uses Genetic Programming to evolve models, in the form of decision trees, which will decide whether it is convenient to perform the offloading of a mobile application on the cloud. The decision is taken on the basis of the parameters and the properties typical of the application, of the user and of the environment, with the support of a tool for simulating both cloud and mobile environments, presented in the next section.

It is necessary to consider that the system is based on a taxonomy of parameters and properties of the mobile systems, defined in [3], which will be used to take decisions in order to build the model that decides the offloading strategy. The taxonomy only considers aspects that influence the offloading process and is based on four different categories: Application (parameters associated with the application itself), User (parameters assigned according to the user needs), Network (parameters concerning the type and the state of the network), and Device (parameters reflecting the hardware/software features of the devices).

The overall software architecture of the system, illustrated in Figure 1, will be helpful in understanding how the framework works.

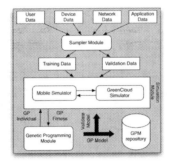

Fig. 1. The overall software architecture of the system

On the top of the architecture, there are the modules containing the data, which will be used by the other components of the system. These different modules will contain a set of data for each of the four taxonomic categories considered. Afterwards, the sampler module will generate the training and the validation dataset, simply randomly combing the data estimated by the above-mentioned models. These two datasets will be used respectively to generate and validate the decision models.

Analyzing the rest of the software architecture, we find the two main modules, used respectively for the simulation and for the inference of the mobile offloading module. The inference part of the designed system consists of a Genetic Programming module, developing a population of models, suitable to decide the possible offloading of a mobile application. The chosen GP system is BoostCGPC *Boost Cellular Genetic Programming Classifier* [2]. One of the advantages of the chosen GP–based module is that it can run on parallel/distributed architectures, permitting time-saving in the most expensive phase of the training process, described in the following. Indeed, each single model of the GP population represents a decision tree able to decide a strategy for the offloading and must be evaluated using the simulation module.

The simulation module consists of the GreenCloud simulator [5] (simulating the cloud part of the offloading process) and of a mobile simulator designed in order to model the mobile device behavior. In practice, each model generated by the GP module is passed to the simulator module, which performs the fitness evaluation directly on the basis of the results obtained simulating the model using the training dataset.

At the end of the process, the best model (or the best models) will form the rules adopted by the offloading engine, which will decide whether an application must be offloaded, considering the defined conditions (user requirements, bandwidth, characteristic of the mobile device and so on). All these models must be validated using the simulation engine with the validation dataset; if the result of this evaluation exceeds a predefined threshold, the model is added to a model repository for future use. The rules used to perform the offloading process are generated using the genetic programming tool. The use of GP supplies the characteristic of adaptivity and the possibility of working with little knowledge of the domain, which is really useful to this particular aim.

2.1   Fitness, Terminals and Functions

As usual, in order to use GP for a particular domain, it is sufficient to choose an appropriate terminal and function set and to define a fitness function. We chose a typical approach to GP for generating decision trees, choosing as terminals simply the two answers, yes or no to the question "Is the process offloadable?". Then, the main parameters/properties that will drive the offloading process are used as functions. For this particular domain, in order to design an appropriate fitness function, it is necessary to take into account the energy wasted, the cost supplied to use the Cloud and the time saved (or wasted) in performing the offload process.

First of all, we define three normalized functions, representing respectively the energy saved, the time saved and the cost saved during the process of offloading (actually the latter is a negative value, as it is a cost not a saving): S_{energy}, S_{time} and S_{cost}.

$S_{energy} = \frac{E_{local} - E_{offload}}{max(E_{offload}, E_{local})}$, i.e. the ratio between the energy saved executing the process on remote servers and the energy necessary to perform the offloading. The energy is computed in accordance with the analysis defined in [6] and the methodology is better detailed in section 3 together with the costs derived from using the cloud resources.

$S_{time} = \frac{T_{local} - T_{offload}}{max(T_{offload}, T_{local})}$, i.e. the ratio between the time saved executing the process on remote servers and the time necessary to perform the offloading.

Differently, the cost function is computed as $S_{cost} = -\frac{C_{offload}}{C_{sup}}$, i.e. the ratio between the cost due to the remote execution and a parameter C_{sup} defining a threshold of cost (if the cost overcomes C_{sup}, S_{cost} becomes -1).

Finally, the fitness is computed as the weighted sum of the three equations described above, using three positive parameters ($p_{energy}, p_{time}, p_{cost}$), modeling the importance we want to give respectively to the energy saving, to the time saving and to the cost saving.

Considering an element T_i (representing an application running on a determined device) of the training set T composed of n tuples, the fitness of this element is computed as

$f(T_i) = p_{energy} * S_{energy} + p_{time} * S_{time} + p_{cost} * S_{cost}$ and consequently the total fitness is given by $f_{tot} = \sum_{i=1}^{i=n} f(T_i)$

3   The Mobile and Cloud Simulator

In this section, the simulator used for the process of offloading is described in detail.

The mobile simulator is written in java and its architecture comprises two modules. The first computes the (time, energy and cost) models that specify hardware characteristics of the mobile devices and the costs of the cloud services. The second module computes the fitness for all the tasks and communicates with the GreenCloud simulator in order to obtain the estimated values concerning the cloud environment (cost, execution time, memory used, etc.).

The main aim of the simulator is to estimate the three important components, which will be used to estimate the goodness (fitness) of a determined model built by the GP system: the time, the energy and the cost associated with that model. The equations used to estimate these three functions are based on the model developed by Kumar [6]. The first element is function of the time required to perform the task entirely on the mobile device and of the time required to perform the same task (or at least part of the task) on the cloud server considering also the overhead associated with the communication; the second element is determined by the energy wasted on the mobile device and the energy consumed performing the offload; finally, the third module represents the cost of the cloud computing services. The latter is computed using GreenCloud [5], which is a simulation environment for energy-aware cloud computing datacenters. It is derived from NS2 (network simulator) and tracks the power use of all the components involved in a datacenter: hosts, communication switches, etc. In our framework, GreenCloud is used to evaluate the execution times of the part of the application offloaded on the servers and consequently the costs necessary to use the servers and the energy wasted. Although the main interest of this paper is on the mobile side, on the Cloud side, we need to simulate the processing delays, the submitting task rates, the impact of mobile data size in the overall performance, in order to identify classes of applications that benefit from the computation offloading.

The time component represents the difference between the time to perform the task locally or remotely. The time of local computation mainly depends on three factors: the average execution time, the probability of interruption and the available memory. A higher probability of interruption corresponds to a large amount of time to complete the task. The available memory has effects on the computation time because the mobile OS performs a time-consuming swapping operation when memory is not sufficient.

In the case of the offload, the time depends on the computation time on the server (obtained by the simulator GreenCloud) that corresponds to the waiting time of the mobile device and the time required to perform the migration of the data (and of part of the application). These delays depend on the type of network, on the latency and on the bandwidth available.

The energy component is obtained from the difference of the energy consumed when the task is executed on the mobile device and the energy consumed when the task runs on the cloud servers. The term, which represents the local energy, is given by the product between the energy consumption of the system (P_c) and the execution time (T_c). The system energy depends on the CPU usage and on the system resources used (GPS, camera, etc.) that are correlated to complexity of the task, available battery and system load.

Using the model proposed by Kumar, we indicate with C the number of instructions required by the computation, with S the speed (instructions for second) of the cloud server and with M the speed of the mobile server. If the data to be transferred between the mobile and the cloud system are D (bytes) and B is the network bandwidth, it takes $\frac{D}{B}$ seconds to transmit and receive data. In addition, the mobile consumes (watts) are indicated with P_c (computing), P_i (idle), and P_{tr} (sending and receiving data). So, the energy consumed on the mobile system will be $P_c * \frac{C}{M}$, the energy consumed for the offloading process and for the computation of the cloud server will be $P_i * \frac{C}{S} + P_{tr} * \frac{D}{B}$ and the effective saving (if positive) in energy of the complete offloading process will be $P_c * \frac{C}{M} - P_i * \frac{C}{S} - P_{tr} * \frac{D}{B}$.

4 Generating Artificial Datasets for Different Kinds of Applications

It is really hard and very costly to measure the behavior and the usage of mobile devices in a real environment. Furthermore, to the best of our knowledge, in the literature, there are no real datasets modeling the behavior of mobile devices. Therefore, we build a tool for building artificial datasets to model a number of realistic mobile scenarios for our experiments. Using this tool, we generated three datasets (named A, B and C). A tuple of each dataset is composed from a set of features, each one modeling a property of the mobile system in accordance with the taxonomy previously defined and the class represents the decision of offloading or not. Most of the features are intuitive and a detailed description can be found in [3]; here we report only three relevant features: *avgtime* represents the average time of execution of the mobile application, *datasize* is the average data size in bytes exchanged by the application, *bandwidth* is the average bandwidth available between the mobile device and the cloud. These features are discretized and can assume the following values: very low, low, medium, high and very high.

A percentage of 70% of the dataset is used as training set and the remainder for testing. A synthetic description of the datasets, together with the typical

Table 1. A synthetic description of the datasets and of the typical applications they model

Dataset	Synthetic Description	Use Cases
A	Average time and datasize properties are generated with a zipf distribution. Probability of interruption property follows a normal distribution.	Applications usually interrupted by an event (i.e. a call, a text message, a notification of another app, etc.). This dataset presents an equal distribution of long/heavy and short/light tasks.
B	Datasize, average time and probability of interruption properties are generated with a normal distribution	Gaming, social networking and messaging applications, presenting a medium/long execution time or computationally intensive.
C	Probability of interruption, network QoS, average execution time, network bandwidth, battery level and cpu available are generated with a zipf distribution. Datasize, network latency, network type, memory available and connectivity are generated with a normal distribution	Most complex scenario (communication, multimedia, sport and shopping applications). They are used frequently and for short time and have very low requirements in terms of time, energy or performance.

applications they represent, are supplied in Table 1 and described in detail in the following. The percentage of tuples, which are classified as offloadable, is reported in Table 2.

Dataset A is modeled using a zipf distribution for the average time and for the datasize property, while the other properties follow a uniform distribution. This choice replicates the case in which most part of the applications have short execution times and very few applications present high execution times, while the probability of interruption follows a normal distribution. This dataset models the common mobile user behavior in which an application is interrupted by an event (a call, a text message, a notification of another app, etc.).

The three main properties in the dataset B (datasize, average time and probability of interruption) follow a normal distribution so that we have a dataset that represents the typical case of the top downloaded apps (mainly game, social and messaging apps), with a similar use behavior. Also in this case, the other properties are generated with a uniform distribution.

As for the third dataset (C), the probability of interruption, the network QoS, the average execution time, the network bandwidth, the battery level and the cpu available are generated using a zipf distribution, while the other properties are generated using a normal distribution. Using this dataset we want to model a more complex environment in which most of the applications are defined by a moderate use of memory and size of data to transmit and average values for network latency and signal strength in 3G networks, which is the most used type of network. For these reasons, more energy is required for the transmission. For values generated with zipf distribution, the applications have low resource available, poor network performance as mean value and most of the applications presents a low use time. These characteristics reproduce a scenario where offloading is less profitable.

It is worth noticing that experts of the domain could find distributions modeling the real behavior of the previously described properties better than how defined in this section; however, the aim of this work is not to define the "best" distributions for the properties of the mobile applications, but to build a framework able to simulate different distributions and understand the behavior in terms of cost, energy and time savings.

Table 2. The different parameters used in the datasets and the resulting percentage of offloadable tasks. Configurations used: C1 ($p_{energy} = 2$, $p_{time} = 0.2$, $p_{cost} = 0.2$), C2 ($p_{energy} = 2$, $p_{time} = 0.2$, $p_{cost} = 1$), C3 ($p_{energy} = 2$, $p_{time} = 1$, $p_{cost} = 1$).

	Dataset A	Dataset B	Dataset C
C1	40%	77%	24%
C2	51%	85%	29%
C3	62%	96%	40%

5 Experimental Section

All the experiments were performed on a Linux cluster with 16 Itanium2 1.4GHz nodes, each having 2 GBytes of main memory and connected by a Myrinet high performance network. As for the BoostCGPC algorithm, we adopted the same parameters used in the original paper [2], and no tuning phase has been conducted. In practice, in each experiment, the BoostGCPC module uses a probability of crossover equal to 0.8 and of mutation equal to 0.1, a maximum depth equal to 17, and a population of 100 individuals per node. The algorithm was run for 5 rounds of boosting on 5 nodes, using 100 generations for rounds. The original training set was partitioned among the 5 nodes. It is worth remembering that the algorithm produces a different classifier for each round on each node, generating a final ensemble of 25 classifiers. A parsimony factor of 0.0001 was used in order to reduce the size of the classifiers. All results were obtained by averaging 30 runs.

In order to evaluate the behavior of different configurations and types of mobile applications besides the classical error measure in the classification task (the ratio between the number of correctly classified cases and the total number of cases) the two standard metrics of *false negative rate* and *false positive rate* developed for network intrusions, have been used. If with normal we indicate the process does not need to be offloaded, the false positive (also called false alarm) rate can be computed as the ratio between the number of normal processes classified as to be offloaded and the total number of normal processes, that is

$$FP = \frac{\#FalseAlarm}{\#TrueNegative + \#FalseAlarm}$$

while false negative is the opposite case (i.e., the number of "to be offloaded" processes classified as normal and the total number of "to be offloaded" processes. These metrics are important because they help to understand which of the two cases is most costly for the offloading process.

5.1 Performance Analysis

In this subsection, a suite of experiments is conducted in order to analyze the behavior of our algorithm for different categories of mobile applications and for different experimental setups. The false positive and false negative rate and the overall error is computed by running the framework on the three datasets described in the previous section (having 15 features and 12,000 tuples each one), by varying the parameters weighting the energy, the cost and the time. In this way, we want to understand if the framework is particularly suitable to a specific distribution or is more oriented toward a specific parameter (i.e. cost), or it is effective to detect the rate of false positives or false negatives.

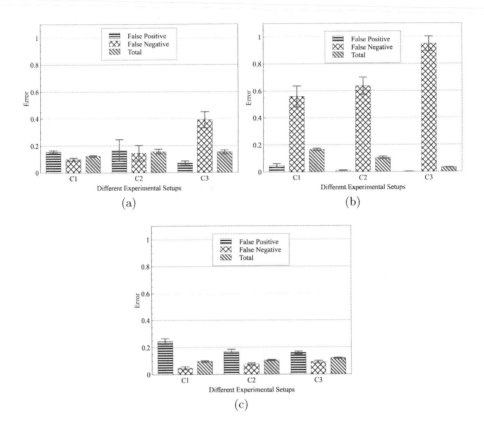

Fig. 2. The different errors (FP, FN and total) respectively for the dataset A (a), B (b) and C (c) with different configurations (C1, C2 and C3)

The results of this evaluation are illustrated in Figures 2 a, b and c. For each dataset, we used three different setup configurations (C1 ($p_{energy} = 2$, $p_{time} = 0.2$, $p_{cost} = 0.2$), C2 ($p_{energy} = 2$, $p_{time} = 0.2$, $p_{cost} = 1$), C3 ($p_{energy} = 2$, $p_{time} = 1$, $p_{cost} = 1$)). The parameters were chosen to give different importance to time and cost components of the fitness function.

The dataset A is composed of applications that require medium values of execution times and hardware requirements are not excessive. The percentage of the tasks that should be executed in offloading or not is well balanced; therefore, the model fits well the data both for the metric of FN and of FP.

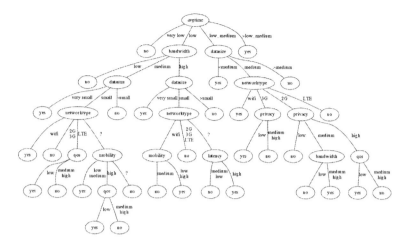

Fig. 3. An example of generated model for the dataset A

On the contrary, the dataset B was created to model applications that have a long execution time and a high use of hardware resources and consequently most of the tasks have benefits in the offloading process. Therefore, the rate of FP is very low, but equally, our model performs well for the FN rate. The dataset C models applications that have a little benefit from using the offloading mechanism. In this scenario, the correct percentage of offloadable tasks is between 20% and 40%. The False Negatives rate is very low because the number of tasks for which do offload is relatively low and they are recognized almost always correctly.

5.2   Analyzing the Models

An example of generated tree for the dataset A is shown in figure 3. It is immediately evident that the execution time, the amount of data to be transmitted and the type of network used for transmission are the main discriminating factors to make offload or not. This is due to the impact that the offloading process has in terms of energy and time taken to perform the offload. It is useful to remember that communication has a significant impact on energy consumption on a mobile device. Indeed, the first and second levels of the tree are sufficient to classify applications with a very short or very long execution times. If the data to be transmitted are low then the task of offloading is preferable. This tree reflects the nature of the applications modeled by this dataset: variables execution time, very different amount of transmitted data and, in general, no predominant trend to make offload or not.

As for the dataset B (figure 4), the percentage of offloadable tasks is predominant. The decision to make or not the offloading depends on the situations in which the power consumption is excessive in relation to the task requirements or to the condition of the battery. For example, tasks with low *avgtime*, medium

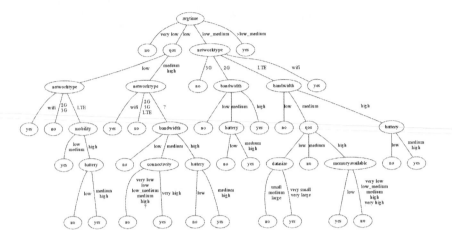

Fig. 4. An example of generated model for the dataset B

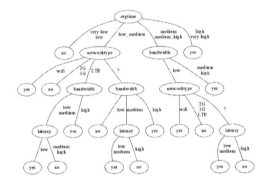

Fig. 5. An example of generated model for the dataset C

network and *qos* and a high-energy network usage do not perform the offloading. The same decision is taken whether the network type is not specified and the device has low battery. As for dataset C (figure 5), composed by a low percentage of tasks that benefits from the offloading, the final decision is mainly determined by the conditions of the network (bandwidth available, network type, latency) or by the amount of data to be transferred. The execution time is only used for the decision only in the rare case of application with a long execution time (i.e. games).

6   Conclusions and Future Work

An automatic approach to generate models for taking decisions on the process of offloading of mobile applications on the basis of the user requirements, of the conditions of the network, of the hardware/software features of the mobile device and of the characteristics of the application is presented. Using a tool for generating artificial datasets, the utility of the framework in simulating different kinds of mobile applications was demonstrated. The rules generated in the form of decision trees result really understandable and supply useful information in deciding whether determined kinds of applications are able to be offloaded and on the main conditions to be evaluated. Future works include to test the framework with real datasets and to verify whether the models obtained work in real environments.

References

1. Buyya, R., Yeo, C.S., Venugopal, S., Broberg, J., Brandic, I.: Cloud computing and emerging it platforms: Vision, hype, and reality for delivering computing as the 5th utility. Future Generation Computer Systems **25**(6), 599–616 (2009)
2. Folino, G., Pizzuti, C., Spezzano, G.: Gp ensembles for large-scale data classification. IEEE Transactions on Evolutionary Computation **10**(5), 604–616 (2006)
3. Folino, G., Pisani, F.S.: A Framework for Modeling Automatic Offloading of Mobile Applications Using Genetic Programming. In: Esparcia-Alcázar, A.I. (ed.) EvoApplications 2013. LNCS, vol. 7835, pp. 62–71. Springer, Heidelberg (2013)
4. Gurun, S., Krintz, C.: Addressing the energy crisis in mobile computing with developing power aware software. In UCSB Technical Report, UCSB Computer Science Department (2003)
5. Kliazovich, D., Bouvry, P., Audzevich, Y., Khan, S.U.: Greencloud: A packet-level simulator of energy-aware cloud computing data centers. In: Proceedings of the Global Communications Conference, GLOBECOM 2010, pp. 1–5. IEEE, Miami (2010)
6. Kumar, K., Yung-Hsiang, L.: Cloud computing for mobile users: Can offloading computation save energy? IEEE Computer **43**(4), 51–56 (2010)
7. Lee, K., Rhee, I., Lee, J., Chong, S., Yi, Y.: Mobile data offloading: how much can wifi deliver? IEEE/ACM Transactions on Networking **21**(2), 536–550 (2013)
8. Liu, J., Kumar, K., Lu, Y-H.: Tradeoff between energy savings and privacy protection in computation offloading. In: Proceedings of the 2010 International Symposium on Low Power Electronics and Design, pp. 213–218. ACM, Austin (2010)
9. Wolski, R., Gurun, S., Krintz, C., Nurmi, D.: Using bandwidth data to make computation offloading decisions. In: 22nd IEEE International Symposium on Parallel and Distributed Processing, IPDPS 2008, pp. 1–8. IEEE, Miami (2008)

EvoCOMPLEX

Common Developmental Genomes Revisited – Evolution Through Adaptation

Konstantinos Antonakopoulos[(⊠)]

Department of Computer and Information Science,
Norwegian University of Science and Technology, Sem Sælandsvei 7-9,
NO-7491 Trondheim, Norway
kostas@idi.ntnu.no

Abstract. Artificial development has been widely used for designing complex structures and as a means to increase the complexity of an artifact. One central challenge in artificial development is to understand how a mapping process could work on a class of architectures in a more general way by exploiting the most favorable properties from each computational architecture or by combining efficiently more than one computational architectures (i.e., a true multicellular approach). Computational architectures in this context comprise structures with connected computational elements, namely, cellular automata and boolean networks. The ability to develop and co-evolve different computational architectures has previously been investigated using common developmental genomes. In this paper, we extend a previous work that studied their evolvability. Here, we focus on their ability to evolve when the goal changes over evolutionary time (i.e., adaptation), utilizing a more fair fitness assignment scheme. In addition, we try to investigate how common developmental genomes exploit the underlying architecture in order to build the phenotypes. The results show that they are able to find very good solutions with rather simplified solutions than anticipated.

Keywords: Common developmental genomes · Evolvability · Cellular automata · Boolean network · L-systems

1 Introduction

In artificial systems, a species can be linked to a certain computational architecture, such as, a cellular automata (CA) [1] or a boolean network (BN) [2]. Here, computational architectures are considered as structures comprising connected computational elements. A computational element may represent a cell (part of a cellular automaton) or a node (part of a boolean network). Most such systems include a specific genetic representation (genotype), a mapping process (genotype-to-phenotype) and have a specific structure as a target (phenotype).

A big challenge in developmental systems is how a genotype-phenotype mapping can work on a class of computational architectures (species), towards scalable systems for complex computation. So, it is important to investigate whether

© Springer-Verlag Berlin Heidelberg 2014
A.I. Esparcia-Alcázar et al. (Eds.): EvoApplications 2014, LNCS 8602, pp. 101–112, 2014.
DOI: 10.1007/978-3-662-45523-4_9

it is possible to exploit the most favorable properties from each species or to combine more than one species in a more efficient way (i.e., a true multicellular approach). To study this concept, an experimental approach was undertaken [3] and [4], giving rise to common developmental genomes.

Common developmental genomes are genomes constructed in a modular way (chromosomes), making it possible to develop and evolve more than one species, towards a *common* goal [3],[5]. In [3], it was investigated whether common developmental genomes can favor the evolvability of different species. The species studied therein were cellular automata and boolean networks. Evaluation of the fitness was done by averaging the partial fitnesses of the species involved. Even though common genomes exhibited superior ability to evolve and adapt to the environment than genomes evolved separately for each species, the fitness evaluation scheme in [3] needs some reconsideration. For example, a CA with a fitness 0.1 and a BN with a fitness 0.9, would have an average fitness of 0.5. On a different case, with the CA having a fitness 0.5 and the BN having a fitness 0.5, we will also get an average fitness 0.5. As such, there is no way to discriminate better from worse individuals in a population. Even still, they are all assigned the same fitness score.

In this paper, we continue the study of [3]. The goal herein is to test the ability of common developmental genomes to adapt when the goal changes over evolutionary time (i.e., adaptation), facilitating a more fair fitness assignment scheme. Through this new fitness evaluation scheme we aim at assigning a more fair fitness to the evolving species but also, and perhaps more importantly, since the genetic information (genotype) is common for all species, the scheme may act as a means to indirectly apply evolutionary pressure towards the inferiorly evolving species. In addition, we analyze the structures of the best phenotypes by visual inspection and investigate how common developmental genomes exploit the underlying architectures in order to build their solutions.

The rest of the article is laid out as follows. The developmental model is given at Section 2. Section 3 give a brief description of the emergent dynamics in artificial systems. Section 4 present the experimental setup. Results are given in Section 5, with the conclusion at Section 6.

2   The Developmental Model

In this section, the genetic representation and the developmental model is given in brief. For a detailed description, see [5]. Figure 1, shows the genome constructed by two parts or *chromosomes*. The first chromosome creates the cells / nodes of the species whereas the second chromosome generates the connections. Each chromosome is governed by rules. The rules for node / cell creation are different from those for connectivity.

The rules of the first chromosome describe cell processes like growth, differentiation and apoptosis and are used during the development process (ontogeny). The rules of the second chromosome express the connectivity and are used for developing the connections of the boolean network. To express the rules in the chromosomes, an L-system is used as a developmental model.

Fig. 1. The genome is split into two chromosomes: Node- and Connectivity-chromosomes

L-systems are rewriting grammars, able to describe developmental or generative systems and have successfully been used to simulate biological processes [7], [8]. Two separate L-systems are used in the representation. The first L-system processes the first chromosome rules where a second L-system deals with the connectivity rules of the second chromosome.

2.1 The L-system for the First Chromosome

The L-system used here is context-sensitive. As such, development is using the strict predecessor/ancestor to determine the applicable production rule. The rules are able to incorporate all the cell processes of a species. Table 1(a), shows the type of symbols used by the L-system of the first chromosome.

Table 1. (a) Symbol table for nodes/cell creation, (b) Symbol table for creating connectivity

(a)			(b)	
Symbol	Description		Symbol	Description
a	Add (growth)		x	Node (different from y)
b	Add (growth)		y	Node (different from x)
c	Add (growth)		+	Connect forward
d	Delete (apoptosis)		−	Connect backwards
X	Substitute (differentiation)		→	Production
Y	Substitute (differentiation)			
→	Production			

Symbol a is the *axiom*. Apart from the symbols a, b, and c, which perform *growth* of the phenotype, symbol d performs *apoptosis*, aiming at the deletion of the current rule (i.e., cell/node). Symbols X and Y, represent the *differentiation* process, replacing the predecessor cell/node. For example, for X→Y the outcome will be Y. The length of each rule is 4 symbols (i.e., 4x8bits=32bits). For node/cell generation the L-system runs for n timesteps and then stops. As such, the intermediate phenotypes generated by development are of variable size. Figure 2a, gives an example of a first chromosome L-system.

Detailed example with step-by-step development of a 2D-CA architecture can be found at [5].

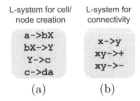

L-system for cell/ node creation	L-system for connectivity

(a)   (b)

Fig. 2. (a) L-system rule set for node/cell generation, (b) L-system rule set for connectivity

2.2   The L-system for the Second Chromosome

The rules are able to generate the connections necessary for the wiring of the nodes. They contain symbols which when executed by the L-system, result in creating a connection forward or backwards from the current node. Each node in the network has unique numbering; current node holds number zero and any nodes starting from the current node forward have positive numbering. Nodes existing from the current node backwards, have negative numbering. As such, there is a need to differentiate between the current and the next node, using different symbols but also to describe when a connection will be created forward or backwards from the current node.

The length of connectivity rules is also four. The L-system uses a D0L (i.e., with zero-sided interactions). The second chromosome L-system is shown at Figure 2b. Symbols are explained in Table 1(b).

The *axiom* rule for the second chromosome is x→y. Then, development continues looking for rules of type xy→+value, or xy→-value. In short, these two rules imply that if two different (distinct) nodes are found (x≠y), it creates a connection forward (if the rule includes a '+'), or similarly a connection backwards (if the rule includes a '-'). The field value is encoded in the genotype and denotes the node number of the newly created connection. If value=0, a self-connection is created to the current node. Detailed example with step-by-step development of a boolean network architecture is presented at [5].

2.3   The Genetic Algorithm for Common Genetic Representation

A genetic algorithm (GA) is utilized to create and evolve the chromosome rules. Since there are two separate L-systems involved in development, the evolutionary process will be consisted of two phases: a. the creation of nodes and b. the creation of the connections. Mutation and single-point crossover are used as genetic operators. Mutation may occur anywhere inside the 4-symbol rule, such as the production symbol (→) remains undistorted after mutation. Single-point crossover between two parents always takes place at the position of the production symbol in the rule. The evolutionary cycle ends after a predetermined number of generations.

3   Emergent Dynamics in Artificial Systems

In biology, development is a process starting from a zygote and develops into a multicellular organism. Similarly, in the artificial domain, development simulates this biological process; from an given initial condition, the zygote, through an iterative developmental process, it can develop into a final structure (phenotype). Assuming the developmental process is deterministic, i.e,. the outcome of development is defined by the initial zygote (genome), some initial condition and a developmental mapping, then an initial configuration (or a set of configurations) exists and is sufficiently defined by the developmental genome and the initial conditions [6].

Any sparsely connected computational architecture (i.e., CA, BN, etc.) can be represented in the space time domain. Phenotypic structures can be shown as nodes and their transitions in time can be shown as developmental paths from the zygote to the final organism. Development of a structure comprise developmental steps (DS). Each DS may include one or more developmental processes proposed by the model (Section 2). Development starts with the zygote (initial genome).

Fig. 3. Developmental path of a structure shown as a trajectory

Figure 3 shows the path of development of a non-uniform 2D-CA. White cells are considered empty whereas colored cells represent the CA rule of the particular cell. Solid lines represent consecutive developmental steps (DS 10-11 and DS 99-100). Non-consecutive developmental steps are represented by dashed lines (zygote-DS 10 and DS 11-99). The path from the zygote until DS 10 has gone through 10 different intermediate phenotypic structures. Similarly, the path from DS 11 until DS 99 has produced 88 different intermediate phenotypic structures. DS 100 has a loop back to DS 99; this type of behavior is a *cycle attractor* which indicates whether the structure is stable or not. The path until DS 99 represents a *transient period* or phase. The structure at DS 100 is the final phenotype.

The behavior of the system is described by the initial state and the trajectory of all 100 developmental steps of the example. Each developmental step is further analyzed into state steps (SS). A state includes cell/node information giving a snapshot of instantaneous behavior. As such, state steps provide information about the emergent behavior of intermediate and final phenotypes in the space/time domain.

The descriptions on emergent dynamics explained above, are useful to better understand the definitions of the computational goals for the common developmental genomes (Sections 4.3 and 4.4).

4 Experimental Setup

For the experiments, a 6x6 2D-CA and a N=36 BN is used. The size chosen for the CA is the minimum possible. By choosing a smaller lattice size, there will be too many dependencies in the cell states of the CA. Also, the maximum number of nodes/cells in the species should allow for easy, visual explanation of the final phenotypic structures. The larger the size of the species, the harder it is to visually interpret their structure.

For the two species to be comparable, they must have the same state space or the same amount of possible states. Since the size of each architecture is 36 and each cell/node can take 2 different distinct values (boolean), the total state space for each species is 2^{36}. The number of outgoing connections per node is $K = 5$. When the number of outgoing connections exceeds five, a self-connection to the originating node is created instead. The number of incoming connections per node is limited only by the total number of nodes found in the network $(N - 1)$.

For each individual, a random initial state is created and fed into the architecture. We use a total number of 36 rules for node generation and connectivity (i.e., 32x36=1152bits). Each rule can be reused during L-system development. The GA program drives a single population of 20 individuals. Development runs for 100 timesteps (DS) for each individual. In each DS, behavior is defined by 1000 state steps (SS). *Generational mixing* is used as global selection mechanism and *fitness proportionate* for parental selection. Mutation rate is set to .0009 and crossover rate to .001. We run a total of 20 experiments of 10000 generations each. Evaluation of phenotypes is given by the cell types and functionality of Table 2.

Table 2. Cell types and functionality

Cell Type	Function name
a	NAND
b	OR
c	AND
d	IDENTITY CELL
X	XOR
Y	NOT

4.1 Fitness Assignment Scheme

The new fitness evaluation scheme used is described in four steps:

- Run the first 20% of evolutionary time using normal fitness evaluation (final fitness is the average of the fitnesses of CA and BN), e.g., $fitness_{total} = (fitness_{CA} + fitness_{BN})/2$
- In the next 20% – 50% of time and if the partial fitnesses differ more than 30%, there is an extra 10% of fitness credit assigned to the species with the higher fitness. For example if CA has a 30% higher fitness than BN, then $fitness_{total} = [(fitness_{CA} + (fitness_{CA} * 0.1)) + fitness_{BN}]/2$

– In the next 50% – 70% of time, species are evolved using normal fitness evaluation, e.g., $fitness_{total} = (fitness_{CA} + fitness_{BN})/2$
– In the final 70% – 100% of time and if the partial fitnesses differ more than 30%, there is an extra 10% of fitness credit assigned to the species with the higher fitness. For example, if BN has a 30% higher fitness than CA, then $fitness_{total} = [(fitness_{BN} + (fitness_{BN} * 0.1)) + fitness_{CA}]/2$

The highest assigned fitness score is 100 and the lowest is 2 with a worst-case of 0.1. The final fitness for the common developmental genome is the average of the fitness of the species involved. If, for example CA's fitness is 50 and BN's fitness is 20, the final fitness of the common developmental genome will be 35.

4.2   Studying the Dynamic Behavior

To study the evolvability of computational properties, the system must be able to target different behavior on the architectures chosen (CA and BN). Their behavior can be evolved through the study of various dynamic problems i.e., stable point attractor, short attractors or long repetitive/chaotic behavior.

The computational problems chosen here describe some basic dynamic behavior for CA and BN and the goal is generally expected to be reached. Though, the problems as such are of minor importance since we are mainly after the ability of common developmental genomes to adapt during evolution.

4.3   First Problem Definition

Evolution searches for a cycle attractor of size 2-160, at generations 1 - 5000. A minimal cycle attractor can be found as early as in SS 2, that is, behavior is stabilized and the final structures are phenotypes obtained at SS 1 and SS 2. On the other extreme, a maximally big cycle attractor may be found as late as in SS 1000-160=840. Best fitness score is assigned for cycle attractors of size 80. Here, no fitness credit is assigned for cycle attractors found at an earlier or later stage i.e., a cycle attractor can occur after any transient phase. Fitnesss distribution is given at Figure 4(a).

4.4   Second Problem Definition

After generation 5000, the evolutionary goal change. From generation 5000 - 10000, evolution searches for a transient phase of size 1-200, followed by a cycle attractor of 2-160 steps. Best fitness score is assigned for transient phase 100 and cycle attractor 80. This is a harder problem than the previous one, considering that the total number of states / developmental step is 1000. No credit is given for point attractors following a transient phase. Here, separate fitnesses are assigned for the transient phase and the cycle attractor. The final fitness is estimated by averaging their respective fitnesses, e.g., for the CA will be $fitness_{CA} = (fitness_{transient} + fitness_{cycleattractor})/2$. The fitness distribution for this problem is shown at Figure 4(b).

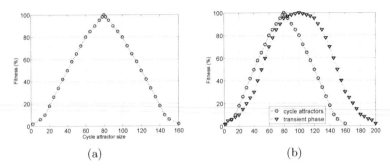

Fig. 4. Fitness distributions plots: (a) Cycle attractors, (b) Transient phase & cycle attractor

5   Results

Figure 5 shows the average fitness evaluation of common developmental genomes over all runs. The 'AVG' line shows the average fitness of both species (CA and BN). The 'CA' line shows the average fitness of the cellular automata only and the 'BN' line gives the average fitness of the boolean network.

The first problem (search for cycle attractor) is studied at generations 1-5000. During this period, both CA and BN are able to find fairly good solutions. After generation 2000, the effect of the new fitness assignment scheme can be observed. BN is constantly being credited with an extra 10% of fitness due to its fitness difference to the CA. This credit assignment in one of the species in common developmental genomes, can indirectly act as a means of evolutionary pressure for the other species, since they share the same genetic information. Though, the performance of the CA remains constant until the very end. It is not until generation 4600, where an improvement in performance for both species occurs.

The second problem (search for transient period & cycle attractor) is examined at generations 5001-10000. At generation 5001, the genome still contains genetic information optimized for the previous problem (generation 5000). So, the same genetic information acts as a basis for the second problem, which initially gives only average solutions. After generation 7000 the new assignment scheme gets into effect. This is evident from a sharp fitness increase for both species. Here, the performance of BN has an impact in the performance of the CA (generation 7350).

Figure 6 shows some evolutionary steps of one of the best CA runs over time. Solid line shows consecutive generations where dashed lines delineate more than one generation steps. The figure, shows some of the best evolved phenotypes for the first problem (gen.2-5000). From generation 5001, the target changes and the genome tries to adapt to the newly set goal, with a clear impact in the fitness. Some of the phenotypes for the second problem are shown for generations 5001, 8500 and 10000.

The model managed to find several perfect solutions for the first problem, but also, many good solutions for the second problem. The solutions achieved by

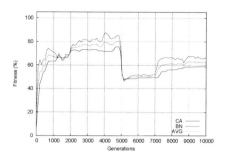

Fig. 5. Fitness evaluation of common developmental genomes (averaged)

Fig. 6. Some of the best intermediate and final phenotypes of a CA evolution over time

the developmental model with the CA, extended out exploiting the complete CA lattice for both the problems investigated. In addition, development produced maximally big genomes at the very beginning of the process (not shown). As we will see in the next paragraph, this is not the case for the evolved BN phenotypes.

Figure 7 shows two of the best evolved BN solutions for the first problem at generation 5000. Both solutions solved this problem perfectly (fitness 100), but with a quite different structure. The solution at Figure 7(a), shows a network where each node has at least two connections to other nodes and at least one self-connection.

The numbers at the nodes indicate the node number and the connections are shown in black solid lines. Since there is no explicit positional information for the nodes of the BN, the node numbers indicate their sequential position (next, previous node). The arrow at the end of each connection, indicates the flow of information between the originating and destination nodes.

On the other hand, the solution at Figure 7(b), shows a network where one node is rather influential (node nr.1), since the outcome of the majority of the nodes in the network, is dependent on the outcome of node nr.1. Self-connections are rare since most of the connections point to a different node than the originating node.

Some of the near-perfect solutions given by evolution (fitness > 80), include networks with a rather small number of nodes (not shown). All perfect solutions (fitness 100), involved networks having the maximum number of nodes allowed by the model (N=36). This suggests that development initially tries to seek solutions

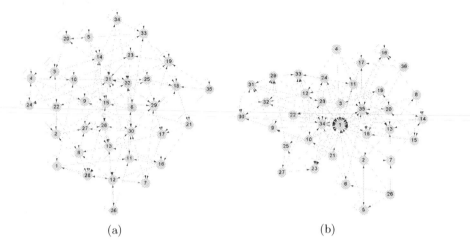

Fig. 7. Two of the best evolved boolean networks for the first problem (generation 5000, fitness 100)

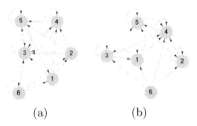

Fig. 8. The best evolved BNs for the second problem (generation 10000, fitness 76)

using less number of nodes and then extends the networks by introducing more nodes in the network. This shows an unexpected emergent behavior of the system since the developmental model was not designed as such.

Figure 8 shows the best evolved BN solutions for the second problem at generation 10000. Both solutions have a rather small number of nodes (N=6) and most of the nodes have at least one self-connection. Other, less than perfect solutions provided networks having the max number of nodes (N=36).

At generation 5001, the goal changes and evolution finds near perfect solutions with networks of similar size as before. At the end of evolution, the solutions included networks with a rather simplified structure. The latter shows that the developmental model is able to give both complex and more simplified solutions, depending on the goal sought.

Next, we investigate how common developmental genomes exploit the underlying architectures, in order to build the final solutions. To achieve this, we focus on the variation of the nodes/cells during evolution. Here, we are interested only in the change of the value of the cell/node, not if the change has a

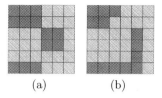

(a)   (b)

Fig. 9. Amount of CA structures that is computing (light gray) versus their static parts (dark gray). (a) First problem, (b) Second problem.

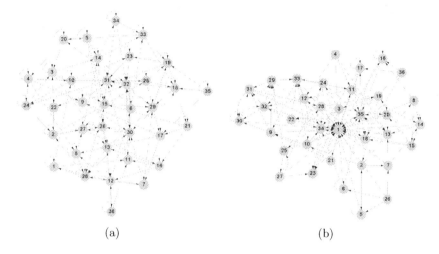

(a)   (b)

Fig. 10. Computing parts of BN phenotypes for the two of the best evolved networks for the first problem

positive (i.e., fitness increase), or a neutral (i.e., equal fitness) impact to the fitness. Cells/nodes performing rarely any computation ($\prec$30% of the evolutionary time) are considered static, where cells/nodes computing more than 30% of the time is considered that they are actively contribute to the final solution.

Figure 9 shows two 2D-CA of size 6x6. The light-gray colored cells indicate cells that compute. As such, a total of 70% approximately of the CA structure is actually computing during evolution. Similarly, the dark-gray colored cells indicate cells that are static, constituting a total of 30% of the structure.

Next, Figure 10 shows the two best evolved networks for the first problem (as in Figure 7). The nodes of the networks that are computing are shown in dark gray color. Figure 10(a) indicates that approximately 55.6% of the network is computing with the rest 44.4% of the network being static. Similarly, Figure 10(b), shows that a total of approximately 70% of the network is actually active. The BN solutions found, give quite different statistics; the first network solution involve more self-connections/node than the network solutions for the second problem. Self-connections contribute to the network's neutrality and this can partially have an impact on the amount of the network that is actually active. Regarding the second problem (network solutions of Figure 8), all the nodes in the networks found to be computing and no static nodes are observed.

6   Conclusion

In this work, we extended a previous study by looking at how common developmental genomes can evolve computational architectures when the goal changes over time (evolution through adaptation). The focus here was to evolve CA and BN computational architectures with simple cycle attractor with transient phase problems as a computational goal and a more fair fitness assignment scheme. Also, it was investigated how common genetic representation is being exploited during development, sometimes exhibiting emergent behavior during phenotype construction. Common developmental genomes where able to adapt fairly well to each problem, considering the number of available state steps during development. In addition, they were able to exploit a large part of the underlying architectures having on average more than 55% of the total number of cells/nodes actively computing, for both problems studied.

References

1. Bidlo, M., Vasicek, M.: Evolution of cellular automata with conditionally matching rules. In: Congress on Evolutionary Computation (CEC 2013), pp. 1178–1185 (2013)
2. Bull, L.: Artificial symbiogenesis and differing reproduction rates. Artificial Life **16**(1), 65–72 (2010)
3. Antonakopoulos, K., Tufte, G.: On the Evolvability of Different Computational Architectures using a Common Developmental Genome. In: Rosa, A., Dourado, A., Madani, K., Filipe, J., Kacprzyk J. (eds.) IJCCI 2012, pp. 122–129. SciTePress Publishing (2012)
4. Antonakopoulos, K., Tufte, G.: Is Common Developmental Genome a Panacea Towards More Complex Problems? In: 13th IEEE International Symposium on Computational Intelligence and Informatics (CINTI 2012), pp. 55–61 (2012)
5. Antonakopoulos, K., Tufte, G.: A Common Genetic Representation Capable of Developing Distinct Computational Architectures. In: IEEE Congress on Evolutionary Computation (CEC 2011), pp. 1264–1271 (2011)
6. Tufte, G.: The discrete dynamics of developmental systems. In: IEEE Congress on Evolutionary Computation (CEC 2009), pp. 2209–2216 (2009)
7. Lindenmayer, A.: Developmental Systems without Cellular Interactions, their Languages and Grammars. Journal of Theoretical Biology **30**(3), 455–484 (1971)
8. Lindenmayer, A., Prusinkiewicz, P.: Developmental Models of Multicellular Organisms: A Computer Graphics Perspective. In: Langton, C.G. (ed.) Proceedings of ALife, pp. 221–249. Addison-Wesley Publishing (1989)

Investigation of Genome Parameters and Sub-transitions to Guide Evolution of Artificial Cellular Organisms

Stefano Nichele[✉], Håkon Hjelde Wold, and Gunnar Tufte

Department of Computer and Information Science,
Norwegian University of Science and Technology,
Sem Selandsvei 7-9, 7491, Trondheim, Norway
{nichele,gunnart}@idi.ntnu.no, haakonhw@stud.ntnu.no

Abstract. Artificial multi-cellular organisms develop from a single zygote to complex morphologies, following the instructions encoded in their genomes. Small genome mutations can result in very different developed phenotypes. In this paper we investigate how to exploit genotype information in order to guide evolution towards favorable areas of the phenotype solution space, where the sought emergent behavior is more likely to be found. Lambda genome parameter, with its ability to discriminate different developmental behaviors, is incorporated into the fitness function and used as a discriminating factor for genetic distance, to keep resulting phenotype's developmental behavior close by and encourage beneficial mutations that yield adaptive evolution. Genome activation patterns are detected and grouped into genome parameter sub-transitions. Different sub-transitions are investigated as simple genome parameters, or composed to integrate several genome properties into a more exhaustive composite parameter. The experimental model used herein is based on 2-dimensional cellular automata.

Keywords: Artificial Development · Evolution · Complexity · Emergence · Cellular Automata

1   Introduction

Evolved artificial developmental (EvoDevo) systems have shown many favorable features that are also present in natural biological systems, such as the ability to evolve robust genomes [1]. However, robustness and evolvability may not be always rowing in the same direction. A biological organism may be considered robust if, after genome mutations, it keeps the same ability or functional properties. In contrast, evolvability is a property that promotes genetic variation in order to produce adaptive evolution, being able to evolve through natural selection. One may think that too high robustness would not provide enough genetic diversity whereas too high evolvability would cause more disadvantageous mutations, thus annihilating adaptation. In EvoDevo systems, small changes in the genome often lead to completely different emergent phenotypes. It is particularly difficult to understand which changes will be produced to the developing organism by each genetic operator, e.g. mutation, crossover, and which phenotypic traits will be affected. As such, evolutionary algorithms

© Springer-Verlag Berlin Heidelberg 2014
A.I. Esparcia-Alcázar et al. (Eds.): EvoApplications 2014, LNCS 8602, pp. 113–124, 2014.
DOI: 10.1007/978-3-662-45523-4_10

spend a relevant amount of time generating low fitness solutions that may not give any genetic contribution to the population and thus being often discarded. We investigate if genome information could be used to guide evolution. Our results indicate that genome parameters could predict the developing behavior based on genome composition and thus help to guide evolutionary search in the right area of the search space, where the sought behavior is more likely to be found.

The article is laid out as follows: background information and motivation is presented in Section 2. In Section 3 the developmental model used in the experiments is presented. Section 4 describes Lambda genome parameter, meaning and usage. The experimental setup is illustrated in Section 5. In Section 6 and 7 the results of the experiments are presented together with the discussion. Section 8 concludes the work.

2   Motivation and Background

Artificial developmental systems can be considered as complex systems [2], where there is no central controller and the developed artificial organisms are the result of an emergent process out of the local interactions of simple cells. Many developmental systems target specific phenotypic structures or structural properties [3], whether some others execute a particular computational task that emerges out of the development of the machine' structure [4]. Programming an artificial developmental system to produce such emergent computation cannot be done using traditional engineering approaches. One solution could be to exploit nature's way of tackling problems, namely evolution by natural selection. Evolutionary algorithms have been widely used as population-based metaheuristic optimization algorithms [5]. In general, those evolutionary techniques do not make any assumption about the underlying fitness landscape. An indirect genotype-to-phenotype mapping can result in two very similar genotypes developing into two very different phenotypes. A developmental mapping may be represented by a function that maps elements in the genotype space to elements in the phenotype space. Such spaces may have regions where small distances between genotypes are preserved into small differences between resulting phenotypes, whether in some other regions distances are hardly preserved at all [12]. In practice, small mutation can have a huge impact on the emergent phenotype. This can be problematic if solutions are to be discovered by evolutionary algorithms. Having a genome parameter that may predict the emergent behavior could be useful to reduce phenotypic distance. Such information could contribute to guide evolutionary search throughout the solution space, where the target phenotype may plausibly appear.

3   Evolution and Development

The relation between natural evolution and development in biological systems is still a fairly unexplored area [13]. Investigation of natural evolution makes it hardly possible to obtain experimental proofs due to the time scale of evolution. In evolved artificial systems there is no such problem. It is possible to execute experiments in a reasonable time and investigate different evolutionary factors that may influence on developmental paths. However, there is a lack of knowledge of what kind of information must be present in the genome in order to obtain a sought phenotypic behavior. We try to exploit genome regulatory information in a simple developmental model and investigate if such information could contribute to guide evolution in the vast solution space, i.e. toward where the target developmental trajectory is more likely to emerge.

3.1   Cellular Developmental Model

The developmental model used herein is based on cellular automata, i.e. synchronized cellular updates, parallel operation and discrete cell states. As such, the totality of regulative inputs can be coded completely in the genome (this does not imply that all of the genome information is expressed in the phenotype). To be able to have a complete regulatory network for all possible input states the model needs to be minimalistic. However, some features are not reduced to the minimum. The number of cell states is set to three instead of two. This was done to keep the concept of multicellular organism and cells differentiation, i.e. two types of cells in addition to the cells that are defined to be dead (void/quiescent). To be able to keep the principle of a growing (expanding) organism there is a constraint on how a cell can come "alive". This constrain is to only allow cells that have at least one neighbor expressing a cell type different from void to be able to come alive. The organisms develop in a two dimensional grid world, starting from a single cell placed in the grid (zygote). The placement of the first cell is of no importance as the grid uses cyclic boundary conditions. The local cellular communication is based on von-Neumann neighborhood (5 neighbors) and includes only cell type information, i.e. no environmental influence. With three cell types multicellularity is possible and at the same time the number of all possible cellular states in the defined neighborhood is not extremely large, i.e. max 243 (or 3^5). A developing organism will consist of different construct of these three cells. A more detailed description on the developmental model is given in [7, 8].

L	R	U	D	C	$C_{(t+1)}$
0	0	0	0	0	0
0	0	0	0	1	{0,1,2}
0	0	0	1	0	{0,1,2}
0	0	0	1	1	{0,1,2}
0	0	1	0	0	{0,1,2}
:	:	:	:	:	:
1	1	1	1	1	{0,1,2}
0	0	0	0	2	{0,1,2}
0	0	0	2	0	{0,1,2}
0	0	0	2	1	{0,1,2}
0	0	0	2	2	{0,1,2}
:	:	:	:	:	:
2	2	2	2	2	{0,1,2}

Fig. 1. Genome developmental table: regulatory input and cellular actions

The table in Figure 1 is a scaled down illustration of all possible regulatory combinations. For the first entry in the table, i.e. all regulatory inputs set to 0, the output of the development process is fixed at 0. This is done to fulfill the stated constraint related to growth. All other regulatory inputs have a possibility of regulating the cell to be at any of the available cell types, indicated by the triplet *{0, 1, 2}*.

Figure 2 shows an example of a developing organism. At Development Step (DS) 0 the organism consists of only a single cell of type 1 (the zygote), at DS 1 the first cell has divided and differentiated into three cells of type 2. At DS 2 – DS 4 the change in phenotypic structure along the developmental path can be observed. The last shown organism is at DS 2000000.

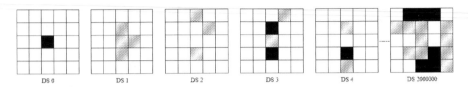

Fig. 2. Example of developing organism at intermediate development steps

3.2   Quantification of Phenotypes

Having defined genetic information for the cellular model, a quantifiable measure has to be identified for the developed organisms. Properties that can be used need to provide information on the developing organism as a whole and the occurring phenotypic changes [11]. For a given organism, the initial cell (zygote) follows a developmental path and after a transient phase reaches an attractor, i.e. a final stable state or a self-reorganizing cycle. A complete trajectory identifies the whole lifecycle of the organism [6, 8] together with morphology, size and behavior changes. Trajectory length is an abstract measure that does not code for any computational task, e.g. majority, synchronization or a given phenotypic structure, since moving from node to node in a trajectory is the computation. For the scope of this research, no specific problem is implied and generalization is crucial. As such, trajectory length is the chosen metric of phenotypic complexity.

3.3   Evolution of Genome Information

In the model described earlier, the gene regulatory information is composed by the cell state of the five cells in the neighborhood. The evolvable information is then represented by the column C(t+1) in Figure 1, which describes the outcome of the gene regulation process. Moreover, such explicit representation of all possible cellular actions opens the possibility to identify sub-groups of developmental rules (sub-transitions):

- Growth rules: sub-transitions that represent a void cell (type 0) becoming alive (type 1 or type 2);
- Differentiation rules: one of the alive cells switches to the other alive cell type;
- Death rules: one of the alive cell types becomes void;
- No-change rules: the cell does not change its state.

Death sub-transitions are a special case of differentiation rules where alive cells differentiate to quiescent cells. This group of transitions is also used to calculate Lambda parameter, as described in the following section.

The developmental trajectory from zygote to multi-cellular organism can be represented by the state transition in Figure 2. Such trajectory produces a genome activation pattern at each development step that can be measured in terms of sub-transitions activated in the genome. For example, from DS 0 to DS 1 only one differentiation sub-transition is activated, together with three growth sub-transitions and twenty one no-change sub-transitions. No death sub-transitions are triggered.

4   Lambda Genome Parameter

Parameters obtained from the genome information can be used to estimate the dynamic developmental behavior of the emerging organisms. Langton [6] tried to find a relation between CA behavior and a parameter λ. He observed that the basic functions required for computation (transmission, storage and modification of information) are more likely to be achieved in the vicinity of phase transitions between ordered and disordered dynamics (edge of chaos). He hypothesized that it is easier to find rules capable of complex computation in a region where the value of λ is critical. Since the developmental model is composed by 3^5 regulatory combinations, all the possible regulatory inputs and relative outputs (growth, differentiation, death or no action) are fully specified in the developmental table. In order to calculate λ, it is necessary to define a quiescent state, the void cell (type 0) in our case. Lambda is defined as follows:

$$\lambda = \frac{K^N - n}{K^N} \tag{1}$$

λ can be calculated according to Equation 1, where n represents the number of transitions to the quiescent (dead) state, K is the number of cells types (three in our case) and N is the neighborhood size (five in the Von Neumann neighborhood). In this way, the value of λ is based only on local properties of the neighborhood and in particular the cellular actions that are present in every cell.

Previous works [6, 7] have shown a clear relation between Lambda parameter and developed organisms' trajectory length. In particular, it is possible to identify a parameter space interval where organisms are more likely to have long life cycles. As such, Lambda (or other genome parameters) could be used to guide evolution when the target fitness is based on organisms' developing trajectories, as the work herein.

As shown in Equation 1, Lambda is determined by the ratio of sub-transitions in the developmental table that lead to the quiescent state over the total number of sub-transitions in the regulatory table. As such, λ takes into account only developmental rules that describe a cell death, i.e. one of the alive cell types becomes void. In other words, it does not consider other sub-transition groups (growth, differentiation, no-change). Lambda can be considered a single sub-transition genome parameter.

4.1   Genome Parameter Sub-transitions

Lambda parameter has been shown to be able to differentiate different developmental behaviors (transient, attractor and trajectory length) for boolean CAs [6, 9, 10] and with organisms with 3 cell types [7, 8]. When the number of possible cell states gets bigger, Lambda may not be able to capture genome properties related to transitions to the chosen quiescent states. This is due to the presence of a growing number of sub-transition classes. Lambda's meaning would then be loose and be interpreted just as one of the many sub-transition classes in the genome table. On the other hand, there exist many sub-transitions parameters that hold the same parameter distribution as Lambda. Such sub-transition parameters could be then composed to create a custom parameter that captures the same genome properties as Lambda does.

5   Experimental Setup

In the experiment herein the presented developmental model with organism size of 4x4 cells is used. This leads to a theoretical maximum trajectory length and attractor length of 3^{16} development steps.

The genetic algorithm uses a population of 24 genotypes with elitism. The 8 worst individuals are replaced in each generation by newly generated offspring, selected through proportionate selection. Each two selected genotypes undergo one-point uniform crossover with probability 0.7 and mutation with probability 0.02 per gene. The genotype initial population is initialized with void genomes, i.e. all the transitions in the developmental table lead to the quiescent state. This means that the resulting phenotypes are the most unfit and difficult to evolve, i.e. dead organisms that end-up in a point attractor after a single development step. This is done to provide an even starting point for comparison.

In the standard GA (used as reference), the fitness is proportional to the developed trajectory length (the longer the fitter). In the GA that uses Lambda genome parameter contribution in the fitness function, the combined fitness (CFitness) is calculated as follows:

$$CFitness = Fitness + Fitness \times \frac{Abs(HiLambda - Lambda)}{HiLambda} \times ratio \qquad (2)$$

In Equation 2, the used ratio is 0.2 [1] and HiLambda represents the Lambda value where the longest trajectory length is more likely to be found (0.66 in our model), i.e. critical Lambda [6].

6   Genome Parameter to Guide Evolution

In this first experiment, performances of a conventional genetic algorithm are compared to a GA that encapsulates Lambda in the fitness function. The chosen trajectory length targets are set as 1000, 5000, 10000 and 15000 development steps (average over 1000 runs for target 1000, average over 20 runs for the other targets due to runtime). Results are shown in Figures from 3 to 6 respectively. In all the four considered cases, the effect of Lambda in fitness is clearly visible.

---

[1] The ratio that gave best results for GA with λ in fitness from randomized genomes is 0.05. Otherwise 0.2 is used in all the plotted results.

In Figure 3 the target trajectory length was set as 1000 development steps. The conventional GA performs better than the one with Lambda contribution in the fitness function for few generations. From generation 17 the effects of Lambda driving evolution are more evident and the algorithm converges faster toward the target.

Table 1. Comparison of reference GA and GA with Lambda contribution in the fitness function. Target trajectory length is 1000 development steps. Avg over 1000 runs.

GA	Void genomes (plotted)		Randomized genomes	
Reference GA	443,60	-	372,00	-
Lambda fitness	365,62	-17,57%	351,33 [1]	-5,56%

Table 1 shows numerical results when trajectory length target is 1000 development steps. This is analyzed from two different initial conditions: void initialized genomes (all the transitions in the developmental table lead to the quiescent state and the organism are the most unfit, plotted in Figure 3) and randomly initialized genomes (not plotted here). From void genomes the reference GA needs 443,6 generations on average (over 1000 runs), whether Lambda parameter in the fitness function is 17,57% faster (unpaired 2-tail t-test, p<0,0001). From randomized genomes the latter is still 5,56% faster, finding solutions in 351,33 generations on average compared to 372 generations needed by the conventional GA (it is important to mention that the GA with Lambda in fitness with void initialization is even faster than the reference GA with randomized initialization).

The same trend is shown in Figure 4, where the target was longer. Here the difference in convergence speed is more accentuated. Results in Figure 5 and 6 confirm that there is a point where the two lines cross each other. After that specific generation the algorithm with Lambda contribution converges faster than the conventional approach. It is clear that the ability of Lambda to detect longer trajectories in certain areas of the parameter space is beneficial when trajectory length is the target behavior. In all the presented scenarios, both approaches show an asymptotic tail towards 0 (minimum distance from target fitness). The difference is in the speed of convergence to the asymptotic target distance. Lambda in the fitness function is promising.

As a side experiment, λ was used outside the fitness function with a conventional GA. In such experiment λ was used as a discard parameter where genomes were discarded after selection if the parameter value was not matching a defined interval of acceptance. Here the results were not promising and in some cases the system was not evolvable.

7   Genotype Sub-transitions

Lambda genome parameter measures sub-transitions in the genome developmental table that lead to the quiescent state. Other sub-transitions are present in the genome table, i.e. growth, differentiation and no-change. Here it is investigated if other sub-transition classes could replace Lambda in forecasting the emergent behavior, thus being able to be used in multi-cellular developmental systems with more cell types. In such case, Lambda may represent too few genotype properties, thus not being able to

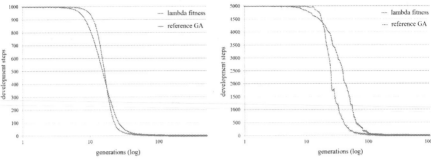

Fig. 3. Comparison of reference GA and GA with Lambda contribution in the fitness function. Target trajectory length is 1000 development steps. Distance from target (y) over generations (x). Avg over 1000 runs.

Fig. 4. Comparison of reference GA and GA with Lambda contribution in the fitness function. Target trajectory length is 5000 development steps. Distance from target (y) over generations (x). Avg over 20 runs.

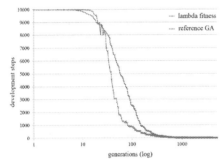

Fig. 5. Comparison of reference GA and GA with Lambda contribution in the fitness function. Target trajectory length is 10000 development steps. Distance from target (y) over generations (x). Avg over 20 runs.

Fig. 6. Comparison of reference GA and GA with Lambda contribution in the fitness function. Target trajectory length is 15000 development steps. Distance from target (y) over generations (x). Avg over 20 runs.

drive evolution. Moreover, several sub-transitions could be used together to compose custom parameterizations of the rule-space.

Figure 7 shows an example of sub-transition classes' activation patterns for a specific developed organism, successfully evolved in the previous set of experiments. Here each line represents one of the sub-transitions (growth in red, death in blue, differentiation in green and no-change in purple). The plot shows the number of cells that trigger a specific sub-transitions class in each development step. Pattern repetitions may indicate that an attractor has been reached or that same pattern repetition happens in different areas of the grid world where the organism is developed. This may indicate self-regulation based on topologic properties. The top-line (purple) shows activation of no-change sub-transitions, which is often the most used sub-class, whether growth (red) and death (blue) are often overlapping and seem to have a similar trend.

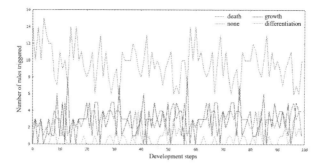

Fig. 7. Sub-transitions (growth, death, differentiation, no-change) activation pattern (y) over the generations (x) for the given example organism

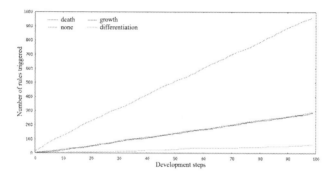

Fig. 8. Cumulative sum of sub-transitions activation pattern for the given example organism

Figure 8 plots the cumulative sub-transition usage during development, for the same given organism. It is clear that growth rules and death rules have to be balanced. This was observed with target trajectories of different lengths. Differentiation rules and no-change rules did not show any specific trend.

Figure 9 plots developed trajectory lengths for 100000 randomly generated genotypes. As such, the distribution of transition rules in the genotype is scrambled and distributed in the rule sub-transition space. In Figure 9 only death sub-transitions are considered. The plot shows a similar distribution to Lambda parameter, since the death sub-transitions capture the same genome properties as Lambda. Figure 10 plots the same organisms when the considered genome parameter is differentiation sub-transitions. Here the relation between the considered sub-parameter and trajectory length is weaker and organisms are less concentrated around the critical parameter value. Same results were obtained for other sub-transition groups.

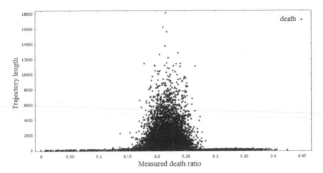

Fig. 9. Death sub-transition parameter distribution (x) and resulting trajectory length measured as #development steps (y). 100000 organisms.

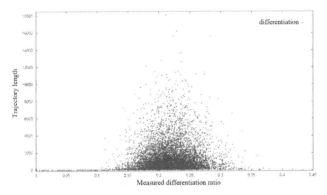

Fig. 10. Differentiation sub-transition parameter distribution (x) and resulting trajectory length measured as #development steps (y). 100000 organisms.

In Figure 11 a composed sub-parameter is considered, namely the difference between number of death and growth sub-transitions. It is evident that when growth and death rules are balanced it is possible to develop long trajectories (as the target in our experimental work). On the other hand, when those sub-transitions are not balanced, the organism produces a very short trajectory cycle. This information may be important at the design stage of an EvoDevo system, when Lambda is not able to characterize the behavioral regime due to a larger number of available cell types. In such case, Lambda would be no more than one out of the many sub-transition groups, thus lacking a clear relation between trajectory length and the parameter space.

Finally, Figure 12 shows a zoomed-in plot of the same 100000 generated organisms in Figure 9, 10 and 11, where genomes with unbalanced death-growth difference develop short trajectories. In contrast, balanced rule-sets develop longer trajectories, being able to filter-out unfit genomes. That was not possible if only a single sub-transition class was considered. It is important to highlight that Lambda is a single-transition parameter.

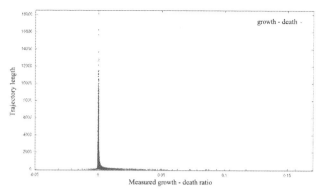

Fig. 11. Growth-Death sub-transition parameter distribution (x) and resulting trajectory length measured as #development steps (y). 100000 organisms.

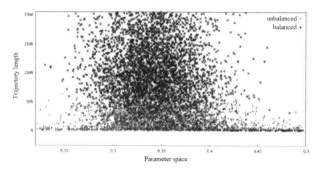

Fig. 12. Genomes unfiltered vs. genome filtered with growth-death sub-transition parameter

8   Conclusion

The presented experiments investigated how to exploit genotype information of artificial cellular organism to guide evolution in favorable areas of the solution space, where the sought phenotypic behavior is more likely to be found. Genome information has been used to calculate Lambda genome parameter. Such parameter was incorporated into the fitness function to speed-up convergence to the target trajectory, as shown in the plots in Figure 3, 4, 5 and 6, for different target trajectory lengths. Previous work [8] has shown that other parameters besides Lambda, e.g. Sensitivity [14], Mean Field Parameters [15], have similar abilities to forecast emergent behaviors. Thus, it may be interesting to extend the investigation and compare results obtained with other parameters.

The used genome representation allowed identifying genome sub-transitions other than those used to calculate Lambda (transitions to the quiescent state). The identified sub-transition groups (growth, differentiation, death, no-change) can be considered single transition parameters and thus used as Lambda. They can also be composed together to produce a multiple-transition genome parameter when Lambda may not be able to characterize the phenotype behavior due to increased number of cell types. In particular, death-growth transition difference has been shown to be well suited to identify artificial organisms that produce long trajectory, as in Figure 11, and filter out organisms with short trajectories, as shown in Figure 12. It may be interesting to investigate sub-transitions' potential the same way as Lambda was used here.

The approach used herein shows that exploiting genome information during evolution could increase the evolvability of the system, when there is an indirect genotype to phenotype mapping and fitness is a measure of phenotypic properties.

As a future work, it may be possible to investigate the robustness of solutions evolved with a fitness measure based on both phenotype and genotype information. In particular, how fragile evolved organisms are to external perturbation, both at genotype level, i.e. mutations in the rule table, and at phenotype level, i.e. perturbation of the system state during development.

References

1. Wagner, A.: Robustness and evolvability: a paradox resolved. Proceedings of the Royal Society B - Biological Sciences **275**(1630), 91–100 (2008)
2. Bar-Yam, Y.: Dynamics of complex systems. Studies in Nonlinearity, p. 864. Westview Press (1997)
3. Miller, J.F.: Evolving developmental programs for adaptation, morphogenesis, and self-repair. In: Banzhaf, W., Ziegler, J., Christaller, T., Dittrich, P., Kim, J.T. (eds.) ECAL 2003. LNCS (LNAI), vol. 2801, pp. 256–265. Springer, Heidelberg (2003)
4. Tufte, G., Haddow, P.C.: Towards development on a silicon-based cellular computation machine. Natural Computation **4**(4), 387–416 (2005)
5. Glover, F., Kochenberg, G.A.: Handbook of metaheuristics. International Series on Operations Research and Management Science, p. 570. Springer (2003)
6. Langton, C.G.: Computation at the edge of chaos: phase transitions and emergant computation. In: Forrest, S. (ed.) Emergent Computation, pp. 12–37. MIT Press (1991)
7. Tufte, G., Nichele, S.: On the correlations between developmental diversity and genomic composition. In: 13th Annual Genetic and Evolutionary Computation Conference, GECCO 2011, pp. 1507–1514. ACM (2011)
8. Nichele, S., Tufte, G.: Genome parameters as information to forecast emergent developmental behaviors. In: Durand-Lose, J., Jonoska, N. (eds.) UCNC 2012. LNCS, vol. 7445, pp. 186–197. Springer, Heidelberg (2012)
9. de Oliveira, G., de Oliveira, P., Omar, N.: Definition and application of a five-parameter characterization of one-dimensional cellular automata rule space. Artificial Life **7**, 277–301 (2001)
10. de Oliveira, G., de Oliveira, P., Omar, N.: Guidelines for dynamics-based parameterization of one-dimensional cellular automata rule space. Complexity **6**(2) (2001)
11. Kowaliw, T.: Measures of complexity for artificial embryogeny. In: GECCO 2008, pp. 843–850. ACM (2008)
12. Rothlauf, F.: Locality, distance distortion, and binary representations of integers. Working Paper 11/2003. University of Mannheim
13. Pollard, T.D.: No question about exciting questions in cell biology. PLoS Biol. **11**(12), e1001734 (2013). doi:10.1371/journal.pbio.1001734
14. Binder, P.M.: Parametric ordering of complex systems. Physical Review E **49**(3), 2023–2025 (1994)
15. Li, W.: Phenomenology of nonlocal cellular automata. Journal of Statistical Physics **68**(5–6), 829–882 (1992)

Training Complex Decision Support Systems with Differential Evolution Enhanced by Locally Linear Embedding

Piotr Lipinski[✉]

Computational Intelligence Research Group, Institute of Computer Science,
University of Wroclaw, Wroclaw, Poland
lipinski@ii.uni.wroc.pl

Abstract. This paper aims at improving the training process of complex decision support systems, where evolutionary algorithms are used to integrate a large number of decision rules in a form of a weighted average. It proposes an enhancement of Differential Evolution by Locally Linear Embedding to process objective functions with correlated variables, which focuses on detecting local dependencies among variables of the objective function by analyzing the manifold in the search space that contains the current population and transforming it to a reduced search space. Experiments performed on some popular benchmark functions as well as on a financial decision support system confirm that the method may significantly improve the search process in the case of objective functions with a large number of variables, which usually occur in many practical applications.

1 Introduction

Contemporary intelligent systems often consist of a large number of independent subsystems integrated into one application. Different subsystems may be based on different principles, may use different technologies, may process different data, may be trained on different datasets with different paradigms. Merging a number of independent subsystems increases the total efficiency and the total liability of the entire intelligent system.

Simple examples of such complex intelligent systems include decision support systems [7], [9], classifier systems [15], multi-agent systems [4], [16] and rule-selection systems [5], [12], which are composed of a number of independent decision entities, agents or rules, integrated using evolutionary algorithms into one consistent system. Evolutionary algorithms often determine the optimal parameters for the integration of independent subsystems, such as their importance factors or weights of their impact to the overall system.

Since the number of components in contemporary complex systems is large, the search space of integration parameters has a high dimension, which constitutes a bottleneck for many optimization algorithms. Although, in general, the different subsystems are usually assumed to be independent, in fact, there are

© Springer-Verlag Berlin Heidelberg 2014
A.I. Esparcia-Alcázar et al. (Eds.): EvoApplications 2014, LNCS 8602, pp. 125–137, 2014.
DOI: 10.1007/978-3-662-45523-4_11

often some dependencies between them and between their results. Taking these dependencies into consideration during the optimization process may lead to a significant reduction in the computing time and may also result in increases of the overall efficiency of the entire system.

In such cases, although the objective function $F : \mathbb{R}^n \rightarrow \mathbb{R}$ is formally a function of n variables, some of them are correlated, either globally over the entire search space or locally over a certain subspace containing a global optimum of the objective function F, so the original objective function F may be replaced with another function $G : \mathbb{R}^k \rightarrow \mathbb{R}$ of k variables and a mapping $\Phi : \mathbb{R}^n \rightarrow \mathbb{R}^k$, where $k \leq n$, which maps n-dimensional vectors $\mathbf{x} \in \mathbb{R}^n$ into k-dimensional vectors $\mathbf{y} \in \mathbb{R}^k$ in such a way that $F(\mathbf{x}) = G(\mathbf{y})$.

Therefore, the problem of optimizing the objective function F over the search space $\mathbb{R}^n$ may be reduced to the problem of optimizing the objective function G over the search space $\mathbb{R}^k$, where $k \leq n$, which usually leads to significant reductions in the optimization algorithm.

Although there are numerous techniques of detecting global dependencies among variables over the entire search space, usually in a preprocessing phase, such as the Principal Component Analysis [17], the Linear Discriminant Analysis [17], the Multidimensional Scaling [1], as well as their extensions capable of discovering non-linear dependencies, there has been little research on local dependencies over neighborhoods of optimal solutions and detecting them during runtime of the optimization algorithm [10].

The approach presented in this paper is inspired by Estimation of Distribution Algorithms [6] that try to regard the population of candidate solutions as a data sample with a probability distribution approximating the probability distribution describing optimal solutions. Similarly, the population of candidate solution may be used to detect correlations among variables, reduce the search space and simplify the optimization problem.

This paper proposes an improvement of Differential Evolution [2] for objective functions with locally correlated variables, which is capable of discovering local dependencies among variables of the objective function and locally reducing it to another objective function of a smaller number of variables, using Locally Linear Embedding [13].

This paper is structured in the following manner: Section 2 discusses the principles of Locally Linear Embedding and its application to the current population in evolutionary algorithms. Section 3 proposes Differential Evolution Enhanced by Locally Linear Embeddings. Section 4 presents a preliminary evaluation of the approach on some popular benchmark functions and Section 5 discusses some experiments on a financial decision support system. Finally, Section 6 concludes the paper.

2   Locally Linear Embedding in the Search Space

Let $\mathcal{P} = \{\mathbf{x}_1, \mathbf{x}_2, \ldots, \mathbf{x}_N\} \subset \mathbb{R}^d$ be a population of N individuals, where each individual $\mathbf{x}_i = (x_{i1}, x_{i2}, \ldots, x_{id})^T \in \mathbb{R}^d$, for $i = 1, 2, \ldots, N$, is a data point in the search space $\Omega = \mathbb{R}^d$, where d is the dimensionality of the optimization problem.

We may investigate the manifolds in Ω that contain the population. In the pessimistic case, the population is chaotic and widespread across the entire search space without any significant dependencies, so the only one reasonable manifold to consider is the entire search space itself. In the optimistic case, the population may be chaotic, but focused on a certain manifold in the search space, possibly of a lower dimensionality than the entire search space. It may happen when some variables of the objective function are correlated, so there are some dependencies between values of genes in the chromosome.

It is worth noticing that such dependencies may be local, occurring only in a certain region of the search space, e.g. in the neighborhood of a local or global optimum of the objective function, where the current population focuses on, so they usually cannot be discovered by popular preprocessing methods before the evolution process starts.

Figure 1 presents a classic example illustrating the approach. The subplot (a) presents the population $\mathcal{P}$ in the original search space $\mathbb{R}^3$ with colors denoting the values of the objective function. It is easy to see that all the individuals lie in a certain manifold in the search space, the so-called Swiss-Roll manifold, presented in the subplot (b). Although the manifold is embedded in the 3-dimensional search space, it is actually a 2-dimensional manifold homeomorphic to a rectangle, so the original population may be transformed from the original search space a reduced search space $\mathbb{R}^2$ (in fact, to a rectangle embedded in $\mathbb{R}^2$), presented in the subplot (c). Finally, exploiting the original manifold by the evolutionary algorithm is equivalent to exploiting the reduced search space.

Assume that the population lies in a certain manifold in the search space. Although the manifold is embedded in the d-dimensional search space, it may be homeomorphic to another manifold of a lower dimensionality. However, the homeomorphism may not be obvious and discovering it may not be simple, especially in the case of local and non-linear dependencies.

One of the possible approaches, based on the Locally Linear Embeddings (LLE) [13], is first to determine the K nearest neighbors of each individual in the population, then to approximate each individual by a linear combination of its K nearest neighbors, and finally to map the population to a data space of the lower dimensionality l so that the mapping of each individual was approximated by the linear combination of mappings of its K nearest neighbors with the same linear coefficients as in the original data space.

First, for each individual $\mathbf{x}_i \in \mathcal{P}$, we determine its K nearest neighbors in the population $\mathcal{P}$, which may be formulated as finding a sequence of indices $n_1^{(i)}, n_2^{(i)}, \ldots, n_K^{(i)} \in \{1, 2, \ldots, N\} \setminus \{i\}$ such that

$$dist(\mathbf{x}_i, \mathbf{x}_{n_1^{(i)}}) \leq dist(\mathbf{x}_i, \mathbf{x}_{n_2^{(i)}}) \leq \ldots \leq dist(\mathbf{x}_i, \mathbf{x}_{n_K^{(i)}}) \leq dist(\mathbf{x}_i, \mathbf{x}_j), \quad (1)$$

for all $j \in \{1, 2, \ldots, N\} \setminus (\{i\} \cup \{n_1^{(i)}, n_2^{(i)}, \ldots, n_K^{(i)}\})$, where $dist$ is a distance function in the search space Ω (usually the euclidean distance in $\mathbb{R}^d$).

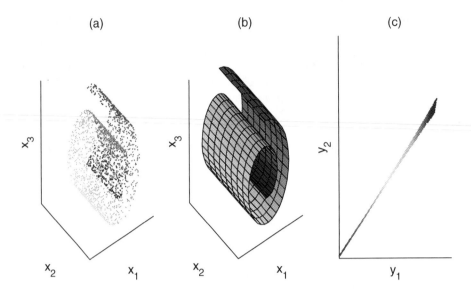

Fig. 1. An example of a 2-dimensional population embedded in the 3-dimensional search space: the population in the original search space (subplot (a)), the manifold defined by the population (subplot(b)), the population in the reduced search space (subplot (c))

Second, for each individual $\mathbf{x}_i \in \mathcal{P}$, we approximate it by a linear combination of its K nearest neighbors, which may be formulated as finding linear coefficients $w_1^{(i)}, w_2^{(i)}, \ldots, w_K^{(i)} \in \mathbb{R}$ minimizing the error function

$$||\mathbf{x}_i - \tilde{\mathbf{x}}_i||^2, \quad \text{where} \quad \tilde{\mathbf{x}}_i = \sum_{k=1}^{K} w_k^{(i)} \mathbf{x}_{n_k^{(i)}}, \tag{2}$$

under the constraint $\sum_{k=1}^{K} w_k^{(i)} = 1$.

Third, we try to construct a mapping from the original search space to the reduced search space so that the mapping of each individual was approximated by the linear combination of mappings of its K nearest neighbors with the same linear coefficients as in the original search space, which may be formulated as finding a reduced population $\mathcal{R} = \{\mathbf{y}_1, \mathbf{y}_2, \ldots, \mathbf{y}_N\} \subset \mathbb{R}^l$, where each reduced individual $\mathbf{y}_i = (y_{i1}, y_{i2}, \ldots, y_{il})^T \in \mathbb{R}^l$, for $i = 1, 2, \ldots, N$, is a data point in the reduced search space $\mathbb{R}^l$, minimizing the error function

$$\sum_{i=1}^{N} ||\mathbf{y}_i - \tilde{\mathbf{y}}_i||^2, \quad \text{where} \quad \tilde{\mathbf{y}}_i = \sum_{k=1}^{K} w_k^{(i)} \mathbf{y}_{n_k^{(i)}}, \tag{3}$$

under the constraint $d^{-1}\mathbf{Y}^T\mathbf{Y} = \mathbf{I}$, where $\mathbf{Y} \in \mathbb{R}^{l \times N}$ is the matrix with columns $\mathbf{y}_i$ and $\mathbf{I} \in \mathbb{R}^{N \times N}$ is the identity matrix (the constraint requires that the covariance matrix of the mapped individuals is the identity matrix).

3   Differential Evolution Enhanced by Locally Linear Embeddings

Algorithm 1 presents an overview of the Differential Evolution Enhanced by Locally Linear Embeddings (DEELLE) for an objective function $F : \mathbb{R}^n \to \mathbb{R}$ of non-linearly correlated variables.

DEELLE begins with generating a random population $\mathcal{P}_0$ of N individuals and evaluating it. In the main evolution loop, for each individual $\mathbf{x}$ from the current population $\mathcal{P}_t$, called the target vector, a new vector $\mathbf{v}$, called the donor vector, is created, then the donor vector is recombined with the target vector forming a new vector $\mathbf{u}$, called the trial vector, and finally, if the trial vector outperforms the target vector, it replaces it in the next population, as in classic DE [2]. In some main evolution iterations, DEELLE performs a subevolution, which analyses the current population, transforms it to a reduced search space, and performs the same routine as the main evolution, but on the selected manifold only.

The main evolution and the subevolution is run in such a way that first a number of main iterations is performed in the entire original search space to move the population to some promising regions of the search space, then a number of subevolution iterations is performed in a selected manifold and then the population is restored to the original search space in order to ensure whether the manifold corresponded to a neighborhood of the global optima or not. Few next main iterations may correct the population and move it to some other promising regions of the search space, and then a number of subevolution iterations exploit the new manifold.

3.1   Search Space and Population Reduction

The subevolution starts with determining the manifold in the search space $\mathbb{R}^d$ that contains the current population $\mathcal{P}_t$ and transforming it to a reduced population $\mathcal{R}_0$ based on Locally Linear Embeddings [13].

First, for each individual $\mathbf{x}_i \in \mathcal{P}_t$, its K nearest neighbors in the current population $\mathcal{P}_t$ are determined. Let $n_1^{(i)}, n_2^{(i)}, \ldots, n_K^{(i)}$ be the indices of the successive nearest neighbors of the individual $\mathbf{x}_i$.

Second, for each data point $\mathbf{x}_i \in \mathcal{P}_t$, linear coefficients $w_1^{(i)}, w_2^{(i)}, \ldots, w_K^{(i)}$ are determined by minimizing the error function (2), which may be transformed, taking into consideration the constraint $\sum_{k=1}^{K} w_k^{(i)} = 1$, to

$$||\mathbf{x}_i - \tilde{\mathbf{x}}_i||^2 = ||\sum_{k=1}^{K} w_k^{(i)}\mathbf{x}_i - \sum_{k=1}^{K} w_k^{(i)}\mathbf{x}_{n_k^{(i)}}||^2 = ||\sum_{k=1}^{K} w_k^{(i)}(\mathbf{x}_i - \mathbf{x}_{n_k^{(i)}})||^2 = ||\sum_{k=1}^{K} w_k^{(i)}\mathbf{z}_k||^2,$$

$$(4)$$

Algorithm 1. Differential Evolution Enhanced by Locally Linear Embeddings (DEELLE)

$\mathcal{P}_0 = $ Random-Population(N)
Population-Evaluation($\mathcal{P}_0, F$)
$t = 0$
while not Termination-Condition($\mathcal{P}_t$) **do**
  for all $\mathbf{x} \in \mathcal{P}_t$ **do**
    pick randomly distinct $\mathbf{x}_1, \mathbf{x}_2, \mathbf{x}_3$ from $\mathcal{P}_t \setminus \{\mathbf{x}\}$
    $\mathbf{v} = \mathbf{x}_1 + \alpha \cdot (\mathbf{x}_2 - \mathbf{x}_3)$
    $\mathbf{u} = $ Binomial-Recombination($\mathbf{v}, \mathbf{x}$)
    if $F(\mathbf{x}) \leq F(\mathbf{u})$ **then**
      $\mathbf{u}$ will replace $\mathbf{x}$ in $\mathcal{P}_{t+1}$
    end if
  end for
  Population-Evaluation($\mathcal{P}_{t+1}, F$)
  $t = t + 1$
  if Subevolution-Starting-Condition() **then**
    Search-Space-Reduction()
    $\mathcal{R}_0 = $ Population-Reduction($\mathcal{P}_t$)
    $s = 0$;
    while not Subevolution-Termination-Condition($\mathcal{R}_s$) **do**
      for all $\mathbf{x} \in \mathcal{R}_s$ **do**
        pick randomly distinct $\mathbf{x}_1, \mathbf{x}_2, \mathbf{x}_3$ from $\mathcal{R}_s \setminus \{\mathbf{x}\}$
        $\mathbf{v} = \mathbf{x}_1 + \alpha \cdot (\mathbf{x}_2 - \mathbf{x}_3)$
        $\mathbf{u} = $ Binomial-Recombination($\mathbf{v}, \mathbf{x}$)
        if $F(\mathbf{x}) \leq F(\mathbf{u})$ **then**
          $\mathbf{u}$ will replace $\mathbf{x}$ in $\mathcal{R}_{s+1}$
        end if
      end for
      Reduced-Population-Evaluation($\mathcal{R}_{s+1}, F$)
      $s = s + 1$
    end while
    Search-Space-Restoring()
    $\mathcal{P}_t = $ Population-Restoring($\mathcal{R}_{s-1}$)
  end if
end while

---

where $\mathbf{z}_k = \mathbf{x}_{n_k^{(i)}} - \mathbf{x}_i$. Defining the matrix $\mathbf{Z} \in \mathbb{R}^{d \times K}$ as the matrix with columns $\mathbf{z}_k$ and the vector $\mathbf{w} \in \mathbb{R}^K$ as the vector with coordinates $w_k^{(i)}$ (certainly, the matrix $\mathbf{Z}$ and the vector $\mathbf{w}$ depends on i, but we omit it here for the sake of simplicity of the notation), the error function (2) becomes

$$|| \sum_{k=1}^{K} w_k^{(i)} \mathbf{z}_k ||^2 = ||\mathbf{Z}\mathbf{w}||^2 = (\mathbf{Z}\mathbf{w})^T (\mathbf{Z}\mathbf{w}) = \mathbf{w}^T \mathbf{Z}^T \mathbf{Z} \mathbf{w} = \mathbf{w}^T \mathbf{V} \mathbf{w}, \qquad (5)$$

where $\mathbf{V} = \mathbf{Z}^T \mathbf{Z} \in \mathbb{R}^{d \times d}$. Moreover, the constraint $\sum_{k=1}^{K} w_k^{(i)} = 1$ may be transformed to $\mathbf{1}^T \mathbf{w} = 1$, where $\mathbf{1} \in \mathbb{R}^K$ is the vector of ones.

Therefore, in order to minimize the error function (2), the Lagrange multiplier method may be used, i.e. the following equation system, with the Lagrange multiplier λ, must be solved:

$$\frac{\partial \mathbf{w}^T \mathbf{V} \mathbf{w}}{\partial w_i} = \lambda \frac{\partial \mathbf{1}^T \mathbf{w}}{\partial w_i}, \tag{6}$$

for each $i = 1, 2, \ldots, K$ with the constraint $\mathbf{1}^T \mathbf{w} = 1$.
Since

$$\nabla \mathbf{w}^T \mathbf{V} \mathbf{w} = 2 \mathbf{V} \mathbf{w}, \quad \text{and} \quad \nabla \mathbf{1}^T \mathbf{w} = \mathbf{1}^T, \tag{7}$$

the equation system (6) is equivalent to the matrix equation

$$2 \mathbf{V} \mathbf{w} = \lambda \mathbf{1}^T, \tag{8}$$

thus, if $\mathbf{V}$ is invertible,

$$\mathbf{w} = \frac{\lambda}{2} \mathbf{V}^{-1} \mathbf{1}^T, \tag{9}$$

and λ must be adjusted to fulfil the constraint $\mathbf{1}^T \mathbf{w} = 1$. If $\mathbf{V}$ is not invertible, the error function should be modified by some regularization component [13] and minimized in a similar way.

Third, reduced individuals $\mathbf{y}_1, \mathbf{y}_2, \ldots, \mathbf{y}_N \in \mathbb{R}^l$ are determined by minimizing the error function (3). Assume at the beginning that $l = 1$ and then each $\mathbf{y}_i$ is just a real number. Thus, the error function (3) may be transformed to

$$\sum_{i=1}^{N} ||\mathbf{y}_i - \tilde{\mathbf{y}}_i||^2 = \sum_{i=1}^{N} ||\mathbf{y}_i - \sum_{k=1}^{K} w_k^{(i)} \mathbf{y}_{n_k^{(i)}}||^2 =$$

$$= \sum_{i=1}^{N} (\mathbf{y}_i^2 - \mathbf{y}_i \sum_{k=1}^{K} w_k^{(i)} \mathbf{y}_{n_k^{(i)}} - \sum_{k=1}^{K} w_k^{(i)} \mathbf{y}_{n_k^{(i)}} \mathbf{y}_i + (\sum_{k=1}^{K} w_k^{(i)} \mathbf{y}_{n_k^{(i)}})^2) =$$

$$= \sum_{i=1}^{N} (\mathbf{y}_i^2) - \sum_{i=1}^{N} \sum_{k=1}^{K} \mathbf{y}_i w_k^{(i)} \mathbf{y}_{n_k^{(i)}} - \sum_{i=1}^{N} \sum_{k=1}^{K} w_k^{(i)} \mathbf{y}_{n_k^{(i)}} \mathbf{y}_i + \sum_{i=1}^{N} (\sum_{k=1}^{K} w_k^{(i)} \mathbf{y}_{n_k^{(i)}})^2) =$$

$$= \mathbf{Y}^T \mathbf{Y} - \mathbf{Y}^T (\mathbf{W} \mathbf{Y}) - (\mathbf{W} \mathbf{Y})^T \mathbf{Y} + (\mathbf{W} \mathbf{Y})^T (\mathbf{W} \mathbf{Y}) =$$

$$= \mathbf{Y}^T (\mathbf{I} - \mathbf{W}) \mathbf{Y} - (\mathbf{W} \mathbf{Y})^T (\mathbf{I} - \mathbf{W}) \mathbf{Y} =$$

$$= (\mathbf{Y}^T - (\mathbf{W} \mathbf{Y})^T)(\mathbf{I} - \mathbf{W}) \mathbf{Y} = \mathbf{Y}^T (\mathbf{I} - \mathbf{W})^T (\mathbf{I} - \mathbf{W}) \mathbf{Y} = \mathbf{Y}^T \mathbf{M} \mathbf{Y},$$

where $\mathbf{Y} \in \mathbf{R}^{l \times N}$ is the matrix with columns $\mathbf{y}_i$, $\mathbf{W} \in \mathbf{R}^{N \times N}$ is the matrix with elements $w_{ij} = w_k^{(i)}$ if $\mathbf{x}_j$ is the k-th nearest neighbor of $\mathbf{x}_i$ and $w_{ij} = 0$ otherwise, $\mathbf{I} \in \mathbb{R}^{N \times N}$ is the identity matrix, and $\mathbf{M} = (\mathbf{I} - \mathbf{w})^T (\mathbf{I} - \mathbf{w}) \in \mathbb{R}^{N \times N}$.

Therefore, in order to minimize the error function(3) under the constraint $d^{-1} \mathbf{Y}^T \mathbf{Y} = \mathbf{I}$, the Lagrange multiplier method may be used, i.e. the following equation system, with the Lagrange multiplier λ, must be solved:

$$\frac{\partial \mathbf{Y}^T \mathbf{M} \mathbf{Y}}{\partial \mathbf{y}_i} = \lambda \frac{\partial d^{-1} \mathbf{Y}^T \mathbf{Y}}{\partial \mathbf{y}_i}, \tag{10}$$

for each $i = 1, 2, \ldots, N$ with the constraint $d^{-1}\mathbf{Y}^T\mathbf{Y} = \mathbf{I}$.

Since

$$\nabla \mathbf{Y}^T \mathbf{M} \mathbf{Y} = 2\mathbf{M}\mathbf{Y} \quad \text{and} \quad \nabla d^{-1}\mathbf{Y}^T\mathbf{Y} = 2d^{-1}\mathbf{Y}, \tag{11}$$

the equation system (10) is equivalent to the matrix equation

$$\mathbf{M}\mathbf{Y} = \lambda d^{-1}\mathbf{Y}, \tag{12}$$

thus, $\mathbf{Y}$ is an eigenvector of the matrix $\mathbf{M}$. As the error function (3) is being min-imized, the eigenvector $\mathbf{Y}$ should correspond to the smallest non-zero eigenvalue of the matrix $\mathbf{M}$. In order to generalize the calculation for $l > 1$, the succes-sive eigenvectors of the matrix $\mathbf{M}$ should be taken to determine the successive coordinates of the mappings $\mathbf{y}_i$ [13].

Finally, the reduced population $\mathcal{R}_0$ consists of mappings $\mathbf{y}_i$ of individuals $\mathbf{x}_i$ from the original population $\mathcal{P}_t$.

3.2   Reduced Population Evaluation

Although the evolutionary operators of the subevolution are derived from the main evolution without modifications, i.e. only the chromosome length changes, the problem occurs in evaluating the reduced population. In the literature con-cerning LLE, [13], a few solutions are suggested to restore a data point from the reduced data space to the original data space.

In DEELLE, evaluating a reduced individual $\mathbf{y} \in \mathbb{R}^l$, begins with finding the mapping of an original individual from the current population $\mathcal{P}_t$ closest to the reduced individual, i.e. determining the index $i \in \{1, 2, \ldots, N\}$ minimizing the distance $\|\mathbf{y} - \mathbf{y}_i\|$. Next, the reduced individual $\mathbf{y}$ is approximated by a linear combination of mappings $\mathbf{y}_{n_1^{(i)}}, \mathbf{y}_{n_2^{(i)}}, \ldots, \mathbf{y}_{n_K^{(i)}}$ of the K nearest neighbors of the closest original individual $\mathbf{x}_i$. Finally, the restored individual $\mathbf{x} \in \mathbb{R}^d$ corresponding to the reduced individual $\mathbf{y}$ is defined as a linear combination of the K nearest neighbors $\mathbf{x}_{n_1^{(i)}}, \mathbf{x}_{n_2^{(i)}}, \ldots, \mathbf{x}_{n_K^{(i)}}$ of the closest original individual $\mathbf{x}_i$ with the same linear coefficients as in the reduced search space and the objective function for the reduced individual is approximated by the objective function of the restored individual.

3.3   Search Space and Population Restoring

After termination of the subevolution, the current reduced population $\mathcal{R}_t$ is restored to the original search space by applying the same procedure as during the reduced population evaluation, described in the previous subsection.

4   Experimental Evaluation on Popular Benchmark Functions

A preliminary evaluation of the approach proposed was performed on a number of classic benchmark functions usually used in testing evolutionary algorithms for continuous problems [18]. The first part of benchmark functions concerns the classic De Jong test suite composed of the unimodal function F_1, the discontinuous function F_3 and the noisy function F_4 [18]. The second part of the benchmark functions includes other popular benchmark functions, such as the Rastrigin function F_6, the Schwefel function F_7, and the Griewangk function F_8 [18].

$$F_1(\mathbf{x}) = \sum_{i=1}^{n} x_i^2 \qquad\qquad F_6(\mathbf{x}) = 10n + \sum_{i=1}^{n}(x_i^2 - 10\cos(2\pi x_i))$$

$$F_3(\mathbf{x}) = \sum_{i=1}^{n} \lfloor x_i \rfloor \qquad\qquad F_7(\mathbf{x}) = 418.9829n - \sum_{i=1}^{n} x_i \sin(\sqrt{|x_i|})$$

$$F_4(\mathbf{x}) = \sum_{i=1}^{n} i x_i^4 + \mathcal{N}(0,1) \qquad F_8(\mathbf{x}) = 1 + \sum_{i=1}^{n} \frac{x_i^2}{4000} - \prod_{i=1}^{n} \cos(x_i/\sqrt{i})$$

Each classic benchmark function $F : \mathbb{R}^n \to \mathbb{R}$ was extended by a mapping $\Psi : \mathbb{R}^m \to \mathbb{R}^n$, for $m > n$, so that the actual objective function $f : \mathbb{R}^m \to \mathbb{R}$, called the m-dimensional deceptive objective function, was a composition of the mapping Ψ and the classic benchmark function F, i.e. $f(\mathbf{x}) = F(\Psi(\mathbf{x}))$. It is easy to see that variables of the final objective function f were correlated (although the objective function f was formally a function of m variables, the real dimensionality of the optimization problem was $n < m$) and the improvement mechanism proposed in this paper might have a chance to reduce the search space. Both, the linear mappings Ψ with a random matrix $\mathbf{A} \in \mathbb{R}^{n \times m}$ and a random vector $\mathbf{b} \in \mathbb{R}^n$, where $\Psi(\mathbf{x}) = \mathbf{Ax} + \mathbf{b}$, and the non-linear mappings Ψ based on polynomial functions with random parameters, were considered.

Furthermore, k-deceptive objective functions were defined by the analogy to the k-deceptive objective functions used for evaluating the ECGA algorithm [3]: the entire chromosome $\mathbf{x}$ was divided into blocks of successive k genes, then a chosen k-dimensional deceptive objective function was evaluated on each block, next the values of the deceptive objective function on all the blocks was summed and finally returned as the results of the k-deceptive objective function.

Each experiment concerned a classic benchmark function transformed to a k-deceptive benchmark function with the final chromosome length $d = 50, 100$, or 250, divided into blocks of $k = 25$ genes, where on each block, the k-dimensional deceptive benchmark function based on a n-dimensional classic benchmark function, for $n = 5, 10$, or 15, was evaluated. Parameters of the transformation Ψ extending the n-dimensional classic benchmark function to a k-dimensional deceptive benchmark function were generated randomly for each experiment. Such an optimization problem was solved twice: once with the locally linear embeddings mechanism turned off, and once with turned on. In both cases, the population size was $N = 500$ and the parameter $\alpha = 0.5$. The original algorithm run for 2500 iterations. The improved algorithm run for 2500 iterations in total: main evolution was run for 100 iterations, then subevolutions was run for 400 iterations, and it was repeated 5 times. In the LLE part, $K = 25$ nearest neighbors were used. Thus, during their run, both algorithms evaluated the same number of individuals.

Table 1 presents a summary of results for all the benchmark functions. In order to compare the original algorithm with the improved one, for each experiment, the difference between the best found solution and the actual optimum of the objective function was evaluated for each algorithm. The difference for

Table 1. Summary of results on popular benchmark functions

		linear mappings Ψ					non-linear mappings Ψ					
d	n	f_1	f_3	f_4	f_6	f_7	f_8	f_1	f_3	f_4	f_6	f_7	f_8
50	5	24.66	5.23	385.99	8.10	99.06	8.98	20.12	3.59	717.10	15.82	16.48	19.49
50	10	15.13	4.13	85.62	22.21	30.80	7.55	15.80	3.62	317.57	16.68	11.08	13.86
50	15	11.58	2.80	325.49	10.09	34.46	2.97	7.20	3.37	7.45	2.42	37.99	5.86
100	5	17.83	3.92	197.89	16.30	24.83	7.20	16.14	4.03	98.68	8.55	31.09	20.76
100	10	5.79	3.02	44.30	8.13	49.84	3.58	7.18	2.94	77.16	7.53	19.32	5.40
100	15	3.68	1.97	14.26	2.44	67.19	3.13	1.45	1.50	36.03	3.12	23.42	3.79
250	5	5.60	1.75	61.84	7.12	95.25	3.20	6.09	2.40	49.23	8.59	27.95	7.12
250	10	1.54	1.43	9.14	2.39	43.17	1.56	1.93	1.21	10.73	1.35	38.62	1.38
250	15	1.05	1.07	3.39	0.82	20.15	1.04	0.72	0.94	3.21	1.09	13.34	0.92

the original algorithm was divided by the difference for the improved one and noted in Table 1. Therefore, the values below 1 mean that the original algorithm found a better approximation of the optimum of the objective function than the improved one, while values above 1 correspond to the opposite case. It is easy to see that the improved algorithm outperformed the original one in most cases.

5   Practical Evaluation on a Decision Support System

Some experiments were also performed on real-world problems, such as constructing optimal weights for a rule-based decision support system, where the weights are highly dependent due to existing similarities in the decision rules.

For practical evaluation of the approach proposed, a stock market trading decision support system, discussed in details in [7] and similar to the system with binary encoding presented in [9], was studied. Evolutionary algorithms were used in the system to combine a number of stock market trading rules into one trading expert being a weighted average of particular trading rules with the weights determined by an evolutionary algorithm as a solution to an optimization problem with an objective function relating to a performance of the trading expert over a certain training period.

A stock market trading rule is a function $f : \mathcal{K} \mapsto s \in \mathbb{R}$ that maps a factual financial knowledge $\mathcal{K}$ (e.g. financial time series of recent stock price quotations) to a real number s encoding a trading signal (low values denote a sell signal, high values denote a buy signal). Examples of such trading rules may be found in Technical Analysis [11].

A stock market trading expert $e : \mathcal{K} \mapsto s \in \mathbb{R}$ is a weighted average of a number of defined trading rules $f_1, f_2, \ldots, f_d$, available in the decision support system, with weights $w_1, w_2, \ldots, w_d \in \mathbb{R}$.

For a given training period, the trading expert may be evaluated in a type of simulation. It starts with an initial capital: an initial amount of cash and an initial number of stocks. In successive days of the training period, the trading expert produces a trading signal. If it is a buy signal, a part of available cash is invested in stocks. If it is a sell signal, a part of available stocks is sold. Each transaction is charged with a transaction fee. Finally, the efficiency of the trading expert is defined by the Sharpe ratio [14] of daily return rates.

Therefore, constructing efficient trading experts is an optimization problem of finding the weights vector $\mathbf{w} \in \mathbb{R}^d$ maximizing the efficiency measure being the Sharpe ratio over a given training period.

Due to the large number of trading rules in the decision support system (in experiments, $d = 500$), the dimension of the search space is excessively large and constitutes a bottleneck for many optimization algorithms. However, many trading rules are similar, based on similar financial principles, so the variables of the objective function seems to be correlated [8]. Thus, applying the dimensionality reduction mechanism proposed in this paper may significantly improve the efficiency of the evolutionary search process.

Experiments were performed on 10 datasets. Each dataset concerned one stock chosen from the CAC IT 20 index of the Paris Stock Exchange, a training period from January, 2, 2009 to November, 30, 2009 (234 trading days) and a set of selected 500 trading rules, based on technical analysis indicators [11]. Each optimization problem was solved twice: once with the locally linear embeddings mechanism turned off, and once with turned on. Parameters of the algorithms were the same as discussed in the previous section.

Table 2 presents a summary of results on learning the financial decision support system for the 10 datasets. The second and the third column contain the objective function values for the best solution found by the original and the improved algorithm, respectively. Both algorithm found similar solutions, perhaps the quasi-optima, so the values are similar. The forth and the fifth column contain the objective function values for the best solution found after 500 iterations. Finally, the sixth column contains the improvement factors described

Table 2. Summary of results on learning a financial decision support system for 10 datasets concerning one stock chosen from the CAC IT 20 index of the Paris Stock Exchange

Stock	DE	DEELLE	DE-500	DEELLE-500	Improvement
Alcatel-Lucent	28.17	28.19	23.63	27.61	1.17
Alstom	19.83	19.99	17.86	19.11	1.07
Cap Gemini	20.98	21.04	17.48	20.68	1.18
France Telecom	10.83	10.76	8.49	10.65	1.25
Legrand	22.96	23.04	22.01	22.74	1.03
Neopost	19.38	19.42	17.09	18.46	1.08
Schneider Electric	25.77	25.93	23.94	25.88	1.08
STMicroelectronics	19.97	20.76	15.45	20.13	1.30
TF1	25.04	25.45	19.86	24.68	1.24
Vivendi	15.87	16.13	11.93	16.08	1.35

in the previous section (the same as presented in Table 1), i.e. the fifth column divided by the fourth column. It is easy to see that the improved algorithm outperformed the original one, but the improvement was lower than in the case of simple benchmark functions discussed in the previous section.

6   Conclusions

This paper proposes an improvement of Differential Evolution for objective functions with non-linearly correlated variables, which tries to detect non-linear local dependencies among variables of the objective function by analyzing the manifold in the search space that contains the current population and transforming individuals to a reduced search space using Locally Linear Embeddings.

A preliminary evaluation performed on some popular benchmark functions confirmed that the method may significantly improve the search process, especially in the case of complex objective functions with a large number of variables, which usually occur in many practical applications.

Further evaluation on a financial decision support system, where the proposed algorithm was used to learn the trading system and discover the importance weights for the trading rules, confirmed the preliminary results. Applying Locally Linear Embeddings led to a significant improvement of the evolutionary algorithm, however, the improvement rate was lower than in the case of simple benchmark functions.

References

1. Cox, T., Cox, M.: Multidimensional Scaling. Chapman & Hall (2001)
2. Das, S., Suganthan, P.N.: Differential Evolution: A Survey of the State-of-the-Art. IEEE Transactions on Evolutionary Computation $15(1)$, 4–31 (2011)
3. Harik, G.: Linkage Learning via Probabilistic Modeling in the ECGA, IlliGAL Research Report, no. 99010. University of Illinois at Urbana-Champaign (1999)
4. Hilletofth, P., Lattila, L.: Agent based decision support in the supply chain context. Industrial Management & Data Systems $112(8)$, 1217–1235 (2012)
5. Ishibuchi, H., Yamamoto, T.: Fuzzy rule selection by multi-objective genetic local search algorithms and rule evaluation measures in data mining. Fuzzy Sets and Systems $141(1)$, 59–88 (2004)
6. Larranaga, P., Lozano, J.A.: Estimation of Distribution Algorithms. Kluwer Academic Publishers (2002)
7. Korczak, J., Lipinski, P.: Evolutionary Building of Stock Trading Experts in a Real-Time System. In: Congress on Evolutionary Computation, pp. 940–947 (2004)
8. Lipinski, P.: Dependency Mining in Large Sets of Stock Market Trading Rules. In: Enhanced Methods in Computer Security, Biometric and Intelligent Systems, pp. 329–336. Kluwer Academic Publishers (2005)
9. Lipinski, P.: A Stock Market Decision Support System with a Hybrid Evolutionary Algorithm for Many-Core Graphics Processors. In: Guarracino, M.R., et al. (eds.) Euro-Par-Workshop 2010. LNCS, vol. 6586, pp. 455–462. Springer, Heidelberg (2011)

10. Lipinski, P.: Evolution Strategies for Objective Functions with Locally Correlated Variables. In: Fyfe, C., Tino, P., Charles, D., Garcia-Osorio, C., Yin, H. (eds.) IDEAL 2010. LNCS, vol. 6283, pp. 352–359. Springer, Heidelberg (2010)
11. Murphy, J.: Technical Analysis of the Financial Markets, NUIF (1998)
12. Nojima, Y., Ishibuchi, H.: Multiobjective genetic fuzzy rule selection with fuzzy relational rules. In: IEEE International Workshop on Genetic and Evolutionary Fuzzy Systems, pp. 60–67 (2013)
13. Roweis, S., Saul, L.: Nonlinear Dimensionality Reduction by Locally Linear Embedding. Science **290**, 2323–2326 (2000)
14. Sharpe, W.: Capital Asset Prices: A Theory of Market Equilibrium under Conditions of Risk. Journal of Finance **19**, 425–442 (1964)
15. Sirlantzis, K., Fairhurst, M.C., Guest, R.M.: An evolutionary algorithm for classifier and combination rule selection in multiple classifier systems. In: 16th International Conference on Pattern Recognition, pp. 771–774 (2002)
16. Wang, M., Wang, H., Xu, D., Wan, K.K., Vogel, D.: A web-service agent-based decision support system for securities exception management. Expert Systems with Applications **27**(3), 439–450 (2004)
17. Webb, A.: Statistical Pattern Recognition. John Wiley, London (2002)
18. Whitley, D., Rana, S., Dzubera, J., Mathias, K.: Evaluating evolutionary algorithms. Artificial Intelligence **85**(12), 245–276 (1996)

A Memetic Framework for Solving Difficult Inverse Problems

Maciej Smołka$^{(\boxtimes)}$ and Robert Schaefer

AGH University of Science and Technology,
Al. Mickiewicza 30, 30-059 Kraków, Poland
{schaefer,smolka}@agh.edu.pl

Abstract. The paper introduces a multi-deme, memetic global optimization strategy *Hierarchic memetic Strategy* (HMS) especially well-suited to the solution of a class of parametric inverse problems. This strategy develops dynamically a tree of dependent populations (demes) searching with the various accuracy growing from the root to the leaves. The search accuracy is associated with the accuracy of solving direct problems by hp–adaptive Finite Element Method. Throughout the paper we describe details of exploited accuracy adaptation and computational cost reduction mechanisms, an agent-based architecture of the proposed system, a sample implementation and preliminary benchmark results.

Keywords: Inverse problems · Hybrid optimization methods · Memetic algorithms

1 Motivation

Inverse problems form an important area of the contemporary research related to fundamental problems in science and engineering (see *e.g.* [1]). Among its numerous applications one can find such activities as oil and gas explorations, material processing and others. A quite general definition of the inverse problem is to find a value of a parameter $\omega^* \in \mathcal{D}$ realizing

$$\min_{\omega \in \mathcal{D}} \{f(u_o, u(\omega)) : \ A(u(\omega)) = 0\} \tag{1}$$

where A is a *direct problem operator*, $u(\omega) \in U$ is the direct solution corresponding to ω, $u_o \in \mathcal{O}$ is an observation (typically a measured quantity related somehow to the direct solution) and $f(\mathcal{O}, U) \longrightarrow \mathbb{R}_+$ is *a misfit functional*. In a typical situation U is a Sobolev space and $A : U \longrightarrow U'$ is a differential operator between U and its conjugate. When solving such problems one usually faces some significant obstacles. One of them is the ill-conditioning, i.e. a small change

The work presented in this paper has been partially supported by Polish National Science Center grants no. DEC-2012/07/B/ST6/01229 and DEC-2011/03/B/ST6/01393.

A.I. Esparcia-Alcázar et al. (Eds.): EvoApplications 2014, LNCS 8602, pp. 138–149, 2014.
DOI: 10.1007/978-3-662-45523-4_12

in parameters sometimes results in a big change in results. Other noticeable difficulties are the multi-modality, i.e. the non-uniqueness of solutions, and possible low regularity of the misfit functional. Both of them significantly reduce the usefulness of computationally relatively inexpensive convex optimization methods (such as gradient-based ones), because in the lack of the misfit differentiability their use is problematic in general and, even worse, in the case of multiple local optima they do not deliver the guarantee of finding the global one.

There exist some methods to overcome those difficulties. One of the most popular is the misfit regularization (see *e.g.* [2]) providing a modified version of the misfit, which is regular and convex (hence unimodal). This can be a very effective technique, however it is not very useful when the considered inverse problem is inherently multimodal and we need to find all minima. On the other hand, a careless use of the regularization can lead to the replacement of the original problem solution with an artificial solution of the over-regularized misfit. A different way is to use a stochastic global optimization methods from simple Monte Carlo type to more sophisticated single- and multi-deme genetic searches (see *e.g.* [3–5]). Such methods may handle irregularity and multimodality, but the price is the high computational cost and the low accuracy. Another possibility is to perform multiple convex searches from a set of points generated randomly (multistart strategy). Such methods might be additionally improved by the sophisticated post-processing leading to the reduction of a random sample from which local methods are started or the early suspension of non-promising local searches (see *e.g.* [6,7]).

The authors intend to synthesize slightly diverse ideas of the inverse analysis arising from the following sources.

Hierarchic Genetic Strategy (HGS). This strategy develops dynamically a tree of dependent *demes* i.e. sub-populations of the total multiset of various type individuals created by the strategy. The root-deme performs the most global search with a low accuracy. The search performed by demes located deeper in the tree is more localized and more accurate. See [8] for details and [9] for HGS floating point encoding implementation. An important HGS extension going towards the effective solving of the inverse parametric problems is the hp–HGS strategy (see [10] and references therein) which combines HGS with the hp-adaptive Finite Element Method (hp–FEM) [11]. This strategy offers the advantageous computational cost resulting from the common scaling of the hp–FEM error according to the various accuracy of HGS inverse search in the root deme, branch demes and leaf demes. The hp–HGS asymptotic guarantee of finding all extremes and the computational cost reduction rate are discussed in [10].

Memetic algorithms (see *e.g.* [12]) allow to compose various techniques into a single population-based stochastic strategy in order to obtain more efficiency and flexibility. Candidate solutions are represented as software agents, other agents are responsible for governing populations, which leads to the idea of the computing Multi-Agent System (MAS) (see *e.g.* [13,14]). The first attempt to apply agents in profiling of HGS demes is described in [15]. An example of solving inverse parametric problem by an Evolutionary Multi-Agent System (EMAS) can be found in [16]. The paper [17] shows a different way of a memetic enhancement of genetic search by introducing 'gradient mutation' into the genetic solving of inverse problems coming from the computational mechanics.

Clustered Genetic Search (CGS) tries to extract the knowledge from the genetic sample (the population) or a sequence of samples in order to approximate central parts of local extreme's basins of attraction (see *e.g.* [7]). CGS follows the simple strategy introduced by Törn [6], which performs a density clustering of the uniformly sampled population undertaking the elitist selection.

The solution proposed in this paper, called *Hierarchic Memetic Strategy* (HMS) combines all mechanisms described above in a form of a loosely coupled tree of searching demes. The novelty of our proposition consists of the intensive profiling of searching process towards essential decreasing of computational cost and exploring multiple extremes. This profiling utilize intensively the knowledge about the solving problem extracted from the evolving demes and their current structure.

2   HMS Architecture

The main idea of the HMS is to provide a global optimization tool especially suited to solving difficult inverse problems. Their difficulty lies in their inherent multi-modality as well as the nontrivial computational cost of a direct problem solution, which is necessary for evaluating the misfit. Nevertheless, they also have some features we can take advantage of. First of all, their global minimum value is well-known (and equal to 0), which can be used in e.g. the construction of stopping conditions for stochastic evolution. Second, in some important cases the cost of the direct problem solution can be modulated by an assumed accuracy of the solution: it is the case of hp-FEM direct solvers [11].

As a global optimization tool the HMS tries to combine the high-level exploratory ability with the accuracy and efficiency of a local optimization method. Contrary to two-phase methods in which the global phase is followed by local searches, the HMS goes 'memetic way', i.e. intermixes local-optimization-oriented mechanisms into a global stochastic search machinery. The global part follows the multi-population evolutionary approach introduced by the HGS [8]. Namely the global search is performed by a collection of genetic populations. The populations can evolve in parallel, but they are not mutually independent. The structure of the dependency relation is hierarchical (i.e. tree-like, see Fig. 1) with a restricted number of levels. The HGS proved to have considerable exploratory capabilities together with a good search accuracy especially with floating-point phenotype encoding [9]. The HMS, naturally, tries to retain these abilities at the same time going beyond the HGS in some aspects. First of all, it adds local optimization to the set of operations applied to the genetic individuals. But this is done with care in order to avoid the premature population convergence on one hand and the high cost of running instances of a local method from inappropriate points on the other hand. Namely some genetic individuals (but not necessarily all of them) receive an identity and some intelligence hence becoming

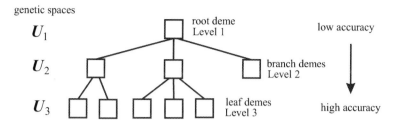

Fig. 1. HGS-like evolutionary population tree

independent agents in a multi-agent system (MAS), and the decision of performing the local search becomes their own responsibility. Moreover the demes are
managed by special controller agents. Note that this is somewhat similar but at
the same time significantly different from the Globally Balanced HGS (GB-HGS)
[15] where only demes have corresponding agents. The idea of turning a passive
genetic individual into an intelligent agent has some further consequences. We
have to redefine the genetic operations in such a way that they can be applied
to agents and while there is no big problem with the mutation and the crossover
(but one has to note that in this case a new agent is activated), the selection
cannot be performed in the simple genetic (or evolutionary) way. Namely we
follow the lines of the EMAS [13,14], thus performing an operation analogous to
the proportional selection but realized as a two-agent rendezvous.

In the sequel we shall present the structure of the HMS starting from a
description of HMS agent types.

2.1   HMS Agent Types

Master Agent (MA). As a global system coordinator it is started as a first agent
in the HMS MAS. Its responsibilities include performing the system initialization
including the activation of other basic agents, i.e. the Objective Agent and a
Local Agent of the deme-tree root. After the initialization, the Master Agent
starts the global loop of deme coordination and checks if the global stopping
condition is satisfied. It is shown in the following algorithm:

1: create OA
2: create root location node
3: **repeat**
4:     receive proposals from DAs and choose one
5: **until** global stop condition is satisfied.

Deme Agent (DA). It is a deme-tree node coordinator. Each deme has an associated level of computational accuracy stored as a property of the corresponding
Local Agent. In fact Deme Agent is an abstract class with two different special-
izations: Evolutionary Agent and Local Agent.

Evolutionary Agent (EA). This is a simple (passive) evolutionary population owner. Periodically, after receiving the permission from the Master Agent it lets its population evolve for a fixed number of generations (this is called a *metaepoch*) and then sprouts a new deme from the current best individual unless the sprout condition is not satisfied (see the algorithm below). Note that similar agents form the structure of the GB-HGS [15]. The Evolutionary Agent algorithm may be presented in the following way.

```
 1: create initial deme population
 2: repeat
 3:     send a proposal to MA
 4:     if MA has accepted the proposal then
 5:         evolve owned population for a fixed step number
 6:         if the best individual satisfies the sprout condition then
 7:             create new child DA
 8:         end if
 9:     end if
10: until local stop condition is satisfied
```

Local Agent (LA). The Local Agent owns a population of Computational Agents and acts as their action local scheduler. Namely it receives action proposals from Computational Agents, selects one of them according to a probability distribution, send a proposal to the Master Agent and if the proposal is accepted, lets the selected Computational Agent perform its action (see the algorithm below). The Local Agent's responsibilities include also some action coordination, such as checking if a pending sprout action is allowed. The Local Agent algorithm is presented below.

```
 1: create initial deme population
 2: repeat
 3:     send CFP to all active CAs
 4:     receive action proposals from CAs and choose one
 5:     send a proposal to MA
 6:     if MA has accepted the proposal then
 7:         if CA action creates new individual then
 8:             create new CA
 9:         else if chosen action is SPROUT then
10:             if sprouting can be performed then
11:                 create new child DA
12:             end if
13:         end if
14:     end if
15: until local stop condition is satisfied
```

Computational Agent (CA). It is an *active* individual of the HMS genetic population. It owns an immutable genotype consisting of an encoded domain point (a chromosome) and a level of the computational precision. The precision level must be consistent with the owning Local Agent's level. The mutable part of a

Computational Agent's state includes a nonnegative memetic parameter called *life energy*. The life energy is exchanged during a Computational Agent action execution such that the total energy remains constant within each deme. Only agents with the positive life energy are considered active (alive) and take part in the system evolution. Namely there exists a pool of actions from which an active Computational Agent can choose one at a time to perform. The available action pool size depends primarily on the agent's life energy but can be affected by other parameters as well. The action selection is determined by a given probability distribution. Finally, the action is performed only if permitted by the owning Local Agent (see the algorithm below).

1: request objective computing from OA
2: **while** life energy > 0 **do**
3:     receive CFP from owning LA
4:     choose an available action
5:     send the proposal to LA
6:     **if** received permission from LA **then**
7:         perform chosen action
8:         update life energy
9:     **end if**
10: **end while**

There is an energy quantum related to each action, which is spent (during GET it can sometimes be gained) by a Computational Agent during the action execution. Currently the following actions are considered (cf. [14]): GET, MUTATE, CROSSOVER, LOCOPT and SPROUT.

The GET action is the above-mentioned kind of the distributed selection. It is a two-agent stochastic duel during which the proper quantum energy moves from the loser to the winner. A Computational Agent with a lower (i.e. better because closer to the global minimum) objective value has more chances to win. MUTATE and CROSSOVER are straightforward counterparts of corresponding genetic (or evolutionary) operations, like e.g. the normal mutation and the arithmetic crossover. The SPROUT action is inspired by the child branch sprouting operation, which is fundamental in the HGS [8]. In the HMS it produces a new deme together with its Local Agent and an initial population of Computational Agents. The probability of selecting SPROUT increases with the decreasing value of the objective. Obviously SPROUT makes no sense at the leaf level, where it can be optionally replaced with LOCOPT. The LOCOPT is a local optimization method execution started from the agent's decoded chromosome. In the current realization LOCOPT is allowed only at the leaves and, as in the case of SPROUT, the probability of its selection is high for Computational Agents with the low objective value.

Objective Agent (OA). In the real HMS use case (i.e. in solving inverse problems) the objective value is computed externally by a specialized direct solver. The responsibility of an Objective Agent (typically one in the whole system) is to provide a proper solver gateway, i.e. to execute the solver process (or several parallel processes) properly and to transfer the input data to the solver and the solver output back to the HMS. Additional Objective Agent activities may include: caching solver results, solver instance pooling (in the case of the parallel execution) and scheduling objective computations according to a sophisticated optimizing policy (e.g. a diffusion-based one [18]).

2.2 Population Structure

As it was stated before the HMS genetic population is decomposed into dependent demes forming a dynamically-changing tree of the fixed maximal depth m. Genetic individuals, i.e. Computing Agents, located at the tree levels close to the root perform the chaotic and inaccurate search, whereas going towards the leaves the search becomes more and more focused and the accuracy is increased (see Fig. 1). The variability of the search accuracy results from the diversity of the genotype encoding precision used at different tree levels. The latter of course depends on the encoding type. In the case of the binary encoding (as in the Simple Genetic Algorithm) it can be achieved by the binary genotype length variation, whereas in the case of the real number encoding (as in the Simple Evolutionary Algorithm) it can be realized by the appropriate phenotype scaling. The latter case is used in the prototype implementation of the HMS so we present here some details. The description follows the ones presented in papers [9,15].

In the real number encoding both phenotypes and genotypes are vectors from $\mathbb{R}^N$. We assume that the solution domain is a box $\mathcal{D} = [a_1, b_1] \times \cdots \times [a_N, b_N]$ and we take a sequence of scaling factors $\eta_i \in \mathbb{R}$ such that $\eta_1 > \eta_2 > \ldots \eta_{m-1} > \eta_m = 1$. Then the genetic universum at the tree level j is

$$U_j = \left[0, \frac{b_1 - a_1}{\eta_j}\right] \times \cdots \times \left[0, \frac{b_N - a_N}{\eta_j}\right] \tag{2}$$

and the encoding mapping at the level j is defined as

$$\mathcal{D} \ni x \longmapsto \left\{\frac{x_k - a_k}{\eta_j}\right\}_{k=1}^N \in U_j. \tag{3}$$

Moreover we define the scaling mapping $scale_{i,j} : U_i \ni x \mapsto \frac{\eta_i}{\eta_j} x \in U_j$. In such a genetic universa the search at lower levels is more chaotic (because the mutation acts stronger) and less precise (the loss of precision is caused by limitations in the real number representation). One can use various genetic operators in such an encoding, but among the most important one can find the normal mutation $y_i = x_i + \mathcal{N}(0, \sigma_j^{mut})$ for $i = 1, \ldots, N$, where $\mathcal{N}(0, \sigma_j^{mut})$ is a normally-distributed random variable with the standard deviation σ_j^{mut} set separately for each level j, and the arithmetic crossover $y_i = x_i^1 + \mathcal{U}([0,1])(x_i^2 - x_i^1)$ for $i = 1, \ldots, N$, where $\mathcal{U}([0,1])$ is a random variable distributed uniformly over the interval $[0,1]$. Both operators are used in our sample implementation. Furthermore we exploit the classical fitness-proportional (roulette-wheel) selection in passive populations (on Evolutionary Agents) additionally preserving the best individual of each generation. A newly sprouted deme's population is sampled according to the N-dimensional Gaussian distribution centered at the properly encoded fittest individual of the parent process with the diagonal covariance matrix with values $(\sigma_j^{sprout})^2$ on the diagonal. The sprout cannot be performed in population P at level j if there exists a population P' at level $j+1$ such that $|\overline{y} - scale_{i,i+1}(y)| < c_j$, where y is the best individual in P, $\overline{y}$ is the average phenotype of P' and c_j is a branch comparison constant.

Finally, it should be mentioned that the further utilization of the knowledge gathered during the multi-level enhanced genetic evolution is possible by means of the clustering technique, in which better approximation of attraction basins of the local minima can be developed allowing yet more precise application of local optimization methods.

3   Sample Implementation

As our algorithmic framework is sophisticated, agent-based one, it also poses several challenges for the implementation task. Two main goals were especially considered during the design phase: flexibility and efficiency.

Flexibility. It was quite obvious from the beginning that HMS, being a framework, should be extensively configurable, which means that it has to embrace changes in such aspects as various particular sub-algorithms (*e.g.* the computation of CA action probabilities), local and global stopping conditions, local optimization methods, objective approximations etc. All such issues are addressed primarily by the extensive use of appropriate design patterns (such as Strategy or Proxy). Some aspects of configurability are obtained through the inclusion of scripting capabilities into the solid Java skeleton, namely some sub-algorithms can be defined in separate JavaScript scripts. There is also a higher level of flexibility reached by HMS. Through the foundation on the Java Agent Development Framework JADE [19] (in version 4.2) it obtained a potential ability of distributed deployment. The use of JADE is justified by its de facto standard position in the multi-agent middleware area and the relative easiness to write code controlling concurrent agents communicating through asynchronous message passing. JADE's FIPA standard compliance encouraged us to base HMS agent communication protocols on the FIPA solutions as well. Both the location selection performed by the Master Agent with the cooperation of Local Agents and the Computational Agent selection conducted by a Local Agent are a modifications of the FIPA Contract-Net protocol. Another example is the multiple use of the FIPA Request protocol (e.g. requesting the objective value from the Objective Agent by a Computational Agent).

Efficiency. A message-intensive multi-agent system may seem not very suitable for numerical computations. However, one should consider that in our real use case the cost of solving a direct problem dominates the other costs, including agent thread allocation and asynchronous message passing, by far. Hence our main effort is to reduce the number of the direct solver calls and decrease the cost of the particular direct solution as far as possible (and this is obtained through the presented analysis) instead of looking for a more time-effective implementation environment, which would lack other above-mentioned desired features.

4   Benchmark Tests

Some preliminary benchmark tests were performed. Their aim was basically to prove the HMS abilities to find the global minimum with the assumed accuracy in comparison with an already-tested effective tool: GB-HGS [15]. Namely we took the best accuracy obtained by GB-HGS in the optimization of two popular benchmark functions and treated this accuracy as the goal for HMS. The chosen type of tests (i.e. the tests with an assumed accuracy) influenced the setting of the HMS stopping conditions. Namely the global stopping condition was satisfied if a leaf approached the global minimum with the given accuracy, whereas a leaf stopping condition was satisfied if the leaf approached the global minimum or if a fixed number of its consecutive metaepochs were ineffective, i.e there was no significant change in the leaf's population average fitness. As the active populations do not use the basic notion of metaepoch, for stopping condition definition we use performing the number of steps equal to the current population size instead.

As benchmarks we chose the 20-dimensional Rastrigin function over the box $[-512, 512]^{20}$ and the 10-dimensional Ackley path function over the box $[-30, 30]^{10}$. Both test were repeated 10 times. The tree had 2 levels. At the root level an Evolutionary Agent (i.e. a passive population) was run, whereas at the leaf level we executed Local Agents together with populations of Computational Agents (i.e. active individuals capable of performing the local optimization). The normal mutation and the arithmetic crossover were used as the genetic operations. To make the comparison more clear in both benchmarks most of HMS execution parameters was set exactly (or almost exactly) as in GB-HGS.

In 10D Ackley function minimization we assumed the accuracy of 0.01 (in this case the obtained accuracy was much better). The execution parameters for 10D Ackley function are summarized in Tab. 1. Note that the metaepoch length parameter is not directly applicable to Local Agents (see above). Similarly, the population size in this case is not constant, in our simulations it varied between 10 and 30. The objective call statistics are shown in Tab. 2. The cost of a local method application is included in the leaf level cost. Note that the average fitness call number in the case of GB-HGS shows only the order of the actual quantity but nothing more is available in [15]. In [15], however, one can also find results of minimizing 10D Ackley function by means of the Simple Evolutionary Algorithm (SEA). It turns out that SEA after 10^7 fitness calls approaches the minimum with the accuracy about 5, which is obviously far from the HMS's achievement.

In Rastrigin 20D we assumed the accuracy of 1000 (note that this time the number of local minima is really huge). The execution parameters are summarized in Tab. 3 (the meaning of the parameters is the same as in the Ackley

Table 1. HMS execution parameters (Ackley 10D)

	Root level	Leaf level
Population/initial population	50	10
Metaepoch length	50	-
Encoding scale η_j	4.0	1.0
Mutation rate	0.1	0.03
Crossover rate	0.5	0.5
Mutation standard deviation σ_j^{mut}	4.0	0.8
Sprout standard deviation σ_j^{sprout}	10.0	2.0
Sprout minimal distances c_j	12.0	2.4

Table 2. Average number of objective evaluations (Ackley 10D)

	Root level	Leaf level	Total
GB-HGS			10000000
HMS	147093	4340	151433

Table 3. HMS execution parameters (Rastrigin 20D)

	Root level	Leaf level
Population/initial population	50	10
Metaepoch length	50	-
Encoding scale η_j	5.0	1.0
Mutation rate	0.1	0.03
Crossover rate	0.5	0.5
Mutation standard deviation σ_j^{mut}	68.27	13.65
Sprout standard deviation σ_j^{sprout}	170.675	34.125
Sprout minimal distances c_j	204.81	40.95

Table 4. Average number of objective evaluations (Rastrigin 20D)

	Root level	Leaf level	Total
GB-HGS			10000000
HMS	194899	3570.1	198469.1

case). The fitness call statistics are gathered in Tab. 4. Note that the number of fitness calls is much higher at the root level, which is very advantageous from the point of view of inverse problem solving, because the cost of direct solution is much less then in case of leaves, because of much lower required accuracy.

Finally let us note that more thorough HMS testing should tackle real inverse problems (instead of simple benchmark functions). Such tests, involving oil exploration problems, are planned in the near future.

5   Conclusions

In the paper we have presented a memetic global optimization framework HMS. It can be used in general optimization but its main design goal is to solve inverse problems. The main benefit of the presented framework is a significant reduction of the computational cost together with the ability of the exploration of multiple extreme obtained on the several separate, but perfectly focusing ways, namely (see Sec. 2):

- self-adaptation through construction of a sophisticated deme topology;
- simultaneous error scaling;
- knowledge mining and online search profiling;
- parallel processing.

To develop these features HMS summarizes and improves ideas taken from HGS, hp-HGS and CGS (see Sec. 1).

The preliminary tests show the advantage of HMS over the refined hierarchic genetic strategy GB-HGS dedicated to multimodal problems (number of fitness calls decreases by two orders) as well as over the single deme evolutionary algorithm (here number of fitness call decreases even more). An additional cost decrement can be obtained by the common error scaling and the deme clustering, which were not included in the presented series of tests.

References

1. Tarantola, A.: Inverse Problem Theory. Mathematics and its Applications. Society for Industrial and Applied Mathematics (2005)
2. Engl, H., Hanke, M., Neubauer, A.: Regularization of Inverse Problems. Mathematics and its Applications, vol. 375. Springer, Heidelberg (1996)
3. Pardalos, P., Romeijn, H.: Handbook of Global Optimization (Nonconvex Optimization and its Applications), vol. 2. Kluwer (1995)
4. Chakraborty, U.K. (ed.): Advances in Differential Evolution, vol. 143. Studies in Computational Intelligence. Springer (2008)
5. Cantú Paz, E.: Efficient and accurate parallel genetic algorithms, vol. 2. Kluwer (2000)
6. Törn, A.A.: A search clustering approach to global optimization. In: Dixon, L.C.W., Szegö, G.P. (eds.) Towards Global Optimisation 2, pp. 49–62. North-Holland, Amsterdam (1978)
7. Schaefer, R., Adamska, K., Telega, H.: Genetic clustering in continuous landscape exploration. Engineering Applications of Artificial Intelligence **17**, 407–416 (2004)
8. Schaefer, R., Kołodziej, J.: Genetic search reinforced by the population hierarchy. In: Foundations of Genetic Algorithms 7, pp. 383–399, Morgan Kaufman (2003)
9. Wierzba, B., Semczuk, A., Kołodziej, J., Schaefer, R.: Hierarchical Genetic Strategy with real number encoding. In: Proceedings of the 6th Conference on Evolutionary Algorithms and Global Optimization, pp. 231–237 (2003)
10. Barabasz, B., Migórski, S., Schaefer, R., Paszyński, M.: Multi-deme, twin adaptive strategy hp-HGS. Inverse Problems in Science and Engineering **19**(1), 3–16 (2011)

11. Demkowicz, L., Kurtz, J., Pardo, D., Paszyński, M., Rachowicz, W., Zdunek, A.: Computing with hp Finite Elements II. Frontiers: Three-Dimensional Elliptic and Maxwell Problems with Applications. Chapman & Hall/CRC (2007)

12. Neri, F., Cotta, C., Moscato, P. (eds.): Handbook of Memetic Algorithms. Studies in Computational Intelligence, vol. 379. Springer, Heidelberg (2012)

13. Cetnarowicz, K., Kisiel-Dorohinicki, M., Nawarecki, E.: The application of evolution process in multi-agent world (MAW) to the prediction system. In: Tokoro, M. (ed.) Proceedings of the 2nd International Conference on Multiagent Systems (ICMAS 1996). AAAI Press (1996)

14. Byrski, A., Schaefer, R., Smołka, M., Cotta, C.: Asymptotic guarantee of success for multi-agent memetic systems. Bulletin of the Polish Academy of Sciences: Technical Sciences 61(1), 257–278 (2013)

15. Jojczyk, P., Schaefer, R.: Global impact balancing in the hierarchic genetic search. Computing and Informatics 28(2), 181–193 (2009)

16. Wróbel, K., Torba, P., Paszyński, M., Byrski, A.: Evolutionary multi-agent computing in inverse problems. Computer Science 14(3), 367–383 (2013)

17. Burczyński, T., Orantek, P.: The hybrid genetic-gradient algorithm. In: Proceedings of 3rd KAEGiOG Conference, Potok Złoty, Poland (1999)

18. Grochowski, M., Smołka, M., Schaefer, R.: Architectural principles and scheduling strategies for computing agent systems. Fundamenta Informaticae 71(1), 15–26 (2006)

19. Bellifemine, F.L., Caire, G., Greenwood, D.: Developing Multi-Agent Systems with JADE. Wiley (2007)

EvoENERGY

Customizable Energy Management in Smart Buildings Using Evolutionary Algorithms

Florian Allerding[1]([envelope]), Ingo Mauser[2], and Hartmut Schmeck[1]

[1] Karlsruhe Institute of Technology – Institute AIFB, 76128 Karlsruhe, Germany
{florian.allerding,hartmut.schmeck}@kit.edu
[2] FZI Research Center for Information Technology, 76133 Karlsruhe, Germany
mauser@fzi.de

Abstract. Various changes in energy production and consumption lead to new challenges for design and control mechanisms of the energy system. In particular, the intermittent nature of power generation from renewables asks for significantly increased load flexibility to support local balancing of energy demand and supply. This paper focuses on a flexible, generic energy management system for Smart Buildings in real-world applications, which is already in use in households and office buildings. The major contribution is the design of a "plug-and-play"-type Evolutionary Algorithm for optimizing distributed generation, storage and consumption using a sub-problem based approach. Relevant power consuming or producing components identify themselves as sub-problems by providing an abstract specification of their genotype, an evaluation function and a back transformation from an optimized genotype to specific control commands. The generic optimization respects technical constraints as well as external signals like variable energy tariffs. The relevance of this approach to energy optimization is evaluated in different scenarios. Results show significant improvements of self-consumption rates and reductions of energy costs.

Keywords: Energy Management · Smart Building · Evolutionary Algorithm · Combined Heat and Power Plant · Household Appliances

1 Introduction and Scenario

The world-wide energy supply is currently in a transition phase mainly due to the increasing share of power generation from renewable sources and the accelerated reduction of nuclear based power generation. The German "Energiewende" ("energy transition" [7]) is already causing a tremendous change in the structure of energy supply in Germany. The nuclear power phase-out is supposed to be completed by 2023. Accordingly, the share of photovoltaic power and wind power is increasing. The ambitious targets of the German government are to cover 35 % of electricity consumption in Germany from renewable energy sources by 2020, 50 % by 2030 and at least 80 % by 2050 [7]. In particular, highly decentralized

© Springer-Verlag Berlin Heidelberg 2014
A.I. Esparcia-Alcázar et al. (Eds.): EvoApplications 2014, LNCS 8602, pp. 153–164, 2014.
DOI: 10.1007/978-3-662-45523-4_13

photovoltaic systems in the German grid are causing volatile electricity prices at the European Energy Exchange (EEX) and voltage and congestion problems in the low-voltage grid [12]. This requires advanced management and optimization strategies for the grid as well as for single buildings or households that are enabling flexibility of electricity consumption.

The heterogeneous structure of households and buildings in general with different setups of appliances and the intermittent character of distributed generation or storage systems and new types of large consumers (e.g. electric vehicles) call for a flexible approach towards configuration and optimization. The Energy Management System (EMS) described in this paper has been developed within various research projects at the Karlsruhe Institute of Technology (KIT) and the Research Center for Information Technology (FZI) [3]. It has been deployed in real-world environments such as the Energy Smart Home Lab (ESHL) on KIT's campus[1] and the FZI House of Living Labs (HoLL)[2].

The ESHL consists of a $60m^2$ apartment equipped with a combined heat and power plant (CHP), an air conditioner, thermal storages, intelligent appliances, and an electric car. The scenario of ESHL focuses clearly on residential buildings, whereas the HoLL is a mixed environment of a Smart Home, Smart Offices and Smart Production in a large building. The HoLL is equipped with an extended set of distributed power generation and storage systems, intelligent appliances with wireless communication, building automation systems, and electrical cars. External signals, reflecting the global and local grid state, are sent to the EMS, which is able to adapt the building's energy demand and production automatically without constraining the occupants while complying with their preferences. The electric and thermal loads of appliances and electric cars are being shifted within user-defined degrees of freedom.

The major contribution of this paper is the description and evaluation of a novel approach to energy management, which is extending the approach presented in [2]: Similar to the concept of "plug-and-play", the components with shiftable loads or flexible production send a standardized *problem part* to the evolutionary optimizer, containing a genotypic description, and a local evaluation function. Thus, the components provide all the necessary information and the optimizer can run global optimizations based on the sub-problems. The remainder of this paper is structured as follows. Section 2 introduces energy management in general and state-of-the-art approaches to optimization of energy production and consumption in buildings. Sect. 3 outlines the overall system architecture of the EMS presented in this paper – the *Organic Smart Home* (OSH) – and the technical systems which are used. The unique feature of the OSH is its flexibility in integrating the abstract descriptions of sub-problems as problem parts. This abstraction and the Evolutionary Algorithm are presented in Sect. 4. The simulation setup and evaluation results are depicted in Sect. 5. Finally, the conclusions and an outlook are summarized in Sect. 6.

---

[1] http://www.izeus.kit.edu/english/

[2] http://www.fzi.de/en/fzi-house-of-living-labs/

2   Energy Management and Problem Definition

There are quite a few approaches to autonomous systems for energy management based on optimization techniques for electricity grids. Often, the optimization problem is formulated as a linear programming (LP) [9], mixed integer linear programming (MILP) [1,6,8,11] or mixed integer non-linear programming (MINLP) [4] problem. The EMS described in this paper is not only considering electricity in terms of active power, but also other commodities as reactive power, natural gas, hot and chilled water consumption, and emissions of greenhouse gases. Therefore, it has to take into account multiple objectives in the optimization and to consider the building with all its technical systems, energy production and consumption in various kinds, no matter whether it is electricity or another form of energy. This also includes the shift of energy consumption from one energy carrier to another.

When optimizing the usage of renewable energies in buildings and the electricity production by cogeneration with respect to variable external signals (e.g. load limitation signals) and user preferences, it is important to regard time steps as short as possible to take account of short-time consumption and production peaks. Usually, building simulation and building energy management, which is focusing on thermal energy, use time steps in scale of minutes [5], whereas the OSH works with time steps on a second to second basis. Optimizing this system for a time horizon of several hours would result in a MILP with thousands of constraints and variables, which could usually not be solved within adequate time on normal computers [1]. For that reason and due the fact that embedded systems with limited resources are applied, we use a metaheuristic to find feasible solutions for this optimization problem: an Evolutionary Algorithm (EA).

The energy management problem for an exemplary scenario with shiftable appliances, and a CHP can be formulated as follows: Various external signals are taken into account by the EMS. These include energy price signals for the different commodities, which are consumed or produced in the domain of the EMS, and load limitation signals that are reflecting the current grid state. Based upon these signals, the EMS has to optimize the operating times of delayable appliances and the CHP. Hence, for every specific optimization problem (as already pointed out in [2]) a discrete time horizon $\mathbb{T} = \{0, ..., T\}$, which can be exact to the second, has to be defined. This horizon depends on the current optimization situation and has a variable length.

The user specifies his preferences by providing a latest finishing time d_j for the work-item of a delayable household appliance j, which defines the temporal degree of freedom ($tDoF$):

$$tDoF_j = d_j - r_j - p_j$$

d_j latest time by which the appliance j has to finish its work-item
r_j release time of appliance j
p_j duration of the current work-item of appliance j

The starting time s_j can now be chosen by the EMS variably within this $tDoF$. Accordingly, the constraint for shifting the start time of appliance j is:

$$s_j = r_j + \Delta t \quad \text{with } \Delta t \leq tDoF$$

Based on the specific duration p_j for the appliance j, a binary vector $(a_{j,t})$ can be defined which indicates whether the appliance j is running in a time slot t. Additionally, the vector $(q_{j,i})$ represents the power consumption of the appliance j during its work-item. An example of these two vectors can be formulated as follows:

$$(a_{j,t})_{t\in\mathbb{T}} = \begin{pmatrix} 0\ 0\ 0\ 1\ 1\ 1\ 1\ 1\ 0\ 0\ 0\ 0 \end{pmatrix}^{\mathsf{T}} \quad (q_{j,i}) = \begin{pmatrix} 50\ 700\ 270\ 2100\ 500 \end{pmatrix}^{\mathsf{T}}$$

It has to be ensured that the active time of the work-item of appliance j is as long as its duration p_j:

$$\sum_{t=0}^{T} a_{j,t} = p_j \text{ and } a_{j,t} \in \{0,1\}, \quad \forall j \in J, \forall t \in \mathbb{T},$$

$$\text{as well as} \quad a_{j,t} = 0 \quad \text{for } t < r_j \text{ or } t \geq d_j$$

The operation time of the CHP can be defined by a similar vector (c_t). In addition to this, a second vector indicating the starting times of the CHP (cs_t) is taken into account as shown in the following example:

$$(c_t)_{t\in\mathbb{T}} = \begin{pmatrix} 0\ 1\ 1\ 0\ 0\ 1\ 1\ 0\ 0\ 1\ 1\ 1 \end{pmatrix}^{\mathsf{T}} \quad (cs_t)_{t\in\mathbb{T}} = \begin{pmatrix} 1\ 0\ 0\ 0\ 1\ 0\ 0\ 0\ 1\ 0\ 0\ 0 \end{pmatrix}^{\mathsf{T}}$$

With respect to the constraints for the appliances and the CHP above, the typical inhouse baseload $P_{base}(t)$ and the electrical power at the grid connection $P_{ex}(t)$ can now be calculated as follows:

$$P_{ex}(t) = \underbrace{\sum_{j\in J} a_{j,t} \cdot q_{j,|t-s_j| \bmod p_j}}_{\text{appliances}} + P_{base}(t) - \underbrace{p_{chp} \cdot c_t}_{\text{CHP}}$$

Different variable prices for the commodities, in form of an active power tariff $EP(t)$ and a natural gas tariff $GP(t)$, as well as the gas amount g when the CHP is running and the elevated amount g_s during the starting process of the CHP are being considered. These costs of the commodities as well as the additional costs CO_{ol} for load limitation violations of variable lower limit $L_l(t)$ and upper limit $L_u(t)$ for consumption $EP_{grid}(t)$ and feed-in $EP_{feedIn}(t)$ are calculated in the following way:

$$CO_{gas} = \sum_{t=0}^{T} GP(t) \cdot (g \cdot c_t + g_s \cdot cs_t)$$

$$CO_{el} = \sum_{t=0}^{T} P_{ex}(t) \cdot \left(EP_{grid}(t) \cdot {}_{[P_{ex}(t)\geq 0]} + EP_{feedIn}(t) \cdot {}_{[P_{ex}(t)<0]} \right)$$

$$CO_{ol} = \sum_{t=0}^{T} pf_u \cdot (P_{ex}(t) - L_u(t)) \cdot \left(EP_{grid}(t) \cdot {}_{[P_{ex}(t)\geq L_u(t)]} \right) +$$

$$\sum_{t=0}^{T} pf_l \cdot (L_l(t) - P_{ex}(t)) \cdot \left(EP_{feedIn}(t) \cdot {}_{[P_{ex}(t)<L_l(t)]} \right)$$

The variables pf_u and pf_l describe the penalty factors for the violation of upper and lower load limit. Finally, the optimization objective can now be formulated as:

$$min(CO_{sum}) = min(CO_{el} + CO_{ol} + CO_{gas})$$

This fitness function $min(CO_{sum})$ is used by the approach presented in this paper.

3 Organic Smart Home

The architectural design of the OSH is based on the generic *Observer/Controller Architecture* (O/C Architecture) [10] as already introduced in [3]. The O/C Architecture implies a regulatory feedback mechanism, which constitutes one way to achieve controlled self-organization in technical systems. The O/C Architecture uses a set of sensors and actuators to measure system variables and to influence the *System under Observation and Control* (SuOC). O/C Architecture and SuOC form the so called *organic system* [10]. Multiple local O/C-loops enable responses to the behavior and the status of different local agents and their interactions. The global O/C-loop activates reactions in order to control the global behavior emerging from interactions between local agents. Every loop consists of an observer and a controller, the former monitoring the status of the system through certain attributes and derivation of situation parameters and the latter influencing the underlying SuOC in an adequate way through aggregation of the derived information and learning methods. The segmentation into global and local units is called *hierarchical* O/C Architecture [10]. This general approach is more closely described in [2,3] and the system architecture is outlined in Fig. 1.

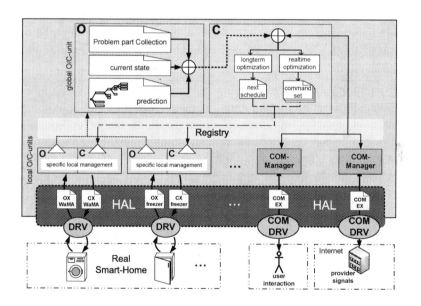

Fig. 1. Organic Smart Home – architectural overview

In between the local O/C-units and physical hardware components or simulation agents is the Hardware Abstraction Layer (HAL), which realizes the abstraction from the manufacturer specific protocols and communication media of the components, as introduced in [3]. Data of the SuOC is filtered in the local

O/C-units and passed to the global O/C-unit, which aggregates all information into the current state of the system and calculates a prediction for the future state within the next optimization horizon.

Based on the predictions by the local O/C-units, the global O/C-unit calculates an optimized schedule for the components in the building. This schedule defines actions and procedures for all devices which may be controlled by the OSH. Nevertheless, the schedule may be overridden by the local O/C-units, if the user forces so or certain circumstances require immediate action. This could be the case if, e.g., the temperature of a thermal energy storage is falling below a defined threshold level. The OSH considers various input values for the optimization: energy prices, load limitation, objectives defined by the user, the observed behavior, status of devices and storages, and external factors (e.g. weather). The OSH has been deployed on KIT's ESHL and at the FZI's HoLL showing that it can be used for both simulations and real-world applications.

4   Sub-problem Based Optimization by Evolutionary Algorithms

Households and buildings have usually heterogeneous configurations and differing optimization objectives. Therefore, a "plug-and-play" approach for the integration of different appliances, decentralized power plants, and other energy-related devices into the optimization of an EMS is introduced. For every device, a specific sub-problem is defined by modeling abstract *Problem Parts (PP)* which can be generically used in the global optimization of the building. Every sub-problem has a device-specific encoding, representing the sub-problem using a bit string of a specific length, even though the length of the bit string may vary from 0 bit to hundreds of bits per sub-problem. This abstract representation of a sub-problem as bit string provides the "plug-and-play" capabilities in the global optimization, because every specific sub-problem is abstracted to a structurally identical representation.

For instance, household appliances have usually some degree of freedom (*DoF*) as introduced in Sect. 2. This may either be a temporal degree of freedom (*tDoF*), which is applicable for delayable appliances, or an energy-related degree of freedom (*eDoF*), which is applicable for devices having variations of the same programs or are able to use different alternative energy sources. Appliances with a *tDoF* include dishwashers, washers, and dryers with time preselection. The *eDoF* could be used in appliances using, for example, either electricity or gas (this could also be achieved indirectly by using hot water provided by a central hot water supply) for the heating phase in their programs, which could be the case in dishwashers, washing machines, dryers, and heating, ventilation and air conditioning (HVAC) systems. These *DoFs* are modeled as PPs.

These PPs are exchanged using a common interface, which allows to handle the heterogeneous PPs of the different devices in order to solve the global optimization problem of energy management in the household. The PP contains length and instance of the bit string as well as the function *evaluate()*, which

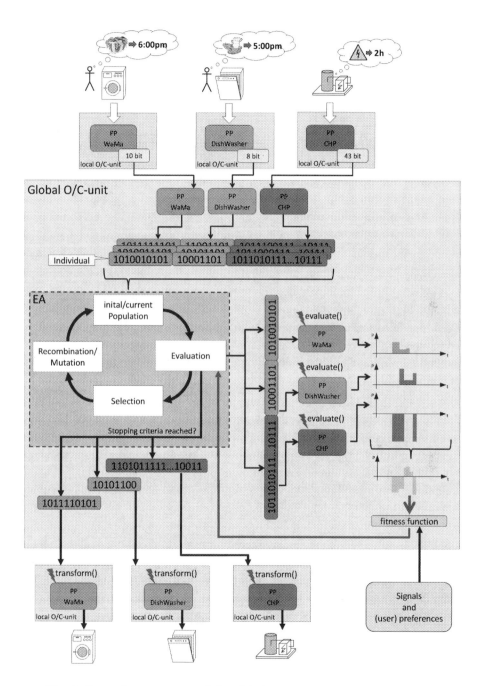

Fig. 2. Exemplary execution of the global optimization process in the OSH

returns the expected load profile of the appliance as a function of the current instance of the bit string. The second function *transform()* allows to re-transform the abstract representation into a specific solution for the sub-problem, which can then be handled by the corresponding device. The methods *evaluate()* and *transform()* consider specific constraints, which are, for instance, the maximum runtime of a CHP.

A concrete process of the global optimization based on the PPs using an EA with a binary representation is depicted in Fig. 2. Based on the architecture of the OSH, presented in Sect. 3, the PPs are constructed in the local O/C-units which are specific for a class of appliances. In the simplified scenario in Fig. 2 the user fills up a washing machine with laundry in the morning and defines that the laundry has to be washed by 6:00pm. Additionally, the dishwasher has to be finished by 5:00pm. In this example, the CHP has to run at least 2h during the current optimization period in order to fulfill the thermal demand of the building. In case of the washing machine a PP will be formulated in the local O/C-unit, where in the present example the encoding for the defined starting time of the washing machine will need 10 bits.

This abstracted PP will now be communicated to the global O/C-unit together with the PPs from the other appliances. The amount of PPs in the global O/C-unit represents the abstracted global optimization problem in the building for the current optimization period. Based on the bit-count of every PP the individuals of the initial population for the evolutionary algorithm can be created randomly as shown in Fig. 2. For the evaluation of every individual, the individual is split up into different parts, which are representing the encoding of the different PPs. The PP has the method *evaluate()* to calculate the resulting load profile by the given encoding. For every PP and therefore every appliance a partial load profile will be created this way. These partial profiles will now be combined to the resulting expected load curve in the household by the given configuration of the individual. Based on that curve, the given signals, and user preferences, the *fitness value* can be calculated using the *fitness function*.

This evolutionary cycle will run until the stopping criteria has been reached. In the present approach the stopping criteria is a given maximum number of generations. The best configuration will be separated into specific bit strings. These bit strings are combined with the PPs and are communicated back to the local O/C-units. In the local O/C-units every abstracted problem will now be transformed to the specific phenotype by the method *transform()* of the PP. This solution, in case of the washing machine a shifted starting time within its degree of freedom, will then be communicated to the physical appliance. For the other appliances the process can be considered as analog to the washing machine. In the following we present two concrete examples for PPs, the first one for appliances like dishwashers and the second one for a CHP as they are modeled in Sect. 2. For appliances with a *tDoF*, the length of the encoded bit string can be formulated as follows:

$$\text{bit string for } tDoF: \quad k \quad \text{bits with} \quad k = \lceil \log_2(tDoF) \rceil$$

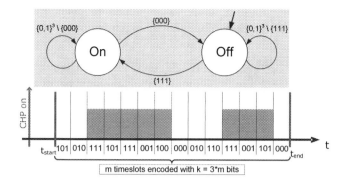

Fig. 3. Exemplary binary encoding of a CHP and its automaton

Taking into account an *eDoF*, supplementary m bits are required:

$$\text{bit string for } eDoF: \quad m \quad \text{bits with} \quad m = count(\text{alternative profiles})$$

$$\text{bit string for } tDoF \text{ and } eDoF: \quad n \quad \text{bits with} \quad n = k + m$$

This bit string of length n will now be communicated to the global O/C-unit in addition to the current expected load profile for the function *evaluate()*. In contrast to the appliances, a CHP usually runs discontinuously, because it sometimes produces more thermal energy and sometimes more electricity than necessary. Fig. 3 shows an exemplary approach for encoding the bit string in order to integrate the CHP into the global optimization using a PP. A finite optimization horizon between t_{start} and t_{end} is given. This interval is segmented into time periods where every time period is encoded with 3 bits, showing a stable behavior in simulations. Regarding the automaton in Fig. 3 the CHP starts running *(On)* if the bits are equal to 111. Otherwise it stays in the state *Off* and vice versa for the other state. Due to this a smoother behavior of the CHP can be reached. The electric generation, the thermal model of the CHP, and the warm water as well as the heating demand have to be integrated into the PP to realize the *evaluate()* function.

5   Simulation and Results

Initially, a set of simulation runs has been executed in order to calibrate the parameters of the EA. Fig. 4 depicts the outcomes for different mutation and crossover probabilities. Fig. 4(a) shows the results of 10 generations with 100 individuals (1000 evaluations), whereas Fig. 4(b) shows those of 20 generations with 100 individuals (2000 evaluations). Increasing the number of generations improves the simulation results significantly. The best results are obtained by a mutation probability of 0.05 and a crossover probability of 0.6. The actual simulation results are based upon more than 200 simulation runs, each simulating a household consisting of five appliances and a CHP for one year with a different

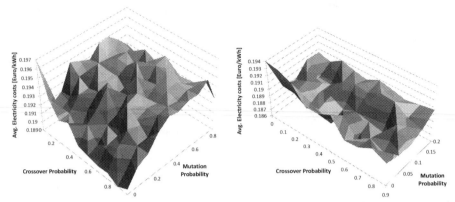

(a) Avg. electricity costs (1000 evaluations) (b) Avg. electricity costs (2000 evaluations)

Fig. 4. Variation of mutation and crossover probabilities (full opt.)

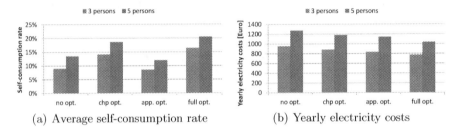

(a) Average self-consumption rate　　　　(b) Yearly electricity costs

Fig. 5. Simulation results of different setups

set of parameters. The starting times of five simulated appliances have been generated based on typical usage hours. The temporal degree of freedom varies from 0 seconds for hob and oven to up to several hours for dishwasher, washing machine and dryer. The variable electricity tariff has been generated based on a standard load profile and ranges from 0.12 to 0.44 Euro with a mean value of 0.28 Euro per kWh. The feed-in tariff for the CHP of 0.05 Euro per kWh is slightly lower than the current tariff in Germany, in order to avoid unnecessary operation times of the CHP. The load limitation has been set to 3 kW and the penalty factors pf_u and pf_l are set to a value of 1, which doubles the costs for loads that are exceeding the load limitation. In this setup, the EA uses binary tournament selection, single-point-crossover with two offspring and bit-flip-mutation using an elitist (μ,λ)-strategy with a rank based survivor selection.

　　Simulation results show that the optimization of the CHP and the appliances is able to decrease the average expenses for electricity by up to 18 % (see Fig. 5(b)) without increasing the costs for natural gas. The self-consumption rate is increased from 9 to 17 % for a household size of 3 persons and from 13 to 20 % for a household size of 5 persons (see Fig. 5(a)). This demonstrates the

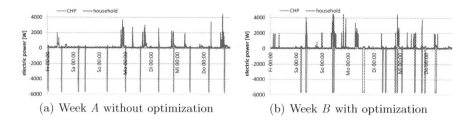

(a) Week A without optimization   (b) Week B with optimization

Fig. 6. Real world results during a trial phase in the ESHL

ability of the optimization in reducing energy costs as well as the successful abstraction of the optimization problem presented in this paper. Non-optimized results (*non-opt.*) have been obtained by starting all appliances immediately, disregarding their potential *DoFs*, and controlling the CHP only according to the temperature thresholds of the thermal storage. Nevertheless, the simulations also show that the improvements of both energy expenses and self-consumption rate are only possible if CHP and appliances are optimized together (*full opt.*). Optimizing the CHP alone (*chp opt.*) does increase the self-consumption rate, though reducing the costs only slightly. The optimization of the appliances (*app. opt.*) leads to a greater decrease of electricity costs. However, it slightly decreases the self-consumption rate (see Fig. 5).

A similar setup using the calibrated parameters mentioned above has been evaluated in a trial phase with probands in the ESHL in 2013. The comparison of a week with and a week without optimization (see Fig. 6) visualizes the synchronization of the CHP and the load of the household. Hereby, the optimization was able to reduce the electricity costs by 23 %.

6   Conclusions and Outlook

In this paper we presented an approach to a "plug-and-play" energy management for Smart Buildings, which can be used for simulations as well as for real-world applications. Optimization problems of the devices are abstracted into sub-problems, which are solved by an EA with respect to variable tariffs, load limitation signals and constraints of appliances and the CHP. The simulation results show that expenses for electricity in this setup could be reduced by up to 18 % using the *tDof* of the appliances and the flexibility of the CHP. Additionally, the simulations show that optimizing either CHP or appliances alone is not sufficient, while the combined optimization of both increases the self-consumption rate and decreases energy costs significantly. This way we were able to show the capabilities of the sub-problem based optimization in energy management. The results of the simulation have been verified using a real-world scenario with test persons. A systematic variation of parameters for the EA shows that the numbers of generations and individuals as well as the mutation and crossover probabilities have to be carefully adjusted in order to obtain good results. This indicates the potential for introducing a meta-evolution which may automatically adjust the parameters for different setups, e.g., varying household sizes, building types, or combinations of devices. In extension of the setup in this paper, further devices can easily be integrated into the optimization. This includes interruptible appliances, hybrid appliances, PV systems with battery storage, electrical cars, heat pumps, chillers and water heaters.

References

1. Abras, S., Ploix, S., Pesty, S., Jacomino, M.: A multi-agent home automation system for power management. In: Cetto, J.A., Ferrier, J.-L., Costa dias Pereira, J.M., Filipe, J. (eds.) Informatics in Control Automation and Robotics, vol. 15. LNEE (LNCS), pp. 59–68. Springer, Heidelberg (2008)
2. Allerding, F., Premm, M., Shukla, P.K., Schmeck, H.: Electrical Load Management in Smart Homes Using Evolutionary Algorithms. In: Hao, J.-K., Middendorf, M. (eds.) EvoCOP 2012. LNCS, vol. 7245, pp. 99–110. Springer, Heidelberg (2012)
3. Allerding, F., Schmeck, H.: Organic smart home: architecture for energy management in intelligent buildings. In: Proceedings of the 2011 Workshop on Organic Computing. ACM (2011)
4. Babu, C., Ashok, S.: Peak load management in electrolytic process industries. IEEE Transactions on Power Systems (2008)
5. Crawley, D.B., Hand, J.W., Kummert, M., Griffith, B.T.: Contrasting the capabilities of building energy performance simulation programs. Building and Environment (2008)
6. Di Giorgio, A., Pimpinella, L.: An event driven smart home controller enabling consumer economic saving and automated demand side management. Applied Energy (2012)
7. Federal Ministry of Economics and Technology (BMWi): Germany's new energy policy - Heading towards 2050 with secure, affordable and environmentally sound energy, Berlin (2012)
8. Ha, D.L., Joumaa, H., Ploix, S., Jacomino, M.: An optimal approach for electrical management problem in dwellings. Energy and Buildings (2012)
9. Mohsenian-Rad, Leon-Garcia, A.: Optimal residential load control with price prediction in real-time electricity pricing environments. Transactions on Smart Grid (2010)
10. Müller-Schloer, C., Schmeck, H., Ungerer, T.: Organic Computing - A Paradigm Shift for Complex Systems. Birkhauser Verlag AG (2011)
11. Sou, K.C., Weimer, J., Sandberg, H., Johansson, K.H.: Scheduling smart home appliances using mixed integer linear programming. In: Decision and Control and European Control Conference (CDC-ECC). IEEE (2011)
12. Zipf, M., Möst, D.: Impacts of volatile and uncertain renewable energy sources on the german electricity system. In: European Energy Market (EEM). IEEE (2013)

Dynamic Programming Based Metaheuristic for Energy Planning Problems

Sophie Jacquin[1,2]([✉]), Laetitia Jourdan[1,2], and El-Ghazali Talbi[1,2]

[1] Inria Lille - Nord Europe, DOLPHIN Project-team, 59650 Villeneuve dAscq, France
sophie.jacquin@inria.fz
[2] Université Lille 1, LIFL, UMR CNRS 8022, 59655 Villeneuve dAscq cedex, France

Abstract. In this article, we propose DYNAMOP (DYNAmic programming using Metaheuristic for Optimization Problems) a new dynamic programming based on genetic algorithm to solve a hydro-scheduling problem. The representation which is based on a path in the graph of states of dynamic programming is adapted to dynamic structure of the problem and it allows to hybridize easily evolutionary algorithms with dynamic programming. DYNAMOP is tested on two case studies of hydro-scheduling problem with different price scenarios. Experiments indicate that the proposed approach performs considerably better than classical genetic algorithms and dynamic programming.

1 Introduction

Energy planing problems such as hydro-scheduling problem (HSP) aims to find a schedule of outflows in a hydro-electric network composed of reservoirs, turbines and pumps that maximizes the profit (or minimizes the cost). Dynamic programming (DP), an algorithm based on the search of the best path on a graph of states [2] can be used to solve hydro-scheduling problems. But in this case, the size of the graph grows quickly with the number of time periods, the number of reservoirs and their capacities. So in practice it is not possible to use it directly. Nevertheless, some adaptations of dynamic programming have been proposed for this kind of problems [3–5], but they are very specific to each problem and only allow to deal with problems of relatively small size. Metaheuristic algorithms, such as genetic algorithms (GA) could be a solution to overcome the aforementioned difficulties. They have been used to solve hydro-scheduling problems [6–10] . However genetic algorithms tend to converge prematurely and the optimization process can be stuck at a local optimum. Besides, genetic algorithms also take a large number of iterations to reach the global optimal solution. In the case of hydro-scheduling problems, the flaws of this method could be partially explained by the dynamic structure of the problem.

An interesting way to solve such problems is to hybridize dynamic programming and metaheuristics. A first attempt was made in [11] where a local search and DP were combined to form Discrete Differential Dynamic Programming (DDDP). The method replaces the small neighborhood of the local search (LS)

© Springer-Verlag Berlin Heidelberg 2014
A.I. Esparcia-Alcázar et al. (Eds.): EvoApplications 2014, LNCS 8602, pp. 165–176, 2014.
DOI: 10.1007/978-3-662-45523-4_14

by a bigger one defined as a restriction of the graph of states around the path defined by the current solution. And then the best neighbor is chosen by using DP in this restricted graph. This method has been generalized to the hybridization of any exact method with LS in [12]. Another hybridization between LS and DP is proposed in [13] and is called dynasearch. The main idea of dynasearch is using traditional definiton of neighborhood while allowing several moves within one iteration. The best sequence of possible moves for one iteration is chosen by using DP. Some hybridizations between DP and GA have also been proposed : the method proposed in [14] can be used for all permutation problems, the hybridization is to use DP in the crossover operator to find the best solution having some common characteristics with the parent solutions. In [15,16] DDDP is applied starting from trial solutions constructed from some solutions given by a GA. These different hybridizations give promising results. However it seems that it has never been tried to use a representation of a sequence of states in a genetic algorithm. In the proposed approach to solve the hydro-scheduling problem, called DYNAMOP for DYNAmic programming using Metaheuristic for Optimizations Problems, a genetic algorithm based on a representation taking into account the dynamic structure of HSP is used. This representation models a solution as a path in the graph of states (the same as in dynamic programming), each gene will then be a state traversed by the path. This representation allows a greater separability of the fitness function in terms of genes. The fitness is the sum of the edge values and a change on a gene only modifies two edges. This could result in a better locality properties in the recombination and mutation of the genotypes. In addition, this partial separability allows to apply an iterative evaluation and and hence to speed up the computation time of the fitness. Another great advantage of this representation is that it allows to build hybridization with DP easily. In the following section, the hydro-scheduling problem is detailed. Then DYNAMOP is introduced and its specificities are explained. Section 4 presents the experimental protocol and the datasets. In section 5 the results are presented and discussed. Finally a conclusion about the potential of this method and perspectives are given.

2   Hydro-Scheduling Problem Description

The objective is to find a scheduling of water outflow in a hydroelectric system that maximizes the benefits. The considered hydroelectric system is here a network of several reservoirs. For each tank, the water outflow is directed to a single other tank passing through one or several turbines. On top of turbines, there is exactly one pipe out of each tank to discharge water without using it. Figure 1 gives two examples of hydroelectric networks.

Thereafter it will be noted $r_{i,t}$ the spilled water of reservoir i at time t without being used and $q_{j,t}$ the water used for the turbine j. Therefore, the scheduling should fix the values of $r_{i,t}$ and $q_{j,t}$. The benefit to maximize is described as follows:

$$profit = \sum_{t=1...T} \sum_{i=1...N} \sum_{j \in T_i} price_{t,j} \times prod_j(q_{j,t}, V_{i,t}),$$

where T denotes the number of hours in the time period, N the number of tanks and T_i the set of turbines that are supplied by tank i, $price_{t,j}$ is the price of the energy producted by turbine j at time t, it could correspond to the spot contract or to a purchasing obligation. The production function $prod_j$ of a turbine j not only depends on the flow $q_{j,t}$ but also on the amount of water on the corresponding tank at time t $V_{i,t}$. This function is very irregular, it is neither linear nor convex regarding to the decision variables. Actually it is described as follows:

$$prod_j(q, V) = \sum_{l \in Int_{V,j}} \sum_{k \in Int_{q,j}} (a_{j,k,l} \times (min(B_{j,k+1}, q) - B_{j,k}) \mathbb{1}_{V \in l} \times \mathbb{1}_{q \geq B_{j,k}}),$$

where

- $Int_{V,j}$ is the set of intervals of definition of the function regarding to V.
- $Int_{q,j}$ is the set of intervals of definition of the function regarding to q.
- $B_{j,k}$ is the lower bound of the kth interval of the production function according to the rate q.
- $a_{j,k,l}$ is a linear coefficient of the production function.

Some constraints have to be respected:

1. Reservoirs storage constraints:

$$V_{min,i,t} \leq V_{i,t} \leq V_{max,i}.$$

The minimum limit is dependent on time as, for example, during drought period of summer it could be necessary to store more water. A natural inflow $NI_{i,t}$ for each reservoir i at each time t is taken into account to compute $V_{i,t}$.

2. Constraints of max and min flow in pipes:

$$r_{min,i} \leq r_{i,t} \leq r_{max,i}.$$

3. For each turbine i a constraint of minimal production:

$$prodMin_i \leq prod_i(q_{i,t}, V_{j,t}),$$

where j corresponds to the supply reservoir of turbine i.

4. Constraint of maximum outflow for each turbine i:

$$q_{i,t} \leq q_{max,i}(V_{j,t}).$$

This maximal limit is depending on the amount of water on the supply tank of turbine i.

5. At the end of the time horizon the amount of water in each reservoir i must be the same than the initial amount:

$$V_{i,T} = Vinit, i.$$

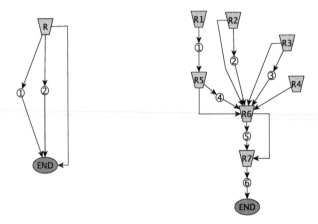

Fig. 1. Hydroelectric network case 1 and 2. Tanks are represented by trapezoids, turbines by circles and pipes by edges.

3   DYNAMOP

The main idea of DYNAMOP is to use a GA to run through the graph of states of DP. Dynamic programming is a method based on Bellman Principle of Optimality [1]. It is used to solve optimization problems by creating a sequence of decisions $(d_i)_{i=1..N}$ such that the choice of d_k can have an impact on the choice of d_p $(p > k)$. Besides, this method can be seen as the search of a shortest path in a graph of states previously constructed (see [2]). Solutions in the proposed genetic algorithm are represented as path of the graph of states. As explained previously this methodology is proposed in order to overcome the difficulties associated with a more classical GA or with the use of a DP. To construct the individuals used in DYNAMOP, the states and the edges have to be specified (see section 3.1). Then some evolutionary operators adapted to this kind of representation are proposed.

3.1   Representation

A solution is represented by the corresponding path in the graph of states. The graph of states is similar to the one used for dynamic programming and that is defined as follow:

- A state S_t is totaly defined by a vector $(q_{S_t,i})_{i=1..N}$ where $q_{S_t,i}$ is the total amount of water having been dispatched from tank i until t. The initial state S^* is defined by the zero vector, and the final state S_T is also fixed since the constraints on final amount on tanks imply:

$$q_{S_T,i} = \sum_{t=1..T} NI_{i,t} + \sum_{j \in \delta_i^+} q_{S_T,j}.$$

where δ_i^+ is the set of tanks flowing into the tank i.

– There is an edge between two states S_t and S_{t+1} iff for all tank i $q_{i,S_t} \leq$ $q_{i,S_{t+1}}$. The edge is evaluated by the value of the best profit that it is possible to obtain passing from S_t to S_{t+1}. If it is not possible to pass from S_t to S_{t+1} without violating constraints on pipes a penalty is added.

In practice a solution will be encoded in form of a table giving for each time t the corresponding vector of outflow $q_{s,t}$ except for the initial state (which is invariant). On top of that the edges values are also stored which will allow to use a delta evaluation. Figure 2 illustrates this representation process for the simple case of one reservoir.

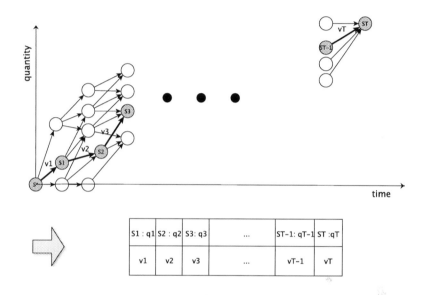

Fig. 2. Representation

Initialization: Initializing of such an individual is made iteratively (regarding to the time period t) by randomly choosing, a feasible state S_t among those for which the edge $S_{t-1} - S_t$ exist.

Fitness Function and Constraint Handling: The fitness function is the sum of the values of edges. Due to the fact that these values are saved, after applying an evolutionary operator, only edges that have been modified by this operator have to be recomputed.

The value of an edge $S_{t-1} - S_t$ is the sum on i of $v_{i,t}$, where $v_{i,t}$ is the best benefits that can be done by discharging the amount of water $qty = q_{i,S_t} - q_{i,S_{t-1}}$ of tank i plus a penalty if the constraints on pipe can not be satisfied. This penalty increases linearly with the error. When it is necessary to solve a dispatch problem between many turbines, $v_{i,t}$ is computed by solving a mixed integer linear program (MILP) with CPLEX.

3.2 Crossover

The idea of the crossover between two paths P_A and P_B is to replace a portion of P_A by a portion of P_B and vice versa. The lenght of the portion is randomly chosen. Let S_{t1}^B and S_{t2}^B the states of start and end of the portion of replacement. The transition from state S_{t1-1}^A to S_{t1}^B or from S_{t2}^B to $S_{t_2+1}^A$ could be impossible. However there always exist some states of P_A from which S_{t1}^B can be joined and states that can be joined from $S_{t_2}^B$. This is because of the uniqueness of the initial and final states. So the transition between P_A and S_{t1}^B will always exist and be constructed by finding the state of P_A the closest of S_{t1-1}^A from which it is possible to join S_{t1}^B and randomly build a path between these two states.

Figure 3 shows the crossover process in the simple case of a single tank. The black path and the white path are recombined to form two offspring. The transition paths are the gray ones.

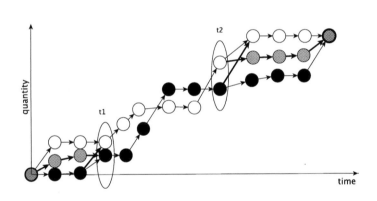

Fig. 3. Crossover process

3.3 Mutations

Two different mutations are designed.

A Switch Mutation: The mutation is to modify one state of the path. The state S_t to modify is selected randomly. The new state S_t' is selected randomly among all states adjacent to S_{t-1} and S_{t+1}. If there exists some states that allow to respect the bound constraints on pipes, one of them is preferred.

A Hybrid Ameliorative Mutation: The main idea is to randomly select two states of the path P separated by L locus and to replace the intermediate states by those of a better path between these two states. This better sub-path is computed in choosing randomly a tank and in computing the better way to use the water used in P for this tank during the L time periods considering that the outflow of other tanks remain unchanged. So, DP is used in a graph of states restricted in length and width. This is similar to the idea of finding the best neighbor in the DDDP [11] where the reduction of the width of the graph is used to define the neighborhood. The step-size used for DP is set in advance.

4   Experimental Protocol

The hydroelectric networks used for the study are those of Figure 1.

4.1   A Basic Genetic Algorithm for Comparison

To be able to compare our algorithm we also propose a genetic algorithm with more classical representation and operators. It will be noted BGA for Basic Genetic Algorithm.

In this version solution is represented as vector of $N \times T$ elements of $[0,1]$. The first T elements give information on the scheduling of the first tank then the following T elements give information on the scheduling of the second tank, etc.. For a tank i each element gives the percentage of the amount of available water that is used on top of the minimum required quantity. This minimum quantity is the quantity that has to be discharged in order to respect the minimum bound on the reservoir content. It allows to obtain a solution that will always respect the bounds constraints on tanks. So, It is a kind of dynamic representation that allows to avoid proposing unrealistic solutions, where more water is discharged than the tank contains. This representation has also been used in [17] for the same kind of problem, except that it has been done with a binary representation.

The evolutionary operators chosen are very classical in GA. The crossover is a 2-points crossover, and the mutation is to randomly choose a gene and to change its value by a quantity randomly chosen in $[0,1]$.

4.2   Cases of Study

The first case study is to find the schedule of outflows in a hydro-electric network composed of a single tank, two turbines and a pipe as shown in Figure 1. Tank capacity is very large and the outflow is not limited on the pipe. Therefore with a discretization step of $20m^3/s$ for the flow rate the number of states in the graph of states for one year horizon is 3×10^6. This number is important as the evaluation of edges (adapted to any number of turbines) is time consuming.

The second case corresponds to the second network presented in Figure 1. In this case the outflows on pipes and turbines have bounds that are depending to the upstream tank content. This restricts the search space but complicates finding feasible solutions. As the size of the graph of states grows exponentially with the number of tanks, even with a large step of discretization this case is not solvable by dynamic programming in a reasonable time (9×10^{11} states in the graph for a coarse discretization).

4.3 Parameter Setting

Proper settings of a GAs parameters are required to achieve the best performance. For this reason, a sensitivity analysis was carried out for each algorithm, to determine the effect of the crossover rate, the mutation rate, the population size and the replacement strategy. Two strategies of replacement are tested. The first one consists of replacing the whole current generation by the offspring and applying weak elitism. The second strategy is to generate N_o offspring and to apply a strong elitism. In this case the number of offspring has also to be set. This analysis is done thanks to Irace [18]. Irace is a package for R (a statistical software) that implements the iterated racing procedure. This procedure is an extension of the Iterated F-race procedure. Its main purpose is to automatically configure optimization algorithms by finding the most appropriate settings given a set of instances of an optimization problem. Here the instances were 10 different price scenarios. For each algorithm and each case the parameters are first set for a period of one day and then the size of the population and of the offspring is reanalyzed for each time period.

5   Results

Each algorithm is tested on the two cases of study on different time horizons. DYNAMOP is also tested without using the hybridization, this version will be denoted DYNAMOP-H. DYNAMOP-H uses the same parameters as DYNAMOP except that the hybrid mutation does not occurred. For each test 10 runs have been made with a maximum time as stopping criteria. The results are presented in Tables 1 and 2. On top of GA, a Mixed Integer Linear Program (MILP) and a DP are also applied in order to have an idea to the optimal solution when it is possible.

For each algorithm the mean of the solution for the 10 runs is given in the line "Mean" the standard deviation between these different solutions is given in the line "std". The line "Best" gives the best result over the 10 runs. The line "Gap" gives a percentage which is : $\frac{Best_{found} - Best_{algo}}{Best_{found}} \times 100$. Where $Best_{found}$ is the best feasible solution found for the problem, and $Best_{algo}$ is the best solution obtained by the algorithm tested. The value of $Best_{found}$ is noted in bold in the table. The line "Computation time" gives the execution time of each methods in seconds. Futhermore, for each simulation, Kruskall Wallis test is applied to the samples obtained on different runs followed by a post hoc test in order to compare the different algorithms.

5.1   First Case: Simple Hydro System

In Table 1, we can notice that if we compare the three genetic algorithms results to dynamic programming results the performance are quite different. For 720h horizon of planification, DYNAMOP-H and BGA have quite similar results and their gap with the DP solution is more than 16%. Whereas DYNAMOP is not far from the DP solution (only 1.7% of difference in a time twice shorter). In this case, the hybridization improves the results a lot although the time used by the algorithm is the half of that is used by DP. A Kruskal Wallis test applied to the samples obtained on different runs followed by a post hoc test allows to confirm the superiority of DYNAMOP on the two other algorithms with a risk of 0.01%.

For 8760h horizon of planification, we can observe a real gap between all the genetic algorithms. The representation used in both version of DYNAMOP and DYNAMOP-H allows to have a gap of 32.34% whereas BGA is at 54.24%. With an hybridization with DP, the performance of the algorithm is really improved and DYNAMOP is near the optimal solution found by DP. The gap is then only at 3.27% with a computation time that is 4 times less than DP. The significance of the results is again confirmed by the statistical tests with a risk of 0.01 %. The results are promising for the simple hydro system. In next section, we test DYNAMOP with a more complex hydraulic system.

Table 1. Results on first case: Simple hydro system. The best solutions found are bolded and used to compute the gaps.

planification horizon		BGA	DYNAMOP	DYNAMOP-H	DP
720h	Mean $(\times 10^6)$	2.3524	2.9391	2.3548	**3.0999**
	std $(\times 10^6)$	0.1540	0.0651	0.1866	
	Best $(\times 10^6)$	2.5949	3.0473	2.6007	
	Gap	16.29 %	1.7%	16.11 %	0 %
	Time (s)		2420		5030
8760h	Mean $(\times 10^7)$	1.4549	3.0620	2.1428	**3.2209**
	std $(\times 10^7)$	0.0123	0.0410	0.031	
	Best $(\times 10^7)$	1.4740	3.1156	2.1793	
	Gap	54.24 %	3.27 %	32.34 %	0%
	Time (s)		20000		79376.82

5.2   Second Case: Multi-reservoirs Hydro System

In this second case, the system has several reservoirs. On top of that it has strict constraints on minimum and maximum rates on pipes and turbines that make it difficult to find a feasible solution. In Table 2, different simulations are presented with a different planning horizon (24h, 720h and 8760h). The solutions given in the last column of this table are obtained by solving a MILP with the software CPLEX. For the 24 h period, this solution is the optimal one. For the period of

720 h this solution is not the optimal one, because the program is stopped before reaching the optimal solution due to a lack of memory. So it is the best feasible solution found before the program has to stop. For the period of one year the data size is too big to obtain any result with DP or with CPLEX (denoted NA in the table).

As before, all the evolutionary algorithms have the same amount of time to solve the problem.

We can first remark that in some case, the classical genetic algorithm (BGA) is not able to find a feasible solution and so gives negative result. In this specific case, the proposed representation allows to find easily feasible solutions.

Table 2. Results on second case: Multi-reservoirs hydro system. The best solutions found are bolded and used to compute the gaps.

planification horizon		BGA	DYNAMOP	DYNAMOP-H	MILP
24h	Mean ($\times 10^4$)	-5.6342	4.3049	4.2850	**4.4786**
	std	417.2407	272.035	257.921	
	Best ($\times 10^4$)	-5.5642	*4.3524*	4.3132	
	Gap	-	2.8 %	3.69%	0 %
	Time (s)		1650		3030.129
720h	Mean ($\times 10^6$)	2.1507	2.5848	2.5785	0.0553
	std	65054.11	7671.21	10662.3	
	Best ($\times 10^6$)	2.2474	**2.5956**	2.5912	
	Gap	13%	0%	0.17%	97%
	Time (s)		20000		345656.23
8760h	Mean ($\times 10^7$)	1.6683	2.6022	2.5565	NA
	std	292521.6	1849345 0	1319762	
	Best ($\times 10^7$)	1.7010	**2.8071**	2.7133	
	Gap	39.4%	0%	3.34%	
	Time (s)		40000		-

For a 24h planification horizon a test of Kruskal Wallis allows to say that there is a significant difference between the 3 algorithms with a risk of 0.01%. Then the test post hoc shows that the difference is significant with a risk of 0.01% between BGA and DYNAMOP in the hybrid and non hybrid version, whereas there is no significant difference between DYNAMOP and DYNAMOP-H. This is consistent with the numerical results that show that DYNAMOP outperformed BGA with or without hybridization. Actually, the gap with the optimal solution is less than 3% for DYNAMOP whereas BGA cannot find any feasible solution.

Similarly for a 720h horizon there is a statistical difference between BGA and the two versions of DYNAMOP with and without hybridization but there is no statistical difference between DYNAMOP and DYNAMOP-H. In 17 times less from time that MIP, DYNAMOP allows to obtain a feasible solution that is 47 times better. The difference between the solution given by DYNAMOP and the solution given by BGA is to 13%, so DYNAMOP is highly better than BGA.

For a larger time horizon, 8760h which corresponds to a time horizon of one year, the MILP is not able to find a solution with CPLEX. This is denoted by NA in the table 2. Again DYNAMOP provides the best results. Statistically the difference between DYNAMOP and DYNAMOP-H is not significant, but DYNAMOP and DYNAMOP-H are statistically better than BGA. The difference between the best solution provided by DYNAMOP and the best solution provided by BGA is 39.4%.

In this case of study the impact of the hybridization is not substantial, actually it is not surprising because it could modify only the schedule of one of the 7 tanks.

6   Conclusion

In this paper we have presented DYNAMOP, an original approach using evolutionary algorithms to guide dynamic programming. This approach has many advantages and allows to overcome the drawbacks of DP and classical GA. Firstly, due to the use of a path representation of a solution, the hybridization with dynamic programming is easy to realize and allows to significantly improve the obtained results. This hybrid approach shows its efficiency and effectiveness in solving real instances associated to the problem. However, even without hybridization, the representation itself is advantageous, indeed DYNAMOP-H outperformed BGA when the size of the problem becomes bigger. This could be due to the fact that the better separability of the fitness function regarding to the genes leads to a better logic in the recombination of individuals. This greater separability also allows to apply an incremental evaluation, only the values of the modified edges have to be recomputed after applying an evolutionary operator. This allows to speed up the fitness computation and then allows obtaining more generation than with a classical genetic algorithm (BGA) in the same time.

Such an algorithm offers great potential to solve a large set of other combinatorial problems. Actually this methodology could be generalized to any problem which holds the Bellman property. It involves many different cases of applications, such as graph routing problems, sequencing problems, selection problems, partitioning problems, distribution problems, production or inventory problems or string processing problems. Therefore, we believe that extending DYNAMOP methodology to solve problems with dynamic structure could be a new and interesting line of research.

References

1. Bellman, R.E.: Dynamic Programming. Princeton University Press (1957)
2. Lew, A., Mauch, H.: Dynamic Programming. Springer (2006)
3. Wall, A.: Hall and Buras. The dynamic programming approach to water resources development. Journal of Geophysical Research **66**, 517–520 (1961)

4. Ferrero, R.W., Rivera, J.F., Shahidehpour, S.M.: A dynamic programming two-stage algorithm for long-term hydrothermal scheduling of multireservoir systems. IEEE Transaction on Power System **13**(4), 1534–1540 (1998)
5. Yakowitz, S.: Dynamic programming applications in water resources. Water Resources Research **18**, 673–696 (1983)
6. Wardlaw, R., Sharif, M.: Evaluation of genetic algorithms for optimal reservoir system operation. Journal of Water Resources Planning and Management **125**, 25–33 (1999)
7. Wardlaw, R., Sharif, M.: Multireservoir systems optimization using genetic algorithms: Case study. Journal of Computing in Civil Engineering **14**, 255–263 (2000)
8. Kumar, S., Naresh, R.: Efficient real coded genetic algorithm to solve the non-convex hydrothermal scheduling problem. International Journal of Electrical Power & Energy Systems **29**, 738–747 (2007)
9. Orero, S.O., Irving, M.R.: A genetic algorithm modelling framework and solution technique for short term optimal hydrothermal scheduling. IEEE Transactions on Power Systems **13**, 501–518 (1998)
10. Zoumas, C.E., Bakirtzis, A.G., Theocharis, J.B., Petridis, V.: A genetic algorithm solution approach to the hydrothermal coordination problem. IEEE Transactions on Power Systems **19**, 1356–1364 (2004)
11. Heidari, M., Te Chow, V., Kokotovifa, P.V., Meredith, D.D.: Discrete differential dynamic programing approach to water resources systems optimization. Water Resources Research **7**(2), 273–282 (1971)
12. Sniedoviech, M., Voss, S.: The corridor method: a dynamic programming inspired metaheuristic. Control and Cybernetics **35**, 551–578 (2006)
13. Congram, R.K., Potts, C.N.: An iterated dynasearch algorithm for the single-machine total weighted tardiness scheduling problem. INFORMS Journal on Computing **14**, 52–67 (1998)
14. Yagiura, M., Ibaraki, T.: The use of dynamic programming in genetic algorithms for permutation problems. European Journal of Operational Research **92**, 387–401 (1996)
15. Park, Y.M., Park, J.B., Won, J.R.: A hybrid genetic algorithm/ dynamic programming approach to optimal long-term generation expansion planning. Elservier Science **20**, 295–303 (1998)
16. Tospornsampan, J., Kita, I., Ishii, M., Kitamura, Y.: Optimization of a multiple reservoir system operation using a combination of genetic algorithm and discrete differential dynamic programming: a case study in mae klong system, thailand. Paddy and Water Environment **3**(1), 29–38 (2005)
17. Miranda, V., Srinivasan, D., Proena, L.M.: Evolutionary computation in power systems. Elservier Science **20**, 89–98 (1998)
18. Lpez-Ibez, M., Dubois-Lacoste, J., Sttzle, T., Birattari, M.: The irace package, iterated race for automatic algorithm configuration. Technical report, IRIDIA (2011)

Looking for Alternatives: Optimization of Energy Supply Systems without Superstructure

Mike Preuss[1][✉], Philip Voll[2], André Bardow[2], and Günter Rudolph[3]

[1] Chair of Information Systems and Statistics, ERCIS, WWU Münster,
Münster, Germany
mike.preuss@uni-muenster.de
[2] Institute of Technical Thermodynamics, RWTH Aachen University,
Schinkelstr. 8, 52062 Aachen, Germany
{philip.voll,andre.bardow}@ltt.rwth-aachen.de
[3] Computational Intelligence Group, TU Dortmund, Dortmund, Germany
guenter.rudolph@tu-dortmund.de

Abstract. We investigate different *evolutionary algorithm* (EA) variants for structural optimization of energy supply systems and compare them with a deterministic optimization approach. The evolutionary algorithms enable structural optimization avoiding to use an underlying superstructure model. As result of the optimization, we are interested in multiple good alternative designs, instead of the one single best solution only. This problem has three levels: On the top level, we need to fix a structure; based on that structure, we then have to select facility sizes; finally, given the structure and equipment sizing, on the bottom level, the equipment operation has to be specified to satisfy given energy demands. In the presented optimization approach, these three levels are addressed simultaneously. We compare EAs acting on the top level (the lower levels are treated by a *mixed-integer linear programming* (MILP) solver) against an MILP-only-approach and are highly interested in the ability of both methods to deliver multiple different solutions and the time required for performing this task.

Neither state-of-the-art EA for numerical optimization nor standard measures or visualizations are applicable to the problem. This lack of experience makes it difficult to understand why different EA variants perform as they do (e.g., for stating *how* different two structures are), we introduce a distance concept for structures. We therefore introduce a short code, and, based on this short code, a distance measure that is employed for a *multidimensional scaling* (MDS) based visualization. This is meant as first step towards a better understanding of the problem landscape. The algorithm comparison shows that deterministic optimization has advantages if we need to find the global optimum. In contrast, the presented EA variants reliably find multiple solutions very quickly if the required solution accuracy is relaxed. Furthermore, the proposed distance measure enables visualization revealing interesting problem properties.

© Springer-Verlag Berlin Heidelberg 2014
A.I. Esparcia-Alcázar et al. (Eds.): EvoApplications 2014, LNCS 8602, pp. 177–188, 2014.
DOI: 10.1007/978-3-662-45523-4_15

1   Introduction

We address the problem of synthesizing energy supply systems with regard to time-dependent heating and cooling demands. This problem can be treated on several different scales from a single building to urban systems. In the present study, we focus on medium-scale problems, e.g., an industrial site or a university campus comprising of several, but not very many buildings. In this class of problems, the energy demands are distributed spatially, so that heating and cooling can be supplied in both centralized and distributed fashion. Of course, any mixture between these two extremes may be suitable – as is usually the case.

Energy supply systems incorporate energy conversion plants (e.g., boilers), energy distribution infrastructure (e.g., heating pipelines and power cables), and energy storages. The synthesis of these integrated systems is a complex problem that has to be considered on three levels [2] (Fig. 1): on the top level, the *synthesis* level, the structure or configuration of the energy system is fixed; on the intermediate level, the *design* level, the technical specifications of the employed technical components have to be specified (e.g., nominal capacities and operating limits); finally, on the bottom level, the *operation* level, technical components' operation modes need to be specified for each instant of time. The three decision levels directly influence each other, and thus, for optimal synthesis, all three levels must be considered simultaneously.

For the optimization-based synthesis of energy supply systems, most commonly superstructure-based optimization methods are employed [5].The general superstructure optimization problem for energy supply systems synthesis is given by a mixed-integer nonlinear programming (MINLP) problem:

$$\min_{s,d,o} f(s,d,o), \quad \text{s.t.} \quad h(s,d,o) = 0, \quad g(s,d,o) \leq 0, \quad s \in S, d \in D, o \in O \quad (1)$$

where the values of the decision variable vectors s, d, and o must be determined to minimize the objective function f. The decision variables are part of the continuous and/or integer variables space S, D, and O, which represent the synthesis (i.e., (non-)existence of a unit), design (i.e., unit sizing, etc.), and

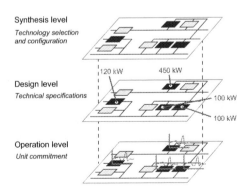

Fig. 1. Hierarchically-structured problem of energy systems synthesis on three levels

operation (i.e., flow rates, on/off-status of a unit, etc.) decision variable spaces, respectively.

It is crucial to understand that the designer has to decide *a priori* which alternatives should be included in the superstructure: On the one hand, the designer thereby runs the risk to exclude the optimal solution from consideration; on the other hand, to circumvent this problem, excessively large superstructures can be employed, which however lead to prohibitive computational effort for the solution of the optimization problem [4].

To avoid these issues, recently two methods have been proposed for the automated optimization-based synthesis of energy supply systems; an automated superstructure-based synthesis methodology [8] and an automated superstructure-free synthesis methodology [7]:

a) The superstructure-based synthesis methodology employs algorithms for automated superstructure generation and deterministic optimization. To find the optimal solution of a synthesis problem, this methodology performs successive superstructure expansion and optimization to continuously increase the number of units embedded in the superstructure until the final superstructure incorporating the optimal solution is found.

b) The superstructure-free methodology simultaneously generates and optimizes candidate solutions in search for the optimal solution. The methodology is based on a knowledge-integrated evolutionary algorithm that applies a handful of generic replacement rules for the evolution of solution structures.

In this work, linearized MILP formulation is employed for synthesis of energy supply systems [7]. For reasonably small test cases, synthesis problems can then be solved exactly in seconds or minutes, but for large-scale problems, the solution can take up to hours. However, if the structure is fixed – as is the case for the candidate solutions arising in the superstructure-free approach – the underlying design and operation problems can usually be solved as an MILP in a matter of seconds. In case of the superstructure-free approach, the problem is not solved exactly, however, it might be faster to find a very good solution heuristically than to wait for the optimum generated through deterministic search. But the main asset of the metaheuristic search is that we obtain several good solutions in one run. This is a major benefit for real-world planning problems because a single solution has only limited significance, , and thus decision makers usually prefer to obtain several promising alternatives that can be further evaluated with regard to further constraints arising in practice (e.g., changing constraints such as energy tariffs and energy demands).

The main task of this work is to investigate under which conditions a metaheuristic has advantages when compared to exact optimization algorithms for the type of structural problems we are dealing with, especially if several alternative solutions are desired. Therefore, first, the test case is described in detail in §2. We will experimentally compare an exact solution and the metaheuristic optimization in §6. However, we start with describing the superstructure-free synthesis methodology in §3. In order to quickly recognize the produced structures and be able to compute a distance between possible alternatives, we define a shortcode, and based on that, a distance measure between structures in §4. Being equipped with a distance matrix, we can establish a *multidimensional scaling* (MDS) based visualization of our non-numerical search space in order to get a first idea of difficulties this problem contains and use this in order to select suitable optimization techniques. In §5, the different employed EA approaches are introduced and the different ways to solve an MILP by means of a solver alone (based on an successively extended superstructure) or in combination with an EA are explained.

2   Test Case

The test case represents a real-world problem from the pharmaceutical industry. The test case has already been analyzed in detail in [7]. The analyzed site consists of six building complexes housing offices, production and research facilities (Fig. 2). A public road separates the considered site into main site (A) and secondary site (B). On site A, all building complexes are connected by a central heating and cooling network. In the base case, site B is not connected to the cooling network, but only to the heating network. The connection of site B to the cooling network on site A is not allowed due the public road. Both sites are connected to the regional natural gas grid (gas tariff: 6 ct/kWh) and the regional electricity grid (electricity tariff: 16 ct/kWh; feed-in tariff: 10 ct/kWh). Electricity generated by the combined heat and power (CHP) engines can be used on-site to meet electricity demands or to run compression chillers, or else it can be fed to the regional electricity grid. All heat generators have to be installed on site A.

The described site has time-varying demands for heating, cooling, and electricity. modeled by monthly-averaged demand time series. The annual demands for electricity, heating, and cooling amount to 47.7 GWh, 28.1 GWh, and 27.3 GWh, respectively. The demand profiles are symmetric around the summer months July

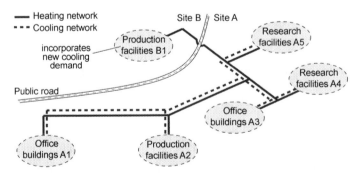

Fig. 2. Schematic plant layout of the considered site. On site A (main site), a central heating and cooling network connects five building complexes. The building complex on site B (secondary site) is only connected to the central heating network. Establishing new connections between both sites is impossible due to a separating public road. [7]

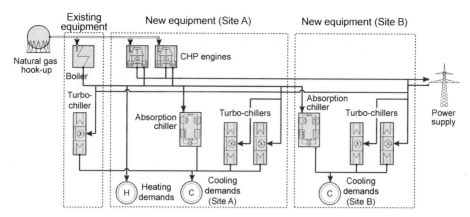

Fig. 3. Optimal flowsheet of the real-world synthesis problem. For simplicity, the electricity demand is not shown in the figure. [7]

and August. Thus, they are further simplified by aggregation to only six time steps.In addition, the minimum and maximum demands are taken into account. These demands occur only during few hours per year, however, it is important to incorporate them in the demand profiles to guarantee adequate equipment sizing. In total, the energy demands are modeled by eight time steps including the peak-load time steps.

The existing supply system consists of three boilers, one CHP engine, and three compression chillers. However, one boiler and one compression chiller cannot be further operated, and thus require substitution. Next to the given component types, we will also consider absorption coolers.

The optimal solution installs existing as well as new equipment. The optimal net present value adds up to $-46.99 \cdot 10^6$ EUR (Table 1) improving the base case by 39 %.

Table 1. Economic parameters of base case and NPV-optimal solution [7]

solution	NPV / 10^6 EUR	investments / 10^6 EUR	energy cost / 10^6 EUR p.a.	maintenance cost / 10^6 EUR p.a.
base case solution	−76.36	0	11.27	0.11
NPV-optimal solution	−46.99	2.35	6.44	0.22

3   Superstructure-Free Synthesis Methodology

The superstructure-free synthesis methodology proposed by [8] employs a hybrid optimization algorithm combining metaheuristic with deterministic optimization [6]. Metaheuristic optimization is realized by an evolutionary algorithm employing a mutation operator that randomly replaces substructure from a candidate solution by alternative structures. This approach allows for simultaneous alternatives generation (on the synthesis level) and optimization (on the design and operation levels). The mutation operated is based upon a hierarchically-structured graph, the so-called *energy conversion hierarchy* (ECH) that classi-fies the considered energy conversion units according to their functions. This enables an efficient definition of all reasonable connections between the regarded technologies. Thus, a minimal set of generic replacement rules is then sufficient to employ structural mutation for the generation of any solution structure. For more details on this concept, the reader is kindly referred to [8].

The general mathematical programming problem for single-objective opti-mization based synthesis of energy supply systems is given by (1). Here, the decision variable vectors s, d, and o are part of the continuous and/or integer variable spaces S, D, and O, which represent the synthesis, design, and opera-tion decision variable spaces, respectively. The three synthesis levels feature an inherent hierarchical structure, and thus the mathematical programming formu-lation can be decomposed into an upper level dealing with the synthesis, and a lower level dealing with the design and operation. Thus, the mathematical programming formulation can be reformulated as

$$\min_{s} \ \hat{f}(s), \quad \text{s.t.} \ \min_{d, o} \ f^{(s)}(d, o).$$

Instead of explicitly modeling structural decisions in a superstructure, the presented mutation operator is embedded in an evolutionary algorithm that con-tinuously evolves new configuration alternatives to perform optimization on the synthesis level. For equipment sizing and operation, rigorous MILP optimization is used as local refinement strategy; i.e., for each configuration alternative gener-ated by mutation, an MILP problem is solved to identify the optimal equipment sizing and operation that maximizes the net present value. With net present value $C_{t_{\mathrm{CF}}}$ as objective function, the problem formulation of the hybrid opti-mization is given by

$$\max_{\sigma} \ \hat{C}_{t_{\mathrm{CF}}}(\sigma), \qquad \sigma \in \Sigma, \quad \text{s.t.} \ \max_{d, o} \ C_{t_{\mathrm{CF}}}^{(\sigma)}(d, o), \tag{2}$$

where σ represents a structure evolved by mutation, and Σ represents the set of all possible structures.

In this paper, the hybrid optimization is based on the MILP formulation presented by [7]. However, it should be noted again that the generic component-based modeling enables to use any other programming formulation as well.

4 Shortcode and Distance Measure

To simplify recognition of structures contained in actually evaluated solutions, a shortcode is defined that provides the types and numbers of the employed energy conversion plants. Note that the topology is omitted from this notation, so that it is possible that two solutions appear to be identical but have different topolo-gies and thus different target values. The four different technology types boiler, absorption chiller, compression chiller, and combined heat and power (CHP) engine are matched to the tokens Bo, AC, CC, and CE, followed by the number of plants per type encoded in a structure. As an example, Bo1CC1 represents a structure that embeds one boiler and one compression chiller.

On base of this short code, we define a distance function over the different structures to obtain a numerical value. The function is given in (3) and resembles the euclidean distance with each of the four types (in alphabetical order, AC=1, Bo=2, CC=3, and CE=4), with N_{i1} and N_{i2} denoting the two structures. Two structures that embed a certain type of technology or not are considered more diverse than two structures that incorporate the same types of technologies but in different numbers. Thus, the second term in (3) with the signum function makes sure that the distance of two structures containing 0 and 1 units of a specific technology type are considered larger than for 1 and 2 or higher unit numbers.

$$dist_1(N_1, N_2) = \sqrt{\sum_{i=1}^{4}(|N_{i1} - N_{i2}| + \operatorname{sgn}(|N_{i1} - N_{i2}|))^2} \qquad (3)$$

For so-called retrofit optimization, where a number of plants is already installed, it is necessary to add means that reveal if a plant is new or retained from the base case. We express the difference in the shortcode by writing existing plants with small letters, such that AC1ac1bo2 denotes one new and one existing absorption chiller and two boilers. The distance function is adjusted appropriately in (4) with the introduction of n_1 und n_2 for the existing plants. The correction factor r (set to 2) in the last term connects old and new plants of the same types by adding the sum of these as additional 'dimension'.

$$dist_2(N_1, N_2, n_1, n_2) := \left(\sum_{i=1}^{4}(|N_{i1} - N_{i2}| + \operatorname{sgn}(|N_{i1} - N_{i2}|))^2 \right.$$
$$\left. +(|n_{i1} - n_{i2}| + \operatorname{sgn}(|n_{i1} - n_{i2}|))^2 + r(|N_{i1} + n_{i1} - N_{i2} - n_{i2}|)^2 \right)^{1/2} \qquad (4)$$

We obtain figure 4 by computing a distance matrix from 100 randomly chosen solutions by means of $dist_2$ and then using multidimensional scaling (MDS) as dimension reduction technique in order to map it into a 2-dimensional space. The best solutions are found in the middle, on the border to several invalid regions. Note that invalid solutions have the same objective function values, and thus evalution of these solutions provides no information for the optimization method on the search direction to reach an area of valid solutions. However, the chosen distance function appears to be meaningful because the resulting topology looks intuitive (as expected, similar structures are mapped to the same region of the target area).

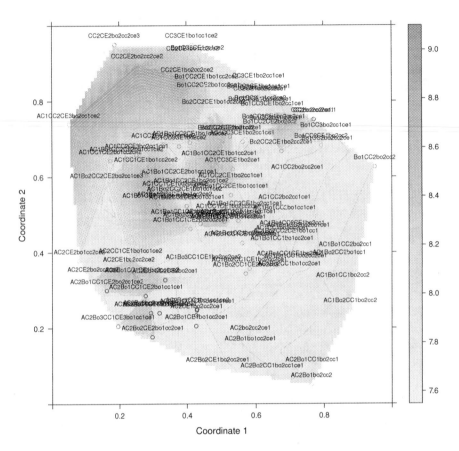

Fig. 4. Multidimensional scaling (MDS) based visualizaton of a random sample of size 100. The contour reveals the (log10 transformed) objective function values (NPV) of the different solutions, with invalid ones having a cost of $\text{\euro}10^9$.

5   MILP Solving and Evolutionary Approaches

As explained in §2, we are dealing with a 3-level hierarchical problem that may be approached in two very different ways: 1) by means of an MILP solver that solves a series of successively extended superstructure-based optimization problems (in the following referred to as the *purely MILP-based approach*) to return the exact global optimum (in case it can be solved) – however, depending on the problem size at considerably computational cost, i.e. long solution times; and 2), by means of a superstructure-free EA (in the following referred to as the *mixed approach*) that works on the top synthesis level of the optimization problem and uses an MILP solver to determine the solutions for the underlying design and operation levels. In both cases, the necessary computing times are usually much smaller for infeasible solutions, however, the computing times for feasible solutions can vary significantly due to the different complexities of the underlying design and operation problems. From sensitivity analyses concerning result stability under shifts in demand data (introducing new time steps or changing values of existing time steps), we know that the optimal solution can easily vary by up to 2%. For this reason, we do not necessarily have to find the global optimal solution, but we strive for solutions with at most 1% deviation from the global optimum. In case of the combined approach, the same accuracy is required for the lower level MILP optimization.

As MILP solver, we employ SCIP [1], version 3.0.0, one of the fastest available non-commercial solvers. Note that exchanging the solver with a quicker commercial solver will reduce computing times for both approaches approximately by a factor of 10, according to our tests.

In our first tests with the mixed approach, we found that a lot of precious running time is lost by re-evaluating already considered solutions. Therefore, a tabu search-like [3] list of forbidden structures is implemented for all metaheuristics to follow. During the algorithm run, we keep track of the shortcodes for evaluated solutions. New solution candidates are produced by applying the mutation operator described in §3. However, they are only evaluated if they are either not yet contained in the list, or if 10^3 successive attempts fail to obtain an untested structure. Note that the topologies of solution candidates are not regarded, and multiple topologies may map to the same shortcode. It thus makes sense to allow the evaluation of a candidate with an already recorded shortcode as it may have a different topology. However, at least at the beginning of a run, this rarely happens because many different plant combinations are available.

In order to roughly estimate the size of the set of different structures (neglecting differences in the topology), we first consider the choice of already existing plants. We can choose any combination of 0 to 2 boilers, one or none CHP engine, and 0 to 2 absorption chillers, leading to $3 \cdot 2 \cdot 3 = 18$ possibilities. Let us assume that for each of these, we can add up to 10 new plants of $4 + 1$ types (AC, Bo, CC, CE, and *none*). Drawing 10 times from this set with replacement and without considering order results in $\frac{(n+k-1)!}{(n-1)!k!} = \frac{(5+10-1)!}{(5-1)!10!} = 1001$ possibilities for the added plants. This results in $18 \cdot 1001 - 1 = 18017$ type combinations without taking the topology into account. However, this is only a rough estimate because we allowed for a greater number of new plants, but this was only rarely realized during our relatively short runs as it requires a high number of successive mutations into one direction.

As algorithm types, we consider random search, random walk (implemented as (1,1)-EA), a (10+10)-EA and a (50+10)-EA, each of these utilizing a tabu list as described above. The reasoning behind using a population was to enable more parallelized search. Our EA employs an evolution strategy (ES) type selection, structural mutation as described above in §3, and no recombination.

6   Experimental Comparison

The two goals of the algorithm comparison are to find out, a) which metaheuristic-based approach reliably detects at least one near-optimal solution (objective value

$\leq 1\%$ from global optimum) faster than the integrated MILP-based approach, and b) which of the approaches can be recommended concerning the number of good alternatives it produces quickly.

Pre-experimental planning. During first tests, we found that, in most cases, 30 seconds suffice to solve the design and operation problem for a given structure. Therefore, the maximum time for this solution phase is constrained to 30 seconds. This means that the concerned evaluations return an objective value that is worse than it will be if the underlying optimization problem is solved to global optimality. On the other hand, we save precious time as the overall run length should be less than one day (24 h).

An additional test with a (1+1)-EA revealed that it usually gets stuck very early, and thus is mostly not able to reach the desired objective function value level. This may be surprising because the (1+1)-EA was allowed to perform restarts. However, it can be explained with the relatively short run length that did not enable more than a small number of restarts. This variant is therefore disregarded in the following.

Setup. The purely MILP-based (deterministic) approach is run until the desired accuracy of 1% is reached; the corresponding solution time is recorded. The 4 mixed approaches are run 10 times until 3000 evaluations have been spent. Note that the actual computing time for this is limited by $0.5\,\text{minutes} \cdot 3000 = 1500$ minutes. However, the true computing time varies between runs and usually takes about 60% of this value (the time consumed by the underlying MILP-solving cannot be predicted). The average number of mutations is set to 1.5 for the random walk and population-based EAs.

Task. A mixed approach is considered reliable only if it produces a solution within the 1% bound before reaching the time spent by the purely MILP-based approach in *every* run. We consider one metaheuristic better than another if it consistently provides more satisfactory solutions within a smaller average time.

Results/Visualization. For the given problem, the purely MILP-based approach via SCIP needs 619 minutes to reach the 1% bound. This is depicted as red line in the diagrams for the mixed approaches in fig. 5. Each row of the plot represents one of the 10 runs, and blue dots each stand for one (structurally different) solution with satisfactory quality. The number on the bottom right corner of each plot denotes the average number of satisfactory solutions obtained over the runs, at the top right corner the average time for reaching a satisfactory solution is depicted.

Observations. Random search generates only few satisfactory solutions, whose generation is not even necessarily faster than the solution provided by the purely MILP-based approach. Random walk, (10+10)-EA and (50+10)-EA produce many near-optimal solutions, however on average at proportionally larger computation times. We would like to add that during the runs, technical problems with SCIP were observed because it sometimes (in about 1 of 500 cases) crashed during the design and operation level optimization.

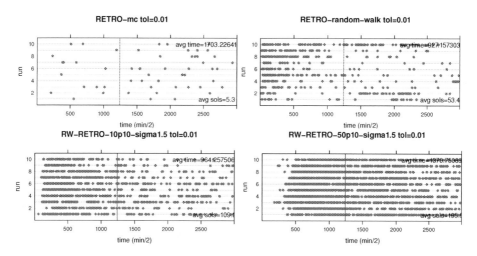

Fig. 5. Performance comparison of different random search and EA variants (all with tabu list), from left to right and top to bottom: random search, random walk, (10+10)-EA and (50+10)-EA. The red line represents the required time of the purely MILP-based approach to reach the desired accuracy. The blue dots each represent one satisfactory solution provided by the mixed approach.

Discussion. From the results we deduce that random search is obviously not the method of choice, as it is unreliable and does not generate many satisfactory solutions. The other three algorithms each have different strenghts: the (tabu list enhanced) random walk provides good solutions very quickly, but obtains much fewer of them if compared to the (10+10)-EA and the (50+10)-EA. With the two criteria given above, it is not possible to take a decision between them, they are uncomparable. If only response time is considered, the (tabu list) random walk appears best, if more solutions are needed, the slightly slower (10+10)-EA is recommended.

7   Conclusions

We compare several EA variants that employ an underlying MILP solver in order to solve a structural optimization problem without using superstructure models to a MILP-only approach that solves a series of successively extended superstructure models. The latter may have an advantage if we need to find the exact global optimum, while some of the proposed tabu-list enhanced EA variants reliably find multiple solutions very quickly if the required accuracy is relaxed a bit. Furthermore, our distance measure enables a visualization that reveals interesting problem properties. This should be helpful for improving the optimization process in the future. Additionally, we need to carefully analyze the distribution of the obtained solutions.

References

1. Achterberg, T.: SCIP: solving constraint integer programs. Mathematical Programming Computation **1**(1), 1–41 (2009)
2. Frangopoulos, C.A., von Spakovsky, M.R., Sciubba, E.: A brief review of methods for the design and synthesis optimization of energy systems. Int. J. Appl. Therm. **5**(4), 151–160 (2002)
3. Glover, F.: Future paths for integer programming and links to artificial intelligence. Comput. Oper. Res. **13**(5), 533–549 (1986)
4. Kallrath, J.: Mixed integer optimization in the chemical process industry: Experience, potential and future perspectives. Chem. Eng. Res. Des. **78**(6), 809–822 (2000)
5. Liu, P., Georgiadis, M.C., Pistikopoulos, E.N.: Advances in energy systems engineering. Ind. Eng. Chem. Res. **50**(9), 4915–4926 (2011)
6. Puchinger, J., Raidl, G.R.: Combining Metaheuristics and Exact Algorithms in Combinatorial Optimization: A Survey and Classification. In: Mira, J., Álvarez, J.R. (eds.) IWINAC 2005. LNCS, vol. 3562, pp. 41–53. Springer, Heidelberg (2005)
7. Voll, P., Klaffke, C., Hennen, M., Bardow, A.: Automated superstructure-based synthesis and optimization of distributed energy supply systems. Energy **50**, 374–388 (2013)
8. Voll, P., Lampe, M., Wrobel, G., Bardow, A.: Superstructure-free synthesis and optimization of distributed industrial energy supply systems. Energy **45**(1), 424–435 (2012)

Multi-material Compositional Pattern-Producing Networks for Form Optimisation

Ralph Evins[1,2]([⊠]), Ravi Vaidyanathan[3], and Stuart Burgess[4]

[1] Empa, Swiss Federal Laboratories for Materials Science and Technology,
Überlandstrasse 129, 8600 Dübendorf, Switzerland
ralph.evins@empa.ch
[2] Chair of Building Physics, Swiss Federal Institute of Technology ETH Zürich,
ETH-Hönggerberg, 8093 Zürich, Switzerland
[3] Imperial College London, South Kensington Campus, London, UK SW7 2AZ
[4] University of Bristol, Tyndall Avenue, Bristol, UK BS8 1TH

Abstract. CPPN-NEAT (Compositional Pattern Producing Networks and NeuroEvolution for Augmented Topologies) is a representation and optimisation approach that can generate and optimise complex forms without any pre-defined structure by using indirect, implicit representations. CPPN is based on an analogy to embryonic development; NEAT is based on an analogy to neural evolution. We present new developments that extend the approach to include multi-material objects, where the material distribution must be optimised in parallel with the form.

Results are given for a simple problem concerning PV panels to validate the method. This approach is applicable to a large number of problems concerning the design of complex forms. There are many such problems in the field of energy saving and generation, particularly those areas concerned with solar gain. This work forms a first step in exploring the potential of this approach.

Keywords: CPPN · NEAT · Form · Multi-material

1 Introduction

1.1 Engineering Form Optimisation

Form is used here to refer to the physical shape of an object, and form optimisation refers to the process of finding optimal or high-performing forms for engineered objects, measured against some metric. Optimisation of form is more challenging than optimising specific design parameters, as form may be represented in many ways, making the design space almost infinite. This paper presents new developments to a systematic way of automatically generating and evolving forms to find areas of optimal performance.

© Springer-Verlag Berlin Heidelberg 2014
A.I. Esparcia-Alcázar et al. (Eds.): EvoApplications 2014, LNCS 8602, pp. 189–200, 2014.
DOI: 10.1007/978-3-662-45523-4_16

1.2   Form Representation

Form representations can be divided into two approaches. Direct representations relate the set of variables being optimised (the genotype) to the associated form (the phenotype) in a way that is constant throughout the optimisation process. Classes and types of form are broadly defined at the beginning of the process through the choice of a particular representation (shapes or mathematical functions) with a fixed number of parameters (also called degrees-of-freedom). The representation used implicitly affects the forms generated: some forms will be completely unobtainable, and others will be complicated to describe and therefore difficult to discover. Direct representations are appropriate for simple optimisations where the design space is limited to an easily-describable set of forms. Imam [4] discussed a variety of direct representation types, including independent nodes, design elements, super curves and superposition of shapes.

Indirect representations, by contrast, use a mapping from genotype to phenotype that changes as part of the form-finding process. Indirect representations have no predefined set of parameters. Instead they generate a means of representing a form in parallel with the parameters that define it. Types of indirect representation include generative (generating functions that map parameters to forms) and ontogenic (based on iterative mapping transformations). For generative representations, Bentley and Kumar [2] used the term embryogeny: the process of growth that defines how a genotype is mapped onto a phenotype. They discuss three types of generative encoding: external (pre-stated, a form of direct representation), explicit (inherent in the data structure, like a list of instructions) and implicit (interactive, dynamic rules that depend on context). Bentley and Kumar found that for the problem they selected, implicit embryogenies performed best.

Another approach to indirect form representation is the related field of topology optimisation. This is concerned with broad classes of shape (e.g. number of sides, number of holes). It uses a discrete selection field over a fixed domain, analogous to the discrete voxels used in this work. An objective function is minimised over this selection field using a variety of methods, for example the Evolutionary Structural Optimisation approach [8] progressively eliminates low-stress material from the structure. The approaches used in topological optimisation are tightly linked to structural engineering issues, and are not easily adaptable to problems in other fields, especially if analytical objective functions are not available (i.e. when using black-box simulations).

The indirect representation used in this work is Compositional Pattern Producing Networks (CPPN) with the optimisation method NeuroEvolution for Augmented Topologies (NEAT), which are explained in detail in the following section. CPPNs were proposed by Stanley [6]; NEAT was originally developed by Stanley and Miikkulainen [7]. This work builds upon that of Clune and Lipson [3], who developed a 3-dimensional formulation of CPPN-NEAT. CPPN-NEAT has been used on few real problems: to interactively generate artwork, as demonstrated in the website picbreeder [5], and to evolve forms for simulated robots [1].

1.3 Application to the Energy Field

It has been established by Clune and Lipson [3] that CPPN-NEAT can generate a diverse range of interesting forms. The methods developed here could be applied to any problem which seeks to optimise abstract forms for objectives evaluated using black-box simulations. There are many such problems in the field of energy research; one particularly relevant area is energy use in buildings, where architectural desires closely interact with engineering requirements.

This paper applied the method developed to a problem concerning a photovoltaic (PV) collector. It is a very simple validation problem, which seeks to establish whether the breadth and diversity of solutions produced by CPPN-NEAT can produce reasonable answers to a specific problem. However, if combined with other constraints, for example the problem of building-integrated PV, this approach could provide a way to find high-performing, highly diverse forms that solve a real design problem.

2 Form Generation Method

2.1 Compositional Pattern Producing Networks (CPPNs)

Compositional Pattern Producing Networks (CPPNs), proposed by Stanley [6], are based upon the biological processes that guide embryonic development: chemical gradients provide information to new cells regarding their position in the overall structure, which influences how they develop. Stanley [6] details the following desirable properties obtainable via such developmental processes: repetition; repetition with variation; symmetry; imperfect symmetry; elaborated regularity; preservation of regularity.

The steps in the CPPN process is given below. The predefined coordinate system is discretised at a chosen resolution over a chosen domain, and the value of a function is calculated for every point x, y, z. The presence or absence of material at a given location is determined by whether the output of that function is above or below a threshold. For an x, y, z coordinate system, the result is a set of voxels (3 dimensional pixels). Further processing may then be conducted to obtain a smooth form from the rectilinear cubic voxels. In this work, an isosurface was generated surrounding the voxel set: each point where a voxel is present has a value of 1, and points where no voxel is present have a value of 0; the isosurface was formed for the value 0.5. The resulting surface consists of triangular planar faces.[1]

---

[1] It is necessary to threshold the output of the CPPN, which is a continuum across the complete x, y, z domain, in order to produce a binary distinction between solid and void. Because the function must be evaluated at discrete points, this results in a set of voxels whose dimensions correspond to the sampling interval. These must then be smoothed using an appropriate method (here the MatLab isosurface algorithm) to obtain planar faces. The impact of threshold value, sampling interval and smoothing process is an interesting topic for future investigation.

- For n points in the discrete domain:
    - Evaluate network using coordinates x, y, z as values of input nodes.
    - If result is greater than threshold, assign solid voxel to set V.
- (Apply smoothing algorithm to set of voxels V to get surface of polygons P.)
- Evaluate objective function $f(V)$ (or $f(P)$).

This process of form generation depends on a functional representation that takes a set of coordinate values as an input, and produces an output that governs the form produced. Neural networks are an ideal means of representing such a function. Each coordinate dimension is an input node to the network, along with a bias node that is set to 1. Each link in the network has a weight by which its value is multiplied. Each intermediate node has a functional transformation associated with it, selected from a set of available functions (linear, sine, cosine, square...). If there are multiple links into a node, their values are summed. The output node of the network then produces the numerical output of the function.

An illustration of the process is given in Figure 1, which extends into 3D the example used by Stanley [6] and Clune and Lipson [3], describing by means of a CPPN an insect body with several bulbous sections. For simplicity, each dimension is used by one function only, and the results are then summed. The square function is used on the dimensions x and z, thus giving a circular cross section when these are summed (since a circle in that plane has an equation of the form $x^2 + z^2 = r^2$). The cosine function is applied to the y dimension, causing periodic repetition along the long axis.

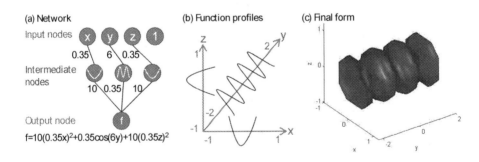

Fig. 1. Example of the CPPN process. (a) Network of nodes, connections, functions and weights. (b) Profiles obtained for each dimension based on the functions used in the network. (c) The final form produced by the network is an isosurface fitted to the set of voxels defined by $f(x, y, z) > threshold$.

2.2 NeuroEvolution of Augmenting Topologies (NEAT)

Since CPPN describes a form by means of a particular network (nodes, connections, functions and weights), in order to evolve object forms, it is necessary to evolve network representations. The method used here is NeuroEvolution for

Augmented Topologies (NEAT), originally developed by Stanley and Miikku-lainen [7] for evolving neural networks but also commonly applied to CPPN problems. The steps are given below

- Initialise network (random connections and weights).
- Assign species (used in selection process).
- Evaluate CPPN (see above).
- For each generation:
    - Check for stagnation or refocus.
    - For each space in new population:
    - Select parents (based on shared fitness of species).
    - Generate new individual by crossover (splice networks) and mutation (Add node, add connection, change function, perturb weight).
    - For each individual in new population:
        - Assign species.
        - Evaluate CPPN.
    - Select individuals to continue.

The method begins with a very simple network (just input nodes, bias node and output node, directly connected) and increases its complexity by adding connections and nodes, mutating connection weights and node function types, and crossing over network segments. The number of input nodes is equal to the number of dimensions of the CPPN. This may be 2D, 3D or include other pos-sibilities like distance from centre. There is only one output node. Recurrence in networks is not used at all in this work (it was found by Clune and Lipson [3] to produce highly fractal forms). The process of crossover is complicated in variable-structure representations: it is necessary to know which segments of two individuals can be interchanged without breaking connectivity or introducing spurious deformity. This is achieved in NEAT by means of historical innovation tracking: each alteration to a network is recorded, and this historical informa-tion allows only correctly-aligned network segments to be exchanged (a process termed artificial synapsis, see [7]). The parameters used are given in Table 1.

2.3   Implementation

The NEAT code used in this work is loosely based on the MatLab implementa-tion by Christian Mayr[2], which was based on the original C++ code of Kenneth Stanley[3]. An improvement here is to construct an explicit function string that is evaluated very easily for each set of inputs. The function string was constructed iteratively by substituting placeholders for upstream nodes, working backwards from the output node.

This approach to form optimisation require a very large number of function evaluations (up to 150,000 evaluations per run). The code was run on the Uni-versity of Bristol Advanced Computing Research Centre machine BlueCrystal.

---

[2] http://nn.cs.utexas.edu/?neatmatlab
[3] http://nn.cs.utexas.edu/?neat_original

Table 1. Parameters used for NEAT algorithm

Maximum generations		10000	[3]		Threshold	10
Population size		15	[3]	Refocus	# generations	100
Selection	Pressure	1.1			Add node	0.25 [3]
	Kill percentage	0.2	[7]		Add connection	0.3 [6]
	Number kill	5	[7]		Change function	0.1
	Number copy	1	[7]		Perturb weight	0.9 [6]
Speciation	Threshold	4			Gene re-enabled	0.25 [6]
	C1	1	[6]	Mutation	Weight cap	-100
	C2	1	[6]		Weight range	-10
	C3	0.4	[6]		Overall	0.75 [6]
	C4	2		Crossover	Interspecies	0.001 [6]
Stagnation	Threshold	10			Multipoint	0.75 [6]
	# generations	15	[7]			

In order to minimize the need for parallel-specific coding, each optimisation run was split across 8 local cores using the Matlab parfor syntax for parallel loops. Separate processors were used for each repeat of a run.

3   Multi-material Formulation

3.1   New Development

The new development presented in this work is the extension of CPPN-NEAT to multi-material forms. Engineered objects usually consist of more than one material, and the interactions between them can have a significant effect on performance. This makes it difficult to determine the optimal placement of each material independently; they must be developed in harmony to take advantage of synergies between them. It is highly desirable that the two materials together should make up the whole form (no holes) and nothing else (no dislocations) so as not to affect the performance of the form-finding process. The CPPN-NEAT method has been extended to allow the evolution of separate material placements in parallel with the overall form-finding process. This has been applied to thin shelled forms, assuming a hollow object consisting of triangular planar panels.

Material placement could be optimised using a lower level optimisation process, i.e. for each proposed form, a second-level optimisation would be performed to determine the optimal placement of the materials. However, this would be computationally much more demanding: if the form optimisation is order O, performing an optimisation of material placement for every evaluated form would be of order O^2. It is much more efficient to optimise both the form and the material division in parallel as part of the same optimisation, this being of order $2O$. This has been achieved by evolving two CPPN representations using a single NEAT loop (separate NEAT processes were used for each CPPN to allow different parameters for each, but both used a common generation iteration). The first network represents the overall form as before; the second network maps the placement of materials onto the form generated by the first network. The second

CPPN is queried only at locations where material is present (as determined by the first CPPN). If the output value from the second CPPN is greater than the threshold it indicates the primary material; if it is less than the threshold it indicates the secondary material. In this way since the network provides a value for all solid locations and no others, holes and dislocations are avoided.

For thin shell objects a mapping has been used that operates on the polygon mesh rather than on the voxel set. This allows the use of local coordinates: the orientation and inclination of each polygon. This permits changes of material between horizontal and vertical, North and South facing and top and bottom sides, independently of position in the overall form. Figure 2(a) shows this mapping: the solid voxels from the form CPPN are used to produce a shell consisting of the set of polygons P, for which the orientation θ and inclination γ values are determined; these are used as the input coordinates to the material CPPN, which provides the primary and secondary material polygons P_1, P_2.

Instead of distinguishing between two discrete material types, some property of the material can be treated as continuously variable. This could correspond to thickness, reinforcement, void ratio, glazing ratio etc. The process for this is very similar to above, but rather than applying a threshold to the output of the material CPPN to give a binary choice, the value is scaled from 0 to 1 to provide the continuous property M for each polygon. This is presented as a second option of the new development (see Figure 2(b)).

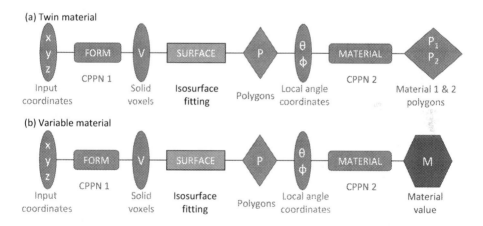

Fig. 2. Process diagrams for using two CPPNs to determine form and material distribution in parallel, for (a) two-material forms and (b) variable-material forms. CPPN 1 produces voxel set V; an isosurface is fitted to V to give polygon set P; CPPN 2 is applied to P to find material division P_1, P_2 or continuous property M.

3.2   Objective Functions

An example problem is used to validate the multi-material formulation in which the second material represents PV panels, and the objective function takes the ratio of energy generated to total cost. Two different options were addressed.

The first option assumed a discrete material distribution, using the formulation in Figure 2(a). A highly simplified calculation is used for the energy generation potential, which was taken as proportional to the total area of PV polygons that are within 55 degrees of South and with an inclination of 0 or greater (i.e. not angled downwards). Cost is taken as the sum of the total area of PV panels multiplied by a price factor (here 10, i.e. the PV panel cost is ten times that of the support), plus the total area of both materials (i.e. the support system). Thus the objective function was:

$$\frac{\sum P_2|_{\theta>125,\,\theta<235,\,\gamma\geq0}}{10\sum P_1 + \sum(P_1 + P_2)} \tag{1}$$

where θ is the angle of orientation of the polygon from north, γ is the angle from horizontal, P_1 is the area of support polygons, and P_2 is the area of PV polygons. For a proper analysis of the energy generated from the PV panels, a more detailed simulation would be necessary. This could be using a table lookup for different angles, if self-shading is ignored, or using a detailed ray tracing simulaton, if self shading is important. Both are beyond the scope of this paper, where the aim is to validate the new material representation with a very simple case.

The second option assumed a variable-material property using the formulation in Figure 2(b), taking the percentage of a polygon surface covered by PV to be a continuous variable. The generation from a polygon was determined by the percentage of PV (the property M) and the cosine of the angle between the polygon normal vector and the optimum alignment vector for the chosen latitude (here taken to be South, 45 degree inclination). Thus the objective function was:

$$\frac{\sum P_2 M \frac{\sqrt{2}}{2}\left(\sin(\theta) - \cos(\gamma)\right)}{10\sum P_1 + \sum(P_1 + P_2)} \tag{2}$$

4   Results

4.1   Two Materials

This case demonstrates two things: that the CPPN-NEAT method can produce forms that respond to the optimisation objective, and that the two-material formulation can also adjust the material distribution in accordance with the objective. Figure 3 shows the final forms from all twenty runs of the two-material case, ordered by fitness value. It is clear that a very wide range of forms can be produced. Nuances of the objective function become apparent, such as the way the isosurface fitting to the voxels affects the range of angles of polygons.

Fitness values ranged from 76.7 to 81.3 with a mean of 79.0 and a standard error of 1.4. The objective can be split into the following components, in rough order of priority: maximise the area of PV panel that is broadly south-facing; minimise the area of PV panel that does not meet the above conditions; minimise the total surface area. There are a number of different approaches evident in the

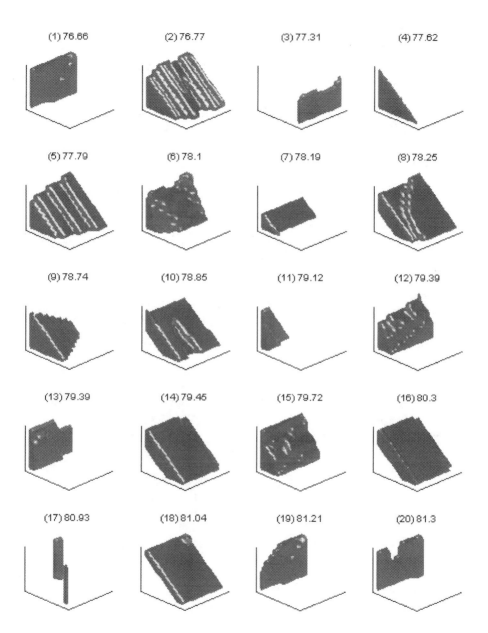

Fig. 3. All final optimised two-material forms with fitness values. Support is red, PV panel material is blue.

solutions found. The greatest total south-facing area is given by an inclined plane, either as a pyramid (solutions 4, 9) or wedge (2, 5, 7); the total surface area can then be reduced by making it thinner (8, 10, 14, 16), culminating in making it as thin as possible (1 voxel) (18). The greatest broadly south-facing area per total surface area is given by a section of a sphere (6); this may be approximated by a section of a cylinder, aligned either horizontally (12, 15) or vertically (17). The simplest form with reasonable performance is a thin obloid (1, 3, 11, 13, 19, 20). Because the PV panels need not face exactly south, there is scope to increase the surface area by adding undulations (2), steps (5, 8, 9, 12) and bulges (1, 10, 19, 20). Similarly the area of the top surface can be increased by including slopes (19) or dips (20). There was no limitation on single-block forms for this problem. However, generally dividing a form adds extra material without increasing south-facing area, and whilst multiple high-performing forms would maintain high fitness they would be likely to require more complex representations than single forms. Only one run resulted in a multiple block solution (17).

Material distribution is clearly adapting to the objective of the optimisation. All forms have the PV panel material predominantly on the south-facing side only none of the forms have any significant PV panel material on the rear or under sides (not shown). There is some variation in how well the PV panel covers the south face, with some obvious gaps (2, 8 10, 15) and missing upper edges (3, 11, 13). In general the material placement errors are low: on average across the 20 solutions, 1.8% by area has 'missing' PV (would fit the criteria but not present) and 0.9% incorrect PV (does not meet the criteria). It is interesting to note that the high-fitness solutions (nearer to number 20) do not have notably lower material placement errors (e.g. the highest error of 7.2% is for solution 18), although the errors are more likely to be in missing south-facing area rather than erroneous non-south-facing areas. There is clearly a balance between the performance of the form and the accuracy of the material distribution.

4.2 Continuously-Variable Material

The second option, to optimise a continuously-variable material parameter, is a more challenging and subtle problem. Because the angle of the surface relative to the average sun position is taken into account in calculating energy gener-ated, it is now more important that the PV should face directly south at 45 degree inclination. This eliminated the curved surfaces from the previous case. Figure 4 shows selected forms from the continuously-variable material option. These examples cover all the forms found: there were three low fitness forms like (1), fourteen mid fitness forms like (2), and the unique forms (3, 4, 5). Fitness values ranged from 54.7 to 78.0 with a mean of 68.9 and a standard error of 5.5. The types repeat many those of the previous section: horizontal cylinder (2), wedge (4) and thin angled plan (3, 5); there is also the notably low-performing horizontal plane (1) where the algorithm was unable to progress beyond the simple plane. This occurred in 4 out of 20 runs, whereas there are no such low-performing solutions in the previous case. Additional complexity is introduced

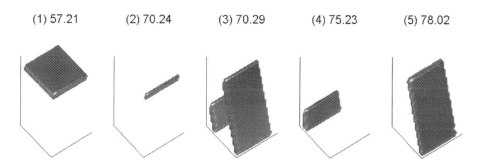

Fig. 4. Selected optimised variable-material shell forms with fitness value

to the problem by the variable-material formulation, which appears to be preventing the algorithm finding good solutions in some cases. The distribution of the PV is sometimes almost binary (1, 2, 4), where the material mapping falls almost entirely to one end of the scale or the other. This is to be expected, as it provides solutions with reasonable performance that have very simple material distributions and are therefore very easy for the algorithm to find. The distribution in form (3) is a gradual progression, with low PV ratio at the bottom and high at the top, demonstrating that the formulation is able to produce this sort of distribution. The highest performing solution (5) uses a precise distribution in which the main face has a high PV ratio (100%), the top edge (at an angle to the sun that is sizeable but less than 90 degrees) has an intermediate ratio, and the rest has a ratio of zero.

5   Conclusions

The multi-material implementation was demonstrated on an example problem concerned with PV panels. The algorithm was successful, generating solutions that combine high-performance forms with appropriate material distributions. For the discrete problem, the diversity of solutions found across 20 runs was large, highlighting the range of shapes and distributions obtainable. This also included solutions that exploited aspects of the process, for example using curved edges to increase surface area. For the continuously-variable problem, there was a greater range of fitness values, showing that the algorithm sometimes fails to find good solutions. It is inevitable that the continuous problem will be harder, but future work could investigate how to overcome this barrier, perhaps by approximating the gradient as bands.

The algorithm is exploring a very large search space, and the great variety of solutions make it useful to compare several runs of the algorithm rather than to take only one solution as indicative. Form optimisation problems are by nature very complicated, and problems may not be solved completely. The algorithms developed can be used to guide the design process, but are unlikely to generate a perfect result.

There are clearly many simpler ways of approaching the problem of form optimisation, especially for the problems examined here. However, the method used offers the potential for breadth and adaptability: the range of forms available is limitless. On that basis, the initial demonstration of the method has been satisfactory: from the vast realm of possible configurations, finding solutions to conceptually simple problems is not trivial. This paper is the first step in developing this approach to indirect form representation and optimisation into a usable method. Future work will extend the application to other cases where complex forms are required, for example the trade-off between winter solar gain, summer solar gain and light availability in passive building design.

Acknowledgments. Funded by the Industrial Doctorate Centre in Systems, Universities of Bristol and Bath, UK (EPSRC Grant EP/G037353/1) and Buro Happold Ltd, UK.

References

1. Auerbach, J.E., Bongard, J.C.: Evolving complete robots with CPPN-NEAT: the utility of recurrent connections. In: Proceedings of the 13th Annual Conference on Genetic and Evolutionary Computation, GECCO 2011, pp. 1475–1482. ACM, New York (2011)
2. Bentley, P., Kumar, S.: Three ways to grow designs: A comparison of evolved embryogenies for a design problem. In: Genetic and Evolutionary Computation Conference, pp. 35–43. Morgan Kaufmann (1999)
3. Clune, J., Lipson, H.: Evolving 3D objects with a generative encoding inspired by developmental biology. SIGEVOlution **5**(4), 2–12 (2011)
4. Imam, M.H.: Three-dimensional shape optimization. International Journal for Numerical Methods in Engineering **18**(5), 661–673 (1982)
5. Secretan, J., Beato, N., D'Ambrosio, D.B., Rodriguez, A., Campbell, A., Folsom-Kovarik, J.T., Stanley, K.O.: Picbreeder: A case study in collaborative evolutionary exploration of design space. Evolutionary Computation **19**(3), 373–403 (2010)
6. Stanley, K.O.: Compositional pattern producing networks: A novel abstraction of development. Genetic Programming and Evolvable Machines **8**(2), 131–162 (2007)
7. Stanley, K.O., Miikkulainen, R.: Evolving neural networks through augmenting topologies. Evolutionary Computation **10**(2), 99–127 (2002)
8. Xie, Y.M., Steven, G.P.: A simple evolutionary procedure for structural optimization. Computers & Structures **49**(5), 885–896 (1993)

EvoFIN

On Evolving Multi-agent FX Traders

Alexander Loginov and Malcolm I. Heywood[(⊠)]

Faculty of Computer Science, Dalhousie University, Halifax, NS, Canada
a.loginov@yahoo.ca, mheywood@cs.dal.ca
http://www.cs.dal.ca

Abstract. Current frameworks for identifying trading agents using machine learning are able to simultaneously address the characterization of both technical indicator and decision tree. Moreover, multi-agent frameworks have also been proposed with the goal of improving the reliability and trust in the agent policy identified. Such advances need weighing against the computational overhead of assuming such flexibility. In this work a framework for evolutionary multi-agent trading is introduced and systematically benchmarked for FX currency trading; including the impact of FX trading spread. It is demonstrated that simplifications can be made to the 'base' trading agent that do not impact on the quality of solutions, but provide considerable computational speedups. The resulting evolutionary multi-agent architecture is demonstrated to provide significant benefits to the profitability and improve the reliability with which profitable policies are returned.

Keywords: Non-stationary · Forex · Genetic Programming · Multi-agent Teams

1 Introduction

Machine learning (ML) has had a widespread impact on the automatic identification of trading agents for identifying profitable trading strategies under stock or currency markets. From the perspective of a generic process, multiple factors should be considered. For example, technical indicators (TI) are used to provide temporal features from which a decision tree (DT) defines the training strategy (e.g., buy–stay–sell). Although the TI might be designed independently before a DT is constructed – such as in the manner that attribute selection might be performed independently of classifier construction – the quality of the resulting trading strategy will be dependent on the quality of the initial set of TI. This sequential dependence has lead authors to adopt various strategies in which:

1. as wide a set of TI are initially included as possible after which the DT selects the most appropriate. For example, [1] used genetic programming (GP) to define the DT and inso doing noted that combinations of TI lead to better currency trading strategies. Other authors report similar findings using different ML paradigms e.g., [2];

© Springer-Verlag Berlin Heidelberg 2014
A.I. Esparcia-Alcázar et al. (Eds.): EvoApplications 2014, LNCS 8602, pp. 203–214, 2014.
DOI: 10.1007/978-3-662-45523-4_17

2. mechanisms are pursued that permit temporal feature construction at the same time as identifying a suitable DT. For example, the coevolutionary approach suggested by [3,4] evolves two populations simultaneously representing TI and DT respectively.

Naturally, the design of TI has a considerable impact on how the trading data is 'interfaced' to the DT. Thus, not only the type of TI, but the parameterization of the TI needs to be considered [5]. Moreover, trading data is non-stationary, thus an agent strategy that is appropriate for one period of trading will become unprofitable under a future period. This has lead to the adoption of various schemes for re-training or incremental evolution e.g., [4,6,7].

Finally, we note that it has been known for a while that in the general machine learning setting, stronger models for regression or classification result when multiple models are combined in an 'ensemble' e.g., [8,9]. Indeed, boosting has been reported for identifying multiple DT in the case of a 'multi-level' framework for stock trading [2].[1] More generally, multiple frameworks have been proposed for the purpose of constructing 'teams' of multiple GP individuals from one or more populations (e.g., [10,11]). However, such approaches assume that the application is stationary, whereas this is frequently observed not to be the case in financial applications [12,13].

Constructing GP teams through some form of voting on some form of streaming data has certainly been previously reported (e.g., [13,14]). However, in this work we take a closer look at specific caveats that make the application of ensemble methods (cf., multi-population architectures) challenging under a trading agent scenario. Specifically, an attempt is made to quantify the following: 1) computational overhead of constructing multiple solutions; 2) non-stationary nature of the task implies that ensemble content is likely to (at best) go stale or (at worst) over-learn, and 3) how to recombine multiple GP solutions (say, one from each population) into a single cohesive solution.

With this in mind, we assume the general framework of FXGP [3,4] for coevolving TI and DT (Section 2) and concentrate on assessing to what degree combining multiple DT from different populations has on the quality of the resulting agent strategy. The computational overhead of maintaining multiple populations is addressed by adopting an approach closer to the 'weak learner' methodology in which we reduce the functionality in the TI and DT, resulting in a threefold speedup in the time to evolve a single population. The non-stationary nature of the task is addressed through the use of the behavioural criteria for triggering re-training, as in the original FXGP framework. In the case of combining solutions from each population, an approach to voting is adopted which enables us to avoid the need to maintain a large number of parallel populations i.e., a computational overhead for real-time operation. Benchmarking is then performed with the original FXGP framework, the proposed simplified framework (sFXGP) and sFXGP deployed to construct multiple agents concurrently.

---

[1] Such a scheme does not naturally carry over to the currency trading scenario investigated here on account of the DT being used for predicting the one-step-ahead return relative to a sample of β-portfolio of stocks.

All benchmarking is performed using the most recent 3 year period available for the EURUSD currency pair i.e., the most widely traded foreign exchange pair.

2   The FXGP Algorithm Overview

FXGP is based on the biological metaphor of symbiosis. Specifically, a host organism aggregates symbionts under an egalitarian transition that is most famously associated with the origin of mitochondria within eukaryotic cells (e.g., [15]). Fitness can potentially be represented at the level of symbiont or host. As we are not interested in attempting to model the transition from (lower level) symbiont to (higher level) host we assume that fitness is only evaluated at the level of the host; thus, providing the basis for host–symbiont fitness to exceed the mere sum of its (symbiont) parts. With this in mind, it is only the host which is explicitly associated with fitness. Symbionts exist for as long as they are used in at least one host. Variation operators have the potential to introduce new symbionts and manipulate symbiont-to-host membership, resulting in a fixed size host (DT) population but variable sized symbiont (TI) population. Within the context of designing trading agents, pursuing a symbiotic coevolutionary enables us to evolve host DT using a representation specifically appropriate for expressing conditions for deploying trading actions (buy, hold, sell); whereas the symbiont population is designed to express TI [3,4]. We take the view that the only 'true' measure of fitness is at the level of the host (i.e., some aggregate measure of trading quality). Thus, TI are only deemed useful if they promote good DT.

The TI population in the original FXGP framework consists of TI of the three following types [3,4]: Value, Moving Average (MA) or Weighted Moving Average (WMA). The MA and WMA types of TI are calculated as follows:

$$MA_i = \frac{\sum_{i=1}^{n} V_i}{n} \tag{1}$$

$$WMA_i = \frac{\sum_{i=1}^{n} \frac{V_i}{i+1}}{\sum_{i=1}^{n} \frac{1}{i+1}} \tag{2}$$

where V_i is a TI value and the TI program assumes the form of linear GP and be composed from any of seven available functions (Table 1).

At the same time, the DT population consists of the individual trees that can include variable number of nodes and each node consists of one of the following conditional statements [3,4]:

- *if($X_i > Y_i$) then else*
- *if(($X_i > Y_i$) and ($X_{i+m} < Y_{i+m}$)) then else*

where X_i and Y_i can be 0, price or a TI and *then* and *else* can be the next node or one of the trading signals (buy, sell or stay).

Table 1. Original set of a TI functions. Functions marked with † are redundant.

Function	Definition
Addition	$R[x] \leftarrow R[x] + R[y]$
Subtraction	$R[x] \leftarrow R[x] - R[y]$
Division	$R[x] \leftarrow R[x] \div 2$
Multiplication†	$R[x] \leftarrow R[x] \times R[y]$
Square root†	$R[x] \leftarrow \sqrt{R[y]}$
Division†	$R[x] \leftarrow R[x] \div R[y]$
Division†	$R[x] \leftarrow 1 \div R[x]$

In addition FXGP assumed an interface to the (stream) trading data in which re-training was triggered by a set of trading criteria (Figure 1) [3,4]. That is to say, after an initial period of training, a champion individual is identified (validation) and deployed for trading until one of three trading criteria flag a deterioration in trading performance. FXGP utilized three criteria: 1) max. single drawdown, 2) max. number of consecutive loss making trades, 2) max. number of bars without variation [3]. At this point a new DT–TI population is coevolved relative to training–validation data leading up to the point of failure (Figure 1). In the case of the FX task, such a scheme was demonstrated to be more effective than continuously evolving against the trading data [4].

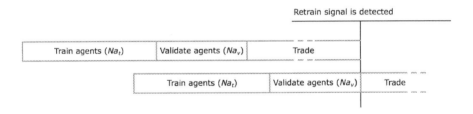

Fig. 1. The Train–Validate–Trade cycle. Independent populations are coevolved during Training partition Na_t and the champion trading agent is selected using the Validation partition Na_v.

3   Multi-agent FXGP

This section describes the new version of the algorithm in which *teams* of FXGP individuals suggest the trading action; hereafter FXGPT. As indicated in Section 1 we perceive several potential pathologies that could detract from realizing the benefits of pursuing a multi-agent / ensemble approach to currency trading. Section 3.1 will address simplifications that we introduce to reduce the computational footprint of the original FXGP framework; hereafter *simple* FXGP (*s*FXGP). FXGPT is then defined relative to *s*FXGP (Section 3.2).

3.1 *simple* FXGP

FXGP as originally defined assumed a set of seven TI functions (Table 1), whereas analysis of the resulting solutions indicated that four of them are redundant (marked with † in the Table 1) and can be removed from the original set. In addition, operations removed from the instruction set, when they were used by FXGP typically resulted in intron behaviour. Thus, multiplication often produced a TI with the wrong scale, whereas two of the division functions and the square root function frequently resulted in illegal operations (e.g. division by zero or square root of negative value). Needless to say, this also removes instruction types that have a longer (computational) latency i.e., division and square root; thus an expected improvement to TI execution, where it is the evaluation of TI that account for the majority of CPU time. Thus, sFXGP will assume the first three TI functions from Table 1.

Originally three types of TI were supported (Section 2), whereas sFXGP will be limited to supporting two types of TI (Table 2). The calculation of the Weighted Moving Average (WMA) requires more computational resources compared to estimation of the Moving Average (MA). At the same time experimentation indicated that the effectiveness of the WMA failed to improve on that using TI based on MA alone, resulting in the simplified set of TI parameters and a smaller search space.

Table 2. TI parameters

Parameter	Description
TI type	Value or Moving Average (MA)
TI scale	TI that crosses 0 or TI that crosses price
Period n	Number of hours (n) in a price history to calculate MA
Shift m	Price m hours back in a history

3.2 Constructing FXGP Teams

FXGP populations are evolved relative to the current historical trading data with trading criteria used to re-trigger training (Section 2). That is to say, each time the retraining criteria flags poor trading behaviour, all populations will be re-evolved. In order to construct multiple sFXGP populations we will concentrate on the interface to the (streaming) data, and assume the following two modes:

Mode 0: Given P independent sFXGP populations, identify one champion trading agent from each using the validation data, Na_v (Figure 2).

Mode 1: As per mode 0, however, all sFXGP individuals passing the validation criteria form the basis for a new population, p^*. This population continues evolution with respect to partition Nt_t (Figure 2). Note that each individual from p^* is still treated as an independent trading agent.

Such a comparison enables us to look at the relative tradeoff between complete independence in identifying team champions (mode 0) versus conducting a final evolutionary cycle in which credit assignment between individual may take place (mode 1).

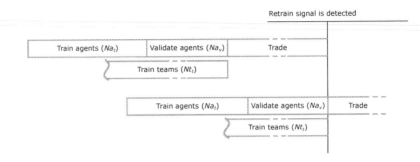

Fig. 2. The team mode Train–Validate–Train–Trade cycle. Independent populations are evolved during Training partition Na_t and a subset of sFXGP individual identified from each using the Validation partition Na_v. The FXGP teams are trained over partition Nt_t (mode 1 only). The point at which retraining is invoked corresponds to three trading criteria.

Post evolution, each trading agent in the team returns one of three actions per trading 'tick' (hourly in this work), where actions are mapped to an integer value using the following assignment: Sell $= -1$; Stay $= 0$; Buy $= 1$. The scheme adopted for combining the recommendation from each agent assumes the following form: $a = \sum_{i \in A} a_i$ where $a_i \in \{-1, 0, 1\}$ corresponds to the three possible actions that each champion can assume and A is the strongest subset of agents from p^* at the last generation. The resulting number line is then re-mapped into one of the three actions using the following rule:

$$\text{IF } (a \geq \gamma) \text{ THEN } (buy) \text{ ELSE IF } (a \leq -\gamma) \text{ THEN } (sell) \text{ ELSE } (hold) \quad (3)$$

Naturally, the value for the threshold γ needs to be defined by the user and remains the same throughout the trading activity. We note that the generic form of this model has been adopted in the past for discretizing the output of (single) neural network trading agents into long and short positions [16] and 'risk management' in the case of boosted DT (γ_0 parameter in [2]).

4   Experimental Setup

4.1   Source Data

The EURUSD tick-by-tick prices[2] were converted into one hour bars and used to define market activity during the period from January 3, 2010 to November

---

[2] http://www.truefx.com

30, 2012. We used the same period of time as in [4] to establish a baseline for comparison. The distribution of floating spreads (the difference between Ask and Bid prices) of the hour bars during trading (Open, High, Low and Close prices) are shown in the Figures 3(a) and 3(b). The results in [4] were obtained with the assumption of a *fixed spread* value of 0.00002 USD based on the FxPro Group average EURUSD spread value.[3]

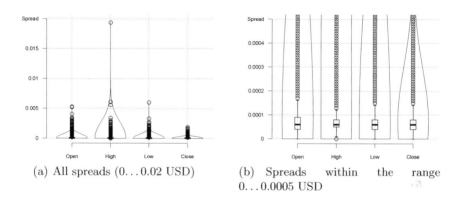

(a) All spreads (0 . . . 0.02 USD)

(b) Spreads within the range 0 . . . 0.0005 USD

Fig. 3. Spreads distributions. Internal box-plot provides quartile statistics. Violin profile characterizes the distribution.

Both versions of the algorithm (unmodified and the version we describe in this work) allow user to specify the *limit spread* value to open the trades. If the spread exceeds the limit, the algorithm will not generate *buy* or *sell* signals to open a new trade. However, if the position was already opened, *buy* or *sell* signals to close an existing position will be generated regardless of the spread value. In this research the spread limit was selected empirically and set to 0.00025 USD for all cases i.e., a less conservative limit (relative to the earlier FXGP work), making the role of policy identification more prominent.

4.2 Parameterization

Both updated versions of the algorithm (*s*FXGP and FXGPT) inherit the parameterization of the original FXGP (as described in [3,4]) with the addition of the parameters, specific for the evolution of teams (Table 3). All runs were performed on a 2.8 GHz iMac computer with Intel Core i7 CPU, 16GB RAM and Mac OS X 10.7.2. Where indicated, use is also made of the Apple GCD enqueue application which identifies tasks for simultaneous execution against the available CPU cores.

---

[3] http://www.fxpro.co.uk

Table 3. Team specific parameters

Parameter	Value	Description
A	3	Number of trading agents in a team (number of independent DT–TI populations)
γ	2	Team's trading signal threshold (Equ. (3))
mode	0 or 1	0 - team is built with champion agents, 1 - team is evolved
teams	100	Teams' population size ($|p^*|$)
teamsGap	25	Number of teams to be replaced in each generation
teamsGnrts	1000	Max number of teams' population generations
teamsPlt	200	Number of generations without best score improvement to stop training
testSize	500	The data partition size to evolve teams (i.e., $Nt_t = Na_v$)

5 Results

The following experiments were performed within this research to distinguish between the various components of the system:

- FXGP – original FXGP version of the algorithm as described in [3,4] i.e., wider range of TI and DT.
- sFXGP – *simple* FXGP version of the algorithm i.e., limited TI and DT (Section 3.1).
- FXGPT(3) – teams formed using three sFXGP champions under teaming mode 0 (Section 3.2).
- FXGPT(3e) – teams formed using three sFXGP champions under teaming mode 1 (Section 3.2)

The results of all three experiments are summarized in the Table 4 where the last line (FXGP†) repeats the best sFXGP result from [4] for a fixed spread of 0.00002 USD. Such a decision can only be made given suitable priori knowledge of the market behaviour. This assumption is not made in the case of sFXGP or FXGPT. Each experiment includes 100 simulation runs. FXGP and sFXGP make *no* use of GCD style parallelization, however, both forms of FXGPT are able to.

Table 4 provides the overview of both the number of profitable runs and the respective quartile statistics. Comparing FXGP to FXGP†indicates that removing the prior knowledge regarding spread limits results in an immediate significant reduction in performance. The simplifications introduced to define sFXGP (from FXGP) have no measurable impact on the quality of trades. Introducing the simplest form of multi-agent behaviour, FXGPT(3) (mode 0: sampling a single champion from each independently evolved population), results in a $\approx 13\%$ improvement to the median score. Introducing evolution using teaming mode 1 (FXGPT(3e)) results in a tightening of the distribution of scores, as well as providing a 50% improvement relative to the single agent case (Table 3). This also

Table 4. Quartile performance of trading agents (pips). FXGP†was the best previous result using the original FXGP algorithm with prior knowledge of spread. FXGP is the same algorithm without accurate spread information. sFXGP, FXGPT(3) and FXGPT(3e) represent the proposed single agent and two 3 agent formulations (mode 0 and 1 respectively).

Algorithm	Profitable runs (%)	Score (pips)				
		min	1st quartile	median	3rd quartile	max
FXGP	73	-3459.0	-63.3	996.2	1905.3	4159.5
sFXGP	74	-3153.8	-94.8	988.5	1917.8	4054.6
FXGPT(3)	78	-2219.2	70.2	1117.3	2144.5	6291.0
FXGPT(3e)	81	-1876.6	288.5	1489.2	2462.8	4362.4
FXGP†	82	-3087.9	383.4	1522.5	2639.5	5298.6

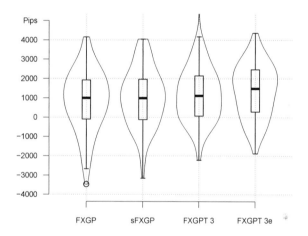

Fig. 4. Distribution of scores in pips over trading simulation period of time. Quartile information appears in the box plot (illustrating the information from Table 4). The contours of the violin mimic the actual distribution of the underlying data.

results in FXGPT(3e) managing to match the performance of FXGP†, where the latter makes use of prior information in selecting an optimal spread.[4]

In order to characterize the computational costs of each algorithm, we report the total number of retraining events and the cost of any single retraining event. Figure 5 summarizes the total count of retraining events over the three year trading period. In the case of both single agent algorithms (FXGP and sFXGP), a significant reduction in the number of retraining events occurs. Given that there was no trading benefit in assuming the (original) FXGP framework over

---

[4] The p-values for a Student t-test at the 95% confidence interval as applied between each pairwise test of FXGPT(3e) against FXGPT(3), sFXGP and FXGP is 0.161, 0.047 and 0.008 respectively.

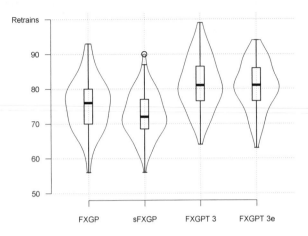

Fig. 5. Distribution of number of retraining events over trading simulation period of time. Box plot define the quartile information and violin the actual distribution.

sFXGP, this reduction in the number of retraining intervals appears to indicate that sFXGP agents are more general. Conversely, there is a significant increase in the number of retraining events when teams of trading agents are assumed (either mode of FXGPT).

Figure 6 summarizes the cost of performing any single retraining event. It is immediately apparent that sFXGP is significantly faster than FXGP as originally conceived. Thus, the cost of supporting multiple types of moving average

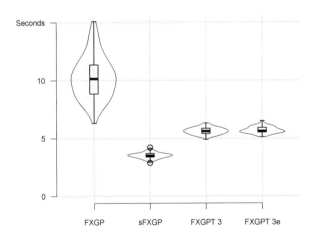

Fig. 6. Distribution of average training times (over a run) per population (FXGP and sFXGP) and per team of three populations (FXGPT)

and division operators as well as a square root operator (TI population) does not result in any better trading performance, while sFXGP reduces the computational overhead by 65 – 70 %. FXGPT is able to maintain the computational overhead at $\approx 40\%$, albeit with use of the coarse grained parallelism available through Apple GCD.[5]

6   Conclusion

We can make following conclusions based on the obtained results:

- The use of real prices with floating spreads (Table 4, sFXGP) significantly affects the trading results and reduces the number of profitable solutions and scores compared to trading with assumed fixed spreads as previously reported (Table 4, FXGP†).
- Both single agent variants (FXGP and sFXGP) return a very similar number of profitable solutions and scores (Table 4). We conclude that the simplifications introduced to sFXGP did not reduce the performance of the algorithm and, at the same time, the training time was reduced by 65% (Figure 6). The average number of retrains was also reduced (Figure 5).
- The use of teams of champion trading agents (Table 4, FXGPT(3)) improves the negative spread of runs compared to that of a single trading agent (Table 4, sFXGP). At the same time the CPU cost for maintaining a team of champion agents is still significantly $\approx 40\%$ lower than that for the original FXGP.
- The use of evolved teams (Table 4, FXGPT(3e)) outperformed all other configurations and demonstrated the best results in all categories: trustability (the percentage of profitable runs) and quartile scores. Indeed, this configuration provides statistically significant improvements over the single population models (95 percentile) and adds > 350 pips to the median performance of FXGPT(3).

Acknowledgments. The authors gratefully acknowledge support from the NSERC CRD grant program (Canada).

References

1. Dempster, M., Payne, T.W., Romahi, Y., Thompson, G.: Computational learning techniques for intraday FX trading using popular technical indicators. IEEE Transactions on Neural Networks **12**, 744–754 (2001)
2. Creamer, G., Freund, Y.: Automated trading with boosting and expert weighting. Quantitative Finance **10**(4), 401–410 (2010)
3. Loginov, A., Heywood, M.I.: On the Utility of Trading Criteria Based Retraining in Forex Markets. In: Esparcia-Alcázar, A.I. (ed.) EvoApplications 2013. LNCS, vol. 7835, pp. 192–202. Springer, Heidelberg (2013)

---

[5] GCD does not facilitate speeding up evaluation of a single population.

4. Loginov, A., Heywood, M.I.: On the impact of streaming interface heuristics on GP trading agents: an FX benchmarking study. In: ACM Genetic and Evolutionary Computation Conference, pp. 1341–1348 (2013)

5. Fernandez-Blanco, P., Bodas-Sagi, D., Soltero, F., Hidalgo, J.: Technical market indicators optimization using evolutionary algorithms. In: ACM Conference Companion on Genetic and Evolutionary Computation, pp. 1851–1858 (2008)

6. Dempsey, I., O'Neill, M., Brabazon, A.: Adaptive trading with grammatical evolution. In: IEEE Congress on Evolutionary Computation, pp. 2587–2592 (2006)

7. Wilson, G., Banzhaf, W.: Interday and Intraday Stock Trading Using Probabilistic Adaptive Mapping Developmental Genetic Programming and Linear Genetic Programming. In: Brabazon, A., O'Neill, M., Maringer, D.G. (eds.) Natural Computing in Computational Finance. SCI, vol. 293, pp. 191–212. Springer, Heidelberg (2010)

8. Freund, Y.: Boosting a weak learning algorithm by majority. Information and Computation **121**(2), 256–285 (1996)

9. Wolpert, D.H.: Stacked generalization. Neural Networks 5(2) 241–259

10. Brameier, M., Banzhaf, W.: Evolving teams of predictors with linear genetic programming. Genetic Programming and Evolvable Machines **2**(4), 381–408 (2001)

11. Soule, T., Komireddy, P.: Orthogonal evolution of teams. In: Riolo, R., Soule, T., Worzel, B. (eds.) Genetic Programming Theory and Practice IV, pp. 79–95. Springer (2007)

12. Larkin, F., Ryan, C.: Modesty Is the Best Policy: Automatic Discovery of Viable Forecasting Goals in Financial Data. In: Di Chio, C., Brabazon, A., Di Caro, G.A., Ebner, M., Farooq, M., Fink, A., Grahl, J., Greenfield, G., Machado, P., O'Neill, M., Tarantino, E., Urquhart, N. (eds.) EvoApplications 2010, Part II. LNCS, vol. 6025, pp. 202–211. Springer, Heidelberg (2010)

13. Mayo, M.: Evolutionary Data Selection for Enhancing Models of Intraday Forex Time Series. In: Di Chio, C., et al (eds.) EvoApplications 2012. LNCS, vol. 7248, pp. 184–193. Springer, Heidelberg (2012)

14. Folino, G., Papuzzo, G.: Handling Different Categories of Concept Drifts in Data Streams Using Distributed GP. In: Esparcia-Alcázar, A.I., Ekárt, A., Silva, S., Dignum, S., Uyar, A.Ş. (eds.) EuroGP 2010. LNCS, vol. 6021, pp. 74–85. Springer, Heidelberg (2010)

15. Margulis, L., Fester, R.: Symbiosis as a Source of Evolutionary Innovation. MIT Press (1991)

16. Dunis, C.L., Laws, J., Sermpinis, G.: Higher order and recurrent neural architectures for trading the EUR / USD exchange rate. Quantitative Finance **11**(4), 615–629 (2011)

Geometric Semantic Genetic Programming for Financial Data

James McDermott[1,2]([⊠]), Alexandros Agapitos[1],
Anthony Brabazon[1,3], and Michael O'Neill[1]

[1] Natural Computing Research and Applications Group,
Complex and Adaptive Systems Lab, University College Dublin, Dublin, Ireland
jmmcd@jmmcd.net, {alexandros.agapitos,anthony.brabazon,m.oneill}@ucd.ie
[2] Management Information Systems, Lochlann Quinn School of Business,
University College Dublin, Dublin, Ireland
[3] Accountancy, Lochlann Quinn School of Business, University College Dublin,
Dublin, Ireland

Abstract. We cast financial trading as a symbolic regression problem
on the lagged time series, and test a state of the art symbolic regression
method on it. The system is geometric semantic genetic programming,
which achieves good performance by converting the fitness landscape
to a cone landscape which can be searched by hill-climbing. Two novel
variants are introduced and tested also, as well as a standard hill-climbing
genetic programming method. Baselines are provided by buy-and-hold
and ARIMA. Results are promising for the novel methods, which produce
smaller trees than the existing geometric semantic method. Results are
also surprisingly good for standard genetic programming. New insights
into the behaviour of geometric semantic genetic programming are also
generated.

Keywords: Automated trading · Commodity · Exchange rate · Index ·
Genetic programming · Semantics · Fitness landscape · Hill-climbing

1 Introduction

Trading on financial markets is an important problem in its own right, and an
interesting and difficult test problem for machine learning methods. It is a source
of unending difficulty because of feedbacks between traders: each trader changes
the environment for others, so no particular solution can win in the long run.

It is common to cast trading as a regression problem, where the goal is to
predict the next price in a time series in terms of the current price and some
lagged prices. Trading proceeds by interpreting negative predictions as short
signals and positive predictions as buy signals.

A standard method of time-series modelling is ARIMA, the auto-regressive
integrated moving average [11]. ARIMA and related methods use linear combinations of the lagged time-series. The autocorrelation is used to indicate which
lags contain significant information, in the form of linear correlations with the

A.I. Esparcia-Alcázar et al. (Eds.): EvoApplications 2014, LNCS 8602, pp. 215–226, 2014.
DOI: 10.1007/978-3-662-45523-4_18

present value. If it is hypothesized that even lags which are not significantly correlated with the present value may contain information which can by taken advantage of by using them non-linearly and in combination, then there is a motivation for using other non-linear regression methods.

Genetic programming symbolic regression (GPSR) is an example. In comparison to a method like ARIMA, GPSR is more flexible, because it allows nonlinear combination of variables. However it is less reliable, due to its stochastic nature. For time series with simple structure, ARIMA will generally be faster and more reliable, and will produce a simpler and more readable model. For more complex time series, GPSR has the potential to out-perform ARIMA.

In recent years, several advances have been made in the state of the art in GPSR. One example is the *geometric semantic genetic programming* (GSGP) approach of Moraglio et al. [9], described in detail in Sect. 3.1. A geometric semantic mutation operator causes the fitness landscape to become a cone, easily searched using hill-climbing. However the GSGP operators bring about a very large increase in the size of the trees produced, so it is interesting to consider variations which avoid creating such large trees while retaining the geometric property. We propose two new mutation operators (see Sect. 3.2). The first, *one-tree* GSGP mutation, is very similar to the standard GSGP mutation operator, but adds less genetic material at each mutation step, helping to keep trees small. The other, *optimal-step* GSGP mutation, also uses this idea, and also chooses an optimal mutation step-size at each step: this may allow the search to approach the optimum much faster, requiring fewer steps, so that again the tree eventually produced has accumulated fewer nodes.

It is interesting to test GSGP in financial trading because it has not yet, to our knowledge, been tested on financial data or on any type of time-series modelling. In this paper we compare ARIMA, GSGP, and a standard GP hill-climber. We run our tests over 3 datasets of 1400 points each, derived from Gold, GBP/USD, and S&P500 markets.

Sect. 2, next, describes some related work. The GSGP methods are described in Sect. 3. Experiments and results are given in Sect. 4; Sect. 5 analyses these results; and Sect. 6 gives conclusions and future work.

2   Related Work

Many authors have used evolutionary methods, and particularly GP, for financial trading: see [2,3] and references therein. Previous work has shown the potential benefit of exploring new GP representations in particular [1]. Out-performing a buy-and-hold strategy was found to be surprisingly difficult by several authors as described by Lohpetch and Corne [5]. They can more reliably out-perform buy-and-hold when trading at a monthly level, with less reliability when trading daily. They do not attempt 5-minute trading as in the current paper.

The GSGP method was developed by Moraglio et al. [9]. It is rooted in the unifying theory of geometric operators [8]. A geometric mutation operator produces new individuals distributed in a ball surrounding the original. A geometric crossover operator produces children distributed in the line segment between the two parents. The radius of the ball, and the line segment, are defined using a suitable metric. In the case of geometric *semantic* GP, the metric is on the semantic space of programs. In this space, each element is a vector of the outputs from some program on the vector of fitness cases. The key achievement of Moraglio et al. [9] in relation to GPSR is to define mutation and crossover operators which are geometric according to Euclidean distance on the semantic space. Because symbolic regression fitness is equivalent to Euclidean distance from the target in the semantic space, the fitness landscape becomes a cone. This means that search will encounter no local optima and can proceed reliably and efficiently, an important step forward for GP.

In fact, the absence of local optima, and the consensus of previous results [9, 12], suggests that a hill-climber is a sufficient search algorithm: a population and a crossover operator are unnecessary. Standard GP, using the subtree mutation operator, also encounters no local optima. For this paper, then, we consider mutation and hill-climbing only.

GSGP has previously been used for symbolic regression on real-world data [12]. However, the results achieved there were no better than predicting a constant for all data points[1]. On the other hand, the fact that the landscape becomes a cone promises very good performance; and results on randomly-generated symbolic regression problems have been very good [9].

One disadvantage of the GSGP operators is that they bring about a very large increase in the size of the trees produced. The mutation operator adds two random trees plus four nodes to the tree at each step. The new variants proposed in the following sections aim to mitigate this.

3   GP, GSGP, and Variations

A key concept in understanding GSGP is *semantic space*. Individuals' values on the vector of fitness cases give their position in semantic space. For example, consider a dataset of three input variables x_0, x_1, and x_2, and one output variable y, with 2 fitness cases:

	x_0	x_1	x_2	y
Fitness case 0	3	4	1	10
Fitness case 1	7	8	2	12

Consider an individual (* x0 x1). Its values on the two fitness cases are $(12, 56)$. These two values give the individual's position in the 2-dimensional semantic space, which is depicted in Fig. 1. The target $y = (10, 12)$ is also a point in semantic space.

---

[1] For example, for a problem in predicting the *bioavailability* of certain drugs [12], the mean of the target values on all fitness cases is approximately 66.4%. Predicting this value for all fitness cases produces a fitness value of 30.4%.

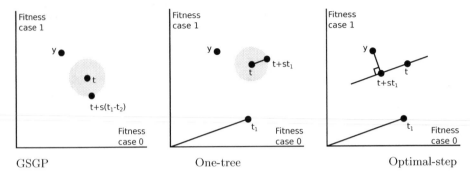

GSGP   One-tree   Optimal-step

Fig. 1. GSGP and variations. Individuals are shown in the semantic space. In a dataset of two fitness cases, an individual's values on the two cases give its position in this space. In GSGP, left, the tree resulting from a mutation is expected to lie in a ball surrounding the original (in semantic space). The same is true of *one-tree* GSGP, centre. In *one-tree optimal-step* GSGP, right, the optimal value of the mutation step size s is found, in order to scale the effect of the new random tree and bring the resulting tree as close to the optimum as possible. The new random tree t_1 is seen as a vector with a fixed direction. Changing the scalar moves the resulting tree back and forth along a line through t parallel with that vector. Choosing the optimal s brings the new point as close as possible to the target y.

3.1   GSGP

The GSGP mutation operator for symbolic regression problems [9] works by taking the difference of two randomly-generated trees t_1 and t_2, scaled by a positive constant s giving the step-size, and combining that with the original tree t, to give a new tree t_{new} as shown in Fig 2.

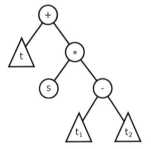

Fig. 2. The new tree produced by the GSGP mutation operator: $t_{\text{new}} = t + s(t_1 - t_2)$

In the semantic space, the new individual is distributed in a ball of radius s, because for each dimension of the semantic space, the added tree $(t_1 - t_2)$ has expected value 0. See Fig. 1. One disadvantage of the operator, mentioned in previous work [12], is that the resulting tree grows by $4 + |t_1| + |t_2|$ nodes per step, where $|\cdot|$ indicates the number of nodes in a tree. The 4 comes from the s, $+$, $-$, and $*$ nodes.

Running for many generations then results in very large trees, which have some disadvantages. They are for practical purposes unreadable. They require very large CPU and memory resources, though correct implementation can mitigate this issue: Moraglio et al. [9] avoid storing the trees themselves by restricting attention to a space of polynomials in which simplification of large trees is automatic; the implementation of Vanneschi et al. [12] uses pointers to previous results; our implementation[2] uses memoisation [7]. Large trees are often also associated with a decrease in generalisation ability (i.e. overfitting), but this is shown by Vanneschi et al. [12] to be bounded above.

3.2   Novel GSGP Variations

It is interesting to consider variations on the GSGP mutation operator, with the goal of avoiding the large trees it produces, but retaining the beneficial geometric property.

We propose a *one-tree* GSGP mutation operator which instead uses only a single new random tree and draws s from a normal distribution centred at 0:

$$t_{\text{new}} = t + st_1$$

For each dimension, the tree st_1 has expected value 0, because of the distribution of s. This operator adds $3 + |t_1|$ nodes per step, so it approximately halves the number of nodes in the eventual result.

We also propose an *optimal-step one-tree* GSGP mutation operator, defined by the same equation as the one-tree operator, which again uses only one new random tree, and again adds $3 + |t_1|$ nodes per step. The difference is that instead of drawing s from a normal distribution, it finds the *optimal* value for s at each mutation event. The optimal value of s is the positive or negative constant which minimises the distance of the resulting tree from the optimum. This value can be calculated by differentiation. In the following, y is the target vector in semantic space, i.e. the vector of target values at the fitness cases; t and t_1 are to be interpreted as the vectors of the corresponding tree's outputs at the fitness cases. Multiplication and other operators are to be interpreted element-wise.

The distance of the resulting tree from the optimum, which we wish to minimise, is $\text{RMSE}(y, t + st_1)$. Minimising RMSE is equivalent to minimising MSE.

$$\begin{aligned}
\text{MSE}(y, t + st_1) &= \text{mean}((y - (t + st_1))^2) \\
&= \text{mean}(((y - t) - st_1)^2) \\
&= \text{mean}((y - t)^2 - 2(y - t)st_1 + s^2 t_1^2)
\end{aligned}$$

---

[2] All code and data used in this study is available for download from https://github.com/jmmcd/PODI.

To find the optimal s, we differentiate with respect to s:

$$d(\text{MSE})/ds = \text{mean}\left(-2(y-t)t_1 + 2st_1^2\right)$$
$$= -2\,\text{mean}((y-t)t_1) + 2s\,\text{mean}(t_1^2)$$

This is zero when:

$$2\,\text{mean}((y-t)t_1) = 2s\,\text{mean}(t_1^2)$$

Therefore the optimum value for s is:

$$s = \text{mean}((y-t)t_1)/\text{mean}(t_1^2)$$

All the values t and t_1 are known; in the symbolic regression setting, the values y are also known. Therefore, the optimal value of s can be calculated. This results in using the new random tree t_1 to always step in the direction of the target vector in semantic space (not guaranteed using the other mutation operators); and to take the step of precisely the right length, to minimise the new distance to the target vector. The process is visualised in Fig. 1.

A GP method using a standard GP mutation operator, or the GSGP or GSGP-one-tree operators, is *black-box*: it requires only the ability to call the fitness function. In contrast, GSGP-optimal-ms requires knowledge of the values y, and so is not a fully black-box method.

3.3   Standard GP

As a control we also used a GP operator which is not geometric in the semantic space: the subtree mutation of standard GP. In our implementation, subtree mutation cuts at any node (even the root), and replaces with a new subtree created using the *grow* method. Again, we use a mutation-only hill-climber. Due to the ability to cut even at the root, the subtree mutation operator can, by itself, reach any point in the search space; and it induces a landscape with no local optima. GP hill-climbing is known to perform surprisingly well [10]. It provides a direct comparison with the GSGP hill-climbers.

4   Experiments and Results

4.1   Trading Strategy

We cast trading on time series as a symbolic regression problem. GP attempts to predict the time series as a function of the lagged variables. More precisely, we use the log-returns time series $L_t = \log(v_t/v_{t-1})$. The goal is to estimate a function $f(x) = L_t, x = (L_{t-19}, L_{t-18}, \ldots, L_{t-1})$.

The predictor is operationalised as a trader with a simple strategy: at each time-step either a long or short position is opened, depending on the sign of the predicted log-return. It is closed at the next time-step and returns are collected. The returns consist of the simple return $r_t = (v_t - v_{t-1})/v_{t-1}$ if the open position was long, or the negative of the simple return if the open position was short. This is summarised by saying the returns are $\mathrm{sgn}(\widehat{L_t})r_t$. The returns are accumulated over time. Such a model is useful only for testing, since it ignores real-world issues such as trading costs and interest.

We also define the classification accuracy $\mathrm{CA} = \#(\mathrm{sgn}(\widehat{L_t}) = \mathrm{sgn}(L_t))/N$, i.e. the proportion of time-steps on which the predicted sign is correct.

4.2 Experimental Setup

Three price histories were used: Gold (GOLD), GBP/USD (GU), and the Standard & Poor 500 index (SP500), each taken at 5-minute intervals for 1400 time-steps. (1-hour data was also considered, but discarded after pilot experiments on the theory that the structure in the time series being exploited by GP was rather short-term.) The data is available for download: see https://github.com/jmmcd/PODI. The log-return at time-step t was calculated as $\log(v_t/v_{t-1})$. The data was split into training and test data (418 test points), omitting the first 19 points for use as lags.

Two baselines were used. For each dataset we calculate an ARIMA model using the R function `auto.arima`, available in the `forecast` package. It automatically chooses the model order to minimise the AIC (Akaike information criterion). For our datasets, it chose ARIMA models as follows: GOLD (3, 0, 3), GU (4, 0, 1), and SP500 (2, 0, 2). The first integer indicates the auto-regression order, the second the degree of differencing, and the third the moving average order. In all cases the degree of differencing is zero, as expected because the log-return time series is stationary. Having chosen these models, it then fits the model using the training sets. Accumulated returns are calculated over the testing set. For each dataset we also calculate the returns accumulated using a buy-and-hold strategy over the testing set.

The GP alphabet consists of one variable for each of 19 lags, the constants -1, -0.1, 0.1, and 1, and the functions +, -, *, /, sin, sqrt, and square. A fitness evaluation budget of 20,000 was used, with 40 generations of 500 individuals each. At each generation a single best individual was selected as the parent of the next generation. For GP subtree mutation, a maximum depth of 12 was used. For GSGP, the mutation step was $s = 0.001$, as used by Moraglio et al. [9] and found to perform well by Vanneschi et al. [12].

Previous work [9,12] has not reported the algorithm or parameters used to generate the trees t_1 and t_2, but it is likely that non-trivial trees are being generated. We use the *grow* algorithm. Pilot experiments found that using a maximum depth of 3 offered no advantage over a maximum depth of 2, so 2 is used in all experiments to be reported (a tree of a single node is counted as depth 0, so maximum depth 2 allows a tree of up to 7 nodes).

The hypotheses to be tested are:

- Can any GP/GSGP methods out-perform the buy-and-hold and ARIMA baselines in trading on test data?
- Which of the GP/GSGP methods performs the best?

4.3   Results

Table 1 shows the main results. For each dataset, the ARIMA and buy-and-hold performance are shown first. For each type of mutation (GP, GSGP, GSGP-one-tree, GSGP-optimal-ms), the best run out of 30 (chosen by classification accuracy on the training set) is then considered. Its classification accuracy on training and test sets is shown. Finally, a 0 or 1 indicates whether its accumulated returns after 50, 100, and then all 418 time-steps of the test data have out-performed *both* ARIMA and buy-and-hold.

Table 1. Results. ARIMA and buy-and-hold performance are shown for each market. For GP, GSGP, and variants, the best result out of 30 runs, as measured by classification accuracy on the training set, is shown. Its classification accuracy on the training set and test set are shown (CA train and CA test), followed by a 0 or 1 indicating whether its returns were better than both ARIMA and buy-and-hold after 50, 100, or all 418 time-steps of the test data.

Market	Method	CA (train)	CA (test)	R@50	R@100	R@End
GOLD5m	Buy and hold	n/a	n/a	-0.00070	-0.00071	0.00026
	ARIMA	0.54	0.54	0.00432	-0.00464	0.01367
	GP	0.61	0.59	0	0	0
	GSGP	0.58	0.57	0	0	0
	GSGP-one-tree	0.57	0.58	1	0	0
	GSGP-optimal-ms	0.58	0.58	1	0	0
GU5m	Buy and hold	n/a	n/a	-0.00040	-0.00005	0.00016
	ARIMA	0.50	0.50	-0.00177	-0.00200	0.00095
	GP	0.56	0.59	0	0	1
	GSGP	0.55	0.59	1	1	1
	GSGP-one-tree	0.57	0.54	1	0	1
	GSGP-optimal-ms	0.58	0.55	1	1	1
SP5005m	Buy and hold	n/a	n/a	0.00000	0.00044	-0.00076
	ARIMA	0.64	0.65	-0.00051	-0.00145	-0.00089
	GP	0.78	0.80	1	0	1
	GSGP	0.65	0.65	0	1	0
	GSGP-one-tree	0.67	0.62	1	0	0
	GSGP-optimal-ms	0.65	0.64	0	0	0

The results show that GP and the GSGP variants can perform well. Classification accuracy is 54-65%, with an exceptional 80%, on the test data: enough to accumulate positive returns in trading and out-perform the classification accuracy achieved by ARIMA. Note that each of GP and the GSGP variants are represented by a single individual here, hence no statistical test is carried out.

However the returns accumulated by the ARIMA method can be quite good, in particular on the GOLD dataset. Its performance near the end of the test data is unbeatable using GP or GSGP variants. The trading performance on the GOLD dataset is shown in Fig. 3. However, in other cases both ARIMA and buy-and-hold can be beaten (indicated by a 1 in the final three columns).

Accumulated returns using the GP/GSGP methods are particularly strong, and more reliable, in the short term – up to about 50 time-steps. This suggests that a good strategy is to retrain the model frequently with up-to-date data. This tends to confirm the previously-stated theory that the 1-hour data is less amenable to GP/GSGP learning.

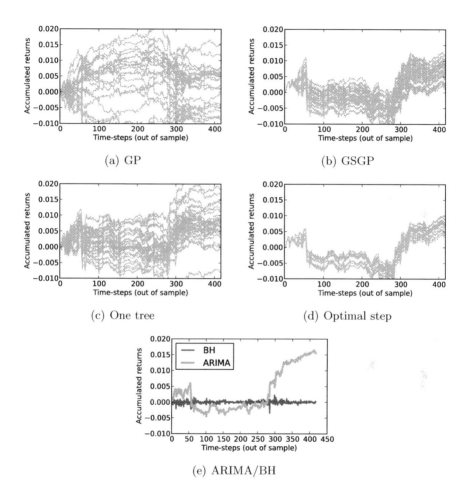

Fig. 3. Returns on the Gold 5-minute data with ARIMA and buy-and-hold shown for comparison. Many of the GP/GSGP variants do well early on, but ARIMA's performance near the end of the trading period is very good.

Fig. 3 shows the accumulated returns on the Gold data only. As shown, ARIMA does well in the first 50 time-steps, then quite badly before achieving large gains near the end. The buy-and-hold strategy does not do well with these datasets, because there is no consistent upward trend. Neither is there a consistent downward trend, so a "sell-and-hold" strategy would not perform well either. Buy-and-hold and "sell-and-hold" are equivalent to predicting constant True and constant False, respectively.

Next, the different GP mutation types were compared. Two out-of-sample criteria were used: the classification accuracy on the test set (higher is better) and the returns after 50 time-steps of the test set (higher is better). Mann-Whitney U tests were used, to avoid requiring an assumption of normality. The significance threshold was $\alpha = 0.05$. For each dataset, 6 pairwise tests were performed (GP v GSGP, GP v GSGP-one-tree, GP v GSGP-optimal-ms, etc.) A Bonferroni correction was applied, in other words p-values were multiplied by 6 to compensate for the multiple tests. Results are shown in Table 2.

Table 2. Comparison of GP mutation types. The ordering of the median value is shown as $<$ if the difference is non-significant and as $<<<$ if significant. GSGP-one-tree is notated as "1t" and GSGP-optimal-ms as "Opt".

Data	Criterion							
GOLD	CA	Opt	$<$	1t	$<$	GSGP	$<<<$	GP
GOLD	R@50	GP	$<<<$	GSGP	$<$	Opt	$<$	1t
GU	CA	GP	$<$	1t	$<<<$	Opt	$<<<$	GSGP
GU	R@50	1t	$<$	Opt	$<<<$	GSGP	$<$	GP
SP500	CA	Opt	$<$	GSGP	$<$	1t	$<<<$	GP
SP500	R@50	Opt	$<<<$	GSGP	$<$	GP	$<$	1t

The two criteria (classification accuracy and Returns@50) often disagreed in the ordering of the values. In fact, results are very mixed: all four mutation types "won" at least once, counting cases where two "winners" tied with non-significant differences. However, in summary it seems that GP has performed quite well, certainly holding its own overall against the GSGP variants; whereas the GSGP-optimal-ms method has not demonstrated any great advantage, at least using these two out-of-sample criteria.

One possible interpretation of the results is that the time series contain a limited amount of structure to be exploited by learning methods, and that both ARIMA and standard GP are sufficient to capture most of this structure. Hence the extra modelling ability of GSGP, seen in previous work, is unneeded.

The improvement in fitness over the generations (not shown for lack of space) is relatively slight for all GP/GSGP methods. Again, this suggests that whatever structure is present is being exploited easily in the early generations, and that longer evolution is not needed.

The computational time required for the different methods was not recorded. However, all GP methods are roughly comparable in this, and are far slower than deterministic methods such as ARIMA.

5   Discussion

One interesting effect of the GSGP variants was observed in pilot experiments. GSGP is "greedy": once added, a subtree cannot be deleted from a GSGP individual. If a subtree displays a division by zero or other "pathological" behaviour known to occur in GP [4], it may be difficult for evolution to counteract, and performance on the entire run may be affected. Usually, such subtrees are simply not selected, so the problem does not arise. However, GSGP and variants are vulnerable to a poor choice of initial individual. If it is chosen randomly, there may be a substantial probability of choosing a subtree of pathological behaviour. Instead, it is safer to select the initial individual from an initial population. Experiments to measure the size of this effect are ongoing.

Previous work has not exhibited any solution trees produced using GSGP methods. The trees produced by [12] were too large to reconstruct on computer, never mind in print. The individuals evolved by [9] used the functions +, -, and * only, so implicit simplification into polynomials was possible, so the trees' "true form" (i.e. the form produced prior to simplification) could be avoided. That simplification is not possible with our alphabet. So, it is interesting to look at an example tree produced using the GSGP-one-tree variant after just three steps (random constants have been rounded off):

```
(+ (+ (+ (* (/ x3 0.1) (sin x0)) (* 1.346 (* (/ x0 x5) (sin -0.1))))
(* -0.0506 (+ (+ x6 x1) x1))) (* 0.165 (sin (sin x3)))).
```

It is a linear combination of random subtrees, with both positive and negative coefficients. GSGP-optimal-ms produces trees of similar form. The original GSGP method also produces a linear combination of random subtrees, though using both addition and subtraction, and with all coefficents equal to 0.001. In fact, it is useful to see GSGP and variants as ad-hoc approaches to generalised linear models (GLMs). This relationship has not been explored in previous work. It suggests that previous research into using GP in a GLM context is of relevance, in particular the Fast Function Extraction system of [6].

The form of trees produced by GSGP and variants may be limiting. They cannot use non-linear behaviour at the root. Although non-linearities arise in the random subtrees, these are crucially never subject to gradual improvement, only re-weighting.

6   Conclusions and Future Work

Although somewhat mixed, our results are perhaps the first positive results using GSGP on real-world data. We have shown that GP, GSGP, and variants can perform well out-of-sample over short time horizons. The novel GSGP variants produce smaller trees, relative to the original GSGP. It is clear that for each setup, some runs (out of 30) are far more successful than others. Therefore, future work will consist of using a validation dataset to pick out the individuals created during the most successful runs, and then trade on the test set only using those. In the meantime, using the best classification accuracy on the training set to choose the best runs seems to work well.

References

1. Agapitos, A., O'Neill, M., Brabazon, A.: Stateful program representations for evolving technical trading rules. In: Proceedings of the 13th Annual Conference Companion on Genetic and Evolutionary Computation GECCO, pp. 199–200. ACM (2011)
2. Brabazon, A., O'Neill, M.: Biologically inspired algorithms for financial modelling. Springer, Berlin (2006)
3. Brabazon, A., O'Neill, M.: Natural computing in computational finance, vol. 1-3. Springer (2008)
4. Keijzer, M.: Improving symbolic regression with interval arithmetic and linear scaling. In: Ryan, C. et al. (eds.): EuroGP 2003. LNCS, vol. 2610, pp. 70–82. Springer Heidelberg (2003)
5. Lohpetch, D., Corne, D.: Outperforming Buy-and-Hold with Evolved Technical Trading Rules: Daily, Weekly and Monthly Trading. In: Di Chio, C., Brabazon, A., Di Caro, G.A., Ebner, M., Farooq, M., Fink, A., Grahl, J., Greenfield, G., Machado, P., O'Neill, M., Tarantino, E., Urquhart, N. (eds.) EvoApplications 2010, Part II. LNCS, vol. 6025, pp. 171–181. Springer, Heidelberg (2010)
6. McConaghy, T.: FFX: Fast, scalable, deterministic symbolic regression technology. In: Genetic Programming Theory and Practice IX, pp. 235–260. Springer (2011)
7. Michie, D.: Memo functions and machine learning. Nature **218**(5136), 19–22 (1968)
8. Moraglio, A.: Towards a geometric unification of evolutionary algorithms. Ph.D. thesis, University of Essex (November 2007). http://eden.dei.uc.pt/~moraglio/
9. Moraglio, A., Krawiec, K., Johnson, C.G.: Geometric Semantic Genetic Programming. In: Coello, C.A.C., Cutello, V., Deb, K., Forrest, S., Nicosia, G., Pavone, M. (eds.) PPSN 2012, Part I. LNCS, vol. 7491, pp. 21–31. Springer, Heidelberg (2012)
10. O'Reilly, U.M., Oppacher, F.: Program search with a hierarchical variable length representation: Genetic programming, simulated annealing and hill climbing. In: Davidor, Y., Schwefel, H.P., Manner, R. (eds.) Parallel Problem Solving from Nature - PPSN III. LNCS, vol. 866, pp. 397–406. Springer, Jerusalem (1994). http://www.springer.de/cgi-bin/search_book.pl?isbn=3-540-58484-6
11. Tsay, R.S.: Analysis of financial time series, 3rd edn. Wiley, Hoboken (2010)
12. Vanneschi, L., Castelli, M., Manzoni, L., Silva, S.: A New Implementation of Geometric Semantic GP and Its Application to Problems in Pharmacokinetics. In: Krawiec, K., Moraglio, A., Hu, T., Etaner-Uyar, A.Ş., Hu, B. (eds.) EuroGP 2013. LNCS, vol. 7831, pp. 205–216. Springer, Heidelberg (2013)

On PBIL, DE and PSO for Optimization of Reinsurance Contracts

Omar Andrés Carmona Cortes[1]([⊠]), Andrew Rau-Chaplin[2], Duane Wilson[2],
and Jürgen Gaiser-Porter[3]

[1] Instituto Federal do Maranhão, São Luis, MA, Brasil
omar@ifma.edu.br
[2] Risk Analytics Lab, Dalhousie University, Halifax, NS, Canada
arc@cs.dal.ca, dwilson@gmail.com
[3] Global Analytics, Willis Group, London, UK
gaiserporterj@willis.co

Abstract. In this paper, we study from the perspective of an insurance company the *Reinsurance Contract Placement problem*. Given a reinsurance contract consisting of a fixed number of layers and a set of expected loss distributions (one per layer) as produced by a Catastrophe Model, plus a model of current costs in the global reinsurance market, identifying optimal combinations of placements (percent shares of subcontracts) such that for a given expected return the associated risk value is minimized. Our approach explores the use bio-inspired metaheuristics with the goal of determining which evolutionary optimization approach leads to the best results for this problem, while being executable in a reasonable amount of time on realistic industrial sized problems.

Keywords: Reinsurance Analytics · Reinsurance Contract Placement · Particle Swarm Optimization · Differential Evolution · Population-Based Incremental Learning · Financial Risk · Optimization

1 Introduction

Risk hedging strategies are at the heart of prudent risk management. Individuals often hedge risks to their property, particularly from infrequent but expensive events such as fires, floods and robberies, by entering into risk transfer contracts with insurance companies. Insurance companies collect premium from those individual with the expectation that at the end of the year they will have taken in more money than they have had to pay out in losses and overhead, and therefore remain profitable or at least solvent. Perhaps not surprisingly insurance companies themselves try to hedge their risks, particularly from the potentially enormous losses often associated with natural catastrophes such as earthquakes, hurricanes and floods. Much of this hedging is facilitated by the global "property cat" reinsurance market [1], where reinsurance companies insure primary insurance companies against the massive claims that can occur due to natural catastrophes.

© Springer-Verlag Berlin Heidelberg 2014
A.I. Esparcia-Alcázar et al. (Eds.): EvoApplications 2014, LNCS 8602, pp. 227–238, 2014.
DOI: 10.1007/978-3-662-45523-4_19

Analytics in the reinsurance market is becoming increasingly complex for at least three reasons. Firstly, factors like climate change are skewing the data in ways that are not fully understood making experience a less useful guide in decision making. Secondly, the global distribution of economic activity is changing rapidly with key supply-chain now having significant exposure to parts of the world where catastrophic risk is less well understood. For example, few in 2011 understood that a Thailand flood event could cost $47 Billion USD in property losses and cause a global shortage of hard disk drives that lasted throughout 2012. Lastly, there is a tendency for risk transfer contracts to become ever more complex, in large part by increasing the number of sub-contracts (called layers) that make up a contract. This in turn makes it increasingly important to have good computational tools that can help underwriters understand the interaction between layers and to decide on placement percentages, that is which layers to buy and how large a share or percentage of them to buy, in order to minimize risk for a given expected return.

In this paper, we study from the perspective of an insurance company the *Reinsurance Contract Placement problem*. Given a reinsurance contract consisting of a fixed number of layers and a set of expected loss distributions (one per layer) as produced by a Catastrophe Model [2], plus a model of current costs in the global reinsurance market, identifying optimal combinations of placements (percent shares of sub contracts) such that for a given expected return the associated risk value is minimized. Our approach is to explore the use of metaheuristics (evolutionary and swarm algorithms) with the goal of determining which approach leads to the best results for this problem, while being executable in a reasonable amount of time of realistic industrial sized problems.

There are many bio-inspired metaheuristics that can be applied to optimize problems like this, such as Particle Swarm Optimization (PSO) [3], Differential Evolution (DE) [4,5], Genetic Algorithms (GA) [6], Evolution Strategies (ES) [7] and Population-Based Incremental Learning (PBIL) [8]. Indeed, the broader area of computational finance is a field that has been gaining attention lately in the evolutionary computation community driven by the increasing availability of financial data for analysis and improvements in computer processing power [9]. Some notable examples of metaheuristics in computational finance include [9], [10], [11], [12].

Recently, risk and reinsurance problems have also been tackled using bio-inspired algorithms such as in [13], [17] and [14]. Here the focus has been on stop loss and ruin predictions, a somewhat different problem than the contract placement problem studied in this paper. The initial work on contract placement [15] which has been applied in an industrial setting used a parallel discretized enumeration method. Unfortunately, while this method worked well when the number of layers was small (for example 2-5 layers), it experienced exponentially growing runtimes as the number of layers is increased. For instance, a problem with just 7 layers and using a discretization of 5% requires more than a week to be solved using an R-based implementation of this method, while problems of more than 7 layers or finer discretization might run for months or years and are therefore practically infeasible. Initial work addressing the Reinsurance Contract Placement problem using evolutionary techniques was described in [16]. The approach taken was to compare the Population-Based Incremental Learning (PBIL) [8] method to the previously studied enumeration method to try and determine if the evolutionary method could find results that were comparable in quality to the exact enumeration approach, and if the use of PBIL would allow larger problems, that is those with more layers, to be solved in a feasible amount of time. While [16] demonstrated that PBIL worked for this problem it generated as many questions as it answered. For example, 1) is PBIL the best approach or would newer evolutionary methods like PSO, or DE be better? 2) How good are the results in high dimensions given that we have no other method to compare against?, and 3) what values for key parameters like number of iterations or population size work best for each method and at what point do the benefits of larger values (and corresponding larger run-times) diminish? It is these questions that this paper sets out to answer. In the remainder of this paper, we first formally define our reinsurance contract placement problem in Section 2. Then we describe the evolutionary methods PSO, DE and PBIL in Section 3. Thereafter, we present a detailed performance analysis comparing our results in terms of quality and performance on real-world data, in Section 4.

2 The Reinsurance Contract Placement Problem

Insurance organizations, with the help of the global reinsurance market, look to hedge their risk against potentially large claims, or losses [1]. This transfer of risk is done in a manner similar to how a consumer cedes part of the risk associated with their private holdings. However, unlike the case of the consumer, who is usually given options as to the type of insurance structures to choose from, the insurer has the ability to set its own structures and offers them to the reinsurance market. Involved in this process are decisions around what the type and the magnitude of financial structures, such as deductibles and limits, as well as the amount of risk the insurer wishes to maintain. The deductible describes the amount of loss that the insurer must incur before being able to claim a loss to the reinsurance contract, the limit describes the maximum amount in excess of the deductible that is claimable and the placement describes the percentage of the claimed loss that will be covered by the reinsurer.

In the reinsurance placement problem an insurer given a fixed number of layers and loss distributions is then faced with the problem of selecting an optimal combination of placements. As with most financial structures, the central problem is in selecting an optimal proportion, or placement, of each layer such for a given expected return on the contracts the associated risk is minimized. This means, from the perspective of the insurer, they wish to maximize the amount claimable for a given risk value. In doing so they minimize amount of loss the insurer may face in a year. This formulation leads to a optimization problem as depicted in Equation 1.

$$maximize \ VaR_\alpha(\mathbf{R}(\pi))$$
$$s.t. \qquad E(\mathbf{R}(\pi)) = a \qquad (1)$$

Given that the expected return a is specified in Equation 1 we can rewrite it as a Pareto Frontier problem as shown in Equation 2, where q is a risk tolerance factor greater than zero. More details about the math involved in this particular optimization problem can be seen in [1], [20] and [16].

$$maximize \ VaR_\alpha(\mathbf{R}(\pi)) - qE(\mathbf{R}(\pi)) \qquad (2)$$

3   Evolutionary/Swarm Algorithms

Evolutionary/Swarm algorithms are population-based stochastic algorithms that originate from nature and provide attractive features for solving both continuous and discrete problems [24]. In this section we briefly describe the three meta-heuristics we will be evaluating for treaty placement problem.

3.1   Differential Evolution

The Differential Evolution (DE) was proposed by Rainer Storn and Kenneth Price in 1995 [4,5] to solve optimization problems [21]. The basic structure of the approach is given in the Algorithm 1, in which F is the scaling vector within the domain $[0, 2]$ and CR is the crossover rate. Initially, a population of real-coded individuals $X_i^D = (x_i^1, x_i^2, ..., x_i^D)$ is randomly created within the domain $[a_i^D, b_i^D]$ where D represents the problem dimension. Then a vector of differences is created based on the equation $x_i' = x_i^3 + F \times (x_i^2 - x_i^1)$, where three member of the population are selected at random, x_i^1, x_i^2 and x_i^3. As we can see, F is used to weight the contribution of the vectors x_i^2 and x_i^3. This calculation is commonly referred as mutation.

Actually, each gene of an individual(n) is chosen taking into account the Crossover Rate (CR), $i.e.$, if the random number is less than CR then the new gen assumes the value computed by the vector of differences, otherwise the new gene is the same of x_i, where i is the index of the individual that can be replaced in the current population. The new individual will replace the current one only if the new one has the best fitness. This strategy is called DE/rand/1/bin. If the best individual is used for creating the vector of differences the strategy is called DE/best/1/bin.

3.2   Particle Swarm Optimization

The particle swarm optimization was firstly proposed by Kennedy and Eberhart [3] also in 1995. The algorithm consists of particles that are placed into the search space. Each particle moves combining some aspects of its own history position and the global position. All particles move around the search space and probably the swarm will move towards the potential optimum in the next iterations.

Generate a population **X** of size n within the domain $[a_i, b_i]$
for $i = 1$ to *pop_size* **do**
    Choose 3 individuals of population x_i^1,x_i^2 and x_i^3
    $x' = x^3 + F \times (x^2 - x^1)$
    for $j = 1$ to D **do**
        Chose a number r at random within $[0, 1]$
        if $(r < CR)$ **then**
            $n_{ij} = x_j'$
        else
            $n_{ij} = x_j$
        end
    end
    if $(f(n_i) < f(x_i))$ **then**
        $x_i = n_i$
    end
end

Algorithm 1. Differential Evolution(DE)

A particle represents a position in the search space as $X_i^D = (x_i^1, x_i^2, ..., x_i^D)$. Further, a particle has a velocity $V_i^D = (v_i^1, v_i^2, ..., v_i^D)$ which is used to determine its new position in the next iteration, where D represents the problem dimension. The new position is determined by means of the Equations 3 and 4, where w represents the inertia weight, c_1 and c_2 are acceleration constants, r_l and r_2 are random number in the range $[0, 1]$, p_i^d is the best position reached by the particle P, and g^d is a vector stores the global optima of the swarm so far.

$$v_i^d = w \times v_i^d + c_1 r_1 \times (p_i^d - x_i^d) + c_2 r_2 \times (g^d - x_i^d) \tag{3}$$

$$x_i^d = x_i^d + v_i^d \tag{4}$$

The Algorithm 2 outlines how PSO works. Initially, the swarm is created at random, where each particle has to be within the domain $[a_i^d, b_i^d]$. Then particles are evaluated in order to initialize the P matrix and the g^d vector, which are the best experience of each particle and the best solution that has been found up to now, respectively. Thereafter, the velocity and the position of a particle are updated within a loop that obeys some stop criteria.

3.3 Population-Based Incremental Learning

Population based incremental learning (PBIL) was first proposed by Baluja [8] in 1994. In the original version of the algorithm, the population were encoded using binary vectors and an associated probability vector, which was then updated based on the best members of a population. Unlike other evolutionary algorithms, a new population is generated at random using the updated probability vector for each generation. Since Baluja's initial work, extensions to the algorithm have been proposed for continuous and base-n represented search spaces [19,22].

Generate a swarm of particles $\mathbf{X}$ of size s from $[a_i^d, b_i^d]$;
for $i = 1$ **to** *swarm_size* **do**
  Evaluate swarm;
  Update the best position g
  Update p of the particles
  for $j = 1$ *to* D **do**
    Update velocity V using Equation 3
    Update position X using Equation 4
  end
end
Verify if the current g is better than the best of the current swarm

Algorithm 2. Particle Swarm Optimization (PSO)

Here we substitute the intervals for equidistant increments in the lower and upper bounds of the search space. The Algorithm 3 describes the discretized PBIL (DiPBIL) method used in this paper in terms of the following tunable parameters: I = Number of Increments (*i.e.* the discretization), LR_2 = Learning Rate in base 2, NLR_2 = Negative Learning Rate in base 2, M_R = Mutation Rate, M_S = Mutation Shift and q = Number of best results to be used in updating. In the same spirit as the original PBIL, the probability matrix is initialized with all increments having an uniform distribution and is updated after every generation with the best combinations member (see Algorithm 1). The updating of each vector in the matrix, however, is done using the base-n method, with an adjusted learning rate and updating function [23]. To ensure more population diversity from across generations, the probability matrix is updated with best member from previous generations as well as the top q members from the current generation. This modifies the updating process as shown in Equation 5, where LF_{ijk} is the ith learning factor, as described in [23], for the kth best result for the jth variable.

for $i = 1$ **to** *pop_size* **do**
  Generate a population $\mathbf{X}$ of size n from P_{ij} ;
  Evaluate $\mathbf{f}$ = fun($\mathbf{X}$);
  Find $\mathbf{x}_G^{best}$ from the current and previous populations;
  Find $\mathbf{x}_i^{best}$ for top q-1 members of the current population;
  Update P_{ij} based on $\mathbf{x}_G^{best} \cup \mathbf{x}_i^{best}$ using LR_N and NLR_N;
end

Algorithm 3. DiPBIL

$$p_{ij}^{NEW} = \sum_{k=1}^{q} p_{ij}^{OLD} \frac{LF_{ijk}}{q} \qquad (5)$$

4   Experimental Results

In this section we compare the reinsurance contract optimization technique against the three algorithms discussed previously, using an anonymized 7 layered real world data set composed by information such as: recoveries, reinstatements, loss table and rate on line (rol). Further, the level of discretization is 5%. Each algorithm was executed 31 trials, thus we can guarantee that the distribution of the outcomes of the experiments follows a normal distribution (central limit theorem) [25], allowing us to make parametric tests. Further, the test has been conducted considering three different number of iterations (500, 1000, 2000) and three population sizes (100, 200, 400), leading the complete experiment to a 837 executions. The parameters were chosen empirically and all tests have been done using R version 2.15.0 and RStudio on a Windows 7 64-bit Operating System running on an Intel i7 3.4 Ghz processor, with 16 GB of RAM. The PBIL algorithm was completely implemented in R language, whereas DE and PSO were obtained from R packages. It is important to notice that the DE package for R uses the strategy DE/best/1/bin. Moreover, the PSO package is based on the implementation of SPSO 2007 [26].

4.1   Quality Analysis

The quality analysis comprises two parts. The first one makes a comparison within each algorithm, *i.e.*, we have tried to identify how the changes on both the number of iterations and the population size affect the precision of a particular algorithm. The second one compares the quality of the solutions between algorithms. All evaluations are supported by Analysis of Variance (ANOVA) and Tukey test. Furthermore, the experiments aim to answer all questions which were done in Section 1.

Comparison Within Metaheuristics. Table 1 presents the mean (average), the best, the worst, and the standard deviation of the risk (in dollars) for the algorithms considering a given expected return, where the best results are emphasized. The mean represents the average on 31 executions and results going toward zero mean lower risk, therefore, better results. Doing so, we are answering the second question. Each algorithm was evaluated for varying population size and number of iterations. The results given by DE were omitted because no differences were found, the outcome -1014986645 was reached regardless the increasing on both the number of iterations and the population size. Thus, considering these results we can state the following observations: (i) The DE algorithm is not sensitive neither to the number of iterations nor to the population size, getting stuck in a local optima; (ii) PSO got some good results, however it can not evolve properly as long as we increase both the number of iterations and the population size, reaching the best value (-1014569720) at least once only with a population size of 100; (iii) PBIL evolves properly and reaches the best solution at least once in all configurations, allowing to find out a good Pareto frontier if necessary.

Table 1. Results in terms of quality for PSO and PBIL

PSO			
500 iterations			
	100 pop	200 pop	400 pop
Mean	**-1014797783**	-1014914071	-1014894134
Worst	**-1014986645**	-1016020335	**-1014986645**
Best	**-1014569720**	-1014694720	-1014699862
Stdev	157117.8977	327431.8272	**136276.6568**
1000 iterations			
Mean	**-1014848734**	-1014912637	-1014931139
Worst	-1014986645	**-1014986645**	**-1014986645**
Best	**-1014569720**	-1014699862	-1014699862
Stdev	157584.0928	127561.8282	**115174.7963**
2000 iterations			
Mean	**-1014964318**	-1014977394	-1014977394
Worst	-1016020335	-1014986645	**-1014986645**
Best	**-1014694720**	-1014699862	-1014699862
Stdev	227266.6245	**51507.73476**	**51507.73476**
PBIL			
500 iterations			
	100 pop	200 pop	400 pop
Mean	-1015360605	-1015127063	**-1014956575**
Worst	-1016280747	**-1016176585**	**-1016176585**
Best	**-1014569720**	**-1014569720**	**-1014569720**
Stdev	723154.6754	552965.2035	**432175.8289**
1000 iterations			
Mean	-1015142297	-1015028435	**-1014924013**
Worst	-1016176585	-1016176585	**-1016020335**
Best	**-1014569720**	**-1014569720**	**-1014569720**
Stdev	617360.1748	503103.4937	**347988.6081**
2000 iterations			
Mean	-1015253346	-1015022019	**-1014959747**
Worst	-1019014085	-1016020335	**-1014986645**
Best	**-1014569720**	**-1014569720**	**-1014569720**
Stdev	904081.2636	364027.6174	**104119.1131**

Comparison Between Metaheuristics. The purpose of this experiment is to compare the performance, in terms of quality, between algorithm, allowing us to answer the first question. In order to do so, we define the number of iterations and vary the population size. Figure 1 shows the average result of each algorithm, where the graphs depict 500, 1000 and 2000 iterations, respectively. Considering the number of iterations, the PSO algorithm presented the best overall results using 500 iterations. An interesting thing to noticed is that as long as we increase both the iteration number and the population size the algorithms tend to present more similar results, however three observations have to be made: (i) PBIL shows clearly how evolve itself as long as we change the population size; (ii) PSO starts presenting better solutions than the other algorithms in the initial configurations, nonetheless the algorithm worse in terms of quality when the population size changes; and (iii) as previously mentioned, DE gets trapped in a local optima. In this context, if we applied an ANOVA test in all of those combinations, the statistical meaning start disappearing when 2000 iterations and population size of 200 are used which ends up answering the third question. In other words, using a population size of 200 or 400 leads to similar outcomes. Moreover, extending this statistical evaluations to the other configurations we will see that PSO and DE some times provide similar quality of solution, whereas PBIL improves the results based mainly on the variation of the population size.

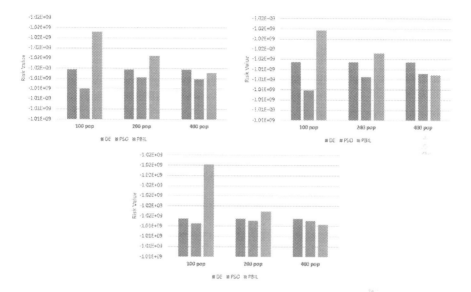

Fig. 1. Results of the different AEs for 500, 1000 and 2000 iterations, respectively

4.2 Performance

It is important to be aware that both DE and PSO have implementations in C language linked with R. Thus, we have used the compiler package [1] from R just in our PBIL code in order to improve its performance as well. Figure 3 presents the performance of the algorithms in terms of elapsed time.

It is clear that DE has the best performance in terms of time. On the other hand, it is not possible to identify if the difference between PSO and PBIL is significant. Thus, in order to compare theses algorithms we did a two-tailed t-test with $\alpha = 0.01$, where t has to be in the range $[-1.645, 1.645]$ for accept the null hypothesis (h_0) we consider as "there are no differences between means". As illustrated in Table 2, we can observe that the null hypothesis is rejected in four

---

[1] The compiler package improves the performance of R code creating a byte-code.

cases as follows: (i) 500 iterations and population size equals to 100: **PBIL**; (ii) 1000 iterations and population size equals to 200: **PSO**; (iii) 1000 iterations and population size equals to 400: **PSO**; and, (iv) 2000 iterations and population size equals to 100: **PBIL**.

Looking at the results we can state the compiler package is more efficient in compiling the outer loop than the inner one, which deals with the population size, this might be the reason why PBIL is faster with small populations and higher number of iterations. Anyway, the PBIL presented a good performance because it is not written in C, but in pure R.

Table 2. A t-test between PSO and PBIL

500 iterations					
	100pop	Stdev	200pop	Stdev	400pop	Stdev
PSO	82.1648	9.7339	159.2845	7.4825	320.1658	13.57
PBIL-C	77.39	8.3282	160.74	46.8142	350.26	101.65
t	**2.0752**		-0.1709		**-1.6339**	
1000 iterations					
PSO	171.5858	12.2129	333.6309	17.7405	656.7248	21.46
PBIL-C	166.58	34.5330	368.35	102.0374	758.53	216.93
t	0.7609		**-1.8665**		**-2.6002**	
2000 iterations					
PSO	414.0819	75.7310	738.6980	77.8075	1475.4380	92.61
PBIL-C	344.11	86.4658	703.9	237.0902	1534.6525	444.91
t	**3.3894**		0.7764		-0.7254	

In spite of using packages, parallel computing represents a viable alternative in order to speedup the Pareto frontier calculation because points are computed independently (one per given expected return). In this context, Figure 2 shows the speedup obtained for each algorithm increasing the thread count. The experiment was conducted in a SunBlade server x6440, with four Quad-core AMD Opteron 8384 (2.7GHz) processors and 32 GB Ram, running Red Hat Enterprise Linux 4.8.

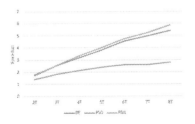

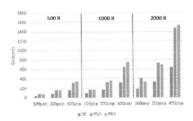

Fig. 2. The achieved speedup increasing the thread count

Fig. 3. Performance of the evolutionary algorithms

As we can see in the Figure 2, the best speedup was reached by the PBIL algorithm, where 8 threads leaded to a speedup close to 6. DE and PBIL had similar outcomes until 4-5 threads and then PBIL start improving a little faster. Whereas PSO presented the worse efficiency when the number of threads were increased.

5   Conclusions

This paper presented an evaluation of three different algorithms (Differential Evolution, Particle Swarm Optimization and Population-Based Incremental Learning) optimizing the problem of the Reinsurance Contract, answering relevant questions. Future implementations include a real multi-objective PBIL, PSO and DE versions, *i.e*, optimizing the risk value and the expected return at the same time. Furthermore, we plan to extend the PBIL approach evaluating the performance gains achievable with an optimized C/OpenMP implementation.

References

1. Cai, J., et al.: Optimal reinsurance under VaR and CTE risk measures. Insurance: Mathematics and Economics **43**, 185–196 (2008)
2. Grossi, P., Kunreuther, H.: Catastrophe Modeling: A New Approach to Managing Risk. International Series on Risk, Insurance and Economic Scurity. Springer (2005)
3. Kennedy, J., Eberhart, R.: Particle swarm optimization. In: Proceedings of the IEEE International Conference on Neural Networks, vol. 4, pp. 1942–1948 (1995)
4. Storn, R., Price, K.: Differential Evolution A simple and efficient adaptive scheme for global optimization over continuous spaces, Technical Report TR-95-012 (March 1995). ftp.ICSI.Berkeley.edu/pub/techreports/1995/tr-95-012.ps.Z
5. Storn, R., Price, K.: Minimizing the real functions of the ICEC 1996 contest by differential evolution. In: Proc. of IEEE International Conference on Evolutionary Computation, Nagoya, Japan (1996)
6. Michalewicz, Z.: Genetic Algorithms + Data Structure = Evolution Programs, 3rd edn Springer (1996)
7. Yao, X., Liu, Y., Lin, G.: Evolutionary programming made faster. IEEE Transactions on Evolutionary Computation **3**(2), 82–102 (1999)
8. Baluja, S.: Population based incremental learning. Technical Report, Carnegie Mellon University
9. Edward Tsang, P.K., Martinez-Jaramillo, S.: Computational finance feature article. IEEE Computational Intelligence Society (2004)
10. Gilli, M., Schumann, E.: Heuristic optimisation in nancial modelling. COMISEF wps-007 (2009)
11. Maringer, D.G., Meyer, M.: CSmooth transition autoregressive models: New approaches to the model selection problem. Studies in Nonlinear Dynamics and Econometrics **12**(1), 1–19 (2008)
12. Krink, T., Paterlini, S.: Multiobjective optimization using Differential Evolution for real-world portfolio optimization. Computational Management Science **8**, 157–179 (2011)

13. Shapiro, A.F., Gorman, R.P.: Implementing adaptive nonlinear models. Insurance: Mathematics and Economics **26**(2–3), 289–307 (2000)
14. Salcedo-Sanz, S., Carro Calvo, L., Claramunt Bielsa, M., Castañer, A., Marmol, M.: An Analysis of Black-Box Optimization Problems in Reinsurance: Evolutionary-Based Approache (2013). Available at SSRN: http://ssrn.com/abstract=2260320 or http://dx.doi.org/10.2139/ssrn.2260320
15. Mistry, S. (n.d.), et al.: Parallel Computation of Reinsurance Models (unpublished manuscript)
16. Cortes, O.A.C., Rau-Chaplin, A., Wilson, D., Gaiser-Porterz, J.: Efficient Optimization of Reinsurance Contracts using Discretized PBIL. In: Proceedings of Data Analytics, London (2013)
17. Posík, P., Huyer, W., Pál, L.: A comparison of global search algorithms for continuous black box optimization. Evolutionary Computation 20, 509–541 (2012)
18. Sebag, M., Ducoulombier, A.: Extending Population-Based Incremental Learning to Continuous Search Spaces. In: Eiben, A.E., Bäck, T., Schoenauer, M., Schwefel, H.-P. (eds.) PPSN 1998. LNCS, vol. 1498, pp. 418–427. Springer, Heidelberg (1998)
19. Bureerat, S.: Improved Population-Based Incremental Learning in Continuous Spaces. In: Gaspar-Cunha, A., Takahashi, R., Schaefer, G., Costa, L. (eds.) Soft Computing in Industrial Applications. AISC, vol. 96, pp. 77–86. Springer, Heidelberg (2011)
20. Mitschele, A., Oesterreicher1, I., Schlottmann, F., Seese1, D.: Heuristic optimization of reinsurance programs and implications for reinsurance buyers. In: International Conference of the German Operations Research Society (2006)
21. Sun, C., Zhou, H., Chen, L.: Improved differential evolution algorithms. In: IEEE International Conference on Computer Science and Automation Engineering, vol. 3, pp. 142–145 (2012)
22. Yuan, B., Gallagher, M.: Playing in continuous spaces: Some analysis and extension of population-based incremental learning. In: CEC 2003, CA, USA, pp. 443–450 (2003)
23. Servais, M.P., Jager, G., Greene, J.R.: Function optimisation using multi-base population based incremental learning. In: PRASA 1997. Rhodes University (1997)
24. Pehlivanoglu, Y.V.: A New Particle Swarm Optimization Method Enhanced With a Periodic Mutation Strategy and Neural Networks. IEEE Transactions on Evolutionary Computation 17(3), 436–452 (2013)
25. Schefler, B.: Statistics: Concepts and Applications. Benjamin-Cummings Pub. Co. (1988)
26. Clerc, M.: A method to improve Standard PSO, Open access archive HAL (2009). Available at http://hal.archives-ouvertes.fr/hal-00394945 (last Visit June 6, 2013)

Algebraic Level-Set Approach
for the Segmentation of Financial Time Series

Rita Palivonaite[(✉)], Kristina Lukoseviciute, and Minvydas Ragulskis

Research Group for Mathematical and Numerical Analysis of Dynamical Systems,
Kaunas University of Technology, Studentu 50-222, LT-51368 Kaunas, Lithuania
{rita.palivonaite,kristina.lukoseviciute,minvydas.ragulskis}@ktu.lt
http://www.personalas.ktu.lt/~mragul

Abstract. Adaptive algebraic level-set segmentation algorithm of financial time series is presented in this paper. The proposed algorithm is based on the algebraic one step-forward predictor with internal smoothing, which is used to identify a near optimal algebraic model. Particle swarm optimization algorithm is exploited for the detection of a base algebraic fragment of the time series. A combinatorial algorithm is used to detect intervals where predictions are lower than a predefined level. Moreover, the combinatorial algorithm does assess the simplicity of the identified near optimal algebraic model. Automatic adaptive identification of quasi-stationary segments can be employed for complex financial time series.

Keywords: Segmentation · Financial time series · Particle swarm optimization

1 Introduction

Financial time series prediction is a challenging task for researchers and practitioners in different fields of science and engineering. Many different techniques are used to analyze time series. Data mining community consider such major tasks as indexing, clustering, classification, segmentation, prediction and summarization [1]. Discovering information from massive data becomes a challenge, which leads to the necessity to present data in reduced form. The dimensionality reduction of the data is the first step to efficiently deal with data mining tasks [2]. Segmentation in time series analysis is often referred to as a dimensionality reduction algorithm. Most time series segmentation algorithms can be grouped into one of the following three categories: sliding windows [3], top-down [4], bottom-up [5]. Segments are usually used for representing financial time series. One frequently used segmentation method is Piecewise Linear Approximation (PLA) [6,7]. PLA has been applied for pattern matching [8] and predicting the trading points [9] in the stock market. In predicting stock movement, financial analysts not only consider the trend identified by the curve but also take into account certain points on the time series data. Segments extracted from financial

© Springer-Verlag Berlin Heidelberg 2014
A.I. Esparcia-Alcázar et al. (Eds.): EvoApplications 2014, LNCS 8602, pp. 239–250, 2014.
DOI: 10.1007/978-3-662-45523-4_20

time series are widely used in trend analysis as well as in predicting future tendency of the price movement. Time series segmentation method based on turning points, which are extracted from the maximum or minimum points of the time series is proposed in [10]. This method generates segments at different levels of details and achieves satisfactory results in preserving higher number of trends compared to other segmentation approach.

A novel time series segmentation algorithm based on algebraic predictor with internal smoothing and an adaptive level-set method for the assessment of prediction errors is presented in this paper. The algebraic prediction method with internal smoothing (APIS) is used to forecast time series, build a model of the process and then use this model for the segmentation of financial time series [11].

2   Preliminaries

Time series prediction is a challenging task in many fields of economics and finance. Despite of plenty forecasting techniques, there is no single method outperforming all others in all situations. In this paper we will use an algebraic one point forward prediction technique. The main difference of the algebraic prediction technique first introduced in [12] and developed in [11] from other alternative time series predictors is in the fact that the algebraic predictor identifies the algebraic complexity of the time series by means of the Hankel rank (or H-rank) of a sequence. The identification of the H-rank will serve as key computational tool in the segmentation procedure of the analyzed time series.

The definition of the H-rank is presented in [12], but we will give a brief overview of the computational techniques used for the identification of H-ranks.

Let S be a sequence of real numbers:

$$S := (x_0, x_1, x_2, \ldots) \tag{1}$$

The Hankel matrix $H^{(n)}$ constructed from the elements of the sequence S is defined as follows:

$$H^{(n)} := \begin{vmatrix} x_0 & x_1 & \cdots & x_{n-1} \\ x_1 & x_2 & \cdots & x_n \\ \cdots & \cdots & \cdots & \cdots \\ x_n & x_{n+1} & \cdots & x_{2n-2} \end{vmatrix} \tag{2}$$

where n denotes the order of the square matrix. The determinant of the Hankel matrix is denoted by $d^{(n)} = \det H^{(n)}$; $n \geq 1$. The H-rank of the sequence is such natural number $m = Hr\,(x_k; k \in Z_0)$ that satisfies the following condition[12]:

$$d^{m+k} = 0 \tag{3}$$

for all $k \in 1, 2, \ldots$, but $d^m \neq 0$.

Let us assume that the H-rank of the sequence is m, $m \leq +\infty$. Then the elements of the deterministic algebraic sequence S are expressed in the form[12]:

$$x_n = \sum_{k=1}^{r} \sum_{l=0}^{n_k-1} \mu_{kl} \binom{n}{l} \rho_k^{n-l}; \; n = 0, 1, 2, \ldots \tag{4}$$

where the characteristic roots $\rho_k \in C$; $k = 1, 2, \ldots, r$ can be determined from the Hankel characteristic equation

$$\begin{vmatrix} x_0 & x_1 & \cdots & x_m \\ x_1 & x_2 & \cdots & x_{m+1} \\ & & \cdots & \\ x_{m-1} & x_m & \cdots & x_{2m-1} \\ 1 & \rho & \cdots & \rho^m \end{vmatrix} = 0; \tag{5}$$

the recurrence indexes of these roots n_k $(n_k \in N)$ satisfy the equality $n_1 + n_2 + \ldots + n_r = m$; coefficients $\mu_{kl} \in C$; $k = 1, 2, \ldots, r$; $l = 0, 1, \ldots, n_k - 1$ can be determined from a system of linear algebraic equations which can be formed from the systems of equalities in Eq. (4), and this system has a unique solution [13].

The algebraic prediction technique in [12] exploits the concept of the H-rank and performs the extrapolation of the reconstructed algebraic model into the future. But a random sequence does not have a rank simply due to an inevitable contamination by noise. Thus special evolutionary computational strategies are developed in [12] for the identification of a closest skeleton algebraic sequence to the real-world time series, but due to variability of forecasted values the algebraic predictor in [12] is applicable for estimation of local minimums and maximums in day-ahead forecasting applications. In this paper for financial time series segmentation task we employ enhanced algebraic method with procedure of internal smoothing (APIS) [11]. Internal smoothing procedure enable reaching a healthy balance between excellent variability of skeleton algebraic sequences and valuable properties of predictors based on the moving averaging method which is widely used in financial time series primary analysis and forecasting.

The forecasting idea is based on the assumption that the sequence $\tilde{S}$ is produced by adding noise to some unknown algebraic sequence:

$$\tilde{S} := (x_0 - \varepsilon_0, x_1 - \varepsilon_1, x_2 - \varepsilon_2, \ldots) = (\tilde{x}_0, \tilde{x}_1, \tilde{x}_2, \ldots) \tag{6}$$

We will try to indentify algebraic relationships in the available observation data and to smooth the forecast before the prediction is done. In order to remove inherent random variation we employ simple moving average smoothing technique:

$$\bar{x}_k = \frac{1}{s} \sum_{s=1}^{s-1} x_{k-i-1} \tag{7}$$

where $\bar{x}_k$ is a smoothed value at the moment k; s is the averaging window. The width of averaging window s should be preselected for each time series, though some general recommendations are given in [11]. It is common that for financial time series forecasting the best result is achieved with $s = 1$, it is so

called the naïve method [14]. In this paper according to these recommendations
we set $s = 1$.

The schematic diagram of the algebraic prediction with internal smoothing
process is illustrated in Fig. 1.

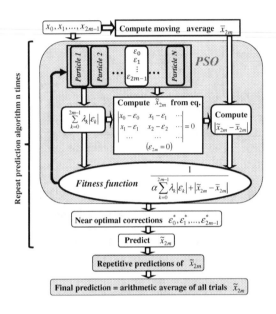

Fig. 1. The illustration of the algebraic prediction with internal smoothing (APIS)
forecasting procedure

Let the H-rank of that unknown algebraic sequence is assumed to be equal
to m; $2m$ observations x_0, x_1, x_2, ..., x_{2m-1} are available for the building the
algebraic model of the process; x_{2m-1} is the value of the observation at the
present moment. The first task is to compute the moving average forecast value
$\bar{x}_{2m}$ with parameter $s = 1$. Secondly, the set of corrections $\{\varepsilon_0, \varepsilon_1, \ldots, \varepsilon_{2m-1}\}$
must be identified before any algebraic predictions could be made.

Evolutionary algorithms will be used to identify the near-optimal set of corrections. Particle swarm optimization (PSO) techniques have been successfully
employed for the identification of the skeleton algebraic sequence in [11]. We will
also use PSO for the selection of a near-optimal set of corrections. Though the
selection of the parameters of PSO remains mostly empirical and depends on
the structure of the fitness function [15], we fix $w = 0.6$ and $c_1 = c_2 = 1.7$ as
recommended by Trelea [16] (c_1 and c_2 are two positive constants, called acceleration constants, representing weightings of the stochastic acceleration terms
that pull each particle toward the *particle's best* and the *global best*; w is the
inertia weight balancing the global and the local search). Due to the indication
that the effect of the population size on the performance of the PSO method is

of minimum significance [17] and most researchers use a swarm size of 10 to 60 [18], we set the swarm size for PSO to 30 particles.

As the black thick arrow in Fig. 1 illustrates, a new set of near-optimal corrections $\{\varepsilon_0, \varepsilon_1, \ldots, \varepsilon_{2m-1}\}$ is generated every time when the PSO algorithm is executed. The next step is to determine the element $\tilde{x}_{2m}$ from the following equality based on the eq. (3), when the H-rank is assumed to be m:

$$\begin{vmatrix} x_0 - \varepsilon_0 & x_1 - \varepsilon_1 & \cdots & x_m - \varepsilon_m \\ x_1 - \varepsilon_1 & x_2 - \varepsilon_2 & \cdots & x_{m+1} - \varepsilon_{m+1} \\ \cdots & \cdots & \cdots & \cdots \\ x_m - \varepsilon_m & x_{m+1} - \varepsilon_{m+1} & \cdots & \tilde{x}_{2m} \end{vmatrix} = 0; \qquad (8)$$

The goal of selecting the set of corrections $\{\varepsilon_0, \varepsilon_1, \ldots, \varepsilon_{2m-1}\}$ is to minimize any distortions from original time series. Therefore, the fitness function for the set of corrections $\{\varepsilon_0, \varepsilon_1, \ldots, \varepsilon_{2m-1}\}$ has to be maximized [11]:

$$F(\varepsilon_0, , \varepsilon_1, \ldots, \varepsilon_{2m-1}) = \frac{1}{\alpha \sum_{k=0}^{2m-1} \lambda_k |\varepsilon_k| + |\tilde{x}_{2m} - \bar{x}_{2m}|}; \; \alpha > 0; \qquad (9)$$

where α is the penalty proportion between the sum of weighted corrections and the difference of forecasts based on skeleton algebraic sequences and moving averages; coefficients λ_k determine the tolerance corridor for the corrections (all corrections would be the same if $\lambda_k = 1/(2m); \; k = 0, 1, \ldots, 2m - 1$) [12].

3   The Construction of the Segmentation Algorithm

3.1   Time Series Prediction Procedure

As mentioned previously, we will use the time series prediction algorithm based on algebraic prediction with internal smoothing (APIS) [11] for the segmentation of the time series. But instead of trying to identify the most appropriate H-rank of the time series at the beginning of the prediction process, we will perform the prediction at different preset values of the H-rank.

In general, the selection of the effective range of H-ranks can be free, though too wide range of H-ranks would raise the computational costs required by the proposed technique. We preselect $2 \leq Hr \leq 10$ for the artificial time series with additive noise. We started with $Hr = 2$ for an elementary arithmetic progression, which is quite acceptable for financial time series segmentation task. On the other hand, the length of the vector of corrections $\{\varepsilon_k\}$ is equal to 20 already at $Hr = 10$ (what raises computational costs of the prediction algorithm and increases the complexity of the identified algebraic model).

The prediction algorithm extrapolates the skeleton sequence by one element into the future: $\tilde{x}_{2m}$ is the algebraic prediction of the sequence $(x_0, x_1, \ldots, x_{2m-1})$ (Fig. 1). Next, we shift the observation window by one element and predict $\tilde{x}_{2m+1}$. The process is continued until the last element of the original data sequence is predicted.

The next step is the selection of the tolerable error level L for the algebraic prediction of the analyzed time series. The basic idea of the proposed technique is straightforward: the preselected algebraic model is sufficiently accurate if extrapolation errors of the prediction are lower than predefined error level L. All continuous time series prediction intervals with extrapolation errors lower than the level L are considered as the segments. Recommendations for selection of tolerable error level for time series segmentation are developed in [19].

3.2   Combinatorial Aspects of the Segmentation Algorithm

The proposed segmentation algorithm is based on two important concepts:

a) The algorithm must automatically identify the longest time interval where the current algebraic model does not produce forecasting errors higher than the predetermined level L;

b) The segmentation algorithm must also evaluate the simplicity of algebraic model in each identified segment.

In other words, the segmentation algorithm should find a conciliation between two extremities which are graphically represented in Fig. 2. The x-axis represents the order of the algebraic model (H-rank), the vertical axis illustrates the adaptive preference of the segmentation algorithm.

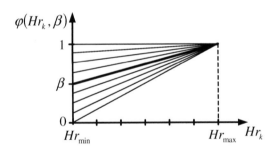

Fig. 2. The schematic diagram of the preference function $\varphi(Hr_k, \beta)$ illustrated by the thick solid line going through points $(Hr_{min}; \beta)$ and $(Hr_{max}; 1)$

The preference function $\varphi(Hr_k, \beta)$ is defined as linear function with parameter β, $0 \leq \beta \leq 1$:

$$\varphi(Hr_k, \beta) = \beta + \frac{Hr_k - Hr_{min}}{Hr_{max} - Hr_{min}}(1 - \beta) \tag{10}$$

The preference function $\varphi(Hr_k, \beta)$ does not assess the simplicity of the algebraic model at $\beta = 1$. On the contrary, the preference function $\varphi(Hr_k, \beta)$ gives the highest priority to the simplest algebraic model at $\beta = 0$. We will use the arithmetic average between these two cases by set at $\beta = 0.5$ (Fig. 2). Then the segmentation procedure can be illustrated by the following example. The longest segment $l_n^{(i)}$ is identified in the first step of the algorithm – note that before taking the decision which segment is given a highest priority we divide the length of each segment by the value of the preference function $\varphi(Hr_k, \beta)$:

$$l_k^{(i)} = \frac{l_k^{(i)}}{\varphi(Hr_k, \beta)} \tag{11}$$

where $l_n^{(i)}$ is the length of the segment, Hr_k – the k-th H-rank, i – an iteration of combinatorial algorithm.

Thus a shorter segment can be given a higher priority than a longer segment if only the algebraic model of the shorter segment is sufficiently simpler compared to the algebraic model of the longer model.

A schematic diagram of combinatorial segmentation algorithm for the identification of longest continuous intervals of successful predictions in the effective range of H-ranks is illustrated in Fig. 3.

The main idea of combinatorial segmentation algorithm is characterized by this illustrative example.

Step 1. Set the level L and perform the algebraic forecasting of the given data at different preselected H-ranks. Mark intervals of the time series where forecasting errors are lower than L. Such marking is schematically illustrated in Fig. 3 (a). Horizontal lines denote continuous intervals for each discrete H-rank (the vertical axis stands for the H-rank). The length of intervals is denoted as $l_k^{(i)}$, where the index k stands for the k-th H-rank and i is the iteration of the segmentation process (at the beginning of the process it is set to zero). As we introduced previously the evaluation of the length of the interval depends on the H-rank: the smaller is the H-rank – the prior is the interval of this H-rank. In this schematic example we set the parameter $\beta = 0.5$ of function $\varphi(Hr_k, \beta)$ (eq. 10). It means that the interval of the lowest H-rank is twice important as the interval of the highest H-rank.

Step 2. Identify the longest continuous interval. Though in our schematic example the interval $(t_2; t_7)$ of the highest H-rank is the longest with length $l_5^{(0)}$, but after evaluation of all segments by the preference function $\varphi(Hr_k, \beta)$, the longest picked interval is $l_1^{(0)}$ (with the lowest H-rank). We considered that the length $l_1^{(0)} = 2 \cdot l_5^{(0)}$ with $\beta = 0.5$. We marked the longest evaluated continuous interval by gray shaded box in Fig. 3 (a).

Step 3. Denote the marked interval as the segment associated to the according H-rank; erase all the information about the other H-ranks above and below the marked segment. The selected segment $(t_0; t_3)$ is marked by a thick solid horizontal line in Fig. 3 (b).

Step 4. With preference function $\varphi(Hr_k, \beta)$ evaluate the longest continuous interval in the zones not occupied by the marked segments (return to the Step 2). Though the longest interval is with the highest H-rank $(t_3; t_7)$ (note that it was truncated after the Step 2), but after evaluation by function $\varphi(Hr_k, \beta)$ it is not considered as the segment. Besides, though the lengths of $l_2^{(1)}$ and $l_3^{(1)}$

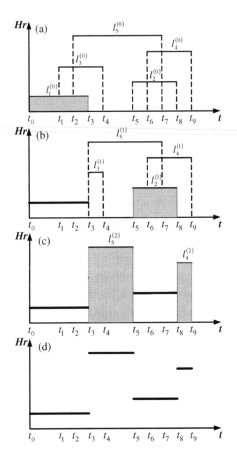

Fig. 3. The illustration of the combinatorial segmentation algorithm. Horizontal lines in part (a) show intervals where algebraic prediction errors are lower than the pre-set level L (the height of a line stands for the appropriate H-rank). The length of the longest weighted interval above the level L for all H-ranks is denoted as $l_k^{(i)}$, where indexes k indicate the k-th H-rank Hr and i indicates the iteration of combinatorial segmentation algorithm. The parameter β is set to 0.5. The gray-shaded area in part (a) illustrates the longest preferred continuous line interval which is associated to a separate segment in part (b). The process is continued through parts (b - d) until the whole sequence is split into separate segments. Thick solid lines represent the result of the segmentation algorithm.

are the same size, the interval $(t_5; t_8)$ is selected due to the lowest H-rank. It is marked as gray shaded box.

Step 5. Erase all the information below and above the selected segment and evaluate the rest segments. At the final step we select two not overlapping intervals $(t_3; t_5)$ and $(t_8; t_9)$ as the last segments.

Finally, the segmentation algorithm identifies four distinct segments $(t_0; t_3)$, $(t_3; t_5)$, $(t_5; t_8)$ and $(t_8; t_9)$ (Fig. 3 (d)). Note that in the real world time series it might be that in some intervals any particular segment could not be selected due to high forecasting errors exceeding the predefined level L.

4   Computational Experiments with Financial Time Series

We test the functionality of the proposed segmentation algorithm using real-world finance time series. We select a standard STLFSI (St. Louis Fed Financial Stress Index) time series describing 230 consecutive measures of the degree of financial stress in the markets (we selected mounthly data range from 1993-Dec-01 to 2013-Mar-31) [20]. Financial STFSI time series is constructed from 18 weekly data series: seven interest rate series, six yield spreads and five other indicators. Each of these variables captures some aspect of financial stress. Accordingly, as the level of financial stress in the economy changes, the data series are likely to move together. Note that vertical axis is transformed to interval $[0; 1]$. Due to specific properties of APIS forecasting method, this transformation ensures lower time series prediction errors[11]. We set parameter $\beta = 0.5$ and the tolerable error level $L = 0.05$ (we consider that algebraic model is sufficiently accurate if extrapolation errors of the prediction are lower than 5 % length of all range of time series data values). The segmentation result of STLFSI time series is presented in Fig. 4. The PSO algorithm is iterated 30 times and the averaged result of APIS is presented.

Our segmentation method has singled out the following mounthly intervals: 1994-May-31 – 1998-Mar-31, 1998-Jul-31 – 2001-Apr-30, 2001-May-31 – 2002-Jan-31, 2002-Mar-31 – 2007-Mar-31, 2008-Nov-30 – 2009-Dec-31, 2010-Jan-31 – 2011-Mar-31, 2011-Apr-30 - 2013-Jan-31.

A comparative assessment of the functionality of the proposed technique with other typical segmentation methods is required in order to understand if our methodology does outperform other methods or not. One of the most commonly used representations is piecewise linear approximation. In the context of data mining, it supports change point detection.

The first comparison is performed with sliding-windows segmentation method. This method is based on growing, usually linear, segment until it exceeds some user-specified criteria. The process repeats with the next data point [3]. Due to comparison we have chosen the same tolerable error level $L = 0.05$. The results of the change point detection are presented in Fig. 4(c). It is clear that linear approximation is not as precise as APIS and approximation errors exceed the pre-set tolerable error level L more common. Naturally, this leads to the higher number of segments. Such approximation becomes greatly over-fragmented for real-world datasets with inevitable additive noise [5].

The second comparison is performed with the bottom-up segmentation method. Starting from the finest approximation, segments are merged until some stopping criterion is met [5]. In our case, the stopping criterion is the maximum error per segment exceeding the preset error level $L = 0.05$. The segmentation results are presented in Fig. 4(d). The bottom-up algorithm is the natural complement to the

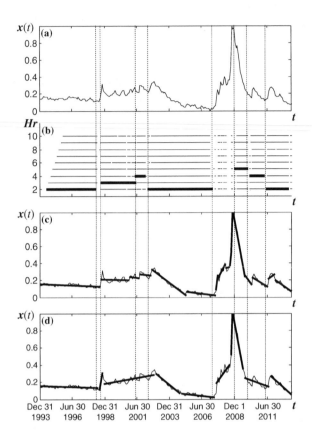

Fig. 4. The segmentation of STLFSI time series. The time series is illustrated in part (a); The result of the segmentation with APIS at tolerable error level $L = 0.05$ is presented in part (b). The result of the segmentation with sliding-windows method is presented in part (c); The result of the segmentation with bottom-up method is presented in part (d).

top-down algorithm. Top-down: the time series is recursively partitioned until some stopping criterion is met. Empirical comparison of the major segmentation algorithms on a very diverse collection of datasets does show that top-down and bottom-up algorithms produce similar results [5] - and thus (due to the space limitations) the results of top-down algorithm are excluded.

Generally, we are able to locate different algebraic relationships while other segmentation methods are approximated only by one type of function, usually by a low order polynomial.

5   Conclusions

Any time series segmentation algorithm must comply with two major requirements: the time series must be approximated by the simplest possible mathematical model (the model identification is a task of the data mining process) and finding change points, which are used as markers between appropriate segments. The main advantage of our proposed method is based on the fact that we do identify algebraic models of the process – but the order of this algebraic model is detected completely automatically. In other words, one does not have to analyze the time series employing different methods and techniques.

The proposed segmentation algorithm reveals that the hidden structure of the time series is able to identify potential changes in the evolution of the process and exploits predictability as a tool for the characterization of complexity. Such predactability can be directly used for the decision-making analysis in financial time series analysis.

Acknowledgments. This research was funded by a grant (No. MIP-100/2012) from the Research Council of Lithuania.

References

1. Esling, P., Agon, C.: Time-series data mining. ACM Computing Surveys (CSUR) **45**(1), 12 (2012)
2. Ralanamahatana, C.A., Lin, J., Gunopulos, D., Keogh, E., Vlachos, M., Das, G.: Mining Time Series Data, Data Mining and Knowledge Discovery Handbook. pp. 1069–1103 Springer, (2005)
3. Qu, Y., Wang, C., Wang, S.: Supporting fast search in time series for movement patterns in multiples scales. In: Proceedings of the 7th International Conference on Information and Knowledge Management, CIKM 1998, pp. 251–258 (1998)
4. Lavrenko, V., Schmill, M., Lawrie, D., Ogilvie, P., Jensen, D., Allan, J.: Mining of Concurrent Text and Time Series. In: Proceedings of the 6th International Conference on Knowledge Discovery and Data Mining, pp. 37–44 (2000)
5. Keogh, E.J., Chu, S., Hart, D., Pazzani, M.: Segmenting time series: a survey and novel approach. Data Mining in Time Series Databasis 57, 1–22 (2003)
6. Keogh, E.J., Pazzani, M.J.: Relevance feedback retrieval of time series data. In: Proceedings of the 22nd Annual International ACM SIGIR Conference on Research and Development in Information Retrieval, Berkeley, California, United States, pp. 183–190 (1999)
7. Li, C.S., Yu, P.S., Castelli, V.: MALM: a framework for mining sequence database at multiple abstraction levels. In: Proceedings of the 7th International Conference on Information and Knowledge Management, Bethesda, Maryland, United States, pp. 267–272 (1998)
8. Zhang, Z., Jiang, J., Liu, X., Lau, W.C., Wang, H., Wang, S.-S., Song, X., Xu, D.: Pattern Recognition in Stock Data Based on a New Segmentation Algorithm. In: Zhang, Z., Siekmann, J.H. (eds.) KSEM 2007. LNCS (LNAI), vol. 4798, pp. 520–525. Springer, Heidelberg (2007)
9. Chang, P.C., Fan, C.Y., Liu, C.H.: Integrating a piecewise linear representation method and a neural network model for stock trading points prediction. IEEE Transactions on Systems, Man, and Cybernetics Part C 39(1), 80–92 (2009)
10. Yin, J., Si, Y.W., Gong, Z.: Financial Time Series segmentation Based On Turning Points. In: Proceedings of 2011 International Conference on System Science and Engineering, Macau, China, pp. 394–399 (2011)

11. Palivonaite, R., Ragulskis, M.: Short-term time series algebraic forecasting with internal smoothing. Neurocomputing (article in press) (2014)
12. Ragulskis, M., Lukoseviciute, K., Navickas, Z., Palivonaite, R.: Short-term time series forecasting based on the identification of skeleton algebraic sequences. Neurocomputing **74**, 1735–1747 (2011)
13. Navickas, Z., Bikulciene, L.: Expressions of solutions of ordinary differential equations by standard functions. Mathematical Modeling and Analysis **11**, 399–412 (2006)
14. Lacina, M., Lee, B.B., Xu, R.Z.: An evaluation of financial analysts and naïve methods in forecasting long-term earnings. Advances in Business and Management Forecasting 8, 77–101 (2011)
15. Eberhart, R.C., Kennedy, J.: Particle swarm optimization: developments, applications and resources. In: Proceedings of IEEE Congress on Evolutionary Computation, Seoul, Korea. pp. 81–86. IEEE Service Center, Piscataway, (2000)
16. Trelea, I.: C.: The particle swarm optimization algorithm: convergence analysis and parameter selection. Information Processing Letters **85**(6), 317–325 (2003)
17. Shi, Y.H., Eberhart, R.C.: Parameter selection in particle swarm optimization. In: Proceedings of Seventh Annual Conference on Evolutionary Programming, San Diego, CA, pp. 591–600. Springer, New York (1998)
18. Kennedy, J., Eberhart, R.C., Shi, Y.H.: Swarm Intelligence. Morgan Kaufman (2001)
19. Palivonaite, R., Lukoseviciute, K., Ragulskis, M.: Algebraic segmentation of short nonstationary time series based on evolutionary prediction algorithms. Neurocomputing **121**, 1354–364 (2013)
20. St. Louis Fed Financial Stress Index News Releases (2013) (accessed November 1, 2013). http://www.stlouisfed.org/newsroom/financial-stress-index

Dynamic Index Trading Using a Gene Regulatory Network Model

Miguel Nicolau$^{(\boxtimes)}$, Michael O'Neill, and Anthony Brabazon

Natural Computing Research and Applications Group, University College Dublin,
Dublin, Ireland
{Miguel.Nicolau,M.ONeill,Anthony.Brabazon}@ucd.ie

Abstract. This paper presents a realistic study of applying a gene regulatory model to financial prediction. The combined adaptation of evolutionary and developmental processes used in the model highlight its suitability to dynamic domains, and the results obtained show the potential of this approach for real-world trading.

1   Introduction

Recent work in the Evolutionary Computation field has seen a surge of interest in Genetic Regulatory Networks (GRNs) as models for computation [1,4,9,10,13]. In nature, GRNs are a key element of temporal gene expression regulation in biological organisms, providing the remarkable capacity of cells to respond to their ever-changing surrounding environment.

GRN-based algorithms combine the adaptive power of evolutionary processes with regulatory mechanisms that differential gene expression provides, leading to life-long conditional adaptation to the environment. This makes these algorithms especially useful for noisy and dynamic environments.

One such dynamic and hard to predict environment are financial markets. In this study, a GRN model is applied to the problem of index trading. Experiments were designed to make this problem as realistic as possible, hence using only raw historical prices and their transformations, and relatively short trading periods, focusing on the dynamic adaptation of the system. The results obtained again highlight the advantages and limitations of current GRN models, and their potential as computational devices, and further pave the future for their continued adaptation in the EC community.

This paper starts with a brief introduction to GRNs and the model used, in Section 2. This is followed by an overview of index trading and the methodology used (Section 3). Section 4 presents and analyses the results obtained, and finally conclusions and future work directions are drawn in Section 5.

2   Artificial Gene Regulatory Model

2.1   Background

Gene Regulatory Networks (GRNs) refer to the complex networks of gene regulation occurring in cell environments. Given a suitable environment, segments of

© Springer-Verlag Berlin Heidelberg 2014
A.I. Esparcia-Alcázar et al. (Eds.): EvoApplications 2014, LNCS 8602, pp. 251–263, 2014.
DOI: 10.1007/978-3-662-45523-4_21

DNA encoding genes are transcribed into RNA strands, which, through a translation process, are used to form sequences of amino-acids, thus creating proteins. Some of these proteins are called *Transcription Factors*, and their role is to help create an environment that either enhances or inhibits the expression of genes. This leads to complex networks of regulation, with genes encoding proteins that themselves enhance or inhibit the expression of proteins from other genes.

2.2   The Model

Typically, artificial GRN models are a broad simplification of their biological counterpart. In this work, a model originally presented by Wolfgang Banzhaf [1] is used; it was shown to exhibit similar dynamics to real world GRNs [2], and has been applied to dynamic control problems (such as the pole-balancing benchmark [13] and index trading [12]).

The model consists of a binary linear genome, which is scanned for 32 bit binary promoter sequences, identifying gene locations. Once a promoter is found, the 2×32 bits preceding it represent two regulatory sites (an enhancer and a inhibitor), and the following 5×32 bits represent the gene contents (used to encode a protein); this is shown in Fig. 1.

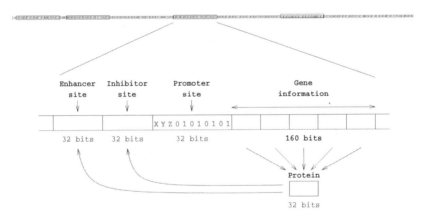

Fig. 1. Bit string encoding of a gene. If a promoter site is found, the gene information is used to create a protein, whose quantity is regulated by the attachment of proteins to the enhancer and inhibitor sites.

Each protein encoded by a gene is a Transcription Factor (TF), that is, it is a regulatory protein, whose role is to affect the rate of expression of all genes (including the one that produced it). Proteins are 32 bit binary sequences, extracted using a majority rule from the 5 sequences of 32 bits that compose the gene information (i.e., if 3 or more equally located bits are set to 1, then the corresponding bit in the protein is also set to 1).

Proteins are bound to regulatory sites via an exclusive-or matching of their respective 32 bit signatures (i.e., the number of different bits in protein signatures and regulatory sites determines the regulatory strength). The enhancing and inhibiting signals regulating the production of each protein p_i are calculated as:

$$e_i, h_i = \frac{1}{N} \sum_{j=1}^{N} c_j \exp(\beta(u_j - u_{max})) \quad , \tag{1}$$

where N is the total number of proteins, c_j is the concentration of protein j, u_j is the number of complementary bits between the (enhancing or inhibitory) regulatory site and protein j, u_{max} is the maximum match observed in the current genome, and β is a positive scaling factor.

The concentration of protein p_i is calculated using a differential equation:

$$\frac{dc_i}{dt} = \delta(e_i - h_i)c_i \quad , \tag{2}$$

where δ is a positive scaling factor (representing a time unit). All the concentrations are normalised at each time step, ensuring that $\sum_i c_i = 1.0$ at all times; this results in competition for resources within the cell environment.

Input and Output. This model has been extended with the notion of inputs and outputs [13], to facilitate its application to computation. In order to encode inputs, extra regulatory proteins (EPs) are injected into the system. These are not produced by any gene, yet also contribute to the regulation of gene expression. They represent the variables required to describe the state of the environment, and their concentrations reflect the (normalised) value of those inputs.

To extract output signals, genes are divided into two classes: TF-genes (genes encoding transcription factors), and P-genes (encoding *product* proteins). The concentration of proteins produced by P-genes can then be used as output signals of the system. The approach taken here is the same as in previous studies [12].

3   Index Trading

In the Financial domain, an index is a composite measure of price changes in a portfolio of shares in a market. Investors who wish to proxy the return of the index can trade it using index funds (EFTs), which offer low expense ratios and high liquidity. These investments are very popular and are the focus of our study.

Evolutionary algorithms have been successfully applied to financial modelling; the reasons for their applicability include their ability to efficiently explore the search space, and uncover dependencies between input variables, leading to their proper inclusion in the final models [5]. Brabazon and O'Neill [3] provide an overview of the application of evolutionary computation to financial modelling.

3.1 Methodology

The trading methodology is based in previous studies [7,12,14], where a trader issues *buy*, *sell*, or *do nothing* signals for each day of the training or test periods. Starting with a capital of $10000, if a buy signal is issued, 10% of the total funds (initial capital plus earnings) are invested in the index; this position is automatically closed after a ten day period. If a sell signal is issued, an investment of 10% is sold short, and also closed after ten days. This ensures that the system cannot overtrade at any point (i.e., issue a trade signal with no funds available)[1].

The profit or loss at the end of each trading period uses a conservative estimate of one-way trading costs and slippage of 0.2% and 0.3%, respectively. Uncommitted funds take into account a risk-free rate of return, which is approximated using the average interest rate over the entire dataset.

3.2 Datasets

The work presented here follows closely the methodology of previous applications of Grammatical Evolution [3,14] and GRNs [12] to index trading, and uses three datasets, from the UK FTSE 100 index, the Japan Nikkei index, and the German Dax index. To keep the results comparable, all data is drawn from the period between 16/4/1991 and 21/10/1996; Fig. 2 plots each dataset. These were divided into four training periods and twelve test periods, of 90 days each, with the latter representing the period where the system has gone *live*.

These datasets highlight the potential risk of overfitting the training period. The FTSE training period exhibits a very unstable, slightly downwards trend, whereas the test period exhibits a clear growth trend. The Dax index shows a slight growth in the training period, with a sudden drop towards the end, which is somewhat consistent with the test period. Finally, the Nikkei training period exhibits a very strong decline in index value, followed by an unstable test period, consisting of medium term upwards and downwards trends.

3.3 Data Preprocessing

In previous studies [3,12], the data was pre-processed prior to evolution, with the raw prices initially transformed into a moving average with a 75 day gap, and then normalised into the range of 0 to 1. However, as the current study focuses on application to real market trading, both of these pre-processing steps are troublesome, as detailed below, and hence were not used.

Moving Average. Working with a moving average smoothes the price curve, but at a cost - the description of trends is also smoothed out. This is exemplified in Fig. 3, for the FTSE market. In the first year of data, for example, the market switches from upwards to downwards trends in a short period of time. This is clearly visible at the beginning of test period 1 (T1), where the index value is

---

[1] In the final 10 days of each period, all trade actions are ignored.

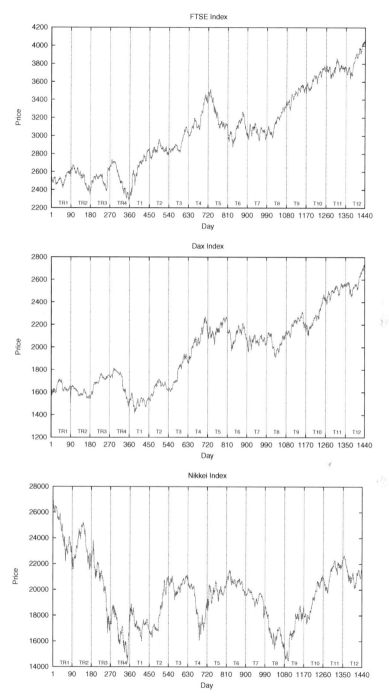

Fig. 2. Plots of the three markets used in this study, along with their training and live (test) periods. Each period consists of 90 traiding days; data ranges from 16/4/1991 to 21/10/1996.

growing, but the $MA(75)$ is still reflecting the previous downwards trend. As the current experiment uses fairly short trading periods (90 days), a 75 day moving average is too slow to indicate the current trend of the index. Working with a smaller value ($MA(10)$) reduces this problem, but as all trading periods are of 10 days, the indication of trends is still sometimes deceptive.

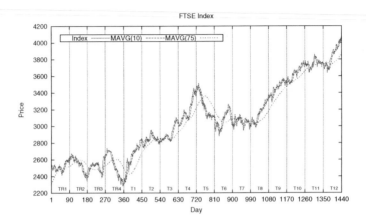

Fig. 3. Index closing values and 10 and 75-day moving average, for the FTSE market

Normalisation. Normalisation can also introduce problems. As the range of future index values cannot be known, a minimum and maximum value must be set for normalisation. On certain markets, this is problematic for model induction, because the range of values encountered in training might be quite different from the range of the test period. Fig. 4 highlights this problem on the FTSE market. As the training period has the range $[2281.0, 2737.8]$, normalising over this range would mean that all normalised values from test period $T2$ onwards would have a capped value of 1.0. Even if the full range of prices $[2281.0, 4073.1]$ were somehow guessed at the start, this would still be problematic, as the training period would only expose the models to a $[0, 0.255]$ range.

3.4   Technical Indicators

Rather than just working with raw and historical market price data, it is typical in the financial domain to derive information from the raw data series into *technical indicators*. These look to predict future price levels, or more generally market trends. Although a potentially infinite number of such indicators may exist, certain classes of indicators are regularly used by investors [7,15]. The following were used in this study[2]:

---

[2] To minimise price range issues, all price data used is logarithmic; the n-day periods used are typical values from the literature.

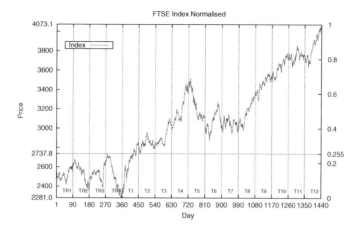

Fig. 4. FTSE index, normalised over the range $[2281.0, 4073.1]$

– **Moving Average Convergence Divergence (MACD)**. The MACD [11] is a popular indicator: it is typically calculated by subtracting the exponential moving average (EMA) of the last 12 days from the 26-day EMA.
– **Relative Strength Index (RSI)**. The RSI is a momentum indicator; it calculates an upward or downward charge per trading period, and returns the ratio of the EMA of these charges [17]. A 14-day RSI is used.
– **Stochastic Oscillator (sOsc)**. This indicator returns the relative location of the current price in relation to its full price range over a period of n days (a 14-day period was used); it tries to predict price turning points [6].
– **Premier Stochastic Oscillator (psOsc)**. The psOsc is based on an 8-day sOsc, which is smoothed using a 5-day double EMA [8]. This smooths and evens out the response to market changes.

4   Setup and Results

4.1   Encoding

The four technical indicators used ($MACD(26, 12)$, $RSI(14)$, $sOsc(14)$ and $psOsc(8, 5)$) were encoded using EPs, as explained in section 2.2. The choice of binary signature for the EPs can influence the system. In previous studies [12], signatures as different as possible from each other were chosen, but this created dependencies between them (i.e., for a regulatory site to fully match one, it had to fully ignore another). To try to minimise these dependencies, the following encodings were used:

$$MACD(26, 12): \texttt{00000000000000000000000000000000}$$
$$RSI(14): \texttt{00000000000000011111111111111111}$$
$$sOsc(14): \texttt{00000000111111110000000011111111}$$
$$psOsc(8, 5): \texttt{00000000111111111111111100000000}$$

The initial rate of expression of all genes in a model was initially the same, and the system was first allowed to settle for a maximum of 100000 regulatory iterations, or until all protein concentrations were stabilised; after this period, the trading session begins. To synchronise the GRN with the trading simulator, a trading signal was extracted every 2000 protein iterations.

To extract a trading signal from the network, the concentration of a given P-gene is used (all P-genes are tested, and the best result is chosen):

$$c_i >= 66\% \rightarrow \text{BUY} \qquad 66\% > c_i > 33\% \rightarrow \text{D/N} \qquad c_i <= 33\% \rightarrow \text{SELL}$$

This methodology thus encodes technical indicators as regulatory proteins, which influence the internal regulatory process of the genome, and therefore influence the resulting concentration of P-genes, which can then be interpreted as a trading signal. It is a very similar process as seen in previous applications of GRNs to time-series datasets [12,13].

4.2   Evolutionary Setup

A $(250+250) - ES$ evolutionary strategy was used to evolve the binary genomes: a population of 250 individuals is used to create 250 offspring, and the best 250 of all parents and offspring are used as the new parent population (a maximum of 100 iterations were allowed). The variation operator used was a bit-flip mutation, set to 1% and adapted by the 1/5 rule of Evolution Strategies [16].

4.3   Evaluation

Two approaches were used when deriving models: the first denominated *Fixed*, and the second *Dynamic*. Each was run independently on the three markets; the training periods (TR1→TR4, see Fig. 2) were used to derive a trading model.

At the end of the evolutionary process, the best *Fixed* approach model is applied to all test periods (T1→T12). The *Dynamic* approach, however, is only tested on period T1; it is then reprocessed in a smaller evolutionary process (50 ES iterations), using a moving window of 4 training periods each time: train in TR2→T1, test in T2; train in TR3→T2, test in T3; and so on.

As noted in Section 3, long term investments tend to produce good returns in historically upwards return indexes. A common passive investment strategy is *Buy & Hold* (B&H), where an investment is made and held for a long time. In order to evaluate the performance of the evolved traders, their performance was compared to a B&H strategy in both the training and test datasets.

As seen in previous studies [3,12,14], it would be inadequate to simply calculate fitness as the profit return, as this does not consider the risk of deploying an evolved trader. A measurement of this risk is provided by the maximum draw-down, that is, the maximum cumulative loss of the system during each of the datasets. This can be incorporated into the fitness calculation by subtracting the maximum cumulative loss from the profit of each period.

4.4   Results and Analysis

For both approaches, 50 independent runs were done for each market. Table 1 shows the best models in each market, chosen by their TR1→TR4 training performance. As expected, both evolved traders do quite well on the train-ing periods, both due to the obvious fact that they were optimised for those periods, but also because of the downwards trend of period TR1→TR4 on all markets (as highlighted in Section 3.2), which hampers the gains of the B&H benchmark.

Once the traders go *live*, the figures change considerably. In upwards trend markets like FTSE and DAX, the B&H benchmark performs very well, and is very hard to improve on that performance; only the dynamic approach was able to achieve better test performance, in the FTSE market. In the Nikkei market, however, with its fluctuating and slightly downwards trend, both traders achieved better performance. The Dynamic trader in particular is on par or superior to similar EC approaches found in the literature [3,12,14].

It is interesting to observe the behaviour of both evolved traders; Fig. 5 plots the best Fixed and Dynamic FTSE traders. As the training period TR1→TR4 has no clear trend, cautious traders that mostly take no risk are evolved, profiting from rate of interest returns in funds not invested. Only the TR4 period exposes the system to a downwards trend.

Once the evolved Fixed trader goes live, it can be seen that it keeps the same cautious behaviour. However, in the periods T1→T12, the market exhibits an upwards trend, which the trader seldom identifies. This is clearly visible in the period T8→T12. The Dynamic trader, however, is constantly exposed to the changing market trend, and adapts to a more aggressive (and profitable) buying behaviour. This is again clearly visible in the period T8→T12, where at each new live period, more and more buy actions are generated.

Although the better approach, the Dynamic trader is not always the best. In the Nikkei market, for example, it is not fast enough to adapt to the insta-bility of the index, leading to periods (T3, T4, T6, T9 and T11) where the Fixed approach generates more profit; these are periods of sudden trend change, where the Dynamic trader has been trained on the previous period. At the end of all test periods, however, the Dynamic trader performance is still clearly superior.

Table 1. Best evolved traders compared to Buy & Hold benchmark, on the FTSE, Dax and Nikkei markets (net profit in dollars)

	Period	FTSE			Dax			Nikkei		
		Buy & Hold	Static	Dynamic	Buy & Hold	Static	Dynamic	Buy & Hold	Static	Dynamic
Train	TR1 (1 to 90)	35.69	209.59	209.59	-1413.58	284.90	284.90	-4094.96	1156.8	1156.8
	TR2 (91 to 180)	-1734.99	137.16	137.16	34.7648	259.92	259.92	-16.34	955.46	955.464
	TR3 (181 to 270)	1100.9	1267.02	1267.02	1267.77	161.96	161.96	-3989.76	2126.39	2126.39
	TR4 (271 to 360)	-2650.98	928.87	928.87	-2341.59	1447.94	1447.94	255.12	2718.93	2718.93
	Total	-3249.38	2542.64	2542.64	-2452.64	2154.72	2154.72	-7845.94	6957.58	6957.58
Test	T1 (361 to 450)	2402.85	227.71	227.71	34.82	-581.02	-581.02	-940.44	175.93	175.93
	T2 (451 to 540)	-124.51	39.19	598.78	289.72	200.16	196.48	2451.63	51.91	450.61
	T3 (541 to 630)	617.82	719.40	799.46	1538.52	363.96	594.47	49.81	57.78	36.78
	T4 (631 to 720)	1206.9	1068.92	1300.30	1317.47	-26.33	1213.62	-2221.33	1393.61	976.81
	T5 (721 to 810)	-2010.04	209.59	285.05	594.23	295.88	319.75	1060.15	-935.99	-605.42
	T6 (811 to 900)	-675.91	247.55	108.72	-1281.42	204.61	249.87	-882.82	214.32	63.37
	T7 (901 to 990)	-181.46	355.13	271.38	-328.61	165.47	220.07	-834.97	-233.17	-174.09
	T8 (991 to 1080)	1239.55	209.59	196.85	520.64	120.79	624.01	-3051.26	2114.46	2159.62
	T9 (1080 to 1170)	337.91	209.59	198.44	55.51	236.78	365.18	1901.6	284.28	-479.75
	T10 (1171 to 1260)	722.71	209.59	564.64	1304.42	217.09	314.08	1136.03	-1475.39	1249.46
	T11 (1261 to 1350)	-23.49	209.59	216.08	412.75	192.73	328.63	653.651	614.37	-282.48
	T12 (1351 to 1440)	795.61	209.59	327.07	669.43	-102.78	516.86	-1021.36	141.93	488.72
	Total	4307.09	3915.443	5094.48	5127.48	1287.34	4362.00	-1699.94	2404.04	4059.56

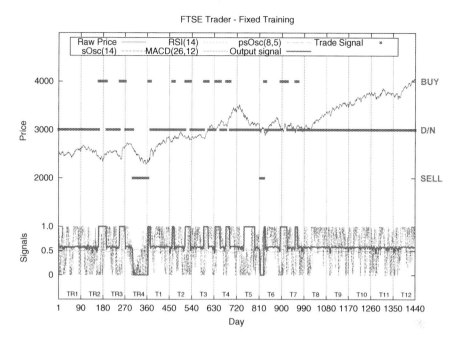

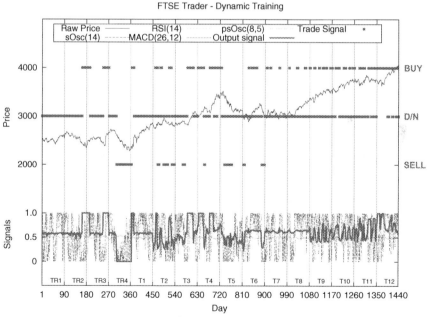

Fig. 5. Best Fixed (top) and Dynamic (bottom) traders for the FTSE market. The top of each plot shows the index value and the generated trade action (buy, sell or do nothing), and the bottom shows the inputs to the GRN (technical indicators) and the generated output signal.

5 Conclusion

In this study, a realistic simulation of applying a GRN model to index trading was presented. Different aspects of feature selection were analysed, and two approaches were applied to three market indexes.

The results obtained show the potential of applying developmental systems to real-world dynamic problems, but also their limitations, The applied developmental system seems unable to adapt to all market fluctuations in unseen data (Static approach), and still requires an extra evolutionary process to adapt to new market tendencies (Dynamic approach). But even the latter approach exhibits signs of overfitting its training data.

Future work will address these issues. The field of Epigenetics shows us that states of cellular organisms can be transmitted to offspring: a similar artificial process could transmit the regulatory state of parents to offspring (in the Dynamic approach), transferring the state of the market to new models, which will trade in later periods. This will allow newly created models to retain a better *historical* state, derived from trading in all previous periods.

References

1. Banzhaf, W.: Artificial regulatory networks and genetic programming. In: Riolo, R., Worzel, B. (eds.) Genetic Programming Theory and Practice, ch. 4, pp. 43–62. Kluwer Publishers, Boston (November 2003)
2. Banzhaf, W., Kuo, P.D.: Network motifs in natural and artificial transcriptional regulatory networks. Biological Physics and Chemistry 4(2), 85–92 (2004)
3. Brabazon, A., O'Neill, M.: Biologically Inspired Algorithms for Financial Modelling. Springer (2006)
4. Cussat-Blanc, S., Bredeche, N., Luga, H., Duthen1, Y., Schoenauer, M.: Artificial gene regulatory networks and spatial computation: A case study. In: Lenaerts, T., et al. (ed.) Proceedings of ECAL 2011, pp. –. MIT Press (2011)
5. Iba, H., Nikolaev, N.: Genetic programming polynomial models of financial data series. In: Proceedings of CEC 2000, vol. 2, pp. 1459–1466 (2000)
6. Lane, G.C.: Lanes stochastics. Technical Analysis of Stocks and Commodities 2(3), 80 (1984)
7. LeBaron, B., Lakonishok, J., Brock, W.: Simple technical trading rules and the stochastic properties of stock returns. Journal of Finance 47(5), 1731–1764 (1992)
8. Leibfarth, L.: Premier stochastic oscillator. Stocks and Commodities V 26(8), 30–36 (2008)
9. Leier, A., Kuo, P.D., Banzhaf, W., Burrage, K.: Evolving Noisy Oscillatory Dynamics in Genetic Regulatory Networks. In: Collet, P., Tomassini, M., Ebner, M., Gustafson, S., Ekárt, A. (eds.) EuroGP 2006. LNCS, vol. 3905, pp. 290–299. Springer, Heidelberg (2006)
10. Lopes, R.L., Costa, E.: ReNCoDe: A Regulatory Network Computational Device. In: Silva, S., Foster, J.A., Nicolau, M., Machado, P., Giacobini, M. (eds.) EuroGP 2011. LNCS, vol. 6621, pp. 142–153. Springer, Heidelberg (2011)
11. Murphy, J.J.: Technical Analysis of the Financial Markets: A Comprehensive Guide to Trading Methods and Applications. Prentice Hall Pr. (1999)

12. Nicolau, M., O'Neill, M., Brabazon, A.: Applying Genetic Regulatory Networks to Index Trading. In: Coello, C.A.C., Cutello, V., Deb, K., Forrest, S., Nicosia, G., Pavone, M. (eds.) PPSN 2012, Part II. LNCS, vol. 7492, pp. 428–437. Springer, Heidelberg (2012)

13. Nicolau, M., Schoenauer, M., Banzhaf, W.: Evolving Genes to Balance a Pole. In: Esparcia-Alcázar, A.I., Ekárt, A., Silva, S., Dignum, S., Uyar, A.Ş. (eds.) EuroGP 2010. LNCS, vol. 6021, pp. 196–207. Springer, Heidelberg (2010)

14. O'Neill, M., Brabazon, A., Ryan, C., Collins, J.J.: Evolving Market Index Trading Rules Using Grammatical Evolution. In: Boers, E.J.W., Gottlieb, J., Lanzi, P.L., Smith, R.E., Cagnoni, S., Hart, E., Raidl, G.R., Tijink, H. (eds.) EvoIASP 2001, EvoWorkshops 2001, EvoFlight 2001, EvoSTIM 2001, EvoCOP 2001, and EvoLearn 2001. LNCS, vol. 2037, p. 343. Springer, Heidelberg (2001)

15. Pring, M.J.: Technical Analysis Explained: The Successful Investor's Guide to Spotting Investment Trends and Turning Points. McGraw-Hill (1991)

16. Rechenberg, I.: Evolutionsstrategie 1994. Frommann-Holzboog, Stuttgart (1994)

17. Wilder, J.W.: New Concepts in Trading Technical Systems. Trend Research (1978)

Analysis of Dynamic Properties of Stock Market Trading Experts Optimized with an Evolutionary Algorithm

Krzysztof Michalak[(✉)]

Department of Information Technologies, Institute of Business Informatics,
Wroclaw University of Economics, Wroclaw, Poland
krzysztof.michalak@ue.wroc.pl

Abstract. This paper concerns optimization of trading experts that are used for generating investment decisions. A population of trading experts is optimized using a dynamic evolutionary algorithm. In the paper a new method is proposed which allows analyzing and visualizing the behaviour of optimized trading experts over a period of time. The application of this method resulted in an observation that during certain intervals of time the behaviour of the optimized trading experts becomes more stable.

Keywords: Trading rules · Dynamic optimization · Usage patterns · Trading expert optimization · Trading expert stability

1 Introduction

Softcomputing methods are commonly used in the context of financial problems. Neural networks are used for time series prediction [8] (sometimes combined with population-based methods [3]) and also for the detection of rare events [12,15]. Evolutionary methods perform well on problems like portfolio optimization [2,10,13] and trading strategies optimization [1,6]. Optimization of trading experts based on stock market trading rules is one of the approaches to developing trading strategies using computational methods [4,14]. Apart from trading expert optimization one of the interesting topics is the analysis of trading rules interactions and usage patterns [9,11].

In this paper dynamic evolutionary optimization approach is used for trading experts optimization. The variability of the experts optimized by the evolutionary algorithm over time is then analyzed and a visualization method is proposed. Results presented in this paper suggest that there exist time periods in which there is little change in the optimal set of trading rules.

2 Dynamic Optimization of Trading Experts

Algorithmic trading requires making decisions about buying and selling financial instruments based on information obtained from the market. Trading experts

© Springer-Verlag Berlin Heidelberg 2014
A.I. Esparcia-Alcázar et al. (Eds.): EvoApplications 2014, LNCS 8602, pp. 264–275, 2014.
DOI: 10.1007/978-3-662-45523-4_22

analyzed in this paper generate "buy" and "sell" signals at consecutive time instants for each stock separately based on technical analysis indicators, stock price, volume, etc. The working of these experts is based on a set of trading rules which generate individual "buy" and "sell" signals using various relationships between the observed values. An example of a trading rule based on two moving averages is presented in Algorithm 1. The "buy" signal is represented by a numeric value "1" and the "sell" signal is represented by a numeric value "-1". A rule can also output "0" which can be interpreted as "no decision". These numeric values are used for calculating composite signals which are based on averages of values returned by many trading rules.

Algorithm 1. An example of a trading rule based on two moving averages.

IN:

$\tau_{fast} = 10$ - the period of the fast moving average

$\tau_{slow} = 80$ - the period of the slow moving average

t - the time instant for which to generate the decision

OUT:

A decision for the time instant t

if $MA_{\tau_{fast}}(t) < MA_{\tau_{slow}}(t)$ **then**
   return -1   // Sell
else
  if $MA_{\tau_{fast}}(t) > MA_{\tau_{slow}}(t)$ **then**
     return 1   // Buy
  else
     return 0   // No suggestion
  end if
end if

In this paper the following structure of a trading expert is used:

$$b_1, \ldots, b_{N_{rules}}, s_1, \ldots, s_{N_{rules}}, \Theta_{buy}, \Theta_{sell} \tag{1}$$

where:

N_{rules} - the number of trading rules,

b_i - a binary variable that determines if the i-th rule is used for generating "buy" signals,

s_i - a binary variable that determines if the i-th rule is used for generating "sell" signals,

$\Theta_{buy}, \Theta_{sell}$ - decision thresholds for "buy" and "sell" decisions respectively.

As presented in Equation (1), trading experts used in this paper turn individual rules on and off separately for generation of "buy" and "sell" signals. Also, the Θ_{buy} and Θ_{sell} decision thresholds are adjusted separately. The individual trading rules generate their own "buy" and "sell" signals represented by numbers -1, 0 or 1. The composite "buy" signal y_{buy} is calculated as an average from those rules for which $b_i = 1$:

$$y_{buy} = \frac{\sum_{i=1}^{N_{rules}} b_i y_i}{N_{rules}} , \tag{2}$$

where:

y_i - the signal generated by the i-th rule.

The composite "sell" signal is calculated likewise. Buy and sell transactions are made when the respective signal exceeds a given threshold ($y_{buy} > \Theta_{buy}$ or $y_{sell} > \Theta_{sell}$). The parameters of an expert can be directly used as a chromosome in an evolutionary algorithm.

The situation in the economy and on the market changes continually. Thus, one can expect that the applicability of various trading rules may change over time. Therefore, the optimization of trading experts can be treated as a dynamic optimization problem. In this paper we assume that changes in the environment occur at certain time instants and the algorithm can evolve for a preset number of generations N_{gen} after each change. This scenario is depicted in Figure 1. Because the situation on the market changes quickly only a limited number of generations can be allowed within each time interval.

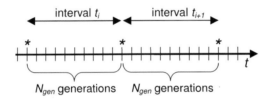

Fig. 1. An overview of dynamic optimization scenario. N_{gen} generations of the evolutionary algorithm are executed between every two changes in the environment.

A well-known fact concerning the dynamic optimization is that in an evolutionary algorithm the population may converge to an optimum for a given time instant which decreases variability in the population and makes it very hard to adapt to new conditions in the time instants that follow. One of the methods of preventing such loss of diversity is the addition of random immigrants [7]. In this paper three methods of introducing random immigrants to the population are presented.

Reinit - the population is initialized randomly for each new interval. This is equivalent to a static optimization - optimizing the trading experts separately for each interval without using any prior knowledge gathered from previous intervals.

Every Interval - random immigrants are added to the population when the optimization starts to handle a new time interval. The number of random immigrants was set to be equal to the population size.

Every Generation - random immigrants are added in the same way as in the **Every Interval** approach, plus some random immigrants are added at the beginning of each generation. The number of immigrants arriving at the beginning of each generation was set to 20% of the population size.

In all the proposed approaches a single-objective evolutionary algorithm with roulette-wheel selection is used. The genetic operators are bit-flip mutation with probability 0.02 for b_i and s_i, polynomial mutation [5] with distribution index 20 for Θ_{buy} and Θ_{sell} and a single-point crossover with crossover probability 0.9. An overview of the evolutionary algorithm used in this paper is given in Algorithm 2.

The $Evaluate(P, t_k)$ procedure evaluates all the specimens in a given population P on data from time interval t_k. The fitness of a specimen that represents trading expert parameters (cf. Equation (1)) is the return obtained when investing during the time interval t_k using the trading signals calculated according to Equation (2). The b_i, s_i, Θ_{buy} and Θ_{sell} parameters are taken from the specimen for which the fitness is calculated.

The optimization of trading experts described in this paper was performed using minute quotations of 50 stocks and ETF shares: AA, AAPL, AIG, ALU, AMD, ANR, BAC, BSX, C, CHK, CSCO, DELL, EEM, EFA, EMC, EWJ, EWZ, F, FAZ, FCX, FXI, GE, GLW, HPQ, INTC, IWM, JPM, MS, MSFT, MU, NOK, NWSA, ORCL, PBR, PFE, QQQ, RF, S, SDS, SIRI, SPY, T, TZA, VALE, VWO, VXX, WFC, XLF, XLI and YHOO. The range of available data contains quotation from the period from 2011.10.17 to 2013.05.20. The above-mentioned companies were selected as 50 companies with the largest total volume of transactions in the available data range.

The dynamic optimization was performed for a number of time intervals t_k, $k \in \{1, \ldots, N_{time}\}$. Each time interval t_k corresponded to an 8-week period starting at the week number k. Therefore, the population was first optimized with respect to the performance on an interval $week_1, \ldots, week_8$, then $week_2, \ldots, week_9$, and so on. The number of time intervals was set to $N_{time} = 76$ with the first day of $week_1$ on 2011.10.17 and the last day of $week_{76}$ on 2013.05.20. Specimen fitness for each time instant t_k was calculated as the overall return obtained by using the trading expert encoded in the specimen over the interval $week_k, \ldots, week_{k+7}$. In this paper intra-day trading was assumed: all the remaining stocks were sold at the end of the day. Commission was set to 0.4% per transaction. In every method a population of 50 specimens was evolved for 30 generations for each time interval t_k.

3   Analysis of Trading Rules Usage

This section analyzes the usage of trading rules in experts optimized using the evolutionary algorithm described in the previous section. In dynamic optimization context an interesting question is how often and in what way does the usage of individual trading rules change over time.

Algorithm 2. An overview of the evolutionary algorithm used for optimization of trading experts.

IN:

    variant - a method of introducing random immigrants to the population

    N_{pop} - number of specimens in the population

    N_{gen} - number of generations

// — In the "reinit" variant the population is initialized —
// — for every interval separately, not only at the beginning —
if variant $\neq$ "reinit" **then**
    $P = \text{InitPopulation}(N_{pop})$
end if

// — Time interval —
for $k = 1 \rightarrow N_{time}$ **do**
    if variant $=$ "reinit" **then**
        // — Initialize new population —
        $P = \text{InitPopulation}(N_{pop})$
    else
        // — Random immigrants —
        $R = \text{InitPopulation}(N_{pop})$
        $P = P \cup R$
    end if
    $\text{Evaluate}(P, t_k)$

    // — Generation —
    for $g = 1 \rightarrow N_{gen}$ **do**
        if variant $=$ "every generation" **then**
            // — Random immigrants —
            $R = \text{InitPopulation}(0.2 * N_{pop})$
            $P = P \cup R$
        end if

        $\text{Evaluate}(P, t_k)$
        $P = \text{Select}(P, N_{pop})$
        $\text{Crossover}(P)$
        $\text{Mutation}(P)$
    end for
end for

To address this question the following method is proposed. For each time interval t_k the population P_k optimized to give the highest return on the interval $week_k, \ldots, week_{k+7}$ is processed. A fraction $P_k^{(best)}$ of $q^{(best)}\%$ best specimens from the population P_k is extracted. For visualization of the usage of trading rules for generating the "buy" signals a matrix $A_{N_{time} \times N_{rules}}$ is calculated in which the k-th row contains average values of parameters b_i found in $P_k^{(best)}$ for $k = 1, \ldots, N_{time}$. For visualization of the usage of trading rules for generating the "sell" signals a similar, but separate matrix is built based on s_i parameters from the same fraction $P_k^{(best)}$ of the population P_k.

Visualization of trading rules usage

For visualization the columns of matrix A are clustered using an agglomerative hierarchical algorithm. In this clustering algorithm the center of a cluster is defined as the average value of those columns of the matrix A that belong to this cluster. The hierarchical clustering algorithm builds a tree structure in which nodes contain nested subsets of columns of matrix A. Each tree node T contains a list of columns $T.C$ and two references $T.left$ and $T.right$ to child nodes. The child nodes represent subsets that were clustered together to form the cluster $T.C$. The structure built by the clustering algorithm is shown in Figure 2.

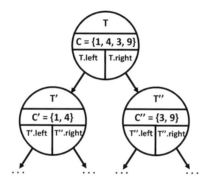

Fig. 2. The structure built by the clustering algorithm

After clustering the *SortNode* procedure is used to change the ordering of columns in all clusters in such a way that there is minimal difference between adjacent columns from neighbouring clusters. The *SortNode* procedure works as follows when called for a tree node T. First, if the $T.left$ and $T.right$ subtrees are non-empty, the procedure is called recursively: *SortNode*($T.left$), *SortNode* ($T.right$). Then, depending of which distance between columns is the smallest one, the *SortNode* procedure reorders columns in child nodes. Using notation shown in Figure 2 we have the $C' = T.left.C$ and $C'' = T.right.C$.

The reordering of columns in child nodes is done according to which of the conditions is found to be true when comparing distances between the first and the last columns of C' and C'':

- if $d(C'.first, C''.first)$ is the smallest, C' is reversed,
- if $d(C'.last, C''.last)$ is the smallest, C'' is reversed,
- if $d(C'.first, C''.last)$ is the smallest, both C' and C'' are reversed,
- if $d(C'.last, C''.first)$ is the smallest, no reordering is performed,

The procedure of construction and clustering of the matrix A is performed separately for parameters b_i and s_i. The clustered matrix can be visualized as a checkerboard plot. Examples of checkerboard plots for the AAPL stock are presented in Figure 3. The plots are based on $q^{(best)} = 20\%$ of populations after 30 generations of the dynamic optimization evolutionary algorithm.

What can be easily seen from the clustered checkerboard plots is that there are many rules that are activated (black areas) or deactivated (white areas) together. Also, it can be observed that there are prolonged periods when no change to the best trading experts is introduced.

From the visual exploration two questions arise. First, how often are the rules used for generation of both "buy" and "sell" signals? Second, what is the stability of the best rule sets generated by the evolutionary algorithm?

The usage of the trading rules for generation of "buy" and "sell" signals

As shown in Equation (1) each trading expert contains separate variables for enabling the "buy" signals from individual rules (the b_i variables) and separate ones for the "sell" signals (the s_i variables). In order to get some insight on how the rules are used (for generating "buy" signals, "sell" signals, both or none) the percentage of specimens in which each of the four situations occurred for each of the rules $i = 1, \ldots, N_{rules}$ was calculated. The observed percentages calculated from 380000 specimens (50 stocks, 10 best specimens ($q^{(best)} = 20\%$), 76 intervals, 10 iterations) are presented in Tables 1-3.

The results shown in Tables 1-3 motivate using separate variables b_i and s_i for determining whether to use individual rules for generating "buy" and "sell" signals. In about 25% of specimens the rules are used for generating both the "buy" and "sell" signals, but equally often the trading expert is optimized towards using distinct rules for generating each of the signals.

The stability of the results produced by the optimal rule sets

Based on the visual exploration of the plots representing the usage of the trading rules with respect to time it can be observed that there exist certain periods of time in which the rules used by the best specimens remain the same.

Figures 4 and 5 present the average return (calculated over 10 iterations) obtained by the best specimens in the population after 30 generations of the

Table 1. The percentages of specimens in which rules were used for generating "buy" signals, "sell" signals, both or none in the populations optimized using the "Every Generation" method

Usage	Mean	Std. dev.
Not used	0.24387	0.01316
Buy	0.25827	0.013
Sell	0.24171	0.013111
Both	0.25614	0.013346

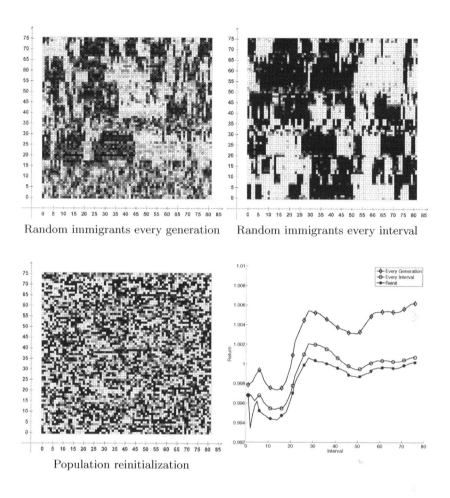

Fig. 3. Visualization of the usage of trading rules for generating "buy" signals for the AAPL stock. Black represents used rules, white represents unused rules.

Table 2. The percentages of specimens in which rules were used for generating "buy" signals, "sell" signals, both or none in the populations optimized using the "Every Interval" method

Usage	Mean	Std. dev.
Not used	0.24205	0.026379
Buy	0.26194	0.026503
Sell	0.2378	0.02493
Both	0.25821	0.026473

Table 3. The percentages of specimens in which rules were used for generating "buy" signals, "sell" signals, both or none in the populations optimized using the "Reinit" method

Usage	Mean	Std. dev.
Not used	0.24395	0.0091361
Buy	0.25763	0.0099813
Sell	0.24265	0.0096086
Both	0.25577	0.0090758

evolution. As can be seen in the graphs, the best results are obtained when random immigrants are added to every generation of the evolutionary algorithm. On the other hand, totally reinitializing the entire population produces the worst results. This suggests that while high diversity is required for the algorithm to be able to track changing optimal rule set, some useful information can be obtained from previous time intervals. This information is lost when the population is reinitialized and the results deteriorate.

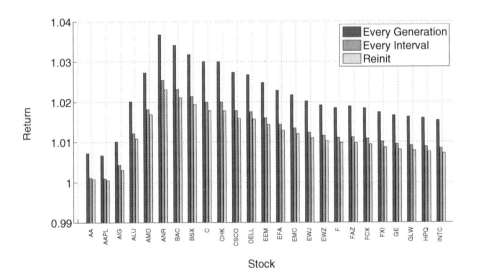

Fig. 4. The average return achieved by the best specimens after 30 generations (stocks AA to INTC)

Figure 6 presents the dependence between the return obtained in time intervals t_k (x axis) and t_{k+1} (y axis), where $k = 1, \ldots, N_{time} - 1$ by specimens that had not changed for at least 3 intervals. Clearly, adding immigrants to every generation causes the optimized rule set to produce similar returns repetitively over several time intervals. In most cases the returns obtained in time intervals

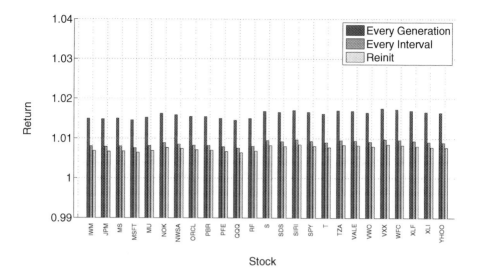

Fig. 5. The average return achieved by the best specimens after 30 generations (stocks IWM to YHOO)

t_k and t_{k+1} are very similar (most of the points are placed near the $y = x$ line). Conversely, when immigrants are only added at the beginning of every interval there is much more difference between the return obtained in interval t_k and interval t_{k+1}. This suggests that when using the Every Interval method the algorithm does not adapt too well and the optimal rule set may remain unchanged even though the obtained returns vary significantly. Note, that in the case of immigrants added to every generation the diversity of the population may be expected to increase, but the returns given by optimized rule sets are less diverse. This can be indicative of a fact, that in the case of immigrants added to every generation the algorithm is not only able to find good solutions more easily than

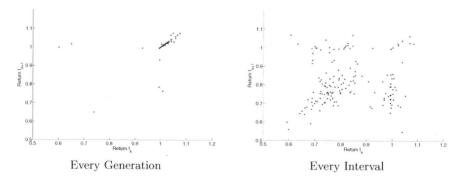

Every Generation   Every Interval

Fig. 6. The dependence between the return obtained in interval t_k (x axis) and interval t_{k+1} (y axis). The specimens that had not changed for at least 3 intervals were used.

in the case of immigrants added once every interval only, but also that the optimized rule sets seem to be more universal i.e. they can produce good results for several consecutive time intervals.

4   Conclusion

In this paper dynamic properties of trading experts optimized using a dynamic evolutionary algorithm were analyzed. A new method of analyzing and visualizing the behaviour of trading experts over a period of time was proposed. The application of this method to trading experts generating decisions for 50 stocks and ETF shares resulted in several observations:

– Introducing additional random immigrants at the beginning of every generation allows the evolutionary algorithm to produce specimens with higher fitness values compared to the algorithm where random immigrants are added only once for every interval at the beginning of the evolution.
– On the other hand, reinitializing the entire population for each new time interval deteriorates the results significantly. This means that despite the large variability of trading rules usage, useful information can be extracted from trading experts optimized for past time intervals.
– Visualization of trading rules usage shows prolonged periods of time when the same set of rules produces the best investment returns.
– The evolutionary algorithm can produce good rule sets that are relatively stable - they produce similar return values for consecutive time intervals.
– Among the fittest specimens the fraction of rules used at the same time for generating "buy" and "sell" signals is approximately $1/4$. This result suggests, that in order to build good trading experts one should allow using trading rules separately for generating "buy" and "sell" signals.

Further work may include development of methods that allow early detection of time intervals during which the optimal set of rules remains the same or very similar. It is worth investigating if the analysis of the stability of optimal trading rule sets could be useful for deciding if a given trading expert should be used for making decision at a given time or not.

References

1. Bauer, R.: Genetic Algorithms and Investment Strategies. Wiley, Chichester (1994)
2. Best, M.J.: Portfolio Optimization. Chapman&Hall/CRC (2010)
3. Cai, X., Zhang, N., Venayagamoorthya, G.K., Wunsch II, D.C.: Time series prediction with recurrent neural networks trained by a hybrid PSOEA algorithm. Neurocomputing **70**(13–15), 2342–2353 (2007)
4. Chiam, S.C., Tan, K.C., Al Mamun, A.: Investigating technical trading strategy via an multi-objective evolutionary platform. Expert Systems with Applications **36**(7), 10408–10423 (2009)

5. Deb, K., Goyal, M.: A Combined Genetic Adaptive Search (GeneAS) for Engineering Design. Computer Science and Informatics **26**, 30–45 (1996)
6. Dempster, M., Jones, C.: A Real-Time Adaptive Trading System using Genetic Programming. Quantitative Finance **1**, 397–413 (2001)
7. Grefenstette, J.J.: Genetic algorithms for changing environments. In: Manner, R., Manderick, B. (eds.) Parallel Problem Solving from Nature, pp. 137–144. Elsevier Science Publisher (1992)
8. Inoussa, G., Peng, H., Wu, J.: Nonlinear time series modeling and prediction using functional weights wavelet neural network-based state-dependent AR model. Neurocomputing **86**(1), 59–74 (2012)
9. Lipinski, P.: Dependency Mining in Large Sets of Stock Market Trading Rules. In: Pejas, J., Piegat, A. (eds.) Enhanced Methods in Computer Security, Biometric and Intelligent Systems, pp. 329–336. Kluwer Academic Publishers (2005)
10. Michalak, K., Filipiak, P., Lipiński, P.: Evolutionary Approach to Multiobjective Optimization of Portfolios That Reflect the Behaviour of Investment Funds. In: Ramsay, A., Agre, G. (eds.) AIMSA 2012. LNCS, vol. 7557, pp. 202–211. Springer, Heidelberg (2012)
11. Michalak, K., Filipiak, P., Lipinski, P.: Usage Patterns of Trading Rules in Stock Market Trading Strategies Optimized with Evolutionary Methods. In: Esparcia-Alcázar, A.I. (ed.) EvoApplications 2013. LNCS, vol. 7835, pp. 234–243. Springer, Heidelberg (2013)
12. Michalak, K., Lipinski, P.: Prediction of high increases in stock prices using neural networks. Neural Network World, 15, **4**, 359–366 (2005)
13. Radziukyniene, I., Zilinskas, A.: Evolutionary Methods for Multi-Objective Portfolio Optimization. In: Proceedings of the World Congress on Engineering 2008, pp. 1155–1159. Newswood Limited (2008)
14. Wang, F., Yu, P.L.H., Cheung, D.W.: Combining technical trading rules using particle swarm optimization. Expert Systems with Applications (in press), Available online 24 October 2013. http://dx.doi.org/10.1016/j.eswa.2013.10.032
15. Yu, L., Wang, S., Lai, K.K., Wen, F.: A multiscale neural network learning paradigm for financial crisis forecasting. Neurocomputing **73**(4–6), 716–725 (2010)

A Comparative Study
on the Use of Classification Algorithms
in Financial Forecasting

Fernando E.B. Otero[✉] and Michael Kampouridis

School of Computing, University of Kent, Chatham Maritime, Kent, UK
{F.E.B.Otero,M.Kampouridis}@kent.ac.uk

Abstract. Financial forecasting is a vital area in computational finance, where several studies have taken place over the years. One way of viewing financial forecasting is as a classification problem, where the goal is to find a model that represents the predictive relationships between predictor attribute values and class attribute values. In this paper we present a comparative study between two bio-inspired classification algorithms, a genetic programming algorithm especially designed for financial forecasting, and an ant colony optimization one, which is designed for classification problems. In addition, we compare the above algorithms with two other state-of-the-art classification algorithms, namely C4.5 and RIPPER. Results show that the ant colony optimization classification algorithm is very successful, significantly outperforming all other algorithms in the given classification problems, which provides insights for improving the design of specific financial forecasting algorithms.

Keywords: Financial forecasting · Classification · Genetic programming · Ant Colony optimization

1   Introduction

Financial forecasting is a vital area in computational finance [13]. There are numerous works that attempt to forecast the future price movements of a stock; several examples can be found in [1].

In this study, we approach the financial forecasting problem as a classification problem [5,14]. In a classification problem, the aim is to create a model that places objects (examples) into pre-defined categories (classes). The model is able to determine the category of an object by analysing patterns (attribute-values) between objects of that category. Classification problems can therefore be viewed as optimisation problems, where the goal is to find the best model that represents the predictive relationships in the data. Classification algorithms can be grouped by the type of the model representation that they produce: as 'black-box' models (e.g., the models produced by support vector machines using kernels and artificial neural networks, which are difficult to interpret); and 'white-box' models (e.g., decision tree and classification rule models, which are more readily

© Springer-Verlag Berlin Heidelberg 2014
A.I. Esparcia-Alcázar et al. (Eds.): EvoApplications 2014, LNCS 8602, pp. 276–287, 2014.
DOI: 10.1007/978-3-662-45523-4_23

interpreted). Since 'white-box' models have the advantage of being easier to interpret, they can be used to further understand the data—i.e., they can be used to understand how the predictions are made by the model. This enhanced understanding leads to a greater degree of trust in the models produced, which is crucial in various domains—e.g., medical and financial domains, where the predictions usually need to be validated by doctors/experts.

In this paper, *our goal is to report and analyse the performance of such 'white-box' models, one from the domain of genetic programming (GP) [8], and one from the field of ant colony optimization (ACO) [3]*. We also compare the performance of these two algorithms with two other state-of-the-art algorithms, namely C4.5 and RIPPER. For the purposes of the GP, we will be using EDDIE [7], an algorithm especially designed for classification financial forecasting problems. For the purposes of ACO, we will be using the Unordered cAnt-Miner$_{\mathrm{PB}}$ [10], which is a classification algorithm.

The remainder of this paper is organised as follows. In Section 2 we discuss the financial forecasting problem and how it can be viewed as a classification problem. Section 3 presents the research goals of this study. The datasets used in our experiments are described in Section 4, while the algorithms are described in Section 5. Section 6 presents and discusses the computational results. Finally, Section 7 concludes this paper.

2   Problem Description

2.1   Financial Forecasting

One of the most common methods used in the financial forecasting area is technical analysis [4]. This method assumes that patterns exist in historical data and that these patterns will repeat themselves. Consequently, it is worth identifying these patterns, so that we can exploit them in the future and make profit. As part of technical analysis, several indicators are used. These technical analysis indicators are formulas that measure different aspects of a given financial dataset, such as trend, volatility and momentum.

An example of such indicators is the Moving Average (MA), which calculates the averages of a given dataset under sliding windows of a fixed length L. One way of using MAs is to compare a short-term MA with a long-term one; for instance, when the short-term MA goes above the long-term one, this would indicate that the market is in an upward trend and thus it would be a good indication to buy.

The above method has been extensively used in both the literature and in the industry. However, what is evident is that both academics and people who work in the industry tend to use very specific L lengths for the indicators; for instance, 20 days is a common short-length period and 50 days is a common long-term period. In [7], it was argued that this method is not very flexible and cannot guarantee that specific pre-specified indicators are necessarily the best ones. For example, nobody can guarantee that a 20 days MA is definitely more effective than a 25 days MA, under all possible datasets.

In our current work, we will be building on the above idea by allowing all algorithms tested in this paper to use any period lengths within a parameterised length $[MinP, MaxP]$, which is set to $[2, 65]$ days. This will add flexibility to all algorithms and enable them to create new indicators. However, one has to keep in mind that this will also add to the complexity of the problem. While traditionally a financial forecasting algorithm would have to deal with a low number of indicators, e.g. 6 technical indicators with two period lengths—a short (20 days) and a long (50 days) term—leading to a total number of 12 indicators, in our framework each algorithm would have to choose among $6 \times 64 = 384$ indicators. Hence, the problem is much more complex than the traditional classification financial forecasting problems, as the number of combinations for all available indicators is much higher.

2.2 The Classification Problem

Each algorithm tested in this work will be attempting to answer the question 'Will the price of the X stock rise by $r\%$ within the next n days?' Thus, the classes are calculated by looking ahead of the closing price for a time horizon of n days, trying to detect if there is an increase of the price by $r\%$. For this set of experiments, n is set to 20 and r to 4%. In other words, the algorithms will be trying to forecast whether the daily closing price is going to increase by 4% within the following 20 days.

Depending on the classification of the predictions, we can have four cases: True Positive (TP), False Positive (FP), True Negative (TN), and False Negative (FN). As a result, we can use the metrics presented in Equations 1, 2 and 3:

Rate of Correctness
$$RC = \frac{TP + TN}{TP + TN + FP + FN} \tag{1}$$

Rate of Missing Chances
$$RMC = \frac{FN}{FN + TP} \tag{2}$$

Rate of Failure
$$RF = \frac{FP}{FP + TP} \tag{3}$$

It should also be noted that we chose to use RMC and RF instead of the more 'traditional' classification Recall and Precision measures, because they are metrics related to the financial forecasting problem. Thus, it would make more sense to an investor to know how many times an algorithm returns FP predictions, because this could have a very negative impact on his portfolio.

3   Research Goals

The goal of this study is to analyse the performance of state-of-the-art classification algorithms when applied to financial forecasting, and compare it to two well-known bio-inspired algorithms, namely EDDIE and Unordered cAnt-Miner$_{PB}$. EDDIE is a GP financial forecasting algorithm, as it was designed specifically for the purposes of financial forecasting and that has been previously successfully applied to datasets from different international markets. The Unordered cAnt-Miner$_{PB}$ algorithm is an established ant colony optimization (ACO) [3] classification algorithm which has been found efficient in discovering comprehensible and accurate classification models [10].

As we discussed in Section 2.2, financial forecasting can be modelled as a classification problem. Thus, we can summarise the goals of this study as follows:

– How do EDDIE and Unordered cAnt-Miner$_{PB}$ compare to state-of-the-art classification algorithms in terms of Rate of Correctness, Rate of Missing Chances and Rate of Failure?
– Can we get insights on the differences in the search behaviour between GP and ACO, based on their performance as classification algorithms in the given financial forecasting problem?

4   Data Preparation

The set of data used in this work is composed of three parts: (i) daily closing price of a stock, (ii) a number of attributes, and (iii) signals. Stocks' daily closing prices can be obtained online on websites such as http://finance.yahoo.com and also from financial statistics databases like *Datastream*.[1] The attributes are indicators commonly used in technical analysis [4]; which indicators to use depends on the user and his belief of their relevance to the prediction. The technical indicators that are used in this work are: Moving Average (MA), Trade Break Out (TBR), Filter (FLR), Volatility (Vol), Momentum (Mom), and Momentum Moving Average (MomMA).[2] Also, as already explained in Section 2, the signals are calculated by looking ahead of the closing price for a time horizon of n days, trying to detect if there is an increase of the price by $r\%$.

As we are approaching the financial forecasting problem as a classification problem, the training set is created using the daily closing price of a stock for a fixed time window. For each training day (each example in our training set), we calculate the aforementioned technical indicators MA, TBR, FLR, Vol, Mom and MomMA for the periods from 2 to 65 days—the predictor attributes values of the problem. There are 384 predictor attribute in total: 6 indicators and 64 possible periods ($6 \times 64 = 384$). We also calculate the signals for each of the training days by 'looking ahead' if the value of the stock increased by $r\%$ or not (0=no increase, 1=increase)—the class attribute values of the problem. The test set is created in a similar fashion, with the difference that the test set is used

---

[1] Available at: http://thomsonreuters.com/datastream-professional/

[2] We use these indicators because they have been proved to be quite useful in developing decision trees in [9]. Of course, there is no reason not to use other information like fundamentals or limit order book. However, the aim of this work is not to find the ultimate indicators for financial forecasting.

```
<Tree> ::= If-Then-Else <Condition> <Tree> <Tree> | Decision
<Condition> ::= <Condition> AND <Condition> |
        <Condition> OR <Condition> |
        NOT <Condition> |
        <VarConstructor> <RelationOperation> Threshold
<VarConstructor> ::= MA period | TBR period | FLR period | Vol period
        | Mom period | MomMA period
<RelationOperation> ::= ">" | "<" | "="
Terminals:
        MA, TBR, FLR, Vol, Mom, MomMA are function symbols
        Period is an integer within a parameterised range, [MinP, MaxP]
        Decision is an integer, Positive or Negative implemented
        Threshold is a real number
```

Fig. 1. The Backus Normal Form of EDDIE 8

only to evaluate the performance of the algorithm and the algorithms have no access to the test set during training.

Using the above procedure, we created 25 datasets. These datasets consist of daily closing prices from 18 stocks from FTSE 100, and 7 international indices. The 18 FTSE 100 stocks are: Aggreko, Amlin, Barclays, British Petroleum (BP), Cadbury, Carnival, Easyjet, First, Hammerson, Imperial Tobacco, Marks & Spencer, Next, Royal Bank of Scotlland (RBS), Schroders, Sky, Tesco, Vodafone and Xstrata. The 7 indices are: Athens Stock Exchange (Greece), DJIA (USA), HSI (Hong Kong), MDAX (Germany), and NASDAQ (USA), NIKEI (Japan), and NYSE (USA). For each of the datasets, the training set is 1000 days and the test set 300.

5   Algorithms

5.1   EDDIE

EDDIE 8 is a Genetic Programming (GP) [8] financial forecasting algorithm, which learns and extracts knowledge from a set of data. After feeding the data to the system, EDDIE creates and evolves a population of decision trees. Figure 1 presents the Backus Normal Form (BNF) (grammar) of EDDIE 8. As we can see, the root of the tree is an If-Then-Else statement. The first branch is either a boolean (testing whether a technical indicator is greater than/less than/equal to a *threshold*), or a logic operator (AND, OR, NOT), which can hold multiple boolean conditions. The Then and Else branches can be a new tree, or a decision, to buy or not-to-buy (denoted by 1 and 0). The *threshold* is a real number, which is randomly generated within the range of the minimum and maximum values of the respective indicator.

As we can observe from the grammar in Figure 1, there is a function called 'VarConstructor', which takes two children. The first one is the indicator, and the second one is the 'Period'. 'Period' is an integer within the parameterized range [MinP, MaxP] that the user specifies. The advantage of this approach is that it makes the GP more dynamic, as EDDIE 8 is not constrained to pre-specified

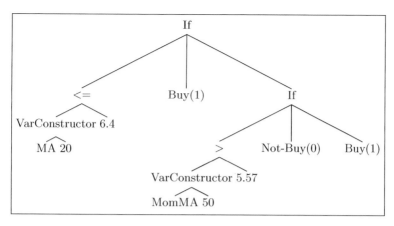

Fig. 2. Sample decision tree generated by EDDIE 8. As we can see, if the *20 days MA* is less than or equal to *6.4*, then the user is advised to buy; otherwise, the user is advised to consult another tree, which is located in the third branch ('else-branch') of the tree. This tree checks if the 50 days Momentum Moving Average is greater than 5.57; if it is, it advises to not-buy, otherwise to buy.

periods, as is usually the case in literature and industry. As a consequence, it is up to the GP and the evolutionary process to look for the optimal periods values from the period range provided. For instance, if this range is 2 to 65 days, then EDDIE 8 can create Moving Averages with any of these periods, e.g., 20 days MA, 25 days MA, and so on. Furthermore, the periods are leaf nodes and are thus subject to genetic operators, such as crossover and mutation. A sample tree of EDDIE 8 is presented in Figure 2. The periods 20 and 50 of the figure's sample tree are leaf nodes; the advantage of this being that the GP can replace them with more effective periods, which might have come up during the evolutionary process.

EDDIE's fitness function is a weighted formula, combining Equations 1-3:

$$ff = w_1 * RC - w_2 * RMC - w_3 * RF \qquad (4)$$

where w_1, w_2 and w_3 are the weights for RC, and the financial-based metrics RMC and RF. These weights are given in order to reflect the preferences of investors. For instance, a conservative investor would want to avoid failure; thus a higher weight for RF should be used. For the experiments in this paper, the focus is on strategies that mainly target correctness and reduced failure.

5.2   Unordered cAnt-Miner_PB

Unordered cAnt-Miner_PB [10] is an ACO classification algorithm that employs an improved sequential covering strategy [11] to search for the best set of classification rules. The use of this improved strategy avoids the potential problem of rule interaction arising from the greedy nature of the sequential covering commonly

```
IF MA_20 <= 6.4 THEN Buy(1)
IF MA_20 > 6.4 AND MM_50 > 5.57 THEN Buy(0)
IF MA_20 > 6.4 AND MM_50 <= 5.57 THEN Buy(1)
```

Fig. 3. Sample of a set of classification rules representing the same conditions of EDDIE's tree from Figure 2

used by rule induction algorithms. Instead of creating a rule and then determine its consequent (the prediction of the rule) based on the majority class value of the covered training examples, as the majority of ACO classification algorithms, an ant creates rules for each class value in turn using as negative examples all the examples associated with different class values. The advantage of discovering a set of classification rules (unordered rules) is that the order in which the rules are discovered is not important to the interpretation of the individual rules, in contrast to rule induction algorithms that discover a list of classification rules (ordered rules). A sample of a set of classification rules is presented in Figure 3.

In summary, the Unordered cAnt-Miner$_{PB}$ works as follows. Each ant starts with an empty set of rules and iteratively adds a new rule to this set. In order to create a rule, an ants adds one term at a time to the rule antecedent by choosing terms to be added to the current partial rule based on their values of the amount of pheromone (τ) and a problem-dependent heuristic information (η). After a rule is created and pruned, it is added to current set of rules and the training examples correctly covered by the rule are removed. At the end of an iteration, when all ants have created a set of rules, the best set of rules (determined by the highest predictive accuracy on the training data) is used to update pheromone values, providing a positive feedback on the terms present in the rules—the higher the pheromone value of a term, the more likely it will be chosen to create a rule. This iterative process is repeated until a maximum number of iterations is reached or until the algorithm stagnates.

Since the consequent of a rule is fixed during its creation, the Unordered cAnt-Miner$_{PB}$ uses a class-specific heuristic information[3] and dynamic discretisation procedure of continuous values. Hence, when a particular indicator value is selected (e.g., *20 days MA*), the algorithm determines the threshold value by looking at the training data and selecting the one that gives the highest information gain, instead of choosing them in a random way as EDDIE does. Therefore, the selection of threshold values in the Unordered cAnt-Miner$_{PB}$ algorithm is tailored for the current available data—only suitable values are considered as candidate threshold values to create indicator conditions.

---

[3] The heuristic information represents a priori information about the quality of the candidate components of the antecedent of a rule and it is used in the stochastic rule construction process. The Unordered cAnt-Miner$_{PB}$ uses the information gain measure [12] as the heuristic information.

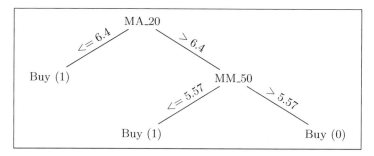

Fig. 4. Sample decision tree generated by C4.5 representing the same conditions of EDDIE's tree from Figure 2

5.3 C4.5 (J48)

J48 is Weka's implementation [14] of the well-known C4.5 algorithm [12]. The C4.5 algorithm, probably the most known decision tree induction algorithm, employs an entropy-based criterion in order to select the best attribute to create a node. C4.5 has been successfully applied to a wide range of classification problems and it is usually used on evaluative comparisons of new classification algorithms.

5.4 RIPPER (JRip)

JRip is Weka's implementation [14] of the RIPPER algorithm [2]. RIPPER sequentially creates a set of rules that is subject to a global post-processing step by implementing a rule induction procedure with a reduced error pruning strategy [12]. The final set of rules created by JRip has a similar structure than the one created by the Unordered cAnt-Miner$_{PB}$ algorithm (Figure 3).

6   Results

The experiments were carried out using 25 datasets created using the procedure described in Section 4. The parameters used for both stochastic algorithms are: EDDIE 8 {max. initial depth = 6, max. depth = 8, generations = 50, population size = 500, tournament size = 2, reproduction probability = 0.1, crossover probability = 0.9, mutation probability = 0.01, w_1 = 0.6, w_2 = 0.1, w_3 = 0.3} and Unordered cAnt-Miner$_{PB}$ {colony size = 5, evaporation factor = 0.90, minimum number of examples = 10}. The other algorithms were used with the default values proposed by their correspondent authors, which typically represent robust values that work well across different datasets. We did not attempt to optimise the parameters to individual datasets. Since both EDDIE 8 and Unordered cAnt-Miner$_{PB}$ are stochastic algorithms, each algorithm is run 50 times for each dataset; C4.5 and RIPPER are deterministic algorithms, hence they are run once per dataset.

Table 1. Summary of the results concerning the rate of correctness (RC). The best RC value for a given dataset is in bold.

	EDDIE 8	U-cAnt-Miner$_{PB}$	C4.5	RIPPER
Aggreko	0.549	**0.594**	0.573	0.450
Amlin	0.518	**0.523**	0.453	0.467
Athens	**0.535**	0.515	0.467	0.413
Barclays	**0.549**	0.533	0.503	0.470
BP	0.533	**0.534**	0.467	0.510
Cadbury	**0.654**	0.625	0.527	0.553
Carnival	0.506	0.500	**0.587**	0.503
DJI	0.653	**0.696**	0.670	0.667
Easyjet	0.451	**0.564**	0.540	0.550
First	0.509	0.506	**0.593**	0.577
Hammerson	0.533	0.524	0.507	**0.593**
HIS	0.603	**0.687**	0.573	0.627
Imperial Tobacco	0.566	**0.630**	0.593	0.567
Marks & Spencer	0.500	0.572	0.527	**0.660**
MDAX	0.492	0.499	**0.503**	0.487
NASDAQ	0.549	**0.594**	0.573	0.450
Next	0.465	**0.595**	0.470	0.450
NIKEI	0.516	0.556	**0.617**	0.380
NYSE	0.546	**0.564**	0.563	0.500
RBS	0.529	0.569	0.567	**0.493**
Schroders	0.570	0.602	0.493	**0.643**
Sky	0.516	**0.599**	0.583	0.427
Tesco	0.613	**0.621**	0.587	0.600
Vodafone	0.501	0.555	**0.633**	0.450
Xstrata	0.607	**0.685**	0.677	0.590

The results of our experiments are presented in Table 1 for Rate of Correctness; Table 2 for Rate of Missing Chances; and Table 3 for Rate of Failure. For EDDIE 8 and Unordered cAnt-Miner$_{PB}$ algorithms, a value on those tables corresponds to the average value measured over the 50 runs of the algorithm. Table 4 presents the results of the non-parametric Friedman statistical test with the post-hoc Hommel's test [6]. The information presented in Table 4 corresponds to the average rank (first column), where the lower the rank the better the algorithm's performance, and the adjusted p_{Homm} value. Statistically significant differences amongst the algorithm with the best rank (the control '(c)' algorithm) are determined by the p_{Homm} value: if the p value is less than 0.05, the difference in the rank is statistically significant at the $\alpha = 0.05$ level—i.e., the algorithm with the best rank significantly outperforms the other algorithm.

Our results showed that the Unordered cAnt-Miner$_{PB}$ algorithm achieved the best average rank in terms of both Rate of Correctness (RC) and Rate of Missing Chances (RMC), outperforming all the other algorithms with statistically significant differences. It achieved the best RC value in 13 out of the 25 datasets and the best RMC value in 23 out of 25 datasets. Both C4.5 and EDDIE 8 achieved similar results for RC and RMC, while RIPPER was the worst performing algorithm. The results for Rate of Failure (RF) did not show any significant differences between the algorithms; all algorithms achieved similar average ranks.

The results provide interesting insights of the strengths the Unordered cAnt-Miner$_{PB}$ algorithm when compared to EDDIE. Both algorithms are stochastic

Table 2. Summary of the results concerning the rate of missing changes (RMC). The best RMC value for a given dataset is in bold.

	EDDIE 8	U-cAnt-Miner$_{PB}$	C4.5	RIPPER
Aggreko	0.283	**0.164**	0.426	0.427
Amlin	0.429	**0.294**	0.457	0.531
Athens	0.252	**0.159**	0.276	0.394
Barclays	0.444	**0.355**	0.500	0.464
BP	0.421	**0.346**	0.474	0.438
Cadbury	0.166	**0.145**	0.350	0.433
Carnival	0.153	**0.142**	0.239	0.337
DJI	0.161	**0.013**	0.062	0.118
Easyjet	0.458	0.668	**0.404**	0.498
First	0.530	0.498	**0.403**	0.461
Hammerson	0.382	**0.233**	0.331	0.396
HIS	0.267	**0.002**	0.248	0.150
Imperial Tobacco	0.449	**0.182**	0.355	0.452
Marks & Spencer	0.474	0.263	0.435	**0.253**
MDAX	0.204	**0.031**	0.397	0.493
NASDAQ	0.416	**0.267**	0.396	0.584
Next	0.477	**0.206**	0.482	0.568
NIKEI	0.300	**0.008**	0.062	0.677
NYSE	0.207	**0.157**	0.364	0.525
RBS	0.373	**0.281**	0.332	0.370
Schroders	0.328	**0.065**	0.276	0.309
Sky	0.469	**0.317**	0.497	0.626
Tesco	0.287	**0.231**	0.429	0.278
Vodafone	0.303	**0.231**	0.261	0.380
Xstrata	0.259	**0.044**	0.122	0.244

Table 3. Summary of the results concerning the rate of failure (RF). The best RF value for a given dataset is in bold.

	EDDIE 8	U-cAnt-Miner$_{PB}$	C4.5	RIPPER
Aggreko	0.514	0.522	**0.509**	0.508
Amlin	**0.405**	0.427	0.469	0.450
Athens	**0.533**	0.539	0.576	0.621
Barclays	**0.397**	0.431	0.443	0.480
BP	**0.337**	0.363	0.400	0.363
Cadbury	**0.331**	0.359	0.403	0.354
Carnival	0.631	0.631	**0.593**	0.659
DJI	**0.285**	0.298	0.303	0.287
Easyjet	0.305	0.284	**0.266**	0.276
First	0.285	0.305	0.241	**0.224**
Hammerson	0.427	0.444	0.449	**0.350**
HIS	**0.293**	0.312	0.332	0.316
Imperial Tobacco	**0.293**	0.335	0.318	0.311
Marks & Spencer	0.388	0.365	0.367	**0.284**
MDAX	0.513	**0.507**	0.508	0.526
NASDAQ	0.305	0.314	**0.282**	0.359
Next	0.392	**0.337**	0.380	0.377
NIKEI	0.452	**0.410**	0.597	0.477
NYSE	0.445	0.435	**0.411**	0.458
RBS	0.386	0.369	**0.359**	0.420
Schroders	0.365	0.388	0.438	**0.290**
Sky	0.335	0.304	**0.222**	0.407
Tesco	0.284	0.295	**0.235**	0.299
Vodafone	0.514	0.480	**0.410**	0.558
Xstrata	0.281	0.295	**0.275**	0.303

Table 4. Statistical test results according to the non-parametric Friedman test with the Hommel's post-hoc test. Statistically significant differences at the $\alpha = 0.05$ level are in bold.

Algorithm	Average Rank	Adjusted p_{Homm}
(i) Rate of Correctness		
U-cAnt-Miner$_{PB}$ (c)	1.76	–
C4.5	**2.52**	**0.0374**
EDDIE 8	**2.72**	**0.0171**
RIPPER	**3.00**	**0.0020**
(ii) Rate of Missing Chances		
U-cAnt-Miner$_{PB}$ (c)	1.12	–
C4.5	**2.68**	**5.1E-9**
EDDIE 8	**2.88**	**2.8E-6**
RIPPER	**3.32**	**1.9E-5**
(iii) Rate of Failure		
EDDIE 8 (c)	2.26	–
C4.5	2.34	0.8265
U-cAnt-Miner$_{PB}$	2.52	0.8265
RIPPER	2.88	0.2685

algorithms, which can perform a more global search than the deterministic C4.5 and RIPPER algorithms. While EDDIE is a GP algorithm tailored for financial forecasting, it does not use heuristics to guide the search. In this sense, the search of the GP is 'blind', using the training examples just as an oracle: it can query the quality of a solution on the training data, but it does not 'look' into the training data to shape the solutions. The Unordered cAnt-Miner$_{PB}$ is an ACO algorithm, which uses the information gain of the predictor attributes as heuristic information in the rule construction process. It also incorporates a dynamic discretisation procedure to find threshold values to create the indicator conditions (e.g., `MA_20 < 6.4`); and the consequent (decision) of the rules are fixed during creation, so the conditions selected to create the antecedent are relevant for this particular consequent. In summary, it uses more information available from the training data to guide the search.

Given our findings, we hypothesise that in order to improve EDDIE's performance, there is a need to incorporate more background information to the GP search. While the creation of the conditions can be left to the GP, the choice of the value of the decision can be determined using the training data. A similar procedure can be applied to the selection of threshold values, where instead of selecting values at random, the values can be selected based on the training data. In this way, the GP search is focused in finding a good structure to represent the conditions, and there is less pressure for the GP to find the correct values to be used as the decision and threshold.

7   Conclusion

In this paper we presented a comparative study of different classification algorithms in financial forecasting. Our first research goal was to analyse the performance of state-of-the-art classification algorithms and compare their performance to two well-known bio-inspired algorithms: EDDIE, a GP algorithm designed specifically for financial forecasting; and Unordered cAnt-Miner$_{PB}$ (U-cAnt-Miner$_{PB}$), an ACO algorithm designed for classification. Our results show that the U-cAnt-Miner$_{PB}$ algorithm was significantly better than all the other algorithms tested. Regarding our second research goal, we identified potential strengths of the U-cAnt-Miner$_{PB}$ search, when compared to EDDIE: the use of a data-driven procedures to determine the prediction of the classification rules and to determine threshold values for the indicator conditions.

As a future research direction, we aim to investigate whether heuristics procedures, such as the ones used by U-cAnt-Miner$_{PB}$, can be applied to GP algorithms, like EDDIE, and lead to improved solutions. Our hope is that the GP's search can benefit from using such data-driven processes, and select the thresholds and decision values in a more sophisticated manner.

References

1. Chen, S.H.: Genetic Algorithms and Genetic Programming in Computational Finance. Springer-Verlag New York, LLC (2002)
2. Cohen, W.: Fast effective rule induction. In: Proceedings of the 12th International Conference on Machine Learning, pp. 115–123. Morgan Kaufmann (1995)
3. Dorigo, M., Stützle, T.: Ant Colony Optimization. 328 pages MIT Press (2004)
4. Edwards, R., Magee, J.: Technical analysis of stock trends. NYIF (1992)
5. Fayyad, U., Piatetsky-Shapiro, G., Smith, P.: From data mining to knowledge discovery: an overview. In: Advances in Knowledge Discovery & Data Mining, pp. 1–34. MIT Press (1996)
6. García, S., Herrera, F.: An Extension on "Statistical Comparisons of Classifiers over Multiple Data Sets" for all Pairwise Comparisons. Journal of Machine Learning Research **9**, 2677–2694 (2008)
7. Kampouridis, M., Tsang, E.: EDDIE for investment opportunities forecasting: Extending the search space of the GP. In: Proceedings of the IEEE World Congress on Computational Intelligence, Barcelona, Spain pp. 2019–2026 (2010)
8. Koza, J.: Genetic Programming: On the programming of computers by means of natural selection. MIT Press, Cambridge, MA (1992)
9. Martinez-Jaramillo, S.: Artificial Financial Markets: An agent-based Approach to Reproduce Stylized Facts and to study the Red Queen Effect. Ph.D. thesis, CFFEA, University of Essex (2007)
10. Otero, F., Freitas, A.: Improving the Interpretability of Classification Rules Discovered by an Ant Colony Algorithm. In: Proceedings of the 2013 Genetic and Evolutionary Computation Conference, pp. 73–80. ACM Press (July 2013)
11. Otero, F., Freitas, A., Johnson, C.: A New Sequential Covering Strategy for Inducing Classification Rules With Ant Colony Algorithms. IEEE Transactions on Evolutionary Computation **17**(1), 64–76 (2013)
12. Quinlan, J.R.: C4.5: programs for machine learning. Morgan Kaufmann Publishers Inc., San Francisco, CA, USA (1993)
13. Tsang, E., Martinez-Jaramillo, S.: Computational finance. IEEE Computational Intelligence Society Newsletter, 3–8 (2004)
14. Witten, H., Frank, E.: Data Mining: Practical Machine Learning Tools and Techniques, 2nd edn. Morgan Kaufmann (2005)

Pattern Mining in Ultra-High Frequency Order Books with Self-Organizing Maps

Piotr Lipinski[1]([✉]) and Anthony Brabazon[2]

[1] Computational Intelligence Research Group, Institute of Computer Science,
University of Wroclaw, Wroclaw, Poland
lipinski@ii.uni.wroc.pl
[2] Natural Computing Research and Applications Group, Complex and Adaptive
Systems Laboratory, University College Dublin, Dublin, Ireland
anthony.brabazon@ucd.ie

Abstract. This paper addresses the issue of discovering frequent patterns in order book shapes, in the context of the stock market depth, for ultra-high frequency data. It proposes a computational intelligence approach to building frequent patterns by clustering order book shapes with Self-Organizing Maps. An experimental evaluation of the approach proposed on the London Stock Exchange Rebuild Order Book database succeeded with providing a number of characteristic shape patterns and also with estimating probabilities of some typical transitions between shape patterns in the order book.

1 Introduction

Analyzing ultra high-frequency data still remains a grand challenge for contemporary time series analysis, usually because of the large amount of data required to be processed and because of the noisy nature of the data. However, insights gleaned from ultra high-frequency data is crucial for understanding market microstructure. As noted by Goodhart and O'Hara [2]: ... *the issue of learning from high frequency data is fundamental to understanding market behavior* ... (p. 80).

Since the early days of market microstructure research, a considerable amount has been uncovered about the behaviour of markets under differing forms of regulation. Some of the classical and best-known stylised facts arising from early market microstructure research on the NYSE or LSE are the intraday patterns which arise on trade volume, price volatility and bid-ask quote spreads, which typically exhibit a 'reverse J' intraday seasonality pattern. Another issue which has become clear from the literature on market microstructure is that the measurement of returns and their associated volatility is particularly difficult at high frequencies, due to microstructure noise. However, as noted by Engle et al. [1], measurement of facets of liquidity such as market depth (and its associated variability) is much easier than measuring the volatility of returns at high frequencies (as the latter is contaminated by microstructure noise) and this suggests that

A.I. Esparcia-Alcázar et al. (Eds.): EvoApplications 2014, LNCS 8602, pp. 288–298, 2014.
DOI: 10.1007/978-3-662-45523-4_24

liquidity risk metrics could be a useful supplement when attempting to design and evaluate potential high-frequency trading strategies.

In this study we employ data drawn from the LSE Rebuild Order Book database and aim to address the issue of frequent patterns in order book shapes in the context of the market depth, which indicates the quantity of an asset on offer at each tick level in the order book. Initially, it focuses on an examination of a number of possible definitions of order book shapes facilitating a further clustering of order book shapes and the discovery of frequent patterns. In addition to providing useful insight which could assist with theory development, this knowledge could prove useful for the design of trade execution strategies, or more generally, for the design of trading strategies via enhanced understanding of trading costs and the likely carrying capacity of a strategy.

The remainder of this paper is organised as follows. Section 2 provides a short introduction to the LSE Rebuild Order Book database. This is followed in Section 3 by a short discussion on the order book shape concept which is used in this study. Section 4 proposes a method of clustering order book shapes and discovering shape patterns, followed in section 5 by a discussion on frequent order book patterns discovered. Section 6 refers to the issue of dynamic transitions between different shape patterns in the order book and estimating their probabilities. Section 7 summarizes the computational experiments, and the paper is concluded in section 8, with some suggestions for future work being provided.

2   Order Book Data

The London Stock Exchange Rebuild Order Book (LSE ROB) database contains intraday order information and trading data for all order book driven securities on the LSE. For each trading day, it provides all orders on the order book at the beginning of the trading day (the opening position), details of all orders entered onto and deleted from the order book during the trading day, details of all modifications to visible orders and changes to orders resulting from executions, as well as details of all manual and automatically executed trades. It facilitates the reconstruction of the LSE order book system.

In this research, we extracted order book snapshots from the LSE ROB database for a selected list of 100 securities with the highest number of orders registered over a chosen 15-day period (from April 1, 2010 to April 15), selected from 1977 securities available in total. For some basic statistics, the highest number of orders registered for a single security was 1652471 (RIO TINTO). There were 109501999 orders registered over the period under study in total. The total volume of the database for the period under study was about 15GB. As the LSE ROB database was published as a set of raw text files, which were usually unsorted, the extraction of the order book snapshots required some efficient algorithms such as the B-Trees routines, mainly for sorting and searching.

Snapshots were extracted for each selected security, for each 5 seconds of each trading day and were used later to form order book shapes, described in the next section, and to discover some characteristic patterns in order book shape. It is worth noticing that each snapshot contained all the bid and ask orders registered on the stock market and not yet deleted or executed until the snapshot time, not only the 5 best bid and 5 best ask orders, as published in many popular financial services.

3 Order Book Shape

The shape of the order book is defined on the basis of the best bid and ask offers in the order book.

Consider a snapshot of the current order book at certain time t containing the list of all the bid and ask orders registered on the stock market and not deleted until time t. The bid and ask orders may be aggregated in such a way that the all the orders with the same price are listed together with the total volume. Let $(p_1^{(B)}, v_1^{(B)})$, $(p_2^{(B)}, v_2^{(B)})$, ..., $(p_{h_B}^{(B)}, v_{h_B}^{(B)})$ be the list of aggregated bid orders, sorted decreasingly according to the price, where $p_i^{(B)}$ is the price and $v_i^{(B)}$ is the volume of the i-th aggregated bid order and h_B is the length of the list. Let $(p_1^{(A)}, v_1^{(A)})$, $(p_2^{(A)}, v_2^{(A)})$, ..., $(p_{h_A}^{(A)}, v_{h_A}^{(A)})$ be the list of aggregated ask orders, sorted increasingly according to the price, where $p_i^{(A)}$ is the price and $v_i^{(A)}$ is the volume of the i-th aggregated ask order and h_A is the length of the list.

Figure 1 illustrates some characteristics of the order book snapshot. Figure 1(a) presents a bar diagram of order prices, i.e. the sequence $p_{15}^{(B)}, \ldots, p_1^{(B)}$, $p_1^{(A)}, \ldots, p_{15}^{(A)}$. Figure 1(b) presents prices after subtracting the mean price. Figure 1(c) presents prices after subtracting the mean price and dividing by it. It is easy to see that the shapes of order prices cannot well characterize the order book snapshot, because the prices of orders are rather similar with only some minor regular differences.

Figure 1(d) presents a bar diagram of order volumes, i.e. the sequence $v_{15}^{(B)}, \ldots,$ $v_1^{(B)}, v_1^{(A)}, \ldots, v_{15}^{(A)}$ and Figure 1(e) presents volumes after dividing by the total volume of the order book. It is easy to see that the shapes of order volumes are more irregular than prices and may contain some interesting knowledge

Therefore, in our research, we focus on order book shapes combining the price information with the volume information and we define the order book shape of the size $2h$, for some $h \in \mathbb{N}$ lower or equal to h_A and h_B, as the vector

$$\mathbf{s} = (s_h^{(B)}, s_{h-1}^{(B)}, \ldots, s_1^{(B)}, s_1^{(A)}, \ldots, s_{h-1}^{(A)}, s_h^{(A)}) \in \mathbb{R}^{2h}, \tag{1}$$

where

$$s_i^{(B|A)} = (p_i^{(B|A)} - \bar{p}) \frac{v_i^{(B|A)}}{\bar{v}}, \quad \bar{p} = \frac{p_1^{(B)} + p_1^{(A)}}{2}, \quad \bar{v} = \sum_{i=1}^{n} v_i^{(B)} + \sum_{i=1}^{n} v_i^{(A)}. \tag{2}$$

Figure 1(f) presents the order book shape of the size 30. Additional examples of order book shapes may be found on Figure 4, Figure 5 and Figure 6 described later.

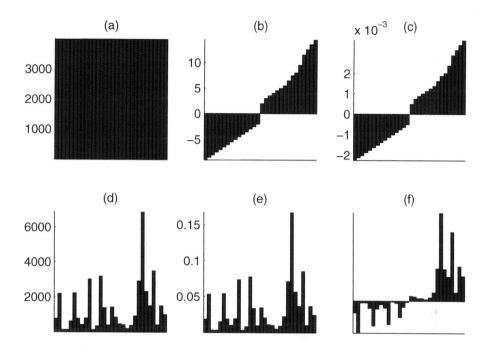

Fig. 1. The order book snapshot of the RIO TINTO company from the London Stock Exchange (ISIN GB0007188757) for April 1, 2010 9:00:00: (a) 15 best bid (increasingly, i.e. the worst first) and 15 best ask (increasingly, i.e. the best first) prices, (b) prices after subtracting the mean price, (c) prices after subtracting the mean price and dividing by the mean price, (d) volumes of 15 best bid and 15 best ask aggregated orders, (e) volumes after dividing by the total volume of the order book, (f) the shape of the order book.

4   Discovering Shape Patterns

Each order book shape of size $2h$ may be treated as a data point in the data space $\mathbb{R}^{2h}$. Similarities between order book shapes may be found by applying some clustering techniques, such as Self-Organizing Maps (SOM) [4] by Kohonen, to the cloud of the data points.

A Self-Organizing Map consists of M so-called codebook vectors, $\mathbf{v}_1, \mathbf{v}_2, \ldots,$ $\mathbf{v}_M \in \mathbb{R}^{2h}$ embedded in the data space and a topology structure in a form of a regular two dimensional hexagonal lattice defining a neighborhood relation for the codebook vectors. Figure 2(a) and (b) illustrates the neighborhood relation on a plane and Figure 2(c) illustrates it in the data space (projected to two dimensions). Therefore, the codebook vectors, connected each to other according to the neighborhood relation, form an elastic net embedded in the data space, which will be adjusted to the given data sample in the training process in order to fold onto the cloud of given data points.

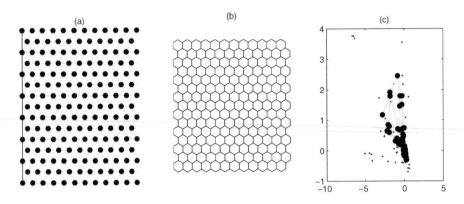

Fig. 2. A Self-Organizing Map with 180 codebook vectors: (a) the hexagonal lattice of the size 15×12 defining the neighborhood relation for the codebook vectors, (b) the lattice where each cell corresponds to one codebook vector and adjoining cells correspond to neighbor codebook vectors, (c) the codebook vectors embedded in the data space (projected to two dimensions)

First, the training algorithm places the codebook vectors in a regular grid on the plane defined by the two first principal components of the given data sample. Next, in successive iterations of the training algorithm, one data point $\mathbf{s}$ is randomly picked from the given data sample, distances between each codebook vector $\mathbf{v}$ and the picked data point $\mathbf{s}$ are evaluated and the nearest codebook vector $\mathbf{u}$, the so-called Best Matching Unit (BMU), is determined. The BMU and its neighbor codebook vectors are moved towards the picked data point $\mathbf{s}$ using the updating formula

$$\mathbf{v} := \mathbf{v} + \alpha \cdot \theta(\mathbf{s}, \mathbf{u}, \mathbf{v}) \cdot (\mathbf{s} - \mathbf{v}), \tag{3}$$

where $\mathbf{v}$ is the codebook vector to be updated, $\mathbf{s}$ is the selected data point, α is a learning coefficient decreasing in successive iterations of the training algorithm and $\theta(\mathbf{s}, \mathbf{u}, \mathbf{v})$ is a neighborhood function determining the size of the movement, usually $\theta(\mathbf{s}, \mathbf{u}, \mathbf{v})$ is larger for $\mathbf{v}$ close to $\mathbf{u}$ according to the neighborhood relation and smaller for other codebook vectors. The training algorithm iterates adjusting the net to the data sample either for a set number of iterations or until the net fits the given data sample sufficiently well.

Assigning each data point from the given data sample to the nearest codebook vector defines a clustering of the given data sample, where data points assigned to the same codebook vector constitute a cluster.

Self-Organizing Maps were applied to order book shapes to split them into a number of groups and try to find some frequent shape patterns characteristic to each group.

The data sample consisted of $N = 21600$ order book shapes corresponding to the order book snapshots of the RIO TINTO company from the London Stock

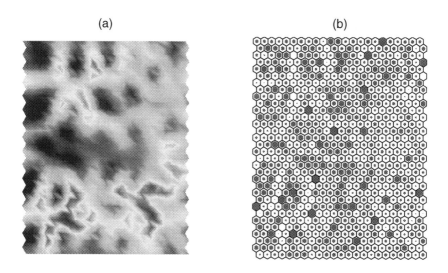

Fig. 3. Results of clustering the 21600 order book shapes with a Self-Organizing Map of 736 codebook vectors with the hexagonal topology of the size 32×23: (a) the hits diagram presenting the number of order book shapes in each cluster, (b) the U-Matrix presenting the distances between codebook vectors in the data space

Exchange (ISIN GB0007188757) from April 1, 2010 to April 9, 2010 (5 working days) taken each 5 seconds from 9:00:00 to 14:59:55 each day. Each order book shape was a vector of length $d = 30$ in the data space $\mathbb{R}^{30}$. Self-Organizing Maps with $M = 736$ codebook vectors and the Gaussian neighborhood function θ were used.

Figure 3(a) presents the hits diagram of the SOM. Each cell corresponds to one codebook vector and adjoining cells correspond to neighbor codebook vectors. Cells are filled according to the number of order book shapes assigned to the codebook vector, i.e. an empty cell denotes that no order book shapes were assigned to the codebook vector, while a full cell denotes that many order book shapes were assigned to the codebook vector. It is easy to see that there is a number of large clusters grouping many similar order book shapes and a number of small clusters grouping few order book shapes. Future studies focus on the large clusters, because they reveal more general similarities, while the small clusters may be rather incidental.

Figure 3(b) presents the U-Matrix of the SOM, which shows the distances between codebook vectors in the data space. The red color denotes that adjoining codebook vectors are far apart, while the blue color denotes that adjoining codebook vectors are close. It is easy to see that the majority of the large clusters are well separated and well established in the data space.

5   Frequent Order Book Patterns

Although all the order book shapes in a cluster are closer to the codebook vector
of that cluster than to of another, particular order book shapes may significantly
differ. In order to define significant order book patterns, we investigate the large
clusters and differences between a certain number of order book shapes nearest
to the codebook vector of the cluster representing the order book pattern. If
the majority of the shapes in the cluster is similar each to other, the pattern is
well-established. If not, the pattern is rather insignificant.

Figure 4 presents three order book shapes assigned to the first largest cluster,
namely the 1st, 50th and 100th order book shape nearest to the codebook vector
of the cluster. Figure 5 and Figure 6 presents the same concerning the third and
the fifth largest cluster, respectively. It is easy to see that the order book shapes
within each cluster are similar. Certainly, in each cluster, there might be some
order book shapes different from the other and far from the codebook vector

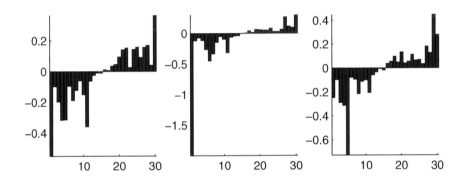

Fig. 4. Three order book shapes from the first largest cluster: the 1st, 50th and 100th
order book shape nearest to the codebook vector of the cluster

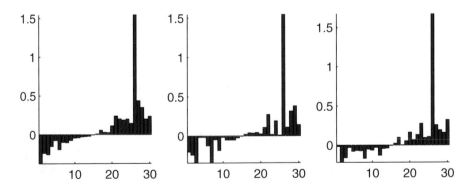

Fig. 5. Three order book shapes from the third largest cluster: the 1st, 50th and 100th
order book shape nearest to the codebook vector of the cluster

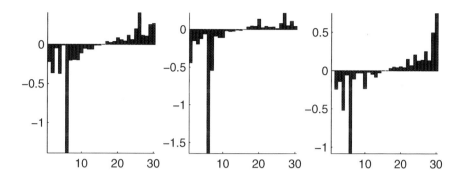

Fig. 6. Three order book shapes from the fifth largest cluster: the 1st, 50th and 100th order book shape nearest to the codebook vector of the cluster

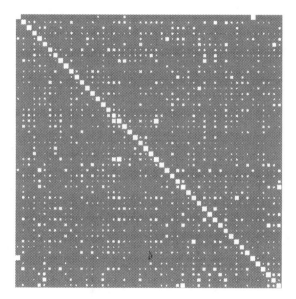

Fig. 7. The Hinton diagram of the transition probability matrix for 50 largest clusters of order book shapes

of that cluster, which was assigned to that cluster only because of that the other codebook vectors were even farer, but focusing on a selected number of order book shapes nearest to the codebook vector may guarantee that they are consistent.

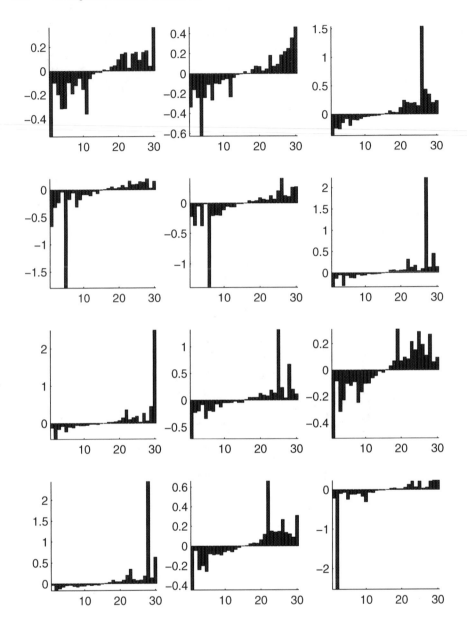

Fig. 8. The 12 most frequent order book patterns discovered on the order book snapshots of the 100 instruments from the London Stock Exchange with the highest numbers of order registered during the period from April 1, 2010 to April 15, 2010

6 Transitions Between Order Book Patterns

In further research, we focus on the 50 largest clusters, defined respectively by the codebook vectors $\mathbf{v}_1, \mathbf{v}_2, \ldots, \mathbf{v}_{50}$, and the 100 order book shapes $\mathbf{s}_1^{(k)}, \mathbf{s}_2^{(k)}, \ldots,$ $\mathbf{s}_1 00^{(k)}$ nearest to the codebook vector $\mathbf{v}_k$, for each $k = 1, 2, \ldots, 50$.

First, for each cluster $k = 1, 2, \ldots, 50$ and for each successive shape $i = 1, 2, \ldots, 100$ in the cluster, let $t_0^{(k,i)}$ denote the time when the order book shape occurred and let $t_l^{(k,i)} > t_0^{(k,i)}$ denote the earliest time after $t_0^{(k,i)}$ when any shape of the l-th cluster occurred ($t_l^{(k,i)} = -1$ if no shape from the l-th cluster occurred after $t_0^{(k,i)}$), for each $l = 1, 2, \ldots, 50$. Let $\delta_{i,k,l} = 1$ if $0 < t_l^{(k,i)} - t0^{(k,i)} < 300$, i.e. if the first shape from the l-th cluster occurred within 5 minutes after the i-th shape from the k-th cluster, and $\delta_{i,k,l} = 0$ otherwise.

Next, a transition probability matrix $\mathbf{T} \in \mathbb{R}^{50 \times 50}$ with elements t_{kl} may be defined by

$$t_{kl} = \frac{1}{100} \sum_{i=1}^{100} \delta_{i,k,l}, \tag{4}$$

which corresponds to the frequency of the event that after a shape from the k-th cluster, a shape from the l-th cluster will occur within 5 minutes.

Figure 7 presents the Hinton diagram of the transition probability matrix $\mathbf{T}$. Each cell of the Hinton diagram corresponds to a cell of the transition probability matrix $\mathbf{T}$ and the size of the square in the cell of the Hinton diagram corresponds to the value in the cell of the transition probability matrix $\mathbf{T}$ (large squares - values close to 1, small square - values close to 0).

One may see that probabilities of transitions between some patterns are high, while between other are low. The high values on the diagonal of the matrix mean that occurring a shape of the same cluster within 5 minutes has a large probability, which is rather obvious, because changing the order book shape in a short time requires the occurance of a large order, which is not common.

Probabilities of transitions between order book patterns might be further used in financial decision support systems for automatic trading to predict some changes on the stock market.

7 Summary of Experiments

In the previous sections, we focused on the order book snapshots of the RIO TINTO company (being the equity with the highest number of orders registered during the period from April 1, 2010 to April 15, 2010) from April 1, 2010 to April 9, 2010 (5 working days) taken each 5 seconds from 9:00:00 to 14:59:55 each day. Experiments on other instruments were also performed and results are rather similar.

Figure 8 presents 12 most frequent patterns discovered on the order book snapshots of the 100 instruments from the London Stock Exchange with the highest numbers of orders registered during the period from April 1, 2010 to April 15, 2010.

In all the experiments discussed here, the order book shapes of the size 30 were investigated, however different size of the shapes may be also considered. Popular financial services usually publish order book snapshots with 5 best bid and 5 best ask orders, so order book shapes of the size 10 were also studied, but the results obtained were worse, perhaps because of the fact that shorter shapes do not allow us to distinguish as many patterns as longer shapes.

8   Conclusions and Perspectives

In this paper, we present the results of initial research on order book shape, frequent patterns in these shapes, dependencies between these patterns and knowledge extraction from order book shape.

Additional research is needed to improve the clustering techniques for discovering common patterns and in order to increase their reliability. It may be achieved by studies on the intra-cluster similarities and inter-cluster dissimilarities. Using additional outlier detection methods may also eliminate some small clusters corresponding to patterns arising due to noisy data. Reducing dimensionality, especially in the case of shapes of larger sizes, may improve the quality of clustering as well as making the computational process faster.

Order book shape patterns may constitute an interesting source of knowledge for financial decision support systems for automatic trading. However, more effort is needed to incorporate the knowledge extracted, for instance the transition probabilities, into expert trading systems.

Some extensions of order book shape may be also studied, such as dynamic order book shape, i.e. a sequence of a number of successive order book shapes revealing a certain phenomena of the stock market, such as the behavior of the stock market after a large order is put onto the order book.

References

1. Engle, R., Fleming, M., Ghysels, E., Nguyen, G.: Liquidity and Volatility in the U.S. Treasury Market: Evidence From A New Class of Dynamic Order Book Models. http://www.unc.edu/maguilar/metrics/Giang.pdf, (accessed February 21 2012)
2. Goodhart, C., O'Hara, M.: High frequency data in financial markets: Issues and applications. Journal of Empirical Finance 4, 73–114 (1997)
3. Heston, S., Korajczyk, R., Sadka, R.: Intraday patterns in the crosssection of stock returns. Journal of Finance 65(4), 1369–1407 (2010)
4. Kohonen, T.: Self-Organizing Maps. Springer (2000)
5. Lee, Y., Fok, R., Liu, Y.: Explaining intraday pattern of trading volume from the order flow data. Journal of Business Finance and Accounting 28(3), 199–230 (2001)
6. McInish, T., Wood, R.: An analysis of intraday patterns in bid-ask spreads for nyse stocks. Journal of Finance 47(2), 753–764 (1992)
7. O'Hara, M.: Market Microstructure Theory. Blackwell, Oxford (1995)
8. Tian, G., Guo, M.: Interday and intraday volatility: additional evidence from the shanghai stock exchange. Review of Quantitative Finance and Accounting 28(3), 287–306 (2007)

EvoGAMES

Multi-Criteria Comparison of Coevolution and Temporal Difference Learning on Othello

Wojciech Jaśkowski[✉], Marcin Szubert, and Paweł Liskowski

Institute of Computing Science, Poznan University of Technology,
Poznań, Poland
{wjaskowski,mszubert,pliskowski}@cs.put.poznan.pl

Abstract. We compare Temporal Difference Learning (TDL) with Coevolutionary Learning (CEL) on Othello. Apart from using three popular single-criteria performance measures: (i) generalization performance or expected utility, (ii) average results against a hand-crafted heuristic and (iii) result in a head to head match, we compare the algorithms using performance profiles. This multi-criteria performance measure characterizes player's performance in the context of opponents of various strength. The multi-criteria analysis reveals that although the generalization performance of players produced by the two algorithms is similar, TDL is much better at playing against strong opponents, while CEL copes better against weak ones. We also find out that the TDL produces less diverse strategies than CEL. Our results confirms the usefulness of performance profiles as a tool for comparison of learning algorithms for games.

Keywords: Reinforcement learning · Coevolutionary algorithm · Reversi · Othello · Board evaluation function · Weighted piece counter · Interactive domain

1 Introduction

The board game of Othello constitutes a non-trivial interactive domain, which has become a popular testbed for evaluating and comparing different computational intelligence algorithms [1–3]. The most popular algorithms used for learning Othello-playing strategies include *competitive coevolutionary learning* (CEL) [4] and *temporal difference learning* (TDL) [5]. TDL is a well-recognized example of reinforcement learning [6], in which the playing agent aims to find a value function for predicting chances of winning a game from a particular state. CEL, on the other hand, searches the space of strategies directly by maintaining a set of candidate solutions that compete against each other and are randomly tweaked by means of evolutionary operators such as mutation or crossover. The essential difference between TDL and CEL is that TDL guides the learning using the whole course of the game while CEL uses only the final game outcome.

Since both CEL and TDL can be applied to the same problem of learning game-playing strategies, it is not surprising that they have been the subject

© Springer-Verlag Berlin Heidelberg 2014
A.I. Esparcia-Alcázar et al. (Eds.): EvoApplications 2014, LNCS 8602, pp. 301–312, 2014.
DOI: 10.1007/978-3-662-45523-4_25

of comparative investigations. In one of the first such comparisons for Othello, Lucas and Runarsson [1] found out that when learning strategies represented with simple weighted piece counters "TDL learns much faster than CEL, but properly tuned CEL can learn better playing strategies". However, Szubert et al. [7] showed that the difference between TDL and CEL largely depends on the performance measure used: CEL and TDL perform similarly when playing against a random player, but TDL is superior to CEL when compared against a heuristic hand-crafted player. These results were confirmed also for a non-linear, complex n-tuples strategy representation [8], for which CEL is substantially worse than TDL while a hybrid of CEL and TDL works even better [3]. Interestingly, in the context of Backgammon game, Darwen showed that CEL can beat TDL [9].

Therefore, the general conclusions of the results of research comparing CEL and TDL are not clear and they depend, among others, on selected objective performance measure whether this is a fixed hand-crafted opponent, a random player or a round robin tournament [3]. This insight led to devising performance profiles [10], a multi-criteria method for comparison players and algorithms. Performance profiles allow to analyze and present graphically the performance of different players when facing opponents of various strength. Thus performance profile conveys much more information about player's characteristics than the commonly used single-criteria performance measures which are prone to compensation due to aggregation of results: the awards received in interactions with a certain group of tests can cancel out the penalties incurred in interactions with another group of tests.

Our main contribution in this paper is the comparison of CEL and TDL using the multi-criteria performance measure based on performance profiles. In this way we are able to precisely pin-point performance differences between the strategies learned by the two analyzed algorithms and explain the differences in results obtained on single-criteria performance measures. We notice that it is easy to misjudge relative algorithms strength basing only on a single-criteria performance measure.

2 Othello

2.1 Game Rules Description

Othello is a perfect information, zero-sum, two-player strategy game played on a 8×8 board. There are 64 identical disks which are white on one side and black on the other. The game begins with each player having two disks placed diagonally in the center of the board. Players alternate placing disks on the board, with the black player moving first. A move is legal if the newly placed piece is adjacent to an opponent's piece and causes one or more of the opponent's pieces to become enclosed from both sides of a horizontal, vertical or diagonal line. The enclosed disks are then flipped. The game ends when neither player has a legal move. A player who has more pieces on the board wins. If both players have the same number of pieces, the game ends in a draw.

2.2   Weighted Piece Counter (WPC) Strategy Representation

We represent strategies using WPC, a simple, linear board state evaluation function, which indicates how desirable a given board state is. WPC assigns weight w_i to board location i and uses scalar product to calculate the value f of a board state $\mathbf{b}$: $f(\mathbf{b}) = \sum_{i=1}^{8 \times 8} w_i b_i$, where b_i is 0, $+1$ or -1 for empty location, black piece or white piece, respectively. The players interpret $f(\mathbf{b})$ in a complementary manner: the black player prefers moves leading towards states with a higher value, whereas lower values are favored by the white player.

All algorithms considered in this paper employ WPC as a state evaluator in 1-ply setup: given the current board state, the player generates all legal moves and applies f to the resulting states. The state gauged as the most valuable determines the move to be made. Ties are resolved at random.

3   Coevolutionary Learning

Coevolutionary algorithms [11] are variants of evolutionary computation in which an individual's fitness depends on other individuals. Similarly to the evolutionary one, coevolutionary algorithm use mechanisms such as selection and variation that mimic the natural evolution. The driving force of coevolutionary algorithms is the continuous Darwinian *arms race* taking place between one or two competing populations [12]. The difference between coevolutionary and evolutionary methods lies in the evaluation phase, when the fitness of individuals is assessed. Evolutionary algorithms that solve optimization problems have access to the objective function of a problem, thus individuals' fitness is directly computed. In coevolutionary algorithms, individuals' fitness is typically only estimated by aggregating results of multiple interactions between individuals from the maintained populations.

In this paper we use a one-population variant of competitive coevolution and apply it to learn Othello board evaluation function. The algorithm uses mutation as the only variation operator while fitness of an individual is defined as a sum of two values: i) the average result of games played against other individuals from the population (a round robin tournament) and ii) the average result of games played against a sample of random WPC players. This particular coevolutionary algorithm has been recently found superior to a typical one-population coevolution [10].

4   Temporal Difference Learning

Temporal Difference Learning (TDL) is a reinforcement learning (RL) method which has become a popular approach for elaborating game-playing strategies [1,2,13]. The use of RL techniques for such applications stems from modeling a game as a sequential decision problem, where the task of the learner is to maximize the expected reward in the long run (game outcome).

In this paper we use $TD(\lambda)$ algorithm [5], which solves prediction learning problem that consists in estimating the future behavior of an unknown system from the past experience. Learning occurs whenever systems state changes over time and is based on the error between the temporally successive predictions. Its goal is to make the preceding prediction to match more closely the current prediction (taking into account distinct system states observed in the corresponding time steps). Technically, at a certain time step t, prediction P_t can be considered as a function of two arguments: current system state and the vector of weights $\mathbf{w}$. The $TD(\lambda)$ algorithm is expressed by the following weight update rule:

$$\Delta\mathbf{w}_t = \alpha(P_{t+1} - P_t)\sum_{k=1}^{t}\lambda^{t-k}\nabla_w P_k,$$

where α is the learning rate, and λ is the decay parameter, which influences the magnitude of changes applied to all the preceding predictions within a single learning episode. When applied to the problem of learning game-playing strategy represented as WPC, P_t estimates the chances of winning from the game state $\mathbf{b}_t$, by mapping the outcome of the WPC function f to a closed interval $[-1, 1]$ using hyperbolic tangent, so that $P_t = tanh(f(\mathbf{b}_t))$.

The process of learning consists of applying the above formulas to the WPC vector after each move of a self-play game. During game play, moves are selected on the basis of the most recent evaluation function. Othello is a deterministic game, thus the course of the game between two deterministic players is always the same. This feature reduces the number of possible states a learner can explore, which makes learning ineffective. To remedy this situation, at each turn, a random move is forced with a certain probability ϵ. As a result, players are confronted against a wider spectrum of possible behaviors.

5   Experimental Setup and Parameters Tuning

In order to fairly compare the algorithms, we set them up so that their total computational effort is the same and it is equal to $2,000,000$ training games. To evaluate a given algorithm we measure the performance of its *best-of-run* player. In CEL this is the individual from the last generation with the highest fitness, while in TDL this is simply the only learning player. Since both considered algorithms are stochastic, we compare their average results over 100 runs.

Instead of selecting arbitrary values of parameters for CEL and TDL, we perform a series of preliminary experiments to optimize them. As the optimization goal we use the performance measure of *generalization performance* [14] (also known as expected utility [10]). Generalization performance of a player is defined as its expected score over all possible opponents. To approximate this measure we compute the average game result of the player against $50,000$ random players. A random player is a random weighted piece counter player that weights are drawn uniformly at random from a fixed interval of $[-1, 1]$. In each game players are rewarded 1 point for a win and 0.5 point for a draw.

5.1   Temporal Difference Learning

The $TD(\lambda)$ algorithm described in Section 4 has two parameters: learning rate α and decay $\lambda \in [0, 1]$. Additionally, since the algorithm learns on the basis of self-play games, there is another important parameter — random move probability ϵ. The results of different combinations of α and ϵ for $\lambda = 0$ are presented in Table 1.

Table 1. The results obtained by TDL players for different α and ϵ. Generalization performance values are presented in percent points.

$\alpha =$	.01	.02	.03	.04	.05	.06	.07	.08	.09	.1
$\epsilon = .0$	81.4	82.3	84.2	84.0	84.3	82.1	79.9	75.4	71.5	72.0
$\epsilon = .05$	84.0	81.1	82.7	86.2	**87.9**	87.7	87.4	87.4	87.0	86.8
$\epsilon = .1$	84.4	81.5	82.4	84.4	87.3	87.7	87.2	86.4	85.4	85.4
$\epsilon = .15$	84.9	82.7	82.2	83.3	86.1	87.8	86.7	85.5	84.6	84.5

On the basis of these results we chose $\alpha = 0.05$ and $\epsilon = 0.05$ as the best parameters. In the second stage, we checked different values of decay λ. However, changing λ did not provide statistically better results than those obtained with $\lambda = 0$. This observation confirms previous results [2].

5.2   Coevolution

CEL has several quantitative and qualitative parameters. The former include population size, random sample size, mutation probability and mutation range, while the latter mutation and selection operators. The weights of the individuals in the initial population were drawn at random from the $[-0.1, 0.1]$ interval.

For each of the parameters we considered several possible values. We chose to test six population sizes and six random sample sizes: 4, 10, 20, 50, 100, 200. We selected four selection strategies:

- *tournament selection,* with tournament size 5,
- *stochastic universal sampling* [15], a variant of a roulette-wheel selection that guarantees that the frequency of selection for each individual is consistent with its expected frequency of selection,
- $(\mu + \lambda)$ evolutionary strategy, where $\mu = \frac{1}{2}popsize$ and $\lambda = \frac{1}{2}popsize$, and
- (μ, λ) evolutionary strategy, *where* $\mu = \frac{1}{2}popsize$ and $\lambda = popsize$.

Additionally, we considered *Gaussian mutation* and *uniform mutation*. These mutation operators perturb each weight of the WPC with probability p by adding to it a random value drawn uniformly from the interval $[-r, r]$ in case of uniform mutation, or from $\mathcal{N}(0, \sigma)$ for Gaussian mutation. For parameters p, r, and σ we considered values of .05, .1, .2, .3, .4, .5, .6, .7, .8, .9 and 1.0.

Results

We carried out the tuning of CEL parameters in two stages. In the first stage, we fixed the mutation operator to Gaussian mutation with $p = 0.1$ and $\sigma = 0.25$ and focused on finding the best selection strategy and best values of population size and random sample size. For this purpose, we evaluated all $6 \times 6 \times 4 = 144$ combinations of population size, random sample size and selection operators.

The results of optimization are shown in Fig. 1. On this basis, we decided to use (μ, λ)-ES, population size of 20 and random sample size of 200.

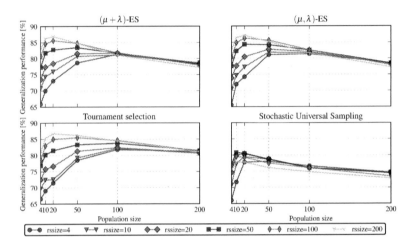

Fig. 1. The impact of population size, random sample size and selection operator on the generalization performance of CEL. The values are presented in percent points.

In the second stage, we evaluated Gaussian mutation and uniform mutation for every combination of mutation probability, mutation operator and their parameters, $7 \times 7 \times 2 = 98$ experiments in total. Surprisingly, we have found no evidence of any statistical differences between either the mutation types or their parameters with the sole exception of the combination of Gaussian mutation with $\sigma = .05$ and $p \in \{.05, .1\}$ that were statistically (t-test, $\alpha = 0.05$) inferior to other combinations. As a result, for the rest of the experiments we use Gaussian mutation with $p = 1.0$ and $\sigma = 1.0$.

6   Comparison of Coevolution and Temporal Difference Learning

6.1   Single-Criteria Comparison

We start the comparison between CEL and TDL by applying three commonly used [1,16,17] single-criteria performance measures:

- *generalization performance* — the average performance against randomly generated WPC players (see Section 5).
- *heuristic performance* — the average performance against a "standard" hand-crafted WPC heuristic player [3,18]. Since this player is deterministic, following earlier work [1], we force players to make random moves with probability $\epsilon = 0.1$, and thus we slightly alter the game definition.
- *head to head* — indicates how well a set of players copes in games against players from another set.

Table 2. Comparison of CEL and TDL using three performance measures: i) generalization performance, ii) heuristic performance, and iii) the result of head to head match. The results are shown in percent points, where 100% means getting all possible points (winning all games). Values of generalization performance and heuristic performance are accompanied by 95% confidence intervals. Note that the results of head to head match sum up to 100%.

	Performance measure [%]		
Algorithm	generalization	heuristic	head to head
Coevolutionary Learning (CEL)	86.97±0.21	32.31±0.62	21.2
Temporal Difference Learning (TDL)	87.26±0.32	46.14±0.96	78.8

Table 2 presents the results for CEL and TDL using the above-described single-criteria performance measures. To compute generalization performance and heuristic performance we played 50,000 games for each best-of-run player. The results were averaged over 100 best-of-run players for each algorithm.

The comparison using the three single-criteria performance measures is equivocal. The performance measure of generalization performance shows no statistical difference between CEL and TDL (t-test, $\alpha = 0.01$). However, TDL is clearly superior to CEL when playing against a heuristic player and in a head to head match. Can we then claim with a confidence that TDL is "better" than CEL?

6.2 Multi-Criteria Comparison with Performance Profiles

Performance Profiles. Single-criteria methods of performance evaluation do not draw a clear picture of the relative performance of analyzed methods. To better understand the characteristics of compared methods we use *performance profiles* [10]. They compare performance of players using sets of opponents of various strength, treating the result of match against opponents of each such set as a separate performance criteria.

To prepare a performance profile, we first generate a number of opponents and group them into bins according to their strength. To this aim, we randomly generated about 1,000,000 players (opponents) by sampling WPC weights uniformly and independently from the $[-1, 1]$ interval. Next, the generalization performance of each opponent was estimated by taking average from the results of games 2,000 against random WPC strategies. The range of possible performance values, i.e., $[0\%, 100\%]$, is then divided into 100 bins of equal 1%-performance width, and each opponent is assigned to one of these bins based on its generalization performance.

However, finding extremely strong or weak strategies in this way is very difficult, if not impossible. To overcome this, the strongest (performance $> 81\%$) and the weakest (performance $< 13\%$) opponents were obtained using multiple independent runs of evolutionary learning with random sampling [10]. In this way, we were able to fill 93 bins $(4\% - 96\%)$, each one of containing $1,000$ opponents. Note that building the opponents database is computationally expensive. However, once created, it can be reused[1].

The set of opponents partitioned into bins form the basis for building performance profiles. The player to be assessed plays games against all the opponents from each bin, and the average game outcome is plotted against the bins. Performance profile is a multi-criteria performance evaluation method since the performance of a given player is measured separately on every bin, each being a different criterion.

Results. We apply this multi-criteria method to inspect the best-of-run individuals of the two algorithms considered in this paper. The resulting performance profiles are presented in Fig. 2. Since we have 100 runs per algorithm, we average the profiles over 100 best-of-run players. A point of coordinates (x, y) in a plot means that the best-of-run individuals have on average performance y when playing against opponents of performance x. For example, the performance of CEL is nearly 95% for opponents with performance of 20%. The whiskers in the plots mark 95% confidence intervals.

The decreasing trend in each data series confirms the intuition that it is harder to win against stronger opponents than against the weaker ones.

The most important observation from the plots is that TDL players are significantly better when facing the strong opponents. Moreover, the stronger the opponents the wider the performance gap between CEL and TDL players. On the other hand, CEL players are better than TDL players against the weakest opponents. For example, CEL players win nearly 98% games against the weakest opponents in our database of performance of 4%, while TDL players win only 94% games against them.

6.3 Discussion

In Section 6.1 we showed that there is no statistical difference in generalization performance between CEL and TDL, but TDL is better than CEL in a game against a hand-crafted heuristic player and in a head to head tournament. Performance profiles could explain this discrepancy.

---

[1] The data and Java code for creating performance profiles for Othello are available at http://www.cs.put.poznan.pl/wjaskowski/projects/performance-profiles.

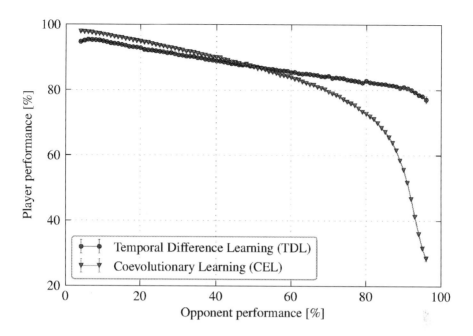

Fig. 2. Performance profiles of coevolutionary learning (CEL) and temporal difference learning (TDL). Each point (x, y) means player performance y against opponents of performance x. Confidence intervals for each point are less than 1%. Right side of the plot indicates that TDL copes much better than CEL against stronger opponents.

First, we can see that in Fig. 2 CEL and TDL curves cross at about 50%, both obtaining performance about 87% at this point. This value precisely matches the generalization performance results obtained by CEL and TDL (cf. Table 2), because the 50%-bin contains average players of performance equal to a random WPC player.

Second, we should realize that the heuristic performance and the result in head to head match determine how a player copes against strong opponents, rather than average ones. Performance profile analysis confirms that TDL fares much better than CEL against strong opponents (cf. Fig 2).

Third, what the three single-criteria performance measure miss is that CEL is better than TDL for weaker opponents.

The three single-criteria measures are like three points sampled from a signal; we can hypothesize about its shape, but they are not enough to fully understand it. Performance profiles allow us to not only understand the single-criteria results but also to see the trade-offs between TDL and CEL.

7   Strategies Comparison

The average performance against particular type of opponents allows us to draw conclusions about the superiority of some approaches over others, but it says

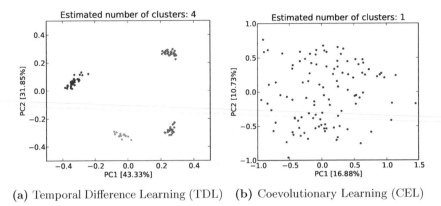

(a) Temporal Difference Learning (TDL)   (b) Coevolutionary Learning (CEL)

Fig. 3. Learned strategies represented as points in the PCA-reduced space. Different colors indicate clusters identified by the mean-shift algorithm.

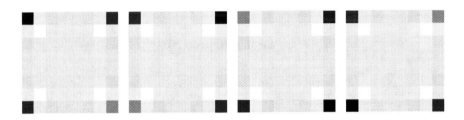

Fig. 4. WPC strategies produced by TDL corresponding to centers of the clusters identified by the mean-shift algorithm (cf. Fig. 3) illustrated as Othello boards with locations shaded accordingly to corresponding weights

nothing about the weights of elaborated WPC strategies. For this reason, we investigate the distribution of final strategies learned by TDL and CEL.

To analyze the WPC strategies, we treat them as points in a 64-dimensional space. First, we linearly scale all their weights to $[0, 1]$ interval. Finally, we clustered them using the mean-shift algorithm [19]. Figure 3 illustrates the results of clustering the strategies produced by TDL and CEL in a two dimensional space, which was obtained by applying PCA (Principle Component Analysis). For TDL, we can clearly see four clusters, while CEL strategies are randomly spread in the space. It appears that the players produced by CEL are much more diversified than those produced by CEL.

Selected WPCs are presented graphically in weight-proportional gray-scale in Figures 4 and 5 for TDL and CEL, respectively. In the figures darker squares denote larger weights, which correspond to more desirable board locations.

Interestingly, TDL strategies exhibit some symmetries. In particular, the corners are the most desirable, while their immediate neighbors have very low weights. The only difference between these four strategies is the weight in one

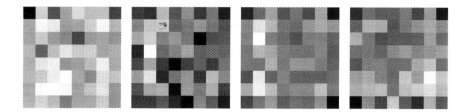

Fig. 5. Selected WPC strategies found by CEL and illustrated as Othello boards with locations shaded accordingly to corresponding weights. The first two strategies from the left are the most distant ones in the 64-dimensional space, the third one is the centroid of the set of all CEL strategies while the right-most one is the best strategy with respect to the generalization performance.

of the board corners — it is significantly lower than in the other three corners. In contrast, CEL strategies are less symmetrical and, apart from the typically black corners, they do not exhibit any regularities nor symmetries.

8   Conclusions

This study presents an evidence that while temporal difference learning (TDL) and coevolutionary learning (CEL) obtain similar results against average opponents, TDL copes much better against stronger ones. This was observed using single-criteria performance measures, but the full picture was only revealed using multi-criteria performance profiles. The characteristics of the strategies learned by TDL and CEL differ significantly and this is reflected in strategy weights.

Despite their usefulness, performance profiles have some limitations. Their computation requires numerous opponents of specific performances to be prepared, what is computationally expensive. Therefore, profiling game-playing strategies seems to be only possible for simple and linear representations (like WPC) and for games which can be quickly played (1-ply only). Nevertheless, such settings are perfectly acceptable when the emphasis of the research is put not on the absolute performance of the players, but on the learning algorithms.

Acknowledgments. This work has been supported by the Polish National Science Centre grant no. DEC-2013/09/D/ST6/03932. M. Szubert has been supported by Polish Ministry of Science and Education, grant no. 2012/05/N/ST6/03152.

References

1. Lucas, S.M., Runarsson, T.P.: Temporal difference learning versus co-evolution for acquiring othello position evaluation. In: IEEE Symposium on Computational Intelligence and Games, 52–59 IEEE (2006)
2. van den Dries, S., Wiering, M.A.: Neural-Fitted TD-Leaf Learning for Playing Othello With Structured Neural Networks. IEEE Transactions on Neural Networks and Learning Systems **23**(11), 1701–1713 (2012)

3. Szubert, M., Jaśkowski, W., Krawiec, K.: On scalability, generalization, and hybridization of coevolutionary learning: a case study for othello. IEEE Transactions on Computational Intelligence and AI in Games **5**(3), 214–226 (2013)
4. Axelrod, R.: The evolution of strategies in the iterated prisoner's dilemma. In: Davis, L., (ed.) Genetic Algorithms in Simulated Annealing, London pp. 32–41 (1987)
5. Sutton, R.S.: Learning to predict by the methods of temporal differences. Machine learning **3**(1), 9–44 (1988)
6. Sutton, R., Barto, A.: Reinforcement learning, Vol. 9. MIT Press (1998)
7. Szubert, M., Jaśkowski, W., Krawiec, K.: Learning board evaluation function for othello by hybridizing coevolution with temporal difference learning. Control and Cybernetics **40**(3), 805–831 (2011)
8. Lucas, S.M.: Learning to play Othello with N-tuple systems. Australian Journal of Intelligent Information Processing Systems, Special Issue on Game Technology **9**(4), 01–20 (2007)
9. Darwen, P.J.: Why co-evolution beats temporal difference learning at backgammon for a linear architecture, but not a non-linear architecture. In: Proceedings of the 2001 Congress on Evolutionary Computation, Vol. 2, pp. 1003–1010. IEEE (2001)
10. Jaśkowski, W., Liskowski, P., Szubert, M., Krawiec, K.: Improving coevolution by random sampling. In: Blum, C. (ed.) GECCO'13: Proceedings of the 15th Annual Conference on Genetic and Evolutionary Computation, pp. 1141–1148. ACM, Amsterdam (2013)
11. Popovici, E., Bucci, A., Wiegand, R.P., de Jong, E.D.: Coevolutionary Principles. In: Handbook of Natural Computing. Springer (2011)
12. Nolfi, S., Floreano, D.: Coevolving Predator and Prey Robots: Do Arms Races Arise in Artificial Evolution? Artificial Life **4**(4), 311–335 (1998)
13. Tesauro, G.: Temporal difference learning and td-gammon. Communications of the ACM **38**(3), 58–68 (1995)
14. Chong, S.Y., Tino, P., Yao, X.: Relationship between generalization and diversity in coevolutionary learning. IEEE Transactions on Computational Intelligence and AI in Games **1**(3), 214–232 (2009)
15. Baker, J.E.: Reducing bias and inefficiency in the selection algorithms (1985)
16. Chong, S.Y., Tino, P., Ku, D.C., Xin, Y.: Improving Generalization Performance in Co-Evolutionary Learning. IEEE Transactions on Evolutionary Computation **16**(1), 70–85 (2012)
17. Szubert, M., Jaśkowski, W., Krawiec, K.: Coevolutionary temporal difference learning for othello. In: IEEE Symposium on Computational Intelligence and Games, Milano, Italy, pp. 104–111 (2009)
18. Samothrakis, S., Lucas, S., Runarsson, T., Robles, D.: Coevolving Game-Playing Agents: Measuring Performance and Intransitivities. IEEE Transactions on Evolutionary Computation **99**, 1–15 (2012)
19. Comaniciu, D., Meer, P., Member, S.: Mean shift: A robust approach toward feature space analysis. IEEE Transactions on Pattern Analysis and Machine Intelligence **24**, 603–619 (2002)

Evolving Evil: Optimizing Flocking Strategies Through Genetic Algorithms for the Ghost Team in the Game of Ms. Pac-Man

Federico Liberatore$^{(\boxtimes)}$, Antonio M. Mora, Pedro A. Castillo,
and Juan Julián Merelo Guervós

Departamento de Arquitectura y Tecnología de Computadores. CITIC-UGR,
ETSIIT, University of Granada, Granada, Spain
federico.liberatore@urjc.es,
{amorag,pacv,jmerelo}@geneura.ugr.es

Abstract. Flocking strategies are sets of behavior rules for the interaction of agents that allow to devise controllers with reduced complexity that generate emerging behavior. In this paper, we present an application of genetic algorithms and flocking strategies to control the Ghost Team in the game Ms. Pac-Man. In particular, we define flocking strategies for the Ghost Team and optimize them for robustness with respect to the stochastic elements of the game and effectivity against different possible opponents by means of genetic algorithm. The performance of the methodology proposed is tested and compared with that of other standard controllers. The results show that flocking strategies are capable of modeling complex behaviors and produce effective and challenging agents.

Keywords: Flocking Strategies · Genetic Algorithms · Artificial Intelligence · Ms. Pac-Man · Videogames · Evolutionary Computation

1 Introduction

The game of Ms. Pac-Man was released in 1981 and, albeit similar to the original Pac-Man, it features a female protagonist, new maze designs, and several other gameplay changes over the original game, such as a stochastic event that reverses the direction of movement of the ghosts. Videogames such as Ms. Pac-Man are an ideal testbed for computational intelligence (CI) methods as they allow for the confrontation of multiple intelligent agents in a simple, yet challenging, context. A Ms. Pac-Man vs Ghosts competition has been run since 2009 [12]. Participants can submit controllers for either Ms. Pac-Man or the Ghost Team. During the competition, the controllers are ranked according to the results of random matches between two controllers of the same kind (e.g., Ghosts controllers) against two other controllers of the opposite kind (e.g., Ms.Pac-Man controllers). The controllers of each type that get the best score win the match and increase their rank. The competition is won by the controller of each kind having the highest rank.

© Springer-Verlag Berlin Heidelberg 2014
A.I. Esparcia-Alcázar et al. (Eds.): EvoApplications 2014, LNCS 8602, pp. 313–324, 2014.
DOI: 10.1007/978-3-662-45523-4_26

As the Ghost Team is a group of individuals that perform simple actions (i.e., moving up, down, left, or right), it seems a natural proving ground for algorithms based on the paradigm of Swarm Intelligence (SI). For this reason, in this work an evolved controller for the Ghost Team based on Genetic Algorithms (GAs) and Flocking Strategies (FSs) is proposed. FSs [17] consist of simple rules for the interactions of the agents that determine the next move of a ghost according to its distance to the other agents in the game. Despite their simplicity, FSs often result in complex emerging behaviors which, in turn, might result in a performance improvement or lead to a more entertaining gameplay. GAs are used to design FSs for the Ghost Team that are effective at minimizing Ms. Pac-Man final score and that are also robust with respect to the stochastic elements of the game. To the best of the authors knowledge this is the first work to actually applying flocking algorithms to the game of Pac-Man. Our objective is to understand how the proposed methodology would perform in comparison to controllers that use different approaches.

2   Ms. Pac-Man. The Game and the Problem

The game of Pac-Man needs no presentation. Since its release in 1980 many variants have been proposed and Ms. Pac-Man was one of them. Released in 1981, Ms. Pac-Man presented several features that extended on the original game, such as a female character, new maze designs, and several game-play changes.

In this game, Ms. Pac-Man has to collect all the pills in the maze while avoiding the four ghosts chasing her. If Ms. Pac-Man is touched by a ghost the player loses one life, Ms. Pac-Man is relocated at the initial position, and the ghosts respawn from the center of the maze. The *powerpills* turn the ghosts vulnerable for a short time, allowing Ms. Pac-Man to "eat" them. When a ghost gets eaten, it disappears from the game and respawns at the center of the maze after a certain amount of time. As the levels are cleared, the game becomes more difficult by changing certain parameters such as respawn time, length of time the ghosts are vulnerable, and ghosts' speed. Differently from the game of Pac-Man, this game has elements of randomness, firstly included to make the game more engaging. In fact, occasionally there is a global reversal event when all the ghosts suddenly change direction.

Given its multiple challenges, the game has been chosen for the Ms. Pac-Man vs Ghosts competition, a game AI competition where participants can submit controllers for both Ms. Pac-Man and the Ghost Team. The aim of Ms. Pac-Man agents is to maximize the final score, while the aim of Ghost Team controllers is to minimize it. The version of the game implemented for the competitions differs slightly from the original one. A thorough description of the game rules can be found in [18]. For the purposes of this work, the relevant restrictions for the Ghost Team are briefly enlisted in the following:

- A ghost can never stop and, when it is in a corridor, it can only move forward.
- A ghost can choose its direction only at a junction. Specifically, a ghost can only move into a corridor different from the one it is coming from. As a result, a ghost cannot turn back on itself.

- Every time a ghost is at a junction the controller has to provide a direction (i.e., UP, DOWN, LEFT, or RIGHT) from the set of feasible directions, i.e., those directions corresponding to corridors different from the one the ghost is coming from. If no direction or an unfeasible direction is returned by the controller, the game framework chooses a random direction from the set of feasible directions.
- At every tick of the game all the ghosts obligatorily reverse their direction according to a small random probability, set in the game implementation to 0.005.
- After 2000 game ticks, a level is considered completed: Ms. Pac-Man is rewarded with the points of the remaining pills and the game moves on to the next level.

3   Background and State of the Art

In this section, the main techniques applied in the development of this work are briefly described, along with some relevant bibliography.

SI [3] is the term used to describe the type of coordinated intelligence that arises from the collective behavior of decentralized, self-organized systems, either natural or artificial. SI techniques have been widely used in many fields including medicine, robotics, defense, astronomy, optimization, telecommunication, art, cinematography, and videogames. Flocking refers to a SI technique proposed by Reynolds [17] for the coordinated movement of multiple AI agents. Originally, flocking algorithms have been developed to mimic lifelike behaviors of groups of beings such as herds of animals and schools of fishes. A flocking system typically consists of a population of simple *agents* (or *boids*) interacting locally with one another depending on the distance between them. The agents follow very simple steering behaviors:

- *Separation* makes the agent steer away from close flock mates.
- *Alignment* makes the agent steer toward the average heading of the flock.
- *Cohesion* makes the agent steer toward the average position of distant flock mates.

Despite the lack of a centralized control structure dictating how individual agents should behave, the interactions between such agents lead to the emergence of "intelligent" global behavior, unknown to the individual agents [21]. Due to this desirable property, the easiness of implementation, and the reduced computational cost, flocking algorithms have been extensively applied to many fields, such as cinematography, art, medicine, etcetera. A presentation of flocking algorithms applications in videogames can be found in [19] and [16].

In the last years, a number of works regarding the Ghost Team have been proposed. Nguyen and Thawonmas [14,15] presented a controller based on Monte Carlo Tree Search where the behavior of Ms. Pac-Man is simulated. Their controller won the Ms. Pac-Man Versus Ghost Team Competition held in 2011. Svensson and Johansson [22] exploited the behavior emerging capabilities of

Influence Maps. A different line of research is pursued by Sombat *et al.* [20] that analyzed Ms. Pac-Man matches to classify Ghost Team controllers according to their enjoyability and, therefore, understand the attribute that a NPC should posses for players to be engaged. In the last decade, a number of EAs have been proposed to address different aspects of the game of Pac-Man. One of the first works in the subject is the paper by Gallagher [8] that optimized rule-based fine state machines through population-based incremental learning to devise an adaptive Pac-Man agent. More recently, Galvan-Lopez [9] explored and compared the performance of two types of Grammatical Evolution (GE) mappings to generate controllers for Ms. Pac-Man. Alhejali and Lucas [1] applied Genetic Programming (GP) to evolve a diverse set of behaviors using different versions of the game. The resulting controller proved to be competitive with the best reactive controllers reported at the time. In a subsequent article [2], the same authors extended their work by applying a "training camp framework" to GP, where a set of specialized behaviors is evolved according to specific training scenarios. A different approach is presented by Brandstetter and Ahmadi [4] that proposed a GP-based controllers that relies exclusively on information retrieval terminals rather than action-issuing terminals. Thawonmas [23] applied a GA to optimize the parameters of the Ms. Pac-Man controller ICE Pambush 3, winner of the IEEE CEC 2009 Ms. Pac-Man competition. A number of authors made use of EAs to design neural network-based controllers, both for Ms. Pac-Man [5,11] and the ghosts [10]. Gagne and Congdon [7] evolved rule-based intelligent agent for the ghost team. Finally, Cardona *et al.* [6] explored competitive co-evolution techniques to generate at the same time optimal Ms. Pac-Man and Ghost Team controllers.

In this work, an offline GA is applied to a flocking model for the Ghost Team, in order to improve its decision engine, which will be used later during game. To the best of the authors' knowledge, this is the first time FS have been applied to the game of Ms. Pac-Man.

4   Ghost Team AI: Evolutionary Flocking

In this section the evolutionary FS model developed for designing controllers for the Ghost Team is described. In the flocking system described, each one of the four ghosts is an independent agent. Nevertheless, all the ghosts determine their movement according to the same FS, as explained in the following.

4.1   Generalized Flocking Strategies

We define a Flocking Rule (FR) for boids (ghosts, in this case), ϕ, as a set of two vectors, ϕ^d and ϕ^m, that jointly describe the steering behavior of a ghost under certain conditions. Each FR considers a number N of concentric ring-shaped neighborhoods centered on the ghost. The limits of each neighborhood are specified by vector $\phi^d \in \mathbb{N}^N$; please note that the elements of vector ϕ^d are always sorted in ascending order as they represent the radii of the concentric neighborhoods . The last element of this vector, ϕ_N^d, is set to ∞ by default to cover the whole space. Vector $\phi^m \in [-1, 1]^N$ defines the magnitude of the steering force applied on the ghost when an agent falls into one of the neighborhoods.

To find the steering force on an agent A, located at position v_a, resulting from the interaction with agent B, located at position v_b, the difference vector v_δ and the Euclidean distance δ between the two agents are calculated:

$$v_\delta = v_b - v_a \tag{1}$$

$$\delta = \|v_\delta\| \tag{2}$$

To identify the magnitude ϕ_N^m we need to determine the neighborhood $0 < n \leq N$ where agent B belongs, by applying the following condition:

$$\phi_{n-1}^d < \delta \leq \phi_n^d \tag{3}$$

where $\phi_0^d = 0$. Finally, the steering force on agent A resulting from the interaction with agent B is given by:

$$f^B = \phi_n^m \cdot \frac{v_\delta}{\delta} \tag{4}$$

A negative magnitude corresponds to the behavior of separation, while a positive magnitude corresponds to the behavior of cohesion. No alignment behavior is included in this strategy model as it would make the ghosts very predictable.

Differently from the basic flocking algorithm where only one type of agent is considered, in the game Ms. Pac-Man a variety of different actors are present. Also, the ghosts can be in different states (e.g., normal or edible). To be effective, a strategy for the Ghost Team should take into account at least all the elements presented to the player on the screen. Let S be the set of possible ghost states:

$$S = \{\text{HUNTER, HUNTED, BLINKING}\} \tag{5}$$

$HUNTER$ is the "normal" state of a ghost (i.e., kills Ms. Pac-Man if touched). When Ms. Pac-Man eats a powerpill all the ghosts become $HUNTED$ for a certain length of time (i.e., is killed by Ms. Pac-Man on contact). When this period is about to expire, every ghost blinks to warn the player; we call this state $BLINKING$. Let A be the set of all the actors in the game:

$$A = \{\text{PACMAN, POWERPILL, HUNTER, HUNTED, BLINKING}\}$$

$HUNTER$, $HUNTED$, and $BLINKING$ refers to ghosts in that state. We can now define a Flocking Strategy (FS) for the Ghost Team, Φ, as:

$$\Phi : S \times A \to \phi$$

A FS is a function that, given a ghost state and the type of actor considered, returns the flocking rule that has to be applied to calculate the steering force on the ghost resulting from the interaction with the actor.

As explained in Section 2, every time a ghost is at a junction the game needs to calculate its next move. The controller based on the FS provides the next move by following the steps illustrated in Algorithm 1.

Algorithm 1. Flocking Strategy-based Ghost Controller.

$s \leftarrow$ status of the current ghost G;
$v_a \leftarrow$ position of the current ghost G;
for all actor b in the game **do**
    $\phi \leftarrow \Phi(s,b)$; {Determine the Flocking Rule to be applied.}
    $v_\delta \leftarrow v_b - v_a$; {Calculate the difference vector (Equation 1).}
    $\delta \leftarrow \|v_\delta\|$; {Calculate the Euclidean distance (Equation 2).}
    $n \leftarrow n'|\phi^d_{n'-1} < \delta \leq phi^d_{n'}$; {Identify the neighborhood (Equation 3).}
    $f^b \leftarrow \phi^m_n \cdot \frac{v_\delta}{\delta}$; {Compute the steering force (Equation 4).}
end for
$f \leftarrow \sum_b f^b$; {Calculate the total steering force.}
{Translate the steering force in a ranking for the next ghost direction as follows:}
UP $\leftarrow -f_2$;
DOWN $\leftarrow f_2$;
LEFT $\leftarrow -f_1$;
RIGHT $\leftarrow f_1$;
return the feasible direction (see restrictions in Section 2) having maximum rank;

4.2   Devising Optimized Flocking Strategies by Means of GAs

In this work we are dealing with a two-player competitive game with stochastic elements. A FS could be manually designed by an expert with decent results. Nevertheless,given as the number of parameters and the inherent complexity of the game, it is desirable to automatize the definition of an effective strategy by means of an optimization algorithm. Given the characteristics of the problem and the reduced number of constraints involved, GAs appear to be a sensible choice.

In the following, the elements comprising the GA implemented are described.

Initial Population. Each individual is represented by a FS Φ. The initial population is created as a random set of FSs defined as:

$$\forall s \in S, a \in A, i = 1, \ldots, N, \quad \phi^d_i \sim U(\phi^d_{i-1}, \infty) \tag{6}$$

$$\forall s \in S, a \in A, i = 1, \ldots, N, \quad \phi^m_i \sim N(0, 1/3), \phi^m_i \in [-1, 1] \tag{7}$$

The elements of ϕ^d have a uniform distribution, while the elements of ϕ^m have a truncated normal distribution. The parameters of the normal distribution have been set so as to generate most of the magnitudes close to zero and assign similar probabilities to the appearance of cohesion, separation, and no interaction behaviors.

Fitness Function. The definition of the fitness function is one of the most critical aspects in a GA. The proposed optimization algorithm should generate Ghost Team strategies that perform well against any possible Ms. Pac-Man strategy and, at the same time, should be resilient to the random ghosts reverse direction events (see Section 2). To achieve this result, each flocking strategy is pitted against two different Ms. Pac-Man controllers included in the Ms. Pac-Man vs Ghosts competition framework: *StarterPacMan* (SPM) and *NearestPillPacMan* (NPPM) (for a description of the controllers, please refer to the competition framework documentation[1]). The game is simulated 30 times for each Ms. Pac-Man controller. Thanks to that we can take advantage of the central limit theorem to compute a relatively precise 95% confidence interval of the final score obtained by the Ms. Pac-Man controllers. This is done to minimize the effect of noise present in this problem and in videogames in general [13]. In fact, due to the stochastic elements of the game, the same FS could perform very well sometimes and quite bad some others. Let μ_{SPM}, σ_{SPM}, μ_{NPPM}, σ_{NPPM} be the average score obtained by controller SPM in the 30 runs, the standard deviation of the SPM's scores, the average score obtained by controller NPPM in the 30 runs, and the standard deviation of the NPPM's scores, respectively. The upper limits of the confidence intervals for the scores of the two controllers are:

$$\overline{\text{CI}}_{\text{SPM}} = \mu_{\text{SPM}} + Z \cdot \frac{\sigma_{\text{SPM}}}{\sqrt{30}} \tag{8}$$

$$\overline{\text{CI}}_{\text{NPPM}} = \mu_{\text{NPPM}} + Z \cdot \frac{\sigma_{\text{NPPM}}}{\sqrt{30}} \tag{9}$$

where Z is the 95% percentile of the standard normal distribution. Therefore, 95% the Ms. Pac-Man controllers should get score below the upper limits of the confidence intervals. Our objective is to obtain a Ghost Team controller that minimizes these two values. The fitness function is defined as the average of the confidence intervals' inverses:

$$\text{FITNESS} = \frac{1}{\overline{\text{CI}}_{\text{SPM}}} + \frac{1}{\overline{\text{CI}}_{\text{NPPM}}} \tag{10}$$

Selection, Recombination, and Mutation. After all the individuals (FSs) of the current generation have been evaluated, the offspring will be generated. For each Φ to be generated, two individuals Φ_1 and Φ_2 are chosen by *roulette-wheel selection* (i.e., every member of the population has a probability of being chosen proportional to its fitness). The children individual Φ is created by random recombination of the parameters of parents Φ_1 and Φ_2:

$$\forall s \in S, a \in A, i = 1, \ldots, N, \quad \phi_i^d = \text{rand}(\phi_i^d \in \Phi_1(s,a), \phi_i^d \in \Phi_2(s,a)) \tag{11}$$

$$\forall s \in S, a \in A, i = 1, \ldots, N, \quad \phi_i^m = \text{rand}(\phi_i^d \in \Phi_1(s,a), \phi_i^d \in \Phi_2(s,a)) \tag{12}$$

where *rand* is a function that returns a random value chosen among its arguments.

During the recombination, mutations can occur with probability p^{mut}. When a mutation happens, the current parameter is re-initialized to a random value, according to Equations 6 and 7. The mutation probability p^{mut} is determined dynamically. Initially, its value is set to $p^{\text{mut}} = 0.00125$. At each iteration t, its value changes depending on the coefficient of variation of the current population fitness, c_v:

$$c_v = \frac{\sigma_{FITNESS}^t}{|\mu_{FITNESS}^t|} \tag{13}$$

---

[1] http://www.pacman-vs-ghosts.net/, last visited on February 6, 2014

where $\mu^t_{FITNESS}$ and $\sigma^t_{FITNESS}$ are the current population fitness' average and standard deviation, respectively. c_v measures the degree of variability of the population in terms of fitness. When the variability is low, we increment the mutation probability to introduce new chromosomes in the genetic pool of the population. When the variability is too big, the mutation probability is set to a low initial value:

$$
p_t^{mut} = \begin{cases} 0.00125 & \text{if } c_v > 0.6 \\ p_{t-1}^{mut} & \text{if } 0.3 < c_v \le 0.6 \\ 2 \cdot p_{t-1}^{mut} & \text{if } 0.2 < c_v \le 0.3 \\ 4 \cdot p_{t-1}^{mut} & \text{if } 0.1 < c_v \le 0.2 \\ 8 \cdot p_{t-1}^{mut} & \text{if } c_v \le 0.1 \end{cases} \tag{14}
$$

Once the recombination is done, vectors ϕ_i^d and ϕ_i^m are sorted in ascending order with respect to the values of ϕ_i^m to preserve their feasibility. In fact, by definition vector ϕ_i^m are required to be always sorted in ascending order, and the recombination and the mutation operators might generate vectors that do not comply with this rule.

5   Experiments and Results

In this section, it will be tested how well a GA evolved controller performs, compared to non-evolutionary strategies. The standard Ghost Team controllers included in the competition framework will be used as a comparative basis. In the experiments, the GA described in the previous chapter has been run for 50 generations with a population of 50 candidate strategies. At each iteration, the next generation was constituted by 49 recombined individuals plus the best solution of the current generation.

All the algorithm have been implemented in Java within the framework provided for the Ms Pac-Man vs Ghosts competition. The final program run on a Intel(R) Core(TM) i5-2500K @ 3.3GHz with four cores and 4GB of RAM. Each experiment run on a single core and made use of less than 300MB of memory.

The first experiment performed regards the comparison of the performance of the Ghost Team controllers obtained with different values of the parameter N (i.e., the number of neighborhoods considered in the Flocking Rules). The best strategy found with a certain number of neighborhoods should be at least as good as those found with a lower number of neighborhoods, as the solution space of the former is bigger and contains the others'. Nevertheless, as the number of neighborhoods increases, the solution space increases substantially, that in turn could affect the actual performance of the GA. In this section we use the inverse fitness, FITNESS$^{-}1$, as a measure of performance as it is easier to interpret than the fitness function that takes values close to zero. Being the inverse of the fitness value, a lower FITNESS$^{-}1$ value corresponds to a better controller, and vice-versa.

Table 1 shows the performance of the evolved controllers over 10 runs of the GA with $N = 1, \ldots, 5$. Each column is associated to a different number of neighborhoods. The first row displays the inverse fitness of the best individual found. The second row presents the average controllers fitness; the standard deviation

Table 1. Performance of the controllers for the Ghost Team obtained by the GA using different numbers of neighborhoods.

	$N = 1$	$N = 2$	$N = 3$	$N = 4$	$N = 5$
Best FITNESS⁻1	783.38	726.84	815.66	766.96	720.20
Avg. FITNESS⁻1	871.30±55.45	861.57±70.13	876.31±65.06	905.86±62.66	863.17±72.15
Worst FITNESS⁻1	951.75	969.20	1,032.39	986.48	980.50
Avg. CPU time (s)	1373±150.66	1484.3±122.01	1561±193.94	1562.60±109.90	1473.00±74.02

is also reported after the plus-minus sign. Next, the third row illustrates the fitness value of the worst controller found. Finally, the last row reports the average optimization CPU time in seconds over the 10 runs and the corresponding standard deviation. By observing the table some conclusions can be drawn.

- The best controller is obtained when $N = 5$. This result suggests that increasing the complexity of the FS benefits the controller.
- No clear pattern can be identified in the values taken by Best FITNESS⁻1, nor Avg. FITNESS⁻1, with respect to variations in the value of N. This could be due to the increased complexity in the search space resulting from the high number of parameters to be optimized by the GA.
- The gap between the best and the worst fitness in each column and the fitness standard deviation suggest that the problem presents many local optima in the solution space.

When playing against the best Ghost Team controller obtained by the GA it is possible to observe interesting behaviors. A sample video[2] shows the best Ghost Team controller pitted against the Ms. Pac-Man controller *StarterPac-Man*, included in the competition framework. The video illustrates that, despite the lack of explicit coordination between them, the ghosts show complex strategic behaviors:

- Initially, Blinky (red ghost) and Inky (blue ghost) entrap Ms. Pac-Man in a small corridor. It can be observed that Pinky (pink ghost) is not heading directly toward Ms. Pac-Man using the shortest route, therefore allowing room for alternative strategies.
- In the second round, Blinky chases Ms. Pac-Man and pushes her through the tunnel, at the end of which Pinky is waiting for her. It is interesting to notice that, would Ms. Pac-Man have chosen to move away from the tunnel, she would have moved toward a conveniently located Inky.
- In the last round, Ms. Pac-Man eats a powerpill. Immediately, the ghosts flee in the opposite direction. After getting caught, Blinky takes advantage of the situation to interpose between Ms. Pac-Man and the vulnerable ghosts. This forces Ms. Pac-Man to take a detour and waste precious time, which results in Ms. Pac-Man losing the game because of a recently invulnerable-turned Pinky.

---

[2] https://www.youtube.com/watch?v=I9rL0jUwHhk, visited on February 6, 2014

Without including complex rules, which is a desirable feature in this type of problems (i.e., AI in games), the proposed methodology generates emerging behaviors. This, in turn, results in the ghosts behaving in a "intelligent" fashion although they are not explicitly programmed with this objective in mind.

In the next experiment, we compare our controllers to the five Ghost Team controllers included in the competition framework. Their FITNESS$^-$1 values, computed exactly as per the GA solutions, are illustrated in Table 2.

Table 2. Performance of the standard Ghost Team controllers included in the competition framework

Controller	AggressiveGhosts	Legacy	Legacy2TheReckoning	RandomGhosts	StarterGhosts
FITNESS$^-$1	1893.13	2210.94	1429.20	4200.70	1603.49

According to these results, the best controller is *Legacy2TheReckoning*, followed by *StarterGhosts*. Nevertheless, their FITNESS$^-$1 value is twice that of the best evolved FS found, approximately. These results support the claim that FSs are a viable option for the definition of intelligent controllers.

6   Conclusions and Future Work

In this paper, a new controller for the Ghost Team based on FSs is proposed. FSs are sets of behavior rules that determine the next move of an agent as a force resulting from the interaction of the agents in the game. A GA is presented to design optimized strategies offline. The fitness function evaluates each individual by pitting it against two Ms. Pac-Man controller 30 times, so as to avoid noise in the function. Parents are chosen by roulette-wheel selection and the children are generated by random recombination of the parents' chromosomes. The mutation probability is adaptive and increases when the population is homogeneous, while it decreases when the population is too heterogeneous. The methodology has been empirically tested: the fitness of the best individual found by the GA has been compared to the fitness of the five standard controller included in the competition framework. The results show that FSs model complex behaviors and that the GA successfully optimize the design of the ghosts controller, producing effective and challenging agents.

This work is just scratching the surface and there is still a lot to be investigated. Some possible future lines of research are highlighted in the following. The fitness function can be easily extended by including more Ms. Pac-Man controllers. This should result in a Ghost Team controller that performs better against a wider range of opponents. By considering in the GA fitness function the best Ms. Pac-Man controllers that took part to the competitions, it would be possible to generate Ghost Team controllers that are capable of tackling the best known Ms. Pac-Man strategies.

Moreover, it would be interesting to compare the controllers obtained by applying the presented methodology with the best Ghost Team controllers that took part to the Ms. Pac-Man vs Ghosts competition. This would allow us to really understand the limits of FSs.

The GAs as a means to optimize FSs have proven to be satisfactory. Nevertheless, the recombination step causes abrupt changes in the solutions' parameters and might generate individuals that are very different from the initial ones. It would be interesting to investigate the effectiveness of optimization methods that allows for small changes in the solutions parameters. Particle Swarm Optimization (PSO) algorithms might be a sensible choice. In fact, on top of making few or no assumptions about the problem, PSO algorithm are particularly effective with problems that are noisy and present many multiple optima, such as this one.

Acknowledgments. This work has been supported in part by CANUBE (CEI2013-P-14) and ANYSELF (TIN2011-28627-C04-02), awarded by the Spanish Ministry of Science and Innovation. Liberatore's research was financed by the Government of Spain (TIN2012-32482). All the supports are gratefully acknowledged. In addition, Liberatore would like to thanks the GeNeura research group at University of Granada for their kind hospitality.

References

1. Alhejali, A., Lucas, S.: Evolving diverse Ms. Pac-Man playing agents using genetic programming. In: Proceedings of the 2010 UK Workshop on Computational Intelligence (UKCI 2010), pp. 1–6 (2010)
2. Alhejali, A., Lucas, S.: Using a training camp with Genetic Programming to evolve Ms. Pac-Man agents. In: Proceedings of the 2011 IEEE Conference on Computational Intelligence and Games (CIG 2011), pp. 118–125 (2011)
3. Beni, G., Wang, J.: Swarm intelligence in cellular robotic systems. In: Robots and Biological Systems: Towards a New Bionics?. NATO ASI Series F: Computer and Systems Sciences, vol. 102, pp. 703–712 (1993)
4. Brandstetter, M., Ahmadi, S.: Reactive control of Ms. Pac Man using information retrieval based on Genetic Programming. In: Proceedings of the 2012 IEEE Conference on Computational Intelligence and Games (CIG 2012), pp. 250–256 (2012)
5. Burrow, P., Lucas, S.: Evolution versus Temporal Difference Learning for learning to play Ms. Pac-Man. In: Proceedings of the IEEE Symposium on Computational Intelligence and Games (CIG 2009), pp. 53–60 (2009)
6. Cardona, A., Togelius, J., Nelson, M.: Competitive coevolution in Ms. Pac-Man. In: Proceedings of the 2013 IEEE Congress on Evolutionary Computation (CEC 2013), pp. 1403–1410 (2013)
7. Gagne, D., Congdon, C.: FRIGHT: A flexible rule-based intelligent ghost team for Ms. Pac-Man. In: Proceedings of the 2012 IEEE Conference on Computational Intelligence and Games (CIG 2012), pp. 273–280 (2012)
8. Gallagher, M.: Learning to play Pac-Man: an evolutionary, rule-based approach. In: Proceedings of the 2003 Congress on Evolutionary Computation (CEC 2003), pp. 2462–2469 (2003)
9. Galván-López, E.: Comparing the performance of the evolvable πGrammatical Evolution genotype-phenotype map to Grammatical Evolution in the dynamic Ms. Pac-Man environment. In: Proceedings of the 2010 IEEE Congress on Evolutionary Computation (CEC 2010), pp. 1–8 (2010)

10. Jia-Yue, D., Yan, L., Jun-Fen, C., Feng, Z.: Evolutionary neural network for ghost in Ms. Pac-Man. In: Proceedings of the 2011 International Conference on Machine Learning and Cybernetics (ICMLC 2011), vol. 2, pp. 732–736 (2011)
11. Lucas, S.: Evolving a neural network location evaluator to play Ms. Pac-Man. In: Proceedings of the IEEE Symposium on Computational Intelligence and Games (CIG 2005), pp. 203–210 (2005)
12. Lucas, S.: Ms. Pac-Man versus ghost-team competition. In: Procedings of IEEE Symposium on Computational Intelligence and Games (CIG 2009), p. 1 (2009)
13. Mora, A.: Fernández-Ares, A., Guervós, J.M., García-Sánchez, P., Fernandes, C.: Effect of noisy fitness in real-time strategy games player behaviour optimisation using evolutionary algorithms. Journal of Computer Science and Technology **27**(5), 1007–1023 (2012)
14. Nguyen, K., Thawonmas, R.: Applying Monte-Carlo Tree Search to collaboratively controlling of a Ghost Team in Ms. Pac-Man. In: Proceedings of the 2011 IEEE International Games Innovation Conference (IGIC 2011), pp. 8–11 (2011)
15. Nguyen, K., Thawonmas, R.: Monte Carlo Tree Search for collaboration control of ghosts in Ms. Pac-Man. IEEE Transactions on Computational Intelligence and AI in Games **5**(1), 57–68 (2013)
16. Rabin, S.: Artificial Intelligence: Agents, Architecture, and Techniques. In: Introduction to Game Development, 2nd edn., pp. 521–557. Charles River Media (2010)
17. Reynolds, C.: Flocks, herds and schools: a distributed behavioral model. Computer Graphics **21**(4), 25–34 (1987)
18. Rohlfshagen, P., Lucas, S.: Ms. Pac-Man versus Ghost Team CEC 2011 competition. In: Proceedings of the 2011 IEEE Congress on Evolutionary Computation (CEC 2011), pp. 70–77. IEEE Press (2011)
19. Scutt, T.: Simple swarms as an alternative to flocking. In: AI Game Programming Wisdom, pp. 202–208. Charles River Media (2002)
20. Sombat, W., Rohlfshagen, P., Lucas, S.: Evaluating the enjoyability of the ghosts in Ms. Pac-Man. In: Proceedings of the 2012 IEEE Conference on Computational Intelligence and Games (CIG 2012), pp. 379–387 (2012)
21. Spector, L., Klein, J., Perry, C., Feinstein, M.: Emergence of collective behavior in evolving populations of flying agents. In: Proceedings of the Genetic and Evolutionary Computation Conference (GECCO 2003), pp. 61–73 (2003)
22. Svensson, J., Johansson, S.: Influence Map-based controllers for Ms. PacMan and the ghosts. In: Proceedings of the 2012 IEEE Conference on Computational Intelligence and Games (CIG 2012), pp. 257–264 (2012)
23. Thawonmas, R.: Evolution strategy for optimizing parameters in Ms Pac-Man controller ICE Pambush 3. In: Proceedings of the 2010 IEEE Symposium on Computational Intelligence and Games (CIG 2010), pp. 235–240 (2010)

Procedural Content Generation Using Patterns as Objectives

Steve Dahlskog[1](✉) and Julian Togelius[2]

[1] Malmö University, Ö. Varvsgatan 11a, Malmö, Sweden
steve.dahlskog@mah.se
[2] IT University of Copenhagen, Rued Langaards Vej 7, 2300 Copenhagen, Denmark
julian@togelius.com

Abstract. In this paper we present a search-based approach for procedural generation of game levels that represents levels as sequences of *micro-patterns* and searched for *meso-patterns*. The micro-patterns are "slices" of original human-designed levels from an existing game, whereas the meso-patters are abstractions of common design patterns seen in the same levels. This method generates levels that are similar in style to the levels from which the original patterns were extracted, while still allowing for considerable variation in the geometry of the generated levels. The evolutionary method for generating the levels was tested extensively to investigate the distribution of micro-patterns used and meso-patterns found.

1 Introduction

The study of Procedural Content Generation (PCG), i.e. how game content such as levels, items, quests and characters can be created algorithmically, is currently one of the most active topics within academic research on artificial and computational intelligence in games. A large variety of methods have been proposed to generate an even larger variety of types of game content, subject to various objectives and constraints [1]. The work is motivated both by a real industry need for lowering the cost and saving time of content production and enabling endless user-adaptive games, and by academic interest in formalising game design and building creative machines. A recent "vision paper" for PCG research lists a number of open research challenges [2]. One of them is to learn to imitate style: could you build a content generator that was shown a number of examples of the creative output of a human or team of humans, and that then learned to produce more artefacts in the same style that were clearly original but still recognisably of the same style?

Another active research area has been that of game design patterns. A design pattern is a general concept, which has its roots in architecture, but has been applied both to software design and to game design. Game design patterns have so far been identified manually, and the investigation on how to integrate patterns into PCG has just started.

© Springer-Verlag Berlin Heidelberg 2014
A.I. Esparcia-Alcázar et al. (Eds.): EvoApplications 2014, LNCS 8602, pp. 325–336, 2014.
DOI: 10.1007/978-3-662-45523-4_27

In this paper we demonstrate how practical game design patterns can be combined with procedural content generation to generate game levels that imitate a certain design style, and report the results of a series of experiments using a platform game benchmark. We have previously analysed the classic game *Super Mario Bros.* (SMB) [3] and suggested a collection of patterns and a PCG tool that produce levels by randomly picking copies of these patterns and modifying them according to a desired length and difficulty level [4].

Our prototype is based on evolutionary computation, where we will search the solution space of combinations of simple building blocks for levels that contain structures at a higher level. This way, we introduce a certain measure of control and constrain the shape of the final level through both the objective function and the choice of building blocks, while allowing a significant amount of variation. In the prototype the representation is relying on existing content in SMB, namely on one tile wide *vertical slices*, which we will also refer to as *micro-patterns*. The micro-patterns are extracted from the original SMB levels. A level is simply a sequence (or string) of micro-patterns — this applies both to the original levels and our generated levels. However, not any sequence is interesting but in our prototype we search for specific sequences or patterns that exists in the original game. These sequences will we refer to as *meso-patterns* and they are our search objective for our evolutionary approach.

We have previously reported initial work on this idea in a workshop paper [5]. Compared to that paper, the current paper describes a more mature system, and reports more in-depth results with several variations of the fitness function and a better characterisation of the generator output.

1.1 Background

In the seventies, Alexander et al. proposed a pattern language for architectural application on all levels (regions, cities, neighbourhoods, buildings and rooms) thus allowing everybody the ability to express design. Not only structural and material issues are covered but also life experience like the *Street Cafe*-pattern. The pattern language consists of a set of problems in an environment together with a core solution to its corresponding problem [6] thus giving a designer a tool to handle reoccurring problems. This powerful idea has spread to other areas like object-oriented software development where Gamma et al. have defined a set of templates for solving general design and programming problems [7]. In the context of games have Björk and Holopainen suggested an extensive collection of patterns for game design [8]. Similarly, others have looked into game mechanics [9] and specific game contexts like FPSs [10], RPGs [11], and action games [12]. There have also been some attempts to formulate abstract level design patterns that can be specialised to concrete metrics for different level types [13].

Procedural content generation refers to the (semi-)automatic process of creating game content. One common approach to PCG is the search-based approach, to use evolutionary computation or other stochastic global search/optimisation algorithms [14] for searching the content space. An oft-encountered trade-off in PCG is between control and variation. Methods that have a high variation in output according to some measure usually afford little designer control. Variation can be measured as *expressive range*, the variation along relevant metrics of generated artefacts [15, 16]. Control comes in several flavours: control over style, player experience, difficulty or even playability (e.g. specifying that there is a path from start to end of a level).

1.2   Examples of Patterns

Because of the limited space available we can only briefly mention the patterns that were found [4] in (SMB). The patterns can be grouped into 5 groups; 1) Enemies and hordes, (single and multiple variations), 2) Gaps (single, multiple, variable length, combined with enemies and structures), 3) Valleys (a boxed-in area with structures, possible combined with enemies), 4) Multiple paths (structures horizontally dividing game space combined with enemies and rewards) and 5) Stairs (structures supporting vertical repositioning combined with enemies and gaps). In figure 2 we can see two instances of the 3-Horde pattern (Enemies) and in figure 1 we have a 3-Horde-pattern, a Pillar Gap-pattern and a Enemy-pattern.

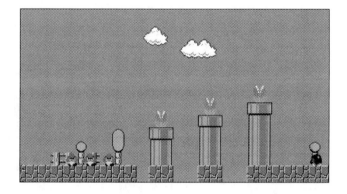

Fig. 1. Three consecutive patterns in SMB

2   Rationale

Our application domain in this paper is the classic 2-dimensional platformer, *Super Mario Bros.* (SMB) [3] and our generator is implemented using the Java-based Mario AI Benchmark[1] [17].

The levels of SMB could be seen as 2D matrices where the cells contain various items such as blocks, coins, enemies, etc.; this is also the internal representation of levels in the Mario AI benchmark. Mario (when small) has the size

---

[1] The benchmark is based on the clone *Infinite Mario Bros* by Markus "Notch" Persson.

of 1 cell, and most levels have a length of 100-300 cells and a height of 20 cells. A slice, or micro-pattern, is simply a vertical column of this array – a subarray with length 1. By analysing the levels of the original SMB, we have identified a library of such slices. New levels could be created by combining slices from this library, drawn at random. Such levels would have some similarity to the original levels, as they would not contain any slices that did not exist in the original game. They would not, for example, contain slices where enemies stack on top of each other or the player starts in mid-air. However, these levels would be uninteresting at best, and probably unplayable, as they might contain too long gaps, unclimbable walls, long stretches of nothing, and generally no discernible structure. However, in the space of all possible sequences of slices there should be many permutations that are well-designed, playable levels that are similar to the original SMB levels not only on micro level but also on meso- and macro-levels. How can we find those levels? In order to guarantee playability we punish unplayable sequences.

2.1   Representation

Our level representation is a sequence of symbols of length 200, where each symbol stands for a specific *micro-pattern* (a vertical slice) taken from the original human created content. The slice is one tile wide and in our example we have a slice containing a Goomba standing on a ground tile. This tile could be copied in sequence two or three times to make a 2-Horde or 3-Horde pattern (as in fig. 2).

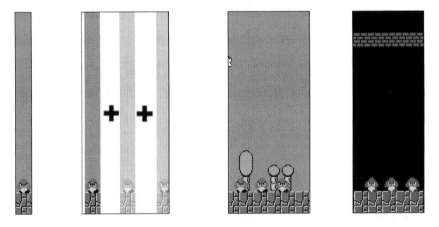

Fig. 2. To the far left we have a vertical slice (micro-pattern) with a Goomba on low ground. To the left a sequence of copies of the same slice making up a 3-Horde meso-pattern that in the original game can be found quite often as in World 8, Level 1 seen to the centre-right and in World 1, Level 2 to the far right.

By adding new slices the solution space grows. The levels of the original SMB contain fewer than 200 slices like this. In our representation, we use an alphabet consisting of 23 frequently occurring micro-patterns. Most of the slices come from unique-looking levels like W1L2 (the first level under ground) and are not reused elsewhere in the game. The advantage of the representation is the ease with which one can generate a level either by the constructive or the generate-and-test approach [14]. One could for example base a constructive PCG algorithm on a *phrase-structure grammar* with pre-checked production rules or by randomly picking slices and evaluate according to constraints. However, we will suggest another approach in the next section.

2.2   Evolutionary Algorithm

The search-based approach taken in this paper is based on a fitness function that rewards the presence of meso-patterns, the higher presence the likelier a member is selected. We apply a simple $\mu + \lambda$ evolution strategy where $\mu = \lambda = 100$ is combined with single-point mutation and one-point crossover. In other words, of a population of 200 we apply *selection* (discarding half of the population), *reproduction* (keeping half of the population and using pairwise breeding to generate new members), *recombination* (fixed one-point-crossover) and *mutation* (the slice at a randomly chosen position in the level has its symbol replaced by a randomly chosen slice).

2.3   Fitness Function

In order to understand how our micro- and meso-patterns interact in the search space we implemented three fitness functions (FF 1-3). The fitness functions were designed in the following way; FF1) a simple uniform reward value for every *unique pattern*, FF2) a simple uniform reward value for *every occurrence of patterns*, and finally FF3) a non-uniform reward weighted value for every occurrence of patterns. The first fitness function worked as a validation of the strings indicating that they could be found (i.e. more than one out of our meso-patterns can be found). The second fitness function was used to explore the frequency of how meso-patterns "appear" in the search space (i.e. how common are the different meso-patterns). The third fitness function was used to explore how the use of weighted values affects the frequency of meso-patterns.

In order to have some input on the weights to use we chose a simple strategy of calculate a weight by inverting the average occurrence of the patterns giving an infrequent pattern a high weight and a frequent pattern a low weight. By doing so, we propose that we can counter the effect of normal distribution while picking random symbols during the task of initiating and mutating the members of the population. Another issue this strategy would counter, is the varying complexity that the individual patterns have. If we would continue to use a uniform reward strategy for the fitness function, complex strings would run a greater risk to be starved to death in our population due the space it takes over uncomplicated patterns (i.e. short patterns are easily fitted into a member in relation to a long pattern). In order to find different variations of the patterns we designed a set of 43 strings of symbols in different categories of the patterns (i.e. 5 categories of patterns and 23 patterns [4]). These strings, (which we will refer to as rules) were used for a simple linear search, covering each member of the population in each generation.

3   Results and Evaluation

We performed the experiments in three stages. First, we evolved a large number of levels using the "unique patterns" version of the evaluation function (FF1). We then repeated this experiment using the "all occurrences" version of the evaluation function (FF2). Based on these runs, we evaluated which micro-patterns were most commonly used, and which meso-patterns were most commonly found. These evaluations were used to calculate the weights for a weighted version of the fitness function (FF3). The third and final experiment, using the weighted version of the evaluation function, aimed to see if we could bring about that all patterns were found in a more balanced way.

3.1   Finding Patterns

For each fitness function, we made 1000 independent runs and recorded the fitness values based on the strings. The fitness value worked as a simple "count a rule when it is fulfilled", but only the first time it occur in a level for FF1, for every time it occurred in FF2 and with weighted values in FF3. We can see that

Table 1. Fitness value variation for 1000 levels counting fitness value based on rules; only one occurrence (FF1), multiple occurrences (FF2) and weighted multiple occurrences (FF3)

Generations	MIN	MAX	MEAN	DEV.	MED.
0 (FF1)	3	8	4.61	0.81	5
10 (FF1)	5	11	7.47	1.02	7
100 (FF1)	8	27	14.94	2.51	15
500 (FF1)	8	31	18.18	3.17	18
1000 (FF1)	9	31	18.97	3.23	19
0 (FF2)	4	10	5.7	1.12	6
10 (FF2)	7	18	11.17	1.74	11
100 (FF2)	13	86	36.98	10.46	37
500 (FF2)	16	183	68.62	30.17	63
1000 (FF2)	18	227	82.17	37.38	73
0 (FF3)	4	202	77.83	36.16	77
10 (FF3)	8	301	121.92	62.83	118
100 (FF3)	20	1030	264.07	149.64	241
500 (FF3)	34	2361	430.33	348.98	337
1000 (FF3)	34	2449	486.20	401.76	374

the evolutionary approach manages to find more meso-patterns over time. In order to measure the effect of our efforts of guiding the evolution to find more elaborate patterns we recorded which rules were present in the best member out of our 1000 runs (see table 2).

Measuring the occurrences of a rule in large population should give an indication on how complicated it is to generate an instance of a meso-pattern (rule) in relation to the micro-patterns. Several of the meso-patterns use the same micro-patterns and since the micro-patterns initial occurrence is based on equal chance to be present in the population and a member we can be certain that, given enough time, the search-based approach will affect the distribution of micro-patterns.

Table 2. Found patterns (rules) in FF1-FF3 together with the calculated weight for FF3 based on 1000 runs

Pattern	Mesa		Straight	Multi-way									
Occurrence in FF1	682	686	1001	239	193	50	93	68	193	168	239	197	132	136
Average in FF1	0.68	0.69	1.00	0.24	0.19	0.05	0.09	0.07	0.19	0.17	0.24	0.20	0.13	0.14
Occurrence in FF2	498	480	523	25	83	221	329	11	83	37	25	13	120	127
Average in FF2	0.5	0.48	0.52	0.03	0.08	0.22	0.33	0.01	0.08	0.04	0.03	0.01	0.12	0.13
Weight	2.01	2.08	1.91	40	12.05	4.53	3.04	90.91	12.05	27.03	40	76.92	8.33	7.87
Occurrence in FF3	1042	1118	1317	574	264	317	40	559	264	298	574	589	697	687
Average in FF3	1.04	1.12	1.32	0.57	0.26	0.32	0.04	0.56	0.26	0.30	0.57	0.59	0.70	0.69

Pattern	Enemy			Hordes								Gaps			
Occurrence in FF1	2605	1198	572	2606	1208	525	920	931	1007	1007	892	111	286	269	286
Average in FF1	2.61	1.20	0.57	2.61	1.21	0.53	0.92	0.93	1.01	1.01	0.89	0.11	0.29	0.27	0.29
Occurrence in FF2	13751	10411	1897	13584	8678	722	3694	4995	8209	8209	3563	14	83	68	132
Average in FF2	13.75	10.4	1.9	13.6	8.68	0.72	3.69	5	8.21	8.21	3.56	0.01	0.08	0.07	0.13
Weight	0.07	0.1	0.53	0.07	0.12	1.39	0.27	0.2	0.12	0.12	0.28	71.43	12.05	14.71	7.58
Occurrence in FF3	*444*	50	8	*444*	*33*	*16*	*0*	90	93	93	0	1720	*44*	*33*	88
Average in FF3	0.44	0.05	0.01	0.44	0.03	0.02	0.00	0.09	0.09	0.09	0.00	1.72	0.04	0.03	0.09

Pattern	Valley			Stair					Pipes					
Occurrence in FF1	87	81	61	845	846	664	705	716	66	47	43	46	61	67
Average in FF1	0.09	0.08	0.06	0.85	0.85	0.66	0.71	0.72	0.07	0.05	0.04	0.05	0.06	0.07
Occurrence in FF2	17	14	17	355	352	257	289	287	28	14	9	14	8	10
Average in FF2	0.02	0.01	0.02	0.36	0.35	0.26	0.29	0.29	0.03	0.01	0.01	0.01	0.01	0.01
Weight	58.82	71.43	58.82	2.82	2.84	3.89	3.46	3.48	35.71	71.43	111.1	71.43	125	100
Occurence in FF3	193	178	162	1233	1197	1110	915	1025	5	43	57	**12**	966	30
Average in FF3	0.19	0.18	0.16	1.23	1.20	1.11	0.92	1.03	0.01	0.04	0.06	0.01	0.97	0.03

For FF1, the distribution of fulfilled rules show promise on only 12 of the rules (with occurrence value of 845–2605) and all rules have been fulfilled. However, this is not sufficient to answer the question on how easy they are to find in relation to each other. It is possible that the more complex rules are starved to death in an evolutionary search. In order to explore this we ran FF2 and counted multiple occurrences. The effect of counting multiple instances gives the conclusion that Enemies and Hordes starves most other rules (except two instances of Multi-way and only mildly two other Multi-way). Problematically as it is, we apply weights for FF3 to counter the multiple-occurrence starvation effect. The weights were calculated as the inverse function ($\frac{1}{x}$ when $x \neq 0$) of the average occurrence. The result for FF3 show positive effect for most of the meso-patterns (26 out of the 43 rules) except for the Gaps-, Enemy- and Horde-patterns for which the result, on the other hand, is absolute catastrophic (in table 2 the negative change is indicated in italic).

4   Expressive Range

Smith & Whitehead [15] introduced the concept of *expressive range* of a level generator and suggested a set of possible metrics that illustrates diversity of the generated content. For PCG-tools it is interesting to show if the tool is able to generate content that is not identical. *Linearity* and *Leniency* were suggested as metrics for platform levels.

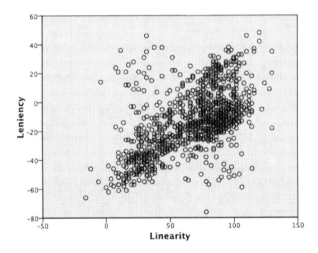

Fig. 3. The distribution of levels generated with FF1 on the two expressivity dimensions

We have implemented versions of these metrics thus: Leniency is calculated across the whole level with +1 for gaps and enemies, and the reverse for the opposite −1 (for jumps with no gap associated, because jumps associated with danger is harder than jumps without danger). Linearity will be counted from the lowest point of the level, due to the fact that most micro patterns are connected to that and therefore all micro patterns forcing the player to jump due to a height difference of more than 1 tile will be considered as raising the non-linearity of the level.

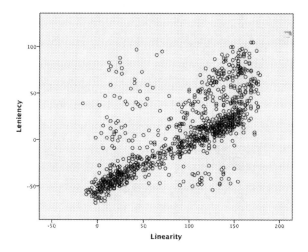

Fig. 4. The distribution of levels generated with FF2 on the two expressivity dimensions

In figure 3, 4 and 5 we show a density plot based on the two metrics; leniency (LEN) and linearity (LIN) with 1000 generated levels for the fitness functions 1, 2 respectively 3 (FF1-3). FF1 have an expressive range in LEN of -75 to $+50$ with a concentration of levels around -20 to ± 0 as well as an expressive range in LIN of -20 to $+130$ with a concentration in the range $+50$ to $+100$. FF2 gives LEN: -75 to $+100$ and LIN: -20 to $+170$. FF2 has two clusters; LEN/LIN -75 to $-25/ \pm 0$ to $+50$ and -25 to $30/ + 85$ to 160. Comparing the two fitness functions (FF1 & FF2) expressiveness yields that FF2 can generate both more difficult and more linear levels. The correlation that may exist is due to the gap and enemy placement in linear space in SMB (and in the micro-patterns) and it is more apparent due to the higher alignment to meso-patterns in FF2 than in FF1, which is more affected by the normal distribution in the variation of micro-patterns and get a less apparent cluster and range. FF3, however differ on all ranges; LEN: -105 to $+80$ & LIN -50 to $+160$. The two clusters; LEN/LIN: -100 to $-30/-25$ to $+25$ and -30 to $+20/+50$ to 130, are less apparent divided from each other and most of the individual members are not spread out as thin as before. The weighted fitness value gives a wider expressive range but the levels are more close if we observe the outliers suggesting that we could say that the *expressive spread* is affected with weighted patterns. The levels are more easy but also less linear. This is no surprise due to the low presence of meso-patterns of Gap-, Enemy- and Horde-type.

5   Discussion

Our approach could be viewed from a level designer's standpoint if we see the design process as handled by our three pattern levels; 1) at the micro-level,

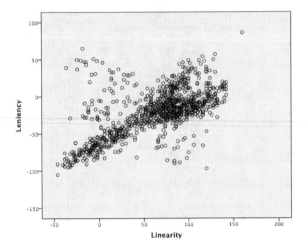

Fig. 5. The distribution of levels generated with FF3 on the two expressivity dimensions

Fig. 6. An example of a generated level

which contain the smallest representation level, in our approach the vertical slices function, 2) at the meso-level, where the combined slices in a certain order function to solve the challenges the designer wants to expose to the players to, and 3) at the macro-level handling the flow and overall (play-)experience of a level and/or game. If we implemented a planner that solved the issue of deciding on order of meso-patterns, difficulty (perhaps with the aid of metrics like leniency), training and educating the player, the full task of the level-designer, namely; to "... use a toolkit or 'level editor' to develop new missions, scenarios, or quests for the players. They lay out the components that appear on the level or map and work closely with the game designer to make these fit into the overall theme of the game" [18], could be solved for an entire game or genre.

In our fitness functions FF2 and FF3, we used weighted sums of the meso-pattern counters. There are well-known problems with fitness functions based on weighted sums, in particular that not all components are maximised at the same rate. An alternative would be to treat the problem as a multi-objective optimisation problem, and use specially designed evolutionary algorithms for this purpose. However, most such algorithms are designed for only a handful of objectives, which is problematic as our problem has dozens.

6   Conclusion

In this paper, we have introduced a pattern-based level generator for plat-form games. The general principle is to identify both micro-patterns and meso-patterns in the original game levels, represent new levels as combinations of micro-patterns and search for such combinations that express as many meso-patterns as possible. This way, micro-patterns are used as building blocks and meso-patterns as objectives. This principle, and the generator based on it, can easily be extended to a large range of different game types and game content types. To validate and explore the workings of our prototype level generator, we ran experiments with three different variations of our fitness function. We found that the generator could easily find certain patterns whereas others where harder to find, but that a rebalancing made it possible to find other patterns, sometimes at the cost of more frequent patterns.

Acknowledgments. We would like to thank Noor Shaker for the generated level image.

References

1. Shaker, N., Togelius, J., Nelson, M.J. (eds.): Procedural Content Generation in Games: a Textbook and an Overview of Current Research (2013). http://www.pcgbook.com
2. Togelius, J., Champandard, A.J., Lanzi, P.L., Mateas, M., Paiva, A., Preuss, M., Stanley, K.O.: Procedural content generation: Goals, challenges and actionable steps. In: Dagstuhl Seminar 12191: Artificial and Computational Intelligence in Games, Dagstuhl (2013)
3. Nintendo: Super Mario Bros. [Digital game] (1985)
4. Dahlskog, S., Togelius, J.: Patterns and Procedural Content Generation: Revisiting Mario in World 1 Level 1. In: Proceedings of the First Workshop on Design Patterns in Games, DPG 2012, pp. 1:1–1:8. ACM, New York (2012)
5. Dahlskog, S., Togelius, J.: Patterns as Objectives for Level Generation. In: Proceedings of the Second Workshop on Design Patterns in Games, DPG 2013 (2013)
6. Alexander, C., Ishikawa, S., Silverstein, M.: A pattern language - Towns, Buildings, Construction. Oxford University Press, New York (1977)
7. Gamma, E., Helm, R., Johnson, R., Vlissides, J.: Design Patterns Elements of Reusable Object-Oriented Software. Addison-Wesley, Reading (1994)
8. Björk, S., Holopainen, J.: Patterns in Game Design. Cengage Learning (2005)
9. Adams, E., Dormans, J.: Game Mechanics: Advanced Game Design. Voices That Matter. Pearson Education, Limited (2012)
10. Hullett, K., Whitehead, J.: Design Patterns in FPS Levels. In: FDG 2010: Proceedings of the Fifth International Conference on the Foundations of Digital Games, pp. 78–85. ACM, New York (2010)
11. Smith, G., Anderson, R., Kopleck, B., Lindblad, Z., Scott, L., Wardell, A., Whitehead, J., Mateas, M.: Situating Quests: Design Patterns for Quest and Level Design in Role-Playing Games. In: Si, M., Thue, D., André, E., Lester, J., Tanenbaum, J., Zammitto, V. (eds.) ICIDS 2011. LNCS, vol. 7069, pp. 326–329. Springer, Heidelberg (2011)

12. Cermak-Sassenrath, D.: Experiences with design patterns for oldschool action games. In: Proceedings of the 8th Australasian Conference on Interactive Entertainment: Playing the System. IE 2012, pp. 14:1–14:9. ACM, New York (2012)
13. Liapis, A., Yannakakis, G.N., Togelius, J.: Towards a generic method of evaluating game levels. In: Proceedings of the AAAI Artificial Intelligence for Interactive Digital Entertainment Conference (2013)
14. Togelius, J., Yannakakis, G., Stanley, K., Browne, C.: Search-based procedural content generation: A taxonomy and survey. IEEE Transactions on Computational Intelligence and AI in Games **3**(3), 172–186 (2011)
15. Smith, G., Whitehead, J.: Analyzing the expressive range of a level generator. In: Proceedings of the 2010 Workshop on Procedural Content Generation in Games. PCGames 2010, pp. 4:1–4:7. ACM, New York (2010)
16. Shaker, N., Yannakakis, G., Togelius, J.: Crowdsourcing the aesthetics of platform games. IEEE Transactions on Computational Intelligence and AI in Games **5**(3), 276–290 (2013)
17. Karakovskiy, S., Togelius, J.: The mario ai benchmark and competitions. IEEE Transactions on Computational Intelligence and AI in Games **4**(1), 55–67 (2012)
18. Fullerton, T.: Game Design Workshop - A Playcentric Approach to Creating Innovative Games, 2nd edn. Morgan Kaufmann, New York (2008)

Micro and Macro Lemmings Simulations Based on Ants Colonies

Antonio González-Pardo$^{(\boxtimes)}$, Fernando Palero, and David Camacho

Computer Science Department, Universidad Autónoma de Madrid, Madrid, Spain
{antonio.gonzalez,david.camacho}@uam.es, fernando.palero@inv.uam.es
http://aida.ii.uam.es

Abstract. Ant Colony Optimization (ACO) has been successfully applied to a wide number of complex and real domains. From classical optimization problems to video games, these kind of swarm-based approaches have been adapted, to be later used, to search for new meta-heuristic based solutions. This paper presents a simple ACO algorithm that uses a specifically designed heuristic, called common-sense, which has been applied in the classical video game *Lemmings*. In this game a set of *lemmings* must reach the exit point of each level, using a subset of finite number of skills, taking into account the contextual information given from the level. The paper describes both the graph model and the context-based heuristic, designed to implement our ACO approach. Afterwards, two different kind of simulations have been carried out to analyse the behaviour of the ACO algorithm. On the one hand, a micro simulation, where each ant is used to model a lemming, and a macro simulation where a swarm of lemmings is represented using only one ant. Using both kind of simulations, a complete experimental comparison based on the number and quality of solutions found and the levels solved, is carried out to study the behaviour of the algorithm under different game configurations.

Keywords: Lemmings video game · Micro and Macro simulations · Ant Colony Optimization algorithms

1 Introduction

Bio-inspired computation has been widely used in different areas from combinatorial optimization problems to stochastic search in a huge number of application domains. From industrial or engineering applications [10] to theoretical developments [13], they have been applied to study new bio-inspired approaches able to deal with *NP-complete*, or *NP-hard*, problems [1]. From the set of different methods and techniques that can be considered as bio-inspired: Artificial Neural Networks, Fuzzy Logic, Evolutionary Computation and Swarm Intelligence, this paper will be focused on the later.

Swarm Intelligence (SI) algorithms are focused on the collective behaviour of self-organizing systems [14], where the iterations among individuals generate

© Springer-Verlag Berlin Heidelberg 2014
A.I. Esparcia-Alcázar et al. (Eds.): EvoApplications 2014, LNCS 8602, pp. 337–348, 2014.
DOI: 10.1007/978-3-662-45523-4_28

collective knowledge based on social colonies [17]. Some examples of this type of algorithms are *Ant Colony Optimization* (ACO) [4,7,11,12]; *Particle Swarm Optimization* (PSO) [20]; *Bee Colony Optimization* (BCO) [18]; *Bird Flocking* [23] or *Bacterial Foraging* [9]. In these algorithms, the population travels through the solution space in order to obtain the best solution to the problem. Each solution is evaluated by a quality function and the resulting value is used to guide the whole population, or swarm, to the optimal solution. This quality function is usually designed as part of the meta-heuristic used by this kind of algorithms.

From the different available methods related to Swarm Intelligence, the selection of ant colonies (ACO) algorithms has been made taking into account two main characteristics. On the one hand, ACO algorithms work with a *population* that allow us to make a simple analogy between the concept of a swarm of creatures, and the ants used to model and solve the problem. On the other hand, the video game selected (*Lemmings Game*) has several characteristics that makes particularly interesting the application of ACO algorithms, such as the possibility to include some physics in the context-based information, to have a set of finite skills which can be used to model an optimization problem, or the necessity to find the optimum path taking into account previous features, among others (see Section 2 for a detailed description).

The increasing interest in the utilization of different techniques in video games [22] from areas like Artificial Intelligence (AI), Computational Intelligence (CI) or Machine Learning (ML), has originated a wide number of game-based software platforms. In these platforms different classical video games, such as Pac-Man (Ms Pac-Man [21]), Tetris [5], Mario Bros (Platformer AI [24,25]), Mastermind [2], Asteroids (Physical Traveller Salesman Problem [6]) or Starcraft (StarCraft [3]) among others, have been adapted as a new benchmark environment for testing classical and new methods from previous areas. The *Lemmings Game* is a popular proven NP-hard puzzle game [8] that can be used as a benchmark for CI algorithms. In spite of the popularity that this game obtained in the 1990s, few research has been applied to it.

This paper presents a simple ACO algorithm that uses a specifically designed heuristic to be applied in the Lemmings video game, where a set of creatures (Lemmings) must reach the exit point of each level using a subset of finite number of skills. The heuristic designed, named **common-sense**, takes into account the "contextual information" that must be used in this game to solve a level. In order to do that, each level is represented as a *contextual graph* where the edges store the allowed movements inside the world. The goal of the algorithm is to assign the best skills in each position on a particular level, to guide the Lemmings to reach the exit. The *common-sense heuristic* allows to select the best skill to be applied by the Lemming in a particular level, using the current state of the level represented by this contextual graph. The paper describes both, the contextual graph model designed and the common-sense heuristic.

On the other hand, two different kind of simulations have been carried out to analyse the behaviour of the ACO algorithms. It has been designed a **micro**

simulation, where each ant is used to model a Lemming, and a **macro simulation** where a complete swarm of Lemmings is represented using only one ant. In the micro simulations two different approaches have been used: the first one only allows one action from each Lemming per step, therefore any Lemming must take into account the previous modifications made by the rest of the Lemmings. In the second kind of micro simulations, a set of parallel modifications (one per Lemming available) is made in the same step, so these actions ignore the context information from the environment. In the macro simulations, only the first Lemming of the swarm can execute an action in a step, whereas the rest of the Lemmings must follow the "leader".

Finally, the paper provides a complete experimental evaluation between these three different kinds of simulations, based on the number and quality of solutions found, and the number and complexity of the levels solved. The main goal of these experiments will be to analyse the behaviour of the meta-heuristic designed, when different modifications are applied in the contextual graph that have been designed to model a level game.

The rest of the paper is structured as follows: Section 2 provides a detailed description of the Lemmnings video game; Section 3 presents the basics on both, the model design to implement the *contextual graph*, and the main features of the ACO algorithm proposed; Section 4 analyses the two different simulations approaches (micro and macro) considered in this work; Section 6 provides a complete description of the experimental settings, and the results obtained from the simulations; finally, Section 5 summarizes the conclusions and introduces some futures lines of work.

2   The Lemmings Video Game

The *Lemmings* are creatures that need to be saved. In each level, Lemmings start in a specific point of the stage and must be guided to the exit point by the player. They live in a two-dimensional space and are affected by **gravity**. They start walking in a specific direction until they find an obstacle. In this case the Lemming will change the direction and walk back. In the case where the Lemming encounters a hole, it will fall down. The only two ways, considered in this work, by which a Lemming can die is by falling beyond a certain distance, or by falling from the bottom of the level. In order to make Lemmings to reach the exit point, players have a set of *skills* that must be assigned (not necessarily all of them) to the Lemmings. Using these skills, Lemmings can modify the environment creating tunnels, or bridges, and thus creating a new way to reach the exit. Following, the basic skills that can be used by any lemming, and the basic features to build the game levels are described.

On the one hand, there are eight different skills, with different features, that are shown in Table 1. Some of these skills have *No Restrictions* (NR). This means that although the number of times that these skills can be assigned is limited, once it is assigned to the Lemming, it does not have any restriction to use it (i.e. Climber or Floater) several times in the same level. Other are *Restricted* (RE)

Table 1. Lemmings skills and basic features (NR:No Restrictions, NE: No Exit, and RE: Restricted)

Skill	Description	Features
Climber	A Lemming given the climber skill can scale vertical walls	NR
Floater	This skill allow the Lemming to open an umbrella if it falls beyond a high distance, avoiding its dead.	NR
Exploder	The Lemming will explode after a short delay	NE
Blocker	Using this skill, a Lemming will halt and the rest of Lemming will turn around	NE
Builder	The Lemming with this skill will build a bridge of a specific length	RE
Basher	To create horizontal tunnels if the environment allows it	RE
Miner	This skill is similar to the previous one, but in this case the tunnel is dug in diagonal direction	RE
Digger	The Lemming will dig vertically downwards until it found air or a solid material	RE

skills, so the Lemming only can use it a maximum number of times (i.e. Builder, Miner or Digger). For example, if the a Lemming has to dig in two separated locations this lemming must be assigned the Digger skill twice. Finally, there are some skills that do *Not* allow to reach the *Exit* (NE) to the Lemming, because the Lemming will die (i.e Exploder), or because it will not be able to make more movements (i.e. Blocker).

On the other hand, in the Lemmings' world there are a huge number of materials, but all of them can be grouped into two different classes: the ones that can be modified (i.e. it can be dug) and the ones that cannot be altered. In the former type, skills like *Basher*, *Miner* and *Digger* are allowed. In the case that a Lemming is digging and finds a material that cannot be dug, the Lemming will stop digging and start walking. Furthermore, each game level has its own skill configuration, where each skill can be used (i.e. assigned) a maximum number of times. It is not necessary to use all of the skills in the levels. Based on both kind of materials, editable and non editable, three different kinds of levels have been designed:

– **Easy**. These levels use both kind of materials, and the human-likes solution is a short path (few lemmings actions) with few skills are required to reach the exit. When non editable material is used, the lemmings colonies are "guided" to the exit because those skills related to "digging" abilities cannot be used (therefore the search space is reduced).
– **Medium**. In these kind of levels, both materials can be used and the solutions can be a mixture of actions. In the level, it is possible to find parts with a high level of freedom for the lemmings (they can use all of the available skills), and some other parts where the number of skills that can be used are reduced.

– **Hard**. These type of levels only use editable materials, and the solution to reach the exit needs from a large number of skills and actions (large solution paths) to be taken.

The Lemmings' game can be considered an interesting research video game problem specially for optimization algorithms. Three main objectives are necessary to optimize in this game: to save the maximum number of Lemmings in each level, to minimize the use of skills needed to reach the exit of the level, and finally to find the best path that allows to save as many Lemmings as possible using the less number of skills.

The Lemmings' game have been studied in [19]. In this work, authors apply a genetic algorithm to solve the different levels and the goal is the study of how the individuals initialization can affect to the performance of the GA.

Summarizing, the Lemmings video game provides (at least) two new interesting features. On the one hand, the video game provides different kind of terrains, that the algorithm must take into account to avoid a premature dead of the lemming, or to decide an adequate selection from the available skills. This characteristic provides an interesting "context" that should be handled by the algorithm (for instance, by using a constraint-based modelling of the environment or a meta-heuristic to select the best skill). On the other hand, the game itself needs from the management and control of a *colony* of Lemmings. It is necessary to coordinate those lemmings to look for the best solution (which is based on a mixture of different goals).

3   The ACO Approach for the Lemmings Video Game

The Lemmings Game can be seen as a *Constraint Satisfaction Problem (CSP)*, where the variables (denoted as X) represent the different positions of the levels, and the possible values (D) represent are the skills that Lemmings can execute in each position. The set of constraints, C, is composed by the number of lemmings that must be saved, the maximum number of skills that can be applied in each level, or the different destination from a given position taking into account the applied skill (i.e. given a position the set of possible destination nodes is different whether the skill is **Builder** or **Digger**). In order to execute an ACO algorithm to solve a CSP, traditionally authors model the CSP as a graph where the nodes represent the variable/value pairs ($< variable, value >$) and the edges connect those nodes whose variable X are different.

The problem with this representation is the size of the resulting graph. In this work, the model used to represent CSP as a graph is the one described in [15]. If the Lemmings level is mapped into a graph using the classical approach for each position, the resulting graph would have eight nodes (each of them represents the action that can be applied in the corresponding position). With the approach used in this work, each node only represents a position and the ants are in charge of selecting a specific skill to be applied in this position.

The adaptation of a Lemmings level into the simplified approach is performed in two different phases. First of all, the level is represented in a two-dimensional representation that contains information about the starting point, the exit point and the terrain information of the level. In Figure 1 there are shown an original lemmings level (Figure 1(a)) and the simplification of this level into a two-dimensional representation (Figure 1(b)). This representation is mapped into a constraint-based graph as Figure 1(c) shows. The constraint-based graph, or **contextual graph**, contains as many nodes as squares are contained in the two dimensional representation and the edges represent the default movement that ants can performed. It is important to note that the application of different skills in the graph will produce the creation of new edges in the graph, thus ants deal with a dynamic graph.

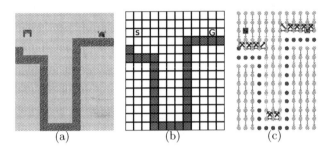

Fig. 1. An easy Lemmings level. The Figure a) shows one of the Lemmings level designed for the experiments carried out in this paper, the Figure b) shows a two dimensional representation of this level where only the starting and exit point, and the walls are represented. Finally, the Figure c) shows the constraint-based graph model for this level.

This work uses a classical ACO approach to search for the best paths of the levels. In this case, the nest of the colony is located in the node that represents the level starting point (marked as a "S" node in Figure 1(c)), and the food is located in the node that represents the level exit point (marked as a "G" node in Figure 1(c)). From the nest, ants start building their own local solution while they travel through the graph. In order to do that, each ant executes the behaviour shown in Algorithm 1.

The first step in the algorithm corresponds to the heuristic information retrieval (line 2). In this work, a heuristic called *Common-Sense* has been used. Using this heuristic, ants can perceive the environment (i.e. ants know the type of terrain of the surrounding nodes) and filter the skills that they can apply depending on this environment. For example, given an ant if the type of the node where the ant is placed and their surrounding are *Air*, the ant knows that the Lemming is falling and a possible skill to apply is **Floater** but not **Builder**. Once the ants have the values for the different skills, corresponding to the heuristic function and the pheromones, the decision of selecting one of them is computed using the classical proportional selection.

Algorithm 1. ACO algorithm for the Lemmings game

Parameter: A contextual graph.
          A Swarm $\mathcal{S}w$ composed by $\mathcal{L}$ Lemmings
          A set of available skills $\mathcal{S}k$
Result: A path plan $\mathcal{P}$ to reach the Exit $\mathcal{G}$, from the Start $\mathcal{S}$.

1 **foreach** $l_i \in \mathcal{L}$ **do**
2       $HeuristicSkillList \leftarrow$ getSkillsUsingHeuristic
3       $PheromoneValues \leftarrow$ getPheromoneValues
4       $newAction \leftarrow$ selectAction($HeuristicSkillList, PheromoneValues$)
5   **if** $newAction \neq currenAction$ **then**
6   **if** $newAction$ $canBeExecuted$ **then**
7   putPheromone
8   updateRemainingActions
9             $currentAction \leftarrow newAction$
10   add $currentAction$ to $\mathcal{P}$
11   **end**
12   **end**
13   goToNextNodeAccordingTo($currentAction$)
14 **end**

---

4   The Micro and Macro Lemmings Simulations

In [16], some initial experiments were made using the common-sense heuristic and a simplified contextual graph.In our initial experiments, the model and the heuristic were compared (using some few levels and a simple configuration) against a Genetic Algorithm approach. No modifications were allowed in the contextual graph during the simulation process and the experimental results were used to demonstrate the feasibility of the approach. In this new work, the contextual graph will be modified by the ants (Lemmings) inside a simulation step, considering (or not) the context of the level.

Therefore, two different kinds of simulations have been carried out to analyse the behaviour of the ACO algorithm. On the one hand, a *micro simulation*, where each ant is used to model a Lemming, and a *macro simulation* where a complete swarm of Lemmings is represented using only one ant. The main characteristics of both simulations can be summarized as follows:

1. In the *micro simulations* two different approaches have been used: "one to one sequential" ($1to1_S$) and "one to one parallel" ($1to1_P$). In the $1to1_S$ simulations, only one action (the application of one skill) from each Lemming is allowed per step. Therefore, any Lemming must take into account the modifications than the rest of the Lemmings previously have made in the environment, so this kind of simulation can be considered as contextual-based, because the actions previously made by others Lemmings will affect to the current (scheduled) Lemming decision. In the $1to1_P$ simulations, in each step all of the available Lemmings can make one action ignoring the

contextual information from the environment. The main difference between both kind of algorithms is related to the contextual graph modification, the first one will provide a smooth modification of the graph, increasing the importance of the common-sense heuristic. The second approach will allow a fast modification of the graph, so the relevance of the meta-heuristic will be lower in the solution process.

2. In the *macro simulations*, denoted as $1toN$ (one to N), only the first Lemming from the swarm can execute an action (skill) in a particular step, whereas the rest of the Lemmings must follow the "leader" [16]. This kind of simulations provides a semi-static modification of the contextual graph. The graph is slowly modified, so the relevance of the meta-heuristic and the pheromone values will be increased. The parallel simulation is similar to the $1to1_S$ ones, but the latter allows to explore better the solution space (any Lemming has an opportunity to apply an skill), whereas the first reduce the solution space by following a particular Lemming leader.

Previous simulations allows to analyse the behaviour of our approach by modifying three essential features: how fast the graph could be modified, how affects the contextual information to the searching process, and finally the importance of the pheromone concentration in the searching process. Table 2 shows a summary of both, the simulations designed and their basic features.

Table 2. Lemmings simulations and their related basic features.

Simulation	Graph modification	Contextual inf.	Num. Pheromones
$1to1_S$	medium	high	high
$1to1_P$	high	low	low
$1toN$	low	very high	very high

5   Experimental Results

Fifteen different levels[1] have been designed, by hand, to measure the efficiency our approach under different simulations configurations. The complexity of the levels is based on the size of the level, the different blocks contained into each level, the distance from the entry point to the exit point, the number of skills needed to solve the level, the type of terrains contained in the levels, etc. In this work, three different complexity levels are considered: easy, medium and hard, and 5 different levels have been designed per category. All the experiments have been repeated 50 times, using the described contextual graph and the common-sense heuristic. In each experiment, the ant colony is composed by 100 ants that execute during 500 steps. The evaporation rate of the system is 1% and α and β parameters (needed to measure the influence of the heuristic and the pheromone values) are fixed to 1. The number, and quality of the different found paths (solutions), have been used to compare the performance of our approach.

---

[1] http://aida.ii.uam.es/researchers/facultystaff/gonzalez-pardo-antonio/

The quality of any solution is composed by the number of lemmings that reach the exit (Eq. 1), the time needed to solve the problem (2) and the number of skills used (Eq. 3). The goal is to maximize the number of lemmings saved while the time needed to solve the problem and the number of skills used are minimized, but instead of facing this multi-objective problem, Eq. 4 is used and the goal is to maximize it.

$$S(p) = TotalLemm - Blockers - ExplodedLemmings \qquad (1)$$

$$T(p) = MaxTime - ExpendedTime \qquad (2)$$

$$A(p) = TotalActGiv - ActionUsed(p) \qquad (3)$$

$$Q(p) = \frac{T(p) + A(p) + S(p)}{MaxTime + TotalActGiv + TotalLemm} \qquad (4)$$

Table 3 and Figure 2, shows the results of our approach with the three different simulations carried out. Figure 2 shows the number of different paths (solutions) found by each algorithm, whereas Table 3 shows the average and standard deviation of the solutions quality.

Table 3. Average and standard deviation of the best solutions found by the ACO algorithm under different simulation configurations. These results have been obtained executing the different algorithms 50 different times.

Level	Complexity	$1to1_S$	$1to1_P$	$1toN$
1	Easy	**0,86 ± 0,009**	0,69 ± 0,084	0,65 ± 0,089
2	Easy	**0,88 ± 0,021**	0,85 ± 0,032	0,83 ± 0,040
3	Easy	**0,94 ± 0,038**	0,94 ± 0,012	0,90 ± 0,024
4	Easy	**0,82 ± 0,021**	0,78 ± 0,030	0,77 ± 0,030
5	Easy	**0,96 ± 0,015**	0,95 ± 0,008	0,94 ± 0,019
6	Medium	**0,91 ± 0,005**	0,88 ± 0,031	0,85 ± 0,040
7	Medium	**0,94 ± 0,000**	0,89 ± 0,027	0,86 ± 0,037
8	Medium	0 ± 0,000	0,90 ± 0,020	**0,91 ± 0,044**
9	Medium	0 ± 0,000	**0,93 ± 0,006**	0,63 ± 0,018
10	Medium	0,69 ± 0,034	0,69 ± 0,093	**0,78 ± 0,110**
11	Hard	0 ± 0,000	0 ± 0,000	**0,67 ± 0,052**
12	Hard	0 ± 0,000	0 ± 0,000	**0,88 ± 0,050**
13	Hard	0,72 ± 0,061	**0,91 ± 0,013**	0,75 ± 0,034
14	Hard	0,78 ± 0,002	0,82 ± 0,029	**0,90 ± 0,052**
15	Hard	± 0,000	**0,95 ± 0,003**	0,94 ± 0,020

Analyzing the quality of the solutions (Table 3) the $1to1_S$ approach obtains better solutions that $1to1_P$ and $1toN$ in easy and medium levels. This is produced by two different reasons. On the one hand, with easy and medium levels the solution approach is not as bigger as the one in hard levels. So a sequential depth-first search is able to find good solutions, in the maximum number of simulation steps allowed. In this kind of levels is better to strongly use the contextual information than to make a wide parallel search. On the other hand, $1to1_S$ approach performs a depth-first search in the solution space, while $1to1_P$ and $1toN$ algorithms make a breadth-first search.

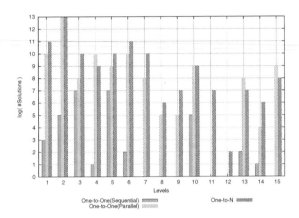

Fig. 2. The figure shows the number of different solutions found by the algorithms. The Y axis represent the $\log_2$ of the different solutions found by the algorithms.

The Figure 2 shows the number of different paths that each algorithm is able to identify. In general, $1toN$ and $1to1_P$ finds more paths than $1to1_S$. This effect is produced because the solution space is more explored by the $1toN$ and $1to1_P$ than $1to1_S$. In a single execution of $1to1_P$ and $1toN$, the number of parallel searches are equals to the number of ants that compose the colony, while in $1to1_S$ al the ants compose a single search. Comparing $1to1_P$ and $1toN$ can be seen that $1toN$, in general, finds more different paths that $1to1_P$. This is an expected results because although both algorithms make a breadth-first search, $1toN$ makes more parallel searches than $1to1_P$.

6   Conclusions

This paper analyses the behaviour of three different ACO-based approaches related to the automatic solving level problem in games. The application domain of this work is the well-known Lemmings game, where a set of Lemmings need to apply different skills in order to reach the exit. Three different categories of levels have been designed, with five levels per each category. The complexity of each level is defined by the size of the level, the number of available skills that can be applied, and the different types of terrains that compose the level.

The three different approaches considered in this work are: *macro simulations*, denoted as $1toN$ (one to N) where a swarm of lemmings is represented using only one ant, and two *micro simulations* denoted as $1to1_S$ and $1to1_P$. In the $1to1_S$ simulations, only one action (the application of one skill) to each Lemming is allowed per step. Also, the Lemmings share the context, this means that any modification performed by one Lemming is visible to the rest of them, so the contextual information will be used by the rest of the Lemmings. However, in the $1to1_P$ simulations, in each step all of the available Lemmings can make one action, therefore they can ignore the contextual information from the environment. One of the main differences between previous approaches (macro and micro) is related to the global behaviour of the searching algorithm for those kinds of simulations. In $1toN$ and $1to1_P$ the algorithm makes a parallel search because they allow the application of different skills at the same time with different lemmings. On the other hand, the $1to1_S$ approach is likely a sequential search because the Lemmings must apply their skills in order taking into account the contextual information.

From the experimental results shown in Table 3 and Figure 2, two main conclusions can be summarized. On the one hand, for easy and some (few) medium levels, the $1to1_S$ approach obtains the highest quality solutions because in those simple levels the ants are able to find short paths (solutions) from the exit using the contextual information. However, once the complexity of the level is increased, this approach has problems to find good quality solutions, or even a solution. In these levels the parallel approaches, $1toN$ and $1to1_P$, find the best solutions. From both approaches, the $1toN$ simulation, is able to find solutions for all the levels considered. This means that the contextual information, used through the common-sense heuristic, guides efficiently the algorithm enabling it to solve the hardest designed levels.

Acknowledgments. This work has been partly supported by Spanish Ministry of Science and Education under grant TIN2010-19872 (ABANT) and Savier project (Airbus Defense & Space project, FUAM-076914).

References

1. Abraham, A., Ramos, V.: Web usage mining using artificial ant colony clustering and linear genetic programming. In: The 2003 Congress on Evolutionary Computation, CEC 2003, vol. 2, pp. 1384–1391 (December 2003)
2. Berghman, L., Goossens, D., Leus, R.: Solving mastermind using genetic algorithms. Computers & Operations Research **36**, 1880–1885 (2009)
3. Blickle, T., Thiele, L.: A comparison of selection schemes used in evolutionary algorithms. Evolutionary Computation **4**(4), 361–394 (1996)
4. Blum, C., Merkle, D.: Swarm Intelligence: Introduction and Applications, 1st edn. Springer Publishing Company (2008) (incorporated)
5. Chen, X., Wang, H., Wang, W., Shi, Y., Gao, Y.: Apply ant colony optimization to tetris. In: Proceedings of the 11th Annual Conference on Genetic and Evolutionary Computation (GECCO), pp. 1:1741–1:1742 (2009)
6. Coldridge, J., Amos, M.: Genetic algorithms and the art of zen. Technical report, Manchester Metropolitan University (2010)
7. Colorni, A., Dorigo, M., Maniezzo, V.: Distributed optimization by ant colonies. In: European Conference on Artificial Life, pp. 134–142 (1991)
8. Cormode, G.: The hardness of the lemmings game, or oh no, more np-completeness proofs. In: Proceedings of Third International Conference on Fun with Algorithms, pp. 65–76 (2004)

9. Das, S., Biswas, A., Dasgupta, S., Abraham, A.: Bacterial foraging optimization algorithm: theoretical foundations, analysis, and applications. Foundations of Computational Intelligence **203**, 2355 (2009)

10. Das, T.K.: Bio-inspired algorithms for the design of multiple optimal power system stabilizers: Sppso and bfa. IEEE Transactions on Industry Applications 44(5) (September/October 2008)

11. Dorigo, M.: Ant colony optimization: A new meta-heuristic. In: Proceedings of the Congress on Evolutionary Computation, pp. 1470–1477. IEEE Press (1999)

12. Engelbrecht, A.P.: Computational Intelligence: An Introduction, 2nd edn. Wiley Publishing (2007)

13. Akan, O.B., Dressler, F.: Bio-inspired networking: From theory to practice. IEEE Communications Magazine, 177–183 (November 2010)

14. Farooq, M.: Bee-Inspired Protocol Engineering: From Nature to Networks. Springer (2008) (incorporated)

15. Gonzalez-Pardo, A., Camacho, D.: A new csp graph-based representation for ant colony optimization. In: 2013 IEEE Conference on Evolutionary Computation, June 20–23, vol. 1, pp. 689–696 (2013)

16. Gonzalez-Pardo, A., Camacho, D.: Environmental influence in bio-inspired game level solver algorithms. In: Zavoral, F., Jung, J.J., Badica, C. (eds.) IDC 2013. SCI, vol. 511, pp. 157–162. Springer, Heidelberg (2013)

17. Karaboga, D.: An idea based on honey bee swarm for numerical optimization. Techn. Rep. TR06 Erciyes Univ. Press Erciyes, 129(2) p. 2865 (2005)

18. Karaboga, D., Basturk, B.: A powerful and efficient algorithm for numerical function optimization: artificial bee colony (abc) algorithm. J. of Global Optimization **39**, 459–471 (2007)

19. Kendall G., Spoerer, K.: Scripting the game of lemmings with a genetic algorithm. In: Proceedings of the 2004 IEEE Congress on Evolutionary Computation, pp. 117–124 (2004)

20. Kennedy, J., Eberhart, R.: Particle swarm optimization. In: Proceedings of the Congress on Evolutionary Computation, vol. 4, pp. 1942–1948 (1995)

21. Martin, E., Martinez, M., Recio, G., Saez, Y.: Pac-mant: Optimization based on ant colonies applied to developing an agent for ms. pac-man. In: Proceedings of the Symposium on Computational Intelligence and Games (CIG), pp. 1:458–1:464 (2010)

22. Miikkulainen, R., Bryant, B.D., Cornelius, R., Karpov, I.V., Stanley, K.O., Yong, C.H.: Computational intelligence in games. In: Computational Intelligence: Principles and Practice (2006)

23. Reynolds, C.W.: Flocks, herds and schools: A distributed behavioral model. SIGGRAPH Comput. Graph. **21**, 25–34 (1987)

24. Shaker, N., Togelius, J., Yannakakis, G.N., Weber, B.G., Shimizu, T., Hashiyama, T., Sorenson, N., Pasquier, P., Mawhorter, P.A., Takahashi, G., Smith, G., Baumgarten, r: The 2010 mario ai championship: Level generation track. IEEE Trans. Comput. Intellig. and AI in Games **3**(4), 332–347 (2011)

25. Togelius, J.: Mario ai competition. In: Lanzi, P.L. (ed.) CIG. IEEE (2009)

Fast Evolutionary Adaptation
for Monte Carlo Tree Search

Simon M. Lucas[✉], Spyridon Samothrakis, and Diego Pérez

University of Essex, Colchester, UK
sml@essex.ac.uk

Abstract. This paper describes a new adaptive Monte Carlo Tree Search (MCTS) algorithm that uses evolution to rapidly optimise its performance. An evolutionary algorithm is used as a source of control parameters to modify the behaviour of each iteration (i.e. each simulation or roll-out) of the MCTS algorithm; in this paper we largely restrict this to modifying the behaviour of the random default policy, though it can also be applied to modify the tree policy.

This method of tightly integrating evolution into the MCTS algorithm means that evolutionary adaptation occurs on a much faster time-scale than has previously been achieved, and addresses a particular problem with MCTS which frequently occurs in real-time video and control problems: that uniform random roll-outs may be uninformative.

Results are presented on the classic Mountain Car reinforcement learning benchmark and also on a simplified version of Space Invaders. The results clearly demonstrate the value of the approach, significantly outperforming "standard" MCTS in each case. Furthermore, the adaptation is almost immediate, with no perceptual delay as the system learns: the agent frequently performs well from its very first game.

1 Introduction

Monte Carlo Tree Search (MCTS) is a powerful selective search method that has had a profound impact on Game AI since its introduction in 2006 by a number of researchers; see the recent survey paper by Browne et al [3] for more details of its history, algorithm, variations and applications.

One of the most appealing features of MCTS is that it can operate without the need for any heuristic: it works reasonably well in its vanilla form on a variety of problems. However, it is also well known and not surprising that the appropriate use of heuristics can significantly boost performance, and all leading Go programs use these.

MCTS selectively builds an asymmetric tree. The algorithm works by following a tree policy until it finds a node to expand, at which point it performs a roll-out (also called play-out or simulation) until the end of the game (or until some other stopping condition is met). The value found at the end of the roll-out is then back-propagated up the tree, updating the mean value and the number of visits to each node. Perhaps the most popular tree policy is based on the Upper

© Springer-Verlag Berlin Heidelberg 2014
A.I. Esparcia-Alcázar et al. (Eds.): EvoApplications 2014, LNCS 8602, pp. 349–360, 2014.
DOI: 10.1007/978-3-662-45523-4_29

Confidence Bounds equation (UCB) which for MCTS is known as UCT (Upper Confidence bounds for Trees). This aims to optimally balance exploitation (visit the child of the current node with the best mean value, left term in equation 1) versus exploration (visit the least explored child, right term in equation 2).

$$UCB1_c = \mu_c + k\sqrt{\frac{\ln N}{n_c}} \qquad (1)$$

where k is an exploration constant, N is the number of times the parent has been visited, and for child c, μ_c is the mean value and n_c the number of visits.

Although some efforts have already been made to incorporate automated learning procedures into MCTS, the current state of the art usually involves a great deal of hand-programming and leaves some important problems largely unanswered, namely:

- The action-space may be too fine-grained; it may be necessary to work in some space of macro-actions in order to perform well. Designing the macro-actions could be done by evolution.
- Uniform random roll-outs may cause insufficient exploration of the state space. They may all end in a similar or even identical degree of failure, rendering them devoid of information. In the worst case, the μ_c values for each child may be identical, meaning there is nothing to exploit.

In this paper we address the second of these problems: this is important since it will aid the development of general video game bots able to play a wide range of games to a high standard without being explicitly programmed for any particular game. This is useful for providing an automatic range of opponents for new video games, and also for evaluating automatically designed video games. Although there have been some very interesting efforts along these lines, for instance [15] [4] [5], the richness of the games that have been evolved so far has been arguably limited by the intelligence of the evolved bots [15], or the NPC rules [4] or the search algorithms used to evaluate them [5].

2   Related Research

Silver et al [13] incorporated temporal difference learning (TDL) into an MCTS algorithm, and drew the distinction between the transient values learned by the MCTS procedure and the long-term heuristic information learned by TDL.

Robles et al [11] used a similar procedure for learning in Othello, where they used TDL to learn a value function both for controlling the tree policy and for controlling the roll-outs.

Although TDL utilises more of the available information during learning than evolution [6], evolution can be more robust due to its direct emphasis on the end goal (such as winning the most games) rather than some proxy of this such as minimising the residual errors.

Evolutionary learning has also been used to tune MCTS algorithms. Benbassat and Sipper [2] used Genetic Programming, in conjunction with MCTS, for several classic games such Othello and Dodgem. In their work, each individual in the evolutionary algorithm represents a function that evaluates a board position. During the rollout step of MCTS, each move is chosen by selecting the action that maximizes the value of the next board state, according to this function.

Independently, Alhejali and Lucas [1] used evolution to tune the weights of the heuristic value function used to guide the roll-outs in an MCTS Pac-Man player. In both these approaches evolution was able to improve on the default MCTS performance, though in both cases the evolutionary algorithm was applied at the level of the individual, where each fitness evaluation involved playing one or more complete games. This approach leads to relatively expensive evolutionary runs, since for most games reasonable standard MCTS players cannot operate much faster than real-time. The approach developed in this paper is very different, since now each roll-out contributes immediately to the fitness evaluation of the policy that guided it.

The main use of the fast evolutionary adaptation used in this paper is to bias the simulation or roll-out policy after the tree policy has found a leaf node to expand. Most previous ways of doing this have relied on the information gained from the simulations; a good example is the recent work by Powley et al [10], where they learn n-gram models to bias the roll-outs. This works well when the simulations are informative, but breaks down when the simulations all terminate in identical or very similar values.

The approach developed in this paper is intended to complement the roll-out mining methods by initially hypothesizing useful "directions" for the roll-outs to take in the absence of any evidence. As the evidence accumulates, the aim is for the evolutionary algorithm to adapt the distribution of roll-out policies accordingly.

One of the most general approaches for optimizing MCTS algorithms is that of Maes et al [7] where they formulate a grammar for describing a general class of Monte Carlo Tree Search algorithms and then search the space induced by that grammar to find high performance ones. However, as with most other methods this requires relatively extensive evaluation in order to determine the fitness of each algorithm instance.

Recently MCTS has found application in video games, with Ms Pac-Man being a good example [12], supported by strong results in competitions both for controlling the Pac-Man agent [9] and the ghost team [8]. However, all these cases relied on some hand-designed heuristics such as disallowing Pac-Man reversals during roll-outs. This was found to be necessary since if the Pac-Man is allowed to reverse then it makes insufficient progress through the maze due to excessive dithering.

This is analogous to the problem observed running vanilla MCTS on the Mountain Car problem described below, and in this case is easily solved by the fast evolutionary adaptation approach.

3   Fast Evolutionary MCTS

The main contribution of this paper is the introduction of a new approach to using an evolutionary algorithm to rapidly adapt the behaviour of an MCTS algorithm. The main idea is to tightly integrate evolution's fitness evaluation process with the MCTS algorithm. Previous evolutionary approaches (e.g. [2], [1]) have been loosely coupled in the sense that each fitness evaluation was based on the performance of the MCTS agent over an entire game or set of games, where the MCTS agent was seen as a black box with a set of tunable parameters.

In the Fast Evolutionary method each iteration (roll-out) of the MCTS algorithm contributes directly to a statistical evaluation of an individual, where each individual is characterised by a vector of parameters. As a result of this change the evolutionary algorithm has access to a much higher bandwidth of information and consequently is able to adapt more rapidly.

Within this fast evolutionary approach there are at least two distinct ways in which it could work: evaluate each individual within the same MCTS tree, or create a new MCTS tree for each individual.

The former approach aggregates the statistics of each individual within the same tree and has the advantage of throwing nothing away. The latter approach is more wasteful since each time an individual is discarded from the population all the statistics are lost; however it can also be used more flexibly and can be used to search the space of different macro-actions for example. In this paper we limit the investigation to the former approach.

Algorithm 1 outlines the main steps. The *while* loop describes the MCTS algorithm executed in order to make each decision. Here the condition is listed as being within a computational budget: this could be measured as elapsed time or as a fixed number of iterations.

For each iteration a parameter vector w is drawn from the evolutionary algorithm by calling evo.getNext() as shown on line 2. Line 3 initialises a statistics object to track the performance of this control vector. The *for* loop (line 4) is there to enable a particular MCTS control policy to be sampled K times before returning its performance statistics to the evolutionary algorithm. There are many statistics that can be used to rate how well an MCTS algorithm is performing: our basic statistics object includes calculation of the mean, standard deviation, min and max. All these can be important, though in this initial study we only use the mean. Alternatively, the K parameter can be seen as the responsibility of the evolutionary algorithm, in which case the *for* loop can be removed.

The parameter vector could be used to control both the tree policy and the default policy as indicated on lines 5 and 6 respectively, with the default policy being used to generate a roll-out that ends in a state with the value of Δ. Apart from the influence of the control parameters, the MCTS algorithm operates as normal with line 7 showing the backup of the tree statistics. Line 8 indicates the statistics object S being updated with the roll-out value Δ.

After running the MCTS algorithm for the allowed computational budget, the *while* loop exits. The algorithm returns the estimate of the best control vector found to date via a call to *evo.getBest()* (line 12). This suggests another use case for the algorithm: to find good control vectors and then use these to *fix* the bias. In the results tables below we refer to this mode of use as *Pre-Evolved*.

Algorithm 1. Fast Evolutionary MCTS. The evolutionary algorithm provides a source of parameter sets used to control the MCTS algorithm.

---

   input   : Parameter K, the number of roll-outs per fitness evaluation, v_0 is root state
   output : weight vector **w** and action a

   ;   *// initialize evolutionary algorithm* evo,
1 **while** *within computational budget* **do**
2 | Set **w** ← EVO.GETNEXT()
3 | Initialise statistics object S.
4 | **for** $i := 1$ *to* K **do**
5 | | v_l ← TREEPOLICY($v_0, T(w)$) ;   *// Tree policy is influenced by* $T(w)$
6 | | Δ ← DEFAULTPOLICY($s(v_l), D(w)$) ;   *// Default policy is influenced by* $D(w)$
7 | | BACKUP(v_l, Δ)
8 | | UPDATESTATS(S, Δ)
9 | **end**
10 | EVO.SETFITNESS(**w**, S)
11 **end**
12 Return **w** ← *evo.getBest*()
13 Return a ← *recommend*(v_o)

Finally, the algorithm returns the selected action for the current root state using a recommendation policy (line 13), which is usually different from the tree policy. In this paper we mainly choose the action with the highest mean value, though for Space Invaders we also experimented with biasing the recommendation directly.

3.1 Biasing Rollouts

The main idea here is to use features associated with a given state to bias the action selection process. The biasing process works as follows: we map from state space S to feature space F with N features and then from feature space to a probability distribution over the set of actions. This is currently implemented using a hand-coded feature space for each problem. There are A actions available and the relative strength a_i of each action i is then calculated as a weighted sum of feature values. The weights are stored in a matrix W where entry w_{ij} is the weighting of feature j for action i:

$$a_i = \sum_{j=1}^{N} w_{ij} f_j \tag{2}$$

These relative action values then feed into a softmax function in order to calculate the probability $P(a_i)$ of taking each action.

$$P(a_i) = \frac{e^{-a_i}}{\sum_{j=1}^{A} e^{-a_j}} \tag{3}$$

The bias is therefore controlled by two things: the features and the weight matrix W. As previously mentioned, for the moment the features are hand-coded though in future they could be evolved using GP or auto-constructed in some other way. The weight matrix is evolved: every roll-out is biased using a W drawn from the evolutionary algorithm.

4   Test Problems

For proof of concept we choose two initial test problems: Mountain Car and Space Invaders. The first one is a simple reinforcement learning problem, but one that MCTS with uniform roll-outs fails on badly. Space Invaders is a more interesting challenge, and even the simplified version used in this paper involves precise shooting of fast moving targets (the aliens move quickly when there are only a few left), and strategic considerations regarding the order in which to shoot the aliens. In each case the MCTS tree policy was UCB1 with the exploration constant k set to 0.3 after some experimentation. The algorithm ran for 200 iterations per action selection. When calculating the mean values of each child in the UCT tree we tried scaling the scores to be in a smaller range, but this tended to degrade performance.

We used a $(1 + 1)$ Evolution Strategy (ES) for the evolutionary algorithm (i.e. the source of roll-out control vectors). This is the simplest possible choice, and most likely far from optimal. A better choice might be to use a bandit-based algorithm in order to maintain a multi-modal distribution of roll-out policies. Nonetheless, even the (1+1) ES is able to produce some interesting results.

4.1   Mountain Car

The mountain car problem is a classic reinforcement learning benchmark problem; here we use a version identical to that described by Sutton and Barto [14] (page 214) apart from limiting the number of steps per episode to 500 instead of 2,500. The problem is illustrated in Figure 1: the aim is to reach the line at the top of the hill on the right, but the engine has insufficient force to overcome gravity. The state of the system is fully specified by two scalar values: position s and velocity v. The state space is small but continuous and there are many ways of constructing features for this. For these experiments we take the most direct approach and simply use s and v scaled to be in the same range from -1 to $+1$. The three possible actions are accelerate left, neutral and accelerate right.

The difficulty of any particular instance of this problem depends on the initial state. For example, if the car starts close to the goal with a large velocity towards the goal then many action sequences will lead to success. All experiments in this paper used a start state of $(s = -0.3, v = 0)$. Starting in this way, close to the centre of the valley and with zero velocity, is relatively hard and a few oscillations are required in order to reach the goal. We limit the number of steps in each episode to 500, and the score (to be minimised) is simply the number of steps taken to reach the goal, or 500 if the goal was never reached. Configured in this way MCTS with uniform random roll-outs reaches the goal around 1 in 30 episodes.

4.1.1   Analysing Trajectories

Figure 2 shows 20 random roll-outs using (a) uniform random actions and (b) random actions biased by Equations 2 and 3, where the weights of matrix W were drawn from a Gaussian distribution with zero mean and a standard deviation of 5. Each illustrative roll-out lasted for 1,000 steps (though for the experiments, we limited episode length to 500). This clearly illustrates the value of the approach. When taking uniform random moves none of the roll-outs reached the goal and therefore, in the standard mountain car reward scheme, would each have a value of -1000 (-1 for each step).

The biases introduce a more directed policy: sometimes this is even worse than the uniform policy but sometimes it is much better, and plot (b) shows several trajectories reaching the goal.

4.1.2   Results

Table 1 shows three sets of results based on the roll-out bias. Each roll-out ran until a terminal state was reached. Uniform roll-outs perform worst, with a mean of 497 and only 4 successes out of 100. The fast evolutionary method (Fast-Evo) reaches the goal in all but one case. From the 100 fast evolutionary runs we saved the bias matrix W with the best result and performed 100 trials with this Pre-Evolved bias. This gave the best result with a mean of 99 and no failures.

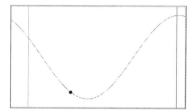

Fig. 1. A depiction of the mountain car reinforcement learning benchmark. The objective is to get to the top of the hill on the right, but the force of the engine is insufficient to directly overcome gravity. To solve the problem (depending on the start state) it is usually necessary to accelerate away from the goal and up the left hill before accelerating toward the goal.

4.2   Space Invaders

Space invaders was released by Taito in 1978 and is one of the classic arcade games of all time, taking gameplay to new levels. There is still significant interest in developing better versions of this type of game, as evidenced by the highly playable and commercially successful Space Invaders Extreme published by SquareEnix for the Sony PlayStation Portable (PSP). The original ROM code is available on line and can be played using the Multi Arcade Machine Emulator (MAME). We encourage the interested reader to try this: the original game is superior to all of the clones we have found on the Web.

Table 1. Mean scores and standard errors for each method based on 100 trials each. The score is the number of steps taken to reach the goal state, so lower scores are better. Each episode was terminated after 500 steps, so the worst possible score is 500. An episode was deemed successful if it found the goal in under 500 steps.

Roll-out	Mean Score (s.e.)	Successes
Pre-Evolved	99 (2.8)	100
Fast-Evo	233 (13)	99
Uniform Random	497 (1.8)	4

Suitable MCTS agents could be used to play-test variations of these games to assess the difficulty of each level and also to feed into the fitness function when automatically evolving new variants. However, in this paper we use the game as an initial benchmark.

Figure 3 shows a screenshot with an MCTS software agent playing the game. This version has the following features:

- The same number of aliens as the original game: 55 arranged in 11 columns, 5 rows.
- Similar movement patterns. On each tick of the game loop just one alien is moved, each missile is moved, and the player cannon is moved. This leads to the dog-legged movement pattern that can be observed in the original game, and naturally leads to the effect of the aliens moving more quickly as more are shot - with extremely fast movement when just one alien is left. Note that many clones of the game ignore this feature and move the aliens together in lock-step.

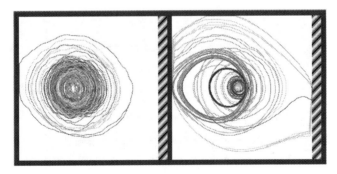

Fig. 2. Random roll-outs through the two-dimensional state space (position: horizontal, velocity: vertical) of the Mountain Car problem: (a) uniform random roll-outs are unlikely to reach the goal and wander through the state-space with no purpose. (b) biased roll-outs encourage more purposeful trajectories through state space, some of which may reach the goal. The set of goal states is shown as the hatched area to the right of each plot.

- Currently there are no alien missiles: the game is over either when an alien lands (reaches the bottom of the screen) or when all the aliens have been shot.
- The aliens are of three types (as with the original game) differing only in the score for shooting each one: scores are 10, 20, 30 for cyan (bottom two rows), magenta (next two rows) and blue (top row) respectively.
- No alien flying saucers along the top. In the original game these were worth between 50 and 300 points, and one strategy involved shooting out some middle columns in order to ensure a clear shot at the flying saucers. Our version is currently missing these.

Despite the limitations compared to the original game, the version used in this paper is nonetheless an appropriate challenge for the MCTS players under study. Actually, the game required some tuning in order to make the difficulty suitable for clearly distinguishing between weak and strong players. We did this by slowing down the speed of the player's missiles[1], and by lowering the starting point of the block of aliens. The latter difficulty adjustment happens in the original game, with the aliens starting lower down as the levels progress. This means they have to be cleared in a more constrained order to prevent them from landing.

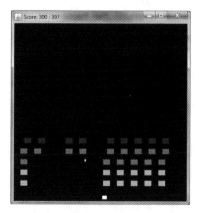

Fig. 3. A Space Invaders game in progress. The aim of this is to shoot all the alien invaders before they land. In this cut-down version there are no bases and the invaders do not drop missiles. Nonetheless when play-testing the game we found that clearing the level required a reasonable level of shooting skill and also that a suitable strategy be employed such as shooting away the end columns first. In the depicted game the AI player has made the mistake of shooting away too many of the central aliens, and the aliens look set to land.

---

[1] Only one player missile can be fired at a time so this limits the rate at which aliens can be shot, and increases the punishment for missing, since the player must wait until the missile has left the top of the screen before firing the next one.

Here the problem of constructing suitable features is much more complicated than for the mountain car problem. There are many elements to good Space Invaders strategy, and sometimes it is desirable to shoot away the end columns, but on other occasions emergency measures are needed and to avoid immediate death it is necessary to shoot away the aliens closest to landing. After some agonising over the best choice of features we made some initial experiments with just a single feature! We call this *nearest edge column displacement* and calculate it as follows. First, we find the minimum (leftmost) and maximum (rightmost) x-coordinates of the set of aliens. We then pick the one closest to the player's missile cannon and subtract the x-coordinate of the cannon.

The fact that this worked rather well was a surprise, but provides interesting insight into the nature of biasing roll-outs for MCTS. The fact is that MCTS is already a powerful adaptive algorithm, and the roll-out bias is just needed to nudge it into more interesting regions of the search space. It may be unnecessary for the roll-out bias to be especially clever.

There are six possible actions, formed by the cartesian product of the movement actions {left, dontMove, right} and the firing action {dontShoot, shoot}. Since there is only one feature this leads to 6 weights to learn in the matrix W.

4.2.1   Results

We tested a number of approaches. Given the simplicity of the parameters to learn, we were able to include a hand-coded set of parameters. The intuition behind these is to bias the roll-outs in order to move to the closest end column most of the time, firing occasionally.

When designing the roll-out bias by hand we also observed a frustrating aspect of this process: although the roll-outs were biased, the behaviour of the agent very often failed to reflect this. The reason for this is that the actions involving more movement may not necessarily lead to better scores, and hence may not be selected at the root level.

In order to force the effect of the bias we also created an option of adding the bias directly into the recommendation policy (i.e. the move actually chosen to play). We refer to this as $\mu + Q$ action selection. We were also interested to see the effects of not using MCTS at all, but simply playing uniform random moves, or random moves according to the hand-coded bias.

Each roll-out ran to a maximum depth of 50 from the root or until the end of the game, whichever condition was met first. This meant that every move in the game required a maximum of 10,000 game-ticks to be simulated; in our simulator this achieves real-time performance at 50 frames (actions) per second.

Table 2 shows the mean and standard error of these variations. The difference in scores between methods is significant (*t*-test, p $= 0.01$) if separated by a horizontal line. The MCTS approaches are described by the roll-out policy and the recommendation policy. The biases are: Q_{hand}: hand-designed, Q_{evo}: evolved for each of the 100 trials using Algorithm 1 and Q_{prevo}: a fixed high scoring bias matrix selected from the 100 trials of the Q_{evo} method. The Q_{evo} approach sometimes (about 5 - 10% of the time) obtains the maximum score of 990; we just selected an arbitrary one of these solutions to fix the Q_{prevo} bias.

The results are interesting. The first thing to note is that the non-MCTS methods perform poorly: clearly it is not enough just to make uniform or biased random moves. Secondly, the best MCTS approach was the hand-coded one with action selection bias. Interestingly, evolution was able to find some good solutions, but not on every run (remember here that an evolutionary run corresponds to a single game being played). The high performance of Q_{prevo} is very encouraging.

Table 2. Mean scores and standard errors for each method based on 100 games each. The maximum possible score is 990. The minimum possible score is zero.

Roll-out	Action selection	Mean Score (s.e.)
Q_{hand}	$\mu + Q_{hand}$	953 (20)
Q_{prevo}	μ	885 (11)
Q_{hand}	μ	877 (17)
Q_{evo}	μ	683 (19)
Uniform Random	μ	674 (16)
Q_{evo}	$\mu + Q_{evo}$	593 (23)
—	Uniform Random	127 (5.1)
—	Biased Random Q_{hand}	119 (6.2)

5   Conclusions

This paper introduced a novel fast evolutionary algorithm for adapting Monte Carlo Tree Search. The algorithm has an important role to play in real-time control problems and video games where uniform random roll-outs may be uninformative. To counter this the evolutionary algorithm is used as a source of roll-out policy control vectors to encourage more decisive simulations that explore more diverse parts of the state space. When it works this enables the MCTS algorithm to work with more informative statistics.

We tested the algorithm on the Mountain Car RL benchmark, and on a reduced but interesting version of space invaders. The algorithm learns extremely quickly and can adapt the roll-outs to great effect during the playing of a single game. The estimated best control-vectors can also be used to fix the bias for a set of runs, a process we call pre-evolving the bias, and this led to good results on both problems under test.

So far the algorithm has been learning a small number of parameters — just six in each case, yet appropriate setting of these was sufficient to significantly improve performance on both test problems. Future work includes more thorough testing of the method, including cases involving complex feature sets with large numbers of parameters to tune.

Given the fact that simple features can lead to significant performance boosts, and the fact that they can be evaluated so rapidly, this suggests that GP could work well for automated feature construction.

References

1. Alhejali, A., Lucas, S.: Using Genetic Programming to Evolve Heuristics for a MonteCarlo Tree Search Ms Pac-Man Agent, In: IEEE Conference on Computational Intelligence and Games, pp. 65–72 (2013)
2. Benbassat, A., Sipper, M.: EvoMCTS: Enhancing MCTS-Based Players through Genetic Programming, In: IEEE Conference on Computational Intelligence and Games, pp. 57–64 (2013)
3. Browne, C., Powley, E., Whitehouse, D., Lucas, S., Cowling, P., Rohlfshagen, P., Tavener, S., Perez, D., Samothrakis, S., Colton, S.: A Survey of Monte Carlo Tree Search Methods. IEEE Transactions on Computational Intelligence and AI in Games **4**(1), 1–43 (2012)
4. Cook, M., Colton, S.: Multi-faceted Evolution of Simple Arcade Games. In: IEEE Conference on Computational Intelligence in Games (CIG), pp. 289–296 (2011)
5. Cook, M., Colton, S., Raad, A., Gow, J.: Mechanic Miner: Reflection-Driven Game Mechanic Discovery and Level Design. In: IEEE Conference on Computational Intelligence in Games (CIG), pp. 284–293 (2013)
6. Lucas, S.: Investigating learning rates for evolution and temporal difference learning. In: IEEE Symposium on Computational Intelligence and Games, CIG 2008, pp. 1–7 (December 2008)
7. Maes, F., St-Pierre, D., Ernst, D.: Monte Carlo Search Algorithm Discovery for Single-Player Games. IEEE Transactions on Computational Intelligence and AI in Games **5**(3), 201–213 (2013)
8. Nguyen, K.Q., Thawonmas, R.: Monte Carlo Tree Search for Collaboration Control of Ghosts in Ms. Pac-Man. IEEE Transactions on Computational Intelligence and AI in Games **5**(1), 57–68 (2013)
9. Pepels, T., Winands, M.: Enhancements for Monte-Carlo Tree Search in Ms Pac-Man. In: IEEE Conference on Computational Intelligence and Games (CIG), pp. 265–272 (2012)
10. Powley, E.J., Whitehouse, D., Cowling, P.I.: Bandits all the way down: UCB1 as a simulation policy in Monte Carlo Tree Search. In: IEEE Conference on Computational Intelligence in Games (CIG), pp. 81–88 (2013)
11. Robles, D., Rohlfshagen, P., Lucas, S.M.: Learning Non-Random Moves for Playing Othello: Improving Monte Carlo Tree Search. In: Proceedings IEEE Conf. Comput. Intell. Games, Seoul, pp. 305–312 (2011)
12. Samothrakis, S., Robles, D., Lucas, S.: Fast Approximate Max-n Monte Carlo Tree Search for Ms Pac-Man. IEEE Transactions on Computational Intelligence and AI in Games **3**(2), 142–154 (2011)
13. Silver, D., Sutton, R.S., Müller, M.: Sample-Based Learning and Search with Permanent and Transient Memories. In: Proceedings 25th Annu. Int. Conf. Mach. Learn., pp. 968–975, Helsinki (2008)
14. Sutton R., Barto, A.: Introduction to Reinforcement Learning. MIT Press (1998)
15. Togelius, J., Schmidhuber, J.: An Experiment in Automatic Game Design. In: IEEE Symposium on Computational Intelligence and Games, pp. 111–118 (2008)

Automatic Camera Control: A Dynamic Multi-Objective Perspective

Paolo Burelli[1] and Mike Preuss[2]([⊠])

[1] Department of Architecture, Design and Media Technology,
Aalborg University Copenhagen, Copenhagen, Denmark
`pabu@create.aau.dk`
[2] European Research Center for Information Systems (ERCIS),
Westfälische Wilhelms-Universität Münster, Münster, Germany
`mike.preuss@uni-muenster.de`

Abstract. Automatically generating computer animations is a challenging and complex problem with applications in games and film production. In this paper, we investigate how to translate a shot list for a virtual scene into a series of virtual camera configurations — i.e automatically controlling the virtual camera. We approach this problem by modelling it as a dynamic multi-objective optimisation problem and show how this metaphor allows a much richer expressiveness than a classical single objective approach. Finally, we showcase the application of a multi-objective evolutionary algorithm to generate a shot for a sample game replay and we analyse the results.

1 Introduction

Three-dimensional computer animation is an established technique employed in the production of films, video-games, commercials and many other visual media. The idea behind 3D computer animation is to produce a virtual environment, containing elements such as lights, objects and buildings, and animate these elements while rendering the frames of a video from a specific point of view within the environments. Producing an animation, like an animated film or a game cut-scene, is a rather complex task, involving 3D modelling, animation, camera work, lighting and a number of other technical and artistic tasks. Such productions often require the work of several professionals for a span of several months. On the other hand, In the last two decades, the availability of cheap or free animation tools and the advent of customisable game engines has produced a drastic change in the demography of the virtual film makers [14]. New forms of the film medium became popular, such as machinima or game replays, created by non-professional or semi-professional cinematographers or game players.

Automating the generation of an animation or parts of it is potentially beneficial as a mean to reduce the costs of professional productions as well as to increase the quality of amateur ones. Furthermore, many of the problems connected with the automation of the cinematographic process in animations are present also in computer games — e.g. effective viewpoint animation, lighting,

© Springer-Verlag Berlin Heidelberg 2014
A.I. Esparcia-Alcázar et al. (Eds.): EvoApplications 2014, LNCS 8602, pp. 361–373, 2014.
DOI: 10.1007/978-3-662-45523-4_30

shot definition and selection — making this a common basic problem for most virtual reality applications. In particular, the problem of virtual camera placement and animation is a common basic virtual reality problem which has received a lot of attention from different researchers throughout the last two decades [9]. Automatic camera control can be described as the process of finding optimal camera positions and movements in a virtual three dimensional environment given a set of requirements describing how the produced images should look like.

In the state-of-the-art of automatic camera control the problem is modelled as a real-valued optimisation problem in which the search space is defined by the possible combinations of different camera parameters (e.g. position, rotation or field of view) and the objective function is based on the level of satisfaction of a series of high-level and environment-independent requirements, such as the visibility of a particular object or the size of that object on the screen. The problem has been addressed from two perspectives: off-line generation of shots from static environments and real-time animation of camera parameters in dynamic and interactive environments.

For off-line generation of shots, the optimisation process is executed until an optimal configuration of the camera is found at each frame that needs to be generated. This approach can be used to generate static pictures; however it is not suitable for dynamic scenes either in real-time or off-line, as each shot is considered as a separated optimisation problem; therefore, subsequent optimisations might end up with very different optimal solutions and this would result in a flickering, unstable view. In the second group of approaches, the search process is performed while the virtual scene is changing — e.g. the game is played. These approaches have been successfully employed in games [4,5] and are particularly suitable for real-time tracking of optimal cameras in interactive and unpredictable virtual environments. However, due to their reactive nature, they are ill suited in situations where the optimum at a certain moment is not necessary the best solution. This is often the case in automatic camera control, in which many types of shot constraint the movement of the camera — e.g. the camera shout be fixed in one position while the characters move. In these situations the camera should be configured so that is can maximise the satisfaction of the requirements for the whole length of the shot.

The limitations of the current approaches constrain the applicability of the available automatic camera control methods; for this reason, we propose a novel approach based on multi-objective optimisation in dynamic environments. The proposed method is designed for off-line calculation of camera configuration sequences that can be used to visualise a computer animation, a game replay or to automatically place camera view-points during the design of a game level. Given a virtual environment, a set of events over time and a shot list — i.e. a list of shot description with starting condition and ending condition — the proposed method executes multiple multi-objective optimisations at key events or key points in time. The resulting solutions from each optimisation are subsequently used to identify the solution (or sequence of solutions) for each shot.

While the problem is dynamic, the computation of the solutions is executed off-line — i.e. after the dynamic actions is has taken place — therefore, the problem is tackled as a sequence of static problems rather than as a single dynamic optimisation problem. By addressing the camera optimisation problem from this perspective, it is possible to select solutions not only based on their instant quality, but also based on their overall performance in the shot. Furthermore, uding multi-objective optimisation, it is possible to generate different types of shots, both static and dynamic, just by changing the principle used to select the solutions from the pool of possible solutions given by the various optimisation sequences. For instance a static shot, can be picked by finding the camera configuration which is for the longest period of time on the Pareto front during the shot.

We demonstrate the application of the approach in a 3D shooter game as a mean to automatically produce cinematographic replays of the game actions. The resulting animations are showcased and evaluated both visually and numerically against a generic single objective optimisation approach, showing that the multi-objective approach performs extremely well and shall be pursued in future works.

2   Related Work

Since the introduction of virtual reality, virtual camera control attracted the attention of a large number of researchers (refer to [9] for a comprehensive review). Early approaches focused on the mapping between the degrees of freedom (DOF) for input devices to 3D camera movement [22]. While these metaphors are currently still common in many virtual reality applications, direct manipulation of the several degrees of freedom of the camera soon demonstrated to be problematic for the user, leading researchers to investigate how to simplify camera control [12,16].

In parallel to the research on control metaphors, a number of researchers investigated the automation of the camera configuration process. Automatic camera control identifies the process of automatically configuring the camera in a virtual environment according to a set of requirements. It is a non-linear automatic control problem [18]: the system's input are the requirements on composition and motion, while the internal state of the system is defined by the camera parameters — e.g. position and rotation. The first seminal works addressing automatic camera control according to this model [1,13,15] defined the concept of frame constraint and camera optimisation. These approaches require the designer to define a set of required frame properties which are then modelled either as an objective function to be maximised by the solver or as a set of constraints that the camera configuration must satisfy. These properties describe how the frame should look like in terms of object size, visibility and positioning.

Olivier et al. [15] modelled these properties — also known as frame constraints [1] — as a series of objective functions describing how much each property is satisfied by a certain camera configuration. The different objective functions are combined linearly to produce a single objective function which can be optimised either in a static environment or in a dynamic one. A variety of algorithms have been employed in the two cases including, among others, Genetic Algorithms [15, 17] and Particle Swarm Optimisation [6] for static scenes, and Hill Climbing [4] and Artificial Potential Fields [7] for real-time optimisation in dynamic scenes. The first two approaches are used to generate still images with specific composition characteristics, while the last two are designed to animate a camera in real-time interactive virtual environment — e.g. computer games.

Among other applications for automatic camera control emerged also the automatic generation of animated films or cinematographic game replays. Dominguez et al. [11] and Cheong et al. [8] investigated the process of automatically analysing a game log to generate a sequence of shot descriptions that can be used to visualise the actions recorded in the game log. Finding the best camera configurations that fit the shot description poses a slightly different problem than the previously described ones, making classical single objective approaches not suitable. The problem is an off-line dynamic optimisation problem, that requires to find a sequence of camera configurations that optimise a given set of requirements over time in a changing virtual environment.

Using a static single-objective optimisation approach per each frame would produce sequences of camera configurations with potentially very different parameters — i.e. the camera would be jumping from one position to a potentially very different one in one frame —; moreover, there would be no possibility to control the camera's dynamic behaviour to produce, for instance, static shots as the camera will always move to the next optimal position. A local search algorithm might reduce the jerkiness of the produce animation, guaranteeing a continuity from one solution to the next one; however, such an approach would not necessarily produce the best camera configurations and it is heavily dependent on the initial configuration.

In this article, we approach this problem as a dynamic multi-objective optimisation problem. Thanks to the diversity of the solutions that can be generated trough this approach, it is possible to produce hight quality camera solutions in dynamic environment, while having full control over the dynamic behaviour of the solution. This makes possible to generate from the same set of frame constraint, different types of shots — e.g static or dolly —. In the rest of the document, we explain the details of this approach and we showcase the advantages of such approach over the current state-of-the art.

3   Multi-Objective Camera Optimisation

Even for a static optimization problem with multiple objectives, a multi-objective approach would have an advantage over a single-objective, weighted approach: depending on the shape of the Pareto front (the set of all optimal compromises for which it is not possible to further improve in one objective without deteriorating), there are situations in which any weighted approach cannot reach the front at the position that is indicated by the concrete weights, while a multi-objective algorithm can do that.

But even if we do not experience such a situation, a multi-objective approach has its advantages: its solution set is well spread over all possible weightings, such that it should contain appropriate solutions even if the problem changes slightly. A single-objective algorithm would come up with good solutions for each concrete case, but even with the same weighting, if the front changes because the problem changes, these solutions would be in a different region of the objective space, and thus most likely also somewhere else in the decision space. This would severely hamper transferability: we cannot find a good compromise solution that works well for all the points in time of a dynamic setting.

It is our basic assumption that the spread of the multi-objective result set allows for easier detection of such transferable solutions which work quite well for all time steps of a dynamic problem than the highly specialized result sets of weighted single-objective optimization runs. The results of the case study that is presented in the next section will show if this is indeed the case. Of course, the multi-objective approach also has a disadvantage because spreading a population over a Pareto front shall be more costly than approaching just a single point on the front. However, in an offline setting as the one we treat here this disadvantage should not be too much of a problem, as there is no realtime constraint that enforces providing a solution hastily. Note that the difference between both approaches is a principle one: letting the single-objective approach run longer does not help because we may get a little bit nearer to the front, but still our best solutions would all be very similar.

In the following, we will in short explain the multi-objective algorithm we employ and then fix a criterion that enables assessing the quality of a single solution over multiple time steps, which is by nature a multi-objective measuring problem.

Our algorithm of choice is the SMS-EMOA [2], because it is known to deal well with a higher number of objectives (more than 3), and usually outperforms older approaches as the NSGA-II [10] on these settings. However, these two algorithms are conceptually not much different, we can still use the variation operators of the NSGA-II[1].

The striking differences are that a) the SMS-EMOA uses the dominated hypervolume within its selection step, and that b) only one solution is generated in every iteration and the worst is removed. This is more greedy than for the NSGA-II, but it has been shown that this leads to a false local optimum (of the multi-objective problem) only in very rare, hard to construct cases (see [3]). The hypervolume is based on the objective value differences to a fixed (bad) reference point.

Constraints can be added in a straightforward way into the algorithm, we follow the approach of a modified selection scheme as utilized in [20]: search points within infeasible regions get a penalty that resembles the distance to the next feasible region. During the selection phase, individuals that carry the highest penalties are always removed first, disregarding the quality of their other

---

[1] This refers to the *simulated binary crossover* (SBX) and *polynomial mutation* (PM) operators from [10] with (near) default parameter values of $\eta_c = 20$ and $\eta_m = 15$.

objective values. We therefore never remove a valid individual in the presence of an invalid one.

If we want to detect which of a given set of solutions is most suitable over multiple time steps and thus multiple slightly different problems, we need to define a measure and base it on a multi-objective notion. It is unlikely to find a solution that is near to specific points that are selected from different fronts by a weighting if the fronts themselves move. Thus, we relax this requirement and strive for single points that are at least very near to all fronts, regardless of which region of the front they approximate. So they are at least near optimal in some sense, even if not optimal concerning the given weighting. Our measure is related to the generational distance as defined in [21], although this was intended to assess the quality of complete populations (front approximations) and not single points. Also see [19] for a list of other frequently used measures in the multi-objective context.

At first, we need a (not necessarily optimal) reference front for every problem instance (time step) that is considered. By definition, none of the contained solutions can dominate any other.[2] For a given test point and a given front, we find all members of the reference front that dominate it or are dominated (note that a point can either dominate or be dominated by one or multiple points of the reference front, but not both). Points that are incomparable (neither dominated nor dominate) are assigned a value of 0. If the test point dominates some points, we choose the one of them with the highest Manhattan distance (added differences per objective) and assign to it the negative value of this distance. If it is dominated, we do the same but with a positive value. Then, we iterate over the reference fronts and sum up the resulting values. This criterion is to be minimized: a value of 0 means that it is situated on all reference fronts, a negative value that it is on average better than the fronts, and a positive value means that it is on average worse than the fronts.

Note that by applying such measure, we virtually create a higher dimensional problem: if we have 5 objectives per front and 5 time steps, the resulting problem would have 25 dimensions. In principle, one could try to directly achieve a good solution by solving this 25 dimensional problem. However, present multi-objective algorithms are not at all good at working in such a setting, and it is not very likely that alternatives will emerge soon.

4   Case Study

The objective of this article is to investigate the applicability of the multi-objective optimisation to the automatic generation of cinematics. Therefore, inspired by the article by Dominguez at al. [11] on automatic generation of game replays, we employ an instance of this problem to evaluate the advantages and disadvantages of our approach. In this case-study, we have modified an existing

---

[2] A point dominates another in the objective space if it at least as good as the second point in all objectives and better in at least one.

action game called Angry Bots[3], so that we could log all the actions and position of the 3D element during a game session and we could replay these using a custom view-point. The game used in this study is an action/shooter game, in which the player controls a humanoid avatar and must explore a science fiction dungeon while been attacked by various forms for enemies. The player can move around the area and shoot at the enemies.

We recorded a short 5 seconds sequence, in which the player is approached by an enemy (both can be seen in Fig.1j). The objectives that the algorithms have to optimise correspond to the satisfaction of the following requirements for the camera:

- Full visibility for the avatar.
- Full visibility for the enemy.
- The enemy should be viewed from the back — i.e. the vantage angle should be equal to 180° horizontally and 0° vertically.
- The enemy should cover half of the screen — i.e. the projection size should be equal to 0.5.
- The enemy should be portrayed in the bottom left corner of the screen — i.e. the frame position should be equal to 0.3 both horizontally and vertically.

Each requirement has a satisfaction value that depends on the comera configuration picked as solutions. Each of these satisfaction values is defined between 0 (completely satisfied) and 1 (completely unsatisfied), and corrispond to and objective function which has to be minimised. For a fully detailed description of the objective function corresponding to each of these requerements, please refer to [5].

On this short game log, we have applied a multi-objective approach based on SMS-EMOA and a single-objective approach based on a standard genetic algorithm to produce a static and a follow version of the shot. In a static shot, the camera does not move for the whole shot sequence, while in a follow shot the camera moves to keep close track of the subjects on the screen.

While the GA employs elitism selection, a mutation rate of 0.5, and a crossover rate of 0.8, both algorithms (SMS-EMOA mutation/crossover parameters were given in sec. 3) run with a population of 50 individuals. The GA is allowed to run 2000 generations, summing up to 10^5 evaluations, and the SMS-EMOA runs up to 50000 evaluations but many more generations (producing only one new individual per generation). While the multi-objective approach uses the 5 objectives given above in their original form, the GA equally weights them and thus optimizes their mean value. However, for the visibility objectives, we constrained the SMS-EMOA in a way that values worse than 0.9 (0 being optimal) for these two objectives were regarded as infeasible. Not doing so would mean that we encourage the algorithm to also search for solutions were avatar or enemy or both are not visible at all, which is clearly undesired. The reference point for the SMS-EMOA was set to $(1, 1, 1, 1, 1)$, which means that the maximal hypervolume measure value is 1, and this would be attained by a single best solution that resides at $(0, 0, 0, 0, 0)$, meaning that it is optimal in all objectives.

---

[3] Unity Technologies - http://unity3d.com/gallery/demos/live-demos#angrybots

4.1   Optimal Solution Difference Estimation

At first we are interested in seeing how different the optimal solutions over the whole sequence of 5 seconds actually are. As the front approximation obtained by means of a multi-objective approach contain much more information on a problem instance than the end population of a single-objective algorithm (as it tends to converge to a very small region of the search space), we ran the SMS-EMOA 10 times on the start time (0 seconds) and re-evaluated the final populations (which contain very different, but in the Pareto sense near optimal solutions) over the successive time steps after 1, 2, 3, and 4 seconds. The S-metric (hypervolume) measures degrade from 0.954 to 0.634, 0.299, 0.163, and 0.074. We deduce that the problem instances at the different time steps are quite different, and that good solutions for time 0 are probably quite bad for the last time steps. We can also state that the obtained final fronts usually contained between 40 and 50 individuals (50 being the theoretical maximum, the whole population is spread over the Pareto front). This means that the 5 different objectives are at least partly in conflict (not necessarily all combinations of them), and that it is highly unlikely that a solution that achieves the optimum for all 5 objectives exists.

4.2   Static and Follow Shot Comparison

We now embark on numerically and visually comparing the results of the single- and multi-objective approach for the static and follow shot. Such a comparison is not trivial, because the two approaches have very different properties concerning the provided solution set: while the MO-approach generates a whole population of different solutions in every run, the GA comes up with only one and slight variations of it. Selection of a suitable solution thus is no issue for the GA, but it is for the SMS-EMOA. Thus, in addition to comparing the results of one MO run and one GA run (each repeated for the 5 time steps), we also have a look at the behavior of the single-objective approach if run 10 times (50 runs altogether), taking only the best obtained solution for each time step into account. This should on the one hand make the results more valuable from a statistical viewpoint, and on the other hand allow conclusions concerning the achievable improvement if for the single-objective approach also a larger pool of solutions exists.

The considered performance measure for both shot types is the *average best fitness value* (ABFV), which here resembles sum of the fitness values over the 5 objectives, averaged over the 5 time steps. For the static shot, only one solution is selected and the average is computed over this single solution. For the follow shot, we select the best solution returned for each time step on the GA side, and the best (in terms of averaged objectives) solution returned by the SMS-EMOA for the first time step, and the subsequently nearest solutions contained in the fronts for the next time steps.

The results of the comparison are displayed in table 1, also containing the variance over the 10 GA runs as last column. The corresponding screenshots for

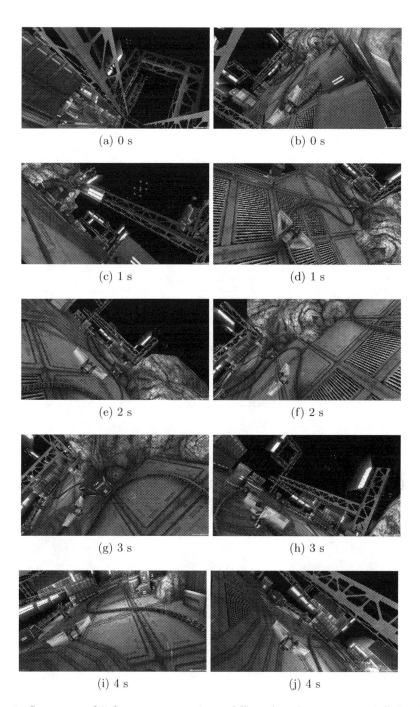

Fig. 1. Sequences of 5 frames representing a follow shot. Images a,c,e,g,i (left side) are produced using single-objective approach, while images b,d,f,h,j (right side) are produced with a multi-objective approach.

Table 1. Average objective values (ABFV) for the two approaches, static and follow shot

shot	MO	GA best	GA average	GA avg. variance
static	0.849	1.031	1.827	0.146
follow	0.466	0.810	1.341	0.557

the follow shot are provided in figure 1. We can state that the multi-objective approach leads to better results than the single-objective one on the average, and even if only the best GA solution from 10 runs is considered.

For the static shot, the visual difference is not really perceivable, it is therefore not depicted. In the follow shot, the solutions provided by the single objective are often very different, which is a big disadvantage for a video (meaning that the camera would need to make fast movements across very different solutions). This gets especially clear while looking at the first 3 frames, where the scene is shot from pretty different angles.

The multi objective approach solves this problem, because there is a large set of near-optimal but different solutions to choose from, and we can reason in objective space level. It is thus possible to find a set of solutions with minimal objective space distance, corresponding to small visual differences. In consequence, this makes the shot sequence much more smooth. Whereas the single-objective approach may lead to a video with jumpy and unsteady camera, the multi-objective approach enables a much more smooth and coherent camera positioning.

4.3   Front Approximation Distance Comparison

As a last test, we would like to know how far the single solutions generated in 10 × 5 GA runs and 5 SMS-EMOA runs are located from the Pareto front approximations obtained by the SMS-EMOA runs (as an average over the time steps). This tells us something about the stability of single solutions over the time steps, and also about the potential improvements that can be made (if we obtain solutions below the front). As measure, we employ the average Manhattan distance to the most dominating/dominated point as laid out in section 3. This comparison is again difficult to conduct fairly, as the MO algorithm provides many solutions per run and the GA only one. The overall number of solutions considered is 220 for the SMS-EMOA, and 50 for the GA.

The results are contained in table 2 and show that the GA sometimes achieves very good solutions, but mostly converges to much worse solutions than the MO approach. The best overall solution is provided by one GA run and is slightly better than the best MO generated one. As can be guessed from the high standard deviation, it is good on average because it gets below the front for at least one time step (actually, it does so for 2 time steps). However, if we review the average GA performance (averaged over each of the 10 run groups, each

Table 2. Average front distance (Manhattan) and averaged distance standard deviations over the 5 time steps for the GA and SMS-EMOA approaches

MO	MO sd	GA best	GA best sd	GA average	GA avg. sd
3.444	0.438	2.876	1.159	6.445	0.453

containing 5 runs over the different time steps), we recognize that such an event rarely happens. On average, the best GA solution is about a factor 2 farther apart from the consecutive fronts than the best MO solution (and consistently so because the average standard deviation is much lower).

We can state that in terms of average distance to the 5 consecutive time step fronts, the GA is not very stable: it may sometimes come up with very good solutions, but usually remains far from the front. However, the single very good GA solution shows that the fronts themselves are far from optimal, it should be possible to improve them, e.g., by tuning the parameters of the SMS-EMOA. This may also be done for the GA of course, but again, we deduce that the big advantage of the MO approach lies in the multitude of solutions generated per run. There seems to be a good chance that we find a suitable solution for very different applications within the delivered Pareto front approximation.

5   Conclusion

We have tested the multi-objective approach to automated camera positioning proposed in this paper for different shot types and have also conducted 2 additional tests in order to find out a) how complete Pareto front approximations generated for one time step degrade for subsequent time steps of a dynamic scene, and b) what solution quality can be expected for multiple single-objective runs in relation to the Pareto front approximations generated by our multi-objective approach.

As this it a first study in the direction of automated generation of dynamic shots for dynamic scenes, it is clear that the performance of both approaches can be improved, e.g. by tuning or the selection of more suitable algorithms (as the CMA-ES as a most capable algorithm for the single-objective case) or search operators. However, the tackled problem is multi-objective even if only one time step is considered, and it gets only higher-dimensional (in objective space) for multiple time steps. Therefore, applying a multi-objective algorithm seems most appropriate, and indeed it shows that the high number of good but different solutions obtained from running a multi-objective algorithm pays off: it is much more likely to find suitable solutions for multiple purposes in the result set of a multi-objective algorithm than to do so even for several runs of a single-objective algorithm (which would be more costly in terms of computation time).

This work shall be extended in various ways: our implementation of different types of shots is preliminary, we ought to find better heuristics to select the most appropriate solutions, and also describe other types of shots and conduct more rigorous tests on more and different scenes. However, the key advantage of the proposed multi-objective approach is that we can reason on the fronts and in the objective space. Thus we can make informed choices when picking solutions for different shots.

References

1. Bares, W.H., McDermott, S., Boudreaux, C., Thainimit, S.: Virtual 3D camera composition from frame constraints. In: ACM Multimedia, pp. 177–186. ACM Press, Marina del Rey (2000)
2. Beume, N., Naujoks, B., Emmerich, M.: SMS-EMOA: Multiobjective selection based on dominated hypervolume. European Journal of Operational Research **181**(3), 1653–1669 (2007)
3. Beume, N., Naujoks, B., Preuss, M., Rudolph, G., Wagner, T.: Effects of 1-Greedy-Metric-Selection on Innumerably Large Pareto Fronts. In: Ehrgott, M., Fonseca, C.M., Gandibleux, X., Hao, J.-K., Sevaux, M. (eds.) EMO 2009. LNCS, vol. 5467, pp. 21–35. Springer, Heidelberg (2009)
4. Bourne, O., Sattar, A., Goodwin, S.: A Constraint-Based Autonomous 3D Camera System. Journal of Constraints **13**(1–2), 180–205 (2008)
5. Burelli, P.: Interactive Virtual Cinematography. PhD thesis, IT University of Copenhagen (2012)
6. Burelli, P., Di Gaspero, L., Ermetici, A., Ranon, R.: Virtual Camera Composition with Particle Swarm Optimization. In: Butz, A., Fisher, B., Krüger, A., Olivier, P., Christie, M. (eds.) SG 2008. LNCS, vol. 5166, pp. 130–141. Springer, Heidelberg (2008)
7. Burelli, P., Jhala, A.: Dynamic Artificial Potential Fields for Autonomous Camera Control. In: AAAI Conference on Artificial Intelligence in Interactive Digitale Entertainment Conference. AAAI, Palo Alto (2009)
8. Cheong, Y.-G., Jhala, A., Bae, B.-C., Young, R.M.: Automatically Generating Summary Visualizations from Game Logs. In: AAAI Conference on Artificial Intelligence in Interactive Digitale Entertainment, pp. 167–172 (2008)
9. Christie, M., Olivier, P., Normand, J.-M.: Camera Control in Computer Graphics. Computer Graphics Forum **27**, 2197–2218 (2008)
10. Deb, R., Pratap, R., Agarwal, S.: A fast and elitist multi-objective genetic algorithm: NSGA-II. IEEE Trans. on Evolutionary Computation **6**(8) (2002)
11. Dominguez, M., Young, R.M., Roller, S.: Design and Evaluation of Afterthought, A System that Automatically Creates Highlight Cinematics for 3D Games. In: AAAI Conference on Artificial Intelligence in Interactive Digitale Entertainment (2011)
12. Drucker, S.M., Zeltzer, D.: Intelligent camera control in a virtual environment. In: Graphics Interface, pp. 190–199 (1994)
13. Jardillier, F., Languénou, E.: Screen-Space Constraints for Camera Movements: the Virtual Cameraman. Computer Graphics Forum **17**(3), 175–186 (1998)
14. Lowood, H.: High-performance play: The making of machinima. Journal of Media Practice **7**(1), 25–42 (2006)
15. Olivier, P., Halper, N., Pickering, J., Luna, P.: Visual Composition as Optimisation. In: Artificial Intelligence and Simulation of Behaviour (1999)
16. Phillips, C.B., Badler, N.I., Granieri, J.: Automatic viewing control for 3D direct manipulation. In: ACM SIGGRAPH Symposium on Interactive 3D Graphics, pp. 71–74. ACM Press, Cambridge (1992)

17. Pickering, J.: Intelligent Camera Planning for Computer Graphics. PhD thesis, University of York (2002)
18. Pontriagin, L.S.: Mathematical Theory of Optimal Processes. Interscience Publishers (1962)
19. Sarker, R., Coello, C.A.C.: Assessment methodologies for multiobjective evolutionary algorithms. In: Evolutionary Optimization. International Series in Operations Research & Management Science, vol. 48, pp. 177–195. Springer, US (2002)
20. Togelius, J., Preuss, M., Beume, N., Wessing, S., Hagelbäck, J., Yannakakis, G.N., Grappiolo, C.: Controllable procedural map generation via multiobjective evolution. Genetic Programming and Evolvable Machines **14**(2), 245–277 (2013)
21. Van Veldhuizen, D.A., Lamont, G.B.: Evolutionary computation and convergence to a pareto front. In: Koza, J.R. (ed.) Late Breaking Papers at the Genetic Programming 1998 Conference. Stanford University Bookstore (1998)
22. Ware, C., Osborne, S.: Exploration and virtual camera control in virtual three dimensional environments. ACM SIGGRAPH **24**(2), 175–183 (1990)

Co-Evolutionary Optimization of Autonomous Agents in a Real-Time Strategy Game

Antonio Fernández-Ares[✉], Antonio M. Mora, Maribel García-Arenas,
Juan Julián Merelo Guervós, Pablo García-Sánchez, and Pedro A. Castillo

Departamento de Arquitectura y Tecnología de Computadores,
Universidad de Granada, Granada, Spain
antares.es@gmail.com,
{amorag,mgarenas,jmerelo,pgarcia,pedro}@geneura.ugr.es

Abstract. This paper presents an approach based in an evolutionary algorithm, aimed to improve the behavioral parameters which guide the actions of an autonomous agent (bot) inside the real-time strategy game, Planet Wars. The work describes a co-evolutionary implementation of a previously presented method GeneBot, which yielded successful results, but focused in 4vs matches this time. Thus, there have been analyzed the effects of considering several individuals to be evolved (improved) at the same time in the algorithm, along with the use of three different fitness functions measuring the goodness of each bot in the evaluation. They are based in turns and position, and also in mathematical computations of linear regression and area regarding the number of ships belonging to the bot/individual to be evaluated. In addition, the variance of using an evolutionary algorithm with and without previous knowledge in the co-evolution phase is also studied, i.e., respectively using specific rivals to perform the evaluation, or just considering to this end individuals in the population being evolved. The aim of these co-evolutionary approaches are mainly two: first, reduce the computational time; and second find a robust fitness function to be used in the generation of evolutionary bots optimized for 4vs battles.

1 Introduction

Planet Wars is a very famous Real-Time Strategy game (RTS), introduced in Google AI Challenge 2010[1] as a framework where the contenders could create their own autonomous players (bots). A match in the game takes place on a map that contains several planets (neutral, enemies' or owned), having everyone an associated growth rate and number of hosted ships. The aim of the game is to defeat all the ships in the opponent's planets. At the end of the match, the winner is the player that remains alive, or that which owns more ships if more than one survives (a limit of turns is reached). This is a pseudo-turn-based game, rather than a real-time one, since it considers one second micro-turns for the bots decide their next set of actions, which then happen at the same simulated time.

---

[1] http://planetwars.aichallenge.org/

© Springer-Verlag Berlin Heidelberg 2014
A.I. Esparcia-Alcázar et al. (Eds.): EvoApplications 2014, LNCS 8602, pp. 374–385, 2014.
DOI: 10.1007/978-3-662-45523-4_31

Our first approach in this field was the so-called GeneBot [1], which is an evolutionary approach for the improvement of a bot's decision engine. It consists in a set of parametrised rules that model the behaviour of the bot, and which was defined by an expert human player. Then, a Genetic Algorithm (GA) was applied offline (not during the game) for evolving these parameters.

GeneBot was designed and optimized for 1 vs 1 battles, using a turn-based fitness function. It evaluated all the individuals in the population by playing five different matches (in five different maps) against a sparring bot provided by the competition, trying to avoid with these repetitions the noisy factor present in this problems (videogames) [2].

Thus, the fitness value for an individual could dramatically vary in different matches, because it depends on the pseudo-stochastic opponent's actions, and also on its own non-deterministic decisions.

In this paper, the aim is to face 4vs matches, trying to define an evolutionary approach which improves the cited behavioural engine (set of rules) to this type of play. Thus, a co-evolutionary method has been proposed.

Co-evolutionary algorithms (CEA) [3] are those which consider different groups of potential solutions (individuals) evolving inside an environment, sometimes interacting with it, and at the same time, being affected by it. Every set of individuals which interact with the environment in the same way is called a *specie*. In CEAs several species (usually two) are able to live and evolve in the same environment grouped in populations.

The fitness of the individuals is usually calculated using some individuals of other populations, according to the dependencies between species (interactions among populations). Depending on these interactions the CEAs are classified in:

– *Competitive co-evolutionary algorithms* [4], where the fitness of an individual depends on competition with other individuals from other species.
– *Cooperative co-evolutionary algorithms* [5], where the aim is to find individuals from which better environment can be constructed. The fitness of an individual depends on its ability to cooperate in solving the target problem with individuals from other species.

In this work, both types have been implemented since the evolution is performed following two different shapes for the four contenders in every match (in the evaluation step): on one approach two of the contenders are individuals being evolved at a specific generation, and the other two opponents with a fixed Artificial Intelligence (AI) engine. On the other approach, four different players corresponding to four individuals being evolved are considered. These are respectively baptised as *previously knowledge-based* approach and *non-previously-knowledge-based* one. So, according to the previous taxonomy, both algorithms are competitive in the fitness calculation step and cooperative regarding the problem solving (find the best agents for this type of battles).The aim of using co-evolution is mainly to reduce the computational time, since a set of individuals are evaluated at a time (two or four, depending on the approach).

Moreover, three different fitness functions are also tested in the work, having three different types: one based in the bot's position and number of turns;

another one based in the computation of a linear regression based on the percentage of ships with respect to the total; and the last calculating the integral of the function which represents these numbers.

Several experiments have been conducted analyzing the robustness of the different fitness functions, and the influence and performance of the previous knowledge consideration (or not) in the evolution.

2   State of the Art

Evolutionary Computation (EC) has been widely applied in the videogames area, including the RTS games, in different issues, such as: automated tactics generation [6], decision making improvement [7], or parameter optimisation in behavioural engines [9]. This work is enclosed in the latter category, since it considers a set of rules, initially defined by an expert, which model a bot's AI in the RTS Planet Wars. These rules are optimised regarding the set of parameters which determine how the bot behaves. This kind of improvement was previously performed by the authors by means of off-line (before the game) Evolutionary Algorithms [1,8]. In the present paper the optimisation have been performed using a Co-Evolutionary approach.

Co-Evolutionary Algorithms (CEAs) have been previously used in this scope, initially regarding puzzle and board games such as Backgammon [10], or Go [11]. The first work proposed a very simple hillclimbing algorithm to evolve a population of neural networks, playing among them as rivals, in a competitive co-evolutionary approach. The latter paper presented a co-evolutionary learning approach which performed well once the EA was correctly tuned, moreover, this method yields better players to solve small Go boards since every individual is evaluated against a diverse population of rivals. In the same line, there are some other works in the card games area, such as [12], aimed to create Poker agents, considering a co-evolution process in which the players are part of the learning process. This meant a difficult process to get robust strategies, due to the variation in opponents, but the results shown to fit with some recommended strategies according experts. The aim of the present work is to conduct a study implementing a similar co-evolutionary approach, being competitive in the fitness calculation, but cooperative since all the opponents are also part of the same learning process (same population).

In recent years, this type of EAs has been also applied to videogames, enclosed in the Computational Intelligence (CI) branch of AI. For instance Togelius et al. [13] studied the co-evolution effects of some populations in car racing controllers, comparing the performance of a single population against various, implementing both generational and a steady-state approaches. Avery and Michalewicz introduced in [14] a co-evolutionary algorithm (for the game TEMPO) which used humans as rivals for the individuals in the evolutionary process. Cook et al. [15] presented a cooperative co-evolutionary approach for the automated design of levels in simple platform games. And recently Cardona et al. [16] studied the performance of a competitive algorithm for the simultaneous evolution of controllers to both Ms. PacMan and the Ghost Team which has to chase her.

Regarding the RTS scope, there are also several related works, such as the study by Livingstone [17], who compared several AI-modelling approaches for RTS games, and proposed a framework to create new models by means of co-evolutionary methods. He considered two levels of learning in a hierarchical AI model (inside an own-created RTS), evolving at the same time different partners in different strategic levels, so it was a cooperative approach. It is different to the one proposed here, since in the present work the co-evolution occurs at the same level for all the individuals. The work by Smith et al. [18] presents an analysis on how a co-evolutionary algorithm can be used for improving students' playing tactics in RTS games. Other authors proposed using co-evolution for evolving team tactics [19]. However, the problem is how tactics are constrained and parametrised and how the overall score is computed. Nogueira et al. [20] considered in a recent publication the use of a Hall of Fame as a set of rivals (in the evaluation function) inside a co-evolutionary algorithm to create autonomous agents for the RTS RobotWars. This is an approach based in a self-learning algorithm as the one we are proposing, but focused in a subset of individuals (the elite) which can have a negative effect in the generalisation factor or the bots' knowledge. We have tested our method considering different rivals, in different studies. One of them is a previously optimized (and good-performing) bot, in order to deal with the so-called previous knowledge (Section 3.1).

3   Cooperative and Competitive Evolution: Co-Bots

There are two types of co-evolution attending to the interaction between the individuals in the population: cooperative and competitive. In this paper, it is described a co-evolutionary algorithm that considers both sides.

Thus, on the one hand, there are simulated 4 on 4 battles where several bots fight for the same goal: win the battle. That means that every bot competes against each other, or in EA-based concepts, every individual in the population competes for perpetuating its species. On the other hand, the cooperative factor arises because every 4 on 4 battle is *all versus all*, so a single individual could have assistance from others for *killing* a (temporary) common rival, since at the end, only one must remain (the winner).

In addition, in the GA the individuals are sharing *knowledge*, because they are *living* (and fighting) together. If the population is improved, the new off-spring *born* of the previous parents will behave better.

One of the main problems of using EAs for training bots in this problem is the huge amount of computational time needed for the evaluation, since it consists in a simulation of several complete battles (in five different and representative maps), moreover a reevaluation process will be performed in every generation (of every individual). The aim of both processes is dealing with the noisy nature of the fitness function due to the pseudo-stochasticity of the problem [2].

Theoretically, the use of a co-evolutionary approach would allow to reduce the number of simulations needed, because the individuals are evaluated in *groups*.

For instance, in a population of 100, the use of co-evolution considering two individuals per evaluation would reduce the number of evaluations in a half.

We will test two different approaches, considering both *4 bots simulations* and *2 bots simulations*. The use of two or four individuals of the population in the experiments depends respectively on the use (or not) of previous knowledge.

3.1   Previous Knowledge vs Auto-Generated Knowledge

In this work we understand as previous knowledge the consideration of a rival evolved in a precedent work [1], *GeneBot*, which proved to be a very competent rival in 1 on 1 battles. This bot will be used as a part of the evaluation process in 4vs battles. The aim is to study the influence of this so-called 'previous knowledge' in the performance of the proposed Co-Evolutionary Genetic Algorithm (Co-GA). To this end, several experiments have been conducted considering an approach in which two of the rivals are GeneBots, and some others in which all the rivals are individuals of the population being evolved. These are:

- **Co-evolution with Previous Knowledge:** In this case, battles between two individuals of the population versus two of the best bots (GeneBots) have been simulated in the evaluation process. It is expected that the Co-Bots are able to learn the basis of the GeneBots, and improve for be better rivals in 4 on 4 battles. To this end the algorithm rewards bots that, at least, win in a battle against GeneBots. Since the approach will evaluate Co-Bots in groups of two, the running time of this approach, will not be reduced in a great factor during the training phase of the bots.
- **Co-evolution with Auto-generated Knowledge:** In this case, battles with four individuals of the population have been tested. For this approach the knowledge is included into the individual when it fights in previous battles, i.e., the rivals are included in the learning process. In this approach a considerable running time reduction with respect to the previous one is expected, because the number of evaluations has been reduced to the half.

3.2   Fitness Functions

In previous works, a bot was evaluated always versus the same bot (a reference bot), several times (in different maps). The fitness function is defined depending of the result of the battle (if the bot wins all its battles or loses in any of them) and the number of turns needed for ending the game. For two bots, A and B the fitness was defined as Fig. 1a shows.

This fitness works well for 1vs1, but in this work we have redefined it for 4vs matches. Moreover two additional evaluation functions have been proposed.

Fitness Based in Position and Turns. This fitness is the natural evolution of the previous one, applied to 4 bots battles. Again, the evaluations are done in several maps. In this case, both the position (1th to 4th) of the bot in the battle, and the number of turns needed, are included into the formula.

We define the term *ferocity*, regarding a bot that wins all its battles. This factor is included in the fitness computation as the sum of turns the bot has

```
A, B ∈ Population
if A WINs always then
    if B LOSEs some battle then
        A is better than B
    else if A take less turns than B then
        A is better than B
    else
        B is better than A
    end if
else
    if B WINs always then
        B is better than A
    else if A take less turns than B then
        B is better than A
    else
        A is better than B
    end if
end if
```

(a) Fitness considered in 1 vs 1 battles

```
A, B ∈ Population
if A average position < B average position then
    A is better than B
else if A average position > B average position then
    B is better than A
else
    if A,B is always 1^th then
        if A take less turns than B then
            A is better than B
        else
            B is better than A
        end if
    else
        if A take less turns than B then
            B is better than A
        else
            A is better than B
        end if
    end if
end if
```

(b) Fitness considered in 4vs battles

Fig. 1. Fitness functions based in turns and positions

needed to win. This sum is considered to select the best bot when more than one wins all its battles, since a bot that wins in less turns is better than other that wins needing more. In some other cases, the sum of turns is called *sturdy*, and opposite to the *ferocity*, it is desirable a bot that take more turns in being defeated. In Fig. 1b there is a formal definition of this fitness.

In this fitness, we are only interested in the final result (position and number of turns). We do not include in the analysis how the bot has reached them. The problem of this function is that the consideration of two different terms makes it difficult the comparison between different evaluations. In order to let easier comparisons two other fitness functions have been defined.

Both of them are based in the percentage of ships belonging to each player in every turn. They are normalized considering the total number of ships in the game for that turn (including neutrals ships in neutral planets). For each player, we have a different *cloud* of ships.

Below, are described the two alternatives to deal with this cloud of points for the fitness function: the use of slopes and areas.

Fitness Based in Slope. For this fitness, a square regression analysis is computed in order to transform the cloud of points into a simple line. The line is represented as $y = \alpha \times x + \beta$, where α and β are calculated as shown in Equations 1 and 2, computing a least squares regression. For every bot in the simulation we calculate α and (*slope*). This *slope* is the fitness of every bot for that simulation.

$$\alpha = \frac{\sum_{i=1}^{n}(X_i - \bar{X}_i)(Y_i - \bar{Y}_i)}{\sum_{i=1}^{n}(X_i - \bar{X}_i)^2} \tag{1}$$

$$\beta = \bar{Y} - \alpha\bar{X} \tag{2}$$

Theoretical maximum and minimum values are set for this fitness. An optimum bot that wins in the first turn, has an ideal slope of 1, so this is the maximum value of our fitness. On the other hand, a bot that loses in the first turn, has a slope of -1. Thus, if we calculate the *slope*, we know if the bot

$WINs$ ($slope > 0$) or $LOSEs$ $slope < 0$. The values of the different battles are summed to compute the global $slope$. Then, the bot with the highest value will be the best is each turn or battle.

3.3 Fitness Based in Area

In this case, the integral of the curve of the bot's live-line is used for calculating the area that is 'covered' by the fitness cloud of points (see Equation 3). This $area$ is normalized considering the number of turns, and thus it represents the average percentage of ships during the battle for each player.

$$area = \frac{\int_0^t \% ships(x)dx}{t} \tag{3}$$

As in previous case, maximum and minimum values has been set for this fitness. If an optimal bot wins in the first turn, the area of each live-line is close to 1, so this is the maximum value of the fitness. Otherwise, if a bot loses in the first turn, its live-line area is close to 0. In this case, we do not extract additional about which bot wins the battle, because the area of the live-line is not related with the winner of the battle. Thus, we are losing some information.

4   Experiments and Results

Several experiments have been conducted in order to study different issues of the proposed approaches, but having in mind that the main objective is the improvement of bots using a co-evolutionary algorithm. The set of parameters considered in the Co-GA are: 100 individuals, 200 generations, 0.6 crossover prob., 0.1 mutation prob., 20 elitism, and 2-tournament size. For each one of the presented approaches (combinations of fitness functions and knowledge-related methods), ten executions of the Co-GA have been performed.

As a first set of results, the average time consumed in the run of every generation is plotted in Fig. 2. The values are, as expected, reduced in a half in the previous knowledge approach (2 individuals per evaluation), and in 3/4 in the auto-generated knowledge (4 individuals per evaluation). This could be non-surprising results, but there should be considered than the original method evaluated 1vs1 battles, which are usually finished in less time than 4vs matches.

The second analysis concerns the fitness evolution. To this end the best, worst, median and average (with standard deviation) fitness values are studied. In Fig. 3 it can be seen the corresponding values to the best execution in every case, i.e. that of the 10 runs which obtained the considered as the best bot.

In auto-generated knowledge fitness (Fig. 3b) it can be observed an homogeneous distribution throughout the generations, because the individuals are learning all of all, so the differences among them remain equal (in some limits) along the whole evolutionary process. That figure shows a high variability (or oscillations) in the best fitness graph, due to the rivals (in evaluation) are included in the learning process, so the population is not adapted to a common behavioural

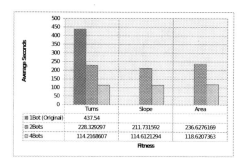

Fig. 2. Average time per generation (secs)

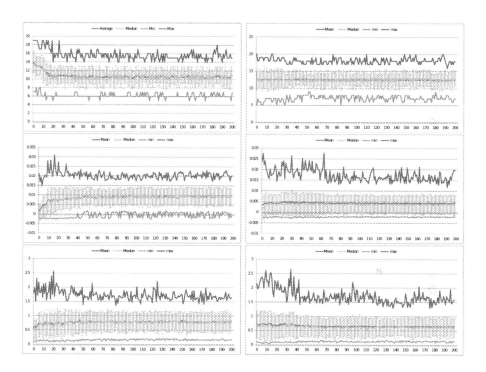

(a) Methods with previous knowledge: (b) Methods with auto-generated knowl-
from top to down Turns/Position, Slope edge: from top to down Turns/Position,
and Area   Slope and Area

Fig. 3. Best, worst, average, median and Std.Dev for fitness in every generation

pattern, but every individual must learn to compete against (potentially) N-1
different bots. This means that the best individual varies frequently.

In the case of previously knowledge fitness (Fig. 3a), it can be noticed a
slight improvement, on the average fitness in the first generations. This happens
because more and more individuals are able to beat the bots considered as rivals

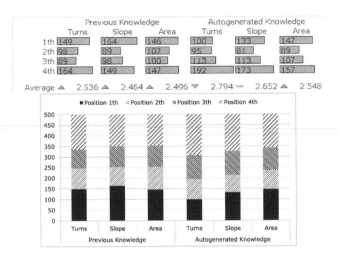

Fig. 4. Results (positions) of 500 4vs battles between 3 GeneBots and a bot per each method

(GeneBots), an expected result. In addition, and due to this behavioural pattern to fight with, the evolution of the best fitness presents less variations.

Anyway, the noisy nature of the fitness function due to the problem itself [2], remains here and this means that traditional evolution graphs (fitness improvement with slight variations along generations) could not be obtained.

Next a comparison between the methods has been performed. The fitness computation function is different for each method, so they can not be directly compared (as they have different magnitudes). So it is necessary to perform simulations in a wide range of maps and enemies to study how good they are.

First a fool bot (GoogleBot) has been chosen to simulate 400 battles. In these battles, every bot obtained by Co-GA has to fight against 3 of these bots. The results have been excellent, with 100% of victories of the Co-Bots against them.

Then, a tough set of rivals has been considered, being three copies of the best bot previously obtained in other work, namely three GeneBots. 500 battles against them have been simulated, and the results are shown in Fig. 4. The best average results are obtained for the Co-Bots obtained using previous knowledge, since they were trained to deal with at least two of them during the evolution. However, the scenario here is quite different since there is another GeneBot as rival. As a general result, in both cases, the worst performance is achieved considering turns/position based fitness.

To study whether the bots actually achieved by the turn-based fitness are really less competitive, we have conducted a simulation (3 vs 3) matching the three bots achieved by the three fitness methods using, separately per knowledge approach. Fig. 5a shows the results for each knowledge method. It is complemented with the summed results plotted in Fig. 5b, which shows the sum per

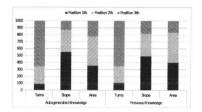

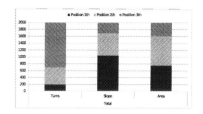

(a) Results (positions) per knowledge approach

(b) Total sum of results (same positions) per fitness method, considering both knowledge approches

Fig. 5. Results of 1000 3 vs 3 battles between the obtained bots

fitness method (for the two knowledge approaches). As it can be seen the bots obtained with the fitness based in turns/positions perform clearly worse than the others.

Finally, the top four of the yielded bots are tested in 500 battles between them. There is one bot per fitness function, without considering the turn-based ones (since they are worse). Fig. 6 shows how the bots have performed and their position in the battles. As it can be seen Slope-based Co-Bots are better than Area-based ones. Similarly, bots trained with previous knowledge, perform better than those with auto-generated knowledge.

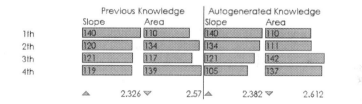

Fig. 6. Results (positions) of 500 4vs battles matching the four best bots obtained (one per approach)

5   Conclusions and Future Work

This paper presents some cooperative co-evolutionary approaches for improving autonomous agents for playing the RTS game Planet Wars. They are trained for 4 on 4 battles, considering two types of evaluation: based in previous knowledge (i.e. against a previously obtained bot), and with auto-generated knowledge (i.e. the rivals are included in the learning process). In addition three different fitness functions have been tested for each method: a position/turns based one, linear regression model and area computation, regarding the number of ships belonging to the bot/individual to be evaluated in the last cases.

The first remarkable result is the significant reduction of the training time needed, due to the use of co-evolution.

It has been shown that a position/turn-based fitness function is less effective for training than one based on the study of curve resources (ships in this paper), in co-evolutionary approaches. Regarding the two mathematical fitness, the one based on the slope has proven to be slightly better, possibly due to a better representation of the bots victories against losses. Another interesting result point to that the use of previous knowledge can make a difference, but not very significant. In the future it may be interesting to go deep in the study on the real influence of the previous knowledge.

Moreover this paper opens up new lines of research on the proposed problem. Such as the study of different ways for extracting knowledge from the population for co-evolution, for example the use of a Hall of Fame as proposed by the authors in [20], or the study of other mathematical fitness approximations. Regarding the co-evolution, it could be studied a competitive approach in which there could be different subpopulations devoted to improve different controllers for agents.

Acknowledgments. This paper has been partially funded by projects CANUBE (CEI2013-P-14) and ANYSELF (TIN2011-28627-C04-02). The authors would also like to thank the FEDER of European Union for financial support via project "Sistema de Información y Predicción de bajo coste y autónomo para conocer el Estado de las Carreteras en tiempo real mediante dispositivos distribuido" (SIPEsCa) of the "Programa Operativo FEDER de Andalucía 2007-2013".

References

1. Fernández-Ares, A., Mora, A.M., Merelo, J.J., García-Sánchez, P., Fernandes, C.: Optimizing player behavior in a real-time strategy game using evolutionary algorithms. In: IEEE Congress on Evolutionary Computation (CEC 2011), pp. 2017–2024 (2011)
2. Mora, A.M., Fernández-Ares, A., Merelo, J.J., García-Sánchez, P., Fernandes, C.M.: Effect of noisy fitness in real-time strategy games player behaviour optimisation using evolutionary algorithms. J. Comput. Sci. Technol. **27**(5), 1007–1023 (2012)
3. Paredis, J.: Coevolutionary computation. Artif. Life **2**(4), 355–375 (1995)
4. Rosin, C.D., Belew, R.K.: New methods for competitive coevolution. Evol. Comput. **5**(1), 1–29 (1997)
5. Potter, M.A., De Jong, K.A.: A cooperative coevolutionary approach to function optimization. In: Davidor, Y., Männer, Reinhard, Schwefel, Hans-Paul (eds.) PPSN 1994. LNCS, vol. 866, pp. 249–257. Springer, Heidelberg (1994)

6. Ponsen, M., Munoz-Avila, H., Spronck, P., Aha, D.W.: Automatically generating game tactics through evolutionary learning. AI Magazine **27**(3), 75–84 (2006)

7. Jang, S.H., Yoon, J.W., Cho, S.B.: Optimal strategy selection of non-player character on real time strategy game using a speciated evolutionary algorithm. In: Proceedings of the 5th IEEE Symposium on Computational Intelligence and Games (CIG 2009), pp. 75–79. IEEE Press, Piscataway (2009)

8. Fernández-Ares, A., García-Sánchez, P., Mora, A.M., Merelo, J.J.: Adaptive bots for real-time strategy games via map characterization. In: 2012 IEEE Conference on Computational Intelligence and Games, CIG 2012, pp. 417–721. IEEE (2012)

9. Fernández-Ares, A., Mora, A.M., Merelo, J.J., García-Sánchez, P., Fernandes, C.M.: Optimizing Strategy Parameters in a Game Bot. In: Cabestany, J., Rojas, I., Joya, G. (eds.) IWANN 2011, Part II. LNCS, vol. 6692, pp. 325–332. Springer, Heidelberg (2011)

10. Pollack, J.B., Blair, A.D.: Co-evolution in the successful learning of backgammon strategy. Mach. Learn. **32**, 225–240 (1998)

11. Runarsson, T.P., Lucas, S.M.: Co-evolution versus self-play temporal difference learning for acquiring position evaluation in smallboard go. IEEE Trans. Evol. Comput. **9**(6), 628–640 (2005)

12. Thompson, T., Levine, J., Wotherspoon, R.: Evolution of counter-strategies: Application of co-evolution to texas hold'em poker. In: IEEE Symposium on Computational Intelligence and Games (CIG 2008), pp. 16–22. IEEE (2008)

13. Togelius, J., Burrow, P., Lucas, S.M.: Multi-population competitive co-evolution of car racing controllers. In: IEEE Congress on Evolutionary Computation (CEC 2007), pp. 4043–4050 (2007)

14. Avery, P.M., Michalewicz, Z.: Adapting to human game play. In: IEEE Symposium on Computational Intelligence and Games (CIG 2008), pp. 8–15 (2008)

15. Cook, M., Colton, S., Gow, J.: Initial Results from Co-operative Co-evolution for Automated Platformer Design. In: Di Chio, C., et al. (eds.) EvoApplications 2012. LNCS, vol. 7248, pp. 194–203. Springer, Heidelberg (2012)

16. Cardona, A., Togelius, J., Nelson, M.: Competitive coevolution in Ms. Pac-Man. In: IEEE Congress on Evolutionary Computation (CEC 2013), pp. 1403–1410 (2013)

17. Livingstone, D.: Coevolution in hierarchical ai for strategy games. In: IEEE Symposium on Computational Intelligence and Games (CIG 2005). IEEE (2005)

18. Smith, G., Avery, P., Houmanfar, R., Louis, S.: Using co-evolved rts opponents to teach spatial tactics. In: IEEE Symposium on Computational Intelligence and Games (CIG 2010), pp. 146–153 (2010)

19. Avery, P., Louis, S.: Coevolving team tactics for a real-time strategy game. In: IEEE Congress on Evolutionary Computation (CEC 2010), pp. 1–8 (2010)

20. Nogueira, M., Cotta, C., Fernández-Leiva, A.J.: An Analysis of Hall-of-Fame Strategies in Competitive Coevolutionary Algorithms for Self-Learning in RTS Games. In: Nicosia, G., Pardalos, P. (eds.) LION 7. LNCS, vol. 7997, pp. 174–188. Springer, Heidelberg (2013)

Sharing Information in Adversarial Bandit

David L. St-Pierre[1,2]([✉]) and Olivier Teytaud[2]

[1] Montefiore Institute, Department of Electrical Engineering and Computer Science,
Liège University, 4000 Liège, Belgium
dlspierre@ulg.ac.be
[2] TAO, Inria, Université Paris-Sud, UMR CNRS 8623, Paris, France

Abstract. 2-Player games in general provide a popular platform for research in Artificial Intelligence (AI). One of the main challenges coming from this platform is approximating a Nash Equilibrium (NE) over zero-sum matrix games. While the problem of computing such a Nash Equilibrium is solvable in polynomial time using Linear Programming (LP), it rapidly becomes infeasible to solve as the size of the matrix grows; a situation commonly encountered in games. This paper focuses on improving the approximation of a NE for matrix games such that it outperforms the state-of-the-art algorithms given a finite (and rather small) number T of oracle requests to rewards. To reach this objective, we propose to share information between the different relevant pure strategies. We show both theoretically by improving the bound and empirically by experiments on artificial matrices and on a real-world game that information sharing leads to an improvement of the approximation of the NE.

Keywords: Bandit problem · Monte-Carlo · Nash Equilibrium · Games

1 Introduction

2-Player games in general provide a popular platform for research in Artificial Intelligence (AI). One of the main challenges coming from this platform is approximating the Nash Equilibrium (NE) over zero-sum matrix games. To name a few games where the computation (or approximation) of a NE is relevant, there is Rock-Paper-Scissor, Battleship, partially observable variants of Chess [4,10], and all games with a simultaneous metagaming part (e.g. choosing a deck in a card game) or simultaneous moves [12]. Such a challenge is not only important for the AI community. To efficiently approximate a NE can also help solving several real life problems. One can think, for example, of financial applications [5] or psychology [7].

While the problem of computing a Nash Equilibrium is solvable in polynomial time using Linear Programming (LP), it rapidly becomes infeasible to solve as the size of the matrix grows; a situation commonly encountered in games. Thus, an algorithm that can approximate a NE faster than polynomial time is required. [3,6,8] show that it is possible to ϵ-approximate a NE for a zero-sum game by

© Springer-Verlag Berlin Heidelberg 2014
A.I. Esparcia-Alcázar et al. (Eds.): EvoApplications 2014, LNCS 8602, pp. 386–398, 2014.
DOI: 10.1007/978-3-662-45523-4_32

accessing only $O(K\frac{\log(K)}{\epsilon^2})$ elements in a $K \times K$ matrix. In other words, in far less than the total number of elements in the matrix.

The early studies assume that there is an exact access to reward values for a given element in a matrix. It is not always the case. In fact, the exact value of an element can be difficult to know, as for instance when solving difficult games. In such cases, the value is only computable approximately. [1] considers a more general setting where each element of the matrix is only partially known from a finite number of measurements. They show that it is still possible to ϵ-approximate a NE provided that the average of the measurements converges quickly enough to the real value.

[11,12] propose to improve the approximation of a NE for matrix games by exploiting the fact that often the solution is sparse. A sparse solution means that there are many pure (i.e. deterministic) strategies, but only a small subset of these strategies are part of the NE. They used artificial matrix games and a real game, namely *Urban Rivals*, to show a dramatic improvement over the current state-of-the art algorithms. The idea behind their respective algorithms is to prune uninteresting strategies, the former in an offline manner and the latter online.

This paper focuses on further improving the approximation of a NE for zero-sum matrix games such that it outperforms the state-of-the-art algorithms given a finite (and rather small) number T of oracle requests to rewards. To reach this objective, we propose to share information between the different relevant strategies. To do so, we introduce a problem dependent measure of *similarity* that can be adapted for different challenges. We show that information sharing leads to a significant improvement of the approximation of a NE.

The rest of the paper is divided as follow. Section 2 formalizes the problem and introduces notations. The algorithm is defined in Section 3. Section 4 evaluates our approach from a theoretical point of view. Section 5 evaluates empirically the proposed algorithm and Section 6 concludes.

2   Problem Statement

We now introduce the notion of Nash Equilibrum in Section 2.1, define a generic bandit algorithm in Section 2.2 and Section 2.3 states the problem that we address in this paper.

2.1   Nash Equilibrium

Consider a matrix M of size $K_1 \times K_2$ with rewards bounded in $[0,1]$, player 1 chooses an action $i \in K_1$ and player 2 chooses an action $j \in K_2{}^1$. In order to keep the notations short and because the extension is straightforward, we will assume that $K_1 = K_2 = K$. Then, player 1 gets reward $M_{i,j}$ and player 2 gets reward $1 - M_{i,j}$. The game therefore sums to 1. We consider games summing to 1 for commodity of notations, but 0-sum games are equivalent. A NE of the

---

[1] From here on in, we will do a small abuse of notation by stating $K_p = [[1, K_p]]$ $\forall$ player p and where $[[\cdot, \cdot]]$ represents a discrete set.

game is a pair (x^*, y^*) both in $[0, 1]^K$ such that if i and j are chosen according to the distribution x^* and y^* respectively (i.e $i = k$ with probability x_k^* and $j = k$ with probability y_k^* with $k \in K$), then neither player can expect a better average reward through a change in their strategy distribution.

As mentioned previously, [11,12] observe that in games, the solution often involves only a small number of actions when compared to the cardinality of the set K. In other words, often $\{i; x_i^* > 0\}$ and $\{j; y_j^* > 0\}$ both have cardinality $<< K$. The sparsity assumption is not a necessity to ensure convergence, but it makes convergence faster.

2.2   Generic Bandit Algorithm

The main idea behind a bandit algorithm (adversarial case) is that it iteratively converges towards a NE. Bandit algorithms have the characteristic of being 'anytime', which means they can stop after any number of iterations and still output a reasonably good approximation of the solution. For a given player $p \in P$ where $P = [[1, 2]]$ for a 2-player game, each possible action is represented as an arm $a_p \in K_p$ and the purpose is to determine a probability distribution θ_p over the set of actions, representing a mixed (randomized) strategy as a probability distribution over deterministic (pure) strategies.

During the iteration process, each player selects an arm from their own set of actions K_p, forming a pair of action (a_1, a_2), according to their current distribution θ_p and their selection policy $\pi_p(\cdot)$. A selection policy $\pi_p(\cdot) \in K_p$ is an algorithm that selects an action $a_p \in K_p$ based on the information at hand. Once the pair of action (a_1, a_2) is selected, a reward r_t is computed for the tth iteration. Based upon the reward, both distributions θ_1 and θ_2 are updated. A detailed description of the selection policies and the distribution updates used in this paper are provided in Section 3.

Such a process is repeated until the allocated number of iterations T has been executed. Afterward, the action to be executed consists in choosing an arm $\hat{a}_p$ according to the information gathered so far. The pseudo code for a generic bandit algorithm up to the recommendation of $\hat{a}_p$ is provided in Algorithm 1.

2.3   Problem Statement

In most of the bandit literature, it is assumed that there is no structure over the action set K_p. Consequently, there is essentially only one arm updated for any given iteration $t \in T$. In games however, the reasons for sharing information are threefolds. First, each game possesses a specific set of rules. As such, there is inherently an underlying structure that allows information sharing. Second, the sheer number of possible actions can be too large to be efficiently explored. Third, to get a precise reward r_t can be a difficult task. For instance, computing r_t from a pair of arms (a_1 and a_2) can be time consuming or/and involve highly stochastic processes. Under such constraints, sharing information along K_p seems a legitimate approach. Given $\psi = (\psi_1, \psi_2)$ that describes some structure of the game, we propose an algorithm α_ψ that shares information along the set of

---

Algorithm 1. Generic Bandit Algorithm. The problem is described through the "get reward" function and the action sets. The "return" method is formally called the recommendation policy. The selection policy is also commonly termed exploration policy.

Require: $T > 0$: Computational budget
Require: $P = [[1, 2]]$: Set of players
Require: K_p: Set of actions specific for each $p \in P$
Require: π_p: Selection policy
  Initialize θ_p: Distribution over the set of actions K_p

  for $t = 1$ to T **do**
    Select $a_p \in K_p$ based upon $\pi_p(\theta_p)$ (for $p \in [[1, 2]]$)
    Get reward $r_t = getReward(a_1, a_2)$: player 1 receives r_t and player 2 receives $1 - r_t$.
    Update θ_p using r_t (for $p \in [[1, 2]]$)
  end for
  Return $\hat{a}_p$

---

actions K_p. To do so, we propose to include a measure of similarity $\psi_p(\cdot, \cdot)$ between actions of player p. Based upon the measure $\psi_p(\cdot, \cdot)$, the algorithm α_ψ shares the information with all other arms deemed similar. The sharing process is achieved by changing the distribution update of θ_p.

3   Selection Policies and Updating Rules

As mentionned in Section 2.2, a selection policy $\pi(\cdot)$ is an algorithm that selects an action $a_p \in K_p$ based upon information gathered so far. There exist several selection policies in the context of bandit algorithms, [9] studied the most popular, comparing them in a Monte-Carlo Tree Search architecture. Here we develop a variant of a selection policy $\pi(\cdot)$ relevant in the adversarial case called $EXP3$ [3]. Throughout this section, the reference to a specific player p is avoided to keep the notation short.

Section 3.1 describes the $EXP3$ selection policy. Section 3.2 presents a recommendation policy, $TEXP3$ [12] dedicated to sparse Nash Equilibria. Finally, Section 3.3 introduces the notion of similarity and define our new updating rule.

3.1   EXP3

This selection policy is designed for adversarial problems. For each arm $a \in K$, we gather the following quantities:

- t_a, the number of simulations involving arm a, or its visit count.
- θ_a, the current probability to select this arm
- w_a, a weighted sum of rewards

The idea is to keep a cumulative weighted sum of reward per arm and use it to infer a distribution of probability over the different arm. An interesting fact is that it is not the probability θ_a that converges to the Nash, but the counter t_a. More formally, every time an arm a receives a reward r_t, the value w_a is updated as follows:

$$w_a \leftarrow w_a + \frac{r_t}{\theta_a} \tag{1}$$

for the player which maximizes its reward (r_t is replaced by $1 - r_t$ for the opponent).

At any given time, the probability θ_a to select an action a is defined as:

$$\theta_a \simeq (1 - \gamma) \frac{\exp(\eta w_a)}{\sum\limits_{k \in K} \exp(\eta w_k)} + \frac{\gamma}{C}, \tag{2}$$

where $\eta > 0$ and $\gamma \in]0; 1]$ and $C \in \mathbb{R}$ are three parameters to tune. $\simeq$ stands for "is proportional to".

3.2   TEXP3

This recommendation policy is an extension of $EXP3$. It is a process that is executed only once before choosing $\hat{a}$, the arm to be pulled. Basically, it uses the property that, over time, the probability to pull an arm a, given by the ratio $\frac{t_a}{T}$, that is not part of the optimal solution will tend toward 0. Therefore, for all arms $a \in K$ deemed to be outside the optimal solution, it artificially truncates these arms. The decision whether an arm is part of the NE is based upon a threshold c. Following [12], the constant c is chosen as $\max\limits_{a \in K} \frac{(T \times t_a)^\alpha}{T}$, where $\alpha \in]0, 1]$. If the ratio $\frac{t_a}{T}$ of an arm $a \in K$ is below such threshold, it is removed and the remaining arms have their probability rescaled accordingly.

3.3   Structured EXP3

As mentioned previously, one of the main reason for sharing information is to exploit a priori regularities that are otherwise time consuming to let an algorithm find by itself. The core idea is that simliar arms are likely to produce similar results. The sharing of information is mostly important in the early iterations because afterwards the algorithm gathers enough information to correctly evaluate each individual relevant arms.

EXP3 uses an exponential at its core combined with cumulative rewards. One must be careful about the sharing of information under such circumstance. The exponential makes the algorithm focus rapidly on a specific arm. The use of cumulative reward is also problematic. For example, sharing several times a low reward can, over time, mislead the algorithm into thinking an arm is better than one that received only once a high reward. To remedy this situation, we only share when the reward is interesting. To keep it simple, the decision whether to share or not is made by a threshold ζ that is domain specific.

Lets define $\varphi_a \subseteq K$ as a set of arms that are considered similar to a based upon the measure $\psi(a, k)$, i.e. $\varphi_a = \{k; \psi(a, k) > 0\}$. If $r_t > \zeta$, for all $k \in \varphi_a$ we update as follow:

$$w_k \leftarrow w_k + \frac{r_t}{\theta_k}. \tag{3}$$

The probability θ_k to select an action k is still defined as:

$$\theta_k \simeq (1-\gamma)\frac{\exp(\eta w_k)}{\sum\limits_{k' \in K} \exp(\eta w_{k'})} + \frac{\gamma}{C}, \tag{4}$$

where $\eta > 0$, $\gamma \in]0;1]$ and $C \in \mathbb{R}$ are three parameters to tune. In the case where $r_t \leq \zeta$, the update is executed following (1) and (2).

4   Theoretical Evaluation

In this section we present a simple result showing that structured-EXP3 performs roughly S times faster when classes of similar arms have size S. The result is basically aimed at showing the rescaling of the update rule.

A classical EXP3 variant (from [1]) uses, as explained in Alg. 2, the update rule

$$\theta_a = \gamma/C + (1-\gamma)\frac{\exp(\eta w_a)}{\sum\limits_{k \in K} \exp(\eta w_k)},$$

$$\text{where} \quad C = K, \gamma = \min(0.8\sqrt{\frac{\log(K)}{Kt}}, 1/K) \text{ and } \eta = \gamma.$$

Note that the parameters γ and η depend on t, removed for shorter notation.

The pseudo-regret L after T iterations is defined as:

$$L_T = \max_{k \in K} \mathbb{E}\left(\sum_{t=1}^{T} r_t(k) - r_t\right)$$

where r_t is the reward obtained at iteration t and $r_t(k)$ is the reward which would have been obtained at iteration t by choosing arm k at iteration t. Essentially, the pseudo-regret is non-negative, and is zero if we always choose an arm that gets optimal reward. With this definition, EXP3 verifies the following[1,2]:

Theorem 1: Pseudo-regret L of EXP3.
Consider a problem with K arms and 1-sum rewards in $[0,1]$. Then, EXP3 verifies

$$L_T \leq 2.7\sqrt{TKln(K)}.$$

It is known since [6] that it is not possible to do better than the bound above, within logarithmic factors, in the general case.

We propose a variant, termed Structured-EXP3 or $sEXP3$, for the case in which for each arm a, there is a set φ_a (of cardinality S) containing arms similar to a. Under mild assumptions upon φ_a, the resulting algorithms has some advantages over the baseline EXP3. The parameters γ and η for $sEXP3$ are defined by Eq. (5) ($C = K$ is preserved, as in EXP3).

$$\gamma = \min(0.8\sqrt{\frac{S\log(K/S)}{Kt}}, S/K) \text{ and } \eta = \gamma/S. \tag{5}$$

Algorithm 2. The EXP3 algorithm as in [1] (left) and TEXP3, sEXP and sTEXP3 variants (right). Strategies are given for player 1. Player 2 use $1 - r_t$ instead of r_t.

for each iteration $t \in [[1, T]]$ do
   Selection policy π: choose arm a
     with probability θ_a (Eq. 4).
   Get reward r_t.
   Update ω_a: $w_a \leftarrow w_a + \frac{r_t}{\theta_a}$.
   if sEXP3 or sTEXP3 and $r_t < \zeta$
then
     for each $b \in \varphi(a) \setminus a$ do

$$w_b \leftarrow w_b + \frac{r_t}{\theta_b}.$$

     end for
   end if
end for

for each iteration $t \in [[1, T]]$ do
   Selection policy π: choose arm a
     with probability θ_a (Eq. 4).
   Get reward r_t.
   Update ω_a:

$$w_a \leftarrow w_a + \frac{r_t}{\theta_a}.$$

end for
Recommendation: choose arm $\hat{a}$ with probability $n_T(a) = \frac{t_a}{T}$.

if TEXP3/sTEXP3 then
   if $t_a/T \leq c$ then
     Set $t_a = 0$.
   end if
   Rescale t_a: $t_a \leftarrow t_a / \sum_{b \in K} t_b$.
end if
Recommendation: choose arm $\hat{a}$ with probability $n_T(a) = \frac{t_a}{T}$.

In other words, γ is designed (as detailed in the theorem below) for mimicking the values corresponding to the problem with K/S arms instead of K arms and η is designed for avoiding a too aggressive pruning.

The following theorem is aimed at showing that parameters in Eq. (5) ensure that Structured-EXP3 emulates EXP3 on a bigger problem with a particular structure.

Theorem 2: Structured-EXP3 and Pseudo-regret.
Consider a problem where there are K' classes of S similar arms i.e. $K = K' \times S$ (arms from different classes have no similarity); φ_a is the set of arms of the same class as arm a. Assume that all arms in a class have the same distribution of rewards, i.e. $a \in \varphi_b$ implies that a and b have the same distribution of rewards against any given strategy of the opponent. Set $\zeta = -\infty$. Then, Structured-EXP3 verifies

$$L_T \leq 2.7\sqrt{T(K/S)ln(K/S)},$$

where S is the cardinal of φ_a (whereas the EXP3 bound is $2.7\sqrt{TKlnK}$).
Proof: For this proof, we compare the Structured-EXP3 algorithm with K arms including classes of S similar arms (i.e. $\forall a \in [[1, K]], \varphi_a = S$) and an EXP3 algorithm working on an ad hoc problem with K/S arms. The ad hoc problem is built as follows.

Instead of arms $A = [[1, K]]$ (ordered by similarity, so that blocks of S successive arms are similar) for the Structured-EXP3 bandit, consider arms $A' = [[1, S + 1, 2S + 1, \ldots, K - S + 1]]$ for the EXP3 bandit. Consider the same reward as in the Structured-EXP3 bandit problem.

Any mixed strategy on the EXP3 problem can be transformed without changing its performance into a mixed strategy on the Structured-EXP3 problem by arbitrarily distributing the probability of choosing arm $k \in A'$ onto arms $[[k, k + 1, \ldots, k + S - 1]] \subset A$.

Let us use $\theta'_{a'}$, the probability that EXP3 chooses $a' \in A'$; and $\omega'_{a'}$, the sum of rewards associated to $a' \in A'$ for EXP3 (notations with no "prime" are for Structured-EXP3). We now show by induction that

- $\omega_a = S \times \omega'_{a'}$ for $a \in A$ similar to $a' \in A'$ when EXP3 and Structured-EXP3 have the same history[2];
- $\theta_a = \frac{1}{S}\theta'_{a'}$ for $a \in A$ similar to $a' \in A'$.

The proof is based on the following steps, showing that when the induction properties hold at some time step then they also hold at the next time step. We assume that $\omega_a = S \times \omega'_{a'}$ (for all $a' \in A'$ similar to a) at some iteration, and we show that it implies $\theta_a = \frac{1}{S}\theta'_{a'}$ at the same iteration (also for all $a' \in A'$ similar to a) and that $\omega_a = S \times \omega'_{a'}$ at the next iteration (also for all $a' \in A'$ similar to a). More formally, we show that

$$\forall (a, a') \in A \times A', a \in \varphi_{a'}, \omega_a = S \times \omega'_{a'} \tag{6}$$

$$\text{implies } \forall (a, a') \in A \times A', a \in \varphi_{a'}, \theta_a = \frac{1}{S} \times \theta'_{a'} \tag{7}$$

and at next iteration Eq. (6) still holds. The properties of Eq. (6) and Eq. (7) hold at the initial iteration (we have only zeros) and the induction from one step to the next is as follows:

- **Let us show that Eq. (6) implies Eq. (7), i.e. if, for all a, ω_a for Structured-EXP3 is S times more than $\omega'_{a'}$ for $a' \in A'$ similar to a, then the probability for Structured-EXP3 to choose an arm $a \in A$ similar to $a' \in A'$ is exactly S times less than the probability for EXP3 to choose a'.** The probability that Structured-EXP3 chooses arm a at iteration t given an history $a_1, \ldots, a_{t-1}$ of chosen arms with rewards $r_1, \ldots, r_{t-1}$ until iteration $t-1$ is

$$\theta_a = (1 - \gamma)\frac{\exp(\eta w_a)}{\sum_{k \in K} \exp(\eta w_k)} + \frac{\gamma}{K}, \tag{8}$$

which is exactly S times less than the probability that EXP3 chooses arm $\lfloor(a-1)/S\rfloor +1$ given a history $\lfloor(a_1 - 1)/S\rfloor+1, \lfloor(a_2 - 1)/S\rfloor+1,\ldots,\lfloor(a_{t-1} - 1)/S\rfloor + 1$. Thus,

$$\theta_a = \frac{1}{S}\theta'_{a'}.$$

---

[2] The set of arms are not the same in Structured-EXP3 and EXP3. By same history we mean up to the projection $a \to a' = \lfloor(a - 1)/S\rfloor + 1$.

This is the case because the S additional factor in w_a is compensated by the S denominator in Eq. (5) so that terms in the exponential are the same as in the Structured-EXP3 case; but the numerator is S times bigger. This concludes the proof that Eq. (7) holds.

– We now show that **the probability that Structured-EXP3 chooses an arm in $[[a', a' + 1, \ldots, a' + S - 1]]$ similar to $a' \in A$ is the same as the probability that EXP3 chooses $a' \in A'$ (given the same history).** The update rule in Structured-EXP3 ensures that $w_a = w_b$ as soon as a and b are similar. So the probability of an arm of the same class as $a \in A$ to be chosen by Structured-EXP3 is exactly the probability of $a' \in A'$ (similar to A) being chosen by EXP3:

$$\sum_{a \text{ similar to } a'} \theta_a = \theta'_{a'}. \tag{9}$$

– **Let us now show that Eq. (6) and Eq. (7) implies Eq. (6) at the next iteration, i.e. the weighted sum of rewards w_a for $a \in A$ is S times more than the weighted sum of rewards $w'_{a'}$ for a similar to a' (given the same histories).** This is because (i) probabilities that Structured-EXP3 chooses an arm a among those similar to an arm a' is the same as the probability that EXP3 chooses a' (given the same history), as explained by Eq. (9), and (ii) probabilities used in the update rule are divided by S in the case of Structured-EXP3 (updates have K at the denominator). This concludes the induction, from an iteration to the next.   □

5   Experiments

This section describes a set of experiments that evaluates the quality of our approach. The first testbed is automatically generated sparse matrices and the results are presented in section 5.1. The second testbed, presented in section 5.2, is the game Urban Rivals (UR), an internet card game. Throughout this section, we used 3 baselines: $EXP3$, $TEXP3$ and $Random$. The parameters γ, η and C were tuned independantly for each testbed (and each algorithm) to ensure they are performing as good as they can. For the automatically generated sparse matrices, the set of parameters that gave the best results are $\eta = \frac{1}{\sqrt{t}}$, $\gamma = \frac{1}{\sqrt{t}}$, $C = 0.65$ and $\alpha = 0.8$. In the game Urban Rivals, the best values found for the parameters are $\eta = \frac{1}{\sqrt{t}}$, $\gamma = \frac{1}{\sqrt{t}}$, $C = 0.7$ and $\alpha = 0.75$.

As a reminder, we add the prefix s when we exploit the notion of distance. The distance $\psi(\cdot, \cdot)$ is specific to the testbed and is thus defined in each section.

5.1   Artificial Experiments

First we test on automatically generated matrices that have a sparse solution and contain an exploitable measure of distance between the arms. We use matrix M defined by $M_{i,j} = \frac{1}{2} + \frac{1}{5}(1 + cos(i \times 2 \times \pi/100))\chi_{i \mod \omega} - \frac{1}{5}(1 + cos(j \times 2 \times$

$pi/100))\chi_{j\ mod\ \omega}$, where $\omega \in \mathbb{N}$ is set to 5 and M is of size 50×50. The distance $\psi(\cdot,\cdot)$ is based on the position of the arm in the matrix. It is defined such that the selected arm a and $k \in K$ have a similarity

$$\psi(a,k) = \begin{cases} 1 & \text{if } (k' - a')\ mod\ \omega = 0 \\ 0 & \text{otherwise,} \end{cases} \tag{10}$$

where k' and a' are the position of respectively k and a in the matrix M. The set φ_a includes all k where $\psi(a,k) = 1$. At any $t \in T$ the reward is given by the binomial distribution $r_t \sim B(20, M(i,j))$, where 20 is the number of Bernoulli trials with parameter $M(i,j)$. The threshold ζ is fixed at 0.8 and for any given T, the experiment is repeated 100 times.

Figure 1 analyses the score (%) in relation to the maximal number of iterations T of our approach playing against the baselines. Figure 1(a) presents the results of $sEXP3$ and $EXP3$ playing against the baseline $Random$. Figure 1(b) shows $sTEXP3$ and $TEXP3$ also playing against the baseline $Random$. Figure 1(c) depicts the results of $sEXP3$ playing against $EXP3$ and $sTEXP3$ playing against $TEXP3$.

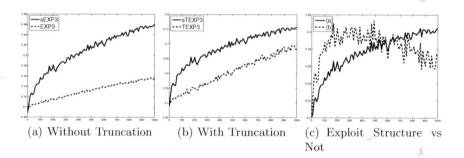

(a) Without Truncation   (b) With Truncation   (c) Exploit Structure vs Not

Fig. 1. Performance (%) in relation to the number of iterations T of our approach compared to different baselines. Each of the 99 different positive abscissa is an independent run, so the null hypothesis of an average ordinate $\leq 50\%$ is less than 10^{-29}. We see that (a) sEXP3 converges faster than EXP3 (in terms of success rate against random), (b) sTEXP3 converges faster than TEXP3 (in terms of success rate against random), (c.a) sEXP3 outperforms EXP3 (direct games of sEXP3 vs EXP3) and (c.b) sTEXP3 outperforms TEXP3 (direct games of sTEXP3 vs TEXP3).

Figure 1(a) shows that $sEXP3$ significantly outperforms $EXP3$. It requires as little as $T = 30$ iterations to reach a significant improvement over $EXP3$. As the maximal number of iterations T grows, $sEXP3$ still clearly outperforms its counterpart $EXP3$.

Figure 1(b) shows again a clear improvement of exploiting the structure (as in $sTEXP3$) versus not (as in $TEXP3$). It requires $T = 30$ iterations to reach a significant improvement. The score in Figure 1(b) are clearly higher than in Figure 1(a), which is in line with previous findings. Moreover, a Nash player would score 87.64% versus the *Random* baseline. The best score 75.68% is achieved by $sTEXP3$ which is fairly close to the Nash, using only 1 000 requests to the matrix.

The results in Figure 1(c) are in line with Figure 1(a) and 1(b). The line representing $sEXP3$ versus $EXP3$ (labeled (a) in reference to Figure 1(a)) shows that even after $T = 1\,000$ iterations, $EXP3$ does not start to close the gap with $sEXP3$. The line representing $sTEXP3$ versus $TEXP3$ shows that it takes around $T = 500$ iterations for $TEXP3$ to start filling the gap with the algorithm that shares information $sTEXP3$. Yet even after $T = 1\,000$ it is still far from performing as well.

Overall for this testbed, the sharing of information greatly increases the performance of the state-of-the-art algorithms. The good behavior of sparsity techniques such as TEXP3 is also confirmed.

5.2   Urban Rivals

Urban Rivals (UR) is a widely played internet card game, with partial information. As pointed out in [12], UR can be consistently solved by a Monte-Carlo Tree Search algorithm (MCTS) thanks to the fact that the hidden information is frequently revealed. A call for getting a reward leads to 20 games played by a Monte-Carlo Tree Search with 1 000 simulations before an action is chosen. Reading coefficients in the payoff matrices at the root is quite expensive, and we have to solve the game approximately.

We consider a setting in which two players choose 4 cards from a finite set of 10 cards. We use two different representations. In the first one, each arm $a \in K$ is a combination of 4 cards and $K = 10^4$. In the second representation, we remove redundant arms. There remain $K = 715$ different possible combinations if we allow the same card to be used more than once in the same combination.

There are two baseline methods tested upon UR, namely $EXP3$ and $TEXP3$.

The distance $\psi(\cdot, \cdot)$ is based on the number of similar cards. It is defined such that the selected arm a and $k \in K$ have a distance $\psi(a, k) = 1$ if k and a share more than 2 cards and 0 otherwise. The set φ_a includes all k where $\psi(a, k) = 1$. At any $t \leq T$ the reward r_t is given by 20 games played with the given combinations. The threshold ζ is fixed at 0.8 and for any given T.

For a given number of iterations T, each algorithm is executed 10 times and the output is saved. To compute the values in Figure 2, we play a round-robin (thus comparing 10×10 different outputs) where each comparison between two outputs consist in repeating 100 times the process of selecting an arm and executing 20 games.

Figure 2 presents the score (%) in relation to the maximal number of iterations T of our approach playing against their respective baselines. Figure 2(a) presents the results of $sEXP3$ playing against $EXP3$. Figure 2(b) shows $sTEXP3$ playing against $TEXP3$. In both cases, we present the results for 2 different representations ($K = 10^4$, and $K = 715$).

Figure 2(a) shows that $sEXP3$ significantly outperforms $EXP3$ independently of the representation since the values are far behind 50%. Even at the

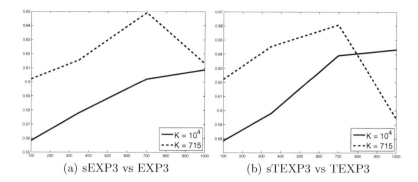

(a) sEXP3 vs EXP3   (b) sTEXP3 vs TEXP3

Fig. 2. Performance (%) in relation to the number of iterations T of our approach compared to different baselines. Standard deviations are smaller than 1%. We see that (a) sEXP3 outperforms EXP3 in both versions (game with 10K arms and game with 715 arms) (b) sTEXP3 outperforms TEXP3 in both versions (game with 10K arms and game with 715 arms).

lowest number of iterations ($T = 100$), there is a significant improvement over $EXP3$ with both representations ($K = 10^4$ and $K = 715$). As the maximal number of iterations T grows, $sEXP3$ still clearly outperforms its counterpart $EXP3$. Moreover, Figure 2(a) shows that the representation impacts greatly on the quality of the results. The discrepancy between the two lines is probably closely related to the ratio $\frac{T}{K}$. For instance, when $T = 1\,000$ and $K = 10^4$ the score is equal to 60.88%. If we compare such a result to $T = 100$ and $K = 715$, a ratio $\frac{T}{K}$ relatively close, the score (60.22%) is rather similar.

Figure 2(b) shows that $sTEXP3$ significantly outperforms $TEXP3$ independently of the representation since the values are also far beyond 50%. The conclusion drawn from Figure 2(b) are quite similar to the ones from Figure 2(a). However, the sudden drop at $T = 1\,000$ and $K = 715$ indicates that $TEXP3$ also start to converge toward the Nash Equilibrium, thus bringing the score relatively closer to the 50% mark.

For the game UR, it seems that sharing information does also greatly improve the performance of the state-of-the-art algorithms.

6   Conclusion

In this paper, we present an improvement over state-of-the-art algorithms to compute an ϵ-approximation of a Nash Equilibrium for zero-sum matrix games. The improvement consist in exploiting the similarities between arms of a bandit problem through a notion of distance and share information among them.

From a theoretical point of view, we compute a bound for our algorithm that is better than the state-of-the-art by a factor roughly based on the number of similar arms.

Moreover, empirical results on the game of Urban Rival and automatically generated matrices show a significant better performance of the algorithms that share information compared to the ones that do not. This is when results are compared on the basis of EXP3 parameters that are optimized on the application.

As future work, the next step is to create a parameter free version of our algorithm, for instance by automatically fixing the parameter ζ. Also, so far we solely focus on problem where the total number of iterations T is too small for converging to the NE. As the maximal number of iterations T gets bigger, there would be no reason for sharing information anymore. A degradation function can be embedded into the updating rule to ensure convergence. We do not know for the moment whether we should stop sharing information depending on rewards (using ζ; if the game is symmetric, this implicitly eventually stops sharing), depending on iterations (using a limit on t/T) or more sophisticated criteria.

References

1. Audibert, J., Bubeck, S.: Minimax policies for adversarial and stochastic bandits. In: 22nd Annual Conference on Learning Theory (COLT), Montreal (June 2009)
2. Auer, P.: Using confidence bounds for exploitation-exploration trade-offs. The Journal of Machine Learning Research 3, 397–422 (2003)
3. Auer, P., Cesa-Bianchi, N., Freund, Y., Schapire, R.E.: Gambling in a rigged casino: the adversarial multi-armed bandit problem. In: Proceedings of the 36th Annual Symposium on Foundations of Computer Science, pp. 322–331. IEEE Computer Society Press, Los Alamitos (1995)
4. Ciancarini, P., Favini, G.P.: Monte carlo tree search in kriegspiel. Artif. Intell. 174(11), 670–684 (2010)
5. Grenadier, S.R.: Option exercise games: An application to the equilibrium investment strategies of firms. Review of financial studies 15(3), 691–721 (2002)
6. Grigoriadis, M.D., Khachiyan, L.G.: A sublinear-time randomized approximation algorithm for matrix games. Operations Research Letters 18(2), 53–58 (1995)
7. Hedden, T., Zhang, J.: What do you think i think you think?: Strategic reasoning in matrix games. Cognition 85(1), 1–36 (2002)
8. Lipton, R.J., Markakis, E., Mehta, A.: Playing large games using simple strategies. In: Proceedings of the 4th ACM Conference on Electronic Commerce, pp. 36–41. ACM (2003)
9. Perrick, P., St-Pierre, D., Maes, F., Ernst, D.: Comparison of different selection strategies in Monte-Carlo tree search for the game of Tron. In: Proceedings of the IEEE Conference on Computational Intelligence and Games (CIG 2012), Granada, Spain (2012)
10. Russell, S., Wolfe, J.: Efficient Belief-State AND-OR Search, with Application to Kriegspiel. In: IJCAI, pp. 278–285 (2005)
11. St-Pierre, D.L., Louveaux, Q., Teytaud, O.: Online Sparse Bandit for Card Games. In: van den Herik, H.J., Plaat, A. (eds.) ACG 2011. LNCS, vol. 7168, pp. 295–305. Springer, Heidelberg (2012)
12. Teytaud, O., Flory, S.: Upper Confidence Trees with Short Term Partial Information. In: Di Chio, C., et al. (eds.) EvoApplications 2011, Part I. LNCS, vol. 6624, pp. 153–162. Springer, Heidelberg (2011)

The Structure of a Probabilistic 1-State Transducer Representation for Prisoner's Dilemma

Jeffrey Tsang[(✉)]

Department of Mathematics and Statistics, University of Guelph, Guelph, Canada
jeffrey.tsang@ieee.org

Abstract. In the study of evolutionary game theory, a tool called the fingerprint was developed. This mathematical technique generates a functional summary of an arbitrary game-playing strategy independent of representational details. Using this tool, this study expands the boundaries of investigating an entire small state space of strategies, to wit the probabilistic 1-state tranducers, as a representation for playing iterated Prisoner's Dilemma. A sampled grid of 35,937 strategies out of the continuous cube was used: they are fingerprinted and pairwise distances computed. A subsampled grid of 4,913 strategies was analyzed using metric multidimensional scaling. The results show that the known 3-dimensional manifold can be embedded into around 4–5 Euclidean dimensions without self-intersection, and the curvature of the fingerprint metric with respect to standard distance is not too extreme; there is also similarity with analogous results on other state spaces.

1 Introduction

The mathematical game is an easily understood model for simulating various interactions, whether cooperative or competitive. In theoretical work, the absolute simplest game, a simultaneous, symmetric two-move game (e.g. Prisoner's Dilemma) is already difficult to understand. To preserve possibilities for complex strategies, we iterate the game, allowing response and counter-response to your opponent. A commonly used method of experimentation is via evolutionary game theory, by using (co)evolutionary algorithms to generate an unlimited population of strategies.

To enable analysis, the concept of fingerprinting is presented in a series of papers [1–3]: this turns the strategies into normal mathematical functions recording the strategy's behaviour against a continuous set of reference strategies, after which handling them becomes much easier. This has led to studies in evolutionary time and population size [8], the effect of noise [4,5], and representational sensitivity [6,7] among other parameters.

The model in [2] was updated in [15], avoiding some problems in the original specification, which include discontinuities and pairs of indistinguishable strategies. One main thrust of the latter paper is that we can define a distance on the space of fingerprints, thus quantifying the notion of "similar" strategies.

© Springer-Verlag Berlin Heidelberg 2014
A.I. Esparcia-Alcázar et al. (Eds.): EvoApplications 2014, LNCS 8602, pp. 399–410, 2014.
DOI: 10.1007/978-3-662-45523-4_33

Investigating the entirety of representations for evolutionary games is extremely difficult: to have any chance of encountering interesting strategies, sufficient power has to be given to the representation, along with the inevitable combinatorial explosion. This is exacerbated by considering *probabilistic* strategies: now the space is inherently continuous and only sampling is possible. We attempt here to analyze the most basic probabilistic space: that of the memoryless, equivalently reactive or probabilistic 1-state transducers.

This can be represented succinctly as the unit cube; we will sample a grid of 35,937 strategies from it and see whether the known cube structure (in genotype space) is preserved under fingerprint distance (in phenotype distinction). We can also look into what curvature is imposed by phenotypic distance, and whether there exist nontrivial pairs of small fingerprint distance but large parameter distance.

The rest of this paper is organized as follows: the fingerprint definition is briefly given in Section 2, the experimental methodology is detailed and described in Section 3, the results and interpretations follow in Section 4, and finally the discussion and conclusions are reported in Section 5.

2   Background

As developed in [15] and used in [16,17], the fingerprint operator used in this study is based on the length-weighted probability of each move pair occuring, when the agent plays against a parametrized k-state probabilistic finite state transducer probe. We will restrict our consideration to memoryless, or 1-state machines, which can be parametrized as $(x, y, z) \in [0, 1]^3$, where x is the probability of cooperating on the initial move, y is the probability of cooperating in response to a cooperate, and z the probability of cooperating in response to a defect.

The operator takes as input a *specification* of a game playing agent P, which is a function ρ_P that gives the probability the agent plays as an input move history s (a string of moves) up to its length, given that its opponent plays as another input move history w (of length 1 shorter due to the simultaneity of the game) as directed. That is, $\rho_P(s, w) = \Pr(\forall i\ P$ plays s_i in turn $i \mid \forall j$ opponent plays w_j in turn $j)$. Call the parametrized opponent $O_1(\boldsymbol{v})$ with $\boldsymbol{v} = (x, y, z)$, and define $\rho_{O_1(\boldsymbol{v})}$ similarly.

Denote by $\mathcal{F}_P$ the output of the operator on P; the (m_1, m_2)th component of the fingerprint function is defined as

$$\mathcal{F}_P(\boldsymbol{v})_{m_1 m_2} = \sum_{n=1}^{\infty} \mu(n) \sum_{\substack{(s,w) \text{ has length } n-1 \\ s \text{ ends with } m_1 \\ w \text{ ends with } m_2}} \rho_{O_1(\boldsymbol{v})}(wm_2, s)\rho_P(sm_1, w)$$

the first sum is the two-way probability the players play (m_1, m_2) respectively on the nth move, weighting that by a given function $\mu(n)$. For special properties, we will use the family of geometric distributions: $\mu(n; \alpha) = (1-\alpha)\alpha^{n-1}$, $\alpha \in [0, 1)$, at $\alpha = 0.8$ in continuity with prior work [15,17].

For agents representable by finite state transducers (such as ours), we can create the following Markov chain: the state space is $Q \times \{C, D\}^2$, the states of the agent adjoined with the last moves of P then O_1. The transition matrix T has entries $(q_1, m_1, m_2) \to (q_2, m_3, m_4)$ equal to $\Pr(P$ transitions from q_1 to q_2 outputting m_3 on input $m_2) \times \Pr(O_1$ outputs m_4 on input $m_1)$.

The fingerprint function is then

$$\mathcal{F}_P(x, y, z; \alpha)_{m_1 m_2} = (1-\alpha)\chi_{m_1 m_2}^T (I - \alpha T(y, z))^{-1} Q_0(x)$$

where $\chi_{m_1 m_2}$ be the indicator vector whose entry is 1 if the state indexed has last move-pair (m_1, m_2), 0 otherwise, and $Q_0(x)$ is the initial state probability vector of P.

Now that the strategies have been transformed into mathematical functions, we can define the distance between two fingerprints using the $\mathcal{L}_1$ distance (also named statistical, or total variation [9]):

$$\|\mathcal{F}_{P1} - \mathcal{F}_{P2}\| = \int_{[0,1]^3} \sum_{m_1 m_2} |(\mathcal{F}_{P1} - \mathcal{F}_{P2})(x, y, z)_{m_1 m_2}| \, dx dy dz$$

3   Methodology

We will study a probabilistic 1-state finite transducer representation for playing iterated Prisoner's Dilemma. This can be described by $(x, y, z) \in [0, 1]^3$, where x is the probability of cooperating on the initial move, y is the probability of cooperating in response to a cooperate, and z the probability of cooperating in response to a defect.

As we have mentioned, this is the continuous unit cube, hence we must sample the space. We will use a grid of 33 values $\{0, \frac{1}{32}, \frac{2}{32}, \ldots, \frac{31}{32}, 1\}$ for each parameter, a total of $33^3 = 35,937$ strategies. Each of these 35,937 strategies was fingerprinted, computed using the matrix formula using the LAPACK linear algebra package into a 4-component function of y, z for $x = 0, 1$ at $\alpha = 0.8$, a value found in previous studies to have good separation properties [16].

Approximate pairwise distances are calculated with a composite third order product Gaussian cubature method (4 points at $(\pm 1/\sqrt{3}, \pm 1/\sqrt{3})$ for the region $[-1, 1]^2$, see [14]) with a grid of 512×512 evenly spaced squares (1,048,576 evaluation points). These are summed in a binary divide-and-conquer fashion to decrease roundoff error. From results in previous studies [17], the integration error is at most on the order of 10^{-10}, where distances are bounded above by 1. For all intents and purposes, the integral is basically exact.

Since this dataset consists of over 645 million numbers, we simply cannot use cubic or worse analysis methods. Several tests on the structure of this space can still be performed though.

One simple test is whether there are pairs of strategies that differ in the parameter values (genotype) but not in fingerprint distance (phenotype). This

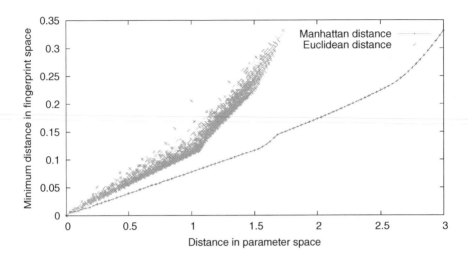

Fig. 1. Minimal fingerprint distance, over all pairs of strategies at a given distance in parameter space, as measured using $\mathcal{L}_1$ or normal $\mathcal{L}_2$ distance

is a direct linear search through the dataset, minimizing the fingerprint distance for a given parameter distance. A second test is through hierarchical clustering: we can plot the distance between each pair of clusters as they are merged and possibly detect strong jumps, which would indicate abnormalities in the structure. For this purpose we use the standard UPGMA (unweighted pair group with arithmetic mean) algorithm [13].

A final test on the full dataset directly measures the curvature of the space. We have two distinct methods of moving from strategy A to strategy B: we can take the straight line in fingerprint space, which is well-defined as a space of mathematical functions. On the other hand, we can also take the straight line in *parameter* space, which is just the unit cube. We can then quantify how a straight line in genotype space is distorted into a curve via phenotypic expression.

Having done extensive tests on the dataset, we note that since this is fundamentally a sampled space, we can without restriction downsample until more expensive analysis tools are within range. We subsample with a grid of 17 values $\{0, \frac{1}{16}, \frac{2}{16}, \ldots, \frac{15}{16}, 1\}$ for each parameter, reducing to $17^3 = 4,913$ strategies.

It is now feasible to use standard metric multidimensional scaling to embed these points into the Euclidean plane. This works by minimizing the *stress* loss function

$$\sum_{i,j}(\delta_{i,j} - d_{i,j})^2$$

where $\delta_{i,j}$ is the true distance between strategies i, j, and $d_{i,j}$ is the distance between the points on the plane representing i, j. The stress majorization SMA-COF algorithm [12] is used for this purpose, with the best fit chosen from around 1,000 runs starting at uniformly random initial points.

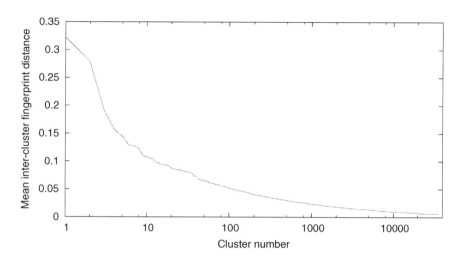

Fig. 2. Averaged inter-cluster distances at the joining of each cluster as done by the UPGMA algorithm. Note the logarithmic x axis.

After the points are placed in $\mathbb{R}^n$, many more analysis techniques can be employed. We will rotate the points using principal component analysis: this aligns the axes to be uncorrelated with ordered variance. With this, we can attempt to find explanatory variables in the strategies themselves that form the most important dimensions in strategy space.

4   Results

4.1   Parameter Distance vs. Minimum Fingerprint Distance

We tabulate the minimum fingerprint distance for some values of parameter distance in the unit cube, as measured using the Manhattan distance (absolute sum over coordinate differences or the $\mathcal{L}_1$ distance) or the normal Euclidean distance ($\mathcal{L}_2$) in Figure 1. That is, we take all pairs of (parameter distance, fingerprint distance), and sort on the first value. For all pairs with the same parameter distance, we find the strategies with the minimal fingerprint distance and plot that. The diameter of the cube is 3 in $\mathcal{L}_1$, and $\sqrt{3}$ in $\mathcal{L}_2$.

The graph for Euclidean distance is more cluttered due to the much larger possible values of distances achievable; in Manhattan distance all possible distances are multiples of $\frac{1}{32}$. The main result of this graph is that there are clearly no nontrivial parameter pairs that are indistinguishable under the fingerprint distance: in fact, there is a piecewise linear trend, indicating the distances have some direct correlation to each other.

We can thus conclude that the basic structure of genotypic space is preserved under the phenotypic measurement of fingerprint distance — the cubic shape does not have self-intersections or other extremely weird distortions.

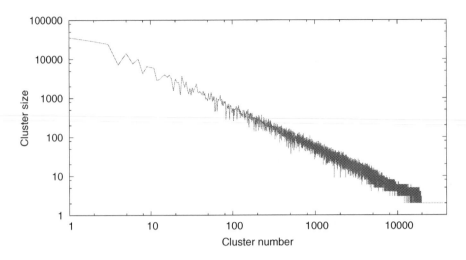

Fig. 3. Cluster size at the joining of each cluster as done by the UPGMA algorithm. Note the log-log scales of both axes.

4.2 Hierarchical Clustering

We plot here the mean inter-cluster distance at the joining of the nth and $n+1$th clusters in the operation of the UPGMA algorithm in Figure 2. Recall that UPGMA recursively joins the two clusters with the minimal inter-cluster distance; after the joining, the distance between any two clusters is defined to be the arithmetic mean of all the distances between any point in the first cluster and any point in the second. The distance increases smoothly as the later clusters are grouped; no obvious jumps or other discontinuities appear in the earlier clusters, which would indicate unusual structure.

We also plot the cluster size after joining the nth and $n+1$th clusters in Figure 3, on a log-log scale. The linear trend is now extremely clear: this is highly consistent with the space being essentially evenly distributed, with UPGMA mostly joining clusters in a balanced manner. Once again we confirm that there are no extraordinary deformations of the cubic structure.

4.3 Curvature of the Parameter Space

We have a full 3-dimensional sampled grid in the unit cube. We can pick a value for x, z, hold them fixed, and consider the points for the grid-sampled values of $y = 0, \frac{1}{32}, \frac{2}{32}, \ldots, \frac{31}{32}, 1$. Since we know all pairwise distances, we can find the distance as traced by this 32-segment line, versus the distance directly (in fingerprint space) between the two points for $y = 0, 1$. These two distances are plotted against each other (for all sampled values of x, z) in Figure 4. The identity function, which represents a straight line, is also plotted for comparison and reference.

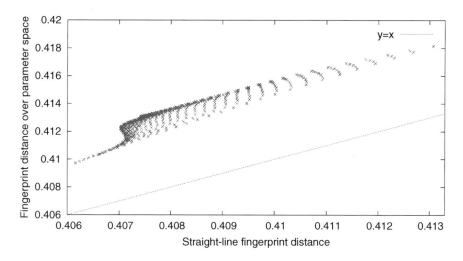

Fig. 4. Plot of the straight-line fingerprint distance between $y = 0$ and $y = 1$ holding x, z fixed, versus the total fingerprint distance as traced by the curve using the grid-sampled values of y. The identity function is given for reference.

Note that due to the functional symmetry of the space between y and z, the graph for z is identical; also since the fingerprint is explicitly linear in x, there is no curvature at all from changing x.

Several salient points can be gleaned from that figure: first, that the distances for completely flipping y lie in the relatively narrow band of 0.406 to 0.413; that there is some curvature in the parameter space due to the fingerprint metric, but that it is on the order of 1% and so is negligible.

4.4   Multidimensional Scaling

We can repeat the multidimensional scaling algorithm with different numbers of dimensions allowed for the points: the error obviously monotonically decreases as we use more dimensions, but when the improvement starts vanishing we can claim this is the essential dimension of the dataset. This is shown in Figure 5.

As expected, dimensions beyond 3 contribute little to the embedding; the 4th gives a small improvement, the 5th and 6th a tiny one, and all further dimensions do not improve the result at all. A commonly quoted goodness-of-fit statistic is Kruskal's normalized stress, computed as

$$\sqrt{\frac{\sum_{i,j}(\delta_{i,j} - d_{i,j})^2}{\sum_{i,j} \delta_{i,j}^2}}$$

which is unity for the trivial solution for putting all the strategies in one single point. Stress below 0.05 is considered good [11]; our stress for embedding into $\mathbb{R}^2$ is 0.0498, into $\mathbb{R}^3$ is 0.0234, into $\mathbb{R}^6$ is 0.0200.

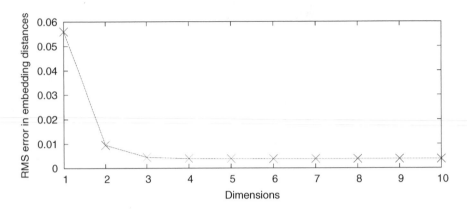

Fig. 5. The best-fit root mean square error in embedding the pairwise distance matrix for the 17^3 points into $\mathbb{R}^n$, for various n. For comparison the root mean square of the distances themselves is 0.1916.

The reason the error does not decrease towards 0 is that the data, computed under $\mathcal{L}_1$, is inherently not Euclidean and cannot be exactly embedded into Euclidean space of any dimension whatsoever. This residual error, which is relatively small, is some measure of the non-Euclidean property of our data.

We will take the best 2-dimensional fit and plot it in Figure 6.

4.5   Colouring Scheme

We describe the colouring schema used in the left scatterplot of Figure 6. Since our strategies are a sampling of the unit cube, we can assign each strategy a colour in the RGB space to succinctly distinguish each of them visually. The method is simple: we let x ($\in [0, 1]$) be the red channel, y be the green channel, and z be the blue channel.

To avoid using colours that are too close to white and hence invisible, we proportionally reduce the channels if their sum is above 1. Thus the 8 deterministic strategies are given the major colours:

- (0,0,0): ALLD, always defect — black
- (1,0,0): C-ALLD, cooperate first move, then defect thereafter — red
- (1,1,0): TFT, tit-for-tat — yellow
- (0,1,0): D-TFT, defect first move, then tit-for-tat — green
- (0,1,1): D-ALLC, defect first move, cooperate thereafter — cyan
- (0,0,1): PSY, psycho (reverse tit-for-tat) — blue
- (1,0,1): C-PSY, cooperate first move, then psycho — magenta
- (1,1,1): ALLC, always cooperate — white (scaled to light grey)

Also, to emphasize the outer faces of the cube, we change the point glyphs depending on the parameters. If all the parameters are extremal (0 or 1) — one of the deterministic corners, we use a double cross; if two of three are extremal,

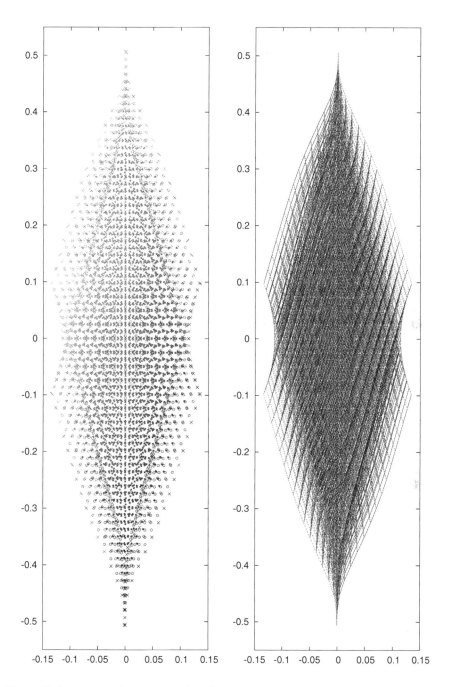

Fig. 6. Left: scatter plot of the reduced grid of 4913 strategies, projected to 2D with metric MDS. For colouring and point glyphs see section 4.5; axes are rotated to principal components, positive orientation is arbitrary. Right: connectivity network of the same. Variation along x, y and z only are red, green and blue lines respectively.

that is we are on an edge of the cube, we use a cross; if one is extremal, that is we are on a face, we use an open circle. For the rest of the points, in the interior of the cube, we use a closed circle.

6 of the 8 deterministic strategies, except C-ALLD and D-ALLC, are clearly marked as corners in this space. The edge network of the outside of the cube is also visible. One feature of note is that C-ALLD and D-ALLC are asymmetrically off to one side (in the horizontal direction). This is actually different from prior results [17], but upon closer inspection, particularly the edges that connect to it, it is a complete artifact.

Notice that the edge from the opposite horizontal corner that connects to these strategies ends up not going to C-ALLD (or D-ALLC), but to its mirror position in the horizontal direction. This shows that C-ALLD and D-ALLC are actually corners in the third dimension, and forced by using only two dimensions, they are swept to one side with a resultant huge jump in the edge.

The right side of Figure 6 shows the connectivity network of the unit cube (changing one parameter by one step, holding the other two fixed). Varying only x, y, and z is shown by the grid of red, green, and blue lines respectively. The symmetry between y and z is clearly shown, the green lines running diagonally from top-right to bottom-left, the blue lines from top-left to bottom-right.

It is likely that the combination of increasing both y and z by one grid value corresponds to a move directly upwards. Conversely, if we increase y by one notch and lower z by one, that looks to be a move directly horizontally. We will test these hypotheses in the upcoming section.

These lines are mostly straight, except for the mentioned huge jumps into C-ALLD and D-ALLC, visible as marked bends. x, the probability of initially cooperating, creates mostly curved lines, most marked in between TFT and D-TFT (PSY and C-PSY respectively). From comparison to Figure 4, where the red lines are actually exactly straight, it is clear it is another form of imprecision. Although distorted, the structure of the cube can still be seen through this grid.

4.6   The Principal Components of the Space

For our final analysis, we will take the 6-dimensional MDS embedded points, rotated using principal component analysis, and attempt to correlate the parameter variables with the important dimensions of the space.

It turns out that we can quantitatively calculate the rotated dimensions of the space easily. The leading dimension can be predicted by $(1 - \alpha)x + \alpha\frac{y+z}{2}$, which can be seen to be the α-geometrically weighted probability of cooperating against a completely random opponent (our α is 0.8). The second dimension can be predicted by $y - z$, which can be seen to be the difference in probability of cooperation depending on the opponent's last move, or "responsiveness". The third dimension can be predicted by $\frac{x}{1-\alpha} - \frac{y+z}{2\alpha}$, which is harder to interpret, but it *subtracts* the probability of cooperation between the first move and the subsequent moves.

The Pearson linear correlation coefficient between these three predictors and the actual MDS-found coordinate values were computed. The leading dimension is predicted with correlation 0.999946, the second with correlation 0.984808, and the third 0.991375. These values are extraordinarily high, indicating that we have indeed found the correct interpretation of these dimensions.

5   Discussion and Conclusions

We have studied a basic probabilistic 1-state transducer representation for Prisoner's Dilemma. Notwithstanding that this space is too simplistic to have many interesting strategies, we can build on knowledge from the smaller state spaces to generalize to the larger, far more intractable ones.

Multiple independent tests were applied to a 35,937-point grid of the continuous cube for this space, with all results in concord with the conclusion that the genotype (parameter space) — phenotype (strategic behaviour as measured by the fingerprint) distinction for this space indeed exists, but is not a severe effect.

No null mutation-pairs (identical phenotype but distinct genotype) were found, meaning the known cubical structure can be embedded into usual space without self-intersection. The results from running the UPGMA clustering algorithm do not show any significant level of structural detail, which is to be expected from a continuous sampling grid. Also, the parameter space is found to be slightly curved with respect to the fingerprint distance, but not highly so.

Multidimensional scaling on a subsampled grid reveal a lot more about the structure. First, we know it has a true dimension of 3; it can be very well embedded into $\mathbb{R}^3$, and there is no improvement after about 6 dimensions. This tells us that the fingerprint distance does indeed mostly respect the metric structure of the cube.

From directly plotting the 2-dimensional embedded points, we can see that the deterministic automata form the corners of the space as expected, but since we are coercing a 3-dimensional object into 2 dimensions, several artifacts appear. Notably, the deterministic strategies C-ALLD and D-ALLC are essentially mapped to two points at once, with a resulting discontinuity in the cube; also the known-straight lines from varying the x parameter are completely curved, even more so than the nonlinear y, z parameters.

Lastly, we have found a fully quantitative explanation for the three (hence all) most important dimensions in the space: they correspond to general cooperativity, responsivity to the opponent, and change in cooperativity from the first to subsequent moves.

For future work, we would like to continue investigating other relatively small state spaces and either discover new dimensions to game-playing strategies, or prove their similarity.

Acknowledgments. The author would like to thank Rajesh Pereira, University of Guelph. This work was made possible by the facilities of the Shared Hierarchical Academic Research Computing Network (SHARCNET:www.sharcnet.ca) and Compute/Calcul Canada.

References

1. Ashlock, D., Kim, E.-Y.: Techniques for analysis of evolved prisoner's dilemma strategies with fingerprints. In: Proceedings of the 2005 Congress on Evolutionary Computation, pp. 2613–2620 (2005)
2. Ashlock, D., Kim, E.-Y., von Roeschlaub, W.K.: Fingerprints: enabling visualization and automatic analysis of strategies for two player games. In: Proceedings of the 2004 Congress on Evolutionary Computation, pp. 381–387 (2004)
3. Ashlock, D., Kim, E.-Y.: Fingerprinting: visualization and automatic analysis of Prisoner's Dilemma strategies. IEEE Transactions on Evolutionary Computation 12(5), 647–659 (2008)
4. Ashlock, D., Kim, E.-Y., Ashlock, W.: Fingerprint analysis of the noisy Prisoner's Dilemma using a finite state representation. IEEE Transactions on Computational Intelligence and AI in Games 1(2), 157–167 (2009)
5. Ashlock, D., Kim, E.-Y.: Fingerprint analysis of the noisy Prisoner's Dilemma. In: Proceedings of the 2007 Congress on Evolutionary Computation, pp. 4073–4080 (2007)
6. Ashlock, D., Kim, E.-Y., Leahy, N.: Understanding representational sensitivity in the iterated Prisoner's Dilemma with fingerprints. IEEE Transactions on Systems, Man and Cybernetics C 36(4), 464–475 (2006)
7. Ashlock, D., Kim, E.-Y.: The impact of cellular representation on finite state agents for Prisoner's Dilemma. In: Proceedings of the 2005 Genetic and Evolutionary Computing Conference, pp. 59–66 (2005)
8. Ashlock, W., Ashlock, D.: Changes in Prisoner's Dilemma strategies over evolutionary time with different population sizes. In: Proceedings of the Congress on Evolutionary Computation 2006, pp. 297–304 (2006)
9. Gibbs, A.L., Su, F.E.: On choosing and bounding probability metrics. International statistical review 70(3), 419–435 (2002)
10. Ishibuchi, H., Ohyanagi, H., Nojima, Y.: Evolution of strategies with different representation schemes in a spatial iterated Prisoner's Dilemma game. IEEE Transactions on Computational Intelligence and AI in Games 3(1), 67–82 (2011)
11. Kruskal, J.B.: Multidimensional scaling by optimizing goodness of fit to a nonmetric hypothesis. Psychometrika 29(1), 1–27 (1964)
12. de Leeuw, J.: Applications of convex analysis to multidimensional scaling. In: Barra, J.R., et al. (eds.) Recent Developments in Statistics. pp. 133–145. North-Holland, Amsterdam, (1977)
13. Sneath, P.H.A., Sokal, R.R.: Numerical Taxonomy: The Principles and Practice of Numerical Classification. Freeman, CA (1973)
14. Stroud, A.H.: Approximate Calculation of Multiple Integrals. Englewood Cliffs, Prentice-Hall, NJ (1971)
15. Tsang, J.: The parametrized probabilistic finite state transducer probe game player fingerprint model. IEEE Transactions on Computational Intelligence and AI in Games 2(3), 208–224 (2010)
16. Tsang, J.: The structure of a depth-3 lookup table representation for Prisoner's Dilemma. In: Proceedings of the IEEE Conference on Computational Intelligence in Games 2010, pp. 54–61 (2010)
17. Tsang, J.: The structure of a 3-state finite transducer representation for Prisoner's Dilemma. In: Proceedings of the IEEE Conference on Computational Intelligence in Games 2010, pp. 307–313 (2013)

Tree Depth Influence in Genetic Programming for Generation of Competitive Agents for RTS Games

Pablo García-Sánchez[⊠], Antonio Fernández-Ares, Antonio M. Mora,
Pedro A. Castillo, Jesús González, and Juan Julián Merelo Guervós

Department of Computer Architecture and Technology and CITIC-UGR,
University of Granada, Granada, Spain
pgarcia@atc.ugr.es

Abstract. This work presents the results obtained from comparing different tree depths in a Genetic Programming Algorithm to create agents that play the Planet Wars game. Three different maximum levels of the tree have been used (3, 7 and Unlimited) and two bots available in the literature, based on human expertise, and optimized by a Genetic Algorithm have been used for training and comparison. Results show that in average, the bots obtained using our method equal or outperform the previous ones, being the maximum depth of the tree a relevant parameter for the algorithm.

1 Introduction

Real Time Strategy (RTS) games are a type of videogame where the play takes action in real time (that is, there are not turns, as in chess). Well-known games of this genre are Age of Empires[TM] or Warcraft[TM]. In this kind of game the players have units, structures and resources and they have to confront with other players to win battles. Artificial Intelligence (AI) in these games is usually very complex, because they are dealing with many actions and strategies at the same time.

The *Planet Wars* game, presented under the Google AI Challenge 2010[1] has been used by several authors for the study of computational intelligence in RTS games [1–3]. This is because it is a simplification of the elements that are present in the complex games previously mentioned (only one type of resource and one type of unit).

The objective of the player is to conquer enemy and neutral planets in a space-like simulator. Each player has planets (resources) that produce ships (units) depending on a growth-rate. The player must send these ships to other planets (literally, crashing towards the planet) to conquer them. A player win if he is the owner of all the planets. As requirements, the limit to calculate next actions (this time window is called *turn*[2]) is only a second, and no memory about the

---

[1] http://planetwars.aichallenge.org/
[2] Although in this work we are using this term, note that the game is always performed in real time.

© Springer-Verlag Berlin Heidelberg 2014
A.I. Esparcia-Alcázar et al. (Eds.): EvoApplications 2014, LNCS 8602, pp. 411–421, 2014.
DOI: 10.1007/978-3-662-45523-4_34

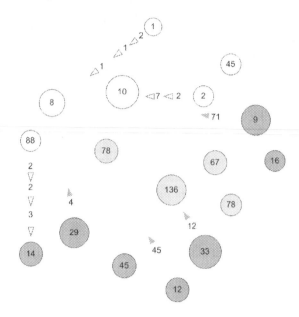

Fig. 1. Example of execution of the Player Wars game. White planets and ships are owned by the player and dark gray ones are controlled by the enemy. Clear gray are neutral planets (not invaded).

previous turns must be used. Figure 1 shows a screen capture of the game. The reader is referred to [1–3] for more details of the game.

In this work Genetic Programming (GP) is used to obtain agents that play the Planet Wars game. The objective of GP is to create functions or programs to solve determined problems. Individual representation is usually in form of a tree, formed by operators (or *primitives*) and variables (*terminals*). These sets are usually fixed and known. The genome size is, therefore, variable, but the maximum size (depth) of the individuals is usually fixed, to avoid high evaluation costs. GP has been used to evolve LISP (LISt Processing) programs [4], or XSLT (eXtensible Stylesheet Language Transformations) scripts [5], among others.

We try to solve the next questions:

- Can a tree-generated behaviour of an agent defeat an agent hand-coded by a player with experience and whose parameters have been also optimized?
- Can this agent beat a more complicated opponent that is adapted to the environment?
- How does the maximum depth affect the results?

The rest of the work is structured as follows: after the state of the art, the description of our agent is presented in Section 3. Then, the experimental setup conduced with the GP is shown (Section 4). Finally, results, conclusions and future works are discussed.

2   State of the Art

RTS games have been used extensively in the computational intelligence area (see [6] for a survey).

Among other techniques, Evolutionary Algorithms (EAs) have been widely used in computational intelligence in RTS games [6]. For example, for parameter optimization [7], learning [8] or content generation [9].

One of these types, genetic programming, has been proved as a good tool for developing strategies in games, achieving results comparable to human, or human-based competitors [10]. They also have obtained higher ranking than solvers produced by other techniques or even beating high-ranking humans [11]. GP has also been used in different kind of games, such as board-games [12], or (in principle) simpler games such as Ms. Pac-Man [13] and Spoof [14] and even in modern video-games such as First Person Shothers (FPS) (for example, Unreal[TM] [15]).

Planet Wars, the game used in this work, has also been used as experimental environment for testing agents in other works. For example, in [2] the authors programmed the behaviour of a *bot* (a computer-controlled player) with a decision tree of 3 levels. Then, the values of these rules were optimized using a genetic algorithm to tune the strategy rates and percentages. Results showed a good performance confronting with other bots provided by the Google AI Challenge. In [3] the authors improved this agent optimizing it in different types of maps and selecting the set of optimized parameters depending on the map where the game was taking place, using a tree of 5 levels. These results outperformed the previous version of the bot with 87% of victories.

In this paper we use GP to create the decision tree, instead of expert human gaming experience to model it, and the resulting agent is compared with the two presented before.

3   Proposed Agent

The proposed agent receives a tree to be executed. The generated tree is a binary tree of expressions formed by two different types of nodes:

- *Decision*: a logical expression formed by a variable, a less than operator ($<$), and a number between 0 and 1. It is the equivalent to a "primitive" in the field of GP.
- *Action*: a leave of the the tree (therefore, a "terminal"). Each decision is the name of the method to call from the planet that executes the tree. This method indicates to which planet send a percentage of available ships (from 0 to 1).

The different variables for the decisions are:

- *myShipsEnemyRatio*: Ratio between the player's ships and enemy's ships.

- *myShipsLandedFlyingRatio*: Ratio between the player's landed and flying ships.
- *myPlanetsEnemyRatio*: Ratio between the number of player's planets and the enemy's ones.
- *myPlanetsTotalRatio*: Ratio between the number of player's planet and total planets (neutrals and enemy included).
- *actualMyShipsRatio*: Ratio between the number of ships in the specific planet that evaluates the tree and player's total ships.
- *actualLandedFlyingRatio*: Ratio between the number of ships landed and flying from the specific planet that evaluates the tree and player's total ships.

The decision list is:

- *Attack Nearest (Neutral—Enemy—NotMy) Planet*: The objective is the nearest planet.
- *Attack Weakest (Neutral—Enemy—NotMy) Planet*: The objective is the planet with less ships.
- *Attack Wealthiest (Neutral—Enemy—NotMy) Planet*: The objective is the planet with higher lower rate.
- *Attack Beneficial (Neutral—Enemy—NotMy) Planet*: The objective is the more beneficial planet, that is, the one with growth rate divided by the number of ships.
- *Attack Quickest (Neutral—Enemy—NotMy) Planet*: The objective is the planet easier to be conquered: the lowest product between the distance from the planet that executes the tree and the number of ships in the objective planet.
- *Attack (Neutral—Enemy—NotMy) Base*: The objective is the planet with more ships (that is, the base).
- *Attack Random Planet*.
- *Reinforce Nearest Planet*: Reinforce the nearest player's planet to the planet that executes the tree.
- *Reinforce Base*: Reinforce the player's planet with higher number of ships.
- *Reinforce Wealthiest Planet*: Reinforce the player's planet with higher grown rate.
- *Do nothing*.

An example of a possible tree is shown in Figure 2. This example tree has a total of 5 nodes, with 2 decisions and 3 actions, and a depth of 3 levels.

The bot behaviour is explained in Algorithm 1.

4   Experimental Setup

Sub-tree crossover and 1-node mutation evolutionary operators have been used, following other researchers' proposals that have used these operators obtaining good results [15]. In this case, the mutation randomly changes the decision of

```
if(myShipsLandedFlyingRatio <0.796)
    if(actualMyShipsRatio <0.201)
        attackWeakestNeutralPlanet(0.481);
    else
        attackNearestEnemyPlanet(0.913);
else
    attackNearestEnemyPlanet(0.819);
```

Fig. 2. Example of a generated Java tree

```
At the beginning of the execution the agent receives the tree;
tree← readTree();
while game not finished do
    // starts the turn
    calculateGlobalPlanets();// e.g. Base or Enemy Base
    calculateGlobalRatios();// e.g. myPlanetsEnemyRatio
    foreach p in PlayerPlanets do
        calculateLocalPlanets(p);// e.g. NearestNeutralPlanet to p
        calculateLocalRatios(p);// e.g actualMyShipsRatio
        executeTree(p,tree);// Send a percentage of ships to destination
    end
end
```

Algorithm 1. Pseudocode of the proposed agent. The tree is fixed during all the agent's execution

a node or mutate the value with a step-size of 0.25 (an adequate value empirically tested). Each configuration is executed 30 times, with a population of 32 individuals and a 2-tournament selector for a pool of 16 parents.

To test each individual during the evolution, a battle with a previously created bot is performed in 5 different (but representative) maps provided by Google is played. Hierarchical fitness is used, as proposed in [2]. Thus, an individual is better than another if it wins in a higher number of maps. In case of equality of victories, then the individual with more turns to be defeated (i.e. the stronger one) is considered better. The maximum fitness is, therefore 5 victories and 0 turns. Also, as proposed by [2], and due to the noisy fitness effect, all individuals are re-evaluated in every generation.

Two publicly available bots have been chosen for our experiments[3]. The first bot to confront is *GeneBot*, proposed in [2]. This bot was trained using a GA to optimize the 8 parameters that conforms a set of hand-made rules, obtained from an expert human player experience. The second one is an advanced version of the previous, called *Exp-Genebot* (Expert Genebot) [3]. This bot outperformed Genebot widely. Exp-Genebot bot analyses the distribution of the planets in the

---

[3] Both can be downloaded from https://github.com/deantares/genebot

map to chose a previously optimized set of parameters by a GA. Both bots are the best individual obtained of all runs of their algorithm (not an average one).

After running the proposed algorithm without tree limitation in depth, it has also been executed with the lower and average levels obtained for the best individuals: 3 and 7, respectively, to study if this number has any effect on the results. Table 1 summarizes all the parameters used.

Table 1. Parameters used in the experiments

Parameter Name	Value
Population size	32
Crossover type	Sub-tree crossover
Crossover rate	0.5
Mutation	1-node mutation
Mutation step-size	0.25
Selection	2-tournament
Replacement	Steady-state
Stop criterion	50 generations
Maximum Tree Depth	3, 7 and unlimited
Runs per configuration	30
Evaluation	Playing versus Genebot [2] and Exp-Genebot [3]
Maps used in each evaluation	map76.txt map69.txt map7.txt map11.txt map26.txt

After all the executions we have evaluated the obtained best individuals in all runs confronting to the bots in a larger set of maps (the 100 maps provided by Google) to study the behaviour of the algorithm and how good are the obtained bots in maps that have not been used for training.

The used framework is OSGiLiath, a service-oriented evolutionary framework [16]. The generated tree is compiled in real-time and injected in the agent's code using Javassist[4] library. All the source code used in this work is available under a LGPL V3 License in http://www.osgiliath.org.

5   Results

Tables 2 and 3 summarize all the obtained results of the execution of our EA. These tables also show the average age, depth and number of nodes of the best individuals obtained and also the average population at the end of the run. The average turns rows are calculated only taking into account the individuals with a number of victories lower than 5, because this number is 0 if they have won the five battles.

As can be seen, the average population fitness versus Genebot is nearest to the optimum than versus Exp-Genebot, even with the lowest depth. Highest

---

[4] www.javassist.org

Table 2. Average results obtained from each configuration versus Genebot. Each one has been tested 30 times.

		Depth 3	*Depth 7*	*Unlimited Depth*
Best Fitness	Victories	**4.933** ± 0.25	4.83 ± 0.53	4.9 ± 0.30
	Turns	244.5 ± 54.44	466 ± 205.44	266.667 ± 40.42
Population Ave. Fitness	Victories	**4.486**± 0.52	4.43 ± 0.07	4.711 ± 0.45
	Turns	130.77± 95.81	139.43 ± 196.60	190.346 ± 102.92
Depth	Best	3 ± 0	5.2 ± 1.78	6.933 ± 4.05
	Population	3 ± 0	5.267 ± 1.8	7.353 ± 3.11
Nodes	Best	7 ± 0	13.667 ± 7.68	22.133 ± 22.21
	Population	7 ± 0	13.818 ± 5.86	21.418 ± 13.81
Age	Best	**8.133** ± 3.95	5.467 ± 2.95	5.066 ± 2.11
	Population	**4.297** ± 3.027	3.247 ± 0.25	3.092 ± 1.27

Table 3. Average results obtained from each configuration versus Exp-Genebot. Each one has been tested 30 times.

		Depth 3	*Depth 7*	*Unlimited Depth*
Best Fitness	Victories	4.133 ± 0.50	4.2 ± 0.48	**4.4** ± 0.56
	Turns	221.625 ± 54.43	163.667 ± 106.38	123.533 ± 112.79
Population Ave. Fitness	Victories	3.541 ± 0.34	3.689 ± 0.37	**4.043** ± 0.38
	Turns	200.086 ± 50.79	184.076 ± 57.02	159.094 ± 61.84
Depth	Best	3 ± 0	5.2 ± 1.84	6.966 ± 4.44
	Population	3 ± 0	5.216 ± 0.92	6.522 ± 1.91
Nodes	Best	7 ± 0	12.6 ± 6.44	18.466 ± 15.46
	Population	7 ± 0	13.05 ± 3.92	16.337 ± 7.67
Age	Best	4.266 ± 5.01	4.133 ± 4.26	**4.7** ± 4.72
	Population	3.706 ± 0.58	3.727 ± 0.62	**3.889** ± 0.71

performance in the population is also with the depth of 3 levels. On the contrary, confronting with Exp-Genebot the configuration with unlimited depth achieves better results. This make sense as more decisions should be taken because the enemy can be different in each map.

In the second experiment, we have confronted the 30 bots obtained in each configuration again with Genebot and Exp-Genebot, but in the 100 maps provided by Google. This experiment has been used to validate if the obtained individuals of the proposed method can be competitive in terms of quality in maps not used for evaluation. Results are shown in Table 4 and boxplots in Figure 3. It can be seen that in average, the bots produced by the proposed algorithm perform equal or better than the best obtained by the previous authors. Note that, even obtaining individuals with maximum fitness (5 victories) that have been kept in the population several generations (as presented before in Tables 2 and 3) cannot be representative of a extremely good bot in a wider set of maps that have not been used for training. As the distributions are not normalized, a Kruskal-Wallis test has been used, obtaining significant differences in turns for the experiment versus Genebot (p-value = 0.0028) and victories in Exp-genebot (p-value = 0.02681). Therefore, there are differences using a maximum depth in the generation of bots. In both configurations, the trees created with 7 levels of depth as maximum have obtained the better results.

Table 4. Results confronting the 30 best bots attained from each configuration in the 100 maps each

Configuration	Average maps won	Average turns
Versus Genebot		
Depth 3	47.033 ± 10.001	133.371 ± 16.34
Depth 7	48.9 ± 10.21	**141.386 ± 15.54**
Unlimited Depth	50.23 ± 11.40	133.916 ± 10.55
Versus Exp-Genebot		
Depth 3	52.367 ± 13.39	191.051 ± 67.79
Depth 7	**58.867 ± 7.35**	174.694± 47.50
Unlimited Depth	52.3 ± 11.57	197.492 ± 72.30

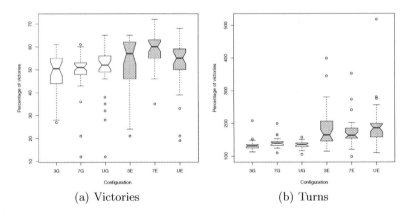

(a) Victories   (b) Turns

Fig. 3. Average of executing the 30 best bots in each configuration (3, 7 and U) versus Genebot (G) and Exp-Genebot (E)

To explain why results versus Genebot (a weaker bot than Exp-Genebot) are slightly worse than versus Exp-Genebot, even when the best individuals produced by the GP have higher fitness, it is necessary to analyse how the best individual and the population are being evolved. Figure 4 shows that best individual using Genebot reaches the optimal before Exp-Genebot, and also the average population converges quicker. This could lead to over-specialization: the generated bots are over-trained to win in the five maps. This is due because these individuals are being re-evaluated, and therefore, they are still changing after they have reached the optimal.

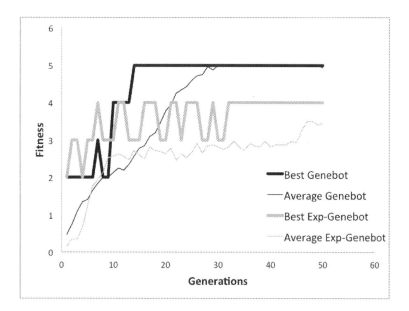

Fig. 4. Evolution of the best individual and the average population during one run for depth 7 versus Genebot and Exp-Genebot

6   Conclusions

This work presents a Genetic Programming algorithm that generates agents for playing the Planet Wars game. A number of possible actions to perform and decision variables have been presented. Two competitive bots available in the literature (Genebot and Exp-Genebot) have been used to calculate the fitness of the generated individuals. These two bots were the best obtained from several runs and the behaviour to be optimized was extracted from human expertise. Three different maximum depth for the trees have been used: 3, 7 and unlimited. Results show that the best individuals outperform these agents during the evolution in all configurations. These individuals have been tested against a larger set of maps not previously used during the evolution, obtaining equivalent or better results than Genebot and Exp-Genebot.

In future work, other rules will be added to the proposed algorithm (for example, the ones that analyse the map, as the Exp-Genebot does) and different enemies will be used. Other games used in the area of computational intelligence in videogames, such as Unreal^{TM} or Super Mario^{TM} will be tested.

Acknowledgments. This work has been supported in part by FPU research grant AP2009-2942 and projects SIPESCA (G-GI3000/IDIF, under Programa Operativo FEDER de Andalucía 2007-2013), EvOrq (TIC-3903), CANUBE (CEI2013-P-14) and ANYSELF (TIN2011-28627-C04-02).

References

1. Lara-Cabrera, R., Cotta, C., Fernández-Leiva, A.J.: A procedural balanced map generator with self-adaptive complexity for the real-time strategy game planet wars. In: Esparcia-Alcázar, A.I. (ed.) EvoApplications 2013. LNCS, vol. 7835, pp. 274–283. Springer, Heidelberg (2013)
2. Mora, A.M., Fernández-Ares, A., Guervós, J.J.M., García-Sánchez, P., Fernandes, C.M.: Effect of noisy fitness in real-time strategy games player behaviour optimisation using evolutionary algorithms. J. Comput. Sci. Technol. **27**(5), 1007–1023 (2012)
3. Fernández-Ares, A., García-Sánchez, P., Mora, A.M., Guervós, J.J.M.: Adaptive bots for real-time strategy games via map characterization. In: 2012 IEEE Conference on Computational Intelligence and Games, CIG 2012, Granada, Spain, September 11–14, pp. 417–721. IEEE (2012)
4. Koza, J.R.: Genetically breeding populations of computer programs to solve problems in artificial intelligence. In: Proceedings of the 2nd International IEEE Conference on Tools for Artificial Intelligence, pp. 819–827 (1990)
5. Garcia-Sanchez, P., Merelo, J.J., Laredo, J.L.J., Mora, A.M., Castillo, P.A.: Evolving xslt stylesheets for document transformation. In: Rudolph, G., Jansen, T., Lucas, S., Poloni, C., Beume, N. (eds.) PPSN 2008. LNCS, vol. 5199, pp. 1021–1030. Springer, Heidelberg (2008)
6. Lara-Cabrera, R., Cotta, C., Fernández-Leiva, A.J.: A review of computational intelligence in rts games. In: FOCI, pp. 114–121. IEEE (2013)
7. Esparcia-Alcázar, A.I., García, A.I.M., García, A.M., Guervós, J.J.M., García-Sánchez, P.: Controlling bots in a first person shooter game using genetic algorithms. In: IEEE Congress on Evolutionary Computation, pp. 1–8. IEEE (2010)
8. Stanley, K.O., Bryant, B.D., Miikkulainen, R.: Real-time neuroevolution in the nero video game. In: IEEE Transactions on Evolutionary Computation, pp. 653–668 (2005)
9. Mahlmann, T., Togelius, J., Yannakakis, G.N.: Spicing up map generation. In: Di Chio, C., et al. (eds.) EvoApplications 2012. LNCS, vol. 7248, pp. 224–233. Springer, Heidelberg (2012)
10. Sipper, M., Azaria, Y., Hauptman, A., Shichel, Y.: Designing an evolutionary strategizing machine for game playing and beyond. IEEE Transactions on Systems, Man and Cybernetics Part C: Applications and Reviews **37**(4), 583–593 (2007)
11. Elyasaf, A., Hauptman, A., Sipper, M.: Evolutionary design of freecell solvers. IEEE Transactions on Computational Intelligence and AI in Games **4**(4), 270–281 (2012)
12. Benbassat, A., Sipper, M.: Evolving both search and strategy for reversi players using genetic programming, 47–54 (2012)

13. Brandstetter, M., Ahmadi, S.: Reactive control of ms. pac man using information retrieval based on genetic programming, 250–256 (2012)
14. Wittkamp, M., Barone, L., While, L.: A comparison of genetic programming and look-up table learning for the game of spoof, 63–71 (2007)
15. Esparcia-Alcázar, A.I., Moravec, J.: Fitness approximation for bot evolution in genetic programming. Soft Computing **17**(8), 1479–1487 (2013)
16. García-Sánchez, P., González, J., Castillo, P.A., Arenas, M.G., Guervós, J.J.M.: Service oriented evolutionary algorithms. Soft Comput. **17**(6), 1059–1075 (2013)

EvoHOT

Diagnostic Test Generation for Statistical Bug Localization Using Evolutionary Computation

Marco Gaudesi[1], Maksim Jenihhin[2], Jaan Raik[2], Ernesto Sanchez[1],
Giovanni Squillero[1(✉)], Valentin Tihhomirov[2], and Raimund Ubar[2]

[1] Politecnico di Torino, Torino, Italy
{marco.gaudesi,ernesto.sanchez,giovanni.squillero}@polito.it
[2] Tallinn University of Technology, Tallinn, Estonia
{maksim.jenihhin,jaan.raik,raimund.ubar,
valentin.tihhomirov}@ati.ttu.ee

Abstract. Verification is increasingly becoming a bottleneck in the process of designing electronic circuits. While there exists several verification tools that assist in detecting occurrences of design errors, or bugs, there is a lack of solutions for accurately pin-pointing the root causes of these errors. Statistical bug localization has proven to be an approach that scales up to large designs and is widely utilized both in debugging hardware and software. However, the accuracy of localization is highly dependent on the quality of the stimuli. In this paper we formulate diagnostic test set generation as a task for an evolutionary algorithm, and propose dedicated fitness functions that closely correlate with the bug localization capabilities. We perform experiments on the register-transfer level design of the Plasma microprocessor coupling an evolutionary test-pattern generator and a simulator for fitness evaluation. As a result, the diagnostic resolution of the tests is significantly improved.

Keywords: Diagnostic test pattern generation · Design error localization · Evolutionary computation · MicroGP · ZamiaCAD

1 Introduction

It is widely acknowledged that verification is consuming the major part of the design cycle of electronic circuits [1]. In turn, most of the verification effort is spent in the loop of locating and correcting the design errors [2]. Therefore, solutions allowing the designer to quickly pin-point the root causes of bugs would significantly decrease the cost of the entire design process.

In order to address this problem, several formal [3-5] and simulation-based [6-8] design error localization approaches have been developed in the past. The formal approaches have high reasoning power and many of them do not require test stimuli. However, their scalability is low, and therefore, they can only be applied to small portions extracted from the real design project, or oversimplified parts. The simulation-based approaches scale reasonably with the size of the design and are limited mainly by the speed of simulation. However, the results are highly dependent on the

© Springer-Verlag Berlin Heidelberg 2014
A.I. Esparcia-Alcázar et al. (Eds.): EvoApplications 2014, LNCS 8602, pp. 425–436, 2014.
DOI: 10.1007/978-3-662-45523-4_35

quality of the test stimuli applied. Thus, it is imperative to develop efficient diagnostic test pattern generation methods to increase the accuracy of the simulation-based bug localization.

In this paper, we consider *statistical bug localization*, an approach that has been successfully applied both to software [7, 8, 10] and hardware [11] debugging. The general rationale behind the statistical localization lies in collecting and analyzing the pass/fail data of the simulation traces and supplementing these with HDL (hardware description language) code level structural information of the design. Based on this analysis, reasoning on bug locations is carried out.

As mentioned above, the efficiency of this reasoning is highly dependent on the quality of input stimuli. Moreover, adding new stimuli to the existing ones may in fact adversely affect the localization accuracy. Thus, there is a need for approaches providing generation of diagnostic tests that allow accurate bug localization by statistical approaches. The initial promising results on assessing diagnostic capability of diagnostic tests for automated statistical bug localization have been presented in [12], however it did not consider particular approach for diagnostic test stimuli generation.

Evolutionary Computation (EC) has been used by the Computer Aided Design community for years, also involving it for the tasks of *automatic test-pattern generation* and *semi-formal verification*. The main obstacle that prevented the exploitation of EC in bug localization was the difficulty of defining a suitable fitness function: a bug is either caught or not caught, with no intermediate state.

In this paper, we propose an approach for diagnostic test generation for statistical bug localization using evolutionary computation. For this purpose we exploit a general-purpose evolutionary toolkit µGP (also spelled *MicroGP*) and investigate dedicated diagnostic capability metrics to be used as the fitness function. The flow starts from a previously existing functional test set provided by the designer and iteratively generates new test stimuli increasing the diagnostic properties of the test set. The approach does not address diagnosis of a specific design error but rather attempts to generate a test that has a high diagnostic resolution throughout the complete RTL design implementation (i.e. hardware description language code).

The advantage of such flow is twofold. First, it significantly saves the test generation time by avoiding experiments for a specific bug to be carried out iteratively during the evolutionary optimization process. Second, it provides a more flexible test set that can be reused even in the case of later modifications to the code while still yielding high overall diagnostic resolution. To the authors' knowing, this is the first approach to generate diagnostic tests for statistical bug localization implementing evolutionary methods.

The paper is organized as follows. Section 2 presents an overview of the related works in the field of diagnostic test pattern generation for locating design errors. Section 3 summarizes the bug localization implementing design analysis framework zamiaCAD. In Section 4, the general diagnosis concept is explained and the diagnostic metrics are presented. Section 5 sketches the evolutionary optimization tool µGP. and explains the diagnostic test pattern generation flow. Experimental results are provided in Section 6. Finally, Section 7 concludes the paper.

2   Overview of Related Works

Several works on Diagnostic Test Pattern Generation (DTPG) have been proposed in the past. Deng et al. [13] propose mutant-based DTPG combined with Bounded Model-Checking (BMC) for generating test stimuli assisting statistical bug localization. The approach is prohibitively time consuming since the number of injected mutants is extremely high and both, BMC and the diagnosis algorithm have to be executed in a loop for all the mutants. Bernardi et al. [14] apply evolutionary algorithms in DTPG for manufacturing defects. However, the task of diagnosing defects in integrated circuits is fundamentally different from locating design errors that is addressed here.

Evolutionary diagnostic test pattern generation requires a suitable fitness function. Abreau et al. [15] and Repinski et al. [16] have studied the effect of different diagnosis metrics. However, these metrics are targeted towards minimizing the error candidates to be corrected by formal design error correction methods and they are not targeting DTPG. In [12] Tihhomirov et al. proposed metrics for assessing the diagnosis capabilities of the test set. The work shows good correlation with the localization accuracy but does not consider the DTPG step. Lisherness et al. introduced metrics to assess the quality of functional tests [17]. However, the metrics are optimized towards coverage and not the diagnostic resolution.

In this paper, we formulate for the first time diagnostic test pattern generation for design errors as an evolutionary algorithm using the diagnostic metrics as the fitness function. The main challenges to be addressed include selecting a suitable metric as a fitness function for EC and to generate a test that has a high diagnostic resolution throughout the complete design implementation in terms of HDL code.

3   Statistical Bug Localization with zamiaCAD

The bug localization method described here has been implemented on top of an open source RTL design and debug framework zamiaCAD [18]. The front-end of zamiaCAD includes a parser and an elaboration engine that both support full VHDL-2002 standard specification and a set of VHDL-2008 extensions. On the back-end side, the framework allows design simulation, static analysis and other applications for debug. zamiaCAD has an Eclipse IDE plug-in based graphical user interface for advanced design entry and navigation. The framework is highly optimized for scalability and performance and is capable of handling very large industrial multi-core designs consisting of tens of millions of VHDL code lines [19].

The statistical bug localization method assumes that design verification has been performed and an erroneous behavior at observable outputs of the design has been detected. Figure 1 presents the statistical bug localization flow. The method is based on four main phases: (1) static slicing, (2) dynamic slicing, (3) statistical suspiciousness ranking of the HDL code items and, an optional, (4) cone inspection phase. First, the design is simulated in order to obtain the list of executed statements and information about passed and failed test cases from the test set. A test case is considered to be passed if the simulated output responses match with expected ones and it is regarded as failed otherwise. Then, *static slicing* is performed based on generating reference graphs. Subsequently, *dynamic slicing* reduces the debugging analysis to all the code items that actually affect the design's faulty behavior for a given test case. Finally, the *statistical suspiciousness ranking* assigns a *suspiciousness score* to each code item based on its presence in the dynamic slices and on the information of passed/failed test cases. Intuitively, if a code item occurs very frequently in executions revealing the error, it is very likely to contain a bug. The ranking is performed for the statement items in the HDL code. In order to reveal the bug locations more accurately, the suspiciousness ranking can be performed hierarchically considering also the branches and conditions that the highly ranked statements may have.

In this paper, we consider debugging as a process of locating the failure, with the correction task being left to the designer. After the latter has received the ranked list of code items the following task is to localize the root cause of the erroneous behavior. Likely locations for bugs are in those code items having the highest suspiciousness scores in the list. In a simple case the designer has to inspect code items at the top of the ranked list, whose score is higher than a preselected threshold value $S_{threshold}$.

However, there exist cases where the statistical ranking does not directly pin-point the root location of the error. The main reasons for this is either very sophisticated nature of the bug (e.g. a long complex sequential scenario required for bug activation) or more often weak diagnostic properties of the diagnostic test. The issue is specifically addressed in this paper.

In case if the automated statistical bug localization fails zamiaCAD also allows application of the *cone inspection* phase. Our previous case studies show that often it is possible to locate the bug by activating depth-limited forward and backward cones from the signals included to the highest ranked items. Therefore, the diagnostic test quality used for statistical ranking is also crucial for this step.

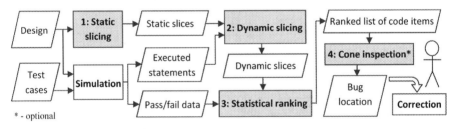

Fig. 1. Statistical bug localization in ZamiaCAD

4   Diagnostic Metrics for Statistical Bug Localization

In the following we propose two metrics for assessment of the diagnostic capability of the given test to locate bugs in the given design. Both metrics can be used by evolutionary methods as fitness functions in generation of high quality tests for design error diagnosis.

The metrics described below reflect the cause-effect relationships between the error hypotheses and the expected test results derived from simulation of the design for the given test.

4.1   Cause-Effect Relationships Between Errors and Test Results

Let us describe first how we model the cause-effect relationships between error-hypotheses and the expected test results.

Consider the approach based on statistical suspiciousness ranking criterion proposed in [11], which is based on design simulation with the given diagnostic test set. Let the diagnostic test set T consist of n tests, $T = (t_1, t_2,... t_n)$, and the design's HDL code C consist of m code items $C = (c_1, c_2,... c_m)$. Without loose of generality under code items we will consider the design statements. Consider a table $D = \| d_{i,j} \|$ where $d_{i,j} = 1$ if the test t_i is covering the code item c_j, and $d_{i,j} = 0$ otherwise. Such a table can be derived by finding the dynamic slices in the HDL code for all the tests of T by simulation.

Let us interpret the table D as a hypothetic Bug Table where $d_{i,j} = 1$ has a meaning of the hypothesis that the test t_i covers the statement c_j in the design description, and does not covet it in case of $d_{i,j} = 0$. An example of such a Bug Table is given in Table 1.

Let $T_F \subseteq T$ be the subset of failed tests, and $T_P \subseteq T$ be the subset of passed tests for the given simulation experiment for a given buggy design. Obviously, $T = T_P \cup T_F$ and $T_P \cap T_F = \varnothing$. Denote by $T(c_i)$ the subset of tests which cover the code item c_i.

Table 1. A Bug Table for error localization in a design

	t_1	t_2	t_3	t_4	t_5	t_6	S(i)
c_1	1	1					0,5
c_2		1	1			1	0,33
c_3		1	1	1			0
c_4					1		0
c_5	1	1	1			1	1	0,6
c_6	1					1	1	1

4.2   Ranking of Suspected Bug Candidates

The statistical *suspiciousness score* for ranking the HDL code item i as the bug candidate during the design error localization is calculated by the following Formula (1):

$$S(i) = \frac{\dfrac{Failed(i)}{TotalFailed}}{\dfrac{Failed(i)}{TotalFailed} + \dfrac{Passed(i)}{TotalPassed}} \qquad (1)$$

where $S(i)$ is the suspiciousness score value of the code item c_i, $Passed(i) = | T_P \cap T(c_i) |$ and $Failed(i) = | T_F \cap T(c_i) |$ are the counts of passing and failing tests that covered the code item c_i in the dynamic slice (depicted in the rows of table D), while $TotalPassed = |T_P|$ and $TotalFailed = |T_F|$ are the total numbers of the passing and failing tests in the complete diagnostic test, respectively. The value of $Failed(i)/TotalFailed$ can be interpreted as the conditional probability of the error in the code item c_i for the given test result, and the value of $Passed(i)/TotalPassed$ can be interpreted as the conditional probability of the correctness of the code item c_i for the given test result. Accordingly, the value of $S(i)$ can be interpreted as the conditional probability that the code item c_i is faulty for the given test result. Let us introduce a threshold $S_{threshold}$ determining the code items c_i with scores $S(i) \leq S_{threshold}$ that should not be considered as the bug location candidates. In case of Formula (1) the default value for $S_{threshold}$ is 0.5.

In Table 1, the entries in the column $S(i)$ correspond to the suspiciousness score values for all the code items (conditional probabilities), given the tests t_1, t_5 and t_6 have failed. In the process of design error diagnosis, the ranking of the code items as being the faulty candidate will proceed according to the values $S(i)$.

4.3   Statistical Assessment of Diagnostic Capability with WHATIF Method

Previous experience has demonstrated the efficiency of Formula (1) is guiding the bug localization process [11]. When looking for the suitable fitness function for evaluation the diagnostic capability of the given test to be used in evolutionary test generation we may mimic real diagnosis procedures using the information in table D and derive estimations of the diagnostic capability for the given tests from it.

Such a procedure is described in [12] as a WHATIF algorithm which is based on using Formula (1) for statistical assessment of suspiciousness scores for the mimicked test experiments targeting bug localization. We refer to *WHATIF* because it consecutively estimates the quality of the given diagnostic test for each of the code items by performing probabilistic simulation of diagnosis experiments i.e. AS IF a bug is located in one of the code items.

For assessment of the test set T, calculate for each code item c_i the conditional suspiciousness score values $S(i|j)$ in condition that the tests in $T(c_j)$ have failed. The values of $S(i|j)$ can be interpreted as conditional probabilities $P(c_i|c_j)$ of errors in c_i, given the tests in $T(c_j)$ have failed.

Let us consider a threshold $S_{threshold}$ for $S(i|j)$. If $S(i|j) > S_{threshold}$ then include c_i into the suspected error candidates together with c_j. Otherwise c_i is not included. Denote the number of all error candidates for the case of failed $T(c_j)$ as $W(c_j)$. Based on the values of $W(c_j)$ we can assess the diagnostic capability of the given test set as the average of bug candidates over all sub-tests $T(c_j)$ as

$$W(T) = \frac{1}{n} \sum_{j=1}^{n} W(c_j) \qquad (2)$$

The lower the value of $W(T)$ the better diagnostic capability the given test set has.

4.4   GENERIC Coverage-Based Approach to Assessment of Diagnostic Resolution

An alternative heuristic procedure for calculating the suspiciousness score values can be derived by interpreting the entries in table D in a way where $d_{i,j} = 1$ means that if the test t_i has passed, the statement c_j, it cannot be an error candidate. We use here a simplifying hypothesis that possible bugs can be related only to single statements, and not to combinations of them. Regarding the general case of multiple errors, the entries of $d_{i,j} = 1$ are overestimated (the bug in c_j covered by t_i in reality may not be able to cause t_i to fail).

Consider again the table D with n columns for sub-tests and m rows for statements. If all columns are different then the diagnosability is evaluated as equal to 1 (denoting the best resolution where the result of the diagnostic procedure at a failing test will be exactly a single buggy statement), otherwise we can calculate the average diagnosability as follows.

Let M_k be a subset of rows which are equivalent. If a subset M_k contains k rows, it means that the result of the diagnosis provides k statements as indistinguishable error candidates. Let q be the number of different subsets M_k. where $1 \leq q \leq n$. The average diagnosability of the design by the given test T can be calculated as

$$G(T) = \sum_{j=1}^{q} \frac{|M_j|}{q} \qquad (3)$$

The value of $G(T)$ means the number of average diagnostic resolution as a measure for estimating the diagnosability of the design for the given test set used for debugging.

5   Evolutionary Diagnostic Test Pattern Generation

Evolutionary Computation (EC) has been little, but steadily, used by the *Computer Aided Design* community during the past 20 years. In the early works of the 1980s, it was mainly seen as a means to optimize numeric coefficients; in the 1990s, the first Evolutionary Algorithms (EAs) eventually gathered recognition. As the complexity of the circuits dramatically increased, evolutionary heuristics started to be seen as promising alternatives to classic approaches. Researchers proposed EA-based methodologies for several well-known NP-hard problems, such as *placement, floorplanning*, and *routing* [20]. Since 2000, the possibility to evolve full assembly programs was also exploited [21].

EAs have long been demonstrated as efficient stimuli generators for *automatic test-pattern generation* and *semi-formal verification*. Evolutionary computation is based on the idea of promoting imperceptible differences that produce small, yet quantifiable, differences in the fitness. Such a smooth fitness functions is easily definable when the goal is test, because the number of detected faults or other standard metrics can be used. Tackling verification, researchers usually resorted to proxy measures like code coverage metrics [22, 23]. The main obstacle that prevented the exploitation of EC in bug localization was the difficulty of defining a suitable fitness function: a bug is either caught or not caught, with no intermediate state.

The concept of *statistical bug localization* enables the definition of a rather smooth fitness function: the amount by which a test program will increase or decrease the diagnostic power of an existing test set. Thus, an EA can be used to add a single element to an existing test suite. Then, the process might be iterated by adding more content, until a stopping condition is eventually met.

5.1 Evolutionary Optimizer μGP

The EA used in the experiment is μGP (also spelled *MicroGP*), a general-purpose evolutionary toolkit developed at Politecnico di Torino [24, 25]. μGP allows a high degree of customization of evolutionary operators, stop criteria, and algorithm parameters. Internally it represents an individual as a multi-graph, where each node roughly corresponds to a locus of the genome. It is interesting to notice that, differently from most EAs, loci can be occupied by alleles with different characteristics, e.g. integer, float or fixed values, and the probability of appearance of each allele can be tuned.

In μGP, the internal parameter *mu* (μ) indicates the size of the population; *lambda* (λ) the number of genetic operators applied at each step, and, thus, indirectly the offspring size; *tau* (τ) the number of individuals in the tournament selection used to select the parent individuals; and *sigma* (σ) the initial strength of the genetic operators, tweaking the similarity between parents and offspring.

μGP implement quite a large variety of genetic operators that can handle the specific characteristics of the individuals' genome: different mutations (single parent), and crossovers (multiple parents). Moreover, two operators mimic *differential evolution* to efficiently handle real-valued parameters, and one operator perform a pseudo exhaustive search on a single parameter. All different operators are activated with a specific probability.

Self-adaptation in EA can be used to shift the focus of the algorithm between exploration and exploitation, depending on the state of the search, improving both the efficiency and the quality of the result. In μGP, the mechanism also regulates all activation probabilities, rewarding the most effective operators. Moreover, the self-adaptation mechanism tweaks σ, regulating the difference between parent and offspring. As a result, the only parameters that need to be set by the user are μ, λ, and τ. However, default values are usually appropriate and no tuning is necessary.

5.2 Evolutionary Diagnostic Test Set Generation Flow

The general flow of the evolutionary diagnostic test generation is presented in Figure 2. It is composed of two main parts: an Evolutionary Algorithm (EA) represented by μGP and an EVALUATOR represented by the zamiaCAD framework.

First, a Test Set is composed of the original functional test, i.e. a set of programs manually developed by the processor designers themselves. Then, an evolutionary optimizer devises a set of new test programs by evolving a population of candidate solutions. The usefulness of each candidate test program is evaluated with respect to the existing Test Set by the zamiaCAD framework and is reported back to the μGP core in form of fitness values. The best individual from the population, i.e. the one with the highest fitness, is added to the Test Set. Then, the process iterates.

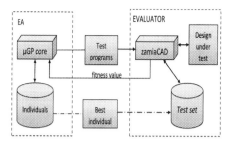

Fig. 2. A general flow of the evolutionary system developed in this work

The evolutionary optimizer evolves the population until some stopping condition is met - usually a *steady state* condition is detected (i.e., non-improvement is recorded for a given number of generations). The outer loop, on the other hand, is repeated until the *Test Set* reaches a satisfying diagnostic capability.

6   Experimental Results

We have performed experiments on an open-source RTL VHDL design of a MIPS-I architecture microprocessor Plasma [26] available from the OpenCores.org website. The zamiaCAD framework was used as an environment to elaborate and simulate the RTL design and served as the evaluator while evolutionary diagnostic test generation was performed by μGP. Both frameworks are open-source and available under the GNU Public License.

μGP is fully controlled by XML configuration files. The most critical one defines the format of the individual. In the current context an individual is an Assembler program, it describes the instructions set architecture of the processor. The configuration file for the Plasma microprocessor consists of about 500 lines, and can be generated almost mechanically from the assembler specification. The other files contain all the variables controlling evolution. As it was mentioned before, the user is not required to modify them since they are self-adapted during the evolution. The only significant parameters were the population size, the number of evolutionary operators and the tournament size. They were set to, respectively, $\mu = 30$, $\lambda = 20$, and $\tau = 2$ (corresponding to a roulette wheel on linearized fitness).

The Plasma RTL VHDL design has in total 1068 concurrent and sequential statements (4,618 lines of VHDL code without libraries). Its original functional test T^O created by the designer for the verification purposes was split into 26 independent test programs and was used as a starting point for the diagnostic test generation.

In the experiment to improve the diagnostic properties of the test set T^O, we have extended it with 10 additional tests by the following three approaches:

1) *pseudorandom* test generation resulting in the diagnostic test set T^R

2) μGP-based test generation using *WHATIF metric W(T)* as a fitness function, resulting in the diagnostic test set T^W

3) μGP-based test generation using *GENERIC metric G(T)* as a fitness function, resulting in the diagnostic test set T^G.

Here the resulting diagnostic tests T^R, T^W, T^G each consist of 36 test programs. The pseudorandom test generation exploits the infrastructure of μGP and relies on its Assembler templates for the Plasma design.

To evaluate real bug localization quality by the different test sets we introduced for the Plasma design 46 realistic bugs. They were latter injected one at a time and the automated statistical localization procedure as described in Section 3 was performed. An example of such bug is shown in Figure 3.

```
case c_mux is
<snip>
  when C_FROM_IMM_SHIFT16 =>
    reg_dest_out <= c_bus;  -- BUG! Should be reg_dest_out <= imm_in & ZERO(15 downto 0);
  when others =>
    reg_dest_out <= c_bus;
  end case;
```

Fig. 3. An example design error *Bug_bus-mux_101-cbus* in the Plasma RTL design

Table 2. Experimental results for diagnostic test generation

Diagnostic quality	Diagnostic tests			
	T^O	T^R	T^W	T^G
# of programs	26	36	36	36
$W(T) \downarrow$	266.86	279.90	262.57	(285.68)
$G(T) \uparrow$	54.00	82.00	(64.00)	103.00
Real quality $\downarrow$	29.02	29.89	22.78	22.24
Time: TPG Assessment	-	1s	2h 27m	1h 50m
	39s	54s	54s	54s
Localization	38m	53m	53m	53m

Table 2 presents the experimental results. The diagnostic quality of each test T^O T^R, T^W, T^G was measured using the *WHATIF W(T) and GENERIC G(T)* metrics. Where the lower the $W(T)$ value the better, and $G(T)$ is the opposite. *Real quality* is the worst number of candidates that need to be considered in average to locate the 46 bugs. Here, if n bug location candidates all have the same score S_n and they are preceded by m candidate locations with higher scores then we consider that our localization result for the actual bug location with S_n to be on the $(m+n)^{th}$ place, i.e. the worst case. The Assessment time reported is the time required to calculate $W(T)$ and $G(T)$for the generated diagnostic tests and the *Localization* time is the time spent on performing statistical localization of all the 46 case-study bugs. The experiments were run on a workstation with Intel Core i5 2.9GHz, 16GB RAM.

As an example consider the following individual results for the localization of the bug *Bug_bus-mux_101-cbus* shown in Figure 3 by the diagnostic test sets. Using T^O has immediately allowed zamiaCAD to assign the actual bug location with the highest suspiciousness score 1.0, i.e. place it to the first rank group of candidates. The size of this group was 34. It means that the engineer has to check in the worst case 34 candidates to get to this location. Test sets T^R, T^W, T^G had changed the size of this group from 34 to 42, 15 and 18 respectively. Therefore T^W was the best improved diagnostic test for this particular bug localization.

The experimental results demonstrate (a) accuracy of the proposed metrics for diagnostic capability assessment, (b) efficiency of μGP to optimize diagnostic tests in using the proposed metrics as fitness functions and (c) overall feasibility of the evolutionary system developed in this work.

7   Conclusions

This paper was the first to propose an approach for diagnostic test generation for statistical bug localization using evolutionary computation. For this purpose, we exploited an evolutionary toolkit μGP (MicroGP) and investigated dedicated diagnostic capability metrics integrated into an open source design analysis tool zamiaCAD to be used as the fitness function for the computation. The proposed approach significantly saves the test generation time by avoiding experiments for each bug to be carried out iteratively during the evolutionary optimization process. Second, it supports reuse of the test set in the case of later modifications to the code.

The experimental results on a Plasma processor showed significantly improved diagnostic resolution of localizing design bugs by the test sets generated implementing the proposed approach.

Acknowledgements. The work has been supported in part by EU FP7 STREP project BASTION, Estonian ICT Program project FUSETEST, by European Union through the European Structural and Regional Development Funds, by Estonian SF grants 8478, 9429, and by ELIKO Technology Centre.

References

1. ITRS. International Technology Roadmap for Semiconductors report. http://www.itrs.net/
2. FP6 PROSYD (2004). PROSYD (Property-Based System Design), FP6 funded STREP. http://www.prosyd.org/
3. Peischl, B., Wotawa, F.: Automated Source-Level Error Localization in Hardware Designs. Design & Test of Computers **23**(1), 8–19 (2006)
4. Smith, A., Veneris, A., Viglas, A.: Design Diagnosis Using Boolean Satisfiability. In: Proc. Asia and South Pacific Design Automation Conference (ASPDAC), pp. 218–223 (2004)
5. Chang, K.-H., Wagner, I., Bertacco, V., Markov, I.L.: Automatic Error Diagnosis and Correction for RTL Designs. In: Proceedings International Workshop on Logic and Synthesis (IWLS), pp. 106–113 (May 2007)
6. Liblit, B., Naik, M., Zheng, A.X., Aiken, A., Jordan, M.I.: Scalable statistical bug isolation. ACM SIGPLAN Notices **40**(6), 15–26 (2005)
7. Liu, G., Fei, L., Yan, X., Han, J., Midkiff, S.P.: Statistical debugging: A hypothesis testing-based approach. IEEE Trans. on Software Engineering **32**(10), 831–848 (2006)
8. Wong, W.E., Debroy, V., Choi, B.: A family of code coverage-based heuristics for effective fault localization. J. of Systems and Software **83**(2), 188–208 (2010)

9. Cleve, H., Zeller, A.: Locating causes of program failures. In: Proceedings Int. Conf. on Software Engineering, pp. 342–351 (2005)
10. Jones, J.A., Harrold, M.J.: Empirical evaluation of the Tarantula automatic fault-localization technique. In: Int. Conf. on Automated Software Engineering, pp. 273–283 (2005)
11. Tšepurov, A., Tihhomirov, V., Jenihhin, M., Raik, J., Bartsch, G., Meza Escobar, J.H., Wuttke, H.D.: Localization of Bugs in Processor Designs Using zamiaCAD Framework. In: 13th International Workshop on Microprocessor Test and Verification (MTV 2012) Common Challenges and Solutions (2012)
12. Tihhomirov, V., Tšepurov, A., Jenihhin, M., Raik, J., Ubar, R.: Assessment of diagnostic test for automated bug localization. In: 14th Latin American Test Workshop (LATW), p. 6 (2013)
13. Deng, S., Cheng, K.-T., Bian, J., Kong, Z.: Mutation-based diagnostic test generation for hardware design error diagnosis. In: IEEE International Test Conference (ITC) (2010)
14. Bernardi, P., Sánchez, E.E., Schillaci, M., Squillero, G., Sonza Reorda, M.: An Effective Technique for the Automatic Generation of Diagnosis-Oriented Programs for Processor Cores. IEEE Transactions on CAD of ICs and Systems 27(3), 570–574 (2008)
15. Abreu, R., Zoeteweij, P., van Gemund, A.J.C.: On the Accuracy of Spectrum-based Fault Localization. In: Testing: Academic and Industrial Conference Practice and Research Techniques – MUTATION, TAICPART-MUTATION 2007, pp. 89–98 (2007)
16. Repinski, U., Raik, J.: Comparison of Model-Based Error Localization Algorithms for C Designs. In: Proc. of 10th East-West Design & Test Symposium (2012)
17. Lisherness, P., Cheng, K.-T.: Coverage discounting: A generalized approach for testbench qualification. In: IEEE International High Level Design Validation and Test Workshop (HLDVT), pp. 49–56 (November 9-11, 2011)
18. zamiaCAD framework web page. http://zamiaCAD.sf.net
19. Tšepurov, A., Bartsch, G., Dorsch, R., Jenihhin, M., Raik, J., Tihhomirov, V.: A Scalable Model Based RTL Framework zamiaCAD for Static Analysis. In: IFIP/IEEE International Conference on Very Large Scale Integration (VLSI-SoC), Santa Cruz, USA (2012)
20. Drechsler, R.: Evolutionary Algorithms for VLSI CAD. Springer (1998) ISBN: 978-1-4419-5040-6
21. Squillero, G.: Artificial evolution in computer aided design: from the optimization of parameters to the creation of assembly programs. Computing 93(2-4), 102–120 (2011)
22. Corno, F., Sonza Reorda, M., Squillero, G.: RT-level ITC'99 benchmarks and first ATPG results. IEEE Design & Test of Computers 17(3), 44–53 (2000)
23. Corno, F., Sanchez, E., Sonza Reorda, M., Squillero, G.: Automatic test generation for verifying microprocessors. IEEE Potentials 24(1), 34–37 (2005)
24. Squillero, G.: MicroGP—An Evolutionary Assembly Program Generator. Genetic Programming and Evolvable Machines 6(3), 247–263 (2005)
25. Sanchez, E., Schillaci, M., Squillero, G.: Evolutionary Optimization: the μGP toolkit. Springer (2011) ISBN: 978-0-387-09426-7
26. Plasma CPU project. http://opencores.org/project,plasma

EvoIASP

Evolutionary Algorithm for Dense Pixel Matching in Presence of Distortions

Ana Carolina dos-Santos-Paulino[1], Jean-Christophe Nebel[2],
and Francisco Flórez-Revuelta[2]([✉])

[1] Télécom Physique Strasbourg, Université de Strasbourg,
Bld. Sebastién Brant, F 67400 Illkirch-Graffenstaden, France
`acdossantos@etu.unistra.fr`

[2] Faculty of Science, Engineering and Computing, Kingston University,
Penrhyn Road, Kingston upon Thames, UK KT1 2EE
`{J.Nebel,F.Florez}@kingston.ac.uk`

Abstract. Dense pixel matching is an essential step required by many computer vision applications. While a large body of work has addressed quite successfully the rectified scenario, accurate pixel correspondence between an image and a distorted version remains very challenging. Exploiting an analogy between sequences of genetic material and images, we propose a novel genetics inspired algorithm where image variability is treated as the product of a set of image mutations. As a consequence, correspondence for each scanline of the initial image is formulated as the optimisation of a path in the second image minimising a fitness function penalising mutations. This optimisation is performed by a evolutionary algorithm which, in addition to provide fast convergence, implicitly ensures consistency between successive scanlines. Performance evaluation on locally and globally distorted images validates our bio-inspired approach.

Keywords: Evolutionary algorithm · Dense pixel matching · Unrectified images · Distorted images

1 Introduction

Despite indubitable progress in last decades, success of current image processing algorithms is largely constrained to controlled environments. In addition, attempting to control the huge number of parameters involved in scene variability is a very clumsy and inefficient way of dealing with real-life situations. In contrast, in the field of bioinformatics, dealing with data variability is at the core of most algorithms since genetic mutations are a reality which cannot be ignored. Based on this observation, the authors have worked on a novel genetics-inspired paradigm for image analysis. This new paradigm relies on the idea that by making an analogy between sequences of genetic material and images, image variability can be interpreted as the product of image mutations. Since many computer vision systems rely either on pixel matching or optical flows, this task

© Springer-Verlag Berlin Heidelberg 2014
A.I. Esparcia-Alcázar et al. (Eds.): EvoApplications 2014, LNCS 8602, pp. 439–450, 2014.
DOI: 10.1007/978-3-662-45523-4_36

has been the core of our investigations [14]. The novel dense pixel matching algorithm we proposed based on this paradigm has demonstrated its robustness not only to camera rotation and translation, but also to local and global distortions [14], so that stereo matching can be freed from the constraint of working with rectified images.

Despite these achievements, the proposed algorithm displays two main limitations: lack of consistency between matches of successive scanlines and a high computational complexity due to the selection of a dynamic programming algorithm to optimise pixel matching. In this work, we propose to address those drawbacks by performing optimisation using an algorithm fitting our bio-inspired paradigm, i.e. a cellular evolutionary algorithm.

A cellular evolutionary algorithm (cGA) is a specific type of evolutionary algorithm where the individuals in the populations are connected establishing a neighbourhood relation between them. Particularly, individuals are conceptually set in a toroidal mesh, and are only allowed to recombine with close individuals [1]. This model fits well with the structure of a image composed by neighbouring lines. Besides, the distortion of a line is quite similar to the distortions of the neighbouring lines. This fact introduces a modification to the original cellular evolutionary model: there is not a single fitness function to optimise, but each individual will optimise the distortion for a specific line in the images.

2   Related Work

The main application of dense pixel matching has been 3D reconstruction from a pair of stereo images. A large body of research has been devoted to the scenario which assumes that images have been rectified so that the problem can be reduced to finding correspondences between a pair of scanlines, see reviews [13][15]. Image rectification has been mainly focused on addressing global distortions associated with camera rotation and translation, and lens distortions. Standard approaches include planar [5], cylindrical [10] and spherical [17] rectifications. In addition to their reliance on finding a set of accurate matching points, pixel interpolations and usage of simple camera models, they are not able to deal with local distortions such as those produced by raindrops and dust.

Although the alternative is the design of dense pixel matching approaches which do not require prior image rectification, very few algorithms have been proposed. [18] offered a solution using multi-resolution image correlation. However, since it was developed to address the particular task of 3D reconstruction of a unique convex object, applications have focused on either face or body part modelling [6][2]. [8] offered a variation of a motion estimation algorithm used for JVT/H.264 video coding to perform a 2-dimensional search. However, the lack of contextual constraints makes the matching process particularly difficult in poorly textured regions. More recently, [11] presented a modification of how the cost volume is created during matching which, they claim, can be integrated in any disparity estimation framework. However, since they only present results on slightly misaligned images, behaviour of their approach in more complicated scenarios remains unknown. Finally, we proposed a novel algorithm, whose fitness function was inspired by our genetics-inspired paradigm. Although it has demonstrated robustness to many camera transformations and distortions [14], it suffers from using a dynamic programming approach for optimisation of the pixel matching process. First, disparity maps display horizontal streaking due to the absence of consistency constraint between successive matched lines. Second, it has a high computational complexity ($O(n^3)$, assuming an image of size n^2).

Although dynamic programming techniques based on tree structures [16][3] have been proposed to allow optimisations across both vertical and horizontal dimensions, they do not provide true 2D optimisation since optimisation is performed along a tree structure instead of a whole image. Moreover, they display a higher computational cost and have only been applied to the rectified scenario. As a consequence, we have investigated alternative approaches to optimise our fitness function. Although dense pixel matching using a genetic algorithm has only been proposed in the rectified image scenario [12][4], an elegant approach allowing optimising matching fitness functions has recently shown a 20% quality improvement while performing fast convergence [7]. In this work, we propose to adopt a similar scheme, but adapted to the unrectified scenario.

3   Bio-inspired Algorithm

Data explosion in sequencing of genetic material gives researchers the opportunity to compare sequences of genetic material to establish evolutionary relationship between proteins. Since protein sequences have an average length of 400 characters and mutate through substitution, insertion and deletion of characters, the alignment of a protein pair is not a trivial matter. The 'Needleman-Wunsch' algorithm [9] has provided an effective automatic method to produce an exact solution to the global alignment of two protein sequences which is still at the core of the latest protein search tools. It is based on a dynamic programming (DP) approach which optimises the global alignment of character strings according to a scoring function taking into account possible mutations. In practice, alignments are produced in two steps. First, a 2D scoring matrix is filled where each cell stores the maximum value which can be achieved by extending a previous alignment. This can be done either by aligning the next character of the first sequence with the next character of the second sequence ('match') or extending either sequence by an empty character to record a character insertion or deletion ('gap'). Second, a 'backtracking' process extracts the optimal path in the matrix, which leads to finding the best alignment between the two sequences.

An analogy can be drawn between aligning protein sequences and matching pixels belonging to scanlines, since both tasks aim at establishing optimal correspondence between two strings of characters: the second image of a pair can be seen as a mutated version of the first image where noise, distortions and individual camera sensitivity alter pixel values (i.e. character substitutions); and a different view angle reveals previously occluded data and introduces new occlusions (i.e. insertion and deletion of characters). In earlier work, taking advantage

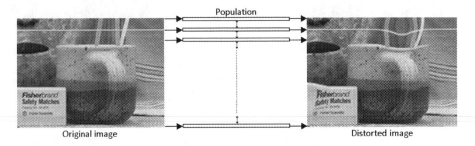

Fig. 1. Each individual in the population represents the path of a scanline in the distorted image. Individuals are linearly connected.

of this analogy, the authors proposed a novel dense pixel matching algorithm able to find correspondence between unrectified images [14]. That approach was shown robust not only to camera rotation and translation, but also to local and global distortions since, instead of restricting itself to finding pixel correspondences between scanlines, it does it between a scanline and an entire image. This was achieved by using a 3D scoring matrix, which allowed taking into account a larger range of 'mutations', see Table 1, so that image distortions could be addressed.

Since pixel matching relies on a DP algorithm operating in a 3D matrix, that approach has a high computational complexity. Moreover, the processing of each scanline independently does not ensure any consistency between matches of neighbouring scanlines. Here, we address those drawbacks by replacing the DP based optimisation by an evolutionary algorithm. Its main principle is the evolution, for each scanline of the first image, of a path within the second image which optimises a scoring function maximising pixel matches and minimising gaps. Moreover, since our evolutionary algorithm relies on recombination between close neighbours, this proposed optimisation implicitly provides consistency between successive scanlines.

4   Evolutionary Proposal

Let I_1 and I_2 be a pair of images composed of n lines, where I_2 is a distorted version of I_1. Each individual in the population represents the path of one line in I_1 (scanline) within I_2 (Fig. 1). Therefore, the number of individuals in the population is equal to the number of lines in the image I_1.

The approach taken is very similar to the behaviour of a linear Cellular Genetic Algorithm with the exception that fitness varies between individuals. However, as neighbouring scanlines have similar distortions, each individual will optimise a similar fitness function. Similarly to cGAs, recombination will take place between close neighbours propagating good solutions to the neighbourhood (Algorithm 1). As a result, the final population will represent distortions between images.

Algorithm 1. Evolutionary process

Initialise the population (see Section 4.3) with a number of individuals equal to the
number of lines in the image
repeat
    Select an individual I at random
    Select a couple of parents I_1 and I_2 in the neighbourhood of I (Section 4.4)
    Recombine I_1 and I_2 by crossover generating I_{new} (Section 4.5)
    Mutate I_{new} (Section 4.6)
    if $fitness(I_{new}) < fitness(I)$ **then**
        Substitute I by I_{new}
    end if
until an ending condition is fulfilled

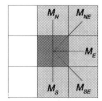

Fig. 2. Different possible matches according to the direction. Stay directions follow the
same nomenclature.

Besides, since the individuals correspond to different lines of the image, the
topology of the population is linear, unlike standard cGAs operating in 2D which
evolve in a toroidal structure. That is coherent, as the first and the last lines of
an image are neither spatially related, nor likely to present a similar distortion
pattern.

4.1 Individual's Representation

Each individual represents the path that a scanline in the original image follows
in the distorted image. Each gene takes one of the 11 values described in Table 1.
A match is achieved when a pixel in the scanline has a correspondence in the
boundaries of the previous pixel in the distorted image. This match can be
located in either the north, south, east, northeast or southeast direction of the
pixel previously analysed (Fig. 2). Moreover, due to distortion or occlusion (if
the images are captured from different view points), a pixel of the original image
may not be found in any of the previously defined adjacent positions or a pixel in
the distorted image may not have any correspondence in the original image. In
the first case, a *stay* (making reference to *stay in the scanline, while moving in
the distorted image*) may be placed in the sequence of directions. In the second
case, a *gap* is placed in the distorted image.

Table 1. Possible gene values, and associated penalties and motions considered in Algorithm 2

Gene values	Representation	Penalty	Motion in the original image	Motion in the distorted image
Match North	M_N	$d(P_{Orig}, P_{Dist})$	$\rightarrow$	$\uparrow$
Match South	M_S	$d(P_{Orig}, P_{Dist})$	$\rightarrow$	$\downarrow$
Match Northeast	M_{NE}	$\sqrt{2} \cdot d(P_{Orig}, P_{Dist})$	$\rightarrow$	$\nearrow$
Match Southeast	M_{SE}	$\sqrt{2} \cdot d(P_{Orig}, P_{Dist})$	$\rightarrow$	$\searrow$
Match East	M_E	$d(P_{Orig}, P_{Dist})$	$\rightarrow$	$\rightarrow$
Stay North	S_N	g	$-$	$\uparrow$
Stay South	S_S	g	$-$	$\downarrow$
Stay Northeast	S_{NE}	$\sqrt{2} \cdot g$	$-$	$\nearrow$
Stay Southeast	S_{SE}	$\sqrt{2} \cdot g$	$-$	$\searrow$
Stay East	S_E	g	$-$	$\rightarrow$
Gap	G	g	$\rightarrow$	$-$

Algorithm 2. Fitness calculation

Let $P_{Orig} = (x_{Orig}, y_{Orig})$ and $P_{Dist} = (x_{Dist}, y_{Dist})$ be the first pixels in associated lines in both the original and the distorted image. Therefore, $x_{Orig} = 1$, $x_{Dist} = 1$ and $y_{Orig} = y_{Dist}$

Set fitness=0

for $i = 1$ **to** *length of the individual* **do**

    Obtain the value V_i for the gene i in the individual

    Increase the fitness with the penalty associated to V_i following Table 1 between P_{Orig} and P_{Dist} where $d(P_{Orig}, P_{Dist}) = \|RGB(P_{Dist}) - RGB(P_{Orig})\|$ and $RGB(P)$ is the RGB value of P

    Update the coordinates for P_{Orig} and P_{Dist} according to the motions described in Table 1

    end for

4.2 Fitness

The fitness function is a measure of the discrepancy between a scanline and its correspondence in the distorted image. It is calculated following Algorithm 2 where successive comparisons are carried out between each pair of pixels that are associated by the path represented by the individual.

We follow the same approach as [14] where matches or stays in NE and SE directions are more penalised since they imply moving by a distance of $\sqrt{2}$ pixels in the image. The value g represents a constant penalty when there is no match.

4.3 Initialisation

Each individual is initialised to represent a trajectory beginning from the left of the distorted image. We propose two types of initialisation strategies: either the selection of a sequence of symbols at random, or the generation of a "locally optimised" path, where the addition of each new symbol relies on keeping the individual fitness minimal.

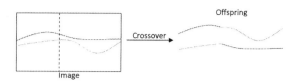

Fig. 3. Illustration of an one-point crossover

The path creation process is completed when (i) the path reaches one of the borders (top, bottom rows or right column) of the distorted image and (ii) it provides correspondence for all pixels of the scanline. If a border is reached first, gaps are included at random positions in the chromosome until all scanline pixels have correspondence. Otherwise, if there is a correspondence for every pixel in the scanline, stay symbols are included at random in the chromosome until the path reaches one of the borders.

4.4   Selection of Parents

As mentioned previously, a new individual I is evolved from a pair of individuals in its neighbourhood[1] . Selection of the parents could be performed in different ways. For instance:

- according to their proximity to I: the probability of an individual to be chosen is calculated according to a gaussian distribution centered in I, or
- according to their fitness using a roulette-wheel method, where the probability of an individual is a function of its fitness and its neighbours' as described by:

$$P_{I_i} = \frac{fitness(I_i)}{\sum_{\forall j \in Neighbourhood(I_i)} fitness(I_j)} \tag{1}$$

4.5   Crossover

Since individuals have different lenghts and representations (paths), which makes their alignments difficult, a typical crossover strategy, where a point (or more) in both parents is selected and the different parts are swapped, is not suitable. Therefore, we propose to select one or more columns in the initial image so that offsprings are generated by swapping the path portions that are defined by those columns (Figure 3). With this procedure, we ensure that each offspring completes a path from the left to the right part of the image.

4.6   Mutation

Mutations produce local changes in the path of an offspring. Those changes can take the following forms:

---

[1] Note that the neighbourhood also includes individual I.

- gene alteration by selecting at random an alternative direction,
- gene deletion,
- gene replication over a contiguous interval of the path,
- simultaneous deletion of a gene pair *gaps/stays* in the scanline, as they correspond to inverse operations, and
- local optimisation by substituting an interval of the path by an optimised path following the methodology presented in Section 4.3.

If the mutation process leads to the generation of an individual whose path does not reach the end of the scanline or one of the borders of the distorted image, it is corrected by employing a process similar to the one presented in Section 4.3. Alternatively, if the path exceeds either the length of the scanline or the distorted image, it is cropped.

5   Experimentation

In order to evaluate our evolutionary based dense pixel matching algorithm we have tested it with different image pairs presenting either global distortions, i.e. distortions affecting the whole image, or local distortions where various distortion filters are applied to different areas of the image. Given that pixel values for each colour channel range from 0 to 255 we have set a penalty $g = 181$, similarly to [14], when a 'gap' or a 'stay' is included in a path. We have also considered all the mutation types stated in Section 4.6 with equal probability. As stopping condition, the evolutionary process finishes if there is no changes in the population for 10,000 generations (i.e. the creation of 10,000 new individuals).

Figure 4 presents matching results between an image 4a and its global sinusoidal distortion 4b. While Figure 4c shows paths representing different individuals in the image, Figure 4d displays how the individuals represent the distortion between the original and the distorted images. All individuals, except those in the top and bottom lines, converged towards very similar distortions. In those border areas, there is no continuity in the distorted stripes. Therefore the algorithm minimises the fitness function by either inserting gaps or jumping to a neighbouring stripe with a similar colour. Finally, Figure 4e shows a reconstruction of the original image using the distorted image and the paths coded in the individuals. The original image is recovered quite satisfactorily, except in the border areas previously mentioned.

Figure 5 shows results for an image pair, proposed by [14], where local distortions were applied on the original image (Figure 5c). Figure 5e and 5f highlight the algorithm's ability to detect and correct the distortion on the rim of the mug. However, in this case, it fails to address the distortion affecting the three straws. One can speculate that, due to the choice of fitness function, the algorithm finds easier to deal with distortions involving matches than gaps or stays.

Next, we studied how the choice of initialisation strategy, see section 4.3, affects performance. As seen in in Figure 6, usage of locally optimised initialisation instead of random one conducts to the generation of an original population which is composed of paths representing quite well the actual distortion. One

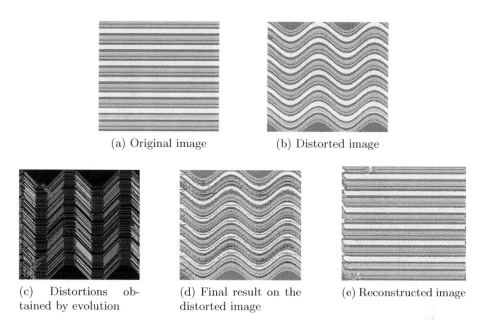

(a) Original image

(b) Distorted image

(c) Distortions obtained by evolution

(d) Final result on the distorted image

(e) Reconstructed image

Fig. 4. Image matching in presence of a global sinusoidal distortion. In (c) colours represent different directions. The reconstructed image (d) is generated by pasting the distorted image pixels according to the path estimated for each line.

Table 2. Comparison between different initialisation methods. Ten runs were carried out with the stripes images using the roulette method with a neighbourhood size 5 to select parents in the crossover.

Percentage of random individuals created	Iterations until convergence (in millions)			Initial fitness	Final fitness		
	Average	Best	σ		Average	Best	σ
0	2.91	2.00	0.74	12,739.58	6,003.22	5,802.13	107.63
50	3.06	2.24	0.54	48,818.54	6,113.75	5,992.04	98.75
100	7.92	5.07	2.23	58,397.66	6,720.27	5,983.65	739.10

may wonder if this optimised initialisation compromises exploration of the solution space and leads to convergence towards a worse fitness. Results in Table 2 reveal that actually optimised initialisation leads to better solutions and faster convergence of the algorithm.

Another important aspect of the algorithm is parents selection. First, Figure 7 shows how the fitness function evolves according to the size of the neighbourhood considered when selecting parents by roulette taking into account the fitness of the individuals. In the case of the stripes image (Figure 7a) where the distortion is global, the larger the neighbourhood the better the results, as good solutions propagate faster. In the case of local distortions (Cones image - 7b), the best result is obtained for a neighbourhood of size 15, whereas there is no significant

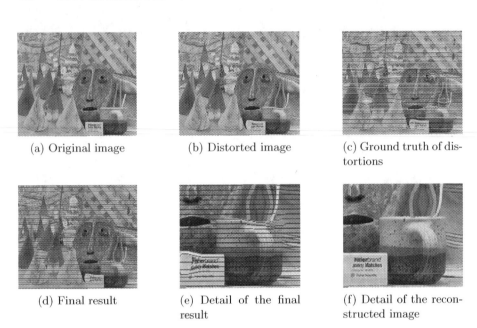

(a) Original image   (b) Distorted image   (c) Ground truth of distortions

(d) Final result   (e) Detail of the final result   (f) Detail of the reconstructed image

Fig. 5. Results obtained with an image with local distortions

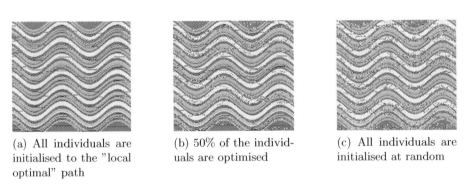

(a) All individuals are initialised to the "local optimal" path   (b) 50% of the individuals are optimised   (c) All individuals are initialised at random

Fig. 6. Initial populations generated from different initialisation methods

difference between usage of sizes 5 and 25. The best neighbourhood seems to be related to the actual size of the distorted areas. These figures also confirm the superiority of locally optimised initialisation over the random one, since in both cases it provides faster convergence towards a lower fitness value. Note that results for random initialisation of all individuals are not shown for the Cones images as they would not fit on the graph.

Second, comparison was performed between two of the methods proposed in Section 4.4 for the selection of parents, i.e. roulette and proximity to the individual to be evolved. As shown on Figure 8, no significant differences are

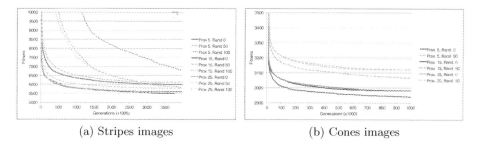

(a) Stripes images   (b) Cones images

Fig. 7. Influence of parents selection and initialisation strategies (*Prox* indicates the number of individuals considered in the neighbourhood and *Rand* the percentage of individuals initialised at random)

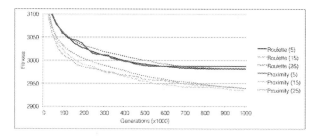

Fig. 8. Influence of the selection method and the neighbourhood size

observed. Therefore, the evolution seems to be more affected by the size of the neighbourhood than the method used to select the parents.

6   Conclusion

We have introduced a novel dense pixel matching algorithm suitable for the unrectified scenario. Based on a bio-inspired approach, our main contribution has been the design of an evolutionary algorithm able to optimise a different fitness function for each scanline while ensuring consistency between neighbouring lines. As demonstrated in experiments involving locally and globally distorted images, the proposed approach is valid, since processing converges towards satisfactory solutions which do not display any horizontal streaking. Moreover, study of different population initialisation and parents selection strategies has revealed that locally optimised initialisation provides a better performance, while the selection of parents is more affected by the choice of the chromosome pool than the method used to extract the actual genitors. As future work, we propose to further develop our system so that it could produce 3D reconstruction in real time from data generated by two uncalibrated video cameras.

References

1. Alba, E., Dorronsoro, B.: Cellular genetic algorithms. vol. 42. Springer (2008)
2. Cockshott, W.P., Hoff, S., Nebel, J.C.: Experimental 3-D digital TV studio. IEE Proceedings of the Vision, Image and Signal Processing **150**(1), 28–33 (2003)
3. Deng, Y., Lin, X.: A Fast Line Segment Based Dense Stereo Algorithm Using Tree Dynamic Programming. In: Leonardis, A., Bischof, H., Pinz, A. (eds.) ECCV 2006. LNCS, vol. 3953, pp. 201–212. Springer, Heidelberg (2006)
4. Han, K.P., Song, K.W., Chung, E.Y., Cho, S.J., Ha, Y.H.: Stereo matching using genetic algorithm with adaptive chromosomes. Pattern Recognition **34**(9), 1729–1740 (2001)
5. Hartley, R.I.: Theory and practice of projective rectification. International Journal of Computer Vision **35**(2), 115–127 (1999)
6. Khambay, B., Nebel, J.C., Bowman, J., Ayoub, A., Walker, F., Donald, H.D.: A pilot study: 3D stereo photogrammetric image superimposition on to 3D CT scan images - the future of orthognathic surgery. The International Journal of Adult Orthodontics and Orthognathic Surgery **17**(4), 331–341 (2002)
7. Kiperwasser, E., David, O., Netanyahu, N.S.: A hybrid genetic approach for stereo matching. In: Proceeding of the 15th Genetic and Evolutionary Computation Conference, pp. 1325–1332. ACM, New York (2013)
8. Nalpantidis, L., Amanatiadis, A., Sirakoulis, G., Kyriakoulis, N., Gasteratos, A.: Dense disparity estimation using a hierarchical matching technique from uncalibrated stereo vision. In: IEEE International Workshop on Imaging Systems and Techniques, pp. 427–431 (2009)
9. Needleman, S.B., Wunsch, C.D.: A general method applicable to the search for similarities in the amino acid sequence of two proteins. Journal of Molecular Biology **48**(3), 443–453 (1970)
10. Roy, S., Meunier, J., Cox, I.J.: Cylindrical rectification to minimize epipolar distortion. In: Proceedings of the 1997 IEEE Computer Society Conference on Computer Vision and Pattern Recognition, pp. 393–399 (1997)
11. Rzeszutek, R., Tian, D., Vetro, A.: Disparity estimation of misaligned images in a scanline optimization framework. In: IEEE International Conference on Acoustics, Speech and Signal Processing, pp. 1523–1527 (2013)
12. Saito, H., Mori, M.: Application of genetic algorithms to stereo matching of images. Pattern Recognition Letters **16**(8), 815–821 (1995)
13. Scharstein, D., Szeliski, R.: A taxonomy and evaluation of dense two-frame stereo correspondence algorithms. Intl. Journal of Computer Vision **47**(1–3), 7–42 (2002)
14. Thevenon, J., Martinez del Rincon, J., Dieny, R., Nebel, J.C.: Dense pixel matching between unrectified and distorted images using dynamic programming. In: Intl. Conference on Computer Vision Theory and Applications, pp. 216–224 (2012)
15. Tippetts, B., Lee, D., Lillywhite, K., Archibald, J.: Review of stereo vision algorithms and their suitability for resource-limited systems. Journal of Real-Time Image Processing, 1–21 (2013)
16. Veksler, O.: Stereo correspondence by dynamic programming on a tree. In: IEEE Computer Society Conference on Computer Vision and Pattern Recognition, vol. 2, pp. 384–390 (2005)
17. Wan, D., Zhou, J.: Self-calibration of spherical rectification for a ptz-stereo system. Image and Vision Computing **28**(3), 367–375 (2010)
18. Zhengping, J.: On the multi-scale iconic representation for low-level computer vision systems. PhD thesis, The Turing Institute and the U. of Strathclyde (1988)

Is a Single Image Sufficient for Evolving Edge Features by Genetic Programming?

Wenlong Fu[1]([✉]), Mark Johnston[1], and Mengjie Zhang[2]

[1] School of Mathematics, Statistics and Operations Research,
Victoria University of Wellington, P.O. Box 600, Wellington, New Zealand
wenlong.fu@msor.vuw.ac.nz
[2] School of Engineering and Computer Science,
Victoria University of Wellington, P.O. Box 600, Wellington, New Zealand
{mark.johnston,mengjie.zhang}@vuw.ac.nz

Abstract. Typically, a single natural image is not sufficient to train a program to extract edge features in edge detection when only training images and their ground truth are provided. However, a single training image might be considered as proper training data when domain knowledge, such as used in Gaussian-based edge detection, is provided. In this paper, we employ Genetic Programming (GP) to automatically evolve Gaussian-based edge detectors to extract edge features based on training data consisting of a single image only. The results show that a single image with a high proportion of true edge points can be used to train edge detectors which are not significantly different from rotation invariant surround suppression. When the programs separately evolved from eight single images are considered as weak classifiers, the combinations of these programs perform better than rotation invariant surround suppression.

Keywords: Genetic Programming · Edge Detection · Gaussian Filter

1 Introduction

In computer vision, a large number of training images are usually required in a machine learning algorithm. In order to reduce the computational cost of learning, one-shot learning has been applied to object recognition [8,23]. After obtaining prior knowledge from existing datasets, such as learnt classifiers or predefined feature distributions, one-shot learning can employ a minimal set of training examples to train new classifiers. The prior knowledge used in one-shot learning is fundamental. In object recognition, the prior knowledge based on predefined features in existing datasets are helpful to effectively train new classifiers based on a few images. For example, the similarity between previously learned classes and new classes have been exploited for the reuse of model parameters [9].

However, edge detection is a subjective task [22,24], and edge features are implicit. Here, edge features in edge detection are functions of raw pixel values in an image relative to a local point, and they are used to classify pixels as edge

© Springer-Verlag Berlin Heidelberg 2014
A.I. Esparcia-Alcázar et al. (Eds.): EvoApplications 2014, LNCS 8602, pp. 451–463, 2014.
DOI: 10.1007/978-3-662-45523-4_37

points or non-edge points. When edge features need to be extracted by Genetic Programming (GP) [13], and only a few training images and their ground truth are provided without predefined features, it is hard to obtain the prior knowledge on these training images from existing datasets because of the unknown characteristics of edge features.

GP has been used to evolve Gaussian-based edge detectors to extract edge features [13]. Gaussian-based edge detection techniques have some advantages for detecting edges, such as filtering noise [1]. In a Gaussian-based GP system [13], a program including Gaussian filters has some ability to extract edges. The domain knowledge, i.e., Gaussian-based edge detection, might be helpful to train new Gaussian-based edge detectors when a small set of training images is used, although there is no prior knowledge from datasets. It is desirable to investigate whether a single training image can be used to train effective Gaussian-based edge detectors using GP.

The overall goal of this paper is to investigate using a single image as the training data to evolve Gaussian-based edge detectors by GP. Note that there are no predefined features for detecting edges, and the Gaussian-based knowledge used in GP comes only from general applications for edge detection. Different from common one-shot learning algorithms [8,9,23], GP selects a single training image without considering the other images in the dataset. When a single training image is used to train GP edge detectors, there is no prior knowledge relative to the training image and its dataset. The performance of the edge detector evolved by GP is strongly dependent on the single image used. In order to investigate the influence from different single training images, eight images from the 20 training image used in [13] are selected as the training data, respectively. Specifically, we investigate the research objectives: (1) whether GP edge detectors evolved by a single training image outperform existing Gaussian-based edge feature extraction techniques, such as the Gaussian gradient and surround suppression [16]; and (2) whether a combination of the GP edge detectors evolved independently from the eight training images can outperform the GP edge detectors evolved by the full 20 images used in [13].

In the remainder of the paper, Section 2 gives some background on Gaussian-based edge detection and related work on GP for edge detection. Section 3 describes how GP is used to evolve Gaussian-based edge detectors. After giving the design of experiments in Section 4, Section 5 presents the results with discussions. Section 6 draws conclusions and suggests future work directions.

2   Background

This section firstly gives some background on Gaussian-based edge detection and then describes related work in edge detection using GP.

2.1   Gaussian-Based Edge Detection

In edge detection, Gaussian filters have been popularly applied for many years [1]. Since varying scales of Gaussian filters have different responses on edges,

Gaussian filters have been used to detect boundaries between different regions [21,27]. Note that a Gaussian filter here does not mean a filter only removing noise. There are different types of Gaussian filters, such as Difference of Gaussians (DoG) and Laplacian of Gaussian (LoG) [21].

Differentiation-based approaches have widely utilised Gaussian filters to extract edge features [1]. Here, we only focus on rotation invariant edge feature extraction in grayscale images. Given a Gaussian filter $g_\sigma(x, y)$ in Equation (1), the gradient magnitude of a Gaussian filter is defined in Equation (4). Here, σ is a *scale* parameter, and x and y are the offset position from a discriminated pixel. The Gaussian gradient filter $\nabla g(x, y)$ combines the horizontal derivative $\frac{\partial g(x,y)}{\partial x}$ (see Equation (2)) and the vertical derivative $\frac{\partial g(x,y)}{\partial y}$ (see Equation (3)).

$$g_\sigma(x, y) = \frac{1}{2\pi\sigma^2} \exp\left(-\frac{x^2 + y^2}{2\sigma^2}\right) \tag{1}$$

$$\frac{\partial g(x, y)}{\partial x} = -\frac{x}{2\pi\sigma^4} \exp\left(-\frac{x^2 + y^2}{2\sigma^2}\right) \tag{2}$$

$$\frac{\partial g(x, y)}{\partial y} = -\frac{y}{2\pi\sigma^4} \exp\left(-\frac{x^2 + y^2}{2\sigma^2}\right) \tag{3}$$

$$\nabla g(x, y) = \sqrt{\left(\frac{\partial g(x, y)}{\partial x}\right)^2 + \left(\frac{\partial g(x, y)}{\partial y}\right)^2} \tag{4}$$

The Canny edge detector [5] is one popular edge detector based on the Gaussian gradient. In the Canny edge detector, after extracting the Gaussian gradient, adaptive thresholding with hysteresis is used to eliminate breaking of edge contours. However, the Canny edge detector is slightly sensitive to weak edges and susceptible to spurious and unstable boundaries with non-significant change in intensity [1,24].

Besides the Gaussian gradient, the second-order derivative has also been employed to extract edge features [1]. The LoG is given in Equation (5). LoG $\nabla^2 g(x, y)$ is a zero-crossing detector [1]. DoG is a second derivative filter [28], approximating LoG well. The DoG is shown in Equation (6), where σ_1 and σ_2 are different scale parameters. Since DoG is based on the difference of two Gaussians $g_{\sigma_1}(x, y)$ and $g_{\sigma_2}(x, y)$, it is a kind of band filter, and suppresses noise with a high spatial frequency, but decreases overall image contrast [21].

$$\nabla^2 g(x, y) = \frac{x^2 + y^2 - 2\sigma^2}{2\pi\sigma^6} \exp\left(-\frac{x^2 + y^2}{2\sigma^2}\right) \tag{5}$$

$$DoG_{\sigma_1,\sigma_2}(x, y) = g_{\sigma_1}(x, y) - g_{\sigma_2}(x, y) \tag{6}$$

In general, one single Gaussian filter is not sufficient to extract edge features. The same type of Gaussian filters have been combined to extract edge features based on responses at different scales [1,3]. Assuming that there are typically varying noise and different types of edges in an image, multi-scale edge detectors employ multiple Gaussian filters to smooth the image. In the multi-scale technique, three directions are generally used. The first direction is from a coarse solution (high σ) to a fine solution (small σ), namely edge focusing [3]. In this direction, firstly, edges are extracted by a Gaussian filter with a high σ, and then the localisation of edges are discriminated by a Gaussian filter with the next smaller σ. The aim of using multi-scale Gaussian filters is to reverse the effect of the blurring caused by large scale Gaussian filters. The threshold at the coarsest level determines the detected edge quality. However, it is hard to set each level scale and choose the threshold in each level [1]. The second direction is from fine to coarse [20]. Since large scale blurs detected edges, the problem of localisation error still exists in the coarse solutions. Again, how to choose scales is not clear. The third direction is to adaptively control scales of Gaussian filters [2]. These scales are adapted to both the local variance and the noise characteristics from a small area in an image. This direction assumes that noise is modelled by a Gaussian distribution with a known variance, and smooths areas based on a scale relative to the estimated Gaussian distribution.

Additionally, different types of Gaussian filters have also been combined for edge detection [15]. In order to detect edges and filter noise, surround suppression [15,16] has been developed. This technique utilises contextual information to suppress responses on textures via combining the Gaussian gradient and the DoG. Surround suppression normally chooses Gabor filters to extract edge features [16]. A two-dimensional Gabor filter can be considered as a Gaussian filter transformed by a sinusoidal function. After applying surround suppression, some noise caused by textures are filtered [24].

2.2   Related Work to GP for Edge Detection

GP has been mainly employed for low-level edge feature extraction. Filter functions were approximated by GP based on one-dimensional step edge responses [17]. These functions are employed to design filters to extract edge features. Pixels in a fixed window of size 13×13 were used as terminals in GP to evolve programs for edge feature extraction based on multiple objectives [30]. The results from GP can compete with the results from the Canny edge detector. Bolis et al [4] used GP to evolve programs to walk in images for searching edges. In hardware design, digital circuits using bits of the pixel intensity in a 4×4 window as inputs were evolved by GP to detect edges [14]. The Sobel detector was approximated by GP using gates as functions and the relationship between a pixel and its neighbours as terminals [18].

Rather than using a moving window, programs based on full images have also been evolved by GP. Four directional shifting operations with one pixel distance, similar to the four macros suggested by Poli [25] for image processing using GP, were used to approximate the Canny detector by GP [7]. A shifting function with more than one pixel distance movement, developed from the shifting operations, was used to evolve low-level edge detectors by GP based on the training images and their ground truth [10,12].

Also, GP has employed normal image operators to construct programs for edge features extraction. Morphological erosion and dilation as terminals were used to detect edges in binary images [26,29]. A rotation variant edge feature was constructed by GP using image filters, and it was combined with texture gradients to train a logistic regression classifier for boundary detection [19]. Three basic features were employed to construct composite edge features by GP, and these composite features combine advantages of three basic features [11].

In summary, when GP is used to extract edge features, the domain knowledge from edge detection used in GP can help to improve detection performance. However, a large set of training images is generally required. How to choose a minimal set of training images needs to be investigated when some degrees of domain knowledge are employed.

3   Gaussian-Based GP System

A Gaussian-based GP system extended from [13] is introduced in this section. The domain knowledge used in Gaussian-based edge detection is employed in the proposed Gaussian-based GP system.

3.1   Terminals Based on Gaussian Models

To rapidly find a Gaussian-based edge detector, the terminal set in the proposed GP system includes the Gaussian gradient, LoG, DoG, and random constants rnd (real numbers) in the range from -10 to 10. The Gaussian gradient, LoG and DoG (on full images) have been developed by human for extracting edge features. In this terminal set, the parameter σ is randomly generated in the range from 1 to 5. Given the small σ in the DoG, we use 2σ in the large scale Gaussian filter. Therefore, the scale range of all Gaussian filters in the DoG is from 1 to 10, and the coarsest scale has the range from 2 to 10. The coarsest scale covers the range from 3 to 6 as suggested in [3] so that more scale values are used in Gaussian filters randomly generated in the GP system.

3.2   Function Set

The full function set is $\{+, -, *, \div, \mathbb{C}, s_{n,m}\}$. Here, $\div$ is protected division, producing a result of 1 for a 0 divisor; $\mathbb{C}$ is a combination function from surround suppression, which takes two arguments; and $s_{n,m}$ is a shifting function to shift its argument (a single two-dimensional matrix input) by n columns and m rows [10].

The definition of $f_1(u,v)\mathbb{C}f_2(u,v)$ involves two steps, where $f_1(u,v)$ and $f_2(u,v)$ are image intensities or outputs of subtrees for a pixel with position (u,v). The first step extracts the neighbours of pixel (u,v) within a 7×7 window from $f_1(u,v)$ and $f_2(u,v)$. The intensities of the neighbours from $f_2(u,v)$ are transformed by Equations (7) and (8), where, x and y (x' and y') are horizontal and vertical offsets, and $\sum_{x',y'}$ is the sum of $positiveN(x',y',f(u,v))$ in the 7×7 window. If $\sum_{x',y'}$ is equal to 0, $normN(x,y,f(u,v))$ will return 0. In the second step, convolution of the intensities of the neighbours from $f_1(u,v)$ and $f_2(u,v)$ is performed to get a final value for $f_1(u,v)\mathbb{C}f_2(u,v)$.

$$positiveN(u,v,f(x,y)) = \max\{f(x+u,v+y),0\} \qquad (7)$$

$$normN(u, v, f(x, y)) = \frac{positiveN(u, v, f(x, y))}{\sum_{u', v'} positiveN(u', v', f(x, y))} \tag{8}$$

3.3   Fitness Function

A fitness function, which has been successfully used in [12], is also employed as the fitness function in our GP system. The fitness function F_d is defined in Equation (10), where o_i is the output of a program for pixel i, v is the threshold for discriminating pixel i as an edge point or a non-edge point, d_1 is a constant, $w_{P,1}$ and $w_{P,2}$ are constant weights, N_i is used to penalise o_i around threshold v, t_i is the ground truth (0 for a non-edge point and 1 for a true edge point), S_{TP} is the number of true edge points correctly predicted, S_T is the number of true edge points, and $\sum_i N_i$ is the sum of N_i for all pixels. We use $v = 0$, $d_1 = 1$, $w_{P,1} = 0.0001$, and $w_{P,2} = 0.001$, the same as [12].

$$N_i = \begin{cases} w_{P,1} & \text{if} \quad o_i \in (v - d_1, v] \quad \& \quad t_i = 0 \\ 1 + w_{P,2} & \text{if} \quad o_i \in (v, v + d_1) \quad \& \quad t_i = 1 \\ 1 & \text{if} \quad o_i \in [v + d_1, \infty) \quad \& \quad t_i = 1 \\ 0 & \text{otherwise} \end{cases} \tag{9}$$

$$F_d = \frac{2S_{TP}}{S_T + \sum_i N_i} \tag{10}$$

3.4   Combinations of Results From Single Training Images

When a set of single images are used to train edge detectors independently, the evolved results might be different. We combine the binary outputs of evolved results from these single training images based on a voting technique. When a fixed random seed is used in the experiments of evolving edge detectors with these single training images, respectively, the initialised populations are the same. The combinations of the results from these single training images are based on the same initialised population, and the results from these images are binary. An evolved edge detector from a single training image is considered as a weak "classifier". In the voting technique, the intensity level for a pixel is increased by one if the pixel is considered as an edge point by an evolved edge detector. Therefore, the highest graylevel of the combination results is the same as the number of single training images used.

4   Experiment Design

The Berkeley Segmentation Dataset (BSD) [22] has been employed to evolve Gaussian-based edge detectors by GP [13]. The BSD dataset provides ground truth for training images and test images, and the training and test images are independent. Each image has 481×321 pixels and comes from the natural world. There are 200 training images and 100 test images. The ground truth are combined from five to ten persons as graylevel images.

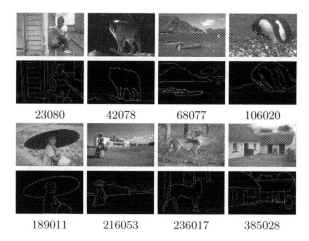

23080   42078   68077   106020

189011   216053   236017   385028

Fig. 1. The eight training images from BSD dataset and their ground truth

In [13], 20 images with rich edge contents as the training data were used to obtain Gaussian-based edge detectors which are better than surround suppression [13]. Here, we select eight images from the 20 images, and Fig. 1 shows the eight images. In the ground truth, black pixels (graylevel 0) are true non-edge points, and white pixels are true edge points. Two images (42078 and 106020) have high contrast intensities between objects and background (expected to be not good for training edge detectors), and the other six images have high proportions of true edge points (expected to be good for training edge detectors).

The parameter values for GP are: population size 200; maximum generations 200; and probabilities for mutation 0.15, crossover 0.80 and elitism (reproduction) 0.05. The maximum depth (of a program) is 8, one larger than the setting in [13]. We perform 30 independent runs for the experiment.

The binary outputs of Gaussian-based edge detectors evolved by GP are directly evaluated without non-maximum suppression and other techniques for linking edge points and removing standalone edge points. Here, binary edges are obtained after using the fixed threshold 0 to indicate positive values for edge points and the others for non-edge points. The popular F-measure [6,22] is employed in the testing phase for performance evaluation. The F-measure $F = \frac{2recall*precision}{recall+precision}$ is a combination of recall and precision. Here, recall is the number of pixels on the true edges correctly detected as a proportion of the total number of pixels on the true edges; and precision is the number of pixels on the true edges correctly detected as a proportion of the total number of pixels detected as edges.

5 Results and Discussion

This section describes the results with discussions. The results from the single training images and their combinations will be compared with the results from 20 images and two existing Gaussian-based edge detectors.

Table 1. Test performance F values (mean $\pm$ standard deviation of 30 runs) for the Gaussian-based edge detectors from the single training images, all eight images (eight), their combinations (voting) based on a single image, the Gaussian gradient (GG), surround suppression (SS), and a set of 20 images (S_{20}), and p-values of the comparisons among these results from t-tests on the BSD test image dataset (100 images)

| | F | p-values | | | | |
		eight	voting	GG	SS	S_{20}
23080	0.5154 ± 0.0238	0.0000 ↓	0.0000 ↓	0.9892	0.0000 ↓	0.0000 ↓
42078	0.4296 ± 0.0590	0.0000 ↓	0.0000 ↓	0.0000 ↓	0.0000 ↓	0.0000 ↓
68077	0.5161 ± 0.0168	0.0000 ↓	0.0000 ↓	0.8071	0.0000 ↓	0.0000 ↓
106020	0.4576 ± 0.0339	0.0000 ↓	0.0000 ↓	0.0000 ↓	0.0290 ↓	0.0000 ↓
189011	0.5187 ± 0.0189	0.0000 ↓	0.0000 ↓	0.3440	0.0000 ↓	0.0000 ↓
216053	0.5327 ± 0.0160	0.0001 ↓	0.0000 ↓	0.0000 ↑	0.0766	0.0000 ↓
236017	0.5093 ± 0.0445	0.0000 ↓	0.0000 ↓	0.4740	0.0016 ↓	0.0000 ↓
385028	0.5243 ± 0.0093	0.0000 ↓	0.0000 ↓	0.0000 ↑	0.0000 ↓	0.0000 ↓
eight	0.5525 ± 0.0203		0.3513	0.0000 ↑	0.0000 ↑	0.0244 ↓
voting	0.5562 ± 0.0068	0.3513		0.0000 ↑	0.0000 ↑	0.0190 ↓
GG	0.5153	0.0000 ↓	0.0000 ↓			0.0000 ↓
SS	0.5381	0.0000 ↓	0.0000 ↓			0.0000 ↓
S_{20}	0.5628 ± 0.0131	0.0244 ↑	0.0190 ↑	0.0000 ↑	0.0000 ↑	

5.1   Overall Results

Table 1 gives the means and standard deviations of the F values on the 100 BSD test images, and the p-values for the comparisons among the Gaussian-based edge detectors from the eight single training images, all eight images together as the training data (eight), their combinations (voting), the 20 images (S_{20}) used in [13], the Gaussian gradient, and surround suppression (SS). Here, the p-values are based on t-tests. Based on significance level of 0.05, ↑ indicates that the relevant item in the first column is significantly better than the relevant item in the first row, and ↓ indicates that the relevant item in the first column is significantly worse than the relevant item in the first row. The results from voting are based on the highest F, and the results from the Gaussian gradient and surround suppression come from [13].

There are five interesting observations from Table 1. Firstly, the results from the eight single training images, except for 216053, are significantly worse than the results detected by surround suppression. However, compared to the Gaussian gradient, only images 42078 and 106020 have significantly worse results, images 216053 and 385028 have significantly better results, and the other four images have no significant differences, in terms of F. It seems that only a few of the single training images can be used as the training data in the GP system for effectively evolving good edge detectors. Secondly, the combinations of the results from the eight training images are significantly improved, compared with the results from each single training image. The combination results based on the simple voting technique are significantly better than the result from surround

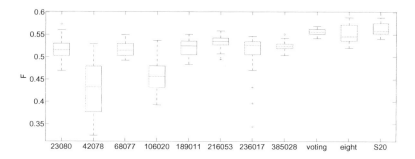

Fig. 2. Boxplot of 30 GP edge detectors' performances on the BSD test image dataset

suppression. Although the combinations are significantly worse than the results from S_{20}, the difference between their means of F is 0.0066 only. Thirdly, in general, the results from a single training image are not stable, such as results from images 42078 and 236017, but image 385028 has very stable test performance. Compared to the results from S_{20}, the results from image 385028 are more stable in terms of the standard deviation of F values. It is possible to use a single image without prior knowledge on a whole dataset to evolve edge detectors which have similar test detection performance. Fourthly, the combinations of the results from the eight training images have very stable test performance (low standard deviation). A potential reason for this is that the eight single images include different edge information so that the combinations can improve the accuracy of predicting edge points. Lastly, the results from using the eight images together are not significantly different from the results using the voting technique. However, the average training time of using one single image is 8861.3 seconds, and the training time of using the eight images is 85738.3 seconds. The total training time of independently using single images is obviously shorter than the training time of using all eight images together.

Fig. 2 gives boxplots of the test performance of these edge detectors on the BSD test image dataset. For the images 42078 and 106020 with high contrast intensities between background and objects, the F values of the evolved edge detectors are located in a large range, and most of these detectors are not good to extract edges. For image 23080, a few of the evolved edge detectors have similar performance to the evolved edge detectors from S_{20}. It seems that a single image can be used to evolve good edge detectors, but how to choose the single image to evolve good edge detectors needs to be further investigated.

5.2 Visual Results

Fig. 3 shows four example detected images from the best evolved edge detector ($F = 0.5731$) from training image 23080, and the best evolved edge detector ($F = 0.5879$) from S_{20} and surround suppression using the threshold with the maximum F. There are no obvious differences between the results detected by the GP edge

Fig. 3. Example detected images by the best GP edge detectors from single training image 23080, S_{20} and surround suppression (SS). Note that GT is ground truth.

detectors from image 23080 and S_{20}. Compared to the detected results from surround suppression, the detected results from single training image 23080 have a higher precision value. The visual results also show that a single training image *can* be used for the GP system to evolve good edge detectors.

5.3 Further Discussion

The results from the eight training images, respectively, show that using a single training image might obtain bad test performance (low F), such as image 42078. Since the 100 BSD test images are generally different from the single training images, a training image with high contrast intensities between background and objects may cause GP to evolve bad edge detectors to extract edges in different test images, such as an image with low contrast intensities between background and objects. However, "high contrast" here is subjective. It is hard to define a quantitative measure to determine whether a single image is good for the GP system to evolve edge detectors. Additionally, what types of natural images could be detected well by the evolved edge detectors with a single training is unknown. Natural images come from various sources, and the training images and test images are grouped by human observations. The training image and test image datasets are generally subjective.

Since there are no predefined features for extracting edges in the GP system, the prior knowledge of a single training image from the whole dataset is difficult to obtain. Different from one-shot learning, using a single image in the GP system is much harder to evolve good candidates. Table 1 shows the differences among the results from the 20 images, the eight images and the voting technique are not obvious, but the computational cost of evolving edge detectors by independently using single images is obviously lower than using a set of images together. Therefore, the voting technique is suggested to extract edge features.

6   Conclusions

The overall goal of this paper was to investigate using single images as the training data to evolve Gaussian-based edge detectors by GP. Based on the results from eight training images, it is possible to use a single training image for GP to evolve Gaussian-based edge detectors which are better than Gaussian gradient and surround suppression on the BSD test image dataset. Although bad edge detectors may be evolved by using a single image only, the voting technique is suggested to effectively combine the edge detectors evolved by independently using single images.

In future work, we will investigate a quantitative measure for effectively selecting single images to evolve edge detectors by GP. How to obtain prior knowledge of a single image from its whole dataset will be investigated for effectively evolving edge detectors when the single image is used as the training data.

References

1. Basu, M.: Gaussian-based edge-detection methods: a survey. IEEE Transactions on Systems, Man, and Cybernetics, Part C: Applications and Reviews **32**(3), 252–260 (2002)
2. Bennamoun, M., Boashash, B., Koo, J.: Optimal parameters for edge detection. Proceedings of the IEEE International Conference on Systems, Man and Cybernetics **2**, 1482–1488 (1995)
3. Bergholm, F.: Edge focusing. IEEE Transactions on Image Processing **9**, 726–741 (1987)
4. Bolis, E., Zerbi, C., Collet, P., Louchet, J., Lutton, E.: A GP Artificial Ant for Image Processing: Preliminary Experiments with EASEA. In: Miller, J., Tomassini, M., Lanzi, P.L., Ryan, C., Tetamanzi, A.G.B., Langdon, W.B. (eds.) EuroGP 2001. LNCS, vol. 2038, pp. 246–255. Springer, Heidelberg (2001)
5. Canny, J.: A computational approach to edge detection. IEEE Transactions on Pattern Analysis and Machine Intelligence **8**(6), 679–698 (1986)
6. Dollar, P., Tu, Z., Belongie, S.: Supervised learning of edges and object boundaries. Proceedings of the IEEE Computer Society Conference on Computer Vision and Pattern Recognition **2**, 1964–1971 (2006)
7. Ebner, M.: On the edge detectors for robot vision using genetic programming. In: Proceedings of Horst-Michael Groβ, Workshop SOAVE 97 - Selbstorganisation von Adaptivem Verhalten, pp. 127–134 (1997)
8. Fei-Fei, L., Fergus, R., Perona, P.: One-shot learning of object categories. IEEE Transactions on Pattern Analysis and Machine Intelligence **28**(4), 594–611 (2006)
9. Fink, M.: Object classification from a single example utilizing class relevance metrics. In: Proceedings of the Neural Information Processing Systems Conference, pp. 449–456 (2004)

10. Fu, W., Johnston, M., Zhang, M.: Genetic programming for edge detection: a global approach. In: Proceedings of the IEEE Congress on Evolutionary Computation, pp. 254–261 (2011)
11. Fu, W., Johnston, M., Zhang, M.: Automatic Construction of Invariant Features Using Genetic Programming for Edge Detection. In: Thielscher, M., Zhang, D. (eds.) AI 2012. LNCS, vol. 7691, pp. 144–155. Springer, Heidelberg (2012)
12. Fu, W., Johnston, M., Zhang, M.: Soft edge maps from edge detectors evolved by genetic programming. In: Proceedings of the IEEE Congress on Evolutionary Computation, pp. 24–31 (2012)
13. Fu, W., Johnston, M., Zhang, M.: Automatic Construction of Gaussian-Based Edge Detectors Using Genetic Programming. In: Esparcia-Alcázar, A.I. (ed.) EvoApplications 2013. LNCS, vol. 7835, pp. 365–375. Springer, Heidelberg (2013)
14. Golonek, T., Grzechca, D., Rutkowski, J.: Application of genetic programming to edge detector design. In: Proceedings of the International Symposium on Circuits and Systems, pp. 4683–4686 (2006)
15. Grigorescu, C., Petkov, N., Westenberg, M.: Contour detection based on nonclassical receptive field inhibition. IEEE Transactions on Image Processing $12(7)$, 729–739 (2003)
16. Grigorescu, C., Petkov, N., Westenberg, M.A.: Contour and boundary detection improved by surround suppression of texture edges. Image and Vision Computing $22(8)$, 609–622 (2004)
17. Harris, C., Buxton, B.: Evolving edge detectors with genetic programming. In: Proceedings of the First Annual Conference on Genetic Programming, pp. 309–314 (1996)
18. Hollingworth, G., Smith, S., Tyrrell, A.: Design of highly parallel edge detection nodes using evolutionary techniques. In: Proceedings of the Seventh Euromicro Workshop on Parallel and Distributed Processing, pp. 35–42 (1999)
19. Kadar, I., Ben-Shahar, O., Sipper, M.: Evolution of a local boundary detector for natural images via genetic programming and texture cues. In: Proceedings of the 11th Annual Conference on Genetic and Evolutionary Computation, pp. 1887–1888 (2009)
20. Lacroix, V.: The primary raster: a multiresolution image description. In: Proceedings of the 10th International Conference on Pattern Recognition, vol. I, pp. 903–907 (1990)
21. Marr, D., Hildreth, E.: Theory of edge detection. Proceedings of the Royal Society of London, Series B, Biological Sciences $207(1167)$, 187–217 (1980)
22. Martin, D., Fowlkes, C., Malik, J.: Learning to detect natural image boundaries using local brightness, color, and texture cues. IEEE Transactions on Pattern Analysis and Machine Intelligence $26(5)$, 530–549 (2004)
23. Miller, E., Matsakis, N., Viola, P.: Learning from one example through shared densities on transforms. In: Proceedings of the IEEE Conference on Computer Vision and Pattern Recognition vol. 1, pp. 464–471 (2000)
24. Papari, G., Petkov, N.: Edge and line oriented contour detection: state of the art. Image and Vision Computing 29, 79–103 (2011)
25. Poli, R.: Genetic programming for image analysis. In: Proceedings of the First Annual Conference on Genetic Programming, pp. 363–368 (1996)

26. Quintana, M.I., Poli, R., Claridge, E.: Morphological algorithm design for binary images using genetic programming. Genetic Programming and Evolvable Machines **7**, 81–102 (2006)
27. Schunck, B.: Edge detection with Gaussian filters at multiple scales. In: Proceedings of the IEEE Workshop on Computer Vision, Representation and Control, pp. 208–210 (1987)
28. Song, D.M., Li, B.: Derivative computation by multiscale filters. Image and Vision Computing **16**(1), 43–53 (1998)
29. Wang, J., Tan, Y.: A novel genetic programming based morphological image analysis algorithm. In: Proceedings of the 12th Annual Conference on Genetic and Evolutionary Computation, pp. 979–980 (2010)
30. Zhang, Y., Rockett, P.I.: Evolving optimal feature extraction using multi-objective genetic programming: a methodology and preliminary study on edge detection. In: Proceedings of the Conference on Genetic and Evolutionary Computation, pp. 795–802 (2005)

Improving Graph-Based Image Segmentation Using Automatic Programming

Lars Vidar Magnusson[(✉)] and Roland Olsson

IT Department, Østfold University College, Halden, Norway
lars.v.magnusson@hiof.no

Abstract. This paper investigates how Felzenszwalb's and Huttenlocher's graph-based segmentation algorithm can be improved by automatic programming. We show that computers running Automatic Design of Algorithms Through Evolution (ADATE), our system for automatic programming, have induced a new graph-based algorithm that is 12 percent more accurate than the original without affecting the runtime efficiency. The result shows that ADATE is capable of improving an effective image segmentation algorithm and suggests that the system can be used to improve image analysis algorithms in general.

Keywords: Image segmentation · Graph algorithm · Evolutionary computation · Automatic programming

1 Introduction

Image segmentation involves partitioning an image into segments or components corresponding to objects in the image. Image segmentation has many applications and is typically used as an early step in a series of image processing techniques. As a result, accurate image segmentation is important; it is likely that it will affect the quality of all image processing that follows. Image segmentation algorithms employ a set of visual cues, such as intensity, texture or shape, to partition an image into its constituent objects. Combining two or more of these cues has been shown to improve the accuracy of an algorithm, but it also requires more processing time. There are also applications for image segmentation that require extremely fast processing, in which case, accuracy has to be sacrificed for runtime performance.

Here we show that it is possible to use evolutionary computation to automatically improve the core algorithm of a highly efficient graph-based segmentation technique [6] – without having to incorporate any additional visual cues, and without altering its overall computational efficiency. By using the ADATE automatic programming system, we have been able to automatically generate a new algorithm with 12 percent better segmentation accuracy on a popular image database.

© Springer-Verlag Berlin Heidelberg 2014
A.I. Esparcia-Alcázar et al. (Eds.): EvoApplications 2014, LNCS 8602, pp. 464–475, 2014.
DOI: 10.1007/978-3-662-45523-4_38

The scientific contributions of this paper can be summarized as follows.

1. An automatically generated and significantly more accurate graph-based image segmentation algorithm that runs as fast as the algorithm on which it was based.
2. Further evidence to support the hypothesis that ADATE can generate new and improve image analysis algorithms in general.

2 Background

Two scientific areas provide the background for this paper. The first is the relatively new machine learning discipline of automatic programming, and the second is the well studied discipline of image segmentation. The following sections present the background considered directly relevant for this paper.

2.1 Automatic Design of Algorithms Through Evolution (ADATE)

ADATE [12] is a system for automatic programming which infers purely functional programs through incremental program transformations – guided by evolutionary principles. The system is capable of inventing auxiliary functions, generating general recursive patterns, and creating and optimizing numerical constants. It can be used either to create entirely new programs, or to improve existing ones.

All programs generated by the ADATE system are evaluated with a user-specified evaluation function – allowing anything from simple input/output pairs to complex simulations. This flexible evaluation system, along with the search-based approach of incremental transformations, make the system useful in many cases where other automatic programming systems would fall short [3,4,9].

The program transformations performed by the ADATE system are grouped into four categories. The first, and most fundamental, category is called *Replacement* (R). A replacement can either replace an entire expression with a synthesized expression, or it can reuse parts of it, as subexpressions. Replacements are separated into two groups to facilitate the evolution process. In one group are the synthesized expressions that change the semantics of the original program. These provide a mechanism for introducing improvements into the program. The replacements in the other group typically maintain the semantics of the original program. More precisely, they do not harm the performance of the original program. These are referred to as *replacements preserving equality* (REQ), and they are important in the evolution process, as they provide a mechanism for doing neutral walks in the search landscape.

The remaining program transformation categories are *Abstraction* (ABSTR), *Case-distribution* (CASE-DIST) and *Embedding* (EMB). These are responsible for creating new auxiliary functions, changing the scope of variables and function, and introducing new function parameters respectively. They maintain the semantics of the original program, and are far less combinatorially challenging than replacements.

The problems are provided to ADATE in *specifications* containing any code needed to run the algorithm, along with any predefined functions, the training instances and the evaluation function that will be used to evaluate the generated programs. ADATE operates using a bare-bone subset of SML [11] called ADATE ML. The language has been stripped of all syntactic sugar to simplify the evolution – essentially reducing the language down to functions and case-expressions.

2.2   Graph-Based Image Segmentation

Graph-based image segmentation is a generic term covering image segmentation algorithms that use a graph-theoretic approach to partition an image into its constituent objects. In this respect, images are typically represented as a graph $G = (V, E)$, where each element in the set of vertices V represents a pixel in the image, and the set E contains edges that connect the vertices in the image according to a neighborhood relation. Each edge has an associated weight that represents some attribute derived from the vertices that it connects.

Wu and Leahy [17] proposed a graph-based data clustering algorithm based on a minimum cut – the set of edges with the smallest weights that partitions a graph into two disjoint subgraphs – and a graph compacting technique. The algorithm employs an efficient multi-terminal network flow algorithm to find the maximum flow between all the nodes in the image graph. This makes it possible to optimally divide the input graph into K regions by removing the edges belonging to the $K - 1$ minimum cuts. The weights in the graph represent the difference in intensity between neighboring pixels in the image being segmented. The runtime performance of the algorithm is polynomial in the number of nodes in the graph, but the algorithm is biased towards small regions.

This shortcoming was addressed by Shi and Malik [15] with the introduction of a *normalized* cut, which normalize the value of each cut using the sum of the weights of the edges between the nodes in a subgraph and the entire graph. This criterion removes the bias towards small regions, but it is computationally inefficient compared to the minimum cut – the decision variant is NP-complete. They show that an approximation can be found by solving a generalized eigenvalue system. This makes the problem tractable, but it still requires long runtimes due to the size of the matrix required to represent the images. Shi and Malik proposed a set of cues suitable for different applications, but only one can be used at any particular time. The framework was extended further by Malik et al. [10] by incorporating a combination of contour and texture cues. They proposed combining the two cues using a simple gating mechanism triggered by the *texturedness* of a region. After an initial over-segmentation, they recalculate the weights and combine regions until a normalized cut threshold is reached.

Felzenszwalb and Huttenlocher [6] introduced a graph-based algorithm for image segmentation that – while operating solely on local attributes – manages to satisfy certain desirable global properties, by producing segmentations that, as defined by the authors, are neither too fine nor too coarse. Unlike the algorithms presented above, this algorithm starts out with each pixel as a separate region and continues to merge regions in a bottom-up fashion. The proposed algorithm employs an adaptive segmentation strategy that keeps track of the similarity of the pixels within a segmented region and the dissimilarity between the different regions. The algorithm is $O(n \log n)$, where n is the number of pixels in the image – a significant improvement over the algorithms above – and most of the time is spent sorting the edges. The proposed algorithm is simple and efficient in its design, and it employs intensity cues only.

Alpert et al. [1] proposed a Bayesian probabilistic framework for combining visual cues. The framework was designed to work with any bottom-up merge based image segmentation algorithm, but it was demonstrated using a Segmentation by Weighted Aggregation (SWA) algorithm as proposed by Galun et al. [7] and Sharon et al. [14]. The algorithm starts with each pixel in the image being represented by a node in the graph. In each iteration, the graph is made coarser by merging seed nodes with their neighbors according to their similarity. A segmentation hierarchy is formed by relating nodes in the coarser graph with the nodes in the previous step. Edge weights are updated recursively by averaging the features, or cues, from earlier steps through weighted aggregation. The algorithm is linear in the number of pixels in the image, but the actual runtime is high due to large matrices and large runtime constants. The two original variants of the SWA algorithm use a wide set of visual cues, whereas the Bayesian framework proposed by Alpert et al. [1] was demonstrated using only intensity and texture cues. The reported runtime for the algorithm with the full featureset [7] is between 5 and 10 seconds on a 400×400 image using a 1.6 Xeon GHz processor.

It is apparent from the research presented above that the algorithm proposed by Felzenszwalb and Huttenlocher [6], though relatively simple both in terms of the overall design and its use of a single intensity cue, is capable of competing with more complex algorithms [2]. As such, it is a good starting point for an attempt to improve a leading image segmentation algorithm using automatic programming. Preliminary work by Huyen and Olsson [8] indicated that the algorithm can be improved. However, this preliminary study had serious limitations. The images used were scaled down to reduce the memory required, and the specification lacked essential features, such as noise filtering, available in the original algorithm. As a consequence, the algorithm is less general than the original and practically useless on the full-sized images. All of these limitations have been addressed in our work to allow the evolution of an algorithm that can perform well even if the conditions change.

3   Experiments

This section describes the most important parts of converting the problem into the proper format for ADATE.

3.1   The Implementation of the Original Algorithm

The original algorithm had to be ported in its entirety to ADATE ML – the language in which ADATE evolves programs. The C++ code provided by

Felzenszwalb and Huttenlocher, in addition to the actual segmentation algorithm, features a Gaussian noise reduction filter and a post-processing step that merges any neighboring components under a certain size. Both these features have been included in our ADATE ML implementation to ensure identical operational semantics for both implementations.

The most important parts of the code in the ADATE ML implementation are located in two functions *main* and *f*, where the definition of the latter contains the code to be modified and improved by ADATE. The *main* function is executed once per image, and is responsible for transforming the pre-processed image data into a graph by letting each pixel be represented by a node, which is connected to its eight immediate neighbors by weighted edges corresponding to the dissimilarity of the pixels. All of the edges are sorted in non-decreasing order, and the data structures used to represent the components during the segmentation process are initialized. Each node in the graph starts out as a component with a threshold corresponding to a constant C that controls how large the resulting segments will be. After these initial tasks, the function invokes the recursive f function to do the actual segmentation, the result of which is post-processed to merge components that are smaller than a certain size.

Every invocation of f selects the next candidate edge from the list of sorted edges. Its weight is compared to the thresholds of the two components that it connects – if they do not belong to the same component already. If the weight W is smaller than the thresholds of both components, the two connected components are merged into a new component, and the threshold of the component is set according to the following equation.

$$T_N = W + \frac{C}{|N|} \ .\tag{1}$$

Here N represents the new component, $|N|$ is the cardinality of N, and T_N is the threshold of N.

The ADATE ML implementation of the algorithm was tested both with a third-party ML compiler and with ADATE's internal compiler before the evolution was started, and it produced the exact same results as the original C++ implementation in both cases.

3.2   The Training and Test Images

There are several image databases available that provide natural images manually annotated by humans, but two of them distinguish themselves from the others in terms of quality, the Berkeley Segmentation Data Set (BSDS) [2] and the Weizmann Segmentation Evaluation Database (WSED) [1]. The way the BSDS evaluates segmentations arguably favors algorithms that are either based on or include some form of edge detection. This makes the dataset unsuitable for evaluating region growing algorithms like the algorithm by Felzenszwalb and Huttenlocher [6]. We therefor chose to use the WSED instead, even though it has fewer images and contains only images with one foreground object.

The dataset contains a total of 100 images with a single foreground object that have been annotated by three or more individuals. Of these 100, 50 were used for training, and 50 were used for testing.

3.3 Measuring the Accuracy of Generated Programs

We have used the same means of measuring the performance of the generated programs that is used in the WSED to determine the accuracy of a segmentation, the F-measure [13] as defined in (2). *Precision* (P) is the ratio of the number of true-positive pixels to the sum of the number of true-positive and the number of false-positive pixels, and *Recall* (R) is the ratio of the number of true-positive pixels to the sum of the number of true-positive and the number of false-negative pixels.

$$F = \frac{PR}{0.5(P + R)} \tag{2}$$

The Felzenszwalb and Huttenlocher algorithm produce segmentations that partition an image into its objects, rather than just foreground and background. To determine the quality of any segmentation the regions are all evaluated and the region with the highest score is selected.

3.4 Selecting the Constant Values

There are three constants in the original algorithm: the standard deviation of the Gaussian noise reduction filter, the threshold for merging components in post-processing, and the constant C that controls the tendency for components to merge.

The standard deviation for the noise filter was set to 0.5, which produced marginally better results on our dataset than the one used by Felzenszwalb and Huttenlocher [6]. The component size threshold for merging components in the post-processing step was not discussed in their article, but it is included in the C++ code provided. We therefore had no reference for choosing this value, and, due to the way the post-processor operates, it could not simply be chosen by optimizing its value. This might interfere with the evolution of an improved algorithm by forcing it to produce suboptimal segmentations to fit the post-processor. Based on this, we decided to use a relative small threshold of 20 to keep the interference with the evolution to a minimum, but at the same time ensure that drastic over-segmentations do not slow down the evaluation.

The third constant C – the only constant used directly in the algorithm – was chosen by running the algorithm on the entire image dataset with values ranging from 500 to 2500. Based on the results, we decided to run our experiments with a value of 1000 for the C constant.

4 Results

In this section the evolved algorithm is presented, along with an analysis of how it behaves and performs in terms of segmentation quality.

4.1   The Improved Algorithm

The program shown in Listing 1 was evolved over only ten generations – an incredibly low number when compared to other problems tackled by ADATE in the past. This shows that it was quite easy for ADATE to improve the Felzenszwalb and Huttenlocher algorithm [6]. We will discuss the changes separately to highlight the semantic difference between the two algorithms, then we will discuss how the changes in semantics collectively affect the behavior of the algorithm.

```
1   fun f( Universe, SortedEdges, Constant ) =
2     case SortedEdges of
3       enil => Universe
4       | econs( CurrentEdge as edge( A, B, W, X ), RestEdges ) =>
5     let
6       val ( ComponentA, ThresholdA ) = find ( A, Universe )
7       val ( ComponentB, ThresholdB ) = find ( B, Universe )
8     in
9       if differentComp( ComponentA, ComponentB ) then
10         if W < ThresholdA andalso W < ThresholdB then
11         let
12           val NewUniverse =
13             updateThresholdValue(
14               ComponentB,
15               W+Constant/
16                 getComponentSize(
17                   if Constant < ThresholdA then
18                     ComponentB
19                   else
20                     ComponentA ),
21                 union( Universe, ComponentA, ComponentB ) )
22         in
23           f( NewUniverse, RestEdges, Constant )
24         end
25         else if W > ThresholdA andalso W > ThresholdB then
26           f( Universe, RestEdges, getComponentSize( ComponentB ) )
27         else
28           f( Universe, RestEdges, Constant )
29       else
30         f( Universe, RestEdges, Constant )
31   end
```

Listing 1. The improved algorithm – written in Standard ML to simplify the syntax.

The two algorithms are identical in terms of semantics until the if-expression on lines 10 through 24. The first case of this if-expression – when the edge weight is smaller than both the thresholds of the components that the edge connects – cause the components to be joined and the threshold to be updated. But, instead of setting the threshold on the new component like in the original algorithm, it is set on the second connected component. The threshold is also calculated differently by no longer using the size of the joined component to divide the constant as in (1), but instead uses the size of one of the connected components – depending on a test to see if the constant is less than the threshold of the first connected component. The new algorithm has also introduced a new test on line 25 that checks whether the edge weight is bigger than both the thresholds of the components that the edge connects. In these situations the value of the constant is changed to the size of the second connected component. This, technically, makes the value a variable, but, for the sake of convenience, we will continue to refer to it as the constant.

The deceptively simple change that sets the new threshold on the second connected component, rather than the joined component, has the obvious effect that only about half the threshold updates will make a difference. Due to the way the components are represented, the second connected component has to be the component with the highest *rank* – a disjoint-set heuristic used to keep the trees shallow [16]. In most cases this translates into to the second connected component being the largest of the two. This is exploited on line 17 where a comparison of the current constant and the threshold of the first connected component determines which size of the components to use to calculate the new threshold. If the constant is equal to or greater than the threshold, the size of the first component is used, and in 98 percent of the cases, the size of this component is equal to or less than the size of the second component.

The new test on line 25 culminates into a recursive call that changes the constant value to the size of the second connected component when the current edge weight is larger than both the thresholds of the connected components. This normally occurs only after the components have been growing for some time, and as a result the new value is normally much larger than the original value. This changes how the algorithm operates on the remaining edges of the image. Any components merged after this will have much higher threshold than normal, essentially marking it with a high degree of variance and drastically increasing the chance of it being merged again.

Whereas the component threshold in the original algorithm is strictly decreasing and inversely proportional to the size of the component, the threshold in the improved algorithm fluctuates depending on the conditions under which two components are joined together. This allows the algorithm to react to patterns that occur during the segmentation.

4.2   Comparison of the Segmentation Quality

The segmentation accuracy of the new algorithm drastically exceeds the segmentation accuracy of the original algorithm. The images in Fig. 1 are some of the examples that showcase the differences between the segmentations produced by the two algorithms.

The first three images are all instances where the new algorithm is far more accurate than the original. In all three images the original algorithm has joined most, if not all, of the foreground object with the background, while the improved

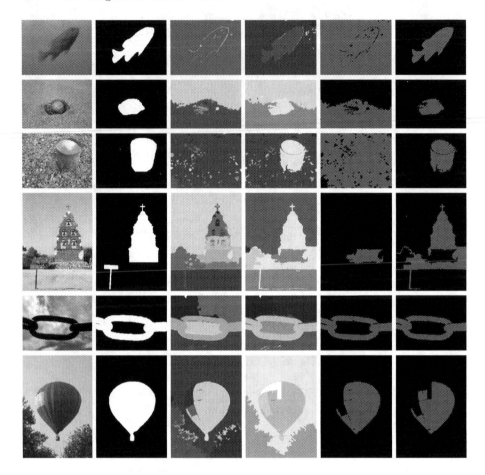

Fig. 1. A selected set of images and their segmentations. From left to right: The original images, the ground-truth images, the segmentation produced by the original algorithm, the segmentation produced by the improved algorithm, the best segment from the original segmentation, and the best segment from the improved segmentation.

algorithm has managed to keep them separate. The segmentation of the fourth image is also improved with the new algorithm, but not by the same amount as the first three. The original segmentation suffers from being over-segmented, while the improved segmentation is an under-segmentation. In the fourth image the score of the segmentation produced by the improved algorithm is slightly lower than the original. In the last image, the reduced quality of the improved algorithm is plainly visible – in the form of an over-segmentation.

4.3   Algorithm Benchmarks

The algorithms were benchmarked separately on both the 50 training images and the 50 test images. We used the same means of measurement as we did during the evolution; we used the F-measure as defined in (2) to determine the accuracy of each segment, and the maximum score to represent the quality of the segmentation.

We tested both algorithms on both the full-sized images and on image reduced in size, where the latter were included to establish whether or not the new algorithm is specialized to the conditions under which it was evolved. The algorithms were all tested using the same noise filter and post-processor settings as during the evolution. The remaining constant were optimized using the 50 training images.

Table 1. The average results from running the two algorithms on the full-sized images. The columns P, R and F represent the average *Precision*, *Recall* and *F-measure* respectively.

Algorithm	Train			Test			Total		
	P	R	F	P	R	F	P	R	F
New	0.79	0.86	0.79	0.81	0.82	0.78	0.80	0.84	0.79
Original	0.75	0.82	0.71	0.76	0.76	0.69	0.75	0.79	0.70

Table 2. The average results from running the two algorithms on the images that have been reduced to a quarter of their original size. The columns P, R and F represent the average *Precision*, *Recall* and *F-measure* respectively.

Algorithm	Train			Test			Total		
	P	R	F	P	R	F	P	R	F
New	0.73	0.79	0.73	0.76	0.81	0.75	0.75	0.80	0.74
Original	0.75	0.76	0.70	0.78	0.78	0.73	0.77	0.77	0.71

The average results from running both algorithms on all the full-sized images can be seen in Table 1. It is apparent from this data that the improved algorithm, on average, outperforms the original algorithm in terms of both precision and recall – yielding an average F-measure 11.5 percent, or 9 percentage points, better than the original. We also did a pairwise comparison of the two algorithms using student-t distribution on the differences, and we can say with 99 percent confidence that the new algorithm is between 1 and 17 percentage points better than the original on the test images.

The benchmark averages are directly comparable to the *one segment coverage test* in Alpert et al. [1] due to using the exact same images and performance measure. Among the algorithms in this test are both the three SWA based algorithms [1,7,14] and the normalized cut with gated intensity and texture cues

[10]. From their results we can see that the algorithm algorithm presented here is still not as good as the two best algorithms [1,7], but it manages to outperform the remaining two [10,14]. All of these algorithms employ two or more cues, and they are, based on their efficiency and reported runtime, an order of magnitude slower.

Alpert et al [1] also tested another very popular algorithm [5] that only uses intensity cues to segment an image. This makes it comparable to the algorithms tested here, but the results show that the accuracy of this algorithm is far worse.

The average results from running the algorithms on the images reduced in size can be seen in Table 2. The improved algorithm outperforms the original here as well, but only by 3.4 percent. Based on the data, this seems to be due to a slight under-segmentation, when compared to the segmentations of the full-sized images.

5   Conclusions

We have successfully been able to improve a leading image segmentation algorithm by using automatic programming, and the new algorithm is both small, efficient and superior to comparable algorithms. The algorithm evolved by ADATE has kept the runtime efficiency of the original algorithm, and the segmentation quality has been improved by 12 percent on full-sized images. This improvement has been achieved without adding any additional visual cues. Instead it has been made possible by the adaptive mechanisms automatically invented by the ADATE system.

The success of our attempt at using ADATE for this purpose provides further evidence that the system is capable of improving state of the art image segmentation algorithms – if not image processing algorithms in general. The ADATE system, through its evolutionary strategy, is highly suitable for problems, like image segmentation, where we typically are looking for the best approximation, not the exact solution. These situations typically require a good heuristic, and the ADATE system has proven several times to be capable of creating customized code to fit this need.

References

1. Alpert, S., Galun, M., Basri, R., Brandt, A.: Image segmentation by probabilistic bottom-up aggregation and cue integration. In: Proceedings of the IEEE Conference on Computer Vision and Pattern Recognition, pp. 1–8. IEEE (June 2007)
2. Arbelaez, P., Maire, M., Fowlkes, C., Malik, J.: Contour detection and hierarchical image segmentation. IEEE Transactions on Pattern Analysis and Machine Intelligence **33**, 898–916 (2011)
3. Berg, H., Olsson, R., Lindblad, T., Chilo, J.: Automatic design of pulse coupled neurons for image segmentation. Neurocomputing 71(10-12), 1980–1993 (2008); Neurocomputing for Vision Research; Advances in Blind Signal Processing

4. Berg, H., Olsson, R., Rusas, P.O., Jakobsen, M.: Synthesis of control algorithms for autonomous vehicles through automatic programming. In: Proceedings of the 2009 Fifth International Conference on Natural Computation, ICNC 2009, vol. 4, pp. 445–453. IEEE Computer Society (2009)
5. Comaniciu, D., Meer, P.: Mean shift: A robust approach toward feature space analysis. IEEE Transactions on Pattern Analysis and Machine Intelligence **24**(5), 603–619 (2002)
6. Felzenszwalb, P., Huttenlocher, D.: Efficient graph-based image segmentation. International Journal of Computer Vision **59**, 167–181 (2004)
7. Galun, M., Sharon, E., Basri, R., Brandt, A.: Texture segmentation by multiscale aggregation of filter responses and shape elements. In: Proceedings of the Ninth IEEE International Conference on Computer Vision, vol. 1, pp. 716–723. IEEE (2003)
8. Vu, H., Olsson, R.: Automatic Improvement of Graph Based Image Segmentation. In: Bebis, G., Boyle, R., Parvin, B., Koracin, D., Fowlkes, C., Wang, S., Choi, M.-H., Mantler, S., Schulze, J., Acevedo, D., Mueller, K., Papka, M. (eds.) ISVC 2012, Part II. LNCS, vol. 7432, pp. 578–587. Springer, Heidelberg (2012)
9. Løkketangen, A., Olsson, R.: Generating meta-heuristic optimization code using adate. Journal of Heuristics 16, 911–930 (2010)
10. Malik, J., Belongie, S., Leung, T., Shi, J.: Contour and texture analysis for image segmentation. International Journal of Computer Vision **43**(1), 7–27 (2001)
11. Milner, R., Tofte, M., Harper, R., MacQueen, D.: The Definition of Standard ML - Revised. The MIT Press (1997)
12. Olsson, R.: Inductive functional programming using incremental program tranformation. Artificial Intelligence **74**, 55–81 (1995)
13. Rijsbergen, C.J.V.: Information Retrieval, 2nd edn. Butterworth-Heinemann, Newton (1979)
14. Sharon, E., Galun, M., Sharon, D., Basri, R., Brandt, A.: Hierarchy and adaptivity in segmenting visual scenes. Nature **442**(7104), 810–813 (2006)
15. Shi, J., Malik, J.: Normalized cuts and image segmentation. IEEE Transactions on Pattern Analysis and Machine Intelligence **22**, 888–905 (2000)
16. Tarjan, R.E.: Efficiency of a good but not linear set union algorithm. Journal of the ACM (JACM) **22**(2), 215–225 (1975)
17. Wu, Z., Leahy, R.: An optimal graph theoretic approach to data clustering: Theory and its application to image segmentation. IEEE Trans. Pattern Anal. Mach. Intell. **15**(11), 1101–1113 (1993)

New Representations in PSO for Feature Construction in Classification

Yan Dai, Bing Xue[✉], and Mengjie Zhang

School of Engineering and Computer Science, Victoria University of Wellington,
PO Box 600, Wellington, New Zealand
{Yan.Dai,Bing.Xue,Mengjie.Zhang}@ecs.vuw.ac.nz

Abstract. Feature construction can improve the classification performance by constructing high-level features using the original low-level features and function operators. Particle swarm optimisation (PSO) is an powerful global search technique, but it cannot be directly used for feature construction because of its representation scheme. This paper proposes two new representations, pair representation and array representation, which allow PSO to direct evolve function operators. Two PSO based feature construction algorithms (PSOFCPair and PSOFCArray) are then developed. The two new algorithms are examined and compared with the first PSO based feature construction algorithm (PSOFC), which employs an inner loop to select function operators. Experimental results show that both PSOFCPair and PSOFCArray can increase the classification performance by constructing a new high-level feature. PSOFCArray outperforms PSOFCPair and achieves similar results to PSOFC, but uses significantly shorter computational time. This paper represents the first work on using PSO to directly evolve function operators for feature construction.

Keywords: Particle swarm optimisation · Feature construction · Classification

1 Introduction

In classification, the quality of the data that is defined by a set of features is an important factor. A classification algorithm usually can not achieve good classification performance using the original feature set. Therefore, feature manipulation techniques are proposed to improve the quality of the feature space, two of which are feature selection and feature construction [11]. Feature selection is to select a subset of original features to reduce the dimensionality and improve the classification performance [7]. Feature construction is a means of enhancing the quality of feature space by constructing new high-level features [6,7]. The constructed feature(s) should be able to discover the hidden relationship between the original low-level features, which is particularly useful when the original features could not provide enough information for classification. This work will mainly focus on feature construction for classification.

© Springer-Verlag Berlin Heidelberg 2014
A.I. Esparcia-Alcázar et al. (Eds.): EvoApplications 2014, LNCS 8602, pp. 476–488, 2014.
DOI: 10.1007/978-3-662-45523-4_39

A constructed feature is usually a function of original low-level features and mathematical operators. Therefore, the selection of the original features and function operators is the key issue in feature construction, but it is a difficult problem due mainly to the large search space. The size of the search space grows exponentially with the number of original features and the candidate operators. As a result, feature construction approaches often suffer from the problem of being stagnation in local optima and computationally expensive. Therefore, a global search technique is needed to develop an effective and efficient feature construction algorithm.

Evolutionary computation (EC) techniques are a group of powerful arguably global search algorithms, which have been successfully applied to many areas [3]. Most of the EC based feature construction approaches rely on genetic programming (GP) due to its tree-like representation [6,9,10]. Particle swarm optimisation (PSO) is a powerful EC technique and is argued to be computationally less expensive than GP [3]. PSO has been used for feature selection [3,14,16], but there is only one work successfully using PSO for feature construction [17]. However, since the original representation in PSO does not allow it to evolve nominal values, the function operators in [17] are selected by a time-consuming inner loop rather than evolved by PSO itself. Therefore, in order to further investigate the use of PSO for feature construction, a new representation scheme needs to be developed to allow PSO itself to select function operators during the evolutionary process.

1.1 Goals

The overall goal of this paper is to propose a new representation scheme in PSO to develop a PSO based feature construction approach to binary classification. To achieve this goal, we develop two new representations named pair representation and array representation, based on which two PSO based feature construction algorithms are developed. We expect each new algorithm to construct a single high-level feature, which can benefit the classification performance either being used solely or combined with the original features. The two proposed algorithms are examined and compared with the first PSO based feature construction approach (PSOFC) [17] on seven commonly used binary classification problems. Specifically, we will investigate:

- whether PSO using the pair representation can automatically construct a new high-level feature to improve the classification performance either by the new feature itself or combined with the original features;
- whether PSO using the array representation can successfully construct a new high-level feature to improve the classification performance and outperforms the pair representation; and
- whether the two new algorithms can use a shorter computational time to achieve similar classification performance to PSOFC.

2   Background

2.1   Particle Swarm Optimisation (PSO)

PSO stimulates social behaviours of birds flocking and fish schooling [5,13]. In PSO, each candidate solution is encoded as a particle. A PSO algorithm starts with randomly initialising a population or swarm of particles. During the evolution of PSO, all the particles move or "fly" in the search space to find the optimal solutions. For any particle i, a vector $x_i = (x_{i1}, x_{i2}, ..., x_{iD},)$ is used to represent its position and a vector $v_i = (v_{i1}, v_{i2}, ..., v_{iD},)$ represents its velocity, where D is the dimensionality of the search space. During the search process, each particle can remember its best position visited so far called personal best (denoted by *pbest*), and the best previous position visited so far by the whole swarm called global best (denoted by *gbest*). Based on *pbest* and *gbest*, PSO iteratively updates the x_i and v_i of particle i to search for the optimal solutions according to Equations 1 and 2.

$$x_{id}^{t+1} = x_{id}^t + v_{id}^{t+1} \tag{1}$$

$$v_{id}^{t+1} = w * v_{id}^t + c_1 * r_{i1} * (p_{id} - x_{id}^t) + c_2 * r_{i2} * (p_{gd} - x_{id}^t) \tag{2}$$

where t shows the tth iteration. $d \in D$ shows the dth dimension. w is the inertia weight, which can balance the local search and global search of PSO. c_1 and c_2 are acceleration constants. r_{i1} and r_{i2} are random constants uniformly distributed in $[0, 1]$. p_{id} and p_{gd} denote the values of *pbest* and *gbest* in the dth dimension. v_{id}^{t+1} is limited by a predefined maximum velocity, v_{max} and $v_{id}^{t+1} \in [-v_{max}, v_{max}]$.

2.2   Related Work on Feature Construction

Feature construction has a long research history and a large number of feature construction approaches have been developed [7]. Based on whether a classification algorithm is included in the evaluation procedure, existing feature construction methods can be broadly divided into two categories, which are wrapper approaches and filter approaches [7]. In wrapper approaches, a classification algorithm is used to evaluate the classification performance of the constructed features. A filter feature construction process is a separate, independent preprocessing stage and the new features are constructed before the classification algorithm is applied to build the classifier [6]. Different filter and wrapper feature construction methods have been developed and more details can be seen in [6,7,11]. Due to the page limit, this section will briefly review typical evolutionary feature construction approaches only.

In evolutionary approaches to feature construction, most of the work relies on GP due to its tree-based representation, which can naturally evolve functions of features and mathematical expressions [6]. Muharram and Smith [9] developed two fitness functions in GP for feature construction, which are based on information gain and gini index, respectively. Experimental results show that the classification performance of four different classification algorithms can be be improved by using the constructed features. Krawiec [6] extends the standard

GP for feature construction framework aiming to preserve the valuable components in GP individuals, which may be destructed by mutation or crossover operators. Neshatian at al. [12] develop a GP based filter feature construction algorithm, where the class dispersion and entropy are used to form the fitness function. Experiments show that these algorithms can improve the classification performance by constructing new high-level features. Later, Neshatian at al. [10] develop a GP based filter system to construct multiple high-level features. New features are constructed by GP with an entropy-based fitness function to maximise the purity of class intervals. Constructing multiple features is achieved by using a decomposable objective function. The experiments show that the constructed features can significantly increase the classification performance.

2.3 PSO for Feature Manipulation

PSO has been used to solve problems in many areas [3, 14–16]. In terms of feature manipulation, PSO has been successfully used for feature selection, but there is only one existing work on PSO for feature construction [17]. Typical PSO based manipulation methods will be reviewed in this section.

Marinakis et al. [8] propose a wrapper feature selection approach based on PSO and K-nearest neighbour (KNN) for a real-world medical diagnosis problem called Pap-smear cell classification. The results show that this method removes around half of the features and achieves good classification performance. Azevedo et al. [1] proposed a wrapper feature selection algorithm using PSO and support vector machine (SVM) for personal identification in a keystroke dynamic system. However, the proposed algorithm obtained a relatively high false acceptance rate, which should be low in most identification systems. Unler and Murat [14] develop a modified PSO algorithm for feature selection. In the proposed algorithm, whether a feature is chosen or not depends on two criteria, which are the *likelihood* calculated by PSO and the relevance of the feature to the already selected features. The experiments show that the proposed algorithm achieves better performance than scatter search and tabu search algorithms. Xue et a. [16] proposed a PSO based multi-objective feature selection approach. Experimental results show that the proposed approach outperforms other three well-known EC based multi-objective feature selection algorithms.

Existing works have shown that PSO can be successfully used for feature selection. However, there is only one existing work to investigate the use of PSO for feature construction [17]. Xue et al. [17] apply PSO to feature construction (PSOFC) to construct a high-level feature, where PSO is used to select original features and a inner loop is used to exhaustively evaluate all the candidate operators to search for an operator for each of the selected features. The experiments have shown that PSOFC can successfully construct a high-level feature to improve the classification performance of three different classification algorithms, i.e. KNN, decision trees (DT), and naïve bayes (NB). However, the operators are not evolved by PSO itself, but selected by the inner loop, which is computationally expensive, especially when the number of features is large. This is due mainly to the major limitation of PSO in feature construction, i.e.

the standard representation does not allow PSO to evolve function operators. Therefore, a new representation scheme is needed in PSO to evolve function operators to further investigate its potential in feature construction.

3   Proposed Approaches

In order to address the major problem in PSO for feature construction, we propose two new representations, which are the pair representation and the array representation. These two new representations allow PSO to directly evolve function operators for feature construction.

3.1   Pair Representation

In this representation, the position shows a candidate solution of the problem, i.e. a constructed feature. The dimensionality of each particle/search space is n, where n is the total number of features in the dataset. Different from the traditional representation in PSO, the meaning/function of each dimension in the pair representation is two-folded. The first one is the probability of a feature being selected and the second one is the operator chosen for this feature if it is selected. By using the pair representation, a PSO based feature construction algorithm is proposed and named PSOFCPair.

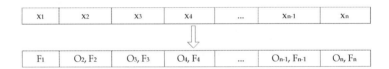

Fig. 1. Pair Representation

Fig. 1 shows a particle in the pair representation. x_i is the value of a particle in the ith dimension with $i \in [1, n]$. F_i represents feature i and O_i represents the operator for feature i. $x_i \in [0, 1]$ represents the probability of F_i being selected. A position determines the selected features and operators, which is regarded as a constructed feature. The selected features and operators are read from left to right and used as input to the feature construction function. The function starts with the first selected feature, followed by a number of pairs of an operator and a selected feature, and ends with the last selected feature. For example, a constructed feature can $F = F_1 * F_3 + F_5 - F_{10}$. Since there is no need to put any operator before the first selected feature, x_1 in the position only determines whether F_1 is selected or not. Note that the order of features in the dataset will not significantly effect the performance of the constructed feature because PSO is expected to automatically evolve the solutions during the evolutionary process and overcome the influence of the features being ordered.

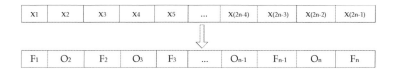

Fig. 2. Array Representation

To determine whether a feature is selected or not, a threshold $\theta \in [0,1]$ is used here. If $x_i > \theta$, F_i is selected. Otherwise, F_i is not selected. If F_i is selected, an operator is needed to select for F_i according to the value of x_i. Given F_i being selected, $\theta < x_i \leq 1$. According to the number of candidate operators, the interval of $[\theta, 1]$ can be divided into a number of sub intervals. The operator is selected according to which sub interval x_i belongs to. For example, if there are four candidate operators, three numbers $(\alpha_1, \alpha_2, \alpha_3)$ can be used here to divide $[\theta, 1]$ into three sub intervals. If $\theta < x_i < \alpha_1$, the first operator is selected. If $\alpha_1 \leq x_i < \alpha_2$, the second operator is selected. If $\alpha_2 \leq x_i < \alpha_3$, the third operator is selected. If $\alpha_3 \leq x_i \leq 1$, the fourth operator is selected.

3.2 Array Representation

The pair representation could allow PSO to be directly used for feature construction without increasing the dimensionality of the search space, but using one variable to determine the selection of both features and operators may limit the search of the their best combination. Therefore, we propose an array representation, where the feature selection and operator selection are determined separately. By using the pair representation, a PSO based feature construction algorithm is proposed and named PSOFCArry.

Fig. 2 shows the position of a particle in the proposed array representation. The dimensionality of the particle is $2n - 1$, where n is the total number of features in the dataset. A dimension is used to determine the selection of either the feature or the operator. The $(2 * i - 1)$th dimension determines whether F_i is selected or not, where $i \in [1, n]$. The $(2 * i - 2)$th dimension determines which operator is selected for F_i, where $i \in [2, n]$ since the first feature does not need any operator. Meanwhile, the operator i is selected only when F_i is selected.

The threshold θ is also used in the $(2*i-1)$th dimension to determine whether F_i is selected or not. θ performs the same way as in the pair representation. According to the number of candidate operators, the interval $[0,1]$ is divided into a number of sub intervals. An operators is selected according to which sub interval x_i in the $(2 * i - 2)$th dimension belongs to, which is the same as in the pair representation.

3.3 Pesuode Code of the Proposed Approaches

Both PSOFCPair and PSOFCArry follow the basic steps in PSO and each of them produces a single high-level feature. An important step in PSOFCPair and

---

Algorithm 1. Pseudo-code of PSOFCArry and PSOFCPair

---
begin
    split the instances into a Training and a Test set;
    initialise x and v of each particle;
    while *Maximum Iterations has been not met* **do**
        construct a new high-level feature for each particle according to the Pair
        or Array representation;
        calculate the classification performance of the constructed high-level
        feature;
        for $i=1$ **to** *Swarm Size* **do**
            update the personal best (*pbest*) of particle i;
            update the global best (*gbest*) of particle i;
        for $i=1$ **to** *Swarm Size* **do**
            for $d=1$ **to** *Dimensionality* **do**
                calculate v_i according to Equation 2
                calculate x_i according to Equation 1
    calculate the classification performance of the constructed feature on the
    test set using 0 as the threshold or using other classification algorithms;
    return *gbest*, the training and testing classification performance.

Table 1. Datasets

Dataset	No. of Features	No. of Classes	No.of Instances
Australian	14	2	690
Ionosphere	34	2	351
WBCD	30	2	569
Sonar	60	2	208
Hillvalley	100	2	606
Musk1	166	2	476
Madelon	500	2	4400

PSOFCArry is the evaluation of a particle, which is shown in Line 1. In both PSOFCPair and PSOFCArry, the algorithm first constructs a new high-level feature according to the low-level features and the operators selected by the particle. The fitness of the particle is evaluated by the classification performance of the newly constructed high-level feature. Since binary classification problems are considered here, we use 0 as the threshold for the constructed feature to determine an instance to be class 1 or class 2. The purpose of using 0 as the threshold for classification rather than using a classification algorithm is to speed up the classification (i.e. the fitness evaluation) process by avoiding a complex process to train a classifier.

4   Design of Experiments

A set of experiments have been conducted to examine the performance of PSOFC-Pair and PSOFCArry on seven binary datasets (see Table 1) chosen from the UCI machine learning repository [4]. The seven datasets are chosen to have different numbers of features and instances. On each dataset, 70% of the instances

Table 2. Operator Selection

PSOFCPair		PSOFCArry	
Interval	Operator	Interval	Operator
[0.5, 0.625)	+	[0.0, 0.25)	+
[0.625, 0.7)	-	[0.25, 0.5)	-
[0.7, 0.825)	*	[0.5, 0.75)	*
[0.825, 1]	/	[0.75, 1]	/

are randomly selected as training examples and the rest 30% are used as the testing set, following the settings in [17] to make a fair comparison.

The parameters in PSOFCPair and PSOFCArry are set as follows [2]: $w = 0.7298$, $c_1 = c_2 = 1.49618$. The swarm size is 30 and the fully connected topology is used. The maximum number of iterations is 100. θ in both PSOFCPair and PSOFCArry is set as 0.5, which means each original feature has 50% probability to be selected for constructing the new high-level feature. Four commonly used function operators in GP for feature construction [11] are used in both PSOFCPair and PSOFCArry, which are "+", "-", "*" and "/" (protected division). The operators are selected according to which interval the corresponding position value falls into and details can be seen in Table 2. The four operators are considered equally important. Therefore, the four intervals in PSOFCPair or PSOFCArry have the same range to ensure that the four operators have the same probability to be selected.

Both PSOFCPair and PSOFCArry are run 50 independent times on each dataset. To test the generality of the constructed feature, three different learning algorithms are used to test its classification performance on the testing set. The three classifiers are DT, KNN with K = 5 and NB. To further test the performance of PSOFCPair and PSOFCArry, they are compared with the first and the only existing PSO based feature construction algorithm (PSOFC) [17].

5   Results and Discussions

The results of PSOFCPair and PSOFCArry are shown in Tables 3 and 4. In the tables, "Org" means all the original features are used for the classification. "CF" means only the single constructed feature is used for the classification. "OrgCF" means the constructed feature and the original features are combined together for classification. "#Fea" represents the total number of features in the datasets. "Best", "Avg" and "Std" represent the best, the average and the standard deviation of the testing classification performance obtained from the 50 runs.

5.1   Results of the PSOFCPair

As can be seen from Table 3, by using only the single constructed feature for classification, DT, KNN and NB can achieve similar or better classification performance than using all the original features on a few datasets only. The results suggest that the simple pair representation in PSO has potential to construct

Table 3. Result of PSOFCPair

Dataset	#Fea	Method	DT			KNN			NB		
			Best	Avg	Std	Best	Avg	Std	Best	Avg	Std
Australian	14	Org	85.99			70.05			85.51		
		CF	77.29	65	4.13	74.4	61.99	4.28	59.9	53.93	1.84
		OrgCF	85.99	85.99	0	74.88	69.05	3.01	85.99	85.34	45.1E-2
WBCD	30	Org	92.98			92.98			90.64		
		CF	95.32	86.5	8.66	95.32	85.94	9.06	61.99	61.41	8.26E-2
		OrgCF	97.08	93.2	92.1E-2	95.91	92.13	4.12	90.64	90.64	0
Ionosphere	34	Org	86.67			83.81			28.57		
		CF	84.76	75.47	5.65	84.76	73.45	5.66	84.76	80.86	2.36
		OrgCF	89.52	86.88	93.8E-2	89.52	84.7	1.57	28.57	28.57	0
Sonar	60	Org	71.43			76.19			53.97		
		CF	69.84	53.14	7.7	65.08	53.05	7.23	47.62	47.62	0
		OrgCF	73.02	71.11	1.42	79.37	66.25	11.9	53.97	53.97	0
Musk1	166	Org	71.33			83.92			42.66		
		CF	67.13	58.95	4.17	64.34	55.37	5.09	60.14	59.38	36.6E-2
		OrgCF	75.52	71.41	58.7E-2	85.31	62.69	13.7	72.73	72.73	0
Hillvalley	100	Org	62.09			56.59			52.2		
		CF	83.79	54.56	7.99	83.52	53.38	7.84	47.8	47.8	0
		OrgCF	85.99	63.47	5.84	83.79	53.56	7.95	52.2	52.2	0
Madelon	500	Org	76.79			70.9			49.49		
		CF	57.31	50.98	2.34	54.23	50.27	1.69	49.49	49.49	0
		OrgCF	77.69	76.79	16E-2	72.44	52.24	5.85	55.51	55.51	1.84E-2

a high-level feature to provide useful information for classification and using only the single constructed needs much less computational time than using the original full set of features. However, the limitation of PSOFCPair is that a feature and its operator share the same value to determine whether the feature is selected or not and which operator is chosen. During the evolution, the shared dimension may not reach the ideal value for both feature and operator selection. Therefore, only using the constructed feature could not improve the classification performance on most cases, but adding it to the original feature set may increase the classification accuracy.

According to Table 3, by adding the constructed feature to the original feature set, the classification performance of all the three classification algorithms (DT, KNN and NB) can be increased. Specifically, the average accuracy of DT is increased on four of the seven datasets and similar on the other three datasets. The best accuracy is higher than using only the original features on six of the seven datasets and the same on one dataset. The performance of using both the constructed feature and the original features on KNN and NB shows a similar pattern to DT, where the classification performance is increased in most cases. These results indicate that adding the constructed feature can provide useful information to the feature set to achieve better classification performance than using only the original features, but the computational time cost by adding only one feature can be safely ignored. Although there is a preprocessing step to constructed the new feature, its computation time is very short (details can be seen in Section 5.3).

5.2   Results of PSOFCArry

According to Table 4, it can be seen that when using only the single constructed high-level feature for classification, the best classification performance of DT is

Table 4. Results of PSOFCArry

Dataset	#Fea	Method	DT			KNN			NB		
			Best	Avg	Std	Best	Avg	Std	Best	Avg	Std
Australian	14	Org	85.99			70.05			85.51		
		CF	88.41	85.05	1.63	87.44	66.59	17.3	76.33	55.21	5.02
		OrgCF	87.92	85.87	98.8E-2	87.92	79.54	4.17	88.89	86.59	67.4E-2
WBCD	30	Org	92.98			92.98			90.64		
		CF	95.91	91.47	2.36	95.91	90.98	2.49	61.4	61.4	0
		OrgCF	97.08	93.45	1.07	95.91	92.65	1.5	90.64	90.64	0
Ionosphere	34	Org	86.67			83.81			28.57		
		CF	83.81	76.71	4.79	85.71	76.32	5.07	87.62	82.32	1.56
		OrgCF	92.38	85.96	3.27	87.62	84.46	1.18	28.57	28.57	0
Sonar	60	Org	71.43			76.19			53.97		
		CF	73.02	63.33	6.14	74.6	61.27	5.45	47.62	47.62	0
		OrgCF	76.19	68.67	4.17	80.95	71.08	6.42	53.97	53.97	0
Musk1	166	Org	71.33			83.92			42.66		
		CF	67.13	58.77	5.29	67.13	57.86	4.39	60.14	59.36	43.5E-2
		OrgCF	73.43	71.32	58.6E-2	84.62	66.99	12.7	72.73	72.73	0
Hillvalley	100	Org	62.09			56.59			52.2		
		CF	99.45	96.98	1.71	99.45	96.87	1.85	50	47.86	31.6E-2
		OrgCF	99.45	97.15	1.51	76.92	62.86	5.34	52.47	52.21	3.81E-2
Madelon	500	Org	76.79			70.9			49.49		
		CF	64.36	57.28	4.16	58.33	53.33	2.34	49.49	49.49	0
		OrgCF	77.05	76.77	24.6E-2	70.9	66.4	8.08	49.49	49.49	0

better than when using all the original features on four of the seven datasets. For example, on the Hillvalley dataset, the classification performance of DT using all the 100 original features is 62.09%. By using only the single constructed features, DT achieved the average classification performance of 96.98% and the best accuracy of 99.45%. The best classification performance of KNN and NB using only the constructed feature is better than using all the original low-level features on most datasets. The results suggests that PSOFCArry can effectively evolve a number of original low-level features and function operators to construct a single high-level feature, which is possible to achieve better classification performance than using all the original features.

According to Table 4, it can be observed that when combing the single constructed feature with the original features, the best classification performance of DT is better than using only the original features on all the seven datasets. The average classification accuracy is similar or better than using only the original features on almost all datasets. KNN and NB shows a similar patter to DT, which is the average accuracy is better or similar on most datasets and the best accuracy is higher than using only the original features on most cases. The results suggest that adding the constructed feature to the original features brings useful information to the feature set, which can help a classification algorithm (DT, KNN or NB) to achieve better classification performance than using only the original features.

5.3   Further Comparisons

Table 5 shows of the classification performance of PSOFCPair, PSOFCArray and PSOFC using DT as the classification algorithm, where "CF" means DT using only the constructed high-level feature and "CFOrg" means the combination of

Table 5. Results of PSOFCPair, PSOFCArray and PSOFC using DT

Feature	Method	Australian		WBCD		Ionosphere		Sonar	
		Ave±Std	Test	Ave±Std	Test	Ave±Std	Test	Ave±Std	Test
CF	PSOFC	85.35±1.13		93.31±1.07		81.01±2.85		63.11±2.26	
	PSOFCPair	65±4.13	-	86.5±8.66	-	75.47±5.65	-	53.14±7.7	-
	PSOFCArray	85.05±1.63	=	91.47±2.36	-	76.71±4.79	-	63.33±6.14	=
	Method	Musk1		Hillvalley		Madelon			
		Ave±Std	Test	Ave±Std	Test	Ave±Std	Test		
	PSOFC	65.96±3.24		85.93±12.5		53.97±4.26E-14			
	PSOFCPair	58.95±4.17	-	54.56±7.99	-	50.98±2.34	-		
	PSOFCArray	58.77±5.29	-	96.98±1.71	+	57.28±4.16	+		
Feature	Method	Australian		WBCD		Ionosphere		Sonar	
		Ave±Std	Test	Ave±Std	Test	Ave±Std	Test	Ave±Std	Test
CFOrg	PSOFC	85.93±66E-2		93.81±1.1		86.55±3.13		71.43±2.8E-14	
	PSOFCPair	85.99±9.9E-14	=	93.2±92.1E-2	-	86.88±93.8E-2	=	71.11±1.42	=
	PSOFCArray	85.87±98.8E-2	=	93.45±1.07	=	85.96±3.27	=	68.67±4.17	-
	Method	Musk1		Hillvalley		Madelon			
		Ave±Std	Test	Ave±Std	Test	Ave±Std	Test		
	PSOFC	71.54±3.09		85.63±12.4		76.79±8.53E-14			
	PSOFCPair	71.41±58.7E-2	=	63.47±5.84	-	76.79±16E-2	=		
	PSOFCArray	71.32±58.5E-2	=	97.15±1.51	+	76.77±24.6E-2	=		

the constructed feature and original features. "Test" shows the results of the statistical significant T-test (Z-test) comparing the classification performance achieved by PSOFC and PSOFCPair(or PSOFCArray). The results of using KNN or NB as the classification algorithm show a similar patter to DT and the results are not listed here due to the page limit. The average computational time (in seconds) of the three algorithms in each run is shown in Table 6.

According to Table 5, when DT using only the constructed feature for classification, PSOFC achieved better performance than PSOFCPair in all cases, better than PSOFCArray in three cases and worse than PSOFCArray in two cases. When using the combination of the constructed feature and the original features, PSOFC achieved slightly better performance than PSOFCPair and similar performance to PSOFCArray. The main reason is that PSOFC using a inner loop for operator selection, which conducts an exhaustive search of all the candidates operators to find the optimal operator for each feature, can obtain a better set of operators. PSOFCPair has a potential limitation due to the use of one dimension for both features and operators. However, the inner loop in PSOFC is time-consuming. From Table 6, it can be observed that the time used by PSOFCPair and PSOFCArray is around 100 times shorter than that of PSOFC. The main reason is that the inner loop in PSOFC causes a much larger number of evaluations than PSOFCPair and PSOFCArray. The operators in PSOFCPair and PSOFCArray are evolved by PSO itself and not need extra calculations. Since the dimensionality of PSOFCArray is higher than PSOFCPair, the computational time used by PSOFCArray is slightly larger than PSOFCPair, but still around 100 times shorter than PSOFC.

Tables 5 and 6 suggest that the new representations in PSOFCPair and PSOFCArray can effectively evolve operators to construct a new high-level feature to achieve similar classification performance to PSOFC, but use significantly shorter computational time.

Table 6. Computation Time used by PSOFCPair,PSOFCArray and PSOFC

Method	Australian	Ionosphere	WBCD	Hillvalley	Musk1	Semeion	Madelon
PSOFCPair	94.6E-2	84.2E-2	54.4E-2	41.6E-2	1.46	2.68	18.8
PSOFCArray	93.3E-2	88E-2	59E-2	44.5E-2	1.93	3.45	25.6
PSOFC	31.4	65.4	47.1	65.6	7.2E2	8.2E2	6.1E4

6   Conclusion and Future Work

The goal of this research was to develop a new representation scheme in PSO for feature construction to construct a high-level feature to improve the classification performance. The goal was successfully achieved by proposing two new representations, which are the pair representation (PSOFCPair) and the array representation (PSOFCArray). PSOFCPair and PSOFCArray were examined and compared with the first and only existing PSO based feature construction algorithm (PSOFC) on seven benchmark datasets. The experimental results show that PSOFCPair increased the classification performance in most cases by adding the constructed feature to the original feature set, but it has a limitation because of using one dimension in the particle for both the feature selection and operator selection. By using a larger dimensionality, PSOFCArray could increase the classification performance by using only the constructed feature and increase the classification performance in almost all cases by adding the constructed feature to the original feature set. PSOFCArray achieved similar classification performance to PSOFC, but used significantly shorter computational time.

This paper is the first work that uses PSO to automatically select original low-level features and function operators for feature construction. In the future, we will further investigate the use of PSO for feature construction and compare its performance with GP based feature construction approaches.

References

1. Azevedo, G., Cavalcanti, G., Filho, E.: An approach to feature selection for keystroke dynamics systems based on PSO and feature weighting. In: IEEE Congress on Evolutionary Computation (CEC 2007), pp. 3577–3584 (2007)
2. Clerc, M., Kennedy, J.: The particle swarm- explosion, stability, and convergence in a multidimensional complex space. IEEE Transactions on Evolutionary Computation **6**(1), 58–73 (2002)
3. Engelbrecht, A.P.: Computational intelligence: an introduction, 2. ed. Wiley (2007)
4. Frank, A., Asuncion, A.: UCI machine learning repository (2010)
5. Kennedy, J., Eberhart, R.: Particle swarm optimization. IEEE International Conference on Neural Networks. **4**, 1942–1948 (1995)
6. Krawiec, K.: Genetic programming-based construction of features for machine learning and knowledge discovery tasks. Genetic Programming and Evolvable Machines **3**(4), 329–343 (2002)
7. Liu, H., Motada, H. (eds.): Feature extraction, construction and selection: A data mining perspective. Kluwer Academic Publishers, Norwell (1998)
8. Marinakis, Y., Marinaki, M., Dounias, G.: Particle swarm optimization for pap-smear diagnosis. Expert Systems with Applications **35**(4), 1645–1656 (2008)

 9. Muharram, M.A., Smith, G.D.: Evolutionary Feature Construction Using Information Gain and Gini Index. In: Keijzer, M., O'Reilly, U.-M., Lucas, S., Costa, E., Soule, T. (eds.) EuroGP 2004. LNCS, vol. 3003, pp. 379–388. Springer, Heidelberg (2004)
10. Neshatian, K., Zhang, M., Andreae, P.: A filter approach to multiple feature construction for symbolic learning classifiers using genetic programming. IEEE Transactions on Evolutionary Computation **16**(5), 645–661 (2012)
11. Neshatian, K.: Feature Manipulation with Genetic Programming. PhD thesis, Victoria University of Wellington, Wellington, New Zealand (2010)
12. Neshatian, K., Zhang, M., Johnston, M.: Feature Construction and Dimension Reduction Using Genetic Programming. In: Orgun, M.A., Thornton, J. (eds.) AI 2007. LNCS (LNAI), vol. 4830, pp. 160–170. Springer, Heidelberg (2007)
13. Shi, Y., Eberhart, R.: A modified particle swarm optimizer. In: IEEE International Conference on Evolutionary Computation (CEC 1998), pp. 69–73 (1998)
14. Unler, A., Murat, A.: A discrete particle swarm optimization method for feature selection in binary classification problems. European Journal of Operational Research **206**(3), 528–539 (2010)
15. Xue, B., Cervante, L., Shang, L., Browne, W.N., Zhang, M.: A multi-objective particle swarm optimisation for filter based feature selection in classification problems. Connection Science (2012)
16. Xue, B., Zhang, M., Browne, W.: Particle swarm optimization for feature selection in classification: A multi-objective approach. IEEE Transactions on Cybernetics **43**(6), 1656–1671 (2013)
17. Xue, B., Zhang, M., Dai, Y., Browne, W.N.: PSO for feature construction and binary classification. In: Proceeding of the Fifteenth Annual Conference on Genetic and Evolutionary Computation Conference, GECCO 2013, 137–144 (2013)

GPU-Based Point Cloud Recognition Using Evolutionary Algorithms

Roberto Ugolotti$^{(\boxtimes)}$, Giorgio Micconi, Jacopo Aleotti, and Stefano Cagnoni

Department of Information Engineering, University of Parma, Parma PR, Italy
{rob_ugo,micconi,aleotti,cagnoni}@ce.unipr.it

Abstract. In this paper, we describe a method for recognizing objects in the form of point clouds acquired with a laser scanner. This method is fully implemented on GPU and uses bio-inspired metaheuristics, namely PSO or DE, to evolve the rigid transformation that best aligns some references extracted from a dataset to the target point cloud. We compare the performance of our method with an established method based on Fast Point Feature Histograms (FPFH). The results prove that FPFH is more reliable under simple and controlled situations, but PSO and DE are more robust with respect to common problems as noise or occlusions.

Keywords: Particle Swarm Optimization · Differential Evolution · Pattern Recognition · GPGPU · Point Clouds

1 Introduction

The recent spread of 3D sensors has strongly increased the number of systems that operate on 3D data to perform operations like motion planning, human-robot interaction, manipulation and grasping.

In this paper, we consider a system which is part of an architecture whose goal is to help users program robotic tasks. To reach this goal, a sub-system for object recognition is required (see Figure 1). It receives input data from a high-resolution planar laser scanner mounted on the wrist of a six degrees of freedom robot arm. The estimated accuracy of the whole measurement chain is about 1.5 cm, the main sources of error being the variable remission of objects and the angle of incidence of the laser. Data undergo several preprocessing steps to refine the acquisition and are then passed to the FPFH (Fast Point Feature Histograms) based recognizer, along with a list of models stored in a database. The output of the recognizer indicates which objects are present in the scene and in which pose. A thorough description of a preliminary version of this system can be found in [12].

In [18] we have shown that bio-inspired metaheuristics like Particle Swarm Optimization (PSO) [5] or Differential Evolution (DE) [17] can successfully perform object recognition and registration.

The main goal of this paper is to present an implementation of the method proposed in [18] to solve the problem of 3D point-cloud registration and recognition. We will assess its performance in several situations and compare our results

© Springer-Verlag Berlin Heidelberg 2014
A.I. Esparcia-Alcázar et al. (Eds.): EvoApplications 2014, LNCS 8602, pp. 489–500, 2014.
DOI: 10.1007/978-3-662-45523-4_40

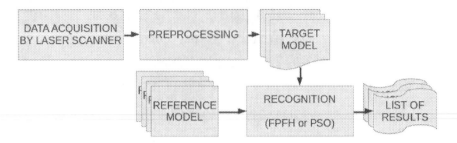

Fig. 1. Representation of the system within which the FPFH recognizer, or the one based on PSO as an alternative, is used

to those obtained using FPFH features. Figure 1 shows that this recognizer can be easily embedded into the existing system.

2   Theoretical Background

In this section, we briefly describe the background of our approach to object recognition without re-introducing PSO and DE, whose descriptions can be found in [1] and [14], respectively.

Point Clouds

A point cloud is a set of three-dimensional points expressed within a certain coordinate system. A point cloud can have several meanings but is usually interpreted as a discrete representation of the external surface of an object. It can be generated artificially, using CAD or 3D editing tools, or by several types of sensors, like, for instance, RGB cameras, depth cameras or laser scanners. Point clouds are often used in object recognition and in many other problems related to the understanding of the environment.

Point-cloud registration is a well-known problem for which many solutions have been proposed. Approaches that inspired our work can be found in [8], where Li et al propose a function based on a Gaussian Mixture distance map and use PSO to optimize it; in [9], where registration of partially overlapped point clouds is achieved by estimating their Extended Gaussian Images; and in [19] where DE is used to register a triangular mesh to a point cloud by minimizing their relative distance.

Model Based Object Recognition

The approach used in this work is an application of the method presented more in depth in [18]. The general process is quite straightforward:

1. A template of the object to recognize is created off-line, defining the available range of deformations to which it can be subject;

2. This model is rotated and deformed during the evolutionary process in order to match, as much as possible, a target under consideration (we used PSO and DE, but other metaheuristics can be used);

3. The process stops when a convergence criterion (e.g. alignment reached, time) is met.

The main goal of this work is to recognize the pose of a known object, so the first step just consists of reading a point cloud from a database of available models. Moreover, the model can only be subject to a rigid transformation, so the search space is defined only by six degrees of freedom (translations and rotations around the three axes). This means that the dimensionality of the search space in which DE and PSO operate is six.

CUDA

Graphic Processing Units (GPUs) contain up to several thousands of cores that can execute the same code at the same time on different data. While originally used only in gaming and computer graphics, their use has recently spread to a very large number of applications [13] following the GPGPU (general-purpose computing on GPU) paradigm, within environments like CUDA or OpenCL.

CUDA (Compute Unified Distributed Architecture) [11] is a general purpose parallel computing environment distributed by nVIDIA^{TM} which exploits the massively parallel computation capabilities of its GPUs. CUDA C/C++ is an extension of the C language that allows development of GPUs routines (named *kernels*), that run in parallel as a number of different CUDA threads, following the Single Instruction Multiple Thread (SIMT) model. Each kernel is executed on different threads, which run all the same code, but on different data. These threads may be grouped into *blocks*. A block can be seen as a group of threads that share the same information and can exploit fast, local memory instead of using the slow, global one.

Algorithms with high arithmetic intensity, low memory requirements and few interactions between independent threads, like evolutionary algorithms (EAs), are very well suited for GPGPU. Therefore, in the last years, many GPU-based implementations of EAs have been presented. The first implementations of PSO and DE based on CUDA were developed in 2009 and 2010, respectively [2,3]; after that, several other implementations have been proposed. Two comprehensive reviews regarding GPU implementations of PSO [6] and DE [7] have been recently presented by Kromer et al.

3   FPFH

Fast Point Feature Histograms [15] (an evolution of PFH [16]) are pose-invariant local features which represent the underlying surface model properties for all the elements composing a point cloud. These features form a full description of a point cloud, therefore they can be used for several tasks, like aligning a target to a reference (registration). These descriptors are computed for each point of a given point cloud and are generated by comparing the normal of a specific point with the normals of the points within a certain radius, which is a fundamental parameter of the algorithm. For a more detailed description, please refer to [16]. Once all descriptors of the two point clouds (target and reference) have been computed, a particular version of the RANSAC algorithm (RANdom SAmple Consensus) [4] is used to find a raw alignment between the clouds. This version is called SAC-IA (SAmple Consensus - Initial Alignment) and is followed by a second step, which attempts to refine the previous alignment, using the Iterative Closest Point algorithm. Eventually, the two transformations found by the algorithms are composed in order to compute the full transformation needed to align the two clouds.

4   Evolutionary Implementation

In this section we describe the fitness function used by PSO and DE, as well as the system's GPU-based implementation. From now on, we will refer only to PSO, but DE could also play exactly the same role.

4.1   Fitness Function

The fitness function used by PSO is relatively straightforward. We compare the target cloud T to be recognized (composed of N_T points), with a reference cloud R extracted from a database, composed of N_R points. This reference is subject to a transformation M encoded by a PSO particle, to obtain $R' = M(R)$. The fitness of a particle is the average of the minimum distances of each point of T to the closest point of the roto-translated reference R'. More formally:

$$F(T, R') = \frac{1}{N_T} \sum_{p \in T} \min_{q \in R'} \left(dist(p, q) \right)$$

where $dist()$ is a valid distance metric between points; in this case we selected the squared euclidean distance.

Each point cloud is expressed within a local reference frame centered around its centroid. A model can do a full rotation around each axis while the range of translation is limited to 10 cm in each direction, which is good enough to satisfy the requirements of the environment we are considering.

4.2   GPU Implementation

The entire system, including the computation of the fitness function, has been implemented on GPU. Several implementation designs have been tested. In the final one, two degrees of parallelism are exploited:

1. The i-th PSO particle represents a possible transformation M_i of the reference R and relies on a CUDA block, so all M_is can be computed in parallel;

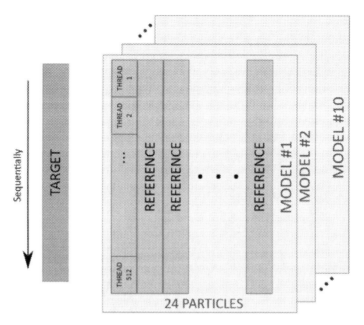

Fig. 2. Scheme of the implementation of the fitness function on CUDA. Target points are computed sequentially. The parallel implementation relies on the fact that each point is compared (potentially) in parallel to all reference models (10 in this case), where each of the 24 PSO particles represents a possible transformation; 512 points are processed simultaneously for each particle.

2. Within each particle (so, within each block), each of many parallel threads processes a limited number of points of R, by firstly computing a portion of the transformed point cloud R' and then comparing it with all points of T.

The points of T are actually processed sequentially, but a significant speedup can be obtained anyway because each of them is compared at the same time to several points of the reference cloud, and to different transformations of R. A further level of parallelization has been tested where each particle is represented by more blocks, and each block considers a sub-portion of T, since different parts of the target can be computed independently. This choice was discarded because it does not bring any speedup of the fitness function computation. This is probably caused by the large amount of resources (especially number of threads) needed for its computation, which prevents a full parallelization and forces the GPU to schedule some CUDA blocks sequentially.

If the target is compared with more than one reference (for instance, to recognize which object has been scanned), a further level of parallelism can be added: several optimization processes can be executed in parallel using different reference models. For the same reason explained in the previous paragraph, the parallelism is not perfect and the difference with respect to a version in which all references are analyzed sequentially is not very significant. Figure 2 outlines how the work is subdivided among CUDA blocks and threads.

The GPU-based implementation of the metaheuristics employed in this paper has been presented in [10][1]. The parallel PSO implementation is structured as three distinct kernels: (i) the first one generates the solutions that is going to be evaluated, (ii) the second one computes the fitness function described before, and (iii) the last one updates the population.

5 Results

We performed the experimented tests on a PC equipped with a 64-bit Intel Core i7 CPU running at 3.40 GHz using CUDA v. 5.0 on an nVidia GeForce GTX680 graphics card with 1536 cores working at 1.20 GHz and compute capability 3.0.

The PSO and DE parameters (unless specified otherwise) were set as in Table 1. They have been chosen by manually generating 40 possible combinations, and testing them on the problem described in the next subsection. The configuration that gave the best average fitness was finally selected. We compared DE and two PSO versions (with global and ring topologies).

Table 1. Parameters used by DE and PSO. Refer to [1] and [14] for the meaning of the parameters

DE	PSO_r	PSO_g
$Cr = 0.9$	$\phi_1 = 1.19$	$\phi_1 = 1.8$
$F = 0.5$	$\phi_2 = 1.19$	$\phi_2 = 0.7$
Exponential Crossover	$\omega = 0.5$	$\omega = 0.72$
Target-to-best Mutation	Ring Topology ($K = 1$)	Global Topology
Population Size = 24	Population Size = 24	Population Size = 24
Generations = 90	Generations = 90	Generations = 90

5.1 Error vs Fitness

We performed several experiments under different conditions. Firstly, we wanted to prove that our fitness function is correct, i.e., a good fitness value actually corresponds to a good match between the reference and the target. In these tests (and in all the following, except the ones presented in Section 5.4), we used the same model (a wooden mallet) as target and as reference, with random roto-translations applied to the target. So, it was actually possible to achieve a perfect matching if the recognition process identified the correct transformation. We define the translation applied to the target as t_T and the rotation as r_T to show that, the closer to (t_T, r_T) the transformation applied to the reference, the better its fitness, i.e. there exists a direct correlation between error and fitness values.

---

[1] The code is available online at http://sourceforge.net/projects/libcudaoptimize/

Figure 3 shows the relationship between errors in the transformation and fitness values. Each point represents an independent repetition of the recognition task. Its position on the graph represents the error in terms of translation (euclidean distance between translation obtained at the end of the experiment and t_T) and rotation (angle between rotation computed and r_T). The color is related to the fitness value: dark colors stand for good (low, since this is a minimization problem) fitness values and light colors represent bad values. As can be seen, the closer a point is to the optimum $(0, 0)$, the darker it is. Computing the correlation coefficient between these two distances and the fitness, the results are 0.825 (translation error) and 0.726 (rotation error) showing a significant direct relationship.

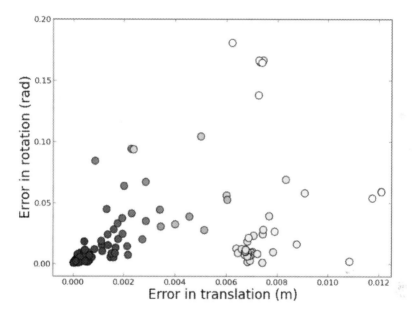

Fig. 3. Relation between error in translation (shown on the x axis of the graph) and rotation (on the y axis) and fitness value (color)

5.2 Time Comparison

We tested different PSO, DE and FPFH parameters (varying the number of generations in the first two, of RANSAC and ICP iterations for the other) in order to see how they behave within different time constraints. We set four different time limits: 0.7 s, 1.3 s, 2.3 s and 3.2 s. Figure 4 shows that FPFH reaches good results very quickly, but cannot improve them any further, while metaheuristics use their exploitation abilities to constantly refine their results. This is confirmed by statistical tests (Friedman test with the Dunn-Sidak correction, $p = 0.01$) which show that within the first two time limits FPFH is statistically better than the other methods considering translation and rotation errors.

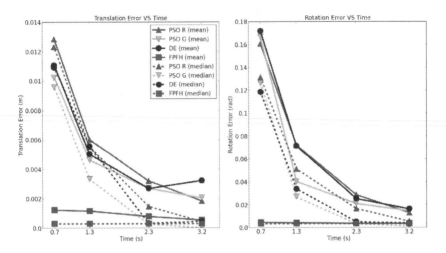

Fig. 4. Error versus processing time allowed for optimization, computed over 100 experiments. Solid lines represent average values, while dotted lines represent medians.

Moreover, PSO/DE have usually a lower median and higher average when compared to FPFH. This result (that will be confirmed in all other tests) proves that evolutionary methods have a better ability of finding more precise solutions, but sometimes they fall in local minima and fail completely. On the contrary, FPFH steadily obtains good results, though worse than the ones obtained in the successful runs of the metaheuristics.

The sequential single-thread CPU implementation of the PSO recognizer takes an average of 60.5 s for 90 generations, which means it is 18.9 times slower than the GPU version. If we parallelize the evolutionary process over the 8 cores available on the CPU, the time needed is reduced to 16.4 s, so the GPU is still 5.1 times faster.

5.3   Noise and Occlusions

In this section, we simulated some situations that can hamper object recognition, like noise and occlusions. We simulated the former by adding to each point of T a random value from a uniform distribution (we chose ranges of 0.001, 0.002, 0.005, 0.01 m), and the latter by removing all points above a certain percentile along a given dimension (we "occluded" 20%, 40%, 60% and 80% of the target). Figure 5 shows that FPFH is less robust to this kind of difficulties than PSO. Starting from an occlusion level of 60%, and for a noise range of 0.01 m, FPFH is significantly worse than all the EA-based methods in translation and rotation errors.

Figure 6 shows, as in Figure 3, how PSO and FPFH react to noise. Each color represents a different value of noise added to the target. It can be seen on the left that there is no clear difference between the different levels of noise

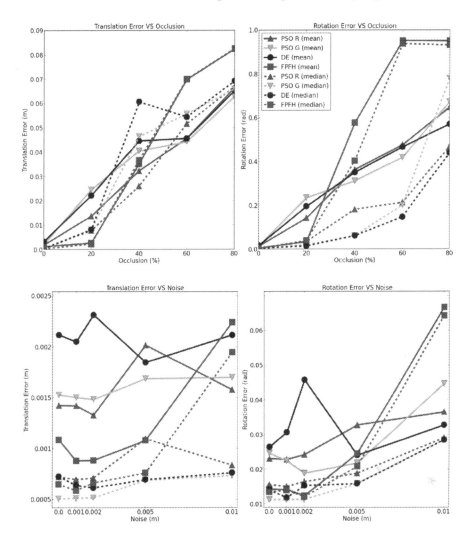

Fig. 5. Variation of errors in the presence of occlusions (top) and noise (bottom) added to the target over 100 experiments. Solid lines represents average values, while dotted lines represents medians.

when using PSO, while, on the right, the points corresponding to different noise levels can be easily clustered as different clouds. In particular, when the noise is low, there is almost no difference among the solutions found but, when noise increases, the dots are scattered over a large area.

5.4 Object Recognition

After assessing the behavior of these two methods under different conditions, we performed some tests on a different problem: object recognition. In this case,

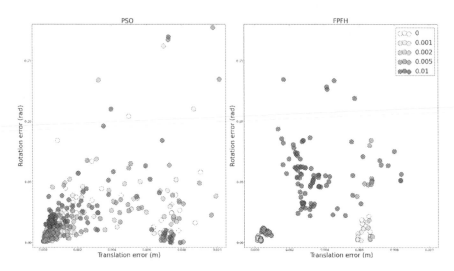

Fig. 6. Errors versus noise level (color) using PSO (left) and FPFH (right) over 100 experiments for each level. The results of FPFH are more consistent, while the ones obtained by PSO are more scattered.

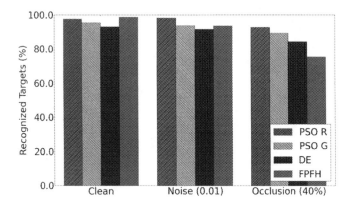

Fig. 7. Percentage of correct recognitions over 500 experiments (50 repetitions for 10 different objects) for every entry of the bar chart. Again, one can see how FPFH performance degrades in the presence of occlusions.

the goal was not only to understand where the object was located, but also to recognize the target object, within a set of ten reference objects: the wooden mallet previously used, a ewer, a burner, a toy horse, a mug and five different boxes of different shapes and sizes. We performed 50 independent tests in which each object was used as target and compared to all the others both under normal conditions and simulating the presence of noise and occlusions. Results are presented in Figure 7.

6   Conclusions

We applied a method based on Particle Swarm Optimization or Differential Evolution to recognize objects acquired with a laser scanner in the form of a point cloud. Each PSO or DE particle encodes a possible roto-translation of a point cloud used as reference; its optimization process tries to minimize the squared euclidean distance between the points of the target and the reference. We compared our method with a well-known method used for this task, FPFH. The main conclusions can be summarized as follows:

- FPFH reaches good results in a very short time, but it is not able to further improve them. Vice versa, the longer the time allowed to run EAs, the better the results they obtain;
- FPFH reaches good results almost always in ideal conditions, while EAs are able to achieve higher precision most of the times, but sometimes fail;
- EAs are more robust to noise and occlusions than FPFH.

As previously stated, PSO and DE parameters were selected among a few manually selected alternatives. It has been largely proved that, in many tasks, a good parameter setting can improve the performance of metaheuristics significantly. As future work, we will try to see if better performance can be achieved by automatically selecting such parameters.

The fitness function currently implemented for PSO can work properly only when the point cloud represents a single target. In some situations, it may be useful to recognize and localize more than one object in the scene at the same time. This can be obtained by moving the focus on the reference instead of focusing on the target: in other words, instead of finding the pose that minimizes the average distance of the points of the target cloud, one should find the transformation that minimizes the same metric regarding the points in the reference cloud. This will be the next step of our work.

References

1. Das, S., Suganthan, P.: Differential Evolution: A Survey of the State-of-the-Art. IEEE Transactions on Evolutionary Computation **15**(1), 4–31 (2011)
2. de Veronese, L., Krohling, R.: Swarm's flight: Accelerating the particles using C-CUDA. In: Proc. IEEE Congress on Evolutionary Computation, pp. 3264–3270 (2009)
3. de Veronese, L., Krohling, R.: Differential Evolution algorithm on the GPU with C-CUDA. In: Proc. IEEE Congress on Evolutionary Computation, pp. 1–7 (2010)
4. Fischler, M.A., Bolles, R.C.: Random sample consensus: a paradigm for model fitting with applications to image analysis and automated cartography. Communications of the ACM **24**(6), 381–395 (1981)
5. Kennedy, J., Eberhart, R.: Particle Swarm Optimization. In: Proc. IEEE International Conference on Neural Networks, vol. 4, pp. 1942–1948 (1995)
6. Kromer, P., Platos, J., Snasel, V.: A brief survey of advances in Particle Swarm Optimization on Graphic Processing Units. In: IEEE World Congress on Nature and Biologically Inspired Computing (NaBIC), pp. 182–188 (2013)

7. Kromer, P., Platos, J., Snasel, V.: A brief survey of Differential Evolution on Graphic Processing Units. In: Symp. on Differential Evolution, pp. 157–164 (2013)
8. Li, H., Shen, T., Huang, X.: Approximately global optimization for robust alignment of generalized shapes. IEEE Transactions on Pattern Analysis and Machine Intelligence **33**(6), 1116–1131 (2011)
9. Makadia, A., Patterson, A., Daniilidis, K.: Fully automatic registration of 3D point clouds. In: Conf. on Computer Vision and Pattern Recognition, pp. 1297–1304 (2006)
10. Nashed, Y.S.G., Ugolotti, R., Mesejo, P., Cagnoni, S.: libCudaOptimize: an open source library of GPU-based metaheuristics. In: Proc. of the Genetic and Evolutionary Computation Conference (GECCO) Companion, pp. 117–124. ACM (2012)
11. nVIDIA Corporation: nVIDIA CUDA Programming Guide v. 5.0. (2012)
12. Oleari, F., Lodi Rizzini, D., Caselli, S.: A low-cost stereo system for 3D object recognition. In: IEEE International Conference on Intelligent Computer Communication and Processing (ICCP), pp. 127–132 (2013)
13. Owens, J.D., Luebke, D., Govindaraju, N., Harris, M., Krüger, J., Lefohn, A.E., Purcell, T.J.: A Survey of General-Purpose Computation on Graphics Hardware. Computer Graphics Forum **26**, 80–113 (2007)
14. Poli, R., Kennedy, J., Blackwell, T.: Particle Swarm Optimization. Swarm Intelligence **1**(1), 33–57 (2007)
15. Rusu, R.B., Blodow, N., Beetz, M.: Fast point feature histograms (FPFH) for 3D registration. In: IEEE International Conference on Robotics and Automation (ICRA), pp. 3212–3217 (2009)
16. Rusu, R.B., Marton, Z.C., Blodow, N., Beetz, M.: Learning informative point classes for the acquisition of object model maps. In: IEEE International Conference on Control, Automation, Robotics and Vision (ICARCV), pp. 643–650 (2008)
17. Storn, R., Price, K.: Differential Evolution - a simple and efficient adaptive scheme for global optimization over continuous spaces. Technical report, International Computer Science Institute (1995)
18. Ugolotti, R., Nashed, Y.S., Mesejo, P., Ivekovič, Š., Mussi, L., Cagnoni, S.: Particle Swarm Optimization and Differential Evolution for model-based object detection. Applied Soft Computing **13**(6), 3092–3105 (2013)
19. Urfalolu, O., Mikulastik, P.A., Stegmann, I.: Scale Invariant Robust Registration of 3D-Point Data and a Triangle Mesh by Global Optimization. In: Blanc-Talon, J., Philips, W., Popescu, D., Scheunders, P. (eds.) ACIVS 2006. LNCS, vol. 4179, pp. 1059–1070. Springer, Heidelberg (2006)

A New Binary Particle Swarm Optimisation Algorithm for Feature Selection

Bing Xue[✉], Su Nguyen, and Mengjie Zhang

School of Engineering and Computer Science, Victoria University of Wellington,
PO Box 600, Wellington 6140, New Zealand
{Bing.Xue,Su.Nguyen,Mengjie.Zhang}@ecs.vuw.ac.nz

Abstract. Feature selection aims to select a small number of features from a large feature set to achieve similar or better classification performance than using all features. This paper develops a new binary particle swarm optimisation (PSO) algorithm (named PBPSO) based on which a new feature selection approach (PBPSOfs) is developed to reduce the number of features and increase the classification accuracy. The performance of PBPSOfs is compared with a standard binary PSO based feature selection algorithm (BPSOfs) and two traditional feature selection algorithms on 14 benchmark problems of varying difficulty. The results show that PBPSOfs can be successfully used for feature selection to select a small number of features and improve the classification performance over using all features. PBPSOfs further reduces the number of features selected by BPSOfs and simultaneously increases the classification accuracy, especially on datasets with a large number of features. Meanwhile, PBPSOfs achieves better performance than the two traditional feature selection algorithms. In addition, the results also show that PBPSO as a general binary optimisation technique can achieve better performance than standard binary PSO and uses less computational time.

Keywords: Binary particle swarm optimisation · Feature selection · Classification

1 Introduction

Feature selection is an important task in classification, which aims to select a subset of features and achieve similar or even better classification performance than using all features [3]. By removing irrelevant or redundant features and selecting only relevant features for classification, feature selection can reduce the dimensionality, simplify the learned classifiers, and/or increases the classification accuracy [3]. Feature selection is a difficult combinatorial problem with a large search space. The size of the search space grows exponentially along with the total number of features in the dataset. Therefore, it is usually impractical to perform an exhaustive search and most of the existing methods suffer from the problem of being computationally expensive or becoming stuck in local optima. Therefore, feature selection tasks need an efficient global search method.

© Springer-Verlag Berlin Heidelberg 2014
A.I. Esparcia-Alcázar et al. (Eds.): EvoApplications 2014, LNCS 8602, pp. 501–513, 2014.
DOI: 10.1007/978-3-662-45523-4_41

Evolutionary computation (EC) techniques are a group of powerful global search algorithms. Particle swarm optimisation (PSO) [8, 13] is a relatively recent EC technique, which is easy to implement, computationally less expensive, and has fewer parameters than other EC algorithms, such as genetic programming (GP) and genetic algorithms (GAs) [4]. Therefore, PSO has gained much attention since it was first proposed [8]. In PSO, each candidate solution is encoded as an individual or a particle in the search space. Each particle i has a position shown by $x_i = (x_{i1}, x_{i2}, ..., x_{iD})$ and a velocity shown by $v_i = (v_{i1}, v_{i2}, ..., v_{iD})$, where D is the dimensionality of the search space. During the evolutionary process, the best previous position of a particle is recorded as the personal best *pbest* and the best position obtained by the population thus far is called *gbest*. PSO searches for the optimal solutions by updating the velocity and the position of each particle according to *pbest* and *gbest*. There are two main categories of PSO, which are continuous PSO [13] and binary PSO (BPSO) [9]. Both continuous PSO and BPSO have been used for feature selection [2, 16, 18].

Feature selection is a binary problem, where BPSO is a more appropriate method than continuous PSO [2]. In BPSO, all elements in the position are either 1 or 0. The velocity in BPSO indicates the probability of the corresponding element in the position vector taking value 1. A sigmoid function is introduced to transform v_{id} to the range of (0, 1). BPSO updates the position and velocity of each particle according to the following formulae:

$$
x_{id}^{t+1} = \begin{cases} 1, \text{if } rand() < \frac{1}{1+e^{-v_{id}^{t+1}}} \\ 0, otherwise \end{cases} \tag{1}
$$

$$
v_{id}^{t+1} = w * v_{id}^t + c_1 * r_{1i} * (y_{id} - x_{id}^t) + c_2 * r_{2i} * (\hat{y}_d - x_{id}^t) \tag{2}
$$

where t denotes the tth iteration. $d \in D$ denotes the dth dimension in the search space. $rand()$ is a random number uniformly distributed in [0,1]. w is inertia weight. c_1 and c_2 are acceleration constants. r_{1i} and r_{2i} are random values uniformly distributed in [0, 1]. y_{id} and $\hat{y}_d$ represent the elements of *pbest* and *gbest* in the dth dimension.

There have been a large number of works on PSO [4], but most of them focus on continuous PSO and there is not much work on BPSO [14] perhaps because there are some limitations on the current standard BPSO. For example, the velocity shows the momentum of a particle's movement in a direction in a particular dimension of the search space. However, this was originally designed for continuous spaces. For binary problems, x_{id} can only be 1 or 0, which means particles cannot keep moving in one direction of a particular dimension. Meanwhile, the parameters in velocity were also designed for continuous PSO. When applying the velocity to BPSO, the parameters cannot produce the effects they were designed for and in fact, they produce an opposite effect compared with in the original continuous PSO (detailed discussions can be seen in [10]). Therefore, the velocity in PSO for continuous space is not meaningful any more in binary space. Since the influence of personal best and global best is reflected through the velocity updating equation, the personal experience and global experience cannot effectively utilised in BPSO. Therefore, in order to address feature selection problems, a new BPSO algorithm is needed.

1.1 Goals

The overall goal of this paper is to develop a new BPSO algorithm for feature selection to select a small feature subset and achieve better classification performance than using all features. To achieve this goal, we propose a new updating mechanism to develop a new BPSO algorithm based on which a new feature selection approach is proposed to reduce the number of features and increases the classification accuracy. Specifically, we will investigate:

 - whether the new feature selection approach can be used to address feature selection problems to reduce the number of features and increase the classification accuracy,
 - whether the new feature selection approach can achieve better performance than two traditional feature selection algorithms, and
 - whether the new BPSO algorithm as a general binary optimisation technique can achieve better performance than the standard BPSO in a shorter computational time.

2 Proposed Approach

To overcome the limitations of standard BPSO [9], we develop a new binary PSO algorithm, where two important issues are considered. The first is to follow the key ideas of the standard (continuous) PSO algorithm, which is that particles are updated according to the best experience of its own (i.e. personal best, *pbest*) and the best experience of its neighbours (i.e. global best, *gbest*). The second is to keep advantages of PSO compared to other EC techniques, i.e. PSO is simple, has fewer parameters and computationally cheaper. Therefore, we aim to develop a new BPSO algorithm, which is simpler than standard BPSO, but has a more powerful search ability.

Since the velocity component in BPSO is not as meaningful as in continuous PSO, we propose a new probability based BPSO named PBPSO, where a "flipping" probability is introduced to replace the velocity to update each particle during the evolutionary process. p shows the "flipping" probability, which is a $D-$dimensional vector. $p_i = (p_{i1}, p_{i2}, ..., p_{iD})$ shows the "flipping" probability for particle i. p_{id} shows the probability of x_{id} being "flipped", i.e. update $x_{id}^{t+1} = 1$ if $x_{id}^t = 0$ or update $x_{id}^{t+1} = 0$ if $x_{id}^t = 1$, where t means the tth iterations in the evolutionary process. The new position updating equation is shown by Equation 3. p is calculated based on the current position of a particle, *pbest* and *gbest*, where the updating formula is shown by Equation 4.

$$x_{id}^{t+1} = \begin{cases} 1 - x_{id}^t, & \text{if } random() < p_{id} \\ x_{id}^t, & otherwise \end{cases} \tag{3}$$

$$p_{id} = p_0 + p_{pd} + p_{gd} \qquad (4)$$

where

$$p_{pd} = \begin{cases} p_1, & \text{if } x_{id}^t \neq y_{id}^t \\ 0, & otherwise \end{cases}$$

and

$$p_{gd} = \begin{cases} p_2, & \text{if } x_{id}^t \neq \hat{y}_d^t \\ 0, & otherwise \end{cases}$$

In Equation 3, $(1 - x_{id}^t)$ is used to update x_{id}^{t+1} from 1 to 0 or from 0 to 1. p_{pd} and p_{gd} reflect the influence of personal best *pbest* and global best *gbest*. p_0, p_1 and p_2 are real numbers in (0,1). $0 < p_0$ is used to ensure that there is always a probability to change the value of x_{id}^t. The values of p_{pd} and p_{gd} are calculated for each dimension in every iteration, but they are not stored through the evolutionary process, which is cheaper than the standard BPSO in terms of memory. $p_0 + p_1 + p_2 = 1$ ensures that when x_{id}^t is different from both y_{id}^t and $\hat{y}_{id}^t$, the probability for x_{id}^t to change equals to 1.

2.1   PBPSOfs for Feature Selection

Based on the proposed PBPSO, a new feature selection approach named PBP-SOfs is developed and the Pseudo-code of PBPSOfs is shown by Algorithm 1. Two key components that need to be shown are the encoding scheme and the fitness function.

In PBPSOfs, the dimensionality (D) of the search space equals to the total number of features in the dataset. So each particle is a D-dimensional binary string, where "1" means the corresponding feature is selected and "0" means the corresponding feature is not selected.

Feature selection has two main objectives, which are maximising the classification accuracy (minimising the error rate) and minimising the number of features. Therefore, a fitness function that combines the two objectives is used in PBPSOfs, which is shown by Equation 5.

$$Fitness = \alpha * Error\,Rate + (1 - \alpha) * \frac{\#Features}{\#All\,Features} \qquad (5)$$

where *Error Rate* represents the classification error rate of the selected features. *#Features* shows the number of selected features and *#All Features* shows the total number of features in the datasets. α and $(1 - \alpha)$ reflect the relative importance of the classification performance and the number of selected features. $\alpha \in (0.5, 1]$ because the classification performance is regarded as more important than the number of features.

Algorithm 1. Pseudo-code of PBPSOfs

Input : p_0, p_1, p_2; P: the population size; T: maximum iterations;
D: dimensionality of search space (i.e. total number of features)

Output: $gbest$ (i.e. selected features), training and testing accuracies of the selected features

begin
   randomly initialise the position each particle;
   for $t=1$ **to** T **do**
      evaluate fitness of each particle;
      for $i=1$ **to** P **do**
         update the $pbest$ of particle i;
         update the $gbest$ of particle i;

      for $i=1$ **to** P **do**
         for $d=1$ **to** D **do**
            if $x_{id}^{t-1} \neq y_{id}^{t-1}$ **then**
               $p_{pd} = p_1$;   // personal experience, *pbest*
            else
               $p_{pd} = 0$
            if $x_{id}^{t-1} \neq \hat{y}_d^{t-1}$ **then**
               $p_{gd} = p_2$;   // neighbourhood's experience, *gbest*
            else
               $p_{gd} = 0$
            $p_{id} = p_0 + p_{pd} + p_{gd}$;
            if $rand < prob$ **then**
               $x_{id} = 1 - x_{id}$;   // x_{id} from 1 to 0 or from 0 to 1
            else
               $x_{id} = x_{id}$

   return $gbest$, training and testing accuracies of the selected features;

---

3 Experiment Design

3.1 Benchmark Techniques

To examine the performance of the proposed algorithm (PBPSOfs), it is compared with a standard BPSO based feature selection algorithm (BPSOfs) [17]. BPSOfs shares the same encoding scheme, fitness function and random seeds with PBPSOfs for fair comparisons.

Two traditional methods are also used to test the performance of PBPSOfs, which are linear forward selection (LFS) [6] and greedy stepwise backward selection (GSBS) [1]. LFS and GSBS were driven from two typical traditional feature selection algorithms, i.e. sequential forward selection (SFS) [15] and sequential backward selection (SBS) [12]. LFS [6] performs a forward selection, but restricts the number of features that are considered in each step. LFS is computationally less expensive than SFS because it reduces the number of evaluations. More

Table 1. Datasets

Dataset	No. of Features	No. of Classes	No. of Instances	Dataset	No. of Features	No. of Classes	No. of Instances
Australian	14	2	690	Zoo	17	7	101
Wisconsin Breast Cancer							
(Diagnostic) (WBCD)	30	2	569	Vehicle	18	4	846
Ionosphere	34	2	351	German	24	2	1000
Hillvalley	100	2	606	Lung	56	3	32
Musk Version1(Musk1)	166	2	476	Sonar	60	2	208
Arrhythmia	279	16	452	Madelon	500	2	4400
Multiple Features	649	10	2000	Isolet5	617	2	1559

details can be seen in [6]. The greedy stepwise based selection method is implemented in Weka [7], which can perform both forward and backward selection [1]. Given that LFS is based on forward selection, the greedy stepwise search is set to be backward to conduct a greedy stepwise backward selection (GSBS). GSBS starts with all available features and stops when the deletion of any remaining feature results in a decrease in classification accuracy.

3.2   Datasets and Parameter Settings

14 datasets were chosen from the UCI machine learning repository [5] to test the performance of PBPSOfs, BPSOfs, LFS and GSBS. The datasets are shown in Table 1. The 14 datasets were chosen to have different numbers of features, classes and instances. For each dataset, the instances are randomly divided into two sets: 70% as the training set and 30% as the test set.

As wrapper approaches, all the algorithms need a learning/classification algorithm. A simple and commonly used learning algorithm [2], K-nearest neighbour (KNN), was used in the experiment and K=5 (5NN). During the evolutionary training process, the classification error rate used in the fitness function is calculated using 10-fold cross-validation on the training set. Note that 10-fold cross-validation is performed as an inner loop in the training process to evaluate the classification performance of a single feature subset on the training set and it does not generate 10 feature subsets. After the training process, the selected features are evaluated on the test set to obtain the testing classification performance of the selected features. A detailed discussion of why and how 10-fold cross-validation is applied in this way is given by [11].

PBPSOfs only involves three parameters, which are p_0, p_1 and p_2. $p_0 = 0.05$ is to make sure that there is always at least a very small probability to update the particle. $p_1 = 0.35$ and $p_2 = 0.65$ are to ensure that the global best has slightly more influence than the personal best. The parameters of BPSOfs are set as follows [13]: $w = 0.7298$, $c_1 = c_2 = 1.49618$. For both BPSOfs and PBPSOfs, the population size is 50, and the maximum number of iterations is 100. The fully connected topology is used. $\alpha = 0.9$ is used in the fitness function to make sure that the classification performance is much more important than the number of features. Both PBPSOfs and BPSOfs have been conducted for 40 independent runs on each dataset.

To test their classification performance, the non-parametric statistical significance test, Wilcoxon test, is performed compare the classification performance of BPSOfs (or PBPSOfs) and that of all features. The significance test is used to compare the classification performance between BPSOfs and PBPSOfs. The significance level is selected as 0.05 (or confidence interval is 95%).

4   Results and Discussions

4.1   Results of PBPSOfs and BPSOfs in Testing Process

Table 2 shows the experimental results of PBPSOfs and BPSOfs on the unseen test sets, where "All" means that all of the available features are used for classification, "AveSize" shows the average number of features selected in the 40 independent runs, "BestAcc", "AveAcc" and "StdAcc" show the best, the average and the standard deviation of the 40 testing accuracies. "Test 1" shows the results of the Wilcoxon significance tests between PBPSOfs (or BPSOfs) and "All", where "+" (-) means PBPSOfs or BPSOfs is significantly better (or worse) than "All", and "=" means they are similar (no significant difference). "Test 2" shows the Wilcoxon significance tests between PBPSOfs and BPSOfs.

Results of BPSOfs. According to Table 2, it can be seen that in most cases (i.e. 12 out of the 14 datasets), the classification performance of the feature subsets selected by BPSOfs is significantly better or similar to that of using all features. In all cases, the average number of features selected by BPSOfs is less than half of the total number of original features. However, on the six datasets with a large number of features (100 or more), the classification performance of BPSOfs is better than using all features on only two datasets.

The results show that BPSOfs with the standard BPSO algorithm can be used to address feature selection problems to reduce the number of features and maintain or even increase the classification performance. However, the results also show the BPSOfs cannot scale well for high-dimensional problems, where feature selection is important and necessary on such problems.

Results of PBPSOfs. From Table 2, it can be seen that the classification performance of the feature subsets selected by PBPSOfs is significantly better than using all features on **all** datasets. In most cases, the average number of features selected by PBPSOfs is less than one third of the total number of features. For example, on the WBCD dataset, PBPSOfs selected only 6.73% (i.e. on average 2.02 of 30) of the original features and achieved significantly better classification performance than using all features.

The results show that PBPSOfs with the new updating mechanism can successfully evolve a smaller feature subset to increase the classification accuracy.

Table 2. Experimental Results in Testing Process

Dataset	Method	AveSize	BestAcc	AveAcc ± StdAcc	Test 1	Test 2
Australian	All	14	70.05			
	BPSOfs	3.18	87.44	82.46 ± 7.3131	+	
	PBPSOfs	2.82	85.51	81.96 ± 7.7095	+	=
Zoo	All	17	80.95			
	BPSOfs	4.15	97.14	95.12 ± 0.6455	+	
	PBPSOfs	3.35	95.24	95.17 ± 0.2508	+	=
Vehicle	All	18	83.86			
	BPSOfs	5.38	86.22	84.21 ± 0.8119	+	
	PBPSOfs	5.02	84.84	84.09 ± 0.434	+	=
German	All	24	68.0			
	BPSOfs	7.9	73.33	68.89 ± 2.0768	+	
	PBPSOfs	5.95	72.67	69.09 ± 1.7842	+	=
WBCD	All	30	92.98			
	BPSOfs	7.92	94.74	93.57 ± 1.2474	+	
	PBPSOfs	2.02	94.74	94.4 ± 0.8049	+	+
Ionosphere	All	34	83.81			
	BPSOfs	8.92	93.33	88.14 ± 2.3128	+	
	PBPSOfs	4.58	91.43	88.45 ± 2.0447	+	=
Lung	All	56	70.0			
	BPSOfs	23.28	90	74.75 ± 7.0666	+	
	PBPSOfs	6.78	80	77.25 ± 5.9108	+	=
Sonar	All	60	76.19			
	BPSOfs	23.02	85.71	78.57 ± 3.4594	+	
	PBPSOfs	14.28	87.3	78.21 ± 3.0323	+	=
Hillvalley	All	100	56.59			
	BPSOfs	39.35	60.16	56.88 ± 1.6322	=	
	PBPSOfs	31.08	61.26	58.25 ± 1.6952	+	+
Musk1	All	166	83.92			
	BPSOfs	75.52	90.91	84.21 ± 2.8401	=	
	PBPSOfs	69.3	88.81	85.38 ± 1.8087	+	+
Arrhythmia	All	279	94.46			
	BPSOfs	99.7	95.14	94.21 ± 0.3937	-	
	PBPSOfs	63.42	95.48	94.71 ± 0.3405	+	+
Madelon	All	500	70.9			
	BPSOfs	243.85	78.59	75.81 ± 1.4905	+	
	PBPSOfs	212.42	81.15	78.91 ± 1.2565	+	+
Isolet5	All	617	98.45			
	BPSOfs	225.15	98.59	98.25 ± 0.1354	-	
	PBPSOfs	169.35	98.87	98.61 ± 0.1248	+	+
Multiple Features	All	649	98.63			
	BPSOfs	237.05	99.1	98.89 ± 0.0923	+	
	PBPSOfs	176.15	99.27	99.01 ± 0.1043	+	+

Comparisons Between PBPSOfs and BPSOfs. From Table 2, it can be seen that on **all** the 14 datasets, PBPSOfs selected a smaller number of features and achieved similar or significantly better classification performance than BPSOfs. The results of the significance tests (Test 2) show that the classification performance of PBPSOfs is similar to BPSOfs in seven cases. Particularly, PBPSOfs is significantly better than BPSOfs on **all** the six datasets with a large number of features, and the number of features is much smaller in PBPSOfs than in BPSOfs. For example, on the Isolet5 dataset, PBPSOfs further reduced around 24.78% of the number of features selected by BPSOfs to reduce the average number of selected features from 225.15 to 169.35, but PBPSOfs significantly increased the classification accuracy. Meanwhile, in almost all cases, the standard deviation values of PBPSOfs is smaller than that of BPSOfs, which shows that PBPSOfs is more stable than BPSOfs.

Table 3. Comparisons with LFS and GSBS

Dataset	Australian			Zoo			Vehicle			German			WBCD			Ionosphere			Lung		
	Size	Acc	T	Size	Acc	T	Size	Acc	T	Size	Acc	T	Size	Acc	T	Size	Acc	T	Size	Acc	T
LFS	4	70.05	+	8	79.05	+	9	83.07	+	3	68.67	=	10	88.89	+	4	86.67	+	6	90.0	-
GSBS	12	69.57	+	7	80.0	+	16	75.79	+	18	64.33	+	25	83.63	+	30	78.1	+	33	90.0	-
Dataset	Sonar			Hillvalley			Musk1			Arrhythmia			Madelon			Isolet5			MultipleF.		
	Size	Acc	T	Size	Acc	T	Size	Acc	T	Size	Acc	T	Size	Acc	T	Size	Acc	T	Size	Acc	T
LFS	3	77.78	=	8	57.69	+	10	85.31	=	11	94.46	+	7	64.62	+	24	98.34	+	18	99.0	=
GSBS	48	68.25	+	90	49.45	+	122	76.22	+	130	93.55	+	489	51.28	+	560	97.16	+			+

The comparisons show that PBPSOfs using the newly developed updating mechanisms can better explore the search space of a feature selection task to further reduce the number of features and simultaneously maintain or increase the classification performance.

Comparisons with LFS and GSBS. Table 3 shows the results of LFS and GSBS. Both LFS and GSBS are deterministic methods, which produce a unique solution/feature subset on each dataset. In the table, "T" shows the results of the significance tests between the classification accuracy of LFS (or GSBS) and PBPSOfs. "+" (or "-") means the PBPSOfs is significantly better than LFS or GSBS. Note that the results of GSBS on the Multiple Features (MultipleF.) dataset are not available because the experiment cannot finish within a week.

According to Table 3, it can be seen that PBPSOfs achieved significantly better classification performance than LFS on nine of the 14 datasets and similar classification performance on four datasets. The best accuracy of PBPSOfs is better than LFS on 13 out of the 14 datasets, although the number of features is larger. PBPSOfs selected a smaller or much number of features than GSBS in all cases and achieved significantly better classification performance than GSBS on 13 out of the 14 datasets. Only on the Lung dataset, the classification performance of LFS and GSBS is better than PBPSOfs. The main reason is that the Lung dataset has a small number of examples, where it is easy to have overfitting problems. PBPSOfs clearly has such a problem because it achieved the training accuracy of 100% in 39 of the 40 independent runs.

4.2   Results of PBPSOfs and BPSOfs in Training Process

Analysing the performance of PBPSOfs and BPSOfs in the training process can further show the search abilities of PBPSO and BPSO as general optimisation techniques rather than specific feature selection algorithms.

Evolutionary Process. We take the Lung and Musk1 datasets as two examples to analyse the evolutionary process. Other datasets show a similar pattern. Figure 1 shows the change of the *gbest* during the evolutionary process, where the horizontal axis shows the number of iterations and the vertical axis shows the average fitness value of the *gbest* in the 40 independent runs.

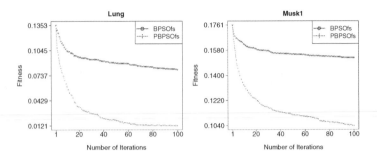

Fig. 1. Evolutionary Process of BPSOfs and PBPSOfs (colour)

According to Figure 1, it can be observed that the *gbest* in PBPSOfs and BPSOfs have the same average fitness value at the first iteration because they were set to start from the same points for fair comparisons. However, even starting from the same points, PBPSOfs using the newly developed updating mechanisms can better explore the solution space to optimise (i.e. minimise) the fitness value to obtain much better results than BPSOfs. Considering the training process only, feature selection is a binary/combinatorial problem with a large and complex search space. The superior performance of PBPSOfs during the training process shows that the proposed PBPSO algorithm can successfully address difficult binary/combinatorial problems, as a general binary optimisation technique (not only specifically designed for feature selection tasks).

Training Performance. Table 4 shows the experimental results of PBPSOfs and BPSOfs from the training process. The average size of the feature subsets in Table 4 is the same as in Table 2 because they are the same feature subsets, but their classification performances are different because they are used on different sets of data, i.e. the training set and test set, respectively. The average computational time of PBPSOfs and BPSOfs are also listed in the last column of Table 4, where the numbers are expressed in minutes.

From Table 4, it can be seen that both PBPSOfs and BPSOfs can reduce the number of features and maintain or even increase the training classification accuracy in almost all cases. Comparing PBPSOfs with BPSOfs, for **all** the fourteen datasets, PBPSOfs selected a smaller number of features than BPSOfs. On 12 out of the 14 datasets, the training classification accuracy of PBPSOfs is similar or significantly better than BPSOfs. Particularly, on **all** the nine datasets with more than 30 features/dimensions, PBPSOfs achieved significantly better performance than BPSOfs, i.e., selected a much smaller number of features and achieved significantly better classification accuracy. For some datasets, e.g. Lung, PBPSOfs has the problem of over-fitting and we will address this in future work.

The results show that PBPSOfs with the newly developed updating mechanisms can improve the search ability over BPSOfs, especially for the high-dimensional problems, where the search space is larger and more complex than low-dimensional problems.

Table 4. Experimental Results in Training Process

Dataset	Method	AveSize	BestAcc	AveAcc ± StdAcc	Test 1	Test 2	Time
Australian	All	14	75.78				
	BPSOfs	3.18	88.2	83.25 ± 7.0772	+		4.91
	PBPSOfs	2.82	86.96	83.41 ± 7.7095	=	=	4.59
Zoo	All	17	86.72				
	BPSOfs	4.15	98.39	97.37 ± 0.3484	+		0.12
	PBPSOfs	3.35	97.99	97.33 ± 0.2327	=	=	0.11
Vehicle	All	18	88.18				
	BPSOfs	5.38	90.54	89.45 ± 0.6187	+		8.48
	PBPSOfs	5.02	90.37	89.44 ± 0.4998	=	=	8.28
German	All	24	80.14				
	BPSOfs	7.9	82.71	80.11 ± 2.3069	=		13.2
	PBPSOfs	5.95	82.71	79.7 ± 1.5259	-	-	12.3
WBCD	All	30	94.97				
	BPSOfs	7.92	96.73	95.6 ± 0.5919	+		4.62
	PBPSOfs	2.02	96.48	95.13 ± 0.396	=	-	3.32
Ionosphere	All	34	85.77				
	BPSOfs	8.92	93.5	91.09 ± 1.1403	+		1.92
	PBPSOfs	4.58	95.53	94.08 ± 0.7378	+	+	1.76
Lung	All	56	81.82				
	BPSOfs	23.28	100	95.68 ± 2.02	+		0.04
	PBPSOfs	6.78	100	99.89 ± 0.7097	+	+	0.02
Sonar	All	60	83.45				
	BPSOfs	23.02	93.1	89.12 ± 1.7137	+		0.97
	PBPSOfs	14.28	94.48	91.03 ± 1.895	+	+	0.77
Hillvalley	All	100	71.46				
	BPSOfs	39.35	73.94	72.28 ± 1.0503	+		50.28
	PBPSOfs	31.08	75.94	73.75 ± 1.0739	+	+	46.1
Musk1	All	166	92.19				
	BPSOfs	75.52	95.5	93.15 ± 1.1531	+		13.96
	PBPSOfs	69.3	97.3	94.83 ± 1.0976	+	+	12.7
Arrhythmia	All	279	94.79				
	BPSOfs	99.7	95.37	94.93 ± 0.2288	+		16.97
	PBPSOfs	63.42	95.86	95.55 ± 0.1657	+	+	12.44
Madelon	All	500	83.24				
	BPSOfs	243.2	87.69	85.93 ± 0.7274	+		991.6
	PBPSOfs	212.42	90.55	88.91 ± 0.6204	+	+	953.63
Isolet5	All	617	99.15				
	BPSOfs	225.15	99.28	99.14 ± 0.0826	=		384.16
	PBPSOfs	169.35	99.49	99.36 ± 0.0643	+	+	328.34
Multiple Features	All	649	99.36				
	BPSOfs	237.05	99.51	99.41 ± 0.0533	+		692.54
	PBPSOfs	176.15	99.63	99.52 ± 0.0542	+	+	551.44

4.3 Analysis on Computational Time

According to Table 4, it can be seen that on datasets with a small number of features or instances, both PBPSOfs and BPSOfs can finish the evolutionary feature selection process in a very short time, which is even less than one minute on the Zoo and Lung datasets. In **all** the 14 benchmark problems, PBPSOfs used a shorter time than BPSOfs. There are two main reasons. The first reason is that the newly developed PBPSO has a simpler updating equation than the standard BPSO. The second reason is that as wrapper approaches, the majority part of the computational time in PBPSOfs and BPSOfs are used on fitness evaluations, which needs to calculate the classification error rate of the selected features. For the same dataset, a large number of selected features needs longer time to calculate the error rate than a small number of selected features. Since PBPSOfs and

BPSOfs have the same number of evaluations during the evolutionary training process and PBPSOfs usually selected a smaller number of features, PBPSOfs is faster than BPSOfs.

5 Conclusions and Future Work

This paper developed a new probability based updating mechanism based on which a new BPSO named PBPSO was proposed. A new feature selection approach named PBPSOfs was developed to maximise the classification accuracy and minimise the number of features. PBPSOfs was examined and compared with a standard BPSO based feature selection approach (BPSOfs) and two traditional feature selection algorithms on 14 datasets of varying difficulty. The experimental results show that PBPSOfs achieved better performance than the two traditional feature selection algorithms. Meanwhile, PBPSOfs outperformed BPSOfs in terms of both the classification performance and the number of features, especially on high-dimensional problems. The performances of PBPSOfs and BPSOfs in the training process show that PBPSO as a general method has better optimisation capability than standard BPSO. Additionally, PBPSOfs is computationally less expensive than BPSOfs due to its simple calculation of the new updating mechanism and selecting a smaller number of features. Overall, the newly developed PBPSO algorithm outperformed the standard BPSO in terms of both the effectiveness and the efficiency.

This work mainly focuses on binary problems, but in future, we will investigate a new PSO algorithm for general discrete problems. We will also further investigate and improve the performance of BPSO by developing new updating mechanisms and new representation or encoding schemes. From the classification point of view, the proposed algorithm may have over-fitting problems, which will also be addressed in future. Meanwhile, we also intend to develop a multi-objective feature selection approach to find a set of trade-off solutions to meet different requirements in real-world applications.

References

1. Caruana, R., Freitag, D.: Greedy attribute selection. In: International Conference on Machine Learning (ICML 1994), pp. 28–36. Morgan Kaufmann (1994)
2. Chuang, L.Y., Chang, H.W., Tu, C.J., Yang, C.H.: Improved binary PSO for feature selection using gene expression data. Computational Biology and Chemistry **32**(29), 29–38 (2008)
3. Dash, M., Liu, H.: Feature selection for classification. Intelligent Data Analysis **1**(4), 131–156 (1997)
4. Engelbrecht, A.P.: Computational intelligence: an introduction, 2nd edn. Wiley (2007)
5. Frank, A., Asuncion, A.: UCI machine learning repository (2010)
6. Gutlein, M., Frank, E., Hall, M., Karwath, A.: Large-scale attribute selection using wrappers. In: IEEE Symposium on Computational Intelligence and Data Mining (CIDM 2009), pp. 332–339 (2009)

7. Hall, M., Frank, E., Holmes, G., Pfahringer, B., Reutemann, P., Witten, I.H.: The weka data mining software: An update. SIGKDD Explorations **11**, 931–934 (2009)
8. Kennedy, J., Eberhart, R.: Particle swarm optimization. In: IEEE International Conference on Neural Networks, vol. 4, pp. 1942–1948 (1995)
9. Kennedy, J., Eberhart, R.: A discrete binary version of the particle swarm algorithm. In: IEEE International Conference on Systems, Man, and Cybernetics (1997), Computational Cybernetics and Simulation, vol. 5, pp. 4104–4108 (1997)
10. Khanesar, M., Teshnehlab, M., Shoorehdeli, M.: A novel binary particle swarm optimization. In: Mediterranean Conference on Control Automation (MED 2007), pp. 1–6 (2007)
11. Kohavi, R., John, G.H.: Wrappers for feature subset selection. Artificial Intelligence **97**, 273–324 (1997)
12. Marill, T., Green, D.: On the effectiveness of receptors in recognition systems. IEEE Transactions on Information Theory **9**(1), 11–17 (1963)
13. Shi, Y., Eberhart, R.: A modified particle swarm optimizer. In: IEEE International Conference on Evolutionary Computation (CEC 1998), pp. 69–73 (1998)
14. Sudholt, D., Witt, C.: Runtime analysis of binary PSO. In: Proceedings of the 10th Annual Conference on Genetic and Evolutionary Computation (GECCO 2008), pp. 135–142. ACM, New York (2008)
15. Whitney, A.: A direct method of nonparametric measurement selection. IEEE Transactions on Computers C-20(9), 1100–1103 (1971)
16. Xue, B., Cervante, L., Shang, L., Browne, W.N., Zhang, M.: A multi-objective particle swarm optimisation for filter based feature selection in classification problems. Connection Science (2012)
17. Xue, B., Zhang, M., Browne, W.N.: New fitness functions in binary particle swarm optimisation for feature selection. In: IEEE Congress on Evolutionary Computation (CEC 2012), pp. 2145–2152 (2012)
18. Xue, B., Zhang, M., Browne, W.: Particle swarm optimization for feature selection in classification: A multi-objective approach. IEEE Transactions on Cybernetics **43**(6), 1656–1671 (2013)

Adaptive Genetic Algorithm to Select Training Data for Support Vector Machines

Jakub Nalepa[✉] and Michal Kawulok

Silesian University of Technology, Gliwice, Poland
{jakub.nalepa, michal.kawulok}@polsl.pl

Abstract. This paper presents a new adaptive genetic algorithm (AGA) to select training data for support vector machines (SVMs). SVM training data selection strongly influences the classification accuracy and time, especially in the case of large and noisy data sets. In the proposed AGA, a population of solutions evolves with time. The AGA parameters, including the chromosome length, are adapted according to the current state of exploring the solution space. We propose a new multi-parent crossover operator for an efficient search. A new metric of distance between individuals is introduced and applied in the AGA. It is based on the fast analysis of the vectors distribution in the feature space obtained using principal component analysis. An extensive experimental study performed on the well-known benchmark sets along with the real-world and artificial data sets, confirms that the AGA outperforms a standard GA in terms of the convergence capabilities. Also, it reduces the number of support vectors and allows for faster SVM classification.

Keywords: Adaptive genetic algorithm · Support vector machines · Training data selection

1 Introduction and Related Work

Support vector machines (SVMs) have been used in various classification problems over the years [6]. SVM determines a hyperplane, defined by a subset of the labeled training samples called support vectors, which separates linearly two classes in the kernel space of high dimensionality. Then, it is used to classify the input data of the same dimensionality as the training set data.

The time and memory complexity of the SVM training ($O(n^3)$ and $O(n^2)$ respectively, where n is the number of samples in the training set) is an important limitation of SVMs in the case of large real-world data sets. Also, the computational complexity of the SVM decision function scales with respect to the number of selected support vectors. Thus, a number of approaches emerged over the years to deal with large and noisy data sets. In the technique proposed by Balcázar et al. [1], a subset of training vectors is drawn randomly. The random selection was the basis of reduced support vector machines introduced by

---

This work has been supported by the Polish Ministry of Science and Higher Education under research grant no. IP2012 026372 from the Science Budget 2013–2015.

A.I. Esparcia-Alcázar et al. (Eds.): EvoApplications 2014, LNCS 8602, pp. 514–525, 2014.
DOI: 10.1007/978-3-662-45523-4_42

Lee and Huang [10]. There exist numerous methods exploiting the geometry information of the training data in the input space, including k-means clustering [4] and crisp clusters with safety regions analysis [9]. The clustering can be performed near the decision boundary to boost its performance. The estimation of the decision boundary, which is unknown before the SVM training, based on the heterogeneity analysis, was proposed by Shin and Cho [14]. The mutual Mahalanobis distances between the training data were studied in [16] to select the vectors closest to the decision boundary. A method operating in the kernel space has been proposed recently [2].

An approach embedding the training data with the convex hulls and analyzing distances between the convex hulls of opposite classes was given by Wang et al. [17]. Reducing training and testing time by interpreting the training set as a graph and applying the β-skeleton algorithm was proposed in [19]. The methods based on the minimum enclosing ball and the smallest enclosing ball with a ring region were discussed in [15,18]. In the active learning techniques operating on an unlabeled set of data, the data labels are determined dynamically [11,13].

Applying evolutionary algorithms for selecting the SVM training set has not been explored extensively. Recently, we proposed a novel genetic algorithm (GA) for this purpose [8]. Noteworthy, this method is not dependent on the training set size, which was a significant drawback of the geometry-based approaches. In the GA, a population of solutions, each representing a subset of $2K'$ (where K' is constant) vectors from the entire training set, evolves with time. It was shown that the GA outperforms random sampling after a very small number of generations. Its important shortcoming is an unclear selection of the chromosome size $2K'$ to avoid the premature search convergence and to cope with noisy data sets. This issue is addressed in the work reported here.

In this paper we propose a new adaptive genetic algorithm (AGA) to select the SVM training set, which incrementally improves a "good" subset of samples from the entire training set. Its parameters are being adapted according to the state of the search. We introduce a new metric of distance between the individuals based on the distribution of vectors in the n-dimensional input space obtained using principal component analysis (where $n < \mathcal{N}$, and $\mathcal{N}$ is a dimensionality of the input data). This measure is used in a proposed multi-parent crossover operator. It is worth noting that the size of an individual $2K$ is also adapted in the AGA, and it is not necessary to estimate it *a priori*. Our work was motivated by the problems related to skin detection. In this field the amount of available data is enormously large and requires a proper selection for the SVM training. An extensive experimental study confirms that the AGA outperforms a standard GA in terms of the convergence capabilities and selection time. Also, it reduces the number of support vectors and allows for faster SVM classification.

The paper is organized as follows. The AGA, along with a new multi-parent crossover operator and the proposed distance measure are presented in Section 2. Section 3 discusses the experimental results. Conclusions and directions for our future work are given in Section 4.

2   Adaptive Genetic Algorithm

In this section we present the proposed adaptive genetic algorithm (AGA) for selecting a valuable training set for SVMs. We discuss a new adaptive multi-parent crossover operator (AMPC), and elaborate on a novel metric used for assessing the distance between individuals, which is incorporated into the suggested AGA.

2.1   Algorithm Outline

In the AGA, the initial population of solutions is generated randomly (Alg. 1, line 1). In each individual, the indexes of vectors forming a subset of the training set T, containing labeled samples belonging to two classes C_1 and C_2, are stored. The length of an individual p_i is given as $\mathcal{L}(p_i) = K(C_1) + K(C_2)$, where $K(C_1)$ and $K(C_2)$ are the numbers of samples from the C_1 and C_2, respectively. To avoid biasing a chromosome by the samples of a single class (e.g., in the case of imbalanced data sets), we assume $K(C_1) = K(C_2) = K$, and $\mathcal{L}(p_i) = 2K$. Thus, $2K$ distinct samples are drawn randomly for N chromosomes. It is worth noting that the size of an individual is independent from the cardinality of T [8].

First, the steady state counters c_B and c_A, along with the steady state flag u_B indicating the change of the best individual's fitness, are initialized (line 2). The c_B and c_A counters depict the number of consecutive generations during which the best fitness η_B and the average fitness η_A have not been improved. Then, the N pairs of chromosomes are determined (line 4) according to the pre-selection scheme (see Section 2.2). A child p_C is generated for each pair of parents using the proposed AMPC. It is mutated with the probability $\mathcal{P}_m$ (line 8), which is based on substituting p_C's vectors from both classes C_1 and C_2 with the random vectors drawn from T. Finally, the fitness $\eta(p_C)$ is determined according to the SVM classification score obtained for the training set T. If the difference between $\eta(p_C)$ and the current best fitness η_B is larger than the minimum improvement threshold ϵ, then η_B is updated (line 11) along with the flag u_B.

The individuals from the children pool and the i-th generation are selected in order to form the $(i+1)$-th generation (line 14). Here, the N best individuals are chosen from the set of size $2N$ containing the individuals from the previous generation and child solutions. The difference between the previous average population fitness η_A^P and the current average fitness η_A is verified, the average steady state counter c_A is increased if necessary, and the η_A^P is updated (lines 16–21). If the numbers of consecutive generations with no improvement in the best fitness η_B and the average fitness η_A exceed thresholds s_B and s_A respectively, then the search is in the steady state (line 25). In order to diversify the search and to avoid the diversity crisis [5], we re-generate a population of size N (line 27). If the number of re-generations surpasses the limit R^C, then the population size is increased according to the increase factor α (line 30). In both re-generation scenarios we copy βN best individuals from the current population and draw the $N - \beta N$ ones randomly. Finally, if the number of re-generations exceeds the limit of re-generations R^I, then the chromosome length is increased by a factor λ, i.e., $\mathcal{L}(p_i) = 2\lambda K$. It is worth noting, that the population is re-generated using the previous $\mathcal{L}^P$ (line 35), and the length of individuals may change to the new

Algorithm 1. Adaptive Genetic Algorithm (AGA).

1: Generate an initial population of size N;   ▷ Random sampling
2: $c_B \leftarrow 0$; $c_A \leftarrow 0$; $u_B \leftarrow$ **false**;   ▷ Initialize the counters c_B and c_A, and flag u_B
3: **while** $(\tau \leq \tau_M)$ **do**
4:     Determine N pairs (p_A, p_B);   ▷ Pre-selection
5:     $u_B \leftarrow$ **false**; $\eta_B \leftarrow 0$;   ▷ Reset u_B flag
6:     **for all** (p_A, p_B) **do**
7:         $p_C \leftarrow$ Crossover(p_A, p_B, p_H);   ▷ AMPC
8:         $p_C \leftarrow$ Mutate(p_C);
9:         $\eta(p_C) \leftarrow$ FindFitness$(p_C, \boldsymbol{T})$;   ▷ Find fitness $\eta(p_C)$
10:        **if** $(|\eta_B - \eta(p_C)| \geq \epsilon)$ **then**
11:            $\eta_B \leftarrow \eta(p_C)$; $u_B \leftarrow$ **true**; $c_B \leftarrow 0$;   ▷ Update η_B and set u_B
12:        **end if**
13:    **end for**
14:    Form the next generation G;   ▷ Post-selection
15:    $\eta_A \leftarrow$ CalculateAverageFitness(G);
16:    **if** $(|\eta_A - \eta_A^P| \leq \epsilon)$ **then**
17:        $c_A \leftarrow c_A + 1$;   ▷ Increase c_A counter
18:    **else**
19:        $c_A \leftarrow 0$;
20:    **end if**
21:    $\eta_A^P \leftarrow \eta_A$;   ▷ Update the previous average fitness η_A^P
22:    **if** (**not** u_B) **then**
23:        $c_B \leftarrow c_B + 1$;   ▷ Increase c_B counter
24:    **end if**
25:    $f_S \leftarrow (c_B \geq s_B)$ **and** $(c_A \geq s_A)$;   ▷ Get steady state flag
26:    **if** f_S **and** $(r \leq R^C)$ **then**
27:        Re-generate population of size N;
28:        $r \leftarrow r + 1$;   ▷ Increase re-generation counter r
29:    **else if** f_S **and** $(r > R^C$ **and** $r \leq R^I)$ **then**
30:        Re-generate population of size αN;   ▷ Increase population size
31:        $r \leftarrow r + 1$;   ▷ Increase re-generation counter r
32:    **else if** f_S **and** $(r > R^I)$ **then**
33:        $\mathcal{L}^{\mathcal{P}} \leftarrow \mathcal{L}$; $\mathcal{L} \leftarrow \lambda\mathcal{L}$;   ▷ Store the current length $\mathcal{L}$ and increase $\mathcal{L}$
34:        $r \leftarrow 0$;   ▷ Reset re-generation counter r
35:        Re-generate population of size N using $\mathcal{L}^P$;
36:    **end if**
37: **end while**
38: **return** solution with the highest fitness η_B;

$\mathcal{L}$ during the AMPC. Thus, the population may contain individuals of various lengths. Finally, the best individual in the last population is returned (line 38), when the execution time of AGA exceeds the limit τ_M (line 3).

2.2 Adaptive Multi-Parent Crossover

In the proposed adaptive multi-parent crossover operator (AMPC), an intermediate child p_{A+B} of the length $\mathcal{L}(p_{A+B}) = \mathcal{L}(p_A) + \mathcal{L}(p_B)$ is generated for each pair of parents p_A and p_B (Fig. 1). Here, we randomized a well-known high-low fit (HLF) pre-selection scheme [7] which proved to be asymptotically best in terms of the GA classification score [8]. For each well-fitted individual p_A (out of $c_h N$ individuals) we select either a well-fitted chromosome or the one from the less-fitted part of the population with the probability $\mathcal{P} = 0.5$. The third parent p_H is selected from the well-fitted part using a tournament selection of size 2. To avoid competing between similar individuals, for the first chromosome p_1 in the tournament we select a second one p_2 such that $d(p_1, p_2) \geq d_m$ (see Section 2.3). Then, the intermediate children p_{A+B} is crossed over with the individual p_H as discussed in [8]. The vectors from p_{A+B} and p_H are drawn to generate a child p_C with probability $\mathcal{P}(p_{A+B})$ and $\mathcal{P}(p_H)$, respectively. Noteworthy, $\mathcal{L}(p_C) = \mathcal{L}$, and $\mathcal{L}$ is adaptively tuned in the AGA (see Alg. 1).

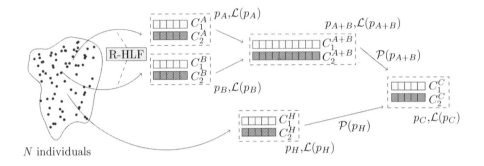

Fig. 1. Adaptive multi-parent crossover

2.3   New Distance Metric Between Individuals

In order to assess the distance between two individuals, i.e., two sets of vectors from the training set $\boldsymbol{T}$, we define a new similarity measure. Here, we compare the distribution of the vectors in each set. First, we transform the $\mathcal{N}$-dimensional input space using principal component analysis (PCA) to select n most discriminating dimensions indicated by the eigenvectors ($\boldsymbol{v}_i$) sorted in the descending order by the corresponding eigenvalues. Subsequently, each i-th dimension is divided into C intervals. The endpoints of the intervals $(r_i^{(0)}, r_i^{(1)}, \ldots, r_i^{(C)})$ are determined so as the same number of vectors from the training set fall into every interval. This splits the training set into C^n clusters, which are assigned with the indices $1, 2, \ldots, C^n$. Each chromosome is characterized by the indices histogram H, and the similarity between two individuals p and q is given: $S(p, q) = (\sum_i \min(h_i^p, h_i^q)) / \min(\mathcal{L}(p), \mathcal{L}(q))$, where h_i^p is the i-th bin of a histogram H_p. Thus, the distance between p and q equals $d(p, q) = 1 - S(p, q)$. The population diversity ϕ is defined as the average distance between the individuals.

The clustering process is illustrated in Fig. 2. Here, for $M = 50$ vectors, the dimensionality was reduced to $n = 2$, and every dimension was split into $C = 5$

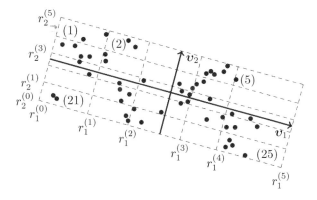

Fig. 2. Cluster identifiers in the PCA feature space

intervals, each containing $M/C = 10$ vectors from the training set. This divided the training set into $C^n = 25$ clusters. This is a fairly simple clustering technique, but we found it sufficient to compare the chromosomes. We have considered to proceed with the clustering directly in the input space, however in the case of high-dimensional data, the number of clusters would become very high even for low values of C, leading to sparse histograms. This was the reason for applying the dimensionality reduction using PCA prior to the clustering.

3   Experimental Results

Extensive computational experiments were performed to compare the performance of AGA with a GA. The AGA was validated using four data sets: 1) *Adult* and *Mushroom* benchmark sets (available at http://archive.ics.uci.edu/ml/datasets.html), 2) real-world *Skin* data derived from the ECU skin image database [12] containing 560732 pixels (as discussed in [8]), and 3) artificial set of *2D* points. Each set is divided randomly into two equinumerous sets, namely the training set T from which the training samples are selected and on which the fitness of individuals is evaluated in AGA, and the validation set V ($|T| = |V|$). Note that for the *2D* artificial set $T = V$. Clearly, the validation sets were not used during the AGA set selection for *Adult*, *Mushroom* and *Skin* data sets, and all the results presented in this paper were obtained for V.

The AGA was implemented in C++ language and the experiments were performed using an Intel Xeon 3.2 GHz computer with 16 GB RAM. We used LIBSVM [3] with RBF kernel: $K\left(\boldsymbol{u}, \boldsymbol{v}\right) = \exp\left(-\|\boldsymbol{u} - \boldsymbol{v}\|^2/\sigma^2\right)$, where σ is the kernel width. SVM parameters (i.e., σ and C) were selected based on a grid search with an exponential step [3]. The kernel parameters are given in Tab. 1. The AGA parameters were tuned experimentally in a similar manner. The following values were used: $N = 10$, $\mathcal{P}_m = 0.3$, $c_h = 0.5$, $\epsilon = 0.001$, $s_a = 3$, $s_b = 5$, $R^C = 1$, $R^I = 2$, $\alpha = 2.0$, $\lambda = 2.0$, $2m = 2K = 20$ (the initial chromosome length $\mathcal{L}$), $\beta = 0.1$, $n = 3$, $\mathcal{P}(p_H) = \mathcal{P}(p_{A+B}) = 0.5$, $d_m = 0.7$, $\tau_M = 60$ min.

Table 1. SVM kernel parameters C and σ for the investigated data sets

Set	C	σ
Adult	1000	0.1
Mushroom	64	4.0
Skin	10	1.0
2D	32	32.0

The results obtained for the AGA along with the results obtained for the GA are given in Tab. 2 for three data sets. The *Mushroom* data set is omitted here, since both the GA with $K = 20m$ and AGA converged to the correct classification ($\eta_B = 100.00\%$) in $\tau < \tau_0 + \Delta\tau$. The corresponding average numbers of support vectors for the *Mushroom* data set are as follows: AGA – 120, GA($K = 20m$) – 200. As mentioned earlier, it is not clearly defined how to specify the chromosome length in the GA. Here, to ensure the fair comparison with the proposed AGA, we run two versions of GA with $K = m$ and $K = 20m$. Also, the population size in GA was set to $N = 40$, which is the maximum number of individuals in a population after the re-generation with increase in the AGA.

Table 2. The best fitness η_B (in %) along with its standard deviation σ among 10 independent AGA executions, the number of support vectors s of the best individual and the generation g, averaged for 10 independent AGA executions, shown for the execution time step $\Delta\tau = 12$ min

Set	τ	AGA $\eta_B \pm \sigma$	s	g	GA, $K = 20m$ $\eta_B \pm \sigma$	s	g	GA, $K = m$ $\eta_B \pm \sigma$	s	g
Adult	τ_0	66.48 ± 4.84	16	—	78.81 ± 0.43	345	—	72.77 ± 2.80	18	—
	$\tau_0 + \Delta\tau$	79.49 ± 0.10	28	111	79.45 ± 0.33	345	3	79.01 ± 0.77	15	62
	$\tau_0 + 3\Delta\tau$	79.50 ± 0.01	52	169	79.91 ± 0.33	339	9	79.12 ± 0.83	15	183
	$\tau_0 + 5\Delta\tau$	79.59 ± 0.17	169	199	80.09 ± 0.22	346	14	79.26 ± 0.44	14	306
Skin	τ_0	84.37 ± 1.31	12	—	88.85 ± 0.31	145	—	86.22 ± 1.12	12	—
	$\tau_0 + \Delta\tau$	88.78 ± 0.13	20	85	89.32 ± 0.09	146	5	88.45 ± 0.16	12	37
	$\tau_0 + 3\Delta\tau$	89.49 ± 0.13	64	154	89.54 ± 0.12	147	14	88.83 ± 0.18	13	108
	$\tau_0 + 5\Delta\tau$	89.87 ± 0.01	114	192	89.57 ± 0.09	147	22	88.98 ± 0.12	13	178
2D	τ_0	80.97 ± 0.91	17	—	97.40 ± 0.12	73	—	84.37 ± 0.85	17	—
	$\tau_0 + \Delta\tau$	98.74 ± 0.17	103	283	98.41 ± 0.15	81	132	92.90 ± 0.47	18	384
	$\tau_0 + 3\Delta\tau$	99.27 ± 0.06	219	328	98.57 ± 0.12	81	395	94.28 ± 0.47	17	1144

It can be noted that the generation of an initial population corresponds to the random sampling approach. Thus, the result η_B in τ_0 is the averaged best fitness among $10N$ random draws, where N is the population size. Clearly, the quality of an initial population depends on the number of training samples in each individual (i.e., the individual length), and the number of random draws (i.e., the population size). Thus, the initial populations were of higher quality for the GA with $K = 20m$. The number of support vectors is incremented more rapidly in the AGA (see s in Tab. 2). It is worth mentioning that the AGA converged quickly to the high-quality training sets, and the increment in the fitness function is significantly larger than in case of the GA, e.g., $\Delta\eta_B \approx 13\%$ in the AGA compared with $\Delta\eta_B \approx 1.2\%$ and $\Delta\eta_B \approx 6.5\%$ in the GA with $K = 20m$ and $K = m$, respectively. The number of generations g in the presented time interval is dependent on the chromosome length. Thus, the g values are the largest for GA with small K. However, the best fitness is not improved significantly. This indicates that the training set cannot be further improved for a given number of samples and corresponding support vectors (see *Skin* and *2D* data sets).

The increase in the number of support vectors highlights the exploration possibilities of the AGA. Once the relatively small solution space region is exploited, the number of training samples is increased. This prevents the search from being stuck in the local minima. The approach of increasing the training set according to the state of search is shown in Fig. 3 for the artificial *2D* data set. Here, the training set samples are visualized as white and black crosses. Similarly, the AGA converges to the very good final results faster than the GA for various K. First, the K value is relatively small and starts increasing when the search progresses. Noteworthy, the maximum number of samples need not to be specified for the AGA (see Fig. 3d) and it is being adapted during the algorithm execution. This makes it possible to tackle the trade-off between the SVM classification accuracy and time by breaking the AGA execution once the desired η_B is obtained, or the maximum number of s is exceeded.

3.1 Sensitivity Analysis on Method Components

A number of factors influence the performance of the proposed adaptive genetic algorithm. In this section we measure the impact of the AGA components on the quality of final SVM training data sets. We analyze the best and average fitness in a population (η_B and $\bar{\eta}$ respectively), its diversity ϕ, the average number of support vectors $\bar{s}$, the number of support vectors of the best individual s, and the average execution time $\bar{\tau}_g$, obtained for three versions of AGA with certain method components removed. The average execution time $\bar{\tau}_g$ depicts the average execution time of a single AGA generation up to the g-*th* generation.

The following versions of the algorithm were analyzed: AGA, AGA with the adaptive pre-selection and multi-parent crossover removed (**No AMPC**), and AGA with the variable chromosome length removed (**No VLC**). In the **No AMPC** version of AGA we replaced the AMPC (see Fig. 1) by the standard high-low fit pre-selection scheme and the crossover operator applied for two parents p_A and p_B [8]. The chromosomes of a constant length $\mathcal{L}$, where $\mathcal{L} = C_1 + C_2 = 2K$, were used in AGA with **No VLC**. Here, we set $K = m + (M - m)/2$, where m and M are the minimum and maximum number of a class vectors in a chromosome in the VLC scheme. The chromosome length settings for each data set are summarized in Tab. 3. We set the initial population size $N = 10$ and $R^I = 1$, so as the maximum population size after the increase equals 20. The other AGA settings remain unchanged. Each data set was split into two sets $\boldsymbol{V}$ and $\boldsymbol{T}$ of equal size. Moreover, we divided the *Mushroom* set so as $|\boldsymbol{T}| = 9\,|\boldsymbol{V}|$ (see *Mushroom* (B)), in order to compare the number of support vectors obtained for both configurations (for *Mushroom* (A) we have $|\boldsymbol{T}| = |\boldsymbol{V}|$).

The experimental results obtained for three versions of AGA are given in Tab. 4. We show the results for various generations g for each data set. It is easy to see that applying the AMPC results in converging to the solutions of higher

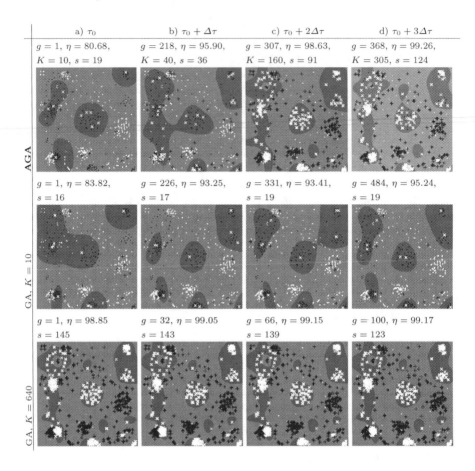

Fig. 3. Examples of training set selection for *2D* data set using AGA, GA with $K = 10$, and GA with $K = 640$, $\Delta\tau = 4$ min

quality faster than using the HLF scheme and standard crossover operator. Even if the randomly drawn initial populations contain better individuals, the AMPC outperforms HLF asymptotically (see e.g., η_B for AGA and **No AMPC**, $g = 200$, *Adult*) in similar time τ. This indicates the better converging capabilities of the AMPC. This is confirmed by the resulting number of support vectors in both configurations – in the AMPC, the last s is slightly larger than for **No AMPC**,

Table 3. The AGA settings for each data set

Set	m	M
Adult	10	320
Mushroom	10	80
Skin	10	400
2D	10	320

Table 4. The best fitness η_B (in %) along with its standard deviation σ among 20 algorithm executions, the average fitness $\bar{\eta}$ (in %), the standard deviation of the population fitness σ_η, the population diversity ϕ, the number of support vectors s of the best individual, the average number of support vectors $\bar{s}$ and the generation g, the average execution time $\bar{\tau}_g$ (in seconds) – the time required for generating the initial population (i.e., the random sampling) is omitted, averaged for 20 independent algorithm executions

Set	g	AGA							No AMPC							No VLC						
		$\eta_B \pm \sigma$	$\bar{\eta}$	σ_η	ϕ	s	$\bar{s}$	$\bar{\tau}_g$	$\eta_B \pm \sigma$	$\bar{\eta}$	σ_η	ϕ	s	$\bar{s}$	$\bar{\tau}_g$	$\eta_B \pm \sigma$	$\bar{\eta}$	σ_η	ϕ	s	$\bar{s}$	$\bar{\tau}_g$
Adult	1	67.35 ± 5.67	53.32	0.09	0.87	18	17	—	68.43 ± 5.07	54.06	0.09	0.87	17	17	—	73.54 ± 4.80	57.30	0.13	0.58	146	145	—
	25	78.65 ± 0.77	71.48	0.03	0.53	18	17	4.1	78.58 ± 0.98	71.66	0.03	0.55	18	17	3.9	79.15 ± 0.41	75.99	0.02	0.40	147	147	34.0
	50	79.17 ± 0.19	74.37	0.03	0.57	17	17	4.4	79.11 ± 0.29	71.64	0.03	0.56	17	17	4.2	79.49 ± 0.29	75.27	0.03	0.43	148	146	41.0
	75	79.32 ± 0.15	73.47	0.03	0.52	24	24	5.1	79.20 ± 0.22	75.68	0.02	0.59	19	20	5.0	79.60 ± 0.31	78.05	0.01	0.42	149	146	42.9
	100	79.36 ± 0.12	73.47	0.03	0.54	28	32	6.1	79.24 ± 0.23	75.99	0.02	0.56	22	26	6.0	79.69 ± 0.28	77.19	0.01	0.44	148	145	43.4
	150	79.43 ± 0.07	75.06	0.03	0.42	67	92	9.7	79.37 ± 0.09	76.81	0.01	0.51	39	56	9.3	79.88 ± 0.31	74.19	0.03	0.43	148	146	44.1
	200	79.97 ± 0.29	76.94	0.02	0.31	229	244	19.3	79.47 ± 0.13	77.03	0.02	0.46	114	147	18.5	79.91 ± 0.29	77.80	0.01	0.44	148	148	44.7
Mush. (A)	1	95.63 ± 1.13	89.66	0.05	0.45	20	20	—	95.22 ± 5.07	88.06	0.06	0.45	20	20	—	99.38 ± 0.21	97.79	0.01	0.24	90	90	—
	20	98.25 ± 0.48	96.66	0.01	0.28	20	20	0.7	98.21 ± 0.98	96.36	0.01	0.28	20	20	0.7	99.87 ± 0.07	99.42	< 0.01	0.20	90	90	3.2
	40	98.69 ± 0.39	97.37	0.01	0.33	22	22	0.9	98.63 ± 0.29	97.67	< 0.01	0.32	25	24	0.9	99.91 ± 0.10	99.44	< 0.01	0.18	90	90	3.5
	60	99.42 ± 0.29	98.51	< 0.01	0.24	40	40	1.1	99.46 ± 0.22	98.73	< 0.01	0.24	39	39	1.0	99.96 ± 0.06	99.45	< 0.01	0.21	90	90	3.6
	80	99.70 ± 0.11	99.07	< 0.01	0.20	61	63	1.3	99.66 ± 0.23	98.77	0.01	0.23	60	58	1.2	99.98 ± 0.04	99.40	< 0.01	0.20	90	90	3.7
	100	99.91 ± 0.11	99.56	< 0.01	0.16	120	127	1.8	99.83 ± 0.09	99.35	< 0.01	0.18	105	107	1.6	99.98 ± 0.04	99.30	0.01	0.20	90	90	3.7
Mush. (B)	1	94.63 ± 1.53	88.64	0.05	0.56	20	20	—	94.70 ± 1.67	87.78	0.06	0.56	20	20	—	97.28 ± 1.01	91.79	0.04	0.50	30	30	—
	10	97.25 ± 0.61	96.11	0.01	0.37	20	20	0.7	98.00 ± 0.45	96.80	< 0.01	0.45	20	20	0.7	99.29 ± 0.35	97.63	< 0.01	0.34	30	30	0.9
	20	98.69 ± 0.49	96.84	0.01	0.40	20	20	0.7	98.65 ± 0.48	96.76	0.01	0.37	20	20	0.7	99.35 ± 0.37	97.97	< 0.01	0.36	30	30	0.9
	40	99.42 ± 0.56	98.23	< 0.01	0.35	30	30	0.8	99.23 ± 0.47	97.65	< 0.01	0.42	26	25	0.8	99.41 ± 0.29	98.07	0.01	0.39	30	30	1.1
	80	99.98 ± 0.05	99.23	< 0.01	0.28	72	72	1.2	99.96 ± 0.11	98.32	0.01	0.34	50	50	1.1	99.80 ± 0.26	98.21	0.01	0.38	30	30	1.2
Skin	1	82.88 ± 2.01	75.02	0.07	0.98	11	12	—	82.98 ± 2.29	73.87	0.06	0.98	12	12	—	87.56 ± 1.89	73.27	0.14	0.78	167	169	—
	25	88.04 ± 0.30	86.39	0.01	0.54	12	12	4.0	87.86 ± 0.58	84.57	0.02	0.59	13	12	4.6	89.55 ± 0.10	88.39	0.01	0.58	179	175	60.4
	50	88.34 ± 0.21	86.30	0.01	0.49	13	15	5.4	88.14 ± 0.70	87.14	0.01	0.65	12	13	5.5	89.66 ± 0.10	87.91	0.01	0.60	181	169	71.6
	75	88.64 ± 0.26	87.31	0.01	0.66	19	19	6.2	88.46 ± 0.35	87.80	< 0.01	0.59	17	19	6.4	89.70 ± 0.06	88.94	< 0.01	0.53	183	174	74.8
	100	89.01 ± 0.12	86.45	0.01	0.63	34	35	7.5	88.76 ± 0.41	87.24	0.01	0.54	30	30	7.7	89.72 ± 0.06	88.79	0.01	0.58	179	172	75.8
	125	89.25 ± 0.13	87.73	0.01	0.61	56	61	9.6	89.18 ± 0.11	87.86	< 0.01	0.57	49	44	9.3	89.72 ± 0.06	86.95	0.02	0.56	181	181	76.0
2D	1	81.02 ± 1.70	74.35	0.05	0.72	17	17	—	81.23 ± 2.16	73.90	0.05	0.72	17	17	—	96.69 ± 0.35	95.01	0.01	0.25	65	65	—
	50	89.69 ± 1.31	85.25	0.02	0.45	18	17	1.3	89.19 ± 1.22	84.81	0.02	0.48	18	17	1.3	97.87 ± 0.23	96.66	< 0.01	0.20	73	70	3.5
	100	93.40 ± 0.75	91.36	0.01	0.36	27	27	1.5	93.12 ± 0.98	90.73	0.01	0.35	27	27	1.5	97.99 ± 0.17	96.89	< 0.01	0.19	73	69	3.7
	200	95.68 ± 0.44	95.68	< 0.01	0.22	49	51	1.8	96.37 ± 0.36	94.89	0.01	0.28	41	43	1.8	98.13 ± 0.14	97.08	< 0.01	0.19	74	72	3.9
	300	98.72 ± 0.11	97.98	< 0.01	0.14	98	95	2.6	98.54 ± 0.57	97.81	< 0.01	0.15	96	92	2.1	98.21 ± 0.11	96.84	< 0.01	0.18	74	71	4.0

which means that the full AGA explores the larger region of the solution space faster, after the currently analyzed region is sufficiently exploited. Thus, the multi-parent crossover contributes significantly to the search performance. Noteworthy, the full AGA and **No AMPC** version of the algorithm managed to converge to very good final results for both version of *Mushroom* data set in similar time. The **No VLC** required noticeably larger execution time for the equinumerous training and validation sets (see $\bar{\tau}$ for *Mushroom* (A) and (B)).

The number of support vectors, both s and averaged $\bar{s}$, drastically increases for the **No VLC** version of AGA. Here, the initial number of training samples for each class in a chromosome is relatively large. This strongly influences the classification time of the SVM. In case of the *Skin* data set, the number of vectors s obtained using the AGA is more than 3 times smaller than using the **No VLC** (the corresponding execution time necessary to converge to this result is almost 8 times lower for the full AGA). However, there exist data sets for which obtaining the high classification score requires a large number of support vectors. In these cases the AGA iteratively increments the training set if necessary. This approach is not possible in the **No VLC** scheme, since the number of vectors ought to be set *a priori* (see *Adult*). It leads to saturating the population with individuals of similar quality (see decreasing σ_η and ϕ), which can cause the diversity crisis. This phenomenon is mitigated by subsequent population re-generations.

4   Conclusions and Future Work

In this paper we proposed a new adaptive genetic algorithm to select a valuable training set for support vector machines. In the presented approach the algorithm settings are being adapted during the execution. It increments the size of the training set when the current region of the solution space is sufficiently exploited for better exploration. We proposed a new multi-parent crossover operator for enhancing the exploration and exploitation capabilities of our approach. We show how adapting the number of training samples in an individual affects the search progress and convergence along with final classification score. A new metric for measuring the distance between two individuals was presented. The metric is based on analyzing the vectors distribution in the feature space obtained using principal component analysis. An extensive experimental study proved that the adaptive genetic algorithm helps reduce the number of support vectors compared with the standard genetic algorithm which decreases the SVM classification time.

Our ongoing research includes incorporating the geometry-based methods into the adaptive algorithm, designing a new memetic algorithm for an efficient training data selection and comparing the proposed algorithms with other state-of-the-art approaches. Also, our aim is to design and implement a parallel version of the algorithm. Finally, we plan to utilize the proposed technique for unlabeled data sets, and to confirm its performance for imbalanced sets.

References

1. Balcázar, J., Dai, Y., Watanabe, O.: A Random Sampling Technique for Training Support Vector Machines. In: Abe, N., Khardon, R., Zeugmann, T. (eds.) ALT 2001. LNCS (LNAI), vol. 2225, pp. 119–134. Springer, Heidelberg (2001)
2. Chang, C.C., Pao, H.K., Lee, Y.J.: RSVM based two-teachers-one-student semi-supervised learning algorithm. Neural Networks **25**, 57–69 (2012)
3. Chang, C.C., Lin, C.J.: LIBSVM: A library for support vector machines. ACM Trans. on Intell. Systems and Technology 2, 27:1–27:27 (2011)
4. Chien, L.J., Chang, C.C., Lee, Y.J.: Variant methods of reduced set selection for reduced support vector machines. J. Inf. Sci. Eng. **26**(1), 183–196 (2010)
5. Corne, D., Dorigo, M., Glover, F., Dasgupta, D., Moscato, P., Poli, R., Price, K.V.: New ideas in optimization, pp. 219–234. McGraw-Hill Ltd. (1999)
6. Cortes, C., Vapnik, V.: Support-Vector Networks. Mach. Learn. **20**(3), 273–297 (1995)
7. Elamin, E.E.A.: A proposed genetic algorithm selection method. In: 1st National Symposium (NITS), pp. 1–8 (2006)
8. Kawulok, M., Nalepa, J.: Support vector machines training data selection using a genetic algorithm. In: Hancock, E. Imiya, A., Kuijper, A. Kudo, M., Omachi, S., Windeatt, T., Yamada, K.: (eds.): SSPR & SPR 2012, LNCS 7626, pp. 557-565. Springer, Heidelberg (2012)
9. Koggalage, R., Halgamuge, S.: Reducing the number of training samples for fast support vector machine classification. Neural Inf. Process. Lett. and Reviews **2**(3), 57–65 (2004)
10. Lee, Y.J., Huang, S.Y.: Reduced support vector machines: A statistical theory. IEEE Trans. on Neural Networks **18**(1), 1–13 (2007)
11. Musicant, D.R., Feinberg, A.: Active set support vector regression. IEEE Trans. on Neural Networks **15**(2), 268–275 (2004)
12. Phung, S.L., Chai, D., Bouzerdoum, A.: Adaptive skin segmentation in color images. In: IEEE Int. Conf. on Acoustics, Speech and Signal Proc., pp. 353–356 (2003)
13. Schohn, G., Cohn, D.: Less is more: Active learning with support vector machines. In: 17th Int. Conf. on Mach. Learn., pp. 839–846. Morgan Kaufmann Inc. (2000)
14. Shin, H., Cho, S.: Neighborhood property-based pattern selection for support vector machines. Neural Comput. **19**(3), 816–855 (2007)
15. Tsang, I.W., Kwok, J.T., Cheung, P.M.: Core vector machines: Fast SVM training on very large data sets. J. of Machine Learn. Res. **6**, 363–392 (2005)
16. Wang, D., Shi, L.: Selecting valuable training samples for SVMs via data structure analysis. Neurocomputing **71**, 2772–2781 (2008)
17. Wang, J., Neskovic, P., Cooper, L.N.: Training Data Selection for Support Vector Machines. In: Wang, L., Chen, K., S. Ong, Y. (eds.) ICNC 2005. LNCS, vol. 3610, pp. 554–564. Springer, Heidelberg (2005)
18. Zeng, Z.Q., Xu, H.R., Xie, Y.Q., Gao, J.: A geometric approach to train SVM on very large data sets. Intell. Sys. and Knowl. Eng. **1**, 991–996 (2008)
19. Zhang, W., King, I.: Locating support vectors via β-skeleton technique. In: Int. Conf. on Neural Inf. Process., 1423–1427 (2002)

Automatic Selection of GA Parameters for Fragile Watermarking

Marco Botta[1]([✉]), Davide Cavagnino[1], and Victor Pomponiu[2]

[1] Dipartimento di Informatica, Università degli Studi di Torino
Corso Svizzera 185, 10149 Torino, Italy
{marco.botta,davide.cavagnino}@unito.it
[2] Department of Radiology, University of Pittsburgh
3362 Fifth Avenue, Pittsburgh, 15213, PA, USA
vpomponiu@acm.org

Abstract. Genetic Algorithms (GAs) are known to be valuable tools for optimization purposes. In general, GAs can find good solutions by setting their configuration parameters, such as mutation and crossover rates, population size, etc., to standard (i.e., widely used) values. In some application domains, changing the values of these parameters does not improve the quality of the solution, but might influence the ability of the algorithm to find such solution. In other application domains, fine tuning these parameters could result into a significant improvement of the solution quality. In this paper we present an experimental study aimed at finding how fine tuning the parameters of a GA used for the insertion of a fragile watermark into a bitmap image influences the quality of the resulting digital object. However, when proposing a GA based new tool to non-expert users, selecting the best parameter setting is not an easy task. Therefore, we will suggest how to automatically set the GA parameters in order to meet the quality and/or running time performances requested by the user.

Keywords: Information hiding · Fragile watermarking · Genetic algorithms · Karhunen-Loève Transform

1   Introduction

The digital revolution of the last decade, in which every piece of information is represented, manipulated, stored and reproduced in digital form, brought about new opportunities along with new challenges. One important issue, that is deserving a lot of attention in the literature, is how to determine if a digital object is genuine, i.e., it has not been altered with respect to its original version.

A possible solution to ensure the protection of the media content is digital watermarking [5]. In general, the watermarking process consists of two phases: the embedding phase and the verification phase. During embedding, the digital host object is modified to carry a watermark signal. Then the watermarked object is released into an environment that may alter it. The aim of the verification is to look for the presence of the watermark into the (possibly) altered object. To improve the security, in case the host object is an image the watermark can be embedded in transform domains like the discrete cosine transform (DCT) or the Karhunen-Loève transform (KLT).

© Springer-Verlag Berlin Heidelberg 2014
A.I. Esparcia-Alcázar et al. (Eds.): EvoApplications 2014, LNCS 8602, pp. 526–537, 2014.
DOI: 10.1007/978-3-662-45523-4_43

The watermark embedded into the host object could be *robust* against manipulations or *fragile*. Fragile watermarking is a particular class of schemes that uses the watermark to alert for any alterations induced to the host signal. There are three main properties required for a fragile watermarking algorithm: 1) the ability of the fragile watermark to detect alterations, 2) the capacity of the fragile watermark to localize the tampered areas and 3) the preservation of the quality of the host signal.

In this paper we evaluate the performance of a Genetic Algorithm (GA) used for embedding a watermark into a bitmap image. The watermark is inserted into a secret space of features extracted from the image, and the GA is used to modify the pixels of the image in such a way that these features contain the intended watermark. In this way, only the entities having knowledge of the secret space will be able to detect modifications to the image by extracting the watermark and comparing it with the one that was inserted, providing a tool to check the authenticity of the image. Moreover, without the knowledge of the secret space it is highly unlikely to successfully tamper (parts of) the image without altering the watermark.

The performance of the GA will be evaluated by varying some of its parameters and measuring the time required for the watermark insertion and the quality of the resulting images. It should be pointed out that in the presented application, the GA is run multiple times, depending on the size of the image to be watermarked, and we must use the best settings that results in lower running times and highest quality. Therefore, after observing the relation among quality, time and GA parameters, we extended the algorithm with the ability to automatically select the appropriate GA parameter settings in order to fulfill the user requirements in terms of quality.

The rest of the paper is organized as follows: in the next section some previous works related to the use of GA for watermarking will be analyzed, while in section 3 the watermarking algorithm will be briefly presented. Section 4 will discuss the experimental results and an analysis of the GA parameters tuning. The final section will draw some conclusions.

2   GA-Based Watermarking Schemes

There are two main techniques to improve the performances of a watermarking system. The first is to use statistical properties during the watermark verification (e.g. in detection). The latter is to employ genetic optimization to find the values of the embedding features that generate almost optimal performances, in terms of imperceptibility and efficacy. This is the most common approach, due to the simplicity of the technique (does not imply mathematical analysis) and the ease in adapting it to many different types of watermarking systems.

Wang et al. [16] optimized a Least Significant Bit (LSB) substitution watermarking method with the use of GA. The insertion works in the spatial domain, and is based on a mapping function that is optimized by a GA in order to find one that achieves both robustness and imperceptibility. The fitness function takes into consideration the distortion induced by the watermark insertion. A similar approach is adopted by Wu et al. [17] who generates optimal mapping functions for finer regions (blocks) of the host image in order to increase the quality of the watermarked image.

Shieh et al. [12] introduce a GA-based watermarking in DCT domain. The watermark insertion is performed via the manipulation of the polarity between the watermark and the DCT coefficients. The GA is employed to find the DCT coefficients that give the optimal trade-off between robustness and image quality. The same strategy was used by Lu et al. [11] for the DWT coefficients to embed the watermark in a color image while Huang et al. [8] adopt a slight variation of [12].

In order to optimize a DCT-based watermarking method Díaz and Romay [6] use a Pareto-based Multi-Objective Genetic Algorithm. The parameters considered for the optimization are the DCT coefficients. The fidelity and robustness are measured directly on the selected coefficients.

Usman et al. [15] present an algorithm that uses the DCT domain for embedding a fragile watermark with the purpose of content integrity. The host image is divided into blocks of size 8×8, and a GA is used to select five DCT coefficients per block for storing the watermark; at the same time, to deal with possible attacks, the non-selected coefficients of the block and of its neighbours are also involved in the watermark embedding. The GA selects the coefficients using a fitness function that considers the distortion w.r.t. the host image.

Aslantas et al. [1] compare some optimization methods by applying them to an algorithm that inserts a fragile watermark into the DCT coefficients of an image. Given that the inverse transformation in the pixel domain may alter some of the inserted bits due to the integer rounding of the pixels, an optimization step is required to restore the correct watermark values. Differential evolution, clonal selection, particle swarm optimization and genetic algorithms are evaluated varying the parameters of each algorithm and comparing the resulting fitness values, computation times and watermark imperceptibility.

Lee and Ho [9] describe the insertion of a fragile watermark in the LSBs of the pixels of an image. The image is divided into blocks that are classified according to the type of edge content (using the discrete cosine transform coefficients). The edge block classification is used in the fitness function of a genetic algorithm employed for the insertion of the watermark bits.

Shih and Wu [13, 14] applied a GA in order to cope with rounding errors that can occur in the DCT coefficients during the embedding stage. The basic issue is that in DCT embedding, integer pixel values are transformed into real value DCT coefficients followed by the insertion of the watermark. Afterwards, the watermarked coefficients are transformed back to integer pixel values by an inverse DCT. However, information might be lost due to rounding errors. The fitness function applied by the scheme is based on the normalized correlation (NC) between embedded and detected watermark and the distortion between host and watermarked images.

3   The Watermarking Algorithm

Some of the previously cited papers compute a linear transform[1] from pixels to a coefficient space (e.g., DCT), also called frequency space or frequency domain, insert the watermark into the coefficients, inverse transform the coefficients into the pixel domain, and then use a GA to improve the quality of the watermarked image by either

---

[1] For a presentation of linear transforms refer to [7].

selecting the best coefficients or optimizing the pixel values in order to solve rounding problems.

The insertion into the coefficients and their inverse transformation are actually not needed when using a GA. Indeed, the GA can be used to optimize pixel values in such a way that when transformed to the coefficient space, the selected coefficients already carry the watermark bits. In the following, we give a description of the algorithm that is an improvement of the one presented in [3], and implements this new idea of not inserting the watermark bits into the KLT coefficients but let the GA free to modify the pixel values in every block in such a way that the watermark extracted from the KLT coefficients is the intended one. Figure 1 shows a block diagram of the watermark embedding scheme.

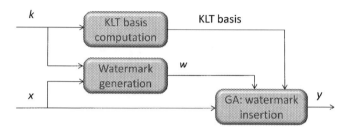

Fig. 1. Block diagram of the watermark embedding

Firstly, a KLT basis is computed from a key image k: its result may be used for watermarking many host images, and is performed only once per key image. The key image, which must be kept secret, is divided into blocks of size $n \times n$ and from the blocks, a Karhunen-Loève basis is derived. This basis defines a linear transformation from the space of pixels to a frequency domain [7]. When a block of $n \times n$ pixels is transformed with this basis, it will produce n^2 coefficients.

In the watermark generation, a cryptographic hash function is applied to a set of pixels of the key image k and of the host image x, to generate a pseudo-random binary sequence that will be used as fragile watermark w for the host image, in order to prevent cut-and-paste attacks, birthday attacks and transplantation attacks [2].

Then, the host image is split into sub-images of size $n \times n$, the watermark is divided into chunks of s bits and each chunk is assigned to one sub-image (for example in raster scan order). For every sub-image, the GA is run and evolves a population of individuals that define a modification of the sub-image pixels, in such a way that when the KLT basis is applied to the sub-image, a secret set of n^2 coefficients is generated, and the s selected coefficients of the KL transformation store the s watermark bits. Thus, an individual of the GA population is composed of n^2 integers (typically in the range [−3, 3]) that added to the pixels produce a modified sub-image. A watermark bit b is extracted from a coefficient c according to the following rule:

$$b = \text{round}(2^{-p}c) \bmod 2 \tag{1}$$

where p is the position (in the binary representation of c) where the watermark bits are stored.

The GA usually runs for a maximum number of generations, but it can be terminated as soon as a viable solution is found. The GA fitness function may take into account many parameters; typically, the distortion of the modified sub-image w.r.t. the original one is a considered factor, and the other is the fact that the modified sub-image should store the s watermark bits. The fitness function F we used for our GA takes into account these two terms: the Bit Error Rate (BER), i.e., the correct extraction of the watermark bits from the KLT coefficients, and the Mean Square Error (MSE), i.e., the distortion w.r.t. the host image:

$$F = \alpha \cdot BER + \min(\beta, MSE) \qquad (2)$$

where $\alpha > \beta$ are chosen so that if $F \leq \beta$ then $BER = 0$; this allows to verify if the GA found a viable solution. Moreover, we adopted the convention the smaller F is, the better the individual.

The result of running the GA optimization on all the host sub-images is the watermark stored in a secret space, so it cannot be easily extracted by an attacker; moreover, any modification to the watermarked image y will result in the modification of one or more watermark bits stored into the coefficients.

A measure of the objective image quality is the Peak Signal-to-Noise Ratio ($PSNR$) computed as $PSNR = 10 \log_{10} \frac{255^2}{m.s.e.}$ (for 256 grey levels images) where $m.s.e.$ is the mean square error between the host image pixels and the watermarked image pixels. The higher this value the better is the resulting watermarked image.

To verify the integrity of a previously watermarked image the secret KLT basis is used to compute the coefficients: from these the watermark bits may be extracted as specified in (1), and compared to the original ones; possibly differing bits reveal a tampering.

4   Experimental Results

Almost all previously cited works did not perform a thorough analysis and tuning of GA parameters, but just reported the used settings. In a previous study [4], we also focused on the analysis of the watermarking algorithm properties, by setting the GA parameters to default values (population size=100, mutation probability p_m=0.05, crossover probability p_c=0.8, terminate if best individual does not change in the last 10 generations or 2000 generations reached) and obtaining good quality results ($PSNR$ between 53 and 54 dB).

Here we evaluate the performances of the proposed algorithm and further investigate whether a wise selection of parameters for the GA may further improve the quality of the resulting watermarked images.

We ran a large number of experiments, for a total of more than 90000 watermarked images, on about 100 different combinations of the four GA parameters we studied in this paper, namely population size, number of stable generations (i.e. the minimum number of generations the best solution found so far by the GA does not improve), mutation and crossover probabilities, and collected quality and running times.

For every parameter combination, we report average values computed by inserting a watermark of 8 bits per block (of size 8×8) into 1000 images taken from OPTIMOL [10]: the images are 256 gray levels bitmaps of 256×256 pixels. All experiments have been performed on a set of workstations, each equipped with 4GB RAM and an Intel(R) Xeon(R) E5410 2.33GHz processor. As a multi-dimensional plot would not be easily readable, we will project some of the results obtained along the dimensions we investigated and show simpler plots.

4.1   Convergence Ability

In this application we faced two aspects of convergence: for some sub-images there is a large number of easy reachable solutions and the GA might premature converge to a local minima, while for other sub-images a solution might not even exist, and the GA does not converge at all. To address the premature convergence issue, we varied the number of stable generations as we report in the following. For what concern the second issue, Figure 2 reports the number of images for which the GA failed to find a solution: with population sizes smaller than 50, even setting 70 stable generations, there are a few images on which the GA fails. We also noted that with mutation probability smaller than 0.03 the algorithm does not find a solution in all the cases, even setting population size = 100 and stable generations = 70.

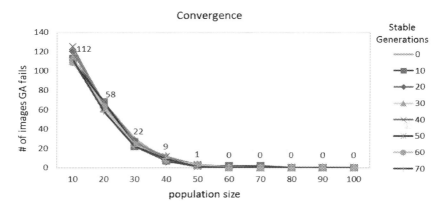

Fig. 2. The covergence of the algorithm vs the size of the population, varying the number of stable generations required to terminate. The labels report the number of images the GA failed for 70 stable generations.

As we would not allow for GA failures (i.e., we want that the watermark is always carried by the image after running the algorithm), we performed experiments and report results for population sizes larger than 50 individuals and $p_m \geq 0.03$.

4.2   Image Quality

The first experiment was aimed at analyzing how smaller populations than the default (100) influence the performances of the algorithm, in order to find an optimal trade-off between quality and running time. Moreover, for every population size, we varied the number of stable generations, from 0 (stops as soon as a solution is found) to 70 (stops when the best solution does not change for 70 consecutive generations), in steps of 10. Figure 3(a) reports the average quality of the watermarked images as a function of population size (different lines) and number of stable generations, by setting $p_c = 0.8$ and $p_m = 0.05$ (similar behaviours were obtained with other combinations of p_c and p_m). As expected, increasing the GA population size slightly improves the quality of the resulting images, but the gain becomes less meaningful for increasingly larger populations. This is probably due to the fact that the exploration ability of the GA in this context does not depend so much on the number of individuals, but rather on other GA parameters. Indeed, as it can be seen from Figure 3(a), the *PSNR* increases by 6 dB for an increasing number of stable generations in which the GA was left running after having reached a solution. This behavior was not anticipated even though it is not really surprising: the fitness function we used has a lot of local minima, so by letting the GA run for longer, a better solution can be found. Anyway, by analyzing the running times (see Figure 3(b)) larger populations and larger number of stable generations result in longer running times. It should be pointed out that there is a linear correlation between *PSNR* and time, on one side, and population size and stable generations on the other side. We will exploit these correlations later on.

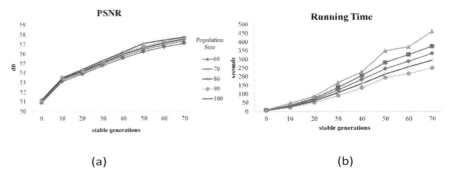

(a)   (b)

Fig. 3. The *PSNR* (a) and Running Time (b) vs the number of stable generations, varying the size of the population, $p_c = 0.8$, $p_m = 0.05$

4.3   Crossover Probability

Figure 4(a) shows the influence of the crossover probability on the image quality. Again, the population size has been set to 100, stable generations to 10 and the mutation probability varies between 0.03 and 0.06. We note that large crossover probabilities do not significantly increase the *PSNR* of the watermarked images, as crossing good individuals better explores solutions that may be quasi optimal. Running times are not very affected by crossover probability (Figure 4(b)), even though $p_c=0.9$ is consistently faster than $p_c=0.8$.

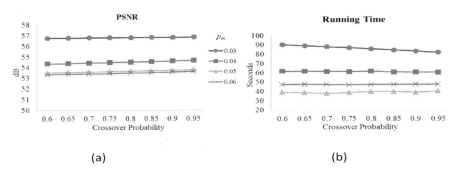

Fig. 4. (a) The watermarked image quality (measured in dB) vs the crossover probability and (b) the average running time for one image vs the crossover probability

4.4   Mutation Probability

Figure 5 reports the quality and running times of the watermarked images when varying the mutation probability used by the GA, and by setting the population size to 100, stable generations to 10 and p_c from 0.6 to 0.9 (in steps of 0.1). As pointed out above for mutation probabilities lower than 0.03, the algorithm does not always find a solution. Both *PSNR* and running times decrease with larger mutation probabilities, so the algorithm is faster but with lower quality. This is due to the fact that once a solution is found, it is likely that it remains the best for the requested stable generations, as new offsprings will undergo mutation at a higher rate and explore far from optimal solutions. There is no significant difference in terms of PSNR, even though $p_c = 0.8$ is faster than the other settings for increasing values of p_m; nonetheless a value of p_m larger than 0.04 worsen the achievable results.

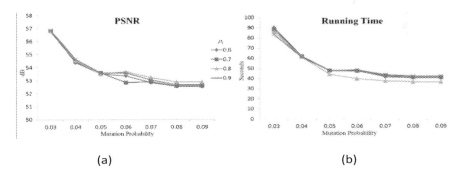

Fig. 5. (a) Quality of the watermarked images (in terms of *PSNR*) vs the probability of mutation. (b) Running time (for a single image) of the insertion algorithm vs the probability of mutation.

4.5   Sensitivity to Modifications

Given that the objective of fragile image watermarking is the detection of unauthorized pixel modifications, a set of tests aimed at verifying the ability of the algorithm to detect modifications to a single pixel in an image block were performed. In particular, we wanted to verify if the images with increased quality (i.e. *PSNR*) obtained from a fine tuning of the GA parameters, were still bearing a watermark able to detect the modification of a single pixel by a single gray level. Figure 6 reports the percentage of image blocks from which an alteration of a single pixel (by ±1 gray level, Figure 6(a), and ±2 gray levels, Figure 6(b)) was detected by the verification algorithm.

As it can be seen the sensitivity does not significantly increase for increasing populations for small number of stable generations, while for larger values of stable generations the sensitivity of the detection algorithm raises of 6-8% for ±1 and 3% for ±2. We can conclude that a larger number of stable generations not only results in higher quality watermarked images, but also increases the probability of detecting alterations.

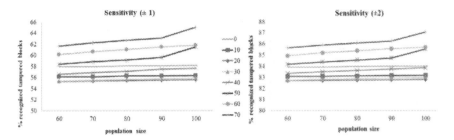

Fig. 6. The percentage of recognized tampered blocks (changing the gray level by ±1 (a) and by ±2 (b)) vs the size of the population, varying the number of generations required for a stable fitness value, $p_c = 0.8$, $p_m = 0.05$

5   Discussion and Conclusions

The GA-based optimization techniques have been efficiently applied in many different watermarking scenarios. A base line watermarking system, due to its modular nature, can be easily extended to incorporate a GA.

However, the use of a GA rises several important concerns such as the dimensionality of the parameters to be adjusted in order to achieve an optimum tradeoff between robustness and quality, the time overhead, and the statistic assumption (i.e., Gaussian) of the host signal and noise source. Moreover, for a non-expert user to optimally set GA parameters is even more difficult.

In this paper, by fine tuning the parameters of the GA, we significantly improved (> 5dB) the performances of a watermarking system without affecting the sensitivity of the embedded watermark, but at the expense of larger computation times. It should be pointed out that from a pure statistical point of view, all the reported results are statistically significant ($p<0.0001$), due to the large number of images used for testing, but from an application point of view, only changes of PSNR greater than 1dB can be considered a real improvement.

From these results, we can provide the user with an easy tool to automatically select the best combination of GA parameters that provides the requested performances.

As shown in the reported graphs, there seems to be a quasi-linear correlation between *PSNR,* on one side, and population size and stable generations on the other
side, so we used a linear regression algorithm to come up with the following formula:

$$PSNR = 1.7906*p_c-87.0244*p_m+0.0265*popsize+0.0757*stableGen+53.8123 \qquad (3)$$

A similar expression can be derived for the expected running time for watermarking an image:

$$time = 96.3561*p_c-466.5239*p_m+1.8742*popsize+5.1698*stableGen-223.1268 \qquad (4)$$

As we obtained slightly better quality results by setting $p_c= 0.9$ and $p_m= 0.03$, from
(3) and (4) one can derive the minimum values of population size and stable generations that provide a given *PSNR* value in the lowest running times.

Figure 7 shows a knob that is presented in the user interface of the application: it
allows the user to set the desired quality of the resulting watermarked image. Depending on this setting, the system automatically selects the best combination of GA parameters, according to the solution of expressions (3) and (4), as outlined above, that
results in the fastest running times.

For instance, if the user sets the knob to 57 dB, the system automatically chooses
p_m=0.03, p_c=0.9, a population size of 70 and number of stable generations = 30, for a
lowest running time of 135.88 seconds. It should be pointed out that the running time
is related to a specific hardware configuration, and it might be lower or greater on the
user's computer. Here it is just used to find the best values of population size and
stable generations and not to predict the running time.

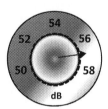

Fig. 7. The knob for selecting the desired quality in dB

As a final consideration, we point out that the overall best performance of our
algorithm is 59.78 dB (p_c=0.9, p_m=0.03, popsize=100, stable generations=50) when
inserting 8 bits-per-block, compared to a best performance among the papers cited in
Section 2 of 57.66 dB, when inserting only 4 bits-per-block. Moreover, it should be
noted that in many cases the comparison with other algorithms is not easy due to the
different payloads and insertion methods used, so we referred to the data reported in
the papers. Anyway, the difference in quality at this level is very significant according
to a statistical t-test ($p<0.001$).

The aim of this study was not only that of finding the GA parameters that deliver
the best performances, but also to analyze how they influence the GA performance in
optimization problems such the one considered here: in our system, we used a standard GA (SteadyStateGA from GALib) that already implements a number of well-
known techniques to control how the population evolves. From our experiments, we

found that changing the common GA parameters, such as mutation and crossover probabilities or population size, does not influence the performances as much as changing the number of stable generations. We think that this is mainly due to the fact that the optimization problem has a large number of solutions, so finding a viable one is pretty simple, but letting the GA running for more generations helps improving the quality of the solution returned. This should be taken into consideration when using GAs in other application domains in which there are a lot of possible solutions.

As future work, we are planning to investigate the implications of automatically choose different GA parameter settings for different sub-images, by predicting the effort necessary to store the watermark bits in each of them, instead of using the same configuration on every sub-image.

References

1. Aslantas, V., Ozer, S., Ozturk, S.: Improving the performance of DCT-based fragile watermarking using intelligent optimization algorithms. Optics Communications **282**(14), 2806–2817 (2009)
2. Barreto, P.S.L.M., Kim, H.Y., Rijmen, V.: Toward secure publickey blockwise fragile authentication watermarking. In: IEE Proceedings - Vision, Image and Signal Processing 2002, vol. 148(2), pp. 57–62 (2002)
3. Botta, M., Cavagnino, D., Pomponiu, V.: KL-F: Karhunen-Loève Based Fragile Watermarking. In: 5th International Conference on Network and System Security NSS 2011, pp. 65–72 (2011)
4. Botta, M., Cavagnino, D., Pomponiu, V.: Fragile watermarking using Karhunen-Loève transform: the KLT-F approach. Accepted for publication in Soft Computing, Springer (2014)
5. Cox, I.J., Miller, M.L., Bloom, J.A., Fridrich, J., Kalker, T.: Digital Watermarking and Steganography, 2nd edn. Morgan Kaufmann Publishers Inc., San Francisco, CA, USA (2008)
6. Díaz, D.S., Romay, M.G.: Introducing a watermarking with a multi-objective genetic algorithm. In: Proceedings of the 2005 conference on Genetic and evolutionary computation (GECCO), pp. 2219–2220 (2005)
7. Gonzalez, R.C., Wintz, P.: Digital Image Processing, 2nd ed. Addison-Wesley Publishing Company (1987)
8. Huang, H.-C., Chu, C.-M., Pan, J.-S.: The optimized copyright protection system with genetic watermarking. Soft Computing **13**(4), 333–343 (2009)
9. Lee, S.-K., Ho, Y.-S.: Fragile watermarking scheme using a simple genetic algorithm. In: International Conference on Consumer Electronics, pp. 190–191 (2002)
10. Li, L.-J., Wang, G., Fei-Fei, L.: OPTIMOL: automatic Object Picture collecTion via Incremental MOdel Learning. In: IEEE Conference on Computer Vision and Pattern Recognition (CVPR), pp. 1–8 (2007)
11. Lu, Yinghua, Han, Jialing, Kong, Jun, Yang, Yulong, Hou, Gang: A Novel Color Image Watermarking Method Based on Genetic Algorithm and Hybrid Neural Networks. In: Greco, Salvatore, Hata, Yutaka, Hirano, Shoji, Inuiguchi, Masahiro, Miyamoto, Sadaaki, Nguyen, Hung Son, Słowiński, Roman (eds.) RSCTC 2006. LNCS (LNAI), vol. 4259, pp. 806–814. Springer, Heidelberg (2006)
12. Shieh, C.-S., Huang, H.-C., Wang, F.-H., Pan, J.-S.: Genetic watermarking based on transform-domain techniques. Pattern Recognition **37**(3), 555–565 (2004)

13. Shih, F.Y., Wu, Y.-T.: Robust watermarking and compression for medical images based on genetic algorithms. Information Sciences **175**(3), 200–216 (2005)
14. Shih, F.Y., Wu, Y.-T.: Enhancement of image watermark retrieval based on genetic algorithms. Journal of Visual Communication and Image Representation **16**(2), 115–133 (2005)
15. Usman, I., Khan, A., Chamlawi, R., Majid, A.: Image Authenticity and Perceptual Optimization via Genetic Algorithms and a Dependence Neighborhood. International Journal of Applied Mathematics and Computer Sciences **4**(1), 37–42 (2007)
16. Wang, R.-Z., Lin, C.-F., Lin, J.-C.: Image hiding by optimal LSB substitution and genetic algorithm. Pattern Recognition **34**(3), 671–683 (2001)
17. Wu, Ming-Ni, Lin, Min-Hui, Chang, Chin-Chen: A LSB Substitution Oriented Image Hiding Strategy Using Genetic Algorithms. In: Chi, Chi-Hung, Lam, Kwok-Yan (eds.) AWCC 2004. LNCS, vol. 3309, pp. 219–229. Springer, Heidelberg (2004)

Classification of Potential Multiple Sclerosis Lesions Through Automatic Knowledge Extraction by Means of Differential Evolution

Ivanoe De Falco[✉]

ICAR-CNR, Via P. Castellino 111, 80131 Naples, Italy
ivanoe.defalco@na.icar.cnr.it

Abstract. In this paper a classifier, designed by taking into account the user–friendliness issue, is described and is used to tackle the problem of classification of potential lesions in Multiple Sclerosis. This tool is based on the idea of making use of Differential Evolution (DE) to extract explicit knowledge from a database under the form of a set of IF–THEN rules, can use this set of rules to carry out the classification task, and can also provide clinicians with this knowledge, thus explaining the motivation for each of the proposed diagnoses. Each DE individual codes for a set of rules. The tool is compared over a database of Multiple Sclerosis potential lesions against a set of nine classification tools widely used in literature. Furthermore, the usefulness and the meaningfulness of the extracted knowledge have been assessed by comparing it against that provided by Multiple Sclerosis experts. No great differences have turned out to exist between these two forms of knowledge.

Keywords: Pattern Recognition · Classification · Differential Evolution · Automatic Rule Extraction · Multiple Sclerosis Diagnosis

1 Introduction

Multiple Sclerosis (MS) is an autoimmune disease characterized by the fact that the immune system acts harmfully on the Central Nervous System [2], causing nerve demyelination. Normally the larger part of MS lesions are small, yet they can sometimes have a diameter of some centimeters. The only way to check the development of this disease consists in clinical examination substantiated by laboratory investigations. Within these latter, magnetic resonance imaging (MRI) is very commonly used to visualize lesions [9].

MRI is currently considered as the most reliable paraclinical test with reference to the issues of diagnosis of the MS disease, evaluation of its evolution, and medical care of its effects. As a matter of fact, the use of MR images as a marker for MS requires the advice of experts and the exploitation of all their knowledge to correctly identify MS lesions.

In general, the process of finding out actual lesions for Multiple Sclerosis can be seen as a pipelining procedure composed by three tasks: the *segmentation* of

© Springer-Verlag Berlin Heidelberg 2014
A.I. Esparcia-Alcázar et al. (Eds.): EvoApplications 2014, LNCS 8602, pp. 538–549, 2014.
DOI: 10.1007/978-3-662-45523-4_44

the MRI images into groups of homogeneous pixels/voxels representing tissues, the *labeling* of those tissues, and finally the actual *classification* step, meaning with this the assignment of each potential lesion detected to one of the possible classes, i.e. either actual lesion or non–lesion.

Yet, this process is very laborious because of the high number of MR images that must be examined and of the variability in the number of MS lesions per image, as well as in their size and spatial distribution. Furthermore, the result of the analysis of an MRI image is a set of potential lesions, some of which are actually lesions whereas others are not. Therefore, it is very important to correctly distinguish among them. This is a typical classification task, that has been up to now carried out prominently by human experts only.

In recent years Clinical Decision Support Systems (CDSSs) are becoming more and more popular in the medical domain, aiming at supporting clinicians in their whole clinical process from diagnosis and investigation to treatment and long-term care. CDSSs have been defined as 'active knowledge systems which use two or more items of patient data to generate case-specific advice' [14].

Among the many tasks that should be dealt with by clinicians, classification [7] is one of the most important and delicate, and is closely related to diagnosis. To point out its significance suffice it to say that a wrong classification leads either to false positive cases, so causing unnecessary worries and medical cares, or, even worse, to false negative diagnoses, which may cause serious illnesses to patients, and even their premature death. So it is not surprising that many classification tools have recently started to be used in the medical domain.

A desirable feature for a classifier is that it should be user–friendly as concerns both its use and the output information it can provide. Of course, this feature becomes even more important when the medical diagnostic process is considered: even if a method can correctly assign patients to diagnoses, it should not be a kind of a black–box or an oracle. Rather, it should provide clinicians with useful information on the reasons why any patient is categorized in the given way.

In this paper a tool, designed by carefully taking the above user–friendliness issue into account, is described and is used to tackle the problem of classification in Multiple Sclerosis. This system is based on Differential Evolution (DE) [11].

It is important to say here that we wish to make reference to the third above mentioned step only, i.e. the classification of potential lesions.

Starting from DE, a classifying tool is designed that can extract explicit knowledge from a database under the form of a set of IF–THEN rules, can use this set of rules to carry out classification, can output the class assigned to each instance, and can also provide clinicians with this knowledge, thus explaining the motivation for each of the proposed diagnoses. Of course, this extracted knowledge should never be seen as a substitute of doctor's experience, rather both as a confirmation of his/her knowledge and as a set of possible suggestions to complement doctor's knowledge, to be clinically validated.

The tool described here is based on *DE* and performs *R*ule *E*xtraction, so it is referenced within this paper as *DEREx*. The originality of the approach presented here lies in the fact that up to now DE has been used in classification tasks in combination with other tools as neural networks e.g. [10], bayes–based methods [13], fuzzy logic tools [1], nearest neighbor [12], and so on, but just seldom has it been applied on its own [8]. More importantly, in all cases in which DE has been used on its own, it has never been assigned the task of extracting by itself classification rules from databases, as it can be noted in [3], where a wide list of applications of DE is reported. Rather, DE is used for other tasks, such as optimizing parameters, optimizing membership functions, etc.

DEREx is used here for multiple sclerosis because recent experiments over other medical databases [4] showed its superiority over other classifiers.

A paramount issue when automatically extracting knowledge from databases is the investigation about whether or not the set of rules found is useful and meaningful for the clinicians. In fact, the extracted knowledge could allow achieving very good classification accuracy, yet it could be very far from the one a doctor would ever use, and it could even be just a kind of a tricky combination of values for the database attributes, without any actual medical meaning. This issue should always be addressed when using one of these rule–extracting tools.

In Section 2 our rule extractor DEREx is shortly described. Section 3 reports on the experimental results on a real Multiple Sclerosis database. The resulting explicit rules are given in Section 4. In Section 5 the extracted knowledge is compared with that provided by Multiple Sclerosis experts. Finally, in Section 6 conclusions are given and future works are outlined.

2   The Rule Extractor: DEREx

To face this problem of supervised classification, we have taken advantage of our DEREx tool [4] to carry out the automatic extraction of a set of explicit IF-THEN rules from the database. This tool relies on Differential Evolution.

Due to lack of space, describing DEREx with sufficient details is here impossible, and reference to [4] should be made. Just to give some necessary information, each solution in the DE population codes for a set of IF–THEN rules, each of which contains AND–connected literals on the database variables. For each class more than one rule can be contained in the individual solution, and these rules can be seen as logically connected in OR. A very important parameter is the maximum number of rules that can be contained in a set, denoted as NR.

During evolution, the fitness of each individual is the percentage of the cases in the training set that are correctly classified by using the set of rules encoded in that individual. Indeterminate items, i.e. the items assignable to either no class or to more than one through the set of rules encoded by the individual being evaluated, are treated as incorrectly classified during training, whereas they are assigned to exactly one class during testing by a recovery mechanism [4].

In the top pane of Fig. 1 the uppermost part says that each DE individual is in this case a vector, containing real values, representing a set of NR classification rules written in sequence in the individual.

The middle part of the top pane shows that each rule is represented by a set of fields. Namely, each rule consists in a *Rule_Active* field, followed by a number of *NV Literal_Representation* groups (where *NV* is the number of variables in the database), and finally by a *Class* field. In the rule, database variables are listed sequentially, meaning that the generic *i*-th *Literal_Representation* deals with the *i*-th variable of the database. *Rule_Active* tells whether or not the rule should be considered during classification. This is decided by comparing the real value contained in this field against a real value Rule Threshold (RT), which is a parameter for our tool: if the former value is higher, then this rule is seen as active in the current individual and should be used in the classification process.

Each *Literal_Representation* field encodes a zero-th order literal, i.e. a literal in which only one variable is contained and is compared with one or two real values by means of relation operators. As shown in the bottom part of the top pane, on its turn this field consists of four fields, each containing a real value, as it is detailed in the following paragraphs.

The first field is the *Literal_Active* field. Similarly to the *Rule_Active* field, it determines whether or not the literal is present in the rule. Also here, a real-valued parameter Literal Threshold (LT) is defined, and the generic literal under account is active if and only if the value in this field is higher than LT.

The second field is called *Literal_Type*. It encodes the relation operator that compares the variable and the constant value(s). We have decided to take the following seven different operators into account: $<, \leq, =, \geq, >, IN, OUT$. The first five operators need one constant value, i.e. C1, whereas the latter two need two constant values C1 and C2. The operator IN checks if the value of the variable contained in the literal is within the numerical range expressed by C1 and C2 in their order of appearance in the individual. The operator OUT, instead, checks if the value taken on by the variable in the literal is outside the range [C1 - C2], meaning that either it is lower than C1 or it is greater than C2.

The third and the fourth fields of the *Literal_Representation* field hold, respectively, the real values for the constants C1 and C2. C1 will be used for each active literal, while C2 only if the *Literal_Type* field contains IN or OUT.

Finally, the *Class* field contains the value representing the class to which all the database instances that satisfy the considered rule are assigned.

The bottom pane of Fig. 1, instead, shows an example for a database with two variables var_1 and var_2, in which we have set $NR = 3$, $RT = 0.50$, and $LT = 0.50$. Starting from the values contained in each field, it can be realized that rules 1 and 3 are active, whereas rule 2 is not. In rule 1, both literals are active, whereas in rule 3 just the literal about var_2 is. Therefore, the DE individual in the figure encodes the following set of rules:

$$IF \ (var_1 \leq 6.14) \ AND \ (var_2 \geq 3.41) \ THEN \ class=2$$

$$IF \ (var_2 \leq 3.12) \ THEN \ class=1$$

3   Experiments

DEREX has been evaluated on a dataset, opportunely anonymized, collected at the Department of Bio-Morphological and Functional Sciences of the University

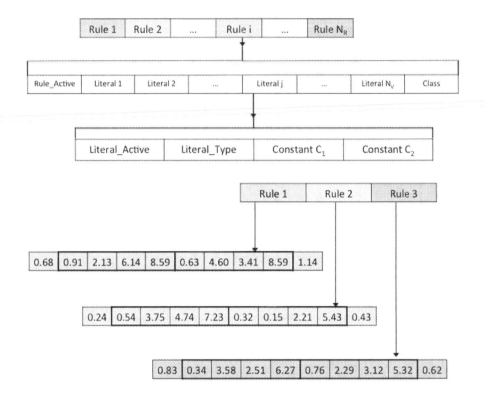

Fig. 1. Top: general structure of individuals in DEREx. Bottom: an example of an individual and its decoding into a set of IF–THEN rules.

Table 1. The sclerosis database

variable	unit range	description
surrounding white matter	0.32 - 1.00	Amount of White Matter enclosing a lesion
compactness	0.31 - 1.98	Degree of compactness of a lesion. For a given shape, compactness is high either if the volume is large or if the enclosing surface is small, i.e. the object is strongly compact
tissue contrast	0.56 - 1.00	Minimum color contrast to detect a WML in the multiparametric space
volume	3 - 10,522	Lesion volume in terms of the number of voxels
sphericity	0.01 - 1.23	Degree of sphericity of a lesion. The more elongated the lesion is and the more it deviates from a sphere, the lower sphericity will be

of Naples Federico II. In particular, starting from MR brain images of 120 patients with clinically definite MS, a multiparametric segmentation procedure has been preliminarily applied to the whole data set in order to identify normal brain tissues or clusters of potentially abnormal white matter voxels, labeled as White Matter Potential Lesions (WMPLs). For each WMPL, the features described in Table 1 represent the actual input data for the DSS.

The resulting database contains 2844 items, 1905 of which represent actual lesions (class 2) and 939 showing no actual lesions (class 1).

As concerns DEREx, a *DE/rand–to–best/1/bin* mutation strategy has been used, and the values for the parameters have been set as follows: population size $N_{Pop} = 30$, number of generations $Gen = 500$, crossover ratio $CR = 0.5$, scale factor $F = 0.5$, $NR = 10$, $RT = 0.50$, and $LT = 0.50$. No preliminary tuning phase has been specifically effected over this sclerosis problem for the choice of these values, rather the same values as in [4] have been used.

In each run 10–fold cross-validation has been carried out, so that, for the generic i-th fold, the i-th 10% of the data, in their order of appearance in the database, is kept for testing, and training takes place on the remaining 90%. For the generic i-th fold the result is represented by the classification accuracy over the related testing set $\%C_{Te}^i$. Then, the result for the whole run is the average, over the 10 folds, of the 10 $\%C_{Te}^i$ values achieved, i.e. $Av_C = \langle \%C_{Te}^i \rangle$.

A total number of 25 runs, each of them being a 10–fold cross-validation, has been effected. The results have been collected in terms of average percentage of correct classification over the testing set over the 25 runs $Av_{CC} = \langle Av_C \rangle$.

As concerns the other classification techniques used in the comparison on this MS problem, reference has been made to the Waikato Environment for Knowledge Analysis (WEKA) system release 3.4 [6] that contains a large number of such techniques, divided into groups (Bayesian, based on functions, lazy, meta-techniques, tree-based, rule-based, other). From each such group at least one representative has been chosen. Due to lack of space, their names are shown in Tab. 2. Three rule–based classifiers have been considered, i.e. OneR, Part, and Ridor, since we are of course more interested in this kind of tools.

Similarly to what was done for DEREx, no preliminary parameter tuning has been carried out for all of the above techniques as well, so the parameter values used for each such method are those set as default in WEKA.

Furthermore, since also for these classification techniques results must be provided in terms of average results over 25 runs, for each of them either the starting seeds or some parameter values have been varied. Actually, RBF, AdaBoost, Part, and Ridor are based on a random starting seed so that the 25 runs for them have been carried out by varying this value. Some other techniques, instead, do not depend on any starting seed, so the 25 runs have been carried out as a function of a parameter typical of the technique: alpha for Bayes Net, globalBlend for KStar, bias for VFI, and minBucketSize for OneR. Finally, NBTree depends neither on an initial seed nor on any parameter, so only one run has been performed for it on the database.

Also for all of these tools 10–fold cross–validation has been carried out.

Table 2 shows the results, achieved by each technique on the database, expressed in terms of Av_{CC}. Namely, for each tool the average accuracy Av_{CC} over the 25 runs, the highest value of Av_C (*best_acc*), and the lowest one (*worst_acc*) are shown. Also the standard deviation *std_dev* is reported for the techniques for which multiple runs are carried out. Finally, the last row of the table reports the rank for each tool based on Av_{CC}.

Table 2. The 10-fold classification accuracy for all the classifiers

	DEREx	Bayes Net	RBF	Kstar	AdaBoost
Av_{CC}	87.49	78.07	82.20	85.60	82.35
$best\_acc$	88.54	78.09	82.24	85.90	82.35
$worst\_acc$	86.90	78.02	82.14	85.27	82.35
std_dev	0.46	0.03	0.04	0.21	0.00
$rank$	1	8	7	5	6

	NBTree	OneR	Part	Ridor	VFI
Av_{CC}	86.81	72.03	87.20	86.14	72.40
$best\_acc$	—	73.91	87.20	87.03	72.40
$worst\_acc$	—	65.30	87.20	85.44	72.40
std_dev	—	2.89	0.00	0.59	0.00
$rank$	3	10	2	4	9

DEREx turns out to be the best tool, the runner-up being Part. It is worth noting that DEREx performs better than all the other rule–based tools.

4   The Advantage of DEREx: The IF-THEN Rules

The clear advantage of DEREx consists in the fact that it provides users with explicit knowledge automatically extracted from the database under the form of IF-THEN rules. In fact, it can straightforwardly express rules to perform diagnosis. Furthermore, DEREx can also perform feature extraction, since the achieved rules may contain some of the database attributes only, which can be seen as an extremely useful support for a correct diagnosis. This has turned out to be true in [4] where seven medical databases have been faced. In this way, physicians are helped with useful information. Of course, their opinion about the correctness and the usefulness of these rules is of paramount importance for medical practice. In the following the best set of rules found for the Multiple Sclerosis problem is reported. Namely, they are those with the highest percentage of correct classification on the testing set achieved on a fold in all the executions.

IF (surrounding_white_matter < 0.81) AND (compactness IN (1.56 - 1.88)) AND (volume IN (7,224 - 10,395)) THEN lesion

IF (surrounding_white_matter > 0.40) AND (compactness ≥ 0.36) AND (tissue_contrast > 0.63) THEN lesion

IF (compactness IN (0.60 - 1.62)) AND (tissue_contrast > 0.65) AND (volume > 8,498) THEN no_lesion

IF (surrounding_white_matter ≥ 0.68) AND (compactness OUT (0.88 - 1.85)) AND (volume ≤ 4,230) AND (sphericity ≥ 0.02) THEN lesion

IF (surrounding_white_matter IN (0.41 - 0.57)) AND (tissue_contrast ≤ 0.58) AND (volume > 1,817) AND (sphericity IN (0.15 - 0.19)) THEN lesion

IF (compactness OUT (1.39 - 1.47)) THEN no_lesion

As it can be seen, the best individual has six active rules, four of which classify for *lesion* and two for *no_lesion*. Thus, even if the OR connector is not

Table 3. Statistics of the best set of rules

	Correct Classification Rate	Sensitivity	Specificity
Training Set	89.11%	89.83%	87.78%
Testing Set	93.43%	90.52%	98.80%

Table 4. Linguistic variables and terms

variable	Terms
surrounding white matter	bit, partially, almost completely, completely
compactness	weak, strong
tissue contrast	little, great
volume	small, medium, large
sphericity	low, moderate, high
tissue structure	normal, abnormal

explicitly present in DEREx, the set of rules performs implicitly an OR over each class by using as many rules as needed to achieve good classification accuracy.

This set of rules has been obtained for fold 7, and its values of correct classification rate, sensitivity, and specificity over both the training set and the testing set are reported in Tab. 3.

5 Comparison Between Extracted Knowledge and Experts' Knowledge

Once we have seen that DEREx is able to extract knowledge that allows classifying with a good accuracy, the question arises whether or not this automatically extracted knowledge is useful, and, even more important, if it is meaningful for experts. To investigate this, we need to compare the knowledge provided by the experts against that provided by DEREx.

The medical knowledge needed to classify WMPLs has been defined in cooperation with a team of physicians, starting from the sclerosis features contained in the faced database, and can be stated, in natural language, as follows. *The tissue composing a WMPL is abnormal if the lesion is somewhat surrounded by WM, characterized by a strong compactness and greatly contrasted in the multiparametric space. The sphericity is moderate or high in small lesions, whereas, as their volume increases, the sphericity starts decreasing progressively. Finally, as volume increases and sphericity starts lessening, a lesion can be surrounded by gradually decreasing WM and its compactness still remains high.*

As it can be seen, the experts' knowledge is based on a fuzzy view, given the use of words such as *somewhat, small, volume increases, starts decreasing, gradually decreasing,* and so on. Furthermore, as it is often the case in the medical domain, this knowledge is based on positive evidence only, i.e. it contains only sentences representing the presence of an actual lesion.

In accordance with this knowledge, the linguistic variables and the fuzzy values shown in Table 4 have been identified.

Table 5. IF–THEN form of experts' knowledge

1) IF [Sphericity is (Moderate OR High)] AND [Compactness is Strong]AND [Volume is Small] AND [TissueContrast is Great] AND [SurroundingWhiteMatter is Completely] THEN [TissueStructure is Abnormal]

2) IF [Sphericity is Moderate] AND [Compactness is Strong]AND [Volume is Medium] AND [TissueContrast is Great] AND [SurroundingWhiteMatter is (AlmostCompletely ORCompletely)] THEN [TissueStructure is Abnormal]

3) IF [Compactness is Strong]AND [Volume is Large] AND [TissueContrast is Great] AND [SurroundingWhiteMatter is (Partially OR AlmostCompletely OR Completely)] THEN [TissueStructure is Abnormal]

4) ELSE [TissueStructure is Normal]

Table 6. Values for the shapes of the trapezoids

Variables	Terms	α_1	α_2	α_3	α_4
Surrounding	Bit	0.32	0.32	0.33	0.38
White	Partially	0.33	0.38	0.40	0.41
Matter	Almost Completely	0.40	0.41	0.46	0.95
	Completely	0.46	0.95	1.00	1.00
Compactness	Weak	0.31	0.31	0.36	0.74
	Strong	0.36	0.74	1.98	1.98
Tissue	Little	0.56	0.56	0.61	0.92
	Great	0.61	0.92	1.00	1.00
Volume	Small	3	3	3,177	3,529
	Medium	3,177	3,529	7,051	7,697
	Large	7,051	7,697	10,522	10,522
Sphericity	Low	0.01	0.01	0.03	0.10
	Moderate	0.03	0.10	1.02	1.03
	High	1.02	1.03	1.23	1.23

These linguistic variables and values have been used to write the three if-then rules aimed at identifying the positive cases, i.e. when a potential lesion is an actual one. Table 5 shows those rules and the default ELSE one.

It is to be noted that the knowledge provided by the experts is in a fuzzy form, whereas that extracted by DEREx contains crisp rules. To effectively compare these two sets of rules, that proposed by DEREx should be reformulated into a fuzzy form. So, it is important to transform the crisp values contained into suitable fuzzy values. To this aim, reference can be made to [5], where a DE tool was used to tune the parameters of a fuzzy system working on this database. Each fuzzy value was there represented as a trapezoid, so four real values were needed to identify the shape of each trapezoid. Those values represent the x–values for the bottom–left, top–left, top–right, and bottom–right vertices of the trapezoid, the y–values being 0 for the bottom vertices and 1 for the top ones. Table 6 shows the results of the tuning of the fuzzy values and the correspondence between the crisp values and the fuzzy ones for each database variable.

By making use of those values, the set of crisp rules found by DEREX and shown in the previous subsection can now be rewritten as shown in Tab. 7.

The correspondence between the two kinds of knowledge can be visually understood by looking at Fig. 2. The figure contains both the sets of fuzzy rules for the presence of lesions only, namely the top pane shows the knowledge

Table 7. Fuzzy form of DEREX knowledge

1) IF (white matter IS (bit surrounded OR partially surrounded OR almost completely surrounded)) AND (compactness IS strong) AND (volume IS large) THEN lesion

2) IF (white matter IS (almost completely surrounded OR completely surrounded)) AND (compactness IS strong) AND (contrast IS great) THEN lesion

3) IF (white matter IS completely) AND (compactness IS weak) AND (volume IS small) AND (sphericity IS (moderate OR high)) THEN lesion

4) IF (white matter IS almost completely) AND (contrast IS little) AND (volume IS (medium OR large)) AND (sphericity IS moderate) THEN lesion

---

1.   IF **(white matter IS (bit surrounded OR partially surrounded OR almost completely surrounded))** AND **(compactness IS strong)** AND **(volume IS large)** THEN lesion

2.   IF **(white matter IS (almost completely surrounded OR completely surrounded))** AND **(compactness IS strong)** AND **(contrast IS great)** THEN lesion

3.   IF (white matter IS completely) AND (compactness IS weak) AND **(volume IS small)** AND **(sphericity IS (moderate OR high))** THEN lesion

4.   IF (white matter IS almost completely) AND (contrast IS little) AND **(volume IS (medium OR large))** AND **(sphericity IS moderate)** THEN lesion

---

*The tissue composing a WMPL is abnormal if the lesion is **somewhat surrounded by white matter**, characterized by a **strong compactness** and **greatly contrasted** in the multiparametric space.*

*The **sphericity is moderate or high** in **small lesions**, whereas, as their **volume** increases, the **sphericity starts decreasing** progressively.*

*Finally, as **volume increases** and sphericity starts lessening, a lesion can be surrounded by **gradually decreasing white matter** and its **compactness still remains high.***

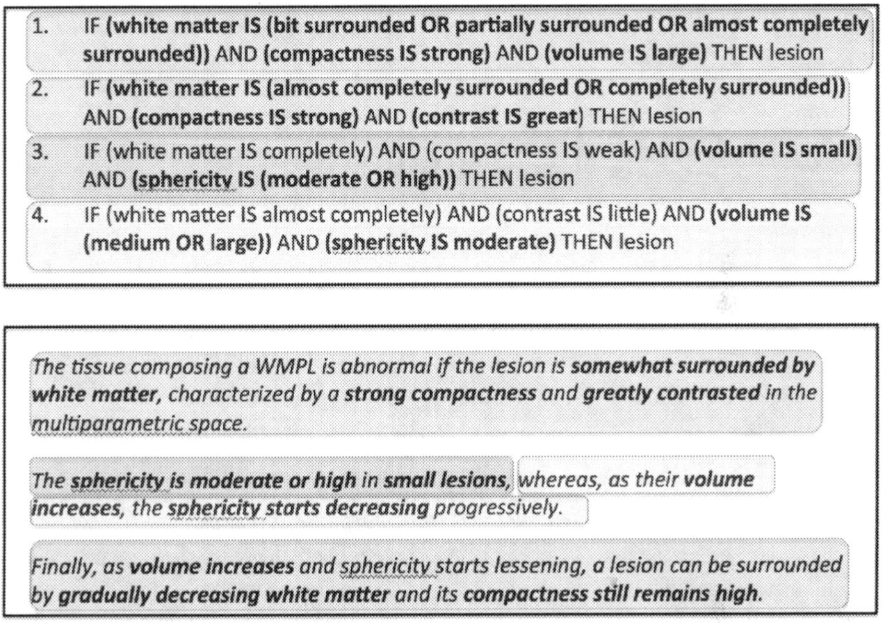

Fig. 2. Extracted knowledge (top pane) and experts' knowledge (bottom pane), and their correspondence

extracted, whereas the bottom one reports the experts' knowledge. In the figure similar concepts are represented by a same color in both sets.

As it can be noted, the rule 1 of DEREx almost completely corresponds to the rule 3 as stated by the experts (both are represented in green color). The variables involved are the same, apart from sphericity that is accounted for by experts whereas DEREx does not mention it, and the fuzzy values taken on by the variables are the same in both cases. Rule 2 found by our system corresponds to rule 1 (blue color represents them both). In this case the correspondence is perfect: the variables involved are the same in both rules, and so are the fuzzy values they take on. Rule 3 of DEREx corresponds to the first part of experts' rule 2 (red color represents them), and the two common variables take on exactly the same values in both rules, whereas DEREx uses two more variables. Finally, rule 4 of DEREx corresponds to the second part of rule 2 (they both are represented in yellow): also in this case DEREx uses two more variables.

In summary, from the analysis of the two kinds of knowledge it appears evident that the knowledge automatically extracted by DEREx is extremely similar to that provided by experts, hence proving that the proposed system is capable of extracting knowledge that is useful and meaningful.

The slight differences in the two sets of rules can be seen as further suggestions for the experts. For example, rule 1 of DEREx, very similar to the third rule by the experts, might suggest the doctors the question whether, in that general frame proposed by their rule, a decrease in sphericity is really important. Vice versa, rule 3 of DEREx might suggest doctors to take into account white matter and compactness too, when volume is small and sphericity is moderate or high.

6   Conclusions and Future Work

In this paper, an approach based on Differential Evolution for the automatic classification of potential lesions in a Multiple Sclerosis database has been followed. Namely, a tool called DEREx has been used, which automatically extracts explicit knowledge from the database under the form of IF–THEN rules containing AND–connected literals on the database variables.

Firstly, DEREx has been run and the most effective set of rules in terms of highest classification accuracy in a ten–fold cross–validation has been found. Secondly, the tool has been compared over the same database against a set of nine classification tools widely used in literature.

The results have proven the viability and the effectiveness of the proposed approach, since this turns out to provide the highest classification accuracy.

The advantage of DEREx consists in providing users with explicit knowledge automatically extracted from the database, since it can straightforwardly express IF-THEN rules to perform diagnosis, differently from many of its competitors.

Attention has been paid to the usefulness of the extracted knowledge, by comparing it against that provided by Multiple Sclerosis experts. Results have shown that the two different kinds of knowledge are actually quite similar, thus proving the quality of the approach followed, at least for this problem.

Future work will involve investigation about the influence of the parameters NR, RT, and LT on solution quality.

Another issue is that DEREx is based on the basic version of DE. Yet, more recently, several enhanced DE versions have appeared that aim at softening the main problem DE suffers from, i.e. that of a limited amount of search moves. So, we aim to use some new versions to further improve DEREx performance.

Moreover, closer cooperation with physicians will be set. This will involve receiving other real databases from them, also with reference to different diseases.

Finally, since physicians make often reference to fuzzy concepts as small, high, etc., the tool will be improved to automatically extract fuzzy rules too.

References

1. Aliev, R.A., Pedrycz, W., Guirimov, B.G., Aliev, R.R., Ilhan, U., Babagil, M., Mammadli, S.: Type-2 fuzzy neural networks with fuzzy clustering and differential evolution optimization. Information Sciences **181**(9), 1591–1608 (2011)

2. Bobholz, J.A., Gremley, S.: Multiple sclerosis and other demyelinating disorders. In: Schoenberg, M.R., Scott, J.G. (eds.) The Little Black Book of Neuropsychology: A Syndrome-Based Approach, pp. 647–662. Springer (2011)

3. Das, S., Suganthan, P.N.: Differential evolution: A survey of the state-of-the-art. IEEE Transactions on Evolutionary Computation **15**(1), 4–31 (2011)

4. De Falco, I.: Differential evolution for automatic rule extraction from medical databases. Applied Soft Computing **13**(2), 1265–1283 (2013)

5. Esposito, M., De Falco, I., De Pietro, G.: An evolutionary-fuzzy dss for assessing health status in multiple sclerosis disease. International Journal of Medical Informatics **80**(12), e245–e254 (2011)

6. Hall, M., Frank, E., Holmes, G., Pfahringer, B., Reutemann, P., Witten, I.H.: The weka data mining software: An update. SIGKDD Explorations **11**(1), 10–18 (2009)

7. Han, J., Kamber, M.: Data mining: concept and techniques. Morgan Kaufmann (2001)

8. Maulik, U., Saha, I.: Automatic fuzzy clustering using modified differential evolution for image classification. IEEE Transactions on Geoscience and Remote Sensing **48**(9), 3503–3510 (2010)

9. Miller, D., Grossman, R., Reingold, S., McFarland, H.F.: The role of magnetic resonance techniques in understanding and managing multiple sclerosis. Brain **121** 3–24 (1998)

10. Özbakir, L., Baykasoğlu, A., Kulluka, S.: A soft computing-based approach for integrated training and rule extraction from artificial neural networks: Difaconn-miner. Applied Soft Computing **10**(1), 304–317 (2010)

11. Price, K., Storn, R.: Differential evolution: Numerical optimization made easy. Dr. Dobb's Journal, 18–24 (1997)

12. Triguero, I., García, S., Herrera, F.: Differential evolution for optimizing the positioning of prototypes in nearest neighbor classification. Pattern Recognition **44**, 901–916 (2011)

13. Wu, J., Cai, Z.: Attribute weighting via differential evolution algorithm for attribute weighted naive bayes (wnb). Journal of Computational Information Systems **7**(5), 1672–1679 (2011)

14. Wyatt, J.C., Spiegelhalter, D.J.: Field trials of medical decision-aids: potential problems and solutions. In: Proceedings of the Annual Symposium on Computer Application in Medical Care, pp. 3–7 (1991)

EvoINDUSTRY

Reducing the Number of Simulations in Operation Strategy Optimization for Hybrid Electric Vehicles

Christopher Bacher[1]([✉]), Thorsten Krenek[2], and Günther R. Raidl[1]

[1] Institute of Computer Graphics and Algorithms,
Vienna University of Technology, Vienna, Austria
{bacher,raidl}@ads.tuwien.ac.at
[2] Institute for Powertrains and Automotive Technology,
Vienna University of Technology, Vienna, Austria
thorsten.krenek@ifa.tuwien.ac.at

Abstract. The fuel consumption of a simulation model of a real Hybrid Electric Vehicle is optimized on a standardized driving cycle using metaheuristics (PSO, ES, GA). Search space discretization and metamodels are considered for reducing the number of required, time-expensive simulations. Two hybrid metaheuristics for combining the discussed methods are presented. In experiments it is shown that the use of hybrid metaheuristics with discretization and metamodels can lower the number of required simulations without significant loss in solution quality.

Keywords: Hybrid Electric Vehicles · Hybrid metaheuristics · Search space discretization · Metamodels

1 Introduction

For the automotive industry these days are game changing. Todays customer expectations and up-coming legal restrictions require the continuous development of vehicles with lower fuel consumptions and less emissions. Ongoing improvement of Internal Combustion Engines (ICEs) is one way to meet this challenge. But increasingly, hybridization of drives is seen as a promising alternative too — especially when the improvement of traditional drives reaches its limits.

The most popular form of hybridization today are different variants of hybrid electric powertrains built into Hybrid Electric Vehicles (HEVs). They integrate an ICE with one or more Electric Machines (EMs) and complement their fuel tank with electro-chemical energy storages (typically). The powertrain structure defines how different machines are able to interoperate; e.g., in a series hybrid the ICE and an EM generate electricity for storage while a second EM propels the vehicle, and in a parallel hybrid all machines are used for propulsion concurrently. Some HEVs, like the HEV considered in this paper, combine multiple concepts.

Operational modes specify the concrete interaction behaviour of a HEV's components. Specific driving situations constrain the allowed operational modes

© Springer-Verlag Berlin Heidelberg 2014
A.I. Esparcia-Alcázar et al. (Eds.): EvoApplications 2014, LNCS 8602, pp. 553–564, 2014.
DOI: 10.1007/978-3-662-45523-4_45

according to internal and environmental factors, like the State of Charge (SOC) of the battery, axle torques or requirements of driving dynamics. Performance and efficiency of HEVs depend strongly on the active mode chosen by the operation strategy for different driving situations. Optimizing the parameters of the operation strategy's decision criteria is therefore of utmost importance for the HEV's fuel efficiency. As specifics of HEVs and operation strategies are often vastly different, experience in manual adjustment is sparse. Therefore, automated algorithmic approaches pose promising alternatives.

In this paper we investigate how to efficiently adjust the (continuous) parameters of a new operation strategy for a "real" HEV[1] by applying metaheuristic optimization methods in combination with metamodels and simple, but effective post-processing techniques.

Our metaheuristic optimization techniques rely on the evaluation of a simulation model of the considered HEV to test different parameter configurations, i.e. candidate solutions, for the operation strategy. Parameter configurations are evaluated by simulating the HEV on a standardized driving cycle defining a required velocity for each second of the cycle. Fuel consumption and SOC of the battery are measured throughout the driving cycle and are used to compute an objective value for a candidate solution, as described in Section 7. Besides measuring these output values of the simulated HEV, the simulation is considered to be a black box function. No further information about the internal state and calculations of the simulation software is currently available to the optimization.

A major challenge for the metaheuristic optimization are the considerably long simulation times, limiting the overall number of simulations which can be performed in practice. For the model at hand the mean simulation time is about seven minutes per candidate solution.Some parameter configurations even lead to simulation times up to twenty minutes, hamstringing the optimization significantly. Further soft constraints in the context of practical application have to be considered. In our concrete case, license restrictions of the simulation software[2] constrain the maximum number of parallel simulations to only eight.

The main goal of this paper is therefore to explore ways to reduce the number of necessary simulations during optimization, while adhering to the solution quality of well known, unmodified reference algorithms. We intend to achieve this by training neural networks and ensemble methods as regression models of the simulations. We also consider how to evaluate the performance of the regression models under the aspect of their integration in the optimization process. Further we exploit a priori characteristics of the search space to limit its effective size. This is done in two ways. First by considering inter-parameter constraints in the form of inequalities and correspondingly repairing infeasible solutions. Second by exploiting the experience that the search space in similar HEV optimization problems often contain many plateaus or areas with shallow slopes. This

---

[1] Due to Non-Disclosure Aggrements we are a not allowed to disclose the actual vehicle.

[2] We use the automotive simulation package GT Suite 7.2 from Gamma Technologies, Inc. http://www.gtisoft.com

observation allows to discretize the continuous domains of the problem to finite sets, without losing significant solution quality.

In Section 2 we give an overview of related work. Section 3 describes the used metaheuristics, and Section 4 details the search constraints. Section 5 introduces the employed regression models, while Section 6 integrates the mentioned modifications into a hybrid, phased metaheuristic. In Section 7 we describe the considered HEV model, its operation strategy and the objective function in more detail and present our experimental results. Finally Section 8 concludes this paper and gives an outline of possible future work.

2   Related Work

Concerning HEV optimization, in [13] a control strategy for a parallel HEV is optimized by Sequential Quadratic Programming (SQP). Optimization is applied on a response surface fit to data from a Design of Experiments (DOE). Their results indicate that building metamodels for simulations of a driving cycle can be done in principle.

Several metaheuristics are studied for a multi-objective HEV optimization in [10]. The methods try to find pareto-optimal solutions that minimize fuel consumption and multiple emission type like CO, Hydrocarbons, and NOx. In contrast, we focus solely on minimizing the fuel consumption.

The current paper builds upon previous work in [15], where a new and effective hybrid metaheuristic — PSAGADO — for fuel consumption optimization has been presented, and the first author's master thesis [3]. The hybrid metaheuristic combines a Particle Swarm Optimization, a Genetic Algorithm, and a Downhill-Simplex to improve the overall performance of the heuristic. Here, we pick up some of the open questions regarding approximation of fitness functions by surrogate models and search space properties.

An overview of basic techniques for simulation-based optimization is given in [1]. The paper describes the use of metamodels/surrogates as replacements for the original simulation, for reducing high computation times, e.g., by using the metamodel as filter for the simulation.

In [12] a framework for combining neural networks with an Evolution Strategy (ES), with Covariance Matrix Adaption (CMA), is proposed. Their strategies are evaluated on a set of standard test functions. Two approaches are described. The first approach, called "controlled individuals", falls back to the original fitness function for a specified fraction of the population, after all individuals have been evaluated with the approximative fitness function. Depending on how the reevaluated individuals are chosen, the approximative fitness function acts as a filter. The second approach is termed "controlled generations", where every few generations the whole population is evaluated with the original fitness function. Further the authors of [12] propose a method for managing the approximative fitness functions and an online training schedule for selecting and weighting new training data, based on the covariance matrix of the ES.

3   Used Metaheuristics

Optimization of the HEV's operation strategy is carried out by population-based metaheuristics. A priori, no information is available which metaheuristic performs best on the given problem, especially with the modifications to reduce running times in place. Based on our experience from [15], the following, well-known metaheuristics have been selected and tested in different usage scenarios, as described in Section 6.

Canonical Particle Swarm Optimization.   As first metaheuristic we consider a Canonical Particle Swarm Optimization (CPSO) in the "velocity update with inertia"-form as described in [17]. Originally proposed in [14], Particle Swarm Optimization (PSO) is a population-based metaheuristic where each particle, i.e. candidate solution, possesses a position x_i and a velocity v_i in the search space. The algorithm proceeds every iteration by evaluating the objective function at positions x_i, updating the velocities according to

$$v_i := \omega v_i + \phi_1 \cdot \mathbf{rand}_{[0,1]} \cdot (x_{L_i} - x_i) + \phi_2 \cdot \mathbf{rand}_{[0,1]} \cdot (x_G - x_i) \qquad (1)$$

where the constants ϕ_1 and ϕ_2 control the influence of their respective terms on the update and $\mathbf{rand}_{[0,1]}$ returns uniform random vectors in $[0,1]$. The velocity update in (1) decreases the velocity in the particle's previous direction, and reorients it towards its local best solution x_{L_i} and global best solution x_G. The updated velocity is used to move each particle to $x_i := x_i + v_i$. We modified the standard algorithm s.t. a particle repositions itself randomly if it has not improved after l iterations.

Evolution Strategy with Active Covariance Matrix Adaption.   An ES with Active Covariance Matrix Adaption (A-CMA)[3] has been implemented, as described in [11]. In each generation the ES samples λ individuals around a mutation center x_w according to a $\mathcal{N}(0, C)$ normal distribution. After evaluating the new population, the mutation center is moved towards the averaged position of the μ best individuals. The direction of the search, stored in C, and the actual step size σ are decoupled and are updated seperately. The covariance matrix C is updated s.t. existing covariance information is reduced and augmented by information from the evolution path p_c and information about the current population Z:

$$C := (1 - c_{\text{cov}})C + c_{\text{cov}}p_c p_c^T + \beta Z \qquad (2)$$

The evolution path p_c stores weighted information about the averaged best search directions of the μ best individuals, over all generations. The population term Z modifies the original covariance matrix by rotating and stretching C towards the μ best individuals and away from the μ worst individuals of the current generation. Constants c_{cov} and β weight the update terms. The update scheme is a variant of [9], with the intent to increase the adaption speed of C, by actively penalizing bad mutation steps.

---

[3] As the algorithm description is rather complex, we recap only the intention of the algorithm. For a complete description we refer to [11].

Sampling Genetic Algorithm. Last but not least, a very simple Genetic Algorithm (GA) is implemented for sampling purposes, which are described in detail in Section 6. The GA controls a population of N individuals x_i, $i = 1, \ldots, N$. In each generation the population is evaluated and a new population is generated. The new population is formed by two mechanisms. The remaining $\lceil R \cdot N \rceil$ individuals, $0 \leq R \leq 1$, are randomly sampled from the search space to introduce variance into the population and to generate a diverse set of training data. The remaining $\lfloor (1 - R) \cdot N \rfloor$ individuals are created by recombination: By a tournament selection of size k, to select two parents x_{p_1}, x_{p_2} are selected and an offspring is derived, by treating the selected parents as corners of a hypercube from within which a point is chosen uniformly at random.

4   Employed Post-Processing Techniques

The developed optimization framework allows to integrate post-processors for modifying solutions generated by the afore-mentioned metaheuristics. Modification of solutions is used to enforce search space constraints, like parameter domains or interdependencies between parameters. Interdependencies occur, for the HEV model at hand, in the form of simple inequalities like $\max_{i \in L} b_i \leq a \leq \min_{j \in U} b_j$ bounding some parameter a by lower bound parameters L and upper bound parameters U. Violation of inequalities renders a solution infeasible for simulation. The post-processor repairs infeasible solutions by assigning parameter a of the violated inequality a feasible random value. Feasible values can be easily determined by considering the parameter's domain and the inequalities to be satisfied.

Besides constraining parameters, a post-processor is used to discretize selected dimensions of the search space. Experience shows that search spaces for HEV models contain many plateaus with solutions of similar fitness. Evaluation of multiple solutions on such a plateau is costly and should therefore be avoided. Discretization supports this, as it limits the domains of the selected parameters to a fixed number of equidistant points. Parameter values are then mapped to the closest discretization point in the parameter's domain.

Currently this mapping is performed in a Lamarckian way i.e. the discretized solution actually replaces the original one. Temporary discretization i.e. mapping only for the evaluation process and retaining the original solution for the optimization process, is also an option which might be considered in future work.

In our implementation discretization points are always equidistantly distributed and their number is adapted during the optimization process, starting with very few points and progressing to a finer resolution of the search space. Different ways to refine the number of discretization points during optimization have been considered, like adapting them according to a linear function every iteration or adapting them only two or three times during optimization, in a step-wise fashion. Discretization makes it reasonable to store all computed solutions in a database, which acts as cache for objective function values. Preliminary experiments have shown that step-wise adaption is beneficial, as the number of cache hits is higher due to the fact that the positions of the discretization points is not modified every iteration.

5   Regression Models as Approximative Fitness Functions

Another way to decrease the number of simulations is to use regression models as approximative fitness functions, as done in [12] and [1]. Information about previous solutions is integrated into regression models to either act as a filter for bad solutions or to stretch the gathered information for several generations. In Section 6 we present hybrid metaheuristics for both approaches.

The range of functions which the regression models can fit to the gathered data is extremely important, as both over- and underfitting may have a negative impact on the optimization performance. As an ideal shape of the regression function cannot be known before the optimization is finished, a heuristic approach has to be considered. Therefore different regression techniques — so called ensemble methods [16] — based on Multilayer Perceptrons (MLPs) are evaluated beforehand and the "best" model is chosen for use.

A typical error function used for regression is the Sum-of-Squares Error:

$$\text{SSE}(\varphi(.), \boldsymbol{X}) = \sum_{i=1}^{|X|} (y_i - \varphi(\boldsymbol{x_i}))^2 \tag{3}$$

The set $\boldsymbol{X}$ denotes all inputs $\{\boldsymbol{x_1}, \dots, \boldsymbol{x_{|X|}}\}$ and target values y_i over which the SSE is computed. The trained regression function $\varphi(.) : \mathbb{R}^d \to \mathbb{R}$ receives the d input parameters of the HEV model as input.

For our purpose, however, SSE is not an appropriate error function for model selection. If the described metaheuristics are considered, it can be seen that the exact objective value of a solution is not required. Rather the order of candidate solutions is important to the metaheuristics' selection criteria.

Therefore Mean Total Order Deviation is proposed as error function:

$$\text{MTOD}(\boldsymbol{X}) = \frac{1}{|\boldsymbol{X}|^2} \sum_{i=1}^{|X|} |\pi_o(\boldsymbol{x_i}) - \pi_\varphi(\boldsymbol{x_i})| \tag{4}$$

Where $\pi_o(\boldsymbol{x_i})$ denotes the rank of solution $\boldsymbol{x_i} \in \boldsymbol{X}$, when all solutions in $\boldsymbol{X}$ are ordered according to their real objective value y_i. Similar, $\pi_\varphi(\boldsymbol{x_i})$ denotes the rank of solution $\boldsymbol{x_i} \in \boldsymbol{X}$, when all solutions in $\boldsymbol{X}$ are ordered according to their predicted objective value $\varphi(\boldsymbol{x_i})$.

MTOD is designed to indicate the mean ordering shift of a solution within the evaluated solution set $\boldsymbol{X}$. Unfortunately, MTOD is inappropriate for classical MLP training methods due to lack of differentiability. Therefore we resort to Sum-of-Squares Error (SSE) for training — under the assumption that SSE is a close approximation of MTOD in many cases — and to MTOD for selection.

MLPs form the base learners for all further methods, as they are able to express a wide range of functions depending on the number of hidden neurons, i.e., neurons between the input and output layer. The considered MLP architectures consist of one or two hidden layers, with different numbers of hidden neurons. Hidden layers use sigmoid activation functions, while the output layer uses a linear activation function. The neural networks are trained with a (modified) Levenberg-Marquardt algorithm [8] provided by the used neural network library ALGLIB[4]

To improve the generalization performance of the regression models, we consider different ensemble methods for combining multiple neural networks. Bagging [4] is the first evaluated approach, which trains multiple models on sets randomly sampled from the original training set X. Bagging then averages the outputs of these models to reduce their variance and to improve generalization performance.

Second, (Stochastic) Gradient Boosting as described in [6] and [5] is adapted for using neural networks. In Gradient Boosting several regression models are used in succession. The first model $\varphi_0(.)$ is the mean over all target values y_i of X. Then different neural networks are trained successively on the errors $(y_i - \varphi_j(x_i))$ and a new candidate regression model is formed by

$$\varphi_j(x) = \varphi_{j-1}(x) + \rho\phi(x), \quad j = 1, \dots, E \tag{5}$$

where ρ weights the newly added model $\phi(.)$ and is determined by treating the SSE as a function of ρ only and setting its gradient to zero. At each step j the candidate with the lowest SSE over the training set X is chosen. The algorithm repeats these steps E-times to build the final model.

Third a partitioning approach similar to [7] is used. The training set X is clustered using the K-means++ algorithm [2] and different neural networks are trained for each cluster $C_k \subset X$. Selecting a neural network for a cluster uses a validation approach. Validation is done by splitting C_k into a training and a validation set and using the validation set for measuring the generalization performance. This is repeated several times and the model architecture with the lowest mean validation error is chosen.

Last a partial simulation and extrapolation approach is explored. The $[0, p]$-fraction of the driving cycle, with $p \in (0, 1)$, is simulated with the HEV model and its output values are recorded, i.e., the fuel consumption. The simulated parameter set x is then augmented with the recorded output values to form $x^{[0,p]}$. The collected set $X^{[0,p]}$ of all $x_i^{[0,p]}$ is then used to train neural networks for predicting the $[p, 1]$-fraction of the driving cycle. Using the additional input data is expected to improve the prediction performance at the cost of higher computation times.

6   A Two-Phase Optimization Approach

We propose an approach for integrating the different metaheuristics, the described post-processing techniques, and regression models into new hybrid metaheuristics. Thereby the optimization is split into two phases.

---

[4] For all (single) neural networks, (ALGLIB (www.alglib.net), Sergey Bochkanov) in version 3.6 is used; accessed: 2013-11-04

The first phase is responsible for aggregating the initial training data. We decided to use the GA from Section 3 for this sampling purpose, as preliminary experiments showed that it produces a more diverse and larger set of training data than the CPSO or the ES. Further we use a step-wise adaption of the number of discretization points, where the times of adjustment correspond to the phases of the optimization algorithm. At the end of this first phase, the different regression models are evaluated. Their performance is measured by averaging the Mean Total Order Deviation (MTOD) values of a 10-fold crossvalidation. The regression model with the lowest validation error is chosen to be used in the optimization. In the second phase the resolution of the search space is enhanced by increasing the number of values per dimensions. Two different approaches for regression model integration have been tested.

A generational approach, similar to the one in [12], in combination with the CPSO is implemented. Optimization uses the regression models as main objective function and switches to the simulation model every m generations. Another integration method pairs the described ES with regression models as filter, as in [1], before passing the best to the simulation model. Far higher numbers of individuals can be sampled this way and only the best κ individuals are simulated each generation.

Further the regression models are updated every τ iterations to include the newly evaluated solutions. For the model update, a regression model with the same architecture as selected at the end of the first phase is used.

7   Experimental Results and Discussion

The considered HEV model possesses an ICE and two EMs — the "generator" and the "motor". ICE and generator are situated on the same shaft, while the "motor" is coupled to the former with a planetary gear set. The HEV is able to operate in two different mode types: pure-electric (EV) and range-extended (ER), with two modes each. The first electric mode uses only the motor-EM for propulsion and is designed for low speeds. The second mode activates both EMs, disables the ICE and decouples it by opening a clutch. It is intended for higher velocities to lower the machine speeds, increasing the efficiency. The first range-extended mode — a so called series mode — targets lower velocities. The motor-EM propels the HEV, while the ICE/generator unit is decoupled from the driving shaft and is solely used to charge the battery. In difference, the second range-extended mode uses a power-split setup, where both ICE and motor-EM are propelling the HEV, but the power output of the ICE is split s.t. the generator-EM is used to charge the battery.

Twelve parameters of the HEV model are optimized. A switch between modes of the same type is performed above specific speeds $speedup_{EV/ER}$ if the axle torque is below specified thresholds $torqueup_{EV/ER}$, respectively. Switching from EV to ER is done at a defined speed $speedmin_{ER}$, which has to be less than $speedup_{ER}$. Further the allowed percental deviation from the initial SOC of the battery $socband$ is optimized. It contributes to the decision of switching between different mode types. Also dependent on the $socband$ is the power used to charge the battery, which is further determined by the interpolation between charge powers for low and high SOC deviations *chargepower*$_{L/H}$. The required charge power is influenced by the decision if the current power demand of the motor-EM is to be covered by the generator, regulated by the *powerdemand* switch, too. Last *generatorpower*$_{min}$ determines the minimal output of the generator-EM. Beside these parameters of the operation strategy, the teeth count of the ring and sun gear of the planetary gear set, connecting the engine- and driving shafts, is optimized too. Ring and sun gear require the constraint that their teeth difference has to be even.

The objective function which shall be minimized sums the HEV's fuel consumption in L/100km and a penalization term for SOC deviations between its initial and final state. The driving cycle we considered for optimization is the standardized EPA US-06[5] driving cycle. The penalization term estimates the fuel needed (measured in L) to charge the battery to the initial SOC state with the integrated ICE/generator unit, if the SOC is lower at the end of the cycle:

$$
\frac{E_{\Delta SOC}}{E_{fuel}\rho_{fuel}} \cdot \frac{100}{G_{eff}} \cdot \frac{10^5}{s_{cycle}} \tag{6}
$$

where $E_{\Delta SOC}$ is the energy equivalent to the SOC difference, $E_{fuel} \approx 43\,\mathrm{MJ\,kg^{-1}}$ denotes the energy density of the fuel, $\rho_{fuel} \approx 0.75\,\mathrm{kg\,L^{-1}}$ the fuel density, G_{eff} specifies the average generator efficiency estimated during simulation and s_{cycle} the length of the driving cycle in m. Penalization is included to favour SOC-balanced solutions, to be comparable to other HEVs. If the SOC is higher at the end than initially, then the penalization term becomes negative and even promotes the solution. The effect is limited by high energy losses during conversion.

A major challenge for proper experimental examination of the optimization problem at hand is the limited number of experiments which we could perform in a reasonable time. The number of simulations was restricted to 16 per iteration.

First, experiments with the unmodified CPSO and the unmodified ES, as described in Section 3, have been performed. Due to high computation times, we have only been able to run 3 experiments per unmodified algorithm. Best solutions for the experiments and information about the number of simulations are given in Table 2. The algorithms' parameters are given in Table 1. For the two-phase optimization the number of discretization points, for each dimension, changes from 6 in the first phase to 16 in the second.

The results for the unmodified metaheuristics clearly indicate that the CPSO dominates the ES. A closer analysis in [3] shows that the ES exhibits problems regarding the solution variance, which we attribute to the existence of plateaus in the search space. The results for the first phase in Table 3 show that the CPSO outperforms the GA if the search space is discretized. Although, the GA generates more distinct solutions — 777 on average — and has therefore been selected as the first phase for all further algorithms.

---

[5] See http://www.fueleconomy.gov/feg/fe_test_schedules.shtml for more information; accessed: 2013-11-11

Table 1. Algorithm parameters

Algorithm	#Iterations	Parameters
unmod. CPSO	200	#Part. $= 16$, $\omega = 0.7298$, $\phi_1 = \phi_2 = 1.496$, $l = 20$
unmod. A-CMA-ES	200	$\lambda = 16$, $\mu = 4$, init. as in [11]
CPSO-Phase I	65	#Part. $= 16$, $\omega = 0.7298$, $\phi_1 = \phi_2 = 2.0$, $l = 20$
GA-Phase I	65	$N = 16$, $R = 0.3$, $k = 2$
CPSO-Phase II	480	as Phase I; $m = 8$, $\tau = 15$
A-CMA-ES-Phase II	60	$\lambda = 100$, $\kappa = 16$, $\mu = 4$, $\tau = 15$

Table 2. Results for the unmodified optimization algorithms

Experiment	Fuel c.	#Sim$_{best}$
unmod. CPSO 1	5.86	3168
unmod. CPSO 2	5.83	1872
unmod. CPSO 3	5.83	2816

Experiment	Fuel c.	#Sim$_{best}$
unmod. A-CMA-ES 1	6.00	528
unmod. A-CMA-ES 2	6.00	2176
unmod. A-CMA-ES 3	6.00	2050

Table 3. Results for Phase I

Experiment	Fuel c.	#Sim$_{best}$
CPSO 1	5.95	320
CPSO 2	6.11	211
CPSO 3	6.02	48
CPSO 4	5.95	105
CPSO 5	5.97	191
CPSO 6	5.96	266
CPSO 7	5.93	148
CPSO 8	6.07	210
CPSO 9	5.96	476
CPSO 10	5.91	87

Experiment	Fuel c.	#Sim$_{best}$
GA 1	6.01	136
GA 2	5.98	501
GA 3	6.04	121
GA 4	6.04	625
GA 5	6.00	727
GA 6	6.06	694
GA 7	5.99	631
GA 8	6.02	594
GA 9	6.00	433
GA 10	6.04	357

Table 4 depicts the best results for each type of regression model. Extrapolation after simulating 75% of the driving cycle clearly outperforms the other models. Nevertheless, due to the still high simulation costs, Bagging has been selected for further experiments.

In the second phase the variants described in Section 6 are evaluated. Preliminary experiments have shown that the CPSO performs better if it is randomly initialized as opposed to starting from a set of good solutions. For the ES, on the other hand, it is beneficial to estimate the mutation center $\boldsymbol{x_w}$, the covariance matrix $\boldsymbol{C}$ and the step size σ from the 30 best solutions and 20 random solutions. The results for the second phase are given in Table 5. Both algorithms have been able to reach solutions below 5.9L/100km. The difference in solution quality compared to the unmodified algorithms is negligible as the HEV model itself exhibits errors at similar magnitude. Comparing the best cases of these algorithms to the unmodified CPSO's best case, then the two-phase optimization with CPSO reaches its best solution at 57.64% and the more consistent

ES variant at 80.07% of the number of simulations. This implies that using discretization and metamodels reduces the required runtime significantly if compared to the unmodified reference algorithms. Further the performance of the ES improved considerably if compared to the unmodified variant. We attribute this to the local search behaviour of the used ES variant.

Table 4. Results for the best regression models per type

Model	Parameters	tMSE	vMSE	tMTOD	vMTOD
Neural network	$L = (12)$, $\omega = 1.0$	1.37	6.25	0.0746	0.0952
Gradient Boosting	$E = 16$, $S = 1.0$	0.16	5.49	0.0330	0.0984
Bagging	$E = 24$, $L = (24, 24)$, $\omega = 1.0$, $S = 1.25$	0.89	5.00	0.0339	0.0783
Partitioning	$O_p = 50\%$, $K = 5$	3.25	15.89	0.0749	0.1298
Partial simulation	$p = 0.25$, $L = (13)$, $\omega = 0.1$	0.01	0.02	0.0615	0.0810
Partial simulation	$p = 0.50$, $L = (13, 13)$, $\omega = 1.0$	0.00	0.01	0.0489	0.0703
Partial simulation	$p = 0.75$, $L = (78)$, $\omega = 1.0$	0.00	0.00	0.0351	0.0387

L — the number of neurons per layer
ω — the value for the weight decay parameter of the training algorithm
O_p — percentage of closest solutions taken from each neighbouring cluster
E — number of (internal) regression models
S — size factor of the new training set sampled from the original training set X

tXXX ... training XXX, vXXX ... validation, $MSE = \frac{1}{|X|} SSE$

Table 5. Results for Phase II

Experiment	Fuel c.	$\#Sim_{best}^{1}$		Experiment	Fuel c.	$\#Sim_{best}^{1}$
CPSO 1	5.93	189 (966)		ES 1	5.87	893 (1670)
CPSO 2	5.97	294 (1071)		ES 2	5.92	803 (1580)
CPSO 3	5.97	535 (1312)		ES 3	5.89	334 (1111)
CPSO 4	5.89	277 (1054)		ES 4	5.90	508 (1285)
CPSO 5	6.10	127 (904)		ES 5	5.87	722 (1499)
CPSO 6	5.97	428 (1205)				
CPSO 7	6.01	46 (823)				
CPSO 8	5.88	302 (1079)				
CPSO 9	5.98	192 (969)				
CPSO 10	5.93	149 (926)				

[1] Numbers in braces give the number of simulations combined with the average number of simulations (777) of the GA in phase I

8   Conclusion and Future Work

We optimized the continuous parameters of an operation strategy for a HEV model based on a real HEV. We explored different ways to reduce the number of simulations required by the optimization by employing search space discretization and metamodels. Search space discretization has proven to be a valuable tool in the presence of search spaces with plateaus. Bagging ensembles have been used to improve the generalization performance and mixing partial simulation and extrapolation yielded even better results. The presented hybrid two-phase metaheuristics have been able to reach similar results as the reference algorithms, while reducing the number of simulations to 57.64% and 80.07%, depending on the metaheuristic. In future work, advanced ways for incorporating metamodels should be studied, like integrating partial simulation into the optimization process, or using metamodels early in the optimization process. Different performance measures for metamodels, e.g., measures capturing the performance for solutions expected to be generated by the algorithms, should be considered.

References

1. April, J., Glover, F., Kelly, J.P., Laguna, M.: Practical introduction to simulation optimization. In: Proceedings of the 2003 of the Winter Simulation Conference, vol. 1, pp. 71–78. IEEE Press (2003)
2. Arthur, D., Vassilvitskii, S.: k-means++: The advantages of careful seeding. In: Proceedings of the Eighteenth Annual ACM-SIAM Symposium on Discrete Algo-rithms. pp. 1027–1035. Society for Industrial and Applied Mathematics, Philadelphia (2007)
3. Bacher, C.: Metaheuristic optimization of electro-hybrid powertrains using machine learning techniques. Master's thesis, Vienna University of Technology, Vienna, Austria (2013)
4. Breiman, L.: Bagging predictors. Machine Learning **24**(2), 123–140 (1996)
5. Friedman, J.H.: Stochastic gradient boosting. Computational Statistics and Data Analysis **38**, 367–378 (1999)
6. Friedman, J.H.: Greedy function approximation: A gradient boosting machine. Annals of Statistics **29**, 1189–1232 (2000)
7. Frosyniotis, D., Stafylopatis, A., Likas, A.: A divide-and-conquer method for multi-net classifiers. Pattern Analysis & Applications **6**(1), 32–40 (2003)
8. Hagan, M., Menhaj, M.: Training feedforward networks with the Marquardt algo-rithm. IEEE Transactions on Neural Networks **5**(6), 989–993 (1994)
9. Hansen, N., Ostermeier, A.: Completely derandomized self-adaptation in evolution strategies. Evolutionary Computation 9, 159–195 (2001)
10. Hu, X., Wang, Z., Liao, L.: Multi-objective optimization of HEV fuel economy and emissions using evolutionary computation. In: Society of Automotive Engineers World Congress and Exhibition, vol. SP-1856, pp. 117–128 (2004)
11. Jastrebski, G., Arnold, D.: Improving evolution strategies through active covari-ance matrix adaptation. In: IEEE Congress on Evolutionary Computation, pp. 2814–2821. IEEE Press (2006)
12. Jin, Y., Olhofer, M., Sendhoff, B.: A framework for evolutionary optimization with approximate fitness functions. IEEE Transactions on Evolutionary Computation **6**(5), 481–494 (2002)
13. Johnson, V.H., Wipke, K.B., Rausen, D.J.: HEV control strategy for real-time opti-mization of fuel economy and emissions. Society of Automotive Engineers Trans-actions **109**(3), 1677–1690 (2000)
14. Kennedy, J., Eberhart, R.: Particle swarm optimization. In: Proceedings of the IEEE International Conference on Neural Networks, vol. 4, pp. 1942–1948. IEEE Press (1995)
15. Krenek, T., Ruthmair, M., Raidl, G.R., Planer, M.: Applying (Hybrid) Metaheuris-tics to Fuel Consumption Optimization of Hybrid Electric Vehicles. In: Di Chio, C., et al. (eds.) EvoApplications 2012. LNCS, vol. 7248, pp. 376–385. Springer, Heidelberg (2012)
16. Mendes-Moreira, J.A., Soares, C., Jorge, A.M., Sousa, J.F.D.: Ensemble approaches for regression: A survey. ACM Comput. Surv. **45**(1), 10:1–10:40 (2012)
17. Poli, R., Kennedy, J., Blackwell, T.: Particle swarm optimization. Swarm Intelli-gence **1**(1), 33–57 (2007)

Hybridisation Schemes for Communication Satellite Payload Configuration Optimisation

Apostolos Stathakis[1]([✉]), Grégoire Danoy[2], El-Ghazali Talbi[3],
Pascal Bouvry[2], and Gianluigi Morelli[4]

[1] Interdisciplinary Centre for Security, Reliability, and Trust,
University of Luxembourg, Walferdange, Luxembourg
`apostolos.stathakis@uni.lu`
[2] CSC Research Unit, University of Luxembourg, Walferdange, Luxembourg
[3] INRIA-Lille Nord Europe, Université Lille 1, Villeneuve-d'Ascq, France
[4] SES Engineering, Betzdorf, Luxembourg

Abstract. The increasing complexity of current telecommunication satellite payloads has made their manual management a difficult and error prone task. As a consequence, efficient optimisation techniques are re- quired to help engineers to configure the payload. Recent works focusing on exact approaches faced scalability issues while metaheuristics provided unsatisfactory solution quality. This work therefore proposes three hybridisation schemes that combine both metaheuristics and an exact method. We focus on the initial configuration problem case and we consider as objective to minimise the length of the longest channel path. Experimental results on realistic payload sizes demonstrate the advantage of those approaches in terms of efficiency within a strict operational time constraint of ten minutes on a single CPU core.

Keywords: Satellite payload configuration · Optimisation · Hybrid metaheuristics

1 Introduction

The communication satellite consists of the payload and the platform. The payload, which plays the main role in the transmission of the signals, includes all the necessary electronic equipment like multiplexers, switches and amplifiers, as well as the receiving and transmitting antennas. The platform consists of all the subsystems that allow the payload to function, like the electric power supply. In the payload the routing of the signals is achieved through reconfigurable switches organised in switch matrices. But the modern operational requirements and the increasing demands of the market have led to large and complex payloads. Numerous amplifiers and large switch matrices are used to ensure flexibility in signal routings and functionality in case of failures (redundancy). As a consequence, the current manual management of the payload, with the use of computerised schematics, is becoming hard and time consuming. Commercial

© Springer-Verlag Berlin Heidelberg 2014
A.I. Esparcia-Alcázar et al. (Eds.): EvoApplications 2014, LNCS 8602, pp. 565–576, 2014.
DOI: 10.1007/978-3-662-45523-4_46

software solutions exist for payload configuration that have built-in optimisers, but as they are closed packages, they do not provide the advantage of the flexibility achieved with the computerised schematics.

To deal with this challenging problem, Stathakis et. al. have proposed an integer linear programming (ILP) model aiming to find solutions using exact methods [8][10]. It was demonstrated though that some instances could not be solved exactly within a time constraint of ten minutes defined by engineers. To overpass this limitation the same authors proposed to apply genetic algorithms for the first time to the considered problem [9] and more instances were solved successfully within the time constraint, with a difference though in the quality of the obtained solutions compared to the optimal ones.

In this article we propose three hybridisation schemes that integrate a local search, a cellular genetic algorithm and the ILP based exact method. We target to solve the real size problem instances within the strict constraint of ten minutes. The experimental results denote the efficiency of the proposed approaches when tackling large payload instances, in both computational time and fitness values.

The remainder of this paper is organized as follows. The next section presents the related works in the subject. Section 3 addresses the considered problem in more details and in Section 4 the proposed hybridisation schemes are detailed. The experimental results are analysed in Section 5 and finally the conclusions and some perspectives for future work are provided.

2   Related Works

In order to meet the modern demands of the market and to achieve the current operational requirements, the satellite industry needs to reach several levels of flexibility as they have been described in [4]. They concern among others flexibility in power allocation (assigning various power levels to channels to cope with traffic allocations), in coverage definition (shape of coverage, number and size of beams in case of multi-beam coverage) and at the channel routing level that we are focusing on. To ensure such flexibility the current payloads are composed with numerous amplifiers and large switch matrices.

The design of the optimal switch matrix topology that will satisfy the given operational requirements is the first optimisation problem which is faced by satellite manufacturers, when constructing the spacecrafts. Switches are expensive components and thus designing a topology that will satisfy all the routing requirements, given a number of channels and amplifiers, while minimising the cost, is of importance. Research works have tackled this design problem, like in [3] where a graph-based analysis is used to minimise the number of needed switches, while ensuring a fault-tolerant switch matrix design.

From the satellite operator point of view, which is of our interest, efficient techniques are also required to find optimal configurations when new operational and business demands arise. Commercial software packages exist, like TRECS [12] and Smartrings [6]. Details concerning the algorithms and the models used by both packages are not accessible due to commercial restrictions.

Smartrings applies a recursive search to compute all possible payload configurations, while the algorithm is controlled by constraints like the number of switches used or the number of the interrupted channel paths. Similarly, TRECS uses an algorithm to find all feasible solutions and sorts them by output signal quality, while rejecting many millions of non-feasible solutions. However those packages lack flexibility. Their closed APIs do not allow efficient interaction and integrations in company workflows. Besides, they use a black-box solver that can not be changed or customised based on the problem that has to be solved, which would allow the application of different single or multi-objective algorithms.

On the academic side, few works have been proposed that deal with the considered problem. In [7] a recursive algorithm was proposed to perform a breadth-first-search (BFS) in order to find all feasible paths that connect channels to amplifiers. Experiments showed the efficiency of the proposed method on a small switch network. However, it can be expected that for larger problems the BFS algorithm will be limited due to its time complexity as every vertex and every edge will be explored in the worst case.

Stathakis et al. [9] proposed and validated an Integer Linear Programming (ILP) optimisation model that can be used for applying single and multi objective algorithms. The model allows the optimisation of specific objectives like the number of switch changes. Instead of enumerating all feasible solutions, the authors aim at a single optimal solution or a set of non-dominated solutions. The same authors extended their mathematical model to minimise the channel interruptions for the reconfiguration problem [10]. As has been demonstrated, not all instances could be solved exactly within the ten minutes constraint. To overcome this limitation metaheuristics were applied for the first time to the considered problem [9], which permitted to solve more instances with a degradation though between their fitness and the one found by the exact.

In this work, we propose novel hybridisation schemes for the considered problem that integrate a local search with a cellular genetic algorithm and the ILP based exact method. The experimental results confirmed the efficiency of those schemes, and thus can be used when tackling even larger payload problem sizes. The proposed methods are high-level relay hybrids according to the taxonomy of hybrid algorithms used in [11].

3   Problem Description

A simplified payload switch matrix example is shown in Fig.1, which is composed by 16 switches. The input channel signals are crossing the switch matrix and are guided for amplification. Different types of switches may be used and each one has different positions allowing different paths. The four possible positions of an R-type switch are shown in Fig.2, whereas the C-type switch has only 2 possible positions. A link (connector between any two payload components) can be used by only a single channel. The switch matrix can have any design topology (not symmetric necessarily) and channels can be placed at any location of the matrix.

The problem of payload configuration can be decomposed into three related subproblems. The first one is the initial configuration problem, which consists in

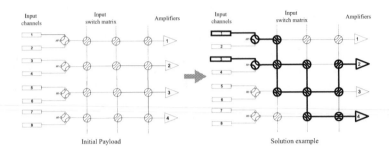

Fig. 1. Simplified initial payload instance and solution that connects channels 1 and 3 to amplifiers 2 and 4

finding an optimal configuration for connecting an initial set of channels in a payload without any pre-connected channels. The second case is the reconfiguration problem, which occurs when there exists a set of pre-connected channel paths that carry services and some additional channels have to be activated. The third one is the restoration problem, which arises when a set of channels is already connected and one or more failures occur to the amplifiers or to the switches. In this case, the channels affected by these failure(s) have to be rerouted through different paths.

In this work we are focusing on the initial configuration problem. More precisely, given a set of channels to connect, the initial payload configuration problem consists in finding the positions of the switches that permit to establish the path from each required channel to an amplifier. Among several important objectives that are of interest, we choose to minimise the length of the longest channel paths. Long paths imply high signal attenuation and they cause restrictions on future reconfiguration processes. In Fig.1 one solution example is shown for connecting channel 1 to amplifier 2 and channel 3 to amplifier 4, where channel 1 follows a path of 7 switch crossings and channel 3 follows a path with 6 switch crossings i.e number of switches used in the path.

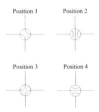

Fig. 2. Positions of one R-type switch

More formally, let k be the number of switches in the switch network and the set C, of size n, the set of channels to connect. Let $path_c, c \in C$ be the length of the channel path c in switch crossings. The solution vector of size k: $P = \{pos_1, \ldots, pos_k\}$ denotes the position of each switch. The objective is to find a solution P which connects the n channels and minimises

$$max_{c \in C}(path_c) \tag{1}$$

4   Proposed Methodology

An illustration of the three schemes with their components is provided in Fig.3. The first one, referred to as LSM, combines a local search with a cellular genetic algorithm. The rest two hybrids, referred to as LSMExB and LSMExP, combine LSM with the ILP based exact method. The local search and cellular genetic algorithm components are presented in the next two subsections. The ILP model is a variation of the one presented in [8]. In the last three subsections, the three hybrids are presented in details.

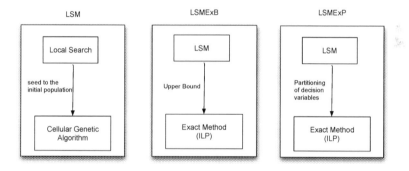

Fig. 3. The three hybrid schemes and their components

4.1   The Local Search Algorithm

The target of the local search algorithm is to find fast approximated payload configurations. The problem is regarded as a permutation problem. Since each path uses an available amplifier and defines positions on the switches, the ordering of channels to connect will influence the quality of the final solution. The next channels will be restricted in both the possible paths, and their final destination (amplifier). For n channels to connect, the solution of the local search algorithm is thus represented as a permutation of size n. We used a simple hill climbing method where starting from a random solution (random permutation), at each iteration the current solution is replaced by a neighbor, using the first improvement strategy. The neighbors are generated with the use of the exchange operator. The local search terminates when there is no improvement. Each solution is evaluated using a greedy method to construct the paths.

A Greedy Method for Constructing Paths. The payload can be represented as a graph $G = (V, E)$, where V is the set of payload components (switches, channels, amplifiers), and E the set of connectors (links) between them. We consider the length of each link to be equal to 1. Each component $u \in V$, has some coordinates (x, y) and at most 4 neighbor nodes (vertices) namely u_s, u_w, u_e, u_n, where s,w,e,n stand for south, west, east and north. The pseudocode of the greedy method used for finding the path of each channel is provided in Algorithm 1. Initially, the destination amplifier is chosen to be the closest available amplifier based on the Manhattan distance. We assume that any channel can be connected to any amplifier. If not, the destination will be chosen among the suitable amplifiers for each channel.

Algorithm 1. Pseudo-code of a greedy method to construct one channel path

---

1: **Input** *channel node c; path_c = {}*
2: *dest = closest_to_c_available_amplifier*
3: *current = switch_node_neighboring_to_c*
4: *path_c.add(current)*
5: *prec_node = channel node c*
6: **while** *(current != dest)* **do**
7:     *next_node = closest_to_dest_available_neighbor*
8:     **if** *(next_node)* **then**
9:         *updateNeighborhood(prec_node, current, next_node)*
10:         *prec_node = current*
11:         *current = next_node*
12:         *path_c.add(current)*
13:     **else**
14:         *path_c.clear*
15:         *break*
16:     **end if**
17: **end while**
18: **if** *(path_c is empty)* **then**
19:     *reset_All_neighbors()*
20: **else**
21:     *dest.available = false*
22: **end if**

The next step is to set as current node the unique switch that is neighbor to the channel and the current node is added to the path (lines 3,4). As precedent node is set the channel node (line 5). To find the next node, the available neighbors of the current node are retrieved and the one which is closest to the destination is selected (line 7). Given the localities of the next and the precedent nodes compared to the current node, the position of the current switch is defined. The *updateNeighborhood* function which is then called (line 9) will update the available neighbors. In this function, the current switch defines which of its neighbors are available from now on. Besides, each of the neighbors of the current switch determines whether the current switch is considered as one of

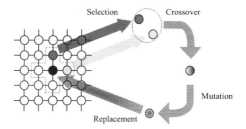

Fig. 4. cGA reproduction cycle with 5×5 population and L5 neighborhood

their available neighbors. The same process is repeated until the destination is reached. If the path can not be found, the neighbors of each switch are reset to the initial status (line 19). As long as a channel path is constructed, the used amplifier is set as not available (line 21).

4.2 The Cellular Genetic Algorithm

The cellular genetic algorithm (cGA) uses a single and structured population [2]. Individuals are spread in a two dimensional toroidal mesh and are only allowed to interact with their neighbors. An illustration of the cGA breeding loop is presented in Fig.4. The individuals are arranged on a 5X5 toroidal grid. The neighborhood of the center individual, linear 5, is presented as dashed lines. The representation of the solution is similar to the one used in [9], i.e. one individual represents the set of positions of all the switches. A binary encoding is used where a switch position is encoded using two bits. The binary vector is thus of size $2 * n$ with n the number of switches in the payload. Each solution describes a unique static graph. To assign a fitness value to the candidate solutions, we use the objective function:

$$F = r_c + \frac{lpl}{1000} \tag{2}$$

where r_c is the number of channels that have not been connected to an amplifier, from the set of n channels to connect, and lpl is the length of the longest found path, i.e. the number of switches used in this path.

4.3 The First Hybrid (LSM)

In the first hybrid, a seed individual provided by the local search is inserted in the initial population of cGA. The rest individuals are created uniformly at random. The global problem is solved by both methods. The two algorithms are applied in sequence. At first the problem is solved using local search and the solution is included to the initial population of the second metaheuristic. According to the taxonomy presented in [11], this hybrid is classified as High Level Relay Hybrid (HRH)(heterogenous, global, general) and is denoted as LSM.

4.4   The Second Hybrid (LSMExB)

The motivation for the second hybridisation scheme comes from the good performance of the cGA as demonstrated in [9]. The solution provided by the LSM can thus be considered as a good upper bound (length of the longest path) for the exact method. We applied this collaborative scheme aiming to improve the hit rate of the exact method (percentage of problems that were solved exactly within ten minutes). Thus, the upper bound of the objective function is set in the ILP model, based on the solution found by LSM and the exact method is then called. The global problem is solved by both methods. The two algorithms are applied in sequence. According to the taxonomy presented in [11], this hybrid is classified as High Level Relay Hybrid (HRH)(heterogenous, global, general) and is denoted as LSMExB.

4.5   Third Hybrid (LSMExP)

In this scheme we propose to partition the decision variables, as indicated in [11]. The decision variables can be partitioned in two sets X and Y. The variables of the set X will be fixed based on the solution found by LSM and the exact method will optimize the problem over the set Y. Hence, the generated problem is subject to free variables in the set Y and freesed variables in the set X. The decision variables that we fix are the positions of the switches based on some paths generated by the solution obtained by LSM. To summarise this hybrid, the global problem is solved by LSM and the partial problem is solved by the exact method. The two algorithms are applied in sequence. At first the problem is solved using metaheuristics, the values of some decision variables are set and the exact method is then called. According to the taxonomy presented in [11], this hybrid is classified as High Level Relay Hybrid (HRH)(heterogenous, partial, general), and is denoted as LSMExP.

5   Experimental Results

In this section we review the performances of the proposed schemes related to the hit rate (percentage of successfully solved instances), the fitness value and the required computational time.

5.1   Experimental Setup

All our experiments were carried out using the HPC facility of the University of Luxembourg, on a single CPU core of an Intel Xeon L5640 at 2.26GHz. The implementation of the metaheuristic algorithms was done using Paradiseo framework v.1.3 [5]. For the exact method CPLEX 12.4.0.0 was used [1].

For the local search and the cGA we used default parameters that are provided in Table 1. The problem instances tackled are the same as in [9], i.e switch matrix with 50 switches and and 23 amplifiers (maximum channels to connect).

Table 1. Parameters used for local search and cGA

	Algorithm	Hill Climbing
LS	Selection Strategy	First Improvment
	Neighbor operator	Exchange
	Population	49, 7×7
	Selection	Binary tournament (BT), Current indiv. + BT
cGA	Neighborhood	L5
	Crossover	DPX, p_c=0.8
	Mutation	Bit flip, $p_m = \frac{1}{chrom\_length}$
	Replacement strategy	Replace if better
	Elitism	1 individual

30 channel instances of size 8, 13, 18 and 23 were randomly selected to connect. For the LSMExP we selected to fix the positions of the switches used by 4, 7, 10 and 12 randomly selected paths respectively.

5.2 Numerical Results

The results obtained after applying the ILP based exact method are displayed in Table 2. The hit rate, which represents for the exact method the percentage of instances that were solved exactly within ten minutes, decreases significantly from 90%, when 8 channels are connected, to 13.333% for the cases of 13 channels to connect. When connecting 18 channels only 6.666% of the instances were solved and none instance for the case of 23 channels (maximum size on a switch matrix with 23 amplifiers).

Table 2. Exact Method

Channels	Hit Rate(%)	Aver. Fitness	Aver. Time(sec)
8	90	$0.00181_{\pm 0.0004}$	$3.199_{\pm 12.896}$
13	13.333	$0.002_{\pm 0}$	$10.67_{\pm 13.647}$
18	6.666	$0.002_{\pm 0}$	$4.525_{\pm 4.122}$
23	0	–	–

Concerning the comparison of LS, cGA and LSM, the average fitness and the hit rate are provided in Table 3. As can be seen the hybrid LSM outperforms the other methods. In terms of hit rate, which in this case denotes the percentage of instances where valid solutions were found (all paths constructed), LSM and cGA have both 100% for the instances of 8, 13 and 18 channels, but LSM has hit rate 82.333% when 23 channels are connected, compared to 80.888% for cGA. The hit rate of LS is 90%, 42.222%, 23.333% and 4.888% for 8, 13, 18 and 23 channels respectively. LSM provides also better fitness values, for example 0.00194 and

0.00304 when 8 and 13 channels are connected compared to 0.00195 and 0.00317 for cGA and for 18 and 23 channels LSM has average fitness 0.00365 and 0.18183 respectively compared to 0.00367 and 0.19879 for cGA. In terms of fitness, LSM outperforms cGA with statistical confidence for the case of 23 channels after performing the Wilcoxon test [13]. LSM has also smaller standard deviation in all cases except for the case of 18 channels. The fitness values of LS itself are 0.10346, 0.69998, 1.18435 and 2.84213 for 8, 13, 18 and 23 channels respectively.

Table 3. Fitness and Hit Rate(%)

#Ch	LS		cGA		LSM	
	Fitness	Hit Rate	Fitness	Hit Rate	Fitness	Hit Rate
8	$0.10346_{\pm 0.3}$	90	$0.00195_{\pm 0.0006}$	100.0	$0.00194_{\pm 0.0005}$	100
13	$0.69998_{\pm 0.69}$	42.222	$0.00317_{\pm 0.0006}$	100.0	$0.00304_{\pm 0.0005}$	100
18	$1.18435_{\pm 0.88}$	23.333	$0.00367_{\pm 0.0007}$	100.0	$0.00365_{\pm 0.0007}$	100
23	$2.84213_{\pm 1.33}$	4.888	$0.19879_{\pm 0.4}$	80.888	$0.18183_{\pm 0.381}$	82.333

The average convergence time of cGA and LSM, which denotes the average time needed by each method to reach the best solution found, is provided in Table 4. LSM converges faster in all cases. The highest difference occurs for 23 channels where LSM converged after 79.48sec and cGA in average after 91.85sec.

Table 4. Metaheuristics - Convergence Time(sec)

Channels	cGA	LSM
8	9.41	5.26
13	27.98	26.94
18	46.81	44.11
23	91.85	79.48

For the next hybrids LSMExB and LSMExP, LSM will run for the time provided in Table 4 and then the ILP based exact method is called so as the total termination condition is ten minutes in all experiments. The comparison between LSMExB and LSMExP in terms of fitness and hitrate is presented in Table 5.

LSMExP method achieved 89.222% hit rate for the maximum case of connecting 23 channels compared to 0% for LSMExB. For 18 channels LSMExP solved 89.444% of instances compared to 6.666% of LSMExB. With LSMExP, the process is significantly accelerated since the exact method is optimising over a subset of the decision variables. LSMExB performed better compared to the ILP based exact method for the case of 13 channels as the hit rate of LSMExB is 16.666% compared to 13.333%. In Table 6 the average fitness is compared

Table 5. Fitness and Hit Rate(%)

#Ch	LSMExB		LSMExP	
	Fitness	Hit Rate	Fitness	Hit Rate
8	$0.00181_{\pm 0.0004}$	90	$0.00191_{\pm 0.0005}$	97.888
13	$0.00260_{\pm 0.0005}$	16.666	$0.00300_{\pm 0.0005}$	93
18	$0.00200_{\pm 0}$	6.666	$0.00363_{\pm 0.0008}$	89.444
23	–	–	$0.00487_{\pm 0.0009}$	89.222

between LSM, LSMExB and LSMExP for the commonly solved instances. We observe that LSMExP provided the optimal solution for these instances (same fitness with LSMExB) and LSM provided solutions of less good quality.

Table 6. Fitness comparison on the commonly solved instances

Channels	LSMExB	LSM	LSMExP
8	$0.00181_{\pm 0.0004}$	$0.00182_{\pm 0.0003}$	$0.00181_{\pm 0.0004}$
13	$0.00260_{\pm 0.0005}$	$0.00261_{\pm 0.0005}$	$0.00260_{\pm 0.0005}$
18	$0.00200_{\pm 0}$	$0.00200_{\pm 0}$	$0.00200_{\pm 0}$

When connecting 8 channels, both LSMExB and LSMExP provided average fitness 0.00181 on the same instances compared to 0.00182 for LSM, and for 13 channels LSM has fitness 0.00261 compared to 0.00260 for the other two hybrids. For the 6.666% instances of 18 channels to connect the three methods had the same performance.

6 Conclusions and Perspectives

In this work we tackled the problem of optimal telecommunication satellite payload configuration. In order to further improve state-of-the-art results and solve the difficult problem instances within ten minutes on a single CPU core, we proposed three hybridisation schemes. The first hybrid (LSM) is a high level relay hybrid that integrates a local search method with a cGA which improved the performance of the metaheuristic. The second hybrid (LSMExB) uses the solution of LSM as an upper bound for the exact method and permitted to solve more problem instances and in much shorter time. The last one (LSMExP) freezes a subset of decision variables based on the best solution obtained by LSM and uses the exact method to optimise the problem over the set of decision variables. With this last hybridisation method, the hitrate of solved instances was significantly increased. Future work will therefore focus on further improving this scheme, for instance by using a more intelligent way of choosing the number and the decision variables to fix. Its scalability will be experimented by using even larger payload instances.

References

1. Ibm ilog cplex. http://www.ilog.com/products/cplex/
2. Alba, E., Dorronsoro, B.: Cellular Genetic Algorithms. Operations Research/Compuer Science Interfaces. Springer, Heidelberg (2008)
3. Amini, O., Giroire, F., Prennes, S., Huc, F.: Minimal selectors and fault tolerant networks. Networks 55(4), 326–340 (2010). http://dx.doi.org/10.1002/net.20326
4. Balty, C., Gayrard, J.D., Agnieray, P.: Communication satellites to enter a new age of flexibility. Acta Astronautica **65**(1–2), 75–81 (2009)
5. Cahon, S., Melab, N., Talbi, E.G.: Paradiseo: A framework for the reusable design of parallel and distributed metaheuristics. Journal of Heuristics 10(3), 357–380 (2004). http://dx.doi.org/10.1023/B:HEUR.0000026900.92269.ec
6. Chaumon, J., Gil, J., Beech, T., Garcia, G.: Smartrings: advanced tool for communications satellite payload reconfiguration. In: 2006 IEEE Aerospace Conference, p. 11 (2006)
7. Gulgonul, S., Koklukaya, E., Erturk, I., Tesneli, A.Y.: Communication satellite payload redundancy reconfiguration. In: 2012 IEEE First AESS European Conference on Satellite Telecommunications (ESTEL), pp. 1–4 (October 2012)
8. Stathakis, A., Danoy, G., Bouvry, P., Morelli, G.: Satellite Payload Reconfiguration Optimisation: An ILP Model. In: Pan, J.-S., Chen, S.-M., Nguyen, N.T. (eds.) ACIIDS 2012, Part II. LNCS, vol. 7197, pp. 311–320. Springer, Heidelberg (2012)
9. Stathakis, A., Danoy, G., Schleich, J., Bouvry, P., Morelli, G.: Minimising longest path length in communication satellite payloads via metaheuristics. In: Proceeding of the Fifteenth Annual Conference on Genetic and Evolutionary Computation Conference, GECCO 2013, pp. 1365–1372. ACM, New York (2013). http://doi.acm.org/10.1145/2463372.2463535
10. Stathakis, A., Danoy, G., Veneziano, T., Schleich, J., Bouvry, P.: Optimising satellite payload reconfiguration: An ILP approach for minimising channel interruptions. In: 2nd ESA Workshop on Advanced Flexible Telecom Payloads. pp. 1–8. European Space Agency (2012)
11. Talbi, E.G.: Metaheuristics - From Design to Implementation. Wiley (2009)
12. TRECS: Transponder reconfiguration system. http://www.integ.com/trecs.html
13. Wilcoxon, F.: Individual Comparisons by Ranking Methods. Biometrics Bulletin **1**(6), 80–83 (1945)

EvoNUM

A Novel Genetic Algorithmic Approach
for Computing Real Roots of a Nonlinear Equation

Vijaya Lakshmi V. Nadimpalli[1(✉)], Rajeev Wankar[2],
and Raghavendra Rao Chillarige[2]

[1] ACRHEM, University of Hyderabad, Hyderabad, 500046, India
nvvlakshmi@gmail.com
[2] School of Computer Information Sciences, University of Hyderabad,
Hyderabad, 500046, India
{wankarcs,crrcs}@uohyd.ernet.in

Abstract. Novel *Pre-processing* and *Post-processing* methodologies are designed to enhance the performance of the classical Genetic Algorithms (GA) approach so as to obtain efficient interval estimates in finding the real roots of a given nonlinear equation. The *Pre-processing* methodology suggests a mechanism that adaptively fixes the parameter-'length of chromosome' in GA. The proposed methodologies have been implemented and demonstrated through a set of benchmark functions to illustrate the effectiveness.

Keywords: Genetic Algorithms · Interval based method · Interval estimates · Tuning GA parameters

1   Introduction

The emerging fields such as soft computing, computational intelligence provide solutions for even complex real world problems through hybridization of various heterogeneous techniques. Here we consider the classical problem of solving a non-linear equation for its roots. There are various conventional numerical methods such as Newton method, Bisection method [1] for solving a nonlinear equation but these methods have many limitations such as sensitivity to initial guess, slow convergence etc. To overcome the drawbacks associated with conventional numerical methods, some meta-heuristic algorithms such as Genetic Algorithms (GA) [2, 3], Particle Swarm Optimization (PSO) [4], Simulated Annealing (SA) [5] have been proposed in the past. Dai et al. [6] utilized mixed GA and quasi-Newton method for solving systems of nonlinear equations. Brits et al [7] proposed a method for finding all roots of systems of nonlinear equations based on the new PSO method called neighborhood best method.

GA are simulation programs [8] that create an environment which would allow only the fittest population to survive. Thus, GA handles a variety of problems and provide some possible solutions and the solutions are represented as chromosomes. The search ability of ordinary GA increases if the GA parameters are tuned suitable to the domain environment. Several approaches are suggested [9-11] to tune GA parameters through explorative methods, fuzzy search methods etc. Uncertainty due to the lack

© Springer-Verlag Berlin Heidelberg 2014
A.I. Esparcia-Alcázar et al. (Eds.): EvoApplications 2014, LNCS 8602, pp. 579–590, 2014.
DOI: 10.1007/978-3-662-45523-4_47

of knowledge about the solution leads to the ill formulation of the problem and its solving strategies. To overcome this, it is essential to acquire knowledge about the function characteristics more precisely through machine learning approaches. The proposed methodology develops GA based knowledge acquisition method for computing all roots in a given closed interval of a nonlinear equation, named as *Pre-processor*. Further, it is coupled with conventional GA along with a *Post-processor* to enhance the accuracy by producing narrow interval estimates for the roots.

Two real numbers are considered to be the interval estimates for a root if the function attains zero at a point in that interval. The aim of the present study is to identify the interval estimates for all the real roots. These interval estimates constitute a sequence of real numbers in the region of interest. It is natural to represent the genes or chromosomes as real numbers for optimization problems of parameters with variables in continuous domains [12]. Hence for the problem of identifying interval estimates in the interested zone $[a, b]$, a chromosome is defined as a finite, monotonically increasing sequence of real numbers starting with 'a' and ending with 'b'. A subinterval $[a_i, a_{i+1}] \subset [a, b]$ of a chromosome is known as potential interval for the function f, if $f(a_i)f(a_{i+1}) < 0$. Further, the number of such potential sub-intervals of a chromosome has been considered as a fitness function. A chromosome is said to be better than other chromosome if it possesses more potential and compact sub-intervals i.e., better fitness value. The uncertainty about the number of roots of the function in the given zone of interest impacts the performance of GA and knowledge about the number of roots of function will significantly improve its performance. Thus a *Pre-processor* is designed as an evolutionary method to learn about the number of roots. If the selected intervals are narrow, then the root computation will be efficient through any interval based root computation method. This lead to another novel *Post-processing* operator for effective enhancement of outcome of GA.

2   Pre-processing Algorithm to Fix the Length of Chromosome (*LC*)

The number of roots for a given nonlinear equation in the region of interest is generally unknown in advance. If *LC* is arbitrarily chosen to be small, then one or more of the existing roots might be lost. Further, with a small *LC*, it is possible that the width of the selected potential intervals may not turn out to be narrow. In general, if *LC* is large, it is not only expected that the number of potential intervals selected are more but also that they are narrow. Considering a large '*LC*' for arbitrary problem influences the resource utilization and computational time, more so when the numbers of roots as well as their distribution over the zone are unknown. These observations made the present study to develop an adaptive procedure to arrive at the apt '*LC*' for any given problem, rather than assuming an arbitrary abnormal value.

We develop the methodology starting with a continuous real valued function $f(.)$ having finite number of simple roots $\alpha_i \in [a, b]$ such that $f(\alpha_i) = 0 \; \forall i = 1, 2, \dots k$. Without loss of generality, assume $a < \alpha_1 < \alpha_2 < \cdots < \alpha_k < b$. f being a continuous function, we have $f(\alpha_i-) = f(\alpha_i) = f(\alpha_i+) \; \forall i$, for each root. Further, by mean value theorem, $\exists \; \delta > 0$ such that $f(\alpha_i - \delta)f(\alpha_i + \delta) < 0$, when $f(\alpha_i) = 0$. Thus one can have a set of points in the interval such as $a < \alpha_1 - \delta_1 < \alpha_1 + \delta_1 < \alpha_2 - \delta_2 < \alpha_2 + \delta_2 < \cdots < \alpha_k - \delta_k < \alpha_k + \delta_k < b$ which brackets all the roots of the $f(.)$. This can be made abstract as $a < x_1 < x_2 < \cdots < x_{2k-1} < x_{2k} < b$. Hence, there are $2k+2$ points in $[a,b]$ producing $2k+1$ intervals as a partition of $[a,b]$, out of these $[x_1, x_2]$, $[x_3, x_4]$ ... $[x_{2k-1}, x_{2k}]$ are 'k' potential intervals containing the roots α_i satisfying the condition $f(x_{2i-1})f(x_{2i}) < 0$, $for\ i = 1,2..k$. One can consider a sequence of numbers of size $n+2$ such that $a = x_0 < x_1 < x_2 < \cdots < x_n < x_{n+1} = b$, as solution to the problem of finding all potential sub intervals that bracket the roots of the function $f(.)$. For this sequence, one can attach a non-negative integer k (referred as potential value) calculated from $k = \sum_{i=0}^{n} \delta(f(x_i)f(x_{i+1}) < 0$ (1), where $\delta(.)$ is Kronecker's delta function. Hence, one can find or construct a sequence that will have the maximum k and this maximum k will turn out to be the number of roots. In this manner one can get the knowledge about the number of roots of given $f(.)$ in the zone of interest $[a,b]$. Discovering the number of roots can be mathematical programming problem given by

$$Max\ k = \sum_{i=0}^{n} \delta(f(x_i)f(x_{i+1}) < 0) \tag{2}$$

Let $U = [a,b]$ and let $P_1, P_2, .. P_m$ be m partitions of U, each of size '$n+2$' with corresponding potential values $k_1, k_2, ... k_m$. Here potential value of a partition corresponds to the number of potential intervals satisfying the condition (1) with respect to $f(.)$ in a considered partition. Let $\Pi(U)$ denote the set of all partitions of U. Define a binary operation $*$ on $\Pi(U)$ such that $P_i * P_j$ consists of the set of intersection of every element of P_i with every element of P_j. The operation $*$ on $\Pi(U)$ is called the product (refinement) of partitions. The following is a recommended *Pre-processing algorithm* to decide about apt size of partition of a given interval $[a,b]$ with the novelty that it starts with the *LC* to be minimum and it fixes the *LC* that is suitable for the given problem. Probability of crossover and mutation P_c, P_m are assigned to be 0.3, 0.1 for all algorithms. The following notation is used in the algorithm.

LC ← Length of Chromosome (or size of the partition).

Max_FV ← Maximum fitness value among all chromosomes (maximum potential value among all partitions).

FV_Refined ← Fitness value obtained though *Post-processing Refinement* technique, i.e., by concatenating all chromosomes in to a single array and then applying the fitness function to select all potential intervals satisfying condition that the product of function values at the end points of each interval is < 0.

Algorithm 1. *Pre-processing algorithm*

// Fixes length of Chromosome //
- Given function $f(.)$ and zone of interest $[a,b]$
- *LC* ← 2 // *Length of Chromosome is initially fixed at 2 //*
- N_1 ← *Population size*
- K_1 ← *Number of generations*

OUTPUT: [*LC_new*] // *Adaptive LC_new that is suitable for the given problem //*

METHOD:

$n \leftarrow LC + 2$ // As default, end points 'a' and 'b' are added to each chromosome //

Step 1: Generate population of N_1 chromosomes, each of length n and store in $A_{N_1 \times n}$

Repeat Step 2 to Step 6 K_1 times in step of 1

Step 2: Fitness function:

   $j \leftarrow 0$

   while $(j < N_1)$

   $j \leftarrow j + 1$

   $X \leftarrow j^{th}$ row of A

   $fv(X) = \sum_{i=1}^{n-1} \delta\big((f(x_i)f(x_{i+1}) < 0)\big)$

   end while

Step 3: Crossover and mutation: Apply crossover (single point) and mutation operators on chromosomes of A, store offsprings in B and then obtain the corresponding fitness value of these offsprings

Step 4: Selection:

   4.1: $C \leftarrow$ Append the population A with offsprings B

   4.2: $A \leftarrow$ Select best N_1 chromosomes (with respective to fitness value) of C

   4.3: $Max\_FV \leftarrow$ maximum among fitness values of chromosomes of A

Step 5: Refinement:

   5.1: $D \leftarrow$ Concatenate all rows of A in to one row, organize in ascending order by removing the duplicates // Will be referred as refined chromosome. //

   5.2: $m \leftarrow$ length of D

   5.3: $FV\_Refined \leftarrow fv(D)$ // where $fv(D) = \sum_{i=1}^{m-1} \delta\big((f(x_i)f(x_{i+1}) < 0)\big)$, fitness value of refined chromosome //

Step 6: if $(FV\_Refined \geq 1.5 * Max\_FV)$

   6.1: $LC \leftarrow 3 * FV\_Refined$

   6.2: $n \leftarrow LC + 2$

   6.3: Generate population of N_1 chromosomes, each of length n and store in $A_{N_1 \times n}$

   6.4: Repeat process from Step 2 to Step 6

      elseif$(K_1 > 2)$ break; // To have at least two generations of GA //

      end if

Step 7: Set $LC\_new \leftarrow 3 * FV\_Refined$

End; //Pre-processing //

3   Post-processor

Generally by employing GA, only one chromosome with maximum fitness value is given as the solution. The prominent advantage of the proposed methodology compared to traditional GA is that the entire knowledge about all chromosomes is utilized by concatenating all the chromosomes to get a more refined partition of $[a, b]$, i.e., if we assume each chromosome to be a partition of $[a, b]$, we are now considering the product of partitions. The following is *Post-processing algorithm* which enhances the efficiency of output of *Conventional_GA*. This algorithm makes root computation efficient by selecting potential intervals enclosing roots, wherein the width of each selected interval is significantly narrow.

Algorithm 2. *Post-processing algorithm*

// Selects potential, narrow intervals enclosing roots //
INPUT:
- Given function $f(.)$ and zone of interest $[a, b]$
- LC_new // Output from Pre-processing algorithm //
- $n \leftarrow LC\_new + 2$ // As default, end points are added to each chromosome //
- $N_2 \leftarrow$ Population size
- $K_2 \leftarrow$ Number of generations
- $E_{N_2 \times n} \leftarrow Conventional\_GA(f(.), n, N_2, K_2, P_c, P_m)$ // random population generated from Conventional GA that is given as output and is stored in $E_{N_2 \times n}$ //

OUTPUT: $[x_{lower}, x_{upper}]$ // x_{lower} and x_{upper} represent the arrays having lower and upper bounds of selected potential intervals that are narrow //

METHOD: Refinement Technique:
Step 1: Concatenate all rows of E in to one row, organize in ascending order by removing the duplicates // Will be referred as refined chromosome //
Step 2: $m \leftarrow length\ of\ E$
Step 3: From array E, pick up x_i's such that $f(x_i)f(x_{i+1}) < 0$, $i = 1,2 \dots m - 1$ and store as $x_{lower} \leftarrow x_i$; $x_{upper} \leftarrow x_{i+1}$ // Selecting intervals from array E such that product of function values at the end points of each interval is negative //
End; // *Post-processing algorithm* //

4   Addressing a Function Possessing Multiple Roots

The procedure developed for functions possessing simple roots needs to be modified to address functions having roots with multiplicity. The following transformation, suggested by [13], converts roots with multiplicity of the problem $f(x) = 0$, as a problem $g(x) = 0$, with simple roots

$$g(x) = \begin{cases} \frac{f(x)}{f'(x)}, & f'(x) \neq 0 \\ 0, & f'(x) = 0 \end{cases} \tag{3}$$

Due to this transformation, every root of $f(x) = 0$ is a simple root of $g(x) = 0$, however every root of $g(x) = 0$ need not be root of $f(x) = 0$. Hence, to address a function having multiple roots, we first make a transformation on $f(x)$. Now, $g(x)$ is considered for the initial population in the place of $f(x)$ in *Pre-processing algorithm*. All the simple roots for $g(x) = 0$ are found through the proposed methodology. Among these roots α_i of $g(x)$, roots satisfying $|f(\alpha_i)| < \epsilon$ are given as the roots for $f(x) = 0$ and the respective multiplicity of each root is found based on conventional method [13].

5 General Algorithm for Function with Known Points of Discontinuity and with Multiple Roots

The real world problems may lead to a situation that $f(.)$ may not be continuous always, further the points and type of discontinuity may not be known. When $f(.)$ has known finite number of points of discontinuity in the region of interest, then the proposed method can be adapted to address discontinuous functions with known points of discontinuity say $\{x_1, x_2, .., x_d\}$. Any discontinuous function can be written as a linear combination of piecewise continuous functions, hence, for known 'd' points of discontinuity, we get $(d + 1)$ intervals, (in each of these intervals, $f(.)$ is continuous), thus the problem is decomposed to $(d + 1)$ problems with respective zone of interest restriction. The following algorithm is an integration of algorithms, namely, *Pre-processing*–to get an estimation of number of roots and *Post-processing*–for selecting the narrow intervals enclosing roots, thereby improving the efficiency of interval based root computation method.

Algorithm 3. Proposed method with *Pre-processing* and *Post-processing* methodologies integrated with Conventional GA

// Finds all interval estimates enclosing all real roots in the given interval $[a, b]$ //

INPUT:
- Given function $f(.)$ and zone of interest $[a, b]$
- d ← Number of points of discontinuity say $\{x_1, x_2, .., x_d\}$
- N_1 ← Population size in *Pre-processing* algorithm
- K_1 ← Number of generations in *Pre-processing* algorithm
- N_2 ← Population size in *Post-processing* algorithm
- K_2 ← Number of generations in *Post-processing* algorithm
- P_c, P_m ← Probability of crossover, mutation
- ϵ ← 10^{-6} *// Tolerance //*

OUTPUT: All potential intervals enclosing roots of transformed function $g(.)$
METHOD:
Step 0: Initialization: i ← 1; LC ← 2; n ← $LC + 2$
Repeat Step 1 through Step 6 while $(i \leq d + 1)$
Step 1: Initialize i^{th} interval $[x_i, x_{i+1}]$ *// $f_i(.)$ is continuous in each of $[x_i, x_{i+1}]$//*
Step 2: $g(x) \leftarrow \frac{f_i(x)}{f_i'(x)}$, if $f_i'(x) \neq 0$ else $g(x) \leftarrow 0$
Step 3: $[LC\_new] \leftarrow Pre-processing\ (g(.), n, N_1, K_1, P_c, P_m)$
Step 4: $n \leftarrow LC\_new + 2$
Step 5: $E_{N_2 \times n} \leftarrow Conventional\_GA\ (g(.), n, N_2, K_2, P_c, P_m)$ *// Here, '$E_{N_2 \times n}$'*
          is random population given as output by applying Conventional_GA//
Step 5: $[x_{i\_lower}, x_{i\_upper}] \leftarrow Post-processing(g(.), E_{N_2 \times n})$
Step 6: $i \leftarrow i + 1$
end while
End; *// Algorithm 3 //*

Thus we get the interval estimates of roots for $g(.)$ and in each of the selected interval above, any bracketing root method such as regula-falsi method [1] can be applied to find all the simple roots of g. Among these roots α_i of $g(x)$, roots satisfying

$|f(\alpha_i)| < \epsilon$ are given as the roots for $f(x) = 0$ and the respective multiplicity of each root is calculated based on conventional method [13].

6   Numerical Experiments

In this section we present 8 examples to illustrate the efficiency and novelty of the proposed method. All computations were done using MATLAB 7.6 on Intel(R) Core(TM) 2 Duo CPU 3.00 GHz Processor and 2 GB RAM. Here tolerance is taken as $\epsilon = 10^{-6}$. Define $gain\ factor = \left(1 - \dfrac{W_w}{W_o}\right) * 100,$ where W_w denotes the sum of widths of selected intervals by applying GA with *Pre-processing* & *Post-processing* techniques and W_o denotes the sum of widths of the selected intervals through conventional GA.

Table 1. A set of bench mark functions and the results with the proposed method are listed below. Here, 'm' in 7th column denotes the multiplicity of root.

Function	Zone	LC_ New Pre- pro	Avg gain %	No. of selected roots			Avg. comp. time per root (sec)
				total	sim- ple	multi- ple	
$f_1 = \sin(\pi x)\cos\left(\dfrac{\pi x}{2}\right)e^x$	[-4.5,4.5]	6	92.75	4	4	-	0.0169
$f_2 = e^x - \dfrac{1}{e^x} - 3x$	[-10, 10]	9	96.99	3	3	-	0.0154
$f_3 = (x-1)^2 \tan(\dfrac{\pi x}{4})$	[-6, 5]	21	96.28	5	3	1 (m=2)	0.0302
$f_4 = \dfrac{Sin^2 x}{\exp\left(\dfrac{x}{2}\right)} - 1$	[-10, 10]	21	95.79	7	7	-	0.0126
$f_5 = \dfrac{2}{3} - (0.1x^{11})\,e^{(2-x^2)}$	[-1 , 1]	9	98.22	3	3	-	0.0183
$f_6 = e^{2\sin(6(x-\pi))} + x - 1$	[-1.5, 2]	15	97.18	5	5	-	0.0131
$f_7 (discontinuous\ function)$ $=$ $-\tan\left(x - \dfrac{\pi}{4}\right), \quad -6 \le x \le -2$ $e^x \sin(10x), \quad -2 < x \le 2$ $(x-5.5)(x-3)^3, \qquad 2 < x \le 6$	{-2, 2} are points of disconti- nuity in [-6,6]	54	96.74	19	16	1 (m=3)	0.0220
$f_8 = \sin(0.2x)\cos(0.5x)$	[-50, 50]	111	96.26	23	15	4 (m=2)	0.0188

From the Table 1, it is apparent that average gain factor is significant with the proposed method and average per root computational time is quite less. We wish to demonstrate through an example f_4 that has 7 simple roots in [-10, 10], the strength of *Pre-processing* in fixing the *LC* adaptive to the problem environment and the strength of *Post-processing* in selecting narrow intervals, thus making root computation efficient with less computational time per root. Further, *Pre-processing* also facilitates to choose the GA parameters such as population size, number of generations in the GA process. Statistical analysis is carried out by repeating each experiment 50 times for varying population size from 10 to 100, in steps of 10.

6.1   Pre-processing – Fixing the LC

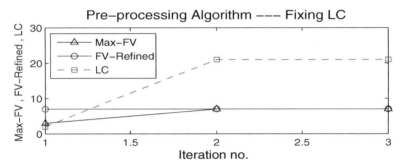

Fig. 1. Explains about the output of *Pre-processing algorithm* that fixes *LC* as 21 for f_4. In the first iteration, $Initial\ LC = 2, Max\_FV = 3, FV\_Refined = 7$, hence, *LC* is reset as $3*7 = 21$. In second iteration, $Max\_FV = 7, FV\_Refined = 7$. As given in *Pre-processing Algorithm*, it continues for one more generation of GA.

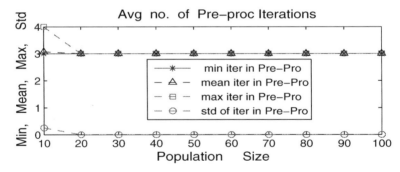

Fig. 2. Displays the average of 50 experiments for minimum, mean, maximum and standard deviation (which tends to zero) of *Pre-processor* iterations. It can be clearly seen that the average number of iterations in *Pre-processing algorithm* $K_1 \leq 4$. Various functions considered by several researchers are taken as test cases and experiments are conducted. It is observed experimentally that more often in *Pre-processing algorithm*, $K_1 \leq 4$.

6.2   Post-processing

Considering f_4 of Table 1 with adaptive $LC = 21$ as input, GA with *Post-processing-Refinement* is carried out, which produces seven non-overlapping potential intervals that are narrow. It is observed that always the number of intervals selected before *Post-processing* is less than or equal to that of number of intervals selected after

Post-processing. Here for this problem, the number of intervals selected before *Post-processing* is 5 whereas, the number of intervals selected after *Post-processing* is 7.

Furthermore, it is observed that *Pre- and Post-processing algorithms* also influence various other parameters of GA such as population size, number of iterations etc. It is found experimentally for various test functions that when we start the GA process with the adaptive *LC*, even though the population size is reduced from $N_2 = 100$ to $N_2 = 75, 50, 25$, this method resulted in selecting maximum number of potential intervals. The statistical analysis of N_2 in GA with respect to mean, maximum, standard deviation of selected intervals facilitates to tune the parameter N_2. Additionally, it is observed through statistical analysis that the number of generations K_2 in GA can also be fine-tuned in a similar way. For the function f_4, mean of selected intervals suggests that all the seven potential intervals are selected even when $K_2 = 2$. Experimental test cases suggest that $K_2 = 3$ worked effectively for majority of functions considered, even for functions possessing dense roots also.

6.3   Comparison Between Conventional GA and Proposed Method for $f_4(x)$

The strength of the proposed methodology can be well understood through the comparison between the conventional GA and proposed method (with *Pre-processing + Post-processing-Refinement*), considering same fitness function in both cases. Since in conventional GA the value of *LC* is unknown, we have selected $LC = 5, 15, 20, 50, 70, 80$ and each experiment is repeated 50 times with varying population size (N_1) from 10 to 100. Now, the same process is repeated with the proposed method (GA with *Pre-processing and Post-processing*) which adaptively fixes *LC* as 21 for this problem. It may be noted that for all the following figures, legend is same as given in Fig. 3.

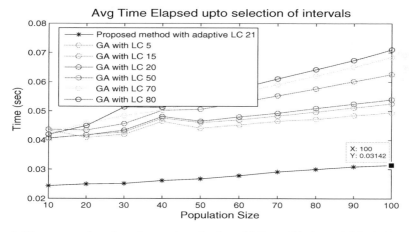

Fig. 3. The average time elapsed up to the selection of "all possible intervals" is depicted here. It can be observed that the average time elapsed to find "all 7 intervals" with adaptive $LC = 21$, for population size $N_2 = 100$ with the proposed method is 0.03142 sec which is much less compared to that of any value of *LC* with conventional GA. This supports the efficiency of *Post-processing.*

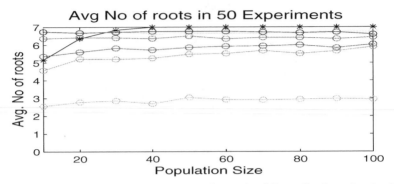

Fig. 4. This figure displays the average number of roots for different N_2. It can be clearly seen that average number of roots found by the proposed method (denoted by '*') is consistent when compared to conventional GA with arbitrary LC.

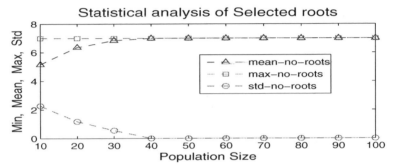

Fig. 5. The statistical analysis about the average of mean, maximum and standard deviation of selected roots with the proposed method indicate that average of standard deviation of selected roots tends to zero for $N_2 > 30$ in GA indicating that all the roots are selected. Thus, the population size N_2 for this problem is suggested to be fine-tuned to approximately 40.

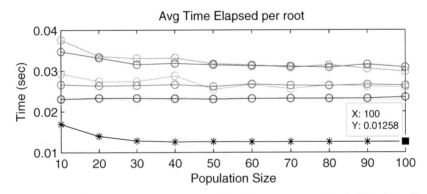

Fig. 6. This figure explains about the comparison between conventional GA with arbitrarily chosen LC and the proposed method with adaptive LC (denoted by '*') with regard to computational time per root. The average computational time per root with proposed method for $N_2 = 100$ is 0.01258 seconds. The very fact that the selected intervals are narrow makes root computation efficient, reducing computational time.

Table 2. The following table depicts the lower and upper bounds of each selected interval with and without *Post-processor* and % of gain factor for each root

Selected Intervals for $f_4(x)$	Selected Intervals –GA with *Pre-processor*, but without *Post-processor*			Selected Intervals–GA with *Pre-processor* and with *Post-processor*			Gain factor= $(1-W_w/W_o)$ *100	Roots
	Interval estimates		Interval Width W_o	Interval estimates		Interval Width W_w		
	Lower	Upper		Lower	Upper			
1	-10.00	-9.3945	0.6055	-9.5304	-9.5084	0.0219	96.3832	-9.5176
2	-9.3945	-7.9416	1.4529	-9.3305	-9.2990	0.0315	97.8319	-9.3275
3	-7.9416	-6.4798	1.4618	-6.4989	-6.4645	0.0343	97.6536	-6.4823
4	-6.4798	-5.1598	1.3200	-6.0789	-6.0140	0.0648	95.0884	-6.0617
5	-5.1598	-3.4636	1.6962	-3.5663	-3.5327	0.0336	98.0191	-3.5642
6	-3.3333	-2.4203	0.9130	-2.5920	-2.5481	0.0438	95.2026	-2.5909
7	-1.6193	-0.7609	0.8584	-0.9203	-0.8373	0.0830	90.3308	-0.9186

It can be observed from the table that the selected intervals with the proposed method with *Post-processing* are very narrow and gain factor is significant, which high lights the novelty of *Post-processing*.

7   Conclusion

The demonstrations reveal that GA coupled with *Pre-processing* module could arrive at apt length of chromosome (LC) even though one starts with LC as two. Further, *Post-processing* (*Refinement*) coupled with GA produces significantly narrow intervals resulting in root computation to be highly efficient   as well as enhances the power of capturing all the roots, i.e., missing a root in the zone of interest has less probability. It is also observed that these novel *Pre-processing* and *Post-processing* modules embedded within the GA help to converge faster, more often less than four iterations.

The sensitivity and robustness of this novel GA has come out by capturing an interval for 31st root of a function $x^2 + \sin\dfrac{1}{x}$ in [0.01, 1.0] besides intervals for all the known 30 roots as reported in [14].

Additionally, it is noticed that *Pre-processing* and *Post-processing algorithms* also influence various other parameters of GA such as population size, number of iterations etc. The work is in progress to analyze the above and its merits and limitations compared with existing methodologies.

Acknowledgements. The authors are grateful to anonymous reviewers and track chairs for helpful suggestions. The first author is thankful to the Director, ACRHEM, UoH and to the Director, HEMRL, Pune for the financial support.

References

1. Numerical Recipes. The Art of Scientific Computing, 3rd edn. Cambridge University Press
2. Holland J.H.: Adaption in natural and artificial systems: an introductory analysis with applications to biology, control, and artificial intelligence. University of Michigan Press
3. Goldberg, D.E.: Genetic Algorithms in Search, Optimization and Machine Learning. Addison-Wesley Publishing
4. Castillo, O., Melin, P., Pedrycz, W. (eds.): Soft Computing for Hybrid Intelligent Systems
5. Annealing, S., Kirkpatrick, S., Gelatt; C.D., Vecchi, M.P.: Optimization. Science, New Series **220**(4598), 671–680 (1983)
6. Dai, J., Wu, G., Wu, Y., Zhu, G.: Helicopter trim research based on hybrid genetic algorithm. In: Proceedings of World Congress on Intelligent Control and Automation, pp. 2007–2011 (2008)
7. Brits, R., Engelbrecht, A.P., van den Bergh, F.: Solving systems of unconstrained equations using PSO. In: Proceedings of International Conference on Systems, Man and Cybermetics, vol. 3, pp. 6–9 (2002)
8. Deb, K.: Multi-objective Optimization Using Evolutionary Algorithms. Wiley (2001)
9. Angelova, M., Pencheva, T.: Tuning Genetic Algorithm parameters to improve convergence time. International Journal of Chemical Engineering **2011**, Article ID 646917, 7
10. Brain, Z., Addicoat, M.: Using Meta-Genetic Algorithms to tune parameters of Genetic Algorithms to find lowest energy Molecular Conformers. In: Proc. of the Alife XII Conference, Odense, Denmark (2010)
11. Yuan, B., Gallagher, M.: A Hybrid Approach to Parameter Tuning in Genetic Algorithms. In: CEC 2005 (2005)
12. Herrera, F., Lozano, M., Verdegay, J.L.: Tackling Real-Coded Genetic Algorithms: Operators and Tools for Behavioural Analysis. Artificial Intelligence Review **12**, 265–319 (1998)
13. Traub, J.F.: Iterative Methods for the Solution of Equations. Prentice Hall, Englewood (1964)
14. Loudas, C.A., Pardalos, P.M. (ed.): Encyclopedia of Optimization, vol. 5, p. 1725. Kluwer Academic Publishers

A Multi-Objective Relative Clustering Genetic Algorithm with Adaptive Local/Global Search Based on Genetic Relatedness

Iman Gholaminezhad[1] and Giovanni Iacca[2]([✉])

[1] Department of Mechanical Engineering, University of Guilan, Guilan, Iran
i.gholaminezhad@gmail.com
[2] INCAS[3], Dr. Nassaulaan 9, 9401 HJ Assen, The Netherlands
giovanniiacca@incas3.eu

Abstract. This paper describes a new evolutionary algorithm for multi-objective optimization, namely Multi-Objective Relative Clustering Genetic Algorithm (MO-RCGA), inspired by concepts borrowed from gene relatedness and kin selection theory. The proposed algorithm clusters the population into different families based on individual kinship, and adaptively chooses suitable individuals for reproduction. The idea is to use the information on the position of the individuals in the search space provided by such clustering schema to enhance the convergence rate of the algorithm, as well as improve its exploration. The proposed algorithm is tested on ten unconstrained benchmark functions proposed for the special session and competition on multi-objective optimizers held at IEEE CEC 2009. The Inverted Generational Distance (IGD) is used to assess the performance of the proposed algorithm, in comparison with the IGD obtained by state-of-the-art algorithms on the same benchmark.

Keywords: Multi-objective optimization · Relative clustering · Genetic relatedness · Inverted generational distance

1 Introduction

According to classic Darwinian theory, natural selection promotes those individuals which behave in their own selfish interests, rather than for the good of their species or for the good of the group in which they live. However, nature offers many examples of social animals (such as eusocial insects, e.g. bees and ants) which do not behave selfishly all the time, but under some conditions they rather tend to cooperate with other members of their colony, for the good of the group as a whole. In fact, in these cases natural selection favors individuals who maximize their genetic contribution to future generations through cooperation with their kin, even if this altruistic behaviour comes with an individual cost [8].

In the last two decades, many evolutionary algorithms (EAs) have been developed based on Darwin's theory and social behaviour, and applied to the solution of complex optimization problems. Successful examples of EAs can be found in

© Springer-Verlag Berlin Heidelberg 2014
A.I. Esparcia-Alcázar et al. (Eds.): EvoApplications 2014, LNCS 8602, pp. 591–602, 2014.
DOI: 10.1007/978-3-662-45523-4_48

particular in the context of multi-objective and dynamic optimization [20, 25]. Nonetheless, rarely EAs have shown the full range of properties exhibited by natural evolution, being instead limited to a coarse and somewhat simplistic approximation of what happens in nature.

A typical technique used to improve multi-objective EAs, as well as swarm intelligence algorithms, is clustering. Clustering is generally considered to facilitate the exploitation process and decrease the computational time to reach convergence. Several examples of clustering-based algorithms exist in the literature. Gong et al. suggested a clustering-based selection strategy of non-dominated individuals by partitioning the non-dominated solutions in each Pareto front into the desired clusters [6]. Tsang and Lau proposed a clustering-based artificial immune system focusing on distributed self-organization, by means of population decomposition and independent evolutionary processes [17]. Moubayed et al. used a clustering-based approach for leader selection in multi-objective particle swarm optimization. In this method better leaders are identified by indirect mapping between objectives and solution clusters [12]. Wang et al. introduced a clustering multi-objective evolutionary algorithm based on orthogonal and uniform design. In this case the orthogonal design generates an initial population of solutions that are scattered uniformly over the search space, while clustering is applied in later stages of the optimization [19]. A similar approach was proposed also by Gao and Zhong, who developed a clustering-based two-phase multi-objective particle swarm optimization in which clustering is applied after a distribution-based generation of the initial population [4].

In this paper we use clustering to build a model of social behaviour and apply it to a multi-objective evolutionary algorithm. As mentioned before, social animals transmit to the next generations not only their own genes, but also - by means of kin selection - their kin's genes (i.e., offspring and/or siblings, which are all characterized by some level of genetic relatedness). In order to develop a simulated model of such behaviour and use it in an optimization algorithm, the first step is to determine the kinship between the individuals in the population, and use it as basis for clustering the whole population into different families. To decompose the current population into different families, each couple of parents must be clustered together with their corresponding offspring (generated by means of crossover and mutation) as well as possible half-siblings (which can be generated because each parent could be selected for reproduction more than once, with different partners). By considering that individuals laying in the same family have some similar genes (i.e., similar variables), it is then possible to design an algorithm in which both family competition and individual competition occur, with the purpose of transmitting individual and kin's genes to the next generations. Here, we use this concept to devise a novel selection strategy which, different from classic selection schemes such as tournament selection or fitness-proportionate selection, embeds naturally local and global search. The proposed multi-objective optimization algorithm based on such strategy, namely Multi-Objective Relative Clustering Genetic Algorithm (MO-RCGA), is tested on ten unconstrained functions taken from the IEEE CEC 2009 benchmark [23], and compared against 15 state-of-the-art multi-objective optimization algorithms.

The rest of the paper is structured as follows: the next section illustrates the working principles of the proposed MO-RCGA, while Section 3 presents the numerical results. Finally, Section 4 concludes this work and suggests possible future research lines.

2 Relative Clustering Genetic Algorithm with Adaptive Local/Global Search

As anticipated in the previous section, the proposed MO-RCGA clusters the individuals into different families, based on their level of kinship (in particular, parents, their children, half-siblings, and cousins lay in the same family). This is done by indexing all parents and their associated offspring produced by recombination and mutation.

Recombination is performed by means of n-point crossover, being n a number between 0 and the individual length (i.e., the problem dimension): for each gene of the parents which are selected for crossover, a uniform random number is drawn in $[0, 1]$; if this number is bigger than a predefined probability of crossover alteration (P_{CA}), the corresponding gene of the two parents are swapped.

In the mutation operator, the genes of each parent can be chosen to mutate depending on a predefined probability of mutation alteration (P_{MA}). If the gene $x_{i,j}$ is selected for mutation (where i and j are respectively the individual and gene index), a uniform random number is drawn within the interval $[-var, +var]$ (being var a given parameter), and the latter number is added to $x_{i,j}$.

Considering the fact that each individual can participate more than once in crossover, its genes may exist in different families. Hence, parents with their associate offspring produced by crossover and mutation, as well as offspring which have only one of the two parents in common (i.e., half-siblings), lay in the same family. By clustering the whole population into different families after the execution of the genetic operators (i.e., crossover and mutation), each family contains individuals which have some similar genes and thus are close to each other in the problem search space.

After such clustering, the algorithm selects the fittest individuals by comparing the individuals from the previous generation with the newly crossed and mutated individuals, and transmits them to the next generation. Selection is performed using the clustered families to choose suitable individuals for reproduction. A first rank-based method is used to select the fittest families. This is done by ranking all families in terms of number of individuals evolved from each family to the next generation. Hence, the higher the number of individuals passed from a family to the next generation, the fittest that family is.

Now, remembering that individuals within the same family are closer to each other than with respect to individuals from different families, it is obvious that choosing for reproduction individuals within the same family (kin selection) is equivalent to perform a local search in the neighbourhood of that family.

The latter is very important especially in the later stages of the optimization, when the algorithm needs to refine the search. On the other hand, if the individuals selected for reproduction are from different families (selfish selection), they are probably far from each other in the search space (especially in the earlier stages of the algorithm), thus allowing for a more global exploration. The latter is more important at the beginning of the optimization process, when the algorithm needs to search for the global optimum region and avoid local optima.

In order to control which strategy must be used, the algorithm adaptively adjusts the probability of local and global search in each generation. At the early iterations, when global exploration is more essential, the algorithm has a higher chance of choosing individuals from different families. Such inter-family selection is performed by comparing the family ranks, so that it is more probable that the selected individual belongs to the highest ranked family (roulette-wheel selection). On the other hand, as the number of iterations increases, the probability of performing intra-family selection (i.e., selecting for reproduction individuals within the same family) is increased. Also in this case, families selected for reproduction are chosen through a rank-based roulette-wheel. It should be noted that for the initial generation, when families do not exist yet, a classic tournament selection scheme is used to select individuals for crossover and mutation.

Basically, by such adaptation of global and local search based on the individual relatedness, the algorithm is able to control the population diversity, a mechanism similar to the classic incest prevention scheme used in the CHC algorithm [3]. To adapt the probability of global and local search smoothly along the generations, we use the following set of equations:

$$range = range_1 + \frac{n_{gen}}{N_{gen}} \cdot (range_2 - range_1) \qquad (1)$$

$$\begin{cases} Prob_G = range \\ Prob_L = 1 - range \end{cases} \qquad (2)$$

where $range_1$ and $range_2$ are predetermined boundary probability values for the global search, while n_{gen} and N_{gen} are respectively the index of the current generation and the maximum number of generations allotted to the evolutionary algorithm. $Prob_G$ and $Prob_L$ indicate respectively the probability of global search and local search.

The flowchart of MO-RCGA is illustrated in Figure 1. For the sake of clarity, we also report its pseudo-code in Algorithm 1. With reference to the pseudo-code, N_{pop} indicates the population size, $rand(0, 1)$ is a uniform random number drawn in $[0, 1]$, and P_C and P_M are respectively the individual probability of crossover and mutation (i.e., the probability that an individual is chosen for crossover and mutation; on the other hand, P_{CA} and P_{MA}, as defined above, are applied at gene level).

3   Numerical Results

In this section, the performance of the proposed MO-RCGA is assessed on the optimization of ten real-parameter multi-objective benchmark functions defined

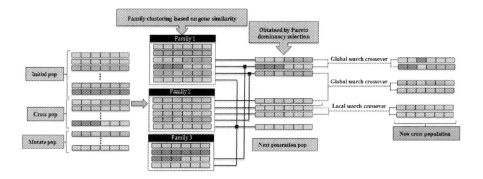

Fig. 1. Flowchart of MO-RCGA

at the CEC 2009 special session on multi-objective optimization [23]. Among these functions, UF1-UF7 are two-objective while UF8-UF10 are three-objective optimization problems. The detailed formulations of the considered test functions are given in [23]. As suggested in the CEC 2009 platform, in the present work the total number of function evaluations N_{fevals} is set as 300000 for each algorithm execution. As also indicated in [23], the population size N_{pop} is set to 100 for two-objective problems and 150 for three-objective functions. It should be noted that the maximum number of generations N_{gen} used in eq. (1) is computed based on the predefined number of function evaluations and population size (i.e., $N_{gen} = N_{fevals}/N_{pop}$). All the other specific parameters of MO-RCGA used in the experimental setup are given in Table 1.

The proposed algorithm has been executed 30 times for each test function, and the average results obtained by MO-RCGA were compared with the results of all the algorithms participating in the CEC 2009 competition [2,5,7,9–11, 13,15,16,18,19,21,22], as well as two more recent multi-objective optimization algorithms [1,14]. The performance indicator used to quantify the quality of the obtained results is the IGD (Inverted Generational Distance) metric [23]. The IGD is defined as follows. Let P^* be a set of uniformly distributed points (in the objective space) along the Pareto Front (PF). Let A be an approximate set of the PF. The IGD is then defined as average distance from P^* to A, namely:

$$IGD(A, P^*) = \frac{\sum_{v \in P^*} d(v, a)}{|P^*|} \tag{3}$$

where $d(v, A)$ is the minimum Euclidean distance between each point v in the PF and all the points in the approximate set A. $|P^*|$ indicates the cardinality of the PF. If $|P^*|$ is large enough to represent the PF well, $IGD(A, P^*)$ can be used as a measure of both diversity and convergence of A to the PF. If the set A is close to the PF and covers it entirely, $IGD(A, P^*)$ will obviously take a low (tending to zero) value. In our experiments, the number of solutions used for computing the IGD (i.e., the cardinality of the approximate set A) is set equal to the population size, therefore 100 for two-objective problems and 150 for three-objective problems.

Algorithm 1. Pseudo-code of MO-RCGA.

// initialization
random initialization of the initial population $\{x_1, x_2, \ldots, x_{N_{pop}}\}$
$n_{gen} = 0$
while $n_{gen} < N_{gen}$ **do**
  // select individuals for reproduction
  if $n_{gen} == 0$ **then**
    for $i = 1 \ldots N_{pop}$ **do**
      tournament selection
    end for
  else
    // family clustering and ranking
    family clustering based on individual kinship
    family ranking based on number of individuals evolved from each family
    // global/local search adaptation
    update of $Prob_L$ and $Prob_G$ according to eq. (1) and (2)
    for $i = 1 \ldots N_{pop}$ **do**
      if $rand(0, 1) < Prob_G$ **then**
        // global search
        rank-based selection from different families
        selection of individuals from the selected families
      else
        // local search
        rank-based selection of a family
        selection of individuals from the selected family
      end if
    end for
  end if
  // genetic operators (reproduction)
  for $i = 1 \ldots N_{pop}$ **do**
    if $rand(0, 1) < P_C$ **then**
      n-point crossover
    end if
    if $rand(0, 1) < P_M$ **then**
      mutation
    end if
  end for
  // Pareto dominance selection
  next generation population selection based on dominance
  $n_{gen} = n_{gen} + 1$
end while

Numerical results are reported in Table 2-3. More specifically, Table 2 shows the minimum (Min), maximum (Max), Mean, and Standard Deviation (SD) of the IGD obtained in the 30 runs of MO-RCGA. Table 3 shows the comparative results of the proposed algorithm with those of the competing algorithms, in the form of mean IGD and its SD obtained through the 30 independent runs. It can be observed that MO-RCGA outperforms in terms of mean IGD all the other algorithms for all the functions except UF7, where it ranks second after the MOEAD algorithm. Finally, Figures 2-11 show the Pareto Front obtained by the proposed algorithm in the best run and the optimal (theoretical) Pareto Front of the ten test problems. It can be seen visually that MO-RCGA is able to detect uniformly the PF on all the test functions, except for the case of UF7 where it fails at covering only the upper leftmost part of it.

Table 2. IGD values obtained with MO-RCGA on functions UF1-UF10 from the CEC 2009 benchmark (30 independent runs)

Table 1. Parameter setting of MO-RCGA

Parameter	Value
$range_1$	0.8
$range_2$	0.2
P_C	1
P_M	0.2
var	0.1
P_{CA}	0.5
P_{MA}	0.2

Function	Minimum	Maximum	Mean	Std. Dev.
UF1	0.00414	0.00431	0.00419	5.22E-04
UF2	0.00407	0.00502	0.00443	1.89E-04
UF3	0.00423	0.00584	0.00491	8.12E-03
UF4	0.00401	0.00522	0.00489	2.66E-04
UF5	0.01283	0.01511	0.01377	5.22E-03
UF6	0.00441	0.00668	0.00536	9.98E-02
UF7	0.00692	0.00882	0.00703	7.32E-03
UF8	0.04308	0.07640	0.0522	3.03E-02
UF9	0.02681	0.03985	0.0297	4.53E-03
UF10	0.06112	0.08321	0.0765	8.24E-03

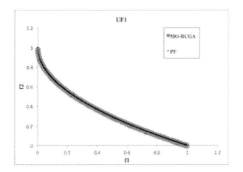

Fig. 2. Final PF set on UF1

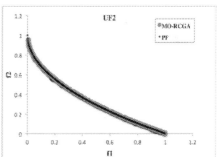

Fig. 3. Final PF set on UF2

Table 3. Comparison of mean IGD and standard deviation (SD) obtained by MO-RCGA and 15 competing algorithms on functions UF1-UF10 from CEC 2009 benchmark (30 runs).

Algorithm	IGD	UF1	UF2	UF3	UF4	UF5	UF6	UF7	UF8	UF9	UF10
MO-RCGA	Mean	**0.00419**	**0.00443**	**0.00491**	**0.00489**	**0.01377**	**0.00536**	0.00703	**0.0522**	**0.0297**	**0.0765**
	SD	**5.22E-04**	**1.89E-04**	**8.12E-04**	**2.66E-04**	**5.22E-02**	**9.9E-02**	7.32E-03	**3.03E-02**	**4.53E-03**	**8.24E-03**
MO-ITLBO	Mean	0.00421	0.00519	0.04681	0.04378	0.07482	0.01144	0.04127	0.06126	0.12379	0.14714
	SD	8.04E-04	1.73E-03	6.48E-03	1.07E-02	8.62E-03	1.01E-02	2.38E-02	1.65E-03	8.97E-02	1.29E-02
MOABC	Mean	0.00618	0.00484	0.0512	0.05801	0.07775	0.06537	0.05573	0.06726	0.0615	0.19499
	SD	NA	NA	NA	NA	NA	NA	NA	NA	NA	NA
MTS	Mean	0.0066	0.00615	0.0531	0.02356	0.01489	0.05917	0.04079	0.11251	0.11442	0.15306
	SD	3.49E-04	5.08E-04	1.17E-02	6.64E-04	3.28E-03	1.06E-02	1.44E-02	1.29E-02	2.55E-02	1.58E-02
DMOEADD	Mean	0.01038	0.00679	0.03337	0.4268	0.31454	0.06673	0.01032	0.06841	0.04896	0.32211
	SD	2.37E-03	2.02E-03	5.68E-03	1.39E-03	4.66E-02	1.03E-02	9.46E-03	9.12E-03	2.23E-02	2.86E-01
LiuLi Algorithm	Mean	0.00785	0.0123	0.01497	0.0435	0.16186	0.17555	0.0073	0.08235	0.09391	0.4691
	SD	2.09E-03	3.32E-03	2.4E-02	6.5E-04	2.82E-02	8.29E-02	8.9E-04	7.33E-03	4.71E-02	1.3E-01
GDE3	Mean	0.00534	0.01195	0.10639	0.0265	0.03928	0.25091	0.02522	0.24855	0.08248	0.43326
	SD	3.42E-04	1.54E-03	1.29E-02	3.72E-04	3.95E-03	1.96E-02	8.89E-03	3.55E-02	2.25E-02	1.23E-02
MOEAD	Mean	0.00435	0.00679	0.00742	0.06385	0.18071	0.00587	**0.00444**	0.0584	0.07896	0.47415
	SD	2.90E-04	1.82E-03	5.89E-03	5.34E-03	6.81E-02	1.71E-03	**1.17E-03**	3.21E-03	5.32E-02	7.36E-02
MOEADGM	Mean	0.0062	0.0064	0.0429	0.476	1.7919	0.5563	0.0076	0.2446	0.1878	0.5646
	SD	1.13E-03	4.3E-04	3.41E-02	2.22E-03	5.12E-01	1.47E-01	9.4E-04	8.54E-02	2.87E-02	1.02E-01
NSGAIILS	Mean	0.01153	0.01237	0.10603	0.0584	0.5657	0.31032	0.02132	0.0863	0.0719	0.84468
	SD	7.3E-03	9.11E-03	6.86E-02	5.12E-03	1.83E-01	1.91E-01	1.95E-02	1.24E-02	4.5E-02	1.63E-01
OW MOSaDE	Mean	0.0122	0.0081	0.103	0.0513	0.4303	0.1918	0.0585	0.0945	0.0983	0.743
	SD	1.2E-03	2.3E-03	1.9E-02	1.9E-03	1.74E-02	2.9E-02	2.91E-02	1.19E-02	2.44E-02	8.85E-02
Clustering MOEA	Mean	0.0299	0.0228	0.0549	0.0585	0.2473	0.0871	0.0223	0.2383	0.2934	0.4111
	SD	3.3E-03	2.3E-03	1.47E-02	2.7E-03	3.84E-02	5.7E-03	2.0E-03	2.3E-02	7.81E-02	5.01E-02
AMGA	Mean	0.03588	0.01623	0.06998	0.04062	0.09405	0.12942	0.05707	0.17125	0.18861	0.32418
	SD	1.03E-02	3.17E-03	1.4E-02	1.75E-03	1.21E-02	5.66E-02	6.53E-02	1.72E-02	4.21E-02	9.57E-02
MOEP	Mean	0.0596	0.0189	0.099	0.0427	0.2245	0.1031	0.0197	0.423	0.342	0.3621
	SD	1.2E-02	3.8E-03	1.32E-02	8.35E-04	3.44E-02	3.45E-02	7.51E-04	5.65E-02	1.58E-01	4.44E-02
DECMOSA-SQP	Mean	0.07702	0.02834	0.0935	0.03392	0.16713	0.12604	0.02416	0.21583	0.14111	0.36985
	SD	3.94E-02	3.13E-02	1.98E-01	5.37E-03	8.95E-02	5.62E-01	2.23E-02	1.21E-01	3.45E-01	6.53E-01
OMOEAII	Mean	0.08564	0.03057	0.27141	0.04624	0.1692	0.07338	0.03354	0.192	0.23179	0.62754
	SD	4.07E-03	1.61E-03	3.76E-02	9.67E-04	3.9E-03	2.45E-03	1.74E-03	1.23E-02	6.48E-02	1.46E-01

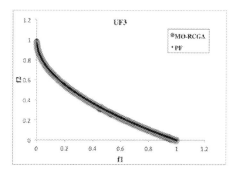

Fig. 4. Final PF set on UF3

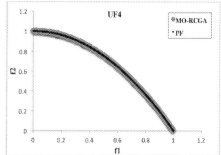

Fig. 5. Final PF set on UF4

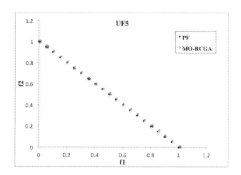

Fig. 6. Final PF set on UF5

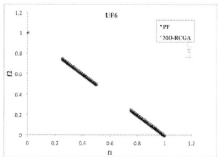

Fig. 7. Final PF set on UF6

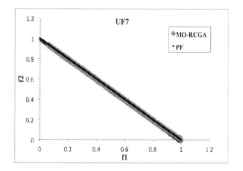

Fig. 8. Final PF set on UF7

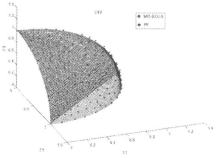
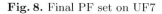

Fig. 9. Final PF set on UF8

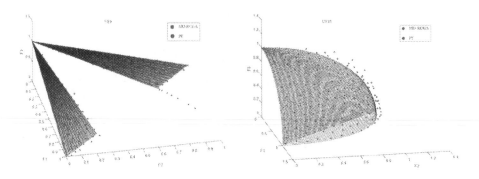

Fig. 10. Final PF set on UF9   **Fig. 11.** Final PF set on UF10

4   Conclusion

In this work we introduced a new algorithm for solving multi-objective optimization problems, namely Multi-Objective Relative Clustering Genetic Algorithm (MO-RCGA). Inspired by the concepts of kin selection and genetic relatedness, the proposed algorithm iteratively clusters the individuals in the population into different families, based on their level of kinship (i.e., parents, offspring and half-siblings). Selection of individuals for reproduction is thus performed at both intra-family and inter-family level. Since individuals within a family have some similar genes and hence are closer to each other in the search space than individuals from different families, by selecting intra-family individuals the algorithm favors local search, while selecting inter-family individuals global search is promoted. An adaptive scheme is presented which balances the two levels of selection during the different stages of the optimization process, thus guaranteeing an optimal trade-off between exploration and exploitation. The performance of MO-RCGA is assessed in comparison with 15 state-of-the-art multi-objective optimization algorithms on ten benchmark functions from the CEC 2009 testbed. Numerical results, expressed in terms of Inverted Generational Distance, show that the proposed algorithm is extremely competitive on all the different functions and against all the considered competing algorithms.

In our future research, we will extend this study on a larger experimental setup, possibly including real-world applications. Also, we will include in the comparison alternative adaptive mechanisms, such as the ensemble of neighbourhood sizes proposed in [24], and we will try to apply the proposed adaptive selection scheme to single-objective optimization. Finally, from an algorithmic point of view, we will try to improve upon the current implementation of MO-RCGA, for example introducing into the algorithm a two-phase scheme including an efficient design of the initial population.

Acknowledgments. INCAS[3] is co-funded by the Province of Drenthe, the Municipality of Assen, the European Fund for Regional Development and the Ministry of Economic Affairs, Peaks in the Delta.

References

1. Akbari, R., Ziarati, K.: Multi-Objective bee swarm optimization. International Journal of Innovative Computing Information and Control **8**(1B), 715–726 (2012)
2. Chen, C.M., Chen, Y.P., Zhang, Q.: Enhancing MOEA/D with guided mutation and priority update for multi-objective optimization. In: IEEE Congress on Evolutionary Computation, pp. 209–216 (2009)
3. Eshelman, L.J.: The CHC Adaptive Search Algorithm: How to Have Safe Search When Engaging in Nontraditional Genetic Recombination. Foundations of Genetic Algorithms pp. 265–283 (1991)
4. Gao, H., Zhong, W.: Multiobjective Optimization Using Clustering Based Two Phase Particle Swarm Optimization. International Conference on Natural Computation **6**, 520–524 (2008)
5. Gao, S., Zeng, S., Xiao, B., Zhang, L., Shi, Y., Tian, X., Yang, Y., Long, H., Yang, X., Yu, D., Yan, Z.: An orthogonal multi-objective evolutionary algorithm with lower-dimensional crossover. In: IEEE Congress on Evolutionary Computation, pp. 1959–1964 (2009)
6. Gong, M., Cheng, G., Jiao, L., Liu, C.: Clustering-based selection for evolutionary multi-objective optimization. In: IEEE International Conference on Intelligent Computing and Intelligent Systems (2009)
7. Huang, V.L., Zhao, S.Z., Mallipeddi, R., Suganthan, P.N.: Multi-objective optimization using self-adaptive differential evolution algorithm. In: IEEE Congress on Evolutionary Computation, pp. 190–194 (2009)
8. Krebs, J.R., Davies, N.B.: An Introduction to Behavioural Ecology. Blackwell Publishing, Inc. (1993)
9. Kukkonen, S., Lampinen, J.: Performance assessment of Generalized Differential Evolution 3 with a given set of constrained multi-objective test problems. In: IEEE Congress on Evolutionary Computation, pp. 1943–1950 (2009)
10. Liu, H.L., Li, X.: The multiobjective evolutionary algorithm based on determined weight and sub-regional search. In: IEEE Congress on Evolutionary Computation, pp. 1928–1934 (2009)
11. Liu, M., Zou, X., Chen, Y., Wu, Z.: Performance assessment of DMOEA-DD with CEC 2009 MOEA competition test instances. In: IEEE Congress on Evolutionary Computation, pp. 2913–2918 (2009)
12. Moubayed, N.A., Petrovski, A., McCall, J.: Clustering-Based Leaders' Selection in Multi-Objective Particle Swarm Optimisation. In: Yin, H., Wang, W., Rayward-Smith, V. (eds.) IDEAL 2011. LNCS, vol. 6936, pp. 100–107. Springer, Heidelberg (2011)
13. Qu, B.Y., Suganthan, P.N.: Multi-objective evolutionary programming without non-domination sorting is up to twenty times faster. In: IEEE Congress on Evolutionary Computation, pp. 2934–2939 (2009)
14. Rao, V., Patel, V.: Comparative performance of an elitist teaching-learning-based optimization algorithm for solving unconstrained optimization problems. International Journal of Industrial Engineering Computations **4**(1), 29–50 (2013)
15. Sindhya, K., Sinha, A., Deb, K., Miettinen, K.: Local search based evolutionary multi-objective optimization algorithm for constrained and unconstrained problems. In: IEEE Congress on Evolutionary Computation, pp. 2919–2926 (2009)
16. Tiwari, S., Fadel, G., Koch, P., Deb, K.: Performance assessment of the hybrid Archive-based Micro Genetic Algorithm (AMGA) on the CEC 2009 test problems. In: IEEE Congress on Evolutionary Computation, pp. 1935–1942 (2009)

17. Tsang, W.W.P., Lau, H.Y.K.: Clustering-Based Multi-objective Immune Optimization Evolutionary Algorithm. In: Coello Coello, C.A., Greensmith, J., Krasnogor, N., Liò, P., Nicosia, G., Pavone, M. (eds.) ICARIS 2012. LNCS, vol. 7597, pp. 72–85. Springer, Heidelberg (2012)
18. Tseng, L.Y., Chen, C.: Multiple trajectory search for unconstrained/constrained multi-objective optimization. In: IEEE Congress on Evolutionary Computation, pp. 1951–1958 (2009)
19. Wang, Y., Dang, C., Li, H., Han, L., Wei, J.: A clustering multi-objective evolutionary algorithm based on orthogonal and uniform design. In: IEEE Congress on Evolutionary Computation, pp. 2927–2933 (2009)
20. Yang, S., Ong, Y.S., Jin, Y. (eds.): Evolutionary Computation in Dynamic and Uncertain Environments, vol. 51. SCI. Springer (2007)
21. Zamuda, A., Brest, J., Bošković, B., Zumer, V.: Differential Evolution with Self-adaptation and Local Search for Constrained Multiobjective Optimization. In: IEEE Congress on Evolutionary Computation, pp. 195–202 (2009)
22. Zhang, Q., Liu, W., Li, H.: The performance of a new version of MOEA/D on CEC 2009 unconstrained MOP test instances. In: IEEE Congress on Evolutionary Computation, pp. 203–208 (2009)
23. Zhang, Q., Zhao, A., Suganthan, P.N., Liu, W., Tiwari, S.: Multi-objective optimization test instances for the CEC 2009 special session and competition. Tech. Rep. CES 487, University of Essex and Nanyang Technological University (2008)
24. Zhao, S.Z., Suganthan, P.N., Zhang, Q.: Decomposition-Based Multiobjective Evolutionary Algorithm With an Ensemble of Neighborhood Sizes. IEEE Transactions on Evolutionary Computation **16**(3), 442–446 (2012)
25. Zhou, A., Qu, B.Y., Li, H., Zhao, S.Z., Suganthan, P.N., Zhang, Q.: Multiobjective evolutionary algorithms: A survey of the state of the art. Swarm and Evolutionary Computation **1**(1), 32–49 (2011)

Noisy Optimization: Convergence with a Fixed Number of Resamplings

Marie-Liesse Cauwet$^{(\boxtimes)}$

TAO (Inria), LRI, UMR 8623 (CNRS - Univ. Paris-Sud), Orsay, France
`marie-liesse.cauwet@inria.fr`

Abstract. It is known that evolution strategies in continuous domains might not converge in the presence of noise [3,14]. It is also known that, under mild assumptions, and using an increasing number of resamplings, one can mitigate the effect of additive noise [4] and recover convergence. We show new sufficient conditions for the convergence of an evolutionary algorithm with constant number of resamplings; in particular, we get fast rates (log-linear convergence) provided that the variance decreases around the optimum slightly faster than in the so-called multiplicative noise model.

Keywords: Noisy optimization · Evolutionary algorithm · Theory

1 Introduction

Given a domain $\mathcal{D} \in \mathbb{R}^d$, with d a positive integer, a noisy objective function is a stochastic process $f : (x, \omega) \mapsto f(x, \omega)$ with $x \in \mathcal{D}$ and ω a random variable independently sampled at each call to f. Noisy optimization is the search of x such that $\mathbb{E}[f(x, \omega)]$ is approximately minimum. Throughout the paper, x^* denotes the unknown exact optimum, supposed to be unique. For any positive integer n, $\tilde{x}_n$ denotes the search point used in the nth function evaluation. We here consider black-box noisy optimization, i.e we can have access to f only through calls to a black-box which, on request x, (i) randomly samples ω (ii) returns $f(x, \omega)$. Among zero-order methods proposed to solve noisy optimization problems, some of the most usual are evolution strategies; [1] has studied the performance of evolution strategies in the presence of noise, and investigated its robustness by tuning the population size of the offspring and the mutation strength. Another approach consists in using resamplings of each individual (averaging multiple resamplings reduces the noise), rather than increasing the population size. Resampling means that, when evaluating $f(x, \omega)$, several independent copies $\omega_1, \ldots, \omega_r$ of ω are used (i.e. the black-box oracle is called several times with a same x) and we use as an approximate fitness value $\frac{1}{r} \sum_{i=1}^{r} f(x, \omega_i)$ in the optimization algorithm. The key point is how to choose r, number of resamplings, for a given x. Another crucial point is the model of noise. Different models of noise can be considered: additive noise (Eq. 3), multiplicative noise (Eq. 4) or a more general model (Eq. 5). Notice that, in Eq. 5 when $z > 0$, the noise decreases to zero near the optimum; this setting is not artificial as we can observe this behavior in many real problems.

© Springer-Verlag Berlin Heidelberg 2014
A.I. Esparcia-Alcázar et al. (Eds.): EvoApplications 2014, LNCS 8602, pp. 603–614, 2014.
DOI: 10.1007/978-3-662-45523-4_49

Let us give an example in which the noise variance decreases to zero around the optimum. Consider a Direct Policy Search problem, i.e. the optimization of a parametric policy on simulations. Assume that we optimize the success rate of a policy. Assume that the optimum policy has a success rate 100%. Then, the variance is zero at the optimum.

1.1 Convergence Rates: Log-Linear Convergence and Log-log Convergence

Depending on the specific class of optimization problems and on some internal properties of the algorithm considered, we obtain different uniform rates of convergence (where the convergence can be almost sure, in probability or in expectation, depending on the setting); a fast rate will be a log-linear convergence, as follows:

$$\textbf{Fast rate: } \limsup_n \frac{\log ||\tilde{x}_n - x^*||}{n} = -A < 0, \tag{1}$$

In the noise-free case, evolution strategies typically converge linearly in log-linear scale, as shown in [5, 7, 8, 15, 18].
The algorithm presents a slower rate of convergence in case of log-log convergence, as follows:

$$\textbf{Slow rate: } \limsup_n \frac{\log ||\tilde{x}_n - x^*||}{\log n} = -A < 0, \tag{2}$$

The log-log rates are typical rates in the noisy case (see [2, 4, 9–11, 16, 17]). Nevertheless, we will here show that, under specific assumptions on the noise (if the noise around the optimum decreases "quickly enough", see section 1.4), we can reach faster rates: log-linear convergence rates as in Eq. 1, by averaging a constant number of resamplings of $f(x, \omega)$.

1.2 Additive Noise Model

Additive noise refers to:

$$f(x, \omega) = ||x - x^*||^p + noise_\omega, \tag{3}$$

where p is a positive integer and where $noise_\omega$ is sampled independently with a fixed given distribution. In this model, the noise has lower bounded variance, even in the neighborhood of the optimum. The uniform rate typically converges linearly in $\log - \log$ scale (cf Eq. 2) as discussed in [2, 9–11, 16, 17]. This important case in applications has been studied in [9, 11, 12, 16] where tight bounds have been shown for stochastic gradient algorithms using finite differences. When using evolution strategies, [4] has shown mathematically that an exponential number of resamplings (number of resamplings scaling exponentially with the index of iterations) or an adaptive number of resamplings (scaling as a polynomial of the inverse step-size) can both lead to a log-log convergence rate.

1.3   Multiplicative Noise Model

Multiplicative noise, in the unimodal spherical case, refers to

$$f(x,\omega) = ||x - x^*||^p + ||x - x^*||^p \times noise_\omega \qquad (4)$$

and some compositions (by increasing mappings) of this function, where p is a positive integer and where $noise_\omega$ is sampled independently with a fixed given distribution. [14] has studied the convergence of evolution strategies in noisy environments with multiplicative noise, and essentially shows that the result depends on the noise distribution: if $noise_\omega$ is conveniently lower bounded, then some standard $(1 + 1)$ evolution strategy converges to the optimum; if arbitrarily negative values can be sampled with non-zero probability, then it does not converge.

1.4   A More General Noise Model

Eqs. 3 and 4 are particular cases of a more general noise model:

$$f(x,\omega) = ||x - x^*||^p + ||x - x^*||^{pz/2} \times noise_\omega. \qquad (5)$$

where p is a positive integer, $z \geq 0$ and $noise_\omega$ is sampled independently with a fixed given distribution. Eq. 5 boils down to Eq. 3 when $z = 0$ and to Eq. 4 when $z = 2$. We will here obtain fast rates for some larger values of z. More precisely, we will show that when $z > 2$, we obtain log-linear rates, as in Eq. 1. Incidentally, this shows some tightness (with respect to z) of conditions for non-convergence in [14].

2   Theoretical Analysis

Section 2.1 is devoted to some preliminaries. Section 2.2 presents results for constant numbers of resamplings on our generalized noise model (Eq. 5) when $z > 2$.

2.1   Preliminary: Noise-Free Case

Typically, an evolution strategy at iteration n:

- generates λ individuals using the current estimate x_{n-1} of the optimum x^* and the so-called mutation strength (or step-size) σ_{n-1},
- provides a pair (x_n, σ_n) where x_n is a new estimate of x^* and σ_n is a new mutation strength.

From now on, for the sake of notation simplicity, we assume that $x^* = 0$.

For some evolution strategies and in the noise-free case, we know (see e.g. Theorem 4 in [5]) that there exists a constant A such that :

$$\frac{\log(||x_n||)}{n} \xrightarrow[n \to \infty]{a.s} -A \tag{6}$$

$$\frac{\log(\sigma_n)}{n} \xrightarrow[n \to \infty]{a.s} -A \tag{7}$$

This paper will discuss cases in which an algorithm verifying Eqs. 6, 7 in the noise-free case also verifies them in a noisy setting.

Remarks: *In the general case of arbitrary evolution strategies (ES), we don't know if A is positive, but:*

- *in the case of a $(1+1)$-ES with generalized one-fifth success rule, $A > 0$ see [6];*
- *in the case of a self-adaptive $(1, \lambda)$-ES with gaussian mutations, the estimate of A by Monte-Carlo simulations is positive [5].*

Property 1. For some $\delta > 0$, for any α, α' such that $\alpha < A$ and $\alpha' > A$, there exist $C > 0$, $C'' > 0$, $V > 0$, $V' > 0$, such that with probability at least $1 - \delta$

$$\forall n \geq 1, C' \exp(-\alpha' n) \leq ||x_n|| \leq C \exp(-\alpha n); \tag{8}$$

$$\forall n \geq 1, V' \exp(-\alpha' n) \leq \sigma_n \leq V \exp(-\alpha n). \tag{9}$$

Proof. For any $\alpha < A$, almost surely, $\log(||x_n||) \leq -\alpha n$ for n sufficiently large. So, almost surely, $\sup_{n \geq 1} \log(||x_n||) + \alpha n$ is finite. Consider V the quantile $1 - \frac{\delta}{4}$ of $\exp\left(\sup_{n \geq 1} \log(||x_n||) + \alpha n\right)$. Then, with probability at least $1 - \frac{\delta}{4}$, $\forall n \geq 1, ||x_n|| \leq V \exp(-\alpha n)$. We can apply the same trick for lower bounding $||x_n||$, and upper and lower bounding σ_n, all of them with probability $1 - \frac{\delta}{4}$, so that all bounds hold true simultaneously with probability at least $1 - \delta$. ☐

2.2   Noisy Case

The purpose of this Section is to show that if some evolution strategies perform well (linear convergence in the log-linear scale, as in Eqs. 6, 7), then, just by considering Y resamplings for each fitness evaluation as explained in Alg. 1, they will also be fast in the noisy case.

Our theorem holds for any evolution strategy satisfying the following constraints:

- At each iteration n, a search point x_n is defined and λ search points are generated and have their fitness values evaluated.
- The noisy fitness values are averaged over Y (a constant) resamplings.
- The jth individual evaluated at iteration n is randomly drawn by $x_n + \sigma_n \mathcal{N}_d$ with $\mathcal{N}_d$ a d-dimensional standard Gaussian variable.

This framework is presented in Alg. 1.

We now state our theorem, under log-linear convergence assumption (cf assumption (ii) below).

Algorithm 1. A general framework for evolution strategies. For simplicity, it does not cover all evolution strategies, e.g. mutations of step-sizes as in self-adaptive algorithms are not covered; yet, our proof can be extended to a more general case ($x_{n,i}$ distributed as $x_n + \sigma N$ for some noise N with exponentially decreasing tail). The case $Y = 1$ is the case without resampling. Our theorem basically shows that if such an algorithm converges linearly (in log-linear scale) in the noise-free case then the version with Y large enough converges linearly in the noisy case when $z > 2$.

Initialize x_0 and σ_0.
$n \leftarrow 1$
while not finished **do**
    for $i \in \{1, \dots, \lambda\}$ **do**
        Define $x_{n,i} = x_n + \sigma_n \mathcal{N}_d$.
        Define $y_{n,i} = \frac{1}{Y} \sum_{k=1}^{Y} f(x_{n,i}, \omega_k)$.
    end for
    Update: $(x_{n+1}, \sigma_{n+1}) \leftarrow \text{update}(x_{n,1}, \dots, x_{n,\lambda}, y_{n,1}, \dots, y_{n,\lambda}, \sigma_n)$.
    $n \leftarrow n + 1$
end while

Theorem 1. *Consider the following assumptions:*

  (i) the fitness function f satisfies $\mathbb{E}[f(x, \omega)] = \|x\|^p$ and has a limited variance:

$$Var(f(x, \omega)) \leq (\mathbb{E}[f(x, \omega)])^z \text{ for some } z > 2; \tag{10}$$

  (ii) in the noise-free case, the ES with population size λ under consideration is log-linearly converging, i.e. for any $\delta > 0$, for some $\alpha > 0$, $\alpha' > 0$, there exist $C > 0$, $C' > 0$, $V > 0$, $V' > 0$, such that with probability $1-\delta$, Eqs. 8 and 9 hold;

  (iii) the number Y of resamplings per individual is constant.

Then, if $z > \max\left(\frac{2(p\alpha' - (\alpha - \alpha')d)}{p\alpha}, \frac{2(2\alpha' - \alpha)}{\alpha}\right)$, for any $\delta > 0$, there is $Y_0 > 0$ such that for any $Y \geq Y_0$, Eqs. 8 and 9 also hold with probability at least $(1 - \delta)^2$ in the noisy case.

Corollary 1. *Under the same assumptions, with probability at least $(1 - \delta)^2$,*

$$\limsup_{n} \frac{\log(\|\tilde{x}_n\|)}{n} \leq -\frac{\alpha}{\lambda Y}$$

Proof of Corollary 1 : Immediate consequence of Theorem 1, by applying Eq. 8 and using $\limsup_{n} \frac{\log(\|\tilde{x}_n\|)}{n} = \limsup_{n} \frac{\log(\|x_n\|)}{\lambda Y n}$. $\qquad\square$

Remarks:

  – **Interpretation:** *Informally speaking, our theorem shows that if an algorithm converges in the noise-free case, then it also converges in the noisy case with the resampling rule, at least if z and Y are large enough.*

- *Notice that we can choose constants α and α' very close to each other. Then the assumption $z > \max\left(\frac{2(p\alpha' - (\alpha - \alpha')d)}{p\alpha}, \frac{2(2\alpha' - \alpha)}{\alpha}\right)$ boils down to $z > 2$.*
- *We show a log-linear convergence rate as in the noise-free case. This means that we get $\log\|\tilde{x}_n\|$ linear in the number of function evaluations. This is as Eq. 1, and faster than Eq. 2 which is typical for noisy optimization with constant variance.*
- *In the previous hypothesis, the new individuals are drawn following $x_n + \sigma_n \mathcal{N}_d$ with $\mathcal{N}_d$ a d-dimensional standard Gaussian variable, but we could substitute $\mathcal{N}_d$ for any random variable with an exponentially decreasing tail.*

Proof of Theorem 1 : In all the proof, $\mathcal{N}_k$ denotes a standard normal random variable in dimension k.

Sketch of proof: Consider an arbitrary $\delta > 0$ and $\delta_n = \exp(-\gamma n)$ for some $n \geq 1$ and $\gamma > 0$.

We compute in Lemma 2 the probability that at least two generated points x_{n,i_1} and x_{n,i_2} at iteration n are "close", i.e are such that $\big|\,\|x_{n,i_1}\|^p - \|x_{n,i_2}\|^p\,\big| \leq \delta_n$; then we calculate the probability that the noise of at least one of the λ evaluated individuals of iteration n is bigger than $\frac{\delta_n}{2}$ in Lemma 3. Thus, we can conclude in Lemma 4 by estimating the probability that at least two individuals are misranked due to noise.

We first begin by showing a technical lemma.

Lemma 1. *Let $u \in \mathbb{R}^d$ be a unit vector and $\mathcal{N}_d$ a d-dimensional standard normal random variable. Then for $S > 0$ and $\ell > 0$, there exists a constant $M > 0$ such that :*

$$\max_{v \geq 0} \mathbb{P}(\big|\,\|u + S\mathcal{N}_d\|^p - v\,\big| \leq \ell) \leq MS^{-d} \max\left(\ell, \ell^{d/p}\right).$$

Proof. For any $v \geq \ell$, we denote $E_{v \geq \ell}$ the set :

$$E_{v \geq \ell} = \left\{x\ ;\ \big|\,\|x\|^p - v\,\big| \leq \ell\right\} = \left\{x\ ;\ (v - \ell)^{\frac{1}{p}} \leq \|x\| \leq (v + \ell)^{\frac{1}{p}}\right\}.$$

We first compute $\mu(E_{v \geq \ell})$, the Lebesgue measure of $E_{v \geq \ell}$:

$$\mu(E_{v \geq \ell}) = K_d \left\{(v + \ell)^{\frac{d}{p}} - (v - \ell)^{\frac{d}{p}}\right\},$$

with $K_d = \frac{(2\pi)^{d/2}}{2 \times 4 \times \cdots \times d}$ if d is even, and $K_d = \frac{2(2\pi)^{(d-1)/2}}{1 \times 3 \times \cdots \times d}$ otherwise. Hence, by Taylor expansion, $\mu(E_{v \geq \ell}) \leq Kv^{\frac{d}{p}-1}\ell$, where $K = K_d\left(2\frac{d}{p} + \sup_{v \geq \ell}\ \sup_{0 < \zeta < \frac{\ell}{v}} \frac{q''(\zeta)}{2}\frac{\ell}{v}\right)$, with $q(x) = (1 + x)^{\frac{d}{p}}$.

• If $v \geq \ell$:

$$\mathbb{P}(\big|\,\|u + S\mathcal{N}_d\|^p - v\,\big| \leq \ell) = \mathbb{P}(u + S\mathcal{N}_d \in E_{v \geq \ell}),$$

$$\leq S^{-d} \sup_{x \in E_{v \geq \ell}} \left(\frac{1}{\sqrt{2\pi}}\exp(-\frac{\|S^{-1}(x - u)\|^2}{2})\right)\mu(E_{v \geq \ell}),$$

$$\leq M_1 S^{-d}\ell,$$

$$\leq M_1 S^{-d}\max\left(\ell, \ell^{d/p}\right).$$

where $M_1 = \frac{K}{\sqrt{2\pi}} \sup\limits_{v \geq \ell} \sup\limits_{x: ||x|| \leq (v+\ell)^{\frac{1}{p}}} \left[v^{\frac{d}{p}-1} \exp\left(-\frac{||S^{-1}(x-u)||^2}{2}\right) \right].$

- If $v < \ell$, $\mathbb{P}(| \ ||u + S\mathcal{N}_d||^p - v| \leq \ell) \leq M_2 S^{-d} \ell^{d/p} \leq M_2 S^{-d} \max\left(\ell, \ell^{d/p}\right),$

where $M_2 = 2^{\frac{d}{p}} \frac{K_d}{\sqrt{2\pi}}$. Hence the result follows by taking $M = \max(M_1, M_2)$. $\square$

Lemma 2. *Let us denote by $P_n^{(1)}$ the probability that, at iteration n, there exist at least two points x_{n,i_1} and x_{n,i_2} such that $| \ ||x_{n,i_1}||^p - ||x_{n,i_2}||^p | \leq \delta_n$. Then*

$$P_n^{(1)} \leq B\lambda^2 \exp(-\gamma' n),$$

for some $B > 0$ and $\gamma' > 0$ depending on γ, d, p, C, C', V, α, α'.

Proof. Let us first compute the probability $P_n^{(0)}$ that, at iteration n, two given generated points x_{n,i_1} and x_{n,i_2} are such that $| \ ||x_{n,i_1}||^p - ||x_{n,i_2}||^p | \leq \delta_n$. Let us denote by $\mathcal{N}_d^1$ and $\mathcal{N}_d^2$ two d-dimensional standard independent random variables, $u \in \mathbb{R}^d$ a unit vector and $S_n = \frac{\sigma_n}{||x_n||}$.

$$P_n^{(0)} = \mathbb{P}\left(| \ ||x_n + \sigma_n \mathcal{N}_d^1||^p - ||x_n + \sigma_n \mathcal{N}_d^2||^p | \leq \delta_n\right),$$

$$= \mathbb{P}\left(| \ ||u + S_n \mathcal{N}_d^1||^p - ||u + S_n \mathcal{N}_d^2||^p | \leq \frac{\delta_n}{||x_n||^p}\right),$$

$$\leq \max_{v \geq 0} \mathbb{P}\left(| \ ||u + S_n \mathcal{N}_d^1||^p - v| \leq \frac{\delta_n}{||x_n||^p}\right).$$

Hence, by Lemma 1, there exists a $M > 0$ such that $P_n^{(0)} \leq M S_n^{-d} \left(\frac{\delta_n}{||x_n||^p}\right)^m$, where m is such that $\left(\frac{\delta_n}{||x_n||^p}\right)^m = \max\left(\frac{\delta_n}{||x_n||^p}, \left(\frac{\delta_n}{||x_n||^p}\right)^{d/p}\right)$. Moreover $S_n \geq V'C^{-1} \exp(-(\alpha'-\alpha)n)$ by Assumption (ii). Thus $P_n^{(0)} \leq B \exp(-\gamma' n)$, with $B = MV'^{-d} C^d C'^{-mp}$ and $\gamma' = d(\alpha - \alpha') + m\gamma - mp\alpha'$. In particular, γ' is positive, provided that γ is sufficiently large.

By union bound, $P_n^{(1)} \leq \frac{(\lambda-1)\lambda}{2} P_n^{(0)} \leq B\lambda^2 \exp(-\gamma' n)$. $\square$

We now provide a bound on the probability $P_n^{(3)}$ that the fitness value of at least one search point generated at iteration n has noise (i.e. deviation from expected value) bigger than $\frac{\delta_n}{2}$ in spite of the Y resamplings.

Lemma 3.

$$P_n^{(3)} := \mathbb{P}\left(\exists i \in \{1, \ldots, \lambda\} \ ; \ \left|\frac{1}{Y}\sum_{j=1}^{Y} f(x_{n,i}, \omega_j) - \mathbb{E}\left[f(x_{n,i}, \omega_j)\right]\right| \geq \frac{\delta_n}{2}\right)$$

$$\leq \lambda B' \exp(-\gamma'' n)$$

for some $B' > 0$ and $\gamma'' > 0$ depending on γ, d, p, z, C, Y, α, α'.

Proof. First, for one point x_{n,i_0}, $i_0 \in \{1, \ldots, \lambda\}$ generated at iteration n, we write $P_n^{(2)}$ the probability that when evaluating the fitness function at this point, we make a mistake bigger than $\frac{\delta_n}{2}$.

$P_n^{(2)} = \mathbb{P}(|\frac{1}{Y}\sum_{j=1}^{Y} f(x_{n,i_0}, \omega_j) - \mathbb{E}[f(x_{n,i_0}, \omega_j)]| \geq \frac{\delta_n}{2}) \leq B' \exp(-\gamma'' n)$ by using Chebyshev's inequality, where $B' = 4Y^{-1}C^{pz}$ and $\gamma'' = \alpha z p - 2\gamma$. In particular, $\gamma'' > 0$ if $z > \frac{2(mp\alpha' - (\alpha - \alpha')d)}{p\alpha m}$; hence, if $z \geq \max\left(\frac{2(p\alpha' - (\alpha - \alpha')d)}{p\alpha}, \frac{2(2\alpha' - \alpha)}{\alpha}\right)$, we get $\gamma'' > 0$.

Then, $P_n^{(3)} \leq \lambda P_n^{(2)}$ by union bound. $\qquad \square$

Lemma 4. *Let us denote by $P_{misranking}$ the probability that in at least one iteration, there is at least one misranking of two individuals. Then, if $z > \max\left(\frac{2(p\alpha' - (\alpha - \alpha')d)}{p\alpha}, \frac{2(2\alpha' - \alpha)}{\alpha}\right)$ and Y is large enough, $P_{misranking} \leq \delta$.*

This lemma implies that with probability at least $1 - \delta$, provided that Y has been chosen large enough, we get the same rankings of points as in the noise free case. In the noise free case Eqs. 8 and 9 hold with probility at least $1 - \delta$ - this proves the convergence with probability at least $(1 - \delta)^2$, hence the expected result; the proof of the theorem is complete. $\qquad \square$

Proof. (of the lemma)

We consider the probability $P_n^{(4)}$ that two individuals x_{n,i_1} and x_{n,i_2} at iteration n are misranked due to noise, so

$$\|x_{n,i_1}\|^p \leq \|x_{n,i_2}\|^p \tag{11}$$

$$\text{and } \frac{1}{Y}\sum_{j=1}^{Y} f(x_{n,i_1}, \omega_j) \geq \frac{1}{Y}\sum_{j=1}^{Y} f(x_{n,i_2}, \omega_j) \tag{12}$$

Eqs. 11 and 12 occur simultaneously if either two points have very similar fitness (difference less than δ_n) or the noise is big (larger than $\frac{\delta_n}{2}$). Therefore, $P_n^{(4)} \leq P_n^{(1)} + P_n^{(3)} \leq \lambda^2 P_n^{(0)} + \lambda P_n^{(2)} \leq (B + B')\lambda^2 \exp(-\min(\gamma', \gamma'')n)$. $P_{misranking}$ is upper bounded by $\sum_{n \geq 1} P_n^{(4)} < \delta$ if γ' and γ'' are positive and constants large enough. γ' and γ'' can be chosen positive simultaneously if $z > \max\left(\frac{2(p\alpha' - (\alpha - \alpha')d)}{p\alpha}, \frac{2(2\alpha' - \alpha)}{\alpha}\right)$. $\qquad \square$

3   Experiments: How to Choose the Right Number of Resampling?

We consider in our experiments a version of multi-membered evolution strategies, the (μ, λ)-ES, where μ denotes the number of parents and λ the number of offspring ($\mu \leq \lambda$; see Alg. 2). We denote $(x_n^1, \ldots, x_n^\mu)$ the μ parents at iteration n and $(\sigma_n^1, \ldots, \sigma_n^\mu)$ their corresponding step-size. At each iteration, a (μ, λ)-ES noisy algorithm : (i) generates λ offspring by mutation on the μ parents, using the corresponding mutated step-size, (ii) selects the μ best offspring by ranking the noisy fitness values of the individuals. Thus, the current approximation of the optimum x^* at iteration n is x_n^1, to be consistent with the previous notations, we denote $x_n = x_n^1$ and $\sigma_n = \sigma_n^1$.

Algorithm 2. An evolution strategy, with constant number of resamplings. If we consider $Y = 1$, we obtain the case without resampling. $\mathcal{N}_k$ is a k-dimensional standard normal random variable.

Parameters : $Y > 0$, $\lambda \geq \mu > 0$, a dimension $d > 0$.
Input : μ initial points $x_1^1, \ldots, x_1^\mu \in \mathbb{R}^d$ and initial step size $\sigma_1^1 > 0, \ldots, \sigma_1^\mu > 0$.
$n \leftarrow 1$
while (true) **do**
    Generate λ individuals indenpendently using :

$$\sigma_j = \sigma_n^{mod(j-1,\mu)+1} \times exp(\frac{1}{2d} \times \mathcal{N}_1)$$
$$i_j = x_n^{mod(j-1,\mu)+1} + \sigma_j \mathcal{N}_d$$

    $\forall j \in \{1, \ldots, \lambda\}$, evaluate i_j Y times. Let y_j be the averaging over these Y evaluations.
    Define $j_1, \ldots, j_\lambda$ so that $y_{j_1} \leq y_{j_2} \leq \cdots \leq y_{j_\lambda}$.
    Update : compute σ_{n+1}^k and x_{n+1}^k for $k \in \{1, \ldots, \mu\}$:

$$\sigma_{n+1}^k = \sigma_{j_k}$$
$$x_{n+1}^k = x_{j_k}$$

    $n \leftarrow n + 1$
end while

Experiments are performed on the fitness function $f(x, \omega) = ||x||^p + ||x||^{pz/2}\mathcal{N}$, with $x \in \mathbb{R}^{15}$, $p = 2$, $z = 2.1$, $\lambda = 4$, $\mu = 2$, and $\mathcal{N}$ a standard gaussian random variable, using a budget of 500000 evaluations. The results presented here are the mean and the median over 50 runs. The positive results are proved, above, for a given quantile of the results. This explains the good performance in Fig. 1 (median result) as soon as the number of resamplings is enough. The median performance is optimal with just 12 resamplings. On the other hand, Fig. 2 shows the mean performance of Alg. 2 with various numbers of resamplings. We see that a limited number of runs diverge so that the mean results are bad even with 16 resamplings; results are optimal (on average) for 20 resamplings.

Results are safer with 20 resamplings (for the mean), but faster (for the median) with a smaller number of resamplings.

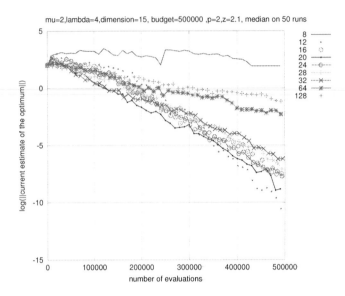

Fig. 1. Convergence of Self-Adaptive Evolution Strategies: Median results

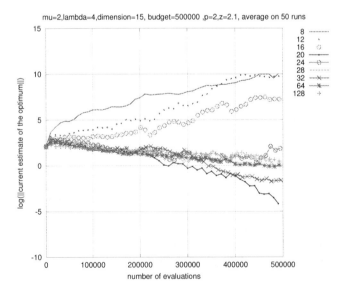

Fig. 2. Convergence of Self-Adaptive Evolution Strategies: Mean results

4   Conclusion

We have shown that applying evolution strategies with a finite number of resamplings when the noise in the function decreases quickly enough near the optimum provides a convergence rate as fast as in the noise-free case. More specifically, if the noise decreases slightly faster than in the multiplicative model of noise, using a constant number of revaluation leads to a log-linear convergence of the algorithm. The limit case of a multiplicative noise has been analyzed in [14]; a fixed number of resamplings is not sufficient for convergence when the noise is unbounded.

Further Work. We did not provide any hint for choosing the number of resamplings. Proofs based on Bernstein races [13] might be used for adaptively choosing the number of resamplings.

Acknowledgments. This paper was written during a stay in Ailab, Dong Hwa University, Hualien, Taiwan.

References

1. Arnold, D., Beyer, H.-G.: Investigation of the (μ, λ)-es in the presence of noise. In: Proc. of the IEEE Conference on Evolutionary Computation (CEC 2001), pp. 332–339. IEEE (2001)
2. Arnold, D., Beyer, H.-G.: Local performance of the $(1 + 1)$-es in a noisy environment. IEEE Transactions on Evolutionary Computation **6**(1), 30–41 (2002)
3. Arnold, D.V., Beyer, H.-G.: A general noise model and its effects on evolution strategy performance. IEEE Transactions on Evolutionary Computation **10**(4), 380–391 (2006)
4. Astete-Morales, S., Liu, J., Teytaud, O.: log-log convergence for noisy optimization. In: Proceedings of EA 2013. LNCS. Springer (2013) (page accepted)
5. Auger, A.: Convergence results for $(1,\lambda)$-SA-ES using the theory of φ-irreducible Markov chains. Theoretical Computer Science **334**(1–3), 35–69 (2005)
6. Auger, A.: Linear convergence on positively homogeneous functions of a comparison-based step-size adaptive randomized search: the $(1+1)$-es with generalized one-fifth success rule (2013) (submitted)
7. Auger, A., Jebalia, M., Teytaud, O.: (x, sigma, eta): quasi-random mutations for evolution strategies. In: EA, p. 12 (2005)
8. Beyer, H.-G.: The Theory of Evolution Strategies. Natural Computing Series. Springer, Heidelberg (2001)
9. Chen, H.: Lower rate of convergence for locating the maximum of a function. Annals of statistics **16**, 1330–1334 (1988)
10. Coulom, R.: CLOP: Confident Local Optimization for Noisy Black-Box Parameter Tuning. In: van den Herik, H.J., Plaat, A. (eds.) ACG 2011. LNCS, vol. 7168, pp. 146–157. Springer, Heidelberg (2012)
11. Fabian, V.: Stochastic Approximation of Minima with Improved Asymptotic Speed. Annals of Mathematical statistics **38**, 191–200 (1967)
12. Fabian, V.: Stochastic Approximation. SLP. Department of Statistics and Probability, Michigan State University (1971)

13. Heidrich-Meisner, V., Igel, C.: Hoeffding and bernstein races for selecting policies in evolutionary direct policy search. In: ICML 2009: Proceedings of the 26th Annual International Conference on Machine Learning, pp. 401–408. ACM, New York (2009)

14. Jebalia, M., Auger, A., Hansen, N.: Log linear convergence and divergence of the scale-invariant (1+1)-ES in noisy environments. Algorithmica (2010)

15. Rechenberg, I.: Evolutionstrategie: Optimierung Technischer Systeme nach Prinzipien des Biologischen Evolution. Fromman-Holzboog Verlag, Stuttgart (1973)

16. Shamir, O.: On the complexity of bandit and derivative-free stochastic convex optimization. CoRR, abs/1209.2388 (2012)

17. Teytaud, O., Decock, J.: Noisy Optimization Complexity. In: FOGA - Foundations of Genetic Algorithms XII - 2013, Adelaide, Australie (February 2013)

18. Teytaud, O., Fournier, H.: Lower Bounds for Evolution Strategies Using VC-Dimension. In: Rudolph, G., Jansen, T., Lucas, S., Poloni, C., Beume, N. (eds.) PPSN 2008. LNCS, vol. 5199, pp. 102–111. Springer, Heidelberg (2008)

A Differential Evolution Framework with Ensemble of Parameters and Strategies and Pool of Local Search Algorithms

Giovanni Iacca[1]([✉]), Ferrante Neri[2,3], Fabio Caraffini[2,3],
and Ponnuthurai Nagaratnam Suganthan[4]

[1] INCAS[3], Dr. Nassaulaan 9, 9401 HJ Assen, The Netherlands
giovanniiacca@incas3.eu
[2] Centre for Computational Intelligence, School of Computer Science
and Informatics, De Montfort University, The Gateway, LE1 9BH Leicester, UK
{fneri,fcaraffini}@dmu.ac.uk
[3] Department of Mathematical Information Technology, University of Jyväskylä,
P.O. Box 35 (Agora), 40014 Jyväskylä yliopisto, Finland
{ferrante.neri,fabio.caraffini}@jyu.fi
[4] School of Electrical & Electronic Engineering, College of Engineering,
Nanyang Technological University, 50 Nanyang Avenue, Singapore 639798, Singapore
epnsugan@ntu.edu.sg

Abstract. The ensemble structure is a computational intelligence supervised strategy consisting of a pool of multiple operators that compete among each other for being selected, and an adaptation mechanism that tends to reward the most successful operators. In this paper we extend the idea of the ensemble to multiple local search logics. In a memetic fashion, the search structure of an ensemble framework cooperatively/competitively optimizes the problem jointly with a pool of diverse local search algorithms. In this way, the algorithm progressively adapts to a given problem and selects those search logics that appear to be the most appropriate to quickly detect high quality solutions. The resulting algorithm, namely Ensemble of Parameters and Strategies Differential Evolution empowered by Local Search (EPSDE-LS), is evaluated on multiple testbeds and dimensionality values. Numerical results show that the proposed EPSDE-LS robustly displays a very good performance in comparison with some of the state-of-the-art algorithms.

Keywords: Differential Evolution · Global Optimization · Ensemble · Parameter Adaptation · Mutation Strategy Adaptation

1 Introduction

Differential Evolution (DE) [24] is a simple, fast and efficient stochastic algorithm with few parameters to tune [4,21]. After the early DE implementations, important efforts have been made to improve the performance by introducing different mutation and crossover strategies [4,5,21,26,36]. The choice of appropriate

© Springer-Verlag Berlin Heidelberg 2014
A.I. Esparcia-Alcázar et al. (Eds.): EvoApplications 2014, LNCS 8602, pp. 615–626, 2014.
DOI: 10.1007/978-3-662-45523-4_50

mutation and crossover strategies (as well as their related control parameters) is not easy due to the complex interaction between them [1]. An inappropriate choice of strategies or parameters may lead to an efficient behaviour of the algorithm. Thus, various empirical guidelines were suggested for choosing a mutation strategy and its associated control parameter settings, see e.g. [17] and [35]. Although these guidelines are rather useful for choosing the mutation parameters, the performance of DE is still sensitive to the combination of the mutation and crossover strategies, with their associated parameters. Furthermore, the best setting of mutation strategy, crossover strategy and control parameters can be different for different optimization problems. Based on these observations, different adaptation schemes have been proposed in the past years, see e.g [1,25,34] to overcome the time consuming trial-and-error procedure and let the algorithm self-adapt to the fitness landscape.

As an alternative to adaptation, in [16] a DE framework with an *ensemble* of mutation and crossover strategies and parameter values (known as EPSDE: Ensemble of Parameters and Strategies in DE) was proposed. EPSDE contains a pool of mutation and crossover strategies along with a pool of values corresponding to each associated parameter which compete to produce successful offspring. Due to its richness of search moves, EPSDE has proved so far extremely successful on many different optimization problems. In different contexts, a similar logic has been employed, see e.g. [32].

In this paper, we extend the concept of ensemble by combining the ensemble of strategies and parameters proposed in [16] with a pool of local search algorithms, as suggested in [30]. More specifically, three different local search algorithms, which co-exist and compete to produce better solutions, are embedded within the EPSDE framework in order to improve upon its performance. The proposed algorithm, referred to as EPSDE-LS, is evaluated on two different benchmarks in comparison with three state-of-the-art optimization algorithms.

The reminder of this paper is organized as follows. Section 2 presents the proposed EPSDE-LS algorithm. Section 3 presents the numerical results. Finally, Section 4 concludes the paper and suggests some possible future developments.

2   Ensemble of Parameters and Strategies Differential Evolution Empowered by Local Search

This paper proposes an extension of the concept of EPSDE in a memetic fashion. More specifically, the proposed algorithm, namely Ensemble of Parameters and Strategies Differential Evolution empowered by Local Search (EPSDE-LS), integrates within a EPSDE framework also a pool of local search algorithms (see Alg. 1). The main motivation behind the proposed design, besides the benefits of DE memetic schemes, see e.g. [12], [19] and [20], is that an a priori design of an algorithm should take into account the features of the optimization problems, such as ill-conditioning, separability, multimodality, see [2] and [11]. Thus, multiple search logics are here blended within the same framework. The algorithm should progressively "learn" how each component can successfully tackle the features of the optimization problem and progressively adapt to the problem and solve it efficiently.

Let us describe the proposed EPSDE-LS more in detail, considering the EPSDE framework first and then the pool of local search algorithms. As described in [16], EPSDE makes use of the following pools of strategies:

– Pool of mutation strategies: $P_{mut} = \{\text{cur-to-pbest}/1, \text{cur-to-rand}/1\}$
– Pool of crossover strategies: $P_{cross} = \{\text{bin}, \text{exp}\}$

In addition to that, two pools of mutation an crossover parameters are defined, namely P_F and P_{CR}. The mutation strategies are defined as:

– DE/cur-to-pbest/1: $x'_{off} = x_i + F\left(x^p_{best} - x_i\right) + F\left(x_s - x_t\right)$
– DE/cur-to-rand/1: $x_{off} = x_i + K\left(x_r - x_i\right) + F\left(x_s - x_t\right)$.

Regarding DE/cur-to-rand/1, it should be observed that the crossover operation is not applied, as this mutation strategy contains an implicit arithmetic crossover, see [25]. On the contrary, when DE/cur-to-pbest/1 strategy is selected, a crossover completes the offspring generation, see [36]. Moreover, x^p_{best} is an individual randomly selected amongst the best $100 \cdot p\%$ where p is a dynamic value that varies between 0 and 1 according to the following rule:

$$p = \lfloor 0.005 \cdot (1 - n_{eval}/N_{eval}) \rfloor \tag{1}$$

where n_{eval} and N_{eval} indicate, respectively, the current and maximum number of fitness evaluation. In this way, at the beginning of the optimization ($n_{eval} = 0$) the mutation uses a random solution among the top 50% individuals in the current population: this guarantees a higher chance of taking a suboptimal solution, thus increasing the exploration pressure. Later on ($n_{eval} \rightarrow N_{eval}$), the percentage of top individuals will progressively decrease, thus making the mutation strategy more exploitative.

The selection of these strategies is motivated by the consideration that they offer diverse and complementary search moves. As a general observation, as highlighted in [21], DE is characterized by a limited amount of search moves. Hence, the employment of multiple mutations and crossover compensates the lack of DE search moves. However, it is important to note that in order to have an effective ensemble, the candidate pools of mutation/crossover strategies and parameters must be chosen so to avoid the unfavorable influences of less effective mutation strategies and parameters [27]. In other words, the strategies and parameters present in the pools should have diverse characteristics, so that they can exhibit distinct performance during different stages of the evolution, as well as when dealing with different problems, see [21].

In the EPSDE framework, the mutation and crossover strategies have been chosen as they correspond to two diverse search logics. More specifically, the DE/cur-to-rand/1 mutation strategy attempts to enhance upon the performance of each population individual by adding to it two randomized vectors:

$$x_{off} = x_i + K\left(x_r - x_i\right) + F\left(x_s - x_t\right). \tag{2}$$

This operation is rather exploratory as it can potentially reach every point of the decision space and each offspring is loosely related to the generating parent (e.g. no sequences of design variables are copied from the parent to the offspring). Conversely, DE/cur-to-pbest/1 is a fairly exploitative mutation strategy as it makes use of a fitness based criterion to increase the selection pressure. Since part of the mutation takes into account only those solutions that display the best fitness values, the mutation excludes some search moves and exploit only those search directions that appear the most promising. In addition, the crossover application makes the offspring more similar to the parent that has generated it, thus further increasing the exploitation. The two crossover strategies allow different degrees of exploration/exploitation balance. The DE/cur-to-pbest/1 mutation followed by exponential crossover is the most exploitative option while the offspring generation by DE/cur-to-pbest/1 mutation and binomial crossover contains a higher exploratory potential, see [31]. The exponential crossover leads to a copy of contiguous design variables while the binomial tends to copy scattered variables. This fact has an impact especially in non-separable problems where the inter-variable interaction can be strong.

Regarding the ensemble coordination and adaptation, EPSDE operates as follows. At the beginning of the optimization, each member in the initial population is randomly assigned a mutation/crossover strategy and the associated parameter values taken from the respective pools. Then, during each generation, the population members (target vectors) produce offspring (trial vectors) using the assigned mutation/crossover strategies and parameter values. If the trial vector is better than the target vector, in the next generation the mutation/crossover strategies—and the corresponding parameter values—are retained, while the trial vector replaces its parent (target vector). Otherwise, the target vector is retained and randomly associated, with equal probability, to new mutation/crossover strategies and associated parameter values from the respective pools. Thus, this mechanism relies on the selection properties of evolution to increase, while the optimization process goes on, the probability of producing offspring by the best combinations of strategies and parameters. In summary, the ensemble is a simple and straightforward self-adaptation where the fittest strategies survive along with the solutions that have generated.

Let us consider now the pool of local search algorithms. The proposed EPSDE-LS employs a pool P_{LS} containing three algorithms, namely Nelder-Mead simplex [18], Powell's conjugate direction method [22], and Rosenbrock's algorithm [28]. As in the case of offspring generation within EPSDE, the pool has been selected in order to empower the algorithm with multiple and diverse search operators.

As an initial note, the three local search algorithms can be divided into two groups. We should remark indeed, that while Powell's and Rosenbrock's algorithms require only an initial point to start the search, the simplex algorithm requires $n + 1$ points. In our case, for the first two algorithms we initialize the initial point to the current best solution in the EPSDE population. In Nelder-Mead algorithm, we instead initialize the first point of polytope to the current best solution, while the remaining n points are initialized randomly. Moreover, while Rosenbrock's and Powell's algorithms are purely deterministic local search operators, Nelder-Mead algorithm contains some randomization features due to the random initialization of n points that generate the polytope. Since these n points can be sampled apart from each other within the decision space, Nelder-Mead algorithm contains some global search features and thus has the potential of jumping outside a basin of attraction and detect new promising search directions. On the contrary, Rosenbrock's and Powell's algorithms tend to exploit the starting solution and detect the closest optimum.

Furthermore, although both Rosenbrock's and Powell's algorithms belong to the same local search category, they present different features in terms of search logic. While Rosenbrock's algorithm follows the local gradient by means of a rotation matrix that changes the coordinate system, Powell's algorithm makes use of the conjugate search directions. This fact causes that Rosenbrock's algorithm performs a single diagonal move while Powell's algorithm performs a diagonal move as the result of n conjugate steps where the fitness has separately been optimized along each direction.

As for the coordination of the local search within the EPSDE framework, we adopted the following scheme. Every F_{LS} generations of the EPSDE framework (being F_{LS} a prefixed parameter, namely the local search activation frequency), the algorithm selects randomly one of the three locals search methods from the pool P_{LS}. The local search is then applied to the individual of the EPSDE population displaying the best performance, with a fixed computational budget (number of fitness evaluations) B_{LS}.

We should note that the employed coordination of local search has been chosen in consideration of the Ockham's Razor in Memetic Computing, i.e. an algorithmic design should be performed avoiding unnecessary components and attempting at first to achieve the desired performance in the simplest way. In this light, the local search activation by random selection of the meme/operator is likely one of the simplest way to perform the design of a hybrid algorithm.

Moreover, a straightforward extension to local search of the ensemble logic cannot be efficiently performed. In EPSDE, the trial of a strategy is based on a single fitness evaluation. On the contrary, in order to observe an improvement with the local search, a certain budget allocation must be considered. Thus, if a reward is given to the most successful local search algorithm, there is a high risk that only one algorithm is used while the remaining two are disregarded. This action would inhibit the logic of multiple and diverse search logics thus resulting in a biased search. In other words, the selection pressure over the successful local search strategy (that is applied in EPSDE with the most successful mutation/crossover strategies) is implicit in this case, since the same operator is anyway applied iteratively until budget exhaustion.

As a final remark, we should note that the choice of performing the local search over the best individual of the population is due to the DE nature/structure of the EPSDE scheme. As shown in [10], DE frameworks appear to work successfully when one solution displays a much better fitness than the average population performance. The best solution, namely super-fit, guides the search and allows quick progression of the population. Thus, if the local search is always applied to the best solution there is the highest likelihood to generate a super-fit individual.

Algorithm 1. EPSDE-LS pseudo-code

---

initialize a pool of mutation strategies P_{mut} and crossover strategies P_{cross}
initialize a pool of scale factors P_F and crossover probabilities P_{CR}
generate N_p individuals of the initial population pseudo-randomly
for $i = 1 : N_p$ **do**
    assign to x_i random strategies/parameters from $\{P_{mut}, P_{cross}, P_F, P_{CR}\}$
    compute $f(x_i)$
end for
$g = 1$
while budget condition **do**
    for $i = 1 : N_p$ **do**
        generate x'_{off} through mutation strategy/parameter associated to x_i
        generate x_{off} through crossover strategy/parameter associated to x_i
        if $f(x_{off}) \leqslant f(x_i)$ **then**
            save index i for replacing $x_i = x_{off}$ (including mutation and crossover strate-
            gies as well as parameters) in the next generation
        else
            assign to x_i new random strategies/parameters from the pools
        end if
    end for
    perform replacements
    $g = g + 1$
    if $(g \bmod F_{LS}) = 0$ **then**
        select a local search algorithm from the pool P_{LS}
        apply it to x_{best}, until the budget condition B_{LS}
    end if
end while

---

3   Numerical Results

In order to assess the performance of EPSDE-LS on a broad set of real-parameter optimization problems, we evaluated the minimization results obtained by the proposed algorithm on two different benchmarks, namely:

- the benchmark used at the CEC 2013 [15], composed of 28 test functions;
- the large-scale optimization benchmark used at CEC 2010 [29], composed of 20 test functions.

Furthermore, we studied the scalability properties of the proposed algorithm testing the CEC 2013 benchmark in 10, 30 and 50 dimensions, and the CEC 2010 benchmark in 1000 dimensions. We compared EPSDE-LS performance (i.e., the quality of the final solutions) with that of the following algorithms:

- Modified Differential Evolution + pBX crossover (MDE-pBX) [13], with pop-ulation size equal to 100 individuals and group size q equal to 15% of the population size;

- Cooperatively Coevolving Particle Swarms Optimizer (CCPSO2) [14], with population size equal to 30 individuals, Cauchy/Gaussian sampling selection probability $p = 0.5$ and set of potential group sizes $S = \{2, 5\}$, $S = \{2, 5, 10\}$, $S = \{2, 5, 10, 25\}$, for experiments in 10, 30 and 50 dimensions, respectively;
- Covariance Matrix Adaptation Evolution Strategy (CMA-ES) [8], with the default parameter setting of the original implementation [7], namely $\lambda = \lfloor 4 + 3\ln(D) \rfloor$, $\mu = \lfloor \lambda/2 \rfloor$, and initial step-size $\sigma = 0.2$.

As for EPSDE-LS, we set $N_p = 50$, $F_{LS} = 200$, and $B_{LS} = 1000$, while the parameter pools were chosen as $P_{CR} = \{0.1, 0.5, 0.9\}$ and $P_F = \{0.5, 0.9\}$. As said before we selected the following pools of strategies: $P_{cross} = \{\text{bin}, \text{exp}\}$ and $P_{mut} = \{\text{cur-to-pbest/1}, \text{cur-to-rand/1}\}$. The local search methods were configured as follows:

- Powell, with 100 fitness evaluations per each bi-directional line search. The Brent's line search algorithm was implemented and configured as in [23].
- Nelder-Mead: reflection coefficient $\alpha = 1$, contraction coefficient $\beta = 0.5$, expansion coefficient $\gamma = 2$ and shrinkage coefficient $\delta = 0.5$.
- Rosenbrock: positive perturbation factor $\alpha = 2$, negative perturbation factor $\beta = -0.5$, and threshold for coordinate system rotation $\epsilon = 10^{-5}$.

For each algorithm, we executed 100 independent runs, with a computational budget of $10000 \times D$ fitness evaluations (where D is the problem dimension), as suggested by the CEC 2013 competition rules. As an additional note, a toroidal handling of the bounds was used for all the algorithms in this study. This means that, given an interval $[a, b]$, if $x_i = b + \zeta$, i.e. the i-th design variable exceeds the upper bound by a quantity ζ, its value is replaced with $a + \zeta$. A similar mechanism was applied for the lower bound.

The entire experimental setup (fitness functions and algorithms) was coded in Java and executed on a hybrid network composed of Linux and Mac computers, using the distributed optimization platform Kimeme [3]. Numerical results, reporting for each test function the average of the fitness error (with respect to the global optimum) obtained by each algorithm at the end of the allotted budget, with its standard deviation, are shown in Tables 1, 2, 3, and 4. Next to the average error, we report the outcome of the Wilcoxon Rank-Sum test [33] applied, with confidence level 0.95, to each pair-wise comparison between the final fitness errors shown by EPSDE-LS (taken as reference) and those shown by the algorithm in the corresponding column name. To simplify the interpretation of this test, we indicate with "=" an acceptance of the null-hypothesis (that the two algorithms under comparison are statistically equivalent from an optimization point of view), and with "+" ("-") a superior (worse) performance of EPSDE-LS with respect to the algorithm in the column label. Finally, the bold face indicates the algorithms showing the best average fitness error.

From the numerical results, it can be seen that the proposed EPSDE-LS outperforms, on a regular basis, the competing algorithms at all dimensionalities. In particular, EPSDE-LS seems particularly competitive against CMA-ES and CCPSO2, while in low-mid dimensionalities (10-50) MDE-pBX shows in many

Table 1. Average Error ± Standard Deviation and Wilcoxon Rank-Sum Test (reference =EPSDE-LS) on CEC2013 [15] in 10 dimensions

	EPSDE-LS	CMAES		MDE-pBX		CCPSO2	
f_1	0.00e+00 ± 0.00e+00	0.00e+00+0.00e+00	=	0.00e+00±2.27e-14	=	3.08e-03±1.05e-01	+
f_2	1.09e+03 ± 1.15e+03	0.00e+00+0.00e+00	-	2.54e+03±5.07e+03	+	1.80e+06±1.21e+06	+
f_3	6.86e+02 ± 2.61e+03	7.69e-02±6.40e-01	-	1.41e+05±1.23e+06	+	7.41e+07±1.12e+08	+
f_4	1.64e+01 ± 1.46e+01	0.00e+00+0.00e+00	-	3.82e+00±3.15e+01	-	1.05e+04±2.69e+03	+
f_5	0.00e+00 ± 0.00e+00	0.00e+00±0.00e+00	=	0.00e+00±7.01e-14	=	2.20e-02±6.13e-02	+
f_6	8.05e+00 ± 3.77e+00	6.95e+00±8.44e+00	-	5.70e+00±4.83e+00	-	4.67e+00±7.85e+00	=
f_7	1.16e+00 ± 6.98e-01	6.36e+13±6.32e+14	+	7.37e+00±1.02e+01	+	3.99e+01±1.26e+01	+
f_8	2.04e+01 ± 1.02e-01	2.04e+01±1.16e-01	=	2.05e+01±9.69e-02	+	2.04e+01±7.48e-02	+
f_9	6.00e+00 ± 1.02e+00	1.51e+01±4.02e+00	+	2.16e+00±1.39e+00	-	5.48e+00±8.99e-01	-
f_{10}	1.44e-01 ± 8.94e-02	1.60e-02±1.36e-02	-	1.06e-01±8.03e-02	-	1.93e+00±9.27e-01	+
f_{11}	1.31e-10 ± 5.64e-10	2.56e+02±2.89e+02	+	2.89e+00±1.72e+00	+	2.76e+00±1.85e+00	+
f_{12}	1.13e+01 ± 4.34e+00	3.30e+02±3.15e+02	+	1.02e+01±4.53e+00	-	3.39e+01±1.02e+01	+
f_{13}	1.55e+01 ± 6.17e+00	2.29e+02±2.76e+02	+	1.94e+01±8.85e+00	+	4.22e+01±8.88e+00	+
f_{14}	3.90e+01 ± 3.62e+01	1.78e+03±4.21e+02	+	1.08e+02±9.77e+01	+	8.67e+01±6.15e+01	+
f_{15}	9.43e+02 ± 2.74e+02	1.78e+03±4.00e+02	+	7.56e+02±2.63e+02	-	1.03e+03±2.70e+02	+
f_{16}	7.49e-01 ± 2.83e-01	3.90e-01±3.24e-01	-	5.74e-01±4.62e-01	-	1.31e+00±2.35e-01	+
f_{17}	1.03e+01 ± 1.08e-01	9.74e+02±3.03e+02	+	1.32e+01±1.92e+00	+	1.79e+01±2.64e+00	+
f_{18}	2.32e+01 ± 5.90e+00	1.03e+03±3.15e+02	+	2.02e+01±5.18e+00	-	5.82e+01±6.30e+00	+
f_{19}	5.43e-01 ± 1.52e-01	1.18e+00±4.76e-01	+	6.57e-01±2.22e-01	-	1.00e+00±3.69e-01	+
f_{20}	2.99e+00 ± 3.46e-01	4.79e+00±2.72e-01	+	2.73e+00±6.04e-01	-	3.59e+00±2.16e-01	+
f_{21}	3.80e+02 ± 6.01e+01	3.87e+02±5.04e+01	=	3.98e+02±1.99e+01	+	3.68e+02±6.68e+01	-
f_{22}	1.73e+02 ± 5.65e+01	2.32e+03±4.07e+02	+	1.77e+02±1.37e+02	=	1.23e+02±6.60e+01	-
f_{23}	1.08e+03 ± 2.89e+02	2.24e+03±4.28e+02	+	8.43e+02±3.48e+02	-	1.37e+03±2.82e+02	+
f_{24}	2.11e+02 ± 1.24e+01	3.73e+02±1.36e+02	+	2.05e+02±5.21e+00	-	2.11e+02±1.80e+01	+
f_{25}	2.12e+02 ± 5.16e+00	2.61e+02±5.29e+01	+	2.01e+02±8.24e+00	-	2.12e+02±1.46e+01	+
f_{26}	1.83e+02 ± 3.10e+01	2.57e+02±1.09e+02	+	1.40e+02±4.16e+01	-	1.71e+02±2.37e+01	+
f_{27}	4.87e+02 ± 5.37e+01	4.01e+02±9.94e+01	-	3.04e+02±1.72e+01	-	4.33e+02±5.71e+01	-
f_{28}	2.96e+02 ± 2.80e+01	1.22e+03±1.13e+03	+	3.04e+02±5.53e+01	+	4.01e+02±1.63e+02	+

cases the lowest average error, although with a larger standard deviation and thus lower robustness. Similarly, in 1000 dimensions CMA-ES obtains in most cases the lowest error, but statistically proves equivalent to EPSDE-LS. All in all, among the selected algorithms, EPSDE-LS shows the best characteristics in terms of robustness and scalability.

In order to give a further insight into the results presented above, we ranked the algorithms under study by means of the Holm-Bonferroni procedure [9], as described in [6], with level of confidence set to 0.05. For the sake of completeness, in this analysis we included also the original EPSDE algorithm [16] (whose results are not reported in Tables 1-4 due to space limitations), executed with the same setting of EPSDE-LS but without pool of local search. Table 5 displays the ranks, z_j values, p_j values, and corresponding δ/j obtained in this way. The rank of EPSDE-LS is shown in parentheses in the table caption. Moreover, we indicate whether the null-hypothesis (that the two algorithms have indistinguishable performances) is "Rejected", i.e. EPSDE-LS statistically outperforms the algorithm under consideration, or "Accepted" if the distribution of values can be considered the same (there is no statistic out-performance). It can be seen that the proposed EPSDE-LS has the highest rank amongst all the algorithms considered in this study. It can be observed also that the null-hypothesis is rejected in all the cases, i.e. the global performance of EPSDE-LS over the two benchmarks is superior to the global performance of all the other algorithms considered in this study.

Table 2. Average Error ± Standard Deviation and Wilcoxon Rank-Sum Test (reference =EPSDE-LS) on CEC2013 [15] in 30 dimensions

	EPSDE-LS	CMAES		MDE-pBX		CCPSO2	
f_1	**0.00e + 00 ± 0.00e + 00**	0.00e + 00 ± 1.18e − 13	=	2.27e − 13 ± 4.86e − 13	+	1.36e − 12 ± 6.01e − 12	+
f_2	1.68e + 06 ± 8.26e + 05	**0.00e + 00 ± 1.54e − 13**	−	2.70e + 05 ± 2.62e + 05	−	2.14e + 06 ± 1.04e + 06	+
f_3	1.03e + 06 ± 2.13e + 06	**9.24e + 01 ± 4.00e + 02**	−	5.19e + 07 ± 1.18e + 08	+	1.13e + 09 ± 1.18e + 09	+
f_4	2.17e + 04 ± 5.55e + 03	**0.00e + 00 ± 1.29e − 13**	−	3.49e + 02 ± 3.18e + 02	−	5.64e + 04 ± 2.09e + 04	+
f_5	**0.00e + 00 ± 3.01e − 14**	9.09e − 13 ± 2.46e − 12	+	1.09e − 10 ± 1.00e − 09	+	3.04e − 07 ± 8.74e − 07	+
f_6	1.05e + 01 ± 5.75e + 00	**4.83e + 00 ± 1.28e + 01**	−	3.41e + 01 ± 2.77e + 01	+	3.44e + 01 ± 2.78e + 01	+
f_7	**2.78e + 01 ± 9.88e + 00**	3.51e + 08 ± 3.49e + 09	+	5.61e + 01 ± 1.90e + 01	+	1.19e + 02 ± 2.33e + 01	+
f_8	**2.10e + 01 ± 6.30e − 02**	2.10e + 01 ± 5.49e − 02	+	2.10e + 01 ± 5.93e − 02	+	2.10e + 01 ± 5.44e − 02	+
f_9	3.14e + 01 ± 1.65e + 00	4.42e + 01 ± 7.09e + 00	+	**2.16e + 01 ± 4.36e + 00**	−	3.02e + 01 ± 2.20e + 00	−
f_{10}	2.60e − 02 ± 1.60e − 02	**2.01e − 02 ± 1.71e − 02**	−	1.81e − 01 ± 1.10e − 01	+	2.00e − 01 ± 9.45e − 02	+
f_{11}	**2.18e − 03 ± 3.82e − 03**	1.05e + 02 ± 2.55e + 02	+	4.68e + 01 ± 1.54e + 01	+	5.76e − 01 ± 6.49e − 01	+
f_{12}	**6.63e + 01 ± 2.02e + 01**	8.08e + 02 ± 9.37e + 02	=	6.91e + 01 ± 2.20e + 01	=	2.13e + 02 ± 5.62e + 01	+
f_{13}	**1.06e + 02 ± 2.51e + 01**	1.65e + 03 ± 1.67e + 03	+	1.50e + 02 ± 3.56e + 01	+	2.58e + 02 ± 4.39e + 01	+
f_{14}	5.69e + 02 ± 2.06e + 02	5.39e + 03 ± 7.64e + 02	+	1.20e + 03 ± 4.25e + 02	+	**6.57e + 00 ± 3.69e + 00**	−
f_{15}	4.71e + 03 ± 8.51e + 02	5.29e + 03 ± 6.36e + 02	+	**4.01e + 03 ± 7.00e + 02**	−	4.03e + 03 ± 4.77e + 02	−
f_{16}	1.63e + 00 ± 4.89e − 01	**1.23e − 01 ± 1.06e − 01**	−	1.32e + 00 ± 8.61e − 01	−	2.40e + 00 ± 4.03e − 01	+
f_{17}	3.27e + 01 ± 7.89e − 01	4.07e + 03 ± 8.51e + 02	+	6.89e + 01 ± 1.24e + 01	+	**3.13e + 01 ± 4.89e − 01**	−
f_{18}	8.87e + 01 ± 2.31e + 01	3.95e + 03 ± 7.79e + 02	+	**8.31e + 01 ± 1.66e + 01**	=	2.44e + 02 ± 5.78e + 01	+
f_{19}	2.46e + 00 ± 5.06e − 01	3.50e + 00 ± 9.05e − 01	+	9.10e + 00 ± 4.94e + 00	+	**8.55e − 01 ± 1.71e − 01**	−
f_{20}	1.19e + 01 ± 5.30e − 01	1.50e + 01 ± 4.97e − 02	+	**1.09e + 01 ± 7.97e − 01**	−	1.39e + 01 ± 4.52e − 01	+
f_{21}	3.00e + 02 ± 7.94e + 01	3.09e + 02 ± 8.58e + 01	+	3.09e + 02 ± 7.63e + 01	+	**2.58e + 02 ± 7.21e + 01**	=
f_{22}	7.70e + 02 ± 2.52e + 02	6.92e + 03 ± 9.35e + 02	+	1.11e + 03 ± 5.46e + 02	+	**1.21e + 02 ± 7.28e + 01**	−
f_{23}	4.86e + 03 ± 6.99e + 02	6.78e + 03 ± 7.36e + 02	+	**4.47e + 03 ± 7.32e + 02**	−	5.26e + 03 ± 7.22e + 02	+
f_{24}	2.79e + 02 ± 7.17e + 00	7.93e + 02 ± 5.89e + 02	+	**2.31e + 02 ± 1.11e + 01**	−	2.81e + 02 ± 1.08e + 01	+
f_{25}	2.92e + 02 ± 5.00e + 00	3.81e + 02 ± 1.54e + 02	+	**2.75e + 02 ± 1.55e + 01**	−	3.03e + 02 ± 6.25e + 00	+
f_{26}	2.16e + 02 ± 5.13e + 01	4.66e + 02 ± 2.24e + 02	+	2.16e + 02 ± 4.31e + 01	+	**2.02e + 02 ± 4.53e + 00**	−
f_{27}	1.09e + 03 ± 4.99e + 01	8.17e + 02 ± 2.09e + 02	−	**6.55e + 02 ± 1.13e + 02**	−	1.07e + 03 ± 1.13e + 02	=
f_{28}	**3.00e + 02 ± 2.16e − 13**	1.94e + 03 ± 3.38e + 03	+	3.11e + 02 ± 1.11e + 02	+	5.43e + 02 ± 5.77e + 02	+

Table 3. Average Error ± Standard Deviation and Wilcoxon Rank-Sum Test (reference =EPSDE-LS) on CEC2013 [15] in 50 dimensions

	EPSDE-LS	CMAES		MDE-pBX		CCPSO2	
f_1	**0.00e + 00 ± 0.00e + 00**	2.27e − 13 ± 0.00e + 00	+	3.32e − 11 ± 2.60e − 10	+	7.05e − 12 ± 3.53e − 11	+
f_2	6.61e + 06 ± 2.72e + 06	**2.27e − 13 ± 0.00e + 00**	−	9.06e + 05 ± 4.90e + 05	−	4.37e + 06 ± 2.29e + 06	−
f_3	7.35e + 06 ± 1.79e + 07	**2.32e + 04 ± 9.57e + 04**	−	1.42e + 08 ± 1.57e + 08	+	3.09e + 09 ± 3.03e + 09	+
f_4	5.51e + 04 ± 9.43e + 03	**2.27e − 13 ± 0.00e + 00**	−	1.09e + 03 ± 8.33e + 02	−	1.08e + 05 ± 3.86e + 04	+
f_5	**1.14e − 13 ± 1.97e − 14**	1.95e − 09 ± 9.17e − 10	+	2.54e − 05 ± 2.52e − 04	+	3.92e − 04 ± 3.89e − 03	+
f_6	4.36e + 01 ± 9.69e − 01	**4.29e + 01 ± 5.98e + 00**	+	5.67e + 01 ± 2.24e + 01	+	4.74e + 01 ± 1.34e + 01	+
f_7	7.50e + 01 ± 1.59e + 01	1.98e + 04 ± 1.96e + 05	+	**6.81e + 01 ± 1.22e + 01**	−	1.43e + 02 ± 2.39e + 01	+
f_8	2.12e + 01 ± 3.93e − 02	**2.11e + 01 ± 3.75e − 02**	−	2.12e + 01 ± 4.36e − 02	+	2.12e + 01 ± 3.86e − 02	=
f_9	6.06e + 01 ± 2.04e + 00	7.66e + 01 ± 8.71e + 00	+	**4.27e + 01 ± 6.99e + 00**	−	5.87e + 01 ± 3.26e + 00	−
f_{10}	5.21e − 02 ± 4.01e − 02	**2.70e − 02 ± 1.55e − 02**	−	4.09e − 01 ± 5.57e − 01	+	2.03e − 01 ± 1.80e − 01	+
f_{11}	**1.86e − 01 ± 2.65e − 01**	2.46e + 02 ± 5.29e + 02	+	1.21e + 02 ± 2.97e + 01	+	9.07e − 01 ± 8.53e − 01	+
f_{12}	**1.53e + 02 ± 3.83e + 01**	2.28e + 03 ± 1.53e + 03	+	1.62e + 02 ± 3.45e + 01	=	4.55e + 02 ± 8.03e + 01	+
f_{13}	**2.44e + 02 ± 4.17e + 01**	3.26e + 03 ± 1.25e + 03	+	3.22e + 02 ± 5.39e + 01	+	5.69e + 02 ± 8.18e + 01	+
f_{14}	7.52e + 02 ± 2.41e + 02	8.74e + 03 ± 1.05e + 03	+	2.79e + 03 ± 8.06e + 02	+	**7.35e + 00 ± 3.55e + 00**	−
f_{15}	9.07e + 03 ± 1.21e + 03	9.04e + 03 ± 8.70e + 02	+	**7.58e + 03 ± 8.01e + 02**	−	8.31e + 03 ± 8.71e + 02	−
f_{16}	2.24e + 00 ± 5.52e − 01	**8.00e − 02 ± 4.27e − 02**	−	1.93e + 00 ± 8.76e − 01	−	2.75e + 00 ± 5.96e − 01	+
f_{17}	5.66e + 01 ± 1.60e + 00	6.84e + 03 ± 1.10e + 03	+	1.79e + 02 ± 3.56e + 01	+	**5.16e + 01 ± 3.28e − 01**	−
f_{18}	1.96e + 02 ± 6.47e + 01	7.01e + 03 ± 9.83e + 02	+	**1.86e + 02 ± 3.17e + 01**	=	4.87e + 02 ± 9.77e + 01	+
f_{19}	4.71e + 00 ± 8.61e − 01	6.26e + 00 ± 1.54e + 00	+	3.94e + 01 ± 1.21e + 00	+	**1.49e + 00 ± 2.32e − 01**	−
f_{20}	2.15e + 01 ± 6.05e − 01	2.50e + 01 ± 9.74e − 02	+	**2.01e + 01 ± 9.17e − 01**	−	2.33e + 01 ± 8.19e − 01	+
f_{21}	6.20e + 02 ± 4.37e + 02	7.95e + 02 ± 3.57e + 02	+	8.91e + 02 ± 3.44e + 02	+	**4.42e + 02 ± 3.45e + 02**	=
f_{22}	9.07e + 02 ± 3.04e + 02	1.18e + 04 ± 1.34e + 03	+	3.22e + 03 ± 1.06e + 03	+	**1.11e + 02 ± 9.60e + 01**	−
f_{23}	9.37e + 03 ± 1.26e + 03	1.18e + 04 ± 9.41e + 02	+	**9.08e + 03 ± 1.05e + 03**	=	1.09e + 04 ± 1.34e + 03	+
f_{24}	3.54e + 02 ± 6.16e + 00	1.74e + 03 ± 1.02e + 03	+	**2.88e + 02 ± 1.56e + 01**	−	3.60e + 02 ± 9.64e + 00	+
f_{25}	3.81e + 02 ± 6.60e + 00	5.07e + 02 ± 2.06e + 02	+	**3.68e + 02 ± 1.48e + 01**	−	3.97e + 02 ± 1.08e + 01	+
f_{26}	3.99e + 02 ± 1.02e + 02	7.71e + 02 ± 8.75e + 02	+	3.55e + 02 ± 7.46e + 01	−	**2.15e + 02 ± 4.95e + 01**	−
f_{27}	1.86e + 03 ± 5.99e + 01	1.32e + 03 ± 3.23e + 02	−	**1.23e + 03 ± 1.49e + 02**	−	1.82e + 03 ± 8.56e + 01	−
f_{28}	6.49e + 02 ± 8.45e + 02	2.80e + 03 ± 4.35e + 03	+	**5.05e + 02 ± 5.99e + 02**	−	7.24e + 02 ± 1.08e + 03	+

Table 4. Average Error ± Standard Deviation and Wilcoxon Rank-Sum Test (reference =EPSDE-LS) on CEC2010 [29] in 1000 dimensions.

	EPSDE-LS	CMAES		MDE-pBX		CCPSO2	
f_1	1.99e + 02 ± 9.10e + 02	6.95e + 04 ± 9.91e + 03	+	1.05e + 09 ± 6.58e + 08	+	**6.47e − 14 ± 1.41e − 13**	-
f_2	3.70e + 02 ± 8.88e + 01	1.01e + 04 ± 4.63e + 02	+	7.02e + 03 ± 2.38e + 02	+	1.36e + 02 ± 1.11e + 02	-
f_3	1.04e + 01 ± 1.32e + 00	1.99e + 01 ± 1.12e − 02	+	1.93e + 01 ± 4.76e − 02	+	**7.34e − 11 ± 1.05e − 10**	-
f_4	3.93e + 11 ± 1.78e + 11	**5.55e + 10 ± 4.75e + 09**	-	3.21e + 12 ± 9.76e + 11	+	2.14e + 12 ± 1.27e + 12	+
f_5	**7.97e + 07 ± 1.29e + 07**	6.65e + 08 ± 1.19e + 08	+	1.54e + 08 ± 2.77e + 07	+	3.92e + 08 ± 7.98e + 07	+
f_6	**1.93e + 01 ± 1.73e − 01**	1.98e + 07 ± 5.87e + 04	+	3.65e + 06 ± 1.75e + 06	+	1.71e + 07 ± 4.45e + 06	+
f_7	**3.24e + 03 ± 1.88e + 04**	3.08e + 06 ± 2.04e + 05	+	6.79e + 06 ± 1.01e + 07	+	7.60e + 09 ± 9.72e + 09	+
f_8	3.47e + 07 ± 2.14e + 07	**4.44e + 06 ± 3.21e + 05**	-	2.03e + 08 ± 1.63e + 08	+	5.46e + 07 ± 4.16e + 07	+
f_9	5.77e + 07 ± 1.96e + 07	**7.27e + 04 ± 1.07e + 04**	-	1.68e + 09 ± 1.00e + 09	+	5.01e + 07 ± 7.68e + 06	-
f_{10}	4.77e + 03 ± 1.76e + 02	1.03e + 04 ± 4.04e + 02	+	7.33e + 03 ± 2.55e + 02	+	**4.57e + 03 ± 2.75e + 02**	-
f_{11}	**1.53e + 02 ± 1.65e + 01**	2.18e + 02 ± 1.77e − 01	+	2.06e + 02 ± 2.40e + 00	+	2.00e + 02 ± 5.98e + 00	+
f_{12}	2.70e + 04 ± 5.91e + 03	**1.64e − 19 ± 4.18e − 20**	-	2.92e + 05 ± 6.60e + 04	+	6.12e + 04 ± 8.14e + 04	+
f_{13}	1.45e + 03 ± 8.16e + 02	**4.53e + 02 ± 6.59e + 01**	-	2.88e + 09 ± 3.17e + 09	+	1.14e + 03 ± 5.42e + 02	+
f_{14}	2.83e + 08 ± 2.44e + 07	**7.69e + 04 ± 1.06e + 04**	-	1.04e + 09 ± 1.97e + 08	+	1.60e + 08 ± 3.35e + 07	-
f_{15}	9.12e + 03 ± 4.17e + 02	1.04e + 04 ± 5.58e + 02	+	**7.44e + 03 ± 2.80e + 02**	-	9.31e + 03 ± 5.52e + 02	+
f_{16}	3.99e + 02 ± 2.34e + 00	3.97e + 02 ± 2.92e − 01	-	**3.84e + 02 ± 1.22e + 00**	-	3.95e + 02 ± 1.45e + 00	-
f_{17}	1.36e + 05 ± 1.42e + 04	**4.17e − 19 ± 7.23e − 20**	-	4.35e + 05 ± 8.33e + 04	+	1.41e + 05 ± 1.44e + 05	+
f_{18}	9.01e + 04 ± 4.09e + 05	**1.59e + 02 ± 1.67e + 02**	-	3.73e + 10 ± 1.95e + 10	+	5.62e + 03 ± 4.13e + 03	-
f_{19}	2.95e + 06 ± 1.90e + 05	**3.38e + 01 ± 1.36e + 01**	-	9.22e + 05 ± 1.06e + 05	-	1.14e + 06 ± 1.22e + 06	-
f_{20}	1.74e + 04 ± 4.61e + 04	**7.51e + 02 ± 9.99e + 01**	-	4.18e + 10 ± 2.02e + 10	+	1.42e + 03 ± 1.19e + 02	-

Table 5. Holm test on the Fitness, reference algorithm = EPSDE-LS (Rank = 3.50e+00)

j	Optimizer	Rank	z_j	p_j	δ/j	Hypothesis
1	MDE-pBX	3.08e+00	-2.36e+00	9.06e-03	5.00e-02	Rejected
2	EPSDE	2.98e+00	-2.90e+00	1.86e-03	2.50e-02	Rejected
3	CCPSO2	2.79e+00	-3.97e+00	3.53e-05	1.67e-02	Rejected
4	CMAES	2.47e+00	-5.75e+00	4.55e-09	1.25e-02	Rejected

4   Conclusions

This paper proposes a Memetic Computing structure composed of a DE framework, which makes use of an ensemble of crossover/mutation strategies and parameters, and a pool of three local search methods.

The ensemble is a simple and efficient self-adaptive technique that allows the successful strategies to be propagated in the future generations while blocking the propagation of unsuccessful strategies. This framework is empowered by a pool of three local search algorithms whose activation is coordinated by a randomized criterion. These three local search algorithms are Nelder-Mead, Powell, and Rosenbrock algorithms. The proposed algorithm has been tested over a diverse testbed in various dimensions ranging from 10 to 1000 and compared against modern meta-heuristics representing the state-of-the-art in optimization. The EPSDE-LS should be considered as a first successful attempt to extend the concept of ensemble to structures composed of multiple local search operators. This algorithmic design has been performed by following the philosophy of Memetic Computing and the simplistic combination of its operators has been inspired by the Ockham's Razor principle applied to algorithmic design. Despite its simplicity in the meme coordination, the resulting algorithm displays a great ability to adapt to diverse fitness landscapes, thus proving a powerful tool for addressing complex optimization problems.

Acknowledgments. INCAS[3] is co-funded by the Province of Drenthe, the Municipality of Assen, the European Fund for Regional Development and the Ministry of Economic Affairs, Peaks in the Delta. The numerical experiments have been carried out on the network of the De Montfort University with the software for distributed optimization Kimeme [3].

References

1. Brest, J., Greiner, S., Bošković, B., Mernik, M., Žumer, V.: Self-Adapting Control Parameters in Differential Evolution: A Comparative Study on Numerical Benchmark Problems. IEEE Transactions on Evolutionary Computation **10**(6), 646–657 (2006)
2. Caraffini, F., Neri, F., Iacca, G., Mol, A.: Parallel memetic structures. Information Sciences **227**, 60–82 (2013)
3. Cyber Dyne Srl Home Page: Kimeme (2013). http://cyberdynesoft.it/
4. Das, S., Suganthan, P.: Differential Evolution: A Survey of the State-of-the-Art. IEEE Transactions on Evolutionary Computation 15(1), 4–31 (2011)
5. Das, S., Abraham, A., Chakraborty, U.K., Konar, A.: Differential Evolution with a Neighborhood-based Mutation Operator. IEEE Transactions on Evolutionary Computation **13**(3), 526–553 (2009)
6. Garcia, S., Fernandez, A., Luengo, J., Herrera, F.: A study of statistical techniques and performance measures for genetics-based machine learning: accuracy and interpretability. Soft Computing **13**(10), 959–977 (2008)
7. Hansen, N.: The CMA Evolution Strategy (2012). http://www.lri.fr/~hansen/cmaesintro.html
8. Hansen, N., Müller, S.D., Koumoutsakos, P.: Reducing the Time Complexity of the Derandomized Evolution Strategy with Covariance Matrix Adaptation (CMA-ES). Evolutionary Computation **11**(1), 1–18 (2003)
9. Holm, S.: A simple sequentially rejective multiple test procedure. Scandinavian Journal of Statistics **6**(2), 65–70 (1979)
10. Iacca, G., Mallipeddi, R., Mininno, E., Neri, F., Suganthan, P.N.: Super-fit and Population Size Reduction Mechanisms in Compact Differential Evolution. In: Proceedings of IEEE Symposium on Memetic Computing, pp. 21–28 (2011)
11. Iacca, G., Neri, F., Mininno, E., Ong, Y.S., Lim, M.H.: Ockham's Razor in Memetic Computing: Three Stage Optimal Memetic Exploration. Information Sciences **188**, 17–43 (2012)
12. Iacca, G., Caraffini, F., Neri, F.: Multi-strategy coevolving aging particle optimization. International Journal of Neural Systems **24**(01), 1450008 (2014)
13. Islam, S., Das, S., Ghosh, S., Roy, S., Suganthan, P.: An Adaptive Differential Evolution Algorithm With Novel Mutation and Crossover Strategies for Global Numerical Optimization. IEEE Transactions on Systems, Man, and Cybernetics, Part B: Cybernetics 42(2), 482–500 (2012)
14. Li, X., Yao, X.: Cooperatively Coevolving Particle Swarms for Large Scale Optimization. IEEE Transactions on Evolutionary Computation 16(2), 210–224 (2012)
15. Liang, J.J., Qu, B.Y., Suganthan, P.N., Hernndez-Daz, A.G.: Problem Definitions and Evaluation Criteria for the CEC 2013 Special Session on Real-Parameter Optimization. Tech. Rep. 201212, Zhengzhou University, Zhengzhou, China (2013)
16. Mallipeddi, R., Suganthan, P.N., Pan, Q.K., Tasgetiren, M.F.: Differential evolution algorithm with ensemble of parameters and mutation strategies. Applied Soft Computing 11(2), 1679–1696 (2011), the Impact of Soft Computing for the Progress of Artificial Intelligence

17. Mezura-Montes, E., Velazquez-Reyes, J., Coello Coello, C.: Modified differential evolution for constrained optimization. In: IEEE Congress on Evolutionary Computation, pp. 25–32 (2006)
18. Nelder, A., Mead, R.: A simplex method for function optimization. Computation Journal **7**, 308–313 (1965)
19. Neri, F., Iacca, G., Mininno, E.: Disturbed Exploitation compact Differential Evolution for Limited Memory Optimization Problems. Information Sciences **181**(12), 2469–2487 (2011)
20. Neri, F., Tirronen, V.: On Memetic Differential Evolution Frameworks: a Study of Advantages and Limitations in Hybridization. In: Proceedings of the IEEE World Congress on Computational Intelligence, pp. 2135–2142 (2008)
21. Neri, F., Tirronen, V.: Recent Advances in Differential Evolution: A Review and Experimental Analysis. Artificial Intelligence Review **33**(1–2), 61–106 (2010)
22. Powell, M.J.D.: An efficient method for finding the minimum of a function of several variables without calculating derivatives. The Computer Journal **7**(2), 155–162 (1964)
23. Press, W., Teukolsky, S., Vetterling, W., Flannery, B.: Numerical Recipes in C, 2nd edn. Cambridge University Press, Cambridge (1992)
24. Price, K., Storn, R.: Differential evolution: A simple evolution strategy for fast optimization. Dr. Dobb's J. Software Tools **22**(4), 18–24 (1997)
25. Price, K.: An Introduction to Differential Evolution. In: Corne, D., Dorigo, M., Glover, F., Dasgupta, D., Moscato, P., Poli, R., Price, K.V. (eds.) New Ideas in Optimization, pp. 79–108. McGraw-Hill (1999)
26. Price, K.V., Storn, R., Lampinen, J.: Differential Evolution: A Practical Approach to Global Optimization. Springer (2005)
27. Qin, A.K., Huang, V.L., Suganthan, P.N.: Differential Evolution Algorithm With Strategy Adaptation for Global Numerical Optimization. IEEE Transactions on Evolutionary Computation **13**(2), 398–417 (2009)
28. Rosenbrock, H.H.: An automatic Method for finding the greatest or least Value of a Function. The Computer Journal **3**(3), 175–184 (1960)
29. Tang, K., Li, X., Suganthan, P.N., Yang, Z., Weise, T.: Benchmark Functions for the CEC'2010 Special Session and Competition on Large-Scale Global Optimization. Tech. rep., University of Science and Technology of China (USTC), School of Computer Science and Technology, Nature Inspired Computation and Applications Laboratory (NICAL): Hefei, Anhui, China (2010)
30. Tirronen, V., Neri, F., Kärkkäinen, T., Majava, K., Rossi, T.: An Enhanced Memetic Differential Evolution in Filter Design for Defect Detection in Paper Production. Evolutionary Computation **16**(4), 529–555 (2008)
31. Weber, M., Neri, F., Tirronen, V.: A Study on Scale Factor/Crossover Interaction in Distributed Differential Evolution. Artificial Intelligence Review **39**(3), 195–224 (2013)
32. Wessing, S., Preuss, M., Rudolph, G.: When parameter tuning actually is parameter control. In: Proceesings of the Conference on Genetic and Evolutionary Computation, pp. 821–828. ACM (2011)
33. Wilcoxon, F.: Individual comparisons by ranking methods. Biometrics Bulletin **1**(6), 80–83 (1945)
34. Zaharie, D.: Control of population diversity and adaptation in differential evolution algorithms. In: Matousek, D., Osmera, P. (eds.) Proceedings of MENDEL International Conference on Soft Computing, pp. 41–46 (2003)
35. Zaharie, D.: Influence of crossover on the behavior of differential evolution algorithms. Appl. Soft Comput. **9**(3), 1126–1138 (2009)
36. Zhang, J., Sanderson, A.: Jade: Adaptive differential evolution with optional external archive. IEEE Transactions on Evolutionary Computation, **13**(5), 945–958 (2009)

An Improved Multiobjective Electromagnetism-like Mechanism Algorithm

Pedro Carrasqueira[1]([✉]), Maria João Alves[2], and Carlos Henggeler Antunes[3]

[1] INESC Coimbra, Coimbra, Portugal
pmcarrasqueira@net.sapo.pt
[2] Faculty of Economics, University of Coimbra / INESC Coimbra, Coimbra, Portugal
mjalves@fe.uc.pt
[3] Department of Electrical Engineering and Computers,
University of Coimbra / INESC Coimbra, Coimbra, Portugal
ch@deec.uc.pt

Abstract. Electromagnetism-like Mechanism (EM) is a population based optimization approach, which has been recently adapted to solve multiobjective (MO) problems (MOEM). In this work, an enhanced multiobjective Electromagnetism-like Mechanism algorithm is proposed (EMOEM). To assess this new algorithm, a comparison with MOEM algorithm is performed. Our aim is to assess the ability of both algorithms in a wide range of continuous optimization problems including benchmark problems with two and three objective functions. Experiments show that EMOEM performs better in terms of convergence and diversity when compared with the MOEM algorithm.

Keywords: Electromagnetism-like mechanism · Multiobjective continuous optimization

1 Introduction

Multiobjective optimization problems arise in different fields, such as engineering design and economics, among others. These problems are, in general, hard to solve due to the number of objective functions, the size and shape of the search space associated with nonlinear and/or combinatorial characteristics. Meta-heuristics are, in general, inspired on natural or physical mechanisms. Population-based meta-heuristics are specially fitted to solve multiobjective optimization problems because they are able to produce a set of solutions in a single run. This is relevant because in multiobjective problems a non-dominated front should be identified. The population-based meta-heuristic Electromagnetism-like Mechanism (EM) was initially designed to solve single objective optimization problems. Later, it has been adapted to multiobjective optimization (MOEM). The Electromagnetism-like Mechanism (EM) was first proposed by [2] and is inspired on the electromagnetism theory. Each point is a charged particle. The charge of a particle depends on its objective function value. The movement of particles resembles the Coulomb's Law. The principle is that the force exerted

© Springer-Verlag Berlin Heidelberg 2014
A.I. Esparcia-Alcázar et al. (Eds.): EvoApplications 2014, LNCS 8602, pp. 627–638, 2014.
DOI: 10.1007/978-3-662-45523-4_51

by one particle on another particle is directly proportional to the product of their charges and is inversely proportional to the distance between the particles. Then, particles move themselves by an attraction-repulsion mechanism. Particles with higher charge values attract other particles while the poor charged particles repel the others. The charge of each particle is influenced by the charge of all other particles. Because of the good performance EM has demonstrated [6] [14], it was extended to solve multiobjective optimization problems (MOEM) [9], in particular to solve a problem of inventory control [10] [11]. As far as we know, these are the only attempts to adapt the EM algorithm to solve multiobjective optimization problems.

In this work we present an Enhanced MOEM algorithm, EMOEM. The main components of the MOEM algorithm [9] are changed and a crowding mechanism to guarantee diversity of solutions is used. We test the new algorithm on benchmark problems and compare its results with those of existing MOEM algorithm. We perform statistical tests to validate results and guarantee the significance of the conclusions.

This paper is organized as follows. In section 2 the fundamental concepts of multiobjective optimization are presented. In Section 3 we propose the new EMOEM algorithm. In Section 4, experimental results are shown. The analysis of results is presented in section 5. The last section provides conclusions and future research directions.

2   Fundamental Concepts of Multiobjective Optimization

A multiobjective optimization problem is defined as

$$
\begin{aligned}
&Min \, \overrightarrow{f}(\overrightarrow{x}) = (f_1(\overrightarrow{x}), f_2(\overrightarrow{x}), \cdots, f_m(\overrightarrow{x})) \\
&S.t. \, \overrightarrow{x} \in \Omega, \\
&\Omega = \{\overrightarrow{x} \in \mathbb{R}^d | g_i(\overrightarrow{x}) \leq 0, \, i = 1, 2, \cdots, p\},
\end{aligned}
\tag{1}
$$

where $f(\overrightarrow{x})$ is the vector of objective functions to optimize, $\overrightarrow{x} = (x_1, x_2, \cdots, x_d)$ is the decision vector, d is the number of variables and $g_i(\overrightarrow{x})$ are the constraints.

Definition 1. *A vector $\overrightarrow{x} \in \Omega$ dominates a vector $\overrightarrow{y} \in \Omega$ and we say $\overrightarrow{x} \preceq \overrightarrow{y}$, if $f_i(\overrightarrow{x}) \leq f_i(\overrightarrow{y})$, $\forall i = 1, \cdots, m$ and $\exists j \in \{1, \cdots, m\} : f_j(\overrightarrow{x}) < f_j(\overrightarrow{y})$.*

If the vector $\overrightarrow{x} \in \Omega$ is strictly better than vector $\overrightarrow{y} \in \Omega$ in all m objective functions, we say $\overrightarrow{x}$ strongly dominates $\overrightarrow{y}$ and we denote $\overrightarrow{x} \prec \overrightarrow{y}$.

Definition 2. *A solution $\overrightarrow{x} \in \Omega$ is said efficient if $\nexists \overrightarrow{y} \in \Omega : \overrightarrow{y} \preceq \overrightarrow{x}$. The corresponding objective point $\overrightarrow{f}(\overrightarrow{x})$ is a non-dominated point.*

The set of all non-dominated solutions to a multiobjective optimization problem is called the Pareto optimal front. Our goal is to approximate the entire Pareto optimal front (PF) of the problem.

3   Multiobjective Electromagnetism-like Mechanism

3.1   MOEM Algorithm

The first attempt to design a MOEM algorithm was presented in [9]. The algorithm is based on three main components: individual charge, total force, and local search procedure. After initializing the initial population, each individual is evaluated to obtain its objective vector. Then, the population is scrutinized to identify the non-dominated individuals, which constitute the initial non-dominated archive. Then, local search, individual charge and force evaluation, and population movement are performed, while a predefined criterion is not met. The MOEM algorithm is described below in algorithm 1.

The local search procedure is applied to each particle of the local archive ($\tilde{S}$). Each variable of the particle is changed by a random value. When all the variables are changed the particle is evaluated. If the new generated particle dominates the old particle, this is replaced. This process is repeated $lsiter$ times for each particle in one generation.

The charge of an individual depends on its objective function values and the ones of all other population members. In MOEM, the charge of a particle i is given by

$$q_i = exp(-d\frac{\min_{\overrightarrow{x}_p \in \tilde{S}} \|\overrightarrow{f}(\overrightarrow{x}_i) - \overrightarrow{f}(\overrightarrow{x}_p)\|}{\sum_{j=1}^{n} \min_{\overrightarrow{x}_p \in \tilde{S}} \|\overrightarrow{f}(\overrightarrow{x}_j) - \overrightarrow{f}(\overrightarrow{x}_p)\|}), \ i = 1, \cdots, n, \qquad (2)$$

where $\tilde{S}$ is the subset of the external archive used in the local search procedure. We obtain the individual forces of each $\overrightarrow{x}_j$ exerts on $\overrightarrow{x}_i$ evaluating the expression (3):

$$\overrightarrow{F}^{ij} = \begin{cases} (\overrightarrow{x}_i - \overrightarrow{x}_j)\frac{q_i q_j}{\|\overrightarrow{x}_i - \overrightarrow{x}_j\|^2} & if \ \overrightarrow{x}_i \prec \overrightarrow{x}_j \\ (\overrightarrow{x}_j - \overrightarrow{x}_i)\frac{q_i q_j}{\|\overrightarrow{x}_i - \overrightarrow{x}_j\|^2} & otherwise \end{cases}, \ j = 1, \cdots, n \ (j \neq i) \qquad (3)$$

The total force exerted on individual i is the sum of individual forces:

$$\overrightarrow{F}^i = \sum_{j \neq i}^{n} \overrightarrow{F}^{ij} \qquad (4)$$

After obtaining the total force vector the movement of each individual i is performed according to expression (5)

$$x_{ir}^{k+1} = \begin{cases} x_{ir}^k + \lambda \frac{F_r^i}{\|\overrightarrow{F}^i\|}(u_r - x_{ir}^k) & if \ F_r^i > 0 \\ x_{ir}^k + \lambda \frac{F_r^i}{\|\overrightarrow{F}^i\|}(x_{ir}^k - l_r) & if \ F_r^i \leq 0 \end{cases}, \ r = 1, \cdots, d \qquad (5)$$

where λ is a random number such that $\lambda \sim U(0,1)$ and l_r, u_r are the lower and upper bounds for each component r of particle $\overrightarrow{x}_i$, respectively.

The non-dominated particles obtained during the algorithm execution are stored in an external archive. In [9], the clustering technique proposed in [13] was used, to maintain the diversity of the non-dominated archive.

Algorithm 1. MOEM pseudo code

1: Initialize iteration counter, $k = 1$
2: Randomly initialize each population individual $\vec{x}_i^k$, $i = 1, \cdots, n$
3: Assess each particle $\vec{x}_i^k$, evaluating $\vec{f}(\vec{x}_i^k) = (f_1(\vec{x}_i^k), f_2(\vec{x}_i^k), \cdots, f_m(\vec{x}_i^k))$, $i = 1, \cdots, n$
4: Insert non-dominated particles into archive $\widetilde{A}$
5: **while** stop criterion is not met **do**
6:     Randomly select the particles to insert into the local archive $\widetilde{S}$ from archive $\widetilde{A}$
7:     Do local search on $\widetilde{S}$
8:     **for** $i = 1, \cdots, n$ **do**
9:         Compute the charge (q_i) of the particle i using (2)
10:        Compute total force $(\vec{F}^i)$ exerted on particle i using (3) and (4)
11:        Move particle i using (5)
12:        Update non-dominated archive $\widetilde{A}$
13:    **end for**
14: **end while**
15: Return non-dominated archive $\widetilde{A}$

3.2   EMOEM Algorithm

We propose herein a new algorithm modifying some of the MOEM main components. Analyzing the charge operator expression in MOEM (2), it can be seen that the number of variables is the factor used to increase charge differences between particles performing significantly different in the objective space. However, when the ratio of the number of variables to population size is small, the problem of small differentiation among particle charges arises, as poor performing particles have very similar charge values to those of good performing particles. Then, in EMOEM the charge factor is modified, using the population size instead of the number of variables. Substituting this factor in (2), the new charge evaluation expression for each particle i of the population in EMOEM is obtained (6).

$$q_i = exp(-n \frac{\min_{\vec{x}_p \in \widetilde{S}} \| \vec{f}(\vec{x}_i) - \vec{f}(\vec{x}_p) \|}{\sum_{j=1}^{n} \min_{\vec{x}_p \in \widetilde{S}} \| \vec{f}(\vec{x}_j) - \vec{f}(\vec{x}_p) \|}), \quad i = 1, \cdots, n. \qquad (6)$$

This change aims at increasing differences among particle charges making them more influenced by the particle's objective function values. Then, charge values of better particles are increased and those of worse particles become lower. This contributes to increase the total force of better particles and inversely decrease the others.

In the MOEM algorithm, each individual moves itself according to expression (5). The individual movement may be performed in a different direction from that indicated by the force vector for two reasons. The first reason is: each coordinate of the force vector is multiplied by the corresponding coordinate of a range vector, the limits of which are $\vec{x}_i$ and one of the variable lower/upper bounds. As the range vector has not all coordinates equal, the direction of the movement is changed. This situation is represented in fig. 1, where a movement of the particle $\vec{x}_i^k = (x_{i1}^k, x_{i2}^k)$ is considered. Since $u_1 - x_{i1}^k \neq u_2 - x_{i2}^k$, then the new position of the particle is out of the direction defined by the force vector. This situation occurs always except when the distance from $\overrightarrow{x}_i$ to the respective bounds is the same in all dimensions. The second reason to deviate the direction of the movement is that the chosen bound depends on the force component sign. There are many situations in which the individual force components have different signs. In such situations different range vectors are used, which deviates the individual from the direction indicated by its force vector. In sum, we conclude that in most cases the direction of movement is different from the direction defined by the force. This may bias the particle movement. The use of a range vector in the original MOEM algorithm guarantees that the new position of a particle always lies within the bounds of the variables, as we can observe in (5). This results from the fact that the term $\lambda \frac{F^i}{\|\overrightarrow{F}^i\|}$ belongs to the range $[0, 1]$. Then the movement is always performed in the direction defined by a linear combination of each component of that vector.

To overcome the limitations of the individual updating process in the MOEM algorithm, a modified update position mechanism is proposed herein. In the new position updating expression, the vector of the allowed range of movement is dropped to guarantee that the movement performed by a particle follows to the direction of its force vector. Then, in the EMOEM algorithm, each particle moves itself according to the expression

$$x_{ir}^{k+1} = x_{ir}^k + \lambda \frac{F_r^i}{\|\overrightarrow{F}^i\|}, \quad r = 1, \cdots, d. \tag{7}$$

where λ is a random uniform value in the interval $[0, 1]$. Since the force vector is normalized, variables should be considered in $[0, 1]$. To satisfy this requirement, a change of variables is performed. Then, before updating the particle position, its variables are mapped onto the $[0, 1]$ interval using the expression

$$x_{ir} \leftarrow \frac{x_{ir} - l_r}{u_r - l_r}, \quad r = 1, \cdots, d. \tag{8}$$

where l_r and u_r are the lower and upper bounds of variable r, respectively. Now it is ensured that each variable of the particle lies in $[0, 1]$ and the particle is ready to be updated. The direction of the movement does not change with the position occupied by the individual in the search space. Then, the movement performed in EMOEM algorithm overcomes the biased situations identified in the MOEM algorithm and at the same time guarantees the feasibility of solutions. In some cases one individual may become infeasible (i.e., outside the bounds) but in such case it is moved to the corresponding bounds. Fig. 2 exemplifies the movement of the particle $\overrightarrow{x}_j^k$ in EMOEM algorithm. The deviation occurring in MOEM, such as in fig. 1, is then corrected.

As in the MOEM algorithm, EMOEM also uses an external archive to store the non-dominated solutions obtained. We use the crowding operator presented in [3] both to substitute one particle of the non-dominated archive when it is full and to select individuals of the non-dominated archive to insert into the local archive. In each of these situations a particle is chosen, by binary tournament, selecting the most crowded individual to be removed from the archive and the least crowded to enter the local archive.

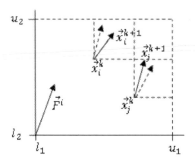

Fig. 1. Update position in MOEM algorithm

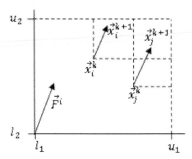

Fig. 2. Update position in EMOEM algorithm

4   Performance Metrics

In multiobjective optimization, the quality of solutions should be assessed in two ways: convergence to the true Pareto Optimal Front and spread of solutions in the non-dominated front obtained. To assess the performance of the proposed EMOEM algorithm we use two performance metrics: Inverted Generational Distance (IGD) and Hypervolume [13]. IGD is the sum of the distances from each point of the true non-dominated front to the nearest point of the non-dominated set found by the algorithm. The hypervolume measures the volume of the space delimited by the non-dominated front obtained and a reference point (generally the nadir point, which is composed by the worst objective function values in the non-dominated set). Both IGD and hypervolume measure convergence and the spread of solutions in the non-dominated front obtained.

Inverted Generational Distance (IGD): Consider P^* a set of points representative of the whole true Pareto Front of the problem and let S be a set of points approximating the Pareto Front. Then, the IGD metric of S relatively to P^* is given by:

$$IGD(S, P^*) = \frac{\sum_{v \in P^*} d(v, S)}{|P^*|}, \qquad (9)$$

where $d(v, S)$ is the Euclidean distance from $v \in P^*$ to the nearest point in S. The lower the IGD metric, the better the approximation set S. Note that we can only use this metric when the Pareto front of the problem is known.

Hypervolume (HV): This metric is evaluated using the algorithm presented in [5]. The bigger the HV value, the better the approximation set.

In order to confirm the significance of the results, a statistical analysis is also conducted. Since the results do not follow a normal distribution, non-parametric tests are used. The Mann-Whitney test is used to compare the algorithms.

5   Experimentation

In this section we present the details of the comparative analysis performed, identifying the problems, the algorithm parameterization, the performance indicators and the methodology used in the experimentation.

We consider 11 problems, 5 from benchmark ZDT [12], 3 from benchmark DTLZ [4] and 3 constrained problems. The problems zdt1, zdt2, zdt3, zdt4 and zdt6 are selected from the benchmark set ZDT. From the group DTLZ, the problems dtlz1, dtlz2 and dtlz3 are selected, considering the case of three objectives. The problems of both groups are unconstrained. The set of problems is completed with the constrained problems CONSTR, SRN and TNK [3].

The IGD and hypervolume indicators are used to assess the performance of the algorithms. We performed 30 independent runs of each algorithm for each problem. The population size was set to 100 individuals and the size of the archive of non-dominated solutions was limited to 100 individuals. The stop criterion adopted was the number of objective function evaluations. The algorithms end when 25000 function evaluations are completed in case of two objective problems, and after 50000 function evaluations for three objective problems.

5.1   Comparative Analysis of EMOEM and MOEM

In figures 3-6, the non-dominated fronts obtained by EMOEM and MOEM algorithms are displayed. As a qualitative indicator we can say that EMOEM performs much better than MOEM both in convergence and spread of solutions in all problems except in TNK, where the results are similar. Observing the graphics of zdt1 and zdt3 problems, it can be seen that most non-dominated solutions computed by the MOEM algorithm are dominated by at least one non-dominated solution obtained by EMOEM. In general, MOEM obtains much less non-dominated solutions and less spread than EMOEM.

Detailed values in tables 1 and 2 confirm the perception given by the graphics. Table 1 presents hypervolume values for both algorithms in all benchmark problems. EMOEM outperformed MOEM in zdt1, zdt2, zdt3, zdt6, CONSTR and SRN problems. EMOEM performed slightly worse in zdt4, dtlz2 and TNK problems.

In table 1, the cases in which the hypervolume median is 0 means that none of the non-dominated solutions obtained by the algorithm is inside the hypercube defined by the non-dominated front of the problem and the reference point. It can be observed that in the case of the zdt2 problem, the MOEM algorithm was not able to solve it in any run (thus its hypervolume is always 0) and EMOEM algorithm could give a good approximation of its Pareto front in some of the runs.

The Mann-Whitney test confirms the significance of the differences registered at $\alpha = 0.05$ level in all problems except in dtlz1 and dtlz3. In these two problems none of the two algorithms achieved the region corresponding to the hypercube defined for hypervolume evaluation, then there are no differences in terms of hypervolume values.

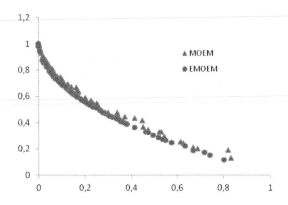

Fig. 3. Problem zdt1

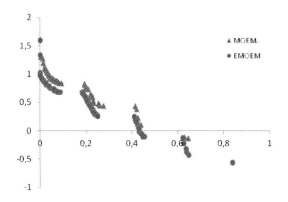

Fig. 4. Problem zdt3

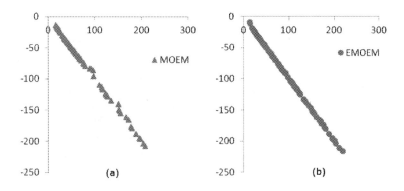

Fig. 5. Problem SRN: (a) MOEM algorithm; (b) EMOEM algorithm

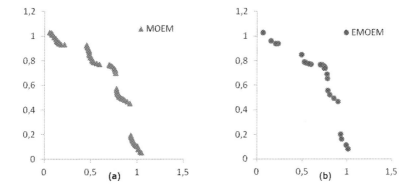

Fig. 6. Problem TNK: (a) MOEM algorithm; (b) EMOEM algorithm

Table 1. Median and Inter-Quartile Range (IQR) of hypervolume values obtained by MOEM and EMOEM algorithms

Problem	EMOEM		MOEM	
	Median	IQR	Median	IQR
zdt1	**0.6114**	0.0321	0.5544	0.1718
zdt2	**0.0828**	0.3040	0.0000	0.0000
zdt3	**0.6705**	0.0751	0.0001	0.1024
zdt4	**0.1077**	0.0107	0.1491	0.0256
zdt6	**0.0053**	0.0087	0.0000	0.0000
dtlz1	0.0000	0.0000	0.0000	0.0000
dtlz2	0.1537	0.0140	**0.2176**	0.0267
dtlz3	0.0000	0.0000	0.0000	0.0000
CONSTR	**3.2852**	0.3925	3.1830	0.0847
SRN	**24616**	130.53	23872	297.03
TNK	0.2979	0.0076	**0.3200**	0.0029

As it can be observed in table 2, MOEM has a great difficulty in generating a large number of non-dominated solutions. EMOEM increases significantly the number of non-dominated solutions generated in all problems except in TNK and it is able to completely fill the archive in most problems.

To compute the IGD metric it is necessary to have a representative set of the true non-dominated front of the problem. Since we do not have the true non-dominated set for the TNK problem, the IGD metric is not evaluated for this problem. In table 3 the results of the IGD performance measure are reported. These results confirm the better performance of EMOEM algorithm in most problems. Although both algorithms have obtained a hypervolume 0 in dtlz1 and dtlz3 problems, in case of the IGD measure MOEM attained better results. The only case in which the results are not significant at $\alpha = 0.05$ level is in zdt4

Table 2. Median and Inter-Quartile Range (IQR) of number of particles in the non-dominated archive at the end of each run of MOEM and EMOEM algorithms

Problem	EMOEM		MOEM	
	Median	IQR	Median	IQR
zdt1	**100**	0	49.5	23.75
zdt2	**10.5**	96	1	1
zdt3	**100**	0.75	20.5	22
zdt4	**33**	12.75	14	3
zdt6	**16**	5	5	2
dtlz1	**99.5**	76.75	6	1.25
dtlz2	100	0	100	0
dtlz3	**24.5**	21	8	2
CONSTR	100	0	100	0
SRN	100	0	100	0
TNK	22	2.75	**100**	0.63

problem, so in this problem the MOEM algorithm is not significantly better than EMOEM.

Table 3. Median and Inter-Quartile Range (IQR) of IGD values obtained in each run of MOEM and EMOEM algorithms

Problem	EMOEM		MOEM	
	Median	IQR	Median	IQR
zdt1	**0.0780**	0.0568	0.1041	0.1231
zdt2	**0.3342**	0.5925	0.7722	0.1257
zdt3	**0.1306**	0.0535	0.8544	0.6901
zdt4	0.5658	0.0136	0.5473	0.0513
zdt6	**0.5643**	0.0574	2.9764	0.6501
dtlz1	8.1697	3.3059	**1.3785**	1.0316
dtlz2	0.2267	0.0179	**0.1763**	0.0205
dtlz3	68.9354	50.297	**17.482**	7.7891
CONSTR	**0.6249**	0.5340	1.1218	0.1394
SRN	**1.4089**	0.1864	2.7933	0.7269

The new EMOEM algorithm performs globally better as it generally obtains better values in both metrics analyzed, improving convergence and spread relatively to MOEM. Only in cases of three-objective problems dtlz1, dtlz2 and dtlz3 a better performance of MOEM algorithm can be observed, but none of the algorithms attains the hypercube defined for the problems dtlz1 and dtlz3. In cases of CONSTR and SRN constrained problems, the EMOEM algorithm is better as it achieves better results than those obtained by MOEM in both metrics.

6   Conclusions and Future Work

The Electromagnetism-like Mechanism has proven to be effective in single optimization [1] [8]. In addition, several modifications of the initial algorithm have been proposed in the literature, which performed better than the initial algorithm in several test problems. However, in the case of multiobjective optimization the results have not been so encouraging. The MOEM algorithm has demonstrated a poor performance in comparison with other representative population-based algorithms in benchmark problems. Our intention has been to redesign the EMOEM algorithm in order to take advantage of the EM ability to solve hard continuous multiobjective optimization problems.

Our motivation to design the EMOEM algorithm derives from experiments in which the MOEM algorithm experienced strong difficulties with several problems. The EMOEM algorithm herein presented is intended to address the bias of individual charge and update position MOEM mechanisms. The behavior of EMOEM represents an improvement relatively to MOEM, increasing the quality of solutions and the number of non-dominated solutions computed.

Future directions of research include designing more effective local search procedures and address more challenging problems. Work is underway to compare EMOEM algorithm with state-of-the-art approaches OMOPSO [7] and NSGA-II [3].

Acknowledgments. This R&D work has been partially supported by the Portuguese Foundation for Science and Technology (FCT) under projects grants MIT/SET/0014/ 2009 and PEst-C/EEI/UI0308/2011, and Project EMSURE (Energy and Mobility for Sustainable Regions, CENTRO 07 0224 FEDER 002004).

References

1. Alikani, M.G., Javadian, N., Tavakkoli-Moghaddan, R.: A novel hybrid approach combining electromagnetism-like method with Solis and Wets local search for continuous optimization problems. Journal of Global Optimization **44**, 227–234 (2009)
2. Birbil, S.I., Fang, S.: An electromagnetism-like mechanism for global optimization. Journal of Global Optimization **25**, 263–282 (2003)
3. Deb, K., Pratap, A., Agarwal, S., Meyarivan, T.: A Fast and Elitist Multiobjective Genetic Algorithm: NSGA-II. IEEE Transactions on Evolutionary Computation **6**(2), 182–197 (2002)
4. Deb, K., Thiele, L., Laumanns, M., Zitzler, E.: Scalable Test Problems for Evolutionary Multiobjective Optimization. In: Abraham, L.J.A. (ed.), Evolutionary Multiobjective Optimization. Theoretical Advances and Applications, pp. 105–145 (2005)
5. Fonseca, C.M., Paquete, L., López-Ibáñez, M.: An Improved Dimension-Sweep Algorithm for the Hypervolume. In: Proceedings of 2006 IEEE Congress on Evolutionary Computation, pp. 1157–1163 (2006)
6. Naji-Azimi, Z., Toth, P., Galli, L.: An electromagnetism metaheuristic for the unicost set covering problem. European Journal of Operational Research **205**, 290–300 (2010)

7. Sierra, M.R., Coello, C.A.C.: Improving PSO-Based Multi-objective Optimization Using Crowding, Mutation and ϵ-Dominance. In: Coello Coello, C.A., Hernández Aguirre, A., Zitzler, E. (eds.) EMO 2005. LNCS, vol. 3410, pp. 505–519. Springer, Heidelberg (2005)

8. Tavakkoli-Moghaddam, R., Khalili, M., Naderi, B.: A hybridization of simulated annealing and electromagnetic-like mechanism for job shop problems with machine availability and sequence-dependent setup times to minimize total weighted tardiness. Soft Computing 13(10), 995–1006 (2009)

9. Tsou, C.-S., Kao, C.-H.: An Electromagnetism-Like Meta-Heuristic for Multi-Objective Optimization. In: Proceedings of 2006 IEEE Congress on Evolutionary Computation, pp. 1172–1178 (2006)

10. Tsou, C.S., Kao, C.-H.: Multi-objective inventory control using electromagnetism-like meta-heuristic. International Journal of Production Research 46(14), 3859–3874 (2008)

11. Tsou, C.S., Hsu, C.-H., Yu, F.-J.: Using multi-objective electromagnetism-like optimization to analyze inventory tradeoffs under probabilistic demand. Journal of Scientific & Industrial Research 67, 569–573 (2008)

12. Zitzler, E., Deb, K., Thiele, L.: Comparison of Multiobjective Evolutionary Algorithms: Empirical Results. Evolutionary Computation 8, 173–195 (2000)

13. Zitzler, E., Thiele, L.: Multiobjective Evolutionary Algorithms: A Comparative Case Study and the Strength Pareto Approach. IEEE Transactions on Evolutionary Computation 3(4), 257–271 (1999)

14. Zhang, C., Li, X., Gao, L., Wu, Q.: An improved electromagnetism-like mechanism algorithm for constrained optimization. Expert Systems with Applications 40, 5621–5634 (2013)

Objective Dimension and Problem Structure in Multiobjective Optimization Problems

Ramprasad Joshi$^{(\boxtimes)}$, Bharat Deshpande, and Paritosh Gote

BITS, Pilani - K K Birla Goa Campus, Zuarinagar 403726, Goa, India
{rsj,bmd}@goa.bits-pilani.ac.in, paritosh.gote@gmail.com

Abstract. Multiobjective optimization seeks simultaneous minimization of multiple scalar functions on $\mathbb{R}^n$. Unless weighted sums are made to replace the vector functions arising thus, such an optimization requires some partial- or quasi-ordering of points in the search space based on comparisons between the values attained by the functions to be optimized at those points. Many such orders can be defined, and search-based (mainly heuristic) optimization algorithms make use of such orders implicitly or explicitly for refining and accelerating search. In this work, such relations are studied by modeling them as graphs. Information apparent in the structure of such graphs is studied in the form of degree distribution. It is found that when the objective dimension grows, the degree distribution tends to follow a power-law. This can be a new beginning in the study of escalation of hardness of problems with dimension, as also a basis for designing new heuristics.

1 Introduction

Multiobjective optimization requires various nontrivial choices of the algorithm designer as well as solution deployer. Acceptable solution criteria themselves are subject to complicated choices affecting many other decisions down the line. Design of evolutionary algorithms for multiobjective optimization involves choosing the search heuristic, designing appropriate representation, designing appropriate variation operators, defining ordering relations, designing selection strategies, and possibly designing adaptation among one or several of all these parameters. Because of the complexity of these choices and designs, and because slight variations in them can produce widely varying behaviours and performances, analysing problem hardness or even defining a problem hardness notion that is not dependent on the semantics and the intuition behind algorithm designs has been a vexatious exercise. We argue here that making the geometric intuition that usually underlies algorithm designs also the basis of analysing problem structure will go a long way in the prediction of problem hardness with respect to specific design primitives in algorithms. For this purpose, studying the partial orders induced by the geometry of problems, and applying probability measure theory, can be a starting point.

© Springer-Verlag Berlin Heidelberg 2014
A.I. Esparcia-Alcázar et al. (Eds.): EvoApplications 2014, LNCS 8602, pp. 639–650, 2014.
DOI: 10.1007/978-3-662-45523-4_52

1.1 Moraglio et al.'s Geometric View of Variation Operators

Moraglio et al., in a series of works (e.g.[4],[3],[6]) have investigated and established a geometric-topological view of the search performed by evolutionary and other population-based heuristic algorithms. They unify the heuristic ideas behind the varied designs of variation (mutation and crossover) operators, and demonstrate that (most) evolutionary algorithms perform convex search, convex in the geometry induced by the neighbourhood structure and metric imposed on the search space by the algorithms' operators.

1.2 A Similar View for Selection Operators

In order to combine such a unified and powerful framework with analyses of problems so that a composite theory of evolutionary computation (of algorithms and problems) can be developed, we propose to use probability measure theory on the spaces of partial- and quasi-order relations that are imposed by the comparison operators and used by the selection operators of evolutionary and other heuristic algorithms. We unify the discrete nature of computed sequences and orders of sampled search points with probability measure theory on the most general continuous search spaces using simple graph models.

The rest of the paper is organized as follows. In Section 2 the basic definitions and their motivation are discussed. Subsequent Section 3 develops elementary tools of analysis of problem structure, especially from probability theory. Section 4 follows up on this development to make a conjecture, which is substantiated by computational experiments described in Section 5. Conclusions (in Section 6) sum up the paper.

1.3 Discovery of the Power Law

Power law distributions (see Clauset et al.[1]) arise in many natural as well as social mass processes, such as the World Wide Web. Among other things, a power law distribution over degrees in a graph indicate a certain scale-freeness[5]. Below (Section 5) we provide evidence that initial populations for optimization problems of many objectives tend to have a power-law distribution over the counts of points dominated by each point, indicating that variation and selection operators that depend on dominance relationships among individuals in the population (e.g. tournament selection) will not be able to distinguish between different solutions and identify niche areas. We investigated only the initial population genrated by uniform random sampling, but it opens up a new way of examining the properties of graphs arising in an optimization by heuristic search process induced by the dominance relationships and following various generative distributions, thereby providing useful information about the hardness of a problem or about tunability of algorithm performance.

2   The Structure of the Explored Search Space

Heuristic (including evolutionary) as well as classical (Newton-like) algorithms explore the search space in an iterative manner: beginning with some initial set of points, they try to figure out, in either geometric, or algebraic, or analytical manner, the next set of points which potentially may be better in the previous set. Similar to the geometric-topological view of Moraglio et al. we here look at the informative structure contained in the explored set of points (either the set under consideration in one iteration or all the points explored till some iteration) by examining the structure of the (transitive) graph that represents the transitive partial order on these points obtained by a strict dominance relation.

2.1   The Search Space

For simplicity, we take a closed bounded Euclidean space $\mathbb{X} \subsetneq \mathbb{R}^n, n \geq 1$ as the *search* space, and a bounded continuous function $f : \mathbb{X} \mapsto \mathbb{R}^m, m \geq 1$ as the multiobjective optimization (minimization) problem. We call $f(\mathbb{X})$ the *objective* space.

2.2   The Partial Order

The partial order we consider is $\prec \subsetneq \mathbb{X} \times \mathbb{X} : x \prec y \Leftrightarrow f_i(x) < f_i(y), i \in \{1, 2, \ldots, m\}$. It is obvious that $\prec$ is a transitive, irreflexive, antisymmetric relation. The transitivity is important to our analysis, in a practical way: it renders making graphs and computing their properties easier. However, it does not take away much of generality: the usual dominance relation that is used extensively in EC literature $x \preccurlyeq y \Leftrightarrow (\forall i \in \{1, 2, \ldots, m\} f_i(x) \leq f_i(y)) \wedge (\exists i \in \{1, 2, \ldots, m\} f_i(x) < f_i(y))$ considers for any given x additionally (to our $\prec$) only a null set of points $y, x \preccurlyeq y$ that has measure 0 as long as the measure is absolutely continuous with respect to the Lebesgue measure. Moreover, in practical floating-point calculations, strict equality comparison does not yield more accurate resutls; it can be counterproductive on the contrary.

2.3   The Graph

We consider the simple directed acyclic graph $G = (V, E)$, for $V \subset \mathbb{X}, |V| < \infty$, induced by the $\prec$ relation: $\forall x \neq y \in V, (x, y) \in E \Leftrightarrow x \prec y$. There are no self loops in G because $\prec$ is irreflexive. G is transitively closed. Such a graph is depicted in figure 1, in which the points are numbered. Thus, in the figure,

$$1 \prec 5, 1 \prec 6; 2 \prec 7, 2 \prec 8 \prec 12 \prec 15; 3 \prec 9 \prec 13, 3 \prec 10 \prec 14; 4 \prec 10 \prec 14, 4 \prec 11.$$

Inset is a possible scenario in a 2-D objective space that can give rise to this graph partially.

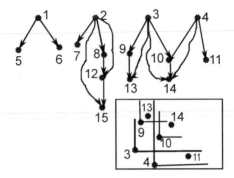

Fig. 1. A Transitive Graph induced by $\prec$

2.4   The Properties of $\prec$ and G Relevant to the Search Space Structure

Any EA (or, many other population-based heuristics too) will make decisions (viz. parental selection, survival selection, variation operators' specific geometry) based on some dominance relationships among the set of points under consideration in one iteration (e.g. a population in a generation in an EA run). "Differentiation" among the population in objective space is a major theme in EA design and performance, as also nearness or similarity between points in the search space. "Locating the pareto-optimal front" means identifying the nearness criteria among the population that lead to differentiation (towards more dominance) of similar or near points from the rest of the search space. For differentiation, one of the criteria used is the "hypervolume", or a rough estimate of the measure $\nu_\prec(x) = \nu(H_x = \{y \in \mathbb{X} : x \prec y\})$ of points H_x dominated by each point x where ν is some volumetric measure, usually taken to be the usual Euclidean volume (Lebesgue measure). Although densities in the search and objective space can be quite different, though related, and can be nonuniform throughout the objective space, the main technique used is taking a reference point in $\mathbb{R}^m$, not necessarily in $f(\mathbb{X})$, and take the Euclidean volume (the Lebesgue measure) of the hypercube defined by the two corners, one the image $f(x)$ of the point x, and the other the reference point, as the hypervolume $hyp(x)$ dominated by x. It is obvious that the $\prec$ relation respects hypervolumes (for a suitable reference point not in the interior of the objective space):

$$H_x \supsetneq H_y \Leftrightarrow x \prec y \Rightarrow hyp(x) > hyp(y). \tag{1}$$

However, we must also take into consideration the fact that algorithms in practice tend to calculate hypervolumes in the objective space. Densities in search and objective spaces can be quite different. We need to take up the question of the relation between the graph G and hypervolumes as calculated by the existing algorithms. Observe that hypervolumes are computed using a reference point in such a way that the putatively dominated sets contain the actual dominated sets, most often properly. The reference point itself must be dominated by every point that dominates anything else in $f(\mathbb{X})$. In other words, the reference point must be well-nigh "high above and outside" the objective space $f(\mathbb{X})$. This makes hypervolume calculations easier. Therefore, in this setting $\forall x \in \mathbb{X}, hyp(x) \geq \nu(H_x)$ where ν is the Lebesgue measure normalized over the search space. Still, because inclusion is equivalent to $\prec$ relation for the dominated sets, and the reference point does not change that inclusion in the first part of (1), the implication in its second part must hold too. Now we can take the $\prec$ relation and its induced graph to represent information that practical heuristic algorithms in EC use for decisions, whether based on ranking or ordering, or based on hypervolumes. For maintaining rigour, however, we confine the discussion to the actual measures of dominated sets.

From the foregoing, it is clear that the hypervolume dominated by a given graph G induced by $\prec$ over f over $\mathbb{X}$, is the total hypervolume (of a union discounting intersections) dominated by the nondominated points, or the vertices of G that have indegree 0. Such points are easily identified by a depth-first (DFS) traversal of G, that follows a directed path in the graph until a potential cycle or a dead-end is visited, restarting at unvisited vertices and down unexplored paths. Such a traversal results in a set of (possibly several, disjoint) tree, in which cycle-forming edges are omitted, and intersecting paths are explored short of the intersecting edge. This set is called a DFS-forest. The nondominated points in a given V of $G = (V, E)$ will be the roots of the trees in this forest. In figure 1, vertices 1,2,3,4 are the roots of DFS trees in and DFS run (regardless of the sequence of vertices taken). If the usual order of natural numbers is taken, then such a DFS run on this graph will yield a DFS forest that is the whole graph except the edge $(4 \rightarrow 10)$.

Let us call the paths in G that go across two disjoint trees in this DFS-forest as *bridges*. Thus in figure 1, the edge $(4 \rightarrow 10)$ is the only bridge. If there are too many bridges in G itself, then the sets dominated by the nondominated points are also intersecting too often. When the bridges are near the roots of the DFS-forest trees, the intersection sets are large too. It can be seen now that the more the disjoint paths in G, the closer (from below) is the total hypervolume dominated by G to the simple sum of the hypervolumes dominated by the nondominated points, because there will be fewer and smaller intersections among the dominated sets. Of course, there is the possibility that the chosen V is such that intersections among the dominated sets are not reflected in the intersecting paths. How is V to be chosen such that this probability is negligible? We address this question in Section 3.

3   Choosing V to Minimize Intersection Without Bridges

The simplest scheme to choose V so that there is a fair correspondence between the number of bridges and intersections of dominated sets is to choose it uniformly randomly. Our next simple proposition tells that the proportion of vertices in V sampled uniformly from any closed connected set of nonzero measure in $\mathbb{X}$ is sharply concentrated around its measure by the uniform probability measure.

Proposition 1. *Let $X \subset \mathbb{R}^n$ be a bounded measurable set and ν be the Lebesgue measure normalized on and restricted to X, such that $\nu(X) = 1$. If V is sampled uniformly at random from X, with $|V| = q < \infty$, then for $Y \subset X$ Borel,*

$$\mathbb{P}[|\{v \in V \cap Y\}| \ge q\nu(Y) + t] \le \exp\left(\frac{-t^2}{2(q\nu(Y) + t/3)}\right)$$

and

$$\mathbb{P}[|\{v \in V \cap Y\}| \le q\nu(Y) - t] \le \exp\left(\frac{-t^2}{2(q\nu(Y))}\right).$$

Proof: Observe that when sampled uniformly, $|\{v \in V \cap Y\}|$ is a binomial random variable that is the sum of the Bernoulli trials over $\mathbf{1}_Y$ with

$$p = \mathbb{P}[x \in Y] = \nu(Y); \; \mathbb{P}[x \notin Y] = 1 - p.$$

So $\mathbb{E}[|\{v \in V \cap Y\}|] = qp = q\nu(Y)$. The result follows from the direct application of Chernoff bounds. $\qquad\square$

Let $u, v \in V$ be two uniformly randomly chosen points, let $\nu(H_u \cap H_v) = h$ and let the number of points in V that are descendents of u, v both be denoted by the random variable N. That means $|\{w \in V \cap H_u \cap H_v\}| = N$. Then by Proposition 1, with $|V| = q$, if $h \ne 0$, $\mathbb{P}[N = 0] \le e^{\frac{-qh}{2}}$. This precisely is an upper bound on the probability of an intersection among dominated sets not being represented by any bridge in the graph G; and this is tight (upto multiplicative fractional constants) by Chernoff bounds. For a large graph, this rapidly diminishes. Hence we can conclude that

Proposition 2. *When there is no bridge in G between DFS trees rooted in two vertices $u, v \in V$, then $H_u \cap H_v = \Phi$, with a high probability $\ge 1 - \epsilon$, wherein $\epsilon \downarrow 0$ as $q \uparrow \infty$.* $\qquad\square$

4   Degree Distribution in a Graph with No Bridges

In each DFS tree (on the graph G obtained as in Section 3 above) containing q_r vertices, the (out-)degrees (in G) of the vertices in the tree are distributed as follows. For each degree in $\{0, 1, \ldots, q_r - 1\}$, the number of vertices with that degree diminishes as the degree rises. With degree $q_r - 1$, there is exactly 1 vertex in the tree, and if there are no bridges, then there is exactly one vertex of degree $q_r - 1$ in G for each DFS tree with q_r vertices. Take $r \in [0, 1]$ and $q_r = qr$. Suppose $r_1, r_2, \ldots, r_k \in [0, 1]$ are the fractions associated with all the k DFS trees of sizes qr_1 etc. in the bridgeless graph G. Then $\sum_i r_i = 1$, and each $r_i = h_i \pm \frac{t_i}{q}$ for some small t_i, where $h_i = \nu(H_{x_i})$, x_i the root of the ith tree. Thus $\sum_i (h_i \pm \frac{t_i}{q}) = 1$. By Proposition 1, the set dominated by the root x_i of a q_{r_i}-tree has this bound:

$$\mathbb{P}[qh_i - t_i < qr_i - 1 < qh_i + t_i] \ge 1 - \exp\left(\frac{-t_i^2}{2(qh_i + t_i/3)}\right) - exp\left(\frac{-t_i^2}{2qh_i}\right).$$

Rearranging and simplifying the inequalities, we get

$$\mathbb{P}\left[r_i - \frac{1+t_i}{q} < h_i < r_i - \frac{1-t_i}{q}\right] \geq 1 - 2\exp\left(\frac{-t_i^2}{2(qh_i + t_i/3)}\right).$$

Now, if k is large and r_i not varying much, then each h_i has to be small. But then the lack of bridges means that the corresponding H_{x_i} are all pairwise disjoint and cover most of the search space, which, with each h_i small, is possible only if the overwhelming majority of x_i lie on the Pareto-optimal front, and their images are as distant as possible in the objective space. This argument needs to be made more rigorous, but we are justified here in claiming that

Conjecture 1. A bridgeless forest of a large number of trees of sizes that do not vary much indicates that a good approximation to the Pareto-optimal front is contained in it.

For an initial graph generated by uniform random sampling, this occurrence is highly unlikely for large m. But for small m, this is plausible. In case of large m, we can expect the more likely scenarios of a large variation in r_i, over small or large k, with a small or large number of bridges. Then the more the bridges, the more uniform is the degree distribution. As the dimension m grows, the variation in r_i will be larger, k larger, and the number of bridges smaller. Trees with large r_i will be less in proportion, and vice versa. Progressively this should lead to a situation that sees a rapid decrease in the number of trees with large size, hence a rapid decrease in the number of vertices with large degree. One would suspect a power-law distribution lurking here. In computational experiments on the DTLZ suite, we found this to be the case. We take a look at those results in Section 5. Note that the discussion of the out-degree distribution carries over with little change to in-degree distribution. Our computational results too confirm this, though we have omitted the graphs due to space constraints here.

5   Computational Experiments and Results

For the DTLZ suite of scalable test problems[2], we generated the graphs G as described in Section 3 above, for 30,000 points chosen uniformly randomly, for each objective dimension 2 through 10. The degree distributions were plotted in a log-log graph to see if power-law behaviour is apparent, which was found to be the case. The out-degree distribution graphs for dimensions 2 and 10, for problems DTLZ1, DTLZ2, DTLZ3, DTLZ4 are shown below (figures 2-5). In each graph, on the x-axis is the logarithm of the out-degree counts (strictly speaking an offset of 1 added, in order to avoid logarithm of 0), going from 10^0 through $10^{4.48}$ for out-degree counts going from 0 to 30,000. The almost-straight line of slope -1 except for DTLZ4 shows the power-law behaviour. The DTLZ4 exception needs explanation, which follows in the next paragraph. It is noteworthy that the graphs gradually take the power-law shapes as the objective dimension grows, though we cannot show all the graphs here. The programs used to carry out this data generation and analysis and the generated graphs are all available with the first author.

In their original paper describing the design of the DTLZ test problems, Deb et al.[2] have explained the goal in the design of DTLZ4 as testing "an MOEA's ability to maintain a good distribution of solutions", resulting in a modification of DTLZ2 that allows "a dense set of solutions to exist near" the plane of intersection of two dimensions in the objective space. This requires good diversity in the initial population itself, and therefore the performance of an MOEA on DTLZ4 in terms of quality of solutions depends sensitively on many parameters chosen at the time of a run. In a product measure absolutely continuous with the Lebesgue measure on the Euclidean space, the measure of points in this intersection region will be null because of the mapping, but their inverse image will be non-null. This will affect the degree distribution in a unique way, because a dense set in the search space will be a set of mutually indifferent points. In figure 6, the dimension 10 in-degree distribution is shown in a similar log-log plot for DTLZ2 and DTLZ4. DTLZ4 is a variation on DTLZ2, and the outlier in the plot for DTLZ4 (near [30,000,8]) shows the effect of the variation, due to the dense set of solutions depicted here, seen in the right-bottom corner.

The specificity of problem structure is even more apparent in the degree-difference graphs shown in the figures 7-10. Here the difference is out-degree minus in-degree. The difference (-30,000 to +30,000) is plotted on the x-axis, and the counts of points having that difference between their out- and in-degrees are plotted on the y-axis. These are **not** log-log plots, and the sharp concentration around the 0 difference is very obvious for the higher dimension. What is remarkable is that DTLZ4 has this concentration even more prominent, and in both lower and higher dimensions.

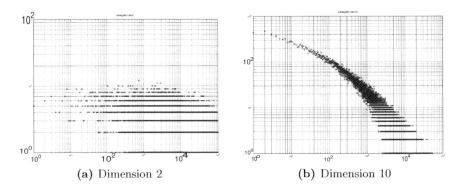

(a) Dimension 2   (b) Dimension 10

Fig. 2. DTLZ1, Out-degree distribution

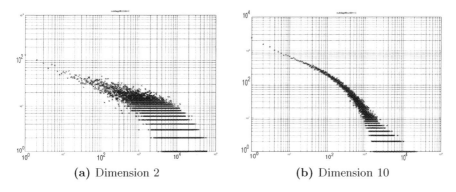

(a) Dimension 2   (b) Dimension 10

Fig. 3. DTLZ2, Out-degree distribution

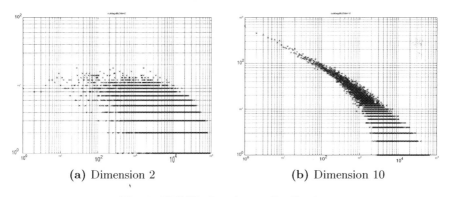

(a) Dimension 2   (b) Dimension 10

Fig. 4. DTLZ3, Out-degree distribution

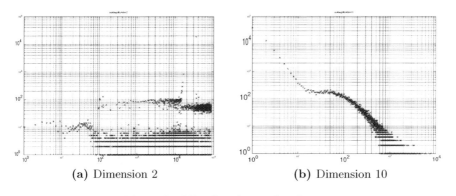

(a) Dimension 2   (b) Dimension 10

Fig. 5. DTLZ4, Out-degree distribution

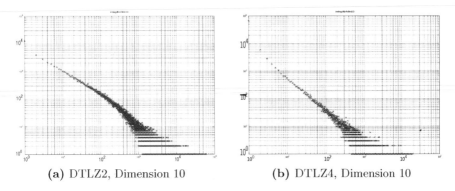

(a) DTLZ2, Dimension 10   (b) DTLZ4, Dimension 10

Fig. 6. DTLZ2 and DTLZ4, In-degree distribution

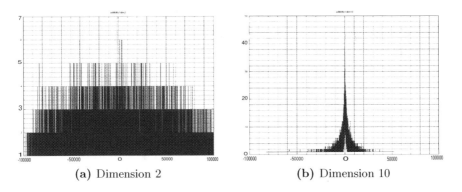

(a) Dimension 2   (b) Dimension 10

Fig. 7. DTLZ1, Degree-difference distribution

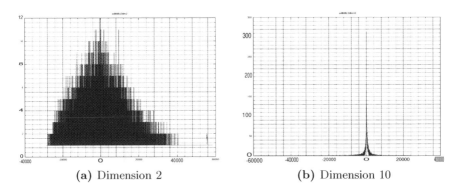

(a) Dimension 2   (b) Dimension 10

Fig. 8. DTLZ2, Degree-difference distribution

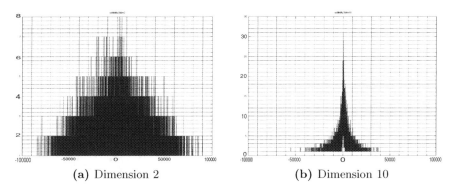

(a) Dimension 2   (b) Dimension 10

Fig. 9. DTLZ3, Degree-difference distribution

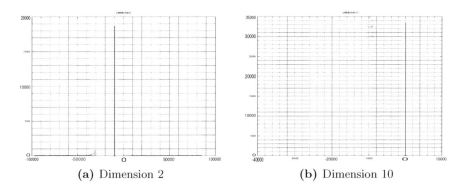

(a) Dimension 2   (b) Dimension 10

Fig. 10. DTLZ4, Degree-difference distribution

6   Conclusions and Future Work

In the graphs, it is apparent that specific problem strucure becomes progressively less important in the degree distribution as the dimension grows. The more the generated points, say 100,000, the more the behaviour is sharply tending towards power-law distribution as the dimension grows. This is not shown here yet. However, even in this there is a variation seen between DTLZ1,2,3 on the one hand and DTLZ4 on the other. This can be a starting point in separating problem-specific and class-general features of test problems and suites.

Examining graphs arising in a similar way but on populations generated by sampling other distributions than the uniform will be a new direction in analysing EA behaviour. Computational experiments with existing MOEAs and analytical framework for a family of distributions progressively sampled by such algorithms will open up the possibility of a new perspective on problem hardness and algorithm performance. The insights thus obtained can be useful in tuning algorithms by assessing the performance during a run.

This is an ongoing work, in which the present paper serves only as a proof-of-concept. Rigorous analysis of the conditions necessary and/or sufficient for obtaining various distributions in the degrees of the partial-order graphs is ongoing, in which other aggregate properties of the graphs are also being considered. For various orders, generated under various conditions such as adaptive or fixed sampling distributions for choosing points, which aggregate properties are preserved will be an interesting question for investigation. Combining this direction of work with Moraglio et al.'s work on algorithms ought to be the main goal in the long run.

References

1. Clauset, A., Shalizi, C.R., Newman, M.E.J.: Power-law distributions in empirical data. CoRR abs/0706.1062v2 (February 2009)
2. Deb, K., Thiele, L., Laumanns, M., Ziztler, E.: Scalable multi-objective optmization test problems. In: Proceedings of the 2002 Congress on Evolutionary Computation, vol. 1, pp. 825–830. IEEE (2002)
3. Moraglio, A.: Abstract convex evolutionary search. In: FOGA. pp. 151–162 (2011)
4. Moraglio, A.: Geometry of evolutionary algorithms. In: GECCO (Companion), pp. 1317–1344 (2012)
5. Newman, M.E.J.: The structure and function of complex networks. CoRR abs/cond-mat/0303516v1 (March 2003)
6. Yoon, Y., Kim, Y.H., Moraglio, A., Moon, B.R.: A mathematical unification of geometric crossovers defined on phenotype space. CoRR abs/0907.3200 (2009)

EvoPAR

Hybrid MPI/OpenMP Parallel Evolutionary Algorithms for Vehicle Routing Problems

Raul Baños[1,2]($\boxtimes$), Julio Ortega[2], and Consolación Gil[3]

[1] Department of Business Administration and Management, Catholic University
of Murcia, Campus de los Jerónimos s/n, E-30107 Guadalupe, Murcia, Spain
`rbanos@ucam.edu`
[2] Department of Computer Architecture and Technology, CITIC-UGR,
University of Granada, C/Periodista Daniel Saucedo s/n, E-18071 Granada, Spain
`jortega@ugr.es`
[3] Department of Informatics, ceiA3, University of Almería,
La Cañada de San Urbano s/n, E-04120 Almería, Spain
`cgilm@ual.es`

Abstract. The traditional fields of improvement in parallelism have
been orientated to experimentation on high-budget equipment, such as
clusters of computers or shared memory machines thanks to their high-
performance and scalability. In recent years, the generalization of multi-
core microprocessors in almost all the computing platforms makes it
possible to take advantage of parallel processing even for the desktop
computer user. This paper analyzes how to improve the performance
of population-based meta-heuristics using MPI, OpenMP, and hybrid
MPI/OpenMP implementations in a workstation having a multi-core
processor. The results obtained when solving large scale instances of
the Capacitated Vehicle Routing Problem with hard Time Windows
(VRPTW) show that, in all cases, the parallel implementations produce
better quality solutions for a given amount of runtime than the sequential
algorithm, and also solutions of similar quality in less runtime.

Keywords: Multi-core processors · Parallel Evolutionary Algorithms ·
MPI · OpenMP · Hybrid MPI/OpenMP · Vehicle Routing Problems

1 Introduction

Heuristics and meta-heuristics have proven to be very effective for complex combinatorial optimization problems appearing in several economic, industrial, and
scientific domains. Nevertheless, these methods often require large runtimes to
obtain high quality solutions when solving large instances of difficult problems.
In this context, parallel processing becomes an interesting tool to reduce the
runtime required to obtain similar quality solutions than those obtained by the
sequential algorithms and/or higher quality solutions than the sequential versions without increasing the runtime required by the latter. Parallel computing
has been successfully applied to improve the performance of bio-inspired heuristic approaches to solve complex optimization problems [17]. While in the past,

© Springer-Verlag Berlin Heidelberg 2014
A.I. Esparcia-Alcázar et al. (Eds.): EvoApplications 2014, LNCS 8602, pp. 653–664, 2014.
DOI: 10.1007/978-3-662-45523-4_53

parallel computing was mainly applied on high cost multiple-processor systems, such as high-performance computer clusters or shared memory architectures, in recent years the introduction of multi-core processors with multi-threading technology in the commercial market [3] has intrinsically implied that parallel processing can be also implemented in low-cost computers and workstations u-sing standard software components [14].

Given a parallel architecture, the decisions to be taken before to parallelize the sequential code are to determine which parallel model is more suitable to implement the algorithm, and the software library to be used. According to the literature [7], the parallel models that are often used to determine the imple-mentation strategy are: (i) The master-worker paradigm, where the master pro-cess divides the work amongst the workers, who complete the required work and return the result to the master. The master then organizes the received information, being the master processor responsible for synchronizing commu-nications, collecting and distributing data, etc.; (ii) the diffusion, also known as fine-grained paradigm, that considers a conceptual population like the master-worker paradigm, but this population contains only a few individuals; (iii) the island-based paradigm, also termed distributed or coarse-grained paradigm, con-sists in dividing the entire population of the sequential algorithm into several sub-populations distributed among different processors. These sub-populations or islands evolve, mainly in isolation, by executing all the steps of the algo-rithm, although it is possible to share information by migrating solutions between islands. The performance of island-based parallelizations is often influenced by two main design parameters: the migration topology and the frequency of these migrations; (iv) hybrid models that combine different implementation strategies.

Two standard software libraries often used for parallel processing are MPI [18] and OpenMP [5]. The MPI (Message Passing Interface) [18] is a portable, effi-cient, and flexible standard specification for the developers and users of message passing libraries. MPI runs on virtually any hardware platform, including those that based on shared, distributed, and hybrid memory architectures, and allows to write parallel programs by providing routines to initiate and configure the me-ssage environment as well as managing some of the tasks of the parallelization, such as decomposing and distributing the starting points of search, moments of communication, synchronization of communications, etc. The OpenMP [5] is a portable and scalable model for specifying shared memory parallelism in Fortran and C/C++ programs in platforms ranging from laptop computers to supercom-puters. The standard OpenMP allows the multi-threaded execution of a program thanks to the fact that compiler directives exploit loop level parallelism using the well-known fork-and-join execution model. Further, it is also possible to use a hybrid programming model which uses OpenMP for parallelization inside the node and MPI for message passing between nodes [6]. In the context of multi-core architectures, the question arises whether it might be advantageous or not to use more than one MPI process with multiple threads running on a node so that there is at least some explicit intra-node communication. The Vehicle Routing Problem and its multiple variants have been extensively tackled by sequential

[4] and parallel [2] meta-heuristics, but no hybrid MPI/OpenMP implementations have been reported for solving the VRPTW. Since both, the OpenMP and the MPI paradigms, have different advantages and disadvantages, and as the VRPTW is a problem whose cost functions are relatively easy to compute but the search space is very large, a priori it is not possible to determine which implementation strategy and software library would obtain the best results.

The paper is organized as follows: Section 2 formally describes the VRPTW. Section 3 presents the framework of this research, including a population-based meta-heuristic (MT-SA) which is parallelized using different parallel models and software libraries. Section 4 presents the results of the empirical analysis carried out in a multi-core workstation, while conclusions are drawn in Section 5.

2   The Vehicle Routing Problem with Time Windows

The Vehicle Routing Problem (VRP) and its multiple variants are NP-hard multi-constrained combinatorial optimization problems that consists in providing goods from a supply point to several geographically dispersed demand points by satisfying a usually large number of constraints. The Vehicle Routing Problem with Time Windows (VRPTW) [9] involves the routing of a set of vehicles with identical capacity stationed at a central depot (logistic center) which operate within a certain time windows and are used to visit and fully supply the demands of set of customers. Routes are designed to start and end at the depot and the total demand met by any route cannot exceed the vehicle capacity. The customers, whose demands can only be supplied once by exactly one vehicle within a certain time window, are placed in diverse geographical locations and have pre-established requirements of goods and service time. The aim is to minimize the total distance travelled by all the vehicles while satisfying the imposed constraints. Some exact methods have been proposed for routing problems, including Lagrange relaxation-based methods, column generation, and dynamic programming [9]. Moreover, meta-heuristics have shown a good performance when solving VRPs [4].

The VRPTW can be modeled as a graph theoretical problem [9]. Let $G = (V, E)$ be a non-directed complete graph, where the vertices $V = \{1, ..., N\}$ correspond to the depot and the customers, and the edges $e \in E\{(i, j) : i, j \in V\}$ to the links between them.

Decision variable

$$X_{ij}^k = \begin{cases} 1 \text{ if vehicle } k \text{ travels from node } i \text{ to node } j \\ 0 \text{ otherwise} \end{cases}$$

Parameters

a_j is the earliest time for customer j to allow the service,
b_j is the latest time for customer j to allow the service,
C_{ij} is the cost for travelling from node i to node j (here, C_{ij} is considered as the distance or time required for travelling from node i to node j),

d_j is the demand at customer j,
K is the maximum number of vehicles that can be used,
N is the number of customers plus the depot (the depot is noted with number 1, and the customers are noted as $2,...N$),
Q^k is the loading capacity of vehicle k.

The objective function is to *minimize*: $TD = \sum\limits_{k=1}^{K} \sum\limits_{i=1}^{N} \sum\limits_{j=1}^{N} X_{ij}^k C_{ij}$ (1)

subject to:

$$X_{ii}^k = 0 \qquad\qquad (\forall i \in \{1, ..., N\}, \ \forall k \in \{1, ..., K\}) \qquad (2)$$

$$X_{ij}^k \in \{0,1\} \qquad\qquad (\forall i,j \in \{1, ..., N\}, \forall k \in \{1, ..., K\}) \qquad (3)$$

$$\sum_{k=1}^{K} \sum_{i=1}^{N} X_{ij}^k = 1 \qquad\qquad (\forall j \in \{2, .., N\}) \qquad (4)$$

$$\sum_{i=1}^{N} \sum_{j=2}^{N} X_{ij}^k d_j \le Q^k \qquad\qquad (\forall k \in \{1, .., K\}) \qquad (5)$$

$$\sum_{k=1}^{K} \sum_{j=2}^{N} X_{1j}^k \le K \qquad\qquad (6)$$

$$\sum_{j=2}^{N} X_{1j}^k - \sum_{j=2}^{N} X_{j1}^k = 0 \qquad\qquad (\forall k \in \{1, ..., K\}) \qquad (7)$$

$$a_j \le s_{kj} \le b_j \qquad\qquad (\forall i,j \in \{1, .., N\}, \forall k \in \{1, ..., K\}) \qquad (8)$$

$$s_{ki} + C_{ij} - L(1 - X_{ij}^k) \le s_{kj} \quad (\forall i,j \in \{1, ..., N\}, \forall k \in \{1, ..., K\}) \qquad (9)$$

Equation (1) is the objective function of the problem. Equation (2) denotes that a vehicle must travel from one node to a different one. Equation (3) indicates that X_{ij}^k is equal to 1 if vehicle k goes from node i to node j, and it is equal to 0 otherwise, i.e. a route between two customers can or cannot be covered by a vehicle. Equation (4) states that a customer is visited once by exactly one vehicle. By specifying the constraint of Equation (5), it is taken into account that for a given vehicle k, the load that has to be transported to complete the routes assigned to such vehicle cannot exceed its capacity Q^k (it is considered that all vehicles have the same capacity, $Q^k = Q$). Equation (6) specifies that there are up to K routes going out of the delivery depot. Equation (7) guarantees that the vehicles depart from and return to the depot. Let s_{kj} be the sum of the distances travelled by vehicle k before arriving at customer j. Equation (8) ensures that time windows are observed. Given a large scalar, L, the inequality represented in Equation (9) specifies that, if vehicle k is travelling from customer i to customer

j, the vehicle cannot arrive at customer j before $s_{ki} + C_{ij}$. As specified by [9], variable s_{kj} corresponds to the time vehicle k starts to service customer j. If vehicle k does not service j, s_{kj} is not calculated. Figure 1 provides an example of how the s_{kj} values are obtained.

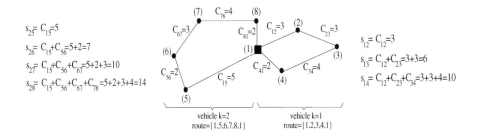

Fig. 1. Determining s_{ki} from a sample solution

3 Algorithms

3.1 The Multi-Temperature Simulated Annealing (MT-SA)

The Multi-Temperature Simulated Annealing (MT-SA) [1] is population-based algorithm that uses mutation operators to vary the individuals of the population, and Simulated Annealing [12] as selection criterion for each individual of the population. Results obtained by MT-SA in single- and multi-objective contexts [1,2] show its good performance when solving vehicle routing problems.

MT-SA manages the population of solutions P using an integer representation. P consists of p individuals (solutions), $P=\{I_1, I_2, \ldots, I_p\}$, where each individual represents the routes travelled by K vehicles to deliver all the customers. Thus, each individual, I_i, is represented by a set of chromosomes, C_{ik}, which consists of a variable number of genes, $C_{ik} = \{1, G_{ik}^1, G_{ik}^2, ..., G_{ik}^l, 1\}$ representing the route of the k-th vehicle in the i-th individual ($2 \leq G_{ik}^j \leq N$). For example, chromosome $C_{3,4} = \{1, 17, 7, 35, 1\}$ indicates that the fourth vehicle of the third individual departs from the depot and visits customers 17, 7, and 35, before returning to the depot, which is represented by identifier 1. The first and last genes are necessary to verify the constraint described in Equation 7.

The initial routes are built by assigning customers to vehicles until all the former are visited by the latter, such that the constraints are fulfilled.

The individuals are optimized by applying ten variation operators often used in this context [9,19]. Some of them are based on choosing one customer and reallocating it in a different visiting order of the same vehicle (the so called Customer random reallocation operator, and the Customer best reallocation operator), other operators modify the vehicle assigned to the customers (Customer random migration, Customer best migration, Customer random exchange, Customer best exchange, Customer exchange with similar time-window), while other operators divide (Route partition), create (New route), or remove (Route elimination) a given route. When applying variation operators, MT-SA accepts or rejects offspring individuals according to the Metropolis criterion [15] often used by Simulated Annealing (SA) [12]. SA optimizes a solution by exposing it to a high initial temperature, Ti, cooling it by means of a cooling rate, $T_{cooling}$, until the temperature falls below a given threshold, T_{stop}. Therefore, better neighbouring solutions are always accepted, whereas worse solutions are accepted with a certain probability, which is dependent on the current temperature, t (when t diminishes, the probability of accepting worse solutions decreases). Our approach considers an interval of initial temperatures $[Ti_{min}, Ti_{max}]$, so that the initial temperature of individual I_1 is Ti_{min}, while individual I_p starts in Ti_{max}, and the others are equally distributed along this interval.

3.2   Parallelization of MT-SA

Since VRPs are very hard problems, there is an increasing interest on the design of faster methods for solving VRPs incorporating parallel processing techniques [4]. Several parallel algorithms have been implemented for solving VRPs [13], including some approaches that have applied parallel simulated annealing using clustered SMP architectures by using OpenMP and MPI [8]. The goal of the parallel implementations presented here is to obtain solutions of a higher quality than the sequential algorithms and also to obtain higher quality solutions than the sequential versions without increasing the runtime required by the latter. With the aim of implementing parallel algorithms that present the same characteristics of the sequential code (a parallel simulation of the sequential code), both the master-worker and the island implementations have been implemented using synchronous communications, i.e. asynchronous message passing (MPI) and the nowait clause (OpenMP) have not been considered. Both paradigms have been adapted to our problem in the following way:

- Master-worker paradigm with OpenMP: the master thread initializes the population of solutions (each one containing a valid set of routes to visit all the customers satisfying the constraints), and, in each iteration, the master thread distributes the p individuals of population P into the number of threads executed (NTH), including itself, so that each thread is in charge of optimizing p/NTH individuals according to the variation operators and the Metropolis function. Once the worker threads have computed their assigned solutions, they return them to the master thread, which computes which is the global best solution, replaces a given percentage of individuals with that solution, and distributes again the work among all the available threads. The master thread is also responsible of controlling the termination condition.
- Island paradigm with MPI: each process initializes and optimizes p/NP individuals autonomously, where NP is the number of processes (islands). Periodically, the best solution of each island is sent to a central process which, temporally, is responsible of determining the global best solution and distributing it between the remaining islands. These islands are responsible for

copying the received solution in a given percentage of solutions of the population, after which they continue the search process. When the termination condition is fulfilled, all the islands send the solutions to the central process, which returns the global best solution.

- Hybrid MPI/OpenMP parallel implementation: the hybrid implementation is based on extending the Island paradigm implemented with MPI, such that the solutions of each island are improved using a parallel scheme based on the master-worker implemented with OpenMP, while MPI is used to establish the communications between the islands by means of message passing.

4   Empirical Analysis

The parallel computer used in our empirical study is a workstation with a single Intel Core 2 Quad Processor Q6600 (4 cores, 2.40 GHz, 1066 MHz front-side bus, 8MB Cache, 4 GB RAM). The sequential algorithm, coded in C++, has been parallelized using MPI (MPICH2 version 1.2.1p1), and OpenMP (version 3.1).

4.1   Test Problems and Parameter Settings

The performance evaluation of the implemented algorithms is analyzed using some of the Gehring & Homberger test problems [10]. In particular, a subset of benchmarks included in the sets of 200, 400, and 600 customers have been considered, as it is displayed in the first column of the tables.

In reference to the parameter settings, the sequential algorithm uses a population of 160 individuals ($|P|=p=160$). The individuals of the population are initialized using the three heuristics described above. The probability of applying a mutation operator is 25%. If mutation is applied, each of the ten mutation variants is applied with a probability that oscillates between 5% and 15% (all them sum 100%). As was previously commented, each individual has its own particular annealing scheduling, so that an initial interval of temperatures $Ti=[1,100]$ and a slow cooling rate ($T_{cooling}=0.995$) is considered, while the minimum temperature is $T_{stop}=0.001$. If the termination condition is not fulfilled and the current temperature falls below T_{stop}, the temperature is reinitialized ($t=Ti$) and the search process continues. When processes or threads communicate to share their best found solutions, the best one is copied in the 25% of the solutions of the population (master-worker paradigm) or each island (island paradigm). According to our experiments, this percentage (25%) is an accurate trade-off between the search process independence derived from the island model and the elitism of the meta-heuristic, while a higher percentage becomes disruptive.

With the aim of analyzing the advantages provided by the multi-core processor, the parallel implementations using the master-worker model with OpenMP, the island paradigm with MPI, and the hybrid MPI/OpenMP implementations are compared in a single processor using several versions having different number of processes and threads. When comparing different algorithms or implementations, it is possible to determine that one technique is better than another one if it obtains a better performance at a given amount of computational cost. For computational optimization practitioners, this cost is typically measured considering a maximum number of fitness evaluations for all the methods, but this criterion assumes that the cost of other operations is either the same or almost the same in both algorithms. However, the VRPTW requires not only the evaluation of the fitness of the solutions and the constraints satisfaction, but also the performance of other expensive operations such as updating the temperature, accepting or rejecting solutions according to the Metropolis criterion, etc. Moreover, it is unknown whether the island paradigm using MPI would expend more clock cycles to perform the message passing than the master-worker parallelization using OpenMP to manage the fork-and-join execution model or not. Thus, the runtime seems to be the best way to measure the computational cost and it has been recently used as termination criterion in the context of routing problems. A total of 15 independent runs with each of these configurations are executed, then analyzing the statistical results obtained.

4.2   Results and Discussion

Table 1 shows the results obtained by 15 independent executions per benchmark of the parallel implementations, when establishing a runtime of 60 seconds as termination criterion. This runtime can be considered an acceptable trade-off runtime in order to compare their performance in fast applications. Columns 2 to 10 in Table 1 provide the average deviation of the solutions obtained by each implementation with respect to the best average results obtained by any configuration (as it is being considered a minimization problem, lower deviation is better, and that implementation having the best mean results is denoted by 0.00%). Each column is marked by two numbers: NP/NTH, where NP indicates the number of processes, and NTH the number of threads. Therefore, column 1/1 denotes the sequential algorithm (MT-SA), columns having values of NP or NTH equal or higher than 2 denote executions of MPI or OpenMP (OMP), respectively, while hybrid MPI/OpenMP implementations correspond to those columns where both, the value of NP and NTH, are equal or higher than 2. The results displayed are the percentage of increment of the average fitness obtained by each configuration in comparison with the best average result. It is observed as, given a fixed number of processes (NP), the use of additional threads increases the quality of the results, but not when the product NP*NTH>4, i.e. a performance degradation is observed in the presence of oversubscription [11]. Similarly, a fixed number of threads (NTH), the use of additional processes increases the quality of the results, but not when the product NP*NTH>4. On overall, the results are obtained by the configuration that uses NP=4 processes and NTH=1 thread, i.e. the parallel implementation that considers the island model with MPI using a number of processes (islands) equal to the number of physical cores available, are slightly better than those obtained by the other parallel versions, while hybrid MPI/OpenMP implementations also obtain good solutions. It can be seen that, when using two processes, the hybrid MPI/OpenMP implementations (columns 7 and 8 of Table 1) outperform to the results obtained by the implementation that only uses MPI (column 6). However, it is seen that the best results are obtained by the configuration NP=4/NTH=1, i.e. a pure MPI implementation. The reason arises from the fact that the population size of each island when using NP=4 is smaller (40 individuals per island) than in case of using NP=1 (160 individuals) or NP=2 (80 individuals). This involves that former configuration is able to perform more iterations within the same runtime (higher intensification), which leads to the rapid convergence of the parallel algorithm.

Table 1. Comparing MT-SA and pMT-SA using different number of processes/islands and threads (15 executions per parallel version and benchmark)

version	Serial	OMP	OMP	OMP	MPI	Hybrid	Hybrid	MPI	Hybrid	(ANOVA)
NP/NTH	1/1	1/2	1/4	1/8	2/1	2/2	2/4	4/1	4/2	p-critical
R1_2_3	22.86	15.86	12.36	13.31	8.73	2.81	3.60	**0.00**	1.45	9.5E-62
R1_2_8	24.34	15.60	13.42	14.07	10.21	3.84	4.28	**0.00**	1.49	1.2E-61
R2_2_3	21.98	14.27	12.20	12.73	9.10	4.75	5.73	**0.00**	1.76	5.3E-55
R2_2_8	27.00	17.99	13.77	12.83	11.42	4.20	4.82	0.36	**0.00**	3.9E-59
C1_2_3	26.67	18.62	14.08	15.39	10.51	4.33	6.22	**0.00**	1.49	4.0E-56
C1_2_8	22.00	15.32	11.32	12.36	8.93	3.91	4.10	0.38	**0.00**	1.9E-48
C2_2_3	31.16	24.58	17.45	20.49	16.95	10.78	10.12	**0.00**	5.92	3.5E-55
C2_2_8	7.87	6.31	6.08	5.86	5.12	4.17	3.15	**0.00**	0.87	4.0E-21
R1_4_3	10.06	7.02	5.30	5.41	7.24	3.58	4.08	**0.00**	2.81	4.4E-41
R1_4_8	7.51	4.33	2.59	2.52	2.94	1.47	1.26	**0.00**	0.13	9.0E-49
R2_4_3	8.03	5.90	3.80	3.78	3.30	1.83	1.24	**0.00**	0.54	2.9E-26
R2_4_8	8.32	6.02	3.39	3.94	2.31	1.60	0.12	0.38	**0.00**	5.9E-33
C1_4_3	5.77	3.73	2.17	1.41	3.33	1.44	1.45	**0.00**	0.54	1.9E-48
C1_4_8	3.35	2.14	1.09	1.14	2.60	1.02	1.26	**0.00**	0.40	1.9E-48
C2_4_3	8.26	5.80	3.75	3.30	4.59	2.34	2.24	**0.00**	1.41	4.9E-35
C2_4_8	3.14	1.62	0.54	0.19	2.27	1.81	1.18	**0.00**	0.18	2.9E-14
R1_6_3	2.49	1.72	0.81	0.78	1.52	0.39	0.43	0.13	**0.00**	4.1E-26
R1_6_8	2.79	2.02	1.17	1.04	1.76	1.01	0.93	0.14	**0.00**	4.1E-26
R2_6_3	4.64	3.04	2.31	1.46	1.70	1.31	1.49	**0.00**	0.24	2.1E-07
R2_6_8	5.58	3.22	2.59	1.53	3.33	1.27	1.99	**0.00**	1.08	2.9E-22
C1_6_3	2.58	1.80	1.24	1.33	1.94	0.66	0.81	0.18	**0.00**	3.4E-28
C1_6_8	1.13	0.80	0.71	0.67	0.41	0.16	0.22	**0.00**	0.20	5.9E-22
C2_6_3	4.27	2.55	1.67	1.66	2.53	1.01	0.58	0.12	**0.00**	4.4E-34
C2_6_8	1.17	0.75	0.92	0.61	0.72	0.34	0.25	**0.00**	0.34	9.9E-06
Average	12.33	8.48	6.31	6.46	5.79	2.81	2.88	**0.08**	0.98	

Whenever several experiments are performed it is important to determine whether or not the variation in the results is significant, i.e. the observed spread of mean values that would not normally arise from the chance variation within groups. With the aim of determining if there is a significant difference between these groups of results obtained in the experiments, which are shown in the first columns, an one-way ANOVA test is applied. Given the typical confidence level

Table 2. Runtime (seconds) required by pMT-SA to obtain a solution of similar quality than that obtained by the serial MT-SA with a runtime of 60 seconds

	1/4 (OMP)		2/2 (Hybrid)		4/1 (MPI)	
	mean	avg. dev.	mean	avg. dev.	mean	avg. dev.
R1_2_3	30.91	3.99	25.17	1.87	30.22	4.36
R1_2_8	34.54	3.29	29.49	3.80	40.34	4.95
R2_2_3	31.34	4.10	24.61	4.00	31.62	7.29
R2_2_8	34.06	2.90	29.07	4.40	36.03	4.62
C1_2_3	29.97	4.75	29.15	3.05	38.27	5.29
C1_2_8	35.61	5.94	30.11	4.13	42.88	9.54
C2_2_3	35.17	4.58	31.56	2.78	40.20	5.65
C2_2_8	38.57	8.39	40.10	8.53	45.58	7.26
R1_4_3	34.30	4.54	42.34	7.79	46.48	5.85
R1_4_8	29.52	3.49	38.52	8.09	40.67	6.33
R2_4_3	33.96	6.83	40.65	7.30	44.00	9.10
R2_4_8	41.73	5.59	49.08	3.93	47.94	3.19
C1_4_3	32.75	4.11	47.83	4.14	42.75	8.08
C1_4_8	34.96	7.02	47.26	4.84	43.81	6.32
C2_4_3	37.30	3.45	45.64	5.95	36.25	4.39
C2_4_8	42.87	7.10	47.39	3.13	45.49	9.34
R1_6_3	29.89	8.57	39.87	4.32	33.38	4.92
R1_6_8	39.31	7.61	45.54	5.84	40.18	7.36
R2_6_3	39.60	8.67	44.72	4.41	44.23	6.15
R2_6_8	31.72	6.18	39.73	5.74	45.25	4.86
C1_6_3	30.32	5.45	38.23	5.01	43.35	4.46
C1_6_8	24.74	9.20	33.69	8.08	30.06	7.84
C2_6_3	28.41	4.80	31.68	6.01	29.79	7.59
C2_6_8	39.10	9.51	32.28	8.06	40.98	8.10

of 95%, the null hypothesis is rejected if the probability value (p-value) is smaller than or equal to the critical value (p-critical=0.05)). The last column of Table 1 show that p-value$\leq$0.05, the null hypothesis is rejected in all cases, i.e. there is a significant variation between the results of the different groups.

Taking into account the previous results, it is now analyzed how the parallel implementations are able to reduce the runtime required to obtain a solution of equal or better quality than the median result obtained by MT-SA after executing 15 independent runs during 60 seconds. Three configurations are analyzed: an OpenMP implementation ({NP=1,NTH=4}), a MPI implementation {NP=4, NTH=1}, and a hybrid OpenMP/MPI implementation {NP=2,NTH=2}. Table 2 shows the mean, and average deviation of the 15 independent runs carried out by these configurations of pMT-SA. These results show that the parallel implementations in all cases need less than 60 seconds to reach a solution of at least the same quality than that obtained by the serial algorithm, i.e. the parallel algorithms obtain an improvement in terms of speedup. At first sight, yielding speedups of 2 could be considered poor in terms of scalability, but it should be considered that MT-SA is a stochastic approach, which is why it is possible that some threads do not perform a given instruction (e.g.: if the conditional expression of a while structure results as false when computed on its own data), and therefore this stream processor is simply put into idle mode during the remaining loops performed by the others. This phenomenon, known as thread divergence [16], often causes serious performance degradation.

5   Conclusions

The generalization of multi-core processors allows us to take advantage of parallel processing even on desktop and laptop computers. The design of efficient methods for solving vehicle routing problems has become an area of research that has attracted much attention due to its influence in transportation, logistics, and supply chain management. Since this problem is NP-hard, most algorithms presented to solve this problem are based on heuristic and meta-heuristic approaches. Nevertheless, whenever the number of customers is very large, it is necessary to apply techniques, such as parallel processing, to improve the efficiency of these heuristics. This paper analyzes the advantages provided by multi-core processors to obtain good quality solutions to the vehicle routing problem with time windows. With this aim, a population-based meta-heuristic based on Simulated Annealing has been parallelized using MPI, OpenMP, and hybrid MPI/OpenMP schemes. Results obtained in a workstation with a multi-core processor show that these parallel implementations outperform the performance of the sequential algorithm. Moreover, it is observed that the use of additional processes and threads often increase the quality of the solutions, but always considering the existence of oversubscription when the number of processes or islands (managed by MPI) multiplied by the number of threads (managed by OpenMP) is higher than the number of available processing cores. As future work, it is planned to analyze the behavior of the parallel algorithms in a cluster, and also to apply them to solve multi-objective formulations of this problem.

Acknowledgments. This work has been partially supported by the Spanish Ministry of Economy and Competitiveness and FEDER funds under project TIN2012-32039. R.Baños also acknowledges the support of a Juan de la Cierva postdoctoral fellowship.

References

1. Baños, R., Ortega, J., Gil, C., Fernández, A., de Toro, F.: A multi-start hybrid algorithm for vehicle routing problems with time windows. In: World Online Conference on Soft Computing in Industrial Applications (2011)
2. Baños, R., Ortega, J., Gil, C., Fernández, A., de Toro, F.: A simulated annealing-based parallel multi-objective approach to vehicle routing problems with time windows. Expert Systems with Applications **40**(5), 1696–1707 (2013)
3. Blake, G., Dreslinski, R.G., Mudge, T.: A survey of multicore processors. IEEE Signal Processing Magazine **26**(6), 26–37 (2009)

4. Bräysy, O., Gendreau, M.: Vehicle routing problem with time windows, part II: Metaheuristics. Transportation Science **39**(1), 119–139 (2005)
5. Chapman, B., Jost van der Pas, R., Kuck (foreword), D.J.: Using OpenMP: Portable shared memory parallel programming. The MIT Press (2007)
6. Chorley, M.J., Walker, D.W.: Performance analysis of a hybrid MPI/OpenMP application on multi-core clusters. Journal of Computational Science **1**(3), 168–174 (2010)
7. Coello, C.A., Lamont, G.B., Van Veldhuizen, D.A.: Evolutionary algorithms for solving multi-objective problems. Genetic and Evolutionary Computation Series. Springer (2007)
8. Czech, Zbigniew J., Mikanik, Wojciech, Skinderowicz, Rafał: Implementing a parallel simulated annealing algorithm. In: Wyrzykowski, Roman, Dongarra, Jack, Karczewski, Konrad, Wasniewski, Jerzy (eds.) PPAM 2009, Part I. LNCS, vol. 6067, pp. 146–155. Springer, Heidelberg (2009)
9. El-Sherbeny, N.A.: Vehicle routing with time windows: An overview of exact, heuristic and metaheuristic methods. Journal of King Saud University (Science) **22**(3), 123–131 (2010)
10. Gehring, H., Homberger, J.: A parallel two-phase metaheuristic for routing problems with time windows. Asia-Pacific Journal of Operations Research **18**(1), 35–47 (2001). http://www.sintef.no/Projectweb/TOP/VRPTW/Homberger-benchmark/
11. Iancu, C., Hofmeyr, S., Zheng, Y., Blagojevi, F.: Oversubscription on multicore processors. In: IEEE International Parallel and Distributed Processing Symposium, pp. 1–11 (2010)
12. Kirkpatrick, S., Gelatt, C.D., Vecchi, M.P.: Optimization by simulated annealing. Science **220**(4598), 671–680 (1983)
13. Le Bouthillier, A., Crainic, T.G.: A cooperative parallel meta-heuristic for the vehicle routing problem with time windows. Computers & Operations Research **32**(7), 1685–1708 (2005)
14. Márquez, A.L., Gil, C., Baños, R., Gómez, J.: Parallelism on multicore processors using Parallel.FX. Advances in Engineering Software **42**(6), 259–265 (2011)
15. Metropolis, N., Rosenbluth, A.W., Rosenbluth, M.N., Teller, A., Teller, E.: Equation of state calculations by fast computing machines. The Journal of Chemical Physics **21**(6), 1087–1092 (1953)
16. Robilliard, D., Marion, V., Fonlupt, C.: High performance genetic programming on GPU. In: Proceedings of the 2009 Workshop on Bio-inspired Algorithms for Distributed Systems, pp. 85–94 (2000)
17. Santander-Jimenez, S., Vega-Rodriguez, M.A., Gómez-Pulido, J.A., Sánchez-Pérez, J.M.: Evaluating the performance of a parallel multiobjective Artificial Bee Colony Algorithm for inferring phylogenies on multicore architectures. In: Proceedings of the 2012 IEEE 10th International Symposium on Parallel and Distributed Processing with Applications, pp. 713–720 (2012)
18. Snir, M., Otto, S., Huss-Lederman, S., Walter, D., Dongarra, J.: MPI: The complete reference. MIT Press, Boston (1996)
19. Tan, K.C., Chew, Y.H., Lee, L.H.: A hybrid multiobjective evolutionary algorithm for solving vehicle routing problem with time windows. Computational Optimization and Applications **34**(1), 115–151 (2006)

Dynamic and Partially Connected Ring Topologies for Evolutionary Algorithms with Structured Populations

Carlos M. Fernandes[1,2(✉)], Juan L.J. Laredo[3], Juan Julián Merelo[2], Carlos Cotta[4], and Agostinho C. Rosa[1]

[1] LaSEEB-ISR-IST, University of Lisbon, Lisbon, Portugal
{cfernandes,acrosa}@laseeb.org
[2] Department of Architecture and Computer Technology,
University of Granada, Granada, Spain
jjmerelo@gmail.com
[3] Faculty of Sciences, Technology and Communications,
University of Luxembourg, Luxembourg City, Luxembourg
juan.jimenez@uni.lu
[4] Departamento de Lenguages y Ciencias de la Computación,
University of Malaga, Malaga, Spain
ccottap@lcc.uma.es

Abstract. This paper investigates dynamic and partially connected ring topologies for cellular Evolutionary Algorithms (cEA). We hypothesize that these structures maintain population diversity at a higher level and reduce the risk of premature convergence to local optima on deceptive, multimodal and NP-hard fitness landscapes. A general framework for modelling partially connected topologies is proposed and three different schemes are tested. The results show that the structures improve the rate of convergence to global optima when compared to cEAs with standard topologies (ring, rectangular and square) on quasi-deceptive, deceptive and NP-hard problems. Optimal population size tests demonstrate that the proposed topologies require smaller populations when compared to traditional cEAs.

1 Introduction

In standard Evolutionary Algorithms (EAs), all individuals are potential partners, i.e., there are no mating restrictions in the population preventing the pair-wise recombination of individuals. In genetics, this behavior is called *panmixia*, and the respective populations are called *panmictic*. For that reason, standard EAs without mating restrictions are also called *panmictic* EAs.

In panmictic EAs, genotypic representation, operators, selection schemes and population size are typical working mechanisms that require design choices. However, a population structure may be also introduced in the design scheme of EAs. The structure then specifies a network of acquaintances over which individuals can interact: mating or selection is restricted to neighborhoods within the network. The non-panmictic EAs that use this scheme are known as *spatially structured* EAs [12]. Spatially structured EAs include fine-grained approaches such as cellular EAs (cEAs) 1

© Springer-Verlag Berlin Heidelberg 2014
A.I. Esparcia-Alcázar et al. (Eds.): EvoApplications 2014, LNCS 8602, pp. 665–677, 2014.
DOI: 10.1007/978-3-662-45523-4_54

and coarse-grained approaches such as island models [3]. In cEAs, the population is distributed in a grid and the interaction is restricted to the the individuals' neighborhood. In island EAs, different subpopulations evolve isolated from each other and occasionally exchange individuals using a predefined strategy which specifies the rate and quantity of information to transfer.

The main disadvantage of island and cellular EAs is that their base-structures require extra designing and tuning effort. In addition, the chosen structure affects the connectivity and the performance of the algorithm. In the case of island models, this added complexity translates in deciding policies for the migration frequency, selection and replacement of migrants and the topology itself. As for traditional cEAs, they use static structures that impose a rigid connectivity between the individuals. The investigation in this paper is an attempt to design a simple dynamic topology for cEAs, with a varying neighborhood degree and an intrinsic clustering behavior that approaches the cEA to an island model. In fact, the resulting structure may be considered a hybridization between a cellular and an island-based EA. This study is restricted to 1-dimensional structures, also known as *ring topologies*. The case of 2-dimensional population structures is left for a future investigation.

In the proposed partially connected ring topology the individuals are distributed in a 1-dimensional grid with size $1 \times Y$, where $1 \times Y > n$ and n is the population size. Therefore, there are $Y - n$ empty nodes or gaps in the network. Every time-step, each individual tries to recombine with one of its left or right neighbors (decided by tournament). If the individual has only one neighbor, it recombines with that neighbor. If there are no neighbors, there is no crossover and only mutation is applied. The structure is dynamic: in each time-step, every solution is allowed to move to neighboring nodes (if there are empty nodes in the individual's neighborhood).

With this scheme different niches may appear and disappear at run-time as the flow of information is interrupted by gaps. However, these gaps change during the run: the resulting cEA has certain resemblance with an island model, with dynamic clusters (or sub-populations) of individuals with varying size. We hypothesize that with this scheme the population diversity decreases at a lower rate (when compared to a standard ring topology), the optimal populations for a high rate of convergence are smaller, and the performance of the cEA on deceptive and hard problems is improved. The results of the experiments confirm the assumptions.

The remaining of the paper is structured as follows: Section 2 gives a background review on cEAs and on the effects of the topology on the diversity; Section 3 describes the proposed partially connected topologies; Section 4 describes the experiments and the results; Section 5 concludes the paper and outlines future lines of work.

2   Background Review

The initial objective of spatially structured EAs was to develop a framework for studying massive parallelization. However, the need to provide traditional EAs with a proper balance between exploration and exploitation motivated several lines of research that explore the potentiality of different population structures in maintaining genetic diversity 11. The primary focus of the field has been on static regular lattices: every individual has a fixed number of potential interaction partners. Additionally, complex population structures have been studied (see 8 and 12), many of them using recent developments in network theory.

In standard cEAs, the most typical population structure is a toroidal 2-dimensional grid with size $X \times Y$. The grid may be square or rectangular. The neighborhood of an individual is then defined according to a radius centered in the individual location. In this paper, we restrict the study to von Neumann neighborhood with radius 1, i.e., the neighborhood of each individual consists of the individual itself and the individuals at adjacent North, East, South and West nodes. When the size of the grid is set to $1 \times Y$ (ring), the neighborhood consists of the individual and its left and right neighbors.

Standard cEAs have some drawbacks: synchronicity (in most cases) and a strong dependence on the problem, since the genetic diversity promoted by a prefixed topology is uncorrelated to the problem structure. In addition, the rigid connectivity of static structures may negatively affect the convergence abilities of the algorithms on some kind of problems, in which genetic diversity is crucial for escaping local optima.

For that reason, dynamic population structures have recently raised the interest of cEAs researchers. To the extent of our knowledge, only three works address explicitly the issue of dynamic population structures in cellular EAs. In 1, Alba and Dorronsoro dynamically change the ratio that defines the neighborhood of interaction. Since the ratio may affect selection pressure, the authors analyze the influence of its value on the balance between exploration and exploitation. However, the base-structure of the cellular EA is maintained throughout the run. In 12, Whitacre et al. focus on two important conditions missing in EA populations: a self-organized definition of locality and interaction epistasis. With that purpose in mind, they propose a dynamic structure and conclude that the two features, when combined, provide behaviors not present in the traditional spatially structured EAs. The most noticeable change is an unprecedented capacity for sustainable coexistence of genetically distinct individuals within a single population. The authors state that the capacity for sustained genetic diversity is not imposed on the population; instead, it emerges as a natural consequence of the dynamics of the system. Laredo et al. 7 proposed a framework for EAs based on peer-to-peer networks 10. Within a simulated network, they model the dynamics of real networks and conclude that their system is able to achieve better performance than traditional EAs on a wide range of problems, while being scalable and resilient to the volatility of nodes in the network.

In this paper we try a different approach. The radius of the neighborhood is fixed, and the typical grid structure is maintained. However, the size of the grid, which is usually set to $X \times Y = n$, is increased so that $X \times Y > n$ and some cells remain unoccupied. With empty cells in the grid, the individuals are then allowed to move to adjacent cells, according to a specific movement rule. Three different movement strategies are tested. The proposed scheme has been inspired by the work on a self-organized population of simple particles described in 2. Recently, a similar structure has been used for defining the interaction network of the Particle Swarm algorithm 6 with promising results 3. The following section describes the original system and its application to the particular case of the cEA.

3   Partially Connected Ring Topologies

As stated above, traditionally, cEAs are structured on 2-dimensional toroidal grids with size $X \times Y$, and the population size n is set to $n = X \times Y$. The main idea of this paper is to use populations structured in grids such that $n < X \times Y$. For that purpose, the dynamic complex system proposed by Fernandes et al. in 2 has been adapted for structuring populations.

---

1. Randomly place n particles in a grid of node with size $X \times Y$
2. Randomly attribute a fitness value to each particle
3. For each particle do
    4. check neighborhood for marks and other particles
    5. if no marks in the neighborhood
        6.   move to a free node in the neighborhood (if any)
    7. if there are marks in the neighborhood
        8.   move to the site of the nearest mark
        9.   leave a mark in the previous site
        10. erase the mark in the new site
11. if stop criteria not met return to 3

Fig. 1. Pseudo-code of the original complex system 2

The algorithm in 2 is a discrete complex adaptive system described by a set of local rules. These rules define the actions of a population of n simple particles that move on a 2-dimensional toroidal grid of nodes with size $X \times Y$. In each time-step, every particle tries to move to an adjacent node. The rules that control the particles' movements and the detailed description of the system are given below (please see also the pseudo-code in Figure 1).

At $t = 0$, the particles are assigned a random *fitness* value in the range $[0,1]$ and randomly distributed in a $X \times Y$ grid of nodes. Then, at each time-step, each particle moves to an adjacent free node (if any), leaving a mark with information on its current status in the previous node.

The particles decide where to go by inspecting their neighborhood. If there are no free nodes in the neighborhood (i.e., all the cells are occupied by particles), the particle stays in that same node until the next iteration. If it finds free nodes, the particle checks for marks. If it finds no marks, it just randomly chooses a destination node between the free neighboring nodes. If marks are found, the particle moves to the node with the most similar mark. Whenever a particle changes its position, it leaves a mark in its previous location. Furthermore, the marks only remain in the *habitat* for one iteration. Communicating, by depositing and following information, is the base-rule of the system.

This simple set of rules leads to a dynamic global behavior that displays signs of self-organization. A structure of particles, formed by clusters and paths, emerges on the habitat. However, these clusters are far from being static and, in a few generations, the distribution of the whole population may change dramatically (while maintaining a typical configuration of clusters and paths). The population's behavior is not ordered (nor chaotic).

The translation of this system to a population structure for cEAs can be straight-forwardly done. For instance, the particles can be the individuals of the algorithm and the marks can be the fitness of the individuals. Moreover, other rules may be easily implemented and tested. In order to investigate the potentiality of partially connected grid topologies, three different movement rules have been used.

1) Fitness-based movement rule (f): as in the original model, the marks are the fitness of the individuals.

2) Similarity-based movement rule (s): the marks are the genotype of the individual that visited the node in the previous iteration; when deciding the destination node, the individual computes the Hamming distance between its own genotype and the mark. Then, it moves to the node that minimizes the Hamming distance. (As in the original model, if there are no marks in the neighbourhood the individual chooses randomly an empty adjacent node).

3) Random movement rule (r): there are no marks and the individuals move to adjacent cells, select randomly amongst the empty ones.

Since the proposed population structure generates islands of individuals, we hypothesize that the genetic diversity of the population is maintained at a higher level (when compared to the standard ring topology). Therefore, exploration is increased and exploitation is performed at the local level by several subpopulations. Such characteristics could benefit the cEA when optimizing deceptive and multimodal hard problems. The results in the following section confirm these hypotheses.

1. For each individual $i \leftarrow 1$ to n:
    1.1. Initialize individual i
    1.2. Evaluate individual i: $f(\overrightarrow{x_i})$
2. Set grid size: $X \times Y$: $X \times Y > n$
3. Place the individuals randomly on the grid
4. For each individual $i \leftarrow 1$ to n:
    4.1. Compute neighborhood
    4.2. Parent 1 is individual i
    4.3. Parent 2 is the best of the neighbors
    4.3 Crossover (parent 1, parent 2)
    4.4. Select randomly one of the offspring: offspring i
    4.5. Mutation (offspring i)
    4.6. Evaluate offspring i: $f(\overrightarrow{x'_i})$
    4.6. Insert offspring i in temporary population P_t
5. For each individual $i \leftarrow 1$ to n:
    5.1. Replace individual i by offspring I if $f(\overrightarrow{x'_i}) > f(\overrightarrow{x_i})$ (maximization problems)
    5.1. Compute empty adjacent nodes.
    5.2. If at least one empty node, select destination node using movement rule.
6. If the stop criterion is not met, go to 4

Fig. 2. cEA on a partially connected grid

The proposed structure and the three update schemes can be applied to the general case of 2-dimensional grid with size $X \times Y$. However, in this paper we restrict the study to the 1-dimensional case and compare the proposed structure to standard ring topologies. The 1-dimensional base-model display interesting properties, which are described in [2]. The system shows a mixture of order and randomness which is typical, for instance, of class 4 cellular automata 5. Some clusters of particles move up or down, while free particles randomly move through the grid until they are "captured" by a cluster. Meanwhile, clusters disaggregate, freeing more "wandering" particles. The main goal and the motivation behind this work are to explore these emergent properties of the model, adding a self-organized dynamics to cEAs that may help them to escape more often from local optima traps.

The resulting cEA is described in Figure 2. Please note that the main differences to a standard cEA are that the grid size is larger than n and that when computing the neighborhood the algorithm may find two, one or zero potential partners, while in the standard ring topology an individual has always two potential partners for recombination. The following section tests the structures on a set of problems with deceptive landscapes and other characteristics that make them hard for standard EAs to solve.

4   Test Set and Results

In order to investigate their performance, the proposed partially connected ring topologies have been tested on trap functions with increasing degree of difficulty. The results were then compared to the standard square, rectangular and ring structures.

A trap function is a piecewise-linear function defined on *unitation* (the number of ones in a binary string) that has two distinct regions in the search space, one leading to the global optimum and the other leading to a local optimum. Depending on its parameters, trap functions may be deceptive or not. The trap functions in these experiments are defined by:

$$F(\vec{x}) = \begin{cases} k, & if\ u(\vec{x}) = k \\ k - 1 - u(\vec{x}), & otherwise \end{cases} \tag{1}$$

where $u(\vec{x})$ is the unitation function and k is the problem size (and also the fitness of the global optimum). With these definitions, order-3 traps are in the region between deceptive and non-deceptive, while order-2 are non-deceptive and order-4 are fully deceptive. Under these settings, it is possible to investigate not only how the algorithms scale on order-k trap functions but also to observe how that performance varies when moving from non-deceptive to deceptive search spaces. For that purpose, l-bit decomposable functions are constructed by juxtaposing m trap functions and summing the fitness of each sub-function to obtain the total fitness, obtaining the so-called $m-k$ trap problems. Then, by increasing m it is possible to investigate how an algorithm scales.

In the first experiments, order-2, -3 and -4 trap functions were constructed by juxtaposing, respectively, 250, 125 and 75 subproblems, generating 500- (2-trap), 375- (3-trap) and 300-bit (4-trap) problems.

All the cEAs used in the experiments are synchronous (i.e., the offspring are placed in a temporal population and replacement is done after every individual generates one child). Parameterization was done after [1]: population size was set to 400; the recombination operator is the double point crossover with $p_c = 1.0$; mutation is bit-flip with $p_m = 1/l$, where l is the chromosome length. Only one offspring is placed in the temporal population (randomly chosen from the set of two children). In the replacement stage, the offspring replaces its parent if it's better.

The stop criteria are: to find the global optimum or to achieve a maximum of 3,000,000 function evaluations. The number of iterations required to meet the best solution is recorded and averaged over 50 runs. A success measure (successful runs) is defined as the number of runs in which an algorithm attains the global optimum.

Please note that the tests are not intended to show that the proposed structure is better than the standard ring topologies in a wide range of problems. We are first interested in understanding the behaviour of the partially connected rings, in general, and their performance on quasi-deceptive and deceptive problems, in particular.

In the proposed topologies, the empty nodes are obstacles for the flow of information through the population, which means that the search is performed by several subpopulations, although highly dynamic. It is expected therefore that the increase in exploration slows down the convergence speed of the algorithms. However, we expect the payoff to be to an increasing robustness, with the partially connected topologies being able to find the global optimum more often.

The results of the experiments on trap functions are shown in Table 1. The first relevant result is that the standard ring topology (1×400) outperforms the other static structures, not only on deceptive and quasi-deceptive functions, but also on the non-deceptive 2-trap function, finding the global optimum in every run. In this function, the partially connected topologies — random (r), fitness-based (f) and similarity-based (s) — also find the optimum in every run. However, they converge more slowly, probably due to their own balance between exploration and exploitation, which favours exploration (when compared to the standard ring). In 3-trap and 4-trap functions the partially connected rings are also slower (in general, they require about 10% more evaluations to reach the optimum), but in this case they converge more often to the global optimum. As expected, the empty nodes in the ring slow down the convergence speed but increase the convergence probability.

In the previous tests, the grid size of the partially connected topologies was set to 1×500. It is expected that the size affects the speed and the convergence rate of the algorithm. A sparser structure increases exploration (at the expenses of convergence speed); with higher exploration the algorithm converges more often to the optimum.

Table 1 shows the performance of the partially connected rings with different ratios between population size and grid size. The population is set to 400 and the grid size is varied from 450 to 800. As in the previous experiments, the stop criteria are reaching the global optimum or 3,000,000 function evaluations. As expected, convergence speed decreases when the grid size is larger. But the number of successful runs also increases with the size of the structure. Increasing exploration slows down the search process but improves the success in reaching the optimum. By adjusting the size, it is possible to balance global and local search.

Table 1. Averaged function evaluations to a solution (AES), successful runs (SR) and averaged best fitness (FIT)

		20×20	10×40	1×400	$1 \times 500\ (r)$	$1 \times 500\ (f)$	$1 \times 500(s)$
2-trap $l = 500$	AES	1084612.8 ±380406.03	892547.4 ±513403.61	567944.0 ±40322.30	620104.0 ±42747.69	608922.4 ±44761.51	622936.0 ±56503.71
	SR	(47)	(38)	**(50)**	**(50)**	**(50)**	**(50)**
	FIT	0.08±0.34	0.24±0.43	**0.00±0.00**	**0.00±0.00**	**0.00±0.00**	**0.00±0.00**
3-trap $l = 375$	AES	-	161066.7 ±21289.96	697671.8 ±108269.7	752178.7 ±81058.45	752853.3 ±83956.6	738248.9 ±146850.3
	SR	(0)	(3)	(39)	(49)	**(50)**	(47)
	FIT	5.86±2,53	3.60±1.94	0.04±0.47	0.02±0.14	**0.00±0.00**	0.06±0.24
4-trap $l = 300$	AES	-	-	773238.7 ±93423.95	842491.0 ±121666.5	845810.5 ±91364.75	869936.8 ±126965.1
	SR	(0)	(0)	(31)	(35)	(38)	**(43)**
	FIT	6.56±2.09	5.06±2.10	0.42±0.57	0.38±0.66	0.30±0.57	**0.16±0.42**

Table 2. Order-4 trap functions. Varying the size of the grid. $n = 400$.

	r	f	s
1×450	**835837.8** **±146794.4** (37)	**774148.6** **±112251.3** (35)	**868514.3** **±214231.8** (35)
1×500	842491.0 ±121666.5 (35)	845810.5 ±139281.9 (38)	869936.8 ±154717.9 (38)
1×600	978195.1 ±108800.1 (41)	984120.0 ±183584.7 (40)	959930.0 ±110843.9 (40)
1×700	1122688.4 ±132330.9 (43)	1126234.2 ±147857.3 (41)	1160488.9 ±176815.8 (45)
1×800	1327351.1 ±118173.3 **(45)**	1343266.7 ±144683.4 **(42)**	1301502.2 ±127471.9 **(45)**

Finding the optimal population size for a given problem is a fundamental step when optimizing the performance of a given EA. In order to investigate the optimal population sizes for the different structures, we have used a selecto-recombinative version of the cEAs (i.e., without mutation) and the bisection method 9 (please note the bi-section method requires EAs without mutation).

The bisection method, described in Figure 3, is a simple but effective technique used to determine the optimal population size of selectorecombinative EAs. For this particular case the threshold T was set to 0.1 and initial population size was set to 50. Every configuration was run for 30 times before updating and the convergence

1. Start with small n
2. Double n until GA convergence criteria is met
3. (min,max)=($n/2,n$)
4. repeat until (max-min)/min < T
    n =(min+max)/2
    if n leads to convergence criteria
        then max = n
    else min = n
5. Compute the statistics for this problem size using population size = max

Fig. 3. The bisection method for determining the optimal population size of a GA

Table 3. Optimal population size and averaged evaluations to a solution

		ring	*p.c.ring* (*r*)	*p.c.ring* (*f*)	*p.c.ring* (*s*)
4-trap $l = 52$	n	200	175	175	175
	AES	29376.0 ±6235.7	30183.7 ±5422.3	**29207.2** **±6796.6**	29830.1 ±6973.7
4-trap $l = 100$	n	350	300	275	300
	AES	111271.4 ±15166.4	100383.2 ±12045.6	**93848.3** **±13075.7**	100306.6 ±11337.6
4-trap $l = 200$	n	600	500	500	500
	AES	401706.1 ±44220.1	**357428.4** **±29096.9**	369945.3 ±45849.2	367833.3 ±39049.3

criteria is met if 29 of those 30 runs converge towards the global optimum. The algorithms were tested with $p_c = 1.0$. Mutation probability was set to 0. After determining the optimal population size, the configuration with that n value was executed for 50 times and the number of evaluations necessary to reach the optimum was averaged over the successful runs. The results (optimal population size and averaged evaluations to a solution with that particular size) are given in Table 3.

The main conclusions are that, as expected, the partially connected topologies require smaller populations than the fully connected ring. In the case of the quasi-deceptive and deceptive functions, smaller populations lead to faster algorithms. Therefore, and according to the results in Tables 2 and 3, we conclude that the proposed topologies are more robust, although slower, when the population size is set to the same value, and faster when the population size is set to a size that assures a convergence rate close to 100%.

A final set of experiments aims at comparing the standard ring cEA with the random movement version of the proposed ring topology on a wider set of problems. For that purpose, MMDP and Trident problems have been added to the test set. Trident functions are *needle in the haystack* problems that exploit the ability of EAs to mix good but significantly different solutions. The fitness function of the Trident used in this work has two components, *base* and *contribution:* $F(\vec{x}) = \text{base}(\vec{x}) + \text{contribution}(\vec{x})$. The base depends on unitation and is described by:

$$base(\vec{x}) = \|2. u(\vec{x}) - 1\|$$ (4)

where l is the chromosome length. The contribution rewards certain configurations of strings that an equal number of 0's and 1's.

Table 4. MMDP. Contribution of each subproblem configuration to the fitness value.

$u(\vec{x})$	0	1	2	3	4	5	6
$F(\vec{x})$	1.000000	0.000000	0.360384	0.640576	0.360384	0.000000	1.000000

Let L be the first half of the binary string x of length l and R the second half. The *contribution* is described by Equation 5:

$$contribution(\vec{x}) = \begin{cases} 2.l, & R = \bar{R} \\ 0, & otherwise \end{cases}$$ (5)

where $\bar{R}$ is the bitwise negation of R. The Trident accepts strings of length $2k$, where $k \geq 2$. For this paper, 64-bit strings were used.

The MMDP is an NP-hard problem that has been designed to be difficult for EAs. Like the trap functions with order ≥ 3, MMDP is deceptive, but it is also multimodal. It consists of k 6-bits subproblems with two global optima and a deceptive attractor in the middle of the fitness landscape. Each subproblem fitness values depend on the unitiation function. Table 4 shows the contribution of each subproblem to the fitness value of a string. For the experiments, 240-bit strings were used.

Table 5. Selecto-recombinative standard ring topology cEA and partially connected ring cEA with random movement. Optimal population size, average evaluations to a solution and Kolmogorov-Smirnov statistical tests with 0.05 level of significance.

	2-trap ($l = 400$)	3-trap ($l = 300$)	4-trap ($l = 200$)	MMDP ($l = 240$)	Trident ($l = 64$)
$1 \times n$	$n = 500$ 455620.7 ±45848.64	$n = 600$ 524524.1 ±80506.1	$n = 550$ 372881.0 ±53921.9	$n = 750$ 520551.7 ±47646.71	$n = 350$ 91374.14 ±36194.35
$1 \times (1.5n)$	$n = 450$ **444171.8** **±32089.3** (+ ~)	$n = 500$ **427207.6** **±34671.3** (+ +)	$n = 475$ **350769.8** **±36278.0** (+ +)	$n = 600$ **466453.1** **±56597.55** (+ +)	$n = 300$ **78352.55** **±19654.27** (+ ~)

The first test determines the optimal population size of each algorithm for each problem using the bi-section method. The standard ring is compared to the partially connected version with random selection of destination nodes. The results are in Table 5. Statistical tests (Kolmogorov-Smirnov statistical tests with 0.05 level of significance) that compare the AES of each algorithm in each function are also given: (+~)

means that the partially connected ring is faster than the standard ring but the differences in the AES values are not statistically significant; (+ +) means that the partially connected ring is better and the differences are statistically significant.

The proposed topology outperforms the AES of the standard cEA in every function. The differences are statistically significant in order-3 and -4 traps and in the MMDP. The algorithm seems to be particularly suited for deceptive problems.

In the second experiment, the cEAs are provided with mutation: mutation probability was set to $1/l$ for every test. The population size of both strategies is set to half of the optimal population size of the standard cEA, in order to investigate how the cEAs behave when the supply of raw building blocks is reduced and part of the genetic diversity is assured by mutation. (The bisection method determines the optimal population size for the selecto-recombinative version of the algorithm. When using mutation, that minimal population, which guarantees a high rate of convergence, may be reduced.) Results are in Table 6.

Table 6. Standard ring topology cEA and partially connected ring cEA with random movement. Evaluations to a solution, successful runs and best fitness.

		2-trap	3-trap	4-trap	MMDP	Trident
$1 \times n$	AES	306562.5 ±56485.3	424021.6 ±77027.02	351001.9 ±67053.15	610437.5 ±408323.2	24027.5 ±5782.976
	SR	(48)	(37)	(27)	(36)	**(50)**
	FIT	0.40±0.20	0.260±0.44	0.60±0.75	0.11±0.18	**0.0±0.0**
$1 \times (1.5n)$	AES	352105.0 ±37759.4	530622 ±87469.522	446441.1 ±89766.2	638250.0 ±243028.4	27895.0 ±6424.288
	SR	**(50)**	**(50)**	**(45)**	**(45)**	**(50)**
	FIT	**0.0±0.0**	**0.0±0.0**	0.12±0.38	0.04±0.12	**0.0±0.0**

With these settings, the success rates of the standard ring are significantly reduced in the deceptive problems, while the partially connected structure attains success rates above 90% in every problem. In the 2-trap and Trident functions the results are similar: there are no statistical differences between the AES values.

A final note on the implementation of the proposed algorithm: Although uniprocessor implementations are common, cEAs have been initially conceived for parallel computing frameworks, in which several processors are structured in a static grid or ring topology. The proposed schemes could model some properties of networks of processors (such as fail or delays in the communication, represented here by empty cells), but they may be hard to implement in a multiprocessor framework. It is necessary to devise a probability-based partially connected ring topology, where the size of the ring is maintained and links between the nodes are connected and disconnected according to probability values, adjacency rules or even self-organized properties. The results described in this section, which show that the proposed partially connected rings for cEAs are able to improve standard structures in hard problems with deceptive landscapes, are promising and motivate future research on alternative models of the proposed scheme that do not requires empty nodes in the network.

5   Conclusions and Future Work

This paper describes a partially connected 1-dimensional cellular Evolutionary Algorithm (cEA). The structure consists of a population of n individuals randomly distributed in a grid with size $1 \times Y$, where $Y > n$. In every time-step, the individuals try to move to adjacent nodes, according to specific rules. The resulting structure displays an island-model behaviour that promotes genetic diversity and reduces the minimum population size that assures a high rate of convergence to a global optimum.

Three movement rules have been tested: random, fitness based and similarity based rules. The results of the different schemes are similar and further investigation is required in order to understand the potential of each one. The most important outcome here is that the partially connected structure significantly improves the success rates of the standard structure on quasi-deceptive and deceptive problems. Optimal population size tests with selecto-recombinative cEAs show that the proposed algorithm requires smaller populations for attaining the optimum, which means that it has a better ability to recombine the raw building-blocks provided by the initial population and maintain genetic diversity.

Two main lines of research are planned for the future. First, we will investigate the behaviour of general 2-dimensional partially connected grids and compare it to square and rectangular static topologies. The second line of research is dedicated to modelling the partially connected rings in a probability-based model, without empty nodes between the individuals. This way, a multiprocessor approach may be implemented.

Acknowledgements. The first author wishes to thank FCT, *Ministério da Ciência e Tecnologia*, his Research Fellowship SFRH/BPD/66876/2009. The work was supported by FCT PROJECT [PEst-OE/EEI/LA0009/2013], Spanish Ministry of Science and Innovation project TIN2011-28627-C04-02, Andalusian Regional Government P08-TIC-03903, CEI-BioTIC UGR project CEI2013-P-14, and UL-EvoPerf project.

References

1. Alba, E., Dorronsoro, B.: The exploration/exploitation tradeoff in dynamic cellular genetic algorithms. IEEE Transactions Evolutionary Computation **9**, 126–142 (2005)
2. Fernandes, C.M., Laredo, J.L.L., Merelo, J.J., Cotta, C., Rosa, A.C.: Towards a 2-dimensional Framework for Structured Population-based Metaheuristics. In: Proceedings of IEEE International Conference on Complex Systems, pp. 1–6 (2012)
3. Fernandes, C.M., Laredo, J.L.L., Merelo, J.J., Cotta, C., Rosa, A.C.: A Study on Time-Varying Partially Connected Topologies for the Particle Swarm. In: Proceedings of the IEEE Congress on Evolutionary Computation, pp. 2450–2456. IEEE (2013)
4. Gordon, V., Whitley, L.: Serial and Parallel Genetic Algorithms as Function Optimizers. In: Proceedings 5th ICGA, pp. 177–183 (1993)
5. Ilachinski, A.: Cellular Automata: A Discrete Universe. World Scientific (2001)
6. Kennedy, J., Eberhart, R.C.: Swarm Intelligence. Morgan Kaufmann, San Francisco (2001)

7. Laredo, J.L.J., Castillo, P.A., Mora, A.M., Merelo, J.J., Fernandes, C.M.: Resilience to churn of a peer-to-peer evolutionary algorithm. International Journal of High Performance Systems Architecture **1**(4), 260–268 (2008)
8. Payne, J.L., Eppstein, M.J.: Emergent mating topologies in spatially structured genetic algorithms. In: Proc. 8th GECCO, pp. 207–214 (2006)
9. Sastry, K.: Evaluation-relaxation schemes for Genetic and Evolutionary Algorithms. Msc Thesis, University of Illinois, Urbana, IL, USA (2001)
10. Steinmetz, R., Wehrle, K. (eds.): Peer-to-Peer Systems and Applications. LNCS, vol. 3485. Springer, Heidelberg (2005)
11. Tomassini, M.: Spatially Structured Evolutionary Algorithms. Springer, Heidelberg (2005)
12. Whitacre, J.M., Sarker, R.A., Pham, Q.: The self-organization of interaction networks for nature-inspired optimization. IEEE Transactions on Evolutionary Computation **12**, 220–230 (2008)

Systolic Genetic Search for Software Engineering: The Test Suite Minimization Case

Martín Pedemonte[1]($\boxtimes$), Francisco Luna[2], and Enrique Alba[3]

[1] Universidad de la República, Montevideo, Uruguay
mpedemon@fing.edu.uy
[2] Universidad de Extremadura, Mérida, Spain
fluna@unex.es
[3] Universidad de Málaga, Málaga, Spain
eat@lcc.uma.es

Abstract. The Test Suite Minimization Problem (TSMP) is a $\mathcal{NP}$-hard real-world problem that arises in the field of software engineering. It lies in selecting the minimal set of test cases from a large test suite, ensuring that the test cases selected cover a given set of elements of a computer program under test. In this paper, we propose a Systolic Genetic Search (SGS) algorithm for solving the TSMP. We use the global concept of SGS to derive a particular algorithm to explicitly exploit the high degree of parallelism available in modern GPU architectures. The experimental evaluation on seven real-world programs shows that SGS is highly effective for the TSMP, as it obtains the optimal solution in almost every single run for all the tested software. It also outperforms two competitive Genetic Algorithms. The GPU-based implementation of SGS has achieved a high performance, obtaining runtime reductions of up to 40× compared to its sequential implementation, and solving all the instances considered in less than nine seconds.

Keywords: Systolic Genetic Search · Evolutionary Algorithms · Parallel Metaheuristics · GPU · GPGPU · Search-based Software Engineering

1 Introduction

Search-based software engineering (SBSE) [6] is one recent field in Software Engineering (SE) that is based in applying search-based optimization techniques, like Evolutionary Algorithms (EAs), to SE problems. SBSE has been applied to problems from all the phases of the software development process, being software testing one of the most addressed issues [6]. Regression testing is the activity performed within the development process to ensure that changes made to an existing piece of software do not introduce errors. When a piece of software evolves, it grows in complexity and size so the number of test cases of the regression test suite also grows. For this reason, the direct execution of the entire test suite can be impracticable. As a consequence, different approaches have been proposed to reduce the effort devoted to regression testing [16]. The Test Suite Minimization Problem (TSMP) is a $\mathcal{NP}$-hard real-world software testing problem that is based on reducing a large

© Springer-Verlag Berlin Heidelberg 2014
A.I. Esparcia-Alcázar et al. (Eds.): EvoApplications 2014, LNCS 8602, pp. 678–689, 2014.
DOI: 10.1007/978-3-662-45523-4_55

test suite ensuring that a set of test goals are satisfied [16]. The goal is to find the minimal number of test cases of the suite that covers a given set of elements of the piece of software that is being tested.

As realistic software programs and the test suite proposed for its testing involve thousands of lines of code and thousands of test cases, exact algorithms are discarded as solution approach of the TSMP. Metaheuristics are our choice here. The point is that even metaheuristics may be highly computationally expensive when addressing such real-world TSMP instances. In order to tackle these problems properly, we make use of parallelism, which comes out as a reliable strategy to speed up the search of those kind of optimizers. Parallel metaheuristics [1] do not only allow to reduce the runtime of the algorithms, but also usually provide new enhanced search engines that allow to improve the quality of results obtained by traditional sequential algorithms. Despite its advantages, there are very few works that use parallel metaheuristics for solving SBSE problems [17,18].

Systolic Genetic Search (SGS) [12,13] is a recently proposed optimization algorithm that combines ideas from systolic computing and metaheuristics. SGS was explicitly designed to exploit the high degree of parallelism available in modern GPU architectures. SGS algorithm has already shown its potential for tackling the Knapsack Problem finding optimal solutions in short execution times in [12,13]. This paper presents a SGS algorithm for the TSMP. Sequential and GPU-based implementations of SGS are studied in order to understand the numerical efficacy of the proposed algorithm and the performance benefits of its deployment on a GPU card. The main contributions of this paper are:

- It presents a new success of SGS for solving an optimization problem in a unexplored domain. The results obtained are also relevant for the TSMP, as SGS is highly effective for solving seven real-world instance of the problem.
- It shows that the GPU-based implementation of SGS is able to achieve a high performance, obtaining a high runtime reduction compared to the sequential implementation for solutions with similar quality.
- It presents an example of new research based on making algorithms specially tailored for the GPU architecture, instead of porting already existing algorithms originally designed for the CPU.

This article is organized as follow. The next section discusses the related papers in the literature. Section 3 formally introduces the TSMP. Section 4 describes the SGS algorithm, how it is instantiated for tackling the TSMP, and its implementation on a GPU. Section 5 presents the details and the analysis of the empirical study. Finally, in Section 6, we outline the conclusions of this work and suggest future research directions.

2   Related Work

Several specific heuristics for the TSMP have been proposed, like a greedy approach [11], the Algorithm H [7] and variations of the greedy algorithm (GR and GRE algorithms) [3]. However, these heuristics have only been used on relatively small test instances. An empirical evaluation was conducted on larger scenarios using randomly generated instances [4]. This evaluation concluded that there is no single technique that is better than the others for all the scenarios considered.

In the last years, the research community has paid more attention to the multi-objective (MO) TSMP than to the single objective (SO) TSMP. It has been proposed a bi-objective formulation [15,17,18] that considers the coverage and the cost (number of code instructions executed in a profiling tool) as the conflicting goals. There is also a three objective formulation [15] that also includes the fault history as a goal. Despite the existence of these formulations, we believe that the SO TSMP is still an interesting problem. The MO formulations are aimed to obtain solutions that allow to reduce the cost by reducing the coverage. However, it does not seem acceptable to reduce the coverage of test goals in a realistic scenario, even within a tight schedule to execute the regression test.

Recently, the optimal solution of several TSMP instances was found by transforming the instances in a Boolean satisfiability (SAT) problem and solving it using a SAT solver [2]. As the runtime of the proposed algorithm is very high, the authors reduced the original instances using a highly aggressive strategy (removing all test cases whose coverage is contained in another test case from the test suite). For this reason, the largest instance addressed has only 215 test cases. Most instances were solved in less than 3 seconds, but for one that required more than 300 seconds. However, the authors did not report the runtime of neither the transformation between TSMP and SAT nor the reduction of the instances.

Although SBSE is usually a computationally demanding area because most problems has to be solved within a tight schedule and the large size of the instances solved, the application of parallelism to SBSE has been scarce. Up to 2011 there were only three works about using distributed memory architecture platforms to speedup the computation of SBSE (a state-of-the-art on this subject can be found in [17]).

Recently, there have been a couple works that use GPUs in order to solve SBSE problems. In [17,18] the MO TSMP is addressed using a GPU to speedup the fitness calculation of a multi-objective EA. In order to do this, the evaluation of the population is transformed into a matrix-matrix multiplication that is programmed by the authors. The proposed implementation in each generation has to transfer the entire population from the CPU to the GPU, evaluate the fitness function on the GPU and transfer the results back to the CPU. It should be noted that transfers between CPU and GPU in both directions is one of the most costly operation for an hybrid CPU-GPU platform.

3   Test Suite Minimization Problem

The Test Suite Minimization Problem (TSMP) is a real-world problem from the field of software engineering [16]. This problem arises in regression testing and belongs to the class of $\mathcal{NP}$-hard problems since it is equivalent to the Minimal Hitting Set Problem. It consists in reducing a test suite by eliminating redundant test cases, and the goal is to select the minimal set of test cases that cover a set of test goals. It is formally defined as follows.

Let $T = \{t_1, \ldots, t_n\}$ be a test suite for a program that consist of n test cases and $R = \{r_1, \ldots, r_m\}$ the set of all the test goals (requirements) that has to be covered with the test cases. Each test case covers several test goals and this relation could be represented by a matrix $M = [m_{ij}]$ of dimension $n \times m$ (coverage matrix), whose entries are either 0 or 1. If $m_{ij} = 1$ the test case i covers the test goal j, otherwise it does not covers the test goal.

The single objective TSMP consists in finding a subset of test cases with a minimum number of elements that covers all the test goals (100% of coverage). The single objective TSMP can be formulated as the integer programming model presented in Equations 1, 2, and 3, being x_i the binary decision variables of the problem that indicate whether the test case i is included or not in the test suite.

$$(\text{TSMP}) \qquad \text{minimize} \quad \sum_{i=1}^{n} x_i \tag{1}$$

$$\text{subject to:} \quad \sum_{i=1}^{n} m_{ij}x_i \geqslant 1, \forall j = 1, \ldots, m \tag{2}$$

$$x_i \in \{0, 1\}, \forall i = 1, \ldots, n \tag{3}$$

4   Systolic Genetic Search

The idea of *Systolic Computing* [9,10] emerged in the late 70's. It consists in a network of simple data processing units connected in a simple and regular fashion allowing data flow between neighboring units. These units, which are called cells, are capable of performing simple operations to data that is then passed through the system. This kind of architecture offers understandable and manageable, but still quite powerful parallelism.

Systolic computing based metaheuristics adapt this idea to optimization using as a basis the systolic computing architecture. This family of algorithms are characterized by the flow of solutions through data processing units following a synchronous and structured plan. Each cell applies operators to the circulating tentative solutions in order to obtain new solutions that continue moving across the processing units. In this way, the circulating solutions are refined again and again by means of simple low complexity search operators. In particular, Systolic Genetic Search (SGS) [12,13] applies adapted evolutionary operators when two solutions meet in a cell in order to refine the tentative solutions.

The rest of this section is structured as follows. First, in the next subsection the SGS algorithm used in this work is described. Then, it is shown how it is instanciated for tackling the TSMP. Finally, the design and implementation of the GPU-based SGS is commented.

4.1   SGS$_B$: A Systolic Genetic Search Algorithm

In order to characterize a systolic computing based optimization algorithm three basic points has to be precisely defined: the interconnection topology of the systolic structure, the data flow of solutions, and the computation of the cells.

In particular, SGS algorithms use a bidimensional grid of cells in which the solutions circulate synchronously through an horizontal and a vertical data flow.

The data flow determines the flavour of the SGS algorithm. In this work, we use the SGS_B flavour (B stands for both flows), in which a solution moving through the vertical data flow that reaches the last row of the grid is passed on to the cell of the first row of the next column of the grid, while a solution moving through the horizontal data flow that reaches the last column of the grid is passed on to the cell of the first column of the next row of the grid. The interconnection topology and solution flows of SGS_B it is shown in Figure 1. Other data flows have been studied in [12,13].

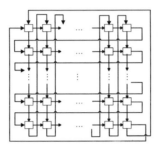

Fig. 1. Interconnection topology and solution flows of SGS_B

The computation performed by the cells is described next. Initially, each cell generates two random solutions which are aimed at moving horizontally and vertically, respectively. At each step of SGS, two solutions enter each cell, one from the horizontal data flow and one from the vertical data flow. Then, it applies adapted genetic operators (crossover and mutation) to generate two new solutions. Later, the cell uses elitism to determine which solution continues moving through the grid for each flow, choosing between the incoming solution and the newly generated one by the genetic operators. The use of elitism is critical, as there is no selection process like in standard genetic algorithms. Finally, each cell sends the outgoing solutions to the next cells of the data flows.

The general idea of the SGS algorithm can be adapted to any solution representation and any particular operator. In this work, since we are addressing a binary problem, we encode the solutions as binary strings, and use bit-flip mutation and two-point crossover as evolutionary search operators.

Even though the idea of SGS is to have a relatively large number of cells in order to allow the algorithm to achieve a good exploration and to take advantage of the parallel computation capabilities offered by devices such as the GPUs, the number of cells should not increase up to values that compromise performance. We consider that a proper balance is to have at least l cells (the length of the tentative solutions). To this end, the length and width of the grid is $\lceil \sqrt{l} \rceil$. If $\lceil \sqrt{l} \rceil$ is an integer, the grid has exactly l cells, otherwise it has some additional cells. In this way, each circulating solution returns to its starting cell in SGS_B after $\lceil \sqrt{l} \rceil \times \lceil \sqrt{l} \rceil$ steps.

The bit-flip mutation operator flips a single bit in each solution of each cell. With the aim of reducing the generation of random numbers during the execution of SGS, the mutation point for each cell is preprogrammed at fixed positions of the tentative solutions, which is defined by considering the location of the cell in the grid. In order to change different bits of the solutions through the grid, the formula for calculating the mutation point of the cell (i, j) is:

$$i \times \lceil \sqrt{l} \rceil + j \mod l \ , \tag{4}$$

where mod is the modulus of the integer division.

As the two-point crossover is applied on each cell, two different crossover point values are chosen randomly for each cell.

4.2 A SGS for the TSMP

In order to tackle the TSMP with a SGS, it is necessary to define a fitness function for this problem. As it is possible to build solutions that are not feasible, i.e., that do not cover all the test goals, the fitness function has to deal with this issue. Our approach applies a penalty function for each test goal that it is not satisfied. Equation 5 shows the fitness function, being k the number of test cases of $\vec{x}$ and c the number of test goals covered by $\vec{x}$.

$$f(\vec{x}) = \frac{n - k}{m - c + 1} \ . \tag{5}$$

4.3 A GPU-Based Implementation of SGS

As a straightforward implementation of the fitness function on the GPU would not properly exploit the massive parallelism available, we followed an idea previously proposed in [17,18] that transforms the evaluation into a matrix-matrix multiplication. However, as there are available libraries that compute linear algebra operations efficiently, we decided to use the matrix-matrix multiplication routine from CUBLAS library. As a consequence, each systolic step requires to invoke two kernels, one for computing the crossover and mutation of the solutions in a cell (`crossoverAndMutation` kernel) and one for completing the fitness calculation and applying the elitist replacement (`fitnessReductionAndElitism` kernel), besides the invocation to CUBLAS. Algorithm 1 presents the pseudocode of the SGS algorithm for the host side (CPU).

All the kernels are implemented following the idea used in [12], in which operations are assigned to a whole block and all the threads of the block cooperate to perform a given operation, i.e. each block processes one cell of the grid. If the solution length is larger than the number of threads in the block, each thread processes more than one element of the solution but the elements used by a single thread are not contiguous. Thus, each operation is applied to a solution in chunks of the size of the thread block.

5 Experimental Results

This section describes the instances of the TSMP used for the experimental study, the parameters setting, and the execution platforms. Then, the results obtained are presented and analyzed.

Algorithm 1. SGS Host Side Pseudocode

1: transfer seed for random number generation to GPU
2: transfer constant data to GPU's global memory
3: invoke `initPop` kernel to initialize population
4: invoke matrix-matrix multiplication from CUBLAS
5: invoke `fitnessReduction` kernel to calculate fitness of the population
6: **for** $i = 1$ **to** *maxGeneration* **do**
7:     invoke `crossoverAndMutation` kernel to compute systolic step
8:     invoke matrix-matrix multiplication from CUBLAS
9:     invoke `fitnessReductionAndElitism` kernel to complete the systolic step
10: **end for**
11: transfer results from GPU to CPU

5.1 TSMP Instances

The instances used in this work are several real world programs that belong to the Siemens benchmark suite [8]. The Siemens benchmark suite is publicly available at the Software-artifact Infrastructure Repository (SIR) website [5]. The suite includes an aircraft collision avoidance system (`tcas`), a statistic computation program (`totinfo`), two priority schedulers (`schedule` and `schedule2`), two lexical analyzers (`printtokens` and `printtokens2`) and a program that performs pattern matching and substitution (`replace`).

Table 1 presents the instances used in this work including the number of test cases and the number of test goals that is directly taken from the benchmark. However, a simple inspection of the coverage matrix shows that there are several test cases that cover exactly the same goals. For this reason, and as we are addressing the single objective TSMP, we preprocessed the instances by removing test cases with exactly the same coverage (Reduced Test Suite Size in Table 1). This process takes less than a second in the same PC that was used in the experimental evaluation. Finally, the table includes the number of test cases of the optimal solution of each instance [2].

Table 1. TSMP instances used in the evaluation and their exact optimal solutions

Instance	Original Test Suite Size	Reduced Test Suite Size	Test Goals	Optimal Solution [2]
`tcas`	1608	8	54	4
`totinfo`	1052	173	117	5
`schedule`	2650	492	126	3
`schedule2`	2710	770	119	4
`printtokens2`	4115	1721	192	4
`printtokens`	4130	1856	195	5
`replace`	5542	2023	208	8

5.2   Algorithms

In addition to the SGS$_B$ algorithm, we have included two algorithms, a simple Genetic Algorithm (GA) with and without elitism, in order to set an actual comparison basis. The GAs have been chosen because they share the same basic search operator (crossover and mutation) that SGS$_B$ so we can properly evaluate the underlying search engine of the techniques. The details of the algorithms used in this work are:

- Simple Genetic Algorithm (SGA): It is a generational GA with binary tournament, two-point crossover and bit-flip mutation.
- Elitist Genetic Algorithm (EGA): It is similar to SGA but children solutions replace parent solutions only if they have a better (higher) fitness value.
- SGS$_B$: The algorithm described in Sect. 4.

5.3   Parameters Setting and Test Environment

The SGA and EGA parameter values used are 0.9 for the crossover probability and $1/l$ for the mutation probability, where l is the length of the tentative solutions (the number of test cases). The population size and the number of generations of both GAs were defined by considering the features of SGS$_B$. For this reason, the population size is $2 \times \lceil\sqrt{l}\rceil \times \lceil\sqrt{l}\rceil$ and the generations are $\lceil\sqrt{l}\rceil \times \lceil\sqrt{l}\rceil$. The number of generations was chosen so that each circulating solution returns to its starting cell in SGS$_B$ after that number of iterations.

The execution platform for the CPU implementation is a PC with a Quad Core Intel i7 2600 processor at 3.40 GHz. with 16 GB RAM using Linux O.S. All CPU implementations were executed as single-threaded applications. The GPU implementations were run in an Nvidia's GeForce GTX 680 (1536 CUDA cores at 1006 MHz., Kepler architecture) connected to the PC used for the CPU executions. CPU and GPU implementations were compiled using the -O3 flag.

All the results reported in the next subsection are averaged over fifty independent runs. The transference times of data between CPU and GPU are always included in the reported total runtime of the GPU version. As the algorithms used in the experimental evaluation are all stochastic, the following statistical procedure [14] has been used to provide statistical significance. If the samples are distributed according to a normal distribution and the variances are homogeneous (homocedasticity), an ANOVA I test is performed; otherwise a Kruskal-Wallis test is performed. All the statistical tests are performed with a confidence level of 95%. As more than two algorithms are considered in the study, a post-hoc phase which consist in a pairwise comparison of all the cases compared using the Bonferroni-Dunn method has been performed. The results are displayed in tabular form, '$\checkmark$' states that there is statistical significance, while '$-$' states that there is no statistically significant differences.

5.4   Experimental Analysis: Numerical Performance

Let us first analyze the numerical efficiency for TSMP of the GPU implementations. Table 2 shows, for each algorithm, its hit rate (i.e., the number of times it

Table 2. Hit rate, numerical efficacy (mean error ± std. dev.) and statistical assesment of GPU versions

Instance	Hit rate			Numerical efficiency			Statistical assessment		
	SGA	EGA	SGS_B	SGA	EGA	SGS_B	SGA-EGA	SGA-SBS_B	EGA-SBS_B
tcas	72%	100%	100%	$0.28_{\pm0.45}$	$0.00_{\pm0.00}$	$0.00_{\pm0.00}$	✓	✓	–
totinfo	8%	100%	100%	$1.16_{\pm0.55}$	$0.00_{\pm0.00}$	$0.00_{\pm0.00}$	✓	✓	–
schedule	0%	48%	92%	$8.52_{\pm2.51}$	$0.58_{\pm0.61}$	$0.08_{\pm0.27}$	✓	✓	✓
schedule2	0%	66%	100%	$9.96_{\pm5.09}$	$0.34_{\pm0.48}$	$0.00_{\pm0.00}$	✓	✓	✓
printtokens2	0%	72%	100%	$14.68_{\pm7.41}$	$0.28_{\pm0.45}$	$0.00_{\pm0.00}$	✓	✓	✓
printtokens	0%	44%	100%	$9.58_{\pm1.99}$	$0.60_{\pm0.57}$	$0.00_{\pm0.00}$	✓	✓	✓
replace	0%	4%	100%	$12.60_{\pm2.49}$	$1.34_{\pm0.59}$	$0.00_{\pm0.00}$	✓	✓	✓

hits the optimal solution), the quality of solutions it reaches (measured in terms of distance to the optimal solution), and the result of the statistical assessment.

The Hit Rate results show that SGS_B is able to always find the optimal solution for all the instances, but schedule (46 out of 50 trials). This means almost full effectiveness (hit rate of 98.8% over then entire testbed). EGA also performs well, finding the optimal solution for all the instances, but it is noticeable that SGS_B is clearly superior to EGA in five instances. On average, EGA reaches a hit rate of 62%. It is remarkable the ability of SGS_B to scale properly with the size of the instances as it has consistently find the optimal solutions regardless of the number of test cases (which ranges from 8 to 2023). Finally, SGA has a poor numerical efficiency and it is only able to find the optimal solution in the two smallest instances.

The next group of columns in Table 2 includes the average number of additional test cases from that of the optimal solution required for each suite to cover 100% program statements in the seven TSMP program instances. Besides confirming the Hit Rate results, these values point out very tight differences between SGS_B and EGA, with statistical confidence though (as shown in the very last columns of the table). SGA has reported the higher (worse) number of test cases. The search engine of SGS_B based on the flow of solutions has allowed this algorithm to identify the region where the optimal solution is located for the considered instances. Within the context of this experimental evaluation, it has been shown that SGS_B provides a highly robust search for the TSMP. The numerical efficiency of the CPU implementations has been also evaluated and roughly the same conclusions are drawn as that of the GPU implementations. However, due to room constraints, they have not been included in this paper.

5.5   Experimental Analysis: Parallel Performance

Since the numerical efficiency of SGA was rather poor, we do not include this algorithm in this study. Table 3 shows the mean runtime and the standard deviation, in seconds, for EGA and SGS_B when executed on CPU. The runtime for tcas instance of the two algorithms is not included in the table as it is below 0.001 seconds, i.e., there are executions which runtime cannot be measured.

Table 3. Runtime in seconds of the CPU versions (mean ± std. dev.)

Instance	EGA	SGS$_B$
totinfo	**0.23 ± 0.01**	0.25 ± 0.01
schedule	**3.71 ± 0.05**	4.46 ± 0.03
schedule2	**11.46 ± 0.11**	13.16 ± 0.06
printtokens2	**157.73 ± 1.44**	253.51 ± 1.28
printtokens	**188.06 ± 1.67**	275.16 ± 1.25
replace	**225.99 ± 1.86**	346.61 ± 1.67

It is pretty clear that EGA has performed much faster than SGS$_B$. Indeed, the larger the TSMP instances the higher the difference in the runtime. This is somewhat surprising as the search engine of the algorithms is built upon the same genetic components. There is a fundamental reason for such results: the fitness function has a variable runtime. For each test case that is included in a tentative solution, it has to be computed which test goals are covered, as a consequence, computing the fitness value of a solution strongly depends on the number of test cases used in the solution. The higher the number of test cases of the solution, the longer the runtime. In this context, we have tracked the runs of the algorithms and it has been shown that EGA converges very quickly to solutions with a few number of test cases due to its elitist strategy, thus making the computation of the fitness function quite fast. SGS$_B$ is also endowed with an elitist mechanism, but it is limited to the scope of the SGS cells and the solution flow. That is, SGS$_B$ promotes a higher solution diversification which, for TSMP, penalizes its runtime.

Now, we analyze the performance of the GPU implementations. Table 4 shows the mean runtime and the standard deviation, in seconds, of EGA and SGS$_B$ executed on a GeForce GTX 680, as well as runtime reduction of each algorithm versus its sequential counterpart. The extremely short execution times of the tcas has driven us to avoid including it here.

Table 4. Performance efficiency of the GPU versions

Instance	EGA		SGS$_B$	
	Runtime in s. (mean ± std.)	Reduction vs. CPU	Runtime in s. (mean ± std.)	Reduction vs. CPU
totinfo	0.031 ± 0.001	7.42	**0.027 ± 0.001**	9.26
schedule	0.210 ± 0.001	17.67	**0.167 ± 0.001**	26.71
schedule2	0.549 ± 0.001	20.87	**0.397 ± 0.001**	33.15
printtokens2	7.858 ± 0.029	20.07	**5.785 ± 0.016**	43.82
printtokens	8.948 ± 0.021	21.02	**6.726 ± 0.023**	40.91
replace	11.112 ± 0.031	20.34	**8.671 ± 0.024**	39.97

The first main conclusion drawn is that SGS_B has the shortest runtime in all the instances studied of the TSMP. Indeed, SGS_B needs only 8.67 seconds for solving the `replace` instance, which is nearly 30% faster than EGA, which follows a similar scheme of implementation. The differences with respect to the CPU implementations has not only vanished, but reversed. The reason for such a result has to do, again, with the computation time of the fitness function: its GPU implementation developed is that suitable for such a massively parallel computing platform that the number of test cases of each solution makes no different in its runtime. This comparison mainly reveals the different performance of the GPU implementation for the search engine of the algorithms, being that of SGS_B faster. This has a clear impact on the runtime reductions: SGS_B has reached a peak of 43.82× for `printtokens2`, and averages 32.3% over the six instances; EGA in turn averages 17.9% (with a maximum value of 21.02% for `printtokens`. We want to remark that we are not providing EGA with a low quality GPU implementation as it runs around 20 time faster.

Although there are several differences between the approach taken in [17,18] and in this work it should be highlighted that the maximal speedup achieved by those authors for the instances considered in this work is 5.26. The most important differences are: they tackle the multi-objective TSMP, while we tackle the single-objective variant; their proposal only uses the GPU to speedup the fitness evaluation, while our proposal implements the whole algorithm in the GPU; and the number of fitness evaluations and the population size are different. Additionally, it should be noted that it is very difficult to evaluate if both CPU-GPU platforms have a similar relative performance.

In summary, the GPU implementation of SGS_B is not only able to reach excellent quality solutions for the TSMP, but it is also able to do it faster. This makes possible to solve real-world software testing environments in which decisions have to be taken within a tight schedule. The improvements in the performance achieved are satisfactory, but there is still room for improvement since the GPU implementation can be further fine tuned to the Kepler architecture.

6   Conclusions and Future Work

In this work, we have proposed a SGS algorithm for solving the single objective TSMP. The experimental evaluation conducted over seven instances from real-world programs, with up to 2023 test cases and 208 test goals, showed that the SGS was able to find the optimal solution on almost every execution, as well as outperforming two GAs for solving instances. The results have also shown that the GPU implementation of SGS speeds up the runtime up to 43 times.

Three main areas that deserve further study were identified. A first issue is to fine tune the GPU implementation of our algorithm for the Kepler architecture. A second line of interest is to evaluate the improved implementation in a Tesla K20 GPU, which is specially designed for high performance computing. And, finally, we aim to evaluate our algorithm with other real-world benchmarks, specially with instances with a larger number of test goals than in this work.

Acknowledgments. M. Pedemonte acknowledges support from Programa de Desarrollo de las Ciencias Básicas, Universidad de la República, and Agencia Nacional de Investigación e Innovación, Uruguay. F. Luna and E. Alba acknowledge partial support from the Spanish Ministry of Economy and Competitiveness and FEDER under contract TIN2011-28194.

References

1. Alba, E., (ed.): Parallel Metaheuristics: A New Class of Algorithms. Wiley (2005)
2. Arito, F., Chicano, F., Alba, E.: On the application of sat solvers to the test suite minimization problem. In: Fraser, G., Teixeira de Souza, J. (eds.) SSBSE 2012. LNCS, vol. 7515, pp. 45–59. Springer, Heidelberg (2012)
3. Chen, T.Y., Lau, M.F.: Heuristics towards the optimization of the size of a test suite. In: Procs. of the 3rd Int. Conf. on Software Quality Management, pp. 415–424 (1995)
4. Chen, T.Y., Lau, M.F.: A simulation study on some heuristics for test suite reduction. Information and Software Technology **40**(13), 777–787 (1998)
5. Do, H., Elbaum, S., Rothermel, G.: Supporting controlled experimentation with testing techniques: An infrastructure and its potential impact. Empirical Softw. Engg. **10**(4), 405–435 (2005)
6. Harman, M., Mansouri, S.A., Zhang, Y.: Search-based software engineering: Trends, techniques and applications. ACM Comput. Surv. **45**(1), 11 (2012)
7. Harrold, M.J., Gupta, R., Soffa, M.L.: A methodology for controlling the size of a test suite. ACM Trans. Softw. Eng. Methodol. **2**(3), 270–285 (1993)
8. Hutchins, M., Foster, H., Goradia, T., Ostrand, T.: Experiments of the effectiveness of dataflow- and controlflow-based test adequacy criteria. In: Proc. of the 16th Int. Conf. on Software Engineering, pp. 191–200 (1994)
9. Kung, H.T.: Why systolic architectures? Computer **15**(1), 37–46 (1982)
10. Kung, H.T., Leiserson, C.E.: Systolic arrays (for VLSI). In: Sparse Matrix Proceedings, pp. 256–282 (1978)
11. Offutt, J., Pan, J., Voas, J.: Procedures for reducing the size of coverage-based test sets. In: Procs. of the Twelfth Int. Conf. on Testing Computer Software (1995)
12. Pedemonte, M., Alba, E., Luna, F.: Towards the design of systolic genetic search. In: IEEE 26th International Parallel and Distributed Processing Symposium Workshops & PhD Forum, pp. 1778–1786 IEEE Computer Society (2012)
13. Pedemonte, M., Luna, F., Alba, E.: New ideas in parallel metaheuristics on gpu: Systolic genetic search. In: Tsutsui, S., Collet, P.: Massively Parallel Evolutionary Computation on GPGPUs. Natural Computing Series, pp. 203–225, Springer (2013)
14. Sheskin, D.J.: Handbook of Parametric and Nonparametric Statistical Procedures, Fifth edition, Chapman and Hall/CRC (2011)
15. Yoo, S., Harman, M.: Pareto efficient multi-objective test case selection. In: Proceedings of the 2007 Int. Symposium on Software Testing and Analysis, pp. 140–150 (2007)
16. Yoo, S., Harman, M.: Regression testing minimization, selection and prioritization: a survey. Softw. Test. Verif. Reliab. **22**(2), 67–120 (2012)
17. Yoo, S., Harman, M., Ur, S.: Highly scalable multi objective test suite minimisation using graphics cards. In: Proceedings of the Third International Conference on Search Based Software Engineering, pp. 219–236 (2011)
18. Yoo, S., Harman, M., Ur, S.: Gpgpu test suite minimisation: search based software engineering performance improvement using graphics cards. Empirical Software Engineering **18**(3), 550–593 (2013)

Optimization of Application Placement Towards a Greener Cloud Infrastructure

Tania Lorido-Botran[✉], Jose Antonio Pascual, Jose Miguel-Alonso, and Jose Antonio Lozano

Intelligent Systems Group, University of the Basque Country, UPV/EHU, Paseo Manuel Lardizábal, 1 20018 Donostia-San Sebastian, Spain
{tania.lorido,joseantonio.pascual,j.miguel,ja.lozano}@ehu.es

Abstract. Cloud infrastructures are designed to simultaneously service many, diverse applications that consist of collections of Virtual Machines (VMs). The policy used to map applications onto physical servers (placement policy) has important effects in terms of application performance and resource efficiency. This paper proposes enhancing placement policies with network-aware optimizations trying to simultaneously improve application performance, resource efficiency and, as a consequence, power efficiency. The per-application placement decision is formulated as a bi-objective optimization problem (minimizing communication cost and minimizing the number of physical servers assigned to the application) whose solution is searched using an evolutionary algorithm with problem-specific crossover and mutation operators. Experiments carried out with a simulator demonstrate how a low-cost optimization technique results in improved placements that achieve all the target objectives.

Keywords: Cloud computing · Tree-network topology · VM placement · Multi-objective optimization · Energy consumption

1 Introduction

In recent years, the utilization of cloud infrastructures to host applications has spread widely. The characteristic that makes these cloud systems so appealing is their elasticity, that is, resources can be acquired on-demand, depending on the time-varying application needs, but paying only for those actually booked (a scheme known as pay-as-yo-go). Virtualization technologies enable the cloud infrastructure to provide such elastic usage. The resources offered by physical servers, organized in several data centers, are provided in the form of abstract compute units that are implemented as Virtual Machines (VMs). Each VM is assigned a pre-configured set of resources: number of cores, amount of memory, disk and network-bandwidth.

Virtualized data centers support a large variety of applications, including batch jobs (scientific applications), and web applications (e.g. an online bookshop or a blog hosting site). Each application is deployed on a set of VMs, which can be allocated to any collection of physical servers in the data center.

© Springer-Verlag Berlin Heidelberg 2014
A.I. Esparcia-Alcázar et al. (Eds.): EvoApplications 2014, LNCS 8602, pp. 690–701, 2014.
DOI: 10.1007/978-3-662-45523-4_56

The problem of assigning a physical location to each VM is known as *VM placement* and it is performed by the manager of the cloud infrastructure. This manager is typically called the Infrastructure-as-a-Service (IaaS) provider.

The challenge for the provider is to host a large and diverse set of applications (VM sets from different clients) in the infrastructure trying to (1) maximize its revenue and (2) provide a good service to the clients. An adequate application placement would be able to maximize the resource usage of physical servers and reduce the energy consumption of the data center, for example by turning off (or setting to idle state) the inactive servers and switches. At the same time, the infrastructure management policies should balance the obtained revenue with the Quality of Service (QoS) agreed with the client, guaranteeing that each application receives the resources payed for.

The VM placement problem has been extensively explored in the literature [11] [12]. Most efforts have been directed towards optimizing the usage of CPU, memory and disk resources, and reducing the energy consumption of physical servers. However, not enough attention has been paid to the utilization of the network. An inappropriate placement of VMs with heavy communication requirements could lead to the saturation of certain network links, with the subsequent negative impact on applications (longer execution or response times). Besides, as stated in [9], the network power has been estimated at 10-20% of the overall power consumption. For this reason, the VM placement policy should try to reduce not only the use of physical servers, but also the use of network links and switches to reduce the total power footprint.

The most common topology of data center networks is a tree of switches arranged in several tiers. The communication latency of any pair of VMs depends on the distance between the physical servers in which they are allocated. This, in turn, depends on their position in the tree. Distance is measured as the number of hops from the sender VM to the recipient one. The collection of VMs forming an application communicate between them following a certain communication pattern. In batch jobs implementing, for example, a scientific computation, the pattern may be all-to-all. In web applications, the VMs are arranged into several layers and there may be intra- and inter-layer communication. Other patterns are possible, depending on the particular characteristics of the application.

Based on the communication pattern of an application, it is straightforward to compute the input/output network bandwidth needed by each VM. The most communicative VM subsets should be placed as *close* as possible (minimizing the distance between them in terms of network hops). This means using the minimum number of physical servers, because intra-server communication is the cheapest. The constraint is that the external aggregated bandwidth required by the all the VMs in a server, from the same or from different applications, cannot exceed the bandwidth of its network connection.

Two examples of VM placement policies that can be used in data centers are first fit (FF) and round robin (RR). Each of them has a different characteristic that makes it appropriate for its use in the data center. The objective of FF is to reduce the number of physical servers in use, saving energy. RR tries to equalize the utilization of all servers to avoid excessive wearing-out of server subsets and thermal peaks. We demonstrate how it is possible to take these policies as starting points and use optimization techniques to improve the benefits for both the infrastructure provider and the application.

The remaining of this paper is organized as follows. After a review of the literature (Section 2), we provide in Section 3 models for cloud applications, data center organizations, and the energy consumed by servers and switches. Then we formulate VM placement as a multi-objective optimization problem (Section 4). We assess the benefits of our approach using the experiments defined in Section 5, whose results are discussed in Section 6. We end in Section 7 with some conclusions and future lines of work.

2   Related Work

Open-source tools for cloud management use rather simple placement policies. For example, Eucalyptus [1] implements FF and RR strategies that only consider the VM requirements and the availability of resources. It also implements a PowerSave policy that is similar to the ranking algorithm available in OpenNebula [4]: choosing first the most used servers (with room for the new demand) with the objective of minimizing the number of used servers and, therefore, the power consumption. Commercial tools for capacity planning, such as NetIQ PlateSpin Recon [3], VMware Capacity Planner [5] and IBM Workload Deployer [2] also focus on maximizing the resource usage and power consumption savings. None of these tools explain how VM placement is carried out.

Neither open-source nor commercial tools consider the impact of network topology and the communication patterns of applications, but it has been analyzed in several research works [7] [8] [9] [11] [12]. For example, Meng et al. [11] propose grouping VMs and servers into clusters, addressing VM placement for each (VM-cluster, server-cluster) pair as a Quadratic Assignment Problem (QAP). The VM clustering tries to maximize the intra-cluster communication and reduce the inter-cluster communication, but all VM-clusters have equal size. The server set assigned to a VM-cluster is fixed. This work does not consider the energy consumed by physical servers. Mann et al. [9] propose an approach similar to ours, but using a greedy heuristic. However, their work does not consider the large variety of applications that can run in the cloud. Georgiou et al. [8] also propose a greedy heuristic to improve the network utilization, but they do not try to consolidate the VMs in the minimum number of physical servers.

3   Application, Data Center and Power Models

This section presents several models that will be later used to define and solve the VM placement problem. First, we present an application model, which covers a wide range of application types that run on cloud environments. Next, we define a general model for describing the interconnection network topology of tree-based data centers. Finally, a power model is introduced to estimate the power consumption of physical servers and switches.

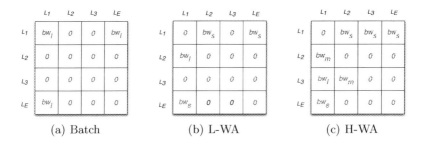

Fig. 1. Simplification of the communication matrix for each application type (defined per layer instead of per VM)

3.1 Modeling Applications

A cloud environment is suitable to run a diversity of applications, formed by a collection of VMs typically organized in one or more layers. The way VMs communicate among them determine the communication pattern of the application.

We propose a simple model that allows us to represent the structure of any kind of application providing a few parameters: number of layers of the application (L), the number of VMs in each layer (N_i being i the layer identifier) and a matrix of the communication needs (or bandwidth, measured in Mb/s) between each pair of VMs i and j ($BW = [bw_{i,j}]$) and with the external world.

For this work, we particularize this model to define two classes of applications: (1) batch jobs, typical of scientific workloads, and (2) web applications. Batch jobs represent the execution of parallel applications, or workflows comprising parallel tasks. The main characteristic of a batch job is the intense internal communication (between tasks-VMs of the same application). In this work, we model them as a single-layer application, with communications following patterns such as all-to-all, neighbour-to-neighbour in a 2D (virtual) arrangement, and neighbour-to-neighbour in 3D.

Web applications are usually implemented using a three-layer architecture: a load balancer that receives end-user requests, a business layer that processes those requests (and replies to them), a and database (DB) or persistence layer. The load balancer distributes the input requests evenly along the VMs of the business layer; it may be implemented on a hardware device, or as a DNS-based redirection—thus, we do not include it in the application model. The number of VMs at the persistence layer depends on the database requirements of the applications. A light workload can be managed by a single DB server that supports both read and write operations; we represent this class of applications as *L-WA*. For applications with heavy database demands (*H-WA*), a master-slave replication scheme may be applied: one of the VMs of the persistence layer is the *master* node that processes all the write operations, while the queries (read operations) are evenly distributed along the remaining VMs in the layer. Whenever a change (write) is done on the master node, it is propagated to the read VMs.

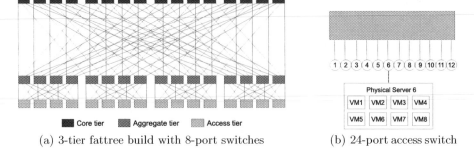

(a) 3-tier fattree build with 8-port switches   (b) 24-port access switch

Fig. 2. Representation of the physical configuration of a data center (network and servers)

IaaS providers offer different types of VMs, with different resource sets. In this work, we will consider small, medium and large instances, with different characteristics only in terms of allotted network bandwidth (in Mb/s): bw_s=50, bw_m=150 and bw_l=300, respectively. Our batch applications use a single layer L_1 of large instances. For L-WA web applications, the business layer (L_1) uses small instances and the database is represented as a single, large VM in layer (L_2). For H-WA applications, the database is modelled as a L_2 layer for reading, with several medium-size VMs, and a single-VM (of large size) layer L_3 for writing. Figure 1 shows the communication pattern between layers for each application type, that is reflected on the BW matrix. The additional layer L_E represents the traffic to/from the Internet and the application itself.

3.2   Describing the Data Center Structure

As stated before, current data centers are usually built using tree-based topologies, such as fat tree and VL-2 [11]. This kind of networks are composed of several tiers of switches (we assume homogeneous switches) and several servers connected to the bottom tier of the tree (the edge or access tier). Each server is divided into several *slots*, where each slot can be a fraction of a core, an entire core or several cores. Application VMs are assigned to different slots of the data center servers. Throughout this work we assume that a VM consumes a slot, and that one slot is equivalent to one core of a multi-core server.

The physical configuration of a data center is defined as the number of servers (P), the number of cores per server (C_p) and the network topology. In particular, a tree-based topology is defined by the number of uplinks and downlinks of the switches $(S_{up}$ and $S_{down})$, the bandwidth (Mb/s) offered by each switch port (S_{bw}) and the number of tiers of the tree (T). The communication latency between two cores i and j depends on the distance between them, measured in terms of *hops*. Matrix $D = [d_{i,j}]$ defines the distance between any pair of cores (actually, the servers to which they belong).

We have focused on data centers built using fat trees as interconnection network, composed of three tiers (as depicted in Figure 2(a)) with the same

Table 1. Parameter values of energy utilization in physical servers and switches

	Consumption at	Server value (W)	Switch value (W)
E_{max}	100% utilization	200	100
E_{idle}	Idle state	10	10
E_{active}	One active core/port	160	31
E_{rem}	Remaining $U_{active} - 1$ cores/ports	40	69

number of switches in each one of them (see Figure 2(b)). We consider that core switches are directly connected to the Internet. In this kind of tree the distance between two servers (matrix D) is computed as follows: cores in the same physical server are at distance 0; servers connected to the same access switch are at distance 2; if aggregation or core switches are required, distance grows to 4 and 6 respectively. The physical configuration of the data center used in this work is: ($P = 1728$ servers, $C_p = 8$ cores, $T = 3$ tiers, $S_{up} = 12$ ports, $S_{down} = 12$ ports, $S_{bw} = 1000$ Mb/s).

3.3 Modeling Power Requirements

Energy is consumed by servers and switches, and also by cooling and energy distribution systems. Reducing power use has direct benefits for the infrastructure provider (lowering the energy bill), while reducing the data center carbon footprint.

PowerNap [10] aims to reduce the consumption of unused servers by switching off memory, disk and other elements. In this work we assume that a strategy like this is used in the data center: unloaded servers and switches operate in an idle state that minimizes energy waste. We define a general model of power utilization of a device (server or switch), inspired in the one provided in [10].

$$E = \begin{cases} E_{idle} & U_{active} = 0 \\ E_{active} + \frac{E_{rem} \cdot (U_{active} - 1)}{U_{total} - 1} & U_{active} > 0 \end{cases}$$

The energy consumption E of a server/switch (in Watts) depends on the number of active cores or ports U_{active}. At idle state, the consumption is equal to E_{idle}. The transition from the idle state to the activation of the first core/port implies an important increase in the energy utilization, because it requires turning on other resources (memory, disk) or internal fans. The consumption of each additional, active core/port is directly proportional to the active number of cores/ports. Table 1 shows the energy consumption values used in this work, for both servers and switches. Values for servers are based on those in [10].

4 Topology-Aware Optimization

The aim of this work is to find a suitable placement for the VMs forming an application onto a set of available cores (slots) in the data center servers. We perform an initial selection of free cores using FF or RR (see Section 5); then, a bi-objective optimization algorithm fine-tunes the VM placement taking into account the communication needs of the application—and the corresponding cost considering the assigned cores and the topology of the data center network.

4.1 Problem Definition

Given an application A with a VM set V of size N, and a subset of available cores $C' \subset C$, where C is the whole set of cores in the data center (note that usually $|C'| >> N$), the VM placement problem involves finding a mapping function φ that assigns each VM, $v \in V$ to a core $c \in C'$:

$$\varphi : V \to C'$$
$$v \mapsto \varphi(v) = c$$

A solution of the VM placement problem has the form $s = (c_1, c_2, \ldots, c_N)$ representing that the VM i has been assigned to core c_i.

Two major selection criteria will be considered to choose a VM placement. First, we favor solutions that minimize communication latency. For this reason, the VM placement will try to allocate the most communicative VMs onto physically close cores, in terms of network distance. The second criterion focuses on reducing the number of servers allocated to the application. An allocation solution that fulfills the first criterion may not satisfy the second one. For example, given an application $A = \{v_1, v_2, v_3, v_4\}$ in which communication occurs between v_1-v_2 and v_3-v_4, the first criterion may place each pair of VMs on a different physical server. However, according to the second criterion, it would be better to place all the VMs in the same server. Both criteria try to improve the use of data center resources, by means of reducing the number of active servers and switches, but the first one specifically tries to benefit the application, optimizing its performance. Placement solutions must obey a restriction: external communication demands by all the VMs assigned to a server cannot exceed the bandwidth of its network link S_{bw}. This constraint does not take into account communication between VMs in the same server.

More formally, we describe VM placement as a bi-objective optimization problem subject to one constraint. The first objective function to minimize is defined as follows:

$$f_1 : \sum_{i,j \in V}^{N} bw_{i,j} \cdot d_{s(i),s(j)} \tag{1}$$

where $d_{s(i),s(j)}$ is the distance between the cores assigned to VMs i and j and $bw_{i,j}$ is the bandwidth required by VMs i and j.

Given the function $\sigma(c) = p$ that returns the server p to which core c belongs to, and a solution s, we define the set of active servers for this solution as $P^s = \{p | \exists i \in \{1, \ldots, N\} \text{ s.t. } \sigma(s(i)) = p\}$. The second objective function to minimize is defined as:

$$f_2 : |P^s| \tag{2}$$

The solutions are subject to the following constraint:

$$\forall p \in P^s : S_{bw} - S^p_{bw} \geq 0 \tag{3}$$

where S_{bw} is the bandwidth available for each physical server and S^p_{bw} is the reserved bandwidth of server i, considering the previously allocated applications and also the new one.

4.2 Multi-objective Optimization with NSGA-II

We have chosen the evolutionary algorithm NSGA-II [6] to solve the multi-objective VM placement problem. A solution or individual is represented as a vector that assigns each VM of the application to one available core. After generating an initial population of N_{pop} individuals, an offspring is created from it applying a crossover and a mutation operator with probability p_{cross} and p_{mut} respectively. The resulting population $2N_{pop}$ is sorted, in order to select the best N_{pop} individuals for the next generation. These steps are iterated along N_{gen} generations. For further information about NSGA-II, please refer to [6].

Guided Crossover. The crossover operator is applied with probability p_{cross}. It combines two individuals to generate a new one, considering the specific characteristics of the problem. Given two parents s_1 and s_2 the crossover operator generates a new child ch as follows. We define $\phi(i, s)$ as the communication cost of VM i in a candidate solution s, considering all the destinations with which it communicates, the corresponding input/output bandwidths, and the distances:

$$\forall i \in \{1, \ldots, N\} : \phi(i, s) = \sum_{j=1, j \neq i}^{N} (bw_{i,j} + bw_{j,i}) \cdot d_{s(i),s(j)} \tag{4}$$

Child ch will be constructed taking from the parents those cores that cause the lowest communication cost. That is, for each VM i, if $\phi(i, s_1) < \phi(i, s_2)$, then core $s_1(i)$ is assigned to VM i of child ch. A correction step to remove any possible repeated position (cores) of each child may be required.

Guided Mutation. The mutation is applied with a probability p_{mut}. There are two types of mutation, that are selected based on another probability p_{mtype}. The first type performs a simple swap between any two elements of the chosen solution, without considering cores in the same server because this change would not affect the values of the objective functions. With probability $1\text{-}p_{mtype}$, the second type of mutation is applied: one of the cores assigned to the solution is replaced with any free core c from the whole network C, selected randomly using a distance-based distribution that favors physically close cores.

Selection Criterion for Solutions in the Pareto Front. The bi-objective optimization algorithm generates a collection of solutions for a given application (Pareto set), with different trade-offs between locality and number of allocated servers. As all Pareto optimal solutions are considered equally good, a selection criterion is required to choose one. We select the solution that is most beneficial for the provider: one that minimizes the *global* number of active servers in the data center P_{active}.

5   Experimental Framework

This section presents the experimental framework used to evaluate the VM placement strategies. The experiments have been performed using an in-house developed scheduling simulator. The initial mapping is generated with a topology-agnostic approach: FF that searches free cores sequentially, always starting at the first one, or RR that also performs a sequential search but starting from the last core used in the previous placement. We then apply the multi-objective optimization over this set of cores. Using this set, the initial population for NSGA-II is generated performing random reorderings of the cores. In all, four VM placement algorithms are considered: FF and RR, without and with optimization, in all cases obeying the bandwidth constraint.

Three initial workload scenarios have been considered, designed to generate low (25%), medium (50%) and high (75%) use of data center resources (servers). Each scenario consists of a sequence of arrival/departure operations (new applications, applications that end). Experiments carried out in the simulator are divided into two phases: first, a warming up until the target load of the scenario is reached and the system arrives to an steady state; then, 10 batches with sets of 1000 operations (equally distributed between arrivals and departures). The simulator gathers different per-batch metrics.

NSGA-II has been used with these parameters: $N_{pop}=100$, $N_{gen}=100$, $p_{cross}=0.8$, $p_{mut}=0.8$ and $p_{mtype}=0.5$. Parameter tuning for the optimization process falls outside the scope of this work. For this parameter configuration, a run of NGSA-II in a desktop PC takes on average just 3". Given the Stochastic nature of the NSGA-II algorithm, we perform five repetitions for each scenario, using the same list of operations as input. Results gathered in the tables are obtained by calculating the mean of those repetitions.

6   Analysis of Results

In this section we discuss the results provided by the simulator, with special focus on the effects that the different placement policies have on applications (which policy is most beneficial in terms of improving communications locality?) and the data center (which policy uses less resources and, therefore, requires less power?). Two approaches are compared, topology-agnostic RR/FF (Without Optimization, WO) and topology-aware RR/FF (with Optimization, O).

Table 2. Values of objective functions, WO - Without Optimization, O - with Optimization

		First fit				Round Robin			
		μ_{f_1}	σ_{f_1}	μ_{f_2}	σ_{f_2}	μ_{f_1}	σ_{f_1}	μ_{f_2}	σ_{f_2}
High	WO	264316.60	32567.10	14.40	2.42	174689.20	19749.78	10.40	0.49
	O	225017.80	32522.66	14.20	2.14	145600.60	18661.38	9.40	0.49
Medium	WO	296971.20	18588.08	16.40	3.26	172445.80	11480.79	8.60	0.49
	O	257856.60	20687.72	15.80	3.12	148800.00	11933.78	8.00	0.00
Low	WO	278839.00	10491.40	19.60	4.08	159689.60	6721.03	7.80	0.40
	O	240159.00	12813.12	17.80	3.37	138890.00	7062.93	7.00	0.00

6.1 Application-Related Metrics

Table 2 gathers the mean μ and standard deviation σ of both objective functions f_1 (communications locality) and f_2 (number of servers assigned to the application). If we focus on topology-agnostic policies, clearly RR is better for applications, as it provides lower communication costs than FF in all scenarios (see f_1 values), while simultaneously providing better (smaller) f_2 values (number of servers per application). The most relevant result, though, is that applying optimization improves values of both objective functions for FF and also for RR.

6.2 Data Center-Related Metrics

The objective functions were designed to have a positive impact on the whole data center as well as on applications. This section evaluates the impact in terms of the number of active physical servers and the power consumption.

Table 3 contains the number of active servers P_{active}. P_{min} is the minimum number of servers that would be necessary to allocate all applications. So, the cost in terms of servers of each VM placement policy can be evaluated as the extra number of servers used relative to P_{min}. FF policy obtains a lower number of extra servers than RR, thus being more appealing for the IaaS provider. The use of optimization makes this number even lower (P_{dif}), while simultaneously improving application-related characteristics.

These benefits in terms of number of active servers translate immediately into lower power requirements for servers. But optimization is focused on communications, and benefits are also expected in terms of reduction of the power required for switching. We have used the energy models described previously to measure power requirements, separately for servers/switches, and total. Results are summarized in Table 4. We see that RR requires more power than FF for servers (globally it uses more servers) but less for switches (makes better use of the network, because individual applications are allocated in fewer servers, and the upper-tier switches are used less). Using optimization we are able to improve both figures and, therefore, the total power required by the data center.

Table 3. Number of active servers in the data center used by the different VM placement strategies

		P_{min}	First fit			Round Robin		
			P_{active}	P_{active}-P_{min}	P_{dif}	P_{active}	P_{active}-P_{min}	P_{dif}
High	WO	1311	1461.20	150.20	33.40	1601.80	290.80	17.60
	O		1427.80	**116.80**		1584.20	**273.20**	
Medium	WO	871	988.20	117.20	22.00	1193.80	322.80	36.40
	O		966.20	**95.20**		1157.40	**286.40**	
Low	WO	429	492.00	63.00	9.40	605.20	176.20	21.20
	O		482.40	**53.40**		584.00	**155.00**	

Table 4. Energy consumption (in Watts) of physical servers and switches. O^* values represent the energy savings with respect to the WO approach.

		First fit			Round Robin		
		E_{server}	E_{switch}	E_{total}	E_{server}	E_{switch}	E_{total}
High	WO	287532.5	30359.4	317891.9	307835.8	24397.9	332233.7
	O^*	4858.7	1322.8	6181.5	2547.7	1412.9	3960.6
Medium	WO	199533.5	22097.8	221631.2	229187.8	17927.0	247114.8
	O^*	3193.2	651.4	3844.6	5256.8	1587.5	6844.4
Low	WO	108183.5	13317.1	121500.6	124508.5	10942.6	135451.1
	O^*	1385.8	325.6	1711.5	3010.6	913.9	3924.5

7 Conclusions and Future Work

Throughout this paper we have demonstrated that a IaaS provider can improve the VM placement policy in use by applying an optimization strategy, with benefits not only for the provider but also for the user. And this optimization can be done at a negligible cost: it is applied when allocating a new application, and it takes a few seconds. Benefits for the provider are measured in terms of used servers and switches, and immediately translate into power demands (resulting in a greener use of the data center). Benefits for the applications are achieved by reducing communication latencies.

This work can be improved in several aspects. One of them is taking into account that providers usually over-subscribe resources: users rarely exploit the 100% of the assigned resources (including cores, memory, network bandwidth, etc.) Therefore it is common practice to assign to a server "extra" slots. This practice rarely affects the QoS perceived by users, although it has to be carefully monitored in the rare event aggregated actual demands exceed server capacity. VM migration is the common solution to this problem, but it does not come for free: it affects QoS and network utilization. We plan to introduce over-subscription and VM migration in our models and experiments.

The elastic capacity of cloud environments allows the applications to dynamically scale the acquired resources (the number of VMs in horizontal scaling) depending on the input workload. Thus, the number of VMs will vary with time and the infrastructure provider should be able to optimize not only the initial placement, but also the addition of new VMs. We plan to adapt our proposal to deal with auto-scalable applications.

Acknowledgments. This work has been partially supported by the Saiotek and Research Groups 2013-2018 (IT-609-13) programs (Basque Government), TIN2013-41272P and COMBIOMED network in computational biomedicine (Carlos III Health Institute). Dr. Pascual is supported by a postdoctoral grant of the UPV/EHU. Mrs Lorido-Botran is supported by a doctoral grant from the Basque Government. Prof. Miguel-Alonso is a member of the HiPEAC European Network of Excellence.

References

1. Eucalyptus, http://www.eucalyptus.com/
2. IBM Workload Deployer, http://www.ibm.com/software/products/us/en/workload-deployer
3. NetIQ PlateSpin Recon, https://www.netiq.com/products/recon/
4. OpenNebula, http://opennebula.org/
5. VMware Capacity Planner, http://www.vmware.com/products/capacity-planner/
6. Deb, K., Pratap, A., Agarwal, S., Meyarivan, T.: A fast and elitist multiobjective genetic algorithm: NSGA-II. IEEE Transactions on Evolutionary Computation **6**(2), 182–197 (2002)
7. Fan, P., Chen, Z., Wang, J., Zheng, Z.: Online Optimization of VM Deployment in IaaS Cloud, In: ICPADS. pp. 760–765 (2012)
8. Georgiou, S., Tsakalozos, K., Delis, A.: Exploiting Network-Topology Awareness for VM Placement in IaaS Clouds, In: CGC. pp. 151–158 (2013)
9. Mann, V., Kumar, A., Dutta, P., Kalyanaraman, S.: VMFlow: leveraging vm mobility to reduce network power costs in data centers. In: Domingo-Pascual, J., Manzoni, P., Palazzo, S., Pont, A., Scoglio, C. (eds.) NETWORKING 2011, Part I. LNCS, vol. 6640, pp. 198–211. Springer, Heidelberg (2011)
10. Meisner, D., Gold, B., Wenisch, T.: PowerNap: eliminating server idle power. ACM SIGPLAN Notices **44**(3), 205–216 (2009)
11. Meng, X., Pappas, V., Zhang, L.: Improving the Scalability of Data Center Networks with Traffic-aware Virtual Machine Placement. In: IEEE INFOCOM. pp. 1154–1162 (March, 2010)
12. Wo, T., Sun, Q., Li, B., Hu, C.: Overbooking-Based Resource Allocation in Virtualized Data Center. In: ISORCW, pp. 142–149 (2012)

GridVis: Visualisation of Island-Based Parallel Genetic Algorithms

Evelyne Lutton[1]([✉]), Hugo Gilbert[2], Waldo Cancino[3], Benjamin Bach[3],
Pierre Parrend[4,5], and Pierre Collet[4]

[1] INRA, UMR GMPA, 1 Av. Brétignières, 78850 Thiverval-Grignon, France
evelyne.lutton@grignon.inra.fr
[2] ENSTA ParisTech, 828, Boulevard des Maréchaux, 91762 Palaiseau Cedex, France
hugo.gilbert@ensta-paristech.fr
[3] INRIA Saclay-Ile-de-France, AVIZ team, Bâtiment 660, 91405 Orsay Cedex, France
waldo.cancino@gmail.com, benjamin.bach@inria.fr
[4] ICube laboratory, Strasbourg University, and ECCE, CS-DC UNESCO UniTwin,
7, rue René Descartes, 67084 Strasbourg, France
pierre.collet@unistra.fr
[5] Schiltigheim, ECAM Strasbourg-Europe 2, Rue de Madrid CS 20013, 67012,
Strasbourg Cedex, France
pierre.parrend@ecam-strasbourg.eu

Abstract. Island Model parallel genetic algorithms rely on various migration models and their associated parameter settings. A fine understanding of how the islands interact and exchange informations is an important issue for the design of efficient algorithms. This article presents GridVis, an interactive tool for visualising the exchange of individuals and the propagation of fitness values between islands. We performed several experiments on a grid and on a cluster to evaluate GridVis' ability to visualise the activity of each machine and the communication flow between machines. Experiments have been made on the optimisation of a Weierstrass function using the EASEA language, with two schemes: a scheme based on uniform islands and another based on specialised islands (Exploitation, Exploration and Storage Islands).

Keywords: Parallel evolutionary algorithms · Island model · Visualisation · EASEA · Grid model

1 Introduction

Island Models are a popular way to parallelise Evolutionary Algorithms: The classical evolutionary model of a single population that performs a community search on an unknown search space is replaced by a set of subpopulations, living their own life in parallel on different machines. This scheme is another way to control the balance between diversity preservation and focus of search:

This work has been funded by the French National Agency for research (ANR), under the grant ANR-11-EMMA-0017, EASEA-Cloud Emergence project 2011, http://www.agence-nationale-recherche.fr/

A.I. Esparcia-Alcázar et al. (Eds.): EvoApplications 2014, LNCS 8602, pp. 702–713, 2014.
DOI: 10.1007/978-3-662-45523-4_57

- It has been proved that having multiple subpopulations helps to preserve genetic diversity, since each island can potentially follow a different search trajectory through the search space[1].
- Global search ability is maintained by periodically exchanging individuals between machines in a process called *migration*.

Migration is thus an important component of islands models, which is controlled by parameters, such as *migration interval* to set the number of generations between two migrations, and *migration size* to define the number of migrating individuals. Due to these additional parameters, it is obvious that a careful parameter setting is a condition to get efficient island models schemes. Theoretical and experimental studies may help to find typical settings, however *ad hoc* tuning remains the favourite method for addressing most of the real life optimisation problems. Visualisation of algorithmic behaviour is the approach that becomes more and more popular for this purpose, as soon as it is able to provide infomation in a condensed, visual, and easily interpretable way [2–4]. The visualisation of evolutionary algorithms is now drawing more and more attention in the community (see for instance the VizGec Workshop series at GECCO conference[1]), and specialised visualisation tools are distributed for various purpose (see Section 2).

In this paper, we present a visualisation tool specifically developed for island-based evolutionary algorithms, called GridVis. Thanks to the EASEA language, communications between machines are collected during execution into log files local to each machine, then grouped, and visualised after execution as a heatmap matrix. Various tools allow examining data at different scales with respect to groups of machines, time or fitness of individual exchanged. Detailed views of the activity of each machine (sending or receiving) are also available.

The remainder of this paper is organised as follows. Section 2 gives an overview of visualisation challenges for evolutionary algorithms, with a focus on what is specific to parallel evolutionary algorithms. Section 2 also presents the EASEA language and its parallel implementation based on an Island Model. GridVis is presented in Section 3, followed by an experimental analysis in Section 4. Results of our experiments are discussed in Section 4.2. Section 5 concludes our work and discusses future research directions.

2   Background

Visualising evolutionary algorithms (EA) is complex, since many different scales and many different objects need to be visualised. Existing tools fall into two major groups: *a)* off-line tools or post-mortem analysis, which try to give an image as precise as possible of all the phenomena which occured during one or several runs [5–8, 8–10], and *b)* on-line tools, which are usually less complex as they monitor what is currently happening during a run [11–15]. The following issues are desirable objectives for EA visualisation [7, 16–18], they consider different levels:

---

[1] http://www.vizgec.ex.ac.uk

- *Individual level:* How to visualise a solution to the problem: both genome and phenotype? How to deal with problem dependent data?
- *Population level:* How to display statistics, convergence, loss of diversity, and lineage of a good solution?
- *Process level:* How to highlight the effects of genetic operators and other parameter settings?
- *Output:* How to visualise the result, particularly in non-standard EAs like multi-objective or cooperative-coevolution EAs?

Visualising parallel and multi-population EAs is a topic which is explored only to a limited extend in the literature so far. For instance, Pohlheim [4] succinctely presents some tools to visualise sub populations and migration effects as 2D coloured plot diagrams.

Stakes in visualising generic parallel processes are depicted in particular in [19–21]. [20] underlines the importance of monitoring asynchronous, distributed algorithms on multiple processors for detecting inconsistencies in the algorithms, to get performance parameters and to develop a conceptual understanding of the algorithm's behaviour. Morrow and Gosh also highlight the computational cost of such a visualisation system if used on-line. Brown et al. [21] report on dynamic visualisations of parallel algorithms for a specific architecture (torus computers), based on a language for encoding optimisation algorithms.

This topic is tightly bound with a broader related research topic: program visualisation. [22], for instance, reports a survey (until 1993) and proposed a taxonomy of program visualisation tools (visualisations for performance tuning, debugging, teaching or understanding the behaviour of programs). A more recent survey of 18 different algorithm visualisation systems [23] focusses on their use in education. It seems clear that the use of a description language makes visualisations less dependent from architecture. GridVis has been developed in a similar spirit, based on the EASEA language described hereafter.

EASEA (for EAsy Specification of Evolutionary Algorithms) [24,25] was initially designed to assist users in producing an evolutionary algorithm from a given problem description. It is based on a C-like language that contains code for the genetic operators (crossover, mutation, initialisation and evaluation) and the genome structure. These functions are written in a dedicated description file, the *.ez file*. Out of them, EASEA generates a complete evolutionary algorithm with potential parallelisation of evaluation over GPGPUs[26], or over a cluster of heterogeneous machines, in the case of an island model. The generated source file for the evolutionary algorithm is user-readable. It can be used as-is, or as a primer, to be manually extended by an expert programmer.

The island model is an efficient and simple way to parallelise evolutionary algorithms [27], because it often results in important speedup. In a cluster of computers, every node, which can be seen as an island, runs a complete evolutionary algorithm, which can be seen as an island. A migration mechanism allows periodically exporting some individuals to the other nodes. EASEA implements islands using

- exchanges between nodes limited by the migration interval, *i.e.* the migration of one individual every n generations , and the migration size, the number of individuals that migrate. This protocol sets up a very lightweight asynchronous communication.
- a loosely connected model that is based on UDP, which allows parallelising over neighbour or distant machines (cluster or grid computing).

Extensions of EASEA to grid and cloud computing are currently under development through the EASEA-Cloud project[2].

3   GridVis

GridVis has been developed in Java, to monitor how the islands communicate: Which machines exchange individuals? When and how much individuals are exchanged? How fit are they? Which machines are the central ones? Are there clusters of exchange? We model the computer cluster that is running the island model, as dynamic network with weighted edges (number and fitness of individuals) and use an adjacency matrix for visualization (Figure 1(a)). Each computer in the cluster appears twice in the matrix, once as row and once as column. Cells in the matrix show information about the exchange between computers during evolution, for example, the amount of individuals exchanged (from row to column). Similar to heat maps [28], exchange is mapped to darkness. Darker cells indicate a higher exchange rate.

While matrix visualizations have recently been applied to dynamic networks [29,30], heatmap visualisations have been used for many different purposes. For evolutionary algorithms visualisation, they have been used for instance for facilitating the exploration and interpretation of Pareto fronts [31]. This visualization scheme has been chosen for the following reasons:

- *Visual simplicity*: Brigthness and colour perception is pre-attentive, and clusters of islands with high exchange rates appear close, due to row and column reordering optimisation.
- *Scalability*: Matrices are well suited for visualising large networks (typical clusters contain about 100 machines) and with many relations between machines (individuals are potentially exchanged between all machines) [32].

Figure 1 shows the GridVis display for a grid of 20 and 100 machines (islands), respectively. The number of individuals sent during a time interval $[t_{MIN}, t_{MAX}]$ from machine i to machine j is given by the grey level of cell (i,j) (white corresponds to no exchange, black is the highest count). Machines are identified by their names on row and columns. The time interval $[t_{MIN}, t_{MAX}]$, which determines the shown exchanges in the matrix, can be dynamically modified using sliders: independently for t_{MIN} (Figure 1(b)) and t_{MAX} (Figure 1(c,d)) and as

---

[2] ANR-11-EMMA-0017, Emergence project 2011, http://www.agence-nationale-recherche.fr/

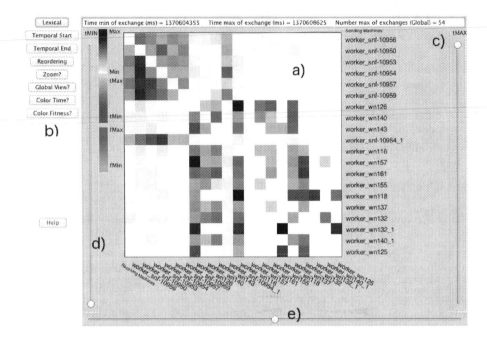

Fig. 1. GridVis Interface visualisation of a grid with 20 machines, using a matrix representation (a). User control is provided by (b) buttons to change the matrix row and column order, and (c,d,e) the shown time interval.

a sliding interval using the bottom bar (Figure 1(e)). Numerical values (in ms for the time) are given in the white frame above the heat map. The following options can be activated on demand, using the buttons in Figure 1(b):

- *Row and column reordering*: Rows and columns can be ordered (i) *lexically*, (ii) by time, or (iii) by similarity of activity. Lexical reordering consists in ordering according to line and column labels. Figure 2(a) illustrates a lexical reordering. The clusters (dark areas in the matrix), which appear using the lexical ordering, indicate that the algorithm choses machines for exchanging individuals, based on the machine's name; nodes of the first cluster had very different names from those of the second. *Temporal reordering* sorts the machines according to when the first individual was sent (Figure 2(b)). *Similarity ordering* tries to place machines (rows and columns) with similar exchange behaviour, close together in order to make sub-clusters of machines visually appearing as dark areas in the matrix. Our ordering optimisation is done using a Traveling Salesman problem (TSP) resolver that takes the number of exchanged individuals as similarity.
- *Zoom*: Individual machines can be selected to get a focussed view, which shows the selected machines only, while using the entire space in the matrix.
- *Grey level rescaling:* each cell has a grey value computed by interpolation between 0 and the maximal number of individuals exchanged in the current

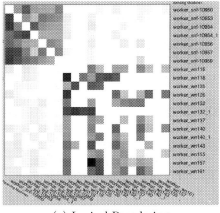 

(a) Lexical Reordering   (b) Temporal Reordering

Fig. 2. Examples for row and column reordering strategies in GridVis. (a) **Lexical reordering**: Here, individuals are almost exclusively exchanged between machines of similar names. (b) **Temporal Reordering**: Here, after a period of exchange between a group of machines (upper-left grey block), some machines worked alone at different times (cells appearing as vertical bars). This effect is due to the grid middelware (Glite) for which the choice of number of islands is controlled but not their synchronisation.

time interval. The grey values are dynamically rescaled when the time interval is changed. The "global view" button cancels this rescaling so that grey levels correspond to the absolute global count of each cell.

- *Colour representation*: The cell colour intensity still represents the number of individuals exchanged, while a colour scale from blue via purple and beige to orange (*time coloring*) represents the time at which the first individual has been exchanged (t_{MIN} is blue and t_{MAX} is orange) (Figure 5(a)). Alternately, the fitness of the exchanged individuals can be shown as a colour ranging from yellow (low fitness) via orange to red (high fitness) (*value encoding*). For each machine we indicate the average best fitness in the considered time interval on the matrix diagonal using that same colour encoding (Figure 5(b)).

Detailed views on the exchange between each pair of machines are available by clicking on the corresponding cell in the matrix. A bar chart as shown in Figure 3(a), indicates *when* individuals have been exchanged in the considered time interval (bars) and *how fit* they have been (colour and length of bars, encoded redundantly). For example, machine j in Figure 3(c) received during three periods, separated by interuptions. At the beginning of each period, many individuals with high fitness are exchanged (red bars). Then rapidly the fitness decreases (the aim is a minimisation of the fitness function). Each period corresponds to the start of a new block of machines. It is obvious that after a while

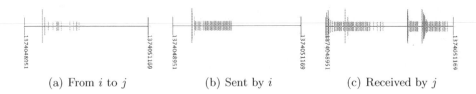

(a) From i to j (b) Sent by i (c) Received by j

Fig. 3. Detailed views visualizing individuals exchanged between two machines, i and j, over time (horizontal bar). Each vertical bar represents an individual, its position on the black horizontal line corresponds to when he was exchanged, received or sent, between t_{MIN} and t_{MAX}. The colours and widths of the bars corresponds to fitness value (long and red is high, short and green is low).

the fitness of exchanged individuals rapidly reaches again the best so far global fitness.

Likewise, clicking a machine's label in the matrix *columns*, shows the same chart indicating when and how much individuals the machine received from the grid (Figure 3(c)). Clicking a machine's name on a *row* shows what it sent (Figure 3(b)).

4   Experimental Analysis

4.1   Setup

Experiments were run using EASEA [33]. The test case aims at **minimising** a Weierstras test function with 10 variables. GridVis has been used to analyse two sets of experiments:

1. *EASEA-Grid experiments*, performed on the Complex Systems Virtual Organization of the European Grid Infrastructure (EGI). Experiments have been performed with 20 and 100 islands. Parameters are given in Table 1.
2. *EASEA-Cluster experiments*, performed on a 24-core machine. In this experiment 15 specialized islands (Exploitation, Exploration and Storage Islands) have been used, according to [24]. Table 2 displays the parameters of each type of island.

For each island connection events have been logged (timestamp, source, destination, individual to be transmitted and its fitness) for each sent/received individual throughout the execution. At the end of each experiment, log-files were collected and grouped in a single file to be displayed by GridVis.

4.2   Results

The *EASEA-Grid experiments* have been used to generate Figures 1 to 3, where de-synchronisation effects have been made evident using a temporal reordering, see figure 2(b). The second set of experiments is analysed below.

Table 1. Parameters for *EASEA-Grid*

Parameter	20-Islands	100-Islands
Nb of generations	1000	500
Population size	2048	512
Crossover probability	0.8	0.8
Mutation probability	0.3	0.3
Surviving parents	100%	100%
Surviving offspring	100%	100%
Elitism	Strong	Strong
Elite	1	1

Table 2. Parameters for *EASEA-Cluster*

| Parameter | Island type | | |
	Exploring	Exploiting	Storing
Nb of islands	10	4	1
Nb of generations	70	70	70
Population size	40	40	40
Mutation probability	0.8	0.7	0.3
Crossover probability	0.8	0.7	0.3
Surviving parents	100%	100%	100%
Surviving offspring	100%	100%	100%
Elitism	Weak	Strong	Strong
Elite	0	1	1

A first global view has been generated for *EASEA-cluster* on Figure 4. Machines 2930 to 2939 are exploring, machines 2940 to 2943 are exploiting, and a single storing machine is used (number 2944). A temporal reordering shows the three clusters (Figure 5(a)), and colour time and colour fitness views (Figures 5(a) and 5(b)) make the different roles of machines types clear.

The following exchange rules have been used *(a)* Exploring machines send their individuals to every machine except the storing machine. *(b)* Exploiting machines send their individuals to every machine except the exploring machines. *(c)* The storing machine receives individuals but does not send any individuals.

Figure 5(a) shows a large cluster of machines (the 10 exploring machines), related by blue cells. They communicate efficiently. The smaller cluster of exploiting machines is in brown, which makes evident that exploiting machines have been started after exploring machines. Figure 5(b) then shows that higher fitness individuals are exchanged in the small cluster of exploiting machines (darker cells), which is coherent with the respective role of exploring and exploiting machines.

Now, let us examine the content of exchanges: as a machine always sends its best individual, the fitness of this individual is an instantaneous image of the state of the corresponding island. Exploring machines decrease their fitness quickly at the beginning of the evolution and then stagnate (Figure 6*(a)*), while exploiting machines improve their solutions later (figures 6*(b)* and 6*(c)*). This

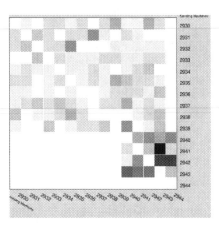

Fig. 4. *EASEA-cluster experiment*: global view for the 15 machines

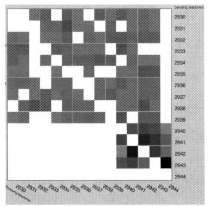

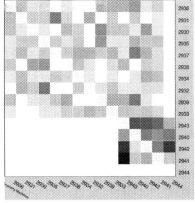

(a) Colour indicating time of interaction (from purple to orange).

(b) Colour indicating fitness (from yellow to red)

Fig. 5. *EASEA-cluster experiment* results. Rows and columns are ordered according to time.

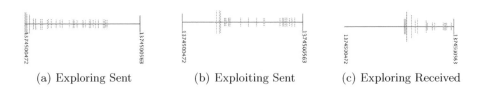

(a) Exploring Sent   (b) Exploiting Sent   (c) Exploring Received

Fig. 6. *EASEA-cluster experiments*: Individuals sent by an exploiting machine (a), sent (b) and received (c) by an exploring machine

fact can be verified on a view visualizing the end of the run (Figure 7): individuals that were sent by exploring machines are coloured red (indicating low performance) while better individuals are manipulated by the exploitation cluster. The role of the storing is to collect best results, it thus only receives dark yellow coloured individuals.

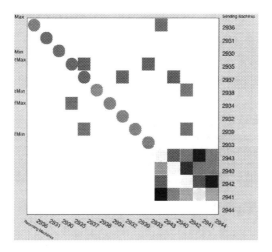

Fig. 7. *EASEA-cluster experiments*: Fitness information about the exchanges, zoom. Yellow areas correspond to better fitness (minisation aim).

5 Conclusions and Future Works

GridVis has proved to be a useful tool to understand the exchange of indivisuals in a grid or on a cluster of machines, runnig an island-based model. The activity of the machine is monitored and the time and quality of the exchanges are easily visualized. The kind of representation that GridVis offers helps the user with characterising a good launch on the grid, thus facilitates the parameters tuning task.

Future work will consider the development of GridVis for dynamic visusalisation, allowing on-line monitoring and parameter adjustments during execution. The integration of GridVis into a development framework based on EASEA for intensive computation purpose will also be considered (within the EASEA-Cloud Emergence project).

References

1. Whitley, D., Rana, S., Heckendorn, R.B.: The island model genetic algorithm: On separability, population size and convergence. Journal of Computing and Information Technology **7**, 33–48 (1999)
2. Lutton, E., Fekete, J.D.: Visual analytics of ea data. In: Genetic and Evolutionary Computation Conference, GECCO 2011. Dublin, Ireland (2011) July 12–16 (2011)

3. Lutton, E., Tonda, A., Gaucel, S., Foucquier, J., Riaublanc, A., Perrot, N.: Food model exploration through evolutionary optimization coupled with visualization: application to the prediction of a milk gel structure. In: From Model Foods to Food Models. DREAM Project's International Conference (June 2013)

4. Pohlheim, H.: AG, D.: Understanding the Course and State of Evolutionary Optimizations Using Visualization: Ten Years of Industry Experience with Evolutionary Algorithms. Artificial Life **12**, 217–227 (2006)

5. Spears, W.M.: An overview of multidimensional visualization techniques. In: Collins, T.D. (ed) Evolutionary Computation Visualization Workshop. Orlando, Florida, USA (1999)

6. Routen, T.: Techniques for the visualisation of genetic algorithms. The First IEEE Conference on Evolutionary Computation. **2**, 846–851 (1994)

7. Shine, W., Eick, C.: Visualizing the evolution of genetic algorithm search processes. In: Proceedings of 1997 IEEE International Conference on Evolutionary Computation, pp. 367–372, IEEE Press (1997)

8. Wu, A.S., Jong, K.A.D., Burke, D.S., Grefenstette, J.J., Ramsey, C.L.: Visual analysis of evolutionary algorithms. In: Proceedings of the 1999 Conference on Evolutionary Computation (CEC 1999). pp. 1419–1425, IEEE Press (1999)

9. Hart, E., Ross, P.: Gavel - a new tool for genetic algorithm visualization. IEEE Trans. Evolutionary Computation **5**(4), 335–348 (2001)

10. Mach, M., Zetakova, Z.: Visualising genetic algorithms: A way through the Labyrinth of search space. In: Sincak, P. - Vascak, J. - Kvasnicka, V. - Pospichal, J. (eds.) Intelligent Technologies - Theory and Applications. Amsterdam, pp. 279–285 IOS Press (2002)

11. Bedau, M.A., Joshi, S., Lillie, B.: Visualizing waves of evolutionary activity of alleles. In: Proceedings of the 1999 GECCO Workshop on Evolutionary Computation Visualization, pp. 96–98 (1999)

12. Bullock, S., Bedau, M.A.: Exploring the dynamics of adaptation with evolutionary activity plots. Artif. Life **12**, 193–197 (2006)

13. Pohlheim, H.: Visualization of evolutionary algorithms - set of standard techniques and multidimensional visualization. In: GECCO 1999 - Proceedings of the Genetic and Evolutionary Computation Conference, San Francisco. CA. pp. 533–540 (1999)

14. Pohlheim, H.: Geatbx - genetic and evolutionary algorithm toolbox for matlab http://www.geatbx.com/

15. Computer, A.K., Kerren, A.: Eavis: A visualization tool for evolutionary algorithms. In: Proceedings of the IEEE Symposium on Visual Languages and Human-Centric Computing. pp. 299–301 (VL/HCC 05 (2005)

16. Parmee, I., Abraham, J.: Supporting implicit learning via the visualisation of coga multi-objective data. In: CEC2004, Congress on Evolutionary Computation, 19–23 June. Volume 1. pp. 395–402 (2004)

17. Collins, T.D.: In: Visualizing evolutionary computation, pp. 95–116. Springer-Verlag New York Inc, New York, NY, USA (2003)

18. Daida, J., Hilss, A., Ward, D., Long, S.: Visualizing tree structures in genetic programming. Genetic Programming and Evolvable Machines **6**, 79–110 (2005)

19. Kohl, J., Casavant, T.: A software engineering, visualization methodology for parallel processing systems. In: Proceedings., Sixteenth Annual International Computer Software and Applications Conference, 1992. COMPSAC 1992. pp. 51–56 (1992)

20. Morrow, T.M., Ghosh, S.: Divide: Distributed visual display of the execution of asynchronous, distributed algorithms on loosely-coupled parallel processors. In: Proceedings Visualization 1993, pp. 166–173 IEEE Computer Society Press (1993)

21. Brown, J., Martin, P., Paku, N., Turner, G.: Visualisations of parallel algorithms for reconfigurable torus computers. In: Proceedings 1998 Australasian Computer Human Interaction Conference, 1998. pp. 152–159 (1998)

22. Price, B.A., Baecker, R., Small, I.S.: A principled taxonomy of software visualization. J. Vis. Lang. Comput. **4**(3), 211–266 (1993)

23. Urquiza-Fuentes, J., Velázquez-Iturbide, J.A.: A survey of successful evaluations of program visualization and algorithm animation systems. Trans. Comput. Educ. **9**(2) (June 2009) 9:1–9:21

24. Maitre, O., Krueger, F., Querry, S., Lachiche, N., Collet, P.: Easea: specification and execution of evolutionary algorithms on gpgpu. Soft Computing **16**(2), 261–279 (2012)

25. Collet, P., Lutton, E., Schoenauer, M., Louchet, J.: Take it EASEA. In: Schoenauer, M., Deb, K., Rudolf, G., Yao, X., Lutton, E., J.J., M., Schwefel, H.P., eds.: Parallel Problem Solving from Nature - PPSN VI 6th International Conference, Paris, France, Springer Verlag (September 16–20 2000) LNCS (1917)

26. Tsutsui, S., Collet, P.: Massively Parallel Evolutionary Computation on Gpgpus. Natural Computing Series, Springer-Verlag New York Incorporated (2013)

27. Alba, E., Tomasini, M.: Parallelism and evolutionary algorithms. IEEE Transactions on Evolutionary Computation **6**(5), 443–462 (2002)

28. Wilkinson, L., Friendly, M.: The history of the cluster heat map. The American Statistician **63**(2), 179–184 (2009)

29. Brandes, U., Nick, B.: Asymmetric relations in longitudinal social networks. IEEE Transactions on Visualization and Computer Graphics **17**(12), 2283–2290 (2011)

30. Bach, B., Pietriga, E., Fekete, J.D.: Visualizing Dynamic Networks with Matrix Cubes. In: SICCHI Conference on Human Factors in Computing Systems (CHI), Toronto, Canada, ACM (April 2014)

31. Pryke, A., Mostaghim, S., Nazemi, A.: Heatmap visualization of population based multi objective algorithms. In: Obayashi, S., Deb, K., Poloni, C., Hiroyasu, T., Murata, T. (eds.) EMO 2007. LNCS, vol. 4403, pp. 361–375. Springer, Heidelberg (2007)

32. Ghoniem, M., Fekete, J.D., Castagliola, P.: A comparison of the readability of graphs using node-link and matrix-based representations. In: Proceedings of the IEEE Symposium on Information Visualization. INFOVIS '04, Washington, DC, USA, IEEE Computer Society pp. 17–24 (2004)

33. Lutton, E., Collet, P., Louchet, J.: EASEA comparisons on test functions: Galib versus eo. In: EA01 Conference on Artificial Evolution, Le Creusot, France (October 2001)

Automated Framework for General-Purpose Genetic Algorithms in FPGAs

Liucheng Guo[1]([✉]), David B. Thomas[1], and Wayne Luk[2]

[1] Department of EEE, Imperial College London, London, UK
{gl512,dt10}@ic.ac.uk
[2] Department of Computing, Imperial College London, London, UK
w.luk@ic.ac.uk

Abstract. FPGA-based Genetic Algorithms (GAs) have been effective for optimisation of many real-world applications, but require extensive customisation of the hardware GA architecture. To promote these accelerated GAs to potential users without hardware design experience, this paper proposes an automated framework for creating and executing general-purpose GAs in FPGAs. The framework contains a scalable and customisable hardware architecture, which provides a unified platform for both binary and real-valued chromosomes. At compile-time, a user only needs to provide a high-level specification of the target application, without writing any hardware-specific code in low-level languages such as VHDL or Verilog. At run-time, a user can tune application inputs and GA parameters without time-consuming recompilation, in order to find a good configuration for further GA executions. The framework is demonstrated on a high performance FPGA platform to solve six problems and benchmarks, including a locating problem and the NP-hard set covering problem. Experiments show our custom GA is more flexible and easier to use compared to existing FPGA-based GAs, and achieves an average speed-up of 30 times compared to a multi-core CPU.

Keywords: Genetic Algorithm · FPGA · Automated Framework

1 Introduction

Genetic algorithms (GAs) are a class of optimisation technique, inspired by natural selection and genetics. GAs have been used to solve an extremely wide range of problems where other methods experience difficulties, including combinatorial optimisation and real-valued parameter estimation [4]. However, complex problems often require many generations to produce a satisfactory solution, meaning CPU-based GAs are often too slow to handle them. CPU-based GAs are also not suitable for many real-time applications due to the unacceptable latency [15].

In order to accelerate GAs, some researchers have adapted them to field programmable gate arrays (FPGAs) [13]. These FPGA-based GAs are shown to be faster than CPU-based GAs in solving many real-world applications [10]. However, existing hardware GAs are mainly written in low-level hardware languages

© Springer-Verlag Berlin Heidelberg 2014
A.I. Esparcia-Alcázar et al. (Eds.): EvoApplications 2014, LNCS 8602, pp. 714–725, 2014.
DOI: 10.1007/978-3-662-45523-4_58

like VHDL or Verilog, that require in-depth knowledge of FPGA architecture and hardware programming. Another problem is that most existing FPGA-based GAs only support one type of chromosome, either binary or real-valued, thus the applicability is limited. To address these issues, this paper proposes an automated unified framework for FPGA-based GAs. The contributions are as follows:

- An automated framework for creating and executing general-purpose GAs in FPGAs: based on user-defined high-level description of an application, the low-level hardware design is generated automatically (section 3.1).
- A novel FPGA architecture for custom GAs: the design is both scalable and customisable, providing a unified platform for both binary and real-valued chromosomes, and also allowing a user to change the parallelism of the architecture (section 3.2 and 3.3).
- A run-time tuning framework: GA parameters and application inputs are changeable without time-consuming recompilation, thus a user is able to tune GA parameters to improve solution quality for future executions with different application parameters (section 4).
- A qualitative comparison of our custom GA with existing FPGA-based designs, showing improved flexibility in hardware architecture and run-time tuning, and increased ability to support complex applications (section 5).
- A quantitative comparison of the accelerated FPGA framework with multi-core CPU, including all I/O and initialisation costs, showing an average speed-up of 30 times while finding the same solutions for six different applications and benchmarks (section 6).

2   Background and Related Work

2.1   Genetic Algorithm

When solving a specific application, GA evolves a population of candidate solutions called individuals towards a better fitness. Before using GA, a user needs to: 1) design the chromosome of an individual; and 2) define the fitness or evaluation function to check the quality of the chromosome. A chromosome contains one or more variables, and is commonly represented as a binary or real values [14]. When the variables are naturally quantized, binary encoding is used to represent chromosomes (called binary GA); when they are continuous, it is more logical to use real values (called real-valued or continuous GA) [12]. The encoding of a chromosome also affects the methods selected for genetic operators, including selection, crossover and mutation.

2.2   Reconfigurable Computing

Many applications have a requirement for high performance. Application-specific integrated circuits (ASICs) are customised for high performance, but they are not flexible after manufacture. Microprocessors provide high flexibility but the performance is likely to be lower than ASICs. Recently, reconfigurable computing that involves FPGAs, combines the flexibility of microprocessors and efficiency of ASICs. The FPGAs contain logic gates and small random-access memories, called Block RAMs (BRAM), which can be configured for specific applications during the compilation process, including synthesis, map, place and route.

However, unlike software, the compilation process is very time consuming and often takes hours to complete, so it is not practical to frequently modify hardware designs. Another big challenge is programmability of FPGAs, as an algorithm needs to be written in low-level hardware languages like VHDL or Verilog, describing registers and logic gates. There are some high-level compilation tools which can reduce the programming effort [7], but even with these tools, it is still difficult for a user without hardware knowledge to create fast and efficient FPGA designs. However, these tools can provide a good intermediate-level target for customisable frameworks, such as our GA system.

2.3   Previous FPGA-Based GAs

GAs have been adapted to FPGAs for improved performance. Since the first reported FPGA-based design [13], there have been many hardware GAs proven to be effective in real-time applications [1,2,6,8–10,13,15]. There are two types of FPGA-based GAs: the application-specific ones are tailored to one specific application, with fixed chromosomes and specific genetic operators [6]; the general-purpose ones can support a wide range of chromosomes and genetic operators for different applications, which are the focus of this paper. For example, a general-purpose GA engine is demonstrated in [10], which shows speed-ups of 5 times over CPU for several GA benchmarks with only binary chromosomes.

However, these previous FPGA-based systems suffer from one or more limitations: 1) a user needs significant hardware architecture knowledge to apply an FPGA-based GA for an application; 2) the system usually supports only one type of chromosome, which is not suitable for different applications; 3) it is not easy to adjust the structure and resource usage, even for an expert, as most of the GA structure is fixed; 4) modifying either GA parameters or application parameters requires recompilation, which usually needs many hours to complete. To address these issues, we propose an automated unified framework for creating FPGA-based general-purpose GAs, which can be easily adapted for new combinatorial or real-valued applications.

3   Automated Framework for General-Purpose GAs

In our framework, a general-purpose GA architecture can be combined with high-level user-defined chromosome and fitness function, to produce a custom GA executable in hardware, providing high performance while retaining functional flexibility. A user without hardware design experience can easily create FPGA-based GA for an application with binary or real-valued chromosomes, and change both GA and application parameters at run-time without recompilation.

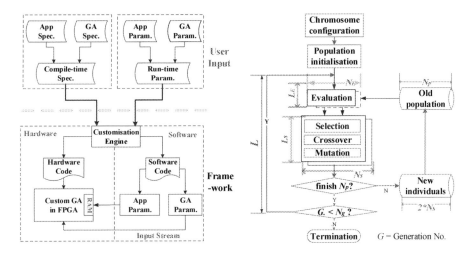

Fig. 1. Automated Framework   **Fig. 2.** Custom GA

3.1 Automated Framework

Figure. 1 provides an overview of the proposed automated framework, show-ing compile-time specification (Spec.) with software on the left, and run-time parameters (Param.) with hardware on the right. The framework requires no hardware programming from users, who only need to define the above high-level inputs for application (App.) and GA. Then the customisation engine, written in Python, automatically combines them and a number of existing files into: 1) hardware code with the compile-time specification, and 2) software code with the run-time parameters. The hardware code is then compiled by a high-level com-pilation tool Maxcompiler to low-level hardware implementation. At run-time the software transfers GA and application parameters to hardware, via input streams and on-chip memories to FPGA.

3.2 FPGA-Based Custom GA

Our framework provides a scalable hardware architecture for FPGA-based GA improved based on [6], which is called "custom GA" in this paper. Each custom GA contains all the hardware and configuration data in order to solve instances of a user's problem. Once compiled, the custom GA can be executed repeat-edly with different application parameters without recompilation, and allows GA parameters, such as mutation rate and random seed, to be varied during execution.

Our custom GA is functionally flexible and scalable, allowing a user to cus-tomise the architecture for hardware resource constraints. In custom GA, the steps of a typical GA are converted into hardware functional units, which are fully pipelined and parallelised. The main units of a custom GA are shown in Fig. 2, labelled by parameters described in Table 1 of section 4.

Chromosome Configuration. A user needs to define the chromosome as an individual in one population, which can be binary or real-valued. Our custom GA provides different genetic operators for the selected chromosome type.

Population Initialisation. The initial population is important in GA, as it may need many generations to produce high fitness individuals from low fitness ones. In our custom GA, there are two approaches to generate initial population. The first one is to use random numbers, which means the initial fitness depends on the random seeds. The second approach is to load a population previously generated by heuristics on a CPU, which is likely to mean a higher starting fitness. It can be transferred to on-chip RAM before execution begins.

Fitness Evaluation. In the custom GA, there are parallel evaluation units to reduce execution time. To simplify the hardware design effort, the fitness function is written in a high-level description language according to simple rules, described in section 4. Section 6 also gives some working examples for different functions.

Selection, Crossover and Mutation (SCM). Selection, crossover and muta-tion units in a custom GA are combined together into a SCM unit due to their close data coupling, making it easier to instantiate replicates for spatial parallelism. Our automated platform provides a extendable library containing different methods of selection, crossover and mutation, allowing a user to cus-tomise them for a specific application. As shown in Table 1, a user can choose the selection method from roulette wheel and tournament selection. For binary chromosomes, a user can select one-point or multi-point crossover to combine different parts from parents, and then choose binary mutation inverting bits in a chromosome. For real-valued chromosome, a user can select blending a crossover, which generates a new value based on a linear mixture of two parents [12], and use real-valued mutation to generate a random value in the range of variables.

It is usually necessary to tune crossover and mutation rates or types for high convergence speed, but in most previous FPGA-based GAs the adjustment requires hardware modification and recompilation, which takes many hours. In contrast, our framework allows users to modify these rates and types at run-time without recompilation (see the examples in section 6).

Random Number Generator. The random number generator plays an important role in many units, including population initialisation and SCM units. Currently the combined tausworthe generator [11], a simple but high-quality pseudo-random number generator, is used in the custom GA. The random seeds can be configured by users at run-time, to explore different number sequences.

3.3   Customisable Parallelism in Custom GA

Parallelism in architecture can reduce the execution time of GAs. As shown in Fig. 2, the number of parallel evaluation units is controlled by N_E, while

Table 1. The Parameters of GA (*C.T*: compile-time, *R.T*: run-time)

C.T.	N_E num of evaluation units	N_S num of SCM units
R.T.	N_g maximal generation	N_p population size
	R_m mutation rate	T_m mutation type ("binary", "real-valued")
	R_c crossover rate	T_c crossover type ("one-point", "multi-point",
	R_s random seed	"blending")
	I_p initial population	T_s selection type ("roulette wheel","tournament")

that of parallel SCM units is defined by N_S. A user can adjust the amount of parallelism by simply changing the two parameters in the input specification, and the framework will automatically compile them to an appropriate hardware.

In Fig. 2, N_p is the population size. If all the individuals in a population are evaluated in the cycle after filling the pipelines, there will be $N_E = N_p$ parallel evaluation instances. The feedback latency will be $L = L_E + L_S$, which are labelled on the left of Fig. 2. In this case, the resource usage will be very large when N_p is big. To solve this problem, we allow evaluation units to process a population over n cycles after filling the pipeline. Therefore, N_E is reduced to N_p/n, and the feedback latency for one generation will be $L' = L_E + L_S + n - 1$, which slightly decreases the performance if $(n-1)$ is far smaller than $L_E + L_S$.

In the same way, we can also adjust N_S to balance the resource usage of SCM units with performance. By tuning N_E and N_S according to the complexity of the evaluation and SCM units, our platform can support complex applications. An example in section 6 shows how this flexibility affects resources and performance.

3.4   Compilation and Execution Reports

There are two reports automatically generated by the framework during compilation and execution. The compilation report presents the results of hardware implementation to the user, including overall resource usage, clock frequency and errors. Errors may be related to the syntax of the input specification, or due to resource exhaustion. Based on the report, the user can decide whether to change N_E or N_S, depending on whether there are any free resources.

During execution, the FPGA will output the best fitness and solutions found over an FPGA-to-CPU stream, making the current best solution immediately available to software. The execution report shows how different configurations and parameters affect performance. It is essentially the "answer" to the problem the user wants to solve, and also contains information suggesting the best configuration for future executions of the problems with different parameters.

4   User Defined Input

When using the framework, users only needs to provide specifications and parameters for their applications and GA, as shown in Table 1. They are represented in a high-level domain specific language, which uses a sub-set of C. We describe the inputs in this section, and present examples in section 6.

Application Specification. There are two compile-time sections in the application specification: 1) $CHROMOSOME$, which describes the names and types of the data elements making up an chromosome; 2) $FITNESS$, which describes the fitness function used to evaluate individuals. The $CHROMOSOME$ sections is declarative, describing data structures, while the $FITNESS$ section contains imperative code, which can combine input parameters and a chromosome to produce a fitness value.

The fitness function is expressed using a sub-set of C which can be automatically compiled into a hardware implementation. The fitness function can contain all standard arithmetic operators (add, mul, etc.) as well as mathematical functions such as sin, log and exp. All components of the chromosome and application parameters are available as implicitly declared variables, which can be read either directly or as array lookups, depending on their types. A user can declare additional temporary variables within the fitness function of any type, and convert expressions between types, for example from fixed-point (int/uint) to floating-point (float/double). A user also can customise the width of an integer for optimisation, for example, uint8 means unsigned 8-bit integer.

The fitness function can contain multiple statements, which are executed sequentially. The statements can be simple assignment, if-else, or for-loops. Due to the underlying compilation strategy, we require that for-loop bounds are statically determined, so that they can later be converted into a streaming representation. These restrictions mean that certain behaviour cannot be expressed, but we show in section 6 that they can be used to capture various common problems.

Application Parameters. Most applications have input parameters passed to the fitness function, which describe a specific instance of the problem, but in the previous FPGA-based GAs, a user has to recompile the design to change them. To save the long compilation time, our single custom GA can support all input problems for an application by changing APP_PARAM section at run-time.

GA Parameters. As seen from Table 1, there are two compile-time and nine run-time parameters for GA. At compile-time, the user can balance the resource usage of evaluation and SCM units, by changing N_E and N_S. At run-time, N_g controls the number of generations generated, while N_p controls the size of one population. T_s, T_c and T_m can be configured for binary or real-valued chromosomes. The framework can also try multiple combinations of run-time parameters, for example trying a list of R_c and R_m to maximize the convergence rate. Changing I_p is also useful if there is a good prior population. These GA parameters can help a user to find a good configuration for a specific application, but they all have sensible default values if a user does not specify them.

5   Qualitative Comparison

We compare the features of previous FPGA-based GAs and our framework in Table 2 [10]. Our custom GA is more flexible and easier to use than the other FPGA-based GAs, resulting in the following advantages:

Table 2. Qualitative Comparisons of FPGA-based GAs (Chrome: Chromosome)

	Year	Chrome.	Run-time GA param.	App. param.	Parallel param.	Initial pop.	App. level	Platform
[13]	1995	binary	-	fixed	-	rand	low	BORDG
[9]	1999	binary	-	fixed	-	rand	low	SFL
[1]	2001	binary	-	fixed	-	rand	low	AXB-MP3
[2]	2001	binary	-	fixed	-	rand	low	Xilinx V1000
[15]	2004	binary	N_p, N_g, R_c, R_m	fixed	-	rand	low	PCI System
[8]	2009	binary	N_p	fixed	-	rand	low	Virtex2 Pro
[10]	2010	binary	$N_p, N_g, R_m,$ R_c, R_s	fixed	-	rand,	low	Virtex2 Pro
ours	2013	binary, real-valued	$N_p, N_g, T_m, R_m,$ T_s, R_s, T_c, R_c, I_p	run -time	N_E, N_S	rand, I_p	high	MAX3 (V6-SXT475)

1. Our framework provides a unified platform for binary and real-valued chromosomes with a flexible structure. There are nine parameters changeable at run-time, including crossover and mutation rates (R_c, R_m), the population size (N_p), generation number (N_g), the random seed (R_s), in particular the selection, crossover and mutation type (T_s, T_c, T_m), application parameters and initial population (I_p), which are all run-time changeable only in our framework. Specifically, the changeable application parameters make it possible to execute different inputs for an application without recompilation. Some platforms also support several run-time parameters, but require the user to have hardware knowledge to change them [10,15].

2. The framework allows a user to decide the number of parallel evaluation (N_E) and SCM units (N_S) at a high level to balance the resource usage with performance, without any manual modification of hardware code. Furthermore, as described in section 3.3, the customisable parallelism makes it possible to support complex applications.

3. The chromosome and fitness function of a new application is defined in a high level description language, making it easy for a user to apply our custom GA, without writing any low-level hardware code using VHDL or Verilog.

6   Experiments

We use our framework to solve six different applications, including a locating problem, the NP-hard set covering problem and four benchmarks. We also show the user's inputs for binary and real-valued chromosomes. The custom GAs are compared against multi-core CPU implementations based on an optimised version of SGA [4]. The CPU-based GAs are executed on Dual 2.67GHZ Intel Xeon X5650 (12 cores, 24 threads) with the POSIX threading library, and compiled with Intel compiler at the highest optimisation level.

6.1   Locating Problem

The locating problem is to find an emergency response unit, which has the best response time to reach any emergency that occurs in a city. Reference [12]

Compile-time specification	Run-time parameters

```CHROMOSOME {float xf,yf;}```
```FITNESS {```
``` float cost = 0.0;```
``` for (int i = 0; i ≤ 9; i ++){```
```   for(int j = 0; j ≤ 9; j ++){```
```   float xn = i + 0.5;```
```   float yn = j + 0.5;```
```   cost += W[i][j]*sqrt((xn - xf)*```
```   (xn - xf)+(yn - yf)*(yn - yf)); }```
``` }```
``` return cost;```
```}```
```GA_PARAM{```$N_E = 2; N_S = 8;$```}```
	```APP_PARAM{ int8 W[10][10] =```
	``` {{0,6,...} {4...}...};}```
	```GA_PARAM{```
	  $N_g = 1,000,000$
	  $N_p = 32$
	  $R_c = 0.6, 0.5, ...$
	  $R_m = 0.01, 0.02, ...$
	  $R_s = $ ```0x1234, 0xffff```
	  T_s: "tournament selection"
	  T_c: "blending crossover"
	  T_m: "real-valued mutation"
	  $I_p = \{(3.1, 4.5),(2.3, 4.8)...\}$
	```}```

Fig. 3. The User Input for Locating Problem

provides an complex example with a 10×10 km city divided into 100 sections. The response unit can be put at any place in the city, so a solution (x_f, y_f) is a floating point coordinate. The cost function is:

$$cost = \sum_{n=1}^{100} w_n \sqrt{(x_n - x_f)^2 + (y_n - y_f)^2} \tag{1}$$

where (x_n, y_n) is the coordinate of the centre of square n and w_n is emergency frequency in square n.

We use real-valued chromosomes, and define high-level specification and parameters in Fig. 3. In the left part showing compile-time specification, the chromosome and application are defined according to the rules described in section 4. The number of parallel evaluation and SCM units can be changed via N_E and N_S. As shown in Fig. 4, we can tune them for resource usage. For example, we reduce N_E of complex evaluation unit from 4 to 2, which slightly decrease performance (5% slower) due to pipelined structure described in section 3.3.

The right part of Fig. 3 shows the run-time parameters, W array is defined as the application parameters. By changing W, we can use the same custom GA to solve multiple input problems without recompilation, which always needs several hours to finish. Then we choose selection, crossover and mutation based on chromosome type. Here we also define a series of run-time parameters to tune convergence speed, the framework will try a full combination of them, including lists of mutation rates (R_m), crossover rates (R_c), and random seeds (R_s). The execution report helps user to find the best configuration for the problem. To compare the execution time with multi-core CPU, we let custom GA run 1,000,000 generations for different population size (N_p). As shown in Fig. 5, our custom GA is 24 times faster than CPU. Although the initial compilation of the custom GA is slow, future executions of the same GA with different parameters require no compilation, and start evaluating immediately.

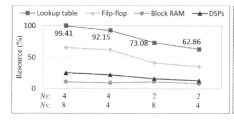
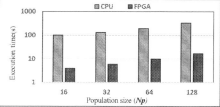

Fig. 4. Resources for various N_E and N_S **Fig. 5.** The execution time for various N_p

Compile-time specification	Run-time parameters

`CHROMOSOME { uintM suite; }`
`FITNESS{`
  `uint cost = 0; uintN cov = 0;`
  `for ( int i = 0; i ≤ M-1; i ++ ){`
    `cov |= suite[i] ? covs[i]: 0;`
    `cost += suite[i] ? costs[i] : 0; }`
  `uint covs_n = countone (cov);`
  `return (p * covs_n - cost);`
`}`
`uint6 countone(uintN cov) {...}`
	`APP_PARAM{ int p = 2,`
	             `uintN covs[M]={...},`
	             `uint cost[M]={...} }`
	`GA_PARAM{`
	  `...`
	  T_c: `"multi-point crossover"`
	  T_s: `"roulette wheel selection"`
	  T_m: `"binary mutation"`
	  I_p = `{0xffff, 0x1, ...}`
	`}`

Fig. 6. The User Inputs for Set Covering Problem

6.2 Set Covering Problem

The set covering problem (SCP) is a classic NP-hard combinatorial optimisation problem, with many practical applications [5]. For example in hardware verification, a suite with M programs can test or cover N functions, and every program has a cost. The relation between them can be represented by an $N \times M$ matrix. The aim of the SCP is to find the lowest cost sub-suite of programs which tests all N functions. For a candidate suite, the fitness is computed as:

$$Fitness = p \times coverage(suite) - cost(suite) \tag{2}$$

where p adjusts the fitness scale, and *coverage* represents how many functions covered. As shown in Fig. 6, the chromosome can be designed as an m-bit binary, the i-th bit of which means whether the i-th program exists in the suite. For FITNESS section, we can define function like *countone*() to calculate the number of 1. In run-time parameters, the coverage array ($cov[M]$), cost array ($cost[M]$) and p are supplied at run-time. We also choose different methods of selection, crossover and mutation from the locating problem. We test an instance of Steiner triple systems (STS_{27}) , which is considered as a hard SCP with a matrix of 117×27 [3]. Our custom GA is 45 times faster than the CPU.

6.3 GA Benchmarks

To test the ability of dealing with numeric computation in our custom GA, we use three GA benchmarks from [10], including binary F6 (BF6), binary F7 (BF7)

Table 3. The GA Benchmarks [10][12]

Name	Fitness function	Parameters
BF6	$4096 + \{[(x^2 + x) \times cos(x)]/220\}$	$0 \leqq x \leqq 65535$
BF7	$32768 + \{56 \times [x \times sin(4x) + 1.25 \times y \times sin(2y)]\}$	$0 \leq x, y \leq 255$
2DS	$65535 - 174 \times \left(150 + \{\prod_{k=1}^{2} \sum_{i=1}^{5} i \times cos[(i+1) \times x_k + i]\}\right)$	$0 \leq x_1, x_2 \leq 255$
F11	$1 + \sum_{n=1}^{N} x_n^2/4000 - \prod_{n=1}^{N} cos(x_n)$	$-10 \leq x_n \leq 10.0$

Table 4. Resources (Res.), Solution Quality and Speed-ups

App.	N_p	N_E	N_S	Res.%	Speed-up	Quality	Description
Locating	32	2	8	73.08	24	96%	real-valued computation
STS_{27}	128	16	16	65.12	45	100%	discrete combinatorics
BF6	32	8	8	26.45	26	100%	
BF7	32	8	8	21.48	25	100%	numeric computation
2DS	32	8	8	68.89	31	100%	
F11	32	8	8	60.05	27	100%	real-valued computation
MEAN	-	-	-	-	30	-	-

and 2-D Shubert function (2DS), and one benchmark called F11 from [12]. As shown in Table 3, these functions have one or more parameters.

6.4 Experiments Summary

Our platform can output the results from FPGA to CPU for comparison. As shown in Table 4, our platform can effectively solve different applications with an average speed up of 30 times, including discrete combinatorics, numeric and real-valued computation. Our custom GA can find a location with 96% of best fitness according to [12] for locating problem, and find the best solutions for all other applications. The clock frequencies of the custom GA is set to a conservative default value of 75MHz, so with longer compile times higher speed-ups are possible. In the Table 4, the resource usages vary by the complexity of an application, the number of evaluation units (N_E) and SCM units (N_S).

Reference [10] gives speed-ups of 5 times over BF6, BF7 and 2DS without reporting exact execution time, so we cannot directly compare its performance with ours. Although based on high-level inputs, our custom GA can still achieve high performance while retaining flexibility, with parallelised and pipelined units.

7   Conclusion and Future Work

GAs are ideal candidates for FPGA acceleration due to their long execution time. To provide an easy way for users to create and execute FPGA-based GAs with binary or real-valued chromosomes, we have proposed and implemented an automated unified framework for general-purpose GAs. The framework contains a scalable and customisable custom GA, which allows a user to tune the resource usage, without directly modifying hardware design. At compile-time, a user just needs to define a high-level specification of an application, including chromosome and fitness function, without writing any hardware code using VHDL. At run-time, the user can change GA and application parameters without waiting for recompilation. When compared with existing FPGA-based GAs, our custom GA has more architectural flexibility, and makes it much easier for users to take advantage of FPGA acceleration. Compared with multi-core CPU over six applications, the average speed-up of the custom GA is 30 times.

In the future, we will allow users to enhance the library in the proposed framework to support more genetic operators. We will also improve the framework by supporting variable length chromosomes, automatic parameter decision and structure tuning due to the flexibility of FPGA platform.

References

1. Shackleford, B., Snider, G., Carter, R.: A high-performance, pipelined, FPGA-based genetic algorithm machine. Genetic Programming and Evolvable Machines **2**(1), 33–60 (2001)
2. Aporntewan, C., Chongstilivatana, P.: A hardware implementation of the compact genetic algorithm. In: Proceedings of the 2001 Congress on Evolutionary Computation, vol. 1, pp. 624–629 (2001)
3. Plessl, C., Platzner, M.: Custom computing machines for the set covering problem. In: Proceedings of 10th IEEE Symposium on Field-Programmable Custom Computing Machines, pp. 163–172 (2002)
4. Coley, D.A.: An introduction to genetic algorithms for scientists and engineers. World Scientific Publishing, Singapore (2003)
5. Balas, E.: A class of location, distribution and scheduling problems: Modeling and solution methods (1982)
6. Guo, L., Thomas, D., Luk, W.: Customisable architectures for the set covering problem. In: Proceedings of International Symposium on Highly Efficient Accelerators and Reconfigurable Technologies (HEART), pp. 69–74 (June 2013)
7. Maxeler Tech, Programming MPC Systems White Paper (2013)
8. Vavouas, M., Papadimitriou, K., Papaefstathiou, I.: High-speed FPGA-based implementations of a genetic algorithm. In: Systems, Architectures, Modeling, and Simulation, pp. 9–16 (2009)
9. Yoshida, N., Yasuoka, T.: Multi-GAP: parallel and distributed genetic algorithms in VLSI. In: Proceedings of IEEE International Conference on Systems, Man, and Cybernetics, vol. 5, pp. 571–576 (1999)
10. Fernando, P., Katkoori, S.: Customisable FPGA IP core implementation of a general-purpose genetic algorithm engine. IEEE Transactions on Evolutionary Computation **14**(1), 133–149 (2010)
11. Ecuyer, P.L.: Tables of maximally equidistributed combined LFSR generators. Mathematics of computation **68**(225), 261–269 (1999)
12. Haupt, R.L., Haupt, S.E.: Practical genetic algorithms. John Wiley & Sons (2004)
13. Scott, S., Samal, A., Seth, S.: HGA: A hardware-based genetic algorithm. In: ACM 3rd International Symposium on Field-Programmable Gate Arrays, pp. 53–59 (1995)
14. Sivanandam, S.N., Deepa, S.N.: Introduction to genetic algorithms. Springer (2007)
15. Tang, W., Yip, L.: Hardware implementation of genetic algorithms using FPGA. In: 47th IEEE Midwest Symposium on Circuits and Systems, pp. 549–552 (2004)

Unreliable Heterogeneous Workers
in a Pool-Based Evolutionary Algorithm

Mario García-Valdez[1][✉], Juan Julián Merelo Guervós[2],
and Francisco Fernández de Vega[3]

[1] Instituto Tecnológico de Tijuana, Tijuana, BC, Mexico
mario@tectijuana.edu.mx
[2] Universidad de Granada, Granada, Spain
jmerelo@geneura.ugr.es
[3] Grupo de Evolución Artificial, Universidad de Extremadura, Mérida, Spain
fcofdez@unex.es

Abstract. In this paper the effect of node unavailability in algorithms using EvoSpace, a pool-based evolutionary algorithm, is assessed. EvoSpace is a framework for developing evolutionary algorithms (EAs) using heterogeneous and unreliable resources. It is based on Linda's tuple space coordination model. The core elements of EvoSpace are a central repository for the evolving population and remote clients, here called EvoWorkers, which pull random samples of the population to perform on them the basic evolutionary processes (selection, variation and survival), once the work is done, the modified sample is pushed back to the central population. To address the problem of unreliable EvoWorkers, EvoSpace uses a simple re-insertion algorithm using copies of samples stored in a global queue which also prevents the starvation of the population pool. Using a benchmark problem from the P-Peaks problem generator we have compared two approaches: (i) the re-insertion of previous individuals at the cost of keeping copies of each sample, and a common approach of other pool based EAs, (ii) inserting randomly generated individuals. We found that EvoSpace is fault tolerant to highly unreliable resources and also that the re-insertion algorithm is only needed when the population is near the point of starvation.

Keywords: Distributed evolutionary algorithms · Cloud computing

1 Introduction

Information technology has become ubiquitous in today's world, sources of computing power range from personal computers and smart-devices to massive data centers. Users can now access vast computational resources available on the Internet using diverse technologies, including cloud computing, peer-to-peer (P2P), and http-based environments. This trend can favor Evolutionary Computation (EC) algorithms as these can be designed as parallel, distributed, and asynchronous systems. Several Evolutionary Algorithms (EA) have been proposed

© Springer-Verlag Berlin Heidelberg 2014
A.I. Esparcia-Alcázar et al. (Eds.): EvoApplications 2014, LNCS 8602, pp. 726–737, 2014.
DOI: 10.1007/978-3-662-45523-4_59

that distribute the evolutionary process among heterogeneous devices, not only among controlled nodes in a in-house cluster or grid but also in those out side the data center, in users' web browsers and smart phones or external cloud based virtual machines. This reach out approach allows researchers the use of low cost computational power that would not be available otherwise, but on the other hand, have the challenge to manage heterogeneous unreliable computing resources. Lost connections, low bandwidth communications, abandoned work, security and privacy issues are all common in these settings.

In this paper the effect of node unavailability in algorithms using the EvoSpace population storage is assessed. EvoSpace [8] is a framework to develop evolutionary algorithms (EA) using heterogeneous and unreliable resources. EvoSpace is based on Linda's tuple space [9] coordination model, where each node asynchronously pulls its work from a central shared memory. The core elements of EvoSpace are a central repository for the evolving population and remote clients here called EvoWorkers which pull random samples of the population to perform on them the basic evolutionary processes (selection, variation and survival), once the work is done, the modified sample is pushed back to the central population. This model contrasts with the use of a global queue of tasks and implementations of map-reduce algorithms, recently favored in other proposals [4,5,12]. Following the tuple space model, when individuals are pulled from the EvoSpace container these are removed from it, so that no other EvoWorker could work on them at same time. This design decision has several known benefits relevant to concurrency control in distributed systems, and also is an effective way of distributing the workload. Leaving a copy of the individual in the population server free to be pulled by other EvoWorkers will result in redundant work and this could be costly if the task at hand is time consuming. EvoWorkers are expected to be unreliable, as they can loose a connection or are simply shut down or removed from the client. When an EvoWorker is lost, so are the individuals pulled from the repository. Depending on the type of algorithm been executed, the lost of these samples could have a high cost. To address the problem of unreliable EvoWorkers, EvoSpace uses a simple re-insertion algorithm that also prevents the starvation of the population pool. Other pool based algorithms normally use a random insertion technique, but we argue this could negatively impact the outcome of the algorithm in some cases.

This work evaluates the effect of the re-insertion algorithm has on the total running time and number of evaluations of a genetic algorithm. Using a benchmark problem from the P-Peaks problem generator, we compare both approaches: (i) the re-insertion previous individuals at the cost of keeping copies of samples, and (ii) inserting randomly generated individuals, with the sometimes beneficial cost of adding diversity to the population. For this experiments we use the same parameters used in an earlier work, in order to compare the performance of the algorithm in similar conditions. EvoSpace was implemented as a web service on the popular Heroku platform and EvoWorkers where simulated using PiCloud, a scientific computing PaaS.

The remainder of the paper proceeds as follows. Section 2 reviews related work. Afterwards, Section 3 briefly describes the proposed EvoSpace framework and gives implementation details the re-insertion process. The experimental work is presented in Section 4. Finally, a summary and concluding remarks are in Section 5.

2   Related Work

Using available Internet resources for EC has been the focus of recent research in the field. The use of volunteer computing using BOINC open source software is used by Smaoui et al. [6] in this case BOINC uses redundancy to deal with the volatility of nodes and unreliability of their results. In this work each BOINC work unit consisted of a fitness evaluation task and multiple replicas were produced and sent to different clients, later when outputs were received a validation step ensured all outputs match. In case of a discrepancy or a time-out from a client, a new job replica was created and sent to another client. The main drawback of this approach was that the master-worker algorithm used was synchronous, so the process had to wait for all jobs to continue to the next generation. Web browsers were used by Merelo et al. [11] using Javascript to implement the algorithm, this has the advantage of not requiring the installation of additional software. In this work the server receives an Ajax request with the best individual obtained from the local evolution in clients, and then responds with additional parameters and the best individual in the population so far. If a client is disconnected no special measures are taken. Several cloud-based EC solutions are based on a global queue of tasks and a Map-Reduce implementation which normally handles failures by the re-execution of tasks [4,5,12].

3   EvoSpace

EvoSpace [8] consists of two main components (see figure 1): (i) the EvoSpace container that stores the evolving population and (ii) EvoWorkers, which execute the actual evolutionary process, while EvoSpace acts only as a population repository. In a basic configuration, EvoWorkers pull a small random subset of the population, and use it as the initial population for a local EA executed on the client machine. Afterwards, the evolved population from each EvoWorker is returned to the EvoSpace container. When individuals are pulled from the container they remain in a phantom state, they cannot be pulled again but they are not deleted. Only if and when the EvoWorker returns the replacement sample phantoms are truly deleted. If the EvoSpace container is at risk of starvation or optionally when a time-out occurs new phantom individuals are re-inserted to the population and available again. This can be done because a copy of each sample is stored in a priority queue used by EvoSpace to re-insert the sample to the central population; similar to games where characters are respawned after a certain time. In the experiments conducted in this work re-insertion occurs when the population size is below a certain threshold. Figure 1 illustrates the main components of EvoSpace.

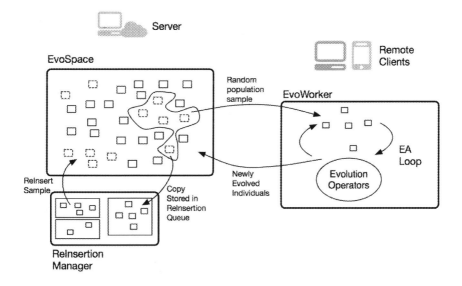

Fig. 1. Main components and dataflow within EvoSpace

3.1   Implementation

Populations of individuals are stored in-memory, using Redis, a key-value database, which was chosen over a relational database system, or other non-SQL alternatives, because it provides a hash based implementation of sets and queues which are natural data structures for the EvoSpace model. The logic of EvoSpace is implemented as a python module and exposed as a web service using Cherrypy http library. The EvoSpace modules are available with a Simplified BSD License from http://github.com/mariosky/EvoSpace.

3.2   Evospace as a Heroku Application

Heroku (http://heroku.com) is a multi-language PaaS, supporting among others Ruby, Python and Java applications. The basic unit of composition on Heroku is a lightweight container running a single user-specified process. These containers, which they call *dynos*, can include web (only these can receive http requests) and worker processes (including systems used for database and queuing, for instance). These process types are the prototypes from which one or more dynos can be instantiated; if the number of requests to the server increases more instances can be assigned on-the-fly. In our case, our CherryPy web application server runs in one web process, when the number of workers was increased we added more dynos (instances) of the CherryPy process.

This model is very different from a VPS where users pay for the whole server; in a process based model, users pay only for the processes they need; being a *freemium* model means also that, if a minimum level of resources is not exceeded, it can be used for free.

Once deployed the web process can be scaled up by assigning more dynos; in our case and in the more demanding configurations of our experiments, the web process was scaled to 20 dynos. Instructions and code for deployment is available at http://www.evospace.org/software.html

3.3   Evoworkers as PiCloud Jobs

PiCloud is a Platform as a Service (PaaS), with deep Python integration; using a library, Python functions are transparently uploaded to PiCLoud's servers as units of computational work they call *jobs*. Each job is added to a queue, and when there is a core available, the job is assigned to it. Both Heroku and PiCloud platforms are deployed on top of Amazon Web Services (AWS) infrastructure in the US-EAST Region. This ensures minimal latency and a high bandwidth communication between the services, and there is no charge for data transfer costs between both services. For the experiments type c1 and c2 Real Time workers where used. The code for the EvoWorkers implementation and experiment data is publicly available from a github repository https://github.com/mariosky/evoPar2014.

4   Experimental Work

4.1   Benchmark

The experiment reported here uses a multimodal problem generator. A P-Peaks generator has been chosen because the problem (and the computing resources needed for the search) can be appropriately scaled. Proposed by De Jong et al. in [2] a P-Peaks instance is created by generating a set of P random N-bit strings, which represent the location of the P peaks in the space. To evaluate an arbitrary bit string $\mathbf{x}$ first locate the nearest peak (in Hamming space). Then the fitness of the bit string is the number of bits the string has in common with that nearest peak, divided by N. The optimum fitness for an individual is 1. This particular problem generator is a generalization of the P-peak problems introduced in [3].

$$f_{P-PEAKS}(\mathbf{x}) = \frac{1}{N}\max_{i=1}^{P}\{N - hamming(\mathbf{x}, Peak_i)\} \tag{1}$$

A large number of peaks induce a time-consuming algorithm, since evaluating every string is computationally hard; this is convenient since to evaluate these type of distributed evolutionary algorithms fitness computation has to be significant with respect to network latency (otherwise, it would always be faster to have a single-processor version). However according to Kennedy and Spears [10] the length of the string being optimized has a greater effect in determining how easy or hard is the problem. In their experiments an instance having P = 200 peaks and N = 100 bits per string is considered to produce a considerably difficult problem.

4.2   Experimental Set-Up

As EvoSpace is only the population store, EvoWorkers must implement the genetic operators. The genetic algorithm executed by EvoWorkers has been implemented using a modified DEAP (Distributed Evolutionary Algorithms in Python) framework [7]. Is important to note that only the basic non-distributed GA library was used. Three methods were added to the local algorithm: getSample() and putBack(); and another for the initialization of the population. The implementation of the local GA simply uses DEAPs methods; for instance to generate the initial population, a local initialize() is called and the population sent to EvoSpace.

The selection of parameters was based on those used in [1]: a tournament size of 4 individuals, a crossover rate of 0.85 and a population of 512 individuals. In [2] a mutation rate equal to the reciprocal of the chromosome length; is recommended, as DEAP uses two parameters they were defined as follows, mutation probability of 0.5 and an independent flip probability of 0.02. For EvoWorkers the parameters were 128 worker generations for each sample, and a sample size of 16. The algorithm stops when reaching the optimum value, or when all workers pulled 100 samples. To simulate unreliable workers each worker was assigned a return sample probability. In the experiments the lower probability was a 30% chance of an EvoWorker returning a sample or an EvoWorker failing 70% of the time; other return sample probabilities where 50%, 70% and 90%. Experiments where carried out for 4, 8 and 16 EvoWorkers. In a pool based asynchronous GAs there is usually no need to wait for a workers job to start a new generation. Although supported by EvoSpace time outs were not chosen as triggers to feed the population with new individuals, the population size was used instead. We believe the population size is a better threshold as it is more critical to the GA performance. In a previous work we found that when the population remaining in the pool was near starvation, the time of completion was increased. For these experiments, the insertion of individuals was triggered when less than 128 individuals remain in the population; the number of individuals feed to the population was 128, or 8 samples when the re-insertion algorithm was used. A summary of the setup is presented in Table 1.

4.3   Results

In this section, results from the experiments are discussed. Figure 2 shows the time required to solution when using four EvoWorkers. For a population of 512 individuals and a sample size of 16, there is no difference in the time required to solution for percentages of 50% and above. Both re-insertion algorithms had comparable times. For 30 percent, both approaches had slight increase in time. For 8 workers (see Fig. 3) there was marginal decrease in overall time; and results where similar to those found in the experiments with 4 workers. Figure 4 shows results for 16 workers, when there was only a 30% chance of returning a sample the rate of re-insertions was high, approximately once every 35 samples. In this case, the insertion of random individuals resulted in a higher time to

Table 1. GA and EvoWorker parameters for experiments

GA Parameters	
Tournament size	4
Crossover rate	0.85
Population Size	512
Mutation probability	0.5
Independent bit flip probability	0.02
EvoWorker Parameters	
Sample Size	16
Generations	128
Other Parameters	
PiCloud Worker Type	Realtime
Number of Workers	4,8,16
Return Sample Probability	30%,50%,90%
Number of Executions	30

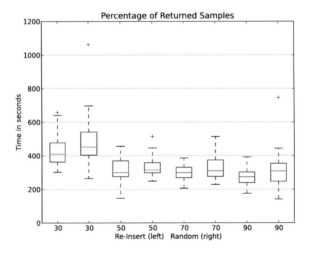

Fig. 2. Time required to solution, 4 Workers

solution. For these experiments when there is not a high rate of re-insertion, both alternatives have similar results, but the re-insertion algorithm is better for situations when there are many starvation conditions. It appears that the insertion of random individuals is not detrimental when there are other evolved individuals in the pool. But when the remaining pool almost consists of random individuals, samples pulled by EvoWorkers need to start the search all over again.

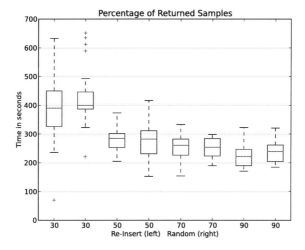

Fig. 3. Time required to solution, 8 Workers

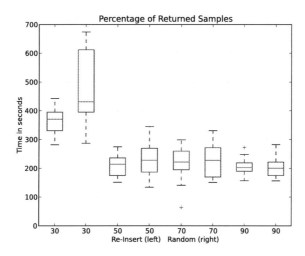

Fig. 4. Time required to solution, 16 Workers

If not many samples are then returned to the pool, the work needed to reach an optimum is increased. Figure 5 also shows the number of evaluations needed to reach an optimum again for 16 workers. Figures 6 and 7 show the time required to solution for 30 and 90 percent of returned samples. For 90% both algorithms had similar speedups when incrementing the number of workers. The marginal speedup obtained for these experiments is related to the population size, but this parameter was not changed. For 30% there was practically no speedup at

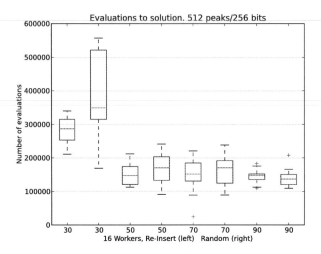

Fig. 5. Number of evaluations needed to solution, 16 Workers

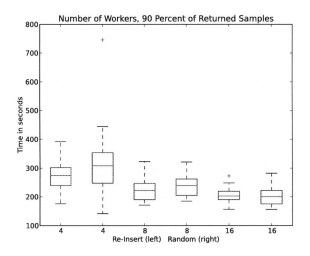

Fig. 6. Time required to solution, 90% of returned samples

all. The re-insert algorithm although not significant, had consistent decrease in time.

Fitness by time was measured as the average from each consecutive sample pulled by each worker. For each sample the average fitness was measured at the start and at the end of the local evolution. Also the minimum and maximum fitness values at start and finish was recorded. Final fitness values are shown in double width lines in figures. Readings used for these figures include all

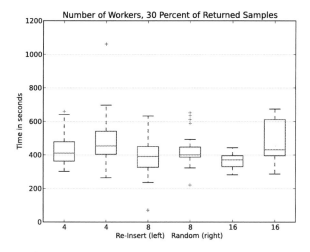

Fig. 7. Time required to solution, 30% of returned samples

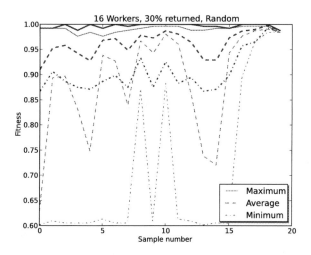

Fig. 8. Fitness by Sample number, 30% of returned samples, 16 Workers, Random Algorithm. For each sample the average fitness was measured at the start (green) and at the end (blue) of the local evolution.

samples, including those that where not returned. Figure 8 shows fitness by time for the random insertion algorithm, as expected initial fitness drops at certain points, when random insertion occurs. Average final fitness is affected by random insertions.Figure 9 shows results for the re-insertion algorithm, with more characteristic curves for this type of algorithms.

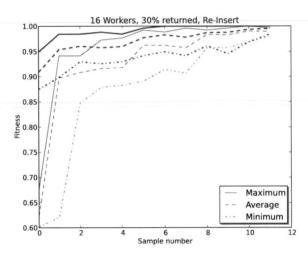

Fig. 9. Fitness by Sample number, 30% of returned samples, 16 Workers, Re-Insert Algorithm. For each sample the average fitness was measured at the start (green) and at the end (blue) of the local evolution.

5   Conclusions and Further Work

The re-insertion algorithm proposed for EvoSpace is a viable alternative to deal with a starving population in pool based GAs, and unreliable EvoWorkers. Using a benchmark problem from the P-Peaks problem generator, the approach was compared against the option of inserting randomly generated individuals. The same parameters and computing resources were used when testing both algorithms with better times reported when using the proposed technique. For experiments where the population size is enough for the number of workers with their sample sizes, plus a buffer to account for loss samples, then both algorithms could be used. However for cases when the number of EvoWorkers is unknown an hybrid approach could be used, insertion of random individuals to gradually increase the population size, and a re-insertion queue to handle lost samples. Further work could be focused on a hybrid approach, and also using heterogeneous computing resources.

Acknowledgments. This paper has been funded in part by projects P08-TIC-03903 (Andalusian Regional Government), TIN2011-28627-C04-02 (Spanish Ministry of Science and Innovation), project 83 (CANUBE) awarded by the CEI-BioTIC UGR. Regional Government Junta de Extremadura, Consejera de Economía, Comercio e Innovación and FEDER, project GRU10029.

References

1. Alba, E., Nebro, A.J., Troya, J.M.: Heterogeneous Computing and Parallel Genetic Algorithms. Journal of Parallel and Distributed Computing **62**(9), 1362–1385 (2002)
2. De Jong, K.A., Potter, M.A., Spears, W.M.: Using problem generators to explore the effects of epistasis. In: Bäck, T., (ed.) ICGA, pp. 338–345. Morgan Kaufmann (1997)
3. De Jong, K.A., Spears, W.M.: An analysis of the interacting roles of population size and crossover in genetic algorithms. In: Proceedings of the 1st Workshop on Parallel Problem Solving from Nature, PPSN I, pp. 38–47. Springer, London (1991)
4. Di Martino, S., Ferrucci, F., Maggio, V., Sarro, F.: Towards migrating genetic algorithms for test data generation to the cloud. In: Software Testing in the Cloud: Perspectives on an Emerging Discipline., pp. 113–135. IGI Global (2013)
5. Fazenda, P., McDermott, J., O'Reilly, U.-M.: A library to run evolutionary algorithms in the cloud using MapReduce. In: Di Chio, C., et al. (eds.) EvoApplications 2012. LNCS, vol. 7248, pp. 416–425. Springer, Heidelberg (2012)
6. Feki, M.S., Nguyen, V.H., Garbey, M.: Parallel genetic algorithm implementation for boinc. In: Chapman, B.M., Desprez, F., Joubert, G.R., Lichnewsky, A., Peters, F.J., Priol, T., (eds.) PARCO, vol. 19. Advances in Parallel Computing, pp. 212–219. IOS Press (2009)
7. Fortin, F.-A., Rainville, F.-M.D., Gardner, M.-A., Parizeau, M., Gagné, C.: DEAP: Evolutionary algorithms made easy. Journal of Machine Learning Research **13**, 2171–2175 (2012)
8. García-Valdez, M., Trujillo, L., Fernández de Vega, F., Merelo Guervós, J.J., Olague, G.: EvoSpace: A Distributed Evolutionary Platform Based on the Tuple Space Model. In: Esparcia-Alcázar, A.I. (ed.) EvoApplications 2013. LNCS, vol. 7835, pp. 499–508. Springer, Heidelberg (2013)
9. Gelernter, D.: Generative communication in linda. ACM Trans. Program. Lang. Syst. **7**(1), 80–112 (1985)
10. Kennedy, J., Spears, W.: Matching algorithms to problems: an experimental test of the particle swarm and some genetic algorithms on the multimodal problem generator. In: The 1998 IEEE International Conference on Evolutionary Computation Proceedings of the 1998 IEEE World Congress on Computational Intelligence, pp. 78–83 (May 1998)
11. Merelo-Guervos, J., Castillo, P., Laredo, J.L.J., Mora Garcia, A., Prieto, A.: Asynchronous distributed genetic algorithms with Javascript and JSON. In: IEEE Congress on Evolutionary Computation, CEC 2008 (IEEE World Congress on Computational Intelligence), pp. 1372–1379 (June 2008)
12. Sherry, D., Veeramachaneni, K., McDermott, J., O'Reilly, U.-M.: Flex-GP: genetic programming on the cloud. In: Di Chio, C., et al. (eds.) EvoApplications 2012. LNCS, vol. 7248, pp. 477–486. Springer, Heidelberg (2012)

EvoRISK

Hyper-Heuristics for Online UAV Path Planning Under Imperfect Information

Engin Akar[1], Haluk Rahmi Topcuoglu[1]($\boxtimes$), and Murat Ermis[2]

[1] Computer Engineering Department, Marmara University, 34722 Istanbul, Turkey
{eakar,haluk}@marmara.edu.tr
[2] Industrial Engineering Department, Turkish Air Force Academy, Yesilyurt,
Istanbul, Turkey
m.ermis@hho.edu.tr

Abstract. Hyper-heuristic techniques are problem independent meta-heuristics that automate the process of selecting a set of given low-level heuristics. Online path planning in an uncertain or unknown environment is one of the challenging problems for autonomous unmanned aerial vehicles (UAVs). This paper presents a hyper-heuristic approach to develop a 3-D online path planning for unmanned aerial vehicle (UAV) navigation under sensing uncertainty. The information regarding the state of a UAV is obtained from on-board sensors during the execution of a navigation plan. The trajectory of a UAV at each region is represented with B-spline curves, which is constructed by a set of dynamic control points. Experimental study performed on various terrains with different characteristics validates the usage of hyper-heuristics for online path planning. Our approach outperforms related work with respect to the quality of solutions and the number of feasible solutions produced.

Keywords: Unmanned Aerial Vehicles · Trajectory design · Hyper-heuristics

1 Introduction

High popularity and increasing application areas require more advanced systems to be developed for Unmanned Aerial Vehicles (UAVs) to enhance success in their missions. Utilization of UAVs in many unsafe operations has also yielded some challenges such as autonomous control, efficient energy use, and communication. A successful path planning algorithm that involves satisfying some constraints while searching for the optimal length path is a necessary element for the autonomy of the air vehicles. In some cases like connection loss with ground station or malfunction of link system, there may be limited information about environment on hand.

The essential properties for motion planning are completeness, which means that the algorithm returns a valid solution if one exists. In the path-planning problem, an exponential growth in complexity exists in the dimension of configuration space [1]. For this reason, heuristic techniques that produce near-optimal or good results in reasonable times are more convenient to apply the problem.

© Springer-Verlag Berlin Heidelberg 2014
A.I. Esparcia-Alcázar et al. (Eds.): EvoApplications 2014, LNCS 8602, pp. 741–752, 2014.
DOI: 10.1007/978-3-662-45523-4_60

A graph based search method is one of the popular approaches for path planning problem. The A* algorithm which is a branch of graph based methods is the most frequently used and well-known search procedure [2]. Application of Delaunay triangulations is another procedure for trajectory planning. After constructing the graph Dijkstra algorithm can be used to determine the optimal path toward target point [3]. The environment can be modeled using the Voronoi map and the optimum path can be obtained by a graph search technique like Dijkstra algorithm [4]. The artificial potential field method is another widely used procedure for autonomous vehicle motion planning [5].

Probabilistic roadmap approach is applicable to mobile agents for motion and trajectory planning. A problem with this method in its basic form is that it has many features, which have to be decided such as the way to sample the space and the local planner to use [6]. Another efficient algorithm for path planning is the Rapidly-Exploring Random Tree approach [7]. Various heuristic techniques such as Ant Colony Algorithm, Particle Swarm Optimization (PSO), Genetic Algorithms [8], and Differential Evolution (DE) are also proposed to get near-optimal or good results.

In this study, we propose a hyper-heuristic based online path planner of a UAV on 3-D terrains that are constructed by various terrain generator algorithms. Since the information about environment is limited or uncertain, the UAV scans a portion of the terrain within the range of its on-board sensors and it generates a subpath that is represented by parametrized B-spline curves. Experimental study by using terrains with different characteristics is conducted in order to present effectiveness of our approach. The results of our hyper-heuristic based solutions are compared with a GA-based reference study [8].

The rest of the paper is organized as follows. Section 2 gives brief information on online path planning. The details of our hyper-heuristic approach are presented in Section 3. Section 4 presents experimental evaluation of our hyper-heuristic based solutions and the related work. Finally, results and conclusion are summarized in Section 5.

2   Online Path Planning Problem

Generating a complete flight path before the mission starts is impossible when the environment is completely unknown or limited information is available. Because, there is no information about the environment in which the UAV flight takes place, the sensors that are embedded on the aircraft is utilized to capture the terrain data in the vicinity. The area that is visible by the UAV is considered as a spherical region. First, this region is identified by calculating the borderlines of the sensor vision. All the height map values that form the map in this limited area are checked. If the distance between the point that UAV is located and the controlled point is smaller than the sensor range, this point is assumed to be visible by the aircraft.

Figure 1 presents an illustration of how online path planning is performed in a given region. First of all, a scan process for capturing the visual data of nearby environment, which is limited with the range of the onboard sensors, is necessary before the flight begins. Therefore, the area bordered with the quarter circle (centered at top-left corner of the region) in Figure 1 is scanned. Then, path-planning algorithm is executed to find a suitable path for each visible region. Following the proper route is built, the aircraft starts to fly towards the border of the currently visible region. When it gets close to the end of the generated path, roughly when it reaches *the three fourths of the subpath* in our case, a new scan operation is initiated to get a new set of surrounding data. Then, the path for the newly captured area is generated. Generation of a new path has to be performed while the aircraft moves from the scanning point to the last point of the current path. This process is repeated until the target position is reached. Thus the complete path is a combination of several smaller path segments.

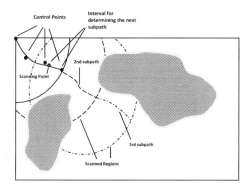

Fig. 1. Online path planning in a region

2.1 Structure of a Subpath

Complex trajectories can be defined easily by means of B-spline curves since they require the coordinate values of its control points [9]. In this study, an individual is a potential solution, i.e., a subpath in the given region, which consists of control points each represented with three floating-point numbers. Those floating point values correspond to the x, y, and z coordinate values of the control points on the 3-D space. There exist a starting and ending point for each individual. At the beginning of path planning, the initial position of the UAV is the starting point of all individuals. The ending point is calculated during individual generation process and may take different values so as to increase the feasibility and the quality of the results. The direction of the UAV is determined by the ending point of the path at each step. The ending point in a step is used as the starting point of the individual in the next step. Before calculating the ending point, the target point is checked if it is located in the sensor range of UAV. If it is visible by the UAV, the ending point is selected as the target position of it.

The most straightforward way to select the end point for the individual at any step is to find the intersection of the line extending between the current position of UAV and target point, within the borders of the sensor scanned area. If the intersection point is not hindered by an obstacle, it may be accepted as the last point of the current flight path. When an obstacle is come across, neighborhood points are controlled repeatedly whether or not they are suitable for UAV passage until the proper point is found. In order to provide the diversity for individuals, different neighbor points may be assigned to different individuals as end points, which helps to increase the feasibility rate in the population.

2.2   Constraints of the Problem

In this study, we consider the following constraints for online path planning:

- The flight path cannot be intersected with the underlying terrain. This is the primary requirement for the flight path to be feasible. This constraint states that any point on the path cannot be under the level of terrain surface.
- The flight path must lie through the area, which satisfies the minimum and maximum flight height constraints of the vehicle.
- UAV maneuvers must be performed at an angle greater than the minimum curvature radius determined in the flight envelope.

2.3   Evaluation Function

Constraints of a feasible UAV trajectory can be included in the evaluation function in the form of penalty values. We adapt the computation of the evaluation function of a subpath given in [8], which consists of 8 terms.

$$f = \sum_{i=1}^{n} w_i f_i \qquad (1)$$

Here, w_i are the weights of each term and f_i are function values related with either constraints or objectives that are described below. The term f_1 calculates the number of discrete curve points located under the ground surface. All the points that form the path are checked one by one, whether they are passing through the terrain. First, elevation of the terrain at the position where the curve point resides is calculated using the heightmap data. This value is compared with the height value of the curve point. If the former value is higher, than the value of this function is incremented. Since, this term reflects the feasibility of the route, its value has to be zero.

The second term is used to calculate the distance penalty of the path, which consists of two parts. The first one is relevant to the minimum (safety) distance between the curve point and the terrain surface. Its purpose is to prevent the UAV flying at a closer height than the allowed minimum distance. To obtain this penalty value, distance of each curve point from the surface is calculated, and difference between this distance value and the specified minimum distance is computed. If the result is less than zero, a penalty value proportional to this difference is added to it. Other consideration of term f_2 is to check the maximum distance of UAV flight path. This penalty value is calculated using the difference between the height of each curve point and the maximum allowable height. This term penalizes the paths that contain points located at higher altitudes than the aircraft can technically fly.

The term f_3 is used to check the minimum curvature radius penalty of the path. This penalty value keeps the UAV acceleration in reasonable limits both in horizontal and vertical directions. First, the angle between two line segments for each successive curve points along the path line is calculated. Secondly, each angle value is checked to see, if it is smaller than the minimum angle. If so, a value proportional to the difference between the calculated angle and the specified minimum angle is added to the result of this function. The term f_4 is the function to calculate length of the path line. The length of the flight path is calculated by adding the distances between two successive curve points.

The term f_5 is related with a potential field value between the starting and the final target point. The term f_6 calculates the distance between the last point of current step and terrain surface so that UAV do not change its direction abruptly, while moving in the next partial step. It helps maintaining feasibility of the path. The term f_7 penalizes the paths being trapped in local optima and guides the aircraft to unexplored areas. The function f_8 calculates another potential field value in order to draw the aircraft toward the final target. If UAV is away from the target, this function produces a constant value. If it gets closer, the output of this term decreases in proportion to the distance between the target and the last curve point of the current step.

Although the evaluation function for the reference study [8] is presented with eight terms as explained above, we consider a more compact representation with five terms where first four terms are same with f_1, f_2, f_3, f_4. In order to represent the last four terms with a single function, we include a new term, f_5^*, for guiding the UAV to the target and keep the length as short as possible.

The term f_5^* penalizes the control points that are far away from the straight path between the starting and ending point in each path step. The straight path is simply the line drawn from initial and final target points. If the calculated curve points are far away from this path, the length of the produced path will be longer. Obtaining the value of this term is achieved by calculating the distance between each control point and the straight path line. A normalization process is carried out to transform the values stated above into $[0, 1]$ range. Since, this is a minimization problem, weighted sum of the normalized values is inverted in the fitness function given in Equation 1.

3   Hyper-Heuristic Based Online Path Planning

Hyper-heuristics are emerging meta-heuristic techniques for automating the process of selecting, applying (or even generating) heuristics to solve hard combinatorial optimization problems [10]. A hyper-heuristic requires a set of low-level heuristics and an objective function where it selects and/or adapts several low-level heuristics during the search for the given combinatorial optimization. Therefore, it operates on search space of heuristics rather than search space of solutions. Hyper-heuristics have been successfully applied to large number of combinatorial optimization problems including personnel scheduling, timetabling, cutting stock and inventory problems [10].

In this paper, we consider *perturbative hyper-heuristics*, which target to improve quality of a candidate solution for the given problem through selecting and applying low-level heuristics. Two separate components of a perturbative hyper-heuristic technique are the i) *heuristic selection mechanism*, and the ii) *move acceptance criteria* [11]. We present the details of selected methods for the two components at the following two subsections, which is followed by the details of low-level heuristics proposed for the UAV path planning problem.

3.1   Heuristic Selection Mechanisms

There are a large number of heuristic selection mechanisms proposed in the literature, where we consider following five heuristics in this study.

- **Simple Random (SR):** In this mechanism, a low level heuristic is selected randomly based on a uniform distribution and it is applied once [12].
- **Greedy (GR):** All low-level heuristics are applied to a candidate individual and the heuristic that generates the best improved solution is selected [12].
- **Random Descent (RD):** It is a variant of the Simple Random case, where each randomly selected heuristic is applied repeatedly until there is no improvement in the solution [12].
- **Choice Function (CF):** This strategy presents a ranking mechanism for low level heuristics [12]. The choice function evaluates an overall score of each heuristic by combining the recent individual performance of the heuristic, recent improvements for consecutive pairs of heuristics and the elapsed time since the heuristic was last applied [12]. In this paper, we apply two types of Choice Function strategy, which are the Straight Choice Function (SC) and the Ranked Choice Function (RC). The former one selects and executes the low level heuristic, which maximizes the choice function. The latter one ranks low-level heuristics based on the choice function. For a portion of the highest ranked heuristics (the best three heuristics in our study), it evaluates change in the objective function; then, it selects the best one.
- **Reinforcement Learning (RL):** Machine learning techniques can be incorporated with hyper heuristics in order to improve the quality of heuristic selection process. A reinforcement learning system interacts with the environment and changes its state with an action based on a defined utility scheme in order to increase its reward [13]. In a reinforcement learning based hyper-heuristic, a utility value is assigned for each low-level heuristic [14]. The heuristic selection phase selects a heuristic based on the utility values, which is followed by a pre-specified reward or punishment process to update the utility value of the selected.

The adaptation rate of low-level heuristics can be set with various strategies (including additive, subtractive, divisional or root based ones), after a reward or a punishment heuristic. Figure 2 shows the transitions between the solutions types considered in our study. As an example, transition "2" represents a change

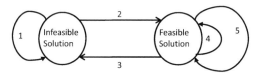

Fig. 2. Utility adaptation operations

from an infeasible solution to a feasible solution after the heuristic applied. It should be noted that there are two transitions between two infeasible solutions. In transition "4", feasibility of the solution does not change; however, the fitness of new solution gets worse. On the other hand, fitness value is improved in transition "5", after the heuristic is applied.

Figure 3 demonstrates corresponding utility adaptation functions considered for our RL-based hyper-heuristics. In these equations, u represents the utility value for any low-level heuristic; k is a promotion variable for rewarding infeasible to feasible conversion, which is equal to 2, 4 or 6 in our experiments. Similarly, is a demotion variable for punishing the action that converts a feasible solution to an infeasible one; and we consider three different values: 1,2 and 3. Finally, n is the maximum utility value. When the utility value takes a value less than the initial utility value or greater than maximum value, it is set to initial and maximum values respectively. The acceptable interval for utility values is equal to $[1..n * |LL|]$, where $|LL|$ is the number of low-level heuristics considered and n is an integer, which is equal to 3 in our experimental study.

```
1: u = u/2      (Infeasible to Infeasible)
2: u = u + k    (Infeasible to Feasible)
3: u = sqrt(u)  (Feasible to Infeasible)
4: u = u - m    (Feasible to Feasible)
5: u = u + 1    (Feasible to Feasible)
```

Fig. 3. Utility adaptation functions of 5 transitions given in Fig. 2

3.2   Criteria for Move Acceptance

In this study, we consider four different move acceptance criteria, which are all move (AM) [12], only improvement (OI) [12], improvement or equal (IE) [12] and exponential Monte Carlo (MC) [15]. The AM case accepts all moves, the OI case accepts only improving moves, and the IE move acceptance mechanism rejects only the worsening moves. The MC strategy accepts all new solutions with better or equal fitness value compared to previous one. Otherwise, a control value is calculated with $e^{z*(f_{new} - f_{old})}$ where z is a constant value (equal to 1 in our computational experiments) for tuning the sensibility of acceptance, f_{new} is the fitness function value for the new solution, and f_{old} is the fitness value of the old solution. Then, a random number is generated between 0 and 1. If the control value is greater than or equal to the random number, the new solution is accepted; otherwise it is rejected.

3.3   Low-Level Heuristics

We utilize eight different low-level heuristics in our study, each of which performs inserting a new control point to the B-spline curve, deleting or updating an existing control point. The first six operations given below are based on heuristics proposed in a recent study related with offline path planning [16].

- **Delete Operation:** In this heuristic, a randomly selected control point is removed from the control point list. The heuristic does not perform any operation, if it reaches minimum number of control points, which is equal to 3 in our computational experiments.

- **Smart Delete Operation:** It deletes the worst control point, where the quality of each control point is computed by the aggregate cost of the related curve segments. It targets to delete the control point, which has highest sub-path length and the highest penalty values due to violating hard constraints. It considers whether the minimum number of control points is achieved or not for the operation.

- **Insert Operation:** A randomly generated point (located within the borders of current sensor scanned region) is added to the control point list. If maximum number of control points is achieved, it does not perform any operation.

- **Smart Insert Operation:** The curve segment that incurs highest cost is determined; a new control point within the boundaries of the current segment is determined and added to the control point list. Like the basic insert operation, it controls whether the maximum control point number is achieved or not after the insertion.

- **Update Operation:** A randomly selected control point is replaced with a randomly generated point located within the borders of current sensor scanned region. It can be also applied for individuals having minimum number of control points.

- **Smart Update Operation:** The control point having the worst fitness value is replaced with a better control point near the optimal path, i.e., the straight line from the starting to the final point within the scanned region.

- **Smooth Turn Operation:** The aim of this operation is to prevent the UAV maneuvering with an angle smaller than the minimum curvature angle, which violates the constraint on minimum curvature radius. It helps to make the path smoother and shorter, as well. The angle at each control point that formed by the successive line segments points is calculated. If any angle is smaller than the minimum turning angle, it is deleted from the control point list (Figure 4.a).

- **Shortcut Operation:** It discovers and fixes the control point that crucially deviates from the optimal path line that lies between the starting and final

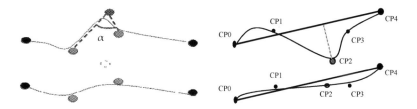

Fig. 4. (a) Smooth turn operation and (b) Shortcut operation

points of the current path. First of all, the control point, which is farthest from the optimal path, is determined by calculating the 3-D distance between each control point and the optimal path. Then, the farthest one is moved to a new point that is closer to the optimal path (Figure 4.b).

4 Experimental Study

In this study, all path planning algorithms are coded in C programming language and experiments are conducted on an Intel Core 2 2.83 GHz machine running Linux operating system. Terrains and 3D testbed for visualization are developed with jMonkey Engine (JME), a Java API that contains several OpenGL based libraries to design 3-D maps for video games. The terrain generator produces height maps for different types of landscapes in different size and forms. The characteristics of the terrain such as flatness or steepness are important for the flight path planning. Therefore, to test the performance of our planner, two types of terrains are considered by using the Hill Algorithm, rough and smooth terrains. The size of terrains used in experiments has been adopted as 128x128. Three different time limits (50, 100 and 200 ms) with four different sensor ranges (16, 24, 32, and 40) on both rough and smooth terrains comprise 24 different test scenarios for each start point and final point pair, where each test scenario is run with 40 trials.

4.1 Pre-Experimentation for Reinforcement Learning

Selection of the most appropriate reinforcement learning (RL) parameters is managed by performing a series of pre-experiments. The utility adaptation functions listed in Figure 3 include two parameters to be determined: i) k for rewarding an action producing an infeasible solution from a feasible, and ii) m for penalizing an action that results in a fitness worsening on a feasible solution.

After a set of experiments, it was observed that the two most frequent value pairs for m and k are $\{m = 1, k = 2\}$ and $\{m = 2, k = 8\}$. We select $\{m = 1, k = 2\}$ pair based on the results for two sensor ranges (32 and 40). Another set of pre-experiments have been carried out to determine the proper values for initial and maximum utility values, which are set with 12 and 24, respectively. In both sets of experiments, a maximum 30 ms is allowed for generating the path for one segment. The size of the surrounding terrain has been chosen as 128x128 and the values 32 and 40 are selected as the onboard sensor range, and each setting has been executed 50 times.

4.2   Results and Discussions

In this section, we present performance comparison of our algorithms with a GA-based reference study [8] for 3-D online path planning by using various test scenarios. The reference study considers B-Spline curve formulation, and it presents two types of crossover operators. Apart from the simple single-point crossover operator, it applies an arithmetic crossover operator with a simple formula to generate the coordinates of the new individual. On the other hand, the reference study employs a non-uniform mutation procedure in which the coordinates of randomly selected point are modified by multiplying with a constant value, in addition to uniform mutation operator.

Table 1. Average fitness value and number of feasible solutions of algorithms on a rough terrain with different sensor ranges

Method	Average Fitness Value				Feasible Solutions			
	16	24	32	40	16	24	32	40
GA	0,0534807	0,0565428	0,0546188	0,0565076	39	40	44	50
RC-AM	0,0508404	0,0525642	0,0516142	0,0518952	50	50	50	50
RC-MC	0,0510116	0,0519878	0,0515696	0,0519768	50	49	50	50
RC-IE	0,0511904	0,0528832	0,0512026	0,0515864	48	49	50	50
RC-OI	0,0511343	0,0531817	0,0520564	0,0523565	49	50	50	50

The results in terms of average fitness value and number of feasible solutions (out of 50 tests) for various sensor ranges on a given rough terrain with time limit value of 100ms are listed in Table 1 for the GA-based reference work and the Rank Choice (RC) cases. Although the other hyper-heuristic cases also outperform the reference work, they are not included in the table due to space limitations. The RC cases produce the best average results among all cases for different sensor range values. The average fitness values generated by GA left behind the hyper-heuristic methods. As can be expected, number of feasible solutions increase with an increase in sensor range. Our hyper-heuristic techniques provide feasible solutions for almost all of the cases.

Boxplot of hyper-heuristics and GA results are depicted in Figure 5 for the case of 100ms time limit with the sensor range of 32. From this graph, it is observed that most of the hyper-heuristic methods outperform the related work. Specifically, Simple Random, Rank Choice and Reinforcement Learning cases generate better results than the GA-based approach.

Another comparison criteria is the change of the fitness value for a given time interval. Generally, the GA method produces slight improvements for the given time intervals and keeps this improvement until the end of time limit. On the other hand, the HH methods may improve the result in any interval; and, they

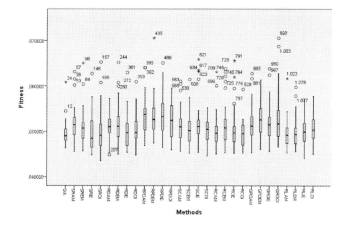

Fig. 5. Comparison of hyper-heuristics with GA on a rough terrain with sensor range of 32

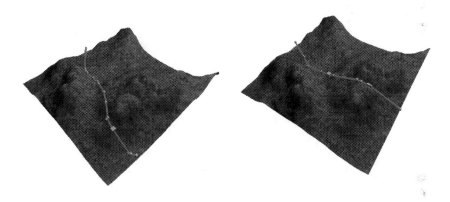

Fig. 6. Sample paths generated with RL-IE and RC-MC methods

produce significant improvements at the initial or earlier stages of each run. In general, HH methods reach the best solution in less than 30 ms.

Finally, we present the result paths of our algorithms on a selected rough terrain in Figure 6. Those paths were produced by the RL method with IE strategy and the RC method with MC strategy, for different destination points.

5   Conclusions

In this paper, we present an online 3-D path planner for the navigation of Unmanned Aerial Vehicles (UAVs) by using hyper-heuristics. Experimental study performed on terrains with different characteristics validates the usage of

hyper-heuristics for online UAV path planning problem, where our approach outperforms related work with respect to quality of solutions and the number of feasible solutions produced.

References

1. Frazzoli, E., Dahleh M., Feron E.: Real-Time Motion Planning for Agile Autonomous Vehicles. In: American Control Conference, Arlington, Virginia, pp. 1–48 (2001)
2. Qi, Z., Shao, Z., Ping, Y.S., Hiot, L.M., Leong, Y.K.: An Improved Heuristic Algorithm for UAV Path Planning in 3D Environment. In: Second International Conference on Intelligent Human-Machine Systems and Cybernetics, Nanjing, Jiangsu, pp. 258–261 (2010)
3. Fu, X., Zhong, L., Gao, X.: Path planning for UAV in radar network area. In: Second WRI Global Congress on Intelligent Systems, Wuhan, pp. 260–263 (2010)
4. Dong, H., Li, W., Zhu, J., Duan, S.: The Path Planning for Mobile Robot Based on Voronoi Diagram. In: Third International Conference on Intelligent Networks and Intelligent Systems, pp. 446–449 (2010)
5. Koren, Y., Borenstein, J.: Potential Field Methods and Their Inherent Limitations for Mobile Robot Navigation. In: Proceedings of the IEEE Conference on Robotics and Automation, Sacramento, California, pp. 1398–1404 (1991)
6. Geraerts, R., Overmars, M.H.: Sampling Techniques for Probabilistic Roadmap Planners. Institute of information and computing sciences, Utrecht University. Technical report, UU-CS-2003-041 (2003)
7. LaValle, S.M.: Rapidly-exploring Random Trees: A New Tool for Path Planning. TR 98–11, Computer Science Dept., Iowa State University (1998)
8. Nikolos, I.K., Valavanis, K.P., Tsourveloudis, N.C., Kostaras, A.N.: Evolutionary Algorithm based Offline/Online Path Planner for UAV Navigation. IEEE Transactions on Systems, Man and Cybernetics - Part B: Cybernetics 33(6), 898–912 (2003)
9. Farin, G.: Curves and Surfaces for CAGD (Computer Aided Graphics and Design): A Practical Guide, 5th edn. Morgan Kaufmann, San Francisco (2001)
10. Burke, E.K., Gendrau, M., Hyde, M., Kendall, G., Ochoa, G., Ozcan, E., Qu, R.: Hyper-heuristics: A Survey of the State of the Art. Journal of Operational Research Society (2013)
11. Ozcan, E., Bilgin, B., Korkmaz, E.E.: A Comprehensive Analysis of Hyper-heuristics. Intelligent Data Analysis 12, 3–23 (2008)
12. Soubeiga, E.: Development and application of hyperheuristics to personnel scheduling, PhD Thesis, School of Computer Science, University of Nottingham, UK (2003)
13. Sutton, R.S., Barto, A.G.: Reinforcement learning: an introduction. The MIT Press (1998)
14. Ozcan, E., Msr, M., Ochoa, G., Burke, E.K.: Reinforcement Learning an Great-Deluge Hyper-heuristic for Examination Timetabling. International Journal of Applied Metaheuristic Computing (IJAMC) 1, 39–59 (2010)
15. Ayob, M., Kendall, G.: A monte carlo hyper-heuristic to optimize component placement sequencing for multi head placement machine. In: Proceedings of the International Conference on Intelligent Technologies (InTech 2003), pp. 132–141. Thailand (2003)
16. Oz, I., Topcuoglu, H.R., Ermis, M.: A meta-heuristic based three-dimensional path planning environment for unmanned aerial vehicles. Simulation 89(8), 903–920 (2013)

Searching for Risk in Large Complex Spaces

Kester Clegg and Rob Alexander[(✉)]

University of York, York, U.K.
{kester.clegg,rob.alexander}@york.ac.uk

Abstract. ASHiCS (Automating the Search for Hazards in Complex Systems) uses evolutionary search on air traffic control simulations to find scenario configurations that generate high risk for a given air sector. Weighted heuristics are able to focus on specific events, flight paths or aircraft so that the search can effectively target incidents of interest. We describe how work on the characterization of our solution space suggests that destructive mutation operators perform badly in sensitive, high dimensional spaces. Finally, our work raises some issues about using collective risk assessment to discover significant safety events and whether the results are useful to safety analysts.

Keywords: Search · Risk · Safety · Air Traffic Control · Simulation · RAMS

1 Introduction and Background

With increasingly complex systems to manage, safety analysts are starting to express concern that large complex systems are becoming too difficult to guarantee safety when part of the system is changed or placed under stress. To help analysts discover hazards within complex systems, the ASHiCS project (Automating the Search for Hazards in Complex Systems) was set up to demonstrate a proof-of-concept tool that would make use of evolutionary search heuristics and simulation to uncover hazards (such as escalating levels of risk) within large complex systems that might otherwise be missed using traditional manual safety analysis.

The combination of simulation and evolutionary search is hardly new; indeed, in many instances of trying to search for novel physical solutions, a simulated environment is an essential part of the search process. Without a rapid build-and-test cycle in virtual environments, it is unlikely that evolutionary search could have been applied to many design problems [1] [2]. However, using search to manipulate simulations of air traffic control (ATC) scenarios is relatively recent, with few practitioners. Part of the reason for this is that the simulation environments are complex, often requiring extensive domain knowledge to understand. Additionally only a small number of fast-time ATC simulations tools are available to academic researchers.

Notwithstanding this, there is recent work in area, particularly by University of New South Wales which has used what was termed the Computational Red Teaming (CRT) Framework to identify patterns in arrival traffic and ground events that lead to delays in dynamic continuous descent arrivals (CDA) scenarios [3]. More recently, the same team has also started to use evolutionary search to look for risk [4] in ATC

© Springer-Verlag Berlin Heidelberg 2014
A.I. Esparcia-Alcázar et al. (Eds.): EvoApplications 2014, LNCS 8602, pp. 753–762, 2014.
DOI: 10.1007/978-3-662-45523-4_61

scenarios, in particular looking at the contribution of air traffic controllers to increased risk. ASHiCS differs in that we search if a specific configuration of the traffic entering the airspace could lead to a hazardous situation by using risk instruments to assess the degradation of safety barriers. Our project also investigates if the search can discover whether the injection of a serious safety incident could overload the air traffic controller (ATCo) workloads for a given traffic input, resulting in rising risk and reduced safety margins.

2   The ASHiCS Search Harness

The ASHiCS search harness generates traffic inputs for the RAMS (Re-organized ATC Mathematical Simulator) Plus air traffic control simulator[1] and analyses the output of each simulation. The RAMS Plus tool (from ISA Software) is used to perform airspace studies and features a capacity and workload simulator, a sector opening hours simulator, a MESEC (multi-executive sector) simulator and a gate-to-gate simulator. Air traffic is generated by specifying the characteristics of each aircraft entering the sector, namely aircraft type, aircraft entry time, its entry and exit flight level and the waypoints specifying its flight path and any level changes.

The traffic input files are created with restrictions on the distribution of aircraft to predetermined flight paths and an enforcement of wake turbulence separation. Once the input files have been created, a non-graphic version of RAMS Plus (i.e. a version that runs without any visualization to speed up simulations) is executed and the outputs analyzed by heuristics in the ASHiCS software.

2.1   Experimental Set Up

The search context is limited to a single en-route air sector containing a number of predetermined flight paths specified using waypoints. Scenarios use a sample size of twenty aircraft whose start times are randomly generated over the span of one hour. Aircraft "appear" outside the sector at cruise speed and do not deviate from their flight path except to resolve a conflict.

The design of the sector is intended to represent two busy en-route flight paths that run north-east to south-west and west to east (hereafter referred to as ns and ew). Each flight path carries a single type of aircraft flying at their typical en-route altitudes and the paths intersect obliquely at the center of the sector; however the flight paths are vertically separated (FL330 and FL190 respectively) so that no conflicts arise. One aircraft is selected at random from the FL330 flight path to undergo an emergency cabin pressure loss event (referred to as CPLoss). This aircraft is assigned a special profile that mimics an emergency descent to FL100. The descent may conflict directly with one or more designated flight paths. CPLoss maintains its planned trajectory on its flight path after reaching FL100. There are also up to three other flight paths (r2, r3 and r4, each at FL230) that intersect at different points in the

---

[1] http://www.eurocontrol.int/eec/public/standard_page/WP_Fast_Time_Simulation_Tools.html

sector. These paths carry just 25% of the traffic, and represent incidental traffic crossing the sector. For ease of implementation, we assume the sector is controlled by a single air traffic controller (ATCo) from FL100 to FL600 with a standard minimum separation of 5nm. The aircraft types, flight paths and flight levels are shown in Table 1:

Table 1. Types of aircraft, flight paths and levels

Aircraft type	Flight path	Flight level
A320	ns	330
DH8	ew, r4	230,190
B737	r2,r3,r4	230
C551	r2,r3,r4	230

Initial Seeding and Aircraft Distribution. The distribution of aircraft between each flight path is decided at random, with the sole restriction that the ns flight path must have at least one aircraft on it to represent CPLoss. The proportion of traffic between the ns and ew flight paths and the lower level paths is split 75:25 in favor of the ns and ew paths. The 25% of traffic on the low level flight paths is allocated one of the r2, r3 or r4 flight paths at random. Aircraft may have their allotted start time adjusted if they are close enough to another aircraft on the same flight path that they would suffer wake turbulence (i.e. less than 120 seconds apart), in which case the following aircraft is moved further back in time to enforce sufficient separation. If several aircraft are initially bunched together, then those aircraft are forcibly separated. This type of traffic configuration and subsequent separation does impinge on the search's ability to manipulate the start times of grouped aircraft, however tightly grouped aircraft can represent a hazard in themselves as they leave fewer options for the resolution of conflicts. As this type of configuration does occur in real-world scenarios we have not excluded it from the search.

Search Parameters. The ASHiCS search harness uses a population of 100 scenarios per generation and typically runs for 300 generations. The search implements what is sometimes termed a "near neighbor, random hill-climber" search. That is, individual scenarios are selected and the aircraft start times are mutated within a set range (generally a few minutes either side of the previous entry time), ensuring that the random sampling of the near neighborhood is constrained. Provided such mutations are not too radical we should be guaranteed that a "near neighbor" of the original scenario is created, as aircraft remain on their flight paths, relatively close to their previous start times. However, to try and ensure that the search has not been unlucky in its initial seeding of random samples (in what is a very large configuration space), we continue to allow a proportion of each population to be generated entirely by random sampling. The split in the population is dictated by a policy of elitism; the top twenty per cent of a generation's scenarios are each mutated to create three "near neighbor copies" and carried over to the next generation. The remaining forty per cent of the population is created from new random samples.

Evolutionary Strategy. The evolutionary strategy for ASHiCS is based primarily on mutation rather than crossover or other combination methods. Our rationale for not selecting crossover is that 'destructive' methods for good gene propagation fare less well than methods that allow gradual changes to a phenotype's fitness depending on problem type [5]. Our choice of population size was partly dictated by the length of time each simulation took, making a very large size impractical. However, despite previous work that suggested large population sizes were essential for complex solution spaces [6] [7], there seems to be a consensus that a destructive means of combining chromosomes (such as crossover) requires larger sample sizes to work effectively [1], whereas non-destructive mutation can work with smaller populations [8]. Our domain may be particularly sensitive to a destructive type operator, as we feel it could neither produce "near neighbor" hill-climbing to allow gradual improvements from an initial starting point, nor would it be able to trace how a scenario could evolve from one that was relatively low risk to one that contained gradually higher levels of risk[2], as the jumps in the search trajectory from a crossover operator are largely arbitrary.

Risk Model. The fitness function uses several outputs from RAMS Plus, including: number of conflicts, number of resolutions, conflict separation percentage[3], total task workload (measured in seconds). Although we recognize that an airborne collision is ultimately the worst possible outcome, using the barrier model from the IRP (Integrated Risk Picture –jointly proposed safety model used by EUROCONTROL and the FAA) [9] and ARMS (Aviation Risk Management Solutions [working group]) [10] allows us to use precursor events to indicate if these barriers have started to deteriorate, increasing the likelihood that a significant safety event (SSE) will occur. Rather than have our search algorithms look for very low frequency events such as air-borne collision (which would represent sudden, huge step changes in severity), we measure the degree of risk by grading the quality of safety barriers that should prevent an accident happening. Under the barrier model, barriers themselves may be composed of multiple factors that degrade in different ways. For example, aircraft separation is an important barrier that degrades by proximity, but not all loss of separation carries the same degree of risk. By creating a "basket of risk measures" related to the states of certain barriers and other indicators, the heuristics can make use of a smooth progressive risk level assessment to direct the search.

Within these measures we also add weightings for specific items of interest. For example, if we want to ensure the additional workload for CPLoss plays a part in our final solution, we must weight conflicts and controller workload tasks associated with CPLoss proportionally greater than those for other aircraft; otherwise scenarios containing incidents elsewhere may outrank it.

---

[2] We have not attempted to incorporate traceability into our search harness as yet, but the choice of a non-destructive operator allows us to keep this as an option for future work.

[3] Defined by RAMS Plus as the percentage of *available separation*, i.e. the "closest point of approach (2D lat. / long.) divided by the largest separation value." In other words, how close two aircraft in conflict got *before* being resolved.

However there are some issues when using a basket of risk measures to define an objective function, which we believe would benefit from wider discussion within the search community. These include:

- High collective risk may not result in discovering a specific event that exceeds safety margins – "hoping" that a scenario with high risk levels will contain a rare or unexpected incident does not appear to be a productive way to search.
- In large configuration spaces, the search can always manipulate inputs to generate some level of risk. Directing the search towards specific targets can be a problem.
- Using a collective measure of risk in a large configuration space makes it difficult to understand the context of the result – i.e. has the search found a unique configuration of input variables that represent this risk, or are there many more variants to discover?

We feel these questions pose generic problems to using search with composite fitness functions in large systems (of systems), but they also raise issues about using search for safety related topics such as risk, which is traditionally assessed using quantifiable, probabilistic reasoning. While we can find hazardous scenarios using search, we may not be able to quantify the result in any meaningful way. Without some characterization of the solution space (e.g. how many hazards does it contain? What is the relationship between different solutions that have similar levels of risk?), safety analysts may not find the results particularly useful.

3   Characterizing the Solution Space

We suspected that our search space was large even before we tried to calculate the input permutations.[4] Large search spaces are termed "high dimensionality" problems when mutation can act on a large number of variables to affect the fitness outcome, traditionally making it difficult to scale evolutionary search to complex design tasks. High dimensionality also causes difficulty when trying to demonstrate that an optimal solution has been found in a given search space [11] [12]. For most real-world problems, this sort of "proof" is impossible to achieve and most practitioners are content to discover a solution which is "good enough". However from a safety perspective it is important to quantify risk to levels that are deemed acceptable to the regulatory authorities, i.e. have we found a rare example of extreme risk, or are there many such examples out there? If the latter can be demonstrated, then there may be a systemic safety problem that needs to be addressed.

These questions are hard to answer unless quantitative descriptions of the solution space can be given, something which is difficult to do with large solution spaces that

---

[4] The size of the search space containing all possible permutations would make an exhaustive search impossible (see appendix of the E.02.05-ASHiCS-D2.2-Method Description Technical Report, available with several other reports from the project at http://ashics.blogspot.co.uk).

cannot be exhaustively searched. We became more concerned about this after we noticed that the ranked fitness scores after several hundred generations contained relatively few high scores in the population. It seemed that the average fitness of the final generations was not being raised in the manner expected of evolutionary computation. This realization led us to try and find out what effect mutation was having on the near neighbors of the fittest individuals.

4   Sensitivity Analysis

By keeping a record of the fitness score of near neighbors that are sampled as part of the hill-climbing algorithm, we can find out how destructive or beneficial our mutations are to each near neighbor of the original scenario. We had noticed that the search often had long plateaus of high fitness (when the best of the previous generation is passed on unchanged to the subsequent generation), during which time it appeared that no mutations of close, high scoring scenarios were able to improve on the previous best fitness score. A sensitivity analysis enables us to compare different mutation rates and see how the mutations were affecting the average.

If most mutations show a significant drop in fitness, it suggests that the original scenario is on or near a peak of high fitness. However, if the summit is narrow and the sides of the peak are steep, then sampling too far from the original will give a rapid drop off in fitness and make it hard to for mutation to find the "sharp point" of highest fitness. If we look at two plots showing a variance in the mutation range value, we can see a marked difference not only in the performance of the search, but also in the effect of mutating copies of the best scenarios.

Fig. 1 shows a sensitivity analysis of run using a mutation range of 300 seconds (i.e. the search can generate a new start time for each aircraft up to 5 minutes before or after its original time). The plot shows fitness values (y axis) of the top ten scenarios of each generation (divide by ten along the x axis to get the actual number of generations). Due to the policy of elitism, the top ten scenarios of a generation are likely to have been generated from one of the top three in the previous generation. As the evolutionary run progresses, we can see that the plateaus becoming longer (plateaus represent no improvement on the previous generation's best scenario) indicating that the search is struggling to improve on the fittest individual. At the beginning of the run, the distance between the fitness scores that the best of a generation and its mutated copies achieve are relatively close together, as we would typically expect from near neighbor sampling of the search space. As the run progresses and higher fitness scores are achieved by the best individual, the gap between the near neighbors and the best individual starts to widen, to the point towards the end of the run where every mutation seems to radically worsen the fitness score of the mutant copy. This type of sensitivity pattern suggests the search landscape is composed of tall, narrow spikes, in which a large mutation is likely to mean the individual is placed beyond the small area of high fitness occupied by the original scenario.

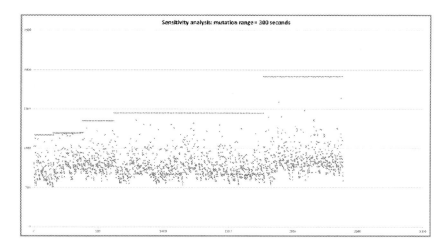

Fig. 1. Sensitivity analysis. Mutation range = 300s.

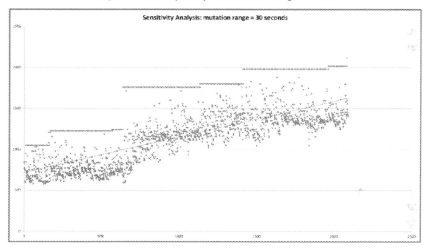

Fig. 2. Sensitivity analysis. Mutation range = 30s.

When we compare this to Fig. 2 which is the same in all respects other than having a much reduced mutation range of 30 seconds (half a minute either side of the original start time), it is immediately obvious that the smaller mutation range has produced a much less destructive effect on the fitness of near neighbors. The overall performance is improved, with a higher final fitness score for the best scenario (which steadily improved over many generations) but also with better average fitness across the population. The gap between the best and its near neighbors indicates that the solution space is highly sensitive to mutation rates. Fig. 1 and Fig. 2 provide us with an intuition of the search space; in that we can see small mutations enable the average fitness of the population to improve, whereas large mutations appear destructive. But how can we be sure that the best scenarios are being genuinely evolved and not

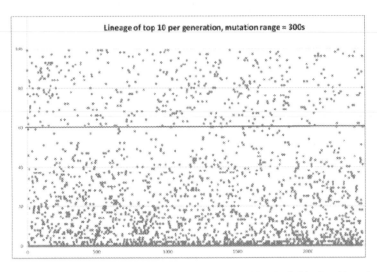

Fig. 3. Lineage of top 10 per generation. Mutation range = 300s. Individuals with an index (y-axis) greater 60 come from random sampling.

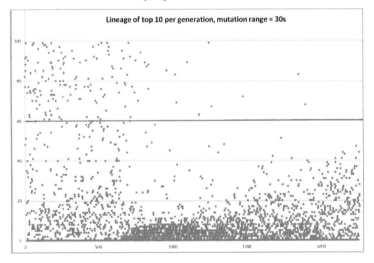

Fig. 4. Lineage of top 10 per generation. Mutation range = 30s. Individuals with an index (y-axis) greater 60 come from random sampling.

chosen from the randomly generated part of the population? By tagging the previous index of selected scenarios, we were able to track a scenario's previous ranking after it had entered the top ten of a particular generation. If the evolutionary search is working effectively, we would expect the proportion of high ranking scenarios coming from the random sector of the population to decrease over time, as evolved scenarios raise their average fitness scores. Fig.3 and Fig. 4 show the lineage of the top ten scenarios from each generation, using the same data as Fig. 1 and Fig. 2. As before, the scatter plots show a number of generations along the x axis, with the lineage (i.e. previous ranking index) of the ten best in each generation on the y axis. Any scenario that comes from an index of over 60 (measured on the y-axis) has come from the random part of the population. We can see that in the case of the poorly perform-ing large mutation rate, the random part of the population continues to supply almost equal numbers of scenarios to the top ten of every generation throughout the run. Over generations there is little drop off in their numbers, which indicates the search is both continuing to select scenarios from the random part of the population and failing to improve them by mutation. Fig. 4 shows the same type of plot but for the smaller mutation range. It shows how over time the search increasingly selects from mutated scenarios, while the contribution from the random part of the population falls off rap-idly and tails off to almost zero in the final stages. The combination of using a sensi-tivity analysis and tracing the lineage of near neighbors gives us some confidence that a non-destructive mutation operator outperforms setting the mutation operator to a large range and offers evidence against the use of destructive operators such as cross-over for this domain.

Observations. However, while we can make qualitative assessments of the solutions discovered by looking at how sensitive the solution space is to mutation rates, we still lack a concrete form of quantitative assessment of the area we are searching. That is to say we cannot say whether the search would find many similar solutions or very few.[5] This is not usually an issue for research into search heuristics; however in the case of searching for risk or safety related factors, it is important as the cost of dealing with risk (usually through the implementation of safety barriers) is often worked out by determining the cost of the outcome multiplied by the frequency of the event occurring. As we are searching for rare events, it would be of interest to not only discover instances of these, but to gain an approximate idea of their frequency for a given configuration of air space. For example, at the intersection of flight paths there may be many ways of producing a conflict between aircraft by adjusting their start times, but while these solutions differ technically, in pragmatic terms the search is not finding anything unique or unexpected. While we believe that evolutionary search can be used to find high risk scenario configurations; there remain some questions about the usefulness of using a collective assessment of risk when trying to qualita-tively assess the search results. High collective risk levels may not point to a specific event that exceeds safety margins. Therefore if we are interested in risk attached to a specific incident, we must weight our heuristics accordingly.

5   Conclusions

In this paper we have described the evolutionary search used by ASHiCS to discover high risk configurations of air sector traffic. We have provided arguments that show the use of destructive operators are unlikely to be effective in the type of high dimen-sional solution space represented by an air sector. The sensitivity analysis suggests that the solution landscape is composed of steep-sided, narrow peaks of high fitness,

---

[5] As each run takes around 26-30 hours (on a Windows 7 64-bit PC, Intel Core 2 Duo 3Ghz, 4GB RAM) it is difficult to generate meaningful statistics using many runs after debugging and experimentation.

in which only very near neighbors are likely to result in a fitness improvement. We believe this is an accurate characterization of the solution landscape, given that adjusting the start times of aircraft by just a few minutes can make a difference to conflict separation of several nautical miles. For our future work, we will increase the complexity of our scenarios by adding thunderstorms represented by transient no-fly zones whose speed, shape and direction are also configured by the search. Our aim will be to target our heuristics towards the late resolution of conflicts caused by the additional vectoring of aircraft to avoid the storm.

References

1. Koza, J., Keane, M., Streeter, M.: Evolving inventions. Scientific American, 52–59 (2003)
2. Fonlupt, C.: Book review: Genetic programming IV: Routine human competitive machine intelligence. Genetic Programming and Evolvable Machines **6**, 231–233 (2005)
3. Alam, S., Zhao, W., Tang, J.: Discovering Delay Patterns in Arrival Traffic with Dynamic Continuous Descent Approaches using Co-Evolutionary Red Teaming. In: 9th ATM Seminar, Berlin (2011)
4. Alam, S., Lokan, C., Abbass, H.: What can make an airspace unsafe? characterizing collision risk using multi-objective optimization. In: IEEE Congress on Evolutionary Computation (CEC), pp. 1–8 (2012)
5. White, D.R., Poulding, S.: A Rigorous Evaluation of Crossover and Mutation in Genetic Programming. In: Vanneschi, L., Gustafson, S., Moraglio, A., De Falco, I., Ebner, M. (eds.) EuroGP 2009. LNCS, vol. 5481, pp. 220–231. Springer, Heidelberg (2009)
6. Goldberg, D.: Genetic algorithms in search, optimization, and machine learning. Addison-Wesley (1989)
7. De Jong, K., Spears, W.: An analysis of the interacting roles of population size and crossover in genetic algorithms. In: Lecture Notes in Computer Science. Springer Berlin / Heidelberg pp. 38–47 (1991)
8. Lima, C., Goldberg, D., Sastry, K., Lobo, F.: Combining competent crossover and mutation operators: A probabilistic model building approach. In Beyer, H.-G. (ed.): Proceedings of the 2005 Conference on Genetic and evolutionary computation (GECCO 2005), New York, pp. 735–742 (2005)
9. Perrin, E., Kirwan, B., Stroup, R.: A Systemic model of ATM Safety: the integrated risk picture. In: 7th ATM Seminar, Barcelona (2007)
10. ARMS Working Group, 2007-2010: The ARMS Methodology for Operational Risk Assessment in Aviation Organisations. (v 4.1, March 2010)
11. Beyer, K., Goldstein, J., Ramakrishnan, R., Shaft, U.: When Is Nearest Neighbor Meaningful? In: Beeri, C., Bruneman, P. (eds.) ICDT 1999. LNCS, vol. 1540, pp. 217–235. Springer, Heidelberg (1998)
12. Merz, P., Freisleben, B.: On the effectiveness of evolutionary search in high-dimensional NK-landscapes. In: IEEE World Congress on Computational Intelligence, Evolutionary Computation Proceedings, pp. 741–745 (1998)
13. Anderson, D., Lin, X.: A collision risk model for a crossing track separation methodology. Journal of Navigation **49**(3), 337–349 (1996)

EvoROBOT

Speeding Up Online Evolution of Robotic Controllers with Macro-neurons

Fernando Silva[1,3]([✉]), Luís Correia[3], and Anders Lyhne Christensen[1,2]

[1] Instituto de Telecomunicações, Lisbon, Portugal
fsilva@di.fc.ul.pt, anders.christensen@iscte.pt
[2] Instituto Universitário de Lisboa (ISCTE-IUL), Lisbon, Portugal
[3] LabMAg, Faculdade de Ciências, Universidade de Lisboa, Lisbon, Portugal
luis.correia@di.fc.ul.pt

Abstract. In this paper, we introduce a novel approach to the online evolution of robotic controllers. We propose accelerating and scaling online evolution to more complex tasks by giving the evolutionary process direct access to behavioural building blocks prespecified in the neural architecture as *macro-neurons*. During task execution, both the structure and the parameters of macro-neurons and of the entire neural network are under evolutionary control. We perform a series of simulation-based experiments in which an e-puck-like robot must learn to solve a deceptive and dynamic phototaxis task with three light sources. We show that: (i) evolution is able to progressively *complexify* controllers by using the behavioural building blocks as a substrate, (ii) macro-neurons, either evolved or preprogrammed, enable a significant reduction in the adaptation time and the synthesis of high performing solutions, and (iii) evolution is able to inhibit the execution of detrimental task-unrelated behaviours and adapt non-optimised macro-neurons.

Keywords: Online evolution · Evolutionary robotics · Artificial neural network · Prespecified behaviours · Neuronal model

1 Introduction

Online evolution is a process of continuous adaptation that potentially gives robots the capacity to respond to task changes and unforeseen circumstances by modifying their behaviour. An evolutionary algorithm (EA) is executed on the robots themselves while they perform their task. The main components of the EA (evaluation, selection, and reproduction) are carried out autonomously by the robots without any external supervision. This way, robots may be capable of long-term self-adaptation in a completely autonomous manner.

The first example of online evolution in a real mobile robot was performed by Floreano and Mondada [7]. The introduction of *embodied evolution* by Watson *et al.* [16] followed, in which the use of multirobot systems was motivated by the speed-up of evolution due to the inherent parallelism in groups of robots that evolve together in the task environment. Over the past decade, different

© Springer-Verlag Berlin Heidelberg 2014
A.I. Esparcia-Alcázar et al. (Eds.): EvoApplications 2014, LNCS 8602, pp. 765–776, 2014.
DOI: 10.1007/978-3-662-45523-4_62

approaches to online evolution have been proposed. Examples include the $(\mu+1)$-online EA of Haasdijk *et al.* [9], mEDEA by Bredeche *et al.* [1], and odNEAT by Silva *et al.* [11]. Notwithstanding, there are still a number of fundamental issues and technological challenges that must be addressed before online evolution becomes a viable approach to adaptation in real robots. The prohibitively long time that the online evolutionary process requires and the fact that ER techniques have not yet scaled to real-world tasks [4] are central impediments to adoption.

In this paper, we introduce a novel approach to the online evolution of neural network-based robotic controllers. We propose the combined use of standard neurons as elementary components, and higher level units that we shall refer to as *macro-neurons*. The macro-neurons are *behavioural building blocks*, either evolved or preprogrammed, that are integrated in the neural architecture before the evolutionary process is conducted. During task execution, both the structure and the parameters of macro-neurons and of the entire ANN are under evolutionary control. In this way, evolution is able to continuously optimise and adapt controllers by using the behavioural building blocks as a substrate.

Our proposed method contrasts with previous approaches in which: (i) ANN outputs are used to execute one out of a finite set of predefined behaviours, either evolved or preprogrammed [3,8,15], which may forestall the synthesis of theoretically optimal controllers, or (ii) ANN-based controllers synthesised through hierarchical decomposition of the task, and structured composition of both evolved and preprogrammed behaviours [4,6,8], which require a substantial amount of experimentation and human intervention. The viability of our method is assessed through a set of simulation-based experiments in which an e-puck-like robot [10] must perform a deceptive and dynamic phototaxis task with three light sources. To the best of our knowledge, this is the first demonstration of unified online evolution of the weights and the ANN topology, and higher level units representing behaviours.

2   Background

In this section, we describe our proposed macro-neuron-based architecture, and we introduce odNEAT, the online neuroevolution algorithm used in this study.

2.1   Specification of Macro-neurons

The main goal in using macro-neurons is to give online evolution behavioural building blocks in order to: (i) synthesise increasingly more complex behaviours by capitalising on the existing ones, both evolved and preprogrammed, and (ii) adapt the structure and the parameters of existing solutions through evolution. Therefore, it is fundamental to specify the behavioural building blocks in a way that enables the evolutionary process to optimise them.

Each macro-neuron M is defined as $\{I_c, O_c, F, P\}$, where I_c is the set of input connections of M, O_c is the set of output connections, F is the function computed by the macro-neuron, and P is the set of parameters of M subject to

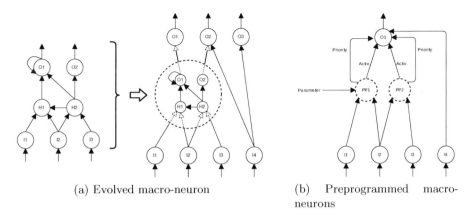

(a) Evolved macro-neuron

(b) Preprogrammed macro-neurons

Fig. 1. Examples of the integration of different types of behavioural building blocks in neural architectures. (a) An evolved ANN-based macro-neuron. (b) Two preprogrammed macro-neurons.

evolution. Each connection $I_{c,i} \in I_c$ contains a weight $w_i \in w$ and transmits to M an input value $x_i \in x$. The computation of M is given by $f(w, x) = y$, where y is the output vector of M. Each $y_j \in y$ is transmitted to other neurons via the corresponding connection $O_{c,j} \in O_c$. Depending on the type of macro-neuron, P refers to different elements. If M is a preprogrammed macro-neuron, P contains the numerical parameters of the behaviour (see below). If M is an evolved ANN, P refers to the connections and neurons that can be manipulated by evolution.

The construction and functioning of neural architectures using macro-neurons is shown in Fig. 1. Figure 1a shows how a previously evolved ANN is translated to a macro-neuron. The connections from the macro-neuron to the output neurons of the network enable evolution to arbitrate and shape the output values of different macro-neurons. Complementary, Fig. 1b illustrates how different preprogrammed macro-neurons are specified. Each macro-neuron transmits two values to each output neuron: (i) a *priority* value, which represents the effective need of the behaviour to execute at a given time, computed based on the input values, and (ii) an *activity* value representing the signal to be sent to the actuators controlled by the output neurons.

The goal of incorporating both priority and activity values in preprogrammed macro-neurons is to add human knowledge to better resolve conflict situations in which different preprogrammed macro-neurons compete for control [2]. In this case, each output neuron considers the activity of the preprogrammed macro-neuron with the highest priority. If no preprogrammed behaviour produces a positive priority value, the output neuron performs the weighted sum of its remaining inputs from standard neurons such as I4 in Fig. 1b.

An important feature of our approach is that macro-neurons are prespecified in the neural architecture before the evolutionary process is conducted. During task execution, online evolution is able to: (i) optimise the *structure* of evolved macro-neurons and of the entire network by adding new neurons and new connections, and by adjusting the connection weights, (ii) adapt the parameters of preprogrammed behaviours such as PP1 in Fig. 1b, and (iii) modulate the execution of macro-neurons by increasing or decreasing the strength of connections such as those related to the priority and activity values. In this way, evolution can, for instance, disable the execution of unnecessary macro-neurons. By combining ANNs and prespecified macro-neurons, either evolved or preprogrammed, we compound: (i) the ANNs' flexibility, robustness, and tolerance to noise [7], (ii) the benefits of each type of macro-neuron, which can be synthesised by distinct evolutionary processes or hand-designed in order to shortcut complex evolutionary processes, (iii) a higher level bootstrap process, which potentially allows robots to adapt to complex and dynamic tasks in a timely manner.

2.2 odNEAT: An Online Neuroevolution Algorithm

NEAT [14] is a state-of-the-art neuroevolution method that evolves the weights and the topology of ANNs. odNEAT [11] is an online, steady-state, decentralised version of NEAT, originally designed for multirobot systems. odNEAT is used in our study because it has shown to enable efficient online adaptation in single robot domains [12]. As we conduct our experiments using one robot, we only describe odNEAT's features with respect to a single agent.

The robot is controlled by an ANN that represents a candidate solution to the task, and maintains a virtual energy level representing its performance. The fitness value is defined as the average of the energy level, sampled at regular time intervals. The robot maintains a population of genomes, the direct genetic encoding of ANNs, and their respective fitness scores in an internal repository. The repository implements a niching scheme comprising speciation and fitness sharing, which allows the robot to maintain a healthy diversity of candidate solutions with different topologies.

In the original definition, odNEAT starts executing with a population of random networks in which each input neuron is connected to every output neuron. When the virtual energy level reaches zero, the current controller is considered unfit for the task. A new genome representing a new controller is created by choosing a parent species from the internal population, and selecting two parents, each one via a tournament selection of size 2. Offspring is created through crossover of the parents' genomes and mutation of the new genome. Once the genome is decoded into a new controller, it is guaranteed a minimum *maturation period* α during which it controls the robot. Mutation is both structural and parametric, as it adds new neurons and connections, and optimises existing parameters such as connection weights and neuron bias values. In this way, odNEAT avoids *a priori* specification of the network topology and can evolve an appropriate degree of complexity for the task.

3   Methods

In this section, we define our experimental methodology, including the robot model, the deceptive phototaxis task, and the experimental setup.

3.1   Robot Model and Behavioural Control

We use JBotEvolver [5], an open-source, multirobot simulation platform and neuroevolution framework for our experiments. The simulated robot is modelled after the e-puck [10], a 75 mm in diameter, differential drive robot capable of moving at a maximum speed of 13 cm/s. The robot is equipped with eight IR sensors for obstacle detection. The IR sensors have a range of 25 cm.[1] Each IR sensor and each actuator is subject to noise, which is simulated by adding a random Gaussian component within ±5% of the sensor saturation value or of the maximum actuation value. The robot is also equipped with an internal sensor that allows it to perceive its current virtual energy level.

During task execution, the robot is controlled by a discrete time recurrent ANN synthesised by odNEAT. The ANN's connection weights ∈ [-5,5] and the activation function is the steepened sigmoid [14]. The inputs of the ANN are the normalised readings from the sensors mentioned above. The input layer consists of 17 neurons: (i) eight for wall detection, (ii) eight for light source detection, and (iii) one neuron for the virtual energy level readings. The output layer contains two neurons, one for setting the signed speed value of each wheel.

3.2   Deceptive Phototaxis

Phototaxis is a standard task in evolutionary robotics, in which robots have to search for and move towards a light source. We study a deceptive and dynamic version of the phototaxis task with three light sources. One source is beneficial to the robot, one source is neutral, and the remaining source is detrimental. The sources are static but they periodically switch their type causing, for instance, the beneficial light source to become neutral or detrimental, and vice versa.

The task requires the robot to perform phototaxis when faced with the beneficial light source, and to perform anti-phototaxis as the alternative action when in close proximity to either the neutral or the detrimental light source. Deceptiveness is introduced by the fact that the three light sources are indistinguishable to the robot's light sensors. The robot must therefore discriminate between different lights based on the temporal correlation between its energy sensor readings and proximity to a given source.

The task environment is illustrated in Fig. 2. The robot operates in a square arena surrounded by walls. The size of the arena is chosen to be 3 x 3 meters. The arena contains four obstacles with dimensions 0.5 x 0.125 meters and one obstacle with dimensions 0.125 x 0.5 meters. The obstacles are of the same material as walls, and increase the difficulty of the task by reducing the area for navigation, and ensuring that there is no straight path between different light sources. The placement and size of the light sources is inspired in the experimental setup of Sperati et al. [13]. The sources have a diameter of 0.32 meters and are positioned symmetrically with respect to the centre of the arena. The distance between the

---

[1] The original e-puck infrared range is 2-3 cm [10]. In real e-pucks, the *liblrcom* library, available at http://www.e-puck.org, extends the range up to 25 cm.

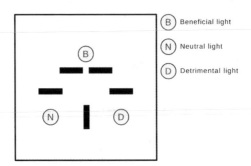

Fig. 2. The task environment. The arena measures 3 x 3 meters. The dark areas denote physical obstacles, while the white areas denote the arena surface on which the robot can navigate. The circular areas represent the different sources.

light sources is set at 1.5 meters. The type of each light source is rotated every five minutes of simulated time in a clockwise manner.

Initially, the robot is placed in a random position. During simulation, the energy level E is updated every 100 ms according to the following equation:

$$\frac{\Delta E}{\Delta t} = \begin{cases} S_r & \text{if } S_r > 0.5 \text{ and near beneficial source} \\ -(S_r + E_c) & \text{if near detrimental source} \\ -E_c & \text{if near neutral source or not close to any source} \end{cases} \quad (1)$$

where S_r is the maximum value of the readings from the light sensors, between 0 (no light) and 1 (brightest light), and E_c is a constant energy consumption value of 0.5. Note that the robot is only rewarded if it is significantly close to the beneficial source, i.e., if $S_r > 0.5$.

3.3 Experimental Setup

We conducted experiments using two types of macro-neurons: evolved ANNs and preprogrammed behaviours. We synthesised three basic primitives of each type: (i) a *move forward* behaviour, executed if there is no obstacle ahead of the robot, (ii) a *turn left* behaviour and (iii) a *turn right* behaviour. The two "turn" behaviours enable turning in the respective direction if there is an obstacle in sensor range. The *move forward* behaviour has access to the readings from the robot's three front sensors. The *turn left* and *turn right* behaviours process the inputs from the three front-right sensors and three front-left sensors, respectively. The macro-neurons are all fully-connected to the output neurons.

The evolved macro-neurons were synthesised using the offline NEAT algorithm [14]. For obtaining each ANN, we conducted 30 independent runs. Each run was performed using a population of 100 genomes and lasted 100 generations. The fitness score of each genome was averaged over 20 samples at each evaluation. After the evolutionary process ended, we post-evaluated the highest scoring controller of each run in 100 samples, and we selected the best controller to form a macro-neuron. The "turn" behaviours were evolved in a T-maze environment. The *move forward* behaviour was evolved in a long corridor.

We developed three preprogrammed macro-neurons functionally similar to the evolved ANNs. As described in Section 2.1, each of these macro-neurons produces priority values and activity values. The *move forward* behaviour executes with fixed priority $p = 0.5$ and transmits activity values $a = 1.0$ to each output neuron, i.e., the robot moves at maximum speed. The *turn left* behaviour produces a priority value p proportional to the distance of the closest obstacle on the front-right side of the robot, and activity values $a_{left} = 0$ and $a_{right} = 0.1$. The *turn right* behaviour operates in a similar manner with respect to the obstacles on the front-left side of the robot, and produces activity values $a_{left} = 0$ and $a_{right} = 0.1$. The priorities of the "turn" behaviours permit a flexible behaviour selection depending on the distance to obstacles, and the activity values enable smooth turns while avoiding an obstacle. Each preprogrammed macro-neuron executes for $exec_{time}$ control cycles of the robot.

Experimental Configuration. We conducted four sets of evolutionary experiments to assess the performance levels of our approach. In the first set of experiments, macro-neurons were not used and odNEAT relied on evolution alone. To provide a meaningful and fair comparison of performance, we conducted a series of preliminary tests to determine the best initial topology for evolution alone. We seeded evolution with a fully-connected hidden layer, and we varied the number of hidden neurons from 1 to 10. We consistently verified better performance when evolution alone started without hidden neurons, i.e., with each input neuron connected to every output neuron ($\rho < 0.05$, Mann-Whitney test). In the second set of experiments, evolution was given access to the three preprogrammed macro-neurons. In the third set of experiments, evolution was seeded with the three evolved macro-neurons. The topology and the connection weights of evolved macro-neurons were also subject to evolution, allowing the behaviours to be adapted during task execution. In the last set of experiments, we evaluated an hybrid approach with access to the preprogrammed *move forward* behaviour and to the evolved "turn" behaviours.

For each experimental configuration, we performed 30 independent runs. Each run lasted 100 hours of simulated time. The virtual energy level of the robot was limited to the range [0,100] energy units. If the virtual energy level reached zero, a new controller was generated and assigned the maximum energy value of 100 units. Crossover was not used. Other parameters of odNEAT were the same as in [11]. The parameter $exec_{time}$ of each preprogrammed macro-neuron was initially set at 1 and subject to a Gaussian mutation with mean 0 and standard deviation of 1. During task execution, $exec_{time}$ was rounded to the nearest integer value. Note that in the case of the "turn" behaviours with low $exec_{time}$ values, it is the consecutive execution of the behaviour while an obstacle is in range that enables the robot to avoid the obstacles.

4   Experimental Results

In this section, we present and discuss the experimental results. We use the Mann-Whitney test to compute statistical significance of differences between sets of results because it is a non-parametric test, and therefore no strong assumptions need to be made about the underlying distributions.

We first compare the performance of the four neural architectures. We analyse: (i) the number of evaluations, i.e., the number of controllers tested by the robot before a solution to the task is found, (ii) the evaluation time elapsed before the solution is synthesised, and (iii) the task performance in terms of fitness score. Evaluation time is measured to complement the number of evaluations. In odNEAT, controllers execute as long as they are able to solve the task, and the duration of evaluations therefore tends to vary (see Sect. 2.2).

The distributions of the number of evaluations and of the evaluation time are shown in Fig. 3. All runs produced controllers well adapted to the periodic changes in the task requirements. The three neural architectures using macro-neurons significantly outperform evolution alone as they require fewer evaluations and shorter evaluation times to synthesise solutions for the task ($\rho < 0.01$, Mann-Whitney). Differences in the number of evaluations and in the evaluation time of architectures using macro-neurons are not significant ($\rho \geq 0.05$).

The most efficient synthesis of controllers occurs when using the evolved macro-neurons, which require an average of 57.60 evaluations and 1.78 hours of evaluation time. Controllers using preprogrammed macro-neurons need 71.50 evaluations and have an evaluation time of 1.91 hours, and the hybrid setup requires an average of 68.53 evaluations and 2.91 hours of evaluation time. Evolution alone requires 201.60 evaluations and 9.50 hours of simulated time. Overall, the results support the conclusion that online evolution can be significantly accelerated by using prespecified behavioural building blocks. Macro-neurons speed up online evolution substantially by reducing the number of evaluations between 69% and 71%, and the evaluation time between 53% and 80%.

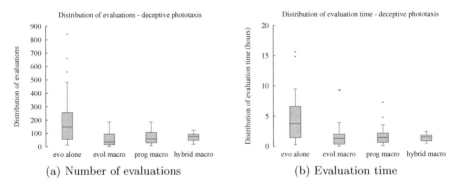

(a) Number of evaluations   (b) Evaluation time

Fig. 3. Distribution of: (a) the number of evaluations necessary to synthesise a solution to the task, and (b) duration of the evaluation period. Outliers above 20 hours in (b) are not shown for better reading of the plot. The missing values are 20.20, 26.96, 54.67, and 77.59 hours, all with respect to evolution alone.

An analysis of the fitness scores of solutions to the task shows that the four neural architectures provide comparable results, with a slight advantage in favour of ANNs synthesised with access to the evolved macro-neurons. Controllers using evolved macro-neurons have an average fitness score of 75.85. In the remaining approaches, which include evolution alone, the average fitness score varies from 67.21 to 69.95. Differences in the fitness scores are not statistically significant across all comparisons ($\rho \geq 0.05$, Mann-Whitney). In this way, using macro-neurons not only allows for a speed-up in the adaptation process, but also leads to the synthesis of competitive and potentially superior performing solutions.

4.1   Dynamics of Neural Architectures

The results described above show that neural architectures using macro-neurons enable a significantly faster adaptation process. In this section, we analyse the topologies of networks evolved in the four experimental configurations in order to determine differences in neural augmentation and dynamics.

The complexity of solutions that solve the task is listed in Table 1. Overall, evolution alone presents the least complex topologies. Despite solving the task with less structure, the number of evaluations and evaluation time are higher, as discussed in the previous section. Given the deceptiveness and complexity of the task, the evolutionary process without access to macro-neurons displays significant difficulties in bootstrapping and finding functioning controllers. Complementarily, ANNs with evolved macro-neurons present the most complex topologies although they require fewer evaluations and shorter evaluation periods. Compared to evolution alone, evolved macro-neurons enable *higher level* bootstrapping as ANNs are seeded with basic general competences for the task. The new connections and new neurons added through evolution augment and adjust both the ANN and the structure of the evolved macro-neurons. The capability to continuously evolve the macro-neurons is particularly important in the case of online evolution as the evolutionary process is given a means to adapt the prespecified behavioural building blocks to the task requirements, and to synthesise more complex behaviours by capitalising on the existing ones.

Final solutions synthesised using preprogrammed macro-neurons are not substantially augmented in terms of neural complexity. The main source of optimisation was the mutation of the connection weights. Online evolution takes advantage of the preprogrammed behaviours' functionality and adjusts primarily the way in which they are used in order to synthesise a solution to the task. Evolution adapts the ANN by: (i) arbitrating the execution of different preprogrammed behaviours for navigation in the environment, and (ii) modulating the excitatory and inhibitory signals of connections related to the operation of the macro-neurons. For instance, when the robot finds the beneficial light source, the programmed behaviours are often inhibited. The robot remains close to the light source by moving around it until the type of the source is changed.

Complementarily, solutions using the preprogrammed *move forward* behaviour and the evolved "turn" behaviours exhibit the two characteristics described above. On one hand, evolved macro-neurons are adjusted and adapted. On the other hand,

Table 1. Neural complexity of the final controllers. Initial complexity, and number of neurons and connections added through evolution (average ± std. dev.)

Experimental configuration	Initial topology		Structure added	
	Neurons	Connections	Neurons	Connections
Evolution alone	19	34	3.23 ± 0.43	6.60 ± 0.77
Evolved macro	39	69	5.80 ± 1.56	12.00 ± 3.16
Preprogrammed macro	22	45	0.17 ± 0.38	0.67 ± 0.84
Hybrid macro	34	60	2.59 ± 0.91	8.31 ± 1.56

evolution optimises when and how the preprogrammed macro-neuron is used in order to maximise task performance.

4.2 Assessing the Robustness of Evolution

In our approach, evolved and preprogrammed behavioural building blocks are prespecified in the neural architecture. In this section, we assess if the online adaptation process is able to inhibit or adapt task-unrelated or non-optimised macro-neurons. We setup two series of experiments, each composed by 30 independent runs. In the first set of experiments, ANNs are initialised with the three evolved macro-neurons and a *do not move* preprogrammed macro-neuron. The preprogrammed macro-neuron continuously produces a priority value $p = 1.0$ and an activity value $a = 0$ to each output neuron, therefore indicating that the most important action is *always* for the robot not to move. In the second set of experiments, neural architectures are initialised only with the three navigation-related evolved macro-neurons. Part of the structure of the evolved macro-neurons is ablated, making them less optimised or even unsuited for the task. Before online evolution is conducted, each connection weight of the evolved macro-neurons is reset to 0 with probability $prob = 0.25$, sampled from a uniform distribution. The goal of the experiment is to analyse the potential costs and the adaptability of online evolution when given access to incomplete and non-optimised macro-neurons.

Table 2 summarises the results of the robustness experiments. Results show that evolution is able to successfully overcome the presence of task-unrelated or non-optimised macro-neurons, either evolved or preprogrammed. In the two setups, solutions are synthesised faster than by evolution alone with respect to the number of evaluations and to the evaluation time ($\rho < 0.01$, Mann-Whitney). In the experimental setup with the *do not move* behaviour, the macro-neuron is preprogrammed and therefore its structure is not subject to optimisation. Evolution is obliged to perform a finer-grain adjustment of connection weights in order to inhibit the outputs of the detrimental macro-neuron, hence the higher number of evaluations and the longer evaluation time.

In the experimental setup using the partially ablated evolved macro-neurons, evolution produces solutions faster but with lower performance when compared to the non-ablated counterparts. In general terms, the ablated macro-neurons cause unadapted solutions to fail rapidly during task execution, hence the low

Table 2. Comparison of results across different experimental configurations. The table lists the average values of each experimental configuration.

Experimental configuration	Evaluations	Eval. time (hours)	Fitness score
Evolution alone	201.60	9.50	67.21
Evolved macro	57.60	1.78	75.85
Evolved + *do not move* macro	73.17	3.13	75.32
Ablated evolved macro	77.33	1.59	69.00

evaluation time. The structure and the parameters of the ablated macro-neurons and of the entire ANN are then progressively optimised until a solution capable of solving the task is synthesised. However, as the ablated evolved macro-neurons are less optimised, the solutions generally yield lower performance levels.

5   Conclusions

In this paper, we introduced a novel approach to the online evolution of robotic controllers. We give evolution direct access to behavioural building blocks pre-specified in the neural architecture as macro-neurons. The structure and the parameters of macro-neurons are under evolutionary control, and they are optimised together with the ANN's weights and topology in a unified manner.

We showed that macro-neurons significantly outperform evolution alone as they enable a substantial reduction in the adaptation time, and the synthesis of high performing solutions. We also showed that distinct types of macro-neurons allow the evolution of solutions in different ways. When using evolved macro-neurons, *both* the macro-neurons and the entire ANN are progressively augmented and adjusted in order to adapt the building blocks to the task requirements. When using preprogrammed macro-neurons, evolution adds significantly less structure to the ANN. The evolutionary process adapts the ANNs by arbitrating the execution of the preprogrammed behaviours, and modulating the input and output signals of the macro-neurons. To conclude, we have also shown that online evolution can successfully: (i) inhibit the execution of detrimental behaviours, and (ii) adapt non-optimised macro-neurons.

The immediate follow-up work includes extending our approach to multirobot systems that exchange solutions to the task [11], in order to potentially facilitate online evolution for real-world complex tasks.

Acknowledgments. This work was partially supported by the Fundação para a Ciência e a Tecnologia under the grants SFRH/BD/89573/2012, EXPL/EEI-AUT/0329/2013, PEst-OE/EEI/LA0008/2013, and PEst-OE/EEI/UI0434/2011.

References

1. Bredeche, N., Montanier, J.M., Liu, W., Winfield, A.F.: Environment-driven distributed evolutionary adaptation in a population of autonomous robotic agents. Mathematical and Computer Modelling of Dynamical Systems **18**(1), 101–129 (2012)

2. Correia, L., Steiger-Garção, A.: A useful autonomous vehicle with a hierarchical behavior control. In: Morán, F., Moreno, A., Merelo, J.J., Chacón, P. (eds.) Advances in Artificial Life. LNCS, vol. 929, pp. 625–639. Springer, Heidelberg (1995)

3. Duarte, M., Oliveira, S., Christensen, A.L.: Automatic Synthesis of Controllers for Real Robots Based on Preprogrammed Behaviors. In: Ziemke, T., Balkenius, C., Hallam, J. (eds.) SAB 2012. LNCS, vol. 7426, pp. 249–258. Springer, Heidelberg (2012)

4. Duarte, M., Oliveira, S., Christensen, A.L.: Hierarchical evolution of robotic controllers for complex tasks. In: IEEE International Conference on Development and Learning and Epigenetic Robotics, pp. 1–6. IEEE Press, Piscataway (2012)

5. Duarte, M., Silva, F., Rodrigues, T., Oliveira, S.M., Christensen, A.L.: JBotEvolver: A Versatile Simulation Platform for Evolutionary Robotics. In: 14th International Conference on the Synthesis and Simulation of Living Systems, pp. 210–211. MIT Press, Cambridge (2014)

6. Fernandez-Leon, J.A., Acosta, G.G., Mayosky, M.A.: Behavioral control through evolutionary neurocontrollers for autonomous mobile robot navigation. Robotics and Autonomous Systems 57(4), 411–419 (2009)

7. Floreano, D., Mondada, F.: Automatic creation of an autonomous agent: Genetic evolution of a neural-network driven robot. In: 3rd International Conference on Simulation of Adaptive Behavior, pp. 421–430. MIT Press, Cambridge (1994)

8. Godzik, N., Schoenauer, M., Sebag, M.: Evolving Symbolic Controllers. In: Raidl, G.R., Cagnoni, S., Cardalda, J.J.R., Corne, D.W., Gottlieb, J., Guillot, A., Hart, E., Johnson, C.G., Marchiori, E., Meyer, J.-A., Middendorf, M. (eds.) EvoIASP 2003, EvoWorkshops 2003, EvoSTIM 2003, EvoROB/EvoRobot 2003, EvoCOP 2003, EvoBIO 2003, and EvoMUSART 2003. LNCS, vol. 2611, pp. 638–650. Springer, Heidelberg (2003)

9. Haasdijk, E., Eiben, A., Karafotias, G.: On-line evolution of robot controllers by an encapsulated evolution strategy. In: IEEE Congress on Evolutionary Computation, pp. 1–7. IEEE Press, Piscataway (2010)

10. Mondada, F., Bonani, M., Raemy, X., Pugh, J., Cianci, C., Klaptocz, A., Magnenat, S., Zufferey, J., Floreano, D., Martinoli, A.: The e-puck, a robot designed for education in engineering. In: 9th Conference on Autonomous Robot Systems and Competitions, pp. 59–65. IPCB, Castelo Branco (2009)

11. Silva, F., Urbano, P., Oliveira, S., Christensen, A.L.: odNEAT: An algorithm for distributed online, onboard evolution of robot behaviours. In: 13th International Conference on Simulation & Synthesis of Living Systems, pp. 251–258. MIT Press, Cambridge (2012)

12. Silva, F., Urbano, P., Christensen, A.L.: Adaptation of Robot Behaviour through Online Evolution and Neuromodulated Learning. In: Pavón, J., Duque-Méndez, N.D., Fuentes-Fernández, R. (eds.) IBERAMIA 2012. LNCS, vol. 7637, pp. 300–309. Springer, Heidelberg (2012)

13. Sperati, V., Trianni, V., Nolfi, S.: Self-organised path formation in a swarm of robots. Swarm Intelligence 5(2), 97–119 (2011)

14. Stanley, K., Miikkulainen, R.: Evolving neural networks through augmenting topologies. Evolutionary Computation 10(2), 99–127 (2002)

15. Urzelai, J., Floreano, D., Dorigo, M., Colombetti, M.: Incremental robot shaping. Connection Science 10(3–4), 341–360 (1998)

16. Watson, R., Ficici, S., Pollack, J.: Embodied evolution: Distributing an evolutionary algorithm in a population of robots. Robotics and Autonomous Systems 39(1), 1–18 (2002)

HyperNEAT Versus RL PoWER for Online Gait Learning in Modular Robots

Massimiliano D'Angelo[1], Berend Weel[2(✉)], and A.E. Eiben[2]

[1] University La Sapienza, Rome, Italy
maxxi.d.angelo@gmail.com
[2] VU University Amsterdam, Amsterdam, The Netherlands
{b.weel,a.e.eiben}@vu.nl

Abstract. This paper addresses a principal problem of *in vivo* evolution of modular multi-cellular robots, where robot 'babies' can be produced with arbitrary shapes and sizes. In such a system we need a generic learning mechanism that enables newborn morphologies to obtain a suitable gait quickly after 'birth'. In this study we investigate and compare the reinforcement learning method RL PoWeR with HyperNEAT. We conduct simulation experiments using robot morphologies with different size and complexity. The experiments give insights into the differences in solution quality and algorithm efficiency, suggesting that reinforcement learning is the preferred option for this online learning problem.

Keywords: Embodied artificial evolution · Modular robots · Artificial life · Online gait learning · Reinforcement learning · HyperNEAT

1 Introduction

The work described in this paper forms a stepping stone towards the grand vision of embodied artificial evolution (EAE) as outlined in [7]. The essence of this vision is to construct physical systems that undergo evolution 'in the wild', i.e. not in a virtual world inside a computer. There are various possible approaches towards this goal including chemical and biological ones. The one behind this study is based on using a mechatronical substrate, that is, robots.

In general, there are two principal forces behind evolution: selection and reproduction. Selection –at least environmental, objective-free selection– is 'for free' in the real world. Therefore, the main challenge for EAE is reproduction, i.e., the creation of tangible physical artifacts with the ability to reproduce. In our case, this means the need for self-reproducing robots. The approach we follow to this end is based on modular robotics with robotic building blocks capable of autonomous locomotion and aggregation into complex 'multicellular' structures in 3D. In this system evolution will not take place in the morphological space of these pre-engineered modules, but in the morphological space of the multicellular organisms. From the perspective of the multicellular robot bodies

© Springer-Verlag Berlin Heidelberg 2014
A.I. Esparcia-Alcázar et al. (Eds.): EvoApplications 2014, LNCS 8602, pp. 777–788, 2014.
DOI: 10.1007/978-3-662-45523-4_63

the basic robots are merely raw material whose physical properties do not change over time.[1]

In [6] a conceptual framework for systems where robot morphologies and controllers can evolve in real-time and real-space is presented. This framework, dubbed the Triangle of Life, describes a life cycle that does not run from birth to death, but from conception (being conceived) to conception (conceiving one or more children) and it is repeated over and over again, thus creating consecutive generations of 'robot children'. The Triangle of Life consists of 3 stages, Birth, Infancy, and Mature Life, cf. Fig. 1.

In this paper we address a fundamental problem in the Infancy stage.
This stage starts when the morphogenesis of a new robot organism is
completed and the 'baby robot' is
delivered. As explained in [6], the
body (morphological structure) and
the mind (controller) of such a new
organism will unlikely fit each other
well. Therefore the new organism
needs some fine tuning.This problem –
the Control Your Own Body (CYOB)
problem– is inherent to evolutionary
ALife systems where both bodies and
minds undergo changes during reproduction.

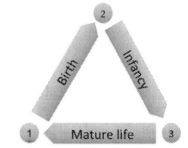

Fig. 1. The Triangle of Life. The pivotal moments that span the triangle and sepa-rate the 3 stages are: 1) Conception: A new genome is activated, construction of a new organism starts. 2) Delivery: Construction of the new organism is completed. 3) Fer-tility: The organism becomes ready to con-ceive offspring.

The work described here addresses the general CYOB problem in a sim-plified form, by reducing it to gait learning. In the modular robots approach the challenge is to find a method that can learn gaits for all different morphologies that can be created with the given modules and can do this quickly. The problem is highly nontrivial, since a modular robot organism has many degrees of freedom, which leads to a very large search space of possible gaits. Furthermore, this learning process must take place on-the-fly, during the real operational period of the robot organisms. The off-line approach, where a good controller is developed (evolved, learned, hand-coded, etc.) before the robot is deployed is not applicable here, because the life cycle of the Triangle is running in a hands-free mode without being paused for intervention by the experimenter.

In our previous work [5] we have applied a reinforcement learning algorithm PoWeR described by Kober and Peters [14] to solve the CYOB problem and investigated the effects of the shape and size of robot organisms on the perfor-mance of the learning method. In this paper we employ an evolutionary approach HyperNEAT [4] that has a good reputation for this type of tasks and compare

---

[1] Nevertheless, evolving the controllers of these elementary robot modules during the operational period is possible.

it with PoWeR. Similarly to [5] we use the learning algorithms with parameter values as recommended by the authors. The grand evolutionary process of the Triangle of Life is not investigated here; it only forms the background context that raises the CYOB problem.

The specific research questions our experiments will try to answer are the following:

1. How do the two approaches compare in terms of the quality of the learned gaits?
2. How do the two approaches compare in terms of the speed of learning?

2   Related Work

The design of locomotion for modular robotics is a difficult problem. As explained by Spröwitz: Locomotion requires the creation of rhythmic patterns which satisfy multiple constraints: generating forward motion, without falling over, with low energy, possibly coping with different environments, hardware failures, changes in the environment and/or of the organism [18].

One of the earliest types is gait control tables as in, for instance, [1] and [19]. A gait control table consist of rows of actuator commands with one column for each actuator, each row also has a condition for the transition to the next row.A second major avenue of research is that of neural networks (NN). In particular for locomotion of robot organisms HyperNEAT is used extensively with several studies showing that HyperNEAT is capable of creating efficient gaits for robots [4,9,20]. HyperNEAT is discussed in more detail in Section 3. Another successful approach that has received much attention is based on Central Pattern Generators (CPG). CPGs model neural circuitry found in vertebrates which output cyclic patterns without requiring a cyclic input [11]. Each actuator in a robot organism is controlled by the output of a CPG, furthermore the CPGs are connected through certain variables which allows them to synchronise and maintain a certain phase difference pattern. Although sensory input is not strictly needed for CPG's, it can be incorporated to shape the locomotion pattern to allow for turning and modulating the speed. This technique has been shown to produce well performing and stable gaits on both non-modular robots [2,18] and modular multi-robot organisms [12,13]. Last, a technique based on artificial hormones has been investigated for the locomotion of modular robot organisms. In this technique artificial hormones are created within robot modules as a response to sensory inputs. These hormones can interact with each other, diffuse to neighbouring modules and act upon output hormones. These output hormones are then used to drive the actuators [10,17]. Furthermore, some techniques in the field of gait learning employ reinforcement learning algorithms, the specific approaches used can range from Temporal Difference Learning (TDL) to Expectation-Maximization (EM). In TDL one seeks to minimize an error function between estimated and empirical results of a controller, in EM controller parameters are estimated in order to maximize the reward gained using it. These algorithms have been used on modular, e.g. [3] and non modular robots, e.g. [16].

Although there is extensive previous work on this issue, we must stress that, of the techniques described above, only the techniques described in [3], [12] and [18] were actually tested on multiple shapes.

3   Experimental Setup

Our primary goal is to compare the reinforcement learning (RL) approach RL PoWER to the population based neural network approach HyperNEAT. Similar to the work in [5] we test both algorithms in various organism morphologies set in a simple environment. These tests are done in simulation using the Webots symulator by Cyberbotics. We use the same adapted YaMoR module [15] as the building blocks for the organisms. The environment for the experiments is an infinite plane, free of obstacles to avoid any extra complexity and the need for supervision. Each experiment starts with the organism lying completely flat at the plane origin.

Nine different robot organisms with different sizes and complexity are defined to examine the generality and scalability of the algorithms. Size and complexity are measured by the number of modules and by the number of extremities, respectively. The experiments are conducted with three complexity levels: organisms with two extremities (I-shape), three extremities (T-shape), and four extremities (H-shape). Each shape is then constructed in three sizes: 7, 11 and 15 modules. A screenshot of the shapes with 7 modules can be seen in Fig. 2, the 11 and 15 module shapes are created by adding modules to the extremities.

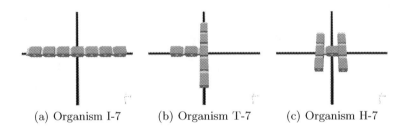

(a) Organism I-7   (b) Organism T-7   (c) Organism H-7

Fig. 2. Robot organisms of size 7

RL PoWeR. We use the RL PoWeR reinforcement learning algorithm described by Kober and Peters [14] to optimise the parameters of a set of cyclic splines, called a policy. In such a policy each spline specifies the angular positions of one of the actuator over time. The use of a set of cyclic splines as the representation was taken from [16].

A cyclic spline is a mathematical function that can be defined using a set of n control points. Each control point is defined by (t_i, α_i) where t_i represents time and α_i the corresponding value. $t_i \in [0, 1]$ is defined as

$$t_i = \frac{i}{n-1}, \forall i = 0, \ldots, (n-1) \tag{1}$$

and $\alpha_i \in [0, 1]$ is freely defined, except that the last value is enforced to be equal to the first, i.e. $\alpha_0 = \alpha_n$. These control points are then used for cyclic spline interpolation using the GSL library. Using GSL it is possible to query a spline for a different number of points than it was defined with, enabling comparison between splines defined with a different number of parameters.

The algorithm starts by creating the initial policy π_0 with as many splines as there are robots (actuators). The algorithm initialises these splines with n values of 0.5 and then adding Gaussian noise. This initial policy is then evaluated after which it is adapted. This adapted controller is evaluated and adapted again until the stopping condition is reached.

Adaptation is done in two steps which are always applied: Exploitation and Exploration. In the exploitation step, the current splines $\hat{\alpha}$ are optimized based on the outcome of previous controllers, this generates a new set of splines.

$$\hat{\alpha}_{i+1} = \hat{\alpha}_i + \frac{\sum_{j=1}^{k} \hat{\Delta}\alpha_{i,j} R_j}{\sum_{j=1}^{k} R_j} \tag{2}$$

where $\hat{\Delta}\alpha_{i,j}$ represents the difference between the parameters of the i-th policy and j-th policy belonging to a ranking of the best k policies seen so far and R_j its reward. In the exploration phase policies are adapted by applying Gaussian perturbation to the newly generated policy.

$$\hat{\alpha}'_{i+1} = \hat{\alpha}_{i+1} + \hat{\varepsilon}_{i+1}, \ \hat{\varepsilon}_{i+1} \sim \mathcal{N}\left(0, \sigma^2\right) \tag{3}$$

where $\hat{\alpha}_{i+1}$ are the parameters after the exploitation step, $\hat{\alpha}'_{i+1}$ the parameters after the exploration step and $\hat{\varepsilon}_{i+1}$ values drawn from a Gaussian distribution with mean 0 and variance σ^2.

Each controller is evaluated for 23.76 seconds (1,485 time steps) after being used for a recovery period of 3.168 seconds (198 time steps) in order to reduce evaluation noisiness as in [8]. The reward R awarded to a controller i is calculated as follows:

$$R_i = \left(100\frac{\sqrt{\Delta_x^2 + \Delta_y^2}}{\Delta_t}\right)^6 \tag{4}$$

where Δ_x and Δ_y is the displacement over the x and y axes measured in meters and Δ_t the time spent in evaluation, as in [16].

The algorithm operating parameters used for the variance and its decay factor are the same as in [16] whereas the others were chosen by hand, without further tuning. Based on our earlier experience, the total number of fitness evaluations was set at 400 and the experiment was repeated for 30 times with organism with different random seeds. An overview of the parameters and the values used in the experiments are described in Table 1.

HyperNEAT. HyperNEAT is a neuroevolutionary method which evolves a neural network connectivity pattern by using a generative encoding called a CPPN. A CPPN is a network of mathematical functions like Sine, Cosine,

Gaussian or Sigmoid, such a network is queried to obtain link weight between nodes of a fixed topology neural network called substrate. An initial population of 25 CPPNs is randomly generated and each CPPN is queried to obtain a connective pattern for an user defined substrate, the resulting neural network is then evaluated. After having carried out the evaluations the initial population is partitioned into species, within each species the best CPPNs are selected and allowed to mate with their fellows in order to create the next generation. The substrate used in our experiments defines a closed-loop gait and is composed of three layers: input, hidden and output layer. Each layer is a $m \times n$ matrix of neural nodes and its size is calculated as $m = (OrganismSize_x * 2) - 1, n = (OrganismSize_y * 2)$ where $OrganismSize_x$ and $OrganismSize_y$ are the sizes of the organism respectively on the x and y axes measured by the number of modules and the extra column is used for additional user defined inputs. The input layer is fed the angular position of each module servo at the previous time step together with a sine wave function value s defined as $s = \sin(\omega t)$ where ω represents the maximal angular velocity of the modules servo and t the current time. The output layer produces the angular positions of each module servo for the current time step. The input and output signals are opportunely scaled to and from the interval $[-1, +1]$.

The controller is evaluated for 23.76 seconds (1,485 time steps) with a recovery time between successive evaluations of 3.168 seconds (198 time steps). These times were chosen because they are multiples of the sine wave period and were found to produce better results and avoid organism flipping because of too harsh transitions between gaits.

The fitness of each controller F_i is calculated as in the original experiment [4] and is defined as

$$F_i = 2^{\left(\Delta_x^2 + \Delta_y^2\right)} \tag{5}$$

where Δ_x and Δ_y is the displacement over the x and y axes measured in meters. Note that although the fitness function defined for both methods are different we present our results with a neutral measurement: the speed of the organism in m/s. The fitness function in our view is an integral part of the method and since we use these methods off-the-shelf we also use the fitness function defined in the original paper.

Table 1. Experiment Parameters

Parameter	Value
Common Parameters	
Recovery Steps	198
Evaluation Steps	1,485
HyperNEAT Parameters	
Population Size	25
Generations	16 or 400
RL PoWER Parameters	
Evaluations	400
Variance	0.008
Variance Decay	0.98
Ranking Size	10
Start Parameters	2
End Parameters	100

To make fair comparisons between RL PoWeR and HyperNEAT, the search efforts must be kept equal. The logical way of achieving this is to use the same number of fitness evaluations which was 400 for RL PoWeR. Working with populations of size 25, this implies 16 generations for HyperNEAT. Intuitively, this is a rather small number to get 'decent' evolutionary development. Therefore, we

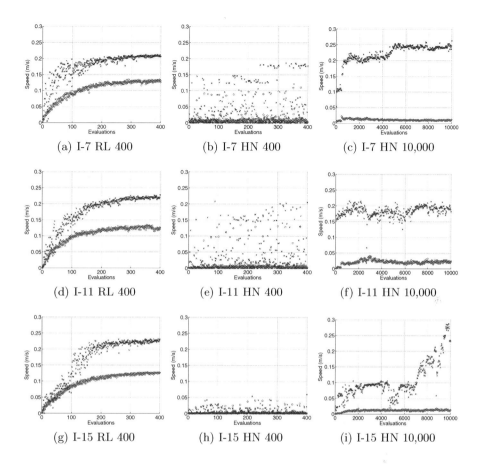

Fig. 3. Controller performance of RL PoWeR (RL) and HyperNEAT (HN) for the I shape (I-7, I-11, I-15). The x axis represents time measured by the number of evaluations, the y axis shows performance measured by the average speed attained (m/s). The top curve (blue) shows the best single run out of the 30 for RL PoWeR and the HyperNEAT run with 400 evaluations. For HyperNEAT with 10,000 evaluations the top curve shows only the best individuals per generation. The lower curve (red) shows the median speed over 30 runs.

also try another policy, keeping the number of generations equal. This means 400 generations, hence $400 \cdot 25 = 10.000$ fitness evaluations. Note, that the progress curves plotting fitness in time for RL PoWeR are converging after 400 evaluations, thus the values for 10,000 are the same.

4   Experimental Results

The performance of the algorithms is exhibited in Figures 3, 4 and 5 for the I, T and H shape respectively. Each Figure contains 9 plots that show two curves: the lower curve (red in colour prints) displays the median speed of the controllers

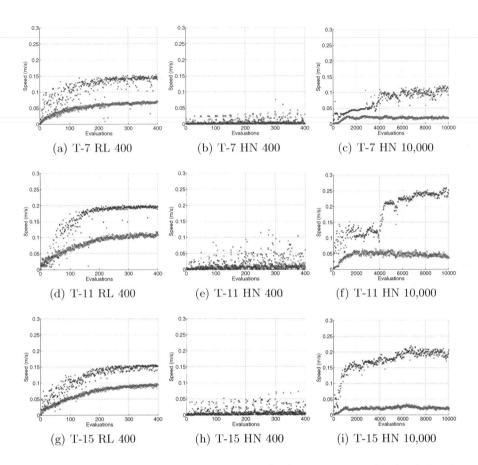

Fig. 4. Controller performance of RL PoWeR (RL) and HyperNEAT (HN) for the T shape (T-7, T-11, T-15). The x axis represents time measured by the number of evaluations, the y axis shows evaluation performance measured by the average speed attained (m/s). The top curve (blue) shows the best single run out of the 30 for RL PoWeR and the HyperNEAT run with 400 evaluations. For HyperNEAT with 10,000 evaluations the top curve shows only the best individuals per generation. The lower curve (red) shows the median speed over 30 runs.

over 30 runs, the top curve (blue in colour) displays the achieved speeds during the best run. To improve readability the top curve for HyperNEAT with 10,000 fitness evaluations only shows the performance of the best individual of each generation. The best runs were selected by the performance at the end of the experiment.

Similarly to our previous research we can see that RL PoWeR manages to reach quite a good performance in both the median and best cases with all shapes and sizes we tested. The algorithm converges within 400 evaluations and has a quite stable performance between consecutive trials, i.e. controllers or gaits. Having stable performance through consecutive controllers is an important trait

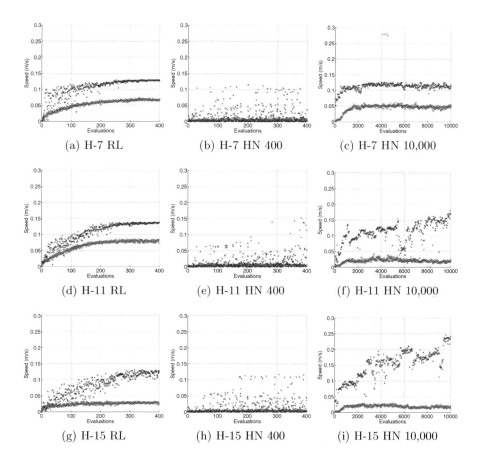

Fig. 5. Controller performance of RL PoWeR (RL) and HyperNEAT (HN) for the H shape (H-7, H-11, H-15). The x axis represents time measured by the number of evaluations, the y axis shows evaluation performance measured by the average speed attained (m/s). The top curve (blue) shows the best single run out of the 30 for RL PoWeR and the HyperNEAT run with 400 evaluations. For HyperNEAT with 10,000 evaluations the top curve shows only the best individuals per generation. The lower curve (red) shows the median speed over 30 runs.

for online learning, where task performance counts from the beginning. A large difference in performance between consecutive gaits implies that poor solutions are being tested as well, and this is clearly disadvantageous for the overall task performance.

The performance of HyperNEAT is quite poor compared to RL PoWeR when using 400 evaluations: even the best controllers in the best run do not reach to the performance of the best run of RL PoWeR in many shapes. 400 evaluations with 25 individuals translates to only 16 generations which is apparently not sufficient. The graphs with 400 evaluations of HyperNEAT also indicate quite large differences in performance of consecutive controllers which is detrimental

Table 2. The table shows the difference in median performance between of RL PoWeR after 400 evaluations and HyperNEAT after 10,000 evaluations. The results of a student's t-test between these median performances showed the difference is significant, the corresponding p values are smaller than 0.01 for each of these tests.

	I	T	H
7	0.10	0.04	0.02
11	0.09	0.05	0.04
15	0.10	0.06	0.02

to the overall performance of the multicellular robot. Running HyperNEAT for 10,000 evaluations, which is 400 generations, leads to much better performance, whereas this is not the case for RL PoWeR (plots omitted here). With 10,000 evaluations the best controllers of the best runs of HyperNEAT now sometimes outperform the best controllers by RL PoWeR. The median performance however is still not as good as that of RL PoWeR.

Table 2 shows the difference between the median performance of RL PoWeR after 400 evaluations and HyperNEAT after 10,000. The median performance of RL PoWeR is significantly higher in all cases with a p value smaller than 0.01. This is mainly due to the larger difference in the performance of consecutive controllers with HyperNEAT. This is not surprising, since HyperNEAT works with populations of 25, which means that it does 25 evaluations before applying selection. This causes a more explorative behaviour where several poor solutions are tested too.

Regarding the influence of different body shapes and sizes, we observed the following. The difference in performance is more pronounced for the I shape than for the T and H shapes. The I shape with RL PoWER has 0.90 - 0.10 m/s higher mean performance than HyperNEAT, which is around 30%-34% of the maximum speed achieved by all controllers (the best performance measured was 0.2946 m/s in a run of HyperNEAT I-15). For the T shape the difference in performance is around 0.05 m/s which is roughly 13%-20% of the maximum speed achieved by all controllers. Both these differences are therefore not only statistically significant, but also meaningful. The difference in performance for the H shape is statistically significant, but less pronounced with 7%-13% of the maximum speed.

Considering the speed of learning we can see that RL PoWeR is much faster in reaching a good performance than HyperNEAT. Although the best performance of HyperNEAT with 10,000 evaluations eventually reaches similar performance to RL PoWeR, it uses 25 times as much search effort to this. Even then the median fitness is not much better than that of RL PoWeR at the end of 10,000 evaluations.

5   Conclusions

In this paper we addressed the Control Your Own Body problem of *in vivo* evolution of modular multi-cellular robots, where robot 'babies' can be produced with arbitrary shapes and sizes. The problem arises in systems where both morphologies and controllers undergo evolution, such as, for instance our Triangle of Life framework, because newly created robot organisms can have bodies and controllers that do not fit well. Therefore, every 'baby robot' needs to learn to control its own body quickly by an online learning method, without grace period.

In this study we reduced this to a gait learning problem and investigated two possible learning approaches: The reinforcement learning algorithm RL PoWeR and the neuro-evolutionary approach HyperNEAT. We took 'off-the-shelf' implementations of these algorithms and conducted simulation experiments on a predefined testbed of robot morphologies with 3 different sizes and 3 levels of complexity.

Regarding the quality of learned gaits we have found that RL PoWeR –that iterates only one single solution– reaches quite reasonable speeds in the median case and good speeds in the best case. HyperNEAT on the other hand seems encumbered by the population of 25 and cannot equal the performance of RL PoWeR within 400 evaluations. After 10,000 evaluations there are some runs that are able to outperform RL PoWeR when looking at the best controller of the best run. However, the median is still much lower than RL PoWeR, because HyperNEAT does more exploration than RL PoWeR, which leads to a larger difference in performance between consecutive controllers. This leads to a lower overall task performance, which is undesirable in online learning.

With regards to the speed of the algorithms, we can see that RL PoWeR is much faster in achieving a high performance than HyperNEAT. Surprisingly this quick convergence does not seem to come at the cost of solution quality as one would expect. To conclude, the main finding of our research is that the RL PoWeR algorithm is the preferable over HyperNEAT for on-line learning.

Further work will be carried out along several lines. First we want to tune the parameters for both the RL PoWER and HyperNEAT algorithms on this problem to improve their performances. Furthermore we will investigate the algorithms stability with regards to failed modules and other disasters. Finally, we would like to validate these results by replicating the experiments using real hardware.

References

1. Bongard, J., Zykov, V., Lipson, H.: Resilient machines through continuous self-modeling. Science **314**(5802), 1118–1121 (2006)
2. Christensen, D.J., Larsen, J.C., Støy, K.: Fault-tolerant gait learning and morphology optimization of a polymorphic walking robot. Evolving Systems (2013)
3. Christensen, D.J., Schultz, U.P., Støy, K.: A distributed andmorphology-independent strategy for adaptive locomotion inself-reconfigurable modular robots. Robotics and Autonomous Systems 61(9),1021–1035 (2013)
4. Clune, J., Beckmann, B.E., Ofria, C., Pennock, R.T.: Evolving coordinated quadruped gaits with the HyperNEAT generative encoding. In: IEEE Congress on Evolutionary Computation (CEC) 2009, pp. 2764–2771. IEEE Press (2009)
5. D'Angelo, M., Weel, B., Eiben, A.E.: Online Gait Learning for Modular Robots with Arbitrary Shapes and Sizes. In: Dediu, A.-H., Martín-Vide, C., Truthe, B., Vega-Rodríguez, M.A. (eds.) TPNC 2013. LNCS, vol. 8273, pp. 45–56. Springer, Heidelberg (2013)

6. Eiben, A.E., Bredeche, N., Hoogendoorn, M., Stradner, J., Timmis, J., Tyrrell, A., Winfield, A, et al.: The triangle of life: Evolving robots in real-time and real-space. In: Lió, P., Miglino, O., Nicosia, G., Nolfi, S., Pavone, M. (eds.) Advances in Artificial Life, (ECAL) 2013, pp. 1056–1063. MIT Press (2013)

7. Eiben, A.E., Kernbach, S., Haasdijk, E.: Embodied artificial evolution. Evolutionary Intelligence 5(4), 261–272 (2012)

8. Haasdijk, E., Eiben, A.E., Karafotias, G.: On-line evolution of robot controllers by an encapsulated evolution strategy. In: IEEE Congress on Evolutionary Computation (CEC) 2010, pp. 1–7. IEEE Press (2010)

9. Haasdijk, E., Rusu, A.A., Eiben, A.E.: HyperNEAT for Locomotion Control in Modular Robots. In: Tempesti, G., Tyrrell, A.M., Miller, J.F. (eds.) ICES 2010. LNCS, vol. 6274, pp. 169–180. Springer, Heidelberg (2010)

10. Hamann, H., Stradner, J., Schmickl, T., Crailsheim, K.: A hormone-based controller for evolutionary multi-modular robotics: From single modules to gait learning. In: IEEE Congress on Evolutionary Computation (CEC) 2010, pp. 1–8. IEEE Press (2010)

11. Ijspeert, A.J.: Central pattern generators for locomotion control in animals and robots: A review. Neural Networks 21(4), 642–653 (2008)

12. Kamimura, A., Kurokawa, H., Yoshida, E., Murata, S., Tomita, K., Kokaji, S.: Automatic locomotion design and experiments for a modular robotic system. IEEE/ASME Transactions on Mechatronics 10(3), 314–325 (2005)

13. Kamimura, A., Kurokawa, H., Yoshida, E., Tomita, K., Kokaji, S., Murata, S.: Distributed adaptive locomotion by a modular robotic system, M-TRAN II. In: Proceedings of 2004 IEEE/RSJ International Conference on Intelligent Robots and Systems (IROS) 2004, vol. 3, pp. 2370–2377. IEEE Press (2004)

14. Kober, J., Peters, J.: Learning motor primitives for robotics. In: IEEE International Conference on Robotics and Automation (ICRA) 2009, pp. 2112–2118. IEEE Press (2009)

15. Möckel, R., Jaquier, C., Drapel, K., Dittrich, E., Upegui, A., Ijspeert, A.: YaMoR and Bluemove - an autonomous modular robot with Bluetooth interface for exploring adaptive locomotion. In: Tokhi, M.O., Virk, G., Hossain, M.A. (eds.) Proceedings of the 8th International Conference on Climbing and Walking Robots (CLAWAR) 2005, pp. 685–692. Springer (2006)

16. Shen, H., Yosinski, J., Kormushev, P., Caldwell, D.G., Lipson, H.: Learning fast quadruped robot gaits with the RL PoWER spline parameterization. Cybernetics and Information Technologies 12(3), 66–75 (2012)

17. Shen, W.M., Salemi, B., Will, P.: Hormones for self-reconfigurable robots. In: Pagello, E., et al. (eds.) Proceedings of the 6th International Conference on Intelligent Autonomous Systems (IAS-6), pp. 918–925. IOS Press (2000)

18. Spröwitz, A., Moeckel, R., Maye, J., Ijspeert, A.J.: Learning to move in modular robots using central pattern generators and online optimization. The International Journal of Robotics Research 27(3–4), 423–443 (2008)

19. Yim, M.: A reconfigurable modular robot with many modes of locomotion. In: Proceedings of International Conference on Advanced Mechatronics, pp. 283–288. Japan Society of Mechanical Engineers, Tokio (1993)

20. Yosinski, J., Clune, J., Hidalgo, D., Nguyen, S., Zagal, J., Lipson, H.: Evolving robot gaits in hardware: the HyperNEAT generative encoding vs. parameter optimization. In: Lenaerts, T., Giacobini, M., Bersini, H., Bourgine, P., Dorigo, M., Doursat, R. (eds.) Advances in Artificial Life, (ECAL) 2011, pp. 890–897. MIT Press (2011)

What You Choose to See Is What You Get: An Experiment with Learnt Sensory Modulation in a Robotic Foraging Task

Tiago Rodrigues[✉], Miguel Duarte, Sancho Oliveira,
and Anders Lyhne Christensen

Instituto de Telecomunicações & Instituto Universitário de Lisboa (ISCTE-IUL),
Lisbon, Portugal
{tiago_luis_rodrigues,miguel_duarte,
sancho.oliveira,anders.christensen}@iscte.pt

Abstract. In evolutionary robotics, the mapping from raw sensory input to neural network input is typically decided by the experimenter or encoded in the genome. Either way, the mapping remains fixed throughout a robot's lifetime. Inspired by biological sensory organs and the mammalian brain's capacity for selective attention, we evaluate an alternative approach in which a robot has active, real-time control over the mapping from sensory input to neural network input. We augment the neural controllers with additional output neurons that control key sensory parameters and evolve solutions for a single-robot foraging task. The results show that the capacity to control the mapping from raw input to neural network input is exploited by evolution and leads to novel solutions with higher fitness compared to traditional approaches.

Keywords: Evolutionary robotics, dynamic sensors, sensor evolution, genome-encoding

1 Introduction

Nature provides different ways in which animals can change the way they perceive their surrounding environment. On the one hand, the raw input can be changed physically at different sensory organs: the diameter of pupils in mammalian eyes changes in order to adjust to varying degrees of luminance [10] or based on the interestingness of the subject [11], and certain mammals, such as cats and dogs, are able to pinpoint the source of a sound by rotating each ear individually [25]. On the other hand, the brain is able to focus on specific sensory stimuli and disregard others, a process known as *selective attention* [9].

In evolutionary robotics (ER), artificial neural networks (ANN) are often used as robotic controllers [20] because of their capacity to tolerate noise [12] such as that introduced by imperfections in sensors and actuators. These controllers are, however, extremely simplified models of a real brain, and usually contain less than a thousand neurons. While humans have sensory organs and brain areas

© Springer-Verlag Berlin Heidelberg 2014
A.I. Esparcia-Alcázar et al. (Eds.): EvoApplications 2014, LNCS 8602, pp. 789–801, 2014.
DOI: 10.1007/978-3-662-45523-4_64

that filter and process stimuli before they reach our consciousness, a typical ANN used in ER is too simple for such a process to take place. The *curse of dimensionality* [5] prevents the use of ANNs with a high degree of complexity, since each additional parameter adds another dimension to the search space. The computational resources required to evolve ANN with complexities that match biological neural networks are not yet available.

In ANN-based ER, the raw sensory inputs are mapped to neural network inputs. The neural network receives inputs mapped to a particular interval, such as [0, 1]. For simple binary sensors like a bumper, the input could be 0 if the bumper is not pressed, and 1 if the bumper is pressed. For more complex sensors that potentially measure continuous quantities, such as an accelerometer or a light level sensor, the optimal mapping might not be obvious and is typically chosen arbitrarily by the experimenter. If the robot has to perform a task in dark environments, it might be beneficial to choose a low maximum range of a light sensor or to use a non-linear mapping. In this way, the network could perceive small variations in luminance.

Inputs from sensors that provide multidimensional data, such as laser scanners and cameras, cannot be fed directly to a neural network. The sensory input, such as a depth map or an image, must first be preprocessed and compressed into a vector with relatively few elements. In [1], for instance, the authors evolve behavioral control for two s-bots [18] to self-assemble. The s-bot is equipped with an omnidirectional camera, and the authors divide its field-of-view into eight non-overlapping cones covering 45° each. The distance to the closest colored object is estimated for each cone and linearly mapped to a neural network input.

In this paper, we propose an approach in which a neural controller has control over the mapping from sensory input to neural input during task execution. The controller is given real-time, direct control over key sensory mapping parameters, namely range and opening angle. We use a foraging task, in which a robot must forage as many preys as possible within a certain amount of time. Our results show that giving a neural controller the capacity to change how it perceives the world improves performance, not only when compared to the traditional approach where the parameters of the sensors are determined a priori by the experimenter, but also when parameters of the sensors are encoded in the controller's genome and therefore are under evolutionary control.

2   Related Work

While many ER studies focus on synthesizing control logic through evolutionary processes [17,20], a substantial amount of work has been devoted to the study of evolutionary processes applied to sensor and morphology optimization. In particular, researchers have experimented with evolving the number, type and position of sensors [3,14–16,21], as well as the sensors' parameters, such as range and opening angle [3,15,21,27].

Balakrishnan and Honavar [3] experimented with putting the range and placement of the sensors under evolutionary control using genome encoding, and compared the results to experiments in which the sensors were fixed a priori. They obtained better results with genome encoding and concluded that the evolution of placement and range of the sensors can lead to more efficient and sometimes counter-intuitive sensor placements. Mark et al. [15] evolved the sensors' opening angle on robots with (i) a fixed number of sensors, and with (ii) a varying number of sensors. They observed that robots with fewer sensors achieved lower fitness scores. In the setup where evolution could add sensors, the authors found that solutions tended to use a large number of sensors. Parker and Nathan [21] co-evolved both the sensor morphology (number of sensors and their placement) and the controller for a hexapod robot. A genetic algorithm was used to optimize a set of control rules and the number of sensors (ultraviolet, infrared and tactile), their placement, and their range. The robot had to explore the environment and find a source of ultraviolet light, while simultaneously avoiding obstacles. Although the authors evolved successful solutions, they found that the evolutionary process consistently ignored infrared sensors and used only tactile and ultraviolet sensors.

Several studies have been conducted in which both the controller and the morphology of the whole robot are optimized by an evolutionary process. These approaches attempt to more accurately mimic how evolution operates in nature, by simultaneously evolving an organism's physical properties and its "brain". Lipson and Pollack [13] demonstrated the evolution of morphology and controller of simple robots that were then fabricated using rapid manufacturing technology. The robots were composed of simple physical building blocks (bars and actuators) and neural building blocks (neurons and synapses), and the goal was to achieve locomotion. Lund et al. [14] studied the concept of *true evolvable hardware* that consists of evolving the number and position of the sensors, body size, wheel radius, wheel base, and motor time constant, which they call the *body plan*, using a simple direct encoding of the physical expressions in the genome. In a different study, Auerbach and Bongard [2] co-evolved both the control and morphology, and they were able to synthesize robots that successfully achieved locomotion. Robots evolved in simple environments displayed significantly more mechanical degrees of freedom on average, than those evolved in more complex environments.

Our approach, although related to the studies discussed above, does not fall into any of these categories. Our controllers can actively change how the world is perceived, but this process is not achieved by modifying the number or position of sensors. While previous studies have shown how controllers can change and adapt to an environment through online evolution [8,24], lifetime learning [7,19], and neuromodulation [23], such changes take place over long time scales because they rely on modifications to synaptic weights and sometimes even to the topology of the neural network [22]. Contrarily, in our approach, controllers can actively change sensor parameters from one control cycle to the next, without modifying synaptic connections or the controller's topology. As we demonstrate in this paper, evolution can exploit the ability to modify how the robot senses the world. As a result, solutions that are able to actively control the mapping from sensory input to neural network input are found to be fitter and less complex than solutions for which the mapping is fixed throughout the robot's lifetime.

3   Methodology

We study an architecture in which controllers are able to change the mapping from sensory input to neural network input in real-time, depending on the robot's internal and external stimulus. We refer to sensors whose parameters are controlled by the network in this way as *dynamic sensors*. The neural controller is augmented with an additional output neuron for each sensor parameter it can modify. An example of such a network can be seen in Figure 1.

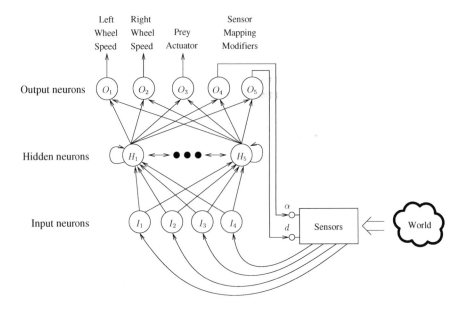

Fig. 1. An example of a neural controller with dynamic sensors. The network is able to control two parameters α and d, which respectively determine the opening angle and the range of four sensors used in the mapping from raw input to neural network input.

We use a foraging task for our experiments: a circular robot with a diameter of 7.5 cm must locate and consume as many preys as possible during its lifetime. The robot has four prey sensors distributed evenly around its circular body. The physical range of the prey sensors is 3 m and their opening angle is 90°. In a typical ER setup, the activation of an input neuron, i, for a prey sensor would be inversely proportional to the distance, d_p, to the closest prey detected by the corresponding sensor, for instance:

$$i = \frac{range - d_p}{range} \tag{1}$$

where the *range* is the maximum physical range of the sensor.

In this study, the neural controllers can change the upper limit of the opening angle and the range used for the mapping from 0 and up to the sensor's maximum physical limit. We scale the activation of the output neurons ($[0, 1]$) controlling a mapping parameter (O_4 and O_5 in Figure 1) to the sensor's range, and use the resulting value as the upper limit when computing the activation of input neurons. Any prey detected by the sensor outside of the range or opening angle set by the controller, is ignored. In this way, the controller can effectively *limit* the sensory inputs that it receives.

We use a pair of output neurons to determine the parameters for all four prey sensors. The mapping from sensory input (distance) to neural network input is always linear and the controller can only decide on the upper limits for the sensors' range and their opening angle. The controller's capacity to change the sensory mapping could, however, easily be extended to allow for individual sensor control, and for more flexibility in terms of the mapping function used.

For our experiments we use JBotEvolver [26], an open source, multirobot simulation platform, and neuroevolution framework. JBotEvolver, the configuration files, and experimental results can be found at: http://biomechineslab. com/dynmic.

4   Experimental Setup

The foraging task is conducted in an 8x8 m arena surrounded by walls. At the beginning of each experiment, the robot is placed in the center of the arena. A total of 35 preys are placed at random locations drawn from a uniform distribution. The robot can consume the preys by moving within a distance of 15 cm and activating its *prey actuator*. Once a prey is consumed, a new prey is created and placed at a random location. The number of preys present in the environment is thus kept constant during an experiment.

The robot is equipped with three actuators and eight sensors. The actuators are composed of two wheels that enable the robot to move at a maximum speed of 10 cm/s, and the prey actuator that enables the robot to consume preys. The sensors are composed of four prey sensors and four wall sensors, distributed evenly around the chassis of the robot. The sensors have a maximum opening angle of 90°. The maximum range is 3 m for the prey sensors and 0.5 m for the wall sensors. The robot model used in this study is not based on any existing physical robot, and our experiments were conducted exclusively in simulation. However, the prey sensors could be implemented based on a complex, multidimensional sensor, such as the omni-directional camera used by the foot-bot [6], while the wall sensors could be implemented using simple infrared or ultrasonic sensors.

If the prey sensors cannot detect any prey within their current range and opening angle, the readings are set to 0. Otherwise the readings are mapped linearly to the ANN inputs based on the distance to the closest prey according to equation (1). For the wall sensors, we use a traditional, linear mapping from raw input to neural network input: the robot has no control over the mapping parameters.

The robot is controlled by a continuous time recurrent neural network [4] with a reactive layer of input neurons, one layer of hidden neurons, and one layer of output neurons. The input layer is fully connected to the hidden layer, which, in turn, is fully connected to the output layer. The input layer has one neuron for each sensor and the output layer has one neuron for each actuator. In our experiments, the robot was able to set both the opening angle and the range of the prey sensors from zero up to their maximum values (90° and 3 m, respectively) at any time. These parameters are controlled by two additional outputs in the neural network. The neurons in the hidden layer are fully connected and governed by the following equation:

$$\tau_i \frac{dH_i}{dt} = -H_i + \sum_{j=1}^{8} \omega_{ji} I_i + \sum_{k=1}^{5} \omega_{ki} Z(H_k + \beta_k) \tag{2}$$

where τ_i is the decay constant, H_i is the neuron's state, ω_{ji} the strength of the synaptic connection from neuron j to neuron i, β the bias terms, and $Z(x) = (1 + e^{-x})^{-1}$ is the sigmoid function. β, τ, and ω_{ji} are genetically controlled network parameters. The possible ranges of these parameters are: $\beta \in [-10, 10]$, $\tau \in [0.1, 32]$ and $\omega_{ji} \in [-10, 10]$. Circuits are integrated using the forward Euler method with an integration step-size of 0.2 and cell potentials are set to 0 when the network is initialized.

Each generation is composed of 100 genomes, and each genome corresponds to an ANN with the topology described above. The fitness of a genome is sampled 10 times and the mean fitness is used for selection. Each sample lasts $3,000$ time steps, which is equivalent to 300 seconds. After all the genomes have been evaluated, an elitist approach is used: the top five genomes are chosen to populate the next generation. Each of the top five genomes becomes the parent of 19 offspring. An offspring is created by applying a Gaussian noise (mean: 0,st.~dev.: 1) to each gene with a probably of 10%. The 95 mutated offspring and the original five genomes constitute the next generation.

In order to evaluate the controllers, we used the following fitness function:

$$F(i) = \phi_i + \Psi_i - \Theta_i \tag{3}$$

$$\Psi(i) = \sum_{s=1}^{\text{time-steps}} \left(\frac{1.5 \text{ m} - C_s}{1.5 \text{ m}} \cdot 5 \cdot 10^{-6} \right) \tag{4}$$

$$\Theta(i) = \sum_{s=1}^{\text{time-steps}} \begin{cases} 10^{-6} & \text{if colliding with wall} \\ 0 & \text{otherwise} \end{cases} \tag{5}$$

where ϕ_i is the number of preys foraged, and C_s is the distance of the robot to the closest prey. The number of preys foraged is the dominant component of the fitness function, while $\Psi(i)$ was used for bootstrapping (the term creates a gradient from the robot to the closest prey), and $\Theta(i)$ was used to prevent the robot from colliding with walls.

We ran a total of 30 evolutionary runs, each lasting $1,000$ generations. After the evolutionary runs had finished, we conducted a post-evaluation with a total of 100 samples of the genome that had obtained the highest fitness in each run. We ran additional experiments to obtain a basis for comparison: (i) a classic setup, where the robot's sensor parameters are fixed, and (ii) a setup, in which the sensor parameters are genome-encoded and therefore under evolutionary control. In the setup with genome-encoded parameters, we added two extra parameters to the existing genome that defined the parameters of the prey sensors, one controls the range and another controls the opening angle. These parameters were subject to mutation over the course of the evolutionary process. For the three setups, we conducted experiments with a varying number of hidden neurons. The hidden neurons ranged from three to ten in order to assess the impact of network complexity on performance and behavior.

5   Results and Discussion

In this section, we present the results of experiments conducted in the three setups: the dynamic sensors setup, the genome-encoded sensors setup, and the fixed sensors setup. The section is divided in three subsections: performance analysis, behavior analysis, and genome complexity analysis.

5.1   Performance

The distribution of fitness scores from the best controllers of the three experimental setups can be seen in Figure 2. We compare the dynamic sensors (three hidden neurons) with the fixed sensors and the genome-encoded sensors (six hidden neurons). We chose these network topologies since they displayed the best performance out of all the network configurations tested (from three to ten hidden neurons). The controllers evolved in the dynamic sensors setup achieved a mean fitness of 25.06 ± 2.27, while in the fixed sensors setup, the controllers achieved a mean fitness of 23.35 ± 1.07, and in the genome-encoded setup, the controllers achieved a mean fitness of 23.40 ± 0.88. The fitness corresponds approximately to the number of preys foraged, which amount to 25.00 ± 2.29, 23.27 ± 1.07, and 23.33 ± 0.897, respectively. Controllers in the dynamic sensors setup outperformed both those envolved in the fixed sensors setup and in the genome-encoded sensors setup (Mann-Whitney U, $p < 0.05$), and had a mean fitness 7% higher than the highest scoring controllers in the other two setups.

In Figure 3, we have plotted the fitness trajectories of best controllers in each setup (left), as well as the mean and standard deviation for the controllers in the dynamic sensors setup and the fixed sensors setup (right). The results

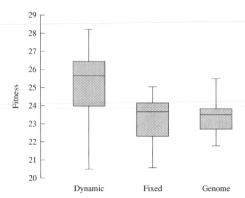

Fig. 2. Distribution of fitness scores achieved by the best controller in 30 evolutionary runs conducted in each of the setups. Each box comprises observations ranging from the first to the third quartile. The median is indicated by a bar, dividing the box into the upper and lower part. The whiskers extend to the farthest data points that are within 1.5 times the interquartile range.

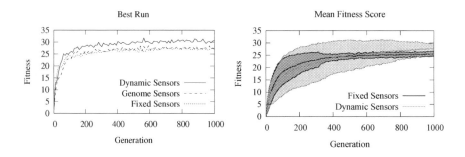

Fig. 3. Left: Fitness trajectories of the highest scoring controllers in each generation for each setup. Right: mean fitness score and standard deviation in each generation for the dynamic sensors setup and the fixed sensors setup.

show that the dynamic sensors setup evolved the controllers with the highest fitness from the 45th generation onward. However, if we compare the mean fitness trajectories, controllers in the dynamic sensors setup have a lower mean fitness than the fixed sensors controllers until the 400th generation. Thereafter, the controllers in the dynamic sensors setup achieve higher fitness scores. The results also show that the dynamic sensors setup yields a higher standard deviation than the fixed sensors setup, which is due to the wide variety of behaviors that are possible in the dynamic sensors setup.

In the following section, we analyze the evolved behaviors in order to determine the reason for the higher performance displayed by the controllers with dynamic sensors.

5.2 Behavior

We performed an analysis of the solutions evolved in the fixed sensors setup and in the genome-encoded setup and found them to be similar. If the robot stops perceiving a prey with its front sensor while moving toward it, the robot turns on the spot until the prey is detected by the front sensor again. The robot's front sensor would, however, often have more than one prey in its field-of-view, and whenever the robot would lose sight of the closest prey, another prey would immediately be detected by the robot's front prey sensor. As a result the robot would not turn on the spot to locate the closer prey, but instead head toward a new prey detected by its front prey sensor.

We analyzed the final sensor parameters of the 30 genome-encoded sensors experiments after evolution had finished, and observed a mean range of 1.95 m $\pm$ 0.23 m, and a mean opening angle of $73°\pm16°$. In most of the runs, relatively large values for the sensor parameters (close to the maximum in many cases) were evolved.

The controllers evolved in the dynamic sensors setup displayed a number of new, interesting solutions in which the capacity to change the sensory mapping parameters was exploited. The best controller sets the opening angle to the

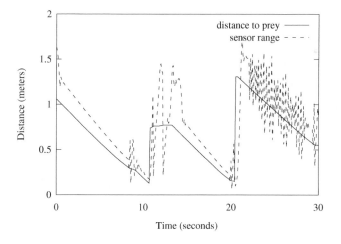

Fig. 4. Comparison between the robot's distance to prey and the sensors' range in a 30-second window, from an experiment with the best controller evolved in the dynamic sensors setup. From 20 s to 30 s, the controller displayed a wider variation of the sensor's range. This pattern of behavior occurred whenever the robot was sensing two preys: one with the front prey sensor, and one with the right prey sensor.

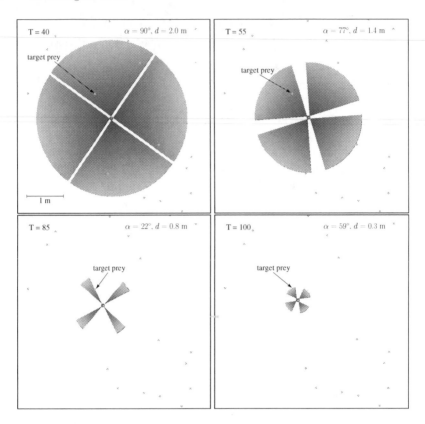

Fig. 5. An example of a foraging behavior with dynamic sensors. Screenshots at timestep T from the same simulation with α and d denoting the opening angle and the range set by the controller. The robot initially uses a long range in order to locate a prey. As the robot starts to move, it begins to adjust both the range and the opening angle of the prey sensors in order to orient itself toward the prey. As the robot approaches, it decreases the opening angle and the range of the sensors until it is close enough to consume the prey.

maximum value of 90° when no prey is detected, and reduces the range as the robot moves closer to a prey. We found that the mean difference between the range of the sensor and the distance to the closest prey in the best controller of the dynamic sensors setup was 11.2 cm, which is only 4% of the maximum physical range of the sensor (see Figure 4). Out of the 30 evolutionary runs, 18 evolved this behavior. In six of the runs, the controllers reduce both the opening angle and the range of the sensor as the robot moves toward the prey. An example of this behavior can be seen in Figure 5. A different evolutionary run produced a behavior that chooses either a backwards movement or a forwards movement, but always with a fixed opening angle of the sensor 90°. When the robot moves backwards toward a prey, it uses a fixed long range. When the robot moves forwards toward a prey, it reduces the sensor range as it gets closer. The solutions evolved in the remaining runs displayed oscillatory behaviors, in which the opening angle and range increase and decrease in cyclic patterns when preys are detected.

5.3   Complexity

For the dynamic sensors setup, we used three hidden neurons but the ANN needs two additional output neurons in order to control the range and opening angle of the sensors. In terms of complexity, the two additional neurons add six more connections to the neural network (two for every hidden neuron), resulting in a total of 59 alleles.

We found that controllers with six hidden neurons displayed the highest performances in both the fixed sensors setup and in the genome-encoded sensors setup. The resulting genomes had respectively 117 alleles and 119 alleles. Of the topologies evaluated in the dynamic sensors setup, we found that controllers with only three hidden neurons displayed the highest performance, which are encoded by genomes with only 59 alleles. The controllers evolved in the dynamic sensors setup thus not only displayed a higher performance but also achieved the highest performance using a simpler solution in terms of genome length.

6   Conclusions

In this paper, we showed how giving a robot the capacity to dynamically change parameters of its sensors can be beneficial not only in terms of the performance of evolved solutions, but also in terms of solution complexity. We gave the controller access to certain sensor parameters, namely the range and opening angle, which the controller was able to change during task execution. The controllers evolved in our experiments were able to outperform both an approach in which the parameters of the sensors were fixed, and an approach in which the sensor parameters were encoded in the genome and subject to evolution.

Giving controllers the capacity to actively control the sensory input to neural network input mapping is fundamentally different from approaches in which sensor parameters are genome-encoded and from approaches in which the robot morphology is under evolutionary control. A controller that has active control over sensory parameters can change the way in which the world is perceived by the robot and essentially limit what it senses. The approach could be extended to other sensors and parameters. In our experiments, only the input mapping for the prey sensors was dynamically changed by the controller. However, multiple sensors could potentially be controlled simultaneously by including additional outputs in the network. In particular, we believe that letting a controller actively modify the mapping from sensory input to neural network input has significant potential for sensors that provide multidimensional inputs such as laser scanners and cameras. The inputs from such sensors must undergo significant preprocessing and compression before they can be fed to a neural controller. It is unlikely that an optimal, static mapping exists in many cases, and in our ongoing work, we are studying the impact of giving controllers greater control over the mapping of complex sensory inputs.

Acknowledgments. This work was supported by Fundação para a Ciência a Tecnologia (FCT) under the grants, SFRH/BD/76438/2011, PEst-OE/EEI/LA0008/2013, and EXPL/EEI-AUT/0329/2013.

References

1. Ampatzis, C., Tuci, E., Trianni, V., Christensen, A.L., Dorigo, M.: Evolving self-assembly in autonomous homogeneous robots: experiments with two physical robots. Artificial Life **15**(4), 465–484 (2009)
2. Auerbach, J.E., Bongard, J.C.: On the relationship between environmental and mechanical complexity in evolved robots. In: International Conference on Artificial Life (ALIFE), pp. 309–316. MIT Press, Cambridge (2012)
3. Balakrishnan, K., Honavar, V.: On sensor evolution in robotics. In: Annual Conference on Genetic Programming, pp. 455–460. MIT Press, Cambridge (1996)
4. Beer, R.D., Gallagher, J.C.: Evolving dynamical neural networks for adaptive behavior. Adaptive Behavior **1**, 91–122 (1992)
5. Bellman, R.: Dynamic Programming, 1st edn. Princeton University Press, Princeton (1957)
6. Dorigo, M., Floreano, D., Gambardella, L.M., Mondada, F., Nolfi, S., Baaboura, T., Birattari, M., Bonani, M., Brambilla, M., Brutschy, A., et al.: Swarmanoid: a novel concept for the study of heterogeneous robotic swarms. IEEE Robotics & Automation Magazine **20**(4), 60–71 (2013)
7. Floreano, D., Dürr, P., Mattiussi, C.: Neuroevolution: from architectures to learning. Evolutionary Intelligence **1**(1), 47–62 (2008)
8. Floreano, D., Mondada, F.: Evolutionary neurocontrollers for autonomous mobile robots. Neural Networks **11**(7–8), 1461–1478 (1998)
9. Fries, P., Reynolds, J.H., Rorie, A.E., Desimone, R.: Modulation of oscillatory neuronal synchronization by selective visual attention. Science **291**(5508), 1560–1563 (2001)
10. Groot, S.G.D., Gebhard, J.W.: Pupil size as determined by adapting luminance. Journal of the Optical Society of America **42**(7), 492–495 (1952)
11. Hess, E.H., Polt, J.M.: Pupil size as related to interest value of visual stimuli. Science **132**(3423), 349–350 (1960)
12. Kam-Chuen, J., Giles, C., Horne, B.: An analysis of noise in recurrent neural networks: convergence and generalization. IEEE Transactions on Neural Networks **7**(6), 1424–1438 (1996)
13. Lipson, H., Pollack, J.B.: Automatic design and manufacture of robotic lifeforms. Nature **406**(6799), 974–978 (2000)
14. Lund, H., Hallam, J., Lee, W.-P.: Evolving robot morphology. In: IEEE International Conference on Evolutionary Computation, pp. 197–202. IEEE Press, Piscataway (1997)
15. Mark, A., Mark, R., Polani, D., Uthmann, T.: A framework for sensor evolution in a population of braitenberg vehicle-like agents. In: International Conference on Artificial Life (ALIFE), pp. 428–432. MIT Press, Cambridge (1998)

16. Mautner, C., Belew, R.K.: Evolving robot morphology and control. Artificial Life and Robotics **4**(3), 130–136 (2000)
17. Meyer, J.-A., Husbands, P., Harvey, I.: Evolutionary robotics: A survey of applications and problems. In: 1st European Workshop on Evolutionary Robotics (EvoRobot), pp. 1–21. Springer, Berlin (1998)
18. Mondada, F., Guignard, A., Bonani, M., Bär, D., Lauria, M., Floreano, D.: Swarmbot: From concept to implementation. In: IEEE/RSJ International Conference on Intelligent Robots and Systems, pp. 1626–1631. IEEE Press, Piscataway (2003)
19. Nolfi, S., Floreano, D.: Learning and evolution. Autonomous Robots **7**(1), 89–113 (1999)
20. Nolfi, S., Floreano, D.: Evolutionary robotics: The biology, intelligence, and technology of self-organizing machines. MIT Press, Cambridge (2000)
21. Parker, G., Nathan, P.: Concurrently evolving sensor morphology and control for a hexapod robot. In: IEEE Congress on Evolutionary Computation (CEC), pp. 1–6. IEEE Press, Piscataway (2010)
22. Silva, F., Urbano, P., Oliveira, S., Christensen, A.L.: odNEAT: An algorithm for distributed online, onboard evolution of robot behaviours. In: International Conference on Simulation and Synthesis of Living Systems (ALIFE), pp. 251–258. MIT Press, Cambridge (2012)
23. Soltoggio, A., Bullinaria, J.A., Mattiussi, C., Dürr, P., Floreano, D.: Evolutionary advantages of neuromodulated plasticity in dynamic, reward-based scenarios. In: International Conference on the Simulation and Synthesis of Living Systems (ALIFE), pp. 569–576. MIT Press, Cambridge (2008)
24. Watson, R., Ficici, S., Pollack, J.: Embodied evolution: Embodying an evolutionary algorithm in a population of robots. In: IEEE Congress on Evolutionary Computation (CEC), pp. 335–342. IEEE Press, Piscataway (1999)
25. Young, E.D., Rice, J.J., Tong, S.C.: Effects of pinna position on head-related transfer functions in the cat. Journal of the Acoustical Society of America **99**(5), 3064–3076 (1996)
26. Duarte, M., Sliva, F., Rodrigues, T., Oliveria, S.M., Christensen, A.L.: JBotEvolver: A Versatile Simulation Platform for Evolutionary Robotics. Proceedings of the International Conference on the Synthesis and Simulation of Living System (ALIFE), pp. 210–211. MIT Press, Cambridge, MA (2014)
27. Zhang, Y., Martinoli, A., Antonsson, E.K.: Evolutionary design of a collective sensory system. In: AAAI Spring Symposium on Computational Synthesis, pp. 283–290. MIT Press, Cambridge (2003)

EvoSTOC

Co-evolution of Sensory System and Signal Processing for Optimal Wing Shape Control

Olga Smalikho[1](✉) and Markus Olhofer[2]

[1] Technische Universität Darmstadt, Darmstadt, Germany
Olga.Smalikho@rtr.tu-darmstadt.de
[2] Honda Research Institute Europe, Offenbach, Germany
Markus.Olhofer@honda-ri.de

Abstract. This paper demonstrates the applicability of evolutionary computation methods to co-evolve a sensor morphology and a suitable control structure to optimally adjust a virtual adaptive wing structure. In contrast to approaches in which the structure of a sensor configuration is fixed early in the design stages, we target the simultaneous generation of information acquisition and information processing based on the optimization of a target function. We consider two aspects as main advantages. First the ability to generate optimal environmental sensors in the sense that the control structure can optimally utilize the information provided and secondly the abdication of detailed prior knowledge about the problem at hand. In this work we investigate the expected high correlation between the sensor morphology and the signal processing structures as well the quantity and quality of the information gathered from the environment.

Keywords: Co-evolution · Neural network · Robust optimization

1 Introduction

Adaptive systems consist of sensors as well as actuators which allow the improvement of systems in reaction to changes in their environment according to a predefined quality measure. The design of such systems is usually driven by the utilization of prior knowledge of the problem at hand in order to generate an effective sensory system which is able to provide all relevant information about the environmental conditions as well as actuator configurations which can generate suitable reactions to improve the system's performance. After the determination of the sensor and actuator configuration a suitable control structure which processes information from the environment to effective actuator signals is generated. This procedure requires a detailed understanding of all phenomena which influence the behavior of the system. One reason is the necessity of knowing what information about the environment is important in order to place the right sensors at the right place. To acquire this knowledge a priori is challenging for a wide variety of tasks. Furthermore, the determination of an optimal overall system is expected to be challenging due to strong interaction between the

© Springer-Verlag Berlin Heidelberg 2014
A.I. Esparcia-Alcázar et al. (Eds.): EvoApplications 2014, LNCS 8602, pp. 805–816, 2014.
DOI: 10.1007/978-3-662-45523-4_65

sensor and actuator configuration with the control system. Therefore it is necessary to solve two tasks. The first is to determine the optimal control structure for the provided information by sensors, and secondly to determine information which optimally suits the control system. In this research we demonstrate the simultaneous evolutionary design of sensor configuration and control structure for the example of a virtual adaptive wing configuration. Based on the evolved designs we investigate the influence of the sensory input dimensionality on the overall system quality. In detail we analyze the trade off between more detailed information which requires the generation of a more complex information processing system and a low dimensional sensory input which is able to acquire a reduced set of environmental information, however requiring a simpler and easier to generate control structure. We demonstrate that both factors are in a trade off relation. Furthermore we invest the co-evolution process of both units and demonstrate the high dependency between sensor and control structure. A variety of similar approaches for the evolutionary design of sensor and actuator configurations have been investigated in the field of evolutionary robotics. Early work in the field of automatic design of a systems by body-brain co-evolution has been reported by Sims [1]. He demonstrated the evolutionary development of the morphology of virtual creatures in a physical simulation fulfilling simple locomotion tasks starting from simple building blocks without any prior knowledge. Parker and Nathan [2] research the design of sensor morphology and controller for a simulated hexapod robot. For this purpose the type of sensors, the heading angle and the range of the sensors as well as the rules for the controller are co-evolved. This method enables the system to extract information from the environment which is relevant to complete a given task by configuring a minimal controller and number of sensors to increase the system's overall efficiency. Bugajska and Schutz [3] co-evolved the shape and strategies in the design of Micro Air Vehicles (MAV). The target, similar to Parker and Nathan, was to find a minimal sensor suite and reactive strategies for navigation and collision avoidance tasks. Sugiura et al. also proposed a system that automatically designs the sensor morphology of an autonomous robot with two kinds of adaptation: ontogenetic and phylo-genetic adaptation[4]. Also Auerbach and Bongard [5] have made extensive research in the field of co-evolution of morphology and control in evolutionary robotics. In their work they implement a growth mechanism to create robots using compositional pattern-producing networks and demonstrate that the concurrent development of the morphological and controller structures of the simulated adaptive robots can give an advantage for the final system performance, compared to the approaches with separate design strategies.

Compared with the reviewed research in evolutionary robotics, we utilize the co-evolution of morphology and information processing structure for the optimal control of an adaptive wing shape. Although the generation of optimal control for adaptive wings is not in the main focus of our research we argue that this problem is a suitable test bed for the research on evolutionary design of adaptive systems. Aerodynamic problems are characterized by highly complex interactions between flow body and flow field which is in most cases difficult to understand in detail. Due to this manual design is generally challenging to achieve. However excellent tools are available for their simulation and the evaluation. In this work we demonstrate that evolutionary methods are able to generate systems which can optimally adapt to environmental conditions, while at the same time we target shedding some light on the precise synchronization of system parts during the developmental process. In comparison to the research [2],[3],[4] we changed the environmental settings randomly in each generation of the evolutionary process and thus obtained a robust adaptive system, able to react during random environmental changes. The target for the development of the adaptive wing is the reduction of the drag the airfoil generates while still creating a minimum of lift. Environmental changes are realized by changes in the angle of attack of the airflow across a wide range. A detailed description of the adaptive wing and the experimental conditions is given in section 2. In section 3 we summarize results of standard design optimization tasks for non-adaptive airfoils in order to generate a baseline for the comparison of the quality achieved by the adaptive system. An airfoil design optimization for a certain number of the fixed environmental conditions, represented in section 3, shows maximal controller potentials for these environmental conditions. In Section 4 we describe the experiments we performed, present results of the experiments and analyze the development process realized. Finally we conclude the paper by a summary of the main findings and an outlook of further work.

2   Framework for Morphology-Controller Co-evolution

In our work we implemented a system, consisting of virtual sensors, actuators and a signal processing structure. The signal processing structure controls the adaptive system under changing environmental conditions by generating actuator signals based on sensor signals derived from the environment. The target has been to achieve a system behavior which reduces the airfoil's drag, calculated in a CFD (computational fluid dynamics) simulation of the resulting airfoil shape while maintaining specified lift value. The actuator signals correspond to changes of the NURBS [6] control points and define the current airfoil shape. The virtual sensors of the system have been defined as pressure sensors, at a given position on the airfoil surface. The values of the virtual sensors correspond to the surface pressure calculated in the CFD simulation and therefore depend on the blade's surface, the angle of attack and the speed of the air flow etc. Fig. 1 (a) shows the described relations between the single parts of the test-framework. With the described setup an adaptive behavior can be realized by the actuators in reaction to the change of the environmental conditions. Furthermore a variable number of sensors or actuators can be easily realized. The described setup serves as a test framework for the simulation of the interactions between control structure and morphology during the operation of the control structure as well during their evolutionary development.

In our work we implemented the two dimensional airfoil by a non-uniform rational B-splines (NURBS) as shown in Fig. 1 (b). The shape of the NURBS

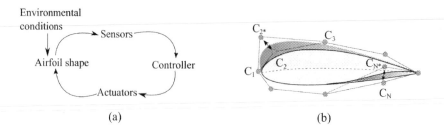

Fig. 1. (a) Adaptive airfoil framework, (b) Example of the airfoil created with NURBS. Airfoil in white, defined by the initial positions of the spline control points. The airfoil shape change (in gray) results from the movements of C_2 and C_N.

curve and with that the shape of the resulting wing profile is determined by the set of spline control points. The splines, defined by its control points C_n, result into a unique two dimensional airfoil shape. By moving the control points in the two dimensional space, a shape change of the airfoil can be achieved. For the simulation of the aerodynamic airfoil characteristics and pressure distribution we used the computational fluid dynamic solver Xfoil[1] because of its high speed which is decisive for optimization tasks (less than 5 seconds). Xfoil calculates different aerodynamic characteristics for the given airfoil geometry and environmental configurations, e.g. angle of attack, Reynolds number etc. In the simulation we change the angle of attack as a variable input of the system in order to generate variations of the airfoil environment. The Reynolds number has been fixed during the optimization($Re = 10^7$). To simulate the sensors we used the distribution of the pressure coefficient over the airfoil surface. The pressure coefficient C_p [7] is defined as a relative pressure throughout a flow field in fluid dynamics. In comparison to a gauge pressure value at the point on the airfoil, the pressure coefficient is dimensionless and independent from effects of the density and speed of the air. We used Xfoil to calculate the profile of the pressure coefficients C_p at 160 points on the airfoil surface. A sensor placed on the airfoil returns a sensor value corresponding to the pressure coefficient at the airfoil surface.

2.1   Controller

The control system is realized by Parker and Nathan [2] as well as Bugajska and Schutz [3] as a reactive system that uses "if...then" rules to control a simulated robot. Haller, Ijspeert and Floreano [8] implemented a controller inspired from the central pattern generators underlying locomotion in animals. In comparison to these approaches we use biologically inspired feed forward neural networks (FFNN). The task of the neural controller is to reduce the drag of the adaptive airfoil system by morphing the airfoil surface. For the implementation the SHARK[2], open-source C++ machine learning library is used. The neural

---

[1] http://web.mit.edu/drela/Public/web/xfoil/
[2] http://image.diku.dk/shark/

network we implemented consists of one input layer, a single hidden layer with sigmoidal activation function and one output layer with a linear activation function. In Fig. 2 a schematic overview of the overall system is given.

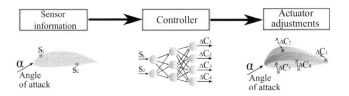

Fig. 2. Schematic view of the overall control structure

3   Baseline Optimization

The target of the baseline optimization has been to find shapes for the airfoils with minimal drag in order to generate a baseline which allows the evaluation of the blade shapes generated by the adaptive system. A second reason for the experiments was to investigate the influence of the number of spline control points on the optimization behavior. To determine the maximal achievable quality of the airfoils conventional evolutionary design optimization was performed. We used a CMA-ES(4,8) strategy with standard population size [9] to find the optimal shapes of the airfoil for the individual angles of attack with lift constraint. Minimal lift constraint has been set to a lift coefficient of NACA 2410 airfoil, $C_l^{min} = C_l^{NACA2410}$. NACA airfoils are the aircraft wing shapes, developed by the National Advisory Committee for Aeronautics in 1948 [10] and define since that time a set of standard airfoil shapes. Fig. 3.a) shows the result of the design optimization with fixed number of spline control points, $C_p = 6$. The maximal thickness of the airfoil was set to the maximal thickness of the NACA 2410 airfoil which is equal to 10% of the chord. For a set of 5 angles of attack the optimal airfoil shapes have been determined experimentally with the resulting drag and lift coefficients given in Table 1. We found specialized solutions for each angle of attack, which have significantly lower drag and higher lift than a single NACA 2410 airfoil being rather robust for wide range of different angles of attack.

The results of the optimization runs can be seen as the maximal achievable performance for the given settings and therefore form the baseline for the evaluation of all further experiments. From here on we concentrate on the sensor-controller optimisation. In a first set of experiments we investigate the influence of the number of spline control points on the optimization results. In the design optimization runs with only 3 variable control points per airfoil we observe a very high improvement of the blade quality in an early phase of the optimization, however with a low final quality. With a higher number of spline control points the airfoil quality improves slower, but the final quality of the airfoil is significantly improved.

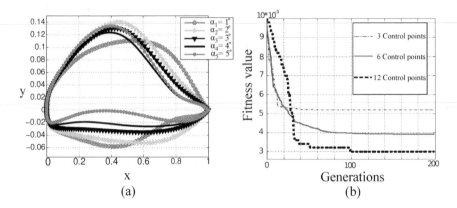

Fig. 3. (a) Optimized airfoil shapes, (b) Averaged quality history of CMA optimisation runs for different number of spline control points. Angle of attack was set to 3°, slightly different start airfoils were used in all 5 of the otherwise identical simulations which were used for averaging.

Table 1. Best baseline performance with 6 spline control points, compared with NACA 2410 airfoil

$\alpha, degree$	$C_d^{opt}10^{-3}$	C_l^{opt}	$C_d^{NACA2410}10^{-3}$	$C_l^{NACA2410}$
1°	3.091	0.401	4.950	0.355
2°	3.192	0.497	5.070	0.467
3°	3.391	0.617	5.390	0.576
4°	3.434	0.845	5.910	0.686
5°	3.860	0.931	6.140	0.791

4   Robust Sensor-Controller Optimization

We implemented the optimization of sensor positions on the airfoil surface and the optimization of neural network weights. We realized the proposed optimization task with a standard Evolution Strategy (ES), developed by Bienert, Rechenberg and Schwefel as well as with a CMA Evolution Strategy [11], [9]. We achieved significantly better results with a standard ES(50,200) with two different self adapted step sizes, for sensor positions and neural network weights adaptation. Detailed results are given in section 4.2.

4.1   System Performance Evaluation

The task for the controller is the improve the airfoil drag after a variation of the inflow angle. Therefore the drag coefficient of the airfoil before any modifications took place C_d^1 is evaluated and after the modification of the airfoil blade C_d^2. The ratio of these two values shows if the neural network outputs realizing an actuator adjustment, perform well and reduce the airfoil drag. The total fitness of the individual has been defined as the sum of the drag coefficient value ratios summed

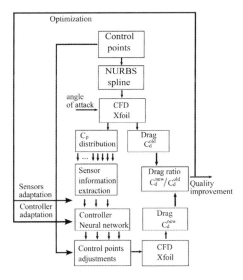

Fig. 4. Overview of the system evaluation

over the set of different angles of attack given in the experimental setup. Fig. 4 shows the structural diagram of individual evaluation. Optimization starts with randomly initiated sensor positions between 0 (trailing edge, wing upper-side) and 2 (trailing edge, wing under-side) and neural network weights, uniformly randomly initialized between -0.01 and 0.01. The trailing edge is defined as rear edge, where the airflow split by the leading edge rejoins [7]. After the change of the angle of attack we evaluated 3 cycles of geometry change in order to let the system convert to a final state. The main reason is that the system goes through a set of partial update steps until the optimal geometry is reached. After the first update the adjusted geometry is therefore likely to be influenced by the shape in the previous step as visible in the final results. The final fitness value for the individual is calculated as the sum of drag value ratios over all tree steps of spline control point adjustments for a single angle of attack and additionally over a cascade of different angles of attack, which however stayed the same during the first experiment. In the second experiment, in each generation a set of angles of attack have been randomly changed between $2°$ and $4°$. The random change was introduced to avoid that only shape transitions which are predefined by the set of given inflow angles are possible. As mentioned, the size of the controller was defined by the number of neurons in the input layer which is equal to the number of sensors, the number of neurons in the output layer equal to the number of actuators and a fixed number of 20 hidden neurons.

4.2 Robust Optimization Results

Fig. 5 shows the filtered fitness curves of the robust optimization described in section 4.1 averaged over 10 runs. The fitness function was defined as following:

$$Fitness(Individual) = \frac{\sum_{\alpha=1}^{N} \sum_{i=1}^{M} \frac{C_d(\alpha,\text{changed airfoil})}{C_d(\alpha,\text{unchanged airfoil})}}{N * M} \tag{1}$$

where M is a number of controller actions for the same angle of attack ($M = 3$) ,α is the angle of attack, N is the total number of angles of attack applied and the individual has been evaluated on, C_d is the drag coefficient. The number of

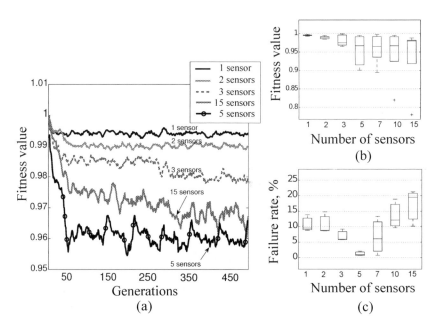

Fig. 5. (a) Robust optimization results filtered with moving average over 10 generations. Fitness curves has been averaged over 10 runs with different starting parameters. (b) Box plot of the optimization runs for each number of sensors, (c) Percentage of the cases in which controller lead to a failure performance, for scenario of 10 random angles of attack between $1°$ and $7°$.

optimization parameters results from the size of system controller (number of neurons in a hidden layer), the number of sensors and actuators (control points of the spline). The total number of parameter is

$$N_{Param} = N_i * N_h + (N_i + N_h) * N_o + N_h + N_o + N_i + N_s \tag{2}$$

where N_i is the number of sensors, N_h the number of neurons in the hidden layer (was fixed to $N_h = 20$), N_o is the number of actuators (was fixed to $N_o = 6$) and N_s is the number of optimization step-sizes ($N_s = 2$). As an example, for the system, using 5 sensors, we need to optimize 283 parameters.

The results show that the system development progress depends on the number of sensors. For the systems, using between 1 and 5 sensors, we observed a clear trend of averaged performance improvement with an enlargement of the sensory system (see Fig. 5 (a) and (b)). Starting with 7 sensors the averaged performance does not improve. Additionally in Fig.5 (c) we see, that on average the failure of controller actions, defined as an action, that lead to an invalid solution, increases gradually for the systems with more than 5 sensors,although the maximal achievable quality given in Fig. 5 (b) is better with a larger sensor number.

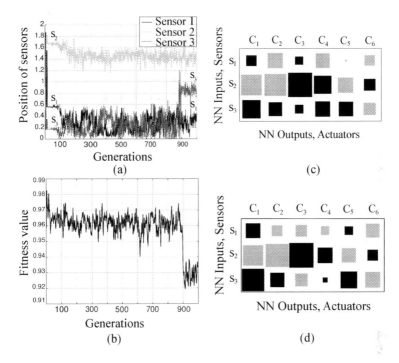

Fig. 6. (a) Development of the position of the sensors during the optimization (b) Optimization of the robust system, using 3 sensors. Evaluation on the random angles of attack between $1°$ and $5°$, Hinton diagrams of the neural controller of the system at generation 800 (c) and 900 (d).

An example of the dynamics of the concurrent sensor-controller adjustment during the optimization experiment is given in Fig. 6. As mentioned, we use single hidden layer, consisting of 20 neurons with sigmoid activation function. To investigate the internal functionality of the neural network as a controller, we visualize converted network connections between sensors and actuators of the adaptive airfoil, omitting the non-linearity of the hidden layer. The connection strengths between neurons have been calculated as following:

$$S_{io} = \frac{\sum_{j=1}^{j=N_h} W_{ij} V_{jo}}{N_h} \tag{3}$$

The variable S_{io} is the converted connection strength between input i and output o, N_h is the number of neurons in a hidden layer, W and V - input and output weights of the neural network. Fig. 6 (c) and (d) show corresponding diagrams of the neural strengths of the system at the 800th and 900th generation. For visualizing of the converted neural connection strengths a Hinton diagrams has been used [12]. The size of the boxes corresponds to the value of the connection strength. The boxes color (gray and black) represents positive or negative sign of the connection strength respectively. The values of the connection strengths lie between zero (no box) and one (box of maximum size). In Fig. 6 (b) we see a significant performance improvement at the generation 900. Fig. 6 (a) shows the development of the sensory system configuration. Sensor 3 changes its position gradually at around the 900th generation. The corresponding change in a controller system can be observed in Fig. 6 (c) and (d). Compared with the controller at generation 800, we can see a significant change of the controller connection strengths at generation 900 for the first and the third sensor. The connections of the second sensor stay nearly constant. Regarding Fig. 6 (a), (b), (c) and (d), a precise sensor-controller adjustment takes place. This results show that the development of the signal measurement and signal processing modules are tightly coupled and precisely coordinated.

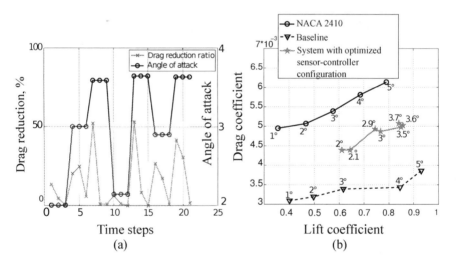

Fig. 7. (a) Percentage of the airfoil drag reduction for a scenario of 7 angles of attack between 2° and 4°, using 7 sensors. (b) Comparison of the robust system performance given in Fig.7 (a) with baseline design optimization in Fig. 3 (a), Tab. 1 and NACA 2410.

Finally we analyzed the results of the robust sensor-controller optimization in Fig. 5. The performance of the optimized system with 7 sensors was again evaluated this time with a set of 7 randomly chosen angles. The result is illustrated in) Fig. 7 (a). As mentioned, the controller adjusts the actuators for the current angle of attack in 3 steps. We observe the drag reduction after almost each controller action. The highest drag reduction takes place in the first of 3 controller actions for the same angle of attack. For example the drag reduction for the angles of attack of 3.5° and 3.6° was above 50% through the first controller adjustment. The fitness value of the system in Fig. 7 (a) is equal to 0.85. Fig. 7 (b) shows a final comparison of the airfoils resulting from a concurrent sensor-controller development, from the standard design optimization and the NACA 2410 airfoil. We observed, that on the test scenario the system with a concurrently optimized sensor and controller configuration does not perform as well as the individual design optimization with respect to a drag, but performs better than NACA 2410 airfoil. Regarding the lift coefficient, the co-evolved system creates higher lift than the profiles of baseline optimization and NACA 2410 for the same angles of attack.

5   Conclusions

This work investigates the generation of an adaptive system realized by an adaptive wing. The system consists of a sensor and actuator configuration as well as a related control structure. The target for the adaptive wing is the minimization of the airfoil drag while the angle in which the air is approaching the airfoil is changed randomly. Sensors as well as the control structure of the adaptive wing design are defined during an evolutionary process, resulting in a concurrent and coordinated development of the overall system. The experimental results demonstrate the expected high correlation between the development of the sensory system and the control systems. Furthermore we observe a strong influence of the number of the environmental sensors, which is related to the amount of information which is available to the control structure, and the final performance of the system. On the one hand the system needs sufficient sensory information defined by the number and position of the sensors for an optimal control strategy in the randomly changing environment. On the other hand the achieved quality of the optimized solution degenerates with very high numbers of optimization parameters, which are determined by the complexity of the control structure which in turn is defined by the number of sensory inputs. Both aspects can be observed in the experimental results. A small number of sensors results in simple and low dimensional control structures which converge quickly in the evolutionary process to a local optimum, yet they have an overall low quality measured by a high drag value due to insufficient sensory information. In the case of a high dimensional sensory input of the system we observe low convergence speed toward an optimum due to the high dimensional optimization problem or even an early convergence to local optima. These results suggest the existence of an optimal number of system parameters for the evolutionary design process. Unfortunately neither the optimal dimensionality of the sensory input nor the optimal number of optimization parameter is known for the problem at hand. Furthermore it is likely that the optimal number of parameters depend on the progress of the optimization process. These findings suggest the necessity of a variable number of free parameters in the system, which is addressed in future work by the realization of a growth process during the evolutionary design process.

Acknowledgments. The authors gratefully acknowledge the support of Giles Endicott and Bernhard Sendhoff and the financial support from Honda Research Institute Europe GmbH.

References

1. Sims, K.: Evolving virtual creatures. In: The 21st Annual Conference, pp. 15–22. ACM Press, New York (1994)
2. Parker, G., Nathan, P.: Co-evolution of sensor morphology and control on a simulated legged robot. In: International Symposium on Computational Intelligence in Robotics and Automation, CIRA 2007, pp. 516–521 (2007)
3. Bugajska, M.D., Schultz, A.C.: Coevolution of form and function in the design of micro air vehicles. In: Evolvable Hardware, 154–166. IEEE Computer Society (2002)
4. Sugiura, K., Akahane, M., Shiose, T., Shimohara, K., Katai, O.: Exploiting interaction between sensory morphology and learning. In: 2005 IEEE International Conference on Systems, Man and Cybernetics, vol. 1., pp. 883–888 (2005)
5. Auerbach, J., Bongard, J.: 12th International Conference on the Synthesis and Simulation of Living Systems (ALife XII) (August 2010)
6. Farin, G.E.: NURBS: From Projective Geometry to Practical Use, 2nd edn. A. K. Peters Ltd., Natick (1999)
7. Anderson, J.: Fundamentals of Aerodynamics. Anderson series, McGraw-Hill Education (2011)
8. von Haller, B., Ijspeert, A.J., Floreano, D.: Co-evolution of Structures and Controllers for Neubot Underwater Modular Robots. In: Capcarrère, M.S., Freitas, A.A., Bentley, P.J., Johnson, C.G., Timmis, J. (eds.) ECAL 2005. LNCS (LNAI), vol. 3630, pp. 189–199. Springer, Heidelberg (2005)
9. Hansen, N.: The CMA Evolution Strategy: A Comparing Review (2006)
10. Jacobs, E.N., Ward, K.E., Pinkerton, R.M.: The characteristics of 78 related airfoil sections from tests in the variable density wind tunnel. Technical Report 460 (1948)
11. Rechenberg, I.: Evolutionsstrategie 1994. Frommann, Stuttgart (1994) Fit via Evolutionsstrategie, Routine von Volker Tuerck vorhanden (1994)
12. Bremner, F., Gotts, S., Denham, D.: Hinton diagrams: Viewing connection strengths in neural networks, vol. 26, pp. 215–218. Springer (1994)

Infeasibility Driven Evolutionary Algorithm with Feed-forward Prediction Strategy for Dynamic Constrained Optimization Problems

Patryk Filipiak[(⊠)] and Piotr Lipinski

Computational Intelligence Research Group, Institute of Computer Science,
University of Wroclaw, Wroclaw, Poland
{patryk.filipiak,lipinski}@ii.uni.wroc.pl

Abstract. This paper proposes a modification of Infeasibility Driven Evolutionary Algorithm that applies the anticipation mechanism following Feed-forward Prediction Strategy. The presented approach allows reacting on environmental changes more rapidly by directing some individuals into the areas of most probable occurrences of future optima. Also a novel population segmentation on exploring, exploiting and anticipating fractions is introduced to assure a better diversification of individuals and thus improve the ability to track moving optima. The experiments performed on the popular benchmarks confirmed the significant improvement in Dynamic Constrained Optimization Problems when using the proposed approach.

1 Introduction

Numerous optimization problems are dynamic in the sense that their objective functions change as time goes by, thus making them difficult to solve. However, recent advances in Computational Intelligence allowed to address Dynamic Optimization Problems (DOPs) with the heuristic approach. The spectrum of Evolutionary Algorithms (EAs) applicable for DOPs has grown significantly within the last few years [2,6,7,10–13,15]. Unlike the classical EAs, they are able to track moving optima and simultaneously explore the search space looking for the newly appearing optima by either introducing or maintaining diversity within a population [10,13,15] or forecasting future promising regions based on the past observations [6,7,12].

Dynamic Constrained Optimization Problems (DCOPs) were defined in [8] as a subclass of DOPs aimed at finding such $x^{(t)} \in \mathbb{R}^d$ for each $t > 0$ that satisfies

$$x^{(t)} = \arg\min\{F^{(t)}(x) : x \in \mathbb{R}^d \ \land \ g_j^{(t)}(x) \leq 0, \text{ for } j = 1, 2, \ldots, m\},$$

where $F^{(t)}$ is the objective function and $g_j^{(t)}$ are the constraint functions. Although lately some EAs for DCOPs were proposed [6,13], Yang et al. [15] identified "a clear gap of studies on constrained and dynamic constrained problems".

Infeasibility Driven EA (IDEA) [14] is one of the algorithms assuring a superior constraint handling by promoting infeasible solutions in order to localize

© Springer-Verlag Berlin Heidelberg 2014
A.I. Esparcia-Alcázar et al. (Eds.): EvoApplications 2014, LNCS 8602, pp. 817–828, 2014.
DOI: 10.1007/978-3-662-45523-4_66

optima on constraint boundaries. Moreover, it is stated in [13] that even though IDEA was originally proposed for Stationary Optimization Problems (SOPs), it has also the ability to deal with some DOPs.

The contribution of this paper is the proposed modification of IDEA named IDEA-FPS. It utilizes the anticipation mechanism that predicts future optima locations based on past observations by following Feed-forward Prediction Strategy (FPS) [7], i.e. it keeps the track of best individuals from past generations and makes predictions about most probable locations of future optima. As the anticipation mechanism the AutoRegressive Integrated Moving Average (ARIMA) model [1] is applied. Also a novel population segmentation into exploring, exploiting and anticipating fractions is proposed to assure a better diversification of individuals and thus improve the ability to track moving optima.

The experiments performed on the popular DCOP benchmarks [5,9] confirmed that IDEA-FPS significantly outperformed IDEA in most of the cases, especially in rapidly changing environments.

2   Infeasibility Driven Evolutionary Algorithm

IDEA [14] was originally proposed to address stationary constrained optimization problems. It maintains a certain fraction of "good" yet infeasible solutions within a population in order to improve an exploration of areas near constraint boundaries. Formally, IDEA evaluates each individual under the two criteria. One criterion is simply an objective function. Another criterion, called *violation measure*, determines to what extent a given solution violates the constraints. Thus IDEA essentially reformulates a single-objective problem into a multi-objective one, so that any two individuals can no longer be compared according to their fitness. Instead, the ranking based on *non-dominated sorting* procedure with *crowding distance* metric (as a tie-breaking rule) is performed as in NSGA-II [3]. It is important to note that crowding distance promotes individuals located in less crowded areas hence it introduces diversity within a population.

Let $M > 0$ be the size of the population P. The main loop of IDEA (presented in Algorithm 1) begins with the random initialization of P then runs $N_{gen} > 0$ iterations, each of which starts with the (re-)evaluation of P.

The heart of IDEA is Sub-IDEA step (Algorithm 2) which essentially runs the entire "evolutionary engine" of the algorithm. It consists of $N_{sub} > 0$ iterations of tournament selection, simulated binary crossover (SBX) and polynomial mutation [14]. As the output Sub-IDEA returns the set C consisting of M offsprings. In order not to confuse iterations of Sub-IDEA step with iterations of the main loop, the former ones will be referred to as *subiterations*.

The key aspect of IDEA is the reduction step. As it is seen in Algorithm 3, the union set of parents P and children C is firstly split into two subsets (S_{feas} and S_{infeas}) based on the feasibility of individuals. Then, both these subsets are ranked separately according to the mentioned NSGA-II ranking. The top $M_{feas} > 0$ individuals among S_{feas} and the top $M_{infeas} > 0$ individuals among S_{infeas} (such that $M = M_{feas} + M_{infeas}$) are chosen to form the new generation

Algorithm 1. Main loop of IDEA.

$P_1 = \text{RandomPopulation}()$
for $t = 1 \rightarrow N_{gen}$ **do**
    $\text{Evaluation}(P_t)$
    $C_t = \text{Sub-IDEA}(P'_t)$
    $P''_t = \text{IDEA-Reduction}(P'_t \cup C_t)$
end for

Algorithm 2. Sub-IDEA step.

$P_1 = P$
$\text{Evaluation}(P_1)$
for $t = 1 \rightarrow N_{sub}$ **do**
    $P'_t = \text{Selection}(P_t)$
    $C_t = \text{Crossover}(P'_t)$
    $C''_t = \text{Mutation}(C'_t)$
    $P_{t+1} = \text{IDEA-Reduction}(P_t \cup C''_t)$
end for
Return $P_{N_{sub}}$

Algorithm 3. IDEA-Reduction of a union $P \cup C$ (where P are parents and C are children), producing an output population P' consisting of $M > 0$ individuals.

$M_{infeas} = size_{infeas} \cdot M$
$M_{feas} = M - M_{infeas}$
$(S_{feas}, S_{infeas}) = \text{Split}(P \cup C)$
$\text{Rank}(S_{feas})$
$\text{Rank}(S_{infeas})$
$P' = S_{feas}(1 : M_{feas}) + S_{infeas}(1 : M_{infeas})$

P'. This sort of a separation is intended to promote the infeasible individuals located near constraint boundaries which otherwise could be eliminated by the feasible ones due to their superiority in violation measure.

3   Feed-forward Prediction Strategy

The Feed-forward Prediction Strategy (FPS) was proposed in [7] as an anticipation mechanism used by Dynamic Queuing Multi-Objective Optimizer (D-QMOO). It assumes that the changes of spatial optima locations in a search space at the consecutive time steps form a pattern that can be fitted with an AutoRegressive (AR) model. As a result, the locations of future optima can be anticipated using this model.

For all time steps $t \in \mathbb{N}_+$, let $x^*_t \in \mathbb{R}^n$ be the argument minimizing $F^{(t)}$, i.e. the location of optimum of $F^{(t)}$. Let $\{X_t\}_{t \in \mathbb{N}_+}$ be the n-dimensional time series of such optima locations, i.e. $X_1 = x^*_1$, $X_2 = x^*_2, \ldots$ Obviously, the exact values of x^*_t aren't known. Instead, an individual $p^*_t \in \mathbb{R}^n$ with the highest fitness among all specimens in a population P_t at time step t is used as the best available approximation of x_t^*. As a result, the accuracy of a prediction model is highly dependent on the efficiency of the EA used. It means that the closer a population can get to the actual optimum at each time step, the more exact locations of future optima can be anticipated. On the other hand, the less effectively EA performs at localizing current optima, the more erroneous anticipations it obtains in return.

It is crucial that models like AR require some $N_{train} > 0$ initial steps for collecting the data and auto-tunning the parameters before they can be used. Thus, any EA would perform equivalently, either with or without using the prediction mechanism, during the initial time steps $t = 1, \ldots, N_{train}$

4   IDEA-FPS

IDEA-FPS is the proposed modification of IDEA that utilizes the ARIMA-based anticipation mechanism following FPS and introduces the novel population segmentation. Apart from maintaining a small fraction of infeasible individuals, as IDEA does, IDEA-FPS performs the repeatable injections of individuals located in the proximity of the anticipated future optima. Also the injections of random immigrants are performed in order to introduce diversity within the population.

A detailed description of IDEA-FPS is given in the following subsections.

4.1   Anticipation Mechanism

The original FPS presented in the previous section was based on the simple AR model. It was parametrized with only a single positive integer p determining the order of autoregression. In IDEA-FPS, the AR model is extended into the more general ARIMA [1] model that often guarantees more accurate forecasts yet requires 3 non-negative integer parameters (p, d, q), where p and q are the orders of autoregression and moving average (respectively) while d is the number of differentiations of consecutive elements. Naturally, AR(p) is equivalent to ARIMA($p, 0, 0$) for all $p > 0$.

A selection of proper values of p, d, q is crucial for balancing an anticipation accuracy and a computational cost. Typically, the greater values of p and q are used, the more accurate forecasts are obtained and the more computation time is needed. However, it is suggested in [1] that ARIMA(p, d, q) typically produces sufficiently accurate forecasts when using the parameters $p, d, q \in \{0, 1, 2\}$ which practically narrows down the spectrum of ARIMA models to 24 variants (excluding cases where $p = q = 0$).

4.2   Population Segmentation

IDEA-FPS retains the feasibility-based population segmentation from IDEA. Simultaneously, it introduces the additional role-based segmentation on: *exploring fraction*, *exploiting fraction* and *anticipating fraction*. Any individual from a given role-based fraction is of course either feasible or infeasible. Similarly, any individual from a given feasibility-based fraction must also belong to either exploring, exploiting or anticipating fraction.

Exploring fraction is built up entirely with random immigrants that are uniformly distributed in the search space. Their randomness prevents a population from trapping into local optima and introduces diversity required for tracking changes in the landscape. *Anticipating fraction* is a group of individuals gathered in the nearest proximity of the predicted location of a future optimum. Providing that a forecast obtained with an anticipation model is accurate, these individuals would become the most contributing ones just after the next environmental change. *Exploiting fraction* in turn is formed with offsprings of both exploring and anticipating individuals from previous generations. It is responsible for a fine-grained search in the areas recognized as promising by the other fractions and for decreasing violation measure of infeasible individuals.

4.3   Algorithm

A pseudo-code of IDEA-FPS is given in Algorithm 4. It begins with a random initialization of $M > 0$ individuals $x_1, \ldots, x_M \in \mathbb{R}^d$ and the empty time series $\{X_t\}_{t \in \mathbb{N}}$. Each iteration $t = 1, \ldots, N_{gen}$ starts with an evaluation of a population P_t, i.e. a computation of fitness and violation measures. Later on, a new exploring fraction comprising of $size_{explore} \cdot M$ random immigrants (where $size_{explore} \in \{0\%, \ldots, 100\%\}$) is injected into P_t. These immigrants replace worst feasible individuals in P_t. If the size of an exploring fraction is greater than the size of a feasible fraction, then also worst infeasible ones are replaced. Note that such replacement strategy promotes infeasible solutions which is one of the key aspects of IDEA as it was mentioned before.

Algorithm 4. Pseudo-code of IDEA-FPS.

$X_0 = (\emptyset)$
$P_1 = \text{RandomPopulation}()$
for $t = 1 \rightarrow N_{gen}$ **do**
   $\text{Evaluation}(P_t)$
   $P_t' = \text{InjectExploringFraction}(P_t, size_{explore})$
   $C_t = \text{Sub-IDEA}(P_t')$
   $P_t'' = \text{IDEA-Reduction}(P_t' \cup C_t, size_{infeas})$
   $p_t^* = \text{BestIndividual}(P_t'')$
   $X_t = (X_{t-1}, \{p_t^*\})$
   if $t \leq N_{train}$ **then**
      $P_{t+1} = P_t''$
   else
      $\widetilde{p_{t+1}^*} = \text{NextBestIndividualAnticipation}(X_t, \text{ARIMA}(p, d, q))$
      $\Phi_{t+1} = \text{AnticipatingFractionDistribution}(\widetilde{p_{t+1}^*}, t)$
      $P_{t+1} = \text{InjectAnticipatingFraction}(P_t'', \Phi_{t+1}, size_{anticip})$
   end if
end for

After invoking standard Sub-IDEA and IDEA-Reduction steps, a *best-of-population* individual p_t^* is selected, i.e. a feasible individual with the highest fitness or (if a feasible fraction is empty) the one with the lowest violation measure. A vector $p_t^* \in \mathbb{R}^d$ is then stored in $\{X_t\}$ as the best approximation of an optimum location at time step t.

For $t = 1, \ldots, N_{train}$ the anticipation mechanism of IDEA-FPS is inactive since best individuals from these generations are used for training the ARIMA model. During this initial period IDEA-FPS behaves like the original IDEA extended with random immigrants injections.

When the condition $t > N_{train}$ is finally satisfied, ARIMA(p, d, q) model is applied to $\{X_t\}$ in order to obtain a forecast concerning the next optimum location $\widetilde{p_{t+1}^*}$.

As a result, the new anticipation fraction is created out of random individuals located in the proximity of $\widetilde{p_{t+1}^*}$. Virtually any continuous probability distribution function can be applied for that purpose. In this paper anticipation fractions are drawn with a d-dimensional Gaussian distribution $\mathcal{N}(\widetilde{p_{t+1}^*}, \sigma_t^2)$ where $\sigma_t = (\sigma_{t,1}, \sigma_{t,2}, \ldots, \sigma_{t,d}) \in \mathbb{R}^d$ with $\sigma_{t,i} = (x_i^{max} - x_i^{min})/100t$ for $i = 1, \ldots, d$ and $x_i^{min} \leq x_i^{max}$.

At the end of the main loop, these new individuals replace worst feasible solutions (and worst infeasible ones if necessary) just like in the case of exploring fraction.

5 Experiments

IDEA-FPS with various ARIMA(p, d, q) models and possible sizes of exploring, exploiting and anticipating fractions was tested on the popular DCOP benchmarks then compared with IDEA.

5.1 Benchmarks

The experiments were performed on the three following benchmarks.

Benchmarks g24 [9] Minimize the function

(a) *g24_1*

$$F^{(t)}(x) = - \left[\sin\left(k\pi t + \frac{\pi}{2} \right) \cdot x_1 + x_2 \right],$$

(b) *g24_2*

$$F^{(t)}(x) = - \left[p_1(t) \cdot x_1 + p_2(t) \cdot x_2 \right],$$

$$p_1(t) = \begin{cases} \sin\left(\frac{k\pi t}{2} + \frac{\pi}{2} \right), & t \mid 2 \\ p_1(t-1), & t \nmid 2 \end{cases}, \qquad p_2(t) = \begin{cases} p_2(\max\{0, t-1\}), & t \mid 2 \\ \sin\left(\frac{k\pi(t-1)}{2} + \frac{\pi}{2} \right), & t \nmid 2 \end{cases}$$

subject to

$$g_1(x) = 2x_1^4 - 8x_1^3 + 8x_1^2 - x_2 + 2 \geq 0,$$
$$g_2(x) = 4x_1^4 - 32x_1^3 + 88x_1^2 - 96x_1 - x_2 + 36 \geq 0,$$

where $x = (x_1, x_2) \in [0, 3] \times [0, 4]$, $t \in \mathbb{N}_+$ and $0 \leq k \leq 2$.

Modified FDA1 [5,6] Minimize the function

$$F^{(t)}(x) = 1 - \sqrt{\frac{x_1}{1 + \sum_{i=2}^{n}\left(x_i - \sin\left(\frac{\pi t}{4}\right)\right)^2}}$$

subject to

$$g_j(x) = \frac{3[x_2 - \frac{1}{2}(\alpha_j + \beta_j)]^2}{2(\alpha_j - \beta_j)^2} - x_1 + \frac{1}{4} \geq 0,$$

$$\alpha_j = \sin\left(\frac{\pi(j+1)}{4}\right), \quad \beta_j = \sin\left(\frac{\pi(j+1)}{4}\right), \quad j \in \{1, 2, 3, 4\}.$$

where $x = (x_1, x_2) \in [0, 1] \times [-1, 1]$ and $t \in \mathbb{N}_+$.

5.2   Performance Measures

An overall efficiency of the analyzed algorithms was assessed with a frequently used *offline performance* measure [10] whereas an accuracy of the anticipation models — with a metric called *Akaike Information Criterion* (AIC) [1].

AIC(L, r) is defined as $-2 \ln L + 2r$, where L is the maximized likelihood for the estimated model and r is the number of input parameters of this model (in the case of ARIMA(p, d, q), $r = p + q + 1$). Note that AIC allows for both computing the expected information loss when using a given anticipation model and in the same time it penalizes a use of too many input parameters which could result in an increase of the computational cost. Thus, it is desirable to always pick ARIMA model with the lowest AIC.

5.3   Setup

In all the experiments a population of 25 individuals was used which is considered a middle-sized population for DCOPs in the literature [10,11]. The crossover and the mutation probability were set to 0.9 and 0.1 (respectively) as suggested in [13]. Violation measure (being the second objective) was defined as the Euclidean distance to the nearest feasible individual.

Each experiment lasted for $N_{gen} = 100$ generations containing a fixed number of $N_{sub} > 0$ subiterations (the exact value of N_{sub} differs in particular cases). The initial $N_{train} = 10$ generations were used for training an anticipation model.

All combinations among $\{0\%, 10\%, 20\%, \ldots, 100\%\}$ of a population size were considered for both exploring and ancitipating fractions. Note that IDEA is a special case of IDEA-FPS with both fraction sizes set to 0% while IDEA-FPS with exploring fraction size = 100% and anticipating fraction size = 0% is indeed the original IDEA with the full re-initialization of a population after each environmental change. For simplicity, the latter case will be referred to as *IDEA with restart*.

Each output presented further in this section is averaged over 50 independent runs with the same input parameters.

5.4   Discussion

Prediction model fitting comprises of setting up an optimal input parameters for a given prediction model. Table 1 summarizes the results of applying ARIMA(p, d, q) with $p, d, q \in \{0, 1, 2\}$ (excluding $p = q = 0$) to IDEA-FPS, tested in benchmarks *g24_1*, *g24_2* and *modified FDA1*. Results are arranged by AIC. In either case, ARIMA(2, 0, 2) gave best results according to AIC. However, ARIMA(2, 1, 2) resulted in slightly better scores on offline performance in *g24_1* and *modified FDA1* being nearly as good when comparing AIC. Generally, models with $p = 2$ together with zero or one differentiation d performed better than the remaining ones. On the other hand, ARIMA(0, d, q) models turned out to be the least effective in both criteria, especially when $d = 2$. This means that selecting a proper value of p played the most important role in fitting the model. A use of non-zero q parameter also had a positive influence although less significant.

Population segmentation affects explicitly the behavior of a whole population. At the first glance an equal-sized segmentation may seem most fair in general. Nevertheless, it is seen in Algorithm 4 that the exploring and anticipating fractions can actually overlap (which gives a large spectrum of contrintuitive possible segmentations) since they are iteratively re-established with consecutive injections of new individuals into the population. In other words, each of the two procedures, i.e. *InjectExploringFraction* at the beginning of a generation and *InjectAnticipatingFraction* at the end of it (providing that $t > N_{train}$), results in a replacement of up to 100% candidate solutions with the new ones.

Table 2 presents offline performances of IDEA-FPS (with $N_{sub} = 2$) obtained in $11 \times 11 = 121$ combinations of $size_{explore}$ and $size_{anticip}$ both in $\{0\%, 10\%, 20\%, \ldots, 100\%\}$. The top three outputs for each benchmark are underlined. It is evident from Table 2 that the rate of exploration had a significant impact on the overall performance of IDEA-FPS in all the analyzed benchmark problems.

Table 1. Partial ranking of ARIMA(p, d, q) with $p, d, q \in \{0, 1, 2\}$ (excluding $p = q = 0$) applied for IDEA-FPS, tested in *g24_1*, *g24_2* and *modified FDA1*; arranged by AIC

	g24_1			g24_2			modified FDA1		
pos.	ARIMA model	offline perform.	AIC	ARIMA model	offline perform.	AIC	ARIMA model	offline perform.	AIC
1.	(2, 0, 2)	-3.796	3.8	(2, 0, 2)	-1.262	122.0	(2, 0, 2)	0.0615	-44.3
2.	(2, 1, 2)	-3.826	7.0	(2, 0, 0)	-1.276	142.1	(2, 1, 2)	0.0678	-36.4
3.	(1, 0, 1)	-3.793	7.2	(2, 0, 1)	-1.262	145.6	(2, 0, 1)	0.0638	21.5
4.	(1, 0, 2)	-3.812	7.3	(2, 1, 1)	-1.237	148.9	(2, 1, 1)	0.0689	25.5
5.	(2, 0, 1)	-3.788	10.9	(2, 1, 2)	-1.238	149.7	(2, 2, 2)	0.0686	46.8
⋮	⋮	⋮	⋮	⋮	⋮	⋮	⋮	⋮	⋮
22.	(2, 2, 0)	-3.713	84.2	(2, 2, 0)	-1.120	221.4	(1, 2, 0)	0.0758	111.6
23.	(1, 2, 0)	-3.726	93.7	(0, 2, 1)	-1.093	221.4	(0, 2, 2)	0.0679	113.7
24.	(0, 2, 1)	-3.649	120.5	(1, 2, 0)	-1.092	255.8	(0, 2, 1)	0.0736	118.0

Particularly, it turned out that the cases with $size_{explore} = 0\%$ performed the least effective every time. On the other hand, the best offline performances were obtained for $50\% \leq size_{explore} \leq 70\%$. Clearly, also the application of an anticipation mechanism noticeably influenced the offline performances. It was especially visible after switching from $size_{anticip} = 0\%$ to $10\% \leq size_{anticip} \leq 30\%$.

Table 2. Offline performance of IDEA-FPS with $N_{gen} = 100$, $N_{sub} = 2$ and various $size_{explore}$ and $size_{anticip}$. The top three results for each benchmark are underlined.

$size_{anticip}$	$size_{explore}$										
	0%	10%	20%	30%	40%	50%	60%	70%	80%	90%	100%
	g24_1										
0%	-3.303	-3.382	-3.451	-3.507	-3.530	-3.571	-3.635	-3.658	-3.473	-3.488	-3.476
10%	-3.324	-3.397	-3.505	-3.570	-3.642	-3.715	-3.743	<u>-3.799</u>	-3.494	-3.489	-3.481
20%	-3.355	-3.458	-3.565	-3.604	-3.692	-3.729	-3.738	<u>-3.766</u>	-3.505	-3.507	-3.482
30%	-3.375	-3.478	-3.577	-3.619	-3.717	-3.747	-3.740	<u>-3.774</u>	-3.491	-3.496	-3.487
40%	-3.383	-3.483	-3.633	-3.647	-3.696	-3.732	-3.727	-3.740	-3.494	-3.490	-3.477
50%	-3.332	-3.454	-3.639	-3.654	-3.743	-3.761	-3.716	-3.743	-3.498	-3.502	-3.478
60%	-3.251	-3.522	-3.639	-3.680	-3.673	-3.740	-3.752	-3.740	-3.488	-3.494	-3.481
70%	-3.294	-3.522	-3.656	-3.669	-3.731	-3.710	-3.747	-3.736	-3.483	-3.487	-3.475
80%	-3.330	-3.665	-3.654	-3.683	-3.691	-3.726	-3.715	-3.732	-3.469	-3.481	-3.492
90%	-3.379	-3.621	-3.695	-3.688	-3.709	-3.722	-3.733	-3.739	-3.725	-3.487	-3.482
100%	-3.336	-3.597	-3.686	-3.708	-3.738	-3.708	-3.755	-3.740	-3.743	-3.727	-3.491
	g24_2										
0%	-0.551	-0.672	-0.848	-0.915	-0.997	-1.053	-1.097	-1.132	-1.154	-1.171	-1.191
10%	-0.880	-0.996	-1.086	-1.131	-1.159	-1.197	-1.222	-1.234	-1.152	-1.163	-1.193
20%	-0.971	-1.050	-1.146	-1.168	-1.199	-1.213	-1.241	-1.251	-1.151	-1.169	-1.188
30%	-0.986	-1.096	-1.164	-1.177	-1.216	-1.228	-1.238	-1.245	-1.157	-1.165	-1.184
40%	-1.039	-1.092	-1.168	-1.184	-1.207	-1.222	-1.230	-1.239	-1.151	-1.158	-1.187
50%	-1.021	-1.109	-1.181	-1.209	-1.220	-1.227	-1.230	-1.236	-1.150	-1.172	-1.184
60%	-1.034	-1.127	-1.180	-1.180	-1.232	-1.236	-1.252	-1.232	-1.153	-1.167	-1.185
70%	-1.037	-1.102	-1.184	-1.200	-1.227	-1.251	-1.238	-1.232	-1.161	-1.163	-1.189
80%	-1.062	-1.129	-1.191	-1.229	-1.225	-1.234	-1.236	-1.241	-1.177	-1.193	-1.188
90%	-1.080	-1.110	-1.197	-1.229	-1.214	-1.238	-1.253	-1.250	-1.249	-1.191	-1.192
100%	-1.052	-1.136	-1.186	-1.216	-1.236	-1.224	<u>-1.266</u>	<u>-1.257</u>	<u>-1.258</u>	-1.256	-1.185
	modified FDA1										
0%	0.149	0.129	0.121	0.114	0.102	0.099	0.089	0.082	0.108	0.107	0.124
10%	0.159	0.131	0.115	0.104	0.091	0.082	0.069	<u>0.062</u>	0.095	0.098	0.123
20%	0.164	0.137	0.112	0.099	0.084	0.072	0.069	0.071	0.093	0.098	0.124
30%	0.167	0.136	0.106	0.092	0.075	<u>0.063</u>	0.066	0.068	0.092	0.096	0.125
40%	0.164	0.127	0.091	0.080	0.072	0.071	0.074	<u>0.065</u>	0.093	0.097	0.124
50%	0.164	0.119	0.089	0.076	0.070	0.072	0.071	0.072	0.093	0.097	0.125
60%	0.153	0.111	0.084	0.078	0.079	0.073	0.072	0.070	0.092	0.097	0.125
70%	0.149	0.097	0.080	0.081	0.076	0.069	0.070	0.071	0.091	0.095	0.123
80%	0.140	0.102	0.092	0.083	0.077	0.072	0.070	0.067	0.092	0.097	0.124
90%	0.153	0.101	0.089	0.080	0.076	0.075	0.068	0.071	0.076	0.097	0.124
100%	0.178	0.108	0.090	0.077	0.082	0.073	0.071	0.071	0.074	0.081	0.125

Table 3. Comparison of offline performances for $N_{sub} = 1, \ldots, 6$ and evaluations of best feasible individuals during a sample run of IDEA-FPS vs. IDEA and IDEA with restart, tested in $g24\_1$, $g24\_2$ and *modified FDA1*

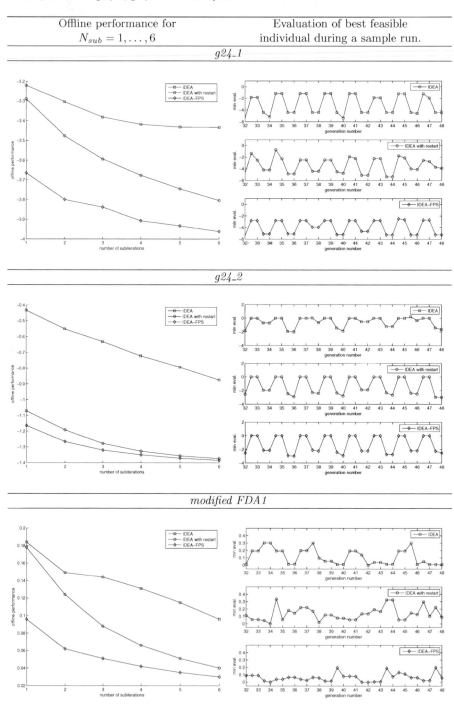

Only in benchmark $g24\_2$ best results were obtained when the size of anticipating fraction approached the level of $size_{anticip} \geq 90\%$. However, in $g24\_2$ global optima tend to jump outside the feasible region which make them less predictable and thus harder to trace.

Number of subiterations is what essentially distinguishes DOPs from iterated SOPs. Table 3 (left column) illustrates the impact of a number of subiterations N_{sub} on the offline performance of IDEA, IDEA with restart and IDEA-FPS. It is clearly seen that the increase of N_{sub} has relatively low influence on the performance of IDEA. Only in $g24\_2$ the scores improved significantly as N_{sub} increased, however the pace of the observed improvement was still considerably slow comparing to IDEA with restart and IDEA-FPS.

Surprisingly large improvement was achieved by IDEA with restart. Within 5 subiterations it nearly approached the level of performance of IDEA-FPS which may lead to the conclusion that the main drawback of IDEA applied for DCOPs is a tendency to get stuck in local optima.

IDEA-FPS outperformed the other two approaches in all the analyzed cases. It is particularly visible for $N_{sub} = 2, 3$ and 4. Injections of exploring and anticipating fractions clearly helped to alleviate the stagnation problem. It is also demonstrated in Table 3 (right column) at the sample runs of the examined algorithms. Periodical fluctuations of best feasible individuals that are visible on the plots relate to rapid reactivity to the environmental changes in $g24\_1$ and $g24\_2$ whereas the distorted irregular variations indicate losing track of global optima. On the other hand, *modified FDA1* is designed in such manner that the ideal run would result in the straight line at the 0 level. Thus, each deviation towards positive values visible on the plots signifies slow reaction to the environmental changes. Note that IDEA with restart hardly approached the 0 level. This implies that global optima in *modified FDA1* are evidently less accessible by purely random individuals then in $g24\_1$ and $g24\_2$. However, an anticipation mechanism of IDEA-FPS allowed for handling well with these difficulties.

Statistical significance of the presented outputs was verified with Wilcoxon test as advised in [4] since nonparametrical test require no assumptions that could be violated when comparing EAs (e.g. independence, normality and homoscedasticity). The pairwise statistical tests confirmed that IDEA-FPS outperformed both IDEA and IDEA with restart at the level of significance $\alpha > 10^{-8}$.

6   Conclusions and Future Work

In this paper a modification of IDEA with an application of the anticipation mechanism following FPS aimed at DCOPs was discussed. In the proposed algorithm (IDEA-FPS) the AR model originally suggested by Hatzakis and Wallace was extended to the more general ARIMA model to obtain more accurate predictions of future optima locations. Also a novel population segmentation was proposed to introduce diversity of individuals thus improve the tracking of moving optima.

Experiments concerning the number of subiterations confirmed that IDEA-FPS significantly outperformed IDEA in rapidly changing environments yet in the cases with $N_{sub} \geq 5$ it was also reasonable to simply use IDEA with restart.

Future works on the performance of IDEA-FPS in handling DCOPs with dynamic constraints are planned in the nearest future. It is also tempting to verify the applicability of other anticipation mechanisms to EAs for DOPs.

References

1. Box, G.E.P., Jenkins, G.M., Reinsel, G.C.: Time series analysis: forecasting and control. Wiley.com (2013)
2. Branke, J.: Evolutionary optimization in dynamic environments. Kluwer Academic Publishers (2001)
3. Deb, K., Pratap, A., Agarwal, A., Meyarivan, T.: A fast and elitist multiobjective genetic algorithm: NSGA-II. IEEE Trans. on Evol. Comput. **6**, 182–197 (2002)
4. Derrac, J., García, S., Molina, D., Herrera, F.: A practical tutorial on the use of nonparametric statistical tests as a methodology for comparing evolutionary and swarm intelligence algorithms. Swarm and Evolutionary Comput. **1**, 3–18 (2011)
5. Farina, M., Deb, K., Amato, P.: Dynamic Multiobjective Optimization Problems: Test Cases, Approximations and Applications. IEEE Trans. on Evolutionary Comput. **8**(5), 425–442 (2004)
6. Filipiak, P., Michalak, K., Lipinski, P.: Infeasibility Driven Evolutionary Algorithm with ARIMA-Based Prediction Mechanism. In: Yin, H., Wang, W., Rayward-Smith, V. (eds.) IDEAL 2011. LNCS, vol. 6936, pp. 345–352. Springer, Heidelberg (2011)
7. Hatzakis, I., Wallace, D.: Dynamic multi-objective optimization with evolutionary algorithms: A forward-looking approach. In: Proc. of the 8th Annual Conf. on Genetic and Evolutionary Computation (GECCO 2006), pp. 1201–1208 (2006)
8. Liang, J.J., Runarsson, T.P., Mezura-Montes, E., Clerc, M., Suganthan, P., Coello Coello, C.A., Deb, K.: Problem definitions and evaluation criteria for the CEC 2006 special session on constrained real-parameter optimization. Nangyang Technological University, Singapore, Tech, Rep. (2006)
9. Nguyen, T., Yao, X.: Benchmarking and solving dynamic constrained problems. In: Proc. of the IEEE Congress on Evolutionary Comput., pp. 690–697 (CEC 2009)
10. Nguyen, T., Yao, X.: Continuous dynamic constrained optimisation - the challenges. IEEE Trans. on Evolutionary Comput. (2012) (accepted paper)
11. Nguyen, T., Yao, X.: Solving dynamic constrained optimisation problems using repair methods. IEEE Trans. on Evolutionary Comput. (2013) (submitted paper)
12. Simões, A., Costa, E.: Evolutionary Algorithms for Dynamic Environments: Prediction Using Linear Regression and Markov Chains. In: Rudolph, G., Jansen, T., Lucas, S., Poloni, C., Beume, N. (eds.) PPSN 2008. LNCS, vol. 5199, pp. 306–315. Springer, Heidelberg (2008)
13. Singh, H.K., Isaacs, A., Nguyen, T.T., Ray, T., Yao, X.: Performance of infeasibility driven evolutionary algorithm (IDEA) on constrained dynamic single objective optimization problems. In: Proc. of the IEEE Congress on Evolutionary Comput. (CEC 2009), pp. 3127–3134 (2009)
14. Singh, H.K., Isaacs, A., Ray, T., Smith, W.: Infeasibility driven evolutionary algorithm for constrained optimization. In: Constraint Handling in Evolutionary Optimization. Studies in Comput. Intelligence, pp. 145–165 (2009)
15. Yang, S., Yao, X. (eds.): Evolutionary Computation for Dynamic Optimization Problems. Studies in Comput. Intelligence, vol. 490. Springer (2013)

Identifying the Robust Number of Intelligent Autonomous Vehicles in Container Terminals

Shayan Kavakeb[(✉)], Trung Thanh Nguyen, Zaili Yang, and Ian Jenkinson

Liverpool Logistics Offshore and Marine Research Institute (LOOM),
School of Engineering, Technology and Maritime Operations,
Liverpool John Moores University, L3 3AF Merseyside, UK
S.Kavakeb@2011.ljmu.ac.uk,
{T.T.Nguyen,Z.Yang,I.D.Jenkinson}@ljmu.ac.uk

Abstract. The purpose of this research is to provide an improved Evolutionary Algorithm (EA) in combination with Monte Carlo Simulation (MCS) to identify the robust number of a new type of intelligent vehicles in container terminals. This type of vehicles, named Intelligent Autonomous Vehicles (IAVs), has been developed in a European project. This research extends our previous study on combining MCS with EAs. This paper has three main contributions: first, it proposes a dynamic strategy to adjust the number of samples used by MCS to improve the performance of the EA; second, it incorporates different robustness measures into the EA to produce different robust solutions depending on user requirements; and third, it investigates the relation between different robust solutions using statistical analyses to provide insights into what would be the most appropriate robust solutions for port operators. These contributions have been verified using empirical experiments.

1 Introduction

The purpose of this research is to identify the robust number of Intelligent Autonomous Vehicles (IAVs) in Container Terminals (CTs)[1]. IAVs belong to a new type of intelligent vehicles developed in a European project named Intelligent Transportation for Dynamic Environment (InTraDE). This is an advanced type of automated vehicles that are able to offer more flexibility than the traditional automated guided vehicles used in ports.

This research is based on our previous research in [4] where we attempted to use an EA to identify the robust number of vehicles in any type of environments where vehicles must shuttle between pickup and delivery points to transport goods. Examples are manufacturing factories, warehouses, and CTs.

In [4], we considered uncertainties in the travel time of vehicles as a major source of uncertainties that has a significant impact on the optimal number of vehicles. Such uncertainties may arise from any breakdowns, collisions, or

---

[1] Note that this research can be applied to identifying the robust fleet size for any type of vehicle in any environment with similar properties.

© Springer-Verlag Berlin Heidelberg 2014
A.I. Esparcia-Alcázar et al. (Eds.): EvoApplications 2014, LNCS 8602, pp. 829–840, 2014.
DOI: 10.1007/978-3-662-45523-4_67

deadlocks. In [4], we developed an evolutionary algorithm combined with the Monte Carlo Simulation (MCS), named FSEA, to identify the optimal number of vehicles that is robust to the changes in travel time of vehicles. Each solution of FSEA represents a particular number of vehicles and the sequence of jobs (with expected duration) that these vehicles need to carry out. To encapsulate uncertainties, whenever FSEA evaluates a particular solution, we use MCS to generate n replications of this solution, of which in each replication some possible uncertainties (e.g. vehicle failures) may occur. Results of n replications are then combined using an aggregation function to produce fitness of individuals. In [4], we adopted the aggregation function commonly used in robust optimisation: averaging the fitness values over all replications. However, just taking the average might not produce the most appropriate robust solution for some specific scenarios. For instance, if the worst case scenario is desired, the worst fitness value received out of n replications should be considered the fitness of individuals. Now, the challenge is how different robust solutions can be produced and then be compared to identify the most appropriate one. More importantly, the process of Monte Carlo sampling is very time consuming. As a result, when being combined with an EA, an MCS will significantly decrease the performance of the EA in terms of computational time. We also observed this behaviour in FSEA in [4]. Therefore, the second challenge in this research is how to improve the performance of an EA when being combined with an MCS.

This research contributes to answering the above questions by proposing some extensions on FSEA. Firstly, to improve performance of combining MCS with EAs, we reduce the number of samples on poor solutions and use more samples on high quality solutions. This can help to reduce the number of samples and improve performance of FSEA significantly. Secondly, we incorporate different aggregation functions in MCS to produce different robust solutions. We then statistically compare those robust solutions to identify the most appropriate robust solutions for port operators.

1.1   Related Literature

Fleet sizing problem (FSP) is one of important design problems in CTs [8,9]. However, it has not received enough attention from the research community. Below is a brief review of research on the FSP in CTs.

The FSP of AGVs was modelled in [10] as a minimum flow problem. They solved this minimum flow problem using a strongly polynomial time algorithm. That research was followed in [11] where an integer programming model was proposed for the fleet sizing of automatic lifting vehicles. The problem was solved using CPLEX commercial solver and validated by conducting a simulation study. In [7], a two-phase algorithm to tackle the problem of fleet sizing and routing of vehicles in Busan port was proposed. In the phase one, the authors determined a lower bound for the required vehicles. In the phase two, using a tabu search algorithm, they checked if there are routes for those lower-bound number of vehicles to do jobs within a given makespan. If such routes are available the fleet size is optimum; otherwise they increase the number of vehicles by one and solve the routing problem until the optimal fleet size is found.

Real applications of optimisation problems usually have uncertain elements [1], [3], [5,6] . This is also the case with the FSP in CTs. However, none of the above research considers any uncertainty. This creates an important gap in fleet sizing research. In this research, we are trying to bridge this gap by producing a range of robust solutions using an EA.

2   IAVs in Container Terminals

This section first explains the transportation tasks in CTs with the IAVs. It then explains an existing approach to model the fleet sizing problem in CTs.

Transportation Tasks in Container Terminals with IAVs. CTs consist of quay side areas where vessels are berthed and stack areas where containers are stacked. A number of quay cranes (QCs) are assigned to vessels to discharge/load containers from/to the vessels. The process of discharging and loading can be greatly facilitated if an IAV is used thanks to its special feature: when being combined with a special table-like frame (to store containers) called a "cassette", an IAV can pickup and drop off a container by itself without having to wait for a crane. This way, we can minimise the waiting time of both cranes and vehicles. In a discharging task, a QC discharges a container from a vessel and then put containers on top of an empty cassette which acts as a buffer of containers. An IAV then can come and collect the loaded cassette and transport it to the storage area. A number of stack cranes (SCs) are assigned to the storage area to stack and unstack containers. The IAV can drop off the loaded cassettes next to a SC and travel back to the QCs for the next discharging tasks. The SC then can come to pickup the container from the cassette and stack it. Once the discharging tasks finishes, the loading tasks starts, i.e. the containers are transported from the stack area to the quay side area. The loading task is similar to the discharging task but in an opposite direction.

Time Window. A time window is a duration between the time that a container is available (release time) and the latest time (due time) that a container must be collected from the cassettes to not cause any delay to QCs.

Containers should be collected from the buffer (i.e. cassettes) within their time windows. To find the possible collection times for a container, we discretized the time window of the container into a number of possible pickup times [11].

A Graph Model for the Fleet Sizing Problem. In [11], the fleet sizing problem in CTs (FSP-CTs) was modelled as a directed graph. This graph shows how containers are collected by vehicles and whether any pair of containers are compatible, i.e. the two containers can be collected sequentially by the same vehicle. Each node in the graph represents a possible pickup time of a container.The graph has also two more nodes, namely the sink and the source nodes. The source is the starting point of all directed paths and the sink is the terminal of all directed paths.

A path from the source node to the sink node is a sequence of containers to be collected by one IAV. The aim is to identify the minimum number of paths covering all the containers. This is equivalent to the minimum number of IAVs. Note that there are two constraints that must be taken into account: 1) each container must be only in one path i.e. it can be collected by just one vehicle; 2) in each path, containers can have only one node i.e. each container can be picked up just once. Fig. 1 shows the graph model for an FSP-CT example. In this example, three containers must be collected. Containers 1 and 3 have two possible pickup times and container 2 has only one pickup time. Node j_{11} corresponds to container 1 at the first pickup time and node j_{12} corresponds to container 1 at the second pickup time. Similarly, container 3 has two nodes in the graph model, j_{31} and j_{32} and container 2 has one node, j_{21}. One solution with two IAVs is shown in this figure. In the solution, containers 1 and 3 are assigned to IAV 1 and container 2 is assigned to IAV 2.

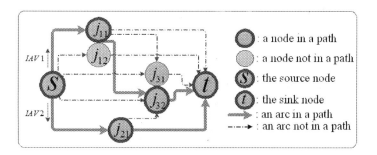

Fig. 1. This figure shows a solution for an FSP-CT with three containers. Containers 1 and 3 have two possible pickup times. Container 2 has only one pickup time. Each node corresponds to one possible pickup time of one container (e.g. container 1 can be picked up at either j_{11} or j_{12}). In this solution, all the three containers are assigned to two IAVs. Containers 1 and 3 are assigned to IAV 1. Container 2 is assigned to IAV 2.

3   An Evolutionary Algorithm to Identify the Robust Number of IAVs

This section briefly explains an evolutionary algorithm, named FSEA, that we developed in [4] to identify the robust number of vehicles. The figures and pseudo-codes in this section are adopted from [4].

Representation. To solve the FSP-CTs by FSEA, we represented a chromosome by a string of pairs of containers: $\{\mathfrak{z}x_1,\ y_1\mathfrak{z};\ \mathfrak{z}x_2,\ y_2\mathfrak{z};\ ...;\ \mathfrak{z}x_n,\ y_n\mathfrak{z}\}$ where for each pair $\mathfrak{z}x_i,\ y_i\mathfrak{z}$, x_i is the pickup time of container i and y_i represents the next container that must be done by the same IAV after container i. Sequences of containers that are assigned to the IAVs can be extracted from this string.

Recombination. To reduce the number of IAVs in individuals, we developed a recombination-based heuristic operator. This operator can decrease the number of IAVs one by one by moving all containers to be done by one selected IAV, named *IAV_delete*, to the list of containers to be done by other IAVs. By removing all the containers to be done *IAV_delete*, this IAV can be eliminated from the list of IAVs i.e. the number of IAVs would be decreased by one. Fig. 2 shows an example of how the heuristic can reduce the number of IAVs.

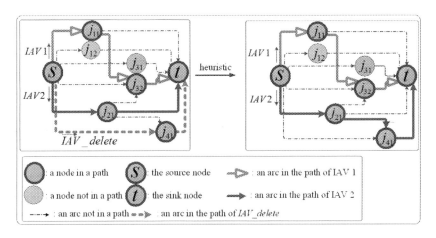

Fig. 2. In this example, the heuristic moves node j_{41} from vehicle 3 to the sequence of containers of IAV 2. By this movement, the number of IAVs decreased from three to two.

Mutation. We also developed a mutation operator similar to the idea of the heuristic. The mutation, however, moves containers between all the IAVs except *IAV_delete*, in a hope that it creates some space to insert containers from *IAV_delete*. Fig. 3 shows how the mutation can help the heuristic to eliminate *IAV_delete*.

Evaluation of Individuals. This subsection explains the Monte Carlo Simulation (MCS) approach in FSEA to evaluate fitness of individuals.

In the static case, i.e. no uncertainty, the total number of IAVs (i.e. the number of paths in the graph model of the FSP-CTs) can be considered the fitness of individuals. In uncertain cases, however, such evaluation may not be totally realistic. It is seen that two individuals can have the same number of IAVs but with different schedules, i.e. sequences of containers are different for the same number of IAVs. Those schedules may behave differently when uncertainties are introduced to the system. To evaluate the robustness of individuals under uncertainties we measured the robustness of the schedule associated with each

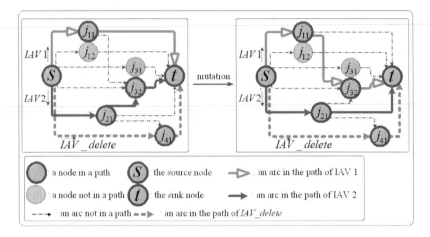

Fig. 3. In this example, if container 3 is moved from IAV 2 to IAV 1, container 4 can be moved by the heuristic from *IAV_delete* to IAV 2. The mutation can move container 3 from IAV 2 to IAV 1 to open up a position for container 4 in IAV 2.

individual. To do so, we developed an MCS which simulates possible uncertainties that may occur to the schedule of an individual. MCS works by estimating failures for the IAVs based on the given failure rates (Algorithm 1).

Algorithm 1. EstimateFailures(λ, $MTTR$, *makespan*)

```
 1: F := 0
 2: t := 0
 3: while t < makespan /*makespan is the due time of the last container*/
 4:     Generate a random exponential value t_e using the parameter λ
 5:     t_f := t_e + t
 6:     t_r := t_f + MTTR /*MTTR is the mean time to repair of IAVs*/
 7:     if t_f < makespan
 8:         F := F ∪ {< t_f, t_r >}
 9:     t := t_r
10: return F
```
where λ is the failure rate of IAVs.

Failures may happen to IAVs and hinder them from transporting their assigned containers. As a result, available IAVs, i.e. the ones that are not in failures, must cover containers of the IAVs that are in failures. If no IAV can cover those containers, additional IAVs must be added to transport the uncovered containers. The total number of additional vehicles is used to measure the robustness of individuals. The higher the number of additional IAVs, the less robust a schedule. MCS replicates n samples of each individual and evaluates the robustness of the schedule of that individual over the n samples. An average of the total number of IAVs over n replications is considered the fitness of an individual. This MCS is extended in this research and it is discussed in Section 4.

4   Extensions on FSEA

This section first explains a new dynamic sampling strategy to improve the performance of FSEA. It then discusses the proposed approach to aggregate results of the samples in MCS to produce different robust solutions.

A New Dynamic Sampling Strategy. As mentioned in Section 3, in FSEA the robustness of individuals are evaluated using MCS. In FSEA, we applied the same number of samples to all individuals, regardless of whether the quality of individuals is good or poor. The higher the number of samples, the more accurate the robustness evaluation of individuals. Evaluating the robustness of poor individuals as accurately as good individuals may not be totally efficient, because those poor individuals would be eliminated in the process of evolution. Therefore, it is a waste of resources. If those poor solutions can be identified and the algorithm spends less time on them, performance of the algorithm can be improved significantly. It is obvious that at the earlier generations the quality of solutions are poor and in the later generations, the quality of solutions are increased. So, we can use a dynamic strategy to adjust the number of samples along with the increase in generations. In this paper, this dynamic strategy will be integrated in a new algorithm named improved FSEA (iFSEA).

iFSEA considers fewer number of samples at the earlier generations and it increases the number of samples step by step during the evolution. The pseudocode for this is shown in Algorithm 2. In this algorithm, an initial number of replications is set as n_0. After g generations it increases the number of replications by s. The number of replications will be increased until it reaches the maximum number samples, n. From that point to the end of the evolution, the number of replications will be kept as n.

Extension on MCS (eMCS). As recalled in Section 3, individuals are evaluated using MCS. MCS evaluates the robustness of individuals by estimating the possible failures of IAVs. MCS in each replication estimates the number of IAVs including the additional IAVs needed to cover failures in each individual. An average of n replications in MCS is considered the fitness of an individual.

In this research, we extend MCS, named eMCS, by considering robustness measures not only an average but also the maximum, minimum, and the most frequently occurred (mode) values of the fleet size as observed out of n replications. Each of those robustness measures can drive the EA to find a different robust solution and hence may be applicable to different scenarios. By using the maximum function, we turn the problem into a minimax problem which looks for the best solution in the worst case scenarios. Specifically, using the Maximum function, our iFSEA will try to minimise the largest fleet size that we can observe when applying eMCS with uncertainties to each individual. For a formal description of minimax problems and their applications in robust optimisation readers are referred to [1].

Algorithm 2. NumberOfReplication(s, g, n, $repNo$, $genCounter$)

```
1: if genCounter % g == 0
2:      if repNo + s > n
3:          return n
4:      repNo := repNo + s
5:      return repNo
6: else
7:      return repNo
```
where $genCounter$ is the current generation of iFSEA, g is the generations interval to increase the number of replications, s is the step to increase the number of replications, n is the maximum number of replications and $repNo$ is the number of replications.

Similarly, by using the mode and minimum functions, iFSEA will try to minimise the most frequently occurred fleet size and the smallest fleet size, respectively, that eMCS observes for each individual under uncertainty. The pseudo-codes for eMCS and iFSEA are in Algorithms 3 and 4 respectively.

5   Experimental Results

This section first compares performance of FSEA and iFSEA. It then statistically compares the robust solutions of iFSEA to identify the most appropriate robust solution for port operators.

Test Cases and Parameter Settings. We selected one European CT as the case study. All settings are from real-world data of this terminal. To create the test cases, we varied the number of QCs and size of buffer. The number of QCs varies from one to three because in this CT at most three QCs can work on one vessel simultaneously. The size of buffer (number of cassettes) under the cranes is varied from 0 to 10. The number of containers to be discharged is 100. In this CT, six stack cranes (SCs) are available and we assume that containers are divided evenly between those SCs. The distances between QCs and SCs are taken from real-world data[2]. The speed of IAVs is considered 4 m/s for empty IAVs and 2 m/s for loaded IAVs. The actual failure rate and mean time to repair (MTTR) for IAVs are not available yet. As a result, we use the same failure rate and MTTR in [2] which are 1.0×10^{-3} failures/sec and 500 sec, respectively. The parameter settings for FSEA and iFSEA are shown in table 1.

---

[2] Due to confidential agreements, we cannot reveal the actual distances.

Algorithm 3. eMCS ($aggregType$)

```
 1: Identify FS, the number of IAVs in the given individual
 2: DF := 0
 3: FSL := 0 /*FSL is a list of additional IAVs*/
 4: repNo := NumberOfReplication()
 5: for j from 1 to repNo
 6:     UC := 0 /*UC is the list of uncovered containers*/
 7:     AV := 0 /*AV is the number of additional vehicles*/
 8:     for i from 1 to FS
 9:         DF := EstimateFailures()
10:         Identify uncovered containers of IAV i based on DF and add
them to UC
11:     for i from 1 to length(UC)
12:         if container UC[i] can be covered by an available IAV k
13:             Assign container UC[i] to IAV k
14:         else
15:             AV := AV + 1
16:             Assign container UC[i] to the new added IAV
17:     FSL := FSL ∪ {FS + AV}
18: switch (aggregType)
19:     case Max:
20:         return the maximum of FSL
21:     case Min:
22:         return the minimum of FSL
23:     case Avg:
24:         return the average of FSL
25:     case Mode:
26:         return the most frequent element of FSL
```

where DF=$\{$ $_i t_f$, t_{ri}, t_f is the time of failure and t_r is the time of repair$\}$ and $repNo$ is the number of replications.

Performance of iFSEA Compared with FSEA. One of the purposes of proposing iFSEA is to improve the computational time of FSEA without decreasing the quality of solutions. To compare quality of solutions of the two algorithms, we applied FSEA and iFSEA to the same test cases. We then used Mann-Whitney to see whether results of the two algorithms are significantly different. The significance level is 95%.

The results showed that there is no significant difference between the solutions of iFSEA and FSEA. The p-values of the statistical analysis are 0.24, 0.48, 0.68 for the test cases of 1, 2, and 3 QCs, respectively. The results show considerable high p-values and it confirms that the quality of solutions is not deteriorated in iFSEA.

Fig. 4 shows differences between the process time of FSEA and iFSEA. It shows that iFSEA in all the cases could solve the problem considerably faster than FSEA.

Algorithm 4. iFSEA(*popSize, m*)

```
 1: Initialize population Pt
 2: Evaluate population Pt by eMCS()
 3: for genCounter from 1 to m /*m is the maximum generations*/
 4:     Select elements from Pt to copy into Pt+1
 5:     for i from 1 to popSize /*popSize is the size of the population*/
 6:         Apply the mutation operator to individual i
 7:         Apply the heuristic operator to individual i
 8:     Evaluate new population Pt+1 by eMCS()
 9:     Pt := Pt+1
10: return the best individual
```

Table 1. Parameters setting for FSEA and iFSEA

	iFSEA					iFSEA & FSEA			
Parameter	n_0	s	g	n	m	$popSize$	λ(failure/sec)	MTTR(s)	other parameters
value	60	20	10	100	100	15	1.0×10^{-3}	500	the same as [4]

Comparison Between Robust Solutions. Results of applying iFSEA to the test cases using different aggregation approaches (e.g. Min, Max, Avg, and Mode) are shown in table 2. Note that a higher number of IAVs may increase productivity under uncertainties, however, it can be expensive to deploy too many IAVs. Therefore, the port operators need an accurate comparison between the robust approaches and based on that they can carefully select the most appropriate robust solution. As a result, we compared the robust approaches using the Mann-Whitney test to provide a tool that can help port operators to identify the most appropriate robust solution.

Table 2. Different robust numbers of IAVs using different aggregation functions

buff. size	1 QC				2 QCs				3 QCs			
	Min	Max	Mode	Avg	Min	Max	Mode	Avg	Min	Max	Mode	Avg
0	7	10	9	8.96	13	17	15	15.55	19	23	21	21.81
1	6	9	8	8.27	12	17	14	14.64	17	22	19	20.25
2	6	9	8	7.51	11	15	13	13.64	15	20	18	18.16
3	6	9	8	7.87	10	14	12	12.32	13	17	15	15.02
4	5	8	7	6.00	9	12	10	10.29	12	17	15	15.49
5	5	8	7	6.76	9	12	11	11.00	12	15	13	13.51
6	5	8	7	6.75	9	11	11	10.85	12	15	14	16.69
7	5	7	7	6.87	9	11	11	10.79	11	14	13	12.53
8	5	7	7	6.67	9	11	10	10.00	10	13	12	11.76
9	5	7	6	6.55	8	9	9	9.44	9	11	10	10.30
10	5	7	5	6.00	8	9	9	9.18	9	11	10	9.00

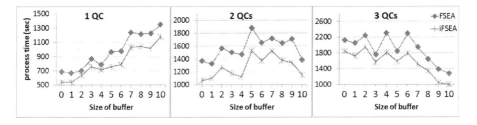

Fig. 4. Results show that in all of the cases iFSEA could solve the problems significantly faster than FSEA

Table 3. Mann-Whitney comparisons of iFSEA using different aggregation functions. The sign "+" or "-" means there is or there is no significant difference, respectively.

Aggre. func.	1QC		2 QCs		3 QCs	
	sig. diff.	p-value	sig. diff.	p-value	sig. diff.	p-value
Min vs Max	+	0.0017	+	0.0354	-	0.0538
Min vs Avg	+	0.0011	+	0.0098	-	0.0790
Min vs Mod	+	0.0470	-	0.1252	-	0.1705
Max vs Min	+	0.0017	+	0.0354	-	0.0538
Max vs Avg	+	0.0409	-	0.2452	-	0.3347
Max vs Mod	-	0.3589	-	0.3347	-	0.2883
Avg vs Min	+	0.0011	+	0.0098	-	0.0790
Avg vs Max	+	0.0409	-	0.2452	-	0.3347
Avg vs Mod	-	0.6410	-	0.5130	-	0.3589
Mod vs Min	+	0.0470	-	0.1252	-	0.1705
Mod vs Max	-	0.3589	-	0.3347	-	0.2883
Mod vs Avg	-	0.6410	-	0.5130	-	0.3589

Table 3 shows which aggregation functions are significantly different from results of the other aggregation functions. For instance, with 1 QC, results of Min are significantly different with the results of Max, Avg, and Mode with the p-values equal 0.0017, 0.0011, and 0.0470, respectively. In contrast, in this case, results of Avg and Max are not significantly different with the p-value equals 0.0409.

The port operators can look at the results of tables 2 and 3 to select the most appropriate number of IAVs. For example, in the case of 1 QCs, Min is not a reasonable choice, because Min is significantly different with Mode and Avg. This means that in a majority of cases the number of IAVs achieved by Min is not enough. In contrast, if the port operators want to be on the safe side, Max is a good option for them. This is because, Max is not significantly different with Mode, meaning that the worst case is also likely the most frequently occurred case. In additions, even though results of Max and Avg in this case are significantly different, the p-value for this case is not considerably high. As a result, for the case with 1 QCs, Max is a reasonable choice.

6 Conclusion

This paper extends our previous research in [4]. In this paper, we developed an evolutionary algorithm combined with the Monte Carlo simulation (FSEA), to identify the robust number of a new type of IAVs in CTs. This paper has the following contributions: 1) it improves performance of the algorithm in [4] by proposing a new dynamic sampling strategy; 2) it proposes four different extensions on Monte Carlo simulation to produce different robust solutions; 3) it statistically evaluates the robust solutions to identify the most appropriate robust solution for port operators.

Acknowledgments. This work was supported by a European project named Intelligent Transportation for Dynamic Environment (InTraDE).

References

1. Beyer, H.G., Sendhoff, B.: Robust optimization-a comprehensive survey. Computer methods in applied mechanics and engineering **196**(33), 3190–3218 (2007)
2. Farling, B., Mosier, C., Mahmoodi, F.: Analysis of automated guided vehicle configurations in flexible manufacturing systems. International Journal of Production Research **39**(18), 4239–4260 (2001)
3. Jin, Y., Branke, J.: Evolutionary optimization in uncertain environments-a survey. IEEE Transactions on Evolutionary Computation **9**(3), 303–317 (2005)
4. Kavakeb, S., Nguyen, T.T.: Identifying the robust number of vehicles in container terminal. Submitted to IEEE Computational Intelligence Magazine (2014)
5. Nguyen, T.T.: Continuous Dynamic Optimisation Using Evolutionary Algorithms. Ph.D. thesis, School of Computer Science, University of Birmingham. http://etheses.bham.ac.uk/1296 (January 2011)
6. Nguyen, T.T., Yang, S., Branke, J.: Evolutionary dynamic optimization: A survey of the state of the art. Swarm and Evolutionary Computation **6**, 1–24 (2012)
7. Pyung Hoi, K., Woon Seek, L., Dong Won, J.: Fleet sizing and vehicle routing for container transportation in a static environment. OR Spectrum **26**(2), 193–209 (2004)
8. Stahlbock, R.: Vob, S.: Operations research at container terminals: a literature update. OR Spectrum **30**(1), 1–52 (2008)
9. Steenken, D., Vob, S., Stahlbock, R.: Container terminal operation and operations research - a classification and literature review. OR Spectrum 26(1), 3–49 (2004)
10. Vis, I.F.A., Koster, R.D., Roodbergen, K.J., Peeters, L.W.P.: Determination of the number of automated guided vehicles required at a semi-automated container terminal. The JORS 52(4), 409–417 (2001)
11. Vis, I.F.A., De Koster, R.M.B.M., Savelsbergh, M.W.P.: Minimum vehicle fleet size under time-window constraints at a container terminal. Transportation Science **39**(2), 249–260 (2005)

A Multi-objective Evolutionary Approach for Cloud Service Provider Selection Problems with Dynamic Demands

Hsin-Kai Chen, Cheng-Yuan Lin, and Jian-Hung Chen[✉]

Dept of Computer Science and Information Engineering,
Chung-Hua University, Hsin-Chu, Taiwan
jh.chen@ieee.org

Abstract. This paper describes a multi-objective evolutionary approach for solving cloud computing service provider selection problems with dynamic demands. In this investigated problem, not only the service purchase costs and transmission costs of service providers are different, but the demands of service requests also change over the given periods. The objective of this problem is to select a number of cloud service provider while optimizing the total service distance, the total number of serviced demand points, the total service purchase costs, and total transmission costs simultaneously in the given continuous time periods. A multi-objective genetic approach with a seeding mechanism is proposed to solve the investigated problems. Four trail benchmark problems are designed and solved using the proposed multi-objective evolutionary algorithm. The results indicate that the proposed approach is capable of obtaining a number of non-dominated solutions for decision makers.

Keywords: Cloud computing · Multi-objective optimization · Dynamic optimization · Evolutionary algorithms

1 Introduction

With the rapid development of computing hardware, high-speed network, web programming, distributed and parallel computing, and other storage technologies, cloud computing has recently emerged as an effective reuse paradigm, where hardware computing power, software functionality, and other computing resources are delivered as integrated services through Internet [1]. There are many global and local commercial cloud service providers, offering various kinds of delivered services such as Infrastructure-as-a-Service (IaaS), Platform-as-a-Service (PaaS) and Software-as-a-Service (SaaS). Recently, the advantages and features of cloud services has arisen the interests of digital entertainment/media/content suppliers to integrate cloud computing services into their content delivery networks [2].

Consider a national-wide area with a number of service request points, the requests at each point usually changes in time; and within this area, a number of cloud service providers with different locations and pricing options of services are available for

© Springer-Verlag Berlin Heidelberg 2014
A.I. Esparcia-Alcázar et al. (Eds.): EvoApplications 2014, LNCS 8602, pp. 841–852, 2014.
DOI: 10.1007/978-3-662-45523-4_68

chosen. From the point view of digital entertainment/media content suppliers, it is an important issue to select suitable cloud computing service providers, which can deliver their contents to massive customers rapidly and smoothly. Therefore, maximizing some expected Quality-of-Service (QoS) indictors and minimizing services related costs are crucial considerations for decision makers. As a result, considering the requirements of content supplier and the conditions of cloud service providers, we formulated such problems to multi-objective dynamic p-median problems in this paper.

The classical p-median problem consists of selecting p facilities in a given space which minimizes the total costs of serving m demand points at a time. P-median problem is prominent combinatorial optimization NP-hard problem in location science and cluster analysis [3-9]. Many exact and heuristic approaches have been proposed for solving p-median problems [3][8][9]. In traditional approaches, the planning of service facility centers usually considers the demand of consumers as constant values. However, it is not true in the real world applications, because the demands of consumers may change by environments and time. The dynamic p-median problem is applicable to all situations modeled by the standard p-median problem whenever demand changes over time in a predictable way.

In this paper, a multi-objective p-median model with dynamic demands which optimizes the total QoS distance, the total number of serviced demand points, the total service purchase costs, and the total network transmission costs is investigated. Considering four different geographical features, we propose an efficient approach based on genetic algorithms for content providers to determine the selection of service providers in different periods and satisfying the dynamic demands of customers. The proposed approach can also provide decision-makers a set of non-dominated solutions for the selection processes.

This paper is organized as follows: Section 2 describes the investigated dynamic p-median problem and multi-objective optimization. Section 3 describes the mathematical model of the investigated problem. Section 4 presents the proposed multi-objective genetic algorithm MOGA for solving investigated problems. Section 5 gives the experimental results and analysis of the proposed algorithm. Section 6 concludes our paper.

2   Related Work

2.1   P-median Problems

The classical p-median problem consists of locating p facilities (medians) in a given space (e.g. Euclidean space) which minimizes the total costs of serving m demand points, where the pair-wise cost of servicing each point from all facilities is given. Each demand point is only served by a single facility and services to demand points are not combinable [3-10].

Exact methods for solving p-median problems include linear programming approaches, dual-based algorithms. However, these exact methods suffer from the curse of dimensionality since the computation costs of calculating all demand points' expectations over all possible future combinations increases exponentially in the number of demand points. Many heuristic approaches have been proposed to solve p-median problems, including greedy heuristic, variable neighbor decomposition search, cooperative parallel variable neighborhood search, and Lagrangian-surrogate heuristic. Modern meta-heuristics have been applied to solve p-median problems as well [8], such as tabu search approaches, simulated annealing approaches and genetic algorithms approaches.

Recently, considering the real-world conditions, various models of p-median problems are proposed in the literature, including stochastic p-median problems, progressive p-median problems [3], dynamic p-median problems, and bi-objective p-median problems [9].

2.2   Multi-objective Evolutionary Optimization

Assume the multi-objective functions are to be minimized. Mathematically, MOOPs can be represented as the following vector mathematical programming problems

$$Minimize \quad F(Y) = \{F_1(Y), F_2(Y), ..., F_i(Y)\}, \tag{1}$$

where Y denotes a solution and $f_i(Y)$ is generally a nonlinear objective function. Pareto dominance relationship and some related terminologies are introduced below. When the following inequalities hold between two solutions Y_1 and Y_2, Y_2 is a non-dominated solution and is said to dominate Y_1 ($Y_2 \succ Y_1$):

$$\forall i : F_i(Y_1) > F_i(Y_2) \wedge \exists j : F_j(Y_1) > F_j(Y_2). \tag{2}$$

When the following inequality hold between two solutions Y_1 and Y_2, Y_2 is said to weakly dominate Y_1 ($Y_2 \succeq Y_1$):

$$\forall i : F_i(Y_1) \geq F_i(Y_2). \tag{3}$$

A feasible solution $Y *$ is said to be a Pareto-optimal solution if and only if there does not exist a feasible solution Y where Y dominates $Y *$, and the corresponding vector of Pareto-optimal solutions is called Pareto-optimal front.

By making use of Pareto dominance relationship, multi-objective evolutionary algorithms (MOEAs) are capable of performing the fitness assignment of multiple objectives without using relative preferences of multiple objectives. Thus, all the objective functions can be optimized simultaneously. As a result, MOEA seems to be an alternative approach to solving the investigated service provider selection problems on the assumption that no prior preference and domain knowledge is available [10-11].

3   Cloud Service Selection Problems with Dynamic Demands

In this paper, the investigated dynamic service provider selection problem (DSPSP) is to select p service providers from n service providers in each season, in order to satisfy the dynamic demands of m service requests from end-users. The following conditions are assumed in this problem:

1) Each service provider has different pricing options for purchasing services and network transmission.

2) Although contents can be deliver to anywhere though internet, end-users still expects no delays during network transmission. Therefore, each service provider has a pre-assumed maximum QoS distance.

3) The number of demand points that a service provider can service is unlimited.

4) The Euclidean distance is used to calculate the distances between demand points and points of service provider.

5) Each demand point can only serviced by a nearest point of service provider within the maximum QoS distance.

6) In order to satisfying the dynamic demands, content supplier may select p different service providers in the next following season.

The investigated problem can be formulated to multi-objective p-median problems with dynamic demands. The objectives of DSPSP are while optimizing four competing objective functions: the total QoS distance, the total number of serviced demand points, the total service purchase costs, and the total network transmission costs.

3.1 Problem Notations

i, j : $i \in \{1,2,3,...m\}$, $j \in \{1,2,3,...,n\}$.

m : The total number of demand points.

n : The total number of service provider points for selection.

L_i : The index of demand points, $L_i = i$.

S_j : The index of the service provider points. Service providers points usually co-locate with some demand points, therefore $S_j \in \{L_1, L_2, ... L_m\}$.

D_j : The maximum QoS distance of the service provider point j.

T : The total service periods.

t_j : The time period that the service provider S_j served, $0 = t_1 < t_2 < ... < t_p < t_{p+1} < T$.

d_{ij} : The distance between L_i and S_j.

md_{ij} : The nearest distance of the demand point L_i between the nearest service provider point, $md_{ij} = min\{d_{ij}\}$.

$w_i(t)$: The demanding function of the demand points L_i at time t, $0 \le t < T$.

w_{ij} : The total demanding amount of the demand point L_i from time t_j to time t_{j+1},

$$w_{ij} = \int_{t_j}^{t_{j+1}} w_i(t)\,dt.$$

A_j : The network transmission cost of the service provider point S_j per demand unit.

C_j : The monthly service purchase cost of the service provider point S_j.

X_i : The serviced index of the demand point L_i. If the demand point service L_i is serviced within the maximum QoS distance of a provider point, then $X_i = 1$, otherwise $X_i = 0$.

Z_j : The selection index of the service provider point S_j. If the service provider point S_j is chosen and serves demand points in the specific time period, then $Z_j = 1$, otherwise $Z_j = 0$.

3.2 Problem Objectives

1. Minimization of QoS distance
2. In the classical p-median problem, the demands in each demands points are usually considered to a constant. However, considering the real-world applications, demands are known to be changed dynamically. Given the demanding function of each demand points, the QoS distance of each demand to its nearest service provider points can be expressed as follows:

$$Minimize\, F_1 = \sum_{j=1}^{n}\sum_{i=1}^{m} w_{ij} \times md_{ij} \times X_i \times Z_j. \tag{4}$$

3. Minimization of network transmission cost

Considering the cloud computing environments, the costs of network transmissions between service provider points and demand points are not fixed. Given the network transmission cost of each service point per time unit, the transmission costs of each facility can be expressed as follows:

$$Minimize\, F_2 = \sum_{j=1}^{n}\sum_{i=1}^{m} w_{ij} \times A_j \times X_i \times Z_j. \tag{5}$$

4. Minimization of service purchase cost

In additional to the network transmission cost, the service purchase cost on a specific service provider point is also an important factor for content suppliers, because the service cost in different service provider point are different. Given the service purchase cost for each service provider points, the total service purchase costs of selected service provider points can be expressed as follows:

$$Minimize\, F_3 = \sum_{j=1}^{n} C_j \times Z_j. \tag{6}$$

5. Maximum of total number of serviced demand points

Because different service providers has different QoS distance, therefore the number of demand points that a service provider points may serviced could be different. Given the maximum QoS distance of each service provider, the number of serviced demand points can be calculated as follows:

$$Maximize\, F_4 = \sum_{i=1}^{m} X_i. \tag{7}$$

3.3   An Illustrative Example

An example is given here to explain our mathematical formation. Assumed that a content supplier plans to select three service provider points (p=3) from six providers (n=6) within twelve months (T=12), in order to service ten demanding points (m=10). The maximum QoS Dj is 3 for all the service provider points. The coordination, demanding function of demand points, the service purchase costs and transmission costs of service provider points are listed in Table 1. Assumed a selection plan for four seasons is determined (as shown in Table 2), three service provider S_2, S_3, S_6 are select in the first season, and finally three service provider S_1, S_3, S_5 are select in the fourth season.

Take the selection plan of Season 4 for example, the total amount of each demand points during Season 4 can be calculated, as shown in Table 3. The distance of each demand point to different service provider points can be calculated, as shown in Table 4. The demand points with Dj are marked as bold. Hereafter, according to all the tables, the objective functions in Season 4 can be calculated, $F_1 = 10.12242$, $F_2 = 1507.5$, $F_3 = 1650$, $F_4 = 8$.

Table 1. The information of demand and service points L_i ,S_j

L_i	S_j	coord.	$w_i(t)$	A_j	C_j
L_1	S_1	(1,8)	10+6t	1	500
L_2	S_2	(2,5)	3+4t	1	700
L_3		(0,9)	16+2t	1	
L_4		(10,2)	25+3t	1	
L_5	S_3	(4,5)	50-2t	1	700
L_6	S_4	(3,7)	99-3t	1	450
L_7	S_5	(12,3)	6+7t	1	450
L_8		(6,16)	24+4t	1	
L_9		(2,10)	10+10t	1	
L_{10}	S_6	(8,4)	5+5t	1	500

Table 2. representation of four selection plan for four seasons

SEASON 1	SEASON 2	SEASON 3	SEASON 4
2, 6, 3	3, 6, 4	5, 4, 3	3, 1, 5

Table 3. The total amount of demands in season 4, according to the selection plan

	t = 0~3	t = 3~6	t = 6~9	t = 9~12
L_1	57	111	165	219
L_2	27	63	99	135
L_3	57	75	93	111
L_4	88.5	115.5	142.5	169.5
L_5	141	123	105	87
L_6	283.5	256.5	229.5	202.5
L_7	49.5	112.5	175.5	238.5
L_8	90	126	162	198
L_9	75	165	255	345
L_{10}	37.5	82.5	127.5	172.5

Table 4. The distance of each demand point to selected service provider points in quarther 4

	$S_3(=L_5)$	$S_1(=L_1)$	$S_5(=L_7)$
L_1	4.24264	**0**	12.083
L_2	2	3.16228	10.198
L_3	5.65685	**1.41421**	13.4164
L_4	6.7082	10.8167	**2.23607**
L_5	**0**	4.24264	8.24621
L_6	**2.23607**	**2.23607**	9.84886
L_7	8.24621	12.083	**0**
L_8	11.1803	9.43398	14.3178
L_9	5.38516	**2.23607**	12.2066
L_{10}	4.12311	8.06226	4.12311

4   The Proposed Multi-objective Genetic Algorithm

In this section, the proposed multi-objective genetic algorithm to find a selection plan within four seasons for DSPSP is described.

4.1   Chromosome Representation

A chromosome has gene information for solving the problem in DSPSP. In the proposed approach, each chromosome of has p genes. When a season is finished, the non-dominated solutions will be selected as seed chromosomes for the initial population of the next season. The chromosome can be regarded as a selection plan for a season.

4.2   Fitness Assignment

We use a generalized Pareto-based scale-independent fitness function (GPSIFF) considering the quantitative fitness values in Pareto space for both dominated and non-dominated individuals [10]. GPSIFF makes the best use of Pareto dominance relationship to evaluate individuals using a single measure of performance. The used GPSIFF is briefly described below. Let the fitness value of an individual Y be a tournament-like score obtained from all participant individuals by the following function:

$$F(X) = Np - Nq + c., \tag{8}$$

where Np is the number of individuals which can be dominated by the individual Y, and Nq is the number of individuals which can dominate the individual Y in the objective space. Generally, a constant c can be optionally added in the fitness function to make fitness values positive. c is usually set to the number of all participant individuals.

4.3   Procedure of MOGA

The procedure of MOGA is written as follows:

Input: population size Npop, recombination probability pc, mutation probability pm, the number of maximum generations Gmax. Current Season Index q=1.
Output: The optimum solutions ever found in P.
Step 1: *Initialization* Randomly generate chromosomes to fill in the population P until Npop individuals are reached. Each chromosome is consists of p genes for a season.
Step 2: *Evaluation* For each individual in the population, compute all objective function values F_1, F_2, F_3.and F_4.
Step 3: *Fitness Assignment* Assign each individual a fitness value by using the equation (8) GPSIFF.
Step 4: *Selection* Select Npop individuals from the population to form a new population using the binary tournament selection without replacement,.
Step 5: *Recombination* Perform the uniform crossover operation with a recombination probability p_c.
Step 6: *One Point Mutation* Apply the one point mutation operators to each gene with a mutation probability p_m. If the mutated gene is duplicated with other genes in the same chromosome, mutate the gene again.
Step 7: *Termination* test If the maximum generations have reached, store all the non-dominated solutions in season q, and then go to Step 8. Otherwise, go to Step 2.
Step 8: *Seeding* q=q+1. If q>4, stop the algorithm. Otherwise, select and copy non-dominated solutions to the initial population of the next season. If the number of non-dominated solutions is greater than the population size Npop, randomly delete solutions until the population size is equal to Npop. Then, go to Step 1.

5   Result and Discussions

5.1   Simulation Environment and Parameter Settings

In this paper, four benchmarks are designed for experiments, as shown in Fig. 1. Each problem has different distribution of demand points on different grid sizes, described as follows:

- Circle: 100 demand points and 36 service providers on a 18*18 grid. The number of providers to be chosen p=10, and the maximum QoS distance $D_j=2.2$.
- Rectangle: Square with empty space. 100 demand points and 36 service providers on a 16*16 grid. The number of providers to be chosen p=10, and the maximum QoS distance $D_j=3$.

- Square: 100 demand points and 36 service providers on a 110*110 grid. The number of providers to be chosen p=10, and the maximum QoS distance $D_j=10$.
- Triangle: 100 demand points and 36 service providers on a 14*14 grid. The number of providers to be chosen p=10, and the maximum QoS distance $D_j=2$.

Ten service providers will be select for each season. The total number of season is 4. The parameter settings of MOGA are listed as follows: population size $N_{pop}=100$, recombination probability $p_c=0.9$, mutation probability $p_m=0.1$, the number of maximum generations $G_{max}=100$. Fifteen independent runs are conducted for each problem.

5.2   Discussions

For each benchmarks, 30 independent runs are conducted using MOGA with seeding mechanism and MOGA without mechanism. Figure 2-5 use boxplot to depict the values F_1 of non-dominated solutions in solving the circle benchmark at different seasons. From these figures, it shows that seeding mechanism can help MOGA obtains better solutions and converge faster. Figure 5-8 use boxplot to depict the values of F_1, F_2, F_3, and F_4 of non-dominated solutions in solving the circle benchmark at the Season 4. Figure 9-12 use boxplot to depict the values of F_1, F_2, F_3, and F_4 of non-dominated solutions in solving the Rectangle benchmark at the Season 4. Due to the page limit, the results of Square and Triangle are not shown in this paper. The results indicate that the proposed MOGA is capable of solving DSPSP and optimize four objectives simultaneously, considering different geographic distribution of demand points.

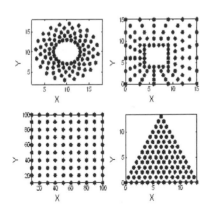

Fig. 1. Distributions of demand points in four benchmark problems

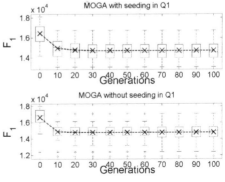

Fig. 2. F_1 of non-dominated solutions for circle benchmark in Season 1

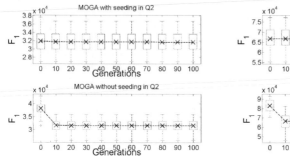

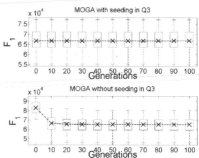

Fig. 3. F_1 for circle benchmark in Season 2

Fig. 4. F_1 for circle benchmark in Season 3

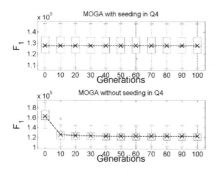

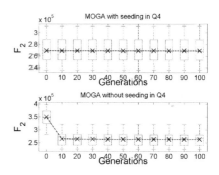

Fig. 5. F_1 for circle benchmark in Season 4

Fig. 6. F_2 for circle benchmark in Season 4

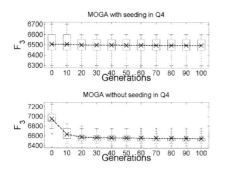

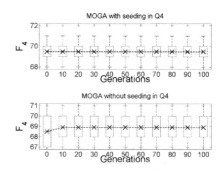

Fig. 7. F_3 for circle benchmark in Season 4

Fig. 8. F_4 for Rectangle benchmark in Season 4

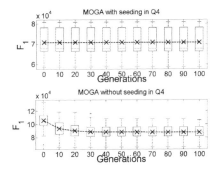

Fig. 9. F_1 for Rectangle benchmark in Season 4

Fig. 10. F_2 for Rectangle benchmark in Season 4

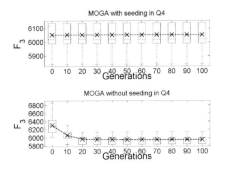
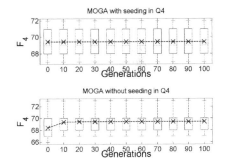

Fig. 11. F_3 for Rectangle benchmark in Season 4

Fig. 12. F_4 for Rectangle benchmark in Season 4

6   Conclusions

In this paper, a multi-objective evolutionary approach is proposed to solve dynamic service provider selection problems. Experimental results demonstrated the proposed approach is capable of optimizing the QoS distance, the total network transmission cost, the total service purchase cost, and the total number of demands points simultaneously. Moreover, the proposed approach can provide mission planers a set of non-dominated solutions for construction plan of service facilities. Our future work is to apply our approach in solving some real cases.

References

1. Foster, I., Zhao, Y., Raicu, I., Lu, S.: Cloud Computing and Grid Computing 360-Degree Compared. In: Proceeding of Grid Computing Environments Workshop, GCE 2008, pp. 1–10, November 12–16 (2008)
2. Li, Y., Shen, Y., Liu, Y.: Utilizing Content Delivery Network in Cloud Computing. In: Proceeding of 2012 International Conference on Computational Problem-Solving (ICCP), pp. 137–143 (October 2012)

3. Drezner, Z.: Dynamic Facility Location: The Progressive p-median Problem. Location Science **3**(1), 1–7 (1995)
4. Own, S.H., Daskin, M.S.: Strategic Facility Location: A Review. European Journal of Operational Research **111**, 423–447 (1998)
5. Wesolowsky, G.O.: Dynamic Facility Location. Management Science **19**(11), 1241–1248 (1973)
6. Wesolowsky, G.O., Truscott, W.G.: The Multiperiod Location-Allocation Problem with Relocation of Facilities. Management Science **22**(1), 57–65 (1975)
7. Francisco, S.D.G., Maria, E.C.: A Heuristic Approach for the Discrete Dynamic Location Problem. Location Science **6**, 211–223 (1998)
8. Pullan, W.: A population based hybrid metaheuristic for the p-median problem. In: Proceedings of IEEE Congress on Evolutionary Computation, pp. 75–82 (June 2008)
9. Arroyo, J.E.C., dos Santos Soares, M., dos Santos, P.M.: A GRASP heuristic with Path-Relinking for a bi-objective p-median problem. In: Proceedings of 10th International Conference on Hybrid Intelligent Systems (HIS), pp. 97–102 (August 2010)
10. Ho, S.-Y., Shu, L.-S., Chen, J.-H.: Intelligent Evolutionary Algorithms for Large Parameter Optimization Problems. IEEE Transaction on Evolutionary Computation **8**(6), 522–541 (2004)
11. Zitzler, E., Thiele, L.: Multiobjective evolutionary algorithms: a comparative case study and the strengthen Pareto approach. IEEE Transaction on Evolutionary Computation **3**(4), 257–271 (1999)

An Object-Oriented Library in JavaScript to Build Modular and Flexible Cross-Platform Evolutionary Algorithms

Víctor M. Rivas[1]([⊠]), Juan Julián Merelo Guervós[2], Gustavo Romero López[2],
Maribel Arenas-García[2], and Antonio M. Mora[2]

[1] Universidad de Jaén, Jaén, Spain
vrivas@ujaen.es
http://vrivas.es/
[2] Universidad de Granada, Granada, Spain

Abstract. This paper introduces jsEO, a new evolutionary computation
library that is executed in web browsers, as it is written in Javascript.
The library allows the rapid development of evolutionary algorithm, and
makes easier the collaboration between different clients by means of individuals stored in a web server. In this work, jsEO has been tested against
two simple problems, such as the Royal Road function and a 128-terms
equation, and analysing how many machines and evaluations it yields.
This paper attempts to reproduce results of older papers using modern
browsers and all kind of devices that, nowadays, have JavaScript integrated in the browser, and is a complete rewrite of the code using the
popular MooTools library. Results show that the system makes easier
the development of evolutionary algorithms, suited for different chromosomes representations and problems, that can be simultaneously executed in many different operating systems and web browsers, sharing the
best solutions previously found.

Keywords: Web browser-based computation · Javascript library ·
Asynchronous communication · Cross-platform evolutionary algorithms

1 Introduction and State of the Art

The Javascript language [1] was introduced in Netscape Navigator in 1995 and
quickly adopted by other web browsers. It soon became a standard proposed by
ECMA International in 1997, with the name of ECMAScript. This interpreted
language gives web navigators (and in fact, many other applications relying on
web engines, like email clients, and lately, since the introduction of `node.js`, any
application) the power to perform any computation apart from the needed to
render HTML code. Despite being a language initially designed to operate over
the Document Object Model (DOM) of a web page, nowadays it has become the
most popular language, due mainly to the fact that, using `node.js`, you need
only one language to create a whole rich internet client-server application.

A.I. Esparcia-Alcázar et al. (Eds.): EvoApplications 2014, LNCS 8602, pp. 853–862, 2014.
DOI: 10.1007/978-3-662-45523-4_69

Javascript offers some good features that can be used for evolutionary computation. First one is related to the interpreter itself, as most applications nowadays run into web browsers; this gives Javascript the opportunity to build web applications that incorporate evolutionary solutions as desktop ones can do. Furthermore, as browsers can be found in most operating systems and devices (from expensive computers to cheap smartphones and tablets), cross-platform interoperability can be yielded with minimum or not effort at all. The second one concerns the intrinsic communicative nature of browsers, i.e., that they are mainly designed to act as clients that send and receives data from web servers. This makes easier the task of running any kind of algorithms in a collaborative way, using many and different hardware and software platforms.

The communicative aspect of web browsers turn them into the clients of application–level networks (ALNs), which are configured as a set of clients/servers (*servents*). Browser based computation can be then considered as belonging to the so called *volunteer computing* [2,3] where volunteer users lend their CPU cycles by means of a downloadable application, and a distributed computation network providing ad hoc computational power is established. SETI@Home is the most well-known ALN, being quite successful [4], it was able to create a virtual computer that processed a high amount of teraflops. Some companies related to volunteer computing, such as Popular Power and others [5], did some experimentation with Java based clients, but none has had commercial success. Volunteer computing has been previously used in evolutionary computation, using frameworks such as DREAM [6], which includes a Java-based virtual machine; peer to peer (P2P) examples also exist, as GOLEM@Home, and G2-P2P [7], in an attempt to avoid bottlenecks produced by the servers.

Usability is also a key feature of these ALN, i.e., its simplicity of use that turns to be the best way to obtain the participation of as many users as possible. In this sense, the use of browsers has many advantages. For instance, users do not have to download any special application (even being a simple screen-saver, as is needed in BOINC, the successor to SETI@Home). Furthermore, users, no matter their technical knowledge, are used to deal with browser interface, i.e, links, forms, layouts, or timeouts. In this sense, using the browser to run this kind of applications do not differ from the way people currently read the newspaper or do the shopping.

In order to create a metacomputer, the existence of an interpreted language in the client like Javascript is only a part of the solution. The other part consists on having an easy, effective way to send and retrieve information from the server in a seamless way. There exist some techniques that allow this kind of communication: AJAX (Asynchronous JavaScript and XML [8]), AJAJ (Asynchronous JavaScript and JSON), and *remoting* using applets or embedded objects. Currently, AJAX and AJAJ are widely used since they can be natively executed by web browsers without using external plugins. As can be seen, they only differ in the way the communication is serialized, as AJAX uses XML[9] to encode both request parameters and data being retrieved, while AJAJ uses JSON.

Both AJAX and AJAJ work using the same basis: an XmlHttpRequest object is created containing a request to the server, and a reference to a *callback* function. As the request is being processed, it generates a series of events that can be asynchronously handled by the *callback* function, which can also access the data returned by the server. Both AJAX and AJAJ provide the ways to use the browser for APLs that create distributed computing systems, since this request-response iterative process does not need to interact with humans, as usually happens in any others distributed computing application. In fact, it even allows to control these APLs from the server with any programming language. Of course, it can also be combined with other distributed programming frameworks, as OSGiLiath [10], a service oriented architecture for evolutionary algorithms.

This paper presents performance measurements on the jsEO (*JavaScript Evolving Objects*, pronounce it yi-see-oh) system, which uses PHP (on the server) and JavaScript on the client. Evolutionary computation, being population based method, is suited for this kind of distributed environment since computation can be distributed among nodes. This can be done both distributing different data portions to every node, or distributing the number of individuals and allowing migration [11]. In the case of jsEO, the genetic algorithm is carried out on the clients, with the server used for interchange of individuals among them. A similar approach was used in [12] as a proof of concept, but without establishing an object-oriented hierarchy, so that new evolutionary algorithms, operators, and/or problems could be developed in an easy, and modular way.

In this work, we have performed some experiments in which clients donate computing power by just loading a web page to find out what kind of performance we can expect from this kind of setup, from the number of machines available to the number of evaluations each one of them usually performs; the results demonstrate this kind of setup is ready to take more computing-intensive experiments without the need of an expensive server or cluster setup.

The rest of the paper is organized as follows: the jsEO library is described next; methodology and experimental setup can be read in section 3, while experiments and results are shown in section 4; finally, discussion, along with future lines work, are exposed in section 5.

2   The jsEO Library

In order to provide a modular, flexible, and object-oriented library, jsEO has been programmed in JavaScript language, making use of the inheritance provided by the MooTools framework, available from http://mootools.net. Following the *evolving objects* methodology, and in the same fashion as pre-existing libraries like EO (written in C++) [13] and JEO (written in Java) [14], jsEO is based on the key point that any object that can be attached some kind of fitness value is a potential candidate for evolution. The jsEO library can de downloaded from anonymo.us/url and it is being developed under the GNU GPLv2 license.

The main advantage of JavaScript is that its virtual machine is included in most (if not all) web browsers. This allows programs written in this language to be executed in billions of computers and other devices like smartphones and tablets. JavaScript was initially designed to operate on the Document Object Model (DOM) browsers generate for every web page they load; thus, content, structure and format style can be dynamically changed while a web page is being visited; however, nowadays the JavaScript standard (ECMAscript) is implemented in many different environments, from standalone interpreters to systems such as the NoSQL database CouchDB.

On the other hand, the main drawbacks of JavaScript arise from the fact that it is interpreted, not compiled, (i.e., slower than desired), it has no access to every resource of the device (e.g. file systems, memory, or output devices), and that its execution can be stopped by web-browsers if it is consuming too many resources; in fact, most browsers put a limit to continuous execution of scripts and will issue a warning if that happens, as was noted by [15].

Fig. 1 shows the class diagram of the library. As can be seen, there exist some abstract class which define the general structure of any evolutionary solution to a given problem. Main class is *jsEO*, which represents any object to which a fitness can be assigned, and, consequently, that can be compared with any other. Starting from *jsEO* class, class *jsEOIndividual* can be derived representing any object that contains a chromosome and, therefore, can be evaluated by means of a fitness function. A *jsEOPopulation* is an aggregation of individuals; it can be used to add, replace or remove individuals, can be sorted, and can be also asked to return a subset of individuals.

In order to build algorithms, operators have to be defined. Any operator inherits from *jsEOOperator*, gets a population as input parameter, and returns a population; thus, it is designed for both operators affecting only one individual and operators acting over a whole population.

Once defined the initial core set of abstract classes (except for *jsEOPopulation*), concrete classes has been derived in order to implement the Standard Genetic Algorithm (*jsEOGA*). This algorithm uses the tournament selector to create sub-populations to which mutator and crossover operators can be applied so that they are made to evolve.

Two special operators have been implemented in order to solve problems in a cooperative environment. The first one, *jsEOSendIndividual*, is intended to send the chromosome and fitness of the best individual to a server where it is stored in case it is best solution found up to the moment. The second one, *jsEOGetIndividual*, makes exactly the opposite: it asks the server for the individual being stored and includes it as a new individual in the population. The communication between the client and the server is done using AJAX technology, and made in an asynchronous way when sending the individual to the server, but in a synchronous way in the case of the *jsEOGetIndividual*. Currently, the server has been programmed in PHP and stores data in a row file, in order to ease the implementation on anyone's server. Every synchronized problem executed with jsEO has to be assigned a unique identifier so that the server can discriminate every task when receiving and sending individuals to the clients.

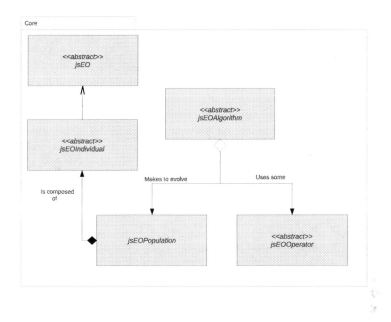

Fig. 1. Class diagram of jsEO. The core package includes some abstract classes (*jsEO*, *jsEOIndividual*, *jsEOAlgorithm*, and *jsEOOperator*) that make easier to develop new evolutionary algorithms by means of inheritance.

3   Methodology and Experimental Setup

The experiments designed to test jsEO include two problems, being the first the 256-bit Royal Road function, while the second is solving a 128-terms equation. In others words, the first one is related to a bit-string chromosome problem, while the second deals with vector of floats. Both problems have been executed as synchronized tasks, and are available at anonymo.us/url. Currently, synchronizing is quite constrained since it is done by means of AJAX connections to a server, without allowing to perform requests from pages hosted on a different one.

Asking for collaboration to run the experiments was done publishing some messages in social nets as Facebook and Twitter, as well as sending an email to a group of about 70 computer-scientist professionals. The user who wanted to participate in the experiments only had to load in his/her browser a web file containing a brief description of the problem and the Javascript library, and the chosen problem was automatically executed. Users were able to select the problem they wanted to execute, to execute it as many time as desired, to change the problem at any moment, and, of course, to stop the execution by closing the browser or loading a new web page.

In order to execute every problem, two new classes were derived from class *jsEOGA*, the first one to deal with bit-string chromosomes, the second one to make evolve vector of floats. The *jsEOGA* is a steady state algorithm, with rank-based selection, and elimination of the worst individuals after joining the current population of every generation with the new individuals created by means of operators. The algorithm stopped after a given number of generations (table 1 shows the parameters used), and incorporated operators for crossover and mutation. In the case of real problem, mutation changes values for new random ones. After every generation, best individual was sent to the server. On the other hand, requesting an individual to the server was done randomly according to the application rate of the corresponding *jsEOGetIndividual* operator. Finally, two different evaluation functions were used, one per problem. In the case of 256-bit Royal Road function, the fitness corresponds to the number of "1111" or "0000" sequences found in the 256-length bit-string. In the case of 128-terms equation, the fitness was the inverse of the value obtained when evaluating a linear equation with 128 real values in the range $(-10, 10)$ composing every chromosome. The exact solution is the one containing the terms that can be downloaded from anonymo.us/url.

Since both problems have been executed in a synchronous way, the best solution can be found in the server, but also in many clients as this individual is sent to the browser as soon as the *jsEOGetInvididual* operator is selected to operate.

Table 1. Parameters used to run the experiments, as in[12]

Parameter	Value
Population size	500
Tournament size	2
Number of generations	50
Operator crossover rate	0.73
Operator mutation rate	0.18
Operator requesting individual rate	0.09
Number of genes affected by mutation	1%
Individuals replaced in every generation	50%
Range for new random real values	
(only for the 128-term equation problem)	$(-10, 10)$

4   Experimental Results

After two days of volunteers executing the algorithms, some results can be drawn gathering data from the web server log file (in this case, Apache log). The log file has been analysed using the free version of WebLog Expert application[1], and the well-known Webalizer application[2].

---

[1] WebLog Expert can be obtained from http://www.weblogexpert.com/
[2] Webalize can be obtained from http://www.webalizer.com

From a potential target of users of more than 500 people, the 128-terms equation has been executed 304 times by 231 different visitors, while the 256-bit Royal Road function has been executed 359 times by 279 visitors. Most of this visits (i.e., executions) were done along a period of approximately 24 hours, but no references about time consumed by every execution have been registered. The algorithms have been executed in up to 128 different combinations of web browser and operating system, any of them in many different versions. As shown in figures 2 and 3, Web browser include Safari, Firefox, Chrome, Internet Explorer, and native browsers for smartphones and tablets; while operating systems include Windows, Linux, MacOS, and Android.

Most used browsers

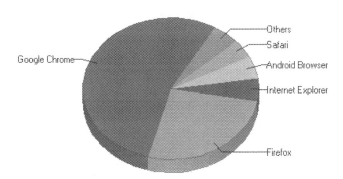

Fig. 2. Summary of browsers used to run the experiments. For any of the browsers, many different versions have been used. For instance, up to 4 different versions of Internet Explorer were found.

As can be seen in table 1, population was composed by 500 individuals, and 50% were replaced in every generation, this means that in every execution 13,000 individuals were evaluated. Consequently, the currently available solutions in the server have been found after 3,952,000 evaluations in the case of the 128-terms equation, and 4,667,000 evaluations for the 256-bit Royal Road function. The solution found for the bit-string problems is composed by 176 characters "0", and 80 characters "1", being its fitness 232. For the real codified problem, the solution yields a fitness of 300,909.09, which corresponds to a value of $3.32E - 06$ when evaluating the equation being solved.

With respect to execution times, some conclusions can be drawn from log files as in every generation the best element has been sent to the server. This way, execution times can be estimated as 50 individuals are sent (one per generation): the fist individual is sent as soon as the first generation is evaluated, and the last one is sent once the new generation has been formed. For 256-bit Royal Road function, the average time required by clients is 97.73 ± 316.21 seconds. Nevertheless, 84% of executions end in less than 60 seconds. With respect to 128-terms equations, results can not be taken into account as we really think

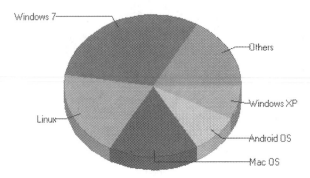

Fig. 3. Set of operating systems that have been used by users visiting the pages containing the experiments. The figures corresponding to Windows include 8 different versions, including the one for phones.

they are wrong. This is probably due to the long string received by the server (containing 128 float numbers), that makes log lines difficult to handle. For instance, according to log file processing, 50% of executions lasted more than 25.9 minutes. In fact, only 23% of the executions would have taken less than 10 minutes to be done. This do not match with some a-posteriori monitored executions, where the time needed to perform the entire algorithm was always between 2 and 7 minutes for different navigators and operating systems.

5   Conclusions, Discussion and Future Work

In this paper we have proved that, without an expensive or far-fetched setup, volunteer computation can achieve high performance, equivalent, at most, to several computers of average performance. The code used to perform the experiment is publicly available and is modular so that creating different experiments is just a matter of writing a new JavaScript fitness function and tuning the GA parameters accordingly.

The experiments have proved that there is a good amount of computational power that can be easily tapped and used for evolutionary computation experiments, however, the nature of jsEO constrains also the way users donate computing power, as well as the number of clients available for an experiment. In this paper we have found some figures, which will undoubtedly vary for other experiments; however, the general shape of the curves will probably be the same, following a very steep decrease from the maximum values obtained.

The GA, being asynchronous, faces some problems that have not been tackled in this paper. What is the best approach to preserve diversity? To generate a new population in each client, and receive immigrants as soon as possible, which are incorporated into the population? Or is it better to create new client populations based on existing populations? What is really the algorithmic contribution of new clients? These issues will be explored as future work. We will also measure the limits of this technology, and test the impact of servers of varying performance and workload on overall performance. Eventually, we will also try to perform a *sneaky* experiment, to check what kind of performance can be expected in that kind of setups.

Acknowledgments. This research has been partially supported by the Spanish Ministry of Science and Innovation through the ANYSELF project, code TIN2011-28627-C04-02. The authors would also like to thank the FEDER of European Union for financial support via project Sistema de Informacin y Prediccin de bajo coste y autnomo para conocer el Estado de las Carreteras en tiempo real mediante dispositivos distribuidos (SIPEsCa) of the Programa Operativo FEDER de Andaluca 2007-2013. We also thank all Agency of Public Works of Andalusia Regional Government staff and researchers for their dedication and professionalism.

References

1. Dionisio, J.D., Toal, R.: Programming With Javascript: Algorithms And Applications For Desktop And Mobile Browsers. Jones & Bartlett Learning (2011)
2. Sarmenta, L.F.G., Hirano, S.: Bayanihan: building and studying Web-based volunteer computing systems using Java. Future Generation Computer Systems **15**(5–6), 675–686 (1999)
3. Anderson, D.P., Korpela, E., Walton, R.: High-performance task distribution for volunteer computing. In: E-SCIENCE 2005: Proceedings of the First International Conference on e-Science and Grid Computing, pp. 196–203. IEEE Computer Society, Washington (2005)
4. Anderson, D.P., Cobb, J., Korpela, E., Lebofsky, M., Werthimer, D.: SETI@home: an experiment in public-resource computing. Commun. ACM **45**(11), 56–61 (2002)
5. Cappello, P., Mourloukos, D.: A scalable, robust network for parallel computing. In: JGI 2001: Proceedings of the 2001 joint ACM-ISCOPE conference on Java Grande, pp. 78–86. ACM Press, New York (2001)
6. Arenas, M., Collet, P., Eiben, A.E., Jelasity, M., Merelo, J.J., Paechter, B., Preuß, M., Schoenauer, M.: A Framework for Distributed Evolutionary Algorithms. In: Guervós, J.J.M., Adamidis, P.A., Beyer, H.-G., Fernández-Villacañas, J.-L., Schwefel, H.-P. (eds.) PPSN 2002. LNCS, vol. 2439, p. 665. Springer, Heidelberg (2002)
7. Mason, R., Kelly, W.: G2–P2P: a fully decentralised fault-tolerant cycle-stealing framework. In: ACSW Frontiers 2005: Proceedings of the 2005 Australasian workshop on Grid computing and e-research, pp. 33–39. Australian Computer Society Inc., Darlinghurst (2005)
8. Brinzarea, B., Dari, C.: AJAX and PHP: Building Modern Web Applications, 2 edn. Packt Publishing (2010)
9. Goldberg, K.H.: XML. Peachpit Press (2009)
10. García-Sánchez, P.: J. González, Pedro A. Castillo, Maribel García Arenas, and Juan Julián Merelo Guervós. Service oriented evolutionary algorithms. Soft Comput. **17**(6), 1059–1075 (2013)
11. Cantú-Paz, E.: Migration policies, selection pressure, and parallel evolutionary algorithms. Journal of Heuristics **7**(4), 311–334 (2001)

12. Merelo, J.J., Castillo, P.A., Laredo, J.L.J., Mora, A., Prieto, A.: Asynchronous distributed genetic algorithms with JavaScript and JSON. In: WCCI 2008 Proceedings, pp. 1372–1379. IEEE Press (2008)
13. Merelo-Guervós, J.-J., Arenas, M.G., Carpio, J., Castillo, P., Rivas, V.M., Romero, G., Schoenauer, M.: Evolving objects. In: Wang, P.P. (ed.) Proc. JCIS 2000 (Joint Conference on Information Sciences), vol. I, pp. 1083–1086 (2000) ISBN: 0-9643456-9-2
14. Arenas, M.G., Foucart, L., Merelo-Guervós, J.-J., Castillo, P.A.: JEO: a framework for Evolving Objects in Java. In: Actas Jornadas de Paralelismo, pp. 185–191. UPV, Universidad Politécnica de Valencia (2001). http://geneura.ugr.es/pub/papers/jornadas2001.pdf
15. Merelo, J.J., García, A.M., Laredo, J.L.J., Lupión, J., Tricas, F.: Browser-based distributed evolutionary computation: performance and scaling behavior. In: GECCO 2007: Proceedings of the 2007 GECCO Conference Companion on Genetic and Evolutionary Computation, pp. 2851–2858. ACM Press, New York (2007)

EvoBIO

What Do We Learn from Network-Based Analysis of Genome-Wide Association Data?

Marzieh Ayati[1]([⊠]), Sinan Erten[1], and Mehmet Koyutürk[1,2]

[1] Department of Electrical Engineering and Computer Science, Case Western Reserve University, 10900 Euclid Ave., Cleveland OH 44106, United States
mxa401@case.edu
[2] Center for Proteomics and Bioinformatics, Case Western Reserve University, 10900 Euclid Ave., Cleveland OH 44106, United States

Abstract. Network based analyses are commonly used as powerful tools to interpret the findings of genome-wide association studies (GWAS) in a functional context. In particular, identification of disease-associated functional modules, i.e., highly connected protein-protein interaction (PPI) subnetworks with high aggregate disease association, are shown to be promising in uncovering the functional relationships among genes and proteins associated with diseases. An important issue in this regard is the scoring of subnetworks by integrating two quantities that are not readily compatible: disease association of individual gene products and network connectivity among proteins. Current scoring schemes either disregard the level of connectivity and focus on the aggregate disease association of connected proteins or use a linear combination of these two quantities. However, such scoring schemes may produce arbitrarily large subnetworks which are often not statistically significant, or require tuning of parameters that are used to weigh the contributions of network connectivity and disease association. Here, we propose a parameter-free scoring scheme that aims to score subnetworks by assessing the disease association of pairwise interactions and incorporating the statistical significance of network connectivity and disease association. We test the proposed scoring scheme on a GWAS dataset for type II diabetes (T2D). Our results suggest that subnetworks identified by commonly used methods may fail tests of statistical significance after correction for multiple hypothesis testing. In contrast, the proposed scoring scheme yields highly significant subnetworks, which contain biologically relevant proteins that cannot be identified by analysis of genome-wide association data alone.

1 Introduction

In recent years, there has been an explosion in genome-wide association studies (GWAS) of complex diseases [6, 22]. These studies have revealed many genetic variants conferring susceptibility to disease. However, GWAS have so far explained a small fraction of the heritability of common diseases and provided limited insights into their molecular mechanisms. A commonly cited reason underlying the limitations of GWAS is the complex nature of diseases, i.e., the interplay among multiple genetic variants in driving disease phenotype [17]. Therefore, many computational

© Springer-Verlag Berlin Heidelberg 2014
A.I. Esparcia-Alcázar et al. (Eds.): EvoApplications 2014, LNCS 8602, pp. 865–876, 2014.
DOI: 10.1007/978-3-662-45523-4_70

methods have been developed to integrate the outcome of GWAS and with other biological data, such as pathways, annotations, and networks, to provide a functional context for the disease association of multiple genetic variants [3,11] and the identification of epistatic interactions [21].

Among computational methods that aim to identify multiple genetic variants associated with diseases, identification of disease-associated functional modules has been commonly used as a powerful tool to gain insights into the systems biology of disease mechanisms [11]. In this application, an important challenge is to define a scoring function that will accurately assess the relevance of a given subnetwork in terms of functional modularity (network connectivity) and disease association. While scoring subnetworks, many of the existing methods ignore the degree of network connectivity and score connected subnetworks of the human PPI network using an aggregate of the disease association of comprising gene products [10,11]. Alternately, some methods incorporate network connectivity by using a linear combination of this aggregate score and the density of the induced subnetwork, using a free parameter to adjust the relative contributions of disease association and network connectivity [15,26]. Subsequently, they identify high-scoring subnetworks using various algorithmic techniques [10,15] and empirically assess the significance of these subnetworks based on permutation tests [3].

Scoring schemes that are based on an aggregate of individual disease association scores are highly influenced by subnetwork size. Indeed, Baranzini *et al.* [3] systematically show that, if correction for multiple hypothesis testing is handled properly, such scoring schemes do not yield statistically significant subnetworks for many diseases. Scoring schemes that incorporate the degree of network connectivity, on the other hand, require tuning of a free parameter to adjust the relative contributions of disease association and network connectivity, making it difficult to apply these algorithms to cases where no training data is available.

In this paper, we propose a scoring scheme that (i) integrates disease association and network connectivity in a parameter-free fashion and (ii) incorporates an approximation of the statistical significance of this integrated score. The key idea of the proposed method is to assess the disease association of each interaction in the network and account for the background disease association as an approximation to statistical significance. In this respect, the proposed approach may be thought of a generalization of Newman's [5] measure of modularity, which was developed for community detection in networks.

We test the proposed scoring scheme on a GWAS dataset for type II diabetes (T2D) and compare its performance with two most commonly used scoring methods. Our results show that subnetworks that are scored highly by the proposed scoring scheme are more likely to be statistically significant as compared to those that are scored high by the other two scoring schemes. We also assess the biological relevance of identified subnetworks in terms of their inclusion of known disease-related proteins that do not exhibit significant disease association based on individual analysis of GWAS data. Our results suggest that the proposed scheme yields parsimonious subnetworks that contain known proteins, as well as those that are not individually significant, but are candidates for further investigation.

2   Methods

The input to the problem of identifying disease-associated functional modules (DAFM) is a graph $G = (V, E, w)$ that represents the human PPI network. Here, V denotes the set of proteins, E denotes the set of pairwise interactions between these proteins, and $w : E \rightarrow \mathbb{R}$ denotes edge weights, where $w(u, v)$ represents the likelihood that proteins $u, v \in V$ interact. The likelihood scores for interactions are usually computed by integrating the outcome of several experimental and computational methods for detecting and predicting protein-protein interactions. In this paper, we use an online tool, MAGNET [13], to score the interactions. Besides the network, we are given a genome-wide association (GWAS) dataset.

Here, our focus is not on assessing the disease association of each variant. We rather assume that the statistical significance of the association of each locus c with the disease is given as a p-value. From these significance values, we compute the association score $r(v)$ of each gene coding for a protein v, by taking the -log of the most significant p-value of the variants that lie within the region of interest for that gene. The objective of the disease-associated functional module (DAFM) identification problem is to identify PPI subnetworks such that:

– the subnetwork is enriched in proteins that are associated with the disease,
– the proteins in the subnetwork are functionally associated with each other.

Consideration of these two criteria together enables identification of functionally modular processes that are associated with the disease. An important challenge in this regard is to develop scoring schemes that can achieve a reasonable balance between these two criteria so that the subnetworks that are assigned statistically significant scores are those that are biologically most meaningful and useful.

2.1   Scoring Subnetworks

In this section, we describe the three scoring schemes that are used in our experimental studies. These scoring schemes are illustrated in Fig. 1. Two of these schemes are based on existing methods for the identification of active subnetworks using gene expression data, and these methods are commonly used in integrating GWAS outcome with PPI networks. The third is a novel scoring method that is based on a measure of modularity in networks [18].

Node-Based Scoring: A popular method for scoring subnetworks is implemented in JactiveModules [10], a Cytoscape plug-in for the identification of "active subnetworks". Since this scoring scheme is based on aggregation of the individual disease association scores of the proteins composing the subnetwork, we refer to it as NODE-BASED scoring. Under this scheme, the connectivity of the subnetwork is imposed as a qualitative constraint to ensure that the proteins in the subnetwork are functionally related. However, the degree of connectivity, hence the degree of functional association among the proteins, is not quantified.

Linear Combination of Node and Edge Scores: Disease association and the degree of connectivity in the network are two criteria that are not readily

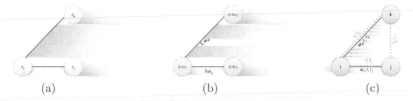

Fig. 1. Illustration of existing and proposed scoring schemes for quantifying the disease association of protein subnetworks: (a) NODE-BASED scoring, (b) LINEAR COMBINATION of node scores and edge scores, (c) the proposed MODULARITY-BASED (MOBAS) scoring scheme. For each method, the score of subnetwork is computed as an aggregate of all quantities in the figure.

comparable. Ma et al. [15] propose a scoring scheme that is based on the LINEAR COMBINATION of node scores and edge weights. This approach has been shown to be more effective than NODE-BASED scoring in the context of identifying "active subnetworks" [15]. However, to the best of our knowledge, it has not found application in the identification of disease-associated subnetworks based on GWAS outcome. An important drawback of this approach is its dependence on a tunable parameter that adjusts the relative weights of node scores and edge weights.

Modularity Based Scoring (MOBAS): The objective in any pattern discovery problem for biological applications is to discover patterns that are *statistically significant*. To this end, it is important to note that "high scoring" does not necessarily mean statistically significant and a scoring scheme should not be overly conservative or overly relaxed, since a conservative scoring scheme may not produce any non-trivial high-scoring patterns and a relaxed scoring scheme may produce high scoring patterns that are not significant. Here, we argue (and show in Section 3) that both NODE-BASED and LINEAR-COMBINATION based scoring schemes are overly relaxed in that they can lead to the identification of very large subnetworks that will achieve high scores just because of their size, since these scoring schemes do not explicitly penalize for the inclusion of more proteins in the subnetwork.

We here propose a novel scoring scheme that integrates degree of network connectivity with disease association in a parameter-free manner by assessing the disease association of each pair of proteins (a potential interaction) in the network. Further, building on Newman's [18] measure of modularity for community detection in networks, the proposed scoring scheme incorporates an approximation of statistical significance into the scoring of subnetworks by taking into account the background disease association scores.

We define the disease association of a pair of proteins $u, v \in V$ as follows:

$$s_{uv} = \begin{cases} w(u,v)r(u)r(v) & \text{if } uv \in E \\ 0 & \text{otherwise} \end{cases}$$

Recall that r_u indicates the likelihood that protein u is associated with the disease of interest. Therefore, s_{uv} provides a measure of the disease association of the interaction between u and v with the disease;

We then define the disease association score of a given subnetwork $Q \subseteq V$ as follows:

$$\sigma_M(Q) = \sum_{u,v \in Q} s_{uv} - \hat{r}_u \hat{r}_v,$$

where $\hat{r}_u$ and $\hat{r}_v$ respectively denote the "background" disease association scores for proteins u and v. We compute these background scores empirically for each protein. For this purpose, we randomize the original GWAS data by permuting the labels of the samples to break the relationship between the genotype and phenotype, while preserving the distribution of genotypes for each locus. We repeat the permutation multiple (N) times such that the number of samples derived from the distribution is sufficiently large and the computation is feasible (we use $N = 100$ in our experiments). In other words, the disease association of subnetwork $Q \subseteq V$ is defined as the linear combination of the differences between the observed and background disease association scores of all potential pairwise interactions in the subnetwork. Note that, it is assumed that an interaction exists between every pair of proteins in the background, therefore any pair of proteins in the subnetwork that do not interact with each other are penalized by a factor of the multiplication of their background association scores. For this reason, groups of proteins that induce a heavily connected subgraph in the PPI network are favored by this scoring scheme.

2.2   Searching for High Scoring Subnetworks

Subnetwork search queries with combinatorial objective functions often lead to NP-hard problems. For this reason, existing methods for identifying disease-associated functional modules use approximation algorithms or heuristics, such as greedy algorithms, simulated annealing [10], genetic algorithms [15], or linear programming based on a continuous approximation [26]. Since our focus here is on the development of a sound scoring function, the algorithm we use to search for high scoring subnetworks should be compatible with those implemented by existing methods, so that the scoring functions can be compared without any algorithmic bias. Here, for simplicity, we implement a greedy algorithm as well.

2.3   Assessment of Statistical Significance

The proposed scoring scheme approximates the statistical significance of subnetworks by accounting for the background distribution of disease association. However, the distributions used in this approximation do not take into account multiple hypothesis testing, since each subnetwork is scored independently. Furthermore, only sample means are incorporated in the scoring function, which may not account for the variability in the distributions of network connectivity and disease association. Consequently, high-scoring modules identified using the proposed scoring scheme are not necessarily significant. For this reason, for all the three scoring schemes that are considered, we assess the statistical significance of all identified subnetworks using empirical distributions generated by running the algorithm on multiple randomized datasets.

We generate the randomized datasets using two different approaches:

1. Random permutation of the phenotypes of samples, with a view to testing the hypothesis that the the high score of each identified subnetwork arises from the correlations between genotype and phenotype.
2. Random permutation of the PPI network, with a view to testing the hypothesis that each high-scoring subnetwork are composed of functionally associated proteins.

Observe that, since the number of hypotheses being tested is equal to the number of potential connected subnetworks of the PPI network, multiple hypothesis testing poses an important challenge in evaluating the significance of identified subnetworks. We tackle this challenge by using the ranking of subnetworks identified on random datasets to generate a null distribution for each subnetwork based on its rank on the original dataset. Namely, for the subnetwork that has the *ith* highest score on the original dataset, we test the hypothesis that the algorithm could discover at least i subnetworks with higher or equal score even if the phenotypes and the interactions in the network were assigned at random. We refer to this measure of significance as the q-value of the subnetwork.

3 Results

In this section, we first describe the datasets used in our experiments. Subsequently, we investigate the statistical significance of the subnetworks identified by the proposed scoring scheme, as well as those identified by aggregation of node scores (NODE-BASED) and linear combination of node and edge scores (LINEAR COMBINATION). We assess the biological relevance of the identified subnetworks using a literature-driven list of genes and processes that have been reported to be associated with T2D. We also perform pathway enrichment analysis to identify the biological processes and pathways potentially associated with T2D. Finally, we investigate the biological relevance of the "novel genes" identified by the scoring gene, namely those that are not known to be associated by the disease, do not show significant disease association according to GWAS data, but are recruited in the significant subnetworks identified by the proposed scoring scheme.

3.1 Datasets and Preprocessing

GWAS dataset: To evaluate the performance of the proposed method, we use a Type 2 Diabetes (T2D) case-control dataset, obtained from Wellcome Trust Case-Control Consortium (WTCCC) [6]. The T2D data contains SNP microarray data for 500000 SNPs on 1999 case and 1504 control samples (1958 British Birth Cohort). For this dataset, we use the genotype calls provided by WTCCC, which were obtained by using CHIAMO.SNPs with > 10% missing genotypes are excluded from the analyses.

Association analysis for individual SNPs: We compute the statistical significance of the association of each SNP with T2D using PLINK[20], a well-established toolkit for whole-genome association analysis.

SNP-gene mapping and association analysis for individual genes: To compute the disease-association for individual genes, we map SNPs to genes by defining the region of interest (ROI) for a gene as the genomic region that extends from 20kb upstream to 20kb downstream of the coding region for that gene. We compute the disease association of each gene as the minimum of the p-values of the SNPs in the region of interest for that gene, that is the p-value of the most significant SNP associated with the gene. We log-transform these values to obtain a disease association score for each gene.

Protein-protein interaction (PPI) dataset: We use a comprehensive human PPI network downloaded from NCBI Entrez Gene Database [16]. This database integrates interaction data from several PPI databases, including HPRD, BioGrid, and BIND. The PPI network contains 56110 interactions among 7692 proteins. We assess the reliability of each interaction in this dataset using MAGNET [13], a web service that uses logistic regression to assign reliability scores to PPIs.

Genes reported to be associated with T2D: In order to assess the biological relevance of identified subnetworks, we use a manually curated database of genes that are reported to be associated with T2D in the literature [12]. This list contains 286 genes. We also use a second database that is generated by using seven independent computational disease gene prioritization methods [23], namely GeneSeeker [8], POCUS [25], G2D [19], PROSPECTR [1], eVOC annotation [24], DGP [14] and SUSPECTS [2].

Pathway enrichment analysis: We also evaluate the subnetworks that are found to be significantly associated with T2D using pathway enrichment analysis. For this purpose, we use Ingenuity Pathway Analysis (IPA), a commercial software that uses a manually curated and highly reliable database of pathway associations to perform pathway enrichment analysis.

3.2   Significance of Identified Subnetworks

In this section, we investigate the statistical significance of the subnetworks identified by each scoring scheme. For this purpose, we compare the scores of highest-scoring subnetworks identified on the WTCCC dataset with that of the highest-scoring subnetworks identified on 100 randomized datasets in which (i) the sample phenotypes are permuted, (ii) PPIs are randomly permuted while preserving the number of interactions for each protein. The results of this analysis are shown in Fig. 2.

The null distribution displayed in Fig. 2 is precisely the distribution used to compute the q-values of each identified subnetworks, as described in Section 2.3.

As seen in top row of Fig. 2, the nine highest scoring subnetworks identified using MoBaS have scores at least one standard deviation above the mean of the top subnetworks identified on randomized datasets. At a q-value threshold of 0.05, two of these subnetworks are detected to be statistically significant. In contrast, all subnetworks identified by LINEAR COMBINATION and NODE-BASED scoring are within one standard deviation of the average score of the top subnetworks identified on randomized datasets. In other words, when the existing genotype-phenotype relationship in the dataset is broken via randomization of samples,

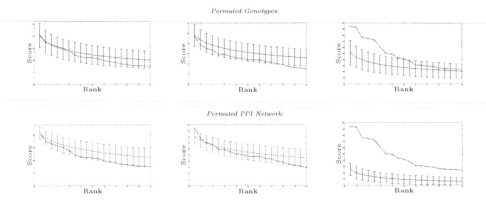

Fig. 2. Statistical significance of high-scoring subnetworks identified using NODE-BASED scoring (first column), LINEAR COMBINATION of node scores and edge scores (second column), and MODULARITY-BASED (MoBAS) scoring (third column). The highest scoring 20 subnetworks identified using each scoring scheme are shown. The x-axis shows the rank of each subnetwork according to their score, the y-axis shows its score. The blue curve shows the scores of the subnetworks identified on the WTCCC-T2D dataset. For each i on the x-axis, the red (green) curve and error bar in the first (second) row show the distribution of the scores of i highest scoring subnetworks in 100 datasets obtained by permuting the genotypes of the samples (permuting the interactions in the PPI networks while preserving node degrees).

LINEAR COMBINATION and NODE-BASED can still detect subnetworks that score high. The respective q-values are shown in Table 1.

Table 1. Statistical significance(q-value) of top two subnetworks identified using each scoring scheme according to the permuted genotype and PPI for WTCCC-T2D

Scoring method	Size	q-value in permuted genotype	q-value in permuted PPI networks
NODE-BASED	187	0.37	0.45
	190	0.70	0.92
LINEAR COMBINATION	41	0.46	0.09
	17	0.79	0.52
MoBAS	14	0.04	< 0.01
	14	0.05	< 0.01

We observe a similar pattern when we compare the subnetworks identified on the original data to those identified on randomly permuted PPI networks. Baranzini *et al.* [3] also investigate this issue systematically on a number of complex diseases and show that, while the subnetworks identified by jActiveModules (NODE-BASED scoring) on some diseases (including multiple sclerosis and rheumatoid arthritis) are significant, many subnetworks that are identified for other diseases

(a)

Gene	p-value
MED17	7.88E-08
MED31	0.0001
POU2F1	0.0002
CDK8	0.0021
ESR1	0.0039
HNF4A	0.0043
BARD1	0.0141
BRCA1	0.0216
MED9	0.0358
MED25	0.0445
MED1	0.0552
MED10	0.0896
MED23	0.0970
MED19	0.3629

(b)

Gene	p-value
MCC	0.0013
STRN3	0.0015
TRAF3IP3	0.0017
FAM40A	0.0020
CTTNBP2NL	0.0042
STK25	0.01041
FGFR1OP2	0.01574
CTTNBP2	0.0230
STK24	0.03524
PPP2R1A	0.0609
PDCD10	0.0657
PPP2CA	0.1232
STRN	0.1642
STRN4	0.1934

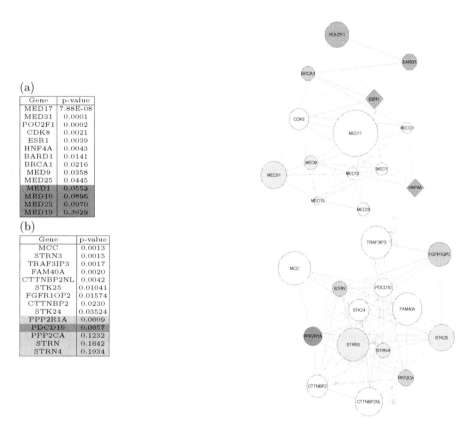

Fig. 3. Two subnetworks that are found to be significantly associated with T2D. The size of each node indicates the significance of the association of the corresponding protein with T2D (r_v). The diamond nodes are those previously reported to be associated with T2D in the literature [12]. The intensity of purple coloring in the nodes indicates the number of computational disease gene prioritization methods [23] that identified the respective gene to be associated with T2D. The individual p-values of each gene in the subnetwork are shown in the table left of the subnetwork. The genes with insignificant p-value ($p > 0.05$) that are known to be related to T2D are highlighted in yellow. The genes with insignificant p-value and are not reported to be related to T2D are highlighted in orange. These genes can be candidates for further investigation.

are not, including those for T2D. Our results stand as a reproduction of these results and suggest that the proposed modularity-based scoring scheme does not suffer from this problem.

To choose significant subnetworks for further investigation, we require statistical significance in terms of both disease association and network connectivity. For this purpose, we compute the q-value of each subnetwork as the maximum of its q-values with respect to permuted genotype and permuted PPI. Consequently, only the two subnetworks identified by the proposed method are deemed statistically significant at a false discovery rate of $q < 0.05$.

3.3   Biological Relevance

In this section, we investigate the biological relevance of the two statistically significant subnetworks ($q < 0.05$) identified by the proposed method. These two subnetworks are shown in Fig. 3. According to Ingenuity Pathway Analysis (IPA) software, the top subnetwork (Fig. 3(a)) is significantly enriched in Estrogen Receptor Signaling ($p < 3.42E-12$) and Glucocorticoid Receptor Signaling ($p < 1.19E-3$). The second subnetwork (Fig. 3(b)) is significantly enriched in Wnt/β-catenin Signaling ($p < 0.01$) and Cell Cycle Regulation by BTG Family Proteins ($p < 2.2E-4$).

The association between a region of the estrogen receptor-α (ESR1) gene and T2D is reported in the literature [9]. Although the p-value of its association with T2D according to GWAS data before correction for multiple hypotheses is moderate ($p < 0.003$), this gene appears in the most significant subnetwork identified by the proposed algorithm. This subnetwork is significantly enriched in Estrogen receptor signaling pathway, which is known to play a crucial role on insulin resistance syndrome [7]. Glucocorticoid excess in vivo has been shown to cause decreased insulin sensitivity and insulin receptor binding in target tissues [4]. The first subnetwork is also enriched in Glucocorticoid Receptor Signaling. As shown in Fig. 3(a), this subnetwork contains nine subunit of mediator complex which has an important role in regulating lipid metabolism linked to major human diseases including type 2 diabetes [27].

The second subnetwork is enriched in Wnt/β-catenin Signalling, which is a well-known pathway related to T2D. STRN, STRN4 and PPP2CA are previously reported to be associated with T2D, but do not have significant p-value according to the association analysis for individual variants (respectively 0.16, 0.19 and 0.12 before correction for multiple hypothesis testing). The subnetwork discovered using the proposed scoring scheme reveals the involvement of these genes in T2D-related processes, demonstrating that network analysis can provide information beyond what can be detected by GWAS data alone.

4   Conclusion

In this paper, with a view to facilitating the identification of disease-associated functional modules, we propose a novel methodology for scoring PPI subnetworks in terms of their association with a complex disease of interest and their network connectivity. Our experimental studies show that objective criteria for scoring subnetworks have to be selected carefully to ensure that the algorithms can detect parsimonious subnetworks that are statistically significant. In particular, we show that, with a carefully designed scoring scheme, network analysis can extract knowledge from GWAS data beyond the scope of the data itself. Namely, the subnetworks identified by the proposed method contain genes that do not exhibit significant association with the disease based on analysis of GWAS data, but are known to have mechanistic role in the disease. Furthermore, the subnetworks identified by the proposed method include genes that are not yet reported to have a role in the disease, are not detected to be significant by GWAS, but have molecular functions that indicate potential involvement in the disease.

The method presented in this paper focuses on a single network pattern: dense subgraphs of the PPI network. However, investigation of different network patterns may provide additional insights on the relationships between different disease-associated genes and molecular mechanisms of these associations. The results reported here are limited to a single disease (T2D) based on a single large scale GWAS. In future work, application of the proposed method to various diseases and reproducibility analyses based on data from multiple cohorts will be crucial in establishing the generalizability of these promising results. The source code of MoBaS is freely available at http://compbio.case.edu/mobas/.

Acknowledgments. We would like to thank Thomas LaFramboise, Yu Liu, Pamela Clark, and Mark Chance for useful discussions. This work was supported in part by US National Science Foundation (NSF) award CCF-0953195 and US National Institutes of Health (NIH) award R01-LM011247. This study makes use of data generated by the Wellcome Trust Case-Control Consortium. A full list of the investigators who contributed to the generation of the data is available from www.wtccc.org.uk. Funding for the project was provided by the Wellcome Trust under award 076113 and 085475.

References

1. Adie, E.A., Adams, R.R., et al.: Speeding disease gene discovery by sequence based candidate prioritization. BMC Bioinformatics, **6** (2005)
2. Adie, E.A., Adams, R.R., et al.: SUSPECTS: enabling fast and effective prioritization of positional candidates. Bioinformatics, **22** (2006)
3. Baranzini, S.E., Galwey, N.W., Wang, J., Khankhanian, P., et al.: Pathway and network-based analysis of genome-wide association studies in multiple sclerosis. Hum. Mol. Genet. **18**, 2078–2090 (2009)
4. Obberghen, E.V., Grunfeld, C., Baird, K., Kahn, C.R.: Glucocorticoid-induced insulin resistance in vitro: Evidence for both receptor and postreceptor defects. Endocrinology **109**, 1723–1730 (1981)
5. Clauset, A., Newman, M.E.J., Moore, C.: Finding community structure in very large networks. Phys. Rev, E 70 (2004)
6. W. T. C. C. Consortium: Genome-wide association study of 14,000 cases of seven common diseases and 3,000 shared controls. Nature **447**, 661–678 (2007)

7. Deng, J.Y., Hsieh, P.S., Huang, J.P., et al.: Activation of estrogen receptor is crucial for resveratrol-stimulating muscular glucose uptake via both insulin-dependent and -independent pathways. Diabetes **57**, 1814–1823 (2008)

8. Driel, M.A., Cuelenaere, K., Kemmeren, P.P., et al.: GeneSeeker: extraction and integration of human disease-related information from web-based genetic databases. Nucleic Acids Res., **33** (2005)

9. Gallagher, C.J., Langerfeld, C.D., Gordon, C.J., et al.: Association of the estrogen receptor-gene with the metabolic syndrome and its component traits in african-american families. Diabetes **56**, 2135–2141 (2007)

10. Ideker, T., Ozier, O., Schwikowski, B., Siegel, A.F.: Discovering regulatory and signalling circuits in molecular interaction networks. Bioinformatics **18**, 233–240 (2002)

11. Jia, P., Zheng, S., Long, J., Zheng, W., Zhao, Z.: dmGWAS: dense module searching for genome-wide association studies in protein-protein interaction networks. Bioinformatics **27**, 95–102 (2011)

12. Lim, J., Hong, K., Jin, H., Kim, Y., Park, H., Oh, B.: Type 2 diabetes genetic association database manually curated for the study design and odds ratio. BMC Medical Informatics and Decision Making (2010)

13. Linderman, G.C., Chance, M.R., Bebek, Gurkan.: MicroArray Gene expression and Network Evaluation Toolkit. Nucl. Acids Res., MAGNET (2012)

14. Lopez-Bigas, N., Ouzounis, C.A.: Genome-wide identification of genes likely to be involved in human genetic disease. Nucleic Acids Res., **32** (2004)

15. Ma, H., Schadt, E., Kaplan, L.M., Zhao, H.: COSINE: COndition-SpecIfic sub-NEtwork identification using a global optimization method. Bioinformatics (2011)

16. Maglott, D., Ostell, J., Pruitt, K.D., Tatusova, T.: Entrez gene: gene-centered information at NCBI. Nucl. Acids Res., **35** (2007)

17. Moore, J.H., Asselbergs, F.W., Williams, S.M.: Bioinformatics challenges for genome-wide association studies. Bioinformatics **26**(4), 445–455 (2010)

18. Newman, M.E.J.: Fast algorithm for detecting community structure in networks. Phys. Rev, E 69(066133) (2004)

19. Perez-Iratxeta, C., Wjst, M., Bork, P., Andrade, M.A.: G2D: a tool for mining genes associated with disease. BMC Genet., **6** (2005)

20. Purcell, S., Neale, B., Todd-Brown, K., Thomas, L., et al.: PLINK: a tool set for whole-genome association and population-based linkage analyses. American Journal of Human Genetics **81**, 559–575 (2007)

21. Ritchie, M.D.: Using biological knowledge to uncover the mystery in the search for epistasis in genome-wide association studies. Annals of Human Genetics **75**(1), 172–182 (2011)

22. Scott, L.J.: A Genome-Wide Association Study of Type 2 Diabetes in Finns Detects Multiple Susceptibility Variants. Science **316**(5829), 1341–1345 (2007)

23. Tiffin, N., Adie, E., Turner, F., et al.: Computational disease gene identification: a concert of methods prioritizes type 2 diabetes and obesity candidate genes. Nucleic Acids Res. (2006)

24. Tiffin, N., Kelso, J.F., et al.: Integration of text- and data-mining using ontologies successfully selects disease gene candidates. Nucleic Acids Res., **33** (2005)

25. Turner, F.S., Clutterbuck, D.R., Semple, C.A.: POCUS: mining genomic sequence annotation to predict disease genes. Genome Biol., **4** (2003)

26. Xia, Y., Wang, Y.: Condition specific subnetwork identification using an optimization model. In: Proceedings of The Second International Symposium on Optimization and Systems Biology, pp. 333–340 (2008)

27. Zhang, Y., Zhao, X., Yang, F.: The mediator complex and lipid metabolism. Journal of Biochemical and Pharmacological Research **1**, 51–55 (2013)

Benefits of Accurate Imputations in GWAS

Shefali S. Verma[1], Peggy Peissig[2], Deanna Cross[2], Carol Waudby[2],
Murray Brilliant[2], Catherine A. McCarty[3], and Marylyn D. Ritchie[1]([⊠])

[1] Center for Systems Genomics, The Pennsylvania State University,
University Park, PA 16802, USA
szs14@psu.edu, marylyn.ritchie@psu.edu
[2] The Marshfield Clinic, Marshfield, WI, USA
Peissig.peggy@securityhealth.org, deanna.cross@unthsc.edu,
{waudby.carol,brilliant.murray}@mcrf.mfldclin.edu
[3] Essentia Institute of Rural Health, Duluth, MN, USA
CMcCarty@eirh.org

Abstract. Imputation methods have been suggested as an efficient way to increase both utility and coverage in genome-wide association studies, especially
when combining data generated from different genotyping arrays. We aim to
demonstrate that imputation results are extremely accurate and the association
analysis from imputed data does not over-inflate the results. Instead imputation
leads to an increase in the power of the dataset without introducing any systematic biases. The majority of common variants can be imputed with very high accuracy ($r^2 > 0.9$) and we validated the accuracy of imputations by comparing
actual genotypes from low-throughput genotyping assays against imputed genotypes. Imputation was performed using IMPUTE2 and the 1000 Genomes cosmopolitan reference panel, which results in about 38 million SNPs. After quality
control and filtering we performed case-control associations with 3,159,556
markers. We show a comparison of results from genotyped and imputed data
and also determine how accurate ancestry is determined by imputations.

Keywords: Imputations · Genome wide association studies · Cataract · Type
2 diabetes · PhenX · 1000 Genomes

1 Introduction

Genome-wide association studies have become the most common study design to
look for regions of the genome that lead to susceptibility for common, complex
traits [1]. Through the evolution of GWAS, we have identified many regions of
the genome that are associated with one or more traits as described by the NHGRI
GWAS Catalog [1]; we have determined that a genome-wide statistical significance p-value threshold of $p < 5 \times 10^{-8}$ is important to control type I error inflation
[2]; replication has become a gold standard to determine the validity of any association result [3]; and we have realized that the effect sizes observed are quite small
and thus in many cases very large sample sizes are necessary to detect associations
[4]. Due to this evolution, much work has been done to combine data from GWAS

© Springer-Verlag Berlin Heidelberg 2014
A.I. Esparcia-Alcázar et al. (Eds.): EvoApplications 2014, LNCS 8602, pp. 877–889, 2014.
DOI: 10.1007/978-3-662-45523-4_71

sometimes using the same genotyping technology on different study populations, but more often different genotyping platforms as well. The resultant combined/or meta-analyzed data is riddled with many SNPs that are   unobserved in one or more studies, and thus the intersection of overlapping SNPs is often a small subset of the whole. However, unobserved genotypes from low-density data can be inferred using imputations [5]. These imputed   data can be used as a proxy to combine data from different genotyping platforms in a joint analysis or meta-analysis.

In addition, these inferred genotypes are often used to test association with disease that cannot be found by genotyping alone due to poor capture of low-density regions in the original genotype array data. We used data from the Marshfield Personalized Medicine Research Project Biobank (PMRP) and linked Electronic Health Record [1] to perform genome-wide imputations and subsequently perform association analysis on genotyped and imputed data to answer two questions: 1) Is the quality of the imputation data comparable to data generated by one or more genotyping platforms 2) Does the imputation provide additional robustness for the detection of disease association signals.

2   Methods

2.1   Subjects and Genotyping

The Marshfield PMRP is a population-based biobank with ~20,000 subjects, aged 18 years and older, enrolled in the Marshfield Clinic healthcare system in central Wisconsin [1]. DNA, plasma, and serum samples are collected at the time the enrollee completes a written informed consent document, with allowance for ongoing access to the linked electronic health records (EHR). PMRP participants also complete questionnaires, including responses regarding smoking history, occupation, physical activity, diet, and a variety of other PhenX measures [6]. The eMERGE network and the Center for Inherited Disease Research (CIDR) at Johns Hopkins University performed the genotyping of the Marshfield PMRP samples using the Illumina Human660W-Quadv1, a platform with total of 560,635 SNPs and 96,731 intensity-only probes. Bead Studio version 3.3.7 was used by CIDR for the genotyping calls. For quality control and data cleaning, the eMERGE quality control (QC) pipeline developed by the eMERGE Genomics Working Group [7] was used. We extracted 4,193 Marshfield samples from eMERGE phase I dataset on which initial QC was already performed and this dataset contained 558,980 markers. Any SNPs from this subset with a minor allele frequency > 5%, SNP call rate > 99%, sample call rate > 99% were used in further analyses. After QC and allele frequency filtering using PLINK [8], a total of 498,195 SNPs were used for imputation in this study.

The molecular fingerprint [8], [9] dataset was a set of 36 SNPs generated on a genotyping panel developed and implemented on the Sequenom platform. This panel was developed as a quality analysis (QA) /QC panel for PMRP and contained at least one polymorphism on every chromosome, inclusion in this panel included at least two instances of disease associated SNPs and a minor allele frequency in the European population of 20%. The whole phenome [9] dataset was also developed on the Sequenom platform and included 15 SNPs. The phenome panel includes candidate SNPs that have a lower MAF in the Caucasian population and is a small panel of candidate genes – not genome-wide, selected for a known associations with one or more phenotypes.

2.2   Methods of Imputation

Genotype imputation is the process of inferring unobserved genotypes in a study sample based on the haplotypes observed in a more densely genotyped reference sample of similar genetic background. After performing the above mentioned quality control procedures and generating a filtered dataset, we used imputation software to impute our data to fill in as many SNPs from the 1000 Genomes dataset as possible.

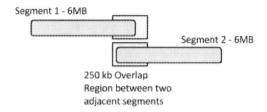

Fig. 1. Representing 6MB segments with 250KB overlap

We performed pre-phasing and imputations using SHAPEIT version 2.r644 (SHAPEIT2) [10] and IMPUTE2[11] software (version 2.3.0) respectively. We based our imputations on the 1000 Genomes Reference Panel Release from March 2012, which includes 1,092 samples across 14 different human populations. IMPUTE2 is a flexible and computationally non- extensive approach as it accounts for certainty in phasing by iterating the steps of imputation in Markov chain Monte Carlo (MCMC) framework and thus separating phasing and imputation steps. For accurate imputations, study and reference panel allele calls need to be on the same physical strand of DNA relative to the human genome reference sequence ("reference"). For strand alignment, we used SHAPEIT2 to check strands and then PLINK to flip strands for markers that are not on same strand as reference ("+" strand). Phasing and imputation were performed as one process in many previous studies, but more recently, the alternative approach of "pre-phasing" has been suggested as a way to maintain imputation accuracy while minimizing computation time, as available reference panels increase in number and in size [12],[13]. Pre-phasing involves phasing the diploid study data prior to imputation and is suggested by mostly any pairing of phasing and imputation software.

The computational arguments for pre-phasing are that (1) imputing into pre-phased haplotypes is much faster than imputing into unphased genotypes and (2) pre-phased data facilitates future updates to imputation, as improved reference panels become available [14]. Although pre-phasing may introduce a small loss of accuracy, due to the lack of incorporating haplotype uncertainty information into the imputation step, the advantages appear to outweigh the disadvantages for most GWAS studies [7]. For phasing, we divided the complete dataset by chromosomes, but we imputed each chromosome in segments so as to improve accuracy over short genomic intervals and also expedite the process by parallelizing jobs over many multi-core computer clusters. We created 6 MB segments over the length of each chromosome as it appears on the reference panel and also segments overlapping the centromere or the terminal ends were then merged into the segments upstream of them (Figure 1). Thus, chromosomes 1-22 were divided into a total of 441 segments for imputations. We used the

IMPUTE2 recommended default buffer size of 250kb for imputations. Imputation jobs were run in parallel on a computer cluster with eight nodes at 40GB of memory. Due to the input of pre-phased haplotypes, the computation time required to impute most segments is approximately one hour or less whereas phasing took about approximately 3 hours. After imputations were complete, all segments were joined together and files were converted to PLINK format by calling genotypes at a probability of 90% for further analysis.

2.3   Phenotyping

All patients were diagnosed for either cataract and/or type 2 diabetes separately in the Marshfield PMRP dataset using electronic phenotyping algorithms. The NHGRI funded eMERGE network (Electronic Medical Records and Genomics) implemented an electronic phenotype algorithm to select cataract cases and controls [6]. Cataracts as a condition were selected by Marshfield Clinic as its primary eMERGE phenotype, and the algorithm, which uses diagnostic and procedure codes, was developed by the Marshfield Clinic Personalized Medicine Research Project (PMRP) investigators [6]. Cases and controls had to meet the following inclusion criteria: Cases- aged 50 years and older at the time of diagnosis or surgery, and Controls – ages 50 years or older at the time of most recent eye exam and had an eye exam in the previous five years. Controls had no diagnostic codes for cataract or evidence of cataract surgery. Cases were identified as "surgical" or "diagnosis only". Surgical cases had undergone a cataract extraction in at least one eye. Diagnosis only cases were required to have either cataract diagnoses on 2 or more dates, or have 1 diagnosis date and NLP/OCR find 1 or more inclusion cataract terms.

Similarly, type 2 diabetes (T2D) patients were also diagnosed by their records from EHR, using an algorithm developed by eMERGE [15]. Expert clinicians experienced with T2D diagnosis carefully designed our algorithm. T2D cases were defined as having the following in their EMR: a T2D ICD-9 medical billing code, information about insulin medication, abnormal glucose or HbA1c levels, or more than two diagnoses of T2D by a clinician. All T2D cases with an ICD-9 code for T1D were removed from further analyses. All control subjects had to have at least 2 clinical visits, at least one blood glucose measurement, normal blood glucose or HbA1c levels, no ICD-9 codes for T2D or any related condition, no history of being on insulin or any diabetes related medication, and no family history of T1D or T2D.

We combined both of these phenotypes and generated a new phenotype "Cataract in Type 2 Diabetes" where cases are defined as people with both cataract and type 2 diabetes, controls are people with either one disease or neither and all others were set to missing. We have 740 cases, 3193 controls, and 260 samples with missing values.

2.4   AssociationAnalysis

Imputed genotypes can be used in many ways for downstream analyses and one such application is to perform   association tests. The goal of this analysis is to demonstrate what, if anything, we gain by using imputed data as   opposed to only using genotyped data. Case and control status were set using binary encoding (cases=1, control=0) and hence we ran logistic regression using PLINK [16] to test for genetic association in cataract in type   2 diabetes patients. Logistic regression is one of the most standard approaches for association analysis in GWAS.   To overcome the risk of population stratification, we adjusted our analysis for first three principal components using SNPrelate [17]. We performed the same analysis in both genotyped and imputed data so   as to compare the results.

3   Results

3.1   Imputation Accuracy

In our study, we validated the accuracy of imputation using two strategies: (1) comparing genotype data from two different genotyping assays (molecular fingerprinting and whole phenome) and (2) performing masked analysis (described more below). Molecular fingerprinting data consists of 36 SNPs and whole phenome consists of 15 SNPs. Each of these genotyping panels was performed on these samples for other association studies; however these data provide an excellent opportunity to validate the imputation based on the GWAS data. We estimated imputation accuracy based on 4,145 and 4,148 out of total 4,193 GWAS samples genotyped from fingerprinting and whole phenome sets, respectively. We compared imputed results with these genotype results by doing concordance checks between the two datasets. Table 1 shows the concordance rate for two groupings of chromosomes between imputed data and either molecular fingerprinting or whole phenome data. The comparisons show that the imputed genotypes are highly accurate with an average of 98.8% concordance (median 99.7%). In fact, all chromosomes had greater than 97% concordance with the exception of chromosome 20 (79.7%) for the molecular fingerprinting.

Table 1. Concordance Rates with Imputed Data

Chromosome	Whole Phenome		Molecular Fingerprint	
	Median	Average	Median	Average
Chr 1 - Chr 10	0.998	0.994	0.997	0.9962
Chr 11 - Chr 22	0.998	0.994	0.996	0.975
Total	**0.998**	**0.994**	**0.997**	**0.985**

IMPUTE2 provides a statistical information metric ("info") whose value ranges from 0 to 1, where 1 means no   uncertainty in imputed genotypes. So we used "info" metric to account for uncertainty and show distributions of   all imputed

SNPs and their accuracy, we plotted a summary of imputation quality metrics of all imputed SNPs. Figure 2 shows the distribution of the "info" quality metric, with a dashed line indicating a potential 0.3 threshold value (a standard threshold used in the field) and Figure 3 summarizes the relationship between the "info" score and minor allele frequency (MAF). The secondary axis indicates the count of SNPs in each MAF bin (0.01 intervals).

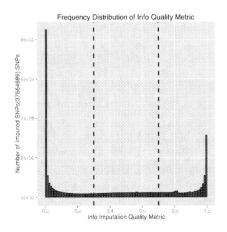
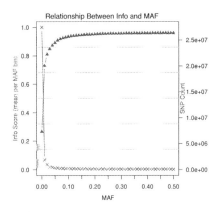

Fig. 2. Summaries of quality metrics at all imputed SNPs. Showing the distribution of the "info" quality metric, with a dashed lines at info 0.3 and 0.7.

Fig. 3. Summarizes the relationship between the "info" score and MAF. The secondary axis indicates the count of SNPs in each MAF bin (0.01 intervals).

Another commonly used approach to asses imputation quality is to "mask" (or hide) a subset of the SNPs genotyped in the study data and then impute these masked SNPs pretending they were unobserved so as to compare these imputed genotypes to the observed actual genotypes. The comparison can be made to either (1) the most likely imputed genotype, yielding a somewhat coarse concordance measure and/or (2) the estimated allelic dosage, yielding a more granular correlation measure. This type of masked analysis is generated from each IMPUTE2 run: each study SNP is removed from imputation in a leave-one-out fashion, imputed, and then compared to the imputation input. Figure 4 represents the concordance and dosage r2 for masked SNPs binned according to MAF in the observed study genotypes (0.01 intervals). This graph shows all SNPs with an info score >0.8. On the secondary y-axes, "SNP count" is the number of SNPs per MAF bin; "% SNP from bin" is the fraction of SNPs in the bin that pass the filter of "info"≥ 0.8. Here we are trying to illustrate the quality of imputation by the fraction of imputed SNPs passing a given quality filter ("info">0.8). Imputation quality is quite high in most MAF bins > 0.05.

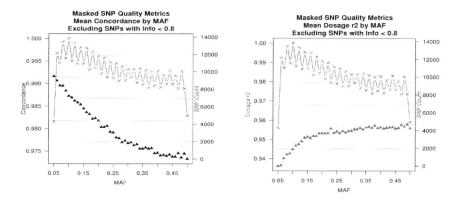

Fig. 4. Quality metrics for all masked SNPs grouped into MAF bins at 0.01 intervals. These plots excludes SNPs with "info" <0.8. On the secondary y-axes, "SNP-count" is the number of SNPs per MAF bin. "%SNP from bin" is the fraction of SNPs in the bin that pass the filter of "info" >=0.8. Note the lower bound of y-axis is >0 for each panel.

3.2   Comparison of Association Results Using Genotyped and Imputed Data

Sample Relatedness. GWAS genotype data was filtered at 99% sample and marker call rate and also all markers with MAF <5% were dropped. Imputed data was filtered at same thresholds with addition filter of info score >0.7 so as eliminate error rate due to imputation. Sample relatedness was evaluated using SNPrelate [17]. A total of 721 individuals were removed after identity- by-descent (IBD) estimation (Figure 4 shows IBD plot for all samples) to create a dataset of unrelated individuals for association analysis. Thus, we have 3,611 total samples: 635 cases, 2743 controls, and 233 missing a phenotype.

Population Structure. For accurate imputations, it is important that the samples from imputed data cluster closely to the reference panel. We performed Principal Component Analysis (PCA) as it has been reliably proven to detect differences between populations [18]. We used a kinship coefficient threshold of 0.125 to identify clusters of closer relatives, and we retained only one subject from each relative cluster. Using R package snpRelate, we calculated 32 principal components (PCs). Principal components were constructed to represent axes of genetic variation across all samples in unrelated adults and pediatric datasets that were LD pruned and also included very common autosomal SNPs (MAF > 5%). Figure 6 shows plot of first two PCs of all non-related samples colored by self-reported ethnicity. Marshfield data is predominantly European descent and we can clearly distinguish that all European samples cluster on same axes. PC1 and PC2 explain only about 0.3% of total variance.

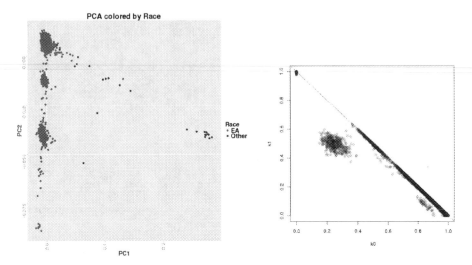

Fig. 5. Principal components analysis (PCA) for all unduplicated samples using autosomal SNPs with missing call rate < 5% and minor allele frequency > 5% that were pruned for both long and short range linkage disequilibrium (n=65355 SNPs). Color-coding indicates self- identified ethnicity.

Fig. 6. Relatedness inference from IBD estimates. Estimates of the IBD coefficents, k0 and k1 are used to infer relatedness. Each point is for a pair of samples and the diagonal line is k0+k1=1.

Association Analysis Results. We performed genome-wide discovery analysis using logistic regression to test the relationship between each SNP and our phenotype following QC and filtering. To minimize the effect of population stratification, we performed the genome-wide association analysis adjusting for first three PCs. A total of 497,799 tests were performed using PLINK's logistic regression method. After the adjustment by the first three principal components, the λgc of the genome-wide association results is 1.0092 representing very minimal differences in underlying population structure between cases and controls. Figure 7 represents quantile-quantile plot for this analysis and Figure 8 depicts the distribution of -log10P-value along all chromosomes in the genotyped data and Table 3 provides list of best signals. The same QC and filtering was performed in the imputed dataset. Association analysis was performed using logistic regression assuming an additive model on a total of   3,159,555 SNPs. After correcting for three principal components in   this dataset as well Cataract in T2D imputed data had an inflation factor of 1.00812 (Q-Q plot shows in Figure 9). In both cases, the quantile-quantile (QQ) plot of the observed P values revealed a good overall fit with the null distribution. Similarly, Figure 10 shows the Manhattan plot of the genome-wide P values of association from imputed data. Taken together, these results clearly indicate that the final association results from our genome-wide discovery analysis are free of inflation effect due to population stratification. Lowest adjusted P-value seen in this case is very similar to genotyped resulted p-value (2.98e-06). Table 4 reports the results for the top 10 most associated SNPs. Our analyses for this paper are not focused much on the discussion of results, instead we want to make clear point that accurate imputation do not create any differential biases and results are not inflated.

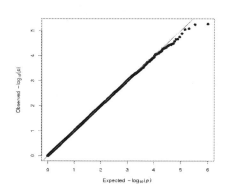

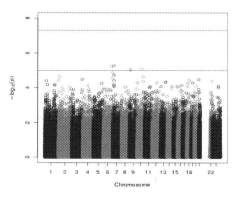

Fig. 7. Q-Q plot

Fig. 8. Manhattan plot with blue line at 1.0e-05 and red line at 1.0e-8 genome wide significance

Table 2. Results for significantly associated SNPs (genotyped data) and the genes that the markers are present in, this table also   provides information on left and right flanking genes

CHR	SNP	UNADJ	GC	GENE	LEFT GENE	RIGHT GENE
7	rs963829	4.91E-06	5.42E-06	N/A	STK31	NPY
6	rs10155709	5.21E-06	5.75E-06	AKAP12	LOC442270	ZBTB2
10	rs4332462	7.56E-06	8.32E-06	N/A	GHITM	LOC642934
9	rs7865126	8.22E-06	9.04E-06	FAM29A	SCARNA8	ADFP
6	rs2983526	1.20E-05	1.32E-05	PDE10A	C6orf118	LOC10013218
7	rs13245518	1.63E-05	1.79E-05	N/A	STK31	NPY
2	rs2304429	2.01E-05	2.19E-05	DNMT3A	LOC729734	LOC10013151
10	rs7903146	2.05E-05	2.23E-05	TCF7L2	LOC143188	hCG_1776259
6	rs844157	2.47E-05	2.69E-05	PDE10A	C6orf118	LOC10013218
3	rs9851100	3.01E-05	3.28E-05	LEPREL1	TP63	LOC391603

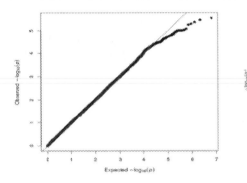

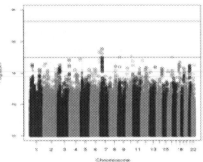

Fig. 9. A. Q-Q plot

Fig. 10. Manhattan plot with blue line at 1.0e-05 and red line at 1.0e-8 genome wide significance

Table 3. Results for significantly associated SNPs (imputed data) and the genes that the markers is present in, this table also   provide information on left and right flanking genes

CHR	SNP	UNADJ	GC	GENE	LEFT GENE	RIGHT GENE
7	rs2813829	2.64E-06	2.90E-06	N/A	STK31	NPY
7	rs2158342	3.19E-06	3.49E-06	N/A	STK31	NPY
6	rs1474718	3.97E-06	4.34E-06	AKAP12	LOC442270	ZBTB2
6	rs10155709	4.73E-06	5.16E-06	AKAP12	LOC442270	ZBTB2
7	rs963829	5.17E-06	5.65E-06	N/A	STK31	NPY
1	rs4332462	7.74E-06	8.42E-06	N/A	GHITM	LOC642934
1	rs8044538	8.60E-06	9.35E-06	N/A	C16orf47	LOC441506
9	rs7865126	9.02E-06	9.80E-06	FAM29A	SCARNA8	ADFP
7	rs156288	9.11E-06	9.90E-06	N/A	STK31	NPY
7	rs156286	9.12E-06	9.91E-06	N/A	STK31	NPY

4   Discussion

The main goals of this paper are to evaluate the accuracy of imputation and to understand how robust association tests are using imputed data above and beyond genotype data alone. Accuracy of imputation was determined using concordance checks with low-throughput genotype data and with an average of over 99% concordance; we can say that imputations using IMPUTE2 are highly accurate. To address the question of utility in association analysis, we used the Cataract in Type 2 Diabetes association results to see coverage of the genome in imputed data versus genotyped data. We were able to replicate association signals on Chromosome 6 and 7 (rs10155709 and rs963829 respectively). Figures 11 and 12 represent a close-up of the association signal at these two loci. These figures show p-values across these two replicated markers for the genotype and imputed SNPs plotted using LocusZoom[19].

The focal SNP in both cases is plotted as a purple diamond and all other data points are colored according to their r_2 with the SNP of focus. We thus identified these two loci associated with cataract in type 2 diabetes at $P<10_{-6}$. The P-value improvements were very marginal from genotyped to imputed data but these results clearly shows that imputation of genotype data using 1000 Genomes reference panel captures a lot more variants of low and rare frequencies as well. This can also be depicted using Phenogram plot [20] as shown in Figure 13 which is representing just the markers that were not genotyped but are covered on genome from imputation. Each black line represents an imputed marker and white space denotes low coverage area. We can clearly see that imputation capture a good amount of genotypes.

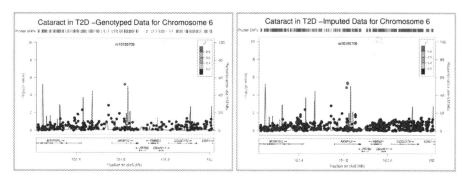

Fig. 11. Chr6 Locuszoom regional plots for association results from - genotyped and imputed data. The focal SNP is plotted as a purple diamond and all other data points are colored according to their r^2 with the SNP of focus.

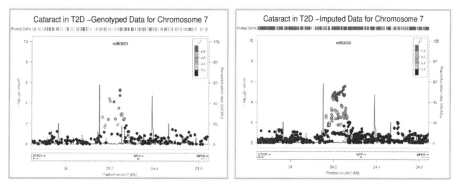

Fig. 12. Chr 7 Locuszoom regional plots for association results from genotyped and imputed data. The focal SNP is plotted as a purple diamond and all other data points are colored according to their r^2 with the SNP of focus.

In summary, imputation based on GWAS genotype data and the 1000 Genomes cosmopolitan reference panel using IMPUTE2 is highly accurate with respect to actual genotype data and can be extremely useful for genome-wide association studies. These techniques continue to be refined and perfected as we learn more about genome structure and human variation. When combining GWAS datasets for meta-analysis or joint analysis, imputation is a robust technique that should be employed.

Phenogram Plot of markers not in genotyped data

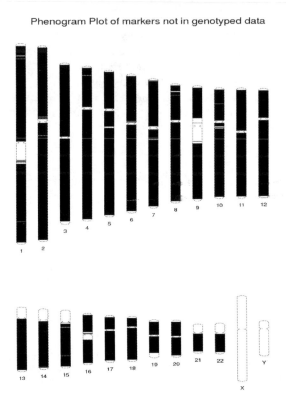

Fig. 13. Phenogram plot representing coverage of genotypes from imputed data (markers not found in genotyped data). Each black line represents an imputed marker and white space denotes low coverage area. ChrX was not imputed so that is left as blank.

References

1. Hindorff, L.A., Sethupathy, P., Junkins, H.A., Ramos, E.M., Mehta, J.P., Collins, F.S., Manolio, T.A.: Potential Etiologic and Functional Implications of Genome-wide Association Loci for Human Diseases and Traits. Proceedings of the National Academy of Sciences of the United States of America **106**, 9362–9367
2. Dudbridge, F., Gusnanto, A.: Estimation of Significance Thresholds for Genomewide Association Scans. Genetic Epidemiology **32**, 227–234
3. Chanock, S.J., Manolio, T., Boehnke, M., Boerwinkle, E., Hunter, D.J., Thomas, G., Hirschhorn, J.N., et al.: Replicating Genotype-phenotype Associations. Nature **447**, 655–660

4. Stranger, B.E., Stahl, E.A., Raj, T.: Progress and Promise of Genome-Wide Association Studies for Human Complex Trait Genetics. Genetics **187**, 367–383

5. Evangelou, E., John P.A.: Ioannidis: Meta-analysis Methods for Genome-wide Association Studies and Beyond. Nature Reviews Genetics **14**, 379–389

6. McCarty, C.A., Wilke, R.A., Giampietro P.F., Wesbrook S.D., Caldwell, M.D.: Marshfield Clinic Personalized Medicine Research Project (PMRP): design, methods and recruitment for a large population-based biobank. Personalized Medicine **2**, 49–79

7. Turner, S., Armstrong, L.L., Bradford, Y., Carlson, C.S., Crawford, D.C., Crenshaw, A.T., de Andrade, M., et al.: Quality Control Procedures for Genome-wide Association Studies. Current Protocols in Human **68**, 1.19.1–1.19.18

8. Cross, D.S., Ivacic, L.C., McCarty, C.A.: Development of a Fingerprinting Panel Using Medically Relevant Polymorphisms. BMC Medical Genomics **2**, 17

9. Cross, D.S., Ivacic, L.C., Stefanski, E.L., McCarty, C.A.: Population Based Allele Frequencies of Disease Associated Polymorphisms in the Personalized Medicine Research Project. BMC Genetics **11**, 51

10. Olivier, D., Marchini, J., Zagury, J.-F.: A Linear Complexity Phasing Method for Thousands of Genomes. Nature Methods **9**, 179–181

11. Marchini, J., Howie, B., Myers, S., McVean, G., Donnelly, P.: A New Multipoint Method for Genome-wide Association Studies by Imputation of Genotypes. Nature Genetics **39**, 906–913

12. Frazer, K.A., Ballinger, D.G., Cox, D.R., Hinds, D.A., Stuve, L.L., Gibbs, R.A., Belmont, J.W., et al.: A Second Generation Human Haplotype Map of over 3.1 Million SNPs. Nature **449**, 851–861

13. Howie, B., Fuchsberger, C., Stephens, M., Marchini, J., Abecasis, G.R.: Fast and Accurate Genotype Imputation in Genome-wide Association Studies through Pre-phasing. Nature Genetics **44**, 955–959

14. Altshuler, D.M., Gibbs, R.A., Peltonen, L., Altshuler, D.M., Gibbs, R.A., Peltonen, L., Dermitzakis, E., et al.: Integrating Common and Rare Genetic Variation in Diverse Human Populations. Nature **467**, 52–58

15. Kho, A.N., Hayes, M.G., Rasmussen-Torvik, L., Pacheco, J.A., Thompson, W.K., Armstrong, L.L., Denny, J.C., et al.: Use of Diverse Electronic Medical Record Systems to Identify Genetic Risk for Type 2 Diabetes Within a Genome-wide Association Study. Journal of the American Medical Informatics Association: JAMIA **19**, 212–218

16. Purcell, S., Neale, B., Todd-Brown, K., Thomas, L., Manuel, A.R.F., Bender, D., Maller, J., et al.: PLINK: a Tool Set for Whole-genome Association and Population-based Linkage Analyses. American Journal of Human Genetics **81**, 559–575

17. Zheng, X., Levine, D., Shen, J., Gogarten, S.M., Laurie, C., Weir, B.S.: A High-performance Computing Toolset for Relatedness and Principal Component Analysis of SNP Data. Bioinformatics **28**, 3326–3328

18. Novembre, J., Stephens, M.: Interpreting principal component analyses of spatial population genetic variation. Nat. Genetics **40**, 646–649

19. Pruim, R.J., Welch, R.P., Sanna, S., Teslovich, T.M., Chines, P.S., Gliedt, T.P., Boehnke, M., Abecasis, G.R., Willer, C.J.: LocusZoom: Regional Visualization of Genome-wide Association Scan Results. Bioinformatics **26**, 2336–2337

20. Pendergrass, S.A., Dudek, S.M., Crawford, D.C., Ritchie, M.D.: Visually Integrating and Exploring High Throughput Phenome-Wide Association Study (PheWAS) Results Using PheWAS-View. BioData Mining **5**, 5

Genotype Correlation Analysis Reveals Pathway-Based Functional Disequilibrium and Potential Epistasis in the Human Interactome

William S. Bush[1(✉)] and Jonathan L. Haines[2]

[1] Center for Human Genetics Research, Department of Biomedical Informatics,
Vanderbilt University, Nashville, TN, USA
william.s.bush@vanderbilt.edu
[2] Institute for Computational Biology, Department of Epidemiology and Biostatistics,
Case Western Reserve University, Cleveland, OH, USA
jonathan.haines@case.edu

Abstract. Epistasis is thought to be a pervasive part of complex phenotypes due to the dynamics and complexity of biological systems, and a further understanding of epistasis in the context of biological pathways may provide insight into the etiology of complex disease. In this study, we use genotype data from the International HapMap Project to characterize the functional dependencies between alleles in the human interactome as defined by KEGG pathways. We performed chi-square tests to identify non-independence between functionally-related SNP pairs within parental Caucasian and Yoruba samples. We further refine this list by testing for skewed transmission of pseudo-haplotypes to offspring using a haplotype-based TDT test. From these analyses, we identify pathways enriched for functional disequilibrium, and a set of 863 SNP pairs (representing 453 gene pairs) showing consistent non-independence and transmission distortion. These results represent gene pairs with strong evidence of epistasis within the context of a biological function.

1   Introduction

In 1912, William Bateson first coined the term epistasis, (from the Greek for standing upon) when he observed an allele at one locus masking the effect of an allele at a second, independent locus [1]. Bateson's concept has also been described as biological epistasis, similar to a biochemist's observation that variation in the physical interaction of biomolecules affects a phenotype [2, 3]. Several years later, R.A. Fisher also used the term epistasis in a statistical context, observing multi-allelic segregation patterns that can be mathematically described as a deviation from additivity in a linear model of genotypes [4]. Given the complexities of known biological pathways that involve numerous inter-molecular interactions, epistasis is presumed to be ubiquitous both statistically and biologically [3]. This belief is driven largely by the notion that networks of gene regulation and protein-protein interaction have a functional endpoint

© Springer-Verlag Berlin Heidelberg 2014
A.I. Esparcia-Alcázar et al. (Eds.): EvoApplications 2014, LNCS 8602, pp. 890–901, 2014.
DOI: 10.1007/978-3-662-45523-4_72

that may be influenced by the simultaneous presence of multiple variants in those genes [3, 5]. Epistasis has been well-documented in model organisms, and was discovered early in the field of genetics. In 1918, Lancefield described a two-locus inheritance pattern for the forked bristle phenotype in Drosophila [6]. A year later, Bridges reported statistical epistasis in Drosophila eye color, where combinations of several different alleles Mendelize with various eye color phenotypes [7]. These alleles influence a biochemical pathway controlling eye pigmentation that was described many years later [8]. More recently, studies of mouse and rat chromosome substitution strains revealed substantial epistasis in over 140 quantitative trait loci [9]. But outside the exploration of these model systems, the concept of epistasis was largely ignored in the field of human genetics. Over the last fifteen years, however, the concept has resurged as the study of common complex human phenotypes has become more prominent.

Epistasis is an attractive concept for complex traits because techniques used to characterize strong single-gene effects (such as linkage analysis) typically fail to consistently identify genomic regions that explain variation in complex traits. Twin studies and family-based segregation analysis establish heritable genetic components to these traits, yet the source of genetic trait variation often remains unknown. One potential source of the unexplained heritability is that a larger proportion of trait variation is due to epistasis -- combinations of genotypes at multiple loci -- rather than single independent loci [10]. Epistasis also fits well with the general notion that complex traits have complex underlying genetic etiologies.

Statistically, the concept of epistasis analysis is very similar in theory to haplotype analysis. Genetically, a haplotype occurs when loci in close physical proximity are linked by a stretch of chromosome and are thus often inherited together. When this occurs in a large population, these loci are said to be in *linkage disequilibrium*, and the alleles of these loci form haplotypes. Because these linked alleles have a high likelihood of being inherited together in the population, the genotypes of these loci are correlated, or alternatively their genotypes are non-independent.

It is also possible that there is correlation between genotypes of loci that are not physically linked on the chromosome. This phenomenon is sometimes referred to as *gametic phase disequilibrium*, as the alleles non-randomly segregate within gametes, but are not physically tethered on the chromosomes [11]. Even though alleles are not linked physically, they may still be linked on some higher biological level that causes the occurrence of the genotypes to be non-independent in the population, presumably by some function that confers a change in evolutionary fitness. We loosely define this phenomenon as functional disequilibrium, and the alleles of these functionally linked loci form a functional psuedo-haplotype.

The work of the International HapMap Project has characterized patterns of linkage disequilibrium among common SNPs in multiple human sub-populations. These patterns are useful for gene mapping studies to determine which portions chromosome (and marker loci) are typically co-inherited within a population, and thus reducing the number of genetic markers needed to effectively capture common variation in the genome. Also, the patterns of linkage disequilibrium established for a population identify haplotypes that can be tested for association with disease phenotypes or other traits. From a broader perspective, the HapMap provides an overview of the structural interdependencies of the human genome, which has given insight into various basic human genetics questions regarding recombination rates [12], segregation distortion [13], genomic regions of selection [14], and even mate choice [15].

Similarly, patterns of functional disequilibrium may exist in human populations that encapsulate common genetic variation into functional (rather than structural) units. These patterns may provide insight into previously unknown interdependencies in biochemical pathways, such as gene expression patterns that detrimentally or beneficially alter pathway kinetics or function. Characterizing functional disequilibrium also builds a better understanding of the general genetic variation in the interactome, and could lead to a new understanding of the biochemistry of these systems.

Functional disequilibrium should also have consequences for disease etiology. Biological pathways likely have distinct genetic architectures that influence overall function, and some genetic architectures may alter susceptibility to disease. Also, alterations in pathway function may influence how environmental exposures are processed, leading to increased or decreased risk of disease upon exposure, such as with nicotine metabolism and lung cancer [16].

As such, a catalog of pathway-based pseudo-haplotypes would be an excellent resource for conducting candidate epistasis studies using genome-wide association data. With these goals in mind, in this work we investigate the presence of functional disequilibrium, observed as correlated genotypes in non-linked SNPs, among a set of core biological pathways from the Kyoto Encyclopedia of Genes and Genomes (KEGG) database.

2   Methods

2.1   Data

For this study, we used publicly available Single Nucleotide Polymorphisms (SNPs) from the Hapmap Phase III dataset. 1,403,896 SNPs genotyped in 57 trios from Utah (Centre d'Etude du Polymorphisme Humain (CEPH) Collection) and 1,484,416 SNPs genotyped in 54 trios from the Yoruba population of Ibadan, Nigeria.

2.2   Domain Knowledge

The Kyoto Encyclopedia of Genes and Genomes [17-19] [accessed 4/27/2009] contains 203 metabolic and regulatory pathways. 183 of these pathways, containing mappings to human genes and of manageable size, were used as gene groups encompassing 4,826 unique genes. Entrez-gene IDs from the KEGG database were mapped to Ensembl gene IDs using the Ensembl database [20]. From these gene groups, 2,096,620 unique gene pairs were constructed by forming all possible pairs of genes within each gene group. Using the Ensembl Variation database, SNPs residing within the Ensembl gene physical (base-pair) start and end were mapped. SNP pairs were created by forming all possible combinations of two SNPs across the two genes. Pairs of SNPs that fall within the same gene, or within 500 KB of each other on the same chromosome were excluded from this analysis as genotypes of these SNPs may be non-independent due to linkage disequilibrium. Two-SNP models were generated using the Biofilter procedure outlined in [21].

2.3   Statistical Analysis

The non-independence of genotypes for each SNP pair was assessed within each dataset using a chi-square test of independence. The chi-square test compares the observed frequency of a genotype combination to the frequency expected if the genotypes are independent. Analysis was conducted using an internally developed C++ program incorporated into the Biofilter framework. Internal software was validated with STATA 10.1.

SNP pairs with genotypes that are non-independent were further analyzed. SNP pairs with a minor allele frequency < 0.10 were excluded from further analysis. We did not filter SNPs based on Hardy-Weinberg Equilibrium tests because unviable or lethal combinations of SNPs could appear out of Hardy-Weinberg Equilibrium if analyzed alone. For the remaining SNP pairs, r^2 correlation coefficients were computed using PLINK software [22, 23]. Using the haplotype transmission disequilibrium test implemented in PLINK, the co-transmission of SNP pairs within CEU and YRI trios was assessed. This test uses a chi-square statistic to measure multi-locus segregation distortion. In this application, the test determines if pathway-based pseudo-haplotypes observed in the parent generation are significantly over- or under-transmitted to offspring in the population, based on the parental haplotype frequencies.

3   Results

3.1   Analysis Overview

To investigate the presence of functional disequilibrium in the human genome, we used a bioinformatics approach to group genes together by functional relationships. 183 pathways from the KEGG database were used to group genes by function, and these gene groups were used to construct SNP pairs that exclude haplotype effects (the SNPs must be > 500 KB apart). Pathway-based SNP pairs were evaluated in the HapMap phase III dataset for Yoruba (YRI) and Caucasian (CEU) populations.

As an initial screen, unrelated individuals (parents) were extracted from the YRI (n=108) and CEU (n=114) datasets and a chi-square test of independence was conducted to assess the correlation between the genotypes of each pathway-based SNP pair. SNP pairs with chi-square statistics > 9.487 ($\alpha = 0.05$, df = 4) were carried forward to the next phase of analysis. To provide additional evidence of functional disequilibrium between the SNP pairs identified in the screen, we conducted a transmission disequilibrium test (TDT) to determine if there was non-independent transmission of pseudo-haplotypes (pathway-based genotype combinations) to off-spring in the sample. Because we are testing transmission of the pseudo-haplotype, this test is independent of the chi-square test used in the initial screen.

Using these analyses, we present pathways potentially enriched for non-independent genotypes in both populations, pathway-based pseudo-haplotypes that show distorted transmission, and an overall collection of gene pairs showing evidence of functional disequilibrium.

3.2   Initial Screen

In the initial screen phase, we evaluated roughly 428 million CEU SNP pairs and 479 million YRI SNP pairs generated from gene combinations found in KEGG pathways. The overall significance rate for the screen was 0.0284 for CEU and 0.0303 for YRI. Both the peptidoglycan biosynthesis (CEU 0.25, YRI 0.15) and atrazine degradation (CEU 0.16, YRI 0.04) pathways had high proportions of significant results, however these two pathways contained relatively few SNP pairs (903 and 2437 respectively). Nearly all of the pathways with high proportions of significant results in the screen were metabolic rather than regulatory pathways. In fact, several large regulatory pathway groups, such as "Pathways in cancer" (CEU 0.0045, YRI 0.0053), axon guidance (CEU 0.0116, YRI 0.0148), tight junction (CEU 0.0145, YRI 0.0186), and focal adhesion (CEU 0.011, YRI 0.0063) had a very low proportion of significant results.

In this screening phase of the analysis, we used a liberal significance threshold ($\alpha = 0.05$). Corrections for multiple hypothesis testing in this setting are difficult due to the correlation between tests; we therefore rely on a two-phase design where results from the initial screen are validated using an independent approach.

3.3   Confirmation

We exploit a unique property of genetic data to conduct a confirmatory analysis; based on Mendel's law of independent assortment, the transmission of two alleles at unlinked loci should be independent. If the potential functional SNP pairs discovered in our screening analysis are transmitted together more or less often than expected by chance, this could further indicate a functional relationship between the loci. Using the full set of 57 CEU trios and 54 YRI trios, we assessed transmission distortion using the haplotype-based TDT for all significant SNP pairs identified in the screening phase. Of the 40,312,276 tests conducted, the TDT identified 1,698,521 (4.21%) significantly distorted haplotype transmissions in CEU. For the YRI samples, 50,175,211 of 2,187,530 (4.36%) tests were significant. The proportion of significant tests by pathway is shown in figure 1.

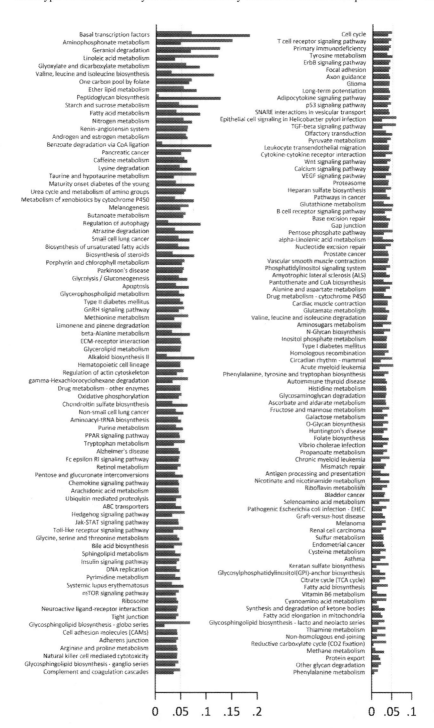

Fig. 1. Distributions of Significant Haplotype TDT. YRI in red, CEU in blue.

3.4   Gene-Gene Pairings with Putative Epistasis

From the results of our genotypic non-independence and pseudo-haplotype transmission tests, we compiled a list of SNP-SNP and subsequent gene-gene pairs that indicate putative epistasis. These SNP-SNP pairs had correlated genotypes and significant pseudo-haplotype TDT statistics in both CEU and YRI samples. The most compelling results are SNP pairs that were correlated in both samples, and also whose haplotypes were identical and similarly distorted in the TDT statistics. 863 of these cases were detected. Of these, 763 SNP pairs contained two intronic SNPs, 98 SNP pairs contained only one intronic SNP (others were coding, within a splice site, or within the 3' or 5' UTR), and only 2 SNP pairs contained two non-intronic SNPs. The two non-intronic SNP pairs are shown in table 1.

Table 1. Two non-intronic SNP pairs showing strong evidence of probable epistasis within biological pathways (pathway 1: Phospatidylinositol signaling, Pathway 2: Olfactory transduction)

SNP Pair	Gene Pair	SNP Type	CEU Freq	YRI Freq	CEU X2	YRI X2	Hap-lotype	CEU TDT	YRI TDT	Path
rs1053454	PIP4K2A	3'	0.41	0.12	0.036	0.032	C	0.026	0.026	1
rs749338	ITPR3	SYN	0.44	0.10			T			
rs2900373	OR13C9	NON	0.19	0.33	0.014	0.044	A	0.029	0.029	2
rs6679056	OR10R2	NON	0.41	0.50			A			

The distribution of gene pairs exhibiting putative epistasis by pathway is shown in figure 2. A database of all significant results from the confirmation phase of this study is also available upon request.

4   Discussion

In this work, we illustrate how a bioinformatics analysis of population-based genetic data can reveal allelic dependencies between genes of biochemical pathways. Just as the physical structure of the chromosome gives rise to correlations among genotypes called linkage disequilibrium, the structure of biochemical systems can likewise give rise to correlations among genotypes that presumably alter offspring viability or evolutionary fitness in some way, a phenomenon we loosely phrase functional disequilibrium. Gene pairs that contain SNPs exhibiting functional disequilibrium are potentially indicative of epistasis in relation to some phenotype.

The results of the initial screen seem to indicate that a higher degree of functional disequilibrium is present in more purely metabolic pathways. Despite this observation, the strongest and most consistent examples of functional disequilibrium occur mostly in regulatory and signaling pathways. Interestingly, pathways with high numbers of implicated gene pairs are heavily involved in nervous signal transduction, such as tight junction, chemokine signaling, and Wnt signaling and general nerve cell function, such as focal adhesion, axon guidance, and regulation of actin cytoskeleton. Several neurological phenotype pathways are well represented in this respect also, such as Alzheimer's disease, Parkinson's disease, and Huntington's disease. Genotypic dependencies among the elements of these disease related pathways should be further investigated, and may lead to new insights into population level risk for these conditions, and for general neurological development.

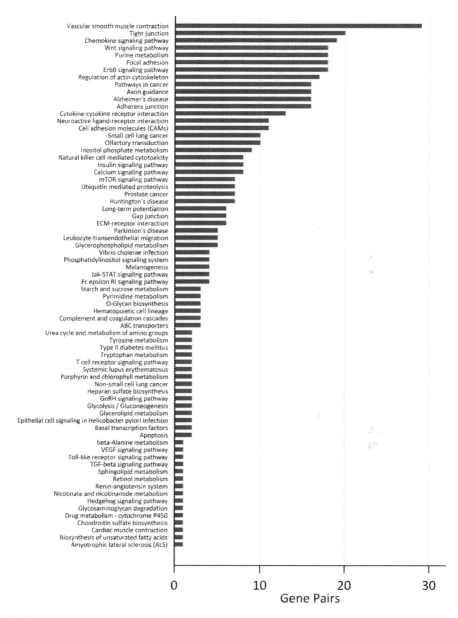

Fig. 2. Distribution of gene-pairs exhibiting strong evidence of epistasis across both CEU and YRI populations, listed by biological pathway

A specific compelling example from this study is the functional disequilibrium between rs1053454, a SNP located in the 3' untranslated region of the 1-phosphatidylinositol-5-phosphate 4-kinase type II alpha gene (*PIP4K2A*)   and rs749338, a synonymous SNP in the inositol 1,4-5-triphosphate receptor type 3 gene (*ITPR3*). These genes function in the phosphatidyinositol signaling pathway (KO:04070), a signal transduction mechanism involved in multiple physiological functions, including neurotransmitter release and other aspects of the nervous system. These two SNPs have non-independent genotypes in CEU and YRI unrelated individuals (CEU $p = 0.0366$, YRI $p = 0.0323$), and the "CT" pseudo-haplotype of these SNPs is significantly and consistently over-transmitted to offspring in both CEU and YRI samples (CEU hap-TDT = 0.026, YRI hap-TDT = 0.026).

Figure 3 illustrates the biochemical relationships between these two genes in phosphatidylinositol signaling pathway.   PIP4K2A converts 1-Phosphatidyl-1D-myo-inositol 5-phosphate to 1-Phosphatidyl-D-myo-inositol 4,5-bisphosphate, which is then converted to Inositol 1,4,5-trisphosphate (IP3) by phospholipase C enzymes (PLC).   IP3 then binds to the IP3 receptor (IP3R) to activate downstream calcium release.   Phosphatidylinositol signaling has been implicated in neuronal function and development[24].

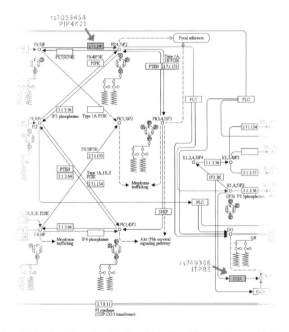

Fig. 3. Putative epistasis in the Phosphatidylinositol Signaling pathway (Adapted from KEGG KO:004070)

There are several important limitations to this work.   There are numerous pathway databases that could be used for this type of analysis.   We chose the KEGG database because it is a well-established and supported collection of biochemical and regulatory pathways.   Other sources of functional information that relate genes could be used as well, and will be explored in future research. We elected to use the phase III Hapmap data only because this data is the most recent large scale collection of genotypes from multiple ethnicities. Using the full collection of Hapmap SNPs was logistically and computationally prohibitive for this work, but is also an area of future research.

The chi-square test of independence is not appropriate for contingency tables with fewer than 5 observations per cell -- a Fisher's exact test should be used in these cases. The computational complexity of a 3x3 Fisher's exact test calculation precluded us from conducting that calculation in these experiments, and instead we filtered the significant results from the chi-square test by minor allele frequency to limit this bias. The haplotype transmission disequilibrium test implemented in PLINK software was intended for true haplotypes of SNPs in linkage disequilibrium on the same chromosome, and performs an expectation maximization (EM) procedure to estimate the chromosomal phase of the haplotypes. When performing the EM procedure on genotypes across chromosomes, the phased haplotype distribution should very closely match the observed multi-locus genotype distribution, and when compared for randomly selected example SNPs they match well. It notable, however, that we are employing this test outside its original design, and the phasing procedure may slightly alter the distribution of transmitted and untransmitted pseudo-haplotypes. Furthermore, it is extremely difficult to assess the false positive rate for this study. Linkage disequilibrium, for example among 10 SNPs of gene 1 and 7 SNPs of gene 2, causes correlations between the tests statistics of all SNP combinations spanning gene1 and gene2.

Finally, for simplicity, we are using the Ensembl definition of a gene region (3' to 5' untranslated region), which does not include upstream or downstream regulatory elements. It is likely that these regulatory elements also contain variants that in combination alter pathway function. These combinations of variants would not be detected in this analysis due to our myopic gene definition.

This work is an initial first step in cataloging correlated collections of functionally related genetic variations in multiple human populations. Future directions include expanding the datasets to include all 11 populations in the Hapmap data, expanding the bioinformatics stores to include protein-protein interaction databases and protein family information, and further refining the statistical analysis of non-independence by conducting multi-locus Hardy-Weinberg Equilibrium tests. Correlated pairs of genetic variants could further be annotated to include evolutionary conservation information, potential gene-based function (such as presence in or near a regulatory sites), and local linkage disequilibrium data. Stored in a public database system, these results could provide insight into new biochemical or regulatory mechanisms, and would provide a set of potential ethnic specific differences in pathway dynamics and function.

Acknoweldgements. This work was supported by National Institutes of Health grants AG19085, AG27944, NS32830, and NS49477.

References

1. Bateson, W.: Mendel's Principles of Heredity. Cambridge University Press, Cambridge (1909)
2. Moore, J.H., Williams, S.M.: Traversing the conceptual divide between biological and statistical epistasis: systems biology and a more modern synthesis. Bioessays **27**, 637 (2005)
3. Moore, J.H.: The ubiquitous nature of epistasis in determining susceptibility to common human diseases. Hum. Hered. **56**, 73 (2003)
4. Fisher, R.A.: Transactions of the Royal Society of Edinburgh **52**, 399 (1918)
5. Moore, J.H., Williams, S.M.: Bioessays **27**, 637 (2005)
6. Lancefield, D.E.: An autosomal bristle modifier affecting a sex-linked character. American Naturalist **52**, 462 (1918)
7. Bridges, C.B.: Specific modifiers of eosin eye color in Drosophila melanogaster. J. Experimental Zoology **28**, 337 (1919)
8. Lloyd, V., Ramaswami, M., Kramer, H.: Not just pretty eyes: Drosophila eye-colour mutations and lysosomal delivery. Trends Cell Biol. **8**, 257 (1998)
9. Shao, H., Burrage, L.C., Sinasac, D.S., Hill, A.E., Ernest, S.R., O'Brien, W., Courtland, H.W., Jepsen, K.J., Kirby, A., Kulbokas, E.J., Daly, M.J., Broman, K.W., Lander, E.S., Nadeau, J.H.: Genetic architechture of complex traits: large phenotypic effects and pervasive epistasis. Proc. Natl. Acad. Sci. USA **105**(50), 19910–19914 (2008)
10. Cordell, H.J.: Detecting gene-gene interactions that underlie dieseases. Nat. Rev. Genet (2009)
11. Wang, X., Elston, R.C., Zhu, X.: The meaning of interaction. Human Heredity **70**, 269 (2010)
12. Frazer, K.A., et al.: A second generation human haplotype map of over 3.1 million SNPs. Nature **449**, 851 (2007)
13. Zollner, S., Wen, X., Hanchard, N.A., Herbert, M.A., Ober, C., Pritchard, J.K.: Evidence for extensive transmission distortion in the human genome. Am. J. Hum. Genet. **74**, 62 (2004)
14. Sabeti, P.C., Varily, P., Fry, B., Lohmueller, J., Hostetter, E., Cotsapas, C., Xie, X., Byrne, E.H., McCarroll, S.A., Gaudet, R., Schaffner, S.F., Lander, E.S.: the International HapMap Consortium, Genome-wide detection and characterization of positive selection in human populations. Nature **449**, 913 (2007)
15. Chaix, R., Cao, C., Donnelly, P.: Is mate choice in human MHC-depedent? PLoS. Genet. **4**, e1000184 (2008)
16. Derby, K.S., Cuthrell, K., Caberto, C., Carmella, S.G., Franke, A.A., Hecht, S.S., Murphy, S.E., Le Marchand, L.: Nicotine metabolism in three ethnic/racial groups with different risks of lung cancer. Cancer Epidemiol. Biomarkers Prev. **17**, 3526 (2008)
17. Kanehisa, M., Goto, S.: KEGG: kyoto encyclopedia of genes and genomes. Nucleic Acids Res. **28**, 27 (2000)
18. Kanehisa, M., Goto, S., Hattori, M., Aoki-Kinoshita, K.F., Itoh, M., Kawashima, S., Katayama, T., Araki, M., Hirakawa, M.: From genomics to chemical genomics: new developments in KEGG Nucleic Acids Res. **34**, D354 (2006)
19. Kanehisa, M., Araki, M., Goto, S., Hattori, M., Hirakawa, M., Itoh, M., Katayama, T., Kawashima, S., Okuda., S., Tokimatsu, T., Yamanishi, Y.: KEGG for linking genomes to life and the envrionment. Nucleic Acids Res. **36**, D480 (2008)
20. Flicek, P., et al.: Ensembl 2008. Nucleic Acids Res. **36**, D707 (2008)

21. Bush, W.S., Dudek, S.M., Ritchie, M.D.: Biofilter: a knowledge-integration system for the multi-locus analysis of genome-wide association studies. In: Pac. Symp. Biocomput., p. 368 (2009)

22. Purcell, S.: PLINK 1.01. Ref Type: Computer Program

23. Purcell, S., Neale, B., Todd-Brown, K., Thomas, L., Ferrieira, M.A.R., Bender, D., Maller, J., Sklar, P., de Bakker, P.I.W., Daly, M.J., Sham, P.C.: PLINK: a tool set for whole-genome association and population-based linkage analyses. Am. J. Hum. Genet. **81**, 559 (2007)

24. Kim, D., Jun, K.S., Lee, S.B., Kang, N., Min, D.S., Kim, Y., Ryu, S.H., Suh, P., Shin, H.: Phospholipase C isozymes selectively couple to specific neurotransmitter receptors. Nature **389**, 290 (1997)

Determining Positions Associated with Drug Resistance on HIV-1 Proteins: A Computational Approach

Gonzalo Nápoles[✉], Isel Grau, Ricardo Pérez-García, and Rafael Bello

Universidad Central "Marta Abreu" de Las Villas, Santa Clara, Cuba
{gnapoles,igrau,ricardop,rbellop}@uclv.edu.cu

Abstract. The computational modeling of HIV-1proteins has become a useful framework allowing understanding the virus behavior (e.g. mutational patterns, replication process or resistance mechanism). For instance, predicting the drug resistance from genotype means to solve a complicated sequence classification problem. In such kind of problems proper feature selection could be essential to increase the classifiers performance. Several sequence positions that have been previously associated with resistance are known, although we believe that other positions could be discovered. More explicitly, we observed that using positions reported in the literature for the *reverse transcriptase* protein, the final decision system exhibited inconsistent mutations. However, finding a minimal subset of features characterizing the whole sequence involve a challenging combinatorial problem. This research proposes a model based on Variable Mesh Optimization and Rough Sets Theory for computing those sequence positions associated with resistance, leading to more consistent decision systems. Finally, our model is validated across eleven well-known *reverse transcriptase* inhibitors.

Keywords: Human Immunodeficiency Virus · Sequence Classification Problem · Drug Resistance · Variable Mesh Optimization · Rough Sets Theory

1   Introduction

More than 20 antiretroviral (ARV) drugs have been licensed to inhibit the function of essential proteins for the HIV life cycle: the protease, the integrase and the reverse transcriptase. For example, the nucleoside/nucleotide reverse transcriptase inhibitors are DNA chain terminators competing with endogenous deoxy-nucleotide triphospates for incorporation into a growing viral DNA chain [1], therefore causing the sequence termination. However, the high rate of replication combined with the high mutability of the virus leads to the rapid emergence of drug-resistant strains undermining the efforts to stop the AIDS pandemic [2]. Although individuals are usually infected with only a single or few original clones, around 10^{10} new virions are produced each day in untreated patients which results in innumerable virus variations, frequently called a quasispecies [3]. For this reason understanding the behavior of this complex retrovirus is decisive for designing more effective therapies. Here machine learning or statistical approaches could be reasonably convenient, complementing the biological knowledge obtained from experimental and clinical assays.

© Springer-Verlag Berlin Heidelberg 2014

A.I. Esparcia-Alcázar et al. (Eds.): EvoApplications 2014, LNCS 8602, pp. 902–914, 2014.

DOI: 10.1007/978-3-662-45523-4_73

Predicting the phenotype resistance to a target drug from the genotype information means to solve a sequence classification problem, which has been addressed by using several machine learning algorithms, such as: artificial neural networks, decision trees, support vector machines, among other techniques [4-8]. Recently, in reference [9] the authors introduced a model based on Fuzzy Cognitive Maps (FCM) for characterizing the influence of sequence sites over the phenotype resistance. Although this research was primarily focused on the causality interpretation, the authors observed that this model reported promising classification accuracies. Inspired by this result, in [10] was performed a study that concluded the superiority of FCM against other approaches for predicting the drug resistance / susceptibility of new mutations. But unexpectedly the global classification rate notably decreased for three classes (susceptible, intermediate and resistant). So, which was the cause of this undesirable behavior?

We suppose that this result is a direct consequence of the feature selection used for reducing the map dimensionality. More explicitly, primary positions associated with resistance were taken from [11-13] by using a biological perspective (positions having high mutability rate). Such features are able to differentiate between susceptible and resistant mutations, but they are not able to efficiently distinguish a resistant mutation from another mutation having intermediate resistance. As a result, the final decision systems computed by using this feature selection showed high inconsistency rate. It means that positions biologically relevant for the classification problems using three classes were omitted, negatively affecting the model accuracy.

However, selecting the set of sequence positions having lowest cardinality that ensures proper consistency involves a difficult combinatorial problem. This paper presents a novel model based on Variable Mesh Optimization (VMO) and Rough Sets Theory (RST) to find positions related with resistance on HIV-1 proteins. More specifically, this research is focused on the reverse transcriptase protein since it has been less studied and it is more difficult to handle. Before doing so, in next section the operators of the VMO metaheuristic are described. Section 3 introduces the proposed algorithm for computing more accurate feature selections by using a new RST-based measure and the selected optimizer. After that, the proposal is validated across eleven well-known reverse transcriptase datasets, whereas in Section 5 comments and future research directions are provided as final contribution of this paper.

2   Variable Mesh Optimization

The VMO metaheuristic is a population-based search method which was designed for solving both discrete and continuous optimization problems [14, 15]. The artificial population is organized as a mesh of nodes, that is, a collection of potential solutions which are normally generated using a random method. During the search process the mesh dynamically expands and contracts itself, moving through the solution space. It involves two stages: the first one is oriented to the generation of new nodes towards local and global optima, and also towards external nodes; whereas the second phase is oriented to the mesh contraction where only best solutions are selected as survivors of the immediate population. For better understanding, next we detail the basic operators describing the discrete VMO, considering a minimization approach.

Step 1) Generating the initial mesh: A common procedure on the population-based metaheuristics is related to the initialization of the artificial agents. Without loss of generality, the population initialization at the beginning of the algorithm execution may be grouped into two major categories: approaches based on pseudo-solutions and random methods. The first approach uses knowledge related to partial solutions, or approximations generated by a simpler algorithm. When this kind of information is not available, then agents are computed by using a random method. The present paper adopts this strategy for generating N_k initial nodes, which are uniformly distributed on the definition range $[a_i, b_i]$ for each variable. The parameter N_k regulates the minimal mesh size, that is, the number of solutions that should be preserved at the cycle $k + 1$, after applying the mesh contraction (or clearing) procedure.

Step 2) Nodes generation towards local optima [14]: This step is related to the mesh expansion process, and its goal is to generate nodes on the neighborhoods of local optima found during the search. For each mesh node n, its K-nearest neighbor nodes are computed (e.g. using the Hamming distance) and the best solution p on this neighborhood is selected (taking into account the fitness value) as a local optimum with respect to its K closest nodes. Hence, a new node n^* arises somewhere between n and p. The proximity of the newly generated node n^* to the current node n or to the local optimum p is subject to a factor μ which is calculated based on the fitness of both nodes n and p, as following equation (1) shows. In this formulation an objective function $f: R^D \rightarrow [0, 1]$ is used to compute the quality of the nodes. Notice that values closest to zero represent high quality solutions. Each component of the node n^* will take either the value of solution n or p. This process is regulated according to the next stochastic rule: "*if Uniform*$(0,1) < \mu_i(n, p)$ *then* $n_i^* = p_i$ *else* $n_i^* = n_i$".

$$\mu_i(n, p) = 1 - 0.5\frac{f(p)}{f(n)} \tag{1}$$

Step 3) Nodes generation towards the global optimum [14]: Here the idea is similar to the semantic of the previous Step 2, but now the threshold μ is calculated taking into account another component: the global best node of the mesh (g) found so far by the algorithm at the current cycle. From the optimization point of view, the goal of this step is to generate new solutions using the information of the mesh, that is, the knowledge of whole population about the fitness landscape. This knowledge allows accelerating the convergence rate, and therefore the global performance. The value assigned to each dimension of the new node n^* is defined through the next stochastic rule: "*if Uniform*$(0,1) < \mu_i(n, g)$ *then* $n_i^* = g_i$*else* $n_i^* = n_i$". Following equation (2) shows how to calculate this threshold using the fitness value of each node. Note that steps related to the generation of new mesh nodes (Step 2 and 3) guarantee a suitable equilibrium between exploration and exploitation of the solution space. However, only using information of optimal solutions the algorithm may prematurely converge to suboptimal solutions, decreasing the metaheuristic performance.

$$\mu_i(n, g) = 1 - 0.5\frac{f(g)}{f(n)} \tag{2}$$

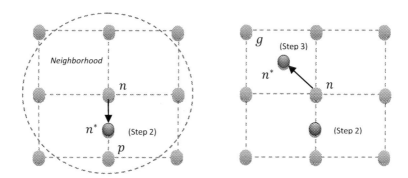

Fig. 1. Mesh expansion during steps 2 and 3 of the VMO metaheuristic: a) nodes generation towards local optima, and b) nodes generation towards the global optimum

Step 4) Mesh expansion [14]: In order to complete the expansion stage, the mesh is stretched from its outer nodes, i.e. using nodes located on the frontier of the current mesh at the k-cycle. The frontier is composed by those nodes having lowest norm (called internal nodes), and by those which greater norm (called external nodes). Here a factor ϖ_i^k is calculated at each cycle, to ensure that the mesh expansion declines all over the search process. The semantic of this procedure is based on the next rule: "*if $Uniform(0,1) < \varpi_i^k$ then $n_i^* = r_i$ else $n_i^* = e_i$*", where r_i denotes a random state for the ith dimension, and e is a node belonging to the mesh frontier (including internal as well as external solutions). The Equation (3) shows how to compute the factor ϖ_i^k, where F_k is the number of evaluations computed at the kth cycle, F_{max} refers to the number of evaluations allowed for the algorithm execution, whereas σ_i^0 represents the initial displacement for each dimension and σ_i^1 is its final value.

$$\varpi_i^k = (\sigma_i^0 - \sigma_i^1) * \frac{F_{max} - F_k}{F_{max}} + \sigma_i^1 \tag{3}$$

Step 5) Mesh contraction [14]: It selects those nodes of the current mesh that will be used as the survivors of the immediate population. Although it is often desirable to select nodes with the best evaluation, it is recommended to apply a clearing procedure to increase the diversity among the nodes. In this paper we use a very simple clearing operator: if two nodes have the same genome (and therefore the same fitness value) then the repeated solution will be replaced by a mutation of the global best individual found so far. For simplicity the number of mutation point is automatically estimated as $m = D/10$, where D is the dimensionality of the optimization problem. Notice that other alternatives may be adopted, although for a discrete search space is preferable to exploit optimal solutions. After that, all nodes are evaluated and those having lowest value will be selected as members of the next mesh. Generally speaking, the VMO metaheuristic has demonstrated to be quite efficient to find minimal reducts in feature selection tasks [14]. That is why we believe that VMO is an apt optimizer to locate the sequence sites associated with drug resistance on HIV proteins.

3   Feature Selection on the Reverse Transcriptase Protein

The present section is oriented to establish the methodology concerning to the feature selection on the HIV-1 reverse transcriptase protein. To do that, we first introduce some basic aspects related to the Rough Set Theory, which plays an important role on the evaluation function that should be optimized. One of the advantages of using this theory for analyzing data is that it is based solely on the original data and does not require any external information. On the other hand, the optimization phase is focused on selecting those sequence positions strongly related with resistance. It means to solve, by using the VMO metaheuristic, a challenging combinatorial problem having $2^{201} - 1$ possible states, given that the reverse transcriptase mutations primarily occur between site 40 and 240. We also present a more competent measure for quantifying the degree of consistency resulting from the future selection at each stage, therefore increasing the accuracy of the proposed methodology.

3.1   Rough Set Theory for Analyzing Inconsistent Information

The Rough Sets Theory (RST) is a suitable technique for modeling uncertainty arising from inconsistency [16]. It uses a pair of approximations to describe a set, which are based exclusively on the original data and does not require any external knowledge. More explicitly, let us suppose an information system $S = (U, A)$, where U is a non-empty finite set of objects called the Universe, whereas A is a non-empty finite set of attributes. So, a decision system is any information system expressed as $DS = (U, A \cup \{d\})$, where $d \notin A$ is the decision attribute. Following equations (4) and (5) show the formalization of the lower and upper approximation for a set $X \subseteq U$ and a subset of attributes $B \subseteq A$. Here $[x]_B$ denotes the set of inseparable objects associated to x (equivalence class) according to the inseparability relation B. The objects in B_*X are categorically members of X, while the objects in B^*X are possibly members of the set X. Notice that this model does not consider any tolerance of errors.

$$B_*X = \{x \in U : [x]_B \subseteq X\} \tag{4}$$

$$B^*X = \{x \in U : [x]_B \cap X \neq \emptyset\} \tag{5}$$

On the basis of the relation of inseparability, the consistency of the decision system can be analyzed. When two inseparable objects belong to different classes of decision, the decision system is said to be inconsistent, otherwise it is consistent. For example, let the partition $Y = \{Y_1, Y_2, \ldots, Y_m\}$ of the universe U according to the values of the decision feature d, where the subsets Y_i are called class of decision. Next equation (6) shows the formulation of the coefficient $Y_B(Y)$ called *quality of classification*, which expresses the relative percentage of objects that can be correctly classified using the inseparability relation B. If $Y_B(Y) = 1$ then the decision system is consistent, hence that there is not any pair of objects in U that is inseparable and that belong to different classes. If $Y_B(Y) < 1$ then the decision system is inconsistent, and the computed value is precisely that, which indicates the degree of consistency. This measure has been successfully used as a heuristic value in feature selection tasks.

$$\Upsilon_B(Y) = \sum_{i=1}^{m} |B_* Y_i| \Big/ |U| \qquad (6)$$

However, this measure could be improved. Frequently the available HIV datasets are strongly imbalanced, meaning that the number of resistant mutations is notably greater than the number of susceptible mutations. For such cases the coefficient $\Upsilon_B(Y)$ could report misleading results. For better understanding of this affirmation, let us consider a decision system having 180 resistant mutations and only 17 susceptible. As well, expect that $|B_* Y_0| = 0$ and $|B_* Y_1| = 178$, where Y_0 denotes the set of susceptible objects, whereas Y_1 is the set of resistant instances. According to the equation (6) the degree of consistency $\Upsilon_B(Y) \approx 0.9$, but it is easy to perceive that only the resistant cases will be correctly classified. For this reason, this paper introduces a new measure called *imbalanced classification quality* (see next equation). It attempts computing the consistency degree for datasets having high ratio between classes.

$$\Upsilon'_B(Y) = \frac{1}{m} \sum_{i=1}^{m} \frac{|B_* Y_i|}{|Y_i|}, |Y_i| \neq 0 \qquad (7)$$

Notice that the coefficient $\Upsilon'_B(Y)$ is very restrictive since it requires proper balance between the cardinality of the lower approximations. This aspect is often desirable for computing high-quality feature selections. It improves the quality of the knowledge-discovery process, which uses this decision system as a learning set, particularly in the construction of classifiers [17]. Following section provides a complete description of the optimization methodology, being able to discover the sequence sites associated with resistance on the HIV-1 reverse transcriptase protein.

3.2   Feature Selection Using VMO and RST

The purpose of the learning algorithm is to generate binary nodes through the discrete VMO metaheuristic defined in previous Section 2. Each node or solution $n \in \{0,1\}^D$ denotes a D-dimensional point on the search space, assuming that D is the number of positions unfolding the reverse transcriptase sequence ($D = |A| = 201$). Thus, the ith position of each node is related to the presence or absence of the ith attribute into the decision system. More specifically, if $n_i = 1$ then the ith attribute should be retained into the decision system as a member of the subset B. If $n_i = 0$ then the ith sequence position should be excluded from the decision system analysis.

In brief, the number of objects belonging to the set B depends on the active sites, that is to say $|B| = |n|$, where $1 \leq |n| \leq |A|$. It attempts to answer a simple question: is the ith sequence position directly associated with the drug resistance target? At the beginning, the learning algorithm uses random nodes, which are generated without preliminary knowledge about the solution search space. This population is iteratively improved using the VMO rules, until the maximal number of generations is reached. At the end, the best sampled solution is returned. But a crucial aspect should still be solved: how to measure the node's quality? Equation (8) shows the objective function used in this paper, considering a minimization approach.

$$f(n) = \phi_1(1 - Y'_{B_n}(Y)) + \phi_2(|B_n|/D) \tag{8}$$

The above objective function has two components: the first factor is oriented to guarantee high level of consistency over the decision system, whereas the second one is focused on reducing the number of active attributes. In this formulation n denotes a mesh node, B_n is the set of sequence positions associated to active components of the current solution n, whereas $D = |A|$ represents the number of possible positions that could be included into the feature selection. An important aspect in this equation is that we use the imbalanced classification quality $Y'_{B_n}(Y)$, instead of using the standard classification quality $Y_B(Y)$. It increases precision of the final feature selection leading to high-quality decision systems. Additionally, we introduce two new parameters $0 < \phi_1, \phi_2 < 1$ for controlling the importance that experts confer to the imbalanced classification quality $Y'_{B_n}(Y)$ regarding the number of selected features.

For the proposed problem we strongly suggest that $\phi_1 > \phi_2$ since the consistency degree of the decision system is a central aspect in classification tasks. Hence, the aim of this learning methodology is to minimize the number of attributes describing the whole protein, but always preserving the knowledge. The objective function $f(.)$ gets its optimal value when a minimal subset of attributes B' is found, and the imbalanced classification quality is equal to 1. It means that the optimal value for the objective function is equal to $\phi_2 |B'|/201$. The closest to $\phi_2 |B'|/201$ the heuristic value, the more desirable the feature selection associated to the node. Following we conducted some experiments across eleven well-known reverse transcriptase inhibitors, showing the reliability of the proposed model in feature selection tasks.

4   Experimental Framework and Simulations

In order to validate the proposal we used 11 reverse transcriptase datasets taken from Stanford Drug Resistance Database [18]. These datasets are grouped into two kinds of reverse transcriptase drugs: nucleoside/nucleotide and non-nucleoside inhibitors. The nucleoside/nucleotide drugs are: Lamivudine (3TC), Abacavir (ABC), Zidovudine (AZT), Stavudine (D4T), Zalcitabine (DDC), Didanosine (DDI), Emtricitabine (FTC) and Tenofovir (TDF); whereas nonnucleoside are: Delavirdine (DLV), Efavirenz (EFV) and Nevirapine (NVP). Before presenting the experimentation framework we introduce a characterization of the inconsistency features of selected datasets, once the feature selection adopted from literature [11-13] is completed.

It should be mentioned that datasets correspond to Antivirogram™ assay but only taking into account the classification problem using three classes. Besides, the reverse transcriptase mutations are often characterized by deletions and insertions resulting in non-homogeneous instances. In order to cope with this situation some methods have been proposed. For example, in [19] the authors introduce a new learning algorithm called Dynamic Backpropagation Through Time which was specifically designed for training Recurrent Neural Networks using variable length instances. But in all the experiments performed next we ignore mutations having more than an amino acid at a sequence position (i.e. only regular instances were considered).

Table 1. Characterization of reverse transcriptase datasets resulting after applying the feature selection adopted from the literature (taking into account both classification problems)

| Drug | Taking into account two classes | | | | Taking into account three classes | | | | |
	#S	#R	$\Upsilon_B(Y)$	$\Upsilon'_B(Y)$	#S	#I	#R	$\Upsilon_B(Y)$	$\Upsilon'_B(Y)$
3TC	18	173	0.9842	0.9415	18	18	155	0.9319	0.9229
ABC	11	43	1.0000	1.0000	11	22	21	1.0000	1.0000
AZT	14	95	0.9724	0.9537	14	21	74	0.7339	0.7250
D4T	29	22	1.0000	1.0000	29	13	9	1.0000	1.0000
DDC	13	14	0.9259	0.9258	13	7	7	0.9259	0.9267
DDI	19	20	0.9487	0.9486	19	10	10	0.6666	0.7403
FTC	4	51	1.0000	1.0000	4	0	51	1.0000	1.0000
TDF	13	10	1.0000	1.0000	10	3	6	0.8947	0.9111
DLV	16	141	0.9044	0.6697	16	32	109	0.6114	0.5179
EFV	11	130	0.9858	0.9506	11	37	93	0.7801	0.7699
NVP	21	182	0.9043	0.5872	21	15	173	0.7129	0.4443

From the above results we can notice that both RST-based measures decreased for datasets using three classes. It suggests that the biological positions reported in the literature are insufficient for characterizing the sequence from the computational point of view. For better understanding, let us analyze the dataset EFV after applying the feature selection described above, considering three classes (susceptible, intermediate and resistant). As a result, the reduced dataset has 60 objects having identical genome but associated to different resistance level. For example, the sequence "VALKNVVN YYGHFM" will be classified as resistant and intermediate at the same time, which evidently is a critical inconsistency that affects the overall performance of machine learning classifiers. This unfavorable behavior is also observed in remaining datasets, mainly associated to highly resistant and intermediate mutations.

The goal of this research is to find a feature selection involving a minimal number of positions ensuring proper consistency. The parameter settings used in this paper is detailed as follow: the number of initial nodes at each cycle is set to 50, the maximum mesh size is $N = 200$, the number of closest neighbors is $K = 3$, whereas the number of iterations adopted for the algorithm execution is set to 400. In addition, the factor controlling the relative importance of the system consistency is $\phi_1 = 0.8$, whereas the weight associated to the node's norm is $\phi_2 = 1 - \phi_1 = 0.2$. The reader should notice that the proposed methodology is mainly oriented to preserve the system knowledge, although it also tries to reduce the number of selected features.

Figures 2-9 show the list of positions found by the proposal for nucleoside/ nucleotide drugs. Due to the stochastic nature involving our model, the optimization phase is performed 30 times for each dataset, and then the best sample is assumed (i.e. the node with lowest norm and also best RST-based measure, having high similarity regarding the sites determined in clinical or experimental studies). Besides, we report mutations that take place in such positions, taking into account datasets information.

Towards this objective, each amino acid sequence is compared with the sequence of a wild-type subtype B laboratory strain, and then the differences between each position reported in datasets and the wild-type sequence are computed.

K	T	A	D	Q	P	M	K	L
65	69	98	123	151	157	184	219	228
R	D	S	E	M	A	V	N	H
N	N	G	N			I	Q	R
		K	S				R	F
		G					E	
		A					T	
		I						

Fig. 2. Mutations observed in sites found as relevant to Lamivudine (3TC), regarding a wild-type laboratory strain. Bold sequence sites denote new positions discovered by the algorithm.

K	K	R	D	I	M	L	K
65	70	83	123	135	184	210	219
R	R	K	E	M	V	W	N
G			N	V			Q
E				T			R
				L			E
							T

Fig. 3. Mutations observed in sites found as relevant to Abacavir (ABC), regarding a wild-type laboratory strain. Bold sequence sites denote new positions discovered by the algorithm.

A	D	K	V	K	I	D	G	R	T
62	67	102	118	122	135	177	190	211	215
V	N	Q	I	E	M	N	A	K	Y
G		R		Q	V	E	S	S	F
E		M		P	T	G	E	D	I
					L			G	E

Fig. 4. Mutations observed in sites found as relevant to Zidovudine (AZT), regarding a wild-type laboratory strain. Bold sequence sites denote new positions discovered by the algorithm.

E	D	F	M	E	T
44	67	77	184	203	215
D	N	L	V	K	Y
	G		I		F
					I

Fig. 5. Mutations observed in sites found as relevant to Stavudine (D4T), regarding a wild-type laboratory strain. Bold sequence sites denote new positions discovered by the algorithm.

F	R		T		M	I	L	
77	83		139		184	202	210	
L	K		R		V	V	W	

Fig. 6. Mutations observed in sites found as relevant to Zalcitabine (DDC), regarding a wild-type laboratory strain. Bold sequence sites denote new positions discovered by the algorithm.

T	V	A	K		V	M	I		L
69	75	98	102		179	184	202		228
K	I	G	Q		D	V	V		H
N		S			I	I			R
D									

Fig. 7. Mutations observed in sites found as relevant to Didanosine (DDI), regarding a wild-type laboratory strain. Bold sequence sites denote new positions discovered by the algorithm.

I	K	K	A	Y		T	M	Q
63	64	70	98	115		165	184	207
K	R	R	G	F		A	V	D
H		S					I	E

Fig. 8. Mutations observed in sites found as relevant to Emtricitabine (FTC), regarding a wild-type laboratory strain. Bold sequence sites denote new positions discovered by the algorithm.

D	F		Q	G	H	R	H
67	77		174	190	208	211	221
G	L		R	A	Y	K	Y
N						T	
						A	

Fig. 9. Mutations observed in sites found as relevant to Tenofovir (TDF), regarding a wild-type laboratory strain. Bold sequence sites denote new positions discovered by the algorithm.

In the above figures plain-text positions denote sequence sites known to contribute to resistance to the target drug. In contrast, bold positions denote new sequence sites found by the proposed algorithm that have been previously associated with resistance to other drugs but not to the explored inhibitor, or they are not frequently considered into the scientific literature [11-13]. It is important to remark that reported positions induce a perfect partition of resistance classes (i.e. the quality of classification is equal to one). It means that the resulting decision system has accurate consistency, which is a desirable feature in prediction tasks. Also the norm of the optimal solutions (number of sequence position associated with drug resistance) is considerably lower than other computational approaches. On the other hand, it is fair to mention that in our research many mutations having deletions or insertions were omitted.

Let us to examine, as an example, discovered positions for Abacavir. For this drug only 8 sequence sites were associated with resistance: 65, 70, 83, 123, 135, 184, 210, and 219. Sites 65, 70, 184, 210, and 219 were confirmed by different mutation panels, but in the literature positions 83, 123 and 135 are rarely considered. Such positions are usually mutated in other HIV subtypes [12, 20, 21] and hence they should be carefully examined. While reference [20] catalogues sites 35, 83, 122, 123, 135, 200 and 211 as non-resistance polymorphic, Kantor and Katzenstein [21] confirmed that mutations at these positions (in particular 43 and 211) may play an essential role in drug resistance evolution and increase viral fitness. It actually confirms the reliability of the proposed model, although deeper biological analysis is still required. Next Table 2 portrays such sequence positions found as relevant to non-nucleoside drugs.

Table 2. Positions found by the proposed methodology as relevant to non-nucleoside drugs

Drug	List of mutations for sites selected by the model as significant for each drug
DLV	98, 101, 103, 106, 108, **135**, 138, **142**, **162**, **173**, **178**, 179, 181, 188, 190, **196**, 219, 225
EFV	**60**, 98, 100, 101, **102**, 103, 106, **123**, **157**, **178**, 181, **184**, 188, 190, **208**, 230, 236
NVP	**65**, **69**, 100, 101, 103, 106, **122**, **123**, 138, **178**, 179, 181, 188, 190, **215**, 230, 236

It should be mentioned that computed positions are not unique, since the convexity of the evaluation function (8) leads to a strong multimodal problem where numerous global optima exist. More explicitly, the model is capable to find several nodes with lowest norm inducing a proper consistency over datasets. Conversely, interesting it is the fact that some unconsidered positions (e.g. 135, 157 or 179) are always found as relevant to nucleoside/nucleotide drugs. It suggests that newly discovered positions are important to the HIV-1 resistance mechanism. What is more, the authors of this research believe that detected mutations in such positions (in combination to other accessory mutations) are responsible to the resistance dissimilarity on non-susceptible sequences. This hypothesis is a result of the characterization of reduced datasets: only using biological evidence we detected inconsistent patterns associated to intermediate and resistant mutations (see Table 1). But using the computational information these contradictions were removed leading to high-quality datasets.

5   Conclusions

Determining the sequence positions associated with drug resistance on HIV proteins is a decisive task to understand the complex behavior of this retrovirus. Many of these positions have been experimentally determined (e.g. from clinical assays), however, this knowledge is not conclusive. Being more precise, in this paper we demonstrated that reduced reverse transcriptase datasets, resulting from primarily sites suggested by biological studies, show inconsistency. It suggests that these positions can distinguish between susceptible and resistant mutations, but they do not efficiently discriminate a resistant mutation from another having intermediate resistance.

Based on these considerations this paper proposed a supervised algorithm to find a more complete characterization of the reverse transcriptase sequence. With this goal in mind we used a relatively new metaheuristic called Variable Mesh Optimization as discrete optimizer. As well we adopted some elements from the Rough Sets Theory to compute the quality of the generated nodes. Simulations results were promising since the proposed methodology confirmed well-known positions, and also found new sites which are rarely associated with drug resistance. Of course, discovered sites should be rigorously studied via biological experiments, although they are a tangible start-point to develop more effective reverse transcriptase inhibitors. Future work will be focused on computing more descriptive patterns from reported positions.

References

1. Tang, M.W., Shafer, W.R.: HIV-1 Antiretroviral Resistance – Scientific Principles and Clinical Applications. Drugs. **72**(9), 1–25 (2012)
2. Kierczak, M., et al.: A Rough Set-Based Model of HIV-1 Reverse Transcriptase Resistome. Bioinformatics and Biology Insights. **3**, 109–127 (2009)
3. Perelson, A.S., et al.: HIV-1 dynamics in vivo: virions clearance in vivo, infected cell life-span, and viral generation time. Science. **271**(5255), 1582–1586 (1996)
4. Beerenwinkel, N., et al.: Computational methods for the design of effective therapies against drug resistant HIV strains. Bioinformatics. **21**, 3943–3950 (2005)
5. Rhee, S.Y., et al.: Genotypic predictors of human immunodeciency virus type 1 drug resistance. PNAS. **103**, 17355–17360 (2006)
6. Woods, M., Carpenter, G.A.: Neural Network and Bioinformatic Methods for Predicting HIV-1 Protease Inhibitor Resistance. Technical Report 02215 (2007)
7. Saigo, H., Uno, T., Tsuda, K.: Mining complex genotypic features for predicting HIV-1 drug resistance. Bioinformatics. **23**, 2455–2462 (2007)
8. Bonet, I., Arencibia, J., Pupo, M., Rodriguez, A., García, M.M., Grau, R.: Multi-Classifier Based on Hard Instances – New Method for Prediction of Human Immunodeficiency Virus Drug Resistance. Current Topics in Medicinal Chemistry. **13**, 685–695 (2013)
9. Nápoles, G., Grau, I., Bello, R., Grau, R.: Two-steps learning of Fuzzy Cognitive Maps for prediction and knowledge discovering on the HIV-1 drug resistance. Expert Systems with Applications. **41**, 821–830 (2014)
10. Grau, I., Nápoles, G., García, M.M.: Predicting HIV-1 Protease and Reverse Transcriptase Drug Resistance Using Fuzzy Cognitive Maps. In: Ruiz-Shulcloper, J., Sanniti di Baja, G. (eds.) CIARP 2013, Part II. LNCS, vol. 8259, pp. 190–197. Springer, Heidelberg (2013)
11. Shafer, R.W.: Genotipic testing for Human Immodeficiency Virus type 1 drg resistance. Clinical Microbiology Reviews. **15**(2), 247–277 (2002)
12. Cane, P., Green, P., Fearnhill, E., et al.: Identification of accessory mutations associated with high-level resistance in HIV-1 reverse transcriptase. AIDS. **21**(4), 447–455 (2007)
13. Johnson, V.A., Calvez, V., Günthard, H.F., et al.: Update of the Drug Resistance Mutations in HIV-1. Topics in HIV Medicine. **21**(1), 6–14 (2013)
14. Bello, R., Puris, A., Falcón, R., Gómez, Y.: Feature Selection through Dynamic Mesh Optimization. In: Ruiz-Shulcloper, J., Kropatsch, W.G. (eds.) CIARP 2008. LNCS, vol. 5197, pp. 348–355. Springer, Heidelberg (2008)
15. Puris, A., Bello, R., Molina, D., Herrera, F.: Variable mesh optimization for continuous optimization problems. Soft Computing. **16**, 512–525 (2012)
16. Pawlak, Z.: Rough sets. Int. J. of Information and Computer Sciences. 11, 341–356 (1982)
17. Bello, R., Verdegay, J.L.: Rough sets in the Soft Computing environment. Information Science. **212**, 1–14 (2012)

18. Rhee, S.Y., et al.: Human immunodeciency virus reverse transcriptase and protease sequence database. Nucleic Acids Research. **31**, 298–303 (2003)
19. Grau, I., Nápoles, G., Bonet, I., García, M.M.: Backpropagation Through Time Algorithm for training Recurrent Neural Networks using variable length instances. Computación y Sistemas. **17**(1), 15–24 (2013)
20. Kearney, M., Palmer, S., Maldarelli, F., et al.: Frequent polymorphism at drug resistance sites in HIV-1 protease and reverse transcriptase. AIDS. **22**(4), 497–501 (2008)
21. Kantor, R., Katzenstein, D.: Drug resistance in non-subtype B HIV-1. Journal on Clinical Virology. **29**(3), 152–159 (2004)

GPMS: A Genetic Programming Based Approach to Multiple Alignment of Liquid Chromatography-Mass Spectrometry Data

Soha Ahmed[1]([✉]), Mengjie Zhang[1], and Lifeng Peng[2]

[1] School of Engineering and Computer Science, Wellington, New Zealand
{soha.ahmed,mengjie.zhang}@ecs.vuw.ac.nz
[2] Victoria University of Wellington, 600, Wellington 6140, New Zealand
lifeng.peng@vuw.ac.nz

Abstract. Alignment of samples from Liquid chromatography-mass spectrometry (LC-MS) measurements has a significant role in the detection of biomarkers and in metabolomic studies.The machine drift causes differences between LC-MS measurements, and an accurate alignment of the shifts introduced to the same peptide or metabolite is needed. In this paper, we propose the use of genetic programming (GP) for multiple alignment of LC-MS data. The proposed approach consists of two main phases. The first phase is the peak matching where the peaks from different LC-MS maps (peak lists) are matched to allow the calculation of the retention time deviation. The second phase is to use GP for multiple alignment of the peak lists with respect to a reference. In this paper, GP is designed to perform multiple-output regression by using a special node in the tree which divides the output of the tree into multiple outputs. Finally, the peaks that show the maximum correlation after dewarping the retention times are selected to form a consensus aligned map.The proposed approach is tested on one proteomics and two metabolomics LC-MS datasets with different number of samples. The method is compared to several benchmark methods and the results show that the proposed approach outperforms these methods in three fractions of the protoemics dataset and the metabolomics dataset with a larger number of maps. Moreover, the results on the rest of the datasets are highly competitive with the other methods.

1 Background

LC-MS is commonly applied to both proteomic and metabolomic experiments. In LC-MS proteomics analysis, the sample is subjected to proteolytic digestion which results in a mixture of peptides. The resulting fraction of peptides mixture is then separated by liquid chromatography [1]. The peptides are then eluted at different retention times and detected by the mass spectrometer after ionization based on their mass to charge ratios [2]. Therefore, the resulting spectrum is a 3D map, called LC-MS map, which consists of mass to charge ratio (m/z), retention time (RT) and ion intensity count (Int). LC-MS can be used for providing quantitative and qualitative information about the proteins in a biological sample

© Springer-Verlag Berlin Heidelberg 2014
A.I. Esparcia-Alcázar et al. (Eds.): EvoApplications 2014, LNCS 8602, pp. 915–927, 2014.
DOI: 10.1007/978-3-662-45523-4_74

[2]. Such information is useful in several applications including system biology, functional genomics and biomarker detection. For these applications to be successful, ideally the m/z and RT of the same molecule at different spectra among the LC-MS replicate runs detected in the same LC-MS platform should be the same. However, this is not always the case. In particular, there is a large shift and sometimes distortion in RT between different runs [2]. In addition, the m/z values show smaller distortion which introduces ambiguity in peak matching in comparative analyses. Moreover, the variations in RT may show non-linear deviations and can be greater than predicted [1]. Therefore, an effective algorithm is required to address two main tasks, the first is to match the peaks arising from the same peptides at different runs within certain m/z and RT windows and the second is to find the correct transformation of the RTs in order to make comparison [3] between the intensity values effectively.

The methods for alignment of LC-MS spectra can be classified into two groups. The first group is the raw-based methods, which select the set of significant peaks from raw data and use these peaks as a reference for aligning the data. These methods can avoid the errors due to feature detection but they have high computational cost [4]. The second group is the peak-based methods where the alignment is done after extracting features and grouping corresponding features (peaks) from different LC-MS runs [2]. However, feature extraction and centroidization can introduce some errors [4]. Therefore, the quality of the alignment algorithm will depend mainly on the quality of these preprocessing paradigms.

Examples of raw-based methods include the hidden Markov Models (HMMs) approach presented in [5], where the alignment of RT and the normalization of the peak intensities were done at the same time. HMMs were used to represent the correct retention times and the parameters of the model were estimated using the maximum likelihood estimation. A star-wise manner alignment of either raw or feature maps was depicted in [1] in the open source platform *OpenMS*. In the first phase, features were matched together using pose clustering followed by linear regression to correct the retention time distortion. In the second phase, the dewarped maps were combined into a consensus map by using the nearest neighbor search. The RANdom SAmple Consensus (RANSAC) algorithm was used in the *MZmine2* [6] framework to find features that fit a non-linear model within a user supplied m/z and RT tolerances. A locally-weighted scatter plot smoothing regression method was used on all the points obtained from RANSAC. Genetic algorithms were used in [7] to predict the RT dewarping function.

Most of these approaches for alignment of LC-MS data focus on solving the pairwise alignment problem, which produces somehow suboptimal results for multiple alignment problems.

Genetic programming (GP) is an evolutionary algorithm which solves a given problem by automatically evolving computer programs (functions) [8]. Initially, GP starts with random programs which are then modified using different genetic operators such as crossover and mutation based on Darwin evolution theory [8]. GP has been successfully used for alignment and forecasting of time series data

[9] and achieved good results. In particular, GP is well known for symbolic regression which provides great potential for aligning LC-MS data. However, GP has not been used for the alignment of LC-MS datasets.

1.1   Goals

The overall goal of this study is to develop a GP based method for multiple alignment of LC-MS peak maps which can correct the distortion of RT in multiple maps simultaneously. The proposed method is composed of two main phases, the first is to match the peaks across multiple maps and the second is to find the best dewarping function for the RT of the matched peaks. The method is tested on one protoemics dataset and two metabolomics datasets and compared against five benchmark algorithms. Specifically we will perform the following:

– develop an appropriate peak matching approach across multiple LC-MS maps with different number of peaks;
– design a GP method to perform multiple-output regression;
– model the terminal set of GP to perform multiple regression simultaneously; and
– investigate whether the new GP method outperforms the conventional alignment methods on these datasets.

1.2   Organisation

The rest of the paper is organised as follows. Section 2 describes the proposed approach and the new GP method. The experimental design, the datasets description and preprocessing are presented in Section 3. Section 4 reports the experimental results along with the discussions. The conclusions and future work are presented in Section 5.

2   The Alignment Approach

The objective of the alignment of LC-MS maps (we refer to each sample or run as a map) is to produce a consensus map which contains matching peaks of the same molecules from each map after transformation of RTs. In other words, the aim is to produce peak lists which have similar m/z and RT values in order to perform comparison of intensity values effectively.

The alignment approach proposed here works with peak data which has a much smaller amount of data than the raw maps. Therefore, it can be used to develop faster dewarping techniques. Figure 1 shows the overview of the proposed alignment approach which starts with taking the peak lists as inputs. The main aim of alignment is to find the possible transformations that maps the RT points of one map (reference map) $(r_1, r_2, ..., r_n)$ to the corresponding points of the other maps $(m_1, m_2, ..., m_x)$. To achieve this objective, the most matched partners must be detected by the peak matching approach which is used as an intermediate step to allow GP to search for the optimal transformation. The peak lists which have different number of peaks are passed to the peak matching

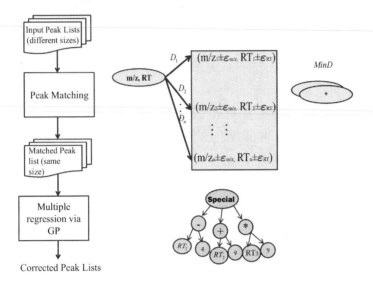

Fig. 1. Overview of the alignment approach

phase to detect the matched peak lists between the reference map and the other maps $((r_1, m_1), (r_2, m_2)....(r_n, m_n))$.

For pairwise alignment, GP can be used directly to evolve the transformation function. However, the multiple alignment of multiple maps requires a different structure of the evolved programs of GP to determine the transformation of the multiple maps. Therefore, a new GP multi-branch tree approach is developed for correcting RTs of multiple maps simultaneously. Finally, GP outputs the corrected peak lists. The two phases of the alignment approach are described below. For presentation convenience, the new approach is called GPMS.

2.1   Peak Matching

The first phase of the approach is to identify the significant matching peaks across all maps. The criteria for peak matching is the distance between the m/z and RT the reference map and the other maps. The procedure for peak matching is as follows:

1. Randomly select a map from the dataset as a reference map $R = (r_1, r_2, ..., r_n)$.
2. For each peak $(m/z_i, RT_i, Int_i)$ in the reference map, find the list of peaks in the next map $M = (m_1, m_2, ..., m_n)$ within a predefined m/z $(m/z_i \pm \varepsilon_{m/z})$ and RT $(RT_i \pm \varepsilon_{RT})$ tolerances and with the same charge.
3. Select the nearest neighbor (1-NN) peak from the list of peaks in the current map with respect to m/z, RT and Int, and add the two peaks as significant peaks of the reference and current maps into the consensus map. The distance between the peaks is measured using the Euclidean distance between m/z, RT and Int. More weight is given to m/z due to the fact that RT and Int

are much more tolerable than m/z. The Euclidean distance is given by:

$$ED = \sqrt{(W_1^2 * (R_{m/z} - M_{m/z})^2 + W_2^2 * (R_{RT} - M_{RT})^2 + W_3^2 * (R_{Int} - M_{Int})^2)}$$

where ED is the Euclidean distance between the two peaks of the reference (R) and the current (M) maps and $W_1 = 0.7$, $W_2 = 0.2$ and $W_3 = 0.1$.

4. Mark the selected peak on the current map as a processed peak so that it will not be selected again as a nearest neighbor to another peak.

5. Repeat step 2- 4 on all the maps until all the peaks in all maps are processed. If there is no corresponding peak found in half of the maps, all significant peaks related to this peak are removed from the significant peak lists.

After identifying the matching peaks across all maps, the list of matching pairs is passed to GP to correct the RT values.

2.2   GP Multi-Branch Regression for Multiple Alignment

Unlike most of the previous RT alignment algorithms, our GP method corrects RTs of all maps simultaneously. The main advantage of this regression GP technique is that it can work efficiently. Another advantage is not having the requirement of a specific *gold standard* reference map for alignment of the rest of the maps. In other words, any map can be selected as a reference to align the rest of the maps. In this approach, we use the tree-based GP [10] for this task but we modified the tree structure as multi-branch tree. In the multi-branch GP approach, each individual is composed of several branches and each branch is responsible for evolving a part of the solution [10,11]. The final solution is integrating all these partial solutions through a special node which represents the root node [12,13]. The number of children of the special node is equal to the number of maps to be aligned. The children of the root node are the functions. The function node can also take other function nodes as its children. The terminal nodes of each branch are the RTs of a specific map and a random constant. The same branch cannot contain RTs from different maps. The structure of the multiple-output regression tree is shown in Figure 2.

   In the rest of the section, we will describe terminal set, function set and the fitness function of the new GP method.

2.3   Terminal and Function Sets

An LC-MS sample is a 3D map composed of the m/z values, RTs and the intensity counts (Ints). The objective here is to correct the RTs of all maps to the corresponding RTs of the reference map. Therefore, the terminal set is composed of the RTs of N maps. We consider each input to GP as N RTs dimensions (equal to number of maps). For example, if we have three maps, each input to the terminal set is composed of three RT variables. We also used a random generated constant in the range of [-10,10] in the terminal set. Hence, our terminal set is composed of RTs values of all maps and random constants values. The function set used for this problem is $F = \{+, -, \times, \%, cos\}$, where

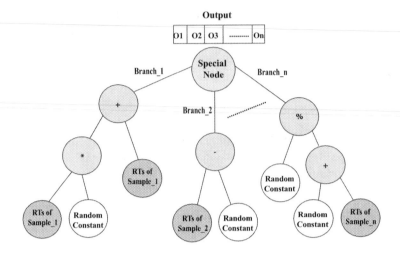

Fig. 2. Tree structure in the Multiple Alignment GP

% is the protected division operator which returns zero if the division is by zero. The aim of using *cos* operator is to evolve non-linear function for prediction and regression of the complex RTs deviations. The outputs (O_i) of each map are collected by the special node which is the root of the tree.

2.4   Fitness Function

For function approximation tasks, the performance can be measured as an error between the predicted and the real target values. As we have multiple outputs, each output corresponds to RTs of one map in the dataset, we calculate the sum of errors between the multiple outputs (which are the estimated outputs of the genetic programs) and the reference map output. The root mean square error (RMSE) is used as a fitness function. Thus the GP framework is to minimize the fitness so that the generated programs lead to minimum error between the RTs to be predicted. The RMSE fitness function is given by:

$$RMSE = \sqrt{\frac{\sum_{i=1}^{N} \sum_{j=1}^{M} (RT_{ij} - \hat{RT}_{ij})^2}{N}}$$

where N and M are the number of maps and the number of RTs to be corrected in each map respectively. RT_{ij} is the ith real RT value of the jth map while $\hat{RT}_{ij}$ is the ith estimated RT value of the jth map by the GP program.

3   Experimental Design

3.1   Data Sets

We tested the proposed approach on one proteomics dataset (P_1) and two metabolomics datasets (M_1, M_2) obtained from the Open Proteomics Database

(OPD) [14] and Lange et al. [1]. Dataset P_1 contains two LC-MS runs with six different fractions and it originates from an *E.coli* sample. For this dataset each fraction is composed of pairs of LC-MS runs. The dataset was analyzed using LC/MS/MS with an ESI ion trap mass spectrometer (ThermoFinnigan Dexa XP Plus). It was exported into mzXML centroided mode and preprocessed using TOPP tools [15] to produce the peak lists which consist of the m/z, RT, intensity values and ignoring the charge states. The numbers of peaks in each fraction run were between 400 to 5800. A partial ground truth was produced using the first fraction of the dataset by linking the LC-MS spectra to the MS/MS of the SEQUEST search. More details about the steps for datasets preparation, analysis, preprocessing and parameters optimisation can be found in [1]. For the two metabolomics datasets, Arabidopsis thaliana leaf tissues were analyzed using two different LC-MS setups. An API QSTAR Pulsar i (Applied Biosystems/MDS Sciex) was used to produce 44 spectra for the M_1 dataset and a MicrOTOF-Q (Bruker Daltonics) to produce 24 spectra for the M_2 dataset. Peak extraction was done using XCMS software [16] resulting in 4000 to 17600 peaks in each spectrum. The ground truth was generated in the same study by selecting the high confident peaks. Those were the peaks found in more than four runs, having the same RT and also showing a high correlation in their peak shapes.

3.2   Genetic Operators and Parameters

The initial populations of GP are generated using the ramped half-and-half method. Each population consists of 1000 individuals in order to reduce the early convergence probability. The tournament selection method is used to select the individuals which can perform well for reproducing the new generations. The size of the tournament is set to 5. The standard crossover and mutation are used here with ratios of 80%, 19% respectively. Elitism is also used with a ratio of 1%. The depth of each individual is kept between 2 and 8. Each evolutionary process stops at the maximum generation 30 unless a perfect error of zero is found. The process is repeated for 30 independent runs. The random seed for each of the 30 runs in each set of experiments are all different. The peak matching phase parameters are as follows: the m/z tolerance and RT tolerance are set to 1.5, 100 respectively for dataset P_1 for all the fractions. For datasets M_1, M_2 the m/z tolerance and RT tolerance are set to 0.011, 20 respectively for both of them. Those parameters were selected after several tuning and they achieved the best results for our method. The GP implementation used in our experiments is the Evolutionary Computing Java-based (ECJ) package [17]. Table 1 describes the run time parameters used in the experiments.

3.3   Benchmark Algorithms

We compared our approach with previous published results of five publicly available benchmark algorithms for alignment of LC-MS maps which are: msInspect [18], MZmine [19], SpecArray [20], XAlign [21] and XCMS [16]. msInspect [18] works in a star-wise manner which aligns all maps with respect to a specific

Table 1. GP run time parameters

Parameter	Value
Initialization method	Ramped Half-and Half
Initial tree Depth	2
Maximum tree depth	8
Generations	30
Mutation probability	19%
Crossover Rate	80%
Elitisim	1%
Population Size	1000
Selection type	Tournament
Tournament Size	5
m/z tolerance	1.5, 0.011,0.011 for P_1, M_1, M_2 respectively
RT tolerance before correction	100, 20, 20 for P_1, M_1, M_2 respectively

reference map, which is the map with minimum number of peaks. The process starts with the selection of the most intense peak within a certain RT tolerance and the removal of the rest of the peaks. After that, pairing the remaining peaks with peaks of similar m/z is performed. Smoothing spline regression is used for dewarping and finally divisive clustering is used to obtain the consensus map. The main disadvantage of this approach is the removal of less intense peaks which might cause the loss of many important peaks. MZmine [19] works by scoring the similarity of all features against a master list and if the score is "good enough" the feature is assigned to the best matched row. MZmine does not perform any transformation of RT. SpecArray [20] schema works as pairwise alignment and combine the pairwise aligned maps into a consensus map until all maps are aligned. SpecArray is not applicable to a dataset with a big number of maps. XAlign [21] also works in a star-wise manner and selects the most intense peaks within a user defined m/z and RT tolerance, the map with the minimum difference to the average RTs is chosen as a reference map. After dewarping the RT, the features with high correlation coefficient are selected to form the consensus map. XCMS [16] works as a multiple alignment approach where peak matching is performed in the first phase by using a fixed interval bin and using kernel density estimation to determine the distribution of the features. Boundaries of regions with features that have similar RTs are selected. Finally non-linear regression is used to correct RTs.

3.4   Performance Evaluation

The performance of the proposed approach is measured through the precision (PR) and recall (RE) measures. Precision is the probability that a found item is relevant, which is in our case the percentage of the correctly aligned peaks among all the peaks aligned by the approach.

$$PR = \frac{\text{Number of correctly aligned peaks}}{\text{Total number of peaks aligned}}$$

Whereas, recall is the probability that a relevant item is found (the percentage of the correctly aligned peaks among the peaks in the ground truth [22]).

$$RE = \frac{\text{Number of correctly aligned peaks}}{\text{Total number of peaks in the ground truth}}$$

The harmonic mean of the precision and recall is measured through the F-measure [22].

$$\text{F-measure} = \frac{2*\text{PR}*\text{RE}}{\text{PR}+\text{RE}}$$

Precision and recall of alignment were calculated using the evaluation script provided by Lang et al. [1].

4   Results and Discussions

4.1   Effectiveness Performance

GPMS is initially tested for the pairwise alignment on P_1 which is available in six different fractions. P_1 shows a large deviation in RT values which is a challenge for the alignment tool to correct the RT. Tables 2 and 3 show the results of the five conventional approaches compared to our approach notated as GPMS. As shown in Tables 2 and 3, GPMS achieved much better performance than msInspect and SpecArray in all the three datasets. GPMS outperformed all other methods in three fractions of P_1. For the first fraction (00), the mean of the 30 runs of GPMS is better than msInspect by 44 % in terms of precision, 30% in terms of recall and 38% in terms of F-measure. For the other approaches GPMS improves the precision by 1-25%, the recall and F-measure by 1-21%. For fraction (20), GPMS achieves similar performance as XCMS and has the third rank after MZmine and XAlign. GPMS performs better than msInspect, SpecArray and XCMS for fraction 40. Furthermore, our new method is the third best after MZmine and XAlign for the same fraction. For fractions (60) and (100), GPMS outperforms all other methods in terms of precision (which reaches 1.00 for fraction (100)) and F-measure. The proposed method has the best recall in fraction (60) while in fraction (100) it has the third best recall after Xalign and XCMS. Finally for fraction (40), the performance of GPMS was slightly better to XCMS and it is the second best after MZmine. In general, for P_1 the proposed method outperforms the other methods in three fractions, the second best in two fractions and third best in one fraction.

For datasets M_1 and M_2 which contain 44 and 24 maps respectively, the challenge for the alignment approach on these complex metabolomics datasets is to assign the most suitable matches and to correct the RT distortion across multiple maps. SpecArray did not manage to produce any results for these complex alignment tasks. As shown in Table 3, GPMS appears to be more powerful in aligning a large number of maps as in the dataset M_1 (44 maps). For M_1, it has better performance than other methods by 1-31% in terms of precision and 2- 49% with respect to F-measure. This suggests that the proposed method can be more powerful for multiple map alignment. The performance of GPMS outperforms msInspect in terms of precision by 41.87%, XCMS by 1% and it is equal to XCMS for M_2. In terms of recall, it is much better than msInspect and SpecArray. GPMS is better than msInspect by 53% and it outperforms SpecArray which did not manage to achieve results in terms of F-measure. Overall, the

Table 2. Proteomics dataset P_1 alignment results

Fraction	Measure	msInspect	MZmine	SpecArray	XAlign	XCMS	GPMS		
							Min	Max	Mean ±St.Dev.
00	Precision	0.38	0.81	0.61	0.82	0.58	0.82	**0.83**	**0.83±0.003**
	Recall	0.52	0.75	0.61	0.82	0.62	0.82	**0.83**	**0.82±0.004**
	F-measure	0.44	0.78	0.61	0.82	0.60	0.82	**0.83**	**0.82±0.004**
20	Precision	0.45	**0.88**	0.62	0.85	0.80	0.80	0.82	0.81±0.0100
	Recall	0.56	**0.87**	0.62	0.85	0.81	0.80	0.80	0.80±0.0000
	F-measure	0.50	**0.87**	0.62	0.85	0.80	0.80	0.81	0.81±0.0060
40	Precision	0.48	**0.90**	0.75	0.87	0.80	0.83	0.84	0.84±0.002
	Recall	0.63	**0.87**	0.75	**0.87**	0.81	0.81	0.81	0.81±0.0
	F-measure	0.54	**0.88**	0.75	0.87	0.80	0.82	0.82	0.82±0.003
60	Precision	0.54	0.84	0.71	0.87	0.75	**0.91**	**0.91**	**0.91±0.000**
	Recall	0.73	0.79	0.71	0.87	0.78	**0.92**	**0.92**	**0.92±0.000**
	F-measure	0.62	0.81	0.71	0.87	0.76	**0.91**	**0.91**	**0.91±0.005**
80	Precision	0.57	**0.94**	0.74	0.90	0.88	0.90	0.90	0.90±0.000
	Recall	0.70	**0.92**	0.74	0.90	0.89	0.89	0.89	0.89±0.000
	F-measure	0.63	**0.93**	0.74	0.90	0.88	0.90	0.90	0.90±0.0040
100	Precision	0.56	0.92	0.77	0.96	0.96	**1.00**	**1.00**	**1.00±0.000**
	Recall	0.82	0.94	0.77	**0.96**	**0.96**	0.94	0.94	0.94±0.000
	F-measure	0.67	0.93	0.77	0.96	0.96	**0.97**	**0.97**	**0.97±0.000**

Table 3. Metabolomics datasets M_1 and M_2 alignment results

Fraction	Measure	msInspect	MZmine	SpecArray	XAlign	XCMS	GPMS		
							Min	Max	Mean ±St.Dev.
M_1	Precision	0.46	0.74	-	0.70	0.70	**0.77**	**0.77**	**0.77±0.003**
	Recall	0.27	0.89	-	0.88	**0.94**	0.89	0.91	0.9±0.004
	F-measure	0.34	0.81	-	0.78	0.80	**0.83**	**0.83**	**0.83±0.001**
M_2	Precision	0.47	**0.84**	-	0.79	0.78	0.79	0.79	0.79±0.001
	Recall	0.23	**0.98**	-	0.93	**0.98**	0.90	0.90	0.90±0.000
	F-measure	0.31	**0.90**	-	0.85	0.87	0.84	0.84	0.84±0.001

performance of GPMS is the second best with respect to precision, third best with respect to recall and F-measure in M_2. In general, GPMS is among the top two methods or even performs best (00, 60, 100 of P_1, M_1).

4.2 Efficiency Performance

Another comparison is done in terms of the run time of each of the methods and the results are shown in Table 4. For all the datasets, GPMS average run time is much better than all other approaches. The computational cost (in terms of time) of GPMS is more lower than the rest of methods, which represents another advantage of GPMS. For all the datasets, GPMS improves the efficiency by an order of magnitude than the rest of the methods except for XCMS. GPMS is also more efficient than XCMS in terms of computational time for P_1 and M_2. Moreover, the efficiency of GPMS for M_2 in one of the runs is also better than XCMS.

Table 4. Comparison of run time of GPMS with other approaches (in seconds)

Dataset	msInspect	MZmine	SpecArray	XAlign	XCMS	GPMS		
						Min	Max	Mean ±St.Dev.
P_1	60	40.2	111	69	54	**4.1**	**9.8**	**6.1±1.20**
M_1	720	1200	-	3060	54	**36.34**	**64.92**	64.92±4.97
M_2	2160	2640	-	2100	348	**81.10**	**94.20**	87.37±3.23

| | Input | | Output | |
	T_0	T_1	T_0	T_1
(SPE T_0 (- (- T_1 9.05) (cos T_1)))	1263.95	1271.96	1263.95	1263.89
	1307.84	1315.58	1307.84	1307.09
	1708.72	1717.28	1708.72	1708.10

(a)

| | Input | | Output | |
	T_0	T_1	T_0	T_1
(SPE T_0 (+ T_1 17.56))	182.95	165.425	182.95	182.98
	111.45	94.12	111.45	111.68
	455.08	438.12	455.08	455.68

(b)

Fig. 3. (a) An evolved model for fraction (00) with some examples of inputs and outputs of the model. (b) An evolved model for fraction (100).

4.3   Interpretation of the Evolved Regression Models

Some examples of the evolved regression models are shown below:

Figure 3 shows some examples of the evolved models for fractions (00) and (100). SPE refers to the special node which is the root node collecting the multiple outputs of the tree. T_0 refers to the RTs of the first map while T_1 refers to the RTs of the second map. The first map (T_0) is selected as the reference map in which the RTs of both maps should be corrected according to it. The dewarping functions of both inputs are determined simultaneously through the multiple branches. As shown in Figure 3 (a), GP managed to determine the correct amount of shift for the RTs of the second map (T_1) through a non linear dewarping model in the second branch of the tree. The RTs of first map (T_0) (the first branch of the tree) is kept the same as it has been selected as the reference map. Some examples are shown in the same figure where the inputs to the models and the mapped outputs after correction shows that GP has successfully aligned the maps with respect to the reference map. The evolved model for fraction (100) is shown in Figure 3 (b) where the GP dewarping function has managed to correct the distortion of RTs through a linear function. Examples of inputs and outputs of fraction (100) are also shown in Figure 3 (b).

5   Conclusions and Future Works

In this paper, we propose a new method for multiple alignment of LC-MS peak data. The proposed method has two phases. In the first phase, the partner peaks across multiple maps are detected in order to form the matched peak lists. In the second phase, the matched peak lists are passed to GP to perform the correction of RTs of all maps simultaneously. The new GP approach is depicted by dividing the tree into multiple branches, in which each branch produces the output dewarping function of each map with respect to the reference map. The proposed GP-based method (GPMS) was tested on one protoemics dataset of six different fractions and two metabolomics datasets. The results show that GPMS achieves better precision, recall and F-measure than five other LC-MS benchmark alignment methods for three fractions of the protoemics dataset and one metabolomic dataset which has larger number of maps. This suggests that GPMS is more powerful in multiple alignment of LC-MS data. The proposed method also shows very competitive results in the rest of the datasets. GPMS in general is always either the best or among the two top methods for these datasets. Furthermore, the proposed GP method is much more efficient in terms of computational time than the benchmark methods.

Although very preliminary, this paper represents the first work of GP for multiple alignment of LC-MS data, and the competitive results of the proposed method encourages us to do further investigation in this direction in the future.

For future works, we will consider merging a clustering scheme to the first phase of the approach. This will relate to another interesting but challenging research direction, i.e. using GP for peak matching through a clustering approach which can match the partner peaks better.

References

1. Lange, E., Gröpl, C., Schulz-Trieglaff, O., Leinenbach, A., Huber, C.G., Reinert, K.: A geometric approach for the alignment of liquid chromatography-mass spectrometry data. Bioinformatics **23**(13), 273–281 (2007)
2. Vandenbogaert, M., Li-Thiao-Te, S., Kaltenbach, H., Zhang, R., Aittokallio, T., Schwikowski, B.: Alignment of LC-MS images, with applications to biomarker discovery and protein identification. Proteomics **8**(4), 650–672 (2008)
3. Lange, E., Tautenhahn, R., Neumann, S., Gropl, C.: Critical assessment of alignment procedures for LC-MS proteomics and metabolomics measurements. BMC Bioinformatics **9**(1), 375–394 (2008)
4. Heidi Vhmaa, Ville R. Koskinen, W.H.: PolyAlign: A versatile LC-MS data alignment tool for landmark-selected and automated use. International Journal of Proteomics, pp. 1–10 (2011)
5. Listgarten, J., Neal, R., Roweis, S., Wong, P., Emili, A.: Difference detection in LC-MS data for protein biomarker discovery. Bioinformatics **23**(2), 198–204 (2007)
6. Pluskal, T., Castillo, S., Villar-Briones, A., Oresic, M.: MZmine 2: Modular framework for processing, visualizing, and analyzing mass spectrometry-based molecular profile data. BMC Bioinformatics **11**, 395 (2010)
7. Palmblad, M., Mills, D.J., Bindschedler, L.V., Cramer, R.: Chromatographic Alignment of LC-MS and LC-MS/MS Datasets by Genetic Algorithm Feature Extraction. Journal of the American Society for Mass Spectrometry **18**(10), 1835–1843 (2007)
8. Poli, R., Langdon, W.B., McPhee, N.F.: A field guide to genetic programming. Lulu Enterprises, UK Ltd. (2008)
9. Ahalpara, D.P.: Improved forecasting of time series data of real system using genetic programming. In: Proceedings of the 12th Annual Conference on Genetic and Evolutionary Computation, GECCO 2010, pp. 977–978. ACM, New York (2010)
10. Smart, W.D., Zhang, M.: Probability based genetic programming for multiclass object classification. In: Proceedings of the 8th Pacific Rim International Conference on Artificial Intelligence, pp. 251–261 (2004)
11. Rodríguez-Vázquez, K., Oliver-Morales, C.: Multi-branches Genetic Programming as a Tool for Function Approximation. In: Deb, K., Tari, Z. (eds.) GECCO 2004. LNCS, vol. 3103, pp. 719–721. Springer, Heidelberg (2004)

12. Zhang, Y., Zhang, M.: A multiple-output program tree structure in genetic programming. In: Proceedings of The Second Asian-Pacific Workshop on Genetic Programming, pp. 1–12 (2004)

13. Defoin Platel, M., Vérel, S., Clergue, M., Chami, M.: Density Estimation with Genetic Programming for Inverse Problem Solving. In: Ebner, M., O'Neill, M., Ekárt, A., Vanneschi, L., Esparcia-Alcázar, A.I. (eds.) EuroGP 2007. LNCS, vol. 4445, pp. 45–54. Springer, Heidelberg (2007)

14. Prince, J., Carlson, M., Lu, R., Marcotte, E.: The need for a public proteomics repository. Nat. Biotechnol. **22**, 471–472 (2004)

15. Kohlbacher, O., Reinert, K., Gropl, C., Lange, E., Pfeifer, N., Schulz-Trieglaff, O., Sturm, M.: TOPP-the OpenMS proteomics pipeline. Bioinformatics **23**(2), 191–197 (2007)

16. Smith, C., Want, E., O'Maille, G., Abagyan, R., Siuzdak, G.: XCMS: processing mass spectrometry data for metabolite profiling using nonlinear peak alignment, matching, and identification. Anal. Chem. **78**(3), 779–787 (2006)

17. White, D.R.: Software review: the ECJ toolkit, 65–67 (2012)

18. Bellew, M., Coram, M., Fitzgibbon, M., Igra, M., Randolph, T., Wang, P., May, D., Eng, J., Fang, R., Lin, C., Chen, J., Goodlett, D., Whiteaker, J., Paulovich, A., McIntosh, M.: A suite of algorithms for the comprehensive analysis of complex protein mixtures using high-resolution LC-MS. Bioinformatics **22**(15), 1902–1909 (2006)

19. Katajamaa, M., Miettinen, J., Oresic, M.: MZmine: Toolbox for processing and visualization of mass spectrometry based molecular profile data. Bioinformatics **22**, 634–636 (2006)

20. Li, X., Yi, E., Kemp, C., Zhang, H., Aebersold, R.: A software suite for the generation and comparison of peptide arrays from sets of data collected by Liquid Chromatography-Mass Spectrometry. Molecular & Cellular Proteomics: MCP **4**(9), 1328–1340 (2005)

21. Zhang, X., Asara, J., Adamec, J., Ouzzani, M., Elmagarmid, A.: Data preprocessing in liquid chromatography/mass spectrometry-based proteomics. Bioinformatics **21**(21), 4054–4059 (2005)

22. Voss, B., Hanselmann, M., Renard, B., Lindner, M., Kthe, U., Kirchner, M., Hamprecht, F.: Sima: simultaneous multiple alignment of lc/ms peak lists. Bioinformatics **27**(7), 987–993 (2011)

An Integrated Analysis of Genome-Wide DNA Methylation and Genetic Variants Underlying Etoposide-Induced Cytotoxicity in European and African Populations

Ruowang Li, Dokyoon Kim, Scott M. Dudek, and Marylyn D. Ritchie[✉]

Center for Systems Genomics, 512 Wartik, The Pennsylvania State University,
University Park, PA, 16802, USA
{rvl5032,duk27,sud23,mdr23}@psu.edu

Abstract. Genetic variations among individuals account for a large portion of variability in drug response. The underlying mechanism of the variability is still not known, but it is expected to comprise of a wide range of genetic factors that interact and communicate with each other. Here, we present an integrated genome-wide approach to uncover the interactions among genetic factors that can explain some of the inter-individual variation in drug response. The International HapMap consortium generated genotyping data on human lymphoblastoid cell lines of (Center d'Etude du Polymorphisme Humain population - CEU) European descent and (Yoruba population - YRI) African descent. Using genome-wide analysis, Huang et al. identified SNPs that are associated with etoposide, a chemotherapeutic drug, response on the cell lines. Using the same lymphoblastoid cell lines, Fraser et al. generated genome-wide methylation profiles for gene promoter regions. We evaluated associations between candidate SNPs generated by Huang et al and genome-wide methylation sites. The analysis identified a set of methylation sites that are associated with etoposide related SNPs. Using the set of methylation sites and the candidate SNPs, we built an integrated model to explain etoposide response observed in CEU and YRI cell lines. This integrated method can be extended to combine any number of genomics data types to explain many phenotypes of interest.

1   Introduction

Genome-wide analysis is a step forward from candidate gene based approaches because it reduces biases associated with candidates' selections. While candidate gene approaches have successfully identified genes involved in cellular mechanisms of drugs, they failed to uncover interactive relationships among the genetic factors that may be explaining much of the variations in drug effects. The cellular susceptibility of the drug is potentially affected by multiple genetic components through non-linear interactions among the components. However, due to the exponential increases of computational calculations when modeling interactive relationships, most research have been focused on finding linear models associated with drug response [1–5]. To uncover the unsolved variances, we propose an integrated genome-wide analysis that

© Springer-Verlag Berlin Heidelberg 2014
A.I. Esparcia-Alcázar et al. (Eds.): EvoApplications 2014, LNCS 8602, pp. 928–938, 2014.
DOI: 10.1007/978-3-662-45523-4_75

identifies interactions among genetic factors from multiple types of genomic data to model the drug response.

The International HapMap Consortium genotyped cell lines of various population groups including trios of European descent (CEU) and Yoruba descent (YRI) [6]. Because these cell lines are publicly available, they have also been used to study methylation patterns at gene promoter regions [7]. Together, genotype variations and methylation levels enable us to study the relationship between these genetic components and drug responses. Previously, through genome-wide analysis, Huang et al. have identified a set of genetic variants that are associated with chemotherapeutic drug induced cytotoxicity in CEU and YRI cell lines, respectively [5]. We used the set of SNPs as dependent variables and methylation levels as independent variables and applied regression models for each unique SNP-methylation combination. We identified SNPs that are correlated with methylation levels, or methylation quantitative trait loci (mQTLs), across the genome using publicly available genome-wide methylation data, generated on the same cell lines [7]. Together, using the genetic variants and correlated methylation levels at gene promoters, we found interactive genetic models that can explain a portion of variability in chemotherapeutic drug response in CEU and YRI cell lines. The integrative models achieved higher explanatory power of drug response in these cell lines than previously published linear models.

Etoposide is a topoisomerase II inhibitor [8] and is used in treatment of cancers including testicular cancer, lung cancer, germinal cancer, endometrial carcinoma, and Kaposi's sarcoma. Treatment with etoposide can lead to severe side effects such as fatigue, bone marrow suppression, diarrhea and acute promyelocytic leukemia [9–11]. Thus, our goal is to identify SNPs and methylation interactions that can best explain the differential etoposide responses in CEU and YRI cell lines. This result paves the way for better understanding of genetic components involved in drug responses, which is a necessary step towards personalized drug prescription for cancer patients.

2   Methods

2.1   Genetic Variants Correlated with Etoposide IC$_{50}$

Huang et al. have identified sets of SNPs that are associated with etoposide IC$_{50}$ in CEU and YRI population, respectively. The inhibition of cell line growth is measured as IC$_{50}$, which is the drug concentration required to stop cell growth by 50%. The method for identifying the SNPs is as follows. A total of 87 and 89 cell lines from HapMap CEU and YRI populations, respectively, were exposed to increasing concentrations of etoposide. SNP genotypes were obtained from the International Hapmap website (HapMap.org) (release 21). Genotyping errors and extreme outliers were removed and only SNPs within 10kb up or downstream of a gene were retained. Quantitative transmission disequilibrium test (QTDT) analysis was performed on Box-Cox transformed IC$_{50}$ values and filtered SNPs with sex as a covariate. Using p < 0.0001 as threshold for significance, 122 and 51 SNPs were significantly associated with etoposide IC$_{50}$ in CEU and YRI, respectively [5]. The associated SNPs were used for subsequent downstream analysis.

2.2   Candidate SNPs and Methylation Levels Association

Gene promoter regions methylation data were generated by Fraser et al. [7]. The data was downloaded from Gene Expression Omnibus database, accession number [GSE27146]. A total of 84 CEU and all (89) YRI cell lines that were tested for etoposide response were used to measure promoter region methylation levels. Over all, methylation levels at 27,578 CpG sites near transcription start sites were measured using the quantitative BeadChip assay (Illumina, San Diego, CA, USA). Several steps, which are described in detail in Fraser et al. [7]. were taken to account for the background noise. Briefly, first, the average background intensity was subtracted from the raw intensity to adjust for sample variations. Then, to minimize batch effects of different arrays, background adjusted raw data were quantile normalized [7].

Regression models were used to test for possible candidate SNPs and methylation level association. Significant CEU and YRI SNPs were tested for their association with methylation in the same respective population. To remove the effect of gender, sex was used as a covariate in the regression model. Using a p-value cut off of 0.0003, 1109 methylation-SNP pairs were significantly associated for CEU and 270 methylation-SNP pairs were significant for YRI, of which 385 and 176 methylation sites were unique, respectively.

2.3   Interactive Model of SNPs and Methylation Levels to Predict Etoposide IC_{50}

The Analysis Tool for Heritable and Environmental Network Associations (ATHENA) is a multifunctional software package that provides machine learning tools to analyze genomics data. The software has been extensively tested and applied in simulation data and real world data with great success [12–15]. The software and its modeling processes have been described previously [16]. Briefly, we used an evolutionary algorithm, grammatical evolution neural network (GENN), to optimize artificial neural networks (ANNs), which are used to model etoposide drug response. The evolution process initiates a set of random models and these random models compete with each other through generations. The "fittest" models, or the models that maximize desired target function, can exchange components of themselves. Through transferring of the components, some models may acquire beneficial components and eventually take over the population pool. This evolution process mimics natural selection where the "fittest model" will survive at the end of evolution. The algorithm is described below.

Step 1: The data is divided into five parts for five cross validations with 4/5 for training and 1/5 for testing.

Step 2: Under population size constraint, a random population of models (ANNs) is generated.

Step 3: All models are evaluated with training data. The models with highest fitness are selected for crossover, mutation, reproduction and migration.

Step 4: Step 3 is repeated for a set number of generations. During this time, new random models are being constantly added into the population to diversify the search space.

Step 5: The best solution at the final generation is tested on the testing data and saved

Step 6: Steps 2-5 are repeated for each cross validation

Step 7: SNPs and methylation probes that appear in at least 3 out 5 cross validation models are saved as consistent variables

Step 8: All consistent variables will be modeled over the entire dataset and results in a final model

The fitness of the model aims to measure how well the model can explain the etoposide drug response, a continuous value. We used R-squared as our fitness metric to represent the percentage of drug response explained by the model. The drug response predicted by the model is scaled using the sigmoid function so that the value is between 0 and 1. As a result, we also scaled the original drug response to be between 0 and 1 using min-max scaling, where

$$Normalized\ D_i = \frac{D_i - \min(D)}{\max(D) - \min(D)} \tag{1}$$

And the R^2 is calculated as:

$$R^2 = \frac{\sum_i^n (D_{predict\ i} - \bar{D})^2}{\sum_i^n (D_i - \bar{D})^2} \tag{2}$$

$$D_i = the\ ith\ value\ of\ drug\ response$$

The final model is an artificial neural network (ANN). ANNs are widely used in data mining field to predict desired outcome. ANNs consist of nodes of input and an output. Each input node is associated with a weight and the weight is generally determined through back-propagation [17]. ANNs can have multiple layers, which make it possible for input nodes to have interactive relationships among themselves. Traditionally, the structure of the network and the input variables need to be defined before optimizing the network. However, this is not the case for genetic analysis because neither the fitness landscape nor the correct variables are known. Evolutionary algorithms can eliminate this deficiency as the network structure and correct variables are evolved automatically, driven by the data [18].

If the variables in the model contain missing values, the samples contain missing values will be removed for that evaluation. To eliminate sample loss, missing values in the SNP genotype data were replaced with 0, making the particular SNP homozygous for its corresponding sample. For 84 CEU samples, there were 176 missing values within 122 SNPs; and for 89 YRI samples there were 86 missing values within 51 SNPs. The replacement represents less than 2% of the data.

3   Results

To ensure validity of the result, each analysis was repeated with a different random seed and GENN population size (Table 1).

Table 1. GENN parameter settings

Parameter	Sample analysis	
Number of processors	16	16
Population size/ processor	20000	3000
Number of generations	2000	2000
Number of migrations	40	40
Crossover probability	0.9	0.9
Mutation probability	0.01	0.01
Random seed	Random 1/Random 2	Random 3/Random 4

Using GENN to identify the most informative SNPs to predict etoposide response, the analysis resulted in several SNPs that consistently appeared in different cross validations with different random seeds and population sizes (Table 2). Each cross validation returned a SNP interaction model that was found to be the best for a subset of cell lines. SNPs that appeared in three out of five cross validations were considered to be interesting.

Table 2. Associated SNPs and methylation in the best model

Probe name	Population	Chromosome	Host gene ID
rs647955	YRI	Chr1	C1QB
rs2605593	YRI	Chr11	C11orf75
rs6944165	YRI	Chr7	LOC647017
rs16905691	YRI	Chr10	PCDH15
cg21931212	YRI	Chr12	C12orf57
rs403029	CEU	Chr10	GATA3
rs1884679	CEU	Chr14	SLC24A4
rs2607839	CEU	Chr10	GRID1
rs9299075	CEU	Chr9	PTPRD

For YRI, the interesting SNPs were rs4770877, rs9730073, rs16905691, rs12113878, and rs9507577. We then integrated SNPs and methylation data so that we could explore interactions between SNPs and methylation levels. Using the same criteria, we identified SNPs rs647955, rs2605593, rs6944165, rs16905691 and methylation probe cg21931212 were consistently associated with etoposide. Sex was included as an input variable, but it was not incorporated in the fittest model. When we analyzed all of the consistent SNPs and methylation probes together, rs647955, rs2605593, rs9730073, rs12113878, rs16905691, and cg21931212 were selected in the final model. The r-square for the final model was $R^2 = 53.75\%$, indicating that the model can explain around 54% etoposide IC_{50} variations in the YRI population. Our model outperformed previous linear SNPs model, which attained a R^2 around 40%5. Figure 1 shows the interaction model between SNPs and methylation for YRI population.

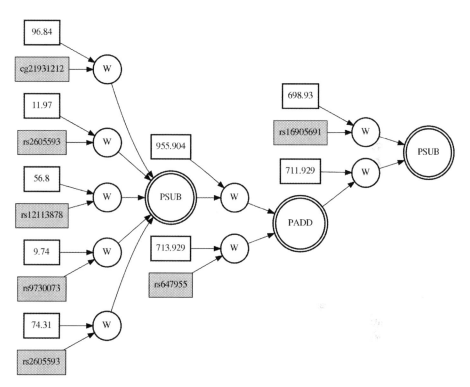

Fig. 1. Final model of SNPs and methylation interactions to predict etoposide IC_{50} in YRI (w: multiplication between constant and variable, PADD: additive node, PSUB: subtractive node)

We did not identify any consistent SNPs and methylation interactions in CEU population. For SNPs only interactions, rs403029, rs1884679, rs2607839, and rs9299075 showed consistent association with etoposide IC_{50}. We again used all of the consistent variables as input to train the final model and the final model included all four SNPs. The r-square for the final model was $R^2 = 46.16\%$, indicating that the model can explain 46% etoposide IC_{50} variations in the CEU population. Figure 2 shows the SNPs interaction model to explain etoposide IC_{50} in CEU.

934   R. Li et al.

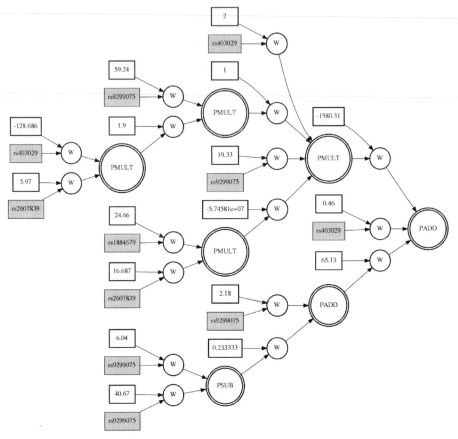

Fig. 2. Final model of SNPs interactions to predict etoposide IC$_{50}$ in CEU (w: multiplication between constant and variable, PADD: additive node, PSUB: subtractive node, PMULT: multiplicative node)

4   Conclusion and Discussion

In this study, we explored interaction relationships among SNPs and between SNPs and methylation levels to model etoposide IC$_{50}$ on HapMap CEU and YRI cell lines. The integrated genome-wide approach demonstrated the ability to combine multiple types of genomics data and identify interactive relationships within and between data sources. Due to the small sample size in this study, the results should be viewed as a proof-of-concept or pilot project for this type of data integration. Future directions will evaluate alternative data fusion techniques with ATHENA on multi-omics data to build meta-dimensional models.

Etoposide is a widely used cancer drug for testicular cancer, lung cancer, germinal cancer, endometrial carcinoma, and Kaposi's sarcoma. However, the drug also has severe side effects for the patients [9–11]. Better understanding of the mechanism of the drug is a crucial step towards personalized prescription of the drug based on patients' genetic makeup. Genetic variations are the most fundamental and the most widely studied genetic factor in relation to the drug response, as Huang et al. previously reported that a group of SNPs were correlated with etoposide IC_{50} in CEU and YRI population. Using the correlated SNPs, they built a linear additive model to explain the variability of IC_{50} in the two populations. Stemming from their multi-genic model, it is logical to hypothesize that etoposide's cellular mechanism could also be comprised of interactive relationship among SNPs. Recent study also suggested that phenotype associated SNPs tend to fall into function-associated regions [19]. Methylation pattern is an important marker for DNA regulatory functions and this led us to explore the interactive relationships between SNPs and methylation levels. Using SNPs and correlated methylation levels, we were able to identify several SNPs and methylation sites that consistently appeared in our models. We applied GENN on these consistent variables to build a final model for each population. For YRI population, we built an interactive model between SNPs and methylation and achieved a R^2 of 54%, exceeding models that only examined linear additive relationships between SNPs. For CEU population, we only identified consistent interactive SNPs variables. Our interaction model with four SNPs resulted in a R^2 of 46%, slightly lower than previously reported R^2 of 55%; potentially due to less number of variables in our model. Based on these results, our genome-wide integrative analysis identified novel interaction relationships between SNPs and methylation sites. This approach can be extended to integrate any number of genomics data to predict or classify a wide range of phenotypes of interest.

Modeling genetic interactions is a complex task, especially when there are a large number of variables. Models produced by GENN are dependent on parameter settings, but they generally contained around ten variables. Evaluating all possible combinations of interactions is impossible given the current computational power, so GENN uses a guided random search to make the search more feasible. In addition, there is variability between samples partitioned in each cross validation. As a result, the fittest model in each cross validations may suffer from inadequate modeling and may not be applicable to other subsets of data. Thus, we utilized a strict requirement to minimize this bias by only keeping variables that appeared in at least 3 out of 5 cross validations, ensuring that the true signal is strong and applicable to different subsets of the data. The trade off of this approach is increased number of false negatives. This is evident when we evaluated SNPs and methylation interactions in CEU population. Because there is a higher number of SNPs and correlated methylation probes in CEU compared to YRI population, the search space exponentially increased. As a result, when modeling interactions between SNPs and methylation, there were many SNPs and methylation probes that appeared in 2 out of 5 cross validations, but none appeared in at least 3. We could potentially miss some true signals by employing a strict consistency requirement, but we are also more confident about our true signals. For YRI population, our final interactive model of SNPs and methylation resulted in a R^2 of 54%, exceeding the previously reported 40% identified in linear model [5].

One should be aware that the interactive relationships produced by GENN are only statistical relationships. Our model uncovered potential genetic variants and methylation sites that could be further validated by functional studies. Some of the genetic variants are unknown but others are found to be relevant through literature search. Genetic variant of rs647955 is located in the C1QB gene. C1QB is known to be involved in systemic lupus erythematosus, an autoimmune disease20. The function of variant rs9730073 is not known, but it was also selected by Huang et al. as one of the final four SNPs used in their linear model for YRI. SNP rs12113878 is located within KLRG2 gene. KLRG2 gene has been found to be associated with prostate cancer aggressiveness and is expressed on subsets of NK/T cells21. Interestingly, rs16905691 is associated with the PCDH15 gene, which is also expressed on NK/T cells. NK/T cells are known to play a key role in defense against tumor development22. Methylation probe cg21931212 lies in C12orf57 gene, which has no known functions. However, recent genome-wide studies have identified the gene to be associated with brain and vision development [23,24]. CEU model SNPs rs9299075 and rs1884679 are located in genes PTPRD and SLC24A4, respectively and both are associated with tumor suppression and identification [25,26]. Many of our modeled genetic variants are associated with cancer and development, which is related to etoposide's drug mechanism. Further study is needed to confirm these relationships.

There are limitations to this study that warrants more future studies on the subject. The study separately analyzed etoposide's response on CEU and YRI cell lines. Previous report has shown that the two cell lines behaved similarly under etoposide [5]. Future analysis plan should include combining the two populations with race adjustment in order to find generalizable models across different cell lines, which will also greatly increase sample size and thus statistical power. It is also known that some of the model SNPs and methylations have linkage disequilibrium (LD) or correlation with each other. Exploring these related genetic factors could reveal more insights on etoposide response. eQTL analysis using gene expressions generated on the HapMap cell lines has also shown significant associations with various chemotherapeutic drug responses [4,5]. It would be interesting to integrate gene expression data as well as methylation data to model the etoposide response in future analysis. Lastly, the method for imputing missing SNPs could incorporate LD information in the future. However, the result in this study should not be affected because less than 2% of the data was missing.

The ultimate goal of this study is to identify potential models that can explain etoposide drug or toxicity response in order to better prescribe treatments to patients and improve clinical knowledge of the treatment. The integrated analysis used in this study has shown that it can identify novel interactions among genetic factors. This approach can also be applied to uncover genetic factors underlying a wide range of other phenotype and diseases.

Acknowledgment. This work was supported by the following grants: NSF Graduate Fellowship via DGE1255832, the PGRN-Statistical Analysis Resource via HL065962, and LM010040.

References

1. Huang, R.S., Duan, S., Kistner, E.O., Hartford, C.M., Dolan, M.E.: Genetic variants associated with carboplatin-induced cytotoxicity in cell lines derived from Africans. Mol. Cancer Ther. **7**, 3038–3046 (2008)
2. Huang, R.S., et al.: Genetic variants contributing to daunorubicin-induced cytotoxicity. Cancer Res. **68**, 3161–3168 (2008)

3. Huang, R.S., et al.: Identification of genetic variants contributing to cisplatin-induced cyto-toxicity by use of a genomewide approach. Am. J. Hum. Genet. **81**, 427–437 (2007)

4. Gamazon, E.R., Huang, R.S., Cox, N.J., Dolan, M.E.: Chemotherapeutic drug susceptibil-ity associated SNPs are enriched in expression quantitative trait loci. Proc. Natl. Acad. Sci. U. S. A. **107**, 9287–9292 (2010)

5. Huang, R.S., et al.: A genome-wide approach to identify genetic variants that contribute to etoposide-induced cytotoxicity. Proc. Natl. Acad. Sci. U. S. A. **104**, 9758–9763 (2007)

6. The International HapMap Consortium: A haplotype map of the human genome. Nature **437**, 1299–13320 (2005)

7. Fraser, H.B., Lam, L.L., Neumann, S.M., Kobor, M.S.: Population-specificity of human DNA methylation. Genome Biol. **13**, R8 (2012)

8. Sinha, B.K., Haim, N., Dusre, L., Kerrigan, D., Pommier, Y.: DNA strand breaks produced by etoposide (VP-16,213) in sensitive and resistant human breast tumor cells: implications for the mechanism of action. Cancer Res. **48**, 5096–5100 (1988)

9. Mistry, A.R., et al.: DNA topoisomerase II in therapy-related acute promyelocytic leuke-mia. N. Engl. J. Med. **352**, 1529–1538 (2005)

10. Ratain, M.J., et al.: Acute nonlymphocytic leukemia following etoposide and cisplatin combination chemotherapy for advanced non-small-cell carcinoma of the lung. Blood **70**, 1412–1417 (1987)

11. Thomson.Micromedex. Drug Inf. Heal. Care Prof. 24th edn. vol. 1, p. 1326 (2004)

12. Holzinger, E., Buchanan, C.: Initialization Parameter Sweep in ATHENA: Optimizing Neural Networks for Detecting Gene-Gene Interactions in the Presence of Small Main Ef-fects. In: Proc. 12th ..., pp. 203–210 (2010). doi:10.1145/1830483.1830519.Initialization

13. Holzinger, E.R., Dudek, S.M., Torstenson, E.C., Ritchie, M.D.: ATHENA Optimization: The Effect of Initial Parameter Settings across Different Genetic Models, pp. 48–58 (2011)

14. Turner, S.D., Dudek, S.M., Ritchie, M.D.: ATHENA: A knowledge-based hybrid backpropagation-grammatical evolution neural network algorithm for discovering epistasis among quantitative trait Loci. BioData Min. **3**, 5 (2010)

15. Holzinger, E.R., et al:. Comparison of Methods for Meta-dimensional Data Analysis Using in Silico and Biological Data Sets, pp. 134–143

16. Holzinger, E.R., et al.: ATHENA: a tool for meta-dimensional analysis applied to geno-types and gene expression data to predict HDL cholesterol levels. In: Pac. Symp. Biocomput., pp. 385–96 (2013). http://www.pubmedcentral.nih.gov/articlerender.fcgi?artid=35 87764&tool=pmcentrez&rendertype=abstract

17. Skapura, D.M.: Building neural networks (1995). http://dl.acm.org/citation.cfm?id=217718

18. Koza, J.R., Rice, J.P.: Genetic generation of both the weights and architecture for a neural network. In: IJCNN 1991, Seattle Int. Jt. Conf. Neural Networks ii, pp. 397–404. IEEE (1991)

19. Dunham, I., et al.: An integrated encyclopedia of DNA elements in the human genome. Nature **489**, 57–74 (2012)

20. Westra, H.-J., et al.: Systematic identification of trans eQTLs as putative drivers of known disease associations. Nat. Genet. **45**, 1238–1243 (2013)

21. Liu, X., et al.: Fine-mapping of prostate cancer aggressiveness loci on chromosome 7q22-35. Prostate **71**, 682–689 (2011)

22. Rouget-Quermalet, V., et al.: Protocadherin 15 (PCDH15): a new secreted isoform and a potential marker for NK/T cell lymphomas. Oncogene **25**, 2807–2811 (2006)
23. Salih, M.A., et al.: A newly recognized autosomal recessive syndrome affecting neurologic function and vision. Am. J. Med. Genet. A **161**, 1207–1213 (2013)
24. Akizu, N., et al.: Whole-exome sequencing identifies mutated c12orf57 in recessive corpus callosum hypoplasia. Am. J. Hum. Genet. **92**, 392–400 (2013)
25. Jiang, Y., et al.: Germline PTPRD Mutations in Ewing Sarcoma: Biologic and Clinical Implications. Oncotarget **4**, 884–889 (2013)
26. Shah, S.P., et al.: Mutational evolution in a lobular breast tumour profiled at single nucleotide resolution. Nature **461**, 809–813 (2009)

Replication of *SCN5A* Associations with Electrocardiographic Traits in African Americans from Clinical and Epidemiologic Studies

Janina M. Jeff[1], Kristin Brown-Gentry[2], Robert Goodloe[2], Marylyn D. Ritchie[10],
Joshua C. Denny[4], Abel N. Kho[5], Loren L. Armstrong[6], Bob McClellan Jr.[2],
Ping Mayo[2], Melissa Allen[2], Hailing Jin[2], Niloufar B. Gillani[2],
Nathalie Schnetz-Boutaud[2], Holli H. Dilks[2], Melissa A. Basford[7],
Jennifer A. Pacheco[8], Gail P. Jarvik[11], Rex L. Chisholm[8], Dan M. Roden[3,7,9],
M. Geoffrey Hayes[6], and Dana C. Crawford[2(✉)]

[1] Charles Bronfman Institute for Personalized Medicine,
Icahn School of Medicine at Mount Sinai, New York, NY, 10029, USA
janina.jeff@mssm.edu
[2] Center for Human Genetics Research, Vanderbilt University, Nashville, TN, 37232, USA
kristin.gentry@healthspring.com, robert.goodloe@gmail.com,
{bob.mcclellan,hailing.jin,nila.gillani,
Nathalie.boutaud,holli.h.dilks,dana.c.crawford}@vanderbilt.edu,
pxm304@case.edu, mjallentn@hotmail.com
[3] Department of Medicine, Division of Clinical Pharmacology,
Vanderbilt University, Nashville, TN, 37232, USA
[4] Department of Biomedical Informatics, Vanderbilt University, Nashville, TN, 37232, USA
josh.denny@vanderbilt.edu
[5] Division of General Internal Medicine,
Northwestern University Feinberg School of Medicine, Chicago, IL, 60611, USA
a-kho@northwestern.edu
[6] Division of Endocrinology, Metabolism, and Molecular Medicine,
Northwestern University Feinberg School of Medicine, Chicago, IL, 60611, USA
{loren-armstrong,ghayes}@northwestern.edu
[7] Office of Personalized Medicine, Vanderbilt University, Nashville, TN, 37232, USA
melissa.basford@vanderbilt.edu
[8] Center for Genetic Medicine, Northwestern University Feinberg School of Medicine,
Chicago, IL, 60611, USA
{japacheco,r-chisholm}@northwestern.edu
[9] Department of Pharmacology, Vanderbilt University, Nashville, TN, 37232, USA
dan.roden@vanderbilt.edu
[10] Department of Biochemistry and Molecular Biology, Penn State University,
University Park, PA, 16802, USA
marylyn.ritchie@psu.edu
[11] University of Washington Medical Center, Seattle, WA, 98195, USA
gjarvik@medicine.washington.edu

Abstract. The NAv1.5 sodium channel α subunit is the predominant α-subunit expressed in the heart and is associated with cardiac arrhythmias. We tested five previously identified *SCN5A* variants (rs7374138, rs7637849, rs7637849,

© Springer-Verlag Berlin Heidelberg 2014
A.I. Esparcia-Alcázar et al. (Eds.): EvoApplications 2014, LNCS 8602, pp. 939–951, 2014.
DOI: 10.1007/978-3-662-45523-4_76

rs7629265, and rs11129796) for an association with PR interval and QRS duration in two unique study populations: the Third National Health and Nutrition Examination Survey (NHANES III, n= 552) accessed by the Epidemiologic Architecture for Genes Linked to Environment (EAGLE) and a combined dataset (n= 455) from two biobanks linked to electronic medical records from Vanderbilt University (BioVU) and Northwestern University (NUgene) as part of the electronic Medical Records & Genomics (eMERGE) network. A meta-analysis including all three study populations (n~4,000) suggests that eight *SCN5A* associations were significant for both QRS duration and PR interval (p<5.0E-3) with little evidence for heterogeneity across the study populations. These results suggest that published *SCN5A* associations replicate across different study designs in a meta-analysis and represent an important first step in utility of multiple study designs for genetic studies and the identification/characterization of genetic variants associated with ECG traits in African-descent populations.

Keywords: Electrocardiographic traits · African Americans · Genetic association study · Electronic medical records · eMERGE · Epidemiology · NHANES

1   Introduction

A necessary step to establish a robust genotype-phenotype relationship in the literature is statistical replication. There are multiple challenges with replication studies, one of which is the phenotypic heterogeneity that exists between the original study and the replication study population(s). Although the use of quantitative traits or intermediate phenotypes for both the discovery and replication study can alleviate some of the expected phenotypic heterogeneity observed for complex diseases, between study differences may not be eliminated. Therefore, it is ideal to include multiple independent studies to confirm a robust genotype-phenotype association.

The quantitative traits examined here are derived from electrocardiograms (ECGs). The ECG is a useful tool in assessing electrical conduction in the heart, and perturbations in the ECG are routinely used to diagnose cardiac arrhythmias, myocardial infarction, pericarditis, and other cardiac abnormalities by measuring and recording the electrical activity of the heart [1]. The ECG begins with the P wave that occurs during atrial depolarization, and represents the electrical impulse from the sinoatrial (SA) node towards the atrioventricular (AV) node that then spreads to the left and right atrium. The PR interval is the time the electrical impulse takes to go to the sinus node to the AV node then to the ventricles (lower chambers of the heart). It is measured from the P wave to the start of the QRS complex. The QRS marks the start of depolarization of the ventricles, and the ST segment represents the ventricle once they have fully depolarized. After depolarization, the left and right ventricles repolarize, represented as the T wave on the ECG. The QT interval represents the time it takes the ventricles to depolarize and repolarize and is measured in the ECG from the start of the QRS complex to the end of the T wave. In this study, we evaluate the associations with PR interval (representing atrioventricular conduction) and QRS duration (representing intraventricular conduction).

Slower cardiac conduction is thought to contribute to cardiac arrhythmias [2]. The PR interval is influenced primarily by body mass index, increased age, and height.

QRS duration is influenced sex and somewhat by body mass index and height [3]. Clinical factors, such as hypertension, cardiac disease, and medications, in addition to genetic factors, can also cause abnormal electrical activity in the heart. Heritability studies suggest that >35% of the variation in ECG traits can be explained by genetics [4-6]. Several genetic association studies of ECG traits have been focused on genes that encode for proteins in voltage-gated ion channels [6-12]. The $NA_v1.5$ sodium channel α subunit is the predominant α-subunit expressed in myocytes and is encoded by the *SCN5A* gene, located on chromosome 3 [11,13]. Genetic association studies have identified variants in the *SCN5A* gene that are associated with long QT syndrome and Brugada syndrome [14-17]. Common variants in *SCN5A* that are associated with longer QRS are also associated with atrial fibrillation [18]. These associations have been reported to explain ~2% of the variation of ECG traits [19].

There have been several candidate gene studies performed in African Americans for *SCN5A* and ECG traits [19-21]. Although there are few genome-wide association studies in African descent populations for ECG traits, there have been at least three GWAS or fine-mapping studies on various ECG traits in African Americans [22-24]. These studies typically include African Americans ascertained from epidemiological longitudinal studies focused on cardiovascular diseases (CVD). In the present study we sought to replicate previously reported associations in *SCN5A* in two study populations of African Americans: the Third National Health and Nutrition Survey (NHANES III, n= 552) and a combined dataset (n= 455) from two biobanks linked to electronic medical records from Vanderbilt University (BioVU) and Northwestern University (NUgene) as part of the Electronic Medical Records and Genomics (eMERGE) network.

2   Methods

2.1   Study Populations and ECG Measurements

African Americans from two study populations were used for the present study (Table 1): the Third National Health and Nutrition Examination Survey (NHANES III) and participants from two biobanks, the Vanderbilt Genome-Electronic Records (VGER) and the Northwestern biobank (NUgene) as part of the eMERGE network [31]. All ECG traits followed a normal distribution and participants with QRS duration >120 m/sec were excluded from all analyses [32].

NHANES III was conducted from 1988-1994 as a complex survey that over-sampled minorities, the young, and the elderly [33]. Biospecimens for DNA extraction were collected in phase 2 of NHANES III (1991-1994). All NHANES participants were interviewed for demographic, socioeconomic, dietary, and health-related data. Additionally, all NHANES study participants undergo a detailed medical examination at a central location known as the Mobile Examination Center (MEC). Electrocardiograms (ECGs) were recorded on adult (40 years of age or greater) men and women in the mobile examination center (MEC) using a standard 12-lead resting ECG [33]. ECGs were recorded using the Marquette MAC 12 (Marquette Medical Systems, Inc, Milwaukee, Wisconsin) (U.S. DHHS, 1996). NHANES

III 12-lead ECG data were recorded with eight independent components of the 12 standard leads simultaneously. ECG data were also sampled at 250 samples per second per channel, giving the availability of multiple simultaneous ECG leads for analysis. This study was limited to self-identified non-Hispanic blacks (referred to here as African Americans) in NHANES III with normal ECG measurements. All procedures were approved by the CDC Ethics Review Board and written informed consent was obtained from all participants. Because no identifying information was accessed by the investigators, Vanderbilt University's Institutional Review Board determined that this study met the criteria of "non-human subjects."

VGER and NUgene are study sites of the National Human Genome Research Institute's electronic MEdical Records and GEnomics (eMERGE) Network [31]. The Vanderbilt study site (VGER) accesses BioVU, which is a collection of DNA samples extracted from discarded blood samples collected for routine clinical care linked to de-identified electronic medical records (EMRs) [34]. The Northwestern biobank, NUgene, combines DNA samples from consented participants with an enrollment questionnaire and longitudinal data from the EMR [31]. Study individuals from both sites were identified using a previously validated algorithm that used ECGs, laboratory data, medication exposures, and natural language processing of clinical notes [35]. Study participants included in this study had a normal ECG without evidence of cardiac disease (or abnormal ECG) before or within one month following the ECG, without concurrent use of medications that interfere with QRS duration, and who did not have abnormal electrolyte values at the time of the ECG. All ECGs had normal Bazett's corrected QT intervals (<450ms), heart rates (between 50-100 bpm), and QRS duration (65-120 ms). All participants were African American indicated by either observer reported (VGER) or self-reported (NUgene) ancestry. Both biobanks were approved by Institutional Review Boards at their respective sites.

2.2   Genotyping and Statistical Analysis

DNA was extracted from crude cell lysates from lymphoblastoid cell lines established for NHANES III participants aged 12 over [36]. We chose five SNPs that were significant at p 1.0E-4 from the original study [19] for genotyping in NHANES III. All genotyping was performed in the Center for Human Genetics Research DNA Resources Core using either Sequenom's iPLEX Gold assay on the MassARRAY platform (San Diego, CA) or Illumina's BeadXpress. All genotype data reported here passed CDC quality control (QC) metrics and are available for secondary analysis through CDC. All statistical analyses in NHANES III were performed using the Statistical Analysis Software (SAS v.9.2; SAS Institute, Cary, NC) either locally or via the Analytic Data Research by Email (ANDRE) portal of the CDC Research Data Center (RDC) in Hyattsville, MD.

Genotyping for VGER and NUgene was performed by the Center for Inherited Disease Research (CIDR) and the Broad Institute. All individuals that met the inclusion criteria (n = 501) were genotyped for >1.1 million SNPs using the Illumina 1M BeadChip at the Broad Institute. Data were cleaned by the eMERGE QC pipeline [37]. There were 46 individuals that did not meet the QC thresholds and were removed from further analysis.

Table 1. Population characteristics. *Original Study data represent data from the Jackson Heart Study abstracted from Jeff et al 2011 [19]. Mean and standard deviation was calculated for ECG traits, age, and sex for African Americans from the epidemiologic (NHANES III) and clinic-based (VGER/NUgene) study populations. Analysis of variance statistical test was performed to determine significant differences across study populations (bolded italicized data denote p<0.001 for all tests).

Trait	Original Study (n= 3,054)*		NHANES III (n= 552)		eMERGE (n = 455)	
	Mean	SD	Mean	SD	Mean	SD
Age (yrs)	*56.5*	*±11.73*	*53.9*	*±11.61*	*46*	*±15*
Sex (% female)	62%	n/a	67%	n/a	77%	n/a
Body mass index (BMI)	not reported		*29*	*±6*	*34*	*±10*
Type 2 diabetes (%)	19%	n/a	8%	n/a	20%	n/a
PR interval (msec)	171.6	±33.02	164.6	±25.56	159	±21
QRS duration (msec)	*92.3*	*±10.12*	*95.5*	*±10.90*	*82*	*±8*

Using standard linear regression, assuming an additive model, we tested each SNP for an association with PR interval and QRS duration. We did not test *SCN5A* variants with heart rate and QT interval since these SNPs were not associated with these traits in the original analysis [19]. All tests were limited to African Americans and adjusted for age and sex. We declared significance at p<0.05 uncorrected for multiple testing. Using a fixed-effects inverse-variance weighted approach, we performed a meta-analysis using the effect sizes, standard errors, and p-values from each study populations using METAL [38]. Pairwise F_{ST} was calculated between the original study and each study population using the Platform for the Analysis, Translation, and Organization of large-scale data (PLATO) [39] (Table 2).

3   Results

We abstracted data from the previously published Jackson Heart Study [19] referred to here as the "original study" for comparison with our population-based (NHANES III) and clinical (eMERGE) collections. We compared the three study populations and observed differences across study populations for age, sex, and ECG measurements (Table 1). On average, eMERGE (46 years) and NHANES III (54 years) participants were younger compared with the original study (57 years). Both eMERGE and NHANES III had more female participants (77% and 67%, respectively) compared with the original study (62%; Table 1). Additionally, the measurements QRS duration and PR interval in eMERGE were shorter compared to the other studies, which is a reflection of the more stringent selection criteria within eMERGE to select subjects without any prior heart disease or abnormalities on their ECG.

To further characterize similarities and differences between the original study and the other two study populations, we first calculated the minor allele frequency and compared these estimates across study populations. Though not statistically significant, NHANES III had a lower minor allele frequency for *SCN5A* rs7374138 (0.15) and rs11129796 (0.08) compared with the original study and eMERGE (Table 2). To further characterize study population differences at these loci, we calculated F_{ST} using the Weir and Cockerham algorithm [25] between the original study and each study site separately for each SNP (Table 2). The fixation index F_{ST} is a measure of population differentiation, and an F statistic >0.15 is indicative as a significant difference between populations. As might be expected, there were no significant differences between studies for any of the SNPs tested at this stringent threshold for population differentiation ($F_{ST}<0.019$, Table 2).

Table 2. Comparison of minor allele frequencies across studies. *Original Study data represent data from the Jackson Heart Study abstracted from Jeff et al 2011 [19]. We calculated three-way F_{ST} for all *SCN5A* SNPs to test for differences between study populations. Abbreviations: minor allele (MA) and minor allele frequency (MAF).

SNP	MA	Original Study* (n= 3,054)	NHANES III (n =552)		eMERGE (n= 455)	
		MAF	MAF	F_{ST}	MAF	F_{ST}
rs7374138	G	0.23	0.15	<0.0001	0.23	<0.0001
rs7637849	A	0.19	0.20	0.014	0.20	<0.0001
rs11129796	T	0.15	0.08	0.019	0.11	0.005
rs7629265	T	0.08	0.09	<0.0001	0.08	<0.0001
rs6768664	G	0.36	0.36	<0.0001	0.38	<0.0001

We performed single SNP tests of association for *SCN5A* SNPs identified in the original study with PR interval and QRS duration in eMERGE and NHANES III [19]. There were no significant associations (p<0.05) observed between *SCN5A* SNPs for any ECG traits in African Americans from NHANES III (Table 3, Figure). Three SNPs (rs7374138, rs7629265, and rs6768664) have a consistent direction of effect compared to the original study, despite not being statistically significant for PR interval. Likewise for QRS duration three SNPs (rs7637849, rs7374138, and rs6768664) have a consistent direction of effect compared to the original study in NHANES III.

To better understand the impact *SCN5A* variation has on these ECG traits, we performed a meta-analysis using the effect estimates from all three study populations (Table 3). All *SCN5A* SNPs were significant (p<0.05) and the direction of effect was consistent with the original study for PR interval. For QRS duration, all *SCN5A* SNPs have a consistent direction of effect; however, rs7629265 and rs6768664 did not meet our liberal significance threshold in NHANES III samples (Table 3). In NHANES III, having two copies of the risk allele "T" for rs7629265 increased QRS duration, whereas in both the original study and in eMERGE; having two copies of the "T" allele decreased the QRS duration.

In contrast, having two copies of the risk allele "G" at rs6768664 is associated with increased QRS duration in both the original study and NHANES III but with decreased QRS duration in eMERGE samples.

4 Discussion

In the present study we replicate and or generalize previously identified *SCN5A* associations in African Americans ascertained from clinical and population-based collections. Associated variants in the clinical-based study population, eMERGE, had a consistent direction of effect with previous studies in African Americans for four of the five SNPs between the two traits. However, in African Americans from the US population-based cohort, NHANES III, several associations had opposing direction of effects, and none of the SNPs tested reached our liberal significance threshold (p=0.05) for any ECG trait.

Here we tested five SNPs: rs7374138, rs11129796, rs7637849, rs7629265, and rs6768664, all located in various *SCN5A* introns. Consistent with published data, three of the five tested SNPs are specific to African-descent populations and are monomorphic or rare in European and Asian-descent populations [19,20,22,24,26]. While there is not a direct biological correlation with the role intronic SNPs have on protein function, intronic regions are known to play an important role in splicing, which could possibly affect protein function. Previous studies report that in African-descent populations one SNP, rs7629265, is in high linkage disequilibrium (LD, r^2 = 0.87) with coding non-synonymous variant, rs7626962 (S1103Y), and has been consistently associated with long QT syndrome [26]. This SNP is associated with PR interval in the combined analysis and is not associated with QRS duration, which is also consistent with the literature [19] (Table 3).

We did not test all *SCN5A* SNPs reported in the literature; as a consequence, there are several important associations we did not test. In spite of this, there are several trends we observed that are consistent with previous studies which suggest testing more SNPs in these regions will likely yield the same results [19,22,24]. Another limitation to this study is sample size. Compared to the previous reports for *SCN5A*, both eMERGE and NHANES III were limited in sample size: n= 455 and n=520, respectively. However, despite this limitation we were able to observe a consistent direction of effect compared to original reports for most *SCN5A* SNPs in African Americans from eMERGE.

In addition to small sample size, differences in study population may explain the lack of replication in NHANES III African Americans. Indeed, there are several similarities and differences across study populations. We sought to replicate associations originally detected in African Americans from the Jackson Heart Study (JHS). The Jackson Heart Study is a longitudinal study collected with the primary objective to identify and explain the disparity of cardiovascular diseases in African Americans [27-29]. As a result, the JHS has more samples with in-depth phenotype information for cardiovascular diseases and related traits compared to the other studies and can possibly include individuals with CVD. Another difference between the NHANES III population compared to the other study populations could be explained by geography. Unlike NHANES III, which is representative of the US population, the JHS is limited to African Americans from the southeastern United States. Similarly, most samples from eMERGE are limited to African Americans that visit the clinic or hospital in the Nashville metropolitan areas, also in the southeastern United States. The prevalence of CVD and related environmental risk factors are disproportionately higher in the southeastern US, which likely makes up majority of the eMERGE samples tested here and all of the JHS samples [30]. Lack of replication in NHANES III might be explained by this difference. Another possibility could be the time in which the study was conducted. Both eMERGE and JHS samples were collected fairly recently (in the past 10 years) compared to NHANES III, which was collected over 20 years ago. There are several environmental factors that have changed since then, such as diet, that might be interacting with these SNPs and thus have an impact on our study and explain our failure to replicate in NHANES III. Other non-genetic risk factors such as age, sex, type 2 diabetes mellitus (T2DM) status, and BMI are associated with ECG traits [3]. Indeed, we did observe significant differences across study populations for age, sex and BMI (Table 1). Study individuals from eMERGE were more likely to be female and were significantly younger compared to the original study and NHANES III. Also, eMERGE study individuals had a higher mean BMI and higher proportion of T2DM cases compared with NHANES III. It is possible that associations between *SCN5A* and ECG traits are modified by environmental factors (such as poor diet and BMI). Additional analyses are needed to statistically assess the impact of gene-environment interactions on this complex trait.

Perhaps the main reason for lack of replication in NHANES III is phenotype definition. It is important to note that despite small sample sizes in the replication cohorts, *SCN5A* associations have a much more consistent direction of effect in eMERGE than do the NHANES III samples compared to the original study (Table 3). One of the main goals of the eMERGE consortium was to successfully replicate GWAS associations in clinical populations, thus accurately identifying phenotypes from electronic medical record (EMR) data was critical. As previously mentioned, eMERGE study participants are limited to ECG measurements in normal range without any evidence of pre-existing heart conditions, laboratory values, or medications that may alter their

ECG results. The algorithm was validated by blinded physician review with a positive predictive value of 97% at both eMERGE sites participating in this study [18]. This stringent phenotype definition was not used in either the original study or NHANES III, and both had longer PR interval and QRS duration compared to eMERGE (Table 1). The broad phenotype definition might have resulted in a loss of power in NHANES III and thus explain why *SCN5A* variants did not replicate. While the original study also had a broad phenotype definition, the loss of power is not as significant given the large sample size, which is almost seven times larger than NHANES III.

Despite these study population differences, most tests of association were significant at p<0.05 after meta-analysis for both PR interval and QRS duration. And, tests of heterogeneity suggested little detectable differences across the studies in this meta-analysis. Overall, our data validate *SCN5A* associations with QRS duration and PR interval in African Americans by meta-analysis. Most importantly, this work highlights the challenge of conducting and interpreting genetic association studies in multiple study populations with differing ascertainment strategies. This latter finding is of particular important in this era of meta-analysis of genetic association studies where study design and phenotypic precision are traded in favor of larger sample sizes for greater power.

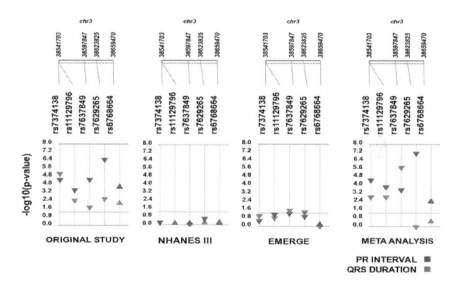

Fig. 1. Association results for *SCN5A* SNPs by study site. We performed single SNP tests of association for five previously identified *SCN5A* SNPs with PR interval (red) and QRS duration (blue). The direction of effect is indicated by the direction of the arrow and the −log p-value is plotted in the y-axis. SNPs are sorted based on location on chromosome 3. SNPs that met our liberal significance threshold p<0.05 are above the line.

Table 3. Association results across three independent African American study populations and meta-analysis results across all study populations. For each test of association, SNP rs number, coded allele (CA), beta, and p-value are given. For the meta-analysis, the Q p-value is also given. *Original Study data represent data from the Jackson Heart Study abstracted from Jeff et al 2011[19].

SNP	CA	Original study (n = 3,054) β (p)	NHANES III (n = 552) β (p)	eMERGE (n = 455) β (p)	Meta Analysis (n~4,000) β (p)	Q P
PR Interval						
rs7374138	G	-4.00 (2.4E-5)	-1.65 (0.40)	-1.94 (0.21)	-3.17 (2.2E-5)	0.37
rs11129796	T	-3.50 (2.4E-4)	0.12 (0.96)	-3.89 (0.05)	-3.14 (1.0E-4)	0.36
rs7637849	A	-4.20 (2.3E-5)	0.11 (0.96)	-3.11 (0.04)	-3.11 (2.0E-4)	0.17
rs7629265	T	-7.80 (2.4E-7)	-4.13 (0.17)	-4.00 (0.08)	-6.32 (5.3E-8)	0.30
rs6768664	G	3.00 (2.4E-4)	0.16 (0.92)	0.16 (0.90)	1.80 (5.0E-3)	0.13
QRS duration						
rs7374138	G	-1.30 (6.2E-6)	-0.70 (0.41)	-1.15 (0.07)	-1.22 (1.0E-3)	0.79
rs11129796	T	-1.10 (2.5E-3)	0.09 (0.94)	-1.40 (0.11)	-1.03 (1.0E-3)	0.52
rs7637849	A	-0.76 (1.2E-2)	-0.39 (0.66)	-1.55 (0.02)	-0.85 (1.3E-6)	0.48
rs7629265	T	-1.50 (1.8E-3)	1.07 (0.82)	-2.08 (0.03)	-0.15 (0.77)	0.01
rs6768664	G	0.67 (9.5E-3)	1.93 (0.73)	-0.20 (0.71)	0.21 (0.45)	0.11

Acknowledgements. This work was supported by NIH U01HG004798 and its ARRA supplements (EAGLE) as well as U01HG004609 (Northwestern University as part of eMERGE); U01HG04603 (Vanderbilt University as part of eMERGE, also serving as the Administrative Coordinating Center). Portions of the dataset(s) used for the analyses described were obtained from Vanderbilt University Medical Center's BioVU, which is supported by institutional funding and by the Vanderbilt CTSA grant UL1 TR000445 from NCATS/NIH. The Vanderbilt University Center for Human Genetics Research, Computational Genomics Core provided computational and/or analytical support for this work. The findings and conclusions in this report are those of the authors and do not necessarily represent the views of the Centers for Disease Control and Prevention.

References

1. Chizner, M.A.: Clinical Cardiology Made Ridiculously Simple. MedMaster, Miami (2004)
2. Capone, R.J., Pawitan, Y., el-Sherif, N., Geraci, T.S., Handshaw, K., Morganroth, J., Schlant, R.C., Waldo, A.L.: Events in the cardiac arrhythmia suppression trial: baseline predictors of mortality in placebo-treated patients. J. Am. Coll. Cardiol. **18**, 1434–1438 (1991)
3. Ramirez, A.H., Schildcrout, J.S., Blakemore, D.L., Masys, D.R., Pulley, J.M., Basford, M.A., Roden, D.M., Denny, J.C.: Modulators of normal electrocardiographic intervals identified in a large electronic medical record. Heart Rhythm **8**, 271–277 (2011)
4. Akylbekova, E.L., Crow, R.S., Johnson, W.D., Buxbaum, S.G., Njemanze, S., Fox, E., Sarpong, D.F., Taylor, H.A., Newton-Cheh, C.: Clinical correlates and heritability of QT interval duration in blacks: the Jackson Heart Study. Circ. Arrhythm. Electrophysiol. **2**, 427–432 (2009)
5. Friedlander, Y., Siscovick, D.S., Weinmann, S., Austin, M.A., Psaty, B.M., Lemaitre, R.N., Arbogast, P., Raghunathan, T.E., Cobb, L.A.: Family history as a risk factor for primary cardiac arrest. Circulation **97**, 155–160 (1998)
6. George Jr., A.L.: Inherited disorders of voltage-gated sodium channels. J. Clin. Invest. **115**, 1990–1999 (2005)
7. George Jr., A.L., Varkony, T.A., Drabkin, H.A., Han, J., Knops, J.F., Finley, W.H., Brown, G.B., Ward, D.C., Haas, M.: Assignment of the human heart tetrodotoxin-resistant voltage-gated Na+ channel alpha-subunit gene (SCN5A) to band 3p21. Cytogenet Cell Genet. **68**, 67–70 (1995)
8. Gouas, L., Nicaud, V., Berthet, M., Forhan, A., Tiret, L., Balkau, B., Guicheney, P., D.E.S.I.R. Study Group: Association of KCNQ1, KCNE1, KCNH2 and SCN5A polymorphisms with QTc interval length in a healthy population. Eur. J. Hum. Genet. **13**, 1213–1222 (2005)
9. Newton-Cheh, C., Eijgelsheim, M., Rice, K.M., de Bakker, P.I., Yin, X., Estrada, K., Bis, J.C., Marciante, K., Rivadeneira, F., Noseworthy, P.A., Sotoodehnia, N., Smith, N.L., Rotter, J.I., Kors, J.A., Witteman, J.C., Hofman, A., Heckbert, S.R., O'Donnell, C.J., Uitterlinden, A.G., Psaty, B.M., Lumley, T., Larson, M.G., Stricker, B.H.: Common variants at ten loci influence QT interval duration in the QTGEN Study. Nat. Genet. **41**, 399–406 (2009)
10. Lai, L.P., Deng, C.L., Moss, A.J., Kass, R.S., Liang, C.S.: Polymorphism of the gene encoding a human minimal potassium ion channel (minK). Gene **151**, 339–340 (1994)
11. Gellens, M.E., George Jr., A.L., Chen, L.Q., Chahine, M., Horn, R., Barchi, R.L., Kallen, R.G.: Primary structure and functional expression of the human cardiac tetrodotoxin-insensitive voltage-dependent sodium channel. Proc. Natl. Acad. Sci. USA **89**, 554–558 (1992)
12. Abriel, H., Kass, R.S.: Regulation of the voltage-gated cardiac sodium channel Nav1.5 by interacting proteins. Trends Cardiovasc. Med. **15**, 35–40 (2005)
13. George Jr., A.L., Iyer, G.S., Kleinfield, R., Kallen, R.G., Barchi, R.L.: Genomic organization of the human skeletal muscle sodium channel gene. Genomics **15**, 598–606 (1993)
14. Wang, Q., Shen, J., Li, Z., Timothy, K., Vincent, G.M., Priori, S.G., Schwartz, P.J., Keating, M.T.: Cardiac sodium channel mutations in patients with long QT syndrome, an inherited cardiac arrhythmia. Hum. Mol. Genet. **4**, 1603–1607 (1994)
15. Bezzina, C., Veldkamp, M.W., van den Berg, M.P., Postma, A.V., Rook, M.B., Viersma, J.W., van Langen, I.M., Tan-Sindhunata, G., Bink-Boelkens, M.T., van Der Hout, A.H., Mannens, M.M., Wilde, A.A.: A single Na(+) channel mutation causing both long-QT and Brugada syndromes. Circ. Res. **85**, 1206–1213 (1999)

16. Schott, J.J., Alshinawi, C., Kyndt, F., Probst, V., Hoorntje, T.M., Hulsbeek, M., Wilde, A.A., Escande, D., Mannens, M.M., Le Marec, H.: Cardiac conduction defects associate with mutations in SCN5A. Nat. Genetics. **23**, 20–21 (1999)

17. Wang, Q., Shen, J., Splawski, I., Atkinson, D., Li, Z., Robinson, J.L., Moss, A.J., Towbin, J.A., Keating, M.T.: SCN5A mutations associated with an inherited cardiac arrhythmia, long QT syndrome. Cell **80**, 805–811 (1995)

18. Ritchie, M.D., Denny, J.C., Zuvich, R.L., Crawford, D.C., Schildcrout, J.S., Bastarache, L., Ramirez, A.H., Mosley, J.D., Pulley, J.M., Basford, M.A., Bradford, Y., Rasmussen, L.V., Pathak, J., Chute, C.G., Kullo, I.J., McCarty, C.A., Chisholm, R.L., Kho, A.N., Carlson, C.S., Larson, E.B., Jarvik, G.P., Sotoodehnia, N., Cohorts for Heart and Aging Research in Genomic Epidemiology (CHARGE) QRS Group, Manolio, T.A., Li, R., Masys, D.R., Haines, J.L., Roden, D.M.: Genome- and phenome-wide analyses of cardiac conduction identifies markers of arrhythmia risk. Circulation **127**, 1377–1385 (2013)

19. Jeff, J.M., Brown-Gentry, K., Buxbaum, S.G., Sarpong, D.F., Taylor, H.A., George, A.L., Roden, D.M., Crawford, D.C.: SCN5A Variation is Associated with Electrocardiographic Traits in the Jackson Heart Study. Circ. Cardiovasc. Genet. **4**, 139–144 (2011)

20. Burke, A., Creighton, W., Mont, E., Li, L., Hogan, S., Kutys, R., Fowler, D., Virmani, R.: Role of SCN5A Y1102 polymorphism in sudden cardiac death in blacks. Circulation **112**, 798–802 (2005)

21. Plant, L.D., Bowers, P.N., Liu, Q., Morgan, T., Zhang, T., State, M.W., Chen, W., Kittles, R.A., Goldstein, S.A.: A common cardiac sodium channel variant associated with sudden infant death in African Americans, SCN5A S1103Y. J. Clin. Invest. **116**, 430–435 (2006)

22. Smith, J.G., Magnani, J.W., Palmer, C., Meng, Y.A., Soliman, E.Z., Musani, S.K., Kerr, K.F., Schnabel, R.B., Lubitz, S.A., Sotoodehnia, N., Redline, S., Pfeufer, A., Muller, M., Evans, D.S., Nalls, M.A., Liu, Y., Newman, A.B., Zonderman, A.B., Evans, M.K., Deo, R., Ellinor, P.T., Paltoo, D.N., Newton-Cheh, C., Beonjamin, E.J., Mehra, R., Alonso, A., Heckbert, S.R., Fox, E.R.: Candidate-gene Association Resource (CARe) Consortium: Genome-wide association studies of the PR interval in African Americans. PLoS Genet. **7**, e1001304 (2011)

23. Butler, A.M., Yin, X., Evans, D.S., Nalls, M.A., Smith, E.N., Tanaka, T., Li, G., Buxbaum, S.G., Whitsel, E.A., Alonso, A., Arking, D.E., Benjamin, E.J., Berenson, G.S., Bis, J.C., Chen, W., Deo, R., Ellinor, P.T., Heckbert, S.R., Heiss, G., Hsueh, W.C., Keating, B.J., Kerr, K.F., Li, Y., Limacher, M.C., Liu, Y., Lubitz, S.A., Marciante, K.D., Mehra, R., Meng, Y.A., Newman, A.B., Newton-Cheh, C., North, K.E., Palmer, C.D., Psaty, B.M., Quibrera, P.M., Redline, S., Reiner, A.P., Rotter, J.I., Schnabel, R.B., Schork, N.J., Singleton, A.B., Smith, J.G., Soliman, E.Z., Srinivasan, S.R., Zhang, Z.M., Zonderman, A.B., Ferrucci, L., Murray, S.S., Evans, M.K., Sotoodehnia, N., Magnani, J.W., Avery, C.L.: Novel Loci Associated with PR Interval in a Genome-Wide Association Study of Ten African American Cohorts. Circ. Cardiovasc. Genet. **5**, 639–646 (2012)

24. Avery, C.L., Sethupathy, P., Buyske, S., He, Q., Lin, D.Y., Arking, D.E., Carty, C.L., Duggan, D., Fesinmeyer, M.D., Hindorff, L.A., Jeff, J.M., Klein, L., Patton, K.K., Peters, U., Shohet, R.V., Sotoodehnia, N., Yong, A.M., Kooperberg, C., Haiman, C.A., Mohlke, K.L., Whitsel, E.A., North, K.E.: Fine-Mapping and Initial Characterization of QT Interval Loci in African Americans. PLoS Genet. **8**, e1002870 (2012)

25. Weir, B.S., Cockerham, C.C.: Estimating F- Statistics for the Analysis of Population Structure. Evolution **38**, 1358–1370 (1984)

26. Splawski, I., Timothy, K.W., Tateyama, M., Clancy, C.E., Malhotra, A., Beggs, A.H., Cappuccio, F.P., Sgnella, G.A., Kass, R.S., Keating, M.T.: Variant of SCN5A sodium channel implicated in risk of cardiac arrhythmia. Science **297**, 1333–1336 (2002)

27. Sempos, C.T., Bild, D.E., Manolio, T.A.: Overview of the Jackson Heart Study: a study of cardiovascular diseases in African American men and women. Am. J. Med. Sci. **317**, 142–146 (1999)

28. Wilson, J.G., Rotimi, C.N., Ekunwe, L., Royal, C.D., Crump, M.E., Wyatt, S.B., Steffes, M.W., Adeyemo, A., Zhou, J., Taylor Jr., H.A., Jaquish, C.: Study design for genetic analysis in the Jackson Heart Study. Ethn. Dis. **15**, S6–37 (2005)

29. Wyatt, S.B., Diekelmann, N., Henderson, F., Andrew, M.E., Billingsley, G., Felder, S.H., Fugua, S., Jackson, P.B.: A community-driven model of research participation: the Jackson Heart Study Participant Recruitment and Retention Study. Ethn. Dis. **13**, 438–455 (2003)

30. Crook, E.D., Taylor, H.: Traditional and nontraditional risk factors for cardiovascular and renal disease in African Americans (Part 2): a project of the Jackson Heart Study investigators. Am. J. Med. Sci. **325**, 305–306 (2003)

31. McCarty, C.A., Chisholm, R.L., Chute, C.G., Kullo, I.J., Jarvik, G.P., Larson, E.B., Li, R., Masys, D.R., Ritchie, M.D., Roden, D.M., Struewing, J.P., Wolf, W.A.: eMERGE Team: The eMERGE Network: a consortium of biorepositories linked to electronic medical records data for conducting genomic studies. BMC Med. Genomics. **4**, 13 (2011)

32. Jeff, J.M., Ritchie, M.D., Denny, J.C., Kho, A.N., Ramirez, A.H., Crosslin, D., Armstrong, L., Basford, M.A., Wolf, W.A., Pacheco, J.A., Chisholm, R.L., Roden, D.M., Hayes, M.G., Crawford, D.C.: Generalization of Variants Identified by Genome-Wide Association Studies for Electrocardiographic Traits in African Americans. Ann. Hum. Genet. **77**, 321–332 (2013)

33. National Center for Health Statistics, Centers for Disease Control and Prevention. Plan and operation of the Third National Health and Nutrition Examination Survey, 1988-1994. Vital Health Stat 1 (1994)

34. Roden, D.M., Pulley, J.M., Basford, M.A., Bernard, G.R., Clayton, E.W., Balser, J.R., Masys, D.R.: Development of a large-scale de-identified DNA biobank to enable personalized medicine. Clin. Pharmacol. Ther. **84**, 362–369 (2008)

35. Denny, J.C., Ritchie, M.D., Crawford, D.C., Schildcrout, J.S., Ramirez, A.H., Pulley, J.M., Basford, M.A., Masys, D.R., Haines, J.L., Roden, D.M.: Identification of genomic predictors of atrioventricular conduction: using electronic medical records as a tool for genome science. Circulation **122**, 2016–2021 (2010)

36. Steinberg, K.K., Sanderlin, K.C., Ou, C.Y., Hannon, W.H., McQuillan, G.M.: Sampson EJ: DNA banking in epidemiologic studies. Epidemiol. Rev. **19**, 156–162 (1997)

37. Zuvich, R.L., Armstrong, L.L., Bielinski, S.J., Bradford, Y., Carlson, C.S., Crawford, D.C., Crenshaw, A.T., de Andrade, M., Doheny, K.F., Haines, J.L., Hayes, M.G., Jarvik, G.P., Jiang, L., Kullo, I.J., Li, R., Ling, H., Manolio, T.A., Matsumoto, M.E., McCarty, C.A., McDavid, A.N., Mirel, D.B., Olson, L.M., Paschall, J.E., Pugh, E.W., Rasmussen, L.V., Rasmussen-Torvik, L.J., Turner, S.D., Wilke, R.A., Ritchie, M.D.: Pitfalls of merging GWAS data: lessons learned in the eMERGE network and quality control procedures to maintain high data quality. Genet. Epidemiol. **35**, 887–898 (2011)

38. Willer, C.J., Li, Y., Abecasis, G.R.: METAL: fast and efficient meta-analysis of genomewide association scans. Bioinformatics **26**, 2190–2191 (2010)

39. Grady, B.J., Torstenson, E., Dudek, S.M., Giles, J., Sexton, D., Ritchie, M.D.: Finding unique filter sets in plato: a precursor to efficient interaction analysis in gwas data. In: Pac. Symp. Biocomput., pp. 315–326 (2010)

General Track

An Effective Nurse Scheduling by a Parameter Free Cooperative GA

Makoto Ohki$^{(\boxtimes)}$ and Satoru Kishida

Graduate School of Engineering, Division of Information and Electronics,
Tottori University, 101, 4 Koyama-Nishi, Tottori, Tottori 680-8552, Japan
{mohki,kishida}@ele.tottori-u.ac.jp
http://www.ele.tottori-u.ac.jp/japanese/labo/denji/

Abstract. This paper describes a technique of penalty weight adjustment for the Cooperative Genetic Algorithm applied to the nurse scheduling problem. In this algorithm, coefficients and thresholds for each penalty function are automatically optimized. Therefore, this technique provides a parameter free algorithm of nurse scheduling. The nurse scheduling is very complex task, because many requirements must be considered. These requirements are implemented by a set of penalty function in this research. In real hospital, several changes of the schedule often happen. Such changes of the shift schedule yields various inconveniences, for example, imbalance of the number of the holidays and the number of the attendance. Such inconvenience causes the fall of the nursing level of the nurse organization. Reoptimization of the schedule including the changes is very hard task and requires very long computing time. We consider that this problem is caused by the solution space having many local minima. We propose a technique to adjust penalty weights and thresholds through the optimization to escape from the local minima.

1 Introduction

General hospital consists of several departments such as the internal medicine department and the pediatrics department. In each department, about fifteen to thirty nursing staffs belong. A chief nurse of the department makes a shift schedule of all nurses in her/his department every month. The chief nurse considers more than fifteen requirements for the scheduling. Such the schedule arrangement, in other words, nurse scheduling, is very complex task. In our investigation, a veteran chief nurse even spends one or two weeks for the nurse scheduling by hand. This means a great loss of work force and time. Therefore, computer software for the nurse scheduling has recently come to be required at the general hospitals [2–6,8–17,19,21]. In the early study [2], the nurse scheduling problem defined as a discrete planning problem is solved by using Hopfield-type neural network. Berrada et al. [3] have proposed a technique to define the nurse scheduling problem as a multi-objective problem and to solve it by using simple optimizing algorithm. The technique by Takabe et al. [4] provides a simple editing tool and simple GA for the nurse scheduling under Visual Basic environment. There are several techniques [5,9,16,21] to make an user modify or select

© Springer-Verlag Berlin Heidelberg 2014
A.I. Esparcia-Alcázar et al. (Eds.): EvoApplications 2014, LNCS 8602, pp. 955–966, 2014.
DOI: 10.1007/978-3-662-45523-4_77

the nurse schedule in the middle or the final stage of the optimization. Burke et al. apply a memetic approach to the nurse scheduling problem [6,12,14,19]. Croce et al. [25] proposes a variable neiborhood search technique for the nurse scheduling. However, the scheduling problem defined in this manuscript is too easy. And the technique is applied to a private hospital in Italy. Real problem of the nurse scheduling in the general hospital is not so easy and very hard to solve.

Some of these techniques are implemented in commercial nurse scheduling software. However, the evaluation technique does not fit to the shift system of our country. Moreover, such a commercial software has not been utilized in most hospitals in fact, because a schedule given by the commercial software is unsatisfactory. Therefore, we have defined the evaluation technique of the nurse schedule [18,20,22].

We have discussed a case that the nurse schedule has been changed in the past weeks of the current month [25]. Such changes yields various inconveniences, for example, imbalance of the number of holidays and attendances. Such an inconvenience causes the fall of the nursing level of the whole nurse organization. Therefore, the inconvenience should be eliminated to make a better schedule. By considering the change of the shift schedule whenever one week passes, the shift schedule is reoptimized in remaining weeks of the current month.

The shift schedule generated by such the commercial software is unsatisfactory. And, many interactions to readjust the schedule are also very complex for the end user. In fact, the nurse schedule is still made by hand of the chief nurse in many general hospitals in our country. The optimization algorithm of such the commercial software is still poor, and moreover, the schedule provided by such the software is hard to revise too. The operation of the software is very complex for end users too, because there are many parameters to be defined by the end users.

In this paper, we discuss about generation and optimization of the nurse schedule by using the Cooperative Genetic Algorithm (CGA) [18]. CGA is a kind of Genetic Algorithm (GA) [1], and a powerful optimizing algorithm for such a combinatorial optimization problem. In the standard GA[1], individuals compete each other and superior individuals are preserved. On the other hand, individuals cooperate each other and the optimization of whole population progresses in CGA. The conventional CGA optimizes the nurse schedule only by using crossover operator, because the crossover has been considered as the only one operation which keeps consistency of relation between chromosomes in the CGA, where the consistency means the numbers of nurses at each shift in this case. Then we have proposed effective mutation operators keeping such the consistency for the CGA [18,20,22]. These mutation operators are activated depending on the optimization speed.

Burke et al. [7] also define a technique to evaluate the nurse schedule. However, the evaluation technique does not fit to a shift system of our country. Therefore, we have defined the evaluation technique of the nurse schedule[18,23,24]. In the real case, there are some cases that nurses come to their office on a different day from the original schedule because of circumstances of other nurse or an emergency. We have discussed such a case that the nurse schedule has been changed in the past weeks of the current month [20,22]. By such the changes, various inconveniences occur, for example, imbalance of the number of holidays and attendances. Such an inconvenience causes the fall of the nursing level of the whole nurse organization. Therefore, such inconvenience should be dissolved to form a better schedule. By considering the change of the shift schedule whenever one week passes, the shift schedule is reoptimized in remaining weeks of the current month.

Reoptimization of the schedule including such the changes is very hard task even by parallel computing techniques [23,24] and then requires very long computing time. We consider that this complexity is caused by that there are many local minima in the solution space of the nurse scheduling problem. If the optimization is caught in the region of the local minimum, some penalty functions stagnate decreasing as still giving greater value. Valley of the local minimum upheaves by increasing weight of such the penalty function. And then, the searching point of the optimization escapes from the local minimum region. We propose a technique adjusting the penalty weights through the optimization when the concerned penalty functions stagnate decreasing. By means of the penalty adjustment, CGA effectively searches the solution space. The optimization finishes in the one-tenth computation time by the conventional technique [22–24]. In addition, a technique of a self adjustment of several parameters, thresholds, of the penalty adjustment technique. By means of this technique, the end user is freed from the onerous task for the definition of various parameters.

2   Genetic Coding of the Nurse Schedule

In CGA for the nurse scheduling, an individual and its group, or the population, are defined shown in Fig.1. The individual chromosome consists of the series of the shift symbols. The shift series consists of 28 fields, since one month includes four weeks in the practical case. The X-th individual expresses one-month schedule of the X-th nurse. In this technique, two or more individuals does not include identical nurse's schedule. In other words, the population expresses the whole schedule of the concerned nurse organization.

3   Basic Algorithm of CGA for Nurse Scheduling

The basic algorithm of the CGA is shown in Fig.2 ([18,20,22]). CGA applies the crossover operator to the population and searches so that a penalty of the whole population becomes small. The crossover operator selects a pair of parent individual from the population. Two child pairs are reconstituted by the two-point crossover. Taking back these child pairs to the original position of the parents, a temporal population is reconstituted. The temporal population is evaluated by the total penalty function E. These procedures are applied to one

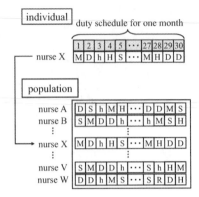

Fig. 1. The X-th individual coded into chromosome denotes one month shift schedule of the X-th nurse. The population includes one month schedules of all nurses. The symbols, D, S, M, h and H, denotes a daytime shift, a semi-night shift, midnight shift, holiday and requested holiday respectively.

hundred parent pairs selected from the population. A population giving the best performance is selected for the next generation.

Since the nurse scheduling problem is particularly difficult to solve, the optimization, which perform the crossover operator only, often stagnates. The crossover operator is superior in ability to local search, but is inferior to global search. When the optimization stagnates for long generation cycles, it is effective to forcibly give small change to the population. Therefore we have proposed a mutation operator activated depending on the optimization speed [22]. The optimization speed $V_E(g)$ at the g-th generation is defined as follows,

$$N_g = g - g_{prim}, \tag{1}$$

$$A_E(g) = \frac{1}{N_g} \sum_{h=0}^{N_g-1} E(g-h), \tag{2}$$

$$V_E(g) = A_E(g-1) - A_E(g), \tag{3}$$

where g_{prim} denotes the generation cycle when the mutation is activated previously. We define two parameters, a guard interval G_g and a speed thleshold ϵ_E [22]. The guard interval is to prevent the activation of the mutation operator for G_g generation cycles after the last activation. The speed threshold is a parameter to detect activation timing. When the optimization speed become less than ϵ_E, the mutation operator activates. The mutation operator randomly selects the day and selects two individuals. One of two giving big value of F_1 is selected in the roulette sellection manner. Another one is randomly selected. And then, these selected shifts are replaced each other. The mutation operator is activated depending on the optimization speed.

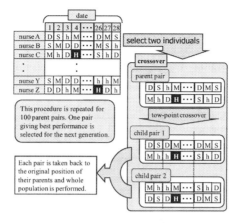

Fig. 2. One generation cycle by the crossover operator

The speed threshold ϵ_E is initialized to 1. We define a counter variable c_{accept} which denotes the number of which the total penalty E is decresed in the previous mutation interval. When the mutation is activated under the following condition,

$$N_g < G_M \wedge c_{accept} = 0, \tag{4}$$

the speed threshold ϵ_E decreases as follows,

$$\epsilon_E := 0.9\epsilon_E. \tag{5}$$

When the mutation is activated under the following condition,

$$N_g = G_M \wedge c_{accept} = 0, \tag{6}$$

the speed threshold ϵ_E increases as follows,

$$\epsilon_E := 1.1\epsilon_E. \tag{7}$$

Otherwise, the speed threshold ϵ_E does not change.

We also have proposed a mutation operator activated periodically in G_M generation cycles[23]. The periodic mutation is advantage on the point that fewer parameter is required to define itself.

4   Evaluation of Nurse Schedule

The chief nurse must consider many requirements for the nurse scheduling. For example, meeting, training and requested holiday must be accepted, where we assume that all the requested holidays have been confirmed by the chief nurse. The semi-night shifts and the midnight shifts should be impartially arranged to all nurses. And arrangement of six or more consecutive days is prohibited. We have summarized all the requirements into the 13 penalty functions [23, 24]. The outline of these penalties are descrived in this paper.

We define the following three penalties concerning on the shift pattern. To evaluate the work load of each nurse i, we define a penalty function F_{1i} for three consecutive days of shift content. It is not preferable for the night shifts to be assigned to some nurse intensively. To suppress this undesirable situation, we define a penalty function F_{2i} to prohibit the X night shift or more for the consecutive Y days. In some hospitals, there are some cases to prohibit a specific shift pattern. If the shift pattern starting from the j-th day of the i-th nurse is prohibited, the penalty f_{3ij} is assigned to 1. We define a penalty function F_{3i}, equal to the sum total of f_{3ij} from $j = 1$ to $j = D$, to implement such the prohibition, where D denotes the number of days of the current month.

We define the following three penalties conserning on the impartiality of the shift and the holliday. The number of the shifts should be impartially assigned to all nurses. A total nursing level falls, if many shifts are concentrated to particular nurses. We define penalty functions F_{4i}, F_{5i} to suppress unevenness of the number of shifts among nurses. The functions F_{4i} and F_{5i} are concerning the numbers of holidays and nught shifts respectivery of the i-th nurse. If the shifts are assigned to particular nurses on many consecutive days, total nursing level falls. We define a penalty function F_{6i} to restrain assignment of the shift on many consecutive shift days of the i-th nurse.

We define the following three penalties conserning on the nursing level. In our algorithm, the number of nurses in each working hours is preserved in any case. However, if new face nurses are intensively assigned on a particular working hours, the nursing level falls. The expert or more skilled nurses should be assigned for keeping nursing level. We define penalty functions F_{7j}, F_{8j} and F_{9j} to evaluate the nursing level on the day time shift, the semi-night shift and the midnight shift respectively.

We define the following three penalties conserning on the nurse combination. The chief nurse also considers affinity between the nurses. Because of bad affinity between a certain nurses assigned to in the same time, there is the case that the nursing level deteriorates remarkably. To restrain such the unfavorable affinity, we define a penalty function F_{10j}. In the midnight shift, the number of assigned nurses is small. If the most of the nurses assigned to the midnight shift are new face, the nursing level at the midnight shift falls remarkably To restrain such the unfavorable situation, we define a penalty function F_{11j}. In general, one or more expert or more skilled nurses should be assigned to the daytime shift and the midnight shift. To restrain such an unfavorable situation, we define a penalty function F_{12j}.

At the real hospital, the shift schedule which optimized before the beginning of the current month is often changed day by day. Such changes of the schedule leads to the falls of the nursing level. To restrain such an unfavorable situation, we reoptimize the shift schedule of the remainder of the current month. On the other hand, with considering the circumstances of the nurses, the shift schedule should not be changed as much as possible. We define a penalty function F_{13} for reoptimizing the shift schedule while having such a dilemma as shown in Fig.3. The penalty function F_{13} performs the difference between the original schedule and the newly optimized schedule of the remainder of the current month.

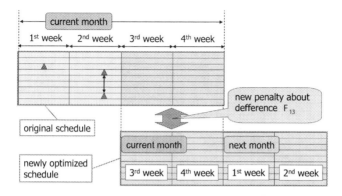

Fig. 3. ermission of the change of the schedule in the past two weeks. The red triangle denotes the schedule change.

Finaly, we perform the shift schedule by the following total penalty function,

$$E = \sum_{i=1}^{M} \sum_{k=1}^{6} h_k F_{ki} + \sum_{j=1}^{D} \sum_{k=7}^{12} h_k F_{kj} + h_{13} F_{13}, \tag{8}$$

where h_k $(k = 1, 2, \cdots, 13)$ denote penalty weights and defined as 1 as a default value.

5   Penalty Adjustment

Reoptimization of the schedule including such the changes is very hard task even by parallel computing techniques ([23, 24]) and then requires very long computing time. We consider that this complexity is caused by that there are many local minima in the solution space. If the optimization is caught in the region of the local minimum, some penalty functions stagnate decreasing as still greater value. To escape from the local minimum area, deforming the solution space is effective.

The shape of the solution space is defined by the penalty function E. By changing the penalty weights, h_k, the shape of the solution space is also deformed. Valley of the local minimum upheaves by increasing weight of a penalty function which stagnates to decrease. And then, the searching point of the optimization moves from the local minimum region. We propose a technique adjusting penalty weight through the optimization when the concerned penalty function stagnate decreasing. We call this technique the Penalty Adjustment (PA). PA is inserted

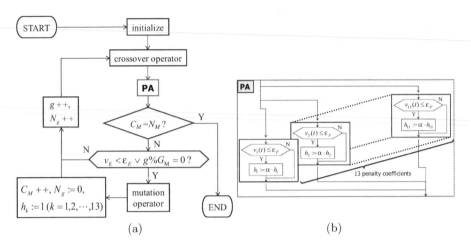

Fig. 4. Optimization flow with the penalty adjustment. (a) whole flow and (b) Primitive operation of the penalty adjustment.

right after the crossover operator as shown in Figure 4 (a) and (b). In this figure, C_M denotes a counter that counts the number of mutation.

Initially, all the penalty weiths h_1—h_{13} are initialized to 1 as a default value. The decreasing speed, $v_k(g)$, of the k-th penalty function, F_k, at the generation cycle g is calculated in PA by the following equations,

$$A_k(g) = \begin{cases} \dfrac{1}{N_g} \displaystyle\sum_{h=0}^{N_g-1} \sum_{i=1}^{M} F_{ki}(g-h) \ (k \le 6), \\ \dfrac{1}{N_g} \displaystyle\sum_{h=0}^{N_g-1} \sum_{j=1}^{D} F_{kj}(g-h) \ (k > 6), \end{cases} \tag{9}$$

$$v_k(g) = A_k(g-1) - A_k(g). \tag{10}$$

As shown in Figure 4 (b),when the decreasing speed of the k-th penalty function, v_k, becomes less than or equal to a penalty threshold ϵ_k, the penalty coefficient h_k is increased by multiplying with a parameter α. The values of α is defined as 1.01. When the mutation is activated, all the penalty weights h_1—h_{13} are initialized to 1 again.

The penalty threshold ϵ_k is initialized to 1. We define a counter variable c_{modify}^k which denotes the number of which the penalty weight h_k is increased in the previous mutation interval. When the mutation is activated under the following condition,

$$c_{modify}^k > 0 \wedge c_{accept} = 0, \tag{11}$$

the penalty threshold ϵ_k decreases as follows,

$$\epsilon_k := 0.9\epsilon_k. \tag{12}$$

When the mutation is activated under the following condition,

$$c_{modify}^k = 0 \wedge c_{accept} = 0, \qquad (13)$$

the penalty threshold ϵ_k increases as follows,

$$\epsilon_k := 1.1\epsilon_k. \qquad (14)$$

Otherwise, the penalty threshold ϵ_k does not change.

6   Practical Experiment

We have tried computational experiment of the nurse scheduling based on the practical situation. In this experiment, the number of the nurses is defined to twenty-three. The shift schedule sufficiently optimized has been announced at the beginning of the current month, and now assume that at two weeks after. We suppose here that there have been several changes in the schedule in the past two weeks. The CGA reoptimizes the shift schedule for the coming four weeks. The schedule on the first two weeks of the objective period has been already announced at the beginning of the current month.

In order to compare exactly, we have tried to optimize the ten times under each condition. Figures 5 (a)—(c) show optimization progresses by using the

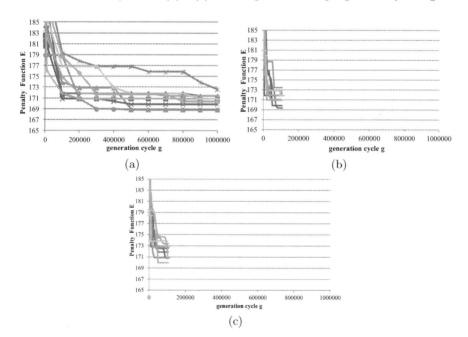

Fig. 5. Optimization progresses. (a) denotes optimization progressions by the periodic mutation operator, (b) denotes optimization progressions by PA with the constant thresholds, $\epsilon_E = 0.01$ and $\epsilon_k = 0.001$ (PA1) and (c) denotes optimization progressions by PA with modification of the speed and the penalty thresholds(PA2).

periodic mutation operator, PA with constant thresholds (PA1) and PA with modification of the speed threshold ϵ_E and the penalty thresholds ϵ_k (PA2). In one trial, the optimization is executed for $N_M = 500$ mutation cycles. The mutation period G_M and the guard interval G_g are defined as 2000 generation cycles and 100 generation cycles respectively. The condition of these parameters provides the best result when using the periodic mutation operator. By means of PA, the optimization finishes in about one-tenth generation cycles by the periodic mutation.

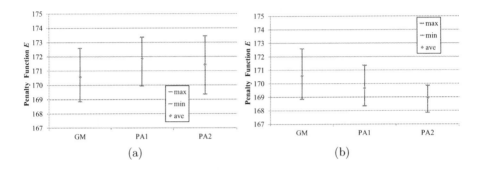

(a)   (b)

Fig. 6. Comparison of the final value of the total penalty function E. "GM" denotes the result given by using the periodic mutation operator. (a) denotes the results after the mutation activates $N_M = 500$ and (b) denotes the results after the optimization is executed for $1,000,000$ generation cycles.

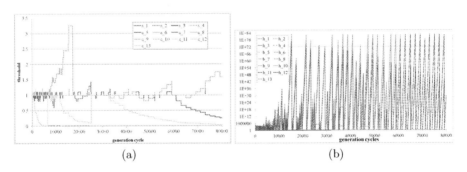

(a)   (b)

Fig. 7. (a) Progress of the speed and the penalty thresholds and (b) progress of the the penalty coefficients. The vertical axes is defined as the logarithmic axes.

Fig.6 shows comparison of the maximum, the average and the minimum value of the ten results under each technique. Compared to the periodic mutation operator, PA is slightly worse. On the other hand, when the optimization is executed for one million generation cycles, PA provieds pretty good results as shown in Fig.6 (b).

Finally, Fig.7 (a) and (b) show an example of the progress of the speed and the penalty thresholds and the progress. The penalty functions that correspond to the threshold has been growing without bounds converge to zero at an early stage of the optimization. Threshold that has declined endlessly is ϵ_E. This means that the optimization stagnates during the mutation cycle.

7 Conclusion

This paper has proposed the technique of the nurse scheduling by using CGA. We have discussed the case that the nurse schedule has been changed in the past weeks. To reoptimize the changed schedule, we have defined a penalty function performing the difference between the original schedule and the optimizing schedule. The reoptimization of the nurse schedule becomes very complex problem. Therefore we need new techniques to search for good schedule effectively. We have proposed a technique adjusting the penalty weights depending on the optimization progress, PA. This technique is implemented with the mutation depending on the optimization speed. By means of PA, the optimization finishes within one-tenth generation cycles by the conventional periodic mutation technique.When the PA is applied to the optimization for one million generation cycles, the splended schedules have been obtained. Thus, the effectiveness of PA is confirmed. In addition, a technique of self adjustment of the speed and the penalty thresholds. By means of this technique, the end user has been freed from the onerous task for the definition of various parameters.

Acknowledgments. This research work has been supported by Tottori University Electronic Display Research Center (TEDREC).

Dr.Ohki would like to thank to cats Civita, Blacky, Blanc and Caramel gave his the healing daily life.

References

1. Goldberg, D.E.: Genetic Algorithm in Search, Optimization and Machine Learning. Addison-Wesley, New York (1989)
2. Goto, T., Aze, H., Yamagishi, M., Hirota, M., Fujii, S.: Application of GA, Neural Network and AI to Planning Problems. NHK Technical report, No.144, pp. 78–85 (1993)
3. Berrada, I., Ferland, J.A., Michelon, P.: A Multi-objective Approach to Nurse Scheduling with both Hard and Soft Constraints. Socio-Econ. Plann. Sci. **30**(3), 183–193 (1996)
4. Takaba, M., Maeda, H., Sakaba, N.: Development of a Nurse Scheduling System by a Genetic Algothm. In: Proc. of 18th JCMI (1998)
5. Ikegami, A.: Algorithms for Nurse Scheduling. In: Proc. of 11th Intelligent System Symposium, pp. 477–480 (2001)
6. Burke, E.K., Cowling, P.: A Memetic Approach to the Nurse Rostering Problem. Applied Intelligence **15**, 199–214 (2001)
7. Burke, E.K., De Causmaecker, P., Petrovic, S., Berghe, G.V.: Fitness Evaluation for Nurse Scheduling Problems. In: Proc. of the 2001 Congress on Evolutionary Computation (2001)

8. Kawanaka, H., Yamamoto, K., Yoshikawa, T., Shinogi, T., Tsuruoka, S.: Automatic Generation of Nurse Scheduling Table Using Genetic Algorithm. Trans. on IEE Japan 122-C(6), 1023–1032 (2002)
9. Inoue, T., Furuhashi, T., Maeda, H., Takabane, M.: A Study on Interactive Nurse Scheduling Support System Using Bacterial Evolutionary Algorithm Enegine. Trans. on IEE Japan 122-C(10), 1803–1811 (2002)
10. Itoga, T., Taniguchi, N., Hoshino, Y., Kamei, K.: An Improvement on Search Efficiency of Cooperative GA and Application on Nurse Scheduling Problem. In: Proc. of 12th Intelligent System Symposium, pp. 146–149 (2003)
11. Cheang, B., Li, H., Lim, A., Rodrigues, B.: Nurse Rostering Problems - a bibliographic survey. Europiean Journal of Operational Research 151, 447–460 (2003)
12. Burke, E.K., De Causmaecker, P., Berghe, G.V., Lnadeghem, H.: The State of the Art of Nurse Rostering. Journal of Scheduling 7, 441–499 (2004)
13. Ernst, A.T., Jiang, H., Krishnamoorthy, M., Owens, B., Sier, D.: An Annotated Bibliography of Personnel Scheduling and Rostering. Annals of Operations Research 127, 21–144 (2004)
14. Burke, E.K., De Causmaecker, P., Berge, G.V.: Novel Meta-Heuristic Approaches to Nurse Rostering Problems in Belgian Hospitals. In: Leung, J. (ed.) Handbook of Scheduling Algorithms, Models and Performance Analysis (2004)
15. Li, J., Aickelin, U.: The Application of Bayesian Optimization and Classifier Systems in Nurse Scheduling. In: Yao, X., Burke, E.K., Lozano, J.A., Smith, J., Merelo-Guervós, J.J., Bullinaria, J.A., Rowe, J.E., Tiňo, P., Kabán, A., Schwefel, H.-P. (eds.) PPSN 2004. LNCS, vol. 3242, pp. 581–590. Springer, Heidelberg (2004)
16. Bard, J.F., Purnomo, H.W.: Preference Scheduling for Nurses using Column Generation. Europiean Journal of Operational Research 164, 510–534 (2005)
17. Özcan, E.: Memetic Algorithms for Nurse Rostering. In: Yolum, I., Güngör, T., Gürgen, F., Özturan, C. (eds.) ISCIS 2005. LNCS, vol. 3733, pp. 482–492. Springer, Heidelberg (2005)
18. Ohki, M., Morimoto, A., Miyake, K.: Nurse Scheduling by Using Cooperative GA with Efficient Mutation and Mountain-Climbing Operators. In: 3rd Int. IEEE Conference Intelligent Systems, pp. 164–169 (2006)
19. Burke, E.K., De Causmaecker, P., Petrovic, S., Berge, G.V.: Metaheuristics for Handling Time Interval Coverage Constraints in Nurse Scheduling. Applied Artificial Intelligence 20(3) (2006)
20. Ohki, M., Uneme, S., Hayashi, S., Ohkita, M.: Effective Genetic Operators of Cooperative Genetic Algorithm for Nurse Scheduling. In: 4th Int. INSTICC Conference on Informatics in Control, Automation and Robotics, pp. 347–350 (2007)
21. Bard, J.F., Purnomo, H.W.: Cyclic Preference Scheduling of Nurses Using a Lagrangian-Based Heuristic. Journal of Scheduling 10, 5–23 (2007)
22. Uneme, S., Kawano, H., Ohki, M.: Nurse Scheduling by Cooperative GA with Variable Mutation Operator. In: Proc. of 10th ICEIS, INSTICC, pp. 249–252 (2008)
23. Ohki, M., Uneme, S., Kawano, H.: Effective Mutation Operator and Parallel Processing for Nurse Scheduling. Studies in Computational Intelligence 299, 229–242 (2010). doi:10.1007/978-3-642-13428-9_10
24. Ohki, M.: Effective Mutation Operator for Nurse Scheduling by Cooperative GA and Its Parallel Processing. In: Proc. of 19th Int. ACM Workshop on Parallel Architectures and Bioinspired Algorithms, pp. 1–8 (2010)
25. Ohki, M., Kinjo, H.: gPenalty Weight Adjustment in Cooperative GA for Nurse Scheduling. In: Proc. of IEEE 2011 Third World Congress on Nature and Biologically Inspired Computing, pp.76–81. IEEE Catalog Number: CFP1195H-CDR (2011) ISBN: 978-1-4577-1123-7

Author Index

Printed in the United States
By Bookmasters